U0915524

湖北统计年鉴

HUBEI STATISTICAL YEARBOOK

2010

（总第26期）

湖 北 省 统 计 局
国家统计局湖北调查总队 编

中国统计出版社
China Statistics Press

(京)新登字 041 号

图书在版编目(CIP)数据

湖北统计年鉴. 2010/湖北省统计局,国家统计局湖北调查总队编
-北京:中国统计出版社,2010.8
ISBN 978-7-5037-6042-6

Ⅰ.①湖… Ⅱ.
Ⅱ.①湖… ②国…
Ⅲ.①统计资料-湖北省-2010-年鉴
Ⅳ.①C832.63-54

中国版本图书馆 CIP 数据核字(2010)第 163375 号

湖北统计年鉴—2010

作　　者 / 湖北省统计局　国家统计局湖北调查总队
责任编辑 / 佘竞雄　邓有成　倪群峰
责任校对 / 倪群峰
封面设计 / 刘亚非
出版发行 / 中国统计出版社
通信地址 / 北京市丰台区西三环南路甲 6 号　中国统计出版社
邮　　编 / 100073
电　　话 / (010)63376907
E - mail / yearbook@gj.stats.cn
印　　刷 / 湖北省统计局印刷厂
经　　销 / 新华书店
开　　本 / 890×1240 毫米　1/16
字　　数 /125 万字
印　　张 / 40.5 印张
印　　数 / 2000 册
版　　别 / 2010 年 8 月第 1 版
版　　次 / 2010 年 8 月第 1 次印刷
书　　号 / ISBN 978-7-5037-6042-6/C·2398
定　　价 / 280.00 元

编辑说明

一、《湖北统计年鉴—2010》是一本信息密集的资料工具书。通过大量数据，全面地分析、记载和反映了湖北省 2009 年经济、社会、科技、文化等方面的发展情况。具有信息量大、权威性强、适用性广等特点。

二、本年鉴包括综合、人口、从业人员和职工工资、固定资产投资、能源生产和消费、物价指数、人民生活、城市概况、农业、工业、建筑业、运输和邮电、国内外贸易、对外经济和旅游、财政、金融和保险业、教育、科技和文化、体育、卫生、社会福利、企业景气与监测、湖北省开发区主要经济指标、武汉城市圈、鄂西生态文化旅游圈、三峡工程湖北库区、县市概况、附录等 24 个部分，城市概况部分系市区资料，不包括市辖县。

三、2010 年的湖北统计年鉴，对部分指标进行了调整改进，增加了鄂西生态文化旅游圈、三峡工程湖北库区、经济普查单位名录库、投入产出表、按美元计价人均 GDP 等指标。

四、本年鉴对过去发表的统计资料重新予以审核，凡与本年鉴资料有出入的，均以本年鉴为准。本年鉴中统计公报的数据为初步测算数，若与年鉴正文数据不一致，请以正文数据为准。

五、年鉴中指标的使用要结合文中的指标解释，以及注解合理使用，以免发生错误。

六、《湖北统计年鉴》公开出版以来，受到国内外读者的爱护与支持，对本年鉴的内容和编辑工作提出了许多宝贵意见，为此，我们特表谢意。由于水平有限，编辑工作中难免有疏误之处，竭诚欢迎读者批评指正。

COMPLIERS NOTES

I. Hubei Statistical Yearbook 2010 (abbreviated as Yearbook hereafter) is an information – intensive reference book. By providing large quantities of data, it has comprehensively analyzed, recorded, and reflected the economic, social, scientific and technological and cultural development of Hubei Province in2009. It is informative, authoritative, and the characteristics of wide applicability.

II. The Yearbook contains 24parts, such as General Survey, Population, Wages of staff, Investment in Fixed Assets, Energy Production and Consumption, Price, People′s Livelihood, Cities Survey, Agriculture, Industry, Construction, Transport and Post Services, Domestic and Foreign Trade, Foreign Economy and Tourism, Finance, Banking and Insurance, Education, Science and Technology and Culture, Sports, Public Health, Social Welfare, Enterprises Survey, Wuhan Urban Circle, Exi Ecological and Cultural Tourism Circle,Hubei Area of The Three Gorges Project,Statistics on Counties and Prefecture, and so on. The part of Cities Survey refers to statistical materials collected in urban areas, information of counties are excluded in this part.

III. The 2010 edition of Hubei Statistical Yearbook has adjusted and improved its item system and added Exi Ecological and Cultural Tourism Circle,Hubei Area of The Three Gorges Project,Number of Corporations, Industrial Activities Units, Hubei 42 Department Input – output Tble in 2007 And so on.

IV. The Yearbook has re – verified the statistical materials published in the past. Any statistics that is not in accordance with those in the Yearbook, please take the statistics in this Yearbook as the standard. All the figures in the Communiqué are preliminary statistics; if any of them is not in accordance with the figures in the body of the Yearbook, please take the latter one as the standard.

V. Please pay attention to the explanation of the items and notes given below when using this Yearbook, so as to avoid any mistakes.

VI. Hubei Statistical Yearbook, since its publication, has received innumerous cares and supports from readers at home and abroad, which have raised many valuable advices and suggestions for the contents and editing of this Yearbook. Therefore, we thank you in particular and we sincerely welcome continued suggestions from the general readers so that the forms and contents of the Yearbook can be further improved.

《湖北统计年鉴－2010》

编委会和编辑出版人员

一、编委会

二、编辑工作人员

Hubei Statistical Yearbook – 2010

EDITORIAL BOARD AND STAFF

目　　录
CONTENTS

6 物 价

PRICE

7　农　　业
AGRICULTURE

8 工业、能源

INDUSTRY AND ENERGY

9　建　筑　业

CONSTRUCTION

10 交通运输、邮电

TRANSPORTATION AND COMMUNICATION, POST SERVICE

11 国内贸易

DOMESTIC TRADE

12　对外经济贸易和旅游

FOREIGN ECONOMY，TRADE AND TOURISM

13 财政、金融、保险

GOVERNMENT FINANCE， BANKING AND INSURANCE

14 科技、教育

SCIENCE，TECHNOLOGY AND EDUCATION

15 文化、体育、卫生、环保

CULTURE, SPORTS, PUBLIC HEALTH AND ENVIRONMENTAL PROTECTION

16 其他社会活动

OTHER SOCIAL ACTIVITIES

17　城市经济与建设

URBAN ECONOMY AND CONSTRUCTION

18 企业景气及重点企业集团

GENERAL OPERATING SITUATION OF ENTERPRISES AND KEY ENTERPRISE GROUPS

19 开发区主要经济指标

MAJOR ECONOMIC INDICATORS OF DEVELOPMAENT ZONE

20 武汉城市圈

WUHAN URBAN CIRCLE

21 鄂西生态文化旅游圈

EXI ECOLOGICAL AND CULTURAL TOURISM CIRCLE

22 三峡工程湖北库区

HUBEI AREA OF THE THREE GORGES PROJECT

23 县域经济

ECONOMY OF CITIES AND COUNTIES

附录 全国分省主要指标

MAJOR INDICATORS BY REGION

2009年湖北省国民经济和社会发展统计公报

湖　北　省　统　计　局
国家统计局湖北调查总队

（2010年1月20日）

2009年是新世纪以来湖北经济发展最为困难的一年，也是面临的挑战最为严峻、付出的努力最为艰辛、发展的道路最不平凡、收获的成效最为显著的一年。自2008年第四季度以来，受国际金融危机严重冲击和全国经济增长明显下滑影响，我省经济发展遇到严重困难。面对严峻复杂的经济形势，省委、省政府认真贯彻落实中央应对国际金融危机冲击的一揽子计划和政策措施，统筹做好保增长、保民生、保稳定各项工作，全省经济逐步复苏向好，各项社会事业全面进步。

一、综合

2009年，全省完成生产总值12831.52亿元，按可比价格计算，比上年增长13.2%，连续6年保持两位数增长。其中：第一产业完成增加值1915.9亿元，增长5.2%；第二产业完成增加值5909.42亿元，增长16.0%；第三产业完成增加值5006.20亿元，增长12.3%。三次产业结构由2008年的15.7∶43.8∶40.5调整为14.9∶46.1∶39.0。在第三产业中金融保险、批发和零售、住宿和餐饮、房地产、交通运输、仓储和邮电及其他服务业分别增长22.8%、16.5%、14.4%、19.6%、3.7%和9.1%。

居民消费价格总指数（CPI）99.6，价格水平下降0.4%，其中：城市下降0.7%，农村与上年水平持平。分类别看，食品类价格上涨0.5%,衣着类价格下降0.8%，家庭设备用品及服务上涨0.2%，医疗保健及个人用品类价格上涨1.4%，交通和通讯价格下降1.7%，娱乐教育文化用品及服务类价格下降1.1%，居住类价格下降2.4%。工业品出厂价格（PPI）下降4.4%,原材料、燃料、动力购进价格下降6.6%，农业生产资料价格下降4.7%。

年末全省从业人员3622万人，比上年末增加15万人，其中城镇就业人员1357万人，比上年末增加20万人。据省劳动和社会保障部门统计，年末城镇登记失业率为4.21%，与上年末基本持平。

经济和社会发展中存在的主要困难和问题有：经济回升基础不稳固，回升态势还不稳定，回升格局还不平衡，节能减排、资源环境与就业的压力仍然较大。

二、农业

全年农林牧渔业增加值达到1915.9亿元，按可比价计算比上年增长5.2%。粮食种植面积401.25万公顷，比上年增加10.58万公顷；棉花种植面积46.01万公顷，减少8.29万公顷；油料种植面积144.83万公顷，增加8.27万公顷。粮食总产量2309.1万吨，比上年增产81.87万吨，增长3.7%；棉花总产量48.05万吨，减产3.29万吨，减6.4%；油料产量314.05万吨，增产28.31万吨，增长9.9%（主要农产品产量见表1）。

2009 年全省主要农产品产量

表 1　　　　单位：万吨

产品名称	产　量	比上年增长%
粮　食	2309.10	3.7
棉　花	48.05	-6.4
油　料	314.05	9.9
花　生	62.74	9.1
油菜籽	236.51	9.8
麻　类	3.82	-19.7
烟　叶	10.90	24.9
茶　叶	14.42	10.7
水　果(不含果用瓜)	400.86	6.2
蔬　菜	2949.57	2.0

全省当年造林面积 16.03 万公顷,比上年增长 5.9%，零星植树达到 1.78 亿株，木材采伐量 170.51 万立方米。畜牧、水产业稳步增长。生猪出栏 3735.49 万头，增长 6.8%；水产品产量达到 338 万吨，增长 7.9%,再创历史新高。农村用电量 104.26 亿千瓦时，比上年增长 6.3%；化肥施用量（折吨）340.26 万吨，增长 3.9%。

三、工业和建筑业

工业生产保持较快增长。全省规模以上工业完成增加值 4742.23 亿元，按可比价格计算，比上年增长 20.1%。其中：国有及国有控股企业完成增加值 1933.09 亿元，增长 11.2%；国有企业增加值 834.42 亿元，增长 7.0%；集体企业增加值 54.63 亿元，增长 16.1%；股份合作企业增加值 23.15 亿元，增长 8.2%；股份制企业增加值 2511.24 亿元，增长 21.1%；外商及港澳台投资企业增加值 1014.56 亿元，增长 26.1%；其他经济类型企业增加值 304.23 亿元，增长 38.9%。轻工业增加值 1464.46 亿元，增长 25.3%；重工业增加值 3277.77 亿元，增长 18.0%。轻重工业结构由 2008 年的 29.0：71.0 变为 30.9：69.1。

工业产品结构改善，高新技术产业增长较快。全省完成高新技术产业增加值 1331.1 亿元，比上年增长 20.5%，占规模以上工业增加值的比重达 28.1%（主要工业产品产量见表 2）。

2009 年主要工业产品产量

表 2

产品名称	单位	产　量	比上年增长%
纱	万　吨	149.36	7.9
布	亿　米	38.62	12.6
化　纤	万　吨	12.08	42.2
卷　烟	亿　支	1278.58	2.6
家用电冰箱	万　台	39.51	36.1
房间空调器	万　台	514.28	4.2
原　煤	万　吨	1063.27	34.2
原　油	万　吨	80.88	-3.6
发电量	亿千瓦小时	1781.75	2.8
#水电	亿千瓦小时	1169.61	-2.2
钢	万　吨	1985.30	0.2
钢　材	万　吨	2172.33	0.8
十种有色金属	万　吨	66.77	-12.7
其中：铜	万　吨	27.16	1.6
水　泥	万　吨	6983.77	17.6
硫　酸	万　吨	733.80	37.1
纯　碱	万　吨	137.61	52.4
烧　碱	万　吨	64.59	31.7
化　肥（折 100%）	万　吨	852.58	40.7
发电设备	万千瓦	206.0	13.7
汽　车	万　辆	119.67	39.1
轿　车	万　辆	49.50	56.1
移动电话机	万　部	831.52	126.2

工业产销衔接较好，经济效益继续提高。全省工业完成销售产值14740.34亿元，增长19.2%，其中：钢铁、汽车、石化、电力、食品五个重点行业实现销售产值超千亿元。工业产品销售率为97.43%。1—11月全省工业经济效益综合指数为229.4，比上年同期提高11.9个百分点。全年全省工业企业实现利润754.22亿元，增长25.2%；其中大中型企业实现利润500.28亿元，增长15.4%。

建筑业发展步伐加快，全年资质以内建筑企业完成施工产值3409.02亿元，增长30.9%；实现利润128.45亿元，增长37.3%；税金96.55亿元，增长19.2%。建筑单位房屋建筑施工面积20771.2万平方米，其中招投标承包面积16572.0万平方米，招投标面为79.8%。建筑企业劳动生产率为15.89万元/人，减少19.3%；新开工房屋建筑施工面积11228.85万平方米，比上年增加535.65万平方米。

四、固定资产投资

全社会完成固定资产投资8211.85亿元，比上年增长41.6%，其中城镇以上项目投资7569.15亿元，增长41.9%；房地产开发投资1200.44亿元，增长34.5%。按经济类型划分，国有经济投资3124.16亿元，增长37.4%；集体经济投资408.91亿元，增长61.4%；城乡私营个体投资1745.62亿元，增长45.3%；其他经济投资2933.16亿元，增长41.7%。按产业划分，全省三次产业投资分别为321.59亿元、3095.14亿元和4795.12亿元，分别增长39.1%、32.0%和48.8%。

全省159个重点建设项目完成投资1145.68亿元，占城镇以上项目投资的15.1%。新增的主要生产能力有：发电机组容量220.9万千瓦、新建高速公路548.45公里、电气化铁路主线正线交付运营里程1039.45公里。

五、国内贸易

全年实现社会消费品零售总额5928.41亿元，增长19.0%。分城乡看，城市实现零售额4128.16亿元，增长17.9%；县及县以下实现零售额1800.25亿元，增长21.6%。分行业看，批发业实现零售额728.95亿元，增长15.9%；零售业4150.26亿元，增长19.9%；住宿和餐饮业795.18亿元，增长19.7%；其他行业254.03亿元，下降2.8%。

六、对外经济

全年实现外贸进出口总额172.29亿美元，比上年下降16.8%，其中：出口99.78亿美元，下降14.8%；进口72.50亿美元，下降19.4%。新批外商直接投资项目268个。全年外商直接投资及其他投资46.88亿美元，比上年增长13.9%，其中外商直接投资36.58亿美元，增长12.7%；外商其他投资9.7亿美元，增长11.6%。对外经济合作业务完成营业额26.3亿美元，新签合同额53.3亿美元，分别增长73.1%和60.8%。

七、交通、邮电和旅游

全年完成货物周转量2808.46亿吨公里，比上年增长4.1%；旅客周转量1096.31亿人公里，增长3.0%。

邮电通信业完成邮电业务总量841.37亿元，增长17.8%。长途光缆线路总长度29200.0万公里；局用交换机达到1732.8万门；固定电话用户1083.3万户，减少95.4万户；移动电话用户达到3136.9万户，新增608.2万户。全省电话普及率为74部/百人。计算机宽带互联网用户361.3万户。

全年国内旅游人数15065.18万人次，比上年增长29.0%；国内旅游收入969.63亿元，增长35.9%。入境旅游人数133.46万人次，比上年增长12.4%。国际旅游外汇收入5.1亿美元，增长15.3%。

八、财政、金融和保险

全年完成财政总收入1533.89亿元，比上年增长14.6%，其中地方一般预算收入814.78亿元，增长14.7%，其中，税收收入616.03亿元,增长14.7%。全年财政支出2107.31亿元，增长27.2%。

年末全省金融机构各项存款余额17678.05亿元，比年初增加4097.52亿元。其中：城乡居民储蓄存款余额8223.41亿元，增加1422.91亿元。金融机构各项贷款余额12057.17亿元，比年初增加3301.98亿元。其中：短期贷款余额3667.02亿元，增加609.10亿元；中长期贷款7100.42亿元，增加2112.35亿元。

全年保费收入372.42亿元，增长17.4%。其中，财产险公司实现保费收入72.76亿元，增长24.8%；人身险公司保费收入299.66亿元，增长15.8%。支付各类赔款及给付82.63亿元，下降3.8%，其中，财产险公司赔款45.62亿元，增长9.8%；人身险公司赔付37.01亿元，下降16.5%。

九、教育和科学技术

年末全省普通高等教育招生39.6万人，在校生124.9万人，毕业生32.8万人；研究生招生3.5万人，在校研究生9.1万人，毕业生2.6万人；各类中等职业教育招生36.7万人，在校生104.2万人，毕业生30.8万人;普通高中招生42.4万人，在校生128.7万人，毕业生45万人；普通初中在校生236.3万人，小学在校生359.3万人，幼儿园在园幼儿83.1万人。

科学研究和技术开发取得新的成果，全年共取得省部级以上科技成果740项。其中,基础理论成果20项，应用技术成果693项，软科学成果27项。全年共签订技术合同5694项，技术合同成交金额77.9亿元，增长24%。

全省科学研究与实验发展(R&D)经费支出178亿元，增长19.4%，占全省生产总值的1.4%。全年安排“863”计划项目298项（课题），经费1.8亿元，“973”计划项目120项，经费11692.11万元。争取国家高技术产业发展项目25个，项目总投资22.5亿元，安排国家资金1.73亿元，银行贷款10.5亿元。

全省具备向社会出具检测报告的产品质量监督检验机构有152个,其中国家产品质量监督检验中心9个。全省通过CNAL认可的检测/校准实验室81家。累计有5257家企业通过ISO9000体系认证；企业获得强制性认证证书5771张。法定计量技术机构有106个，强制检定计量器具130万台件。

全省天气雷达观测站点有10个，卫星云图接受站点17个。地震前兆台站网1个，前兆台站20个；数字测震台网1个，测震台站30个。

十、文化、卫生和体育

全省共有艺术表演团体102个，群艺馆、文化馆111个，公共图书馆107个，博物馆111个，电影放映管理机构111个，放映单位1705个。广播电台11座，电视台12座，有线电视用户803.43万户。全年出版全国性和省级报纸17.76亿份，各类期刊2.65亿册，图书1.45亿册(张)。

全省共有卫生机构10826个，卫生技术人员23.4万人，病床床位17.7万张；卫生防疫、防治机构195个（其中：专科疾病防治所（站、中心）88家，疾病预防控制中心（防疫站）107家），卫生防疫技术人员7473人。

全省运动健儿在国际比赛中共获得冠军17项次、亚军18项次、季军16项次，其中奥运会项目最高水平比赛冠军6项次、亚军3项次、季军1项次；在各类全国比赛中，获冠军56项次、亚军61项次、第三名57项次，其中，全运会项目全国最高水平比赛中冠军14项次、亚军12项次、第三名23项次。全民健身运动蓬勃发展。全年销售体育彩票16.4亿元。

十一、人口、人民生活和社会保障

年末全省常住人口5720万人（指常住本省半年以上人口）。全年出生人口57.8万人，出生率为9.48‰；死亡人口36.58万人，死亡率为6.0‰，人口自然增长率为3.48‰。

城乡居民收入继续增加，城镇居民人均可支配收入14367元，增长9.2%；农民人均纯收入5035.26元，增长8.1%。

社会保障进一步加强，年末全省参加基本养老保险人数980.7万人，比上年增加48.6万人，其中：在职职工709.2万人，离退休人员271.5万人；参加失业保险人数440.3万人；参加医疗保险人数820.7万人，增加105.9万人。年末全省企业参加基本养老保险离退休人员255万人，100%实现了养老金按时足额发放；全年累计领取失业保险金人数13.3万人。

全省城镇居民最低生活保障对象145.2万人，农村居民最低生活保障人数172.5万人，国家抚恤、补助各类优抚对象38.9万人。

社会福利事业不断发展，年末全省各类社会福利收养床位21.1万张，收养18.2万人，城镇社区服务设施7409个。全年销售社会福利彩票31.88亿元。

十二、资源和环境

年末全省耕地面积3323.46千公顷，比上年增加34.13千公顷，增长1.04%。化学需氧量和二氧化硫排放量分别下降1.7%和3.9%，可望提前一年实现“十一五”主要污染物总量控制目标。

长江干流水质总体较好，15个监测断面的水质Ⅰ～Ⅲ类的占100%。与上年相比，长江水质总体无明显变化。

全省17个市、州、直管市、神农架林区中，按二氧化硫、二氧化氮、总悬浮颗粒物或可吸入颗粒物年均浓度综合评价，神农架林区空气质量符合国家一级标准，占重点城市的5.9%；11个城市符合国家二级标准，占重点城市的64.7%；5个城市符合国家三级标准，占重点城市的29.4%。全省达到一级、二级标准的城市占70.6%。

全省累计已发现矿种150种，累计已查明资源储量的矿种92种。2009年国土资源调查及地质勘查新发现矿产地大型1处，中、小型矿产地3处。

全省自然保护区达到63个，其中国家级生态示范区10个；省级自然保护区17个，自然保护区总面积110.6万公顷。

注：本公报所列数据为初步统计数。

STATISTICAL COMMUNIQUE OF HUBEI PROVINCE ON THE 2009 NATIONAL ECONOMIC AND SOCIAL DEVELOPMENT

PROVINCIAL STATISTICAL BUREAU OF HUBEI
HUBEI INVESTIGATION TEAM OF NATIONAL STATISTICAL BUREAU

(20th January 2010)

Since 2009, the new century, the economic development of Hubei's most difficult year, but also the challenges facing the most serious, most hard efforts to develop the road most unusual, most significantly the effectiveness of harvest year. Since the fourth quarter of 2008 has been a serious impact on the international financial crisis and the impact of national economic growth fell significantly, serious difficulties of economic development in our province. The face of severe and complicated economic situation, the provincial government to seriously implement the central response to the international financial crisis package of plans and policy measures, overall good economic growth, ensuring the people's livelihood, maintaining stability of the work, the province's economy gradually recovers to Well, all-round social progress.

I. General Outlook

In 2009, the province completed GDP 1283.15 billion yuan, according to comparable prices, an increase of 13.2% for 6-year double-digit growth. Of which: primary industry added value of 191.59 billion yuan, an increase of 5.2%; the second industry added value of 590.94 billion yuan, up 16.0%; tertiary industry added value of 500.62 billion yuan, an increase of 12.3%. Three industrial structure from 2008 15.7:43.8:40.5 adjusted to 14.9:46.1:39.0. In the tertiary industry in the finance and insurance, wholesale and retail, accommodation and catering, real estate, transportation, storage, post and telecommunications and other services rose by 22.8%, 16.5%, 14.4%, 19.6%, 3.7% and 9.1%.

The consumer price index (CPI) 99.6, the price level decreased by 0.4%, of which: City decreased by 0.7%, unchanged from the previous year in rural areas. Categories Do not look, food prices rose 0.5%, clothing prices fell 0.8%, household equipment and services rose 0.2%, health care and personal products prices increased 1.4%, transport and communication prices fell 1.7%, entertainment, education and culture articles The price of down 1.1%, housing prices fell 2.4% in class. Producer price (PPI) fell 4.4%, raw materials, fuel and power purchase prices fell 6.6%, agricultural production materials prices fell 4.7%.

Million employees across the province in late 3622, an increase of 15 million over the previous year, of which the urban employed 1357 people, an increase of 20 million over the previous year. According to provincial labor and social security department statistics, at the end of the registered urban unemployment rate was 4.21%, essentially flat compared with the previous year.

Economic and social development in the presence of the main difficulties and problems are: the basis for economic recovery is not strong upward trend is not stable, recovery pattern was also uneven, energy conservation, resources and environment and employment pressure is still large.

II. Agriculture

The added value of agriculture, forestry and fisheries throughout the year to reach 191.59 billion yuan, calculated according to comparable prices increased by 5.2% over the previous year. Area of 4.01 million hectares of grain cultivation, 105,800 hectares more than last year; cotton area of 460,100 hectares planted to reduce the 82,900 hectares; oil area of 1.45 million hectares planted increased 82.7 thousand hectares. Total output of 23.09 million tons of grain, yield 818,700 tons over the previous year, an increase of 3.7%; cotton output 480,500 tons, a decrease of 32.9 thousand tons, by 6.4%; oil production 3,140,500 tons, an increase of 283,100 tons, an increase of 9.9% (major agricultural production see table 1).

Table1: Output of Major Farm Products, 2009

Item	Output(10,000 tons)	Increased over 2008(%)
Grain	2309.10	3.7
Cotton	48.05	-6.4
Oil-bearing Crops	314.05	9.9
Peanuts	62.74	9.1
Rapeseed	236.51	9.8
Ramie	3.82	-19.7
Cured tobacco leaf	10.90	24.9
Tea	14.42	10.7
Fruits (Do not contain a fruit to use melon)	400.86	6.2
Vegetables	2949.57	2.0

Afforestation area of the province that year 160,300 hectares, up 5.9% to 178,000,000 sporadic tree planting, timber harvest volume of 1,705,100 m3.

Livestock, aquaculture, growing steadily. Pig slaughter 37,354,900, an increase of 6.8%; aquatic production reached 3.38 million tons, up 7.9%, new record high.

Electricity consumption 10.43 billion kwh, up 6.3%; chemical fertilizer quantity (break tons) 3.40 million tons, an increase of 3.9%.

III. Industry and Construction

Industrial production continued to grow rapidly. The province's industrial added value of the scale was 474.22 billion yuan, according to comparable prices, an increase of 20.1%. Of which: State-owned and state holding enterprises added value of 193.31

billion yuan, up 11.2%; the added value of 83.44 billion yuan of state-owned enterprises, up 7.0%; collective enterprises added value 5.46 billion yuan, up 16.1%; stock cooperative enterprises added value 2.32 billion yuan , an increase of 8.2%; the added value of 251.12 billion yuan joint-stock enterprises, up 21.1%; foreign and Hong Kong, Macao and Taiwan investment enterprises added value of 101.46 billion yuan, up 26.1%; other types of added value of 30.42 billion yuan enterprises, an increase of 38.9%. Light industrial added value of 146.45 billion yuan, an increase of 25.3%; heavy industry was 327.78 billion yuan, an increase of 18.0%. Light and heavy industrial structure was from 2008 into 30.9:69.1 29.0:71.0.

Structural improvements of industrial products, high technology industries grew rapidly. Province completed 133.11 billion yuan added value of high-tech products, up 20.5% over the previous year, accounting for the proportion of above-scale industrial added value up 28.1% (mainly industrial products Table 2).

Table2: Output of Major Industrial Products, 2009

Product	Unit	Output	Increased over 2008(%)
Yarn	10000 tons	149.36	7.9
Cloth	100 million meters	38.62	12.6
Chemical fiber	10000 tons	12.08	42.2
Cigarettes	100 million units	1278.58	2.6
Household refrigerators	10000 units	39.51	36.1
Air condition	10000 units	514.28	4.2
Raw Coal	10000 tons	1063.27	34.2
Crude oil	10000 tons	80.88	-3.6
Electricity	100 million kilowatt-hours	1781.75	2.8
Hydropower	100 million kilowatt-hours	1169.51	-2.2
Crude steel	10000 tons	1985.30	0.2
Rolled steel	10000 tons	2172.33	0.8
Ten kinds of nonferrous metal	10000 tons	66.77	-12.7
Among which：Copper	10000 tons	27.16	1.6
Cement	10000 tons	6983.77	17.6
Sulfuric acid	10000 tons	733.80	37.1
Soda ash	10000 tons	137.61	52.4
Caustic soda	10000 tons	64.59	31.7
Chemical fertilizers（100 percent equivalent）	10000 tons	852.58	40.7
Electricity Generation equipments	10000 kilowatt-10000 hours	206.0	13.7
Motor vehicles	10000 units	119.67	39.1
Car	10000 units	49.50	56.1
Mobile phones	10000 units	831.52	126.2

Good convergence of industrial production and marketing, cost-effective to continue to improve. Province's industrial sales output value of 1474.03 billion yuan to complete, an increase of 19.2%, of which: iron and steel, automobile, petrochemical, power, food sales value of the five key industries over 100 billion yuan. Industrial product sales rate of 97.43%. January-November the province's industrial economic efficiency index was 229.4, compared with same period last year increased by 11.9 percentage points. Annual profits of industrial enterprises throughout the province 75.42 billion yuan, up 25.2%; one medium-sized enterprises realized profits of 50.03 billion yuan, an increase of 15.4%.

Accelerate the pace of the construction industry, the annual qualification to complete construction within the construction output value of 340.90 billion yuan enterprises, up 30.9%; profit 12.85 billion yuan, up 37.3%; taxes 9.66 billion yuan, an increase of 19.2%. Housing construction unit area of 207,712,000 square meters of construction, including bidding contract area of 165.72 million square meters, the bidding side is 79.8%. Construction Labor productivity was 158,900 yuan / person, decreased by 19.3%; newly started housing construction area of 112,288,500 square meters, 5,356,500 square meters more than last year.

IV. Investment in Fixed Assets

Society investment in fixed assets 821.19 billion yuan, up 41.6% over the previous year, of which 756.92 billion yuan investment than urban areas, up 41.9%; real estate development and investment 120.04 billion yuan, an increase of 34.5%. By economic classification, 312.42 billion yuan of state-owned economic investment, up 37.4%; collective investment 40.89 billion yuan, up 61.4%; urban and rural private individual investment 174.56 billion yuan, up 45.3%; other economic investment 293.32 billion yuan, an increase of 41.7%. Classified by industry, the province invested three industries were 32.16 billion yuan, 309.51 billion yuan and 479.51 billion yuan, increased 39.1%, 32.0% and 48.8%.

159 key construction projects throughout the province completed 114.57 billion yuan investment, accounting for more than urban investment of 15.1%. New major production capacity: 2.21 million kilowatts of capacity generating units, the new highway 548.45 km, the main line is electrified railway mileage of 1,039.45 km line delivery operations.

V. Domestic Trade

The whole year, total retail sales 592.84 billion yuan, was an increase of 19.0%. Sub-urban and rural areas, was cities to achieve retail sales of 412.82 billion yuan, up 17.9%; and below the county to achieve retail sales of 180.03 billion yuan, an increase of 21.6%. Different industries, the wholesale and retail sales industry realized 72.90 billion yuan, up 15.9%; retail 415.03 billion yuan, up 19.9%; accommodation and catering industry 79.52 billion yuan, up 19.7%; other industry 25.40 billion yuan, down 2.8%.

VI. Foreign Economic Relations

To achieve total annual imports and exports 17.23 billion U.S. dollars, down 16.8% over the previous year, of which: exports 9.98 billion U.S. dollars, down 14.8%; imported 7.25 billion U.S. dollars, down 19.4%. Newly was approved 268 foreign direct investment projects. Annual foreign direct was investment and other investment 4.69 billion U.S. dollars, up 13.9%, of which 3.66 billion U.S.

dollars of foreign direct investment, up 12.7%; Foreign Investment 970 million U.S. dollars, up 11.6%. Foreign economic cooperation business turnover of 2.63 billion U.S. dollars, new contracts signed 5.33 billion U.S. dollars, up by 73.1% and 60.8%.

VII. Transportation, Post and Telecommunications, Tourism

Annual turnover was of 280.846 billion tons kilometers of cargo, up 4.1%; Passenger 109,631,000,000 kilometers, up 3.0%.

Posts and telecommunications total 84.137 billion yuan of postal and telecommunication services, an increase of 17.8%. The total length of long-distance fiber cable 292 million km; office exchanges reached 17.33 million; 10.83 million fixed telephone users and reduce the 954 000; mobile phone users reached 31.37 million, added 6.08 million. Telephone penetration was rate of the province for the 74 / 100 people. 3.61 million broadband Internet users computer.

150 651 800 Annual number of domestic tourism trips, up 29.0%; domestic tourism income 96.96 billion yuan, an increase of 35.9%. Tourists 1,334,600 passengers, was an increase of 12.4%. International tourism foreign exchange was income 510 million U.S. dollars, up 15.3%.

VIII. Finance, Banking, and Insurance

The total annual was income of 153.39 billion yuan to complete fiscal, up 14.6% over the previous year, of which the local general budget revenue 81.48 billion yuan, up 14.7%, of which 61.60 billion yuan of tax revenue, an increase of 14.7%. Annual expenditure was 210.73 billion yuan, an increase of 27.2%.

At the end of the deposit balance was of financial institutions across the province 1767.805 billion yuan, an increase of 409.75 billion yuan. Of which: savings deposits of urban and rural residents of 822.34 billion yuan, 142.29 billion yuan to increase. Financial institutions loans 1205.72 billion yuan, an increase of 330.20 billion yuan. Of which: short-term loan balance of 366.70 billion yuan, increasing 60.91 billion yuan; long-term loans to 710.04 billion yuan, 211.24 billion yuan to increase.

Annual premium income of 37.242 billion yuan, was an increase of 17.4%. Among them, the financial property and casualty insurance premium was of 7.28 billion yuan, up 24.8%; life insurance company's premium income 29.97 billion yuan, an increase of 15.8%. To pay an indemnity of 8.26 billion yuan, down 3.8%, of which 4.56 billion yuan fiscal compensation insurance companies, an increase of 9.8%; life insurance company Peifu 3.70 billion yuan, down 16.5%.

IX. Education and Science

At the end of the province of higher education enrollment of 39.6 million ordinary students in school 124.9 million, 32.8 million students; graduate enrollment of 3.5 million, 9.1 million people in the graduate school, graduates 2.6 million; various secondary vocational education enrollment 367 000 people, students at 104.2 million, 30.8 million students; high school enrollment of 42.4 million, 128.7 million in students, graduates of 45 million people; ordinary junior high school students 236.3 million, 359.3 million pupils in kindergarten in Park, 83.1 million children.

Scientific research and technological was development to achieve new results, the annual total of more than provincial and ministerial level scientific and technological achievements 740. Among them, 20 the results based on theoretical, applied and technological achievements 693, 27 soft science achievements. Technology contracts were signed the year 5694, technology contracts, turnover 7.79 billion, an increase of 24%.

The province of scientific research and experimental development (R & D) expenditures 17.8 billion, an increase of 19.4%, accounting for 1.4% of the province's GDP. Year arrangement "863" project 298 (topic), was funded 180 million yuan, "973" 120 projects, funding 116.92 million yuan. For national development projects of 25 high-tech industry, the total investment 2.25 billion yuan, 173 million state funds arrangement, bank loan 1.05 billion.

Detection of the province has issued the report to the social product quality supervision and inspection bodies 152, of which the State Quality Supervision and Inspection Center 9. Recognized by the province CNAL was detection / calibration laboratory 81. Total of 5,257 enterprises with ISO9000 system was certification; enterprises to obtain mandatory certification 5771. Authorized measurement institutions 106, mandatory testing of measuring instruments 1.3 million units pieces.

Weather radar sites across the province with 10 satellite cloud map receiving site 17. Network of seismic stations, was a precursor, precursor station 20; digital seismic network one, 30 seismic stations.

X. Culture, Public Health and Sports

The province a total of 102 performing arts organizations, art centers, 111 cultural centers, 107 public libraries, 111 museums, 111 cinema administration, showing unit 1705. 11 radio stations, 12 television stations, cable TV user 8034300. Annual publication of national and provincial newspapers 1.78 billion copies, periodicals 265 million, 145 million books (Zhang).

Health institutions across the province a total of 10,826 health workers, 23.4 million people, 177,000 hospital beds; health and epidemic prevention, prevention and treatment institutions 195 (including: specialist disease control centers (stations, centers) 88, disease prevention and control centers (epidemic prevention station) 107), 7473 were technical staff health and disease prevention.

Province's athletes in international competitions won 17 times the Chinese Communists, runner-up 18 times, third 16 times, including the highest level of Olympic events champion six times, runner-up three times, third place a second; in various national competitions , the winner, 56 times, second place 61 times, third 57 times, which projects the highest national level of the National Games title game 14 times, second place 12 times, third 23 times. Nationwide fitness campaign flourish. Sports Lottery was sales of 1.64 billion yuan the year.

XI. Population, Living Conditions and Social Security

Resident population of the province in late 5720 million (refer to the resident population of the province for more than six months). 57.8 million annual births, birth rate was 9.48 ‰; 36.58 million deaths, mortality rate was 6.0 ‰, the natural population growth rate was 3.48 ‰.

Urban and rural incomes continue to increase, per capita disposable income of urban residents and 14,367 yuan, an increase of 9.2%; rural per capita net income of 5,035.26 yuan, an increase of 8.1%.

Further strengthen social security, at the end of the province participated in basic pension insurance, the number of 980.7 million,

48.6 million more than last year, of which: 709.2 million active employees, retirees 271.5 million; to participate in the number of unemployment insurance, 440.3 million; participate in medical Insurance number 820.7 million, increasing 105.9 million. At the end of the province participated in basic pension insurance company 2.55 million retirees, realized 100% of their pensions in full; annual total number receiving unemployment insurance benefits 13.3 million.

Minimum living guarantee for urban residents across the province object 145.2 million, the number of rural residents living 172.5 million, the state pensions, benefits all entitled groups were 38.9 million people.

The continuous development of social welfare, was at the end of the province adoption of various social welfare beds 211,000, adoption 18.2 million, urban community service facilities in 7409. Annual sales was of 3.19 billion yuan was of social welfare lottery tickets.

XII. Resource and Environment

At the end of 3323.46 thousand hectares of cultivated land throughout the province over the previous year increased 34.13 thousand hectares, an increase of 1.04%. Chemical oxygen demand and sulfur dioxide emissions dropped by 1.7% and 3.9%, is expected to achieve one year ahead of "Eleventh Five" major pollutants amount control target.

Overall good water quality of Yangtze River, the water quality monitoring sections 15 Ⅰ ~ Ⅲ class 100%. Compared with the previous year, was no significant changes in the overall water quality of Yangtze River.

Province's 17 municipal, state, straight city Shennongjia, press sulfur dioxide, nitrogen dioxide, total suspended particles, or an annual average concentration of respirable particulate matter evaluation, Shennongjia meet national air quality standard, accounting for 5.9% of the city; 11 cities meet the national standards, accounting for 64.7% of the city; five cities in line with national levels, accounting for 29.4% of major cities. The province to achieve level 2 standards for accounting for 70.6% was of the city.

Province's total 150 kinds of minerals have been found accumulated reserves of minerals have been identified 92. 2009 land surveys and geological exploration of new mineral deposits found in a large, was medium and small mineral deposits 3.

Up 63 nature reserves across the province, including 10 national ecological demonstration zones; 17 provincial nature reserves, nature reserves total area of 1,106,000 hectares.

Note: All figures in the Communiqué are preliminary statistics.

1 综　合

General Survey

资料整理：周克莉　倪群峰　陶　萍
杨　旸

综　　合

General Survey

从数字看2009年的湖北

Statistic about Hubei in 2009

湖 北 的 地 位

Position of Hubei in the Country

地区生产总值12961.10亿元	Gross Domestic Production:12961.10billion yuan	占全国3.9%
#第三产业5127.12亿元	Tertiary Industry: 458.68 billion yuan	占全国3.6%
人均地区生产总值22677元	Per Capita Regional GDP: 19860 yuan	相当于全国90.0%
全社会固定资产投资总额8211.85亿元	TotaL Investment in Fixed Assets: 579.86billion yuan	占全国3.7%
社会消费品零售总额5928.41亿元	Total Retail Sales of Social Consumption:496.58billion yuan	占全国4.5%
进出口总额172.29亿美元	Total Imports and Exports: 20.57 billion yuan	占全国0.8%
#出口总额99.78亿美元	Total Exports: 11.59billion yuan	占全国0.8%
实际外商直接投资36.58亿美元	Actual Foreign Direct Investment: 3.25 billion yuan	占全国4.1%
粮食产量2309.10万吨	Grain: 22.27 million tons	占全国4.4%
钢产量1985.30万吨	Rolled Steel: 26.95 milliom tons	占全国3.5%
发电量1781.75亿千瓦小时	Electricity: 1794.48 (100 million kWh)	占全国4.8%
城镇居民人均可支配收入14367元	Per Capita Disposable Income of Urban Residents: 13153 yuan	相当于全国83.7%
农村居民人均纯收入5035元	Per Capita Net Incomes of Rural Residents: 4656 yuan	相当于全国97.7%

湖 北 的 人 口

Population of Hubei

常住人口	Population of Permanent residents	5720万人
从业人员	Employment	3622万人
#在岗职工人数	Staff and Workers	680.85万人
出生人口	Birth Population	57.80万人
死亡人口	Death Population	36.58万人
结婚人数	Number of Marriage	565400对
离婚人数	Number of Divorce	81133对
人口密度	Density of Population	328人/平方公里
人口平均期望寿命	Average Life Expectancy	74.0岁

湖 北 的 经 济 发 展

Economic Development of Hubei

		1979—2009年平均增长(%)
地区生产总值	Regional Gross Production	10.6
第一产业	Primary Industry	4.8
第二产业	Second Industry	12.5
第三产业	Tertiary Industry	12.9
全社会固定资产投资	Investment in Fixed Assets	18.3
财政收入	Government Revenue	11.1
货物运输量	Cargo Transport Volume	7.0
社会消费品零售总额	Total Retail Sales of Social Consumption	16.0
出口总额	Total Exports	14.3

湖 北 的 一 天

On Day in Hubei

地区生产总值	Gross Domestic Product	35.51亿元
第一产业	First Industry	4.92亿元
第二产业	Second Industry	16.54亿元
#工业	Industry	14.2亿元
第三产业	Tertiary Industry	14.05亿元
地方财政一般预算收入	Local Government Budgeted Revenue	2.23亿元
货物运输量	Freight Traffic	226.61万吨
竣工房屋面积	Floor Space of Building Completed	26.77万平方米
社会消费品零售总额	Total Retail Sales of Social Consumption	16.24亿元
出口总额	Total Exports	0.27亿美元
出版报纸	Newspapers Published	475.62万份
邮寄函件	Letters and Correspondents Delivered	39.66万件

1-1 土地面积与行政区划

LAND AREA AND ADMINISTRATIVE DIVISION

项 目	Item	单 位	unit	1990	2000	2005	2007	2008	2009
常住人口	Population of the Whole Province	(万人)	(10 000 persons)	5439.29	5960	5710	5699	5711	5720
土地面积	Land Area	(万平方公里)	(10 000 sq.m)	18.59	18.59	18.59	18.59	18.59	18.59
耕地面积	Cultivated Area	(千公顷)	(1000 hectares)	3476.77	3282.96	3161.17	3226.62	3289.33	3308.35
行政区划	Adinimisrtative Division								
省辖市	Municipality	(个)	(unit)	8	12	12	12	12	12
自治州	Prefecture	(个)	(unit)	1	1	1	1	1	1
林区	Forest Zone	(个)	(unit)	1	1	1	1	1	1
县级市	City	(个)	(unit)	22	24	24	24	24	24
省辖行政单位	Adinimistrative Units under the Jurisdiction of Province	(个)	(unit)		3	3	3	3	3
县	County	(个)	(unit)	48	41	39	39	39	40
乡政府	Local Government	(个)	(unit)	1121	476	217	210	207	204
镇政府	Township Government	(个)	(unit)	844	853	737	734	735	740
办事处		(个)	(unit)		145	163	278	285	283
村民委员会	Village Communittee	(个)	(unit)	32765	32400	26678	26045	26101	26051
村民小组	Village Groups	(个)	(unit)	260847	259250	212587	208716	209737	209806

1-2 市、州行政区划

ADMINISTRATIVE DIVISION OF MUNICIPALITIES AND PREFECTURE

单位：个 （2009年底）（by the End of 2009） (unit)

地区	Region	县级市 Cities	县 Counties	区 Districts	乡政府 Village Government	镇政府 Township Government	村民委员会 Villager Communittee	村民小组 Villager Groups
全　省	Total	24	40	38	204	740	26031	209706
武汉市	Wuhan Municipality			13	9	12	2010	18031
黄石市	Huangshi Municipality	1	1	4	1	27	792	7910
十堰市	Shiyan Municipality	1	5	2	43	62	1892	10448
荆州市	Yichang Municipality	3	3	2	13	89	2452	20171
宜昌市	Xiangfan Municipality	3	5	5	22	65	1389	8215
襄樊市	Erzhou Municipality	3	3	3	4	75	2410	14934
鄂州市	Jingmen Municipality			3	3	18	316	4032
荆门市	Xiaogan Municipality	1	2	2	2	50	1395	9956
孝感市	Jingzhou Municipality	3	3	1	23	72	2931	23456
黄冈市	Huanggang Municipality	2	7	1	19	96	4311	36581
咸宁市	Xianning Municipality	1	4	1	12	52	909	10022
恩施自治州	Enshi Prefecture	2	6		46	37	2540	22986
随州市	Suizhou Municipality	1	1	1	3	34	883	8635
仙桃市	Xiantao Municipality	1				15	639	4644
天门市	Tianmen Municipality	1			1	21	767	6721
潜江市	Qianjiang Municipality	1				10	329	2633
神农架林区	Shennongjia Forest Zone				3	5	66	331

注：乡政府、镇政府、村民委员会、村民小组数只涉及农村生产经营单位数

Notes:the number of village government, township government, villager communittee and villager groups only refer to the number of units run by village production operation.

1-3 全省法人、产业活动单位数（2009）

指标名称	Item	合计 Total
总计	Total	328087
一、按登记注册类型分组	**Grouped by Type of Registration**	
内资企业	Inner Funded Enterprises	325727
国有企业	State-owned Enterprises	56450
集体企业	Collective-owned Enterprises	14804
股份合作企业	Share Holding Cooperative Enterprises	2870
联营企业	Joint Funded Enterprises	1098
国有联营企业	State Joint owned Enterprises	142
集体联营企业	Collective Joint-owned Enterprises	455
国有与集体联营企业	State - owned and Collective Joint-owned Enterprises	114
其他联营企业	Other Joint-owned Enterprises	387
有限责任公司	Responsibility Co. Ltd	33454
国有独资公司	State-owned Solely Funded Co.	275
其他有限责任公司	Other Responsibility Co. Ltd	33179
股份有限公司	Share Holding Co.Ltd.	5760
私营企业	Private - owned enterprises	150750
私营独资企业	Private Solely Funded enterprises	72730
私营合伙企业	Private Partnership Enterprises	15981
私营有限责任公司	Private Responsibility Co. Ltd	56784
私营股份有限公司	Private Share Holding Co.Ltd.	5255
其他企业	Others	60541
港、澳、台商投资企业	Hongkong, Macao and Taiwan Funded Enterprises	1133
合资经营企业(港或澳、台资)	Joint Venture with Hongkong, Macao and Taiwan	465
合作经营企业(港或澳、台资)	Cooperate with Hongkong, Macao and Taiwan Funded	33
港、澳、台商独资经营企业	Enterprises Solely Funded by Hongkong, Macao and Taiwan	563
港、澳、台商投资股份有限公司	Share Holding Co.Ltd. With Hongkong, Macao and Taiwan Investment	72
外商投资企业	Foreign Funded Enterprises	1251
中外合资经营企业	Sino - Foreign Joint Funded Enterprises	571
中外合作经营企业	Sino - Foreign Cooperative Funded Enterprises	39
外资企业	Foreign Solely Funded Enterprises	564
外商投资股份有限公司	Foreign Funded Share Holding Co.Ltd.	77
二、按国民经济行业门类分组	**Grouped By Sector**	
农、林、牧、渔业	Farming, Forestry, Animal husbandary and Fishery	5835
采矿业	Mining and Quarrying	5084
制造业	Manufacturing	58561
电力、燃气及水的生产和供应业	Power, Gas and Water Production and Supply	2679
建筑业	Construction	14829
交通运输、仓储和邮政业	Transportaation, Storage and Post	7032
信息传输、计算机服务和软件业	Information Trnsmmision, Computer Service and software	7046
批发和零售业	Wholesale and Retail Sale	68646
住宿和餐饮业	Hotel and Catering	7798
金融业	Banking	1333
房地产业	Real Estate	11468
租赁和商务服务业	Leasing and Commerical Service	18033
科学研究、技术服务和地质勘查业	Scietific research, Polytechnical Service and Geological Prospecting	11243
水利、环境和公共设施管理业	Water Conservancy, Environment and Public Facility Management	3860
居民服务和其他服务业	Resident Service and Others	7721
教育	Education	16918
卫生、社会保障和社会福利业	Health Care, Social Security and Social Welfare	12176
文化、体育和娱乐业	Culture, Sports and Recreation	4476
公共管理和社会组织	Public Management and Social Organizations	63348
国际组织	International Organization	1

NUMBER OF CORPORATIONS, INDUSTRIAL ACTIVITIES UNITS(2009)

法人单位数(个) Corporation Units(units)		产业活动单位数(个) Number of Economic Activities Units (units)	
单产业法人单位 Single-Industry Corperation Units	多产业法人单位 Multi-Industry Corperation Units	合　计 Total	其中：多产业法人所属的产业活动单位 Economic Activities Units under Multi-Industry Corperation Units
306714	21373	409064	102350
304479	21248	405055	100576
48861	7589	98820	49959
14098	706	19020	4922
2727	143	4170	1443
1059	39	1504	445
136	6	186	50
436	19	645	209
109	5	177	68
378	9	496	118
32420	1034	37998	5578
226	49	979	753
32194	985	37019	4825
5262	498	12761	7499
148845	1905	156136	7291
72271	459	73782	1511
15808	173	16340	532
55615	1169	60529	4914
5151	104	5485	334
51207	9334	74646	23439
1079	54	2043	964
445	20	723	278
31	2	36	5
536	27	1002	466
67	5	282	215
1180	71	1987	807
534	37	672	138
37	2	41	4
538	26	1169	631
71	6	105	34
5779	56	7164	1385
4974	110	5429	455
57634	927	60698	3064
2488	191	4147	1659
14539	290	15722	1183
6729	303	9914	3185
6912	134	10142	3230
66744	1902	83878	17134
7609	189	11214	3605
926	407	8771	7845
11140	328	12366	1226
17738	295	19742	2004
10926	317	12650	1724
3682	178	4781	1099
7632	89	8211	579
14444	2474	21377	6933
11026	1150	31401	20375
4349	127	5090	741
51442	11906	76366	24924
1		1	

1－3 续表 continued

(2008)

指 标 名 称	Item	合 计 Total
总 计	Total	293355
一、按登记注册类型分组	**Grouped by Type of Registration**	
内资企业	Inner Funded Enterprises	291165
国有企业	State-owned Enterprises	54899
集体企业	Collective-owned Enterprises	13421
股份合作企业	Share Holding Cooperative Enterprises	2920
联营企业	Joint Funded Enterprises	1030
国有联营企业	State Joint owned Enterprises	134
集体联营企业	Collective Joint-owned Enterprises	433
国有与集体联营企业	State - owned and Collective Joint-owned Enterprises	102
其他联营企业	Other Joint-owned Enterprises	361
有限责任公司	Responsibility Co. Ltd	23789
国有独资公司	State-owned Solely Funded Co.	261
其他有限责任公司	Other Responsibility Co. Ltd	23528
股份有限公司	Share Holding Co.Ltd.	5464
私营企业	Private - owned enterprises	134389
私营独资企业	Private Solely Funded enterprises	70099
私营合伙企业	Private Partnership Enterprises	15683
私营有限责任公司	Private Responsibility Co. Ltd	43848
私营股份有限公司	Private Share Holding Co.Ltd.	4759
其他企业	Others	55253
港、澳、台商投资企业	Hongkong, Macao and Taiwan Funded Enterprises	1060
合资经营企业(港或澳、台资)	Joint Venture with Hongkong, Macao and Taiwan	456
合作经营企业(港或澳、台资)	Cooperate with Hongkong, Macao and Taiwan Funded	31
港、澳、台商独资经营企业	Enterprises Solely Funded by Hongkong, Macao and Taiwan	503
港、澳、台商投资股份有限公司	Share Holding Co.Ltd. With Hongkong, Macao and Taiwan Investment	70
外商投资企业	Foreign Funded Enterprises	1130
中外合资经营企业	Sino - Foreign Joint Funded Enterprises	549
中外合作经营企业	Sino - Foreign Cooperative Funded Enterprises	39
外资企业	Foreign Solely Funded Enterprises	471
外商投资股份有限公司	Foreign Funded Share Holding Co.Ltd.	71
二、按国民经济行业门类分组	**Grouped By Sector**	
农、林、牧、渔业	Farming, Forestry, Animal husbandary and Fishery	24
采矿业	Mining and Quarrying	4862
制造业	Manufacturing	54636
电力、燃气及水的生产和供应业	Power, Gas and Water Production and Supply	2517
建筑业	Construction	12453
交通运输、仓储和邮政业	Transportaation, Storage and Post	6009
信息传输、计算机服务和软件业	Information Trnsmmision, Computer Service and software	6024
批发和零售业	Wholesale and Retail Sale	58526
住宿和餐饮业	Hotel and Catering	7877
金融业	Banking	1074
房地产业	Real Estate	10122
租赁和商务服务业	Leasing and Commerical Service	13630
科学研究、技术服务和地质勘查业	Scietific research, Polytechnical Service and Geological Prospecting	9841
水利、环境和公共设施管理业	Water Conservancy, Environment and Public Facility Management	3760
居民服务和其他服务业	Resident Service and Others	6022
教育	Education	16788
卫生、社会保障和社会福利业	Health Care, Social Security and Social Welfare	12213
文化、体育和娱乐业	Culture, Sports and Recreation	4191
公共管理和社会组织	Public Management and Social Organizations	62786

法人单位数(个) Corporation Units(units)		产业活动单位数(个) Number of Economic Activities Units (units)	
单产业法人单位 Single-Industry Corperation Units	多产业法人单位 Multi-Industry Corperation Units	合　计 Total	其中：多产业法人所属的产业活动单位 Economic Activities Units under Multi-Industry Corperation Units
272667	20688	373013	100346
270584	20581	369780	99196
47484	7415	88285	40801
12744	677	23318	10574
2784	136	4279	1495
996	34	1837	841
128	6	259	131
416	17	938	522
99	3	134	35
353	8	506	153
22877	912	27036	4159
213	48	592	379
22664	864	26444	3780
5018	446	11560	6542
132704	1685	142813	10109
69690	409	74145	4455
15532	151	16445	913
42823	1025	47084	4261
4659	100	5139	480
45977	9276	70652	24675
1009	51	1681	672
437	19	693	256
29	2	42	13
478	25	789	311
65	5	157	92
1074	56	1552	478
520	29	604	84
38	1	42	4
451	20	799	348
65	6	107	42
	24	795	795
4749	113	5254	505
53782	854	56754	2972
2322	195	3929	1607
12262	191	13202	940
5731	278	8881	3150
5896	128	9084	3188
56738	1788	73415	16677
7708	169	11302	3594
682	392	8470	7788
9838	284	10991	1153
13368	262	15275	1907
9568	273	11224	1656
3589	171	4679	1090
5947	75	6482	535
14311	2477	21247	6936
11060	1153	31459	20399
4064	127	4805	741
51052	11734	75765	24713

1-4 国民经济和社会发展总量与速度指标

指 标	单位	Item	unit	总量指标 1978	总量指标 1990
人口与就业		**Population and Employment**			
人口	（万人）	**Population**	**(10 000 persons)**		
年末人口		Population at Year-end		4574.91	5439.29
市镇人口		Urban		690.23	1551.51
乡村人口		Rural		3884.68	3887.78
就业	（万人）	**Employment**			
就业人数		Employment		1910.37	3040.40
职工人数		Staff and Workers		457.34	698.55
#国有单位		State-owned Units		371.56	524.12
本年失业人员就业人数		Unemployed-Reemployees		6.47	17.31
宏观经济		**Marcoeconomy**			
国民核算	（亿元）	**National Accounting**	**(100 million yuan)**		
地区生产总值		Gross Domestic Products		151.00	824.38
第一产业		First Industry		61.11	289.45
第二产业		Second Industry		63.71	313.39
第三产业		Tertiary Industry		26.18	221.54
支出法地区生产总值		Gross Domestic Expenditures			
#最终消费		Final Consumption Expenditures		81.70	535.49
居民消费		Resident Consumption		74.70	434.62
政府消费		Government Consumption Expenditures		7.00	100.87
资本形成总额		Gross Capital Formation		43.11	261.95
固定资本形成		Fixed Capital Formation		31.40	147.13
存货增加		Changes in Stock		11.71	114.82
固定资产投资	（亿元）	**Investment in Fixed Assets**	**(100 million yuan)**		
全社会固定资产投资总额		Total Investment in Fixed Assets		33.58	144.44
#国有单位		State-Owned Units		33.19	100.35
集体单位		Collective-owned Units		0.39	15.59
#房地产开发		Real Estate Development			5.94
财政	（亿元）	**Public Finance**	**(100 million yuan)**		
地方一般预算财政收入		Government Revenue		31.37	77.85
地方财政支出		Local Government Expenditures		29.98	84.82
物价(上年=100)		**Price (prededing year = 100)**			
商品零售价格总指数		General Retail Price Index		100.50	102.90
居民消费价格指数		General consumer Price Index		100.30	104.20
工业品出厂价格指数		Ex-factorty Price Index of Industrial products			109.00
利用外资	（亿美元）	**Utilization of Foreign Capital**	**(100 million dollars)**		
实际外商直接投资		Actual Foreign Direct Investment			0.29
产 业		**Industry**			
农业		**Agriculture**			
乡村从业人员	（万人）	Rural Employment		1525.14	1791.30
农林牧渔业总产值	（亿元）	Gross Output Value of Farming, Forestry, Animal Husbandry and Fishery	(100 million yuan)	84.46	402.23
主要农产品产量	（万吨）	Output of Major Farm Products	(10 000 tons)		
粮食		Grain		1725.63	2475.03
棉花		Cotton		36.67	51.73
油料		Oil-Bearing Crops		23.71	95.75
糖料		Sugar Crops		8.73	34.66
蚕茧		Silkworm Cocoons		0.47	0.79
肉类产量		Output of Meat		64.00	146.85
水产品		Aquatic Products		11.00	70.98

注：1.人口数除1982年、1990年、2000年是以人口普查为基数推算外，1982年及以后为人口抽样调查推算数。

2.2000年以前数据是总人口数，2001年以后数据为常住人口数。

AGGREGATE INDICATORS OF NATIONAL ECONOMIC AND SOCIAL DEVELOPMENT AND THEIR INDICES AND GROWTH RATES

Aggregate Data				速　度　指　标 Indices and Growth Rates								
				2009年比下列各年增长(%) Index (2009 as percentage of the following years)					年平均增长(%) Average Annual Growth Rate			
2000	2005	2008	2009	1978	1990	2000	2005	2008	1979~2009	1991~2009	2001~2009	2006~2009
5950.89	5710.00	5711.00	5720.00	25.0	5.2	-3.9	0.2	0.2	0.7	0.3	-0.4	0.0
2408.49	2466.70	2581.40	2631.20	281.2	69.6	9.2	6.7	1.9	4.4	2.8	1.0	1.6
3542.40	3243.30	3129.60	3088.80	-20.5	-20.6	-12.8	-4.8	-1.3	-0.7	-1.2	-1.5	-1.2
3384.90	3537.00	3607.00	3622.00	89.6	19.1	7.0	2.4	0.4	2.1	0.9	0.8	0.6
677.96	563.93	700.63	680.85	48.9	-2.5	0.4	20.7	-2.8	1.3	-0.1	0.0	4.8
501.11	349.99	296.20	293.12	-21.1	-44.1	-41.5	-16.2	-1.0	-0.8	-3.0	-5.8	-4.3
31.02	51.50	43.49	48.35	647.3	179.3	55.9	-6.1	11.2	6.7	5.6	5.1	-1.6
3545.39	6520.14	11330.38	12961.10	2150.9	661.8	171.3	66.8	13.5	10.6	11.3	11.7	13.7
662.30	1082.13	1780.00	1795.90	321.8	120.9	50.3	22.7	5.2	4.8	4.3	4.6	5.2
1437.38	2810.01	4963.61	6038.08	3796.9	1037.8	217.2	81.7	16.8	12.5	13.7	13.7	16.5
1445.71	2628.00	4586.77	5127.12	4239.2	877.5	185.3	68.9	12.3	12.9	12.7	12.4	13.5
2030.07	3645.71	5829.03	6325.15	1713.9	466.2	151.7	52.7	7.7	9.8	9.6	10.8	11.2
1597.08	2785.42	4225.38	4456.31	1252.3	365.5	125.6	40.4	5.7	8.8	8.4	9.5	8.8
436.00	860.29	1666.65	1868.84	6501.7	956.9	245.6	92.4	12.6	14.5	13.2	14.8	17.8
1882.47	2943.58	5716.36	6827.00	3632.3	1121.9	180.1	100.2	22.3	12.4	14.1	12.1	18.9
1451.85	2804.01	5368.99	6612.85	1915.7	713.5	42.8	-17.3	24.7	10.2	11.7	4.0	-4.6
430.61	139.57	347.37	214.15	194.5	-36.0	-75.9	-18.2	-38.1	3.5	-2.3	-14.6	-4.9
1421.55	2834.75	5798.56	8211.85	24354.6	5585.3	477.7	189.7	41.6	18.6	23.4	18.2	28.6
857.01	1095.71	2237.52	3124.16	9313.0	3013.3	264.5	185.1	39.6	15.0	19.9	11.0	29.3
128.32	79.47	261.45	408.91	104748.7	2522.9	218.7	414.5	56.4	26.1	17.9	4.8	48.0
134.63	447.95	892.67	1200.44		20109.4	791.7	168.0	34.5			26.7	27.1
214.35	375.52	710.24	814.87	2497.6	946.7	280.2	117.0	14.7	11.1	13.2	16.0	21.4
368.77	778.72	1638.03	2090.92	6874.4	2365.1	467.0	168.5	27.6	14.7	18.4	21.3	28.0
97.80	102.10	106.30	98.60	-1.9	-4.2	0.8	-3.4	-7.2				
99.00	102.90	106.30	99.60	-0.7	-4.4	0.6	-3.2	-6.3				
101.70	104.50	106.12	95.55		-12.3	-6.0		-10.0				
9.44	21.85	32.45	36.58		12513.8	287.5	67.4	12.7		29.0	16.2	13.7
1781.70	1931.15	2078.77	2123.29	39.2	18.5	19.2	9.9	2.1	1.1	0.9	2.0	2.4
1125.64	1775.58	2940.47	2985.19	566.4	264.0	109.5	69.8	61.2	6.3	7.0	8.6	14.2
2218.49	2177.38	2227.23	2309.10	33.8	-6.7	4.1	6.0	3.7	0.9	-0.4	0.4	1.5
30.43	37.50	51.34	48.05	31.0	-7.1	57.9	28.1	-6.4	0.9	-0.4	5.2	6.4
269.98	293.90	285.74	314.05	1224.5	228.0	16.3	6.9	9.9	8.7	6.5	1.7	1.7
101.66	42.90	26.47	40.37	362.4	16.5	-60.3	-5.9	52.5	5.1	0.8	-9.8	-1.5
1.22	1.07	1.25	0.61	29.8	-22.8	-50.0	-43.0	-51.2	0.8	-1.4	-7.4	-13.1
271.19	342.63	340.84	367.89	474.8	150.5	35.7	7.4	7.9	5.8	5.0	3.4	1.8
234.34	318.21	313.39	333.90	2935.5	370.4	42.5	4.9	6.5	11.6	8.5	4.0	1.2

Note: 1. Population than in 1982, 1990 and 2000 census as the base is projected, the population in 1982 and beyond as the number of sample projections.

2.2000 before the data on total population, since 2001 data for the resident population.

1-4 续表 1 continued

指 标	单位	Item	unit	总量指标 Aggregate Data 1978	1990
工业		**Industry**			
工业增加值	（亿元）	Added value of Industries	(100 million yuan)		313.24
主要工业产品产量	（万吨）	Output of Major Industrial Products	(10000 tons)		
钢		Steel		307.97	629.25
成品钢材		Rolled-Steel		184.63	533.07
发电量	（亿千瓦小时）	Electricity	(100 million kWh)	91.64	340.39
原煤		Coal		644.01	924.26
农用化肥(折100%)		Chemical Furtilizers		27.62	132.07
化学农药		Chemical Pesicide		2.97	1.07
水泥		Cement		328.65	987.00
化学纤维		Chemical Fiber		0.48	2.48
布	（亿米）	Cloth	(100 million meter)	6.70	14.09
汽车	（万辆）	Moter Vehicles	(10000 Units)	0.80	11.38
建筑业		**Construction**			
建筑业企业职工平均人数	（万人）	Average Number of Employed Persons	(10000 persons)	25.94	41.88
建筑业总产值	（亿元）	Gross Output Value	(100 million yuan)	11.11	49.30
施工房屋面积	（万平方米）	Floor Space of Building Under Construction	(10000 sq.m)	596.00	1684.90
竣工房屋面积	（万平方米）	Floor Space of Building Completed	(10000 sq.m)	297.40	785.90
交通运输		**Transportation**			
货运量	（万吨）	Freight Traffic	(10000 tons)	10199.08	10916.10
#铁路		Railways		3342.00	3901.00
公路		Highways		3382.00	2941.00
水运		Waterways		3096.00	3784.00
客运量	（万人）	Passenger Traffic	(10000 persons)	12009.20	32145.93
#铁路		Railways		2854.00	2107.00
公路		Highways		7429.00	27333.00
水运		Waterways		1722.00	2693.00
港口货物吞吐量	（万吨）	Volume of Freight Handled at Seaports	(10000 tons)		
邮电通信业		**Postal Telecommunication Services**			
邮电业务总量	（亿元）	TotalBusiness Revenue	(100 million yuan)	0.56	4.80
函件	（亿件）	Number of Letters Delivered	(100 million pieces)	1.18	2.39
年末移动电话用户	（万户）	Number of Local Telephone Users	(10000 units)		
国际互联网用户	（万户）	Urban Telephone Users	(10000 units)		
农村电话用户	（万户）	Rural Telephone Users	(10000 units)	4.13	7.07
国内商业		**Domestic Commerce**			
社会消费品零售总额	（亿元）	Total Retail Sales of Consumer Goods	(100 million yuan)	59.84	326.36
对外经济贸易和旅游		**Foreign Trade and Tourism**			
进出口总额	（亿美元）	Total Imports and Exports		1.73	11.90
进口		Imports		0.14	1.18
出口		Exports		1.59	10.72
入境旅游人数	（万人次）	Number of Tourists received	(10000 persons)	1.01	15.57
金融保险	（亿元）	**Banking and Insurance**	(100 million yuan)		
金融机构存款		Deposits of Banking System		42.16	406.56
金融机构贷款		Loans of Banking System		96.78	732.77
国内保险保费收入		Domestic Premium			6.19

总量指标 Aggregate Data				速 度 指 标 Indices and Growth Rates								
				2009年比下列各年增长(%) Index (2006 as percentage of the following years)					年平均增长(%) Average Annual Growth Rate			
2000	2005	2008	2009	1978	1990	2000	2005	2008	1979~2009	1991~2009	2001~2009	2006~2009
1011.78	1847.90	3842.33	4742.23									
895.92	1571.41	2694.81	1958.30	535.9	211.2	118.6	24.6	-27.3	6.1	6.2	9.1	5.7
811.10	1585.85	2962.44	2172.33	1076.6	307.5	167.8	37.0	-26.7	8.3	7.7	11.6	8.2
538.11	1257.19	1794.48	1781.75	1844.3	423.4	231.1	41.7	-0.7	10.0	9.1	14.2	9.1
389.34	478.07	800.11	1063.27	65.1	15.0	173.1	122.4	32.9	1.6	0.7	11.8	22.1
221.11	375.50	634.81	852.58	2986.8	545.6	285.6	127.1	34.3	11.7	10.3	16.2	22.8
5.18	5.03	9.52	10.56	255.6	886.9	103.9	109.9	10.9	4.2	12.8	8.2	20.4
2460.92	4512.53	6178.75	6983.78	2025.0	607.6	183.8	54.8	13.0	10.4	10.8	12.3	11.5
9.82	11.74	11.52	12.08	2416.7	387.1	23.0	2.9	4.9	11.0	8.7	2.3	0.7
17.15	20.89	39.21	38.62	476.4	174.1	125.2	84.9	-1.5	5.8	5.5	9.4	16.6
19.57	46.38	103.2	119.67	14858.8	951.6	511.5	158.0	16.0	17.5	13.2	22.3	26.7
82.76	110.09	137.61	146.02	462.9	248.7	76.4	32.6	6.1	5.7	6.8	6.5	7.3
454.35	1349.32	2710.80	3421.89	30700.1	6841.0	653.1	153.6	26.2	20.3	25.0	25.1	26.2
6256.50	12091.20	18376.5	20499.3	3339.5	1116.6	227.6	69.5	11.6	12.1	14.1	14.1	14.1
3150.10	6896.90	9256.1	10280.7	3356.9	1208.1	226.4	49.1	11.1	12.1	14.5	14.0	10.5
9345.19	49923.52	75777.95	82714	711.0	657.7	785.1	65.7	9.2	7.0	11.2	27.4	13.5
3857.00	8491.00	10202	9839	194.4	152.2	155.1	15.9	-3.6	3.5	5.0	11.0	3.8
2228.00	33481.00	52759	59563	1661.2	1925.3	2573.4	77.9	12.9	9.7	17.2	44.1	15.5
3255.00	7944.00	12681	13305	329.7	251.6	308.8	67.5	4.9	4.8	6.8	16.9	13.8
31593.00	71399.00	89720	96219	701.2	199.3	204.6	34.8	7.2	6.9	5.9	13.2	7.7
3469.00	4615.00	6027	6440	125.6	205.6	85.6	39.5	6.9	2.7	6.1	7.1	8.7
27184.00	66183.00	82532	88703	1094.0	224.5	226.3	34.0	7.5	8.3	6.4	14.0	7.6
679.00	601.00	388	371	-78.5	-86.2	-45.4	-38.3	-4.4	-4.8	-9.9	-6.5	-11.4
4113.46	13992.51	15970.48	16671.77			305.3	19.1	4.4			16.8	4.5
116.60	373.63	715.40	839.18	149753.6	17382.9	619.7	124.6	17.3	26.6	31.2	24.5	22.4
3.62	1.52	1.37	1.45	22.9	-39.3	-59.9	-4.6	5.8	0.7	-2.6	-9.7	-1.2
	1401.00	2528.7	3136.90				123.9	24.1				22.3
	128.00	286.4	361.30				182.3	26.2				29.6
180.00	336.00	401.6	378.0	9052.5	5246.5	110.0	12.5	-5.9	15.7	23.3	8.6	3.0
1789.35	2964.58	5109.73	5928.41	9807.1	1716.5	231.3	100.0	16.0	16.0	16.5	14.2	18.9
32.10	90.92	205.67	172.29	9859.0	1347.8	436.7	89.5	-16.2	16.0	15.1	20.5	17.3
12.79	46.42	89.75	72.50	51685.7	6044.1	466.8	56.2	-19.2	22.3	24.2	21.3	11.8
19.31	44.50	115.92	99.78	6175.5	830.8	416.7	124.2	-13.9	14.3	12.5	20.0	22.4
45.08	82.57	118.75	133.46	13113.9	757.2	196.1	61.6	12.4	17.1	12.0	12.8	12.8
3037.22	8184.96	13439.52	17678.05	41830.9	4248.2	482.0	116.0	31.5	21.5	22.0	21.6	21.2
3147.77	5649.67	8752.41	12057.17	12358.3	1545.4	283.0	113.4	37.8	16.8	15.9	16.1	20.9
60.53	145.08	317.15	372.42		5916.5	515.3	156.7	17.4		24.1	22.4	26.6

1-4 续表 2 continued

指 标	单位	Item	unit	总量指标 Aggregate Data 1978
教育、科技、文化		**Education, Science and Technology and Culture**		
教育		**Education**		
高等学校本专科在校学生	(万人)	Students Enrollment in Institutions of Higher Eductioan	(10 000persons)	4.94
中等专业学校在校学生	(万人)	Students Enrollment in Specialized Secondary Schools	(10 000persons)	5.36
普通中学在校学生	(万人)	Students Enrollment in Regular Secondary Schools	(10 000persons)	372.38
小学在校学生	(万人)	Students Enrollment in Primary Schools	(10 000persons)	765.73
科技		**Science and Technology**		
国有企事业单位各类专业技术人员	(万人)	Scietific and Technological personels	(10 000persons)	22.00
#工程技术人员		Engineering Personel		7.50
文化		**Culture**		
图书出版量	(亿册)	Books Published	(100 million copies)	1.62
杂志出版量	(亿册)	Magazines Issued	(100 million copies)	0.09
报纸出版量	(亿册)	Newspaper Issued	(100 million copies)	1.97
家庭、生活、环境		**Family, People's Lvelihood and Environment**		
家庭		**Family**		
总户数	(万户)	Total Households	(10 000 households)	
城镇居民平均每户家庭人口	(人)	Average Household size in Urban Areas	(person)	4.32
农村居民平均每户家庭人口	(人)	Average Household size in Rural Areas	(person)	6.02
居住		**Housing**		
城镇居民人均住房建筑面积	(平方米)	Per Capita Net Floor Space of Urban Residents	(sq.m)	
农村居民人均住房面积	(平方米)	Per Capita Net Floor Space of Rural Residents	(sq.m)	
生活		**People's Livelihood**		
城镇居民人均可支配收入	(元)	Per Capita Annual Disposbale Income of Urban Residents	(yuan)	325.00
农村居民人均纯收入	(元)	Per Capita Annual Disposbale Income of Rural Residents	(yuan)	110.52
居民储蓄存款余额	(亿元)	Outstanding Amout of Saving Depoists	(100 million yuan)	6.96
工资		**Wages**		
工资总额	(亿元)	Total Wages of Staff and Workers	(100 million yuan)	25.89
职工平均工资	(元)	Average Wages of Staff and Workers	(yuan)	581.00
卫生		**Health Care**		
卫生机构数	(个)	Number of Health Care Organizations	(unit)	5940.00
#医院		Hospitals		1817.00
床位数	(万张)	Number of Hospital Beds	(10 000 units)	11.52
#医院		Hospitals		10.34
卫生技术人员数	(万人)	Number of Medical Technical Personels	(10 000 persons)	14.06
#医生		Doctors		5.82
市政建设		**Urban Civil Construction**		
自来水供水量	(亿立方米)	Volume of Tap Water Supply	(100 million tons)	5.23
公共汽(电)车总数	(辆)	Total Number of Busses (Trolley Busses) and Taxes		1539.00
年末实有道路长度	(公里)	Year-end Length of Paved Roads	(km)	1520.00
绿地面积	(公顷)	Floor Area of Green Zones	(hectare)	4776.00
环境		**Environment**		
污染治理项目本年完成投资	(亿元)	Investment for the Pollusion Treatment projects Completed in this year	(100 million yuan)	
本年施工污染治理项目数	(个)	Number of Pullsion Treatment Items Under Construction in 2006	(unit)	
工业废水排放量	(亿吨)	Volume of Industrial Waste Water Discharged	(100 million tons)	
工业粉尘去除量	(亿吨)	Volume of Industrial Dust Removed	(100 million tons)	

总量指标 Aggregate Data					速度指标 Indices and Growth Rates								
					2009年比下列各年增长(%) Index (2009 as percentage of the following years)					年平均增长(%) Average Annual Growth Rate			
1990	2000	2005	2008	2009	1978	1990	2000	2005	2008	1979~2009	1991~2009	2001~2009	2006~2009
13.04	34.66	101.27	118.49	124.91	2428.5	857.9	260.4	23.3	5.4	11.0	12.6	15.3	5.4
1458.00	27.86	60.60	103.73	104.18	1843.7	-92.9	273.9	71.9	0.4	10.0	-13.0	15.8	14.5
211.56	350.93	446.69	393.44	365.01	-2.0	72.5	4.0	-18.3	-7.2	-0.1	2.9	0.4	-4.9
623.06	667.74	429.19	360.77	359.26	-53.1	-42.3	-46.2	-16.3	-0.4	-2.4	-2.9	-6.7	-4.3
56.10	89.27	82.75	80.42										
24.40	16.50	9.14	7.92										
4.02	2.88	3.46	1.39	2.24	38.3	-44.3	-22.2	-35.3	61.2	1.1	-3.0	-2.8	-10.3
0.73	2.20	1.97	2.29	2.99	3222.2	309.6	35.9	51.8	30.6	12.0	7.7	3.5	11.0
6.24	13.42	19.57	18.80	17.36	781.2	178.2	29.4	-11.3	-7.7	7.3	5.5	2.9	-3.0
		1769.27	1785.92	1791.87				1.3	0.3				0.3
3.47	3.14	2.98	2.96	2.94	-31.9	-15.3	-6.4	-1.3	-0.7	-1.2	-0.9	-0.7	-0.3
4.67	4.11	4.01	4.00	3.99	-33.7	-14.6	-2.9	-0.5	-0.2	-1.3	-0.8	-0.3	-0.1
9.80	13.90	29.92	32.04	32.77		234.4	135.8	9.5	2.3		6.6	10.0	2.3
25.73	30.11	36.05	39.04	40.11		55.9	33.2	11.3	2.7		2.4	3.2	2.7
1427.20	5524.50	8786.00	13153.00	14367.00	4320.6	906.7	160.1	63.5	9.2	13.0	12.9	11.2	13.1
670.80	2268.50	3099.20	4656.38	5035.00	4455.7	650.6	122.0	62.5	8.1	13.1	11.2	9.3	12.9
244.38	1908.80	4465.79	6745.44	8223.41	118052.4	3265.0	330.8	84.1	21.9	25.6	20.3	17.6	16.5
131.24	405.34	653.81	1291.85	1543.21	5860.6	1075.9	280.7	136.0	19.5	14.1	13.9	16.0	23.9
1903.00	7565.00	13330.00	19597.00	23709.00	3980.7	1145.9	213.4	77.9	21.0	12.7	14.2	13.5	15.5
10472.00	11065.00	9459.00	10832.00	10362.00	74.4	-1.1	-6.4	9.5	-4.3	1.8	-0.1	-0.7	2.3
2024.00	2041.00	574.00	592.00	614.00	-66.2	-69.7	-69.9	7.0	3.7	-3.4	-6.1	-12.5	1.7
16.34	14.96	13.96	16.73	18.72	62.5	14.6	25.1	34.1	11.9	1.6	0.7	2.5	7.6
13.16	12.99	9.67	11.32	12.66	22.4	-3.8	-2.5	30.9	11.8	0.7	-0.2	-0.3	7.0
20.92	23.88	21.50	21.72	24.30	72.8	16.2	1.8	13.0	11.9	1.8	0.8	0.2	3.1
8.68	10.30	8.98	8.37	7.99	37.3	-7.9	-22.4	-11.0	-4.5	1.0	-0.4	-2.8	-2.9
23.97	29.83	28.52	29.05	18.68	257.2	-22.1	-37.4	-34.5	-35.7	4.2	-1.3	-5.1	-10.0
3845.00	17621.00	17775.00	19652.00										
5053.00	13096.00	14170.00	16316.00	16279.00	971.0	222.2	24.3	14.9	-0.2	7.9	6.4	2.4	3.5
17480.00	77478.00	56184.00	59576.00	62670.00	1212.2	258.5	-19.1	11.5	5.2	8.7	7.0	-2.3	2.8
1.81	8.52	14.81	16.15	28.13		1454.1	230.2	89.9	74.2		15.5	14.2	17.4
1545.00	851.00	473.00	406.00	318.00		-79.4	-62.6	-32.8	-21.7		-8.0	-10.4	-9.4
16.23	10.67	9.24	9.37	9.13		-43.7	-14.4	-1.2	-2.6		-3.0	-1.7	-0.3
108.00	233.20	378.10	362.12	408.26		278.0	75.1	8.0	12.7		7.2	6.4	1.9

1–5 国民经济和社会发展结构指标
STRUCTURE INDICATORS ON NATIONAL ECONOMIC AND SOCIAL DEVELOPMENT

单位:% (%)

指　标	Item	1978	2000	2005	2008	2009
人口与就业	**Population and Employment**					
人　口	**Population**					
城乡结构	Urban and Rural Structure					
城镇	Urban	14.6	40.2	43.2	45.2	46.0
乡村	Rural	85.4	59.8	56.8	54.8	54.0
性别结构	Sexual Structure					
男	Male	51.3	52.1	51.8	51.8	51.8
女	Female	48.7	47.9	48.2	48.2	48.2
就　业	**Employment**					
产业结构	Industrial Structure					
第一产业	First Industry	77.0	48.0	47.7	47.4	47.0
第二产业	Second Industry	14.1	20.8	20.5	20.2	20.3
第三产业	Tertiary Industry	8.9	31.2	31.8	32.4	32.7
经济类型结构	Structrues by Ownership					
城镇单位从业人员	Staff and Workers Employed in Urban Units					
国有单位	State-Owned	81.2	74.7	62.1	41.5	41.7
城镇集体单位	Collective-Owned	18.8	14.3	8.0	3.6	3.3
其他单位	Others		11.0	29.9	54.9	55.5
宏观经济	**Macroeconomy**					
国民核算	**National Accounting**					
地区生产总值产业结构	Industrial Structure					
第一产业	First Industry	40.5	18.7	16.6	15.7	13.8
第二产业	Second Industry	42.2	40.5	43.1	43.8	46.6
第三产业	Tertiary Industry	17.3	40.8	40.3	40.5	39.6
地区生产总值支出结构	Domestic Expenditures					
最终消费	Total Consumption	54.0	54.0	55.9	49.7	47.8
居民消费	Residents Consumption	49.4	42.4	42.7	36.0	33.7
政府消费	Government Consumption Expenditures	4.6	11.6	13.2	13.7	14.1
资本形成总额	Gross Capital Formation	28.5	50.0	45.1	48.7	51.6
固定资本	Fixed Capital Formation	20.8	38.6	43.0	45.8	49.9
存货增加	Changes in Stock	7.7	11.4	2.1	2.9	1.6
净出口	Net Exports	17.4	-4.0	-1.0	1.6	0.7
投　资	**Investment**					
经济类型结构	Structrues by Ownership					
国有经济	State-Owned	98.8	60.3	38.7	38.6	38.0
集体经济	Collective-Owned	1.2	9.0	2.8	4.5	5.0
其他	Others		30.7	58.5	56.9	57.0
资金来源结构	Structure of Funded Sources					
国家预算资金	State Budgetary Appropriation	77.2	10.0	9.0	9.8	20.9
国内贷款	Domestic Loans	0.4	17.2	16.7	15.4	24.5
利用外资	Foreign Investment		2.0	2.5	1.1	3.5
自筹资金	Fundraising	18.0	54.9	52.7	63.4	45.6
其他投资	Others	4.3	15.9	19.1	10.3	8.7

1-5 续表 1 continued

指 标	Item	1978	2000	2005	2008	2009
财 政	Financial					
地方一般预算支出结构	Local General Budget Expenditure Structure					
#一般公共支出	# General Public Expenditure				16.1	14.8
教育	Education				17.2	15.2
社会保障和就业	Social Security And Employment				17.1	16.5
利用外资	Foreign Investment					
实际外商直接投资结构	Actual Foreign Direct Investment					
合资经营企业	Joint Venture		63.4	40.8	31.3	33.4
合作经营企业	Joint Ventures		3.0	4.8	5.1	5.8
独资经营企业	Sole Proprietorship Business		33.6	34.5	55.8	54.3
外商投资股份制企业	Joint-stock Enterprises With Foreign Investment			0.9	7.8	6.6
产业经济	Industrial Economy					
农 业	Agriculture					
农林牧渔业产值结构	Agricultural Output Value Structure					
农业	Agriculture	77.3	54.7	52.5	47.5	50.6
林业	Forestry	4.9	3.6	2.1	1.7	1.9
牧业	Animal Husbandry	12.8	30.1	30.7	34.3	29.5
渔业	Fisheries	0.8	11.6	13.3	12.7	13.8
农林牧渔服务业	Agriculture Animal Husbandry And Fishery			1.4	3.9	4.1
工 业	Industry					
工业产值按经济类型分	Industrial Output By Type					
#国有企业	# State-owned Enterprises	77.3	35.3	25.3	24.0	22.5
集体企业	Collective Enterprises	22.7	18.4	1.8	1.1	1.0
港澳台商投资企业	Hong Kong, Macao And Taiwan Invested Enterprises		4.2	4.3	4.7	4.6
外商投资企业	Foreign-invested Enterprises		6.8	18.3	18.0	15.2
工业产值按轻重分	Industrial Output Divided By Weight					
轻工业	Light Industry	47.1	38.4	24.8	24.9	27.2
重工业	Heavy Industry	52.9	61.6	75.2	75.1	72.8
建筑业	Building Industry					
建筑业总产值结构	Gross Output Value Structure					
国有经济	State-owned Economy	88.6	58.6	57.6	49.2	47.4
地方	Local	42.8	23.5	19.9	8.9	11.8
部属	Subordinate	45.6	35.1	37.7	40.3	88.2
城镇集体经济	Urban Collective Economy	11.4	27.2	5.2	2.1	2.3
其它经济	Other Economic		14.3	37.3	48.7	50.3
运输业	Transport					
货运量结构	Cargo Structures					
铁路	Railway	32.8	41.3	17.0	13.4	11.9
公路	Highway	33.2	23.8	67.1	69.6	72.0
水运	Water Transport	30.3	34.8	15.9	16.7	16.1

1-5 续表 2 continued

指 标	Item	1978	2000	2005	2008	2009
国内商业	**Domestic Trade**					
社会消费品零售总额结构	Total Retail Sales of Consumer Goods					
#批发零售贸易业	Wholesale and Retail Sale	85.1	61.9	81.5	82.1	82.3
住宿及餐饮业	Hotel and Catering	2.8	10.8	13.1	13.3	13.4
其他	Others	12.1	27.3	5.4	4.6	4.3
对外经济贸易和国际旅游	**Foreign Trade and Tourism**					
进出口总额	Total Imports and Exports					
#出口	Exports	8.1	39.8	51.1	56.4	57.9
进口	Imports	91.9	60.2	48.9	43.6	42.1
海外旅游人数结构	Structure of Tourists					
外国人	Foreigners	47.3	79.3	75.9	78.0	76.2
港澳台同胞	Compatriots from Hongkong, Macao and Taiwan	52.7	20.7	24.1	22.0	23.8
教育、科技、文化	**Education Science and Culture**					
教 育	**Education**					
在校学生结构	Structure of Students Enrollment					
大学生	College and University Students	0.4	3.3	10.4	13.6	14.2
中学生	Secondary School Students	32.6	33.3	45.7	45.1	41.5
小学生	Primary School Students	67.0	63.4	43.9	41.3	40.9
专任教师结构	Full-Time Teacher By Type					
大学	College and Universities	2.9	11.9	17.5	13.9	17.8
中学	Secondary Schools	39.6	38.9	44.5	46.3	38.5
小学	Primary Schools	57.5	49.2	38.0	39.8	30.7
科 技	**Science and Technology**					
各类专业技术人员结构	Structure of Scietific and Technical Personel					
工程技术人员	Engineering Personel	34.2	18.5	11.1		
农业技术人员	Agriculture	5.5	3.4	3.2		
科学研究人员	Scientific Research	6.7	0.6	0.8		
卫生技术人员	Health Care	32.1	20.9	22.8		
教学人员	Teaching	21.5	56.6	62.2		
生活、环境	**People's Livelihood and Environment**					
生 活	**People's Livelihood**					
城镇居民消费结构	Consumption Structutre of Urban Residents					
食品	Food		38.3	39.0	42.2	40.4
衣着	Clothing		11.4	12.0	11.6	11.8
居住	Residence		14.1	10.2	9.6	9.7
其他	Others		36.2	38.8	36.6	38.1
农村居民消费结构	Consumption Structutre of Rural Residents					
食品	Food	70.8	53.2	49.1	46.9	44.8
衣着	Clothing	12.0	4.8	5.1	5.1	5.3
居住	Residence	8.9	11.5	12.8	17.8	18.9
其他	Others	8.3	30.5	33.0	30.2	31.0

1-6　湖北国民经济占全国的比重(2009)
PERCENTAGE OF HUBEI'S NATIONAL ECONOMY IN THE COUNTRY(2009)

指　　标	单位	Item	unit	全　国 Country	湖北 Hubei	湖北占全国的比重(%) Percentage to the Country of Hubei
土地面积	(万平方公里)	Ground space	(10 000 sq.km.)	960.00	18.59	1.9
年末总人口	(万人)	Population	(Year-end)	133474	5720.00	4.3
地区生产总值	(亿元)	Local Gross Production	(100 million yuan)	335352.9	12961.10	3.9
第一产业		First Industry		35477.0	1795.90	5.1
第二产业		Second Industry		156957.9	6038.08	3.8
第三产业		Tertiary Industry		142918.0	5127.12	3.6
人均地区生产总值	(元)	Local Gross Production Per Capita	(yuan)	25188	22677.00	低2511元
全社会固定资产投资	(亿元)	Investment in Fixed Assets	(100 million yuan)	224845.6	8211.85	3.7
#城镇投资		Investment in Cities and Towns		194138.6	7569.15	3.9
#房地产开发		Development of Real Estate		36231.7	1200.44	3.3
地方财政一般预算收入	(亿元)	Government Revenue		68476.88	814.87	1.2
社会消费品零售总额	(亿元)	Total Retail Sales of Social Consumption	(100 million yuan)	132678	5928.41	4.5
进出口总额	(亿美元)	Total Imports and Exports	(100 million dollars)	22072.2	172.29	0.8
#出口		Exports		12016.6	99.78	0.8
实际外商直接投资	(亿美元)	Actual Foreign Direct Investment	(100 million dollars)	900.3	36.58	4.1
普通高等学校本专科在校生	(万人)	Students Enrollment in Institutions of Higher Eductioan	(10 000 persons)	2144.7	124.91	5.8
医院卫生院床位数	(万张)	Number of Hospital Beds	(10 000 units)	441.6	18.72	4.2
卫生技术人员	(万人)	Number of Medical Technical Personnels	(10 000 persons)	539.7	24.30	4.5
#执业(助理)医师		Professional (assisted) Doctors		220.5	1.45	0.7
在岗职工平均工资	(元)	Average Wages of Employed			23709.00	
城镇居民人均可支配收入	(元)	Per Capita Disposable Income of Urban Residents	(yuan)	17174.7	14367.00	低2807.7元
农村居民人均纯收入	(元)	Per Capita Net Incomes of Rural Residents	(yuan)	5153.2	5035.00	低118.2元
居民人均储蓄存款余额	(元)	Deposit Balance Per Capita	(yuan)	19537.00	14388.00	低5149元
工农业主要产品产量	(万吨)	Output of Major Products in Argriculture and industry				
粮食		Grain		53082	2309.10	4.4
棉花		Cotton		637.7	48.05	7.5
油料		Oil-Bearing Crops		3154.3	314.05	10.0
粗钢		Crude steel		56803.29	1958.30	3.4
钢材		Steels		69626.32	2172.33	3.1
原煤		Coal		297300.00	1063.27	0.4
发电量	(亿千瓦小时)	Electricity	(100 million kWh)	37146.5	1781.75	4.8
水泥		Cement		165000.0	6983.78	4.2
农用化肥(折100%)		Chemical Furtilizers		6599.7	852.58	12.9
化学纤维		Chemical Fiber		2730.0	12.08	0.4
布	(亿米)	Cloth	(100 million meter)	740.0	38.62	5.2
汽车	(万辆)	Moter Vehicles	(10 000 units)	1379.5	119.67	8.7

1-7 全省人均国民经济主要指标

MAJOR PER CAPITA INDICATORS OF HUBEI'S NATIONAL ECONOMY

指 标	单位	Item	unit	1990
地区生产总值	(元)	Gross Domestic Product	(yuan)	1541.00
第一产业		First Industry		541.00
第二产业		Second Industry		586.00
第三产业		Tertiary Industry		414.00
地方财政一般预算收入	(元)	Government Revenue	(yuan)	145.54
地方财政支出	(元)	Government Expenditures	(yuan)	158.57
全社会固定资产投资额	(元)	TotaL Investment in Fixed Assets	(yuan)	270.00
社会消费品零售额	(元)	Total Retail Sales of Consumer Goods	(yuan)	610.00
进出口总额	(美元)	Total Imports and Exports	(US.dollars)	22.24
#出口		Exports	(US.dollars)	20.04
农村居民纯收入	(元)	Net Incomes of Rural Residents	(yuan)	671.00
城镇居民可支配收入	(元)	Disposable Income of Urban Residents	(yuan)	1427.00
居民储蓄存款	(元)	Outstanding Amount of Saving Deposits of Urabn And Rural Residents	(yuan)	455.00
在校大学生数	(人/万人)	Number of Students Enrollment in Institutions of Higher Education	(person/10000 persons)	24.38
医院病床数	(张/万人)	Hospital Beds	(bed/10000 persons)	24.50
卫生技术人员数	(人/万人)	Number of Medical Technical Personnels	(person/10000 persons)	39.11
#医 生		Doctors		16.22
主要工农业产品产量	(千克)	Output of Major Industrial and Agricultural Products	(kg)	
粮 食		Grain		467.10
棉 花		Cotton		9.76
油 料		Oil-Bearing Crops		18.07
钢 材		Steel		100.60
原 煤		Coal		174.43
发电量	(千瓦小时)	Electricity	(100 million kWh)	639.62

2000	2005	2006	2007	2008	2009
6293.00	11554.00	13360.00	16386.00	19858.00	22677.00
1164.00	1897.00	2000.00	2419.00	3120.07	3139.69
2525.00	4926.00	5902.00	6964.00	8700.46	10556.08
2540.00	4607.00	5395.00	6822.00	8039.91	8963.50
376.61	658.36	835.01	1036.45	1244.94	1424.60
1647.93	1368.21	1836.36	2205.78	2871.22	3655.45
2498.00	4970.00	6266.00	7960.22	10163.99	14356.38
3144.00	5197.00	5984.00	7072.56	8704.33	10364.35
56.40	159.40	205.88	260.85	360.51	301.21
33.93	78.02	109.78	143.50	203.19	174.44
2268.00	3099.00	3419.00	3997.00	4656.38	5035.00
5524.00	8786.00	9803.00	11485.00	13153.00	14367.00
3209.00	7929.00	8951.00	9534.43	11920.00	14388.00
60.89	177.54	191.58	204.30	207.70	218.37
21.80	23.10	23.50	24.80	27.50	32.73
41.96	37.69	38.23	40.17	41.23	42.49
17.40	14.90	14.90	15.20	15.20	13.97
372.92	382.00	388.00	383.68	390.40	403.69
5.12	6.26	7.87	9.78	9.00	8.40
45.38	51.50	49.10	44.72	50.09	54.90
136.34	278.04	296.35	329.86	519.27	37.98
64.45	83.80	94.90	107.09	140.25	185.89
904.54	2204.00	2273.86	2760.11	3145.00	3114.95

1-8 湖北的一天
ONE DAY IN HUBEI

指标	单位	Item	unit	2000	2005	2007	2008	2009
每天创造的财富		**Daily Production**						
地区生产总值	(亿元)	Gross Domestic Products	(100 million yuan)	9.71	17.86	25.07	31.04	35.51
第一产业		First Industry		1.81	2.96	3.90	4.88	4.92
第二产业		Second Industry		3.94	7.70	11.22	13.60	16.54
第三产业		Tertiary Industry		3.96	7.20	9.95	12.57	14.05
地方财政一般预算收入	(亿元)	Government Revenue	(100 million yuan)	0.59	1.03	1.62	1.95	2.23
粮食	(万吨)	Grain	(10 000 tons)	6.08	5.97	6.27	6.10	6.33
肉类产量	(吨)	Meat	(tons)	7430.00	9387.00	11141.00	9338.08	10055.07
水产品	(吨)	Aquatic Products	(tons)	6420.00	8718.00	10156.00	8586.03	9260.27
钢	(万吨)	Steel	(10 000 tons)	2.45	4.31	4.87	7.38	5.44
成品钢材	(万吨)	Rolled-Steel	(10 000 tons)	2.22	4.34	5.18	8.12	4.88
发电量	(亿千瓦小时)	Electricity	(100 million kWh)	1.47	3.44	4.31	4.92	4.88
水泥	(万吨)	Cement	(10 000 tons)	6.74	12.36	15.24	16.93	19.13
布	(万米)	Cloth	(10 000 meters)	470.00	573.00	846.58	1074.25	1058.08
每天消费量		**Daily Consumption**						
最终消费	(亿元)	Final Consumption	(100 million yuan)	5.56	9.99	13.70	15.97	17.33
居民消费	(亿元)	Resident Consumption	(100 million yuan)	4.37	7.63	10.16	11.58	12.21
城镇居民每人消费性支出	(元)	Per Capita Living Expenditure of Urban Residents	(yuan)	12.72	18.46	23.84	25.97	28.20
#食品消费		Food Consumption		4.88	7.19	9.47	10.95	11.40
农村居民每人生活消费支出	(元)	Per Capita Living Expenditure of Rural Residents	(yuan)	4.26	6.66	8.47	10.01	10.21
#食品消费		Food Consumption		2.27	3.27	4.05	4.69	4.57
政府消费	(亿元)	Government Consumption Expenditure	(100 million yuan)	1.19	2.36	3.53	4.57	5.12
社会消费品零售总额	(亿元)	Total Retail Sales of Consumer Goods	(100 million yuan)	4.90	8.12	11.04	13.60	16.24
每天其他经济活动		**Other Daily Economic Acitivities**						
货物运输量	(万吨)	Freight Traffic	(10 000 tons)	25.60	136.78	160.24	207.61	226.61
旅客运输量	(万人)	Passenger Traffic	(10 000 persons)	86.56	195.61	230.38	245.81	263.61
竣工房屋面积	(万平方米)	Floor Space of Housing Completed	(sq.m)	8.63	18.90	18.09	25.36	26.77
出版报纸	(万份)	Newspapers Published	(10 000 pieces)	367.67	536.16	448.55	515.10	475.62
函件	(万件)	Letters Delivered	(10 000 pieces)	99.00	41.64	34.79	37.56	39.66
进出口总额	(万美元)	Total Imports and Exports	(10 000 US.dollars)	879.45	2490.96	4070.76	5634.79	4720.27
#出口		Exports		529.04	1219.18	2239.39	3175.89	2733.70
实际外商直接投资	(万美元)	Actual Foreign Direct Investment	(10 000 US.dollars)	258.63	598.63	757.87	888.99	1002.10
每天人口变动和婚姻		**Daily Population Changes and Marriages**						
出生人数	(人)	Birhts	(persons)	1582.00	1441.00	1525.75	1533.70	1583.56
死亡人数	(人)	Deaths	(persons)	979.00	940.00	989.59	1082.47	1002.19
结婚对数	(对)	Marriages	(couple)	969.00	1080.00	1329.53	1485.62	1547.95
离婚对数	(对)	Divorces	(couple)	58.00	146.00	180.48	208.23	221.92

1-9　主要年份地区生产总值
GROSS DOMESTIC PRODUCT OF THE MAJOR YEARS

本表按当年价格计算　　(At current price)

年份 Year	地区生产总值(亿元) Total Output (100 million yuan)	第一产业 Primary Industry	第二产业 Secondary Industry	工业 Industry	建筑业 Contruction	第三产业 Tertiary Industry	#金融业 Banking	#房地产业 Real Estate	人均地区生产总值(元) Per Capita GDP (yuan)	人均地区生产总值(美元) Per Capita GDP (yuan)
1952	24.51	13.90	3.83	3.17	0.66	6.78			90.13	34.44
1955	34.05	18.14	7.45	6.25	1.20	8.46			117.88	47.88
1957	48.86	24.33	11.59	9.03	2.56	12.94			162.17	65.87
1962	52.13	29.30	10.63	9.10	1.53	12.20			161.47	65.59
1965	72.43	37.74	21.16	17.36	3.80	13.53			209.26	85.00
1970	88.15	44.41	26.90	21.79	5.11	16.84			221.78	90.09
1975	120.10	53.71	45.48	32.68	12.80	20.91			274.30	139.50
1976	114.64	57.87	34.48	21.33	13.15	22.29			258.35	137.40
1977	131.11	57.52	49.35	39.08	10.27	24.24			291.76	168.65
1978	151.00	61.11	63.71	52.17	11.54	26.18	4.54	1.42	332.03	210.53
1979	188.46	85.15	73.03	58.98	14.05	30.28	5.26	1.62	409.35	273.60
1980	199.38	71.22	91.67	75.63	16.04	36.49	5.51	2.83	427.98	279.67
1981	219.75	87.00	92.85	78.73	14.12	39.90	6.02	3.19	466.32	273.49
1982	241.55	101.73	94.97	82.69	12.28	44.85	6.50	3.10	506.33	267.53
1983	262.58	105.40	106.50	92.19	14.31	50.68	7.09	2.53	543.27	274.98
1984	328.22	126.36	136.50	120.32	16.18	65.36	9.04	3.89	670.97	288.34
1985	396.26	144.44	174.35	152.88	21.47	77.47	10.71	4.61	800.69	272.66
1986	442.04	163.61	187.96	164.93	23.03	90.47	13.68	5.97	881.61	255.33
1987	517.77	183.99	224.53	197.66	26.87	109.25	17.09	7.39	1018.42	273.61
1988	626.52	214.66	271.25	244.17	27.08	140.61	20.82	8.88	1215.93	326.68
1989	717.08	239.07	300.45	276.47	23.99	177.55	28.14	9.18	1373.22	364.72
1990	824.38	289.45	313.39	284.15	29.24	221.54	33.77	11.36	1541.17	322.20
1991	913.38	279.30	359.86	327.50	32.36	274.22	40.30	13.61	1668.03	313.34
1992	1088.39	303.00	444.61	402.59	42.02	340.78	48.07	17.22	1962.45	355.86
1993	1325.83	346.39	537.60	475.44	62.16	441.84	52.22	25.63	2360.53	409.67
1994	1700.92	501.44	657.63	580.80	76.83	541.84	56.83	37.85	2991.33	347.07
1995	2109.38	619.77	780.18	680.92	99.26	709.43	60.86	42.07	3671.41	439.64
1996	2499.77	716.34	923.68	805.53	118.15	859.75	65.37	62.23	4310.98	811.22
1997	2856.47	767.92	1071.86	929.91	141.95	1016.69	69.68	69.65	4883.80	589.13
1998	3114.02	778.22	1199.08	1041.20	157.88	1136.71	74.14	81.78	5287.03	638.60
1999	3229.29	653.99	1314.44	1139.52	174.92	1260.86	78.81	85.01	5452.46	658.65
2000	3545.39	662.30	1437.38	1243.24	194.14	1445.71	81.49	99.40	6293.41	760.22
2001	3880.53	692.17	1574.40	1360.10	214.30	1613.97	88.48	122.49	6866.99	829.65
2002	4212.82	707.00	1709.90	1473.00	236.90	1795.93	96.95	145.17	7436.58	898.46
2003	4757.45	798.35	1956.02	1682.16	273.86	2003.08	107.31	176.80	8378.01	1012.20
2004	5633.24	1020.09	2320.60	1987.50	333.10	2292.55	118.85	204.80	9897.64	1195.83
2005	6590.19	1082.13	2852.12	2478.66	373.46	2655.94	127.32	217.17	11554.00	1410.45
2006	7617.47	1140.41	3365.08	2929.19	435.89	3111.98	174.99	294.73	13360.00	1710.91
2007	9333.40	1378.00	4143.06	3588.00	555.06	3812.34	337.27	409.65	16386.00	2178.55
2008	11328.92	1780.00	5082.07	4391.24	690.84	4466.85	393.05	526.88	19858.00	2859.57
2009	12961.10	1795.90	6038.08	5183.68	854.40	5127.12	479.11	546.11	22677.00	3317.24

1-10 主要年份地区生产总值指数

INDICES OF GROSS DOMESTIC PRODUCT OF THE MAJOR YEARS

按可比价计算，上年=100　　(At comparable price, preceding year = 100)

年份 Year	地区生产总值(%) Total Output (%)	第一产业 Primary Industry	第二产业 Secondary Industry	工业 Industry	建筑业 Contruction	第三产业 Tertiary Industry	#金融业 Banking	#房地产业 Real Estate	人均地区生产总值(元) Per Capita GDP (yuan)
1953	114.0	107.4	129.4	141.0	93.3	122.7			111.6
1955	127.1	135.5	104.9	100.2	139.2	127.1			124.8
1957	107.4	106.4	115.3	109.5	146.0	102.6			104.8
1962	100.9	112.3	84.0	92.7	50.5	94.0			99.0
1965	118.1	111.5	132.5	124.5	196.4	114.9			115.4
1970	126.9	112.2	161.2	151.2	222.0	111.3			123.4
1975	111.4	94.5	139.0	135.2	152.5	116.0			110.0
1976	94.8	107.8	74.4	65.3	103.4	104.0			93.5
1977	115.8	99.1	150.2	185.1	80.1	108.5			114.4
1978	113.5	103.4	128.4	131.9	112.2	107.4			112.2
1979	115.6	118.9	113.1	112.1	118.4	114.4	114.5	112.7	114.2
1980	106.4	86.9	123.5	126.7	107.0	111.0	96.3	160.6	105.1
1981	106.5	113.3	101.5	104.3	87.1	104.9	104.8	108.2	105.3
1982	111.9	115.7	104.7	107.3	88.6	121.6	116.9	105.2	110.6
1983	105.9	99.6	109.9	109.2	115.9	111.5	107.5	80.3	104.6
1984	120.9	114.4	125.0	127.6	106.1	125.2	123.8	149.6	119.5
1985	116.2	108.3	124.7	124.7	124.3	112.4	112.4	112.3	114.8
1986	105.5	103.3	105.2	103.9	116.8	110.2	120.5	122.2	104.1
1987	108.4	103.1	111.3	112.9	99.0	110.7	114.5	113.4	106.9
1988	107.8	94.9	113.7	115.1	101.5	114.3	107.0	105.6	106.4
1989	104.5	105.2	102.1	104.2	81.3	109.3	121.8	93.2	103.1
1990	105.0	107.5	99.0	99.5	92.8	114.8	108.9	109.7	102.5
1991	106.6	95.1	111.1	111.6	106.1	115.4	114.4	114.7	104.2
1992	114.1	108.2	116.6	117.5	107.5	116.9	111.5	117.8	112.6
1993	113.0	105.8	116.7	116.1	123.3	115.3	112.0	119.4	111.6
1994	113.7	107.1	118.8	118.9	117.6	112.4	107.7	127.3	112.3
1995	113.2	108.9	116.1	115.9	118.5	112.7	107.3	121.0	112.0
1996	111.6	104.5	115.5	115.4	116.6	111.3	107.3	116.5	110.5
1997	111.9	106.9	113.4	113.5	112.3	113.5	103.4	110.3	110.9
1998	108.6	99.8	111.2	110.9	113.9	111.5	107.0	117.9	107.9
1999	107.8	101.9	108.2	108.2	107.5	111.0	103.7	106.1	107.2
2000	108.6	102.5	109.1	109.0	110.7	111.5	105.6	116.8	114.2
2001	108.9	102.5	109.9	110.1	108.5	110.8	107.4	122.1	108.5
2002	109.2	102.0	110.1	110.1	110.5	111.4	108.4	114.5	108.9
2003	109.7	105.8	110.2	110.2	110.6	110.8	110.1	119.0	109.5
2004	111.2	106.5	113.6	113.5	114.4	110.6	106.3	114.4	111.0
2005	112.1	104.0	115.2	116.0	109.9	111.8	104.4	103.5	116.7
2006	113.2	105.1	116.0	116.3	115.3	113.5	135.0	129.4	113.2
2007	114.6	104.7	116.7	115.7	123.3	115.9	167.3	132.0	114.7
2008	113.4	106.0	116.6	116.9	114.8	112.4	110.8	115.1	113.2
2009	113.5	105.2	116.8	115.7	123.7	112.3	122.8	111.1	113.3

1-11 主要年份地区生产总值指数

INDICES OF GROSS DOMESTIC PRODUCT OF THE MAJOR YEARS

按可比价计算，1952=100 (At comparable price, 1952 = 100)

年份 Year	地区生产总值(%) Total Output (%)	第一产业 Primary Industry	第二产业 Secondary Industry	工业 Industry	建筑业 Contruction	第三产业 Tertiary Industry	#金融业 Banking	#房地产业 Real Estate	人均地区生产总值(元) Per Capita GDP (yuan)
1953	114.0	107.4	129.4	141.0	93.3	122.7			111.6
1955	121.5	115.8	152.4	168.5	102.2	118.3			114.4
1957	169.6	143.9	280.1	295.3	233.2	172.1			153.0
1962	141.7	130.2	223.9	258.0	116.1	124.2			119.3
1965	205.6	161.5	490.4	538.5	338.9	161.1			161.5
1970	242.6	158.7	705.6	745.9	580.5	202.3			166.0
1975	320.2	185.3	1126.3	1165.1	995.9	259.1			198.9
1976	303.4	199.7	837.8	760.5	1029.9	269.5			185.9
1977	351.4	197.9	1258.5	1407.6	825.1	292.4			212.6
1978	399.0	204.6	1616.5	1857.1	926.0	314.2			238.6
1979	461.3	243.2	1828.2	2082.1	1096.8	359.5	114.5	112.7	272.5
1980	490.8	211.4	2257.6	2637.6	1173.5	398.9	110.3	181.0	286.5
1981	523.0	239.5	2292.0	2751.0	1021.9	418.4	115.6	195.8	301.8
1982	585.4	277.2	2399.3	2950.6	905.2	508.6	135.1	206.0	333.7
1983	620.1	276.1	2637.8	3220.9	1048.9	567.0	145.2	165.4	348.9
1984	749.7	315.9	3297.0	4111.0	1113.2	709.9	179.8	247.5	416.8
1985	871.1	342.0	4111.1	5128.2	1383.1	797.9	202.1	277.9	478.7
1986	919.1	353.1	4326.3	5327.6	1615.8	879.3	243.5	339.6	498.5
1987	996.7	364.1	4816.5	6017.4	1599.1	973.3	278.8	385.1	533.1
1988	1074.3	345.4	5475.9	6925.0	1623.7	1112.1	298.3	406.7	567.0
1989	1122.7	363.3	5592.5	7218.5	1319.6	1215.1	363.4	379.1	584.7
1990	1178.9	390.6	5536.7	7181.9	1224.3	1394.6	395.7	415.8	599.3
1991	1257.2	371.2	6151.9	8018.2	1298.9	1609.6	452.7	477.0	624.3
1992	1434.3	401.6	7175.3	9419.0	1396.0	1881.8	504.7	561.8	703.3
1993	1621.2	424.7	8372.8	10939.2	1720.9	2166.9	565.3	670.8	784.9
1994	1843.3	454.7	9948.0	13008.9	2024.1	2435.8	608.7	854.0	881.6
1995	2086.5	495.2	11547.9	15073.3	2398.9	2740.9	653.4	1033.2	987.5
1996	2327.5	517.4	13342.9	17402.1	2796.6	3050.0	701.2	1204.1	1091.5
1997	2604.6	553.0	15131.7	19753.3	3139.6	3461.5	725.3	1328.7	1211.0
1998	2829.4	549.4	16822.5	21912.2	3576.3	3858.8	776.3	1566.2	1306.3
1999	3048.8	560.1	18195.4	23713.5	3845.1	4285.0	805.2	1661.6	1399.9
2000	3310.6	574.1	19858.1	25847.7	4254.6	4777.6	850.3	1941.2	1598.1
2001	3604.0	588.5	21828.1	28458.3	4618.0	5291.6	913.2	2370.0	1734.3
2002	3936.2	600.2	24038.5	31332.6	5104.3	5892.2	990.1	2713.0	1889.5
2003	4318.6	634.9	26494.8	34517.7	5643.2	6525.7	1090.1	3229.7	2068.1
2004	4802.5	676.2	30099.5	39171.3	6456.0	7218.6	1158.5	3696.0	2294.6
2005	5383.6	703.2	34674.7	45438.7	7095.2	8070.4	1209.5	3825.4	2677.8
2006	6094.2	739.1	40222.6	52845.2	8180.7	9159.9	1632.8	4948.5	3031.3
2007	6984.0	773.8	46939.8	61141.9	10086.8	10616.3	2731.6	6532.1	3476.9
2008	7919.8	820.3	54731.8	71474.9	11579.7	11932.8	3026.7	7518.4	3935.8
2009	8989.0	862.9	63926.7	82696.4	14324.1	13400.5	3716.7	8353.0	4459.3

注：金融业、房地产业指数以1978年为100。

Notes:the indices of banking and real estate are 1978=100

1-12 主要年份地区生产总值构成

COMPOSITION OF GROSS DOMESTIC PRODUCT OF THE MAJOR YEARS

本表按当年价格计算 (At cuurent prices)

年 份 Year	地区生产总值 (%) Total Output (%)	第一产业 Primary Industry	第二产业 Secondary Industry	工业 Industry	建筑业 Contruction	第三产业 Tertiary Industry	#金融业 Banking	#房地产业 Real Estate
1952	100	56.7	15.6	12.9	2.7	27.7		
1955	100	.53.3	21.9	18.4	3.5	24.8		
1957	100	49.8	23.7	18.5	5.2	26.5		
1962	100	56.2	20.4	17.5	2.9	23.4		
1965	100	52.1	29.2	24.0	5.2	18.7		
1970	100	50.4	30.5	24.7	5.8	19.1		
1975	100	44.7	37.9	27.2	10.7	17.4		
1976	100	50.5	30.1	18.6	11.5	19.4		
1977	100	43.9	37.6	29.8	7.8	18.5		
1978	100	40.5	42.2	34.5	7.6	17.3	3.0	0.9
1979	100	45.2	38.8	31.3	7.5	16.1	2.8	0.9
1980	100	35.7	46.0	37.9	8.0	18.3	2.8	1.4
1981	100	39.6	42.3	35.8	6.4	18.2	2.7	1.5
1982	100	42.1	39.3	34.2	5.1	18.6	2.7	1.3
1983	100	40.1	40.6	35.1	5.4	19.3	2.7	1.0
1984	100	38.5	41.6	36.7	4.9	19.9	2.8	1.2
1985	100	36.5	44.0	38.6	5.4	19.6	2.7	1.2
1986	100	37.0	42.5	37.3	5.2	20.5	3.1	1.4
1987	100	35.5	43.4	38.2	5.2	21.1	3.3	1.4
1988	100	34.3	43.3	39.0	4.3	22.4	3.3	1.4
1989	100	33.3	41.9	38.6	3.3	24.8	3.9	1.3
1990	100	35.1	38.0	34.5	3.5	26.9	4.1	1.4
1991	100	30.6	39.4	35.9	3.5	30.0	4.4	1.5
1992	100	27.8	40.9	37.0	3.9	31.3	4.4	1.6
1993	100	26.1	40.5	35.9	4.7	33.3	3.9	1.9
1994	100	29.5	38.7	34.1	4.5	31.9	3.3	2.2
1995	100	29.4	37.0	32.3	4.7	33.6	2.9	2.0
1996	100	28.7	37.0	32.2	4.7	34.4	2.6	2.5
1997	100	26.9	37.5	32.6	5.0	35.6	2.4	2.4
1998	100	25.0	38.5	33.4	5.1	36.5	2.4	2.6
1999	100	20.3	40.7	35.3	5.4	39.0	2.4	2.6
2000	100	18.7	40.5	35.1	5.5	40.8	2.3	2.8
2001	100	17.8	40.6	35.0	5.5	41.6	2.3	3.2
2002	100	16.8	40.6	35.0	5.6	42.6	2.3	3.4
2003	100	16.8	41.1	35.4	5.8	42.1	2.3	3.7
2004	100	18.1	41.2	35.3	5.9	40.7	2.1	3.6
2005	100	16.4	43.3	37.6	5.7	40.3	1.9	3.3
2006	100	15.0	44.2	38.5	5.7	40.8	2.3	3.9
2007	100	14.8	44.4	38.4	6.0	40.8	3.6	4.4
2008	100	15.7	44.9	38.8	6.1	39.4	3.5	4.7
2009	100	13.8	46.6	40.0	6.6	39.6	3.7	4.2

1-13 按支出法计算的地区生产总值

GROSS DOMESTIC PRODUCT BY EXPENDITURE APPROACH

本表按当年价格计算 (At current prices)

年份 Year	地区生产总值(亿元) Gross Domestic Product (100 million yuan)	最终消费 Final Consumption Expenditure	居民消费 Residents Consumption Expenditure	政府消费 Government Consumption Expenditure	资本形成总额 Gross Capital Formation	固定资本形成 Fixed Capital Formation	存货增加 Changes in Inventories	货物和服务净出口 Net Export of Goods and Services
1978	151.20	81.70	74.70	7.00	43.12	31.40	11.72	26.38
1980	200.19	107.79	93.51	14.28	40.10	33.19	6.91	52.30
1985	386.76	240.02	203.23	36.79	135.43	96.71	38.72	11.31
1989	718.07	478.66	398.09	80.57	201.39	115.50	85.89	38.02
1990	818.89	535.49	434.62	100.87	261.95	147.13	114.82	21.45
1991	913.22	597.42	475.85	121.57	281.92	176.32	105.60	33.88
1992	1089.68	689.93	546.61	143.32	355.46	235.63	119.83	44.29
1993	1423.92	876.16	694.49	181.67	512.31	377.95	134.36	35.45
1994	1858.89	1043.25	845.14	198.10	740.13	571.68	168.45	75.51
1995	2364.45	1305.21	1095.97	209.20	973.63	778.25	195.38	85.61
1996	2720.28	1599.74	1346.76	253.00	1191.75	985.03	206.72	-71.21
1997	3107.91	1720.23	1438.12	282.10	1466.81	1102.10	364.71	-79.13
1998	3344.45	1859.97	1518.92	341.10	1614.60	1238.90	375.70	-130.12
1999	3504.01	1887.86	1507.12	380.70	1754.79	1320.10	434.69	-138.64
2000	3760.48	2030.07	1594.08	436.00	1882.47	1451.85	430.62	-152.06
2001	4102.08	2262.67	1767.38	495.30	1884.57	1610.93	273.64	-45.16
2002	4416.88	2499.95	1951.54	548.41	1905.92	1699.78	206.14	11.01
2003	4910.53	2819.24	2188.05	631.20	2037.19	1875.78	161.41	54.10
2004	5633.30	3174.18	2452.62	721.56	2538.77	2325.87	212.90	-79.65
2005	6520.14	3645.71	2785.42	860.29	2943.58	2804.01	139.57	-69.15
2006	7972.33	4245.68	3124.37	1121.31	3634.13	3555.21	78.92	92.52
2007	9550.04	4999.66	3709.69	1289.97	4450.25	4371.14	79.11	100.13
2008	11728.64	5829.03	4225.38	1666.65	5716.36	5368.99	347.37	120.25
2009	13240.42	6325.15	4456.31	1868.84	6827.00	6612.85	214.15	88.27

1-14 按产业分资本形成总额

TOTAL CAPITAL BY TYPE OF INDUSTRY

单位：亿元　　　　本表按当年价格计算

年 份 Year	资本形成总额 Gross Capital Formation	固定资本形成 Fixed Capital Formation	存货增加 Changes in Inventories	第一产业Primary Industry 资本形成总额 Gross Capital Formation	固定资本形成 Fixed Capital Formation	存货增加 Changes in Inventories
1978	43.12	31.40	11.72			
1980	40.10	33.19	6.91			
1985	135.43	96.71	38.72			
1989	201.39	115.50	85.89			
1990	261.95	147.13	114.82			
1991	281.92	176.32	105.60			
1992	355.46	235.63	119.83			
1993	512.31	377.95	134.36			
1994	740.13	571.68	168.45			
1995	973.63	778.25	195.38			
1996	1191.75	985.03	206.72			
1997	1466.81	1102.10	364.71			
1998	1614.60	1238.90	375.70			
1999	1754.79	1320.10	434.69			
2000	1882.47	1451.85	430.62			
2001	1884.57	1610.93	273.64			
2002	1905.92	1699.78	206.14			
2003	2037.19	1875.78	161.41			
2004	2538.77	2325.87	212.90	77.41	78.12	-0.71
2005	2943.58	2804.01	139.57	88.23	93.34	-5.11
2006	3634.13	3555.21	78.92	88.43	107.96	-19.53
2007	4450.25	4371.14	79.11	150.61	149.40	1.21
2008	5716.36	5368.99	347.37	232.56	231.25	1.31
2009	6827.00	6612.85	214.15	282.96	281.59	1.37

(At current price, 100 milliom yuan)

第二产业Secondary Industry			第三产业Tertiary Industry		
资本形成总额 Gross Capital Formation	固定资本形成 Fixed Capital Formation	存货增加 Changes in Inventories	资本形成总额 Gross Capital Formation	固定资本形成 Fixed Capital Formation	存货增加 Changes in Inventories
1106.20	909.79	196.41	1355.16	1337.96	17.20
1188.10	1083.42	104.68	1667.25	1627.25	40.00
1467.11	1327.12	139.99	2078.59	2120.13	-41.54
1811.89	1710.59	101.30	2487.75	2511.15	-23.40
2637.49	2344.35	293.14	2846.31	2793.39	52.92
3064.28	2831.14	233.14	3479.76	3500.12	-20.36

1-15 按支出法计算的地区生产总值指数
INDICES OF GROSS DOMESTIC PRODUCT BY EXPENDITURE APPROACH

按可比价计算 1952=100 (At comparable price, 1952 = 100)

年份 Year	地区生产总值 (%) Gross Domestic Product (%)	最终消费 Final Consumption Expenditure	居民消费 Residents Consumption Expenditure	政府消费 Government Consumption Expenditure	资本形成总额 Gross Capital Formation	固定资本形成 Fixed Capital Formation	存货增加 Changes in Inventories
1952	100.0	100.0	100.0	100.0	100.0	100.0	100.0
1978	488.3	313.7	308.9	369.3	820.0	1396.6	388.5
1980	605.4	388.8	363.4	706.7	663.9	1270.1	209.7
1985	1007.5	736.7	674.8	1492.5	1962.9	3155.5	1067.1
1989	1287.3	969.0	861.3	2284.1	2195.3	3234.3	1416.9
1990	1337.5	1004.9	897.4	2307.0	2504.8	3460.7	1786.7
1991	1344.2	970.7	850.8	2403.9	2595.0	3955.5	1604.4
1992	1471.9	1023.1	870.3	2819.7	2979.1	4806.0	1670.2
1993	1764.8	1242.1	1045.3	3550.0	3598.7	6218.9	1747.0
1994	2075.4	1379.9	1174.9	3802.1	4530.8	8246.3	1920.0
1995	2339.0	1508.3	1302.9	3950.4	5432.4	9945.0	2261.8
1996	2619.7	1702.8	1467.1	4507.4	6475.4	12520.8	2257.2
1997	2902.6	1776.1	1541.9	4584.0	8120.2	14486.6	3634.1
1998	3140.6	1985.6	1697.7	5418.3	9257.0	16775.4	3961.2
1999	3357.3	2130.6	1765.6	6431.5	10099.4	17966.5	4543.5
2000	3629.3	2260.5	1852.1	7055.4	10927.6	19709.2	4738.9
2001	3930.5	2513.7	2042.9	8057.2	10807.4	21542.2	3028.2
2002	4276.4	2795.3	2281.9	8814.6	11099.2	23093.2	2313.5
2003	4618.5	3072.0	2494.1	9890.0	11443.2	24594.3	1753.6
2004	5052.7	3336.2	2683.6	11086.7	13422.9	28775.3	2121.9
2005	5709.6	3726.5	2976.1	12672.1	15288.7	34041.2	1398.3
2006	6531.8	4326.5	3318.4	16600.0	18315.8	42245.1	465.6
2007	7446.3	4785.1	3680.1	18226.8	21667.6	20102.7	450.2
2008	8399.4	5282.8	3952.4	21653.4	25026.1	22575.3	1848.5
2009	9356.9	5689.6	4177.7	24381.7	30606.9	28151.4	1144.2

1-16　三次产业贡献率

PULLING RATE OF THE THREE INDUSTRIES

单位：%　　本表按可比价格计算　　(At comparable price,%)

年　份 Year	地区生产总值 Gross Domestic Product	第一产业 Primary Industry	第二产业 Second Industry	#工　业 Industry	第三产业 Tertiary Industry
1990	100	42.68	-9.84	-4.64	67.16
1991	100	-25.9	65.6	62.7	60.3
1992	100	18.0	48.2	46.4	33.8
1993	100	13.0	53.5	47.7	33.5
1994	100	14.2	59.2	54.7	26.6
1995	100	17.5	54.9	49.8	27.6
1996	100	9.6	62.2	56.7	28.2
1997	100	13.5	53.9	49.8	32.6
1998	100	-1.6	62.8	56.4	38.8
1999	100	5.1	52.2	48.2	42.7
2000	100	5.6	53.0	47.9	41.3
2001	100	5.3	45.2	40.0	49.5
2002	100	3.8	45.1	38.9	51.1
2003	100	9.8	43.4	37.4	46.8
2004	100	9.2	50.4	43.2	40.5
2005	100	6.5	53.5	48.8	40.0
2006	100	6.3	52.4	46.6	41.3
2007	100	4.9	50.9	41.8	44.2
2008	100	6.2	56.0	49.2	37.8
2009	100	5.1	57.9	47.0	37.0

注：产业贡献率指各产业增加值增量与GDP增量之比。

Notes: Industrial contributing rate refers to the ratio of value added of three industries with added value of GDP.

1–17 三次产业拉动率
PULLING RATE OF THE THREE INDUSTRIES

单位：% 本表按可比价格计算 (At comparable price,%)

年 份 Year	地区生产总值 Gross Domestic Product	第一产业 Primary Industry	第二产业 Second Industry	#工 业 Industry	第三产业 Tertiary Industry
1990	5.00	2.1	-0.5	-0.2	3.4
1991	6.6	-1.7	4.3	4.1	4.0
1992	14.1	2.5	6.8	6.5	4.8
1993	13.0	1.7	7.0	6.2	4.4
1994	13.7	1.9	8.1	7.5	3.6
1995	13.2	2.3	7.3	6.6	3.6
1996	11.6	1.1	7.2	6.6	3.3
1997	11.9	1.6	6.4	5.9	3.9
1998	8.6	-0.1	5.4	4.8	3.3
1999	7.8	0.4	4.1	3.8	3.3
2000	8.6	0.5	4.6	4.1	3.6
2001	8.6	0.5	3.9	3.4	4.3
2002	9.2	0.4	4.1	3.6	4.7
2003	9.7	0.9	4.2	3.6	4.5
2004	11.2	1.0	5.6	4.8	4.5
2005	12.1	0.8	6.5	5.9	4.8
2006	13.2	0.8	6.9	6.1	5.5
2007	14.6	0.7	7.4	6.1	6.5
2008	13.4	0.8	7.5	6.6	5.1
2009	13.5	0.7	7.8	6.3	5.0

注：产业拉动率指GDP增长速度与各产业贡献率之乘积。

Notes: Industrial Pulling Rate refers to the products of growwth rate of GDP with Industrial Contributing Rate.

1-18　市、州生产总值(2009)

GROSS DOMESTIC PRODUCT OF CITIES AND PREFECTURES(2009)

单位:亿元　　(100 million yuan)

地　区	Regions	地区生产总值 Gross Domestic Product	第一产业 Primary Industry	第二产业 Secondary Industry	第三产业 Tertiary Industry
武　汉	Wuhan	4620.18	149.06	2142.14	2328.98
黄　石	Huangshi	571.59	45.26	314.12	212.21
十　堰	Shiyan	550.96	66.51	254.76	229.69
宜　昌	Yichang	1272.33	150.70	705.00	416.63
襄　樊	Xiangfan	1201.01	200.21	575.32	425.48
鄂　州	Ezhou	323.71	43.98	179.21	100.52
荆　门	Jingmen	600.10	134.54	265.24	200.32
孝　感	Xiaogan	672.88	145.17	292.20	235.51
荆　州	Jingzhou	709.58	207.22	254.09	248.27
黄　冈	Huanggang	730.19	215.39	273.46	241.33
咸　宁	Xianning	418.45	87.02	179.18	152.24
随　州	Suizhou	341.91	74.91	150.38	116.62
恩施州	Enshi Prefecture	294.26	96.01	79.05	119.20
仙　桃	Xiantao	242.55	47.50	115.57	79.48
潜　江	Qianjiang	234.01	41.19	121.09	71.73
天　门	Tianmen	186.86	47.96	85.58	53.32
神农架	Shennongjia	10.29	1.29	3.95	5.05

1-19　市、州生产总值指数(2009)

INDICES OF GROSS DOMESTIC PRODUCT OF CITIES AND PREFECTURES(2009)

(上年=100,单位:%)　　(preceding year = 100,%)

地　区	Regions	地区生产总值 Gross Domestic Product	第一产业 Primary Industry	第二产业 Secondary Industry	第三产业 Tertiary Industry
武　汉	Wuhan	113.7	101.6	116.0	112.2
黄　石	Huangshi	111.6	103.3	111.4	113.5
十　堰	Shiyan	110.7	106.3	106.8	116.3
宜　昌	Yichang	114.6	105.0	119.0	111.3
襄　樊	Xiangfan	114.6	105.5	117.2	115.8
鄂　州	Ezhou	115.8	106.4	121.5	110.6
荆　门	Jingmen	114.0	106.4	120.5	111.8
孝　感	Xiaogan	114.7	105.0	119.6	115.4
荆　州	Jingzhou	112.6	108.4	116.8	112.0
黄　冈	Huanggang	115.0	107.1	120.0	116.8
咸　宁	Xianning	116.1	102.1	120.1	120.1
随　州	Suizhou	114.0	105.7	114.5	119.7
恩施州	Enshi Prefecture	111.5	104.5	119.3	113.8
仙　桃	Xiantao	115.4	105.0	118.4	117.9
潜　江	Qianjiang	115.3	104.5	119.2	114.3
天　门	Tianmen	114.6	102.1	123.1	113.8
神农架	Shennongjia	108.0	101.1	111.0	108.0

1-20 市、州支出法生产总值(2009)
GROSS DOMESTIC PRODUCT BY EXPENDITURE APPROACH OF CITIES AND PREFECTURES(2009)

单位:亿元 (100 million yuan)

地区	Regions	支出法生产总值 Total Gross Domestic Product by Expenditure	最终消费支出 Final Consumption Expenditure	资本形成总额 Gross Capital Formation	货物和服务净流出 Net Export of Goods and Services
武汉	Wuhan	4623.44	2210.85	3059.15	-646.56
黄石	Huangshi	569.86	295.41	262.33	12.12
十堰	Shiyan	501.86	240.27	221.23	40.36
宜昌	Yichang	1235.44	506.69	693.38	35.37
襄樊	Xiangfan	1143.32	604.20	519.97	19.15
鄂州	Ezhou	323.75	97.35	200.21	26.19
荆门	Jingmen	600.10	294.77	294.58	10.75
孝感	Xiaogan	676.67	262.95	402.72	11.00
荆州	Jingzhou	707.81	401.30	446.09	-139.58
黄冈	Huanggang	730.19	443.26	559.20	-272.27
咸宁	Xianning	418.45	185.46	322.93	-89.94
随州	Suizhou	341.57	182.23	116.20	43.14
恩施州	Enshi Prefecture	294.26	237.31	189.35	-132.40
仙桃	Xiantao	242.56	85.54	130.23	26.79
潜江	Qianjiang	236.06	85.80	145.81	4.45
天门	Tianmen	186.17	96.50	67.27	22.40
神农架	Shennongjia	10.33	5.09	5.94	-0.70

1-21　市、州民营经济增加值

VALUE-ADDED OF PRIVATE ECONOMY IN CITIES AND PREFECTURES

地　区　Regions	增加值(亿元)Value-Added (100 million yuan)		占GDP比重(%) Percentage	
	2008	2009	2008	2009
全　省　Total	**5252.73**	**6174.09**	**46.9**	**47.6**
武汉市　Wuhan	1484.83	1756.44	37.5	38.0
黄石市　Huangshi	322.09	307.57	57.9	53.8
十堰市　Shiyan	230.16	268.52	47.2	48.7
宜昌市　Yichang	588.47	735.40	57.3	57.8
襄樊市　Xiangfan	384.40	495.60	38.3	41.3
鄂州市　Ezhou	135.55	178.45	50.2	55.1
荆门市　Jingmen	253.99	293.24	48.8	48.9
孝感市　Xiaogan	336.24	394.72	56.7	58.7
荆州市　Jingzhou	251.01	292.58	40.2	41.2
黄冈市　Huanggang	338.08	437.89	56.3	60.0
咸宁市　Xianning	220.76	265.36	61.5	63.4
随州市　Suizhou	181.78	216.24	58.6	63.2
恩施州　Enshi Prefecture	89.95	98.18	36.1	33.4
仙桃市　Xiantao	164.87	159.07	70.6	65.6
潜江市　Qianjiang	152.33	152.63	71.9	65.2
天门市　Tianmen	115.83	118.71	61.9	63.5
神农架　Shennongjia	2.39	3.49	30.0	34.0

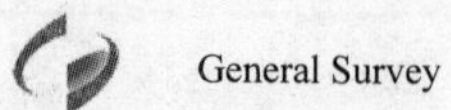

1-22 2007年湖北省42个部门投入产出表

单位：万元

	产 出Output / 投 入Input		中间使用 Intermediate Use 农林牧渔业 Agriculture Animal Husbandry and Fishery	煤炭开采和洗选业 Coal Mining and Dressing
中间投入	农林牧渔业	Agriculture Animal Husbandry and Fishery	4356296.00	22004.01
	煤炭开采和洗选业	Coal Mining and Dressing	13447.61	24320.07
	石油和天然气开采业	Oil and Natural Gas	15603.86	
	金属矿采选业	Metals Mining and Dressing	2330.44	
	非金属矿及其他矿采选业	Non-metallic Minerals and Other Mining and Dressing	69007.63	156.86
	食品制造及烟草加工业	Food manufacturing and tobacco processing industry	825650.08	1464.05
	纺织业	Textile	13632.55	674.24
	纺织服装鞋帽皮革羽绒及其制品业	Textile, leather and feather products industry	16273.91	1089.33
	木材加工及家具制造业	Wood processing and furniture manufacturing	33699.80	88.70
	造纸印刷及文教体育用品制造业	Paper Printing and Educational and Sports Goods	10943.56	378.98
	石油加工、炼焦及核燃料加工业	Petroleum processing, coking and nuclear fuel processing industry	238199.08	6447.69
	化学工业	Chemical Industry	2500160.10	4457.27
	非金属矿物制品业	Non-metallic mineral products industry	76068.21	1907.91
	金属冶炼及压延加工业	Metal smelting and rolling processing industry	336.61	4311.64
	金属制品业	Fabricated metal products	86767.09	546.95
	通用、专用设备制造业	General, special equipment manufacturing industry	120403.44	11723.41
	交通运输设备制造业	Transport Equipment	11886.90	945.56
	电气机械及器材制造业	Electrical Machinery and Equipment	27088.60	1319.24
	通信设备、计算机及其他电子设备制造业	Communications equipment, computers and other electronic equipment manufacturing	6624.01	529.10
	仪器仪表及文化办公用机械制造业	Measuring Instruments and Office Machinery	3055.60	143.67
	工艺品及其他制造业	Artwork and Other Manufacturing	323.50	516.88
	废品废料	Waste waste		128.14
	电力、热力的生产和供应业	Electicity, Gas and Water Production and Supply	249897.63	6100.41
	燃气生产和供应业	Gas Production and Supply	30.60	24.62
	水的生产和供应业	Water Production and Supply	31199.97	5067.64
	建筑业	Building industry	32422.84	35.57
	交通运输及仓储业	Transport and Storage	56842.34	11959.16
	邮政业	Post	2744.41	686.52
	信息传输、计算机服务和软件业	Information transmission, computer services and software	8671.85	1762.32
	批发和零售业	Wholesale and retail trade	124704.30	9061.43
	住宿和餐饮业	Accommodation and Catering Services	24758.09	8962.90
	金融业	Financial sector	89148.20	4202.84
	房地产业	Real Estate		3729.80
	租赁和商务服务业	Leasing and Business Services	7437.04	1917.53
	研究与试验发展业	Research and Experimental Development Industry	251.79	
	综合技术服务业	Integrated Technology Services	13474.30	330.83
	水利、环境和公共设施管理业	Water, Environment and Public Facilities	22443.89	74.62
	居民服务和其他服务业	Resident Services and Other Services	11344.06	578.52
	教育	Education	6396.20	255.18
	卫生、社会保障和社会福利业	Health, Social Security and Social Welfare	10212.69	747.56
	文化、体育和娱乐业	Culture, Sports and Entertainment	4529.43	1255.17
	公共管理和社会组织	Public Management and Social Organization	64091.79	
	中间投入合计	Total intermediate inputs Compensation of Employees	**9188400.00**	**139906.32**
增加值	劳动者报酬	Net Taxes on Production	9579141.68	16577.39
	生产税净额	Depreciation of fixed assets	1136.87	9068.49
	固定资产折旧	Operating Surplus	1357505.48	20718.76
	营业盈余	Total Value	2842215.98	63024.59
	增加值合计	Total investment	**13780000.00**	**109389.23**
	总投入		**22968400.00**	**249295.55**

HUBEI 42 DEPARTMENT INPUT-OUTPUT TABLE IN 2007

(100 million yuan)

中间使用 Intermediate Use					
石油和天然气开采业 Oil and Natural Gas	金属矿采选业 Metals Mining and Dressing	非金属矿及其他矿采选业 Non-metallic Minerals and Other Mining and Dressing	食品制造及烟草加工业 Food manufacturing and tobacco processing industry	纺织业 Textile	纺织服装鞋帽皮革羽绒及其制品业 Textile, leather and feather products industry
	3522.94		6582218.09	727982.76	477793.66
2.34	4064.52	1872.74	21969.05	11475.88	3407.01
			2719.14	67.10	30.32
	22608.23	27.12			
10231.77	174.59	211390.79	9835.39	287.65	450.05
6.71	39.07	29694.92	2275450.36	148196.93	89878.24
10452.22	1706.50	35438.31	38471.55	2839917.92	1577093.41
115.71	7789.09	5285.04	29291.87	119640.12	680020.64
10.40	11583.65	7695.53	5553.66	35593.91	1376.65
72.50	22535.41	44394.07	515225.40	256546.69	147228.68
12958.43	27528.49	64257.45	147104.23	58456.93	68673.64
1078.85	42350.76	160779.80	367131.20	458797.73	81493.54
49.97	141203.12	19172.78	59947.80	15062.07	207.59
1427.24	21299.49	45711.41	37911.42	12250.31	5851.79
4.60	73583.52	341203.05	117107.31	11914.54	7391.33
150.99	64999.98	4081.06	22877.73	33953.99	3419.37
237.49	2845.88	6313.39	11595.69	2076.79	1310.87
1123.74	2018.31	2941.60	25318.21	92668.15	28328.52
27.42	718.16	2874.98	3270.41	3138.02	7191.46
368.49	3649.59	2710.88	14125.89	3719.93	3706.09
22.08	767.26	178.32	6561.39	2751.77	32183.89
9.21	178.16	24.62	507.50		697.70
10829.27	52998.12	59104.43	244717.94	213804.21	79415.02
6.05	1.32		3480.92	3100.15	395.72
213.90	1471.19	8285.26	54704.11	29261.13	13932.01
275.30	5590.83	17754.97	4779.61	1087.51	104.82
3201.28	30114.15	85332.34	203011.60	172045.66	26862.48
226.40	327.94	487.06	3557.00	11828.37	1359.46
1181.67	2609.79	1966.26	27533.26	7568.78	8762.25
1458.83	705.62	906.83	479412.12	156585.90	102141.13
2180.76	13749.08	6245.44	98398.63	6850.00	3554.23
12149.40	28006.10	19839.57	128578.00	43191.69	45840.42
134.21	1210.83	2098.73	171189.07	71175.96	128717.63
182.50	1194.45	1652.49	109525.37	68141.47	64158.04
25.10	40.21	232.13	1703.28	3401.83	623.44
146.38	5621.84	43754.61	109039.30	42281.35	3764.09
64.29	20.99	401.28	293.85	322.93	35.40
5234.92	240.77	33181.64	192482.16	6257.82	98258.72
519.47	46.02	2785.66	3032.53	413.80	82.60
10139.54	26554.68	2890.50	118228.65	999.44	43.27
464.28	783.14	1624.14	2914.82	2189.12	790.05
86983.71	**626453.74**	**1274591.15**	**12250775.49**	**5675006.29**	**3796575.19**
29260.92	135998.05	125739.40	2132838.12	1407980.21	1068920.90
16184.44	44832.00	96709.41	1455979.06	373490.46	125794.39
5946.57	11026.29	64844.19	326350.41	115813.19	92061.43
27612.75	49567.71	53982.66	1560621.58	270205.35	232810.98
79004.68	**241424.06**	**341275.66**	**5475789.16**	**2167489.21**	**1519587.69**
165988.39	**867877.79**	**1615866.81**	**17726564.66**	**7842495.50**	**5316162.87**

1-22 续表1 continued

单位：万元

产出Output \ 投入Input			中间使用 Intermediate Use 木材加工及家具制造业 Wood processing and furniture manufacturing	 造纸印刷及文教体育用品制造业 Paper Printing and Educational and Sports Goods
中间投入	农林牧渔业	Agriculture Animal Husbandry and Fishery	245194.68	193744.72
	煤炭开采和洗选业	Coal Mining and Dressing	1279.41	2722.40
	石油和天然气开采业	Oil and Natural Gas	89.09	846.91
	金属矿采选业	Metals Mining and Dressing		
	非金属矿及其他矿采选业	Non-metallic Minerals and Other Mining and Dressing	39.50	8170.73
	食品制造及烟草加工业	Food manufacturing and tobacco processing industry	551.69	25479.93
	纺织业	Textile	552.41	10651.90
	纺织服装鞋帽皮革羽绒及其制品业	Textile, leather and feather products industry	16468.11	43280.84
	木材加工及家具制造业	Wood processing and furniture manufacturing	275059.72	138674.14
	造纸印刷及文教体育用品制造业	Paper Printing and Educational and Sports Goods	47719.47	859594.32
	石油加工、炼焦及核燃料加工业	Petroleum processing, coking and nuclear fuel processing industry	12838.26	146015.58
	化学工业	Chemical Industry	196072.06	484792.79
	非金属矿物制品业	Non-metallic mineral products industry	1125.26	38707.66
	金属冶炼及压延加工业	Metal smelting and rolling processing industry	19707.87	55904.24
	金属制品业	Fabricated metal products	36140.22	55336.56
	通用、专用设备制造业	General, special equipment manufacturing industry	22741.74	19986.18
	交通运输设备制造业	Transport Equipment	4042.64	7356.40
	电气机械及器材制造业	Electrical Machinery and Equipment	22190.44	32944.72
	通信设备、计算机及其他电子设备制造业	Communications equipment, computers and other electronic equipment manufacturing	6758.23	14638.67
	仪器仪表及文化办公用机械制造业	Measuring Instruments and Office Machinery	643.65	4575.11
	工艺品及其他制造业	Artwork and Other Manufacturing	25039.45	14257.89
	废品废料	Waste waste		51006.59
	电力、热力的生产和供应业	Electricity, Gas and Water Production and Supply	217952.74	160415.39
	燃气生产和供应业	Gas Production and Supply	31.97	614.94
	水的生产和供应业	Water Production and Supply	21428.53	67440.68
	建筑业	Building industry	63.12	301.84
	交通运输及仓储业	Transport and Storage	63814.63	88460.23
	邮政业	Post	1085.52	306.88
	信息传输、计算机服务和软件业	Information transmission, computer services and software	6800.90	12896.05
	批发和零售业	Wholesale and retail trade	39589.90	48657.60
	住宿和餐饮业	Accommodation and Catering Services	1128.46	9314.81
	金融业	Financial sector	25272.75	45874.00
	房地产业	Real Estate	177942.98	21545.81
	租赁和商务服务业	Leasing and Business Services	31826.92	26136.18
	研究与试验发展业	Research and Experimental Development Industry	74.17	1788.60
	综合技术服务业	Integrated Technology Services	20.77	20002.67
	水利、环境和公共设施管理业	Water, Environment and Public Facilities	50.44	596.99
	居民服务和其他服务业	Resident Services and Other Services	113142.79	11411.60
	教育	Education	247.84	5447.77
	卫生、社会保障和社会福利业	Health, Social Security and Social Welfare	386.61	2068.54
	文化、体育和娱乐业	Culture, Sports and Entertainment	256.76	5326.47
	公共管理和社会组织	Public Management and Social Organization		
	中间投入合计	Total intermediate inputs Compensation of Employees	**1635371.68**	**2737295.29**
增加值	劳动者报酬	Net Taxes on Production	486011.99	461383.42
	生产税净额	Depreciation of fixed assets	65619.57	225563.59
	固定资产折旧	Operating Surplus	28580.05	66729.11
	营业盈余	Total Value	148748.65	221296.85
	增加值合计	Total investment	**728960.25**	**974972.96**
	总投入		**2364331.93**	**3712268.25**

(100 million yuan)

中间使用 Intermediate Use					
石油加工、炼焦及核燃料加工业 Petroleum processing, coking and nuclear fuel processing industry	化学工业 Chemical Industry	非金属矿物制品业 Non-metallic mineral products industry	金属冶炼及压延加工业 Metal smelting and rolling processing industry	金属制品业 Fabricated metal products	通用、专用设备制造业 General, special equipment manufacturing industry
	67361.45			3151.10	490.27
99422.38	314460.07	459298.74	508352.47	11571.35	17669.15
986981.01	70108.85	15796.73	5029.22	3169.40	1443.67
	5086.84	382.95	1367207.95	109.62	12249.23
199.22	257506.67	141475.73	55352.60	1016.70	1275.51
320010.48	181542.36	199.68	75700.16	1241.98	190.54
73.50	12456.70	8320.79	763.13	398.23	4115.84
80911.10	156858.64	32025.83	92742.74	5288.15	4290.17
72730.60	123104.37	47916.14	22579.98	2975.86	14083.84
90395.75	318737.21	166925.54	1730.08	43821.02	4746.57
78690.74	573489.68	186001.13	418135.73	34445.28	119241.52
57180.33	3220432.93	381422.06	272212.63	45213.13	199191.61
9731.75	194446.00	787943.78	360982.21	85745.36	100541.64
3165.79	189752.53	546383.87	1787386.53	1145379.71	1392263.77
1826.29	110601.54	115462.41	118670.67	848759.62	536743.89
10264.18	217472.42	226415.97	172354.25	92701.55	676979.11
3490.99	30541.48	60028.66	20156.20	35969.01	19934.87
16684.03	89721.05	88177.93	71806.36	83016.22	153436.17
1104.96	31610.28	26842.19	29339.85	935.27	33246.83
4201.74	32430.96	14756.15	22154.77	1128.54	22414.39
601.74	14813.76	61566.33	6924.96	33296.75	80717.59
	66608.10	6578.87	100436.53	13842.80	29909.59
65075.75	377660.36	232887.68	386794.65	38431.98	114212.16
3676.86	7957.61	37384.56	31984.20	61668.28	116714.04
9442.96	65790.95	12346.79	25347.94	11568.48	23071.68
697.59	3480.03	32614.36	15112.23	132466.92	161329.52
84494.82	309004.54	242469.68	213640.93	61760.89	421055.85
557.46	4742.96	6649.45	766.35	584.57	2957.64
1519.03	48627.11	10450.74	39758.28	3618.88	30885.59
159213.00	371095.31	275958.20	213194.75	109323.60	229072.17
1518.17	33183.86	16080.54	7033.77	3594.45	17295.49
7018.22	66394.58	15062.75	14770.92	4433.54	19015.28
120138.24	539587.88	76206.96	249736.97	155366.77	225755.87
1741.91	115637.24	22217.08	25231.67	2034.67	19598.05
1157.43	18104.79	2066.79	3014.77	924.10	8425.19
4757.15	118193.08	14428.17	2702.14	619.51	46708.65
23.21	10352.61	1744.27	571.14	25.81	598.45
88792.44	209502.12	128163.87	119670.38	36788.67	25375.52
567.25	5832.85	11002.24	50772.66	371.02	2337.13
1832.71	14020.49	52314.14	67103.50	1094.46	52590.16
489.25	9177.37	1764.91	2095.22	684.34	3911.41
2390380.04	**8607489.65**	**4565734.67**	**6979321.45**	**3118537.54**	**4946085.60**
147855.33	1509268.18	1007934.23	1478357.34	801532.78	1579549.33
95301.75	828282.49	558536.71	593672.78	402541.35	689175.26
46114.48	335707.28	223830.29	231632.15	149132.55	134894.27
25527.44	1204071.72	495138.64	713487.94	412065.82	555925.76
314799.00	**3877329.66**	**2285439.87**	**3017150.20**	**1765272.50**	**2959544.62**
2705179.03	**12484819.31**	**6851174.54**	**9996471.65**	**4883810.04**	**7905630.22**

1-22 续表2 continued

单位：万元

产出Output / 投入Input			中间使用 Intermediate Use	
			交通运输设备制造业 Transport Equipment	电气机械及器材制造业 Electrical Machinery and Equipment
中间投入	农林牧渔业	Agriculture Animal Husbandry and Fishery	98422.022	73.142
	煤炭开采和洗选业	Coal Mining and Dressing	2504.84	4228.69
	石油和天然气开采业	Oil and Natural Gas	1573.49	183.61
	金属矿采选业	Metals Mining and Dressing	1068.31	34.13
	非金属矿及其他矿采选业	Non-metallic Minerals and Other Mining and Dressing	1999.09	12.53
	食品制造及烟草加工业	Food manufacturing and tobacco processing industry	38333.49	88.05
	纺织业	Textile	95953.71	254.08
	纺织服装鞋帽皮革羽绒及其制品业	Textile, leather and feather products industry	54766.21	579.19
	木材加工及家具制造业	Wood processing and furniture manufacturing	26373.13	2287.46
	造纸印刷及文教体育用品制造业	Paper Printing and Educational and Sports Goods	158890.56	12735.73
	石油加工、炼焦及核燃料加工业	Petroleum processing, coking and nuclear fuel processing industry	101842.92	9214.22
	化学工业	Chemical Industry	705300.65	214916.71
	非金属矿物制品业	Non-metallic mineral products industry	124772.80	63773.20
	金属冶炼及压延加工业	Metal smelting and rolling processing industry	650094.77	454396.89
	金属制品业	Fabricated metal products	326057.31	260037.92
	通用、专用设备制造业	General, special equipment manufacturing industry	279191.99	78744.92
	交通运输设备制造业	Transport Equipment	630197.28	2334.72
	电气机械及器材制造业	Electrical Machinery and Equipment	89426.92	160601.10
	通信设备、计算机及其他电子设备制造业	Communications equipment, computers and other electronic equipment manufacturing	34589.78	43036.36
	仪器仪表及文化办公用机械制造业	Measuring Instruments and Office Machinery	19659.23	32476.61
	工艺品及其他制造业	Artwork and Other Manufacturing	54916.99	34417.35
	废品废料	Waste waste	15.18	32.05
	电力、热力的生产和供应业	Electricity, Gas and Water Production and Supply	267696.23	69124.96
	燃气生产和供应业	Gas Production and Supply	44308.18	
	水的生产和供应业	Water Production and Supply	22818.11	10302.99
	建筑业	Building industry	489248.46	492.98
	交通运输及仓储业	Transport and Storage	323150.56	39912.97
	邮政业	Post	22612.02	2012.90
	信息传输、计算机服务和软件业	Information transmission, computer services and software	20769.42	5319.45
	批发和零售业	Wholesale and retail trade	922330.69	115421.04
	住宿和餐饮业	Accommodation and Catering Services	43488.48	7349.55
	金融业	Financial sector	111411.12	14900.47
	房地产业	Real Estate	141034.19	102005.29
	租赁和商务服务业	Leasing and Business Services	31058.50	14862.05
	研究与试验发展业	Research and Experimental Development Industry	89113.12	1945.02
	综合技术服务业	Integrated Technology Services	52938.01	1576.54
	水利、环境和公共设施管理业	Water, Environment and Public Facilities	1951.07	109.90
	居民服务和其他服务业	Resident Services and Other Services	38296.40	2250.50
	教育	Education	64017.11	10755.57
	卫生、社会保障和社会福利业	Health, Social Security and Social Welfare	44600.19	5071.54
	文化、体育和娱乐业	Culture, Sports and Entertainment	16857.36	1625.57
	公共管理和社会组织	Public Management and Social Organization		
	中间投入合计	Total intermediate inputs Compensation of Employees	6243649.86	1779497.94
增加值	劳动者报酬	Net Taxes on Production	**1263718.84**	**584442.80**
	生产税净额	Depreciation of fixed assets	**716035.17**	**121439.55**
	固定资产折旧	Operating Surplus	594163.73	38416.49
	营业盈余	Total Value	554673.07	450571.35
	增加值合计	Total investment	3128590.80	1194870.20
	总投入	Total investment	9372240.66	2974368.14

(100 million yuan)

中　间　使　用 Intermediate Use					
通信设备、计算机及其他电子设备制造业 Communications equipment, computers and other electronic equipment manufacturing	仪器仪表及文化办公用机械制造业 Measuring Instruments and Office Machinery	工艺品及其他制造业 Artwork and Other Manufacturing	废品废料 Waste waste	电力、热力的生产和供应业 Electricity, Gas and Water Production and Supply	燃气生产和供应业 Gas Production and Supply
		4151.1	8.84		
3013.98	96.07	619.18		537476.76	1823.22
	0.47			13242.07	54617.76
90.91	3.42	3.18		40264.56	
11.60	4.65	195.10	3962.11		972.19
467.34	46.07	3468.35		184.03	4.35
616.48	121.84	7041.75		2905.26	265.08
1878.89	396.55	20007.96		81545.89	651.37
6425.30	1050.75	146827.34	26373.89	169648.93	324.97
12680.36	6549.43	23348.59	12619.28	9063.76	110608.64
64037.13	17969.34	154520.43		128021.45	2101.83
30700.86	23271.07	76151.08		63220.94	1096.91
100799.02	36734.05	81326.27		10652.79	5350.88
457955.36	10062.25	13267.50		58566.18	8259.42
28122.65	68167.66	45569.61		132004.94	3889.75
7040.45	3845.24	34.13		3639.33	579.74
69836.54	29237.74	13125.92		39303.16	271.48
1016059.05	38812.87	3117.95		6798.24	288.00
20817.48	96617.02	3457.51		56236.86	1422.51
7274.99	284.91	48848.31		14070.57	2266.41
66890.76	15016.38	38495.00	892.06	108495.56	11733.31
65.40	845.50			431.10	602449.60
3635.04	5325.74	12621.04		21252.79	4271.75
859.00	1313.81	637.67		2922.36	341.91
30395.71	22466.04	42663.32		218286.51	7763.60
6230.27	1352.10	3141.38		1292.01	128.07
58043.63	9152.53	3887.82		127479.14	1385.01
58721.29	27184.90	50666.50		300887.00	8673.20
6458.31	5250.63	1558.29		66139.32	1730.16
11683.22	1848.05	638.28		199166.66	3434.94
164680.93	97672.00			29647.17	
4407.82	1815.69	1220.85		243285.84	277.02
3353.22	1049.12			37294.26	123.66
12158.61	25179.76	361.04		48497.33	
255.58	18.69	87.54		46.77	
56465.65	10367.81	1469.56		46931.97	11740.54
25431.12	22065.15	2687.54		226.76	59.90
43002.24	42185.17			670.43	
1535.20	956.88	461.60		1742.17	209.41
2382101.36	624337.32	805678.68	43856.18	2821540.89	849116.55
504896.68	**171281.48**	**138765.94**		**465746.06**	**867004.72**
330459.32	**49883.21**	**51890.12**		**441615.68**	**176720.08**
72782.26	8269.70	17031.67		1042528.88	12593.70
811546.91	73844.35	50164.67	236045.45	1209460.17	503872.94
1719685.17	303278.73	257852.41	236045.45	3159350.79	1560191.43
4101786.53	927616.05	1063531.08	279901.63	5980891.68	2409307.98

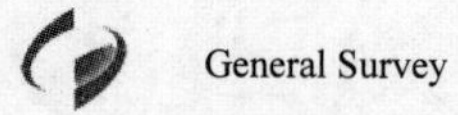

1-22 续表3 continued

单位：万元

投入Input \ 产出Output		中间使用 Intermediate Use	
		水的生产和供应业 Water Production and Supply	建筑业 Building industry
农林牧渔业	Agriculture Animal Husbandry and Fishery		269676.543
煤炭开采和洗选业	Coal Mining and Dressing		32383.98
石油和天然气开采业	Oil and Natural Gas		
金属矿采选业	Metals Mining and Dressing		
非金属矿及其他矿采选业	Non-metallic Minerals and Other Mining and Dressing	4110.78	891354.58
食品制造及烟草加工业	Food manufacturing and tobacco processing industry		7720.10
纺织业	Textile	12.90	10675.24
纺织服装鞋帽皮革羽绒及其制品业	Textile, leather and feather products industry	80.34	174960.81
木材加工及家具制造业	Wood processing and furniture manufacturing	2108.52	115793.25
造纸印刷及文教体育用品制造业	Paper Printing and Educational and Sports Goods	955.05	78266.29
石油加工、炼焦及核燃料加工业	Petroleum processing, coking and nuclear fuel processing industry	5476.25	214741.67
化学工业	Chemical Industry	57817.35	666224.07
非金属矿物制品业	Non-metallic mineral products industry	9854.25	3172142.56
金属冶炼及压延加工业	Metal smelting and rolling processing industry	2554.49	3053577.67
金属制品业	Fabricated metal products	7957.02	474887.91
通用、专用设备制造业	General, special equipment manufacturing industry	40633.70	680075.97
交通运输设备制造业	Transport Equipment	1193.46	273303.30
电气机械及器材制造业	Electrical Machinery and Equipment	10060.54	431251.83
通信设备、计算机及其他电子设备制造业	Communications equipment, computers and other electronic equipment manufacturing	1310.53	25744.18
中间投入 仪器仪表及文化办公用机械制造业	Measuring Instruments and Office Machinery	19595.00	75432.10
工艺品及其他制造业	Artwork and Other Manufacturing	31064.04	321578.99
废品废料	Waste waste		
电力、热力的生产和供应业	Electricity, Gas and Water Production and Supply	57817.09	167352.04
燃气生产和供应业	Gas Production and Supply		
水的生产和供应业	Water Production and Supply	11143.45	19909.94
建筑业	Building industry	2662.56	1251070.10
交通运输及仓储业	Transport and Storage	10078.50	240216.67
邮政业	Post	112.42	2367.46
信息传输、计算机服务和软件业	Information transmission, computer services and software	4748.06	29505.86
批发和零售业	Wholesale and retail trade	19139.50	483820.00
住宿和餐饮业	Accommodation and Catering Services	5663.40	82723.87
金融业	Financial sector	925.45	70004.91
房地产业	Real Estate	30209.52	76921.86
租赁和商务服务业	Leasing and Business Services	2207.94	76053.58
研究与试验发展业	Research and Experimental Development Industry	2.02	
综合技术服务业	Integrated Technology Services	141.66	3082.15
水利、环境和公共设施管理业	Water, Environment and Public Facilities	1922.01	1439.45
居民服务和其他服务业	Resident Services and Other Services	32923.84	30958.59
教育	Education	547.26	2299.50
卫生、社会保障和社会福利业	Health, Social Security and Social Welfare	28357.29	
文化、体育和娱乐业	Culture, Sports and Entertainment	1927.28	28282.99
公共管理和社会组织	Public Management and Social Organization		
中间投入合计	Total intermediate inputs Compensation of Employees	405313.45	13535800.00
增加值 劳动者报酬	Net Taxes on Production	**207746.64**	**3613560.96**
生产税净额	Depreciation of fixed assets	**42186.60**	**684978.67**
固定资产折旧	Operating Surplus	34828.86	208787.44
营业盈余	Total Value	7744.16	643272.93
增加值合计	Total investment	292506.26	5150600.00
总投入	Total investment	697819.71	18686400.00

(100 million yuan)

中　间　使　用 Intermediate Use					
交通运输及仓储业 Transport and Storage	邮政业 Post	信息传输、计算机服务和软件业 Information transmission, computer services and software	批发和零售业 Wholesale and retail trade	住宿和餐饮业 Accommodation and Catering Services	金融业 Financial sector
114988.256			6415.215	511038.502	
4501.77	21.19			29608.40	
				4984.87	
1484.65				1582.50	
33424.48	304.64		63058.25	1080437.51	
11927.10	5.30		8474.97	24545.18	62.13
4163.70	2336.42	8751.84	52332.57	27133.06	30048.09
8252.71	625.16	879.94	7918.76	40651.73	31740.94
13352.63	8734.15	10052.71	63294.53	67955.40	213532.12
1498279.32	8611.90	4955.90	10264.28	106340.49	35119.36
42284.44	463.58	351.26	2774.96	38804.61	21188.67
11127.07	60.93			19980.94	869.28
19193.63			272.11	245.51	417.25
16206.22	656.95	4045.93	11274.92	15230.51	1381.27
18511.60	2113.90	9981.49	68.03	10882.50	9414.71
842507.71	13327.14	2568.93	108427.68	10861.55	28633.00
60388.30	1245.03	149420.28	19248.49	9278.13	7042.95
37603.27	1406.62	157851.77	16818.73	11581.25	82575.04
5444.04	217.22	3478.60	5128.43	8952.28	14435.85
751.70		1654.92		14771.28	
332534.13	4068.86	66323.47	193682.15	122186.15	78855.61
38.73	10.60			31552.84	
6336.15	611.92	5651.93	19489.87	19771.08	19905.92
14232.67	7976.14	8988.23	19681.82	33772.89	17374.15
264814.79	15784.57	4908.77	127076.68	14211.75	80463.67
828.75	8177.46	1456.72	101.45	1244.99	5436.61
27005.13	2339.07	86366.95	15081.74	23200.36	110865.06
298262.97	12492.69	115017.82	175331.89	61320.65	40969.77
110805.88	2879.46	13564.85	132348.48	91943.27	93344.26
470833.20	511.26	37902.59	282674.24	300725.21	145169.11
163451.23	2169.53	61665.41	615363.69	39166.84	124251.07
79383.30	5928.46	24823.36	208867.94	50754.01	131424.98
33468.13	55.63		768.73	305.91	25721.60
32125.30	18.54	3505.27	47144.45	2914.33	9518.23
2269.48		383.49		1008.36	2697.65
129025.37	18407.95	2914.15	249617.91	114718.95	71415.91
134141.92	826.49	13598.71	100606.05	12107.10	62807.65
26533.11		66554.76	41202.40	6467.90	77313.17
31523.12	1947.02	114379.96	42188.58	43861.19	151767.70
194.05	164.24				3537.26
4902200.00	124500.00	982000.00	2647000.00	3006100.00	1729300.00
2379722.02	**116641.12**	**170875.59**	**2471183.56**	**1147982.98**	**856256.61**
630584.19	**12572.15**	**134857.89**	**1067735.24**	**521902.71**	**334421.59**
964215.35	29141.65	513750.76	475945.49	132276.22	180641.28
684278.44	-17954.92	1207115.75	3483235.70	408538.08	2001380.52
4658800.00	140400.00	2026600.00	7498100.00	2210700.00	3372700.00
9561000.00	264900.00	3008600.00	10145100.00	5216800.00	5102000.00

1-22 续表4 continued

单位：万元

产 出Output / 投 入Input			中间使用 Intermediate Use 房地产业 Real Estate	租赁和商务服务业 Leasing and Business Services
中间投入	农林牧渔业	Agriculture Animal Husbandry and Fishery		320.76
	煤炭开采和洗选业	Coal Mining and Dressing		
	石油和天然气开采业	Oil and Natural Gas		1233.19
	金属矿采选业	Metals Mining and Dressing	865.10	
	非金属矿及其他矿采选业	Non-metallic Minerals and Other Mining and Dressing		52.45
	食品制造及烟草加工业	Food manufacturing and tobacco processing industry		327.07
	纺织业	Textile	216.18	144.82
	纺织服装鞋帽皮革羽绒及其制品业	Textile, leather and feather products industry	4502.76	3416.71
	木材加工及家具制造业	Wood processing and furniture manufacturing	42283.42	1247.08
	造纸印刷及文教体育用品制造业	Paper Printing and Educational and Sports Goods	128815.24	64158.05
	石油加工、炼焦及核燃料加工业	Petroleum processing, coking and nuclear fuel processing industry	25330.09	87186.82
	化学工业	Chemical Industry	126890.48	52954.28
	非金属矿物制品业	Non-metallic mineral products industry	1534.67	
	金属冶炼及压延加工业	Metal smelting and rolling processing industry		
	金属制品业	Fabricated metal products	27960.50	47554.18
	通用、专用设备制造业	General, special equipment manufacturing industry	15237.11	3602.36
	交通运输设备制造业	Transport Equipment	9632.30	5141.40
	电气机械及器材制造业	Electrical Machinery and Equipment	63801.60	819.96
	通信设备、计算机及其他电子设备制造业	Communications equipment, computers and other electronic equipment manufacturing	42531.38	23362.53
	仪器仪表及文化办公用机械制造业	Measuring Instruments and Office Machinery	79831.39	2131.60
	工艺品及其他制造业	Artwork and Other Manufacturing	6123.84	4072.33
	废品废料	Waste waste		
	电力、热力的生产和供应业	Electricity, Gas and Water Production and Supply	133378.89	65992.87
	燃气生产和供应业	Gas Production and Supply		
	水的生产和供应业	Water Production and Supply	11242.12	24285.22
	建筑业	Building industry	109541.29	2810.71
	交通运输及仓储业	Transport and Storage	46366.36	87199.06
	邮政业	Post	1491.34	1062.93
	信息传输、计算机服务和软件业	Information transmission, computer services and software	28655.27	17489.04
	批发和零售业	Wholesale and retail trade	28771.78	15363.61
	住宿和餐饮业	Accommodation and Catering Services	46441.36	111988.27
	金融业	Financial sector	180751.47	153924.38
	房地产业	Real Estate	146529.87	132012.10
	租赁和商务服务业	Leasing and Business Services	142470.17	114928.06
	研究与试验发展业	Research and Experimental Development Industry		
	综合技术服务业	Integrated Technology Services	23470.67	87484.14
	水利、环境和公共设施管理业	Water, Environment and Public Facilities	99.56	5620.11
	居民服务和其他服务业	Resident Services and Other Services	67862.68	75112.49
	教育	Education	31440.52	52583.04
	卫生、社会保障和社会福利业	Health, Social Security and Social Welfare	9944.76	93130.47
	文化、体育和娱乐业	Culture, Sports and Entertainment	28813.07	95807.87
	公共管理和社会组织	Public Management and Social Organization	1272.77	43380.08
	中间投入合计	Total intermediate inputs Compensation of Employees	**1614100.00**	**1477900.00**
增加值	劳动者报酬	Net Taxes on Production	2267643.88	506102.72
	生产税净额	Depreciation of fixed assets	507997.80	125969.79
	固定资产折旧	Operating Surplus	326880.89	69404.97
	营业盈余	Total Value	693977.43	154822.52
	增加值合计	Total investment	**3796500.00**	**856300.00**
总投入		Total investment	**5410600.00**	**2334200.00**

(100 million yuan)

中　间　使　用 Intermediate Use					
研究与试验发展业 Research and Experimental Development Industry	综合技术服务业 Integrated Technology Services	水利、环境和公共设施管理业 Water, Environment and Public Facilities	居民服务和其他服务业 Resident Services and Other Services	教育 Education	卫生、社会保障和社会福利业 Health, Social Security and Social Welfare
15172.46	3933.36	583.61	971.74		5736.94
63.51				8544.22	3106.93
			321.16		42.22
855.10		235.68	65.12		242.99
11242.20	708.70				17757.17
818.70	508.60	338.61	282.03		4211.03
251.10	1154.50	449.92	1354.50	2073.50	567.78
8078.10	768.10	1295.22	16846.15	129007.34	4463.60
34991.61	12027.49	3522.74	20532.91	396916.10	16242.32
2507.76	5997.59	1124.67	83.49	10361.98	4786.00
3105.57	1585.51	3265.05	5146.35	11078.21	437574.20
6733.69	544.17	2303.84		3879.21	9332.21
181.81		616.25		766.59	8347.09
545.38	2229.15	905.77	278.59	928.07	20672.58
1263.53	1604.24	1077.35	194.56		61186.72
341.26	1717.02	837.84	3335.86	1421.15	598.19
1092.68	18881.83	621.70	592.69		4401.06
6844.52	8839.55	1275.51	3552.43	135021.31	3918.72
3129.66	2249.45	983.98	3639.88	6608.59	668.70
	851.84	218.18	2797.01	2407.93	1025.20
8361.61	23193.85	12474.32	14894.96	14542.81	36276.69
					5424.13
2519.17	1486.81	1386.14	14410.11	8795.25	16505.70
2305.26	650.64	8140.73	52409.67	24834.80	55497.52
4608.73	19715.14	17218.26	167464.36	57763.66	130413.06
358.56	310.89	623.67	6883.71	333.65	2467.60
18397.24	11654.49	5241.32	16821.55	27360.57	27263.90
9855.41			28955.41	21578.07	108428.66
7376.52	117996.36	13173.32	111507.67	223803.90	19145.04
21120.82	24331.45	12120.99	82901.12	95252.45	35589.39
	2082.44	4310.82	51316.39	89629.37	28533.67
	14246.86	3556.61	78038.47	80997.80	56786.90
	13070.83	1266.28		105959.99	62365.48
20049.81	128012.08	13126.52	62996.55	65506.13	44945.54
	105486.76	93647.10	5574.71	23858.51	4522.18
855.45	2060.38	353.72	261323.06	5885.27	72833.20
9877.14	21678.02	4023.68	115320.85	85819.17	112554.58
544.85	2895.16		147746.02	246124.97	73046.00
6650.79	13604.18	12680.62	8023.49	51769.91	139719.13
	222.59		417.43	869.53	
210100.00	**566300.00**	**223000.00**	**1287000.00**	**1939700.00**	**1637200.00**
162050.06	442260.81	286257.04	1157715.30	2228560.12	613961.00
652.13	48182.83	7341.91	122648.76	1173843.25	532110.11
83346.61	50481.49	16776.10	159998.59	428348.28	214817.72
3551.20	51474.87	206424.95	101637.36	918248.35	138811.18
249600.00	**592400.00**	**516800.00**	**1542000.00**	**4749000.00**	**1499700.00**
459700.00	**1158700.00**	**739800.00**	**2829000.00**	**6688700.00**	**3136900.00**

1-22 续表5 continued

单位：万元

产 出Output / 投 入Input			中 间 使 用 Intermediate Use	
			文化、体育和娱乐业 Culture, Sports and Entertainment	公共管理和社会组织 Public Management and Social Organization
中间投入	农林牧渔业	Agriculture Animal Husbandry and Fishery	625.58	
	煤炭开采和洗选业	Coal Mining and Dressing	237.32	
	石油和天然气开采业	Oil and Natural Gas	45.13	
	金属矿采选业	Metals Mining and Dressing		
	非金属矿及其他矿采选业	Non-metallic Minerals and Other Mining and Dressing	66.20	412.56
	食品制造及烟草加工业	Food manufacturing and tobacco processing industry	66806.25	7918.72
	纺织业	Textile	1062.22	1065.92
	纺织服装鞋帽皮革羽绒及其制品业	Textile, leather and feather products industry	3735.23	8552.05
	木材加工及家具制造业	Wood processing and furniture manufacturing	1009.84	19263.67
	造纸印刷及文教体育用品制造业	Paper Printing and Educational and Sports Goods	17412.58	195321.59
	石油加工、炼焦及核燃料加工业	Petroleum processing, coking and nuclear fuel processing industry	10847.14	114154.31
	化学工业	Chemical Industry	3939.20	10561.97
	非金属矿物制品业	Non-metallic mineral products industry	1337.40	1756.59
	金属冶炼及压延加工业	Metal smelting and rolling processing industry		454.51
	金属制品业	Fabricated metal products	873.30	418.72
	通用、专用设备制造业	General, special equipment manufacturing industry	1624.06	1014.62
	交通运输设备制造业	Transport Equipment	1462.32	12542.16
	电气机械及器材制造业	Electrical Machinery and Equipment	536.22	2848.46
	通信设备、计算机及其他电子设备制造业	Communications equipment, computers and other electronic equipment manufacturing	53925.49	9317.80
	仪器仪表及文化办公用机械制造业	Measuring Instruments and Office Machinery	1928.41	7432.90
	工艺品及其他制造业	Artwork and Other Manufacturing	4928.80	12320.90
	废品废料	Waste waste		
	电力、热力的生产和供应业	Electricity, Gas and Water Production and Supply	13250.12	32554.16
	燃气生产和供应业	Gas Production and Supply	4.53	65.43
	水的生产和供应业	Water Production and Supply	14441.44	6656.95
	建筑业	Building industry	72235.63	13573.40
	交通运输及仓储业	Transport and Storage	37121.46	265064.56
	邮政业	Post	19088.39	36078.82
	信息传输、计算机服务和软件业	Information transmission, computer services and software	23208.37	94178.92
	批发和零售业	Wholesale and retail trade	5422.15	20927.90
	住宿和餐饮业	Accommodation and Catering Services	51812.28	287545.95
	金融业	Financial sector	66308.74	44586.99
	房地产业	Real Estate	8906.15	60350.40
	租赁和商务服务业	Leasing and Business Services	27062.52	243145.10
	研究与试验发展业	Research and Experimental Development Industry	395.58	
	综合技术服务业	Integrated Technology Services		
	水利、环境和公共设施管理业	Water, Environment and Public Facilities	245.35	111317.04
	居民服务和其他服务业	Resident Services and Other Services	6090.83	47159.04
	教育	Education	475.15	110698.97
	卫生、社会保障和社会福利业	Health, Social Security and Social Welfare		201015.51
	文化、体育和娱乐业	Culture, Sports and Entertainment	28301.39	55422.55
	公共管理和社会组织	Public Management and Social Organization	27.26	2100.87
	中间投入合计	Total intermediate inputs Compensation of Employees	**546800.00**	**2037800.00**
增加值	劳动者报酬	Net Taxes on Production	460624.70	3418722.87
	生产税净额	Depreciation of fixed assets	84258.88	26544.25
	固定资产折旧	Operating Surplus	88312.43	892511.32
	营业盈余	Total Value	86203.99	93221.56
	增加值合计	Total investment	**719400.00**	**4431000.00**
	总投入	Total investment	**1266200.00**	**6468800.00**

(100 million yuan)

中间使用 Intermediate Use	最终使用 End-use				
	最终消费支出 Final consumption expenditure				
中间使用合计	居民消费支出 Consumer spending			政府消费支出	合计
	农村居民	城镇居民	小计		
Total intermediate use	Rural residents	Urban residents	Subtotal	Government consumption expenditure	Total
13711877.74	1905592.26	1473410.57	**3379002.83**	863173.87	**4242176.70**
2123565.23	83356.43	30848.37	**114204.80**		**114204.80**
1178129.26	60705.23	207805.81	**268511.04**		**268511.04**
1411969.91		87497.18	**87497.18**		**87497.18**
1709407.71					
5308569.44	2555837.32	8139412.11	**10695249.42**		**10695249.42**
4719448.01	277806.53	1316665.73	**1594472.26**		**1594472.26**
1683531.96	1245402.46	1602347.95	**2847750.41**		**2847750.41**
1358101.71	35183.91	150091.32	**185275.23**		**185275.23**
4399356.19	11544.34	450020.59	**461564.93**		**461564.93**
4624580.06	13822.30	58864.29	**72686.59**		**72686.59**
11245644.07	481942.20	1428068.13	**1910010.33**		**1910010.33**
5517286.76	885587.37	90910.07	**976497.44**		**976497.44**
9695025.80	56473.33		**56473.33**		**56473.33**
4230272.47	70810.71	89668.41	**160479.12**		**160479.12**
3194703.34	292663.70	12839.49	**305503.18**		**305503.18**
2184255.95	118508.27	244127.55	**362635.82**		**362635.82**
1922117.90	363608.46	104190.92	**467799.37**		**467799.37**
1935032.73	294978.98	676786.36	**971765.34**		**971765.34**
605760.74	8154.43	53303.29	**61457.73**		**61457.73**
847170.00	169.88	165655.73	**165825.61**		**165825.61**
269975.05					
4466381.79	129111.87	619239.68	**748351.55**		**748351.55**
952267.87	366707.80	887465.65	**1254173.45**		**1254173.45**
665349.85		31485.32	**31485.32**		**31485.32**
2601691.41	395326.25	671041.70	**1066367.95**		**1066367.95**
4349199.30	97551.31	1046618.60	**1144169.91**	2171.29	**1146341.20**
164062.13	11959.84	7487.74	**19447.58**		**19447.58**
1010032.62	9423.90	723686.15	**733110.05**		**733110.05**
5250623.56		328653.35	**328653.35**		**328653.35**
1909887.53	299627.46	2768429.46	**3068056.92**		**3068056.92**
2937514.77	139033.18	378734.08	**517767.27**		**517767.27**
4116447.65		117980.98	**117980.98**		**117980.98**
2136236.43		117289.32	**117289.32**	21764.90	**139054.22**
418092.17				42719.94	**42719.94**
1110597.47				48102.53	**48102.53**
400181.48		144021.74	**144021.74**	195596.78	**339618.52**
2437467.19	40678.34	287173.03	**327851.37**	63681.44	**391532.81**
1086759.17	205147.90	1222312.42	**1427460.32**	4233068.92	**5660529.24**
1517632.86	20579.13	731793.58	**752372.70**	866894.43	**1619267.14**
918314.86	40904.95	112773.34	**153678.29**	210003.78	**363682.06**
116277.87				6352522.13	**6352522.13**
122440800.00	**10518200.00**	**26578700.00**	**37096900.00**	**12899700.00**	**49996600.00**
48472073.75					
13528720.49					
9867138.36					
23632467.40					
95500400.00					
217941200.00					

1-22 续表6 continued

单位：万元

产 出Output / 投 入Input		最终使用Final use 资本形成总额 Gross capital formation 固定资本形成 Fixed capital formation	存货增加 Increase in inventories
中间投入 农林牧渔业	Agriculture Animal Husbandry and Fishery	2577480.36	16817.60
煤炭开采和洗选业	Coal Mining and Dressing		-141.25
石油和天然气开采业	Oil and Natural Gas		4025.59
金属矿采选业	Metals Mining and Dressing		6885.87
非金属矿及其他矿采选业	Non-metallic Minerals and Other Mining and Dressing		6356.19
食品制造及烟草加工业	Food manufacturing and tobacco processing industry		625664.74
纺织业	Textile		19295.78
纺织服装鞋帽皮革羽绒及其制品业	Textile, leather and feather products industry		2048.11
木材加工及家具制造业	Wood processing and furniture manufacturing	913921.41	2471.85
造纸印刷及文教体育用品制造业	Paper Printing and Educational and Sports Goods		13348.00
石油加工、炼焦及核燃料加工业	Petroleum processing, coking and nuclear fuel processing industry		9598.25
化学工业	Chemical Industry		34601.28
非金属矿物制品业	Non-metallic mineral products industry		5354.13
金属冶炼及压延加工业	Metal smelting and rolling processing industry		46840.69
金属制品业	Fabricated metal products	149808.46	3411.96
通用、专用设备制造业	General, special equipment manufacturing industry	5107813.37	30467.74
交通运输设备制造业	Transport Equipment	6351128.09	54837.17
电气机械及器材制造业	Electrical Machinery and Equipment	530213.01	31160.66
通信设备、计算机及其他电子设备制造业	Communications equipment, computers and other electronic equipment manufacturing	1637399.95	93859.73
仪器仪表及文化办公用机械制造业	Measuring Instruments and Office Machinery	362763.66	-105.94
工艺品及其他制造业	Artwork and Other Manufacturing		3107.47
废品废料	Waste waste		-211.87
电力、热力的生产和供应业	Electricity, Gas and Water Production and Supply		17197.02
燃气生产和供应业	Gas Production and Supply	133052.72	2224.67
水的生产和供应业	Water Production and Supply		984.55
建筑业	Building industry	15018340.65	
交通运输及仓储业	Transport and Storage	2796323.07	-19826.07
邮政业	Post	87153.87	
信息传输、计算机服务和软件业	Information transmission, computer services and software	1184264.92	
批发和零售业	Wholesale and retail trade	4077735.04	-219173.93
住宿和餐饮业	Accommodation and Catering Services	24677.75	
金融业	Financial sector	1599150.71	
房地产业	Real Estate	1160172.98	
租赁和商务服务业	Leasing and Business Services		
研究与试验发展业	Research and Experimental Development Industry		
综合技术服务业	Integrated Technology Services		
水利、环境和公共设施管理业	Water, Environment and Public Facilities		
居民服务和其他服务业	Resident Services and Other Services		
教育	Education		
卫生、社会保障和社会福利业	Health, Social Security and Social Welfare		
文化、体育和娱乐业	Culture, Sports and Entertainment		
公共管理和社会组织	Public Management and Social Organization		
中间投入合计	Total intermediate inputs Compensation of Employees	**43711400.00**	**791100.00**
增加值 劳动者报酬	Net Taxes on Production		
生产税净额	Depreciation of fixed assets		
固定资产折旧	Operating Surplus		
营业盈余	Total Value		
增加值合计	Total investment		
总投入	Total investment		

(100 million yuan)

最终使用End-use 资本形成总额 Gross capital formation 合计 Total	出口 Export	最终使用合计 Total end-use	进口 Import	总产出 Total output
2594297.96	3569530.04	**10406004.70**	1149482.44	**22968400.00**
-141.25	753.58	**114817.13**	1989086.82	**249295.55**
4025.59	1095.82	**273632.44**	1285773.31	**165988.39**
6885.87	16443.06	**110826.11**	654918.23	**867877.79**
6356.19	29523.88	**35880.06**	129420.96	**1615866.81**
625664.74	3002386.51	**14323300.68**	1905305.46	**17726564.66**
19295.78	2157616.73	**3771384.76**	648337.27	**7842495.50**
2048.11	784791.92	**3634590.43**	1959.52	**5316162.87**
916393.27	92939.53	**1194608.02**	188377.80	**2364331.93**
13348.00	14089.95	**489002.88**	1176090.82	**3712268.25**
9598.25	21138.54	**103423.38**	2022824.41	**2705179.03**
34601.28	1206095.83	**3150707.44**	1911532.20	**12484819.31**
5354.13	1151410.87	**2133262.45**	799374.67	**6851174.54**
46840.69	1634434.13	**1737748.15**	1436302.30	**9996471.65**
153220.42	427642.23	**741341.77**	87804.20	**4883810.04**
5138281.11	545140.25	**5988924.54**	1277997.66	**7905630.22**
6405965.26	918660.38	**7687261.46**	499276.75	**9372240.66**
561373.67	268848.61	**1298021.66**	245771.42	**2974368.14**
1731259.68	122082.80	**2825107.82**	658354.02	**4101786.53**
362657.73	78980.08	**503095.54**	181240.22	**927616.05**
3107.47	59649.56	**228582.65**	12221.57	**1063531.08**
-211.87	10433.18	**10221.31**	294.73	**279901.63**
17197.02	827898.42	**1593446.99**	78937.10	**5980891.68**
135277.39	74192.22	**1463643.06**	6602.95	**2409307.98**
984.55		**32469.86**		**697819.71**
15018340.65		**16084708.59**		**18686400.00**
2776496.99	2316832.37	**6239670.56**	1027869.86	**9561000.00**
87153.87	9441.40	**116042.84**	15204.98	**264900.00**
1184264.92	171284.69	**2088659.66**	90092.27	**3008600.00**
3858561.11	1389156.73	**5576371.18**	681894.74	**10145100.00**
24677.75	255425.00	**3348159.67**	41247.20	**5216800.00**
1599150.71	101676.18	**2218594.15**	54108.92	**5102000.00**
1160172.98	21209.95	**1299363.91**	5211.56	**5410600.00**
	101013.79	**240068.01**	42104.44	**2334200.00**
	5793.33	**48513.26**	6905.43	**459700.00**
		48102.53		**1158700.00**
		339618.52		**739800.00**
		391532.81		**2829000.00**
	77.91	**5660607.15**	58666.32	**6688700.00**
		1619267.14		**3136900.00**
	3610.54	**367292.60**	19407.46	**1266200.00**
		6352522.13		**6468800.00**
44502500.00	**21391300.00**	**115890400.00**	**20390000.00**	**217941200.00**

主要统计指标解释

平均增长速度 计算平均增长速度有两种方法：一种是习惯上经常使用的“水平法”，又称几何平均法，是以间隔期最后一年的水平同基期水平对比来计算平均每年增长(或下降)速度；另一种是“累计法”，又称代数平均法或方程法，是以间隔期内各年水平的总和同基期水平对比来计算平均每年增长(或下降)速度。在一般正常情况下，两种方法计算的平均每年增长速度比较接近；但在经济发展不平衡、出现大起大落时，两种方法计算的结果差别较大。

国民经济行业分类 自2003年定期报表开始使用新的《国民经济行业分类》（GB/T4754-2002）该分类是由国家统计局组织修订，经国家质量监督检验检疫总局批准，于2002年5月10日发布实施。这次修订是在1994年分类标准的基础上，参照联合国《全部经济活动的国际标准产业分类》(ISIC/Rev.3)进行的。修订后的《国民经济行业分类》(GB/T4754-2002)共有门类20个，大类95个，中类396个，小类913个。新增门类4个，大类增加3个，中类增加28个，小类增加67个。

企业(单位)登记注册类型 是以在工商行政管理机关登记注册的各类企业为划分对象，以工商行政管理部门对企业登记注册的类型为依据，将企业登记注册类型分为内资企业、港澳台商投资企业和外商投资企业三大类。内资企业包括国有企业、集体企业、股份合作企业、联营企业、有限责任公司、股份有限公司、私营公司和其他企业；港澳台商投资企业和外商投资企业分别包括合资经营企业、合作经营企业、独资经营企业和股份有限公司。对不在工商行政管理部门进行登记注册的行政机关、事业单位和社会团体，主要按其经费来源和管理方式进行划分。

国有企业 指企业全部资产归国家所有，并按《中华人民共和国企业法人登记管理条例》规定登记注册的非公司制的经济组织。不包括有限责任公司中的国有独资公司。

集体企业 指企业资产归集体所有，并按《中华人民共和国企业法人登记管理条例》规定登记注册的经济组织。

股份合作企业 指以合作制为基础，由企业职工共同出资入股，吸收一定比例的社会资产投资组建，实行自主经营，自负盈亏，共同劳动，民主管理，按劳分配与按股分红相结合的一种集体经济组织。

联营企业 指两个及两个以上相同或不同所有制性质的企业法人或事业单位法人，按自愿、平等、互利的原则，共同投资组成的经济组织。联营企业包括国有联营企业、集体联营企业、国有与集体联营企业和其他联营企业。

有限责任公司 指根据《中华人民共和国公司登记管理条例》规定登记注册，由两个以上、五十个以下的股东共同出资，每个股东以其所认缴的出资额对公司承担有限责任，公司以其全部资产对其债务承担责任的经济组织。有限责任公司包括国有独资公司以及其他有限责任公司。

股份有限公司 指根据《中华人民共和国公司登记管理条例》规定登记注册，其全部注册资本由等额股份构成并通过发行股票筹集资本，股东以其认购的股份对公司承担有限责任，公司以其全部资产对其债务承担责任的经济组织。

私营企业 指由自然人投资设立或由自然人控股，以雇佣劳动为基础的营利性经济组织。包括按照《公司法》、《合伙企业法》、《私营企业暂行条例》规定登记注册的私营有限责任公司、私营股份有限公司、私营合伙企业和私营独资企业。

其他企业 指上述企业之外的其他内资经济组织。

与港澳台商合资经营企业 指港澳台地区投资者与内地企业依照《中华人民共和国中外合资经营企业法》及有关法律的规定，按合同规定的比例投资设立、分享利润和分担风险的企业。

与港澳台商合作经营企业 指港澳台地区投资者与内地企业依照《中华人民共和国中外合作经营企业法》及有关法律的规定，依照合作合同的约定进行投资或提供条件设立、分配利润和分担风险的企业。

港澳台商独资经营企业 指依照《中华人民共和国外资企业法》及有关法律的规定，在内地由港澳台地区投资者全额投资设立的企业。

港澳台商投资股份有限公司 指根据国家有关规定，经原外经贸部依法批准设立，其中港、澳、台商的股本占公司注册资本的比例达 25% 以上的股份有限公司。凡其中港、澳、台商的股本占公司注册资本的比例小于 25%的，属于内资企业中的股份有限公司。

中外合资经营企业　指外国企业或外国人与中国内地企业依照《中华人民共和国中外合资经营企业法》及有关法律的规定，按合同规定的比例投资设立、分享利润和分担风险的企业。

中外合作经营企业　指外国企业或外国人与中国内地企业依照《中华人民共和国中外合作经营企业法》及有关法律的规定，依照合作合同的约定进行投资或提供条件设立、分配利润和分担风险的企业。

外资企业　指依照《中华人民共和国外资企业法》及有关法律的规定，在中国内地由外国投资者全额投资设立的企业。

外商投资股份有限公司　指根据国家有关规定，经原外经贸部依法批准设立，其中外资的股本占公司注册资本的比例达 25% 以上的股份有限公司。凡其中外资股本占公司注册资本的比例小于 25%的，属于内资企业中的股份有限公司。

行政机关、事业单位和社会团体　参照企业登记注册类型，主要按其经费来源和管理方式划分。具体规定如下：

⑴行政机关：包括国家机关和政党机关，原则上均列为“国有”。但有特殊规定的，如供销社等，则列为“集体”。

⑵事业单位：包括经国家机构编制部门和有关业务主管部门批准成立的各类事业单位，不包括实行企业化管理的事业单位。事业单位的划分办法如下：

①由国家财政预算拨款或列入财政预算外资金管理以及经费主要来源于国有主管部门或国有上级单位的事业单位，列为“国有”。

②经费主要来源于集体单位的事业单位，列为“集体”。

③公民个人(或个人合伙)开办的事业单位，列为“私营”。

④上述以外的其他事业单位，如果其经费来源不明确，按管理方式进行归类。

⑶社会团体：包括经民政部门批准成立以及未纳入社会团体管理条例范围的工会、妇联等各类社会团体。社会团体的划分办法如下：

①未纳入民政部社会团体管理条例范围的工会、妇联、共青团、青联、工商联、科协、侨联等社会团体，国家拨款设立的基金会或基金管理组织以及经费主要来源于国有业务主管部门或国有上级单位的社会团体，列为“国有”。

②经费主要来源于集体单位的社会团体，列为“集体”。

③公民个人(或个人合伙)开办的社会团体，划为“私营”。

④上述以外的其他社会团体，如果其经费来源不明确，改按管理方式进行归类。

国内生产总值(GDP)　指按市场价格计算的一个国家(或地区)所有常住单位在一定时期内生产活动的最终成果。国内生产总值有三种表现形态，即价值形态、收入形态和产品形态。从价值形态看，它是所有常住单位在一定时期内生产的全部货物和服务价值超过同期投入的全部非固定资产货物和服务价值的差额，即所有常住单位的增加值之和；从收入形态看，它是所有常住单位在一定时期内创造并分配给常住单位和非常住单位的初次收入之和；从产品形态看，它是所有常住单位在一定时期内最终使用的货物和服务价值减去货物和服务进口价值。在实际核算中，国内生产总值有三种计算方法，即生产法、收入法和支出法。三种方法分别从不同的方面反映国内生产总值及其构成。

国民总收入（GNI）　即国民生产总值，指一个国家(或地区)所有常住单位在一定时期内收入初次分配的最终结果。一国常住单位从事生产活动所创造的增加值在初次分配中主要分配给该国的常住单位，但也有一部分以生产税及进口税(扣除生产和进口补贴)、劳动者报酬和财产收入等形式分配给非常住单位；同时，国外生产所创造的增加值也有一部分以生产税及进口税(扣除生产和进口补贴)、劳动者报酬和财产收入等形式分配给该国的常住单位，从而产生了国民总收入的概念。它等于国内生产总值加上来自国外的净要素收入。与国内生产总值不同，国民总收入是个收入概念，而国内生产总值是个生产概念。

三次产业　三产业的划分是世界上较为常用的产业结构分类，但各国的划分不尽一致。我国的三次产业划分是：

第一产业是指农、林、牧、渔业。

第二产业是指采矿业，制造业，电力、煤气及水的生产和供应业，建筑业。

第三产业是指除第一、二产业以外的其他行业。

劳动者报酬 指劳动者因从事生产活动所获得的全部报酬。包括劳动者获得的各种形式的工资、奖金和津贴，既包括货币形式的，也包括实物形式的，还包括劳动者所享受的公费医疗和医药卫生费、上下班交通补贴、单位支付的社会保险费、住房公积金等。对于个体经济来说，其所有者所获得的劳动报酬和经营利润不易区分，这两部分统一作为劳动者报酬处理。

生产税净额 指生产税减生产补贴后的余额。生产税指政府对生产单位从事生产、销售和经营活动以及因从事生产活动使用某些生产要素(如固定资产、土地、劳动力)所征收的各种税、附加费和规费。生产补贴与生产税相反，指政府对生产单位的单方面转移支出，因此视为负生产税，包括政策亏损补贴、价格补贴等。

固定资产折旧 指一定时期内为弥补固定资产损耗按照规定的固定资产折旧率提取的固定资产折旧，或按国民经济核算统一规定的折旧率虚拟计算的固定资产折旧。它反映了固定资产在当期生产中的转移价值。各类企业和企业化管理的事业单位的固定资产折旧是指实际计提的折旧费；不计提折旧的政府机关、非企业化管理的事业单位和居民住房的固定资产折旧是按照统一规定的折旧率和固定资产原值计算的虚拟折旧。原则上，固定资产折旧应按固定资产当期的重置价值计算，但是目前我国尚不具备对全社会固定资产进行重估价的基础，所以暂时只能采用上述办法。

营业盈余 指常住单位创造的增加值扣除劳动者报酬、生产税净额和固定资产折旧后的余额。它相当于企业的营业利润加上生产补贴，但要扣除从利润中开支的工资和福利等。

支出法国内生产总值 是从最终使用的角度反映一个国家(或地区)一定时期内生产活动最终成果的一种方法，包括最终消费支出、资本形成总额及货物和服务净出口三部分。计算公式为：

支出法国内生产总值=最终消费支出+资本形成总额+货物和服务净出口

最终消费支出 指常住单位为满足物质、文化和精神生活的需要，从本国经济领土和国外购买的货物和服务的支出。它不包括非常住单位在本国经济领土内的消费支出。最终消费支出分为居民消费支出和政府消费支出。

居民消费支出 指常住住户在一定时期内对于货物和服务的全部最终消费支出。居民消费支出除了直接以货币形式购买的货物和服务的消费支出外，还包括以其他方式获得的货物和服务的消费支出，即所谓的虚拟消费支出。居民虚拟消费支出包括如下几种类型：单位以实物报酬及实物转移的形式提供给劳动者的货物和服务；住户生产并由本住户消费了的货物和服务，其中的服务仅指住户的自有住房服务和付酬的家庭雇员提供的家庭和个人服务；金融机构提供的金融媒介服务；保险公司提供的保险服务。

政府消费支出 指政府部门为全社会提供的公共服务的消费支出和免费或以较低的价格向居民住户提供的货物和服务的净支出，前者等于政府服务的产出价值减去政府单位所获得的经营收入的价值，后者等于政府部门免费或以较低价格向居民住户提供的货物和服务的市场价值减去向住户收取的价值。

资本形成总额 指常住单位在一定时期内获得减去处置的固定资产和存货的净额，包括固定资本形成总额和存货增加两部分。

固定资本形成总额 指生产者在一定时期内获得的固定资产减处置的固定资产的价值总额。固定资产是通过生产活动生产出来的，且其使用年限在一年以上、单位价值在规定标准以上的资产，不包括自然资产。可分为有形固定资本形成总额和无形固定资本形成总额。有形固定资本形成总额包括一定时期内完成的建筑工程、安装工程和设备工器具购置(减处置)价值，以及土地改良、新增役、种、奶、毛、娱乐用牲畜和新增经济林木价值。无形固定资本形成总额包括矿藏的勘探、计算机软件等获得减处置。

存货增加 指常住单位在一定时期内存货实物量变动的市场价值，即期末价值减期初价值的差额，再扣除当期由于价格变动而产生的持有收益。存货增加可以是正值，也可以是负值，正值表示存货上升，负值表示存货下降。存货包括生产单位购进的原材料、燃料和储备物资等存货，以及生产单位生产的产成品、在制品和半成品等存货。

货物和服务净出口 指货物和服务出口减货物和服务进口的差额。出口包括常住单位向非常住单位出售或无偿转让的各种货物和服务的价值；进口包括常住单位从非常住单位购买或无偿得到的各种货物和服务的价值。由于服务活动的提供与使用同时发生，一般把常住单位从非常住单位得到的服务作为进口，非常住单位从常住单位得到的服务作为出口。货物的出口和进口都按离岸价格计算。

Explanatory Notes on Main Statistical Indicators

Average Annual Growth Rate Two methods for calculating average annual growth rate are applied, one is often called level approach, or the method of calculating geometric average, which is derived by comparing the level of the last year of the interval with that of the beginning year; the other is called accumulative approach or algebraic average or equation method, which is derived by the summation of the actual figure of each year in the interval divided by the figure in the base year. Usually the results calculated by the two methods are fairly close, but they differed sharply when uneven economic development occurred with striking fluctuations in growth.

Industrial Classification of the National Economy The new Industrial Classification of the National Economy (GB/T 4754-2002) is introduced starting from the compilation of 2003 annual statistics. The new revision was based on the 1994 classification and organized by the National Bureau of Statistics taking into consideration of the International Standards of the Industrial Classification of All Economic Activities (ISIC/Rev.3) of the United Nations, and the new Classification was promulgated by the National Administration of Quality Supervision, Inspection and Quarantine on May 10, 2002. The revised version of the Industrial Classification of the National Economy (GB/T 4754-2002) is composed of 20 major divisions, 95 divisions, 396 major groups and 913 groups, including 4 new major divisions, 3 new divisions, 28 major groups and 67 groups.

Registration Status of Enterprises Enterprises are classified into 3 categories, namely domestic-funded enterprises, enterprises with investment from Hong Kong, Macau and Taiwan, and enterprises with foreign investment, in the light of the registration status of an enterprise in industrial and commercial administration agencies. Domestic-funded enterprises include state-owned enterprises, collective-owned enterprises, cooperative enterprises, joint ownership enterprises, limited liability corporations, share-holding corporations Ltd., private enterprises and other enterprises. Included in the enterprises with investment from Hong Kong, Macau and Taiwan and enterprises with foreign investment are joint-venture enterprises, cooperative enterprises, sole investment enterprises and share-holding corporations Ltd. For government agencies, institutions and social organizations which are not requested to be registered in industrial and commercial administration agencies, they are classified mainly by their sources of funds and way of management.

State-owned Enterprises refer to non-corporation economic units where the entire assets are owned by the state and which have registered in accordance with the Regulation of the People's Republic of China on the Management of Registration of Corporate Enterprises. Excluded from this category are sole state-funded corporations in the limited liability corporations.

Collective-owned Enterprises refer to economic units where the assets are owned collectively and which have registered in accordance with the Regulation of the People's Republic of China on the Management of Registration of Corporate Enterprises.

Cooperative Enterprises refer to a form of collective economic units (enterprises) where capitals come mainly from employees as their shares, with certain proportion of capital from the outside, where production is organized on the basis of independent operation, independent accounting for profits and losses, joint work, democratic management, and a distribution system that integrates remuneration according to work with dividend according to capital share.

Joint Ownership Enterprises refer to economic units established by two or more corporate enterprises or corporate institutions of the same or different ownership, through joint investment on the basis of equality, voluntary participation and mutual benefits. They include state joint ownership enterprises, collective joint ownership enterprises, joint state-collective enterprises, other joint ownership enterprises.

Limited Liability Corporations refer to economic units established with investment from 2-50 investors and registered in accordance with the Regulation of the People's Republic of China on the Management of Registration of Corporations, each investor bearing limited liability to the corporation depending on its share of investment, and the corporation bearing liability to its debt to the maximum of its total assets. Limited liability corporations include exclusive state-funded limited liability corporations and other limited liability corporations.

Share-holding Corporations Ltd. refer to economic units registered in accordance with the Regulation of the People's Republic of China on the Management of Registration of Corporations, with total registered capitals divided into equal shares and raised through issuing stocks. Each investor bears limited liability to the corporation depending on the holding of shares, and the corporation bears liability to its debt to the maximum of its total assets.

Private Enterprises refer to profit-making economic units invested and established by natural persons, or controlled by natural persons using employed labour. Included in this category are private limited liability corporations, private share-holding corporations Ltd., private partnership enterprises and private-funded enterprises registered in accordance with the Corporation Law, Partnership Enterprises Law and Interim Regulations on Private Enterprises .

Other Domestic-funded Enterprises refer to domestic-funded economic units other than those mentioned above.

Cooperative Enterprises with Funds from Hong Kong Macau and Taiwan established by investors from Hong Kong, Macau and Taiwan with enterprises in the mainland of China in accordance with the Law of the People's Republic of China on Sino-foreign Cooperative Enterprises and other relevant laws, where the investment or provision of facilities, and the share of profits and risks is stipulated in the cooperative contract.

Enterprises with Sole (exclusive) Investment from Hong Kong, Macau and Taiwan refer to enterprises established in the mainland of China with exclusive investment from investors from Hong Kong, Macau and Taiwan in accordance with the Law of the People's Republic of China on Foreign-Funded Enterprises and other relevant laws.

Share-holding Corporations Ltd. with Investment from Hong Kong, Macau and Taiwan refer to share-holding corporations Ltd. established with the approval from the former Ministry of Foreign Trade and Economic Relations in line with relevant state regulations, where the share of investment from Hong Kong, Macau or Taiwan businessmen exceeds 25% of the total registered capital of the corporation. In case the share of investment from Hong Kong, Macau or Taiwan is less than 25% of the total registered capital, the enterprise is to be classified as domestic-funded share-holding corporation Ltd.

Joint-venture Enterprises with Foreign Investment refer to enterprises jointly established by foreign enterprises or foreigners with enterprises in the mainland of China in accordance with the Law of the People's Republic of China on Sino-foreign Joint Venture Enterprises and other relevant laws, where the share of investment, profits and risks is stipulated in the contract.

Cooperation Enterprises with Foreign Investment refer to enterprises jointly established by foreign enterprises or foreigners with enterprises in the mainland of China in accordance with the Law of the People's Republic of China on Sino-foreign Cooperative Enterprises and other relevant laws, where the investment or provision of facilities, and the share of profits and risks is stipulated in the cooperative contract.

Enterprises with Sole (exclusive) Foreign Investment refer to enterprises established in the mainland of China with exclusive investment from foreign investors in accordance with the Law of the People's Republic of China on Foreign-Funded Enterprises and other relevant laws.

Share-holding Corporations Ltd. with Foreign Investment refer to share-holding corporations Ltd. established with the approval from the Ministry of Foreign Trade and Economic Relations in line with relevant state regulations, where the share of investment from foreign investors exceeds 25% of the total registered capital of the corporation. In case the share of foreign investment is less than 25% of the total registered capital, the enterprise is to be classified as domestic-funded share-holding corporation Ltd.

Government Agencies, Institutions and Social Organizations are classified into following categories by source of funds and way of management taking reference of the registration status of enterprises:

(1) Government agencies: include state and party agencies, classified in principle as state-owned. There are exceptions, such as supply and marketing cooperatives which are classified as collective-owned.

(2) Institutions: include institutions of various types established with the approval by organization and staffing departments of the government, but exclude institutions where enterprise management system is introduced. Institutions are further classified as follows:

(a) Institutions whose main budget is listed in the government budget appropriations or extra-budget funds, or allocated from the budget of their competent government agencies. Such institutions are classified as state-owned.

(b) Institutions whose budget mainly comes from collective units. Such institutions are classified as collective-owned.

(c) Institutions other than those mentioned above whose source of budget is not clear. Such institutions are classified by way of management.

(3) Social organizations: include social organizations established with the approval from the Ministry of Civil Affairs, and organizations that are not covered by social organization management regulations such as trade unions, womens federations etc.. Social organizations are further classified as follows:

(a) Social organizations that are not covered by social organization management regulations of the Ministry of Civil Affairs such as trade unions, womens federations, communist youth leagues, youth associations, industrial and commerce associations, scientists associations, overseas Chinese associations, etc., foundations and fund management organizations established with funds from the state, and social organizations whose funds mainly come from the budget of their competent government agencies. Such institutions are classified as state-owned.

(b) Social organizations whose budget mainly comes from collective units. Such institutions are classified as collective-owned.

(c) Social organizations established by individual or a group of citizens, which are classified as private.

(d) Social organizations other than those mentioned above whose source of budget is not clear. Such organizations are classified by way of management.

Gross Domestic Product (GDP) refers to the final products at market prices produced by all resident units in a country (or a region) during a certain period of time. Gross domestic product is expressed in three different forms, i.e. value, income, and products respectively. GDP in its value form refers to the total value of all goods and services produced by all resident units during a certain period of time, minus the total value of input of goods and services of the nature of non-fixed assets; in other term, it is the sum of the value-added of all resident units. GDP in the form of income includes the income created by all resident units and distributed to resident and non-resident units. GDP in the form of products refers to the value of all goods and services for final consumption by all resident units minus the net exports of goods and services during a given period of time. In the practice of national accounting, gross domestic product is calculated with three approaches, i.e. production approach, income approach and expenditure approach, which reflect gross domestic product and its composition from different aspects.

Gross National Income (GNI) also known as gross national product, refers to the final result of the primary distribution of the income created by all the resident units of a country (or a region) during a certain period of time. The value-added created by the resident units of a country engaged in production activities is distributed, during the primary distribution, mainly to the resident units of that country, while part of it is distributed to the non-resident units in the form of production tax and import duties (minus subsidies to production and import), remuneration for the labourers and property income. At the meantime, a part of the value-added created abroad is distributed to the resident units of the country in the form of production tax and import duties (minus subsidies to production and import), remuneration for the labourers and property income. The concept of gross national income is thus developed, which equals to the gross domestic product plus the net factor income from abroad. Unlike the gross domestic product which is a concept of production, the gross national income is a concept of income.

Three Industries Classification of economic activities into three branches of industries is a common practice in the world, although the grouping varies to some extent form country to country. In China economic activities are categorized into following industries:

Primary industry: refers to agriculture, forestry, animal husbandry and fishery.

Secondary industry: refers to mining and quarrying, manufacturing, production and supply of electricity, water and gas, and construction.

Tertiary industry: refers to all other economic activities not included in primary or secondary industry.

Labourers Remuneration refers to the whole payment of various forms earned by the labourers from the productive activities they are engaged in. It includes wages, bonuses and allowances the labourers earned in monetary form and in kind. It also includes the free medical services provided to the labourers and the medicine expenses, traffic subsidies and social insurance, housing fund paid by the employers. As the individual economy is concerned, since the labourers remuneration is not easily distinguished from the operating profit, both are treated as labourers remuneration.

Net Taxes on Production refers to the difference of the taxes on production minus the subsidies on production. The taxes on production refers to the various taxes, extra charges and fees levied on the production units on their production, sale and business activities as well as on the use of some factors of production, such as fixed assets, land and labour force in the production activities they are engaged in. In contrast to the taxes on production, the subsidies on production refer to the unilateral government transfer to the production units and are therefore regarded as negative taxes on production. They include subsidies on the loss due to implementation of government policies, price subsidies, etc.

Depreciation of Fixed Assets refers to the depreciation of fixed assets of a given period, drawn in accordance with the stipulated depreciation rate for the purpose of compensating the wear loss of the fixed assets or the depreciation of fixed assets calculated in a fictitious way in accordance with the stipulated unified depreciation rate in the national economic accounting system. It reflects the value of transfer of the fixed assets in the production of the current period. The depreciation of fixed assets in various enterprises and institutions managed as enterprises refers to the depreciation expenses actually drawn. In government agencies and institutions not managed as enterprises which do not draw the depreciation expenses, as well as for the houses of residents, the depreciation of fixed assets is the imputed depreciation, which is calculated in accordance with the stipulated unified depreciation rate. In principle, the depreciation of fixed assets should be calculated on the basis of the re-purchased value of the fixed assets. However, there is no actual condition to re-evaluate all the fixed assets in China. Therefore, the above-mentioned methods are temporarily adopted at present.

Operating Surplus refers to the balance of the value added created by the resident units deducting the labourers remuneration, net taxes on production and the depreciation of fixed assets. It is equivalent to the business profit of the enterprises plus subsidies on production, but the wages and welfare expenses paid from the profits should be deducted.

GDP by Expenditure Approach refers to the method of measuring the final results of production activities of a country (region) during a given period from the perspective of final use. It includes final consumption expenditure, total capital formation and net export of goods and services, i.e.:

GDP by expenditure approach = final consumption expenditure + total capital formation + net export of goods and services

Final Consumption Expenditure refers to the total expenditure of resident units for purchases of goods and services from domestic economic territory and abroad to meet the requirements of material, cultural and spiritual life. It excludes the expenditure of non-resident units on consumption in the economic territory of the country. The final consumption expenditure is broken down into household consumption expenditure and government consumption expenditure.

Households Consumption Expenditure refers to the total expenditure of resident households on the final consumption of goods

and services. In addition to the consumption of goods and services bought by the households directly with money, the households consumption expenditure also includes expenditure on goods and services obtained by the households in other ways, i.e. the so-called imputed consumption expenditure, which includes the following: (a) the goods and services provided to the households by the employer in the form of payment in kind and transfer in kind; (b) goods and services produced and consumed by the households themselves, in which the services refer only to the owner-occupied housing and domestic and individual services provided by the paid household workers; (c) financial intermediate services provided by financial institutions; (d) insurance services provided by insurance companies.

Government Consumption Expenditure refers to the expenditure on the consumption of the public services provided by the government to the whole society and the net expenditure on the goods and services provided by the government to the households free of charge or at low prices. The former equals to the output value of the government services minus the value of operating income obtained by the government departments. The latter equals to the market value of the goods and services provided by the government free of charge or at low prices to the households minus the value received by the government from the households.

Total Capital Formation refers to the fixed assets acquired minus those disposed of and the net value of inventory, including the total fixed capital formation and the increase in inventory.

Total Fixed Capital Formation refers to the value of fixed assets acquired minus those disposed of during a given period. Fixed assets are the assets produced through production activities with specified unit value which could be used for over one year, excluding natural assets. Total fixed capital formation can be categorized into total tangible capital formation and total intangible capital formation. The total tangible capital formation include the value of the construction projects, installation projects completed and the equipment, apparatus and instruments purchased as well as the value of land improved, the value of draught animals, breeding stock, animals for milk, wool and for recreational purpose, and the newly increased forest with economic value during a given period. The total intangible capital formation includes the prospecting of minerals, the acquisition of computer software minus the disposal of them.

Increase in Inventory refers to the market value of the change in inventory of resident units during a given period, i.e. the difference of value between the beginning and the end of the period minus the current gains due to the change in prices. The increase in inventory can be positive or negative. A positive value indicates the increase in inventory while a negative value indicates the decrease in stock. The inventory includes the raw materials, fuels and reserve materials purchased by the production units as well as the inventory of finished products, semi-finished products, work-in-progress, etc.

Net Export of Goods and Services refers to the difference of the exports of goods and services minus the imports of goods and services. The imports include the value of various goods and services sold or gratuitously transferred by the resident units to the non-resident units. The imports include the value of various goods and services purchased or gratuitously acquired by the resident units from the non-resident units. Because the provision of services and the use of them happen simultaneously, the acquisition of services by the resident units from abroad is usually treated as import while the acquisition of services by non-resident units in this country is usually treated as export. The export and import of goods are calculated at FOB.

2 总人口

Population

资料整理：王兴华

2-1 总　　人　　口

POPULATION

单位：万人　　(年底数)(number at year-end)　　(10 000 persons)

年份 Year	总人口 Total Population	男 Male	女 Female
1952	2751.20	1427.30	1323.90
1957	3062.41	1579.69	1482.72
1965	3504.54	1793.37	1711.17
1975	4408.15	2261.64	2146.51
1978	4574.91	2348.22	2226.69
1979	4632.78	2376.57	2256.21
1980	4684.45	2401.74	2282.71
1981	4740.35	2430.91	2309.44
1982	4800.92	2464.27	2336.65
1983	4865.73	2501.19	2364.54
1984	4917.75	2532.33	2385.42
1985	4980.19	2565.32	2414.87
1986	5047.83	2603.60	2444.23
1987	5120.27	2640.76	2479.51
1988	5184.94	2673.09	2511.85
1989	5258.83	2712.57	2546.26
1990	5439.29	2805.46	2633.83
1991	5512.33	2839.16	2673.17
1992	5579.85	2875.36	2704.49
1993	5653.48	2913.30	2740.18
1994	5718.81	2947.57	2771.24
1995	5772.07	2959.55	2812.52
1996	5825.13	3004.79	2820.34
1997	5872.60	3016.55	2856.05
1998	5907.23	3032.67	2874.56
1999	5938.03	3031.96	2906.07
2000	5960.00	3102.78	2857.22
2001	5974.56	3 071.52	2903.04
2002	5987.80	3071.52	2903.04
2003	6001.70	3125.70	2876.00
2004	6016.10	3129.60	2886.50
2005	6031.00	3126.47	2904.53
2006	6050.00	3135.11	2914.89
2007	6070.00	3144.26	2925.74
2008	6110.80	3167.45	2943.34
2009	6141.88	3185.46	2956.42

注:总人口除1982年、1990年、2000年是以人口普查为基数推算外，1982年及以后为人口抽样调查推算数。2008年、2009年为户籍人口数。

Note:In addition to the total population in 1982, 1990 and 2000 based on census projections for the base, the population in 1982 and beyond as the number of sample projections. 2008, 2009 was for the household population.

2–2 人口城乡构成

POPULATION

单位：万人 (年底数) (number at year-end) (10 000 persons)

年份 Year	人口数 Total Population	城镇人口 Urban Population	乡村人口 Rural Population
1952	2687.58	271.41	2416.17
1957	3062.41	411.69	2650.72
1965	3504.54	485.06	3019.48
1975	4408.15	626.22	3781.93
1978	4574.91	690.23	3884.68
1979	4632.78	747.92	3884.86
1980	4684.45	786.49	3897.96
1981	4740.35	815.60	3924.75
1982	4800.92	848.76	3952.16
1983	4835.34	873.91	3961.43
1984	4876.07	877.41	3998.66
1985	4930.97	1120.50	3810.47
1986	5047.83	1187.23	3860.60
1987	5120.27	1288.61	3831.66
1988	5184.94	1389.99	3794.95
1989	5258.83	1491.37	3767.46
1990	5439.29	1551.51	3887.78
1991	5512.33	1433.06	4079.27
1992	5579.85	1637.68	3942.17
1993	5653.48	1731.66	3921.82
1994	5718.81	1604.13	4114.68
1995	5772.07	1800.89	3971.18
1996	5825.13	1965.40	3859.73
1997	5872.60	1834.60	4038.00
1998	5907.23	1884.41	4022.82
1999	5938.03	1990.17	3947.86
2000	5960.00	2412.20	3547.80
2001	5658.00	2308.50	3349.50
2002	5672.00	2348.20	3323.80
2003	5685.00	2387.70	3297.30
2004	5698.00	2427.30	2466.70
2005	5710.00	2466.70	3243.30
2006	5693.00	2493.50	3199.50
2007	5699.00	2524.70	3174.30
2008	5711.00	2581.40	3129.60
2009	5720.00	2631.20	3088.80

注：1.人口数除1982年、1990年、2000年是以人口普查为基数推算外，1982年及以后为人口抽样调查推算数。
2.2000年以前数据是总人口数，2001年以后数据为常住人口数。

Notes:a) Population than in 1982, 1990 and 2000 census as the base is projected, the population in 1982 and beyond as the number of sample projections.
b)2000 before the data on total population, since 2001 data for the resident population.

2–3 全省人口自然变动
NATURAL CHANGE OF POLULATION

年 份	人口变动数(万人) Number of Population Changed (10 000 persons)			变动系数(‰) Growth Rates		
Year	出生数 Number of Birth	死亡数 Number of Death	自然增长数 Number of Nature Growth	出生率 Birth Rate	死亡率 Death Rate	自然增长率 Natural Growth Rate
1965	121.48	34.75	86.73	35.10	10.04	25.06
1975	90.80	34.52	56.28	20.74	7.88	12.86
1978	84.91	32.12	52.79	18.67	7.06	11.61
1980	94.84	32.59	62.25	20.36	7.00	13.36
1985	97.83	37.37	60.46	19.95	7.62	12.33
1986	107.09	39.45	67.64	21.01	7.74	13.27
1987	108.56	36.12	72.44	21.43	7.13	14.30
1988	97.62	32.95	64.67	19.08	6.44	12.64
1989	110.13	36.24	73.89	21.09	6.94	14.15
1990	114.40	38.66	75.74	21.60	7.30	14.30
1991	113.34	40.30	73.04	20.70	7.36	13.34
1992	105.60	38.08	67.52	19.05	6.87	12.18
1993	112.55	38.92	73.63	20.04	6.93	13.11
1994	103.31	37.98	65.33	18.17	6.68	11.49
1995	92.96	39.70	53.26	16.18	6.91	9.27
1996	93.24	40.18	53.06	16.08	6.93	9.15
1997	86.62	39.13	47.49	14.81	6.69	8.12
1998	74.09	39.46	34.63	12.58	6.70	5.88
1999	68.52	37.73	30.79	11.57	6.37	5.20
2000	57.76	35.75	22.01	9.71	6.01	3.70
2001	50.84	36.27	14.57	8.51	6.07	2.44
2002	50.10	36.90	13.20	8.38	6.17	2.21
2003	49.50	35.60	13.90	8.26	5.94	2.32
2004	50.66	36.23	14.43	8.43	6.03	2.40
2005	52.60	34.30	18.30	8.74	5.69	3.05
2006	54.80	35.90	18.90	9.08	5.95	3.13
2007	55.69	36.12	19.57	9.19	5.96	3.23
2008	55.98	39.51	16.47	9.21	6.50	2.71
2009	57.80	36.58	21.22	9.48	6.00	3.48

注：1985年以后人口变动系数为人口抽样调查数，其余为公安年报数。

Note: the data of change of population after 1985 was based on census, the rest were from public security annual report.

2–4 全省市、州、县年底人口数（2009）
POPULATION OF CITIES, TOWNS, AND COUNTIES OF HUBEI AT YEAR-END

单位:万人 (10 000 persons)

地 区	Region	户籍人口 Total Population	常住人口 Population of Permnant Residents	地 区	Region	户籍人口 Total Population	常住人口 Population of Permnant Residents
全 省	**Province**	**6141.88**	**5720.00**	竹溪县	Zhuxi County	37.52	33.46
武汉市	**Wuhan City**	**835.55**	**910.00**	房 县	Famg County	48.92	42.15
江岸区	Jiang'an District	67.28	76.73	**宜昌市**	**Yichang City**	**401.37**	**404.55**
江汉区	Jianghan District	47.68	67.39	西陵区	Xilin District	41.83	46.40
硚口区	Qiaokou District	53.17	73.59	伍家岗区	Wujiagang District	15.23	19.35
汉阳区	Hanyang District	54.93	71.30	点军区	Dianjun District	10.57	10.70
武昌区	Wuchang District	113.42	118.10	猇亭区	Huting District	5.03	5.45
青山区	Qingshan District	45.46	52.26	夷陵区	yiling District	52.13	52.00
洪山区	Hongshan District	95.92	116.37	远安县	Yuan'an District	19.49	18.60
东西湖区	Dongxihu District	26.38	39.10	兴山县	xingshan District	18.12	17.50
汉南区	Hannan District	10.73	12.90	归县	Zigui District	38.35	37.60
蔡甸区	Caidian District	44.90	43.65	长阳县	Changyang District	41.39	40.50
江夏区	Jiangxia District	63.70	64.35	五峰县	Wufeng District	20.95	19.60
黄 区	Huangpi District	112.91	89.10	宜都市	Yidu City	39.53	38.95
新洲区	Xinzhou District	99.07	85.16	当阳市	Dangyang City	48.53	48.05
黄石市	**Huangshi City**	**258.56**	**242.61**	枝江市	Zhijiang City	50.22	49.85
黄石港区	Huangshigang district	18.34	21.99	**襄樊市**	**Xiangfan City**	**588.88**	**544.61**
西塞山区	Xisai mountainous area	22.27	25.06	襄城区	Xiangcheng District	46.39	45.61
下陆区	Xialu District	11.33	11.43	樊城区	Fancheng District	71.61	76.10
铁山区	Tieshan District	5.63	6.14	襄阳区	Xiangyang District	103.74	90.90
开发区	Development Zone	13.97	16.76	南漳县	Nanzhang County	59.17	53.30
大冶市	Daye City	85.88	80.70	谷城县	Gucheng County	57.83	50.50
阳新县	Yangxin County	101.14	80.53	保康县	Baokang County	28.75	26.20
十堰市	**Shiyan City**	**353.22**	**324.1**	老河口市	Laohekou City	53.18	48.30
张湾区	Zhangwan District	26.39	28.24	枣阳市	Zaoyang City	111.86	102.20
茅箭区	Maojian District	26.39	28.85	宜城市	Yicheng City	56.35	51.50
丹江口市	Danjiangkou City	49.67	48.13	**鄂州市**	**Ezhou City**	**107.55**	**103.49**
郧 县	Yun County	65.82	57.71	梁子湖区	Liangzihu District	18.24	17.61
郧西县	Yunxi County	51.45	42.84	华容区	Huarong District	25.09	26.01
竹山县	Zhushan County	47.06	42.72	鄂城区	Ercheng District	64.22	59.87

注：常住人口是指常住本地半年以上人口。
Note:The permanent resident population is more than half the local population.

2-4 续表 Continued

单位:万人 (10 000 persons)

地 区	Regions	户籍人口 Total Population	常住人口 Permnant Population	地 区	Regions	户籍人口 Total Population	常住人口 Permnant Population
荆门市	**Jingmen Municipality**	**301.05**	**285.03**	春县	Hanchun County	99.13	89.28
掇刀区	Duodao District	30.01	34.34	黄梅县	Huangmei County	100.36	91.11
东宝区	Dongbao District	37.92	36.26	麻城市	Macheng City	117.99	107.12
京山县	Jingshan County	65.49	57.09	武穴市	Wuxue City	76.60	67.41
沙洋区	Shayang District	62.85	56.42	**咸宁市**	**Xianning City**	**290.62**	**251.63**
钟祥市	Zhongxiang City	104.78	100.92	咸安区	Xian'an District	59.78	55.00
孝感市	**Xiaogan City**	**528.70**	**468.37**	嘉鱼县	Jiayu county	37.08	32.60
孝南区	Xiaonan District	94.85	88.48	通城县	Tongcheng County	49.20	40.28
孝昌县	Xiaochang County	66.47	58.61	崇阳县	Congyang County	46.93	40.70
大悟县	Dawu County	64.43	56.88	通山县	Tongshan county	46.05	37.45
云梦县	Yunmeng County	60.62	51.96	赤壁市	Chibi City	51.58	45.60
应城市	Yingcheng City	63.04	55.99	**随州市**	**Suizhou City**	**257.77**	**220.81**
安陆市	Anlu City	67.21	57.57	曾都市	Zengdu City	63.71	56.50
汉川市	Hanchuan City	112.08	98.88	随县	Sui County	99.75	85.66
荆州市	**Jingzhou City**	**657.12**	**585.40**	广水市	Guangshui City	94.31	78.65
沙市区	Shashi District	63.08	56.78	**恩施州**	**Enshi Prefecture**	**394.92**	**349.10**
荆州区	Jingzhou District	61.77	55.02	恩施市	Enshi City	79.41	75.59
公安县	Gong'an County	102.64	91.76	利川市	Jianli City	88.26	73.51
监利县	Jianli County	144.59	128.8	建始县	Jianshi County	50.97	45.39
江陵县	Jianglin County	41.05	36.79	巴东县	Badong County	49.09	43.93
石首市	Shishou City	64.33	56.81	宣恩县	Xuan'en County	35.35	31.19
洪湖市	Honghu City	93.94	82.65	咸丰县	Xianfeng County	37.59	31.54
松滋市	Songzi City	85.72	76.79	来凤县	Laifeng County	32.21	28.20
黄冈市	**Huanggang City**	**739.61**	**668.64**	鹤峰县	Hefeng County	22.04	19.75
黄州区	Huangzhou City	36.52	34.24	**省直管单位**	**Jurisdictional Area**	**426.93**	**361.69**
团风县	Tuanfeng County	36.84	33.52	仙桃市	Xiantao City	151.76	123.30
红安县	Hong'an County	66.36	60.29	潜江市	Qianjiang City	101.63	93.76
罗田县	Luotian County	62.29	54.98	天门市	Tianmen City	165.51	137.13
英山县	Yingshan County	39.92	36.01	神农架林区	Shennongjian Forest Area	8.03	7.50
水县	Xishui County	103.59	94.68				

主要统计指标解释

人口数 指一定时点、一定地区范围内有生命的个人总和。

年度统计的年末人口数指每年 12 月 31 日 24 时的人口数。

城镇人口和乡村人口 城镇人口是指居住在城镇范围内的全部常住人口；乡村人口是除上述人口以外的全部人口。

出生率(又称粗出生率) 指在一定时期内(通常为一年)一定地区的出生人数与同期内平均人数(或期中人数)之比，用千分率表示。本资料中的出生率指年出生率，其计算公式为：

$$出生率=\frac{年出生人数}{年平均人数}\times 1000‰$$

式中：出生人数指活产婴儿，即胎儿脱离母体时(不管怀孕月数)，有过呼吸或其他生命现象。年平均人数指年初、年底人口数的平均数，也可用年中人口数代替。

死亡率(又称粗死亡率) 指在一定时期内(通常为一年)一定地区的死亡人数与同期内平均人数(或期中人数)之比，用千分率表示。本资料中的死亡率指年死亡率，其计算公式为：

$$死亡率=\frac{年死亡人数}{年平均人数}\times 1000‰$$

人口自然增长率 指在一定时期内(通常为一年)人口自然增加数(出生人数减死亡人数)与该时期内平均人数(或期中人数)之比，用千分率表示。计算公式为：

$$人口自然增长率=\frac{本年出生人数-本年死亡人数}{年平均人数}\times 1000‰$$

$$=人口出生率-人口死亡率$$

Explanatory Notes on Main Statistical Indicators

Total Population refers to the total number of people alive at a certain point of time within a given area.

The annual statistics on total population is taken at midnight, the 3lst of December.

Urban Population and Rural Population Urban population refer to all people residing in cities and towns, while rural population refer to population other than urban population.

Birth Rate (or Crude Birth Rate) refers to the ratio of the number of births to the average population (or mid-period population) during a certain period of time (usually a year), expressed in ‰. Birth rate in the chapter refers to annual birth rate. The following formula is used:

Birth Rate = (Number of Births/Average Number of Population)×1000‰

Number of births in the formula refers to live births, i.e. when a baby has breathed or showed any vital phenomena regardless of the length of pregnancy.

Annual average number of population is the average of the number of population at the beginning of the year and that at the end of the year. Sometimes it is substituted by the mid-year population.

Death Rate (or Crude Death Rate) refers to the ratio of the number of deaths to the average population (or mid-period population) during a certain period of time (usually a year), expressed in ‰. Death rate in the chapter refers to annual death rate. The following formula is used:

Death Rate= (Number of Deaths/Annual Average Number of Population)×1000‰

Natural Growth Rate of Population refers to the ratio of natural increase in population (number of births minus number of deaths) in a certain period of time (usually a year) to the average population (or mid-period population) of the same period, expressed in ‰. The following formula is applied:

Natural Growth Rate of Population = [(Number of Births-Number of Deaths)/Average Number of Population]×1000‰

Natural Growth Rate of Population = Birth Rate-Death Rate

3 就业与工资

Employment and Wages

资料整理：张　蔚　王兴华

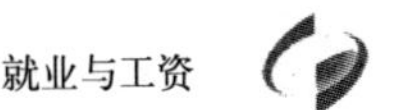

3-1 全社会从业人员

NEMBER OF EMPLOYED PERSONS

单位：万人 (10 000 persons)

年份 Year	合计 Total	按城乡分 Grouped by Areas		按产业分 Grouped by Industries		
		城镇 Urban	乡村 Rural	第一产业 Primary Industry	第二产业 Secondary Industry	第三产业 Tertiary Industry
1952	1020.30	141.60	878.70			
1957	1139.90	173.60	966.30			
1965	1404.20	222.70	1181.60			
1970	1618.50	278.00	1340.80			
1975	1802.50	381.70	1420.80			
1978	1910.40	458.00	1452.30	1470.60	269.00	170.80
1980	1986.90	507.20	1479.70	1453.70	286.30	247.00
1985	2238.10	637.60	1600.50	1383.30	485.40	369.50
1990	3040.40	890.80	2149.60	1859.80	628.50	552.10
1991	3082.70	909.40	2173.30	1897.40	623.00	562.30
1992	3118.60	923.10	2195.50	1869.00	650.90	598.70
1993	3157.60	940.90	2216.70	1818.80	684.60	654.20
1994	3196.90	980.10	2216.80	1760.50	717.10	719.30
1995	3232.50	1015.00	2217.50	1697.00	743.50	792.00
1996	3275.50	1050.80	2224.70	1677.10	746.80	851.60
1997	3311.20	1070.50	2240.70	1663.20	752.00	896.00
1998	3328.20	1093.60	2234.60	1612.50	705.60	1010.10
1999	3358.10	1110.50	2247.60	1612.60	697.80	1047.70
2000	3384.90	1123.80	2261.10	1625.10	702.40	1057.40
2001	3414.50	1148.70	2265.80	1639.00	706.80	1068.70
2002	3443.00	1177.00	2266.00	1652.60	704.10	1086.30
2003	3476.00	1211.00	2265.00	1661.50	712.60	1101.90
2004	3507.00	1245.00	2262.00	1672.90	720.30	1113.80
2005	3537.00	1271.00	2266.00	1687.30	725.00	1124.70
2006	3564.00	1297.00	2267.00	1694.70	732.40	1136.90
2007	3584.00	1322.00	2262.00	1697.00	740.10	1146.90
2008	3607.00	1337.00	2270.00	1707.91	730.42	1168.67
2009	3622.00	1357.00	2265.00	1702.30	736.60	1183.10

3-2 分行业城镇单位从业人员数（2009）

THE NUMBER OF STAFF IN URBAN UNITS BY SECTOR (2009)

单位：人 (person)

行业	Sector	城镇全部单位 All the Units In Urban Area	国有经济单位 State Owned Units	城镇集体单位 Urban Collective Owned Units	其他经济单位 Other Units	城镇私营单位 Urban Private Units
总计	**Total**	**6839898**	**2931210**	**225543**	**1883012**	**1800133**
农、林、牧、渔业	Farming, Forestry, Animal Husbandry and Fishery	167117	151396	4852	1871	8998
采矿业	Mining and Quarrying	187017	60640	10908	33430	82039
制造业	Manufacturing	2109815	291926	47067	895310	875512
电力、燃气及水的生产和供应业	Power, Gas and water production and supply	139457	89905	1010	32850	15692
建筑业	Construction	1079125	190430	79159	451490	358046
交通运输、仓储和邮政业	Transportation, storage and post	376112	252437	11075	72413	40187
信息传输、计算机服务和软件业	Information Transmission, Computer Services and Software	74282	28244	32	29161	16845
批发和零售业	Wholesale and Retail sale	385297	58717	13176	141800	171604
住宿和餐饮业	Hotel and Catering	146110	14730	2695	50700	77985
金融业	Banking	167000	79617	21115	65949	319
房地产业	Real Estate	106937	18385	1295	38458	48799
租赁和商务服务业	Leasing and Commerical Services	72065	29821	3175	15252	23817
科学研究、技术服务和地质勘查业	Scietific Research, polytechnical Service and Geological Prospecting	117341	97662	1229	12472	5978
水利、环境和公共设施管理业	Water Conservance, Environment and Public Facilities Management	88772	76063	5928	2593	4188
居民服务和其他服务业	Resident Service and Others	37919	8836	1959	3049	24075
教育	Education	676415	631465	4142	17295	23513
卫生、社会保障和社会福利业	Health, Social Security and Social Welfare	291396	263119	13229	6831	8217
文化、体育和娱乐业	Culture, Sports and Entertainment	65237	46979	499	4124	13635
公共管理和社会组织	Public Management and Social Organization	552484	540838	2998	7964	684

注：城镇全部单位2009年统计范围含城镇私营单位。（后表未经特别注明均同此口径）

Note: All Statistics of Units in Urban Areas of 2009 including all the private run unit.(The following tables if without specific notes are considered the same standard with this one.)

3–3 分行业在岗职工人数（2009）
NUMBER OF EMPLOYED BY SECTOR (2009)

单位：人 (person)

行业	Sector	城镇全部单位 All the Units In Urban Area	国有经济单位 State Owned Units	城镇集体单位 Urban Collective Owned Units	其他经济单位 Other Units	城镇私营单位 Urban Private Units
总计	**Total**	**6524945**	**2740833**	**207293**	**1776686**	**1800133**
农、林、牧、渔业	Farming, Forestry, Animal Husbandry and Fishery	146796	131129	4798	1871	8998
采矿业	Mining and Quarrying	181074	56391	10658	31986	82039
制造业	Manufacturing	2079956	285856	45688	872900	875512
电力、燃气及水的生产和供应业	Power, Gas and water production and supply	137200	87753	1007	32748	15692
建筑业	Construction	970661	135082	69523	408010	358046
交通运输、仓储和邮政业	Transportation, storage and post	360873	240974	9982	69730	40187
信息传输、计算机服务和软件业	Information Transmission, Computer Services and Software	72335	27549	30	27911	16845
批发和零售业	Wholesale and Retail sale	377734	56419	12433	137278	171604
住宿和餐饮业	Hotel and Catering	139820	13813	2685	45337	77985
金融业	Banking	138774	71044	20845	46566	319
房地产业	Real Estate	105122	17702	1282	37339	48799
租赁和商务服务业	Leasing and Commerical Services	68990	27842	3038	14293	23817
科学研究、技术服务和地质勘查业	Scietific Research, polytechnical Service and Geological Prospecting	109135	90803	1152	11202	5978
水利、环境和公共设施管理业	Water Conservance, Environment and Public Facilities Management	78630	68450	3479	2513	4188
居民服务和其他服务业	Resident Service and Others	36102	7233	1884	2910	24075
教育	Education	646771	604271	3413	15574	23513
卫生、社会保障和社会福利业	Health, Social Security and Social Welfare	280325	252868	12545	6695	8217
文化、体育和娱乐业	Culture, Sports and Entertainment	63064	44989	499	3941	13635
公共管理和社会组织	Public Management and Social Organization	531583	520665	2352	7882	684

3-4 分行业在岗女职工人数（2009）
NUMBER OF FEMALE EMPLOYEES BY SECTOR(2009)

单位：人 (person)

行业	Sector	城镇全部单位（不含私营单位） All the Units In Urban Area	国有经济单位 State Owned Units	城镇集体单位 Urban Collective Owned Units	其他经济单位 Urban Private Units
总计	**Total**	**1683784**	**997184**	**68354**	**618246**
农、林、牧、渔业	Farming, Forestry, Animal Husbandry and Fishery	57976	55624	1673	679
采矿业	Mining and Quarrying	20107	13629	1362	5116
制造业	Manufacturing	448767	90371	18915	339481
电力、燃气及水的生产和供应业	Power, Gas and water production and supply	39092	27282	383	11427
建筑业	Construction	82734	24159	7827	50748
交通运输、仓储和邮政业	Transportation, storage and post	93947	67459	4929	21559
信息传输、计算机服务和软件业	Information Transmission, Computer Services and Software	17360	7902	6	9452
批发和零售业	Wholesale and Retail sale	105687	20936	7146	77605
住宿和餐饮业	Hotel and Catering	39853	8318	1575	29960
金融业	Banking	76169	35079	9628	31462
房地产业	Real Estate	17769	5428	413	11928
租赁和商务服务业	Leasing and Commerical Services	14823	8526	976	5321
科学研究、技术服务和地质勘查业	Scietific Research, polytechnical Service and Geological Prospecting	30514	27118	336	3060
水利、环境和公共设施管理业	Water Conservance, Environment and Public Facilities Management	34692	31008	2895	789
居民服务和其他服务业	Resident Service and Others	4905	2548	803	1554
教育	Education	274963	265392	2065	7506
卫生、社会保障和社会福利业	Health, Social Security and Social Welfare	158962	149100	6101	3761
文化、体育和娱乐业	Culture, Sports and Entertainment	20167	18112	159	1896
公共管理和社会组织	Public Management and Social Organization	145297	139193	1162	4942

3-5 城镇登记失业人数及失业率
NUMBER OF URBAN UNEMPLOYED PERSONS AND UNEMPLOYMENT RATE

单位：万人 (10 000 persons)

年份 Year	本年失业人员就业人数 Unemployed-Reemployees	年末城镇登记失业人数 The Number of Unemployeed in Urban Areas by the End of Year	年末城镇登记失业率(%) Year End Unemployment registered Rate %
1978	6.47	20.03	4.19
1980	30.84	15.54	2.97
1985	17.80	7.31	1.13
1990	17.31	12.66	1.72
1991	18.56	14.20	1.88
1992	20.94	16.89	2.17
1993	22.46	17.96	2.20
1994	21.36	21.06	2.90
1995	24.35	24.45	3.10
1996	21.02	28.25	3.50
1997	23.48	29.83	3.50
1998	23.56	31.33	3.30
1999	28.10	33.10	3.30
2000	31.02	36.64	3.50
2001	44.27	42.15	4.00
2002	46.61	44.66	4.30
2003	44.69	49.34	4.30
2004	43.63	49.37	4.20
2005	51.50	52.60	4.33
2006	55.53	52.56	4.22
2007	45.05	46.72	4.21
2008	43.49	55.07	4.20
2009	48.35	55.25	4.21

3-6 职工平均工资及指数

年份 Year	平均货币工资(元) Average Money Wages (yuan)					指数(上年=100) Indices(preceding year=100)	
	合计 Total	国有经济单位 State Owned Units	城镇集体经济单位 Urban Collective Owned	其他经济单位 Other Units	城镇私营单位 Urban private units	货币工资 Money Wages	国有经济单位 State Owned Units
1978	581.00	592.00	532.00			104.50	104.50
1980	719.00	744.00	619.00			116.00	115.90
1985	1027.00	1082.00	867.00	988.00		115.50	116.30
1990	1903.00	2045.00	1467.00	2259.00		111.70	107.60
1991	2081.00	2213.00	1662.00	2363.00		109.40	108.20
1992	2370.00	2532.00	1837.00	2575.00		113.90	114.40
1993	2933.00	3141.00	2183.00	3248.00		123.80	124.10
1994	4050.00	4348.00	2845.00	4352.00		138.10	138.40
1995	4685.00	4991.00	3308.00	5093.00		115.70	114.80
1996	5099.00	5411.00	3590.00	5754.00		108.80	108.40
1997	5401.00	5741.00	3731.00	5740.00		105.90	106.10
1998	6436.00	6783.00	4748.00	6166.00		108.70	109.10
1999	6991.00	7381.00	5001.00	6681.00		108.60	108.80
2000	7565.00	7989.00	5090.00	7327.00		108.20	108.20
2001	8619.00	9133.00	5677.00	8035.00		113.90	114.30
2002	9611.00	10403.00	6534.00	8180.00		111.50	113.90
2003	10692.00	11806.00	7137.00	8698.00		111.20	113.50
2004	11855.00	13096.00	7608.00	10270.00		110.90	110.90
2005	13330.00	14774.00	8663.00	11572.00		112.40	112.80
2006	15172.00	17078.00	9848.00	13098.00		113.82	115.59
2007	17396.97	21971.00	12921.00	16829.00		114.66	128.65
2008	19596.93	24756.00	14840.00	20293.00		112.65	112.68
2009	23709.00	30028.00	19181.00	23528.00	15615.00	120.98	121.30

注：1998年以后为在岗职工平均工资。2007年以后统计范围含城镇全部私营单位。

AVERAGE WAGES AND INDICES OF STAFF AND WORKERS

指数(上年=100) Indices(preceding year=100)							
城镇集体经济单位 Urban Collective Owned	其他经济单位 OtherUnits	城镇私营单位 Urban private units	实际工资 Real Wages	国有经济单位 State Owned Units	城镇集体经济单位 Urban Collective Owned	其他经济单位 OtherUnits	城镇私营单位 Urban private units
106.40			104.20	103.90	106.10		
116.40			108.60	108.50	109.00		
112.90			104.70	105.40	102.40		
107.10	107.10		107.80	108.30	104.40	103.90	
113.30	104.60		103.00	101.90	106.70	98.50	
110.50	109.00		103.10	103.50	100.00	98.70	
118.80	126.10		106.60	106.80	102.30	108.60	
130.30	134.00		108.70	109.00	102.60	105.50	
116.30	117.00		96.30	95.60	96.80	97.40	
108.50	113.00		95.10	94.00	95.30	99.90	
103.90	99.80		97.60	96.60	95.90	96.60	
109.20	99.10		110.20	110.20	110.80	100.50	
105.30	108.40		110.00	111.00	107.40	110.60	
101.80	109.70		109.30	109.30	102.70	110.80	
111.50	109.70		113.60	114.00	111.20	109.30	
115.10	101.80		112.00	114.40	115.60	102.20	
109.20	106.30		108.80	111.10	106.80	104.00	
106.60	118.10		105.70	105.70	101.60	112.60	
113.90	112.70		109.20	109.60	110.70	109.50	
113.68	113.19		112.03	113.77	111.89	111.40	
131.20	128.49		109.41	122.76	125.19	122.60	
114.85	120.58		105.97	106.00	108.04	113.44	
129.25	115.94		121.84	122.15	130.16	116.76	

Notes:Data after 1998 refers to average wages and indices of employed staff and workers. Statistics of 2007 involves all the private run units in urban areas.

3–7 分行业在岗职工平均工资（2009）

AVERAGE WAGES OF STAFF AND WORKER EMPLOYEED(2009)

单位：元 (yuan)

行业	Sector	城镇全部单位 All the Units In Urban Area	国有经济单位 State Owned Units	城镇集体单位 Urban Collective Owned Units	其他经济单位 Urban Private Units	城镇私营单位 Urban private units
总计	Total	23709.49	30028.00	19181.00	23528.00	15614.76
农、林、牧、渔业	Farming, Forestry, Animal Husbandry and Fishery	14105.00	14443.00	12368.00	12380.00	11938.58
采矿业	Mining and Quarrying	21960.20	38936.00	17319.00	18351.00	16764.21
制造业	Manufacturing	20588.80	35680.00	17723.00	22374.00	14502.86
电力、燃气及水的生产和供应业	Power, Gas and water production and supply	30136.68	32913.00	16144.00	32506.00	15019.88
建筑业	Construction	20712.94	29178.00	16228.00	22238.00	16780.59
交通运输、仓储和邮政业	Transportation, storage and post	25912.09	28938.00	16125.00	26226.00	14984.09
信息传输、计算机服务和软件业	Information Transmission, Computer Services and Software	33947.08	27293.00	17621.00	38658.00	46735.53
批发和零售业	Wholesale and Retail sale	17946.48	22545.00	15107.00	20873.00	14461.69
住宿和餐饮业	Hotel and Catering	15387.87	16806.00	18500.00	17890.00	13780.87
金融业	Banking	44986.46	46664.00	33203.00	52016.00	28031.06
房地产业	Real Estate	24200.66	25177.00	19177.00	24728.00	23642.10
租赁和商务服务业	Leasing and Commerical Services	20809.87	22738.00	16256.00	25725.00	15917.47
科学研究、技术服务和地质勘查业	Scietific Research, polytechnical Service and Geological Prospecting	38465.17	40694.00	28963.00	36014.00	21234.02
水利、环境和公共设施管理业	Water Conservance, Environment and Public Facilities Management	18781.51	19111.00	20024.00	17457.00	13887.84
居民服务和其他服务业	Resident Service and Others	16518.40	28219.00	18182.00	18899.00	13374.75
教育	Education	28709.96	29295.00	26410.00	28645.00	16986.16
卫生、社会保障和社会福利业	Health, Social Security and Social Welfare	27295.45	28433.00	19780.00	22541.00	15023.79
文化、体育和娱乐业	Culture, Sports and Entertainment	24439.46	27427.00	13685.00	29934.00	13770.90
公共管理和社会组织	Public Management and Social Organization	30835.06	31177.00	49510.00	15330.00	9244.15

主要统计指标解释

经济活动人口 指在16周岁及以上，有劳动能力，参加或要求参加社会经济活动的人口。包括就业人员和失业人员。

就业人员 指在16周岁及以上，从事一定社会劳动并取得劳动报酬或经营收入的人员。这一指标反映了一定时期内全部劳动力资源的实际利用情况，是研究我国基本国情国力的重要指标。

各单位的就业人员 指在各级国家机关、政党机关、社会团体及企业、事业单位中工作，取得工资或其他形式的劳动报酬的全部人员。包括在岗职工、再就业的离退休人员、民办教师以及在各单位中工作的外方人员和港澳台方人员、兼职人员、借用的外单位人员和第二职业者。不包括离开本单位仍保留劳动关系的职工。各单位的就业人员反映了各单位实际参加生产或工作的全部劳动力。

城镇私营和个体就业人员 城镇私营就业人员指在工商管理部门注册登记，其经营地址设在县城关镇(含县城关镇)以上的私营企业就业人员，包括私营企业投资者和雇工。城镇个体就业人员指在工商管理部门注册登记，并持有城镇户口或在城镇长期居住，经批准从事个体工商经营的就业人员，包括个体经营者和在个体工商户劳动的家庭帮工和雇工。

城镇登记失业人员 指有非农业户口，在一定的劳动年龄内(16周岁至退休年龄)，有劳动能力，无业而要求就业，并在当地就业服务机构进行求职登记的人员。

城镇登记失业率 城镇登记失业人员与城镇单位就业人员(扣除使用的农村劳动力、聘用的离退休人员、港澳台及外方人员)、城镇单位中的不在岗职工、城镇私营业主、个体户主、城镇私营企业和个体就业人员、城镇登记失业人员之和的比。计算公式为：

$$\text{城镇登记失业率}=\frac{\text{城镇登记失业人数}}{\begin{array}{c}\text{(城镇单位就业人员−使用的农村劳动力−聘用的离退休人员−聘用的港澳台及外方人员)}\\ \text{+不在岗职工+城镇私营业主+城镇个体户主+城镇私营企业及个体就业人员+城镇登记失业人数}\end{array}}\times 100\%$$

职工 指在国有、城镇集体、联营、股份制、外商和港、澳、台投资、其他单位及其附属机构工作，并由其支付工资的各类人员。不包括下列人员：(1)乡镇企业就业人员；(2)私营企业就业人员；(3)城镇个体劳动者；(4)离休、退休、退职人员；(5)再就业的离、退休人员；(6)民办教师；(7)在城镇单位中工作的外方及港、澳、台人员；(8)其他按有关规定不列入职工统计范围的人员。(1998年及以后的数据均为在岗职工数据，其他相关指标如职工工资总额，职工平均工资等指标也从1998年按此口径进行了相应调整)。

国有单位 指资产归国家所有的经济组织。包括按《中华人民共和国企业法人登记管理条例》规定登记注册的非公司制的经济组织，以及中央、地方各级国家机关、事业单位和社会团体。

集体单位 指生产资料归集体所有，并按《中华人民共和国企业法人登记管理条例》规定登记注册的经济组织。

其他单位 包括股份合作单位、联营单位、有限责任公司、股份有限公司、港澳台商投资单位以及外商投资单位等其他登记注册类型单位。

在岗职工 指在本单位工作并由单位支付工资的人员，以及有工作岗位，但由于学习、病伤产假等原因暂未工作，仍由单位支付工资的人员。

工资总额 指各单位在一定时期内直接支付给本单位全部职工的劳动报酬总额。工资总额的计算原则应以直接支付给职工的全部劳动报酬为根据。各单位支付给职工的劳动报酬以及其他根据有关规定支付的工资，不论是计入成本的还是不计入成本的，不论是按国家规定列入计征奖金税项目的，还是未列入计征奖金税项目的，不论是以货币形式支付的还是以实物形式支付的，均包括在工资总额内。

平均工资 指企业、事业、机关单位的职工在一定时期内平均每人所得的货币工资额。它表明一定时期职工工资收入的高低程度，是反映职工工资水平的主要指标。计算公式为：

$$\text{平均工资}=\frac{\text{报告期实际支付的全部职工工资总额}}{\text{报告期全部职工平均人数}}$$

平均工资指数 指报告期职工平均工资与基期职工平均工资的比率，是反映不同时期职工货币工资水平变动情况的相对数。计算公式为：

$$\text{平均工资指数}=\frac{\text{报告期职工平均工资}}{\text{基期职工平均工资}}\times 100\%$$

平均实际工资指数 职工平均实际工资指扣除物价变动因素后的职工平均工资。职工平均实际工资指数是反映实际工资变动情况的相对数，表明职工实际工资水平提高或降低的程度。计算公式为：

$$\text{平均实际工资指数}=\frac{\text{报告期职工平均工资指数}}{\text{报告期城镇居民消费价格指数}}\times 100\%$$

Explanatory Notes on Main Statistical Indicators

Economically Active Population refers to the population aged 16 and over who are capable to work, are participating in or willing to participate in economic activities, including employed persons and unemployed persons.

Employed Persons refer to the persons aged 16 and over who are engaged in social working and receive remuneration payment or earn business income. This indicator reflects the actual utilization of total labour force during a certain period of time and is often used for the research on China's economic situation and national power.

Persons Employed in Various Units refer to all the persons working in government agencies of various levels, political and party organizations, social organizations, enterprises and institutions, and receiving wages or other forms of payment. They include fully-employed staff and workers, re-employed retirees, teachers in schools run by the local people, foreigners and Chinese compatriots from Hong Kong, Macao, and Taiwan working in various units, part-time employees, employees of other units working temporarily at current posts, and employees holding the second job, but exclude staff and workers who have left their working units while keeping their labour contract (employment relation) unchanged. This indicator reflects the total number of laborers actually engaged in production or other operations in various units.

Persons Employed in Private Enterprises and Self-Employed Individuals in Urban Areas Persons employed in private enterprises refer to the persons employed in the private enterprises which have been registered at the departments of industrial and commercial administration and are situated at a county town (i.e. a town where the county government is located) for business operation or at urban areas with the level higher than a county town. The self-employed individuals in urban areas refer to persons who hold the certificates of residence in urban areas or have resided in the urban areas for a long time and have been registered at the departments of industrial and commercial administration and approved to be engaged in individual industrial or commercial business, including self-employed persons as well as helpers and hired labourers who work in the individual households engaged in industrial or commercial business.

Registered Urban Unemployed Persons refer to the persons with non-agricultural household registration at certain working ages (16-50 years for male and 16-45 years for females), who are capable of work, unemployed and willing to work, and have been registered at the local employment service agencies to apply for a job.

Registered Urban Unemployment Rate refers to the ratio of the number of the registered unemployed persons to the sum of the number of persons employed in various units (minus the rural labour force, retirees, and Hong Kong, Macao, Taiwan or foreign employees they employ) laid-off workers in urban units, owners and employees in urban private enterprises, urban self-employed individuals and the registered urban unemployed persons. The formula is as follows:

Registered urban unemployment rate = number of registered urban unemployed persons÷(number of persons employed in urban units - rural labour force employed retirees employed - Hong Kong, Macao, Taiwan or foreign employees employ + laid-off workers + owners and employees in urban private enterprises + self-employed individuals in urban areas + registered urban unemployed persons) × 100%.

Staff and Workers refer to persons working in, and receive payment from units of state ownership, collective ownership, joint ownership, share holding ownership, foreign ownership, and ownership by entrepreneurs from Hong Kong, Macao, and Taiwan, and other types of ownership and their affiliated units. They do not include 1) persons employed in township enterprises, 2) persons employed in private enterprises, 3) urban self-employed persons, 4) retirees, 5) re-employed retirees, 6) teachers in the schools run by the local people, 7) foreigners and persons from Hong Kong, Macao and Taiwan who work in urban units, and 8) other persons not to be included by relevant regulations. (Data of 1998 and afterward refer to fully employed staff and workers. Other related statistics such as total wage bill and average wage are adjusted since 1998 accordingly).

State-owned Units refer to economic units whose assets are owned by the state. Included are non-corporation units registered according to Regulation of the People抯 Republic of China on the Registration of Enterprises and Corporations, state organs, institutions and social organizations at the central and local levels.

Collective-Owned Units refer to economic units registered according to Regulation of the People抯 Republic of China on the Registration of Enterprises and Corporations where the means of production are collectively owned.

Units of Other Types of Ownership refer to units registered with other types of ownership, including cooperative units, joint ownership units, limited companies, share holding corporations, units invested by entrepreneurs from Hong Kong, Macao, and Taiwan, and foreign-invested units.

Fully Employed Staff and Workers refer to persons who work in, and receive wages from their working units, as well as persons who have their work posts, but are temporarily absent from work for reasons of study or on sick, injury or maternal leave and still receive wages from their working units.

Total Wages Bill refer to the total remuneration payment to staff and workers in various units during a certain period of time. The calculation of total wages is based on the total remuneration payment to the staff and workers. Therefore, all the wages and salaries and other payments to staff and workers are included in the total wages regardless of their sources, category, and forms (in kind or cash). (Total wages of staff and workers in this yearbook include only total wages of fully employed staff and workers, excluding the living allowances distributed to those who have left their working units while keeping their labour contract/employment relation unchanged).

Average Wage refers to the average wage in money terms per person during a certain period of time for staff and workers in enterprises, institutions, and government agencies, which reflects the general level of wage income during a certain period of time and is calculated as follows:

Average Wage = Total Wages of Staff and Workers at Reference Time /Average Number of Staff and Workers at Reference Time.

Average Wage Indices refers to the ratio of average wage of staff and workers in the report period to that in the base period, which reflects the change of wage of staff and workers at the different period. It is calculated as follows:

Average Wage Indices = Average Wage of Staff and Workers at Reference Time / Average Wage of Staff and Workers at Base Period x 100%

Average Real Wage Indices average real wage of staff and workers refers to the average wage of staff and workers after removing the effects of the price changes and average real wage indices of staff and workers refers to the change of real wage, which reflects the relative increasing or decreasing level of real wage of staff and workers, which is calculated as follows:

Average Real Wage Indices = Average Wage Indices of Staff and Workers at the Reference Time / Urban Consumer Price Indices at Reference Time × 100%

4 人民生活

Peopole's Livelihood

资料整理：倪群峰　陶　萍　杨　旸
陈艳春　郁　雁

4-1 人民生活水平情况
PEOPLE'S LIVING STANDARD

项　　目	Item	单位	unit	1990	2000	2005	2008	2009
一、城乡就业	Employment							
每一农村劳动力负担人数	Average Person Supported by a Rural Laborer	人	person	1.65	1.49	1.34	1.29	1.28
每一城镇就业者负担人数	Average Person Supported by a Urban Laborer	人	person	1.70	1.73	1.96	1.97	1.99
城镇登记失业率	The Rate of Registered Unemployment	%	percentage	1.70	3.50	4.33	4.20	4.21
二、城乡居民收入	Revenue							
农村居民人均纯收入	Net Income of Rural Residents Per Capita	元	yuan	670.80	2268.50	3099.20	4656.38	5035.26
农村居民人均纯收入指数(1990=100)	Indices of Net Income of Rural Residents Per Capita (1990=100)	%	percentage	100.00	338.20	461.80	693.77	750.64
城镇居民人平年可支配收入	Annual Disposable Income of Urban Residents	元	yuan	1427.15	5524.50	8786.00	13153.00	14367.00
城镇居民人平年可支配收入指数(1990=100)	Indices of Net Annual Disposable Income of Urban Residents (1990=100)	%	percentage	100.00	387.10	615.80	921.59	1006.66
国有职工平均工资	Average Wages of Staff and Workers in State-Owned Units	元	yuan	2045.00	7989.00	14774.00	24756.00	30028.00
三、城乡居民人平消费水平	Consumption Level							
农村居民	Rural Residents	元	yuan	659.00	1302.00	2503.00	3864.00	4137.00
城镇居民	Urban Residents	元	yuan	1341.00	6250.00	8051.00	11780.00	12080.00
四、储　蓄	Savings							
城乡居民人平储蓄存款余额	Balance of Saving Deposits of Rural and Urban Residents Per Capita	元	yuan	455.00	3209.00	7929.00	11920.00	14388.00
五、平均每人居住面积	Floor Area of Housing Per Capita							
城　市(大、中)	Municipalities (Large and Medium-sized)	平方米	sq.m	9.80	13.90	29.90	32.04	32.77
农　村	Rural Areas	平方米	sq.m	25.73	30.11	36.05	39.04	40.11
六、交　通	Transportations							
城镇每百户拥有汽车		辆	set				3.54	4.41
七、文　化	Culture							
每百人每天有报纸	Newspaper Owned Per 100 Persons Every Day	份	unit	3.18	6.17	8.89	9.03	8.32
每人每年有图书、杂志	Books and Magazines Owned Per Capita Anuually	册	unit	8.86	8.54	8.99	6.45	9.14
八、教　育	Education							
学龄儿童入学率	Emrollment Ratio of School-Age Children	%	percentsge	99.04	99.53	99.65	99.85	99.74
每万人口有大学生数	Number of University Students Per 10000 Persons	人	person	23.97	57.49	167.91	207.70	207.15
九、卫　生	Health Care							
每千人有医院病床数	Number of Hospital-Beds Owned By Per 1000 Person	张	unit	2.45	2.18	2.31	2.75	2.21
每千人有医生	Number of Doctors Owned By Per 1000 Persons	人	person	1.62	1.74	1.49	1.52	1.40

注：平均每人居住面积中，城市(大、中)从2002年起为建筑面积，以前年份为居住面积。

Notes: Of Average Housing Areas, it refers to Construction Area of Municipalities (large and medium-sized) since 2002, before2002, it refers to living areas.

4-2 居民消费水平

PEOPLE'S CONSUMPTION LEVEL

年 份 year	居民消费 (亿元) People's Censurption (100 million yuan)	农村居民 rural residernts	城镇居民 wrban residernts	居民消费水平 (元) level of consump- tion (yuan)	农村居民 rural residernts	城镇居民 wrban residernts
1980	93.51	61.47	32.04	201	157	437
1981	106.26	72.84	33.42	225	184	440
1982	126.75	90.67	36.08	266	227	462
1983	141.49	101.17	40.32	293	251	502
1984	172.19	120.41	51.78	352	300	592
1985	203.23	129.78	73.45	411	328	738
1986	247.13	158.31	88.82	493	402	825
1987	271.22	172.47	98.75	533	434	891
1988	328.82	204.21	124.61	638	509	1092
1989	398.09	255.09	143.00	762	630	1218
1990	434.62	273.27	161.35	813	659	1341
1991	475.85	286.08	189.77	869	674	1541
1992	546.61	301.60	245.01	986	706	1926
1993	694.49	357.10	337.35	1236	831	2554
1994	845.14	413.40	431.75	1486	964	3086
1995	1095.97	504.10	591.85	1908	1183	3989
1996	1346.76	594.80	751.99	2323	1396	4892
1997	1438.12	614.90	823.26	2459	1441	5208
1998	1518.92	610.20	908.68	2579	1427	5632
1999	1507.12	558.40	948.69	2545	1302	5802
2000	1594.08	559.10	1034.96	2680	1302	6250
2001	1767.38	585.40	1181.96	2962	1365	7042
2002	1951.54	606.80	1344.70	3263	1418	7899
2003	2188.05	637.70	1550.36	3853	1926	6547
2004	2452.62	700.80	1751.85	4309	2134	7277
2005	2785.42	815.32	1970.10	4883	2503	8051
2006	3124.37	906.15	2218.22	5480	2813	8944
2007	3709.69	1051.82	2657.87	6513	3300	10593
2008	4225.38	1217.95	3007.43	7406	3864	11780
2009	4456.31	1277.72	3178.59	7791	4137	12080

4–3 居民消费水平指数

INDICES OF PEOPLE'S CONSUMPTION LEVEL

(1978年=100)

年 份 year	居民消费 (%) People's Censurption (%)	农村居民 rural residernts	城镇居民 wrban residernts	居民消费水平 (%) level of consumption(%)	农村居民 rural residernts	城镇居民 wrban residernts
1980	117.6	116.1	121.0	115.3	115.2	108.5
1981	134.3	140.4	123.6	130.1	137.9	107.0
1982	156.2	169.2	132.3	149.0	164.2	111.5
1983	172.2	186.6	145.4	162.1	179.7	119.0
1984	196.6	205.4	181.4	183.3	198.7	136.6
1985	218.4	212.2	233.3	201.1	208.2	154.2
1986	253.2	247.7	267.4	229.7	244.3	163.5
1987	263.0	255.1	282.4	235.4	249.4	167.4
1988	268.8	257.1	295.6	237.8	248.6	170.4
1989	278.8	273.6	292.7	243.0	262.6	163.9
1990	290.5	281.2	312.9	247.6	263.3	170.8
1991	275.4	257.6	314.1	229.3	235.7	167.6
1992	281.7	254.0	339.6	231.8	230.5	175.3
1993	338.3	276.9	460.8	274.7	250.1	229.1
1994	380.3	292.4	553.4	304.9	264.6	259.6
1995	421.7	303.5	653.0	334.8	276.3	288.9
1996	474.9	340.2	737.9	373.6	310.0	315.2
1997	499.1	342.9	802.9	389.3	311.8	333.1
1998	549.5	354.6	927.3	425.5	321.8	377.1
1999	571.5	356.0	989.4	440.0	322.1	397.1
2000	599.5	361.0	1062.6	459.8	326.0	420.9
2001	661.3	377.2	1206.1	505.8	341.3	471.0
2002	738.6	391.9	1394.3	564.0	355.3	537.0
2003	807.3	393.9	1578.3	614.7	359.2	595.0
2004	868.7	405.3	1726.7	659.6	372.5	640.2
2005	963.4	458.4	1899.3	729.5	425.0	692.7
2006	1074.2	502.9	2132.9	826.5	480.7	777.9
2007	1191.3	557.2	2365.4	917.4	538.4	853.4
2008	1279.5	599.5	2540.4	984.4	585.8	900.3
2009	1352.4	631.3	2690.3	1038.5	625.0	935.4

注：2003年以前数据根据2004年第一次经济普查资料修订。
Notes:Data before 2003 is Gmended accordity to ecorymic survey 2004.

4-4 城镇居民家庭基本情况

年份 Year	调查户数 (户) Number of Households Surveyed (household)	平均每户家庭人口 (人) Average Number of people Per Household (person)	平均每户就业人口 (人) Number of Employees Per Household (person)	每一就业者担负人数 (人) Average Persons Supported by a Labor (person)
1962	205	5.24	1.67	3.14
1963	240	5.30	1.63	3.25
1964	299	5.36	1.61	3.33
1965	370	5.22	1.60	3.26
1980	571	4.20	2.32	1.81
1981	979	4.21	2.28	1.85
1982	981	4.16	2.32	1.79
1983	980	4.04	2.31	1.75
1984	980	3.97	2.30	1.73
1985	1658	3.84	2.15	1.79
1986	1910	3.76	2.13	1.77
1987	1900	3.73	2.12	1.76
1988	1950	3.61	2.07	1.74
1989	1990	3.52	2.05	1.72
1990	1990	3.47	2.04	1.70
1991	1990	3.45	2.04	1.69
1992	1940	3.36	2.02	1.66
1993	1890	3.29	1.98	1.66
1994	1330	3.23	1.95	1.66
1995	1330	3.22	1.92	1.68
1996	1390	3.24	1.95	1.66
1997	1790	3.23	1.89	1.71
1998	1640	3.19	1.90	1.68
1999	1540	3.15	1.86	1.69
2000	1540	3.14	1.81	1.73
2001	1540	3.10	1.77	1.75
2002	1600	3.07	1.64	1.87
2003	1600	3.06	1.68	1.82
2004	1700	3.03	1.65	1.83
2005	1800	2.98	1.52	1.96
2006	1800	2.96	1.55	1.91
2007	1850	2.95	1.59	1.86
2008	1900	2.96	1.50	1.97
2009	1900	2.94	1.48	1.99

注：由于2002年方法制度重新修订，部分指标有所变化：原“平均每人居住面积”现改为“平均每人建筑总面积”；原“平均每人实际收入”现改为“平均每人总收入”；原“平均每人实际支出”现改为“平均每人总支出”。

BASIC CONDITIONS OF URBAN HOUSEHOLDS

平均每户就业面 (%) Percentage of Employed Persons Per Household (%)	平均每人 Per Capita		平均每人 Per Capita			平均每人建筑面积 (平方米) Average Living Floor Space Per Cappita (sq.m)
	总收入 (元) Actual Income (yuan)	#可支配收入 (元) Disposable Income (yuan)	总支出 (元) Actual Expenditures (yuan)	消费性支出 Living Expenditures	#食品 Food	
31.87	241.1	241.1	245.0	225.8	144.4	
30.75	238.1	238.1	237.2	218.4	133.9	
30.04	232.9	232.9	228.3	211.7	122.7	
30.65	224.3	224.3	218.8	204.4	118.0	3.3
55.24	413.7	413.7	394.2	369.3	210.6	5.1
54.16	456.4	456.4	454.8	422.7	241.2	5.4
55.77	481.4	481.4	460.2	430.7	248.0	5.8
57.18	520.0	511.2	497.6	465.0	273.1	6.5
57.93	599.7	590.6	552.8	516.4	291.1	6.8
55.99	713.3	704.2	693.1	644.2	324.5	7.9
56.65	861.5	851.3	815.5	751.5	387.5	8.2
56.84	960.6	951.8	919.1	836.1	443.2	8.4
57.34	1136.4	1128.1	1153.1	1058.8	538.9	8.9
58.24	1271.6	1262.6	1250.0	1130.7	607.0	9.1
58.79	1437.1	1427.2	1349.4	1220.3	652.4	9.8
59.13	1603.7	1592.9	1538.2	1380.2	717.4	9.6
60.12	1886.4	1874.2	1799.9	1577.7	799.0	9.9
60.18	2453.5	2438.7	2358.1	2097.6	941.5	10.5
60.37	3360.0	3346.0	3588.6	2733.1	1307.1	11.1
59.63	4031.9	4016.7	3977.3	3433.8	1680.6	11.9
60.19	4367.0	4350.2	4290.6	3713.5	1731.4	11.8
58.51	4693.8	4673.2	4549.7	3855.6	1773.6	12.8
59.56	4849.4	4826.4	4903.1	4074.4	1787.7	12.7
59.04	5234.5	5212.8	5333.8	4340.6	1783.4	13.2
57.64	5542.6	5524.5	5643.6	4644.5	1779.4	13.9
57.10	5888.7	5856.0	5774.8	4804.8	1799.4	15.2
53.42	7142.2	6789.0	7159.7	5608.9	2087.8	26.2
54.90	7745.8	7322.0	7551.1	5963.3	2279.6	26.3
54.46	8522.1	8022.8	8076.1	6398.5	2516.2	27.3
51.01	9395.1	8786.0	8582.8	6737.0	2625.4	29.9
52.36	10533.3	9803.0	9839.7	7397.0	2868.4	31.0
53.90	12421.8	11485.0	11476.7	8701.0	3456.0	32.3
50.68	14174.3	13153.0	12471.0	9478.0	3996.0	32.0
50.34	15698.0	14367.0	13868.0	10294.0	4160.5	32.8

Note: The " Average Living Floor Space Per Capita (sq.m) " in the above table was changed into "Average Living Floor Space Per Cappita (sq.m) "; "Actual Income Per Capita (yuan)" into "Average Total Income Per Capita (yuan)"; "Actual Expenditures Per Capita (yuan)" into "Average Total Expenditures Per Capita (yuan)", owing to the changes of items in the reversion of 2006 mearurement system.

4-5 城镇居民家庭收支情况(2009)

单位：元

项目	Item	总计 Total	最低收入户 Lowest Income Households
调查户数(户)	Households Surveyed	1900.00	192.00
比重(%)	Ratio	100.00	10.00
平均每户家庭人口(人)	Average Number of Residents Per Household	2.94	3.47
平均每户离退休人口(人)	Average Number of Retirees Per Household	0.54	0.26
平均每一就业者负担人数(人)	Average Persons supported by a Urban Labor	1.99	2.65
平均每户就业面(%)	Average Employment Rate Per Household	50.34	37.75
平均每人总收入	Per Capita Total Income	15698.11	5513.56
#可支配收入	Disposable Income	14367.48	5002.12
平均每人借贷收入	Income of Loans Per Capita	2742.80	811.91
#提取储蓄存款	Savings Withdrawn	2367.81	589.22
平均每人借贷支出	Expenditures of Loans Per Capita	4070.59	591.48
#存入储蓄款	Money Saved	3513.23	526.14
平均每人总支出	Total Expenditure Per Capita	13868.19	5684.31
#消费性支出	Consumption Expenditure	10294.07	4482.84
一、食品	Food	4160.51	2323.48
粮油类	Oils Class	607.53	379.15
肉禽蛋水产品类	Meat, eggs and aquatic products	1149.20	658.38
蔬菜类	Vegetables	542.84	338.42
调味品	Flavorings	61.93	35.22
糖烟酒饮料	Sugar drink alcohol and tobacco	472.43	231.86
干鲜瓜果类	Dried and Fresh Melons and Fruits	245.60	147.02
糕点、奶及奶制品	Pastries, milk and milk products	236.17	124.81
其他食品	Others	44.22	24.29
饮食服务	Food Service	800.60	384.33
二、衣着	Clothing	1210.32	378.50
服装	Garments	885.63	260.33
衣着材料	Clothing Materials	9.03	3.08
鞋类	Shoes	271.54	98.23
其它衣着用品	Others	37.14	14.53
衣着加工服务费	Clothing Procecing and Service Fees	6.99	2.33
三、居住	Residence	999.49	473.05
住房	Housing	289.00	32.60
水、电、燃料及其他	Water, Electricities, Fuel Materials and Others	665.79	431.73
居住服务	Residence Services	44.69	8.72
三、家庭设备、用品及服务	Facilities, Articals and Services	759.24	222.79
耐用消费品	Durable Consumer Goods	354.79	69.11
室内装饰品	Interrior Decorations	16.95	0.17
床上用品	Bed Articals	57.53	14.29
家庭日用杂品	Daily Use Articals	289.68	131.49
家具材料	Furniture Materials	13.96	3.19
家庭服务	Households Service	26.33	4.53
四、医疗保健	Medicine and Medical Service	694.61	293.09
医疗器具	Medical Equipments	3.15	0.20
保健用品	Health Products	10.91	
药品费	Medicines	331.83	164.68
滋补保健品	Health Care Products	48.43	7.28
医疗费	Medical Service Fees	285.90	117.32
其他	Others	14.40	3.60
五、交通和通讯	Transportation and Communication	953.69	287.54
交通	Transportation	469.21	95.91
通讯	Communication	484.49	191.64
六、娱乐、教育、文化服务	Recreation, Education and Cultural Services	1208.46	428.48
文化娱乐用品	Cultural Recreation Articals	269.42	60.31
文化娱乐服务	Cultural Recreation Services	310.61	53.14
教育	Education	628.43	315.02
八、杂项商品和服务	Miscellaneous Commodities and Services	307.75	75.91
杂项商品	Miscellaneous Commodities	218.70	48.72
服务	Services	89.05	27.20

INCOME AND EXPENDITURE OF URBAN HOUSEHOLDS(2009)

(yuan)

低收入户 Low Income Households	中等偏下户 Medium-Low Income Households	中等收入户 Medium Income Households	中等偏上户 Medium-High Income Households	高收入户 High Income Households	最高收入户 Highest Income Households
191.33	380.83	382.67	379.08	189.50	184.58
10.00	20.00	20.00	20.00	10.00	10.00
3.22	3.17	2.93	2.75	2.66	2.42
0.42	0.53	0.62	0.60	0.53	0.62
2.30	2.11	1.95	1.83	1.62	1.69
43.48	47.32	51.19	54.55	61.65	59.09
7963.36	10399.67	13683.19	18409.85	24503.71	41091.02
7181.57	9430.35	12576.54	16967.64	22309.51	37761.88
1572.69	1342.49	2368.57	3164.26	5256.05	7471.49
1467.37	1192.20	2056.06	2903.84	4378.76	6156.05
1412.41	1830.59	3046.45	4990.39	6957.13	14830.54
1221.74	1621.96	2697.95	4099.51	6166.38	12783.25
7872.70	9623.51	12741.00	16007.77	21875.54	31845.59
6046.05	7354.59	9485.04	12034.22	15441.75	22991.54
2939.54	3391.35	4065.92	4806.00	5645.71	7181.16
470.28	536.00	628.12	681.15	758.72	879.21
847.66	972.29	1143.08	1295.58	1545.41	1866.60
432.96	464.92	545.42	611.58	681.37	834.79
43.39	50.75	61.20	71.96	83.93	103.28
323.72	378.34	469.84	556.29	654.16	830.33
168.94	214.30	242.51	285.24	322.59	382.03
166.21	206.43	227.51	273.46	328.76	378.92
30.30	34.57	43.54	51.49	63.41	76.23
456.09	533.76	704.70	979.27	1207.36	1829.76
579.40	859.15	1101.94	1465.08	2000.65	2783.21
396.50	620.25	803.97	1067.68	1497.23	2090.77
3.38	4.64	8.82	15.09	11.45	19.31
157.32	204.32	250.48	328.07	430.47	558.87
17.50	25.88	29.33	46.80	49.95	102.50
4.70	4.05	9.35	7.45	11.53	11.76
677.70	686.07	812.43	1073.55	1523.95	2590.27
157.20	114.53	101.40	256.49	620.71	1388.04
503.25	551.54	682.97	757.92	814.96	1054.54
17.26	20.00	28.06	59.14	88.28	147.69
358.31	476.31	603.15	794.94	1460.27	2189.04
138.35	188.80	256.90	340.06	770.74	1221.59
1.35	8.87	3.79	16.31	65.60	56.66
18.07	45.49	37.17	63.81	137.30	137.76
188.09	203.10	274.67	337.74	427.08	620.83
1.51	17.46	7.99	13.33	24.05	38.32
10.92	12.60	22.64	23.69	35.50	113.87
415.52	454.28	762.62	823.69	672.80	1763.66
2.03	0.98	0.96	7.87	8.97	2.13
2.23	1.23	12.50	16.06	9.22	47.59
255.96	253.09	368.38	364.70	325.18	698.81
12.64	28.18	47.17	39.69	76.83	189.04
139.39	163.62	320.64	388.42	243.01	739.87
3.26	7.17	12.98	6.95	9.60	86.23
417.14	581.09	844.29	1056.60	1431.75	2941.48
157.69	213.53	386.73	505.64	711.85	1843.67
259.45	367.56	457.55	550.96	719.90	1097.81
529.98	729.05	1040.08	1598.13	2051.02	2881.47
98.16	232.46	183.70	347.35	431.86	695.80
62.44	121.12	229.31	435.90	671.46	947.18
369.38	375.47	627.07	814.87	947.70	1238.49
128.45	177.31	254.62	416.22	655.62	661.25
85.19	124.15	179.25	282.41	522.38	458.94
43.27	53.16	75.37	133.81	133.24	202.32

4-6 城镇居民家庭平均每百户年末耐用品拥有量(2009)

品名	Item		总平均 Total Average	最低收入户 Lowest Income Households
摩托车	(辆) Motorcycles	(unit)	19.00	18.55
助力车	(辆) Auxiliary Drving Bikes	(unit)	11.12	9.37
家用汽车	(辆) Cars for Household Use	(unit)	4.41	2.98
洗衣机	(台) Washing Machins	(unit)	97.46	86.03
电冰箱	(台) Refrigerators	(unit)	98.75	88.20
彩色电视机	(台) Color TV Sets	(unit)	130.45	110.98
家用电脑	(台) Computers	(unit)	57.58	23.21
组合音响	(套) Hi-Fi Stereo Systems	(unit)	29.95	10.41
摄象机	(台) TV Cameras	(unit)	5.38	
照相机	(架) Cameras	(unit)	33.71	7.04
钢琴	(架) Pianoes	(unit)	1.62	
其他中高档乐器	(件) Medium and High-Grade Musical Instruments	(unit)	5.16	0.86
微波炉	(台) Microwave Stove	(unit)	52.84	15.87
空调器	(台) Air Conditioners	(unit)	112.47	50.86
淋浴热水器	(台) Showers	(unit)	82.79	54.24
消毒碗柜	(台) Disinfection cabinet	(unit)	11.29	1.58
洗碗机	(台) Dishwasher	(unit)	0.83	
健身器材	(件) Health Care Instruments	(unit)	3.82	
固定电话	(部) Fixed telephone	(set)	72.40	63.45
移动电话	(部) Mobile Phones	(set)	164.01	108.14

NUMBER OF DURABLE CONSUMER GOODS OWNED PER 100 URBAN HOUSEHOLDS AT THE YEAR-END BY INCOME LEVEL(2009)

低收入户 Low Income Households	中等偏下户 Medium-Low Income Households	中等收入户 Medium Income Households	中等偏上户 Medium-High Income Households	高收入户 High Income Households	最高收入户 Highest Income Households
11.86	26.02	19.84	20.06	16.81	10.58
9.29	12.45	7.28	13.97	12.62	12.05
3.04	1.78	1.22	3.72	8.76	14.85
89.57	96.10	96.28	102.31	100.81	106.77
93.89	94.42	99.41	104.32	100.95	106.63
116.17	127.21	121.34	137.78	145.08	154.96
31.35	50.29	49.52	64.22	84.00	100.94
20.10	26.92	24.56	37.96	34.75	51.91
1.52	2.14	2.56	4.87	14.84	16.50
13.76	24.61	29.73	37.37	55.35	70.99
	0.47	0.58	2.68	1.99	6.24
1.25	5.75	4.26	5.98	8.21	8.33
24.10	44.60	51.88	67.95	74.81	77.40
70.57	87.00	102.51	131.66	155.64	191.39
66.66	72.93	83.64	95.68	96.28	101.48
5.06	4.92	8.65	12.25	20.03	31.92
0.71	0.51	0.48	0.34	2.11	2.59
1.31	0.23	2.08	5.68	9.16	10.65
61.06	68.18	71.39	74.04	81.92	87.42
126.94	154.66	164.64	176.92	197.90	204.06

4-7 城镇居民家庭房屋居住分布情况

URABN HOUSEHOLDS HOUSING CONDITIONS

分　　组	Group	各组户数占总户数比重(%) Percentage of Household in Each Group of the Total Households	
		2008	2009
总　　计	Total	1900	1900
一、房屋产权	Building Property Right		
租赁公房	Leased Pubilc Houses	7.76	7.29
租赁私房	Leased Private Houses	3.01	3.05
原有私房	Original Private Houses	14.87	15.47
房改私房	Private Houses	50.65	51.05
商品房	Commercial Houses	21.55	21.44
其他	Others	2.16	1.69
二、住宅样式	Housing Pattens		
单栋住宅	Sole-Unit Houses	7.29	7.73
四居室	Four-Room Houses	5.03	4.01
三居室	Three-Room Houses	25.56	25.3
二居室	Two-Room Houses	40.65	42.35
一居室	One-Room Houses	5.72	5.06
普通楼房	Ordinary Houses	12.13	11.96
平房及其他	Bungalow and Others	3.62	3.6
三、用水情况	Waters		
独用自来水	Private Tap Water	99.14	99.53
公用自来水	Public Tap Water	0.58	0.19
井、河水	Water from Rivers and Wells	0.28	0.28
其他	Others		
四、卫生设备	Sanitary Faciities		
无卫生设备	Have not	2.3	2.01
有浴室厕所	Toilets with bth-room	80.03	82.01
有厕所无浴室	Toilets without bth-room	15	13.13
公用卫生设备	Public Health Facilities	2.67	2.85
五、取暖设备	Warming Facilities		
无取暖设备	Have not	37.31	36.86
空调设备	Air Conditioner	54.52	56.34
暖　　气	Heater	5.35	5.32
其　　他	Others	2.81	1.49
六、燃料使用情况	Fuel Material Usage Conditions		
煤	Coal	10.47	10.13
罐装液化石油气	LPG cylinders	57.86	56.24
管道液化石油气	LPG Pipeline	4.7	1.94
管道煤气	Piped Coal Gas	8.59	7.23
管道天然气	Gas pipeline	18.1	24.14
其　　他	Others	0.27	0.32
七、通信设备使用情况	Telecommunication Facilities Usage Conditions		
1.每百户固定电话	Per 100 fixed telephone	70.62	72.40
2.每百户移动电话	Mobile Phones Per 100 Households	154.78	164.01

4-8 农民家庭基本情况
BASIC CONDITIONS OF RURAL HOUSEHOLDS

年 份	调查户数 Number of Households Surveyed	常住人口(人) Permanent Residents (person)	平均每户常住人口(人) Average Permanent Residents Per Households (person)	平均每户整半劳动力(人) Average Full-Time and Part-Time Labors Per Household (person)	平均每个劳动力负担人口(人) Average Person Supported by Each Labor (person)
1981	954	5497	5.76	2.67	2.16
1982	948	5364	5.66	2.73	2.08
1983	1470	8267	5.62	2.99	1.88
1984	1510	8317	5.51	3.02	1.83
1985	3300	16473	5.07	2.98	1.71
1986	3300	16432	4.98	2.96	1.68
1987	3300	16195	4.91	2.94	1.67
1988	3300	15966	4.84	2.93	1.65
1989	3300	15567	4.72	2.86	1.65
1990	3300	15411	4.67	2.84	1.65
1991	3300	15094	4.57	2.66	1.72
1992	3300	14900	4.52	2.63	1.71
1993	3300	14651	4.44	2.65	1.67
1994	3300	14466	4.38	2.72	1.61
1995	3300	14447	4.38	2.77	1.58
1996	3300	14053	4.26	2.75	1.55
1997	3200	13453	4.20	2.64	1.60
1998	3200	13239	4.14	2.62	1.58
1999	3200	13082	4.09	2.63	1.55
2000	3300	13557	4.11	2.76	1.49
2001	3300	13490	4.09	2.75	1.49
2002	3300	13420	4.07	2.78	1.46
2003	3300	13385	4.06	2.86	1.42
2004	3300	13356	4.05	2.92	1.39
2005	3300	13228	4.01	2.99	1.34
2006	3300	13259	4.02	3.03	1.34
2007	3300	13186	4.00	3.06	1.30
2008	3300	13163	3.99	3.08	1.29
2009	3300	13151	3.99	3.12	1.28

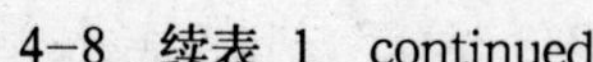

4-8 续表 1 continued

年 份 year	平均每户经营耕地面积(亩) Space of Cultivation land Per Household (mu)	平均每户年末拥有生产性固定资产原值(元) Value of Production Fixed Assets Per Household (yuan)	平均每户年内新建购房屋面积(平方米) Floor Space of Rooms Newly Built Per Household (sq.m)	平均每人年末使用房屋面积(平方米) Lving Space Per Capita (sq.m)
1981	0.52		6.51	15.31
1982	0.57	159.20	5.36	16.45
1983	8.95	389.97	5.65	18.04
1984	8.66	530.20	6.70	19.03
1985	7.60	557.86	8.24	21.18
1986	7.48	610.47	8.45	22.63
1987	7.31	672.87	7.79	23.50
1988	7.04	759.61	4.90	24.15
1989	6.95	819.53	5.50	25.10
1990	6.79	861.91	6.20	25.73
1991	6.58	1068.45	4.56	27.33
1992	6.47	1146.94	4.07	27.94
1993	6.36	1281.66	3.75	25.80
1994	6.69	1542.58	3.91	25.22
1995	6.73	1775.57	4.66	25.92
1996	6.82	2291.60	4.25	26.58
1997	6.56	2688.67	4.98	27.99
1998	6.08	2604.21	4.74	28.38
1999	6.08	2543.61	4.19	29.87
2000	5.93	2482.02	3.48	30.11
2001	5.94	2773.52	2.98	31.19
2002	6.01	2953.37	4.65	31.55
2003	6.03	2989.82	4.01	32.44
2004	6.15	3046.47	2.82	33.68
2005	6.15	4121.20	3.88	36.05
2006	6.12	4297.19	4.22	36.77
2007	6.41	4996.00	3.36	37.96
2008	6.36	5434.99	5.90	39.04
2009	6.51	6368.83	4.40	40.11

4-8 续表 2 continued

年 份	平均每户年末使用房屋价值(元) Value of Per Households Living Space (yuan)	平均每人总收入(元) Total Income Per Capita (yuan)	平均每人纯收入(元) Net Income Per Capita (yuan)	平均每人生活消费支出(元) Living Expenditures Per Capita (yuan)
1981	1249.13	232.64	217.44	183.78
1982	1261.51	311.51	286.07	226.96
1983	1688.93	405.14	299.24	252.47
1984	1786.54	525.86	392.29	305.03
1985	2068.78	569.74	421.24	334.63
1986	2319.44	605.67	445.13	373.53
1987	2514.22	638.64	460.66	408.69
1988	2751.40	710.47	497.84	450.62
1989	3095.15	820.70	571.84	540.13
1990	3545.50	957.01	670.80	607.58
1991	4661.58	936.57	626.92	615.40
1992	4885.77	1015.62	677.82	611.84
1993	5004.02	1135.77	783.18	722.09
1994	5887.81	1690.49	1170.06	1012.95
1995	6729.46	2184.20	1511.22	1245.10
1996	10050.26	2642.45	1863.62	1630.41
1997	11432.61	2913.16	2102.20	1660.13
1998	12966.45	2917.66	2172.24	1699.43
1999	13654.80	2871.62	2217.08	1572.90
2000	13717.28	2930.31	2268.50	1555.61
2001	16007.50	3051.08	2352.16	1649.18
2002	16581.94	3152.80	2444.06	1745.63
2003	19010.48	3307.66	2566.76	1801.63
2004	20254.50	3757.08	2890.01	2088.98
2005	24815.99	4214.81	3099.20	2430.19
2006	27772.00	4574.92	3419.35	2732.46
2007	31696.83	5359.22	3997.41	3090.00
2008	36250.27	6251.22	4656.38	3652.57
2009	41493.01	6642.74	5035.26	3725.40

4–9 农民家庭年人均纯收入及构成

ANNUAL NET INCOME OF RURAL HOUSEHOLDS PERCAPITA AND COMPOSITION

单位：元 (yuan)

指标	Item	2001	2002	2003	2004	2005	2006	2007	2008	2009
全年总收入	Total Revenue	3051.08	3152.80	3307.66	3757.08	4214.81	4574.92	5359.22	6251.22	6642.74
全年纯收入	Annual Net Income	2352.16	2444.06	2566.76	2890.01	3099.20	3419.35	3997.41	4656.38	5035.26
工资性收入	Money Wage	582.60	662.19	706.79	755.23	941.64	1199.16	1451.90	1742.33	1900.69
家庭经营纯收入	House Business Revenue	1676.19	1694.40	1785.27	2051.62	2049.04	2095.10	2395.35	2690.83	2858.38
转移性收入	Transfer Income	80.52	73.38	58.95	66.96	91.71	99.13	116.67	182.40	225.81
财产性收入	Property Income	12.85	14.09	15.76	16.19	16.81	25.91	33.49	40.82	50.37
比重(纯收入=100)	Ratio (net income = 100)									
工资性收入	Money Wage	24.77	27.09	27.54	26.13	30.38	35.07	36.32	37.42	37.75
家庭经营纯收入	House Business Revenue	71.26	69.33	69.55	70.99	66.12	61.27	59.92	57.79	56.77
转移性收入	Transfer Income	3.42	3.00	2.30	2.32	2.96	2.90	2.92	3.92	4.48
财产性收入	Property Income	0.55	0.58	0.61	0.56	0.54	0.76	0.84	0.88	1.00

4–10 农民家庭年人均纯收入分组

RURAL HOUSEHOLDS GROUPED BY ANNUAL NET INCOME PER CAPITA

单位：户 (household)

指标	Item	2001	2002	2003	2004	2005	2006	2007	2008	2009
调查户总计	Total Households Surveyed	3300	3300	3300	3300	3300	3300	3300	3300	3300
200元以下	Below 200 yuan	3	3	2	8	6	9	9	10	29
200–400元	200-400 yuan	5	7	6	11	12	6	9	12	8
400–600元	400-600 yuan	24	36	36	46	30	30	16	17	12
600–800元	600-800 yuan	54	68	64	79	69	61	34	27	22
800–1000元	800-1000 yuan	121	95	102	80	89	77	65	73	29
1000–1500元	1000-1500 yuan	562	468	410	280	269	182	138	115	138
1500–2000元	1500-2000 yuan	706	696	645	431	413	345	237	160	173
2000–3000元	2000-3000 yuan	983	1032	1007	1034	840	787	659	519	478
3000–4000元	3000-4000 yuan	448	495	513	611	702	684	660	559	492
4000–5000元	4000-5000 yuan	212	206	255	339	413	479	510	510	460
5000元以上	5000 yuan and Over	182	194	260	381	457	640	969	1298	1459

4-11 农民家庭年人均经营总收入

ANNUAL TOTAL INCME OF RURAL HOUSEHOLDS PER CAPITA

单位：元 (yuan)

指 标	Item	2001	2002	2003	2004	2005	2006	2007	2008	2009
家庭经营总收入	Total Income of Family Business	2369.01	2394.24	2527.03	2918.92	3167.19	3252.60	3746.03	4287.96	4465.68
农业收入	Farming	1404.75	1430.09	1562.57	1877.48	1933.74	2070.80	2316.71	2546.31	2638.00
林业收入	Forestry	34.80	34.71	31.56	34.10	47.83	54.10	60.37	61.54	59.33
牧业收入	Animal Husbandry	504.77	500.70	517.49	590.41	678.00	580.75	741.27	946.28	901.14
渔业收入	Fishery	108.83	128.40	131.05	144.78	162.28	187.16	215.24	271.92	324.80
工业收入	Industry	65.60	65.06	60.78	47.22	53.92	49.43	46.53	53.95	56.21
建筑业收入	Construction	40.25	35.98	29.95	30.53	57.68	64.86	83.83	99.12	127.73
交通运输邮电业收入	Transportation, Post Services	64.19	59.10	57.61	57.41	80.59	91.21	106.20	116.66	123.48
批零贸易餐饮业收入	Wholesales, Retail Sales and Catering	68.40	66.80	75.63	84.13	99.04	104.48	118.82	133.06	159.22
社会服务和文教卫生业收入	Social Services and Cultural, Educati-onal, and Public Health Services	26.71	25.90	28.19	23.63	32.79	34.93	44.40	44.70	61.25
其他家庭经营收入	Other Family Revenue	50.72	47.51	32.20	29.23	21.32	14.80	12.67	14.42	14.50

4-12 农民家庭年人均生产支出

ANNUAL PRODUCTION EXPENDITURES OF RURAL HOUSEHOLDS PER CAPITA

单位：元 (yuan)

指 标	Item	2001	2002	2003	2004	2005	2006	2007	2008	2009
一、家庭经营费用支出	Expenditures of Family Business	507.42	537.70	602.52	765.03	1038.04	1071.50	1262.04	1493.00	1489.40
农业生产支出	Agricultural Expenditures	252.12	264.14	313.90	394.51	490.41	572.13	663.21	759.00	746.68
林业生产支出	Forestry Expenditures	2.43	2.28	3.24	2.77	6.88	7.00	8.56	6.14	6.69
牧业生产支出	Animal Husbandary Expenditures	164.49	170.24	188.84	256.44	362.15	307.57	369.78	493.71	463.78
渔业生产支出	Fishery Expenditures	34.29	38.35	38.75	51.91	67.00	71.57	77.58	86.30	104.37
工业生产支出	Industrial Expenditures	19.04	19.09	25.24	16.86	19.53	16.80	19.20	14.56	16.37
建筑业支出	Construction Expenditures	2.90	7.49	2.31	2.81	22.14	27.51	32.56	37.45	45.15
交通运输邮电业支出	Expenditures of Transportation and Post Services	16.65	16.23	12.30	11.28	26.09	28.63	36.01	35.09	38.14
批零贸易餐饮业支出	Expenditures of Wholesales, Retail Sales and Catering	9.32	11.02	13.83	23.57	33.11	28.75	42.36	46.38	51.96
社会服务和文教卫生业支出	Expenditures of Social Services and Cultural, Educational, and Public Health Services	3.08	2.91	2.61	3.43	5.88	7.41	9.50	10.76	13.73
其他家庭经营支出	Other Family Expenditures	3.11	5.95	1.50	1.46	4.85	4.17	3.28	3.60	2.53
二、购置生产性固定资产支出	Expenditures of Purchasing Production Fixed Assets	42.71	33.42	41.02	56.75	78.99	70.31	75.47	99.92	148.69
三、税费支出	Expenditures of Taxation	140.17	113.73	90.10	52.08	11.57	14.62	18.22	13.30	11.21

4-13 农民家庭年人均生活消费支出
ANNUAL LIVING EXPENDITURES RURAL HOUSEHOLD OF PER CAPITA

单位：元 (yuan)

指 标	Item	2001	2002	2003	2004	2005	2006	2007	2008	2009
全年总支出	Total Annual Expenditures	2422.68	2520.42	2587.25	3033.24	3675.73	3987.52	4553.70	5384.84	5519.40
生活消费支出	Living Expenditures	1649.18	1745.63	1801.63	2088.98	2430.19	2732.10	3090.00	3652.57	3725.40
一、食品消费	Food Consumption	856.25	872.49	930.98	1076.35	1192.26	1278.80	1479.04	1711.34	1668.35
主 食	Grain	247.05	245.62	232.01	291.96	266.31	279.99	305.79	323.50	320.19
副 食	Non-Staple Food	402.39	406.31	438.72	441.65	519.21	521.06	625.66	771.94	695.66
其他食品	Others	105.23	107.86	144.80	206.65	260.45	291.72	329.14	369.51	392.37
在外饮食	Travelling Catering Service	89.23	101.21	105.31	126.78	136.37	176.71	209.62	237.24	249.14
二、衣着消费	Clothing Consumption	77.28	80.63	80.19	93.52	125.01	146.69	168.64	187.07	195.45
三、居住消费	Residence Consumption	184.53	235.61	223.41	274.10	310.27	377.20	434.91	651.50	702.62
住 房	Housing	95.93	146.64	139.21	183.62	207.47	256.80	292.43	508.63	572.69
电 费	Electricity Fees	24.67	24.45	21.84	24.78	30.44	38.17	46.43	58.77	70.08
燃 料	Fuel	56.69	57.91	52.17	53.06	57.53	66.00	70.34	63.96	39.16
四、家庭设备用品及服务	Famitly facilities and Services	73.77	71.54	73.00	75.11	110.04	135.53	166.25	234.92	229.32
耐用消费品	Durable Consumer Goods	14.55	17.20	26.77	26.22	47.97	65.90	90.40	117.85	133.42
日用杂品	Daily Necessities	47.20	45.11	36.97	38.02	47.85	63.54	69.58	110.17	88.20
五、医疗保健消费	Medicine and Medical Services	87.60	90.51	95.55	110.73	135.37	172.40	178.77	210.36	236.31
医疗保健用品		42.35	38.92	39.28	41.96	56.01	64.76	60.17	64.34	71.18
医疗保健服务费	Health Care Service Fees	40.72	48.14	56.27	68.77	79.36	107.60	118.60	146.02	165.13
六、交通通讯消费	Transportation and Telecommu	88.13	98.92	122.05	162.65	223.16	246.07	281.12	290.44	307.22
交通工具	Transportation	19.70	21.59	29.73	47.44	60.98	74.82	92.97	97.88	108.82
通讯工具	Telecommunication	4.56	7.26	13.85	21.66	26.65	22.13	29.48	26.17	23.71
交通、邮电服务消费		57.18	62.33	78.48	92.20	132.88	149.12	158.66	166.38	174.70
七、文教娱乐用品及服务	Cultural, Educational and Rece Articles and Services	213.61	232.84	223.92	245.68	271.86	292.30	284.13	267.13	281.68
文教娱乐用品	Cultural, Educational and Rece Articles	31.75	35.46	34.76	46.61	52.90	55.12	53.97	53.40	61.71
学杂费	School Fees	174.70	190.68	175.36	176.31	189.93	201.25	185.74	156.51	146.81
技术培训费	Technical Training	2.57	1.85	1.54	5.12	3.09	2.94	5.30	5.23	5.44
文体休闲娱乐费		3.05	2.63	2.09	3.39	4.49	5.92	7.52	11.03	9.92
八、其他商品和服务	Other Commdities and Services	68.00	63.10	52.53	50.85	62.23	83.24	97.13	99.80	104.29

4-14 农民家庭年人均现金收支
ANNUAL CASH REVENUE AND EXPENDITURE OF RURAL HOUSEHOLDS PER CAPITA

单位：元 (yuan)

指　　标	Item	2001	2002	2003	2004	2005	2006	2007	2008	2009
期内现金收入合计	Total Cash Income at Year-End	2180.53	2307.70	2560.51	2971.04	3454.30	3793.20	4498.98	5256.32	5718.37
一、工资性现金收入	Cash Income By Wages	580.55	660.42	704.63	754.47	941.18	1199.10	1454.46	1742.25	1898.93
二、家庭经营现金收入	Cash Income By Family Business	1440.57	1477.16	1719.16	2070.50	2402.70	2470.20	2888.24	3289.11	3532.93
#农业	Farm Products	745.55	752.77	920.54	1197.84	1340.29	1443.51	1655.22	1782.47	1924.84
林业	Forestry Products	17.06	16.89	25.76	29.64	40.17	48.27	56.01	55.94	55.54
牧业	Animal husbandary Products	310.77	317.17	364.41	436.44	522.64	436.72	557.71	722.03	687.14
渔业	Fishery Products	73.32	87.57	126.79	136.17	155.67	182.48	206.85	266.99	320.06
工业	Industry Products	61.60	65.05	58.14	45.73	52.98	48.95	46.53	53.95	56.21
建筑业	Building Industry	34.25	35.98	29.89	30.49	57.68	64.86	83.83	98.93	127.73
交通运输邮电业	Transportation and Post Service	64.19	59.10	57.61	57.41	80.59	91.21	106.20	116.66	123.48
批零贸易餐饮业	Retail Sales and Catering	64.40	66.80	75.63	84.13	99.04	104.48	118.82	133.06	159.22
社会服务和文教卫生业	Social services and cultural and educational sector	26.71	25.90	28.19	23.63	32.79	34.93	44.40	44.70	61.25
其他家庭经营收入	Cash Income of Other Family Business	42.72	49.93	32.20	29.02	20.85	14.79	12.67	14.38	17.46
三、转移性现金收入	Transfer Cash Income	148.51	158.13	124.54	133.17	94.78	102.07	126.97	194.68	243.03
四、财产性现金收入	Property Cash Income	10.90	11.99	12.18	12.90	15.55	21.75	29.31	30.29	39.28
期内现金支出合计	Total Cash Expenditures at Year-End	1994.45	2115.46	2127.96	2482.55	2974.75	3267.10	3740.56	4496.87	4723.52
一、家庭经营费用现金支出	Cash Expenditures By Family Business	446.99	472.03	531.00	683.75	953.96	972.70	1159.13	1383.60	1368.10
购买化肥	Fertilizers Purchases	129.50	130.03	153.48	191.90	215.34	234.63	255.96	340.71	313.95
购买农药	Purchases of Farm Chemical	28.77	28.88	37.35	43.55	51.93	74.54	81.13	94.78	87.72
购买农用薄膜	Purchase of Agricultural Film	3.16	3.05	3.70	4.21	4.82	5.27	5.18	5.42	3.40
二、购买生产性固定资产现金支出	Cash Expenditures of Purchasing Production Fixed Assets	42.71	33.42	41.02	56.75	78.99	70.31	75.47	99.92	148.38
三、税费现金支出	Cash Expenditures of Taxations	133.40	108.12	88.51	51.85	11.55	14.60	18.22	13.29	11.20
四、生活消费现金支出	Cash Expenditures of Living Consumption	1134.77	1242.30	1264.55	1479.46	1813.40	2099.60	2368.68	2857.78	3033.37
五、转移性现金支出	Transfer Cash Expenditures	226.86	243.39	198.55	205.43	105.67	103.54	113.88	133.30	153.91
六、财产性现金支出	Property Cash Expenditures	9.72	16.20	4.33	5.31	10.88	6.23	5.17	8.97	8.33

4-15 农民家庭年人均出售主要农副产品情况
ANNUAL SELLING OF FARM AND SIDELINE PRODUCTS OF RURL HOUSEHOLDS PER CAPITA

品 名	Item		2001	2002	2003	2004	2005	2006	2007	2008	2009
粮 食	(千克) Grain	(kg)	314.93	328.47	299.85	303.46	383.48	391.24	386.98	390.60	422.65
#小 麦	(千克) #Wheat	(kg)	26.77	28.91	31.74	40.06	54.25	77.67	94.39	76.73	62.01
稻 谷	(千克) Paddy	(kg)	259.07	258.20	236.27	234.53	302.70	288.86	268.94	292.78	320.27
棉 花	(千克) Cotton	(kg)	17.62	15.91	11.84	19.60	19.58	24.23	28.52	24.53	26.75
油 料	(千克) Oil Producer	(kg)	46.87	46.91	58.96	79.72	77.73	62.04	61.27	65.14	77.04
糖 料	(千克) Sugar	(kg)	6.25	3.90	5.22	3.99	5.47	6.28	9.16	4.31	4.48
烟 草	(千克) Tobacco	(kg)	2.38	1.91	1.65	1.30	2.34	2.07	1.55	2.11	2.92
蔬 菜	(千克) Vegetable	(kg)	119.59	129.35	145.02	148.96	135.09	133.11	138.89	136.45	133.11
瓜 类	(千克) Melon	(kg)	—	25.09	30.49	26.75	14.21	26.56	16.20	14.80	19.07
水 果	(千克) Fruits	(kg)	55.50	40.05	54.72	66.57	69.54	76.41	82.72	90.38	99.70
茶 叶	(千克) Tea	(kg)	1.11	0.63	0.70	0.80	1.24	1.25	1.56	1.56	1.29
肉 猪	(头) Pigs	(head)	0.33	0.36	0.42	0.35	0.38	0.40	0.33	0.33	0.36
家 禽	(只) Poultry	(head)	1.13	1.74	1.00	1.22	3.07	2.55	2.22	3.71	4.74
猪 肉	(千克) Pork	(kg)	1.94	2.62	3.52	2.08	2.24	2.27	2.19	2.33	2.40
蛋 类	(千克) Eggs	(kg)	5.88	6.51	7.23	8.10	11.98	10.69	8.99	8.25	10.94
水产品	(千克) Aquatic Products	(kg)	17.65	21.59	28.84	25.59	28.59	33.06	35.66	37.33	42.12

4–16 农民家庭主要生活用品购买量

ANNUAL PURCHASES OF ARTICLES FOR BAILY USE OF RURAL HOUSEHOLDS PER CAPITA

品名	Item	2001	2002	2003	2004	2005	2006	2007	2008	2009
粮食 (千克/人)	Grain (kg/person)	—	26.89	30.61	27.53	26.55	26.28	25.72	26.56	27.45
植物油 (千克/人)	Edible Vegetable Oil (kg/person)	1.94	2.52	2.66	2.79	2.89	2.85	3.21	3.55	3.35
动物油 (千克/人)	Edible Animal Oil (kg/person)	0.74	1.29	0.65	0.64	0.73	0.63	0.50	0.47	0.38
蔬菜 (千克/人)	Vegetables (kg/person)	15.38	17.55	14.22	13.97	16.33	16.33	18.82	17.85	16.21
猪肉 (千克/人)	Pork (kg/person)	5.78	6.87	5.94	5.72	6.93	7.46	6.27	6.22	7.04
牛羊肉 (千克/人)	Beef and Mutton (kg/person)	0.30	0.31	0.22	0.28	0.37	0.42	0.49	0.41	0.41
家禽 (千克/人)	Poultry (kg/person)	0.49	0.52	0.66	0.67	0.79	0.79	1.08	1.21	1.16
鲜蛋 (千克/人)	Fresh Eggs (kg/person)	1.19	0.69	0.69	0.57	0.93	0.97	0.97	1.33	1.55
鲜活鱼类 (千克/人)	Fresh Fish (kg/person)	5.52	5.89	6.47	5.81	6.77	7.07	7.69	7.43	7.13
卷烟 (盒/人)	Tobacco (pack/person)	27.99	28.01	26.40	25.72	30.53	30.98	29.06	28.88	27.51
酒 (千克/人)	Wine (kg/person)	7.35	11.30	7.22	8.15	10.13	11.90	12.30	11.70	11.35
水果 (千克/人)	Fruits (kg/person)	5.07	4.44	4.53	5.40	6.84	6.34	6.87	6.80	6.72
服装 (件/人)	Clothing piece/person	1.25	1.72	1.44	1.51	1.81	1.82	1.82	1.99	2.94
鞋类 (双/人)	Footwear (Two/person)	—	—	—	1.32	1.42	1.45	1.35	1.43	1.28
水泥 (千克/人)	Cement (kg/person)	54.45	87.18	64.46	70.88	70.67	108.80	85.93	134.97	137.25
钢材 (千克/人)	Steel (kg/person)	2.25	5.94	3.50	3.76	4.52	6.66	5.84	10.45	10.11
生活用煤 (千克/人)	Coal (kg/person)	57.04	52.58	62.70	58.08	52.97	52.65	49.44	32.82	20.22
电视机 (台/百户)	TV Sets (set/100 households)	3.18	4.64	5.00	7.00	6.88	6.79	5.79	4.95	3.97
洗衣机 (台/百户)	Washing Machine (set/100 households)	0.36	1.06	0.70	0.82	1.85	1.79	1.92	2.73	2.67
电风扇 (台/百户)	Electric Fans (set/100 households)	6.58	7.00	7.55	8.03	8.21	9.73	8.85	9.73	11.45
电冰箱 (台/百户)	Refrigerators (set/100 households)	0.48	0.42	0.42	0.48	1.66	2.67	4.18	5.64	7.06
自行车 (辆/百户)	Bycicle (set/100 households)	4.48	5.61	4.97	6.64	6.05	5.26	5.40	4.83	5.29
摩托车 (辆/百户)	Motocycle (set/100 households)	1.76	2.09	2.13	4.06	4.39	5.00	5.28	4.73	4.26
热水器 (台/百户)	Shower (set/100 households)	0.24	0.21	0.33	0.30	1.24	1.67	2.06	3.11	3.79
电话机 (部/百户)	Telephone Sets (set/100 households)	2.48	3.76	4.12	4.76	5.09	6.15	4.52	4.33	4.37
手机 (部/百户)	Mobile Phones (set/100 households)	0.88	1.88	4.18	7.36	9.64	8.30	12.97	13.82	14.42

4-17 农民家庭年人均主要食品消费量
RURAL HOUSEHOLD ANNUAL CONSUMPTION ON MAJOR FOOD PER CAPITA

单位：千克 (kg)

品 名	Item	2001	2002	2003	2004	2005	2006	2007	2008	2009
一、粮 食	Grain	264.51	260.81	224.30	218.78	212.05	210.06	204.47	190.30	188.94
#小 麦	Wheat	29.67	30.13	22.06	22.52	22.58	23.11	21.80	22.02	19.87
稻 谷	Paddy	208.07	207.42	186.63	182.78	171.47	170.17	168.61	155.37	155.18
二、豆类及豆制品	Bean Products	5.75	7.26	5.58	4.88	6.04	5.87	6.20	5.48	5.49
大 豆	Soy Bean	2.43	3.00	3.09	2.53	2.76	2.73	2.88	2.53	2.52
三、蔬菜及菜制品	Fresh Vegetables and Processed	152.30	153.88	159.76	147.73	152.47	143.75	143.57	132.58	137.04
鲜 菜	Fresh Vegetables	151.54	139.61	151.15	140.34	147.06	138.12	140.57	130.05	134.69
四、油脂类	Oil and Fats	9.69	10.75	9.40	3.52	3.70	3.56	3.77	4.11	3.85
植物油	Edible Vegetable Oil	7.70	8.21	8.75	2.87	2.98	2.89	3.23	3.58	3.39
动物油	Edible Animal Oil	1.99	2.54	0.65	0.64	0.73	0.67	0.53	0.53	0.47
五、肉禽及其制品	Meat and Processed Products	19.73	20.79	23.09	20.81	24.79	25.27	22.70	22.21	22.99
猪 肉	Pork	17.22	18.12	19.50	17.49	20.63	20.91	20.91	17.51	18.14
牛羊肉	Beef and Mutton	0.33	0.35	0.36	0.37	0.44	0.53	0.52	0.50	0.48
家 禽	Poultry	2.01	2.07	2.74	2.48	3.02	2.91	3.30	3.23	3.22
六、蛋类及蛋制品	Eggs and Processed Products	3.95	3.47	3.86	3.99	4.14	4.15	4.17	4.69	4.93
七、奶及奶制品	Milk and Dariy Products	0.21	0.05	0.08	0.11	0.23	0.33	0.50	0.81	1.11
八、水产品	Aquatic Products	6.56	7.31	8.10	7.21	8.11	8.51	9.38	8.71	8.34
鱼 类	Ffish	6.28	7.00	7.74	6.97	7.81	8.18	9.03	8.40	7.97
九、瓜 类		9.10	6.68	9.00	4.99	4.79	8.08	6.28	4.67	5.87
十、酒 类	Liquor and Drinks	8.39	11.51	7.29	8.20	10.17	11.93	12.35	11.76	11.41
#白 酒	Wine Spirit	4.15	7.79	3.68	3.68	3.91	4.06	3.87	3.85	3.94
啤 酒		3.16	3.52	3.53	4.46	6.21	7.83	8.42	7.84	7.40
十一、水果类		10.90	8.19	10.05	9.85	10.62	10.87	11.51	10.37	9.97
十二、坚果及果仁制品	Nuts and Grain Products	0.37	0.31	0.45	0.55	0.76	0.80	0.87	0.97	1.00

4-18 农民家庭每百户主要耐用消费品拥有量
POSSESSION OF DURABLE CONSUMER GOODS PER 100 RURAL HOUSEHOLD

品 名	Item		2001	2002	2003	2004	2005	2006	2007	2008	2009
自行车	(辆) Bicycle	(unit)	110.36	111.33	103.48	102.48	79.09	80.55	73.33	72.45	68.47
电视机	(台) TV Set	(unit)	105.25	110.21	111.27	115.52	110.61	113.06	111.00	113.00	112.88
#彩电	(台) Color TV Set	(unit)	37.58	44.33	56.27	67.97	83.18	92.12	98.82	102.24	105.42
照相机	(架) Camera	(unit)	1.33	1.30	1.79	2.18	1.88	1.76	1.82	2.06	2.58
洗衣机	(台) Washing Machine	(unit)	17.09	20.42	20.12	21.58	26.39	30.12	34.68	37.12	41.70
电冰箱	(台) Refrigerator	(unit)	7.55	8.09	8.52	11.06	14.82	19.18	26.18	30.52	41.36
摩托车	(辆) Motocycle	(unit)	18.39	20.88	25.01	31.42	39.15	45.00	51.45	55.52	59.76
录像机	(台) Videorecorder	(unit)	1.91	1.52	1.18	1.67	0.82	0.76	1.06	0.91	0.52
抽油烟机	(台) Ventilator	(unit)	0.91	1.03	1.06	2.00	3.12	3.72	5.03	6.10	7.70
空调机	(台) Air Conditioner	(unit)	0.42	0.42	1.15	1.48	3.79	5.39	7.61	9.91	12.45
热水器	(台) Shower	(unit)	1.85	3.24	3.70	3.85	6.21	8.79	12.21	16.03	22.73
影碟机	(台) VCD	(unit)	13.12	16.42	23.94	33.24	44.48	51.80	50.64	51.45	50.58
电话机	(部) Telephone Set	(set)	20.00	23.94	31.39	38.64	51.64	57.20	58.36	59.33	55.61
手机	(部) Moblile Phone	(set)	3.82	7.64	20.27	37.12	71.18	90.10	104.67	117.88	134.21
家用计算机	(台) PC	(unit)	0.45	1.42	1.24	1.18	1.09	2.33	2.00	3.00	5.15

4-19 市、州农民年人均纯收入
ANAUAL NET INCOME OF RURAL HOUCEHOLD PER CAPITA IN CITIES AND PREFERCTURES

单位：元 (yuan)

地 区	Region	2001	2002	2003	2004	2005	2006	2007	2008	2009
全 省	Province	2352	2444	2567	2890	3099	3419	3997	4656	5035
武汉市	Wuhan Municipality	3100	3295	3497	3955	4341	4748	5371	6349	7161
黄石市	Huangshi Municipality	2140	2230	2335	2626	2810	3182	3742	4374	4811
十堰市	Shiyan Municipality	1592	1714	1808	1916	1990	2191	2490	2841	3110
宜昌市	Yichang Municipality	2413	2440	2588	2938	3108	3433	4022	4686	5186
襄樊市	Xiangfan Municipality	2479	2564	2658	3060	3191	3519	4114	4880	5440
鄂州市	Ezhou Municipality	2591	2693	2832	3234	3495	3799	4393	5096	5718
荆门市	Jingmen Municipality	2999	2999	3125	3629	3738	4059	4652	5332	5956
孝感市	Xiaogan Municipality	2356	2444	2552	2874	3028	3336	3915	4636	5131
荆州市	Jingzhou Municipality	2303	2408	2502	3002	3108	3502	4140	4889	5464
黄冈市	Huanggang Municipality	2083	2131	2204	2485	2644	2861	3295	3744	4130
咸宁市	Xianning Municipality	2123	2204	2325	2698	2911	3213	3737	4411	4873
随州市	Suizhou Municipality	2298	2455	2565	3017	3223	3581	4177	4967	5457
恩施自治州	Enshi Municipality	1467	1465	1498	1593	1643	1848	2143	2519	2810
仙桃市	Xiantao Municipality	3083	3153	3283	3615	3818	4190	4695	5248	5856
天门市	Tianmen Municipality	2630	2716	2848	3087	3273	3658	4207	4761	5326
潜江市	Qianjiang Municipality	2599	2680	2875	3180	3398	3813	4378	4929	5531
神农架林区	Shennongjia Forest Zones	1330	1465	1594	1906	2164	2394	2850	3330	3707

主要统计指标解释

城镇住户

城镇家庭人口 指居住在一起，经济上合在一起共同生活的家庭成员。凡计算为家庭人口的成员其全部收支都包括在本家庭中。

城镇就业面 指就业人口占家庭人口的百分比。

城镇就业者负担人数 指家庭人口与就业人口之比。

城镇家庭总收入 指家庭成员得到的工薪收入、经营净收入、财产性收入、转移性收入之和，不包括出售财物收入和借贷收入。

城镇家庭可支配收入 指家庭成员得到可用于最终消费支出和其它非义务性支出以及储蓄的总和，即居民家庭可以用来自由支配的收入。它是家庭总收入扣除交纳的所得税、个人交纳的社会保障支出以及记账补贴后的收入。计算公式为：

可支配收入=家庭总收入-交纳所得税-个人交纳的社会保障支出-记帐补贴

城镇家庭总支出 指除借贷支出以外的全部家庭支出。包括消费性支出、购房建房支出、转移性支出、财产性支出、社会保障支出。

城镇家庭消费性支出 指家庭用于日常生活的支出，包括食品、衣着、家庭设备用品及服务、医疗保健、交通和通信、娱乐教育文化服务、居住、杂项商品和服务等八大类支出。

城镇家庭服务性消费支出 指家庭用于支付社会提供的各种非商品性服务费用。

城镇家庭收入分组方法 是将所有调查户依户人均可支配收入由低到高排队，按 10%，10%，20%，20%，20%，10%，10%的比例依次分成：最低收入户、低收入户、中等偏下收入户、中等收入户、中等偏上收入户、高收入户、最高收入户等七组。总体中最低 5%的户为困难户。

恩格尔系数 指食物支出金额在消费性总支出金额中所占的比例。计算公式为：

$$恩格尔系数=\frac{食品支出金额}{消费性总支出金额}\times 100\%$$

农村住户 指农村常住户。农村常住户指长期(一年以上)居住在乡镇(不包括城关镇)行政管理区域内的住户，以及长期居住在城关镇所辖行政村范围内的农村住户。户口不在本地而在本地居住一年及以上的住户也包括在本地农村常住户范围内；有本地户口，但举家外出谋生一年以上的住户，无论是否保留承包耕地都不包括在本地农村住户范围内。

常住人口 指全年经常在家或在家居住 6 个月以上，而且经济和生活与本户连成一体的人口。外出从业人员在外居住时间虽然在 6 个月以上，但收入主要带回家中，经济与本户连为一体，仍视为家庭常住人口；在家居住，生活和本户连成一体的国家职工、退休人员也为家庭常住人口。但是现役军人、中专及以上(走读生除外)的在校学生、以及常年在外(不包括探亲、看病等)且已有稳定的职业与居住场所的外出从业人员，不算家庭常住人口。家庭常住人口主要作为计算农村住户平均每人收入、消费和积累水平及分析家庭人口状况的依据。

整、半劳动力 整劳动力指男子 18 周岁到 50 周岁，女子 18 周岁到 45 周岁；半劳动力指男子 16 周岁到 17 周岁，51 周岁到 60 周岁；女子 16 周岁到 17 周岁，46 周岁到 55 周岁，同时具有劳动能力的人。虽然在劳动年龄之内，但已丧失劳动能力的人，不应算为劳动力；超过劳动年龄，但能经常参加劳动，计入半劳动力数内。常住人口中的职工，若这些职工为劳

动力，就包括在本户的整半劳动力中。

总收入 指调查期内农村住户和住户成员从各种来源渠道得到的收入总和。按收入的性质划分为工资性收入、家庭经营收入、财产性收入和转移性收入。

工资性收入 指农村住户成员受雇于单位或个人，靠出卖劳动而获得的收入。

家庭经营收入 指农村住户以家庭为生产经营单位进行生产筹划和管理而获得的收入。农村住户家庭经营活动按行业划分为农业、林业、牧业、渔业、工业、建筑业、交通运输业邮电业、批发和零售贸易餐饮业、社会服务业、文教卫生业和其他家庭经营。

财产性收入 指金融资产或有形非生产性资产的所有者向其他机构单位提供资金或将有形非生产性资产供其支配，作为回报而从中获得的收入。

转移性收入 指农村住户和住户成员无须付出任何对应物而获得的货物、服务、资金或资产所有权等，不包括无偿提供的用于固定资本形成的资金。一般情况下，是指农村住户在二次分配中的所有收入。

现金收入 指农村住户和住户成员在调查期内得到以现金形态表现的收入。按来源分成工资性收入、家庭经营现金收入、财产性收入、转移性收入。

纯收入 指农村住户当年从各个来源得到的总收入相应地扣除所发生的费用后的收入总和。计算方法：

纯收入=总收入−税费支出−家庭经营费用支出−税费支出−生产性固定资产折旧−赠送农村外部亲友支出−记帐补贴

纯收入主要用于再生产投入和当年生活消费支出，也可用于储蓄和各种非义务性支出。“农民人均纯收入”按人口平均的纯收入水平，反映的是一个地区或一个农户农村居民的平均收入水平。

总支出 指农村住户用于生产、生活和再分配的全部支出。家庭经营费用支出、购置生产性固定资产支出、生产性固定资产折旧、税费支出、生活消费支出、财产性支出和转移性支出。

Explanatory Notes on Main Statistical Indicators

Population of Urban Households refer to members of the household living and sharing economically together. All income and expenditure of the population of the household are included in the income and expenditure of the household.

Proportion of Urban Employment refer to the proportion of employed population to the population of urban households.

Number of Dependents per Urban Employee refers to the ratio between number of persons in urban households and the number of dependents.

Total Income of Urban Households refers to the sum of wage and salary, net business income, income from properties, and income from transfers of members of the households, excluding income from selling of properties and income from borrowings.

Disposable Income of Urban Households refers to the actual income at the disposal of members of the households which can be used for final consumption, other non-compulsory expenditure and savings. This equals to total income minus income tax, personal contribution to social security and sample household subsidy for keeping diaries. Following formula is used:

Disposable income = total household income - income tax - personal contribution to social security - sample household subsidy for keeping diaries

Total Expenditure of Urban Households refer to all expenditure of the households except expenditure on leading. It includes expenditure on consumption, on purchasing or building houses, on transfers, on properties and on social security.

Consumption Expenditure of Urban Households refers to total expenditure of the sample households for consumption in daily life, including expenditure on eight categories such as food, clothing, household appliances and services, health care and medical services, transport and communications, recreation, education and cultural services, housing, miscellaneous goods and services.

Expenditure of Urban Households on Consumption of Services refers to expenditure of households on services of various kinds provided by the society.

Urban Households by Income Group All households in the sample are grouped, by per capita disposable income of the household, into groups of lowest income, low income, lower middle income, middle income, upper middle income, high income and highest income, each group consisting of 10%, 10%, 20%, 20%, 20%, 10% and 10% of all households respectively. The lowest 5% of households are also referred to as poor households.

Engel Coefficient refers to the percentage of expenditure on food in the total consumption expenditure, using the following formula:

Engel Coefficient = (expenditure on food / total consumption expenditure) x 100%

Rural Households refer to resident households in rural areas. Resident households in rural areas are the households residing for more than one year in the areas under the jurisdiction of administration of township governments (excluding county towns), and in the areas under the jurisdiction of administration of villages in county towns. Migrated households residing in the current addresses for over one year with their household registration in other places are included in the resident households of their current addresses. For households with their household registration in one place but all members of the households moving away for living in another place for over one year, they will not be included in the rural households of the area where they are registered, irrespective of whether they still keep their contracted land.

Resident Population refers to population staying at home permanently or for over 6 months during a year and sharing life economically with the household. Members of the household staying away from the household for over 6 months but keeping a close economic relation with the household by sending the majority of income to the household are regarded as resident population of the household. Government staff and workers or retirees living as close members of the household are also considered as resident population. However, servicemen, students of secondary technical schools or schools of higher education and persons with stable jobs and residence outside the household (excluding those visiting relatives or seeking medical service) are not included as resident population of the household. Resident population is used in calculating income, consumption, accumulation on per capita basis of rural households and in analyzing composition of rural households.

Full/Semi Labour Force Full labour force refers to persons capable of work, aged 18-50 for males and 18-45 for females. Semi labour force refers to persons capable of work, aged 16-17 and 51-60 for males and 16-17 and 46-55 for females. Persons at their working ages but not capable of work are not to be included as labour force. Persons not at working ages but participating regularly in work are included in semi labour force. For staff and workers as resident population of the household, they are included as full or semi labour force of the household if they are in the labour force.

Total Income refers to the sum of income earned from various sources by the rural households and their members during the reference period, and is classified as income from wages and salaries, income from household operations, income from properties and income from transfers.

Income from Wages and Salaries refers to income from labour earned by the members of rural households employed by other units or individuals.

Income from Household Operations refers to income by the rural households as units of production and operations. Operations by rural households are classified by economic activities as agriculture, forestry, animal husbandry, fishery, manufacturing, construction, transportation, post and telecommunications, wholesale, retail and catering, social service, culture, education, health, and other household operations.

Income from Properties refers to the income received as returns by owners of financial assets or tangible non-productive assets by providing capitals or tangible non-productive assets to other institutional units.

Income from Transfers refers to the receipt by rural households and their members of goods, services, capitals or rights of assets without giving or repaying accordingly, excluding capitals provided to them for the formation of fixed assets. In general, it refers to all income received by rural households through redistribution.

Cash Income refers to income received by rural households and their members in the form of cash during the reference period. It is classified, by source of income, into income from wages and salaries, cash income from household operations, income from properties and income from transfers.

Net Income refers to the total income of rural households from all sources minus all corresponding expenses. The formula for calculation is as follows:

Net income = total income - taxes and fees paid - household operation expenses - taxes and fees depreciation of fixed assets for production - subsidy for participating in household survey - gifts to non-rural relatives

Net income is mainly used as input for reproduction and as consumption expenditure of the year, and also used for savings and non-compulsory expenses of various forms. "Per capita net income of farmers" is the level of net income averaged by population which reflects the average income level of rural households in a given area.

Total Expenditure refers to total expenses of rural households on production, consumption and redistribution, including expenditure on household operations, on purchase of productive fixed assets, depreciation of productive fixed assets, taxes and fees, expenses on household consumption, expenses on properties and expenses on transfers.

5 固定资产投资

Investment in Fixed Assets

资料整理：柯　超

固 定 资 产 投 资

INVESTMENT IN FIXED ASSETS

2009

全社会固定资产投资完成额	Total Lompleted Investment in Fixed assets	8211.85亿元
城镇投资	Urban Investment	7569.15亿元
#房地产开发	Real Estate Development	1200.44亿元
农村投资	Rural Investment	642.7亿元
#国有经济	State-Owned	3124.9亿元
集体经济	Collective-Owned	411.18亿元
房屋施工面积	Floor Space of Building Under Construction	20142.81万平方米
房屋竣工面积	Floor Space of Building Complete	9772.28万平方米

全社会固定资产投资完成额构成（%）
Composition of Total Completed Investment in Fixed Assets

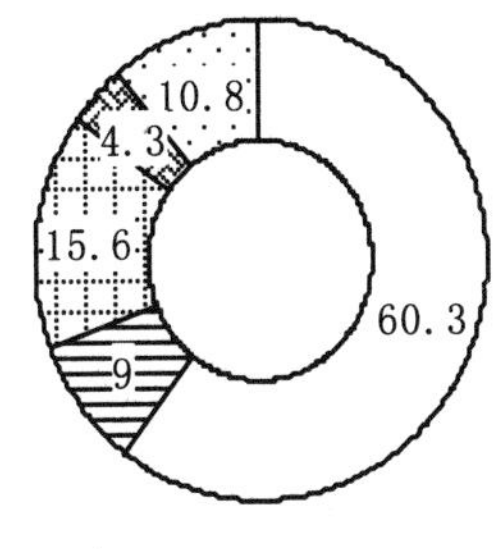

2000

□国有投资　　□集体投资
□私营个体投资　　□外商港澳台商投资
□其他

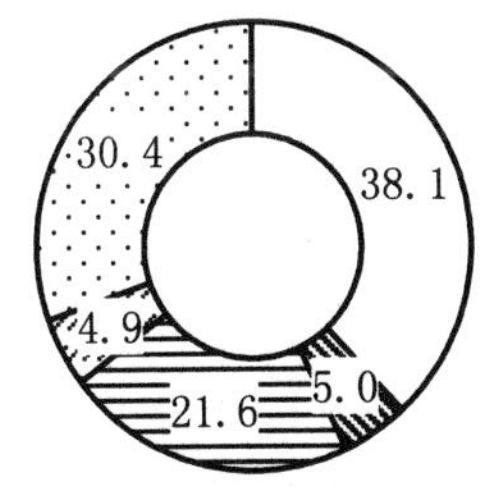

2009

全社会固定资产投资

（亿元）

年份	1995	2000	2001	2002	2003	2004	2005	2006	2007	2008	2009
亿元	827	1422	1552	1695	1884	2356	2835	3573	4534	5799	8212

（年份）

附：全社会固定资产投资完成额构成（%）(Composition of Total Completes Investmaent in Fixed Assets)

		2000	2001	2002	2003	2004	2005	2006	2007	2008	2009
国有投资	State-Owned	60.3	59.2	56.8	47.2	40.4	38.7	41.2	39.9	39.2	38.1
集体投资	Collective-Owned	9	8.1	7.2	5.8	4.5	2.8	3.1	3.4	4.4	5.0
私营个体投资	Individuals	15.6	16.1	15.5	16.1	18.5	19.6	17.8	19.9	20.7	21.6
外商港澳台商投资	Foreign,HK,Macao and Taiwan	4.3	4.1	5	6	6.8	7.4	6.9	6.8	5.9	4.9
其他	Others	10.8	12.5	15.5	24.9	29.8	31.5	31	30	29.8	30.4

5-1 全社会固定资产投资主要指标

指　标	Item	1990	1995	2000
投资总额(亿元)	**Total Investment (100 million yuan)**	**144.44**	**826.50**	**1421.55**
按经济类型分	**Grouped by Ownership**			
国有经济	State-owned Units	100.35	518.76	857.01
集体经济	Collective-owned Units	15.59	72.58	128.32
#农村	Rural	9.59	45.85	98.95
私营个体经济	Individuals	28.50	99.90	221.43
#农村	Rural	23.62	58.67	106.65
联营经济	Joint-Ownership Economic Units		3.63	3.94
股份制经济	Share Holding Co.Ltd.		32.43	86.29
有限责任公司	Limited Liability Corporations		4.39	53.33
港澳台投资经济	Economic Units Funded by Hongkong, Macao and Taiwan		33.60	36.57
外商投资经济	Foreign Funded Enterprise Units		58.72	23.90
其他经济	Others		2.49	10.76
按资金来源分	**Grouped by Source of Finance**			
国家预算内资金	State Budgetary Apporpriations	11.38	58.40	141.48
国内贷款	Domestic Loans	22.22	173.47	243.90
利用外资	Foreign Investment	4.79	88.71	28.28
自筹资金	Fund Raising	92.96	422.92	781.50
其他资金来源	Others	13.09	83.00	226.39
按构成分	**Grouped by Use of Funds**			
建筑安装工程	Construction Installation	92.64	454.40	814.66
设备工器具购置	Purchase of Equipments ad Instruments	41.02	248.50	371.56
其他费用	Ohters	10.78	123.60	235.33
按产业分	**Grouped by Industry**			
#住宅	Residential Housing	39.61	157.18	290.24
第一产业	Primary Industry	12.16	21.88	103.05
第二产业	Second Industry	67.41	401.69	521.58
第三产业	Tertiary Industry	64.87	402.93	796.92
房屋建筑面积(万平方米)	**Floor Space of Building (10000 sq.m)**			
施工面积	Floor Space under Construction	5103.48	8294.84	9920.42
#住宅	Residential Housing	3507.53	5304.79	6831.02
竣工面积	Floor Space Completed	4169.12	5603.20	7508.96
#住宅	Residential Housing	3058.40	3737.81	5417.38
商品房销售面积(万平方米)	**Floor Spaceo of Selling House (sq.m)**	**130.53**	**240.00**	**612.05**

注：2006年全社会投资(城镇投资)不含城镇工矿区私人建房投资(下同)。由于方法制度调整，按可比口径计算，2005年扣除城镇工矿区私人建房投资基数应为2788.92亿元

MAJOR INDICATORS OF TOTAL INVESTMENT IN FIXED ASSETS

2004	2005	2006	2007	2008	2009
2356.38	**2834.75**	**3572.69**	**4534.14**	**5798.56**	**8211.85**
951.73	1095.71	1473.70	1808.61	2273.83	3124.90
105.06	79.47	110.67	155.66	253.32	411.18
65.58	26.55	31.68	44.10	65.02	77.50
436.02	554.27	636.25	900.48	1201.53	1771.61
132.85	135.95	176.87	186.65	190.19	240.48
17.51	19.56	19.42	26.59	15.05	10.73
222.15	232.34	245.27	344.51	462.81	674.54
401.01	557.21	716.16	872.80	1109.43	1606.90
81.72	92.68	119.85	145.53	160.62	197.98
78.18	116.23	127.71	164.84	178.60	202.70
63.00	87.28	123.66	115.12	143.37	211.31
197.03	255.76	378.79	472.98	570.17	711.98
383.78	474.21	708.39	790.84	894.57	1432.98
64.74	71.34	79.32	88.37	57.02	68.33
1182.36	1492.66	1902.71	2470.28	3677.00	4956.65
528.47	540.78	503.48	711.66	599.80	1041.91
1409.25	1696.80	2252.72	2857.31	3568.96	5025.62
537.25	642.86	717.10	896.36	1245.73	1753.28
409.88	495.09	602.87	780.47	983.87	1432.95
433.43	510.04	572.50	709.63	901.26	1127.28
77.55	92.88	107.43	149.40	231.25	321.59
912.93	1086.34	1317.12	1710.59	2344.36	3097.68
1365.90	1655.53	2148.23	2674.15	3222.95	4792.58
13152.08	12572.00	12346.48	13686.34	16417.07	20142.81
9285.64	8401.20	8039.75	8910.75	9896.66	11762.06
9318.34	7863.85	7126.64	7557.62	7551.82	9772.28
7069.45	5627.67	4812.39	5036.19	4679.96	5556.71
1591.81	**1708.02**	**2038.46**	**2538.90**	**1941.62**	**2718.30**

Note: Private housing construction investment in urban mining area was exclued in total investment of 2006. Owing to the adjustment of system, the basic Value should be 2.78892 trillion yuan after private housing construction investment in urban mining area was exclued in total investment of 2005.

5-2 全社会固定资产投资额
TOTAL INVESTMENT IN FIXED ASSETS

单位：亿元 (100 million yuan)

年 份 Year	投资额 Investment	#房地产开发 Real Estate Development	#国有经济 State Owned Units	#集体经济 Collective Owned Units	#私营个体 Individual
1978	33.58		33.19	0.39	
1979	31.53		30.86	0.67	
1980	35.50		34.19	1.31	
"六五"时期 the peroid of the Six-Year Plan	**315.82**		**207.57**	**49.41**	**58.84**
1981	33.48		29.51	3.69	0.28
1982	48.83		34.46	8.45	5.92
1983	56.13		36.69	8.84	10.60
1984	74.47		45.25	10.99	18.23
1985	102.91		61.66	17.44	23.81
"七五"时期 the peroid of the Seven-Year Plan	**680.12**	**5.94**	**435.32**	**94.17**	**150.64**
1986	111.44		66.42	15.89	29.13
1987	140.08		85.32	22.31	32.46
1988	160.46		102.21	24.60	33.64
1989	123.70		81.02	15.78	26.91
1990	144.44	5.94	100.35	15.59	28.50
"八五"时期 the peroid of the Eight-Year Plan	**2211.67**	**253.77**	**1497.69**	**190.04**	**261.87**
1991	168.19	7.88	119.07	19.49	29.63
1992	240.73	12.55	182.86	22.52	35.35
1993	383.18	37.01	275.84	30.62	40.37
1994	593.07	76.20	401.16	44.83	56.62
1995	826.50	121.13	518.76	72.58	99.90
"九五"时期 the peroid of the Nine-Year Plan	**6022.80**	**634.60**	**3425.23**	**573.74**	**943.77**
1996	984.38	118.40	593.32	96.50	124.78
1997	1083.60	126.47	567.60	107.12	160.56
1998	1231.10	131.23	661.94	116.92	194.52
1999	1302.17	123.87	745.36	124.88	242.48
2000	1421.55	134.63	857.01	128.32	221.43
"十五"时期 the peroid of the Ten-Year Plan	**10321.69**	**1354.15**	**4817.55**	**541.41**	**1806.78**
2001	1551.75	151.24	918.21	126.41	249.59
2002	1695.22	178.64	963.18	121.42	263.00
2003	1883.59	239.04	888.72	109.05	303.90
2004	2356.38	337.28	951.73	105.06	436.02
2005	2834.75	447.95	1095.71	79.47	554.27
"十一五"时期 the peroid of the Eleven-Year Plan					
2006	3572.69	564.76	1473.70	110.67	636.25
2007	4534.14	723.73	1808.61	155.66	900.48
2008	5798.56	892.67	2273.83	253.32	1201.53
2009	8211.85	1200.44	3124.90	411.18	1771.61

注：房地产开发投资统计制度从1990年开始建立。
Note: The statistical system of real estate development investment was established in 190

 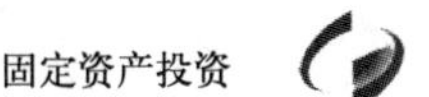

5-3 按登记注册类型分全社会固定资产投资

TOTAL INVESTMENT IN FIXED ASSETS BY TYPE OF REGISTRATION

单位：亿元　　　　(100 million yuan)

指　　标	Item	2007		2008		2009	
		投资额 Investment	#城镇投资 Urban	投资额 Investment	#城镇投资 Urban	投资额 Investment	#城镇投资 Urban
总　计	**Total**	**4534.14**	**4131.26**	**5798.56**	**5332.67**	**8211.85**	**7569.15**
内资企业	Inner Funded Enterprises	4007.54	3801.95	5230.94	4964.97	7513.00	7124.61
国有企业	State-owned Enterprise	1746.00	1697.17	2138.10	2070.64	2886.40	2762.40
集体企业	Collective-owned Enterpr	113.71	71.37	200.57	139.43	351.99	277.09
股份合作企业	Share Holding Cooperativ Enterprises	40.27	38.96	45.26	41.50	47.59	45.39
联营企业	Joint Owned Enterprise	30.10	26.91	25.77	24.99	36.66	35.53
国有联营	State Joint ownership	1.72	1.72	3.24	3.24	14.33	14.33
集体联营	Collective Joint Ownershi	1.79	1.34	7.48	7.37	11.60	11.21
国有与集体联营	Joint State- Collective	10.29	10.20	4.10	3.92	5.10	4.76
其他联营企业	Other Joint Owned Enterp	16.30	13.65	10.95	10.46	5.63	5.23
有限责任公司	Responsibility Co. Ltd	933.59	914.35	1241.93	1224.98	1831.08	1794.34
国有独资公司	State Solely Funded Co.	60.89	60.88	132.50	132.48	224.17	224.17
其他有限责任公司	Others	872.70	853.47	1109.43	1092.50	1606.90	1570.16
股份有限公司	Share Holding Co.Ltd.	344.51	330.66	462.81	443.79	674.54	655.29
私营企业	Private - owned enterprise	684.25	624.83	973.12	893.02	1473.44	1367.33
其他企业	Others	115.11	97.70	143.38	126.62	211.31	187.26
港、澳、台商投资企业	Hongkong, Macao and Ta Funded	145.53	143.87	160.62	159.76	197.98	196.28
合资经营企业	Joint Funded Enterprises	50.97	50.77	52.45	52.29	51.50	51.21
合作经营企业	Cooperative Operation Enterprises	15.35	15.35	0.94	0.94	2.24	2.24
股份有限公司	Share Holding Co.Ltd.	74.97	73.86	96.07	95.49	102.51	101.84
独资经营企业	Solely Funded Enterprise	4.23	3.89	11.17	11.05	41.73	40.99
外商投资企业	Foreign Invested Enterpri	164.84	163.80	178.60	178.01	202.70	200.80
合资经营企业	Joint Funded Enterprises	104.08	103.65	83.49	83.28	117.35	116.09
合作经营企业	Cooperative Operation Enterprises	4.33	4.25	29.09	28.96	13.41	13.34
独资企业	Solely Funded Enterprises	43.46	43.44	54.08	54.00	45.63	45.52
股份有限公司	Share Holding Co.Ltd.	12.98	12.46	11.94	11.78	26.32	25.86
个体经营	Individual Investment	216.23	21.64	228.40	29.92	298.17	47.45
个体户	Individual Self-Employed	204.49	12.79	212.86	16.48	267.07	21.06
个人合伙	Individual Pattenership	11.74	8.85	15.54	13.44	31.10	26.39

5–4 按构成分城镇固定资产投资（2009）
URBAN INVESTMENT IN FIXED ASSETS BY USE OF FUNDS(2009)

单位：亿元 (100 million yuan)

行业	Sector	投资额 Investment	建筑工程 Construction	安装工程 Installation	设备工器具购置 Purchases of Equipments and Instruments	其他 Others
总计	**Total**	**7569.15**	**4111.77**	**464.53**	**1616.89**	**1375.96**
农、林、牧、渔业	Farming, Forestry, Animal Husbandry and Fishery	165.12	89.51	5.91	20.69	49.01
农业	Farming	38.59	21.61	1.27	4.61	11.09
林业	Forestry	22.59	9.10	0.24	0.46	12.79
畜牧业	Animal Husbandry	36.82	20.28	2.35	7.36	6.83
渔业	Fishery	7.00	2.75	0.32	1.07	2.86
农、林、牧、渔服务业	Farming, Forestry, Animal Husbandry and Fishery Services	60.12	35.77	1.73	7.18	15.44
采矿业	Mining and Qarrying	122.93	54.67	12.37	45.49	10.40
制造业	Manufacturing	2320.85	899.31	156.33	1005.85	259.35
农副食品加工业	Food Processing	111.26	48.57	8.41	39.29	14.99
食品制造业	Food Production	78.17	35.39	5.14	27.69	9.95
饮料制造业	Beverage Production	57.52	23.62	4.27	23.07	6.56
烟草制品业	Tobacco Processing	9.10	1.69	0.08	5.02	2.31
纺织业	Textile Industry	89.72	33.98	7.53	39.17	9.04
纺织服装、鞋、帽制造业	Textile Garments, Shoes and Hats Products	55.06	25.55	4.81	19.12	5.57
皮革、毛皮、羽毛(绒)及其制品业	Leather, Furs Down and Related Products	10.80	4.49	0.95	3.70	1.66
木材加工及木、竹、藤、棕、草制品业	Timber Processing and Wwood, Bamboo, Rattan, Palm and Sraw Works	25.30	9.91	2.06	10.63	2.71
家具制造业	Furniture Manufacturing	20.02	11.32	1.81	4.63	2.26
造纸及纸制品业	Papermaking and Paper Products	34.64	13.61	1.80	16.84	2.39
印刷业和记录媒介的复制	Printing and Record Processing	32.75	15.09	1.69	12.07	3.91
文教体育用品制造业	Stationery, Education and Sports Goods	4.89	2.39	0.50	1.57	0.43
石油加工、炼焦及核燃料加工业	Petroleum Processing, Coking Products and Nuclear Fuel Processing	19.62	6.93	2.85	6.74	3.10
化学原料及化学制品制造业	Raw Chemical Material and Chemical Products	223.22	77.96	17.89	97.43	29.95
医药制造业	Medical and pharmaceutical Products	76.85	33.01	6.18	27.02	10.64
化学纤维制造业	Chemical Fibers	3.45	1.38	0.28	1.77	0.02
橡胶制品业	Rubber Products	11.98	5.24	0.80	5.05	0.89
塑料制品业	Plastic Products	56.32	25.64	3.47	21.07	6.14
非金属矿物制品业	Nonmetal Material Products	247.49	89.80	19.78	114.74	23.16
黑色金属冶炼及压延加工业	Smelting and Processing of ferrous Metals	226.75	58.66	13.76	139.18	15.14
有色金属冶炼及压延加工业	Smelting and Processing of Nonferrous Metals	40.74	14.41	2.55	16.29	7.49
金属制品业	Metal Products	113.91	55.58	5.70	42.07	10.56
通用设备制造业	Ordinaryly Machinery Manufacturing	130.25	57.25	10.74	49.78	12.48
专用设备制造业	Special Purpose Equipment Manufacturing	118.95	55.26	5.86	43.70	14.13
交通运输设备制造业	Transportation Equipment Manufacturing	292.62	107.63	14.41	129.36	41.22
电气机械及器材制造业	Electric Machinery and Equipment	95.99	41.29	7.15	39.81	7.74
通信设备、计算机及其他电子设备	Telecommunication Equipment, Computer and Other Electronic Equipment Manufacturing	99.57	30.39	3.64	55.23	10.30
仪器仪表及文化、办公用机械制造	Instruments, Meters, Cultural and Official Machinery	10.42	4.39	0.69	4.47	0.86
工艺品及其他制造业	Handicraft Article and Other Manufacturing	15.43	6.07	1.18	5.96	2.21
废弃资源和废旧材料回收加工业	Waste Resources and Junk Material Recycled	8.06	2.80	0.30	3.39	1.57
电力、燃气及水的生产和供应业	Electric Power, Gas and Water Production and Supply	494.90	152.48	48.30	134.64	159.48
电力、热力的生产和供应业	Electric Power, Steam and Hot Water Production and Supply	398.41	100.40	34.12	111.66	152.23
燃气生产和供应业	Gas Production and Supply	31.61	17.89	4.50	7.63	1.60
水的生产和供应业	Tap Water Production and Supply	64.87	34.19	9.68	15.35	5.65

5-4 续表 continued

单位：亿元 (100 million yuan)

行　　业	Sector	投资额 Investment	建筑工程 Construction	安装工程 Installation	设备工器具购置 Purchases of Equipments and Instruments	其他 Others
建筑业	Construction	30.71	6.33	0.50	20.83	3.05
交通运输、仓储和邮政业	Transportation, storage and Post	957.23	705.04	17.98	92.91	141.30
铁路运输业	Railway Transportation	250.26	189.17	4.54	22.36	34.19
道路运输业	Road Transportation	514.38	429.12	6.70	14.10	64.45
城市公共交通业	Urban Public Transit	67.20	22.51	0.23	18.35	26.11
水上运输业	Waterway Transportation	44.11	22.05	1.56	16.61	3.89
管道运输业	Pipeline Transportation	4.40	1.43	1.06	1.61	0.29
装卸搬运和其他运输服务业	Load and Unload, Carry and Other	9.83	5.79	0.67	2.40	0.97
仓储业	Transportation Storage	53.82	33.96	3.07	6.04	10.75
邮政业	Post	0.97	0.48	0.14	0.19	0.15
信息传输、计算机服务和软件业	Information Transmmision, Computer Service and Software	79.19	20.79	4.74	51.36	2.30
电信和其他信息传输服务业	Telecommunication and Other Information Transmmision Service	66.78	11.08	4.57	49.65	1.48
计算机服务业	Computer Service	2.05	1.45	0.17	0.42	0.01
软件业	Software	10.36	8.26	0.00	1.29	0.81
批发和零售业	Wholesale and Retail Trade	242.32	137.28	24.42	45.26	35.36
住宿和餐饮业	Hotel and Catering Services	152.48	86.31	19.64	31.96	14.56
金融业	Finance	16.13	5.13	1.68	8.54	0.79
银行业	Banking	12.34	3.12	0.93	7.93	0.37
其他金融活动	Other Financial Acitivities	2.16	0.72	0.53	0.50	0.42
房地产业	Real Estate Trade	1365.90	872.44	93.47	25.81	374.18
租赁和商务服务业	Leasing and Commercial Service	128.94	64.19	11.57	12.55	40.62
租赁业	Leasing Service	2.08	0.96	0.01	0.92	0.19
商务服务业	Commercial Service	126.86	63.23	11.57	11.63	40.43
科学研究、技术服务和地质勘查业	Scientific Research, Polytechnical Services and Goelogical Prospecting	46.95	30.52	3.63	7.59	5.21
水利、环境和公共设施管理业	Water Conservancy, Environment and Public Facility Management	827.02	572.82	28.21	35.86	190.14
水利管理业	Water Conservancy Management	112.64	89.38	3.93	6.78	12.55
环境管理业	Environment Management	56.90	40.66	3.45	6.32	6.47
公共设施管理业	Public Facility Management	657.48	442.78	20.83	22.76	171.12
居民服务和其他服务业	Resident Service and Others	19.22	11.48	1.83	3.47	2.44
教育	Education	124.45	91.12	3.83	19.33	10.16
卫生、社会保障和社会福利业	Health Care, Social Security and Social Welfare	74.52	49.25	5.16	14.90	5.21
卫生	Health Care	68.86	44.90	4.73	14.67	4.57
社会保障业	Social Security	1.13	0.86	0.17		0.10
社会福利业	Social Welfare	4.53	3.49	0.27	0.23	0.54
文化、体育和娱乐业	Culture, Sports and Recreation	102.78	59.41	7.43	11.55	24.39
新闻出版业	News Publication	4.04	3.01	0.69	0.25	0.08
广播、电视、电影和音像业	Radio, Television, Film and Stereo	6.51	1.63	1.26	3.37	0.25
文化艺术业	Culture and Arts	29.29	13.93	1.46	1.30	12.59
体育	Sports	18.57	11.45	0.44	1.53	5.15
娱乐业	Receation	44.38	29.39	3.58	5.09	6.32
公共管理和社会组织	Public Management and Social Organizations	297.52	203.68	17.53	28.30	48.01

5-5 按建设性质分城镇固定资产投资（2009）
URBAN INVESTMENT IN FIXED ASSETS BY TYPE OF CONSTRUCTION(2009)

单位：亿元 (100 million yuan)

行业	Sector	投资额 Investment	#新建 New Construction	#扩建 Expension	#改建 Replacement
总计	**Total**	**7569.15**	**4503.38**	**1343.66**	**1331.89**
农、林、牧、渔业	Farming, Forestry, Animal Husbandry and Fishery	165.12	67.61	50.90	43.45
农业	Farming	38.59	17.16	12.12	9.20
林业	Forestry	22.59	7.53	10.00	4.71
畜牧业	Animal Husbandry	36.82	21.97	10.62	3.88
渔业	Fishery	7.00	3.59	1.96	1.45
农、林、牧、渔服务业	Farming, Forestry, Animal Husbandry and Fishery Services	60.12	17.35	16.20	24.21
采矿业	Mining and Qarrying	122.93	28.10	43.42	46.62
制造业	Manufacturing	2320.85	1069.88	562.40	515.99
农副食品加工业	Food Processing	111.26	47.04	33.70	26.89
食品制造业	Food Production	78.17	41.25	23.34	9.68
饮料制造业	Beverage Production	57.52	27.03	16.75	9.85
烟草制品业	Tobacco Processing	9.10	0.24	0.41	1.80
纺织业	Textile Industry	89.72	33.90	26.23	26.46
纺织服装、鞋、帽制造业	Textile Garments, Shoes and Hats Products	55.06	29.36	8.29	15.35
皮革、毛皮、羽毛(绒)及其制品业	Leather, Furs Down and Related Products	10.80	6.85	1.85	1.33
木材加工及木、竹、藤、棕、草制品业	Timber Processing and Wwood, Bamboo, Rattan,Palm and Sraw Works	25.30	9.37	9.76	5.16
家具制造业	Furniture Manufacturing	20.02	10.33	5.55	3.67
造纸及纸制品业	Papermaking and Paper Products	34.64	15.35	8.57	7.35
印刷业和记录媒介的复制	Printing and Record Processing	32.75	15.23	7.17	5.39
文教体育用品制造业	Stationery, Education and Sports Goods	4.89	3.15	0.51	1.14
石油加工、炼焦及核燃料加工业	Petroleum Processing, Coking Products and Nuclear Fuel Processing	19.62	5.97	2.68	8.42
化学原料及化学制品制造业	Raw Chemical Material and Chemical Products	223.22	110.49	41.53	66.85
医药制造业	Medical and pharmaceutical Products	76.85	46.40	16.00	12.94
化学纤维制造业	Chemical Fibers	3.45	1.93	0.28	1.25
橡胶制品业	Rubber Products	11.98	3.40	1.88	6.10
塑料制品业	Plastic Products	56.32	28.23	17.80	7.36
非金属矿物制品业	Nonmetal Material Products	247.49	101.55	66.12	71.95
黑色金属冶炼及压延加工业	Smelting and Processing of ferrous Metals	226.75	73.72	93.47	54.58
有色金属冶炼及压延加工业	Smelting and Processing of Nonferrous Metals	40.74	16.67	6.48	16.04
金属制品业	Metal Products	113.91	60.94	25.31	10.18
通用设备制造业	Ordinaryly Machinery Manufacturing	130.25	61.52	25.87	24.71
专用设备制造业	Special Purpose Equipment Manufacturing	118.95	64.00	26.87	18.03
交通运输设备制造业	Transportation Equipment Manufacturing	292.62	113.41	69.61	71.73
电气机械及器材制造业	Electric Machinery and Equipment	95.99	54.45	16.03	14.09
通信设备、计算机及其他电子设备	Telecommunication Equipment, Computer and Other Electronic Equipment Manufacturing	99.57	68.81	6.66	10.06
仪器仪表及文化、办公用机械制造	Instruments, Meters, Cultural and Official Machinery	10.42	6.56	0.47	1.41
工艺品及其他制造业	Handicraft Article and Other Manufacturing	15.43	6.07	2.05	5.99
废弃资源和废旧材料回收加工业	Waste Resources and Junk Material Recycled	8.06	6.65	1.17	0.25
电力、燃气及水的生产和供应业	Electric Power, Gas and Water Production and Supply	494.90	304.77	76.30	110.20
电力、热力的生产和供应业	Electric Power, Steam and Hot Water Production and Supply	398.41	261.04	56.46	78.59
燃气生产和供应业	Gas Production and Supply	31.61	13.85	3.07	13.74
水的生产和供应业	Tap Water Production and Supply	64.87	29.88	16.77	17.88

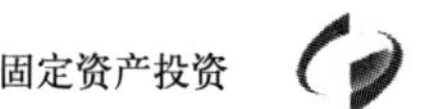

5-5 续表 continued

单位：亿元 (100 million yuan)

行业	Sector	投资额 Investment	#新建 New Construction	#扩建 Expension	#改建 Replacement
建筑业	Construction	30.71	7.21	3.09	1.88
交通运输、仓储和邮政业	Transportation, storage and Post	957.23	636.62	141.91	138.91
铁路运输业	Railway Transportation	250.26	217.10	3.45	29.02
道路运输业	Road Transportation	514.38	300.18	109.64	100.39
城市公共交通业	Urban Public Transit	67.20	53.11	0.57	1.24
水上运输业	Waterway Transportation	44.11	26.21	4.19	3.43
管道运输业	Pipeline Transportation	4.40	4.21	0.14	0.05
装卸搬运和其他运输服务业	Load and Unload, Carry and Other	9.83	5.63	2.59	1.03
仓储业	Transportation Storage	53.82	29.45	20.24	3.49
邮政业	Post	0.97	0.72		0.25
信息传输、计算机服务和软件业	Information Transmmision, Computer Service and Software	79.19	15.90	15.64	27.53
电信和其他信息传输服务业	Telecommunication and Other Information Transmmision Service	66.78	7.40	14.88	25.51
计算机服务业	Computer Service	2.05	0.09	0.51	1.39
软件业	Software	10.36	8.40	0.26	0.63
批发和零售业	Wholesale and Retail Trade	242.32	124.87	48.49	52.28
住宿和餐饮业	Hotel and Catering Services	152.48	73.97	21.60	45.72
金融业	Finance	16.13	3.07	1.72	4.16
银行业	Banking	12.34	1.10	0.88	3.33
其他金融活动	Other Financial Acitivities	2.16	0.67	0.77	0.56
房地产业	Real Estate Trade	1365.90	1335.56	9.21	9.33
租赁和商务服务业	Leasing and Commercial Service	128.94	93.91	9.02	20.74
租赁业	Leasing Service	2.08	0.88	0.41	0.28
商务服务业	Commercial Service	126.86	93.03	8.61	20.45
科学研究、技术服务和地质勘查业	Scientific Research, Polytechnical Services and Goelogical Prospecting	46.95	28.90	7.41	7.17
水利、环境和公共设施管理业	Water Conservancy, Environment and Public Facility Management	827.02	432.71	210.77	167.80
水利管理业	Water Conservancy Management	112.64	37.60	25.56	46.93
环境管理业	Environment Management	56.90	31.02	8.46	16.77
公共设施管理业	Public Facility Management	657.48	364.09	176.75	104.10
居民服务和其他服务业	Resident Service and Others	19.22	9.14	2.51	6.49
教育	Education	124.45	51.35	36.88	16.41
卫生、社会保障和社会福利业	Health Care, Social Security and Social Welfare	74.52	33.71	16.65	16.45
卫生	Health Care	68.86	31.00	14.46	15.74
社会保障业	Social Security	1.13	0.31	0.67	0.15
社会福利业	Social Welfare	4.53	2.40	1.52	0.56
文化、体育和娱乐业	Culture, Sports and Recreation	102.78	56.91	20.88	20.64
新闻出版业	News Publication	4.04	2.36	0.12	1.32
广播、电视、电影和音像业	Radio, Television, Film and Stereo	6.51	1.46	0.81	3.62
文化艺术业	Culture and Arts	29.29	19.31	3.44	5.61
体育	Sports	18.57	13.22	0.09	3.71
娱乐业	Receation	44.38	20.57	16.41	6.38
公共管理和社会组织	Public Management and Social Organizations	297.52	129.20	64.86	80.11

5-6 按控股情况分城镇固定资产投资（2009）
URBAN INVESTMENT IN FIXED ASSETS BY THE SITUATION OF CONTROLLING SHARE HOLDING(2009)

单位：亿元 (100 million yuan)

行业	Sector	投资额 Investment	国有控股 State Share Holding	集体控股 Collective Share Holding	私人控股 Private Share Holding	港澳台商控股 Hongkong, Macao and Taiwan Share Holding	外商控股 Foreign Sgare Holding
总计	**Total**	**7569.15**	**3540.77**	**578.47**	**3016.03**	**177.52**	**133.64**
农、林、牧、渔业	Farming, Forestry, Animal Husbandry and Fishery	165.12	80.51	19.27	64.65	0.58	0.10
农业	Farming	38.59	17.83	7.40	13.36		
林业	Forestry	22.59	17.73	1.07	3.79		
畜牧业	Animal Husbandry	36.82	3.62	2.00	31.11		0.10
渔业	Fishery	7.00	0.67	0.38	5.88	0.08	
农、林、牧、渔服务业	Farming, Forestry, Animal Husbandry and Fishery Services	60.12	40.67	8.43	10.52	0.50	
采矿业	Mining and Qarrying	122.93	53.40	10.48	57.78	0.83	0.44
制造业	Manufacturing	2320.85	485.54	141.45	1556.48	70.91	66.47
农副食品加工业	Food Processing	111.26	2.82	6.84	99.42		2.18
食品制造业	Food Production	78.17	2.37	2.73	67.90	2.17	3.00
饮料制造业	Beverage Production	57.52	2.77	2.62	41.32	4.15	6.66
烟草制品业	Tobacco Processing	9.10	9.03		0.04	0.03	
纺织业	Textile Industry	89.72	8.63	8.58	65.88	2.55	4.07
纺织服装、鞋、帽制造业	Textile Garments, Shoes and Hats Products	55.06	2.80	4.65	46.21	0.76	0.64
皮革、毛皮、羽毛(绒)及其制品业	Leather, Furs Down and Related Products	10.80			6.29	4.51	
木材加工及木、竹、藤、棕、草制品业	Timber Processing and Wwood, Bamboo, Rattan, Palm and Sraw Works	25.30	0.07	2.68	21.56	0.71	0.29
家具制造业	Furniture Manufacturing	20.02	0.30	1.57	16.57	1.01	0.58
造纸及纸制品业	Papermaking and Paper Products	34.64	1.51	1.80	30.89		0.45
印刷业和记录媒介的复制	Printing and Record Processing	32.75	10.94	1.44	19.94	0.43	
文教体育用品制造业	Stationery, Education and Sports Goods	4.89			4.56	0.25	0.08
石油加工、炼焦及核燃料加工业	Petroleum Processing, Coking Products and Nuclear Fuel Processing	19.62	11.18	0.15	5.56		2.73
化学原料及化学制品制造业	Raw Chemical Material and Chemical Products	223.22	48.16	25.34	141.84	5.89	1.99
医药制造业	Medical and pharmaceutical Products	76.85	10.36	4.89	57.23	4.00	0.37
化学纤维制造业	Chemical Fibers	3.45	1.28		2.02	0.15	
橡胶制品业	Rubber Products	11.98	0.44	3.67	7.77		0.11
塑料制品业	Plastic Products	56.32	5.56	3.28	45.34	0.96	1.17
非金属矿物制品业	Nonmetal Material Products	247.49	36.83	16.31	186.55	4.15	3.64
黑色金属冶炼及压延加工业	Smelting and Processing of ferrous Metals	226.75	143.35	7.96	72.02		3.41
有色金属冶炼及压延加工业	Smelting and Processing of Nonferrous Metals	40.74	7.27	0.42	32.21	0.04	0.80
金属制品业	Metal Products	113.91	22.11	4.18	83.01	2.75	1.87
通用设备制造业	Ordinaryly Machinery Manufacturing	130.25	19.93	5.77	99.18	4.69	0.67
专用设备制造业	Special Purpose Equipment Manufacturing	118.95	11.99	5.96	94.24	4.02	2.73
交通运输设备制造业	Transportation Equipment Manufacturing	292.62	100.11	17.12	153.24	6.63	15.52
电气机械及器材制造业	Electric Machinery and Equipment	95.99	3.42	5.47	75.43	1.54	10.12
通信设备、计算机及其他电子设备制造业	Telecommunication Equipment, Computer, Other Electronic Equipment Manufacturing	99.57	18.45	2.73	57.83	17.55	3.01
仪器仪表及文化、办公用机械制造业	Instruments, Meters, Cultural and Official Machinery	10.42	0.91		8.56	0.56	0.39
工艺品及其他制造业	Handicraft Article and Other Manufacturing	15.43	2.92	3.89	8.57	0.04	
废弃资源和废旧材料回收加工业	Waste Resources and Junk Material Recycled	8.06		1.40	5.29	1.38	
电力、燃气及水的生产和供应业	Electric Power, Gas and Water Production and Supply	494.90	398.92	20.90	65.65	6.22	3.20
电力、热力的生产和供应业	Electric Power, Steam and Hot Water Production and Supply	398.41	335.52	13.22	48.16		1.51
燃气生产和供应业	Gas Production and Supply	31.61	17.12	2.75	5.33	6.22	0.20
水的生产和供应业	Tap Water Production and Supply	64.87	46.28	4.93	12.17		1.49

5-6 续表 continued

单位：亿元 (100 million yuan)

行业	Sector	投资额 Investment	国有控股 State Share Holding	集体控股 Collective Share Holding	私人控股 Private Share Holding	港澳台商控股 Hongkong, Macao and Taiwan Share Holding	外商控股 Foreign Sgare Holding
建筑业	Construction	30.71	23.75	0.30	6.65	0.01	
交通运输、仓储和邮政业	Transportation, storage and Post	957.23	831.52	49.91	66.03	9.76	
铁路运输业	Railway Transportation	250.26	249.87	0.10	0.29		
道路运输业	Road Transportation	514.38	462.94	29.36	22.09		
城市公共交通业	Urban Public Transit	67.20	66.11		1.08		
水上运输业	Waterway Transportation	44.11	26.86	2.26	14.85	0.15	
管道运输业	Pipeline Transportation	4.40	2.45	0.60	1.35		
装卸搬运和其他运输服务业	Load and Unload, Carry and Other	9.83	2.79	2.19	4.85		
仓储业	Transportation Storage	53.82	8.94	14.42	20.85	9.61	
邮政业	Post	0.97	0.39		0.58		
信息传输、计算机服务和软件业	Information Transmmision, Computer Service and Software	79.19	56.66	8.62	5.97	4.37	3.57
电信和其他信息传输服务业	Telecommunication and Other Information Transmmision Service	66.78	56.61	0.30	2.11	4.20	3.56
计算机服务业	Computer Service	2.05	0.05	0.27	1.73		
软件业	Software	10.36		8.04	2.13	0.17	0.01
批发和零售业	Wholesale and Retail Trade	242.32	39.60	39.32	159.95	2.35	1.11
住宿和餐饮业	Hotel and Catering Services	152.48	16.98	11.35	113.86	1.47	8.82
金融业	Finance	16.13	11.25	2.64	2.24		
银行业	Banking	12.34	9.71	2.33	0.30		
其他金融活动	Other Financial Acitivities	2.16	0.97	0.13	1.05		
房地产业	Real Estate Trade	1365.90	256.01	146.31	727.20	71.91	41.75
租赁和商务服务业	Leasing and Commercial Service	128.94	92.99	8.01	26.42	1.22	0.30
租赁业	Leasing Service	2.08	0.28	0.54	1.25		
商务服务业	Commercial Service	126.86	92.71	7.47	25.16	1.22	0.30
科学研究、技术服务和地质勘查业	Scientific Research, Polytechnical Services and Goelogical Prospecting	46.95	32.19	2.60	11.59		0.58
水利、环境和公共设施管理业	Water Conservancy, Environment and Public Facility Management	827.02	711.32	46.33	62.24	6.63	0.51
水利管理业	Water Conservancy Management	112.64	106.51	4.43	1.70		
环境管理业	Environment Management	56.90	45.72	3.57	7.09		0.51
公共设施管理业	Public Facility Management	657.48	559.08	38.33	53.45	6.63	
居民服务和其他服务业	Resident Service and Others	19.22	4.10	2.94	12.12	0.06	
教育	Education	124.45	104.81	6.24	13.40		
卫生、社会保障和社会福利业	Health Care, Social Security and Social Welfare	74.52	61.58	5.74	7.21		
卫生	Health Care	68.86	56.45	5.44	6.96		
社会保障业	Social Security	1.13	1.10	0.03			
社会福利业	Social Welfare	4.53	4.03	0.26	0.24		
文化、体育和娱乐业	Culture, Sports and Recreation	102.78	58.88	9.63	26.44	1.03	6.80
新闻出版业	News Publication	4.04	3.80		0.24		
广播、电视、电影和音像业	Radio, Television, Film and Stereo	6.51	3.74	1.73	1.05		
文化艺术业	Culture and Arts	29.29	23.86	2.92	2.51		
体育	Sports	18.57	18.00	0.08	0.49		
娱乐业	Receation	44.38	9.49	4.91	22.16	1.03	6.80
公共管理和社会组织	Public Management and Social Organizations	297.52	220.77	46.42	30.15	0.18	

5-7 按行业分城镇施工投产项目个数（2009）
NUMBER OF URBAN PROJECTS UNDER CONSTRUCTION AND PUT INTO PRODUCTION BY SECTOR(2009)

行业	Sector	施工项目(个) Number of Projects under Construction (unit)	#新开工 Newly Started	全部建成投产项目(个) Completion and Put into Production of All Projects (unit)	项目建成投产率(%) Rate of Completion and Put into Production (%)
总　计	**Total**	**21020**	**17413**	**15041**	**71.6**
农、林、牧、渔业	Farming, Forestry, Animal Husbandry and Fishery	1220	1067	975	79.9
农业	Farming	211	186	179	84.8
林业	Forestry	186	157	153	82.3
畜牧业	Animal Husbandry	312	274	248	79.5
渔业	Fishery	60	55	44	73.3
农、林、牧、渔服务业	Farming, Forestry, Animal Husbandry and Fishery Services	451	395	351	77.8
采矿业	Mining and Qarrying	494	432	359	72.7
制造业	Manufacturing	7090	5667	4914	69.3
农副食品加工业	Food Processing	591	523	447	75.6
食品制造业	Food Production	285	225	201	70.5
饮料制造业	Beverage Production	187	147	111	59.4
烟草制品业	Tobacco Processing	11	9	9	81.8
纺织业	Textile Industry	485	380	352	72.6
纺织服装、鞋、帽制造业	Textile Garments, Shoes and Hats Products	255	209	189	74.1
皮革、毛皮、羽毛(绒)及其制品业	Leather, Furs Down and Related Products	32	21	18	56.3
木材加工及木、竹、藤、棕、草制品业	Timber Processing and Wwood, Bamboo, Rattan, Palm and Sraw Works	120	97	90	75.0
家具制造业	Furniture Manufacturing	96	83	72	75.0
造纸及纸制品业	Papermaking and Paper Products	118	92	82	69.5
印刷业和记录媒介的复制	Printing and Record Processing	100	78	72	72.0
文教体育用品制造业	Stationery, Education and Sports Goods	29	21	20	69.0
石油加工、炼焦及核燃料加工业	Petroleum Processing, Coking Products and Nuclear Fuel Processing	24	16	13	54.2
化学原料及化学制品制造业	Raw Chemical Material and Chemical Products	629	499	460	73.1
医药制造业	Medical and pharmaceutical Products	234	177	145	62.0
化学纤维制造业	Chemical Fibers	13	12	10	76.9
橡胶制品业	Rubber Products	52	46	42	80.8
塑料制品业	Plastic Products	267	229	204	76.4
非金属矿物制品业	Nonmetal Material Products	1000	869	776	77.6
黑色金属冶炼及压延加工业	Smelting and Processing of ferrous Metals	126	95	81	64.3
有色金属冶炼及压延加工业	Smelting and Processing of Nonferrous Metals	89	64	59	66.3
金属制品业	Metal Products	354	289	224	63.3
通用设备制造业	Ordinaryly Machinery Manufacturing	383	295	286	74.7
专用设备制造业	Special Purpose Equipment Manufacturing	400	321	276	69.0
交通运输设备制造业	Transportation Equipment Manufacturing	692	505	381	55.1
电气机械及器材制造业	Electric Machinery and Equipment	266	197	161	60.5
通信设备、计算机及其他电子设备制造业	Telecommunication Equipment, Computer, Other Electronic Equipment Manufacturing	127	79	55	43.3
仪器仪表及文化、办公用机械制造业	Instruments, Meters, Cultural and Official Machinery	36	22	23	63.9
工艺品及其他制造业	Handicraft Article and Other Manufacturing	72	52	48	66.7
废弃资源和废旧材料回收加工业	Waste Resources and Junk Material Recycled	17	15	7	41.2
电力、燃气及水的生产和供应业	Electric Power, Gas and Water Production and Supply	935	714	596	63.7
电力、热力的生产和供应业	Electric Power, Steam and Hot Water Production and Supply	478	344	296	61.9
燃气生产和供应业	Gas Production and Supply	82	59	46	56.1
水的生产和供应业	Tap Water Production and Supply	375	311	254	67.7

5-7 续表 continued

行业	Sector	施工项目(个) Number of Projects under Construction (unit)	#新开工 Newly Started	全部建成投产项目(个) Completion and Put into Production of All Projects (unit)	项目建成投产率(%) Rate of Completion and Put into Production (%)
建筑业	Construction	44	36	33	75.0
交通运输、仓储和邮政业	Transportation, storage and Post	1784	1461	1262	70.7
铁路运输业	Railway Transportation	69	45	34	49.3
道路运输业	Road Transportation	1413	1185	1051	74.4
城市公共交通业	Urban Public Transit	26	16	12	46.2
水上运输业	Waterway Transportation	89	63	50	56.2
管道运输业	Pipeline Transportation	9	7	7	77.8
装卸搬运和其他运输服务业	Load and Unload, Carry and Other	36	35	24	66.7
仓储业	Transportation Storage	134	104	78	58.2
邮政业	Post	6	5	4	66.7
信息传输、计算机服务和软件业	Information Transmmision, Computer Service and Software	270	239	198	73.3
电信和其他信息传输服务业	Telecommunication and Other Information Transmmision Service	245	218	181	73.9
计算机服务业	Computer Service	16	15	13	81.3
软件业	Software	9	6	4	44.4
批发和零售业	Wholesale and Retail Trade	1076	947	833	77.4
住宿和餐饮业	Hotel and Catering Services	775	689	553	71.4
金融业	Finance	95	84	83	87.4
银行业	Banking	70	64	62	88.6
其他金融活动	Other Financial Acitivities	13	11	10	76.9
房地产业	Real Estate Trade	430	361	271	63.0
租赁和商务服务业	Leasing and Commercial Service	253	211	164	64.8
租赁业	Leasing Service	9	8	7	77.8
商务服务业	Commercial Service	244	203	157	64.3
科学研究、技术服务和地质勘查业	Scientific Research, Polytechnical Services and Goelogical Prospecting	170	138	101	59.4
水利、环境和公共设施管理业	Water Conservancy, Environment and Public Facility Management	2372	1857	1611	67.9
水利管理业	Water Conservancy Management	648	512	432	66.7
环境管理业	Environment Management	254	204	165	65.0
公共设施管理业	Public Facility Management	1470	1141	1014	69.0
居民服务和其他服务业	Resident Service and Others	154	136	113	73.4
教育	Education	884	805	718	81.2
卫生、社会保障和社会福利业	Health Care, Social Security and Social Welfare	696	617	522	75.0
卫生	Health Care	605	537	458	75.7
社会保障业	Social Security	19	17	16	84.2
社会福利业	Social Welfare	72	63	48	66.7
文化、体育和娱乐业	Culture, Sports and Recreation	370	327	277	74.9
新闻出版业	News Publication	6	4	2	33.3
广播、电视、电影和音像业	Radio, Television, Film and Stereo	49	44	34	69.4
文化艺术业	Culture and Arts	123	111	95	77.2
体育	Sports	43	37	30	69.8
娱乐业	Receation	149	131	116	77.9
公共管理和社会组织	Public Management and Social Organizations	1908	1625	1458	76.4

5-8 按资金来源和构成分全社会固定资产投资
TOTAL INVESTMENT IN FIXED ASSETS BY SOURCE OF FUNDS AND USE OF FUNDS

年份 Year	按资金来源分 Grouped by Source of Finance					按构成分 Grouped by Use of Funds		
	国家预算内资金 State Budgetary Appropriations	国内贷款 Domestic Loans	利用外资 Foreign Investment	自筹资金 Fund Raising	其他资金来源 Others	建筑安装工程 Construction Installation	设备工器具购置 Purchases of Equipment and Instruments	其他费用 Others
投资额(亿元) Investment(100 million yuan)								
1985	10.99	24.86	0.23	62.28	4.56	67.53	28.67	6.71
1986	13.04	24.14	0.67	69.80	3.79	72.40	31.24	7.81
1987	14.03	29.97	1.50	86.60	7.98	86.83	40.54	12.71
1988	12.77	31.68	3.32	102.70	9.98	100.57	49.28	10.60
1989	9.92	16.55	2.06	85.51	9.66	81.98	33.51	8.22
1990	11.38	22.22	4.79	92.96	13.09	92.64	41.02	10.78
1991	11.83	37.98	5.25	104.41	8.72	108.07	45.11	15.01
1992	12.72	63.14	14.64	131.39	18.85	149.34	68.03	23.36
1993	39.92	86.20	24.74	199.37	32.95	227.25	98.91	57.02
1994	60.87	167.67	38.33	285.54	40.66	361.89	146.12	85.06
1995	58.40	173.47	88.71	422.92	83.00	454.40	248.51	123.59
1996	72.53	206.15	74.86	537.31	93.53	510.52	307.89	165.97
1997	68.08	172.05	51.24	651.08	141.15	600.04	264.16	219.40
1998	85.18	225.95	33.86	703.44	182.66	695.55	323.47	212.08
1999	108.18	207.61	36.57	730.92	218.89	771.24	329.26	201.67
2000	141.48	243.90	28.28	781.50	226.39	814.66	371.56	235.33
2001	174.03	241.96	29.89	874.60	231.27	890.60	419.20	241.95
2002	200.95	280.11	63.22	717.24	433.69	974.73	418.55	301.94
2003	150.20	291.60	57.41	786.40	597.98	1059.98	463.23	360.38
2004	197.03	383.78	64.74	1182.36	528.47	1409.25	537.25	409.88
2005	255.76	474.21	71.34	1492.66	540.78	1696.80	642.86	495.09
2006	378.79	708.39	79.32	1902.71	503.48	2252.72	717.10	602.87
2007	472.98	790.84	88.37	2470.28	711.66	2857.31	896.36	780.47
2008	570.17	894.57	57.02	3677.00	599.80	3568.96	1245.73	983.87
2009	711.93	1432.89	68.32	4956.88	1041.83	5025.62	1753.28	1432.95
构成(%) Composition (%)								
1985	10.7	24.2	0.2	60.5	4.4	65.6	27.8	6.6
1990	7.9	15.4	3.3	64.4	9.0	64.1	28.4	7.5
1995	7.1	21.0	10.7	51.2	10.0	58.6	30.3	11.1
1996	7.4	20.9	7.6	54.6	9.5	62.1	25.9	12.0
1997	6.3	15.9	4.7	60.1	13.0	67.7	22.1	10.2
1998	6.9	18.4	2.8	57.1	14.8	70.2	18.4	11.4
1999	8.3	15.9	2.8	56.1	16.9	63.4	26.5	10.1
2000	10.0	17.2	2.0	55.0	15.8	64.3	23.9	11.8
2001	11.2	15.6	1.9	56.4	14.9	64.8	24.3	10.9
2002	11.9	16.5	3.7	42.3	25.6	64.4	23.6	12.1
2003	8.0	15.5	3.0	41.8	31.7	60.9	23.4	15.7
2004	8.4	16.3	2.7	50.2	22.4	63.9	20.8	15.3
2005	9.0	16.7	2.5	52.7	19.1	59.9	22.7	17.4
2006	10.6	19.8	2.2	53.3	14.1	63.1	20.1	16.8
2007	10.4	17.4	1.9	54.5	15.7	63.0	19.8	17.2
2008	9.8	15.4	1.0	63.4	10.4	61.5	21.5	17.0
2009	8.7	17.4	0.8	60.4	12.7	61.2	21.4	17.4

5–9 国有单位固定资产投资
INVESTMENT IN FIXED ASSETS BY STATE OWNED UNITS

指　　标	Item	2007		2008		2009	
		合计 Total	#房地产开发 Real Estate Development	合计 Total	#房地产开发 Real Estate Development	合计 Total	#房地产开发 Real Estate Development
建设项目	**Number of Construction Projects**						
施工项目　（个）	Projects under Construction (unit)	5346		6494		9622	
全部建成投产项目(个)	Total Projects Completed Put into Operation	3405		4100		6905	
建成项目投产率　(%)	Rate of Projects Completed Put into Operation %	63.7		63.1		71.8	
建设周期　（年）	Construction Cycle (year)	1.57		1.58		1.39	
资金来源　（亿元）	**Tatal Financial Allocation and Loans (100 million yuan)**	**1769**	**64.41**	**2297**	**133.54**	**3354.47**	**248.94**
国家预算内资金	State Appropriation	430.40		447		700.96	
国内贷款	Domestic Loans	400.60	21.10	506	42.36	823.01	121.00
利用外资	Foreign Investment	20.48		14.2		11.74	0.23
自筹资金	Fund Raising	802.2	16.90	1142	63.85	1538.55	52.26
其他资金	Others	115.1	26.41	188	27.33	280.21	75.45
投资总额　（亿元）	**Total Value of Investment (100 million yuan)**	**1809**	**64.41**	**2274**	**128.83**	**3124.90**	**148.61**
按构成分	Grouped by Use of Funds						
#建筑工程	Construction Projects	1094	38.89	1274	73.88	1843.97	80.59
安装工程	Installation Projects	89.69	1.76	109	1.89	142.69	5.09
设备工具器具购置	Purchase of Equipment, Tools and Instruments	314	1.11	398	0.61	476.39	1.44
按产业分	Grouped by Industry						
第一产业	Primary Industry	45.74		72.2		111.72	
第二产业	Second Industry	526.9		644		729.07	
第三产业	Tertiary Industry	1236	64.41	1557	128.83	2284.11	148.61
#住宅	Residential Housing	64.68	47.00	113	78.35	144.60	86.44
按建设性质分	Grouped by Type of Construction						
#新建	New Construction	861.9	64.41	1214	128.83	1630.43	148.61
扩建	Expension	407.3		514		676.83	
改建	Replacement	464.6		435		652.92	
房屋建筑面积（万平方米	**Floor Space of Building (10000 sq.m)**						
施工面积	Floor Space Under Construction	1856	706.64	2377	918.01	2934.68	927.02
#住宅	Residential Buildings	864.3	641.23	1149	810.01	1418.49	792.50
竣工面积	Floor Spaace Completed	828.7	198.57	831	185.51	1361.27	179.14
#住宅	Residential Buildings	357.5	186.18	363	158.22	549.51	165.07

注：建设周期按项目个数计算；本表资金来源均为资金到位数。
Note:Note: The source of finace in this table are the number of funds achieved

5-10 房地产开发投资主要指标

指标	Item	1990	1995	2000
企业个数(个)	**Number of Enterprises (unit)**	**129**	**571**	**1052**
内资	Inner Funded	129	404	848
#国有	State - owned	129	292	380
集体	Collective-owned		51	105
港澳台投资	Funded by Enterprises from Hongkong, Macao and Taiwan		68	149
外商投资	Foreign Funded		99	55
投资完成额(亿元)	**Investment Completed This Year**	**5.94**	**121.13**	**134.63**
按构成分	Grouped by Use of Funds			
#建筑安装工程	Construction Projects	5.45	89.56	99.59
设备工器具购置	Installation Projects		4.47	2.83
按工程用途分	Grouped by Use of Projects			
#住宅	Residential Houses	4.70	61.78	93.15
#经济适用房屋	Economical Houses		7.44	23.53
资金来源	Grouped by Source of Finance	5.94	138.88	117.88
国内贷款	Domestic Loans	1.21	39.01	18.08
利用外资	Foreign Investments		16.35	1.15
自筹投资	Fund Raising	3.72	41.26	47.27
其他投资	Others	1.01	42.26	51.38
房屋建筑面积(万平方米)	**Floor Space of Building (10000 sq.m)**			
施工面积	Floor Space Under Construction	390.11	2049.30	2102.86
#住宅	Residential Buildings	325.82	1299.03	1673.84
竣工面积	Floor Spaace Completed	183.91	518.88	843.55
#住宅	Residential Buildings	156.77	427.19	733.27
土地开发及购置(万平方米)	**Land Development and Purchase (10000sq.m)**			
本年土地开发面积	Area of Land development This Year		903.00	469.28
本年土地购置面积	Area of Land Purchased This Year		719.00	838.12
商品房销售情况	**Selling of Commercial Houses**			
房屋销售面积(万平方米)	Floor Psace of Selling Houses (10000sq.m)	130.53	240.00	612.05
#住宅	Residential Buildings	112.67	211.00	571.04
#经济适用房	Economic Houses		40.00	172.99
商品房销售额(亿元)	Sales Value of Commercial House	6.93	31.00	83.74

注：本表资金来源均为资金到位数。

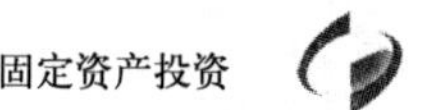

MAJOR INDICATORS OF INVESTMENT IN REAL ESTATE DEVELOPMENT

2004	2005	2006	2007	2008	2009
1917	**1990**	**2170**	**2364**	**3410**	**3460**
1701	1782	1950	2154	3245	3299
246	228	211	200	166	191
91	74	72	74	53	75
137	129	137	128	109	109
79	79	83	82	56	52
337.28	**447.95**	**564.76**	**723.73**	**892.67**	**1200.44**
227.53	315.15	401.78	484.68	668.18	828.62
3.79	4.68	5.90	9.50	11.92	18.51
228.26	317.65	411.00	507.85	660.48	804.16
12.99	13.49	24.89	49.61	68.87	74.37
446.46	513.44	706.19	1004.09	1042.33	1714.76
85.85	100.41	142.42	192.41	227.37	388.45
1.48	1.82	21.27	15.55	10.37	15.83
156.39	186.95	245.44	282.95	448.99	577.76
202.74	224.26	297.06	513.17	355.60	732.71
4055.22	4804.35	5504.08	6552.66	7800.50	9546.53
3354.19	4012.13	4610.94	5513.11	6659.53	7737.46
1532.39	1627.03	1817.70	2099.67	2057.88	2312.11
1329.80	1411.67	1604.83	1814.69	1795.76	2007.34
802.26	941.26	1333.11	974.08	954.48	1361.67
1589.03	1530.64	1544.74	1331.64	1006.16	1000.08
1591.81	1708.02	2038.46	2538.9	1941.62	2718.05
1456.15	1549.19	1915.30	2381.91	1821.31	2576.32
143.81	111.31	103.85	248.97	225.38	176.99
310.36	386.57	520.96	775.16	582.61	960.03

Note: The source of finace in this table are the number of funds achieved

5-11 按登记注册类型分房地产开发投资（2009）

单位：亿元

项 目	Item	总计 Total	内资 Inner Funded	国有 State - owned	集体 Collective -owned	股份合作 Share Holding Cooperation	联营 Joint- Owned	国有独资公司 Solely co.	其他有限责任公司 Responsibility Co. Ltd
企业个数(个)	**Number of Enterprises (unit)**	**3460**	**3299**	**175**	**48**	**26**	**6**	**15**	**1222**
#亏损企业个数	Loss- Making Enterprises	1273	1200	60	13	6		2	469
本年完成投资	**Investment Completed This Year**	**1200.44**	**1095.21**	**141.01**	**14.48**	**11.57**	**2.83**	**7.60**	**435.09**
#土地开发投资	nvestment for Land Development	178.81	156.52	18.49	1.35	3.59	1.55	0.84	56.33
按构成分	Grouped by Use of Funds								
建筑工程	Construction Projects	747.61	670.69	76.58	9.99	4.45	0.99	4.01	279.41
安装工程	Installation Projects	81.02	76.97	4.50	0.60	0.36	0.22	0.59	32.94
设备工器具购置	Purchase of Equipment, Tools and Instruments	18.51	16.42	1.31	0.33	0.03	0.10	0.12	6.82
其他费用	Other Funds	353.31	331.13	58.61	3.55	6.73	1.52	2.87	115.93
#土地购置费	Purchase of Land	161.46	155.77	22.89	0.69	3.16	1.36	1.18	55.34
按构成用途分	Grouped by Use of Projects								
住宅	Residential Buildings	804.16	730.48	81.06	10.13	5.00	2.64	5.38	299.38
#经济适用房	Economical Houses	74.37	73.83	15.46	0.52		0.02	0.78	28.00
别墅、高档公寓	Villa, Top Grade Flat	38.13	22.76	0.01			0.48		17.27
办公楼	Office Building	22.89	21.81	1.44	0.02	1.01		0.02	9.39
商业营业用房	Business Buildings	141.99	135.12	9.15	1.58	2.68	0.16	0.53	63.01
其他	Others	231.40	207.80	49.36	2.75	2.89	0.03	1.67	63.31
本年新增固定资产	**Newly Increased Fixed Assets This Year**	**702.95**	**622.62**	**51.37**	**12.47**	**1.71**	**2.49**	**4.21**	**253.84**
资金来源	**Finance Sources**	**1714.76**	**1547.05**	**240.75**	**11.71**	**14.27**	**6.91**	**8.19**	**654.04**
国内贷款	Domestic Loans	388.45	345.35	118.27	3.42	6.18	0.89	2.73	108.50
利用外资	Foreign Investments	15.83	0.53	0.23					0.28
自筹资金	Fund Raising	577.76	550.11	49.67	6.19	4.13	0.85	2.59	244.16
#自有资金	Self Owned	311.77	300.83	23.19	3.80	3.41	0.81	1.22	137.72
其他资金来源	Others	732.71	651.07	72.58	2.09	3.96	5.16	2.87	301.10
#定金及预收款	Funds Ordered and Pre-received	419.30	373.58	51.08	1.10	1.85	3.23	1.77	169.94
土地开发(万平方米)	**Land Development (10000 sq.m)**								
本年完成开发土地面积	Area of Land development This Year	1361.67	1148.59	71.68	17.04	21.27	4.16	12.00	415.30
待开发土地面积	Area of Land to be Developed	1414.74	1319.89	199.99	6.72	5.70	3.34	1.72	571.16
本年购置土地面积	Area of Land Purchased This Year	1000.08	989.87	62.29	9.00	4.49	5.17	14.51	436.26
本年土地成交价款(亿元)	Value of Land Transaction (100 million yuan)	96.70	96.17	9.01	0.48	2.96	1.28	1.13	43.80

INVESTMENT IN REAL ESTATE DEVELOPMENT BY TYPE OF REGISTRATION(2009)

(100 million yuan)

股份有限公司 Share Holding Co.Ltd.	私营 Private	其他 Others	港澳台商投资 Hongkong, Macao and Taiwan Funded	合资经营 Joint Venture Corperation	合作经营 Cooperative Corperation	独资 Solely Funded	股份有限公司 Share Holding Co.Ltd.	外商投资 Foreign Investment	合资经营 Joint Venture Corperation	合作经营 Cooperative Corperation	独资 Solely Funded	股份有限公司 Share Holding Co.Ltd.
245	**1540**	**22**	**109**	**56**	**2**	**45**	**6**	**52**	**19**	**2**	**29**	**2**
76	564	10	51	31	1	18	1	22	9		12	1
92.10	**385.57**	**4.96**	**71.89**	**15.37**	**1.45**	**41.62**	**13.45**	**33.34**	**13.05**	**6.68**	**13.62**	
13.97	60.27	0.15	15.46	1.72		13.73		6.83	6.23	0.60		
57.95	234.49	2.80	53.17	13.77	1.45	24.51	13.45	23.75	8.25	4.48	11.02	
6.09	31.56	0.11	2.25	0.81		1.44		1.80	1.79		0.00	
1.76	5.95	0.00	0.49	0.16		0.33		1.59	1.57		0.02	
26.30	113.57	2.04	15.98	0.63		15.34		6.21	1.44	2.20	2.57	
10.78	58.79	1.58	3.62			3.62		2.06	0.83		1.24	
71.83	252.22	2.84	48.85	13.09	1.45	20.86	13.45	24.83	11.83	5.06	7.94	
4.37	22.83	1.83	0.14	0.14				0.41	0.41			
0.56	4.44		10.56	5.85	1.45	3.26		4.81	4.19		0.62	
0.61	9.32		1.08	1.08								
9.29	48.32	0.41	2.96	0.38		2.58		3.91	0.91	0.69	2.32	
10.37	75.72	1.71	19.00	0.82		18.18		4.60	0.31	0.93	3.37	
40.60	**251.94**	**4.00**	**50.47**	**6.48**		**43.99**		**29.86**	**8.06**	**4.95**	**16.86**	
118.23	**486.73**	**6.24**	**97.64**	**19.77**	**2.75**	**56.58**	**18.55**	**70.06**	**24.03**	**22.18**	**23.85**	
28.20	75.10	2.07	30.16	2.47	1.65	15.43	10.60	12.94	0.79	8.15	4.00	
	0.02		15.30	0.38	0.50	14.42						
43.33	198.28	0.91	15.11	9.95	0.15	5.01		12.55	3.36	0.48	8.71	
26.99	103.39	0.30	6.32	3.67	0.15	2.50		4.62	2.44		2.19	
46.70	213.33	3.27	37.08	6.96	0.45	21.72	7.95	44.57	19.88	13.55	11.15	
22.89	119.00	2.72	23.41	4.16	0.45	10.86	7.95	22.31	10.10	8.80	3.41	
109.99	493.05	4.10	166.88	27.08	8.39	131.41		46.20	32.72	13.48		
100.21	421.03	10.02	34.12	10.65		23.47		60.73	16.68	38.65	5.39	
54.05	396.58	7.51	7.53			7.53		2.69			2.69	
5.39	30.52	1.58	0.32			0.32		0.21			0.21	

5–12 市、州全社会固定资产投资

TOTAL INVESTMENT IN FIXED ASSETS IN CITIES AND PREFECTURES

单位：亿元 (100 million yuan)

市、州	Cities and Prefectures	2000	2001	2002	2003	2004	2005	2006	2007	2008	2009
全省	**Total**	**1421.55**	**1551.75**	**1695.22**	**1883.59**	**2356.38**	**2834.75**	**3572.69**	**4534.14**	**5798.56**	**8211.85**
武汉市	Wuhan Municipality	461.93	508.44	570.48	645.06	822.20	1055.18	1325.29	1732.79	2222.91	3001.10
黄石市	Huangshi Municipality	40.86	47.53	54.45	69.23	88.30	106.46	138.05	179.85	232.90	343.05
十堰市	Shiyan Municipality	30.90	37.17	45.70	58.68	77.53	103.63	116.61	141.66	185.44	278.35
宜昌市	Yichang Municipality	229.37	248.35	264.91	250.04	271.28	295.80	323.55	390.36	523.46	750.27
襄樊市	Xiangfan Municipality	80.47	87.73	96.78	107.22	130.53	156.62	200.50	265.80	373.77	574.79
鄂州市	Ezhou Municipality	26.10	29.08	32.28	37.51	44.26	55.17	72.05	105.01	150.01	220.60
荆门市	Jingmen Municipality	57.12	56.52	61.72	70.96	86.13	104.15	127.74	153.25	210.08	317.18
孝感市	Xiaogan Municipality	74.67	73.50	81.39	90.21	104.44	121.71	144.82	195.93	270.83	397.26
荆州市	Jingzhou Municipality	81.28	90.28	100.57	96.58	108.23	116.78	149.67	210.75	291.46	435.16
黄冈市	Huanggang Municipality	87.10	92.34	95.35	106.67	130.12	158.56	192.89	258.50	370.85	553.29
咸宁市	Xianning Municipality	44.53	49.22	53.94	62.68	75.28	83.09	103.83	138.38	200.83	301.58
随州市	Suizhou Municipality	22.09	26.01	30.87	36.55	46.47	55.79	70.96	101.92	147.07	208.70
恩施自治州	Enshi Prefecture	31.63	42.62	52.01	58.29	70.03	78.07	87.53	116.09	139.37	182.21
仙桃市	Xiantao Municipality	26.21	29.20	32.32	38.11	46.62	56.14	52.73	64.29	85.24	120.05
潜江市	Qianjiang Municipality	20.88	23.53	23.82	25.73	32.14	40.67	52.61	72.37	88.32	123.96
天门市	Tianmen Municipality	24.53	24.95	26.32	29.46	33.08	41.15	50.81	67.28	86.07	116.51
神农架林区	Shennongjia Forest Zone	1.21	1.90	2.17	2.75	4.07	4.89	5.63	5.63	7.50	10.65
不分地区	Azoanl	80.67	83.56	70.14	97.86	185.67	200.88	357.42	334.29	212.43	277.14

注：2006年全社会投资(城镇投资)不含城镇工矿区私人建房投资(下同)。由于方法制度调整，按可比口径计算，2005年扣除城镇工矿区私人建房投资基数应为2788.92亿元，各市、州全社会投资未做调整。

Note:Private housing construction investment is excluded in total investment in fixed assets in 2006.

5-13 市、州国有单位固定资产投资
INVESTMENT IN FIXED ASSETS BY STATE OWNED UNITS IN CITIES AND PREFECTURES

单位：亿元 (100 million yuan)

市、州	Cities and Prefectures	2000	2001	2002	2003	2004	2005	2006	2007	2008	2009
全省	**Total**	**857.01**	**918.21**	**963.18**	**888.72**	**951.73**	**1095.71**	**1473.70**	**1808.61**	**2273.83**	**3124.90**
武汉市	Wuhan Municipality	269.50	278.65	306.82	301.90	319.36	427.68	556.09	748.71	1072.32	1315.33
黄石市	Huangshi Municipality	23.04	24.89	24.02	22.83	28.14	28.65	30.74	45.70	57.71	106.17
十堰市	Shiyan Municipality	19.12	25.55	30.68	32.56	43.12	51.35	55.42	71.51	76.53	136.88
宜昌市	Yichang Municipality	174.17	193.10	208.50	171.63	151.79	153.75	151.49	163.69	200.93	279.41
襄樊市	Xiangfan Municipality	44.31	51.71	51.89	47.13	45.52	44.45	58.19	63.70	96.61	111.61
鄂州市	Ezhou Municipality	16.98	16.78	17.76	13.90	17.09	19.41	28.87	36.40	62.67	112.80
荆门市	Jingmen Municipality	29.72	28.89	23.46	23.78	23.61	19.63	23.92	37.70	37.64	69.84
孝感市	Xiaogan Municipality	43.66	38.91	40.20	39.21	38.71	37.53	47.57	54.81	74.62	111.71
荆州市	Jingzhou Municipality	39.98	37.42	47.78	36.96	26.06	28.52	41.67	59.14	67.44	130.57
黄冈市	Huanggang Municipality	36.84	38.82	40.76	33.51	35.11	47.02	61.70	79.98	116.76	199.84
咸宁市	Xianning Municipality	27.07	28.36	24.94	22.43	20.27	27.41	39.15	44.53	59.27	103.42
随州市	Suizhou Municipality	9.69	11.46	13.32	15.09	12.65	14.32	21.17	25.71	37.99	70.68
恩施自治州	Enshi Prefecture	19.47	22.65	26.64	24.42	25.60	21.52	32.26	45.29	57.47	88.85
仙桃市	Xiantao Municipality	9.84	10.33	12.15	10.12	9.39	9.65	9.98	9.47	6.54	26.99
潜江市	Qianjiang Municipality	15.81	19.24	17.14	16.68	21.53	19.44	24.19	38.88	38.82	53.64
天门市	Tianmen Municipality	6.84	6.37	5.39	9.11	8.41	11.84	11.94	15.78	28.47	30.47
神农架林区	Shennongjia Forest Zone	1.07	1.56	1.59	1.88	1.80	1.90	2.61	3.18	4.89	8.69
不分地区	Azoanl	69.90	83.52	70.14	65.58	123.57	131.62	276.72	264.43	177.16	168.00

5-14 市、州按经济类型分的全社会固定资产投资（2009）
TOTAL INVESTMENT IN FIXED ASSETS BY OWNERSHIP IN CITIES AND PREFECTURES(2009)

单位：亿元 (100 million yuan)

市、州	Cities and Prefectures	合计 Total	国有经济单位 State Owned Units	集体经济单位 Collective Owned Units	城乡私人 Private Owned Units	其他经济单位 Others
全省	**Total**	**8211.85**	**3124.90**	**411.18**	**1771.61**	**2904.16**
武汉市	Wuhan Municipality	3001.10	1315.33	160.27	392.16	1133.35
黄石市	Huangshi Municipality	343.05	106.17	33.83	96.73	106.32
十堰市	Shiyan Municipality	278.35	136.88	7.83	64.51	69.14
宜昌市	Yichang Municipality	750.27	279.41	18.90	174.63	277.32
襄樊市	Xiangfan Municipality	574.79	111.61	25.16	175.20	262.82
鄂州市	Ezhou Municipality	220.60	112.80	7.34	53.15	47.31
荆门市	Jingmen Municipality	317.18	69.84	17.44	123.60	106.30
孝感市	Xiaogan Municipality	397.26	111.71	29.36	142.10	114.09
荆州市	Jingzhou Municipality	435.16	130.57	23.44	108.13	173.01
黄冈市	Huanggang Municipality	553.29	199.84	39.76	131.39	182.30
咸宁市	Xianning Municipality	301.58	103.42	12.47	82.24	103.45
随州市	Suizhou Municipality	208.70	70.68	9.63	66.62	61.78
恩施自治州	Enshi Prefecture	182.21	88.85	2.14	30.70	60.52
仙桃市	Xiantao Municipality	120.05	26.99	4.13	72.80	16.13
潜江市	Qianjiang Municipality	123.96	53.64	14.10	34.64	21.58
天门市	Tianmen Municipality	116.51	30.47	5.38	21.74	58.92
神农架林区	Shennongjia Forest Zone	10.65	8.69	0.01	1.28	0.68
不分地区	Azoanl	277.14	168.00			109.14

5-15 市、州基本建设投资

INVESTMENT IN INFRASTRUCTION CONSTRUCTION IN CITIES AND PREFECTURES

单位：亿元

(100 million yuan)

市、州	Cities and Prefectures	2000	2001	2002	2003	2004	2005	2006	2007	2008	2009
全省	**Total**	**620.87**	**692.83**	**761.96**	**845.38**	**1171.75**	**1515.21**	**2059.18**	**2623.06**	**3393.06**	**4955.85**
武汉市	Wuhan Municipality	141.12	167.03	197.38	248.28	324.16	507.34	665.77	846.72	1132.30	1511.96
黄石市	Huangshi Municipality	14.13	16.06	18.43	21.81	38.06	61.42	80.31	107.58	135.11	214.79
十堰市	Shiyan Municipality	9.86	13.89	16.65	21.19	34.78	52.63	61.58	78.47	99.94	165.87
宜昌市	Yichang Municipality	167.92	186.79	201.41	176.48	192.94	219.36	226.79	275.39	371.91	547.86
襄樊市	Xiangfan Municipality	27.89	32.49	31.00	31.73	50.13	70.19	108.53	133.85	210.13	310.74
鄂州市	Ezhou Municipality	12.28	13.24	15.66	16.71	21.95	34.93	46.04	66.35	84.44	125.34
荆门市	Jingmen Municipality	14.84	21.11	19.79	22.89	36.02	49.59	68.73	75.34	122.10	207.60
孝感市	Xiaogan Municipality	24.62	25.78	27.22	29.43	47.51	35.68	76.21	119.52	149.33	226.40
荆州市	Jingzhou Municipality	33.55	38.45	45.13	38.41	46.02	50.15	67.60	121.12	173.44	290.16
黄冈市	Huanggang Municipality	22.69	23.23	25.73	33.05	58.47	78.32	106.56	151.82	245.58	413.73
咸宁市	Xianning Municipality	17.90	20.36	22.73	27.87	41.69	38.88	56.29	72.63	117.42	175.98
随州市	Suizhou Municipality	6.97	8.89	12.30	14.97	21.88	28.88	38.96	65.07	96.23	152.87
恩施自治州	Enshi Prefecture	17.39	26.32	36.45	38.93	49.91	50.13	59.22	76.86	90.74	122.32
仙桃市	Xiantao Municipality	6.19	7.31	7.96	8.77	12.32	12.32	21.43	39.62	52.62	89.47
潜江市	Qianjiang Municipality	7.39	5.54	11.58	12.48	19.32	27.60	19.77	26.34	39.40	36.41
天门市	Tianmen Municipality	2.38	2.06	2.01	3.61	12.09	24.45	29.36	43.09	56.79	75.96
神农架林区	Shennongjia Forest Zone	0.82	1.12	1.17	1.75	2.68	4.19	5.13	5.47	7.25	10.40
不分地区	Azoanl	92.93	83.16	69.36	97.02	161.81	169.16	320.90	317.81	208.32	277.99

注：本表口径为50万元以上项目

Note: this form is for 50 yuan project caliber

5-16 市、州技术改造投资

INVESTMENT IN TECHNOLOGY TRANFER IN CITES AND PREFECTURES

单位：亿元

(100 million yuan)

市、州	Cities and Prefectures	2000	2001	2002	2003	2004	2005	2006	2007	2008	2009
全省	**Total**	**245.16**	**290.02**	**320.17**	**383.20**	**534.29**	**531.72**	**625.43**	**807.56**	**1033.28**	**1301.07**
武汉市	Wuhan Municipality	104.52	116.62	129.66	147.72	186.51	176.70	216.04	316.90	406.15	410.32
黄石市	Huangshi Municipality	13.13	16.01	19.92	30.42	35.46	22.92	27.19	38.75	48.91	64.46
十堰市	Shiyan Municipality	8.01	13.67	15.71	15.55	25.99	23.12	18.96	27.66	31.67	46.87
宜昌市	Yichang Municipality	17.39	21.30	23.90	29.95	44.86	32.78	46.91	47.67	65.62	86.65
襄樊市	Xiangfan Municipality	16.52	19.05	21.47	24.14	43.13	39.20	38.80	57.34	70.35	137.43
鄂州市	Ezhou Municipality	6.53	7.55	9.01	12.33	13.91	8.77	15.82	22.88	38.90	64.77
荆门市	Jingmen Municipality	12.62	10.57	14.17	19.42	27.77	31.13	32.42	46.26	52.92	60.57
孝感市	Xiaogan Municipality	12.41	14.19	15.75	18.90	24.88	50.85	35.12	31.16	55.47	79.35
荆州市	Jingzhou Municipality	14.51	16.27	19.76	22.42	26.75	25.54	41.72	42.15	61.98	75.23
黄冈市	Huanggang Municipality	12.58	16.14	16.91	20.95	24.86	21.18	31.01	53.16	56.74	61.45
咸宁市	Xianning Municipality	8.10	8.48	9.30	11.18	13.83	17.30	20.84	25.65	38.68	61.43
随州市	Suizhou Municipality	2.26	3.00	4.08	4.73	9.28	7.63	10.24	10.87	11.45	12.02
恩施自治州	Enshi Prefecture	3.05	3.39	3.13	6.59	7.40	11.38	10.65	11.33	17.30	21.62
仙桃市	Xiantao Municipality	3.46	3.81	4.37	5.22	9.09	14.68	8.62	7.99	8.82	4.75
潜江市	Qianjiang Municipality	7.31	15.81	9.15	8.14	11.08	10.34	29.43	34.02	43.17	81.01
天门市	Tianmen Municipality	2.68	3.23	2.36	3.86	4.52	6.31	14.53	17.26	21.00	29.68
神农架林区	Shennongjia Forest Zone	0.08	0.54	0.73	0.86	1.13	0.33	0.36	0.04	0.05	0.02
不分地区	Azoanl		0.39	0.79	0.82	23.85	31.55	26.77	16.48	4.11	3.43

注：本表口径为50万元以上项目

Note: this form is for 50 yuan project caliber

5-17 市、州房地产开发投资
INVESTMENT IN REAL ESTATE DEVELOPMENT IN CITIES AND PREFECTURES

单位：亿元 (100 million yuan)

市、州	Cities and Prefectures	2000	2001	2002	2003	2004	2005	2006	2007	2008	2009
全省	**Total**	**134.63**	**151.24**	**178.64**	**239.04**	**337.28**	**447.95**	**564.76**	**723.73**	**892.67**	**1200.44**
武汉市	Wuhan Municipality	101.31	115.33	132.50	169.55	233.30	297.99	366.15	459.75	560.36	778.59
黄石市	Huangshi Municipality	2.24	2.55	3.32	4.33	7.64	11.33	16.96	19.66	21.53	25.30
十堰市	Shiyan Municipality	2.84	3.68	6.27	9.47	11.75	20.95	25.18	26.05	28.99	35.73
宜昌市	Yichang Municipality	6.80	6.56	7.80	12.79	20.17	31.70	39.18	48.71	56.68	79.33
襄樊市	Xiangfan Municipality	5.66	7.24	9.08	11.72	17.52	22.09	29.67	36.87	46.21	55.39
鄂州市	Ezhou Municipality	1.22	1.65	1.82	2.34	4.15	6.06	7.84	9.39	10.79	8.11
荆门市	Jingmen Municipality	1.20	1.68	3.50	3.93	4.44	5.31	9.07	11.38	16.84	27.19
孝感市	Xiaogan Municipality	3.83	3.90	4.75	5.37	7.48	9.38	11.26	19.16	28.57	32.40
荆州市	Jingzhou Municipality	3.72	3.93	4.01	6.97	11.58	16.19	18.14	22.20	26.59	32.87
黄冈市	Huanggang Municipality	1.20	1.79	1.93	3.51	6.23	9.08	12.17	23.33	27.38	37.33
咸宁市	Xianning Municipality	0.53	0.73	0.89	1.98	2.58	3.80	7.88	14.60	25.35	39.55
随州市	Suizhou Municipality	0.57	0.69	0.83	2.84	4.20	4.53	6.83	9.11	15.96	17.05
恩施自治州	Enshi Prefecture	0.71	0.64	0.85	1.97	2.96	5.24	8.29	16.22	16.48	16.97
仙桃市	Xiantao Municipality	1.35	0.68	0.65	1.61	2.51	1.96	2.39	2.95	3.92	4.79
潜江市	Qianjiang Municipality	0.22	0.17	0.43	0.35	0.33	0.86	1.32	1.44	2.76	3.57
天门市	Tianmen Municipality	0.13	0.02	0.01	0.31	0.45	1.48	2.44	2.92	4.27	6.27
神农架林区	Shennongjia Forest Zone										

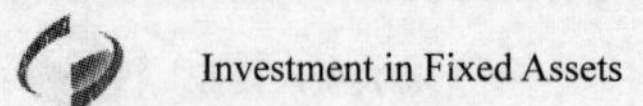

5-18 按国民经济行业分的基本建设投资(2009)

'O THE NATIONAL ECONOMIC CONSTRUCTION OF BASIC INDUSTRY INVE

单位：亿元 (100 million yuan)

行业	sector	全省 Provincial			#地方 Local		
		2007	2008	2009	2007	2008	2009
总 计	**Total**	**2623.06**	**3393.06**	**4955.85**	**2199.14**	**2996.46**	**4495.24**
农、林、牧、渔业	Farming, Forestry, Animal Husbandry and Fishery	77.02	129.84	186.97	76.34	129.54	184.97
农业	Farming	16.88	24.32	39.49	16.81	24.32	38.49
林业	Forestry	11.75	14.75	22.47	11.75	14.75	22.47
畜牧业	Animal Husbandry	13.87	42.72	45.53	13.87	42.72	44.82
渔业	Fishery	4.37	6.27	7.10	4.37	6.27	7.10
农、林、牧、渔服务业	Farming, Forestry, Animal Husbandry and Fishery Services	30.16	41.78	72.38	29.55	41.48	72.08
采矿业	Mining and Qarrying	30.49	40.70	50.17	22.86	36.18	48.01
制造业	Manufacturing	685.97	1055.68	1451.59	650.03	986.37	1407.26
农副食品加工业	Food Processing	32.93	47.32	81.87	32.93	46.17	81.87
食品制造业	Food Production	32.18	42.88	54.67	31.68	42.88	54.67
饮料制造业	Beverage Production	15.30	25.75	34.87	15.30	25.75	34.87
烟草制品业	Tobacco Processing	5.32	1.66	0.47	4.31	1.66	0.47
纺织业	Textile Industry	38.85	49.59	55.70	38.85	49.19	55.70
纺织服装、鞋、帽制造业	Textile Garments, Shoes and Hats Products	21.84	35.30	39.29	21.84	35.30	38.30
皮革、毛皮、羽毛(绒)及其制品业	Leather, Furs Down and Related Products	3.48	4.35	9.91	3.48	4.35	9.91
木材加工及木、竹、藤、棕、草制品业	Timber Processing and Wwood, Bamboo, Rattan, Palm and Sraw Works	10.77	12.96	17.82	10.77	12.96	17.82
家具制造业	Furniture Manufacturing	7.92	18.88	14.55	7.92	18.88	14.55
造纸及纸制品业	Papermaking and Paper Products	12.16	15.46	22.44	12.16	15.46	22.44
印刷业和记录媒介的复制	Printing and Record Processing	10.59	11.57	20.95	10.11	11.16	19.69
文教体育用品制造业	Stationery, Education and Sports Goods	2.58	4.80	3.45	2.58	4.80	3.45
石油加工、炼焦及核燃料加工业	Petroleum Processing, Coking Products and Nuclear Fuel Processing	8.76	2.38	8.07	2.96	2.38	5.23
化学原料及化学制品制造业	Raw Chemical Material and Chemical Products	61.78	105.69	145.85	61.78	105.69	145.85
医药制造业	Medical and pharmaceutical Products	29.29	33.68	54.39	27.78	33.68	54.39
化学纤维制造业	Chemical Fibers	1.43	3.76	2.34	1.43	3.76	2.34
橡胶制品业	Rubber Products	2.55	4.67	7.72	2.55	4.62	7.72
塑料制品业	Plastic Products	16.15	32.69	39.66	16.15	30.19	39.66
非金属矿物制品业	Nonmetal Material Products	71.08	132.20	166.22	71.08	131.05	161.13
黑色金属冶炼及压延加工业	Smelting and Processing of ferrous Metals	9.77	14.47	63.53	9.77	14.47	63.53
有色金属冶炼及压延加工业	Smelting and Processing of Nonferrous Metals	14.60	9.09	25.46	14.60	9.09	25.46
金属制品业	Metal Products	22.56	47.58	79.49	22.15	44.61	79.49
通用设备制造业	Ordinaryly Machinery Manufacturing	43.08	57.27	84.52	40.70	52.51	78.93
专用设备制造业	Special Purpose Equipment Manufacturing	36.44	52.36	85.92	36.21	47.50	84.96
交通运输设备制造业	Transportation Equipment Manufacturing	77.78	139.87	179.00	55.10	90.02	154.60
电气机械及器材制造业	Electric Machinery and Equipment	34.50	55.28	61.45	34.42	55.08	61.45
通信设备、计算机及其他电子设备	Telecommunication Equipment, Computer and Other Electronic Equipment Manufacturing	53.83	80.59	70.78	53.83	79.70	68.91
仪器仪表及文化、办公用机械制造	Instruments, Meters, Cultural and Official Machinery	2.83	6.71	6.63	1.99	6.58	6.33
工艺品及其他制造业	Handicraft Article and Other Manufacturing	3.33	3.45	7.63	3.33	3.45	6.60
废弃资源和废旧材料回收加工业	Waste Resources and Junk Material Recycled	2.30	3.41	6.96	2.30	3.41	6.96
电力、燃气及水的生产和供应业	Electric Power, Gas and Water Production and Supply	306.78	312.72	420.19	159.83	184.69	264.56
电力、热力的生产和供应业	Electric Power, Steam and Hot Water Production and Supply	276.41	266.32	343.16	129.59	139.53	191.10
燃气生产和供应业	Gas Production and Supply	11.08	15.22	25.22	10.95	14.48	22.32
水的生产和供应业	Tap Water Production and Supply	19.29	31.18	51.82	19.29	30.68	51.15

注：本表口径为50万元以上项目

Note: this form is for 50 yuan project caliber

5-18 续表 continued

单位：亿元 (100 million yuan)

行业	sector	全省 Provincial			#地方 Local		
		2007	2008	2009	2007	2008	2009
建筑业	Construction	8.65	16.31	14.02	2.75	9.20	8.67
交通运输、仓储和邮政业	Transportation, storage and Post	580.01	587.83	887.52	390.20	436.81	686.58
铁路运输业	Railway Transportation	187.41	157.73	244.36	2.79	7.44	47.35
道路运输业	Road Transportation	341.81	347.23	490.68	340.99	347.16	490.39
城市公共交通业	Urban Public Transit	10.72	33.36	54.02	10.72	33.36	53.94
水上运输业	Waterway Transportation	11.11	17.03	32.48	7.60	17.03	32.48
管道运输业	Pipeline Transportation	0.30	0.60	4.21	0.30	0.60	2.00
装卸搬运和其他运输服务业	Load and Unload, Carry and Other Transportation	0.80	1.61	8.34	0.80	1.61	7.94
仓储业	Storage	10.94	21.45	50.39	10.32	20.82	49.45
邮政业	Post	0.03	0.26	0.97		0.23	0.97
信息传输、计算机服务和软件业	Information Transmmision, Computer Service and Software	23.17	22.21	31.33	14.58	18.05	25.51
电信和其他信息传输服务业	Telecommunication and Other Information TransmmisionService	20.90	17.59	22.03	12.31	13.44	16.21
计算机服务业	Computer Service	2.04	0.64	1.21	2.04	0.64	1.21
软件业	Software	0.23	3.98	8.09	0.23	3.98	8.09
批发和零售业	Wholesale and Retail Trade	99.26	151.59	179.63	97.42	150.25	178.54
住宿和餐饮业	Hotel and Catering Services	43.52	62.47	99.75	42.90	62.47	95.91
金融业	Finance	2.09	4.50	6.67	1.75	3.02	5.13
银行业	Banking	0.81	2.11	3.76	0.49	0.83	2.51
其他金融活动	Other Financial Acitivities	0.67	1.49	1.45	0.67	1.49	1.45
房地产业	Real Estate Trade	28.32	68.78	138.07	27.74	66.56	136.66
租赁和商务服务业	Leasing and Commercial Service	44.84	75.16	107.94	44.65	75.16	107.40
租赁业	Leasing Service	1.76	0.12	0.81	1.76	0.12	0.81
商务服务业	Commercial Service	43.08	75.04	107.13	42.89	75.04	106.59
科学研究、技术服务和地质勘查业	Scientific Research, Polytechnical Services and Goelogical Prospecting	17.08	29.65	37.89	13.73	23.99	28.16
水利、环境和公共设施管理业	Water Conservancy, Environment and Public Facility Management	386.67	473.63	797.56	379.94	469.17	794.54
水利管理业	Water Conservancy Management	29.42	39.31	113.24	23.60	36.16	110.22
环境管理业	Environment Management	20.17	22.93	50.58	20.17	22.93	50.58
公共设施管理业	Public Facility Management	337.08	411.39	633.73	336.18	410.08	633.73
居民服务和其他服务业	Resident Service and Others	9.57	11.28	15.57	9.57	11.28	15.57
教育	Education	94.34	78.85	109.01	81.54	66.42	91.44
卫生、社会保障和社会福利业	Health Care, Social Security and Social Welfare	23.89	33.69	61.19	23.19	33.03	56.14
卫生	Health Care	22.26	30.49	55.14	21.56	29.83	50.09
社会保障业	Social Security	0.05	0.86	1.13	0.05	0.86	1.13
社会福利业	Social Welfare	1.57	2.34	4.91	1.57	2.34	4.91
文化、体育和娱乐业	Culture, Sports and Recreation	50.41	45.16	87.62	50.41	44.36	87.57
新闻出版业	News Publication	0.57	2.08	3.75	0.57	2.08	3.75
广播、电视、电影和音像业	Radio, Television, Film and Stereo	2.87	2.26	3.50	2.87	2.26	3.45
文化艺术业	Culture and Arts	14.05	12.44	26.48	14.05	12.44	26.48
体育	Sports	14.94	3.39	14.44	14.94	3.39	14.44
娱乐业	Receation	17.97	25.00	39.44	17.97	24.20	39.44
公共管理和社会组织	Public Management and Social Organizations	110.98	193.02	273.17	109.70	189.91	272.62

5-19 按国民经济行业分的技术改造投资（2009）
ACCORDING TO THE NATIONAL ECONOMY INDUSTRY TECHNICAL TRANSFORMATION INVESTMENT(2009)

单位：亿元 (100 million yuan)

行业	sector	全省 Provincial			#地方 Local		
		2007	2008	2009	2007	2008	2009
总　计	**Total**	**807.56**	**1033.28**	**1301.07**	**641.06**	**699.13**	**1021.81**
农、林、牧、渔业	Farming, Forestry, Animal Husbandry and Fishery	9.08	20.28	23.45	9.08	20.28	23.45
农业	Farming	1.38	2.03	2.99	1.38	2.03	2.99
林业	Forestry	0.50	1.89	1.65	0.50	1.89	1.65
畜牧业	Animal Husbandry	1.24	3.25	4.56	1.24	3.25	4.56
渔业	Fishery	0.05	1.53	0.92	0.05	1.53	0.92
农、林、牧、渔服务业	Farming, Forestry, Animal Husbandry and Fishery Services	5.90	11.57	13.34	5.90	11.57	13.34
采矿业	Mining and Qarrying	43.35	49.66	95.44	17.33	23.84	67.61
制造业	Manufacturing	527.61	691.12	789.00	452.31	481.88	644.04
农副食品加工业	Food Processing	16.09	28.57	33.33	16.09	28.57	33.33
食品制造业	Food Production	7.32	15.52	16.76	7.32	15.52	16.76
饮料制造业	Beverage Production	10.23	9.86	22.39	10.23	9.86	22.39
烟草制品业	Tobacco Processing	3.43	4.37	6.97	3.04	4.14	5.44
纺织业	Textile Industry	34.50	33.04	34.64	33.77	32.45	34.64
纺织服装、鞋、帽制造业	Textile Garments, Shoes and Hats Products	7.68	13.22	15.33	7.68	13.22	15.33
皮革、毛皮、羽毛(绒)及其制品业	Leather, Furs Down and Related Products	0.72	1.46	1.03	0.72	1.46	1.03
木材加工及木、竹、藤、棕、草制品业	Timber Processing and Wwood, Bamboo, Rattan, Palm and Sraw Works	7.06	7.12	7.14	7.06	7.12	7.14
家具制造业	Furniture Manufacturing	1.12	2.73	5.06	1.12	2.73	5.06
造纸及纸制品业	Papermaking and Paper Products	7.78	9.70	12.98	7.78	9.70	12.98
印刷业和记录媒介的复制	Printing and Record Processing	2.66	3.91	5.98	2.65	3.91	5.92
文教体育用品制造业	Stationery, Education and Sports Goods	0.07	0.13	0.97	0.07	0.13	0.97
石油加工、炼焦及核燃料加工业	Petroleum Processing, Coking Products and Nuclear Fuel Processing	13.01	11.13	10.77	4.21	2.46	6.37
化学原料及化学制品制造业	Raw Chemical Material and Chemical Products	32.16	63.48	71.51	29.96	63.48	70.98
医药制造业	Medical and pharmaceutical Products	12.07	14.68	20.77	10.36	13.03	18.44
化学纤维制造业	Chemical Fibers	1.48	1.72	1.64	1.48	1.72	1.64
橡胶制品业	Rubber Products	2.60	4.93	4.20	2.08	4.89	4.20
塑料制品业	Plastic Products	7.38	9.87	15.48	6.78	9.87	15.48
非金属矿物制品业	Nonmetal Material Products	32.68	56.13	91.86	32.40	55.64	90.43
黑色金属冶炼及压延加工业	Smelting and Processing of ferrous Metals	154.55	204.87	161.66	154.55	49.43	62.91
有色金属冶炼及压延加工业	Smelting and Processing of Nonferrous Metals	12.11	11.83	14.94	4.84	7.88	13.64
金属制品业	Metal Products	10.84	15.70	27.78	10.36	14.78	27.78
通用设备制造业	Ordinaryly Machinery Manufacturing	26.50	32.76	41.11	26.43	32.76	41.02
专用设备制造业	Special Purpose Equipment Manufacturing	16.37	21.02	21.51	16.01	20.80	19.78
交通运输设备制造业	Transportation Equipment Manufacturing	78.96	83.67	88.16	30.11	47.28	57.72
电气机械及器材制造业	Electric Machinery and Equipment	10.87	11.19	23.31	10.76	11.19	23.31
通信设备、计算机及其他电子设备	Telecommunication Equipment, Computer and Other Electronic Equipment Manufacturing	10.61	12.86	21.52	9.64	12.79	20.02
仪器仪表及文化、办公用机械制造	Instruments, Meters, Cultural and Official Machinery	3.44	2.25	3.07	2.15	1.67	2.70
工艺品及其他制造业	Handicraft Article and Other Manufacturing	2.89	3.31	5.76	2.22	3.31	5.26
废弃资源和废旧材料回收加工业	Waste Resources and Junk Material Recycled	0.44	0.11	1.38	0.44	0.11	1.38
电力、燃气及水的生产和供应业	Electric Power, Gas and Water Production and Supply	48.17	61.42	74.99	34.15	24.55	43.31
电力、热力的生产和供应业	Electric Power, Steam and Hot Water Production and Supply	42.00	51.23	56.33	27.97	14.36	24.65
燃气生产和供应业	Gas Production and Supply	0.72	0.78	5.39	0.72	0.78	5.39
水的生产和供应业	Tap Water Production and Supply	5.45	9.41	13.27	5.45	9.41	13.27

注：本表口径为50万元以上项目
Note: this form is for 50 yuan project caliber

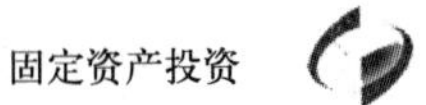

5-19 续表 continued

单位：亿元 (100 million yuan)

行业	sector	全省 Provincial			#地方 Local		
		2007	2008	2009	2007	2008	2009
建筑业	Construction	3.46	5.42		0.34	4.90	1.93
交通运输、仓储和邮政业	Transportation, storage and Post	59.41	57.35		39.24	33.58	56.06
铁路运输业	Railway Transportation	13.11	8.36			0.13	
道路运输业	Road Transportation	22.98	21.81		22.98	21.81	40.79
城市公共交通业	Urban Public Transit	1.23	3.31		1.23	3.31	11.36
水上运输业	Waterway Transportation	20.62	19.76		14.51	4.89	1.27
管道运输业	Pipeline Transportation						0.15
装卸搬运和其他运输服务业	Load and Unload, Carry and Other Transportation	0.20	0.31		0.20	0.31	0.57
仓储业	Storage	0.52	3.79		0.30	3.13	1.93
邮政业	Post	0.01	0.01		0.01	0.01	
信息传输、计算机服务和软件业	Information Transmmision, Computer Service and Software	30.94	39.29		8.40	11.97	6.82
电信和其他信息传输服务业	Telecommunication and Other Information Transmmision Service	28.29	37.15		5.75	9.89	5.66
计算机服务业	Computer Service	0.75	0.69		0.75	0.63	0.73
软件业	Software	1.89	1.45		1.89	1.45	0.42
批发和零售业	Wholesale and Retail Trade	14.07	14.75		13.94	14.47	32.05
住宿和餐饮业	Hotel and Catering Services	7.22	10.57		7.22	10.57	27.85
金融业	Finance	3.48	1.98		1.53	0.44	1.58
银行业	Banking	3.31	1.66		1.36	0.12	1.08
其他金融活动	Other Financial Acitivities	0.16	0.27		0.16	0.27	0.42
房地产业	Real Estate Trade	0.50	2.47		0.25	2.47	2.71
租赁和商务服务业	Leasing and Commercial Service	2.45	3.29		2.00	2.30	10.24
租赁业	Leasing Service	0.18			0.18		0.28
商务服务业	Commercial Service	2.27	3.29		1.82	2.30	9.95
科学研究、技术服务和地质勘查业	Scientific Research, Polytechnical Services and Goelogical Prospecting	2.15	10.43		1.94	5.40	3.99
水利、环境和公共设施管理业	Water Conservancy, Environment and Public Facility Management	30.74	27.90		30.74	27.90	40.02
水利管理业	Water Conservancy Management	4.90	9.73		4.90	9.73	19.40
环境管理业	Environment Management	6.01	5.61		6.01	5.61	4.60
公共设施管理业	Public Facility Management	19.83	12.56		19.83	12.56	16.02
居民服务和其他服务业	Resident Service and Others	1.97	3.33		1.97	1.72	2.55
教育	Education	0.90	2.06		0.84	1.96	5.48
卫生、社会保障和社会福利业	Health Care, Social Security and Social Welfare	5.37	4.74		3.70	4.74	8.05
卫生	Health Care	5.36	4.10		3.69	4.10	7.83
社会保障业	Social Security						
社会福利业	Social Welfare	0.01	0.64		0.01	0.64	0.22
文化、体育和娱乐业	Culture, Sports and Recreation	3.23	5.31		3.23	5.01	8.53
新闻出版业	News Publication	1.22	1.51		1.22	1.20	0.29
广播、电视、电影和音像业	Radio, Television, Film and Stereo	0.74	0.31		0.74	0.31	2.82
文化艺术业	Culture and Arts	0.20	0.08		0.20	0.08	2.08
体育	Sports		1.58			1.58	0.97
娱乐业	Receation	1.06	1.84		1.06	1.84	2.37
公共管理和社会组织	Public Management and Social Organizations	13.47	21.94		12.88	21.16	35.55

5-20 全社会按构成分的投资额

ACCORDING TO THE COMPOSITION OF SOCIAL CAPITAL

单位:亿元 (100 million yuan)

年份 In copies	全省 Provincial			#地方 Local		
	建筑安装工程 Building installation	设备工具器具购置 Equipment tools, equipment purchase	其他费用 Other expenses	建筑安装工程 Building installation	设备工具器具购置 Equipment tools, equipment purchase	其他费用 expenses Other
1978	20.30	9.98	3.30	9.89	4.51	0.48
1980	23.85	9.76	1.89	14.01	4.55	0.97
“六五”时期	**216.19**	**83.11**	**16.52**	**155.63**	**59.71**	**7.43**
1985	67.53	28.67	6.71	54.64	23.00	3.39
“七五”时期	**434.43**	**195.59**	**50.10**	**352.24**	**152.75**	**32.96**
1986	72.40	31.24	7.84	60.18	23.91	4.81
1987	86.83	40.54	12.71	71.79	32.83	7.83
1988	100.58	49.28	10.60	82.40	41.51	7.35
1989	81.98	33.51	8.21	64.30	25.19	5.86
1990	92.64	41.02	10.78	73.58	29.31	7.11
“八五”时期	**1300.95**	**606.68**	**304.04**	**972.09**	**429.78**	**178.69**
1991	108.07	45.11	15.01	86.74	33.68	10.64
1992	149.34	68.03	23.36	119.61	51.46	15.94
1993	227.25	98.91	57.02	174.02	74.17	39.83
1994	361.89	146.12	85.06	261.27	99.72	49.60
1995	454.40	248.51	123.59	330.45	170.75	62.68
“九五”时期	**3392.01**	**1596.34**	**1034.45**	**2593.68**	**1108.81**	**598.32**
1996	510.52	307.89	165.97	392.06	218.14	82.28
1997	600.04	264.16	219.40	405.69	171.97	201.38
1998	695.55	323.47	212.08	556.36	230.59	101.48
1999	771.24	329.26	201.67	594.41	248.78	94.54
2000	814.66	371.56	235.33	645.16	239.33	118.64
“十五”时期	**6031.36**	**2481.09**	**1809.24**	**5317.08**	**1883.69**	**1216.75**
2001	890.60	419.20	241.95	739.97	276.93	124.89
2002	974.73	418.55	301.94	829.11	303.57	155.49
2003	1059.98	463.23	360.38	945.58	363.78	243.47
2004	1409.25	537.25	409.88	1282.71	416.98	307.87
2005	1696.80	642.86	495.09	1519.71	522.43	385.03
“十一五”时期						
2006	2252.72	717.10	602.87	1918.63	601.90	477.07
2007	2857.31	896.36	780.47	2492.24	756.58	660.27
2008	3568.97	1245.73	983.86	3226.13	971.37	819.50
2009	5025.62	1753.28	1432.95	4688.57	1472.47	1253.81

5-21 全社会按国民经济行业分的固定资产投资
ACCORDING TO THE NATIONAL ECONOMY SOCIETY OF FIXED ASSETS INVESTMENT

单位：亿元 (100 million yuan)

行业	sector	全省 Provincial			#地方 Local		
		2007	2008	2009	2007	2008	2009
总　计	**Total**	**4534.14**	**5798.56**	**8211.85**	**3909.09**	**5016.99**	**7417.85**
农、林、牧、渔业	Farming, Forestry, Animal Husbandry and Fishery	149.40	231.25	321.59	148.72	230.95	319.58
农业	Farming	69.65	83.62	117.70	69.58	83.62	116.70
林业	Forestry	15.06	20.11	30.64	15.06	20.11	30.64
畜牧业	Animal Husbandry	17.73	55.76	61.73	17.73	55.76	61.02
渔业	Fishery	6.50	10.49	10.86	6.50	10.49	10.86
农、林、牧、渔服务业	Farming, Forestry, Animal Husbandry and Fishery Services	40.46	61.26	100.67	39.84	60.96	100.37
采矿业	Mining and Qarrying	79.19	102.22	152.35	45.55	71.52	122.36
制造业	Manufacturing	1258.62	1836.59	2406.96	1147.13	1555.08	2203.68
农副食品加工业	Food Processing	51.48	81.56	122.26	51.48	80.41	122.26
食品制造业	Food Production	40.43	60.69	81.27	39.93	60.69	81.27
饮料制造业	Beverage Production	26.07	38.19	62.67	26.07	38.19	62.67
烟草制品业	Tobacco Processing	8.80	6.02	9.29	7.40	5.80	6.39
纺织业	Textile Industry	79.28	89.06	95.00	78.56	87.93	95.00
纺织服装、鞋、帽制造业	Textile Garments, Shoes and Hats Products	32.50	50.57	57.45	32.50	50.57	56.47
皮革、毛皮、羽毛(绒)及其制品业	Leather, Furs Down and Related Products	4.39	6.07	11.10	4.39	6.07	11.10
木材加工及木、竹、藤、棕、草制品业	Timber Processing and Wwood, Bamboo, Rattan, Palm and Sraw Works	19.32	22.26	27.14	19.32	22.26	27.14
家具制造业	Furniture Manufacturing	9.17	21.91	20.66	9.17	21.91	20.66
造纸及纸制品业	Papermaking and Paper Products	20.27	26.58	38.89	20.27	26.58	38.89
印刷业和记录媒介的复制	Printing and Record Processing	14.25	17.03	33.33	13.76	16.62	31.98
文教体育用品制造业	Stationery, Education and Sports Goods	2.70	4.99	5.03	2.70	4.99	5.03
石油加工、炼焦及核燃料加工业	Petroleum Processing, Coking Products and Nuclear Fuel Processing	21.77	16.33	19.62	7.17	5.16	11.88
化学原料及化学制品制造业	Raw Chemical Material and Chemical Products	101.56	176.98	229.44	99.36	176.98	228.91
医药制造业	Medical and pharmaceutical Products	43.44	50.72	77.54	40.22	49.07	75.13
化学纤维制造业	Chemical Fibers	2.91	5.48	3.97	2.91	5.48	3.97
橡胶制品业	Rubber Products	5.34	9.66	12.10	4.82	9.57	12.10
塑料制品业	Plastic Products	26.09	45.96	58.91	25.49	43.46	58.91
非金属矿物制品业	Nonmetal Material Products	107.95	198.20	271.91	107.67	196.56	265.39
黑色金属冶炼及压延加工业	Smelting and Processing of ferrous Metals	165.13	221.06	227.15	165.13	65.61	128.40
有色金属冶炼及压延加工业	Smelting and Processing of Nonferrous Metals	28.52	24.90	41.53	21.25	20.95	40.23
金属制品业	Metal Products	35.19	67.20	117.91	34.27	63.31	117.91
通用设备制造业	Ordinaryly Machinery Manufacturing	71.44	95.58	132.43	68.79	90.51	126.74
专用设备制造业	Special Purpose Equipment Manufacturing	54.00	76.15	120.88	53.41	71.07	117.80
交通运输设备制造业	Transportation Equipment Manufacturing	159.16	231.93	296.08	87.63	145.69	233.29
电气机械及器材制造业	Electric Machinery and Equipment	45.61	74.52	97.51	45.42	74.32	97.51
通信设备、计算机及其他电子设备	Telecommunication Equipment, Computer and Other Electronic Equipment Manufacturing	65.33	94.61	99.57	64.35	93.64	93.14
仪器仪表及文化、办公用机械制造	Instruments, Meters, Cultural and Official Machinery	6.59	9.69	11.59	4.44	8.98	10.92
工艺品及其他制造业	Handicraft Article and Other Manufacturing	7.16	9.02	16.15	6.49	9.02	14.03
废弃资源和废旧材料回收加工业	Waste Resources and Junk Material Recycled	2.78	3.68	8.58	2.78	3.68	8.58
电力、燃气及水的生产和供应业	Electric Power, Gas and Water Production and Supply	359.08	380.39	504.35	198.07	214.73	315.44
电力、热力的生产和供应业	Electric Power, Steam and Hot Water Production and Supply	320.22	321.52	403.86	159.34	157.15	218.53
燃气生产和供应业	Gas Production and Supply	12.67	17.21	32.35	12.54	16.42	29.46
水的生产和供应业	Tap Water Production and Supply	26.19	41.65	68.13	26.19	41.16	67.46

5-21 续表 continued

单位：亿元 (100 million yuan)

行业	sector	全省 Provincial 2007	2008	2009	#地方 Local 2007	2008	2009
建筑业	Construction	13.85	27.12	31.48	4.53	18.09	14.54
交通运输、仓储和邮政业	Transportation, storage and Post	647.86	658.68	989.72	437.14	482.88	767.30
铁路运输业	Railway Transportation	200.58	166.30	250.40	2.85	7.78	47.35
道路运输业	Road Transportation	369.49	376.62	540.26	368.67	376.54	539.84
城市公共交通业	Urban Public Transit	12.58	37.85	67.21	12.58	37.85	67.13
水上运输业	Waterway Transportation	33.07	38.59	45.50	23.13	23.60	41.04
管道运输业	Pipeline Transportation	0.30	1.50	4.40	0.30	0.60	2.18
装卸搬运和其他运输服务业	Load and Unload, Carry and Other Transportation	1.20	2.26	9.83	1.20	2.26	9.43
仓储业	Storage	12.93	26.67	58.87	11.70	25.38	57.27
邮政业	Post	0.07	0.34	1.00	0.04	0.32	1.00
信息传输、计算机服务和软件业	Information Transmmision, Computer Service and Software	55.17	62.98	80.46	24.04	30.89	36.47
电信和其他信息传输服务业	Telecommunication and Other Information Transmmision Service	50.15	55.99	68.06	19.02	23.96	24.06
计算机服务业	Computer Service	2.90	1.33	2.05	2.90	1.28	2.05
软件业	Software	2.12	5.66	10.36	2.12	5.66	10.36
批发和零售业	Wholesale and Retail Trade	131.47	191.08	250.96	129.51	189.43	246.29
住宿和餐饮业	Hotel and Catering Services	70.67	90.71	156.96	69.75	90.71	153.12
金融业	Finance	8.02	6.93	16.80	3.72	3.81	8.53
银行业	Banking	6.12	4.09	12.97	1.85	1.17	4.99
其他金融活动	Other Financial Acitivities	1.13	1.86	2.16	1.13	1.86	2.16
房地产业	Real Estate Trade	899.52	1112.10	1555.29	872.76	1069.60	1353.08
租赁和商务服务业	Leasing and Commercial Service	51.72	85.01	130.75	51.09	84.02	129.48
租赁业	Leasing Service	1.99	0.57	2.21	1.99	0.57	2.21
商务服务业	Commercial Service	49.74	84.45	128.54	49.10	83.46	127.27
科学研究、技术服务和地质勘查业	Scientific Research, Polytechnical Services and Goelogical Prospecting	20.60	42.11	49.67	15.92	30.40	36.60
水利、环境和公共设施管理业	Water Conservancy, Environment and Public Facility Management	436.22	531.44	888.27	429.10	526.98	885.19
水利管理业	Water Conservancy Management	35.84	52.41	139.17	30.02	49.26	136.09
环境管理业	Environment Management	28.54	33.69	61.97	28.14	33.69	61.97
公共设施管理业	Public Facility Management	371.84	445.34	687.13	370.94	444.03	687.13
居民服务和其他服务业	Resident Service and Others	15.28	18.63	22.27	15.28	17.02	22.27
教育	Education	103.76	86.80	129.73	87.32	72.07	106.34
卫生、社会保障和社会福利业	Health Care, Social Security and Social Welfare	35.60	43.19	77.15	33.23	42.51	71.67
卫生	Health Care	33.77	39.24	70.79	31.40	38.57	65.32
社会保障业	Social Security	0.22	0.86	1.13	0.22	0.86	1.13
社会福利业	Social Welfare	1.61	3.09	5.22	1.61	3.09	5.22
文化、体育和娱乐业	Culture, Sports and Recreation	59.29	56.47	108.53	59.29	55.32	108.48
新闻出版业	News Publication	1.79	3.58	4.04	1.79	3.28	4.04
广播、电视、电影和音像业	Radio, Television, Film and Stereo	3.82	2.94	6.96	3.82	2.89	6.91
文化艺术业	Culture and Arts	16.55	14.17	30.65	16.55	14.17	30.65
体育	Sports	14.95	5.59	18.59	14.95	5.59	18.59
娱乐业	Receation	22.17	30.20	48.30	22.17	29.40	48.30
公共管理和社会组织	Public Management and Social Organizations	138.82	234.85	338.55	136.95	230.96	337.27

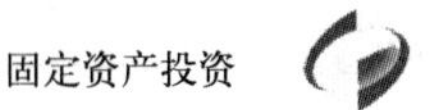

5-22 全社会按三次产业划分的投资额

ACCORDING TO THE THREE INDUSTRIES OF WHOLE SOCIETY OF INVESTMENT

单位：亿元 (100 million yuan)

年份 In copies	全省			#地方		
	第一产业 The first industry	第二产业 The second industry	第三产业 The third industry	第一产业 The first industry	第二产业 The second industry	第三产业 The third industry
1978	**2.24**	**25.28**	**6.06**	**2.24**	**8.80**	**3.85**
1980	2.11	22.75	10.64	2.03	9.98	7.52
“六五”时期	**24.77**	**155.02**	**136.03**	**24.05**	**83.83**	**114.89**
1985	8.37	47.42	47.12	8.09	31.48	41.46
“七五”时期	**49.76**	**335.53**	**294.83**	**47.24**	**245.00**	**245.71**
1986	7.89	50.33	53.22	7.40	34.88	46.62
1987	9.52	70.17	60.39	9.07	52.40	50.98
1988	11.11	85.76	63.59	10.53	67.14	53.59
1989	9.08	61.86	52.76	8.63	44.28	42.43
1990	12.16	67.41	64.87	11.61	46.30	52.09
“八五”时期	**78.98**	**1074.06**	**1058.63**	**73.97**	**674.84**	**831.75**
1991	12.48	77.95	77.76	12.12	55.25	63.69
1992	12.42	121.00	107.31	11.04	87.18	88.79
1993	11.89	170.93	200.36	10.10	114.05	163.87
1994	14.97	302.49	275.61	14.38	173.32	222.89
1995	27.22	401.69	397.59	26.11	220.95	316.82
“九五”时期	**272.08**	**2298.38**	**3452.34**	**271.69**	**1265.99**	**2763.13**
1996	29.76	451.28	503.34	29.73	272.79	389.96
1997	41.02	436.04	606.54	41.02	269.87	468.15
1998	59.48	450.16	721.46	59.48	234.94	594.01
1999	71.22	439.32	791.63	71.22	227.20	639.31
2000	70.60	521.58	829.37	70.24	261.19	671.70
“十五”时期	**416.79**	**3952.90**	**5969.82**	**414.74**	**2724.92**	**5277.86**
2001	77.48	590.01	902.08	77.33	323.55	740.91
2002	80.08	648.81	966.33	79.02	375.77	833.38
2003	88.80	714.81	1079.98	88.35	489.49	974.99
2004	77.55	912.93	1365.90	77.16	684.54	1245.86
2005	92.88	1086.34	1655.53	92.88	851.57	1482.72
“十一五”时期						
2006	107.64	1317.12	2147.93	107.56	1044.17	1845.87
2007	149.40	1710.74	2674.00	148.72	1395.28	2365.09
2008	231.25	2346.32	3220.99	230.95	1859.42	2926.62
2009	321.59	3097.68	4792.58	319.58	2656.02	4442.25

5-23 全社会竣工房屋建筑面积及竣工率
THE FLOOR SPACE OF BUILDINGS COMPLETED ALL SOCIAL AND COMPLETION RATE

年　份 In copies	施工面积(万平方米) Construction area (million square meters)	#住宅 # residential	竣工面积(万平方米) Completion of (million square meters)	#住宅 # residential	竣工率(%) Completion rate (%)	#住宅 # residential
1978	**1343.27**	**513.20**	**666.76**	**280.16**	**49.6**	**54.6**
1980	1951.16	1004.17	1024.51	586.27	52.5	58.4
"六五" 时期			**25700.97**	**19626.87**		
1985	8079.90	5965.71	6899.59	5434.20	85.4	91.1
"七五" 时期			**29202.17**	**22387.23**		
1986	8760.15	6686.78	7754.53	6308.96	88.5	94.3
1987	7922.23	5684.88	6803.61	5233.59	85.9	92.1
1988	7225.98	4892.04	6060.44	4484.69	83.9	91.7
1989	5250.24	3590.22	4414.47	3301.59	84.1	92.0
1990	5103.48	3507.53	4169.12	3058.40	81.7	87.2
"八五" 时期			**23403.26**	**16559.28**		
1991	5300.98	3652.67	4211.39	3157.13	79.4	86.4
1992	5954.84	4066.51	4621.87	3383.72	77.6	83.2
1993	5807.24	3540.57	4050.56	2798.42	69.8	79.0
1994	7158.68	4476.46	4916.24	3482.20	68.7	77.8
1995	8294.84	5304.79	5603.20	3737.81	67.6	70.5
"九五" 时期			**35861.86**	**26378.48**		
1996	8749.65	5581.32	6073.43	4485.82	69.4	80.4
1997	8963.28	5976.86	6430.48	4790.34	71.7	80.1
1998	10485.86	7179.25	7897.96	5792.97	75.3	80.7
1999	10228.93	7219.06	7951.03	5891.97	77.7	81.6
2000	9920.42	6831.02	7508.96	5417.38	75.7	79.3
"十五" 时期			**40164.49**	**29588.06**		
2001	10040.11	7273.21	7716.37	5850.27	76.9	80.4
2002	10301.00	7019.76	7796.76	5583.27	75.7	79.5
2003	10667.78	7276.62	7469.17	5457.42	70.0	75.0
2004	13152.08	9285.64	9318.34	7069.45	70.6	75.9
2005	12572.00	8401.20	7863.85	5627.67	62.6	67.0
"十一五" 时期						
2006	12346.48	8039.75	7126.64	4812.39	57.7	59.9
2007	13686.34	8910.75	7557.62	5036.19	55.2	56.5
2008	16417.07	9896.66	7551.82	4679.96	46.0	47.3
2009	20142.81	11762.06	9772.28	5556.71	48.5	47.2

主要统计指标解释

全社会固定资产投资 是以货币形式表现的在一定时期内全社会建造和购置固定资产的工作量以及与此有关的费用的总称。该指标是反映固定资产投资规模、结构和发展速度的综合性指标，又是观察工程进度和考核投资效果的重要依据。全社会固定资产投资按登记注册类型可分为国有、集体、个体、联营、股份制、外商、港澳台商、其他等。

城镇固定资产投资 指城镇各种登记注册类型的企业、事业、行政单位及个体户进行的计划总投资(或实际需要总投资)50万元及50万元以上的建设项目投资、房地产开发投资、城镇和工矿区私人建房投资。县城及以上区域内发生的投资，县及县以上各级政府及主管部门直接领导、管理的建设项目和企业事业单位的投资均为城镇固定资产投资。

房地产开发投资 指各种登记注册类型的房地产开发公司、商品房建设公司及其他房地产开发法人单位和附属于其他法人单位实际从事房地产开发或经营活动的单位统一开发的包括统代建、拆迁还建的住宅、厂房、仓库、饭店、宾馆、度假村、写字楼、办公楼等房屋建筑物和配套的服务设施，土地开发工程（如道路、给水、排水、供电、供热、通讯、平整场地等基础设施工程）的投资；不包括单纯的土地交易活动。

城镇和工矿区私人建房投资 包括市、县城、城关镇、工矿区所辖范围内的全部私人建房，不论其房主是否系本地的常住户口均应包括。

农村投资 包括在农村区域范围内进行固定资产投资活动的企业、事业、行政单位及农村个人投资。

固定资产投资的资金来源 根据固定资产投资的资金来源不同，分为国家预算内资金、国内贷款、利用外资、自筹资金和其他资金。

(1)国家预算内资金：分为财政拨款和财政安排的贷款两部分。包括中央财政的基本建设基金(分经营性基金和非经营性基金两部分)、专项支出(如煤代油专项等)、收回再贷、贴息资金，财政安排的挖潜改造和新产品试制支出、城建支出、商业部门简易建筑支出、不发达地区发展基金等资金中用于固定资产投资的资金；地方财政中由国家统筹安排的资金等。

(2)国内贷款：指报告期固定资产投资单位向银行及非银行金融机构借入的用于固定资产投资的各种国内借款，包括银行利用自有资金及吸收的存款发放的贷款、上级主管部门拨入的国内贷款、国家专项贷款(包括煤代油贷款、劳改煤矿专项贷款等)、地方财政专项资金安排的贷款、国内储备贷款、周转贷款等。

(3)利用外资：指报告期收到的用于固定资产建造和购置的国外资金(包括设备、材料、技术在内)。包括对外借款(外国政府、国际金融组织贷款、出口信贷、外国银行商业贷款、对外发行债券和股票)、外商直接投资及外商其他投资。不包括我国自有外汇资金(国家外汇、地方外汇、留成外汇、调剂外汇和中国银行自有资金发行的外汇贷款等)。计算利用外资时，需要折算成人民币，折算中所使用的外汇汇率按现汇计算，即按使用外汇时的汇率计算。

(4)自筹资金：指固定资产投资单位报告期收到的，由各地区、各部门及企、事业单位筹集用于固定资产投资的预算外资金，包括中央各部门、各级地方和企、事业单位的自筹资金。

(5)其他资金：指在报告期收到的除以上各种资金之外其他用于固定资产投资的资金，包括企业或金融机构通过发行各种债券筹集到的资金、群众集资、个人资金、无偿捐赠的资金及其他单位拨入的资金等。

固定资产投资按国民经济行业分 根据建设项目建成投产后的主要产品或主要用途及社会经济活动性质来确定国民经济行业。一般情况下，一个建设项目或一个企业、事业单位只能属于一种国民经济行业。

固定资产投资按隶属关系分 是按建设单位或企业、事业、行政单位的主管上级机关确定的。

（1）中央：是指中共中央、人大常委会和国务院各部、委、局、总公司以及直属机构直接领导的建设项目和企业、事业、行政单位。这些单位的固定资产投资计划由国务院各部门直接编制和下达，建设中所需物资、主要设备以及建设中的问题都由中央有关部门安排和解决。

（2）地方：是由省（自治区、直辖市）、地区（州、盟、省辖市）、县（旗、县级市）三级政府及业务主管部门直接领导和管理的建设项目、企业、事业、行政单位。地方项目还包括不隶属以上各级政府及主管部门的建设项目和企业、事业单位，如外商投资企业和无主管部门的企业等。

固定资产投资按建设性质分 根据整个建设项目情况来确定。建设项目的性质一般分为新建、扩建、改建和技术改造、迁建、恢复。房地产开发单位、农村投资、城镇工矿区私人建房投资不划分建设性质。

(1)新建：一般指从无到有“平地起家”开始建设的企业、事业和行政单位或建设项目。现有企业、事业、行政单位一般不属于新建。但如有的单位原有基础很小，经过建设后新增的固定资产价值超过该企、事业、行政单位原有固定资产价值(原值)三倍以上的也应作为新建。

(2)扩建：指在厂内或其他地点，为扩大原有产品的生产能力(或效益)或增加新的产品生产能力，而增建主要的生产车间(或主要工程)、分厂、独立的生产线。行政、事业单位在原单位增建业务用房(如学校增建教学用房、医院增建门诊部、病房等)也作为扩建。

现有企、事业单位为扩大原有主要产品生产能力或增加新的产品生产能力，增建一个或几个主要生产车间(或主要工程)、分厂，同时进行一些更新改造工程的，也应作为扩建。

(3)改建和技术改造：指现有企业、事业单位，对原有设施进行技术改造或更新(包括相应配套的辅助性生产、生活福利设施）的建设项目。现有企业、事业单位为适应市场变化的需要，而改变企业的主要产品种类(如军工企业转产民用品等）的建设项目，应作为改建。原有产品生产作业线由于各工序(车间)之间能力不平衡，为填平补齐充分发挥原有生产能力而增建不增加本企业主要产品设计能力的车间，也应作为改建。技术改造是指企业、事业单位在现有基础上，用先进的技术代替落后的技术，用先进的工艺和装备代替落后的工艺和装备，以改变企业落后的技术经济面貌，实现以内涵为主的扩大再生产，达到提高产品质量、促进产品更新换代、节约能源、降低消耗、扩大生产规模、全面提高社会经济效益的目的。技术改造具体包括以下内容：机器设备和工具的更新改造；生产工艺改革、节约能源和原材料的改造；厂房建筑和公共设施的改造；劳动条件和生产环境的改造等。

固定资产投资按构成分 固定资产投资活动按其工作内容和实现方式分为建筑安装工程，设备、工具、器具购置，其他费用三个部分。

(1)建筑安装工程(建筑安装工作量)：指各种房屋、建筑物的建造工程和各种设备、装置的安装工程。包括各种房屋建造工程；各种用途设备基础和各种工业窑炉的砌筑工程及金属结构工程；为施工而进行的各种准备工作和临时工程以及完工后的清理工作等；铁路、道路的铺设，矿井的开凿及石油管道的架设等；水利工程；防空地下建筑等特殊工程；列入房屋工程预算内的暖气、卫生、通风、照明、煤气等设备的价值及装设油饰工程；列入建筑工程预算内的各种管道(蒸汽、压缩空气、石油、给排水等管道)、电力、电讯电缆导线等的敷设工程；以及各种机械设备的安装工程；为测定安装工程质量，对设备进行的试运工作；房地产开发单位进行的商品房屋开发建设工程、土地开发工程。

在安装工程中，不包括被安装设备本身的价值。

(2)设备、工具、器具购置：指建设单位或企、事业单位购置或自制的，达到固定资产标准的设备、工具、器具的价值。新建单位及扩建单位的新建车间，按照设计或计划要求购置或自制的全部设备、工具、器具，不论是否达到固定资产标准均计入“设备、工具、器具购置”中。

(3)其他费用：指在固定资产建造和购置过程中发生的，除上述几项内容以外的各种应分摊计入固定资产的费用。

施工项目 指报告期内进行过建筑或安装施工活动的项目。凡是报告期内施过工的建设项目，不论施工时间长短，均作为施工项目统计。施工项目个数可以反映一定时期固定资产投资的实际规模，与同期全部建成投产项目个数相比，可以从建设速度的角度反映固定资产投资的效果。根据建设项目施工活动的不同性质，施工项目又分为：本年正式施工项目、本年收尾项目和以前年度全部停缓建项目。

全部建成投产项目 工业项目指设计文件规定形成生产能力的主体工程及其相应配套的辅助设施全部建成，经负荷试运转，证明具备生产设计规定合格产品的条件，并经过验收鉴定合格或达到竣工验收标准，与生产性工程配套的生活福利设施可以满足近期正常生产的需要，正式移交生产的建设项目。非工业项目指设计文件规定的主体工程和相应的配套工程全部建成，能够发挥设计规定的全部效益，经验收鉴定合格或达到竣工验收标准，正式移交使用的建设项目。

新增生产能力(或工程效益) 指通过固定资产投资活动而增加的设计能力(或工程效益)，该指标是以实物形态表现的反映固定资产投资成果的指标，也是考核投资经济效果的重要依据之一。

房屋建筑面积 指房屋建筑物勒脚以上外墙外围的水平截面面积，包括房屋建筑物的有效面积和结构面积。该指标是从实物形态上反映建设规模和建设成果的重要指标之一，也是检查工程形象进度、计算工程造价、分析投资效果、研究施工任务和建筑材料之间平衡情况的重要依据。

住宅建筑面积 指施工和竣工房屋建筑面积中供居住用的房屋建筑面积。

施工面积 指报告期内施工的全部房屋建筑面积。包括本期新开工的面积和上期开工跨入本期继续施工的房屋面积，以及上期已停建在本期恢复施工的房屋面积。本期竣工和本期施工后又停缓建的房屋，其建筑面积仍计入本期房屋施工面积中。

竣工面积 指在报告期内房屋建筑按照设计要求已经全部完工，达到住人和使用条件，经验收鉴定合格(或达到竣工验收标准)，正式移交使用单位的各栋房屋建筑面积的总和。

房屋建筑面积竣工率 指一定时期内房屋竣工面积占同期房屋施工面积的比率。是从房屋建筑施工速度的角度反映投资效果的指标。

新增固定资产 指报告期内已经完成建造和购置过程，并已交付生产或使用单位的固定资产价值。该指标是表示固定资产投资成果的价值指标，也是反映建设进度，计算固定资产投资效果的重要指标。

项目建设投产率 指一定时期内全部建成投产项目个数与同期施工项目个数的比率。该指标是从建设单位建设速度的角度反映投资效果的指标。

固定资产交付使用率 指一定时期新增固定资产与同期完成投资额的比率。该指标是反映固定资产动用速度，衡量建设过程中宏观投资效果的综合指标。由于新增固定资产是较长时期内形成的结果，而投资额则是当年完成的，因此，该指标一般适宜于反映较长时期内固定资产的动用情况。

商品房销售面积 指报告期内出售商品房屋的合同总面积(即双方签署的正式买卖合同中所确定的建筑面积)。由现房销售建筑面积和期房销售建筑面积两部分组成。

商品房销售额 指报告期内出售商品房屋的合同总价款(即双方签署的正式买卖合同中所确定的合同总价)。该指标与商品房销售面积同口径，由现房销售额和期房销售额两部分组成。

经济适用房 指根据地方经济适用房计划安排建设的政策性住宅。经济是指房屋建筑造价和销售价格低于一般商品住宅；适用是指适合中低收入家庭购买使用。经济适用房主要是由国家统一下达投资计划，房地产公司开发，对外销售；用地一般采用行政划拨或招标投标方式，免收土地出让金；对各种经批准的收费减半征收，开发利润不超过3%；销售价格实行政

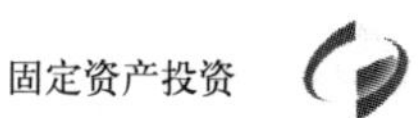

府指导价。该指标可以分析房地产投资结构，反映中低收入家庭商品住宅的供求平衡情况。

Explanatory Notes on Main Statistical Indicators

Total Investment in Fixed Assets in the Whole Country refers to the volume of activities in construction and purchases of fixed assets and related fees, expressed in monetary terms. It is a comprehensive indicator which shows the size, structure and growth of the investment in fixed assets, providing basis for observing the progress of construction projects and evaluating results of investment. Total investment in fixed assets in the whole country includes, by type of ownership, the investment by the state-owned units, collective units, individuals, joint ownership units, share-holding units, as well as investment by businessmen from foreign countries and from Hong Kong, Macao and Taiwan, and by other units.

Urban Investment in Fixed Assets refers to construction projects involving a total planned (or required) investment of 500,000 yuan and over by urban enterprises and institutions of various types of ownership, by administrative units and by individuals, investment in real estate development, and housing investment by individuals in urban areas and in industrial and mining areas. In other words, all investments that take place in county towns and urban areas, investment in construction projects under the direct leadership and management of government agencies at and above county levels and investments by enterprises and institutions at and above county levels are covered in urban investment in fixed assets.

Investment in Real Estate Development refers to the investment by the real estate development companies, commercial buildings construction companies and other real estate development units of various types of ownership in the construction of house buildings, such as residential buildings, factory buildings, warehouses, hotels, guesthouses, holiday villages, office buildings, and the complementary service facilities and land development projects, such as roads, water supply, water drainage, power supply, heating, telecommunications, land leveling and other projects of infrastructure. It excludes the activities in pure land transactions.

Investment in Housing Construction in Urban Areas and in Industrial and Mining Areas refers to all private housing construction under the jurisdiction of cities, county towns and industrial and mining areas, no matter whether the owner of the house is registered as the permanent resident in the locality or not.

Investment in Rural Areas refers to investment in fixed assets by enterprises, institutions and individuals in rural areas.

Sources of Funds for Investment in Fixed Assets include fund from state budget, domestic loans, foreign investment, self-raised funds, and others depending on the source of investment.

(1) Fund from state budget consists of budgetary appropriation and loans from state budget. More specifically, it includes, from the budget of the central government, capital construction fund (operation fund and non-operational fund), special expenses (e.g. expenses on substituting petroleum with coal), loans from repayment, discount fund, expenses on innovation and trial production of new products, expenses on urban construction, expenses on temporary construction by trade departments, development fund for less developed areas, as well as local budgetary fund transferred from the central budget.

(2) Domestic loans refer to loans of various forms borrowed by investing units from banks and non-bank financial institutions during the reference period for the purpose of investment in fixed assets, including loans issued by banks from their self-owned funds and deposit, loans appropriated by higher responsible authorities, special loans by government (including loan for substituting petroleum with coal, special loan for reform-through-labour coal mines), loans arranged by local government from special funds, domestic reserve loan, and working loan, etc..

(3) Foreign Investment refers to foreign funds received during the reference period for the construction and purchase of investment in fixed assets (covering equipment, materials and technology), including foreign borrowings (loans from foreign governments and international financial institutions, export credit, commercial loans from foreign banks, issue of bonds and stocks overseas), foreign direct investment and other foreign investment. Excluded in this category are capitals in foreign exchanges owned by China (foreign exchanges owned by the central and local governments, foreign exchanges retained by enterprises, foreign exchanges by enterprises through regulating mechanism, loans in foreign exchanges issued by the Bank of China with its own fund, etc.). In calculating the utilization of foreign capitals, foreign currencies are converted into Chinese Renminbi applying the current exchange rate when the foreign capitals are actually used.

(4) Self-raised funds refer to extra-budgetary funds for investment in fixed assets received by investing units from central government ministries, local governments, enterprises and institutions, including their self-raised funds.

(5) Others refer to funds for investment in fixed assets received from the sources other than those listed above, including capitals raised through issuing bonds by enterprises or financial institutions, funds raised from individuals and through donations, and funds transferred from other units.

Investment in Fixed Assets by Sector The classification of construction projects by sector is determined by the major products or the purpose of the projects when they are put into production or use, and by the nature of their social economic activities. In general, one project or one enterprise or institution can only be classified into one sector.

Investment in Fixed Assets by Jurisdiction of Management refers to the classification of investment by the competent authorities under which investment is made by construction units, enterprises, institutions or administrative units.

(1) Central investment refers to the investment in projects or by enterprises, institutions or administrative units which are under the direct leadership and management of the CPC Central Committee, the NPC Standing Committee, the State Council and of the national commissions, ministries, agencies and state-owned large corporations. Various ministries and departments of the State Council prepare and implement plans for investment in fixed assets by those departments, and arrange and ensure the supply of materials and key equipment required for the projects.

(2) Local investment refers to the investment in projects or by enterprises, institutions or administrative units which are under the direct leadership and management of departments under the provincial, prefecture and county governments. Also included are projects by foreign-invested enterprises and enterprises without competent managing authorities.

Investment in Fixed Assets by Type of Construction The construction projects in general can be classified, by the type of construction, into new construction, expansion, reconstruction and technical transformation, moving and restoration. However, investment by type of construction is not applied to investment by real-estate development units, investment in rural areas and investment in housing by urban individuals.

(1) New construction in general refers to newly constructed enterprises, institutions, administrative agencies or independent projects from scratch. Construction in the existing enterprises, institutions or agencies is not considered as new construction. In case the assets of the existing unit is quite small, and the value of newly added fixed assets exceeds the original value of assets by three times, the expansion will be considered as new construction.

(2) Expansion refers to construction of new major production workshop, branch factory or independent production line within a factory or in other locations, for the purpose of increasing the production capacity (or improving efficiency) of the original products. Newly constructed houses for the operation of institutions and administrative organizations (such as the newly constructed buildings for teaching in schools, buildings for clinics or wards in hospitals, etc.) are also classified as expansion.

Also included in the expansion are investments by existing enterprises or institutions in building major production line(s) or branch factory(ies) along with some work on innovation, for the purpose of expending the production capacity of original products or producing new products.

(3) Reconstruction refers to construction projects by existing enterprises or institutions in innovation or technical transformation of the old facilities (including auxiliary production equipment and welfare facilities). Also considered as reconstruction is the construction of new workshops by the existing enterprises or institutions to change the variety of products to meet the market demand (such as the production of civil products by defence industries), or to bring the designed production capacity into full play through a more balanced production process on production lines. Technical transformation refers to replacement of old technology or equipment by new technology or equipment, in order to expand the reproduction through improvement of technology contents in production, to improve product quality, to promote new products, to save energy and reduce consumption and to improve overall social-economic efficiency. Contents of technical transformation include: updating of machinery, equipment and tools; reforming production process by using energy or materials saving technology; construction of factory workshops and transformation of public facilities; improvement of working conditions and environment, etc.

Investment in Fixed Assets by Structure By their contents, investment activities are classified into 3 categories, i.e. construction and installation, purchase of equipment and instrument, and other expenses.

(1) Construction and installation (work volume of construction and installation) refers to the construction of various houses and buildings and installation of various kinds of equipment and instruments. They include construction of various houses; equipment foundations, industrial kilns and stoves, and metal structure work; preparation works for project construction, and clearing up works post project construction; pavement of railways and roads, drilling of mines and putting up of oil pipes; construction of projects of water conservancy; construction of underground air-raid shelters and construction of other special projects; value of equipment for heating, sanitation, ventilation, lighting, gas, painting, etc. that are covered by the budget of housing projects; laying out of various pipelines (for steam, compressed air, petroleum, tap water and sewage) and lines for electric power and for communications; installation of various machinery equipment, testing operation for pre-testing the quality of installation projects, and land and other development work conducted by real estate developers for commercial housing. The value of equipment installed is not included in the value of installation projects.

(2) Purchase of equipment and instruments refers to the total value of equipment, tools, and instruments purchased or self-produced which come up to standards for fixed assets by the construction units or investing enterprises or institutions. Equipment, tools and instruments purchased or self-produced for new workshops by newly established or expanded units are categorized as "purchase of equipment and instruments" no matter whether they come up to the standards for fixed assets.

(3) Other expenses refer to expenses occurring during the construction or purchase of fixed assets other than those mentioned above.

Projects under Construction refer to projects with construction and installation activities undertaken in the reference period. All projects that have construction activities undertaken during the reference period are reported as projects under construction irrespective of the length of construction work. The number of projects under construction can reflect the actual size of investment in fixed assets during a given period, and when compared with the number of projects completed and put into use during the same period, it demonstrates the results of investment in fixed assets. Depending on the nature of construction activities, projects under construction can also be classified into projects under construction in current year, winding-up projects in current year and stopped or suspended projects in previous years (with preservation work in current year).

Projects Completed and Put into Use Industrial projects refer to the major projects and accessory facilities completed which result in forming production capacity and have been checked and accepted while the living and welfare facilities have been completed

and can ensure normal production and formally put into production. Non-industrial projects refer to the major projects and accessory facilities completed which possess the designed capacity and have been checked, accepted and formally put into production.

Newly Increased Production Capacity (or Project Efficiency) refers to the increase of designed capacity (or project efficiency) through investment in fixed assets, which reflects the accomplishment of investment in fixed assets in kind and serves as important basis for evaluating the economic efficiency of investment.

Floor Space of Buildings under Construction refers to total floor space of the horizontal section of outer walls above the plinth of the building, including the effective area and the area occupied by the structure. This indicator is one of the important indicators in physical terms to reflect the scale and accomplishment of the construction industry, and important basis for monitoring the progress, calculating the cost, analyzing the efficiency and studying the supply of building materials in relation with the construction projects.

Floor Space of Residential Buildings refers to the floor space of the residential buildings among the total space of buildings under construction or completed.

Floor Space under Construction refers to total floor space of all buildings under construction during the reference period, including floor space of newly started buildings during the reference period, floor space of construction extended from the previous period to the current period, and floor space of construction suspended during the previous period and resumed in the current period. Floor space of construction completed in the current period, and floor space of construction started and then suspended in the current period are also included in the floor space under construction of the current year.

Floor Space of Buildings Completed refers to the floor space of all buildings completed in the reference period, which have been appraised and accepted (or come up to the designed standards) and have been transferred to the owners for use.

Completion Rate of Floor Space of Buildings refers to the ratio of the floor space of buildings completed in certain period of time to the floor space of buildings under construction in the same period. This indicator reflects the investment result from the perspective of the speed of construction.

Newly Increased Fixed Assets refer to the newly increased value of fixed assets, constructed or purchased, that have been transferred to the investors. This is an indicator that demonstrates the results of investment in fixed assets in monetary terms, and an important indicator to reflect the speed of construction and to calculate the efficiency of investment.

Rate of Construction Projects Completed and Put into Use refers to the ratio of the number of construction projects completed and put into use in certain period of time to the number of projects under construction in the same period. This reflects the investment efficiency from the perspective of the speed of projects construction.

Rate of Projects of Fixed Assets Completed and Put into Operation refers to the ratio of the newly increased fixed assets to the total investment made in the same period. This is a comprehensive indicator reflecting the speed of the employment of fixed assets and the investment efficiency at the macro-level. As the newly increase fixed assets is the result of a long period while the investment is completed in the current year, this indicator is expected to be used to reflect the employment of fixed assets over a long period of time.

Area of Commercial Housing Sold refers to total contracted area of commercial housing (i.e. area of floor space as designated in the formal contracts signed by both sides) during the reference time. It constitutes floor space of completed housing and floor space of future housing.

Value of Commercial Housing Sold refer to total value of contracts (i.e. value of sales/purchase for selling/purchase of commercial housing as designated in the contracts signed by both sides) during the reference time. It has the same coverage as the area of commercial housing sold, constituting completed housing and floor space of future housing

Economically Affordable Housing refers to housing constructed according to the state plan for economically affordable housing. Houses of this category featured in low cost in construction and low prices, and therefore are affordable to mid-income or low income households. Economically affordable housing projects are developed by real estate companies under the state investment plan, with the land provided through government allocation or tendering procedures. Developers are exempted from land utilization fees and enjoy another 50% exemption of all other legitimate fees, while their profits are limited to less than 3%, and the completed houses are sold under the government-guided prices. This indicator helps to analyze the investment structure of the real estate industry and the demand and supply of housing for mid or low income households.

6 物价

Price

资料整理：文　峰　李　红　彭惊涛

6-1　物　价　总　指　数（2009）

GENERAL PRICE INDICES(2009)

基　期	Base Period	商品零售价格总指数 General Rtail Price Index	居民消费价格总指数 General Consumption Price Index
以1950年价格为100	The Price of 1950 Equals 100	571.2	864.0
以1952年价格为100	The Price of 1952 Equals 100	506.5	760.0
以1957年价格为100	The Price of 1957 Equals 100	458.6	673.7
以1965年价格为100	The Price of 1965 Equals 100	410.9	592.8
以1970年价格为100	The Price of 1970 Equals 100	414.2	595.0
以1975年价格为100	The Price of 1975 Equals 100	414.7	589.2
以1978年价格为100	The Price of 1978 Equals 100	411.5	587.0
以1980年价格为100	The Price of 1980 Equals 100	387.9	536.0
以1985年价格为100	The Price of 1985 Equals 100	338.2	450.6
以1990年价格为100	The Price of 1990 Equals 100	209.8	284.2
以1995年价格为100	The Price of 1995 Equals 100	112.4	133.7
以1996年价格为100	The Price of 1996 Equals 100	105.8	121.3
以2005年价格为100	The Price of 2005 Equals 100	110.4	112.8
以上年价格为100	The Price of Last Year Equals 100	98.6	99.6

6-2　各市、县物价指数(2009)

PRICE INDICES OF CITIES AND COUNTIES(2009)

(上年=100) (preceding year = 100)

地　区	Region	居民消费价格指数 Consumer Price Index	商品零售价格指数 Retail Price Index	农业生产资料价格指数 Agricultural Production Material Price Index
湖北省	**Hubei Province**	**99.6**	**98.6**	**95.3**
武汉市	Wuhan Municipality	99.4	98.4	
黄石市	Huangshi Municipality	99.5	98.8	
十堰市	Shiyan Municipality	100.8	99.9	
竹山县	zhushan county	100.9	100.2	96.5
宜昌市	Yichang Municipality	100.1	99.8	
宜都市	Yidu Municipality	101.5	100.8	96.1
襄樊市	Xiangfan Municipality	98.7	98.1	
老河口市	Laohekou Municipality	99.5	98.5	98.0
孝感市	Xiaogan Municipality	99.2	99.5	
大悟县	Dawu county	99.8	98.7	96.5
荆州市	Jingzhou Municipality	98.8	97.0	
洪湖市	Honghu Municipality	99.9	99.6	99.5
浠水县	Xishui Municipality	99.4	98.0	99.2
麻城市	Macheng Municipality	99.1	98.2	97.1
咸宁市	Xianning Municipality	99.3	98.8	92.0
崇阳县	Chongyang County	99.9	99.0	92.5
恩施市	Enshi Municipality	100.4	99.8	92.1
天门市	Tianmen Municipality	99.7	98.7	92.8

6-3 全省居民消费、商品零售价格分类指数(2009)

CONSUMER PRICES INDICES AND RETAIL PRICE INDICES BY CATEGORY (2009)

(上年=100) (preceding year=100)

类别	Item	全省 Provincial Indices	城市 Urban Indices	农村 Rural Indices
居民消费价格总指数	**General Consumer Price Index**	**99.6**	**99.3**	**100.0**
*服务项目价格指数	Service Price Index	99.3	98.5	100.8
一、食品	Foods	100.5	100.4	100.6
二、烟酒及用品	Tobacco,Liquor and Articles	101.4	101.8	100.9
三、衣着	Clothing	99.1	99.8	98.0
四、家庭设备用品及维修服务	Household Facilities and Articles	100.2	100.0	100.5
五、医疗保健和个人用品	Medicine and Medical Articles	101.4	101.6	101.2
六、交通和通讯	Transportation and Communication	98.4	98.3	98.5
七、娱乐教育文化用品及服务	Receation, Education and Culture Articles and Services	98.9	98.0	99.9
八、居住	Housing Condition	97.7	95.7	100.1
商品零售价格总指数	**General Price Index**	**98.6**	**98.4**	**98.9**
一、食品	Foods	100.2	100.4	99.9
二、饮料、烟酒	Beverage, Tobacco and Liquor	101.9	102.3	101.5
三、服装、鞋帽	Garments, Shoes and Hats	98.9	99.6	97.9
四、纺织品	Texiles	99.8	100.3	99.4
五、家用电器及音像器材	Household Electric Appliance and Stereo	92.3	88.7	97.5
六、文化办公用品	Stationery and Business Articles	95.4	93.6	98.5
七、日用品	Daily Use Articles	101.8	101.9	101.8
八、体育娱乐用品	Sports and Receation Articles	97.8	95.8	99.8
九、交通、通信用品	Transportation and Communication Articles	92.6	90.8	95.6
十、家具	Furniture	101.8	103.1	99.8
十一、化妆品	Cosmetics	101.2	101.6	100.6
十二、金银珠宝	Gold, Silver and Pearls Jewelery	92.7	91.0	94.9
十三、中西药品及医疗保健用品	Chinese Traditional Medicine, Western Medicines and Health Care Appliances	101.4	102.0	100.7
十四、书报杂志及电子出版物	Books, Newspaper, Magzines and Electronic Publications	106.1	109.0	101.9
十五、燃料类	Fuels	90.7	89.4	92.7
十六、建筑材料及五金电料	Building and Decoration Materials	98.2	99.4	96.7
农业生产资料价格指数	**General Price Index of Means of Agricultural Production**	**95.3**		

6-4　工业品出厂价格指数

EX-FACTORY PRICE INDICES OF INDUSTRIAL PRODUCTS

分　　类	Group Name	上年=100 preceding year=100	1990年=100 1990=100	
		2009	2008	2009
总指数	General Indices	95.55	264.39	252.62
一、按轻重工业分	Grouped by Light Industry and Heavy Industry			
1.轻工业	Light Industry	97.16	197.67	192.06
以农产品为原料	Using Farm Products as Raw Material	97.39	218.06	212.37
以非农产品为原料	Using Non-Farm Products as Raw Material	96.75	141.40	136.80
2.重工业	Heavy Industry	94.69	322.18	305.07
采　　掘	Mining and Quarrying	81.32	648.92	527.70
原　　料	Raw Material	94.09	471.53	443.66
加　　工	Processing	96.36	194.28	187.21
二、按两大部类分	Grouped by Two Sectors			
1.生产资料	Means of Production	94.73	309.75	293.43
采　　掘	Mining and Quarrying	81.32	648.39	527.27
原　　料	Raw Material	93.41	391.96	366.13
加　　工	Processing	96.29	197.44	190.11
2.生活资料	Consumer Goods	98.89	185.72	183.66
食　　品	Foods	99.16	235.79	233.81
衣　　着	Clothing	100.18	182.18	182.51
一般日用品	Daily Use Articles	98.42	174.11	171.36
耐用消费品	Durable Consumer Goods	96.78	68.00	65.81

6-5 原材料、燃料、动力购进价格指数

RAW MATERIAL, FUEL, POWER PURCHASE PRICE INDICES

分类	Group Name	上年=100 preceding year=100	1990年=100 1990=100	
		2009	2008	2009
总指数	General Index	93.38	380.09	354.93
燃料、动力类	Fuel Powers	93.40	567.91	530.43
黑色金属材料类	Ferrous Metal	92.12	335.81	309.35
有色金属材料类	Non-ferrous Metal	83.27	320.29	266.71
化工原材料类	Chemical Materials	86.94	225.61	196.15
木材及纸浆类	Timber and Pulp	91.67	176.41	161.72
建筑材料及非金属矿类	Construction Materials and Non-Metal Mining Industry	95.49	285.25	272.39
其它工业原材料及半成品类	Other Industrial Raw Materials and Semi-Finished Products	97.56	171.22	167.04
农副产品类	Farm and Sideline Products	99.58	334.59	333.18
纺织原料类	Textile Raw Materials	97.20	183.3	178.17

6-6 固定资产投资价格指数

PRICE INDICES OF INVESTMENT IN FIXED ASSETS

分类	Name of Group	上年=100 preceding year=100	1990年=100 1990=100
		2009	2009
总指数	Total Indices	98.8	252.9
建筑安装工程	Construction and Installation	96.8	276.6
设备、工器具	Equipment and Devices	99.0	180.8
其他费用	Others	106.8	299.8

主要统计指标解释

居民消费价格指数 是反映一定时期内城乡居民所购买的生活消费品价格和服务项目价格变动趋势和程度的相对数，是对城市居民消费价格指数和农村居民消费价格指数进行综合汇总计算的结果。该指数可以观察和分析消费品的零售价格和服务价格变动对城乡居民实际生活费支出的影响程度。

城市居民消费价格指数 是反映一定时期内城市居民家庭所购买的生活消费品价格和服务项目价格变动趋势和程度的相对数。该指数可以观察和分析消费品的零售价格和服务项目价格变动对城镇职工货币工资的影响，作为研究职工生活和确定工资政策的依据。

农村居民消费价格指数 是反映一定时期内农村居民家庭所购买的生活消费品价格和服务项目价格变动趋势和程度的相对数。该指数可以观察农村消费品的零售价格和服务项目价格变动对农村居民生活消费支出的影响，直接反映农民生活水平的实际变化情况，为分析和研究农村居民生活问题提供依据。

商品零售价格指数 是反映一定时期内城乡商品零售价格变动趋势和程度的相对数。商品零售价格的变动直接影响到城乡居民的生活支出和国家的财政收入，影响居民购买力和市场供需的平衡，影响到消费与积累的比例关系。因此，该指数可以从一个侧面对上述经济活动进行观察和分析。

农业生产资料价格指数 指反映一定时期内农业生产资料价格变动趋势和程度的相对数。农业生产资料价格指数分为小农具、饲料、产品畜、役畜、半机械化农具、机械化农具、化学肥料、农药及农药械、农机用油、其他农业生产资料十大类。其编制目的是了解农业生产中物质资料投入价格的变动状况，服务于国民经济核算。1994 年以前，农业生产资料价格指数仅仅是商品零售价格指数的一个类别，此后，从商品零售价格指数中分离出来，单独编制。

农产品生产价格指数 是反映一定时期内，农产品生产者出售农产品价格水平变动趋势及幅度的相对数。该指数可以客观反映全国农产品生产价格水平和结构变动情况，满足农业与国民经济核算需要。其中某代表品生产价格指数是通过对全部有出售该产品行为的调查单位的个体指数进行几何平均求得的，类价格指数是通过对其所属的类（或代表品）的价格指数进行加权平均求得的。季度累计价格指数的计算方法与分季指数的计算方法相同。

工业品出厂价格指数 是反映一定时期内全部工业产品出厂价格总水平的变动趋势和程度的相对数，包括工业企业售给本企业以外所有单位的各种产品和直接售给居民用于生活消费的产品。该指数可以观察出厂价格变动对工业总产值及增加值的影响。

原材料、燃料和动力购进价格指数 是反映工业企业作为生产投入，而从物资交易市场和能源、原材料生产企业购买原材料、燃料和动力产品时，所支付的价格水平变动趋势和程度的统计指标，是扣除工业企业物质消耗成本中的价格变动影响的重要依据。

目前，我国编制的原材料、燃料和动力购进价格指数所调查的产品包括燃料动力、黑色金属、有色金属、化工、建材等九大类的近 1800 种产品。

固定资产投资价格指数 是反映一定时期内固定资产投资品及项目的价格变动趋势和程度的相对数。固定资产投资额是由建筑安装工程投资完成额、设备工器具购置投资完成额和其他费用投资完成额三部分组成的。编制固定资产投资价格指数应首先分别编制上述三部分投资的价格指数，然后采用加权算术平均法求出固定资产投资价格总指数。

该指数可以准确地反映固定资产投资中涉及的各类投资品和取费项目价格变动趋势和变动幅度，消除按现价计算的固定资产投资指标中的价格变动因素，真实地反映固定资产投资的规模、速度、结构和效益，为国家科学地制定、检查固定资产投资计划并提高宏观调控水平，为完善国民经济核算体系提供科学的、可靠的依据。

房地产价格指数 是反映一定时期内房地产价格变动趋势和程度的相对数，包括房屋销售价格指数、房屋租赁价格指数、土地交易价格指数和物业管理价格指数。这四套指数的计算方法相似，均采用由下到上逐级汇总的方法。

Explanatory Notes on Main Statistical Indicators

Urban Consumer Price Indices reflect the trend and degree of changes in prices of consumer goods and services purchased by urban households during a given period. It can be used to observe and analyze the impact of price changes in consumer goods and services on wages (in monetary terms) of urban staff and workers, and provide basis for policy-making concerning the living cost and wages of staff and workers.

Rural Consumer Price Indices reflect the trend and degree of changes in prices of consumer goods and services purchased by rural households during a given period. It can be used to observe the impact of change in retail prices of consumer goods and service prices in rural areas on living expenditure of rural households, and to show the changes in the living standard of peasants. It provides basis for analysis and research on condition of life in rural areas.

Retail Price Indices reflect the trend and degree of change in retail prices of commodities during a given period. The change in retail prices of commodities directly affect the living expenditure of urban and rural residents, government revenue, purchasing power of residents and the equilibrium of market supply and demand, and the ratio of consumption to accumulation. Therefore, the retail price indices are useful to analyze the changes of the above economic activities.

Price Indices of Means of Agricultural Production reflect the trend and degree of changes in prices of means of agricultural production during a given period. Price indices of means of agricultural production are composed of 10 categories including small farm tools, feeds, domestic animals for meat, draught domestic animals, semi-mechanized farm machinery, mechanized farm machinery, chemical fertilizers, pesticides and spraying machinery, fuels for farm machinery and other means of agricultural production. Compilation of these indices helps to understand the changes in prices of input into agricultural production and facilitate the compilation of national account statistics. Before 1994, price indices of means of agricultural production was a sub-category in the in the retail price indices of commodities, and it has been compiled separately since 1994.

Indices of Producers' Prices for Farm Products reflect the trend and degree of changes in producers' prices received by farmers when they sell farm products during a given period. These indices depict the change in the level and structure of producers' prices of farm products of the country and meet the needs of agriculture statistics and national account statistics. The producers' price index of a given product is calculated through geometrical mean of individual indices of all surveyed units who sell such product, and the indices of a product category is obtained through weighted mean of price indices of all products in the category. Method for calculating accumulative quarterly indices is the same as for calculating the distinctive quarterly indices.

Ex-factory Price Indices of Industrial Products reflect the trend and degree of changes in general ex-factory prices of all industrial products during a given period, including sales of industrial products by an industrial enterprise to all units outside the enterprise, as well as sales of consumer goods to residents. It can be used to analyze the impact of ex-factory prices on gross output value and value-added of the industrial sector.

Indices of Purchasing Prices of Raw Materials, Fuels and Power reflect changes in the level and degree of prices paid by industrial enterprises when they purchase production input such as raw materials, fuels and power from the market or from other energy or raw materials producing enterprises. These indices provide important basis for measuring the material consumption of industrial enterprises after removing influence of price changes.

At present, close to 1,800 products in 9 categories, including fuels and power, ferrous metals, non-ferrous metals, chemicals, building materials, are covered in China for the survey to produce indices of purchasing prices of raw materials, fuels and power.

Price Indices of Investment in Fixed Assets reflect the trend and degree of changes in prices of investment goods and projects in fixed assets during a given period. The investment in fixed assets consists of three components, namely the investment in construction and installation, the investment in purchases of equipment and instrument, and the investment in other items. Price indices of investment in fixed assets are calculated as the weighted arithmetic mean of the price indices of the three components of investment in fixed assets.

Removing the factor of price change in the aggregates of investment at current prices, this indicator shows the changes in the prices of commodities and fees involved in the investment of fixed assets, and can be used to observe the actual size, growth, structure, and efficiency of investment in fixed assets and provides reliable and scientific data for government planning, management, decision-making, and further improving the current national accounting system.

Price Indices for Real Estate reflect the trend and degree of changes in prices of real estate during a given period, including price indices for selling houses and buildings, price indices for leasing houses and buildings and price indices for land transaction. The methods for the compilation of the three sets of indices are similar in that they all use bottom-up approach under which data are reported from lower level to higher level.

7 农业 Agriculture

资料整理：周克莉

7-1 农村基层组织和农业基本情况

BASIC CONDITIONS OF RURAL GRASSROOTS UNITS AND AGRICULTURE

指　标	Item	1990	1995	2000	2005	2008	2009
农村组织情况　（个）	**Rural Units (unit)**						
乡个数	Township	1121	1040	476	217	207	204
镇个数	Town Governments	844	861	853	737	735	740
村委会个数	Village Committees	3275	32802	32400	26678	26101	26051
村民小组个数	Villager Group	260847	260641	259250	212587	209737	209806
乡村户数、人口	**Rural Households,Population**						
乡村户数　（万户）	Rural Households (10 000 units)	1005.32	1004.21	983.94	1015.72	1038.20	1044.56
乡村人口　（万人）	Rural Population (10 000 persons)	4110.59	4041.67	3947.26	3991.47	4021.05	4008.06
乡村从业人员　（万人）	**Rural Employment (10 000 persons)**	**1791.30**	**1810.44**	**1781.70**	**1931.15**	**2078.77**	**2123.29**
按性别分	Grouped by Sex						
男	Male	944.72	955.74	937.67	1026.48	1105.78	1139.68
女	Female	846.58	854.70	844.03	904.67	972.99	983.61
按行业分	Grouped by Sector						
农林牧渔业	Farming, Forestry, Animal husbandary and Fishery	1453.96	1329.18	1159.13	1101.29	995.76	965.73
工业	Industry	112.29	130.91	116.12	122.41	247.57	301.62
建筑业	Construction	55.33	82.82	104.08	128.43	187.59	211.01
交通运输、仓储业和邮电通讯业	Transportation, Storage, Post and Telecommunication	24.20	35.60	44.61	45.93	58.06	62.30
#仓储及邮电通讯业	Storage, Post and Telecommunication				3.08	5.06	5.45
信息传输，计算机服务和软件业	Information Trnsmmision, Computer Service and Software				2.81	5.05	7.01
批发，零售贸易业	Wholesale and Retail Sales	29.53	55.61	72.07	70.42	92.68	99.81
住宿和餐饮业	Hotel and Food Service				24.69	48.12	52.01
其他非农行业	Other Non- Agriculture Business	115.99	176.32	285.69	432.09	438.88	418.35
国营农林牧渔场从业人员　（万人）	Employees in State-run Agriculture, fores animal husbandry, fishery Farm (10 000 persons)	64.24	59.05	54.94	55.73	56.37	55.68
农业从业人员	Agriculture Employees	38.71	35.59	34.08	35.27	35.92	34.18
非农业从业人员	Non-agriculture Employees	25.53	23.46	20.86	20.46	20.45	21.50
年末实有耕地面积　（千公顷）	**Cultivated Areas (Year-End) (1 000 hectares)**	**3476.77**	**3358.01**	**3282.96**	**3161.17**	**3289.33**	**3308.35**
农业机械总动力　（万千瓦）	Total Agricultural Machinery Power (10 000 kW)	1099.62	1174.34	1414.00	2057.37	2796.99	3057.24
化肥施用量　（万吨）	Consumption of Chemical Fertilizers (10 000 tons)	148.61	228.41	247.08	285.83	327.66	340.26
农村用电量　（亿千瓦小时）	Electricity Consumed in Rural Areas (100 million kWh)	27.21	47.36	60.86	70.09	98.06	104.27
农作物总播种面积　（千公顷）	Total Sown Area (1 000 hectares)	7361.14	7413.71	7584.07	7391.30	7272.33	7527.50
#粮食	Grain Crops	5200.01	4776.65	4156.20	4068.15	3906.69	4012.53
主要农产品产量　（万吨）	**Volume of Major Agricultural Products (10 000 tons)**						
粮食	Grain Crops	2475.03	2463.84	2218.49	2177.38	2227.23	2309.10
棉花	Cotton Crops	51.73	58.60	30.43	37.50	51.30	48.05
油料	Oil-Bearing Crops	95.75	189.44	269.98	293.90	283.56	314.05
肉类产量	Output of Meat	146.83	279.40	271.19	342.63	340.84	367.89
水产品产量	Output of Aquatic Products	70.98	150.91	234.34	318.21	361.90	333.90

注:主要生产品产量2006、2007年数据按农业普查数据进行衔接、调整。
Note:Statistics of output of major farm products of 2006,2007 is adusted according to Second Agriculture Survey.

7–2 主要年份耕地面积

AREAS UNDER CULTIVATION OF THE MAJOR YEARS

单位：千公顷 (1 000 hectares)

年 份 Year	年末实有耕地面积 Cultivated Areas (Year-End)	水 田 Paddy Fields	旱 地 Dry Fields	年内减少 Dereased in Cultivated Areas in This Year	#国家基建占地 Capital Construction	人均占有耕地(公顷) Per Capita Cultivated Area (sq.m) 按乡村人口计算 By Rural Population	按农林牧渔业劳动力计算 By Farming, Forestry, Animal husbandry and Fishery Laborers
1949	2742.58	1765.11	1977.47			0.12	0.29
1952	4015.90	1876.62	2139.28			0.16	0.39
1957	4172.31	1945.05	2227.26			0.16	0.37
1962	4271.33	1847.19	2424.56			0.15	0.39
1965	4239.93	1966.38	2273.55			0.14	0.37
1970	3964.01	1982.20	1981.81			0.11	0.31
1975	3823.00	1996.10	1826.77	54.10		0.10	0.28
1976	3797.21	1991.34	1805.87	58.95			
1977	3779.89	1983.44	1796.45	34.37			
1978	3768.07	1959.63	1808.43	30.77	7.75	0.10	0.28
1979	3754.51	1940.27	1814.24	29.13	5.50	0.10	0.27
1980	3738.51	1929.50	1809.01	35.82	4.69	0.10	0.27
1981	3730.20	1924.66	1805.73	23.64	3.23	0.09	0.26
1982	3718.20	1916.53	1801.67	22.53	2.68	0.09	0.26
1983	3698.74	1907.51	1791.23	28.83	4.93	0.09	0.25
1984	3643.68	1892.89	1750.79	65.23	8.18	0.09	0.25
1985	3584.61	1864.15	1720.46	71.70	8.56	0.09	0.27
1986	3545.00	1847.63	1697.37	49.30	7.30	0.09	0.27
1987	3517.99	1845.17	1672.82	36.16	7.13	0.09	0.26
1988	3498.47	1838.37	1660.10	25.98	4.55	0.09	0.25
1989	3486.57	1858.25	1628.33	17.47	1.83	0.09	0.25
1990	3476.77	1871.77	1605.00	15.60	2.73	0.08	0.24
1991	3458.46	1869.19	1589.27	24.11	4.03	0.08	0.24
1992	3421.57	1845.31	1576.26	41.67	4.95	0.08	0.24
1993	3392.74	1815.75	1576.99	32.84	6.11	0.08	0.24
1994	3375.60	1805.42	1570.18	21.21	3.77	0.08	0.24
1995	3358.01	1780.40	1577.61	21.36	4.23	0.08	0.25
1996	3349.25	1800.00	1549.25	13.80	2.85	0.08	0.26
1997	3342.45	1796.07	1546.38	12.24	2.43	0.08	0.26
1998	3327.16	1788.95	1538.21	19.95	3.83	0.08	0.27
1999	3310.40	1786.34	1524.06	23.08	5.13	0.08	0.27
2000	3282.96	1757.63	1525.33	34.15	5.18	0.08	0.28
2001	3242.85	1742.69	1500.16	46.26	7.76	0.08	0.27
2002	3094.03	1708.58	1385.45	110.10	12.04	0.08	0.27
2003	3033.45	1665.49	1367.96	181.18	7.51	0.08	0.27
2004	3091.75	1789.10	1302.65	39.81	5.36	0.08	0.28
2005	3131.17	1856.17	1305.00	40.70	4.93	0.08	0.28
2006	3201.66	1881.74	1319.92	20.65	5.49	0.08	0.29
2007	3226.62	1890.04	1336.58	21.08	5.67	0.08	0.31
2008	3289.33	1914.07	1375.26	10.68	4.29	0.08	0.33
2009	3308.35	1928.67	1379.68	15.06	5.61	0.08	0.34

注：1996年及以后为农业普查接轨数(下同)。

Notes:Since 1996,the relative targers were in line with the data of agricultural gereral survey (the same as the following tables).

7-3　主要年份农林牧渔业总产值

GROSS OUTPUT VALUE OF FARMING, FORESTRY, ANIMAL HUSBANDRY AND FISHERY

单位：亿元　　当年价格　　(At current price, 100 million yuan)

年　份 Year	农林牧渔业总产值 Gross Output Value of FFAF	农业 Farming	林业 Foresty	畜牧业 Animal Husbandry	渔业 Fishery	农林牧渔服务业 Service Industry for Farming, Forestry, Animal husbandry and Fishery
1949	10.72	7.22	0.69	0.97	0.10	
1952	16.59	12.08	0.79	1.48	0.18	
1957	28.59	20.55	1.46	3.81	0.46	
1962	33.66	26.52	1.71	3.61	0.46	
1965	47.48	37.44	1.98	6.02	0.51	
1970	51.27	40.62	2.07	6.41	0.92	
1975	74.68					
1976	78.87					
1977	78.68					
1978	84.46					
1979	109.85					
1980	94.95	64.70	7.28	17.29	1.46	
1981	111.68	82.78	6.47	14.88	1.61	
1982	128.35	95.32	7.24	17.97	2.12	
1983	134.09	97.53	7.29	20.05	2.96	
1984	169.20	123.09	7.54	26.51	4.79	
1985	192.32	129.61	8.15	39.08	8.18	
1986	219.10	146.79	8.75	43.86	10.77	
1987	249.68	160.13	9.97	54.86	14.19	
1988	297.51	175.12	10.98	80.80	18.83	
1989	335.04	198.56	11.75	91.47	20.66	
1990	402.23	252.92	14.15	98.04	23.88	
1991	405.04	247.01	16.81	102.19	25.06	
1992	435.42	265.53	17.36	110.37	27.59	
1993	501.17	301.99	22.39	134.02	42.77	
1994	786.84	481.82	26.47	219.53	59.01	
1995	988.53	612.12	28.33	268.09	79.98	
1996	1140.76	670.27	33.62	337.02	99.86	
1997	1243.68	711.91	37.33	381.40	113.04	
1998	1222.58	688.06	41.29	371.37	121.86	
1999	1126.10	645.98	40.86	311.43	127.83	
2000	1125.64	615.74	40.24	338.77	130.89	
2001	1172.82	658.26	27.11	352.63	134.82	
2002	1203.30	671.20	28.33	354.84	148.93	
2003	1342.09	733.36	34.78	383.71	170.43	
2004	1695.44	921.59	31.78	514.52	205.68	21.87
2005	1775.58	932.15	37.30	545.40	236.49	24.24
2006	1842.20	995.46	40.50	487.09	221.42	97.73
2007	2296.84	1152.09	41.86	686.19	310.83	105.87
2008	2940.47	1395.76	49.69	1008.65	372.98	113.39
2009	2985.19	1511.49	57.67	881.78	413.14	121.11

7-4 农、林、牧、渔业总产值指数

INDICES OF GROSS OUTPUT VALUE OF FARMING, FORESTRY, ANIMAL HUSBANDRY AND FISHERY

单位：% 上年=100(preceding year=100) (%)

年 份 Year	合 计 Total	农 业 Farming	林 业 Forestry	畜牧业 Animal Husbandry	渔 业 Fishery	农林牧渔服务业 Service Industry for Farming, Forestry, Animal husbandry and Fishery
1978	104.00	103.10	104.90	107.60	94.20	
1980	88.80	83.70	102.80	108.10	111.30	
1985	106.30	101.70	103.00	127.80	133.30	
1986	103.40	100.60	98.50	107.30	129.80	
1987	102.70	101.20	104.50	101.00	120.10	
1988	97.20	93.90	90.60	105.40	105.60	
1989	105.00	104.50	101.60	105.20	108.30	
1990	107.10	108.40	106.00	104.90	106.70	
1991	100.70	97.66	118.80	104.23	104.94	
1992	107.50	107.50	103.27	108.00	110.10	
1993	115.10	113.73	128.97	121.43	155.02	
1994	157.00	159.55	118.27	163.80	137.93	
1995	125.63	127.04	106.99	122.12	135.54	
1996	115.40	109.50	118.67	125.71	124.87	
1997	109.02	106.21	111.04	113.17	113.20	
1998	98.30	96.65	110.61	97.37	107.80	
1999	92.11	93.88	98.95	83.86	104.90	
2000	99.96	95.32	98.48	108.78	102.39	
2001	104.19	106.91	67.37	104.09	103.00	
2002	102.60	101.97	104.50	100.63	110.47	
2003	111.53	109.26	122.77	108.14	114.44	
2004	126.33	125.67	91.37	134.09	120.68	
2005	104.73	101.15	117.37	106.00	114.98	110.84
2006	105.37	109.29	108.58	96.04	109.87	116.05
2007	124.68	115.73	103.36	140.88	140.38	108.33
2008	128.02	121.15	118.17	146.99	119.99	107.10
2009	101.52	108.29	116.10	87.42	110.77	106.81

7-5 农、林、牧、渔业增加值（2009）

VALUE ADDED OF FARMING, FORESTRY, ANIMAL HUSBANDRY AND FISHERY(2009)

单位：亿元 (100 million yuan)

项 目	Item	合 计 Total	农 业 Farming	林 业 Forestry	牧 业 Animal Husbandry	渔 业 Fishery	农林牧渔服务业 Service Industry for Farming, Forestry,Animal husbandry and Fishery
一、总产值(现价)	Gross Output Value(current price)	2985.19	1511.49	57.67	881.78	413.14	121.11
二、中间消耗	Intermedium-Consumption	1196.97	562.95	22.79	415.06	177.31	18.86
三、增加值	Value-Added	1709.50	862.79	32.71	523.84	264.17	25.99

7-6 农、林、牧、渔业总产值指数

INDICES OF GROSS OUTPUT VALUE OF FARMING, FORESTRY, ANIMAL HUSBANDRY AND FISHERY

单位：% 1978年=100(year 1978 =100) (%)

年 份 Year	合 计 Total	农 业 Farming	林 业 Forestry	牧 业 Animal Husbandry	渔 业 Fishery
1978	100.0	100.0	100.0	100.0	100.0
1979	109.6	109.2	101.8	118.8	109.2
1980	97.3	91.4	104.7	127.9	121.5
1981	108.2	102.4	95.4	138.2	134.1
1982	122.6	116.5	104.1	135.6	156.8
1983	122.7	115.9	105.3	160.5	181.2
1984	148.4	140.0	110.6	164.7	254.0
1985	157.7	142.4	114.0	206.2	338.6
1986	163.1	143.3	112.3	263.5	439.5
1987	167.5	145.0	117.3	282.7	527.8
1988	162.9	136.1	106.3	285.5	557.3
1989	171.0	142.3	108.0	301.0	603.6
1990	183.1	154.2	114.5	315.7	644.0
1991	181.7	147.7	125.9	334.0	631.8
1992	194.4	158.7	120.1	360.7	689.3
1993	207.4	168.0	129.5	410.9	936.1
1994	227.8	175.0	152.0	461.7	1203.0
1995	259.9	195.3	156.0	535.1	1530.2
1996	277.6	198.0	168.5	611.1	1732.0
1997	304.0	213.4	179.3	671.6	2007.4
1998	307.3	209.1	204.6	682.3	2164.0
1999	309.5	220.2	196.7	627.9	2270.0
2000	318.1	226.3	194.2	650.4	2324.5
2001	327.6	238.7	141.6	669.6	2382.4
2002	334.2	233.1	145.9	700.2	2677.3
2003	351.8	237.2	167.2	730.8	2824.4
2004	374.7	257.9	153.9	760.8	2979.6
2005	392.4	260.9	180.6	806.4	3425.9
2006	413.5	285.1	196.1	774.5	3764.0
2007	512.7	323.2	202.7	1121.9	4792.7
2008	656.4	392.7	240.6	1649.1	5750.8
2009	666.4	425.3	279.3	1441.6	6370.2

7-7 农作物播种面积

单位：千公顷

年 份 Year	总播种面积 Total Sown Areas	粮食作物 Grain Crops	#小麦 Wheat	#稻谷 Rice	#薯类 Tubers	#玉米 Corn	#大豆 Soybean	经济作物 Economic Crops
1978	7931.05	5544.78	1122.28	2894.63	427.23	403.14	173.43	971.53
1980	7477.06	5352.04	1292.29	2708.22	387.46	406.91	138.94	977.58
1985	7331.71	5108.25	1331.42	2538.57	354.01	374.17	134.64	1280.89
1989	7260.95	5188.95	1341.32	2606.39	389.15	389.03	110.50	1248.15
1990	7361.14	5200.01	1352.10	2636.47	391.90	386.11	164.65	1343.23
1991	7423.92	5194.50	1347.53	2622.79	402.38	395.19	150.61	1414.37
1992	7183.83	4955.35	1287.91	2537.49	392.59	376.18	140.23	1405.87
1993	7125.47	4812.05	1271.23	2377.82	384.33	365.96	181.69	1381.64
1994	7181.43	4797.95	1225.60	2373.26	203.39	373.02	201.52	1456.00
1995	7431.71	4776.65	1179.93	2408.66	397.65	393.77	188.01	1683.56
1996	7579.01	4880.28	1230.14	2448.58	419.53	405.07	174.71	1676.71
1997	7739.21	4944.66	1276.52	2467.51	415.74	400.30	182.51	1689.03
1998	7695.98	4737.15	1212.08	2244.74	431.02	442.84	201.32	1703.80
1999	7788.66	4673.11	1074.43	2284.98	448.72	460.82	207.01	1739.07
2000	7584.07	4156.20	845.10	1995.29	467.61	424.10	224.75	1984.76
2001	7488.99	4015.73	735.85	1953.77	237.75	401.11	218.01	1972.36
2002	7281.61	3816.08	679.02	1888.75	430.61	384.04	217.82	1981.04
2003	7153.24	3572.74	603.43	1808.75	208.56	349.81	196.47	2083.26
2004	7225.13	3817.89	605.08	2084.02	403.79	357.49	186.05	2079.51
2005	7391.30	4068.05	730.61	2162.39	397.75	428.79	179.79	1974.56
2006	7100.59	3902.27	1016.93	1975.07	218.67	431.93	118.40	1825.40
2007	7130.01	3981.43	1096.25	1978.82	219.19	436.34	114.75	1787.79
2008	7272.33	3906.69	1000.57	1978.94	216.09	470.37	206.79	1973.85
2009	7527.50	4012.53	993.36	2045.08	237.93	507.28	195.76	2018.78

注:2006、2007年度农业普查衔接数据。

TOTAL SOWN AREAS OF FARM CROPS

(1 000 hectares)

#棉花 Cotton	#油菜籽 Rape-Seed	#花生 Peanuts	#芝麻 Sesame	#黄红麻 Jute and Ambary	#甘蔗 Sugar-cane	#甜菜 Beet-Roots	#烤烟 Flue-Cured Tobacco	其他作物 Others
593.19	165.27	34.14	102.71	8.39	2.31	0.13	24.75	1414.73
591.67	175.75	40.76	113.51	12.17	1.49	0.12	9.69	1147.44
464.97	361.42	65.94	173.31	94.17	7.85	0.08	37.67	942.56
418.46	452.16	65.74	138.84	30.92	8.48		52.17	823.85
455.92	744.31	63.75	126.85	27.33	8.07	0.01	46.35	817.90
461.55	610.10	61.59	128.17	20.42	8.47	0.02	56.83	815.05
507.19	534.41	64.73	126.32	18.15	10.64	0.02	72.76	822.61
486.06	522.14	79.70	127.24	22.41	15.00	0.03	64.32	931.78
497.58	615.87	86.97	114.77	11.70	15.73		38.69	927.48
502.03	838.82	91.91	110.04	10.83	15.97	0.03	41.16	953.50
474.38	855.26	90.82	107.72	8.59	16.59		51.92	1022.02
480.56	829.80	95.20	107.35	10.10	18.00		70.99	1105.52
431.58	887.01	121.48	113.62	7.94	19.97		48.47	1255.03
310.70	1003.64	143.87	127.14	4.30	23.34		48.32	1376.48
318.07	1158.94	193.42	143.82	3.14	22.17		48.10	1443.11
346.65	1118.06	210.06	129.93	2.65	18.88		40.43	1500.90
286.37	1155.25	206.04	138.88	5.13	19.18		42.90	1484.49
355.02	1174.63	201.11	124.00	2.97	17.24		39.45	1497.24
408.30	1186.10	173.03	111.20	1.36	10.01		39.94	1327.73
360.95	1178.65	171.71	102.52	0.98	9.95		43.68	1348.69
496.40	1001.20	140.10	97.24	0.69	3.70		32.13	1372.92
514.22	927.10	137.80	94.67	0.59	3.60		32.70	1360.79
542.96	1089.61	142.26	92.18	0.50	6.62		46.78	1391.79
460.08	1165.88	183.73	99.64	0.35	10.35		55.87	1496.19

Note:Statistics of 2006 and 2007 are linkage data of Second Agricluture Survey.

7–8 主要农作物播种面积和产量（2009）

TOTAL SOWN AREAS AND OUTPUT OF FARM CROPS(2009)

指　标	Item	播种面积(千公顷) Sown Areas (1 000 hectares)	总产量(吨) Total Output(ton)
农作物总播种面积	**Total Sown Areas of Farm Crops**	**7527.50**	
粮食作物总计	**Total Grain**	**4012.53**	**23091000**
夏粮	Summer Grain	1227.25	3985400
小麦	Wheat	993.36	3316700
大麦	Barley	28.63	106200
蚕豌豆	Broad and Dea Bean	66.28	146700
秋粮	Autumn Grain	2785.28	19105600
稻谷	Rice	2045.08	15919200
#中稻	#Semilate Rice	1271.44	11327600
双季晚稻	Late Double- crop Rice	416.26	2508400
#　稻	#Long-grained Nonglutinous Rice	1653.92	13299200
薯类	Tubers	237.93	848100
玉米	Corn	507.28	2441200
高粱	Sorghum	3.16	12900
粟谷	Millet Grain	0.10	100
其他秋粮	Others	0.46	800
大豆	Soybeans	105.37	255900
杂豆	Miscellaneous Beans	24.11	41900
#绿豆	#Green Beans	17.96	37800
经济作物	**Economic Crops**		
棉花	Cotton	460.08	480530
油料	Oil-Bearing Crops	1455.04	3140500
#花生	#Peanuts	183.73	626187
油菜籽	Rapeseed	1165.88	2365100
芝麻	Sesame	99.64	142100
麻类	Hemp Crops	18.72	38232
#黄麻	#Jute	0.35	1418
麻	Ramie	18.37	36814
糖类	Sugar Crops	10.35	344270
#甘蔗	#Sugarcane	10.35	344270
烟叶	Tobacco Crops	74.59	152069
药材	Crude Drugs	86.23	
花卉园艺	**Flower Gardening**	6.89	
其他农作物	**Others**	**1403.07**	**33045239**
#蔬菜(含菜用瓜)	#Vegetable	1079.25	29795700
瓜果类	Melon and Fruits	96.67	3249539
绿肥	Organic Fertilizer	95.14	

7-9 主要农产品产量

OUTPUT OF MAJOR FARM CROPS

单位：万吨 (10 000 ton)

年 份 Year	粮 食 Grain	夏 粮 Summer Grain	秋 粮 Autumn Grain	棉 花 Cotton	油 料 Oil Bearing Crops	#花 生 Peanuts	#油菜籽 Rapeseed
1949	578.13	101.85	476.28	5.74	13.37	3.17	4.12
1952	747.54	148.81	598.73	12.17	22.34	4.56	7.09
1957	986.08	180.87	805.21	21.02	25.26	11.23	4.86
1962	960.41	246.34	714.07	14.22	18.30	3.81	4.29
1965	1241.34	255.01	986.33	38.29	22.32	5.15	6.76
1970	1268.67	187.06	1081.62	29.64	14.93	4.82	3.94
1975	1561.51	230.10	1331.41	40.61	21.44	5.12	10.65
1978	1725.60	315.04	1410.56	36.67	23.71	4.90	10.72
1980	1536.43	341.32	1195.11	31.63	20.58	5.85	11.59
1985	2216.13	429.58	1786.56	49.22	72.98	13.52	41.14
1989	2370.39	455.26	1915.13	31.28	76.71	14.18	52.56
1990	2475.03	474.96	2000.07	51.73	95.75	12.79	70.90
1991	2244.10	476.20	1767.90	49.11	106.29	11.44	83.75
1992	2426.60	450.90	2022.83	60.99	99.74	15.72	70.86
1993	2325.70	471.87	1853.85	42.50	111.74	20.68	78.35
1994	2422.10	472.70	1949.40	45.00	137.77	24.81	98.07
1995	2463.84	447.20	2016.64	58.60	189.44	27.28	146.24
1996	2484.40	465.24	2019.16	43.01	181.82	30.77	134.88
1997	2634.40	542.60	2091.80	58.09	195.47	31.24	147.53
1998	2475.79	501.69	1974.10	32.50	216.69	42.87	154.76
1999	2451.88	392.71	2059.17	28.15	228.27	48.15	159.97
2000	2218.49	322.39	1896.10	30.43	269.98	53.46	192.40
2001	2138.49	319.14	1819.35	37.35	279.45	63.99	194.79
2002	2047.00	232.27	1841.73	32.26	245.29	72.25	151.40
2003	1921.02	255.65	1665.37	32.50	272.72	68.37	187.10
2004	2100.12	271.24	1828.96	39.54	314.38	63.19	235.12
2005	2177.38	302.49	1874.89	37.50	293.90	60.19	219.15
2006	2099.10	369.08	1730.02	55.20	254.45	48.40	191.83
2007	2185.44	406.44	1779.00	55.73	254.75	48.60	193.30
2008	2227.23	386.24	1840.99	51.30	283.56	49.41	214.89
2009	2309.10	398.45	1910.65	48.05	314.05	62.62	236.51

注：2006、2007年为农业普查衔接数据。
Note:Statistics 2006 and 2007 are linkage data of Second Agriculture Survey.

7-10 人均占有主要农产品产量

PER CAPITA OUTPUT OF MAJOR FARM PRODUCTS

单位：千克/人 (kg/person)

年 份 Year	粮 食 Grain	棉 花 Cotton	油 料 Oil Bearing Crops	猪、牛、羊肉 Output of Pork, Beef and Mutton	水产品 Output of Aquatic Products
1952	275	4.5	8.2		2.9
1957	327	7.0	8.4		4.0
1962	302	4.4	5.8		2.3
1965	359	11.1	6.4		3.3
1970	319	7.5	3.8		2.8
1975	357	9.3	4.9		2.6
1978	379	8.1	5.2		2.4
1980	330	6.8	4.4	11.9	2.9
1985	452	10.0	14.9	20.7	7.6
1989	457	6.0	14.8	26.9	12.8
1990	467	9.8	18.1	27.7	13.4
1991	415	8.9	19.6	29.0	12.9
1992	443	11.1	18.2	31.9	14.9
1993	416	7.6	20.0	35.3	18.1
1994	431	8.0	24.5	41.8	23.0
1995	429	10.2	33.0	48.6	26.3
1996	428	7.4	31.4	40.4	30.1
1997	450	9.9	33.4	44.4	34.6
1998	419	5.5	36.7	44.2	37.0
1999	413	5.0	38.4	44.8	38.6
2000	372	5.1	45.3	45.5	39.3
2001	358	6.3	46.8	48.3	40.5
2002	342	5.4	41.0	49.4	45.4
2003	316	6.5	45.5	51.4	47.8
2004	349	6.6	52.3	54.1	50.2
2005	361	6.2	48.7	56.8	52.8
2006	365	7.4	46.2	42.0	46.7
2007	360	9.2	42.0	42.5	49.1
2008	390	9.0	49.7	49.8	54.9
2009	404	8.4	54.9	64.2	59.1

7-11 蚕、茶、果生产情况

STATISTICS ON SILKWORM COCOONS, TEA AND FRUITS

指 标	Item	1990	1995	2000	2005	2008	2009
蚕茧产量 (万吨)	Silkworm Cocoons (10 000 tons)	0.79	2.24	1.22	1.07	1.25	0.61
茶叶产量 (万吨)	Tea (10 000 tons)	2.84	3.90	6.37	8.50	13.03	14.42
红毛茶	Red Tea	1.52	0.12		0.65	1.09	1.18
绿毛茶	Green Tea	0.55	3.05	5.15	6.72	10.71	11.99
其他茶	Others				0.18	0.22	0.23
园林水果产量 (万吨)	Garden fruit production (10 000 tons)	26.89	114.70	215.68	260.79	377.66	402.15
#苹果	#Apples	1.20	3.21	3.02	1.24	0.89	1.14
柑桔	Citrus	13.08	58.14	94.62	146.26	255.51	274.70
梨	Pears	5.98	26.02		46.80	47.00	46.84
葡萄	Grapes				4.97	33.00	11.12
桃子	Peaches	2.50	14.59	30.87	46.88	51.06	55.66
猕桃	Kiwi fruit				0.85	0.93	0.79
红枣	Dates				2.02	2.27	2.50
柿子	Persimmons				4.77	5.45	5.30
桑园面积 (千公顷)	Area of Mulberry Plantations (1 000 hectares)	14.83					
茶园面积 (千公顷)	Area of Tea Plantations (1 000 hectares)	76.38	113.39	121.02	138.43	184.37	206.41
#当年采摘面积	#Pick Area		7.42		101.62	133.97	149.09
果园 (千公顷)	Area of Orchards (1 000 hectares)	118.04	199.80	233.93	265.05	347.45	367.60
#苹果园	#Apples	6.58	13.66	8.98	3.30	3.34	2.22
柑桔园	Citrus	85.64	98.39	99.13	143.15	211.08	225.63
梨园	Pears	13.96	35.42	33.49	35.90	35.42	38.23
葡萄园	Grapes				4.77	5.85	6.24

7-12 林业生产情况
STATISTICS ON FORESTRY

单位：千公顷 (1 000 hectares)

指　标	Item	1990	1995	2000	2005	2008	2009
造林面积	Build Forestry Areas	221.17	271.63	196.93	186.37	151.35	160.32
用材林	Material Forests	155.13	99.33	75.18	79.47	78.36	79.35
经济林	Economic Forests	34.29	136.69	87.00	39.84	45.79	45.54
防护林	Windbreak Forests	24.09	21.67	28.20	58.72	23.44	35.24
薪炭林	Firewood Forests	5.06	13.72	6.15	6.82	2.72	3.16
特种用途林	Forests for Soecial Puppse	2.60	0.23	0.40	1.53	1.05	1.32
四旁植树(万株)	Planting (10 000 units)	17981.00	27899.00	29934.00	18661.00	18772.87	17859.32
迹地更新面积	Slash Updateing Areas	15.95	29.75	51.29	21.11	22.24	19.21
育苗面积	Raise Seedlings Areas	6.53	7.48	10.82	13.15	11.67	13.45
幼林抚育作业面积	Young Growth Works Areas	264.55	444.75	341.82	405.90	393.91	391.15
成林抚育实际面积	Adult Growth Actual Areas	140.14	353.16	474.31	383.95	403.20	431.73
主要林产品产量（吨）	Output of Forestry Products (ton)						
油桐籽	Tung-Oil Seeds	10623	21507	19418.00	15353	14454	16330
油茶籽	Tea-oil Seeds	23123	13247	17343.00	14337	32831	43920
乌桕子	Tallow Seeds	20704	16190	18145.00	8999	7538	9272
棕　片	palm pieces	2691	3091	4283.00	2193	2259	2423
松　脂	Turpentine	390	1245	3675.00	5251	5247	4479
竹笋干	Bamboo Shoots	253	586	1364.00	2746	4774	4983
板　栗	Chestnut	9388	29005	70818.00	86914	125194	153786
香　菇	Mushroom		10371	20291.00	24620	42852	48927
黑木耳	Jew's-ear	1260	1372	1528.00	12611	15374	14951
白木耳	White Fungus	122	40	147.00	75	142	41
木材采伐量(万立方米)	Output of Timber Cut (10 000 cu.m)	104.90	112.80	116.85	136.00	177.61	169.35
竹材采伐量（万根）	Output of Bamboo Cut (10 000 cu.m)	1237.00	24804.00	26282.00	3609.00	19895.10	22567.50

7-13 畜牧业生产情况
STATISTICS ON LIVESTOCK

指 标		Item		1990	1995	2000	2005	2008	2009
牲畜年末存栏头数	**（万头）**		**(10 000 heads)**						
大牲畜		Large Animals		356.64	413.86	431.50	384.32	319.12	335.56
牛		Cattles and Buffalloes		351.50	409.45	428.38	382.14	317.50	334.01
#良种及改良乳牛		Fine Improved Variety Cows		2.23	2.20		4.69	7.05	5.86
马		Horses		2.56	2.52	1.83	1.58	0.97	0.91
驴		Donkeys		2.28	1.60	0.98	0.44	0.49	0.52
骡		Mules		0.30	0.29	0.30	0.16	0.16	0.12
猪		Hogs		2063.55	2449.11	2132.79	2289.05	2462.40	2546.10
羊	（万只）	Sheep	(10 000 heads)	163.15	263.23	224.80	337.66	387.63	413.23
山羊		Goats		106.72	260.04	223.55	336.97	387.04	412.69
绵羊		Sheep		56.43	3.19	1.25	0.69	0.59	0.54
畜产品产量		**Livestock Products**							
猪牛羊出栏头数	（万头）	Hogs, Sheep and Goats	(10 000 heads)	1805.44	3246.34	3023.96	3841.82	4106.40	4286.86
当年肉猪出栏头数		Hogs		1714.30	2981.48	2714.44	3345.18	3498.30	3735.49
当年出售和自宰的肉用牛		Ox by Sold and Killed		12.44	67.40	104.26	115.49	112.40	118.92
当年出售和自宰的肉用羊	（万只）	Sheep by Slod and Killed	(10 000 heads)	78.70	197.46	205.26	381.15	495.70	551.37
肉类产量	（万吨）	Output of Meat	(10 000 tons)	146.83	279.40	271.19	342.63	392.76	367.01
猪肉		Pork		134.97	239.60	215.84	271.23	292.15	279.90
牛肉		Beef		1.34	8.33	13.80	16.91	18.76	17.03
羊肉		Mutton		1.07	2.78	3.04	6.00	8.12	7.84
禽肉		Poultry		9.45	28.69	38.51	48.49	73.07	61.41
其他禽产品产量	（吨）	Others	(tons)						
牛奶产量		Milk Cow		51933	38214	56400	122223	176720	127900
绵羊毛产量		Sheep's Wool		83.00	14.16	34.57	4.00	0.60	3.10
山羊毛产量		Goats' Wool		15.00	11.01	52.17	16.00	9.87	10.70
蜂蜜		Cashmere		7904	1077	9187	7890	7117	9233
禽蛋	（万吨）	Poultry Eggs	(10 000 tons)	51.87	87.92	102.56	121.25	136.51	144.09

7-14 水产品产量
OUTPUT OF AQUATIC PRODUCTS

指 标	Item	1990	1995	2000	2005	2008	2009
水产品产量 （万吨）	**Output of Aquatic Products (10 000 tons)**	**70.98**	**150.91**	**234.34**	**318.03**	**313.39**	**333.90**
鱼类产量	Fish	67.96	141.44	219.88	277.82	283.62	287.88
虾蟹产量	Shrimp, Prawn and Crab	1.56	3.52	7.51	7.71	34.29	31.71
贝类产量	Shell Fish	1.05	3.39	5.38	1.13	3.23	3.20
其它类产量	Others	0.42	2.56	1.58		3.62	2.79
养殖产量	Artificially Cultivated	60.79	131.69	194.84	274.45	283.13	307.67
捕捞产量	Captured	10.19	19.22	39.50	43.58	30.26	26.20
莲籽产量	Lotus Seed	0.26	0.93	3.02	2.97	3.22	3.48
养殖按水面分类产量(万吨)	Grouped by waters (10 000 tons)	60.79	131.69	193.92	274.45	283.13	307.67
湖 泊	Lakes	9.78	15.24	20.84	28.44	32.51	33.19
水 库	Reservoir	3.88	6.51	8.15	12.52	15.91	19.73
塘 堰	Pools	19.72	31.26	33.05	38.87	27.75	26.60
精 养 池	Fine Cultivated Pools	25.92	73.10	122.96	177.54	182.90	206.31
河 沟	Rivers	1.28	2.25	2.90	6.03	2.32	2.10
其 它	Others	0.21	3.33	6.02	8.03	5.49	1.39
鱼苗产量 （亿尾）	Young Fry (100 million tons)	262.36	373.84	444.01	521.39	643.00	690.00
鱼种产量 （万吨）	Advanced Fry (10 000 tons)	14.15	25.58	38.79	54.04	66.16	77.47
投放鱼种量 （万吨）	Volume of Advanced Fry (10 000 tons)	13.24	25.55	40.16	57.08	65.72	75.77
水产养殖面积 （千公顷）	**Aquatic Raised Areas (1 000 hectares)**						
湖 泊	Lakes	249.71	229.64	196.46	175.34	191.63	196.17
水 库	Reservoir	152.15	144.92	166.07	102.18	93.46	110.77
塘 堰	Pools	153.15	141.09	134.79	119.20	78.56	87.43
精 养 池	Fine Cultivated Pools	55.65	125.88	156.33	220.37	205.49	245.78
河 渠	Rivers	16.63	18.67	20.86	21.89	5.70	5.71
其 它	Others		19.00	32.92	34.56	8.52	3.86

注：2008年为国家核定数据。

Note:Data for 2008 approved a number of countries.

7-15　农业现代化情况

STATISTICS ON AGRICULTURAL MODERNIZATION

单位：千公顷　　(1 000 hectares)

指　标	Item	1990	1995	2000	2005	2008	2009
农业机械化情况	**Statistics on Agricultural Machinery**						
机耕面积	Areas Ploughed by Tractors	1097.23	1247.00	1969.55	2015.93	3886.28	4099.40
机播面积	Seeded Areas by Tractors	47.83	83.38	255.69	233.66	469.45	637.18
机械植保面积	Plant Protection Area by Tractors	1064.75	1783.65	2426.95	2848.66	4035.71	3871.91
机械收获面积	Harvest Area by Tractors	97.56	130.95	643.65	1407.62	2251.94	2554.97
农村电气化情况	**Electrification of Rural Area**						
农村用电量（亿千瓦小时）	Electricity Consumed in Rural Area (100 million kWh)	27.21	47.36	60.86	70.09	98.06	104.27
农用物资使用情况	**Used Agricultural Product Material**						
化肥施用量(折纯量)（万吨）	Consumption of Chemical Fertilizers (10 000 tons)	148.61	228.41	247.08	285.83	327.66	340.26
每亩耕地施用化肥(折纯量)（千克）	Per Mu Consumption of Chemical Fertilizers (kg)	28.50	45.35	50.17	60.28	66.41	87.07
农用塑料薄膜使用量（万吨）	Used Plastic Film (10 000 tons)				5.46	5.91	6.12
农用柴油使用量（万吨）	Used Diesel Oil (10 000 tons)			107.81	41.31	52.45	53.40
农药使用量（万吨）	Used Agricultural Chemical Insecticides (10 000 tons)	4.63	11.24	11.54	11.02	13.84	13.85
农田水利情况	**Irrigation and Water Conservancy**						
有效灌溉面积	Effective Irrigation Area	2324.35	2172.08	2072.53	2064.59	2139.41	2145.99
#机电排灌面积	#Electrical Well		1257.70		1236.11	1321.40	1318.71
占有效灌溉面积的比重（%）	Rate in Effective Irrigation Area (%)		57.9		59.9	61.8	61.4

7–16 主要农业机械和农产品加工机械拥有量

年 份 Year	农业机械总动力(万千瓦) Total Power of Agricultural Machinery(1000 kW)	农用大中型拖拉机(万台) Large and Medium Agricultural Tractors(10 000 units)	农用小型及手扶拖拉机(万台) Mini and Walking Agricultural Tractors (10 000 units)	农用排灌动力机械(万千瓦) Machinery for Machinery for Agricultural Drainage and Irrigation (1000 kW)	农用水泵(万台) Agricultual Water Pump(10 000 units)
1978	616.07	2.80	7.75		21.22
1980	772.53	3.60	10.90		23.70
1985	910.94	5.72	14.62	55.22	21.06
1989	1118.77	8.74	17.49	62.31	21.89
1990	1099.62	8.60	17.70	99.28	24.30
1991	1120.92	8.60	18.30	362.88	24.10
1992	1120.90	8.45	17.92	368.46	23.98
1993	1108.99	7.89	16.99	360.75	23.95
1994	1136.13	7.38	15.72	368.55	24.37
1995	1174.34	7.12	15.47	384.48	26.56
1996	1222.20	7.03	16.47	401.49	27.62
1997	1276.04	7.11	18.50	408.09	28.76
1998	1325.90	7.13	20.60	410.77	29.59
1999	1363.70	7.03	22.67	419.83	32.57
2000	1414.00	6.82	23.63	434.49	35.47
2001	1469.24	6.58	24.88	450.40	40.46
2002	1557.40	6.64	26.68	461.86	43.89
2003	1661.70	6.59	28.23	469.45	45.63
2004	1768.60	6.83	32.09	484.71	50.82
2005	2057.37	7.66	48.39	518.49	55.92
2006	2263.15	8.50	55.69	531.33	71.42
2007	2551.08	9.30	74.12	541.33	82.70
2008	2796.99	10.42	85.23	559.24	87.73
2009	3057.24	11.85	90.84	594.17	87.70

NUMBER OF MAJOR AGRICULTURAL MACHINERY AND MACHINERY FOR PROCESSING FARM PRODUCTS OWNED AT YEAR-END

喷灌机械 (万套) Machinery for Sprinkling (10 000 units)	联合收割机 (台) Combine Hearvesters (unit)	机动脱粒机 (万台) Motorized Huller (10 000 units)	机动喷雾(粉)器 (万部) Motorized Duster (10 000 units)	饲料粉碎机 (万台) Fodder Grinder (10 000 units)	大中型拖拉机配套农具 (万部) Large and Medium Tractors Towing Farm Machinery (10 000 units)	小型拖拉机配套农具 (万部) Mini Tractors Towing Farm Machinery (10 000 units)
0.30	425	15.00	0.78	7.78	4.66	4.92
1.08	602	17.40	1.00	8.20	4.99	7.20
0.73	479	15.22	0.60	5.90	2.39	4.95
0.34	487	12.87		4.81	2.49	9.01
0.31	2335	12.60	3.70	5.60	2.70	10.14
0.34	455	12.50	4.60	5.55	3.00	11.87
0.60	390	12.35	4.70	5.32	3.86	12.30
0.48	345	11.97	4.77	5.12	3.05	11.64
0.47	346	11.39	5.29	5.50	2.91	12.38
0.72	312	11.25	6.44	5.32	2.85	15.48
0.72	553	12.33	6.74	8.70	3.05	23.02
7.75	1521	11.11	7.36	8.79	3.63	29.46
0.80	2338	11.56	8.27	9.65	4.33	37.75
0.71	2559	11.56	8.00	10.48	4.80	42.84
0.85	2704	12.25	8.70	10.73	4.81	37.48
1.01	3363	12.79	9.07	12.60	5.22	41.12
1.08	5722	12.81	9.72	9.59	5.97	46.44
1.17	6708	12.62	10.26	12.33	6.21	49.03
1.20	10585	12.88	11.86	15.01	7.45	59.31
1.55	16085	14.33	15.98	23.88	9.36	96.69
1.75	22407	12.54	25.44	26.37	11.18	111.02
1.81	29803	13.14	30.58	27.04	12.96	149.08
2.23	34983	12.99	35.41	29.94	15.49	169.69
2.21	41904	15.37	38.40	33.46	20.37	178.55

7-17 市、州乡村劳动力
RURAL LABORFORCE IN CITIES AND PREFECTURES

单位：万人 (10 000 person)

市、州	Municipalities and Prefecrures	2008	农林牧渔业劳动力 Laborforce in Farming, Forestry, Animal Husbandry and Fishery	工业劳动力 Laborforce in Industry	2009	农林牧渔业劳动力 Laborforce in Farming, Forestry, Animal Husbandry and Fishery	工业劳动力 Laborforce in Industry
全　省	Province	2078.77	996.76	247.57	2123.29	965.73	301.62
武汉市	Wuhan Municipality	137.78	62.33	17.18	136.74	56.18	19.98
黄石市	Huangshi Municipality	71.51	27.12	17.52	34.61	24.16	25.65
十堰市	Shiyan Municipality	130.15	59.38	9.14	134.72	59.3	10.63
荆州市	Jingzhou Municipality	217.08	122.62	22.2	223.42	116.6	38.5
宜昌市	Yichang Municipality	156.75	80.08	15.01	159.84	80.94	17.42
襄樊市	Xiangfan Municipality	193.85	98.56	25.73	195.62	93.49	29.01
鄂州市	Ezhou Municipality	39.74	22.63	4.72	39.86	21.42	5.09
荆门市	Jingmen Municipality	97.53	55.92	13.74	99.33	49.95	21.5
孝感市	Xiaogan Municipality	215.52	90.95	31.3	220.45	89.61	34.85
黄冈市	Huanggang Municipality	288.87	127.02	32.86	298.26	123.43	35.39
咸宁市	Xianning Municipality	97.67	43.72	9.18	100.16	44.2	10.73
随州市	Suizhou Municipality	98.12	39.84	17.33	100.54	43.13	18.03
恩施自治州	Enshi Prefecture	182.74	96.33	10.23	183.42	95.64	11.39
仙桃市	Xiantao Municipality	64.57	27.52	9.72	64.39	26.74	11.04
天门市	Tianmen Municipality	54.51	25.97	6.52	55.35	25.16	6.41
潜江市	Qianjiang Municipality	29.60	14.28	4.95	30.50	14.36	5.73
神农架林区	Shennongjia Forest Zone	2.77	1.49	0.24	2.77	1.42	0.27

7–18 市、州耕地面积

CULTIVATED AREA OF CITIES AND PREFECTURES

市、州	Municipalities and Prefecrures	1990		1995		2000		2009	
		年末耕地面积（千公顷）Cultivated Area at Year-end(1 000 hectares)	人平耕地（亩）Cultivated Area Per Capita(Mu)	年末耕地面积（千公顷）Cultivated Area at Year-end(1 000 hectares)	人平耕地（亩）Cultivated Area Per Capita(Mu)	年末耕地面积（千公顷）Cultivated Area at Year-end(1 000 hectares)	人平耕地（亩）Cultivated Area Per Capita(Mu)	年末耕地面积（千公顷）Cultivated Area at Year-end(1000 hectares)	人平耕地（亩）Cultivated Area Per Capita(Mu)
全省	Province	3476.78	0.96	3358.00	0.88	3282.96	0.83	3308.35	0.87
武汉市	Wuhan Municipality	240.11	0.54	225.75	0.48	217.84	0.40	206.20	0.34
黄石市	Huangshi Municipality	84.08	0.60	39.70	0.41	79.32	0.48	90.69	0.56
十堰市	Shiyan Municipality	207.27	0.95	194.44	0.86	181.54	0.79	170.41	0.79
荆州市	Jingzhou Municipality	480.48	1.31	590.98	1.11	432.58	1.03	462.69	1.19
宜昌市	Yichang Municipality	275.72	1.07	264.98	0.10	257.71	0.94	230.31	0.85
襄樊市	Xiangfan Municipality	429.00	1.26	415.64	1.14	412.96	1.09	433.72	1.19
鄂州市	Ezhou Municipality	44.33	0.73	40.90	0.61	40.28	0.59	41.25	0.60
荆门市	Jingmen Municipality	240.96	1.34	122.00	1.54	256.53	1.29	254.65	1.34
孝感市	Xiaogan Municipality	296.41	0.83	289.86	0.75	247.10	0.74	260.64	0.83
黄冈市	Huanggang Municipality	335.85	0.77	317.96	0.68	312.36	0.65	333.62	0.75
咸宁市	Xianning Municipality	150.46	0.93	188.78	0.79	145.94	0.81	154.67	0.92
随州市	Suizhou Municipality	99.63	1.52	98.10	0.98	136.58	0.85	137.52	93.00
恩施自治州	Enshi Prefecture	291.61	1.22	288.70	1.16	280.59	1.11	256.87	1.10
仙桃市	Xiantao Municipality	108.29	1.17	104.50	0.98	98.68	1.01	90.84	1.11
天门市	Tianmen Municipality	110.63	1.08	108.50	1.71	107.62	1.00	108.30	1.18
潜江市	Qianjiang Municipality	73.39	1.27	69.02	0.63	66.99	1.01	69.77	1.12
神农架林区	Shennongjia Forest Zone	8.57	1.66	8.20	1.54	8.35	1.54	6.20	1.24

7-19 市、州农、林、牧、渔业总产值及指数

GROSS OUTPUT VALUE AND ITS INDICES OF FARMING, FORESTRY, ANIMAL HUSBANDRY AND FISHERY OF CITIES AND PREFECTURES

市、州	Municipalities and Prefecrures	绝对数(亿元) Absolute Number (100 milion yuan)			指数(%) Indices (%)		
		1995	2000	2009	1995	2000	2009
全　省	Province	988.53	1125.64	2985.19	114.10	102.80	101.52
武汉市	Wuhan Municipality	94.34	126.94	251.79	112.00	105.30	100.02
黄石市	Huangshi Municipality	23.75	27.63	72.17	109.00	104.20	101.47
十堰市	Shiyan Municipality	43.43	44.65	111.94	106.70	111.10	105.50
荆州市	Jingzhou Municipality	178.07	147.69	383.45	112.30	91.00	103.60
宜昌市	Yichang Municipality	80.26	97.19	250.56	116.40	102.60	102.70
襄樊市	Xiangfan Municipality	155.08	158.15	366.00	113.00	93.50	97.10
鄂州市	Ezhou Municipality	18.42	13.92	79.54	123.20	106.70	99.20
荆门市	Jingmen Municipality	103.56	100.13	231.72	115.30	103.00	97.50
孝感市	Xiaogan Municipality	124.45	111.63	260.59	115.00	90.70	103.30
黄冈市	Huanggang Municipality	119.17	127.48	325.82	108.90	102.40	99.50
咸宁市	Xianning Municipality	47.61	52.87	140.18	110.80	104.50	98.40
随州市	Suizhou Municipality	30.07	58.06	131.79	112.60	141.50	100.10
恩施自治州	Enshi Prefecture	48.32	76.78	152.45	111.00	102.30	102.10
仙桃市	Xiaotao Municipality	37.47	39.01	83.20	125.90	102.20	101.60
天门市	Tianmen Municipality	41.58	33.15	72.50	122.00	100.40	127.05
潜江市	Qianjiang Municipality	28.61	30.58	70.00	127.60	101.90	110.12
神农架林区	Shennongjia Forest Zone	0.84	0.99	2.30	103.20	87.10	109.12

注：本表产值按当年价格计算，指数按不变价格计算；全省合计数为调整数，故市、州相加不等于合计数。

Notes:The data of in this table is caculated at current prices of output valul,and the data of indices is calulaled at constort prices therefore,the total of provice is an adiusted number,and that of municipalities and prefecture if added are not egual to the total number.

7-20 市、州农、林、牧、渔业产值（现价）（2009）

GROSS OUTPUT VALUE OF FARMING, FORESTRY, ANIMAL HUSBANDRY AND FISHERY OF CITIES AND PREFECTURES (AT CURRENT PRICES)(2009)

单位：亿元 (100 million yuan)

市、州	Municipalities and Prefecrures	合计 Total	农业 Farming	林业 Forestry	牧业 Animal Husbandry	渔业 Fishery	农林牧渔服务业 Service Industry for Farming, Forestry, Animal Husbandry and Fishery
全省	Province	2985.19	1511.49	57.67	881.78	413.14	121.11
武汉市	Wuhan Municipality	251.79	138.81	1.39	64.78	45.52	1.29
黄石市	Huangshi Municipality	72.17	28.55	2.05	22.42	18.31	0.84
十堰市	Shiyan Municipality	111.94	64.79	4.16	35.82	6.26	0.92
荆州市	Jingzhou Municipality	383.45	168.96	3.23	90.84	115.73	4.69
宜昌市	Yichang Municipality	250.56	129.96	3.13	94.00	21.38	1.69
襄樊市	Xiangfan Municipality	366.00	180.91	5.21	154.70	16.86	8.32
鄂州市	Ezhou Municipality	79.54	26.18	0.67	19.54	32.92	0.22
荆门市	Jingmen Municipality	231.72	106.85	3.68	75.53	40.36	5.30
孝感市	Xiaogan Municipality	260.59	114.12	5.82	95.65	40.04	4.96
黄冈市	Huanggang Municipality	325.82	158.05	9.44	104.61	46.06	7.67
咸宁市	Xianning Municipality	140.18	69.79	7.44	37.83	23.63	1.49
随州市	Suizhou Municipality	131.79	74.42	3.71	45.19	6.28	2.19
恩施自治州	Enshi Prefecture	152.45	92.30	4.63	53.76	0.63	1.14
仙桃市	Xiaotao Municipality	83.20	30.81	0.70	20.01	30.17	1.52
天门市	Tianmen Municipality	72.50	34.08	0.22	21.34	15.46	1.40
潜江市	Qianjiang Municipality	70.00	31.89	0.62	21.31	14.80	1.38
神农架林区	Shennongjia Forest Zone	2.30	1.47	0.07	0.71	0.01	0.04

注：全省数字第二次农业普查后国家统计局重新核定数，故今年州汇总不等于全省。

Note:Note: The number of the second province after the National Bureau of Statistics agricultural census the number of re-approved, it summarizes the state does not mean the province this year.

7–21 市、州农、林、牧、渔业中间消耗（2009）
INTERMEDIATE-CONSUMPTION OF OF FARMING, FORESTRY, ANIMAL HUSBANDRY AND FISHERY OF CITIES AND PREFECTURES(2009)

单位：亿元 (100 million yuan)

市、州	Municipalities and Prefecrures	合计 Total	农业 Farming	林业 Forestry	牧业 Animal Husbandry	渔业 Fishery	农林牧渔服务业 Service Industry for Farming, Forestry, Animal Husbandry and Fishery
全省	Province	1196.97	562.95	22.79	415.06	177.31	18.86
武汉市	Wuhan Municipality	102.73	55.82	0.58	28.97	16.81	0.55
黄石市	Huangshi Municipality	26.91	10.20	0.72	9.64	5.88	0.47
十堰市	Shiyan Municipality	45.43	25.44	2.23	15.13	2.19	0.43
荆州市	Jingzhou Municipality	176.23	73.12	1.26	45.27	51.33	2.25
宜昌市	Yichang Municipality	99.86	47.42	1.14	41.73	8.79	0.78
襄樊市	Xiangfan Municipality	165.78	84.26	2.14	66.12	8.96	4.32
鄂州市	Ezhou Municipality	35.56	13.52	0.44	7.90	13.55	0.15
荆门市	Jingmen Municipality	97.18	39.52	1.39	38.52	16.18	1.57
孝感市	Xiaogan Municipality	115.42	45.27	2.31	47.37	18.33	2.15
黄冈市	Huanggang Municipality	110.44	48.66	3.58	39.18	15.80	3.24
咸宁市	Xianning Municipality	53.61	24.60	3.23	15.33	9.78	0.66
随州市	Suizhou Municipality	56.88	32.76	1.62	20.57	1.49	0.43
恩施自治州	Enshi Prefecture	56.44	36.02	1.56	18.30	0.16	0.39
仙桃市	Xiaotao Municipality	35.69	10.36	0.54	11.89	12.32	0.58
天门市	Tianmen Municipality	24.54	13.63	0.14	6.72	3.63	0.42
潜江市	Qianjiang Municipality	28.81	12.12	0.33	10.12	5.64	0.60
神农架林区	Shennongjia Forest Zone	1.01	0.75	0.03	0.21		0.02

注：全省中间消耗为省级核算数，故市、州相加不等于合计数。

Note:The statistics of Intermedium Consumption is checked by Provincial Statistical Burea,thus the total of municipalities and prefecture do not equal to the total of the whole province.

7-22 市、州农、林、牧、渔业增加值（2009）
VALUE ADDED OF FARMING, FORESTRY, ANIMAL HUSBANDRY AND FISHERY OF CITIES AND PREFECTURES(2009)

单位：亿元 (100 million yuan)

市、州	Municipalities and Prefecrures	合计 Total	农业 Farming	林业 Forestry	牧业 Animal Husbandry	渔业 Fishery	农林牧渔服务业 Service Industry for Farming, Forestry, Animal Husbandry and Fishery
全省	Province	1709.50	862.79	32.71	523.84	264.17	25.99
武汉市	Wuhan Municipality	149.06	82.99	0.81	35.81	28.71	0.73
黄石市	Huangshi Municipality	45.26	18.36	1.33	12.78	12.43	0.37
十堰市	Shiyan Municipality	66.51	39.34	1.93	20.69	4.06	0.49
荆州市	Jingzhou Municipality	207.22	92.83	1.97	45.58	64.40	2.44
宜昌市	Yichang Municipality	150.70	82.54	2.00	52.68	12.59	0.90
襄樊市	Xiangfan Municipality	200.21	96.65	3.08	88.58	7.90	4.01
鄂州市	Ezhou Municipality	43.98	12.66	0.24	11.64	19.37	0.07
荆门市	Jingmen Municipality	134.54	67.33	2.30	37.01	24.12	3.73
孝感市	Xiaogan Municipality	145.17	68.85	3.52	48.29	21.71	2.81
黄冈市	Huanggang Municipality	215.38	109.39	5.86	65.43	30.26	4.43
咸宁市	Xianning Municipality	86.58	45.19	4.21	22.50	13.85	0.83
随州市	Suizhou Municipality	74.91	41.66	2.09	24.62	4.78	1.76
恩施自治州	Enshi Prefecture	96.01	56.28	3.07	35.44	0.47	0.75
仙桃市	Xiaotao Municipality	47.50	20.44	0.15	8.12	17.85	0.94
天门市	Tianmen Municipality	47.96	20.45	0.08	14.62	11.82	0.98
潜江市	Qianjiang Municipality	41.19	19.77	0.29	11.19	9.15	0.78
神农架林区	Shennongjia Forest Zone	1.29	0.72	0.03	0.50	0.01	0.03

注：全省数为省级核算数，故分市州汇总不等于全省。

Note:The statistics of the whole province is checked by Provincial Statistical Burea, thus the total of municipalities and prefecture do not equal to the total of the whole province.

7–23 市、州农业机械拥有量（2009）

市、州	Municipalities and Prefecrures	农业机械总动力（万千瓦特） Total Power of Agricultural Machinery (10 000kW)	大中型农用拖拉机 混合台 Number of Mixed Machinerys	大中型农用拖拉机 万千瓦特 (10 000kW)	小型及手扶拖拉机（台） Mini and Walking Agricultural Tractors (unit)
全省	Province	3057.24	118572	358.41	908358
武汉市	Wuhan Municipality	207.4	7630	18.88	14941
黄石市	Huangshi Municipality	64.86	4877	13.76	3587
十堰市	Shiyan Municipality	124.16	2755	7.27	6791
荆州市	Jingzhou Municipality	403.57	12513	53.90	64234
宜昌市	Yichang Municipality	231.45	8838	23.71	62116
襄樊市	Xiangfan Municipality	474.17	21889	65.25	328205
鄂州市	Ezhou Municipality	49.73	1939	3.95	3225
荆门市	Jingmen Municipality	326.53	15606	49.76	227428
孝感市	Xiaogan Municipality	195.96	10108	31.10	18691
黄冈市	Huanggang Municipality	208.79	9701	22.52	13867
咸宁市	Xianning Municipality	127.98	3861	10.70	8563
随州市	Suizhou Municipality	160.75	5430	7.83	78953
恩施自治州	Enshi Prefecture	155.88	3162	13.16	4667
仙桃市	Xiaotao Municipality	107.01	2150	7.67	19843
天门市	Tianmen Municipality	130.18	3364	11.91	27311
潜江市	Qianjiang Municipality	82.01	4602	16.76	25813
神农架林区	Shennongjia Forest Zone	6.8	147	0.27	123

注：2009年农用汽车指标含低速载货汽车和三轮汽车。

NUMBER OF AGRICULTURAL MACHINERY OWNED OF CITIES AND PREFECTURES(2009)

大中型机引农具（部） Large and Medium Tractor Towing Farm Machinery(unit)	小型及手扶拖拉机机引农具（部） Mini and Walking Tractors Towing Farm Machinery(unit)	农用水泵（台） Agricultural Water Pump (unit)	机动脱粒机（台） Motorized Huller (unit)	农用汽车（辆） Agricultural Vehicle (unit)
203695	1785460	877020	153747	230286
8062	20716	39905	8811	19773
5219	4316	17591	4453	1969
4477	18700	24328	31266	18497
33550	48816	124242	4999	27839
14078	186493	93799	18224	25618
50164	657100	48480	12370	44826
3505	8616	14135	4839	2579
24351	373073	70611	2507	8335
15896	50174	190320	8927	12001
14477	30785	51828	17381	21013
5379	12115	34182	5336	10568
857	10620	19301	20603	10750
5161	298654	64044	2827	15599
4299	6179	49511	4036	4923
5928	27587	21716	1800	3746
8292	30974	12921	5368	1793
	542	106		457

Note:This car targets with low agricultural truck and three cars.

7-24 市、州主要农作物产量（2009）

单位：万吨

市、州	Municipalities and Prefecrures	粮食 Grain	稻谷 Rice	小麦 Wheat	玉米 Corn	薯类 Tubers	大豆 Soybean	棉花 Cotton
全省	Province	2309.10	1591.92	331.67	244.12	84.81	25.59	48.06
武汉市	Wuhan Municipality	135.89	105.82	6.44	12.39	5.39	2.87	3.22
黄石市	Huangshi Municipality	61.64	46.63	3.15	3.92	5.77	0.79	0.61
十堰市	Shiyan Municipality	115.21	26.39	24.68	37.80	19.73	4.22	0.01
荆州市	Jingzhou Municipality	370.45	321.59	32.83	5.59	3.18	3.34	13.16
宜昌市	Yichang Municipality	158.00	68.64	13.84	49.56	21.57	1.93	2.96
襄樊市	Xiangfan Municipality	438.25	187.96	176.19	50.97	11.12	2.55	4.54
鄂州市	Ezhou Municipality	34.06	28.44	1.56	0.55	1.87	0.53	0.56
荆门市	Jingmen Municipality	251.40	185.40	43.03	13.28	3.59	4.64	4.05
孝感市	Xiaogan Municipality	228.87	184.82	33.25	1.35	5.23	2.20	3.24
黄冈市	Huanggang Municipality	315.16	272.37	21.41	2.11	13.66	3.04	7.13
咸宁市	Xianning Municipality	112.51	94.22	1.16	7.41	7.16	1.16	0.27
随州市	Suizhou Municipality	149.85	105.01	37.15	0.90	4.92	0.40	1.49
恩施自治州	Enshi Prefecture	160.65	41.26	2.38	61.93	49.68	3.76	
仙桃市	Xiaotao Municipality	71.21	57.36	5.83	3.22	1.27	2.11	2.65
天门市	Tianmen Municipality	60.05	42.44	11.45	1.53	1.61	2.61	4.72
潜江市	Qianjiang Municipality	38.87	27.44	7.92	1.57	0.69	1.12	4.04
神农架林区	Shennongjia Forest Zone	2.10	0.05	0.10	1.08	0.77	0.08	

OUTPUT OF MAJOR FARM CROPS OF CITIES AND PREFECTURES(2009)

(10 000tons)

油料 Oil Bearing Crops	花生 Peanuts	油菜籽 Rapeseed	芝麻 Sesame	麻类 Hemp Crops	麻 Ramie	糖类 Sugar Crops	甘蔗 Crane	烟叶 Tobacoo Crops	烤烟 Tobacco
314.05	62.62	236.51	14.21	3.82	3.68	34.43	34.43	15.21	10.90
19.05	3.91	12.43	2.72	0.42	0.42	7.69	7.69		
7.69	0.65	6.01	1.03	0.77	0.77	0.11	0.11		
9.96	2.06	6.23	1.56			0.66	0.66	1.83	1.73
54.01	0.44	52.49	1.07	0.07	0.01	6.49	6.49		
23.08	2.96	19.63	0.40			0.31	0.31	1.82	0.97
32.69	16.01	15.37	1.31	0.09	0.09	3.75	3.75	1.68	
5.80	0.38	4.86	0.56	0.04	0.04	0.51	0.51		
36.25	8.04	27.27	0.94			2.50	2.50		
23.19	6.77	15.67	0.75			1.46	1.46		
47.90	13.20	33.05	1.62	0.56	0.54	3.31	3.31		
8.26	1.46	6.20	0.60	1.81	1.81	4.87	4.87		
6.47	3.36	2.46	0.65			0.47	0.47		
7.98	1.20	6.24	0.06			0.05	0.05	9.84	6.48
11.89	0.21	11.26	0.42	0.01		1.21	1.21		
11.20	1.32	9.67	0.22			0.65	0.65		
11.31	0.48	10.67	0.16			0.39	0.39		
0.04		0.03						0.04	0.04

7–25 市、州大牲畜、羊、猪年末存栏、出栏、肉产量（2009）

市、州	Municipalities and Prefecrures	大牲畜存栏（万头） Large Animals in Stock(10 000 heads)	牛 Cattles and Bufflaoes	羊存栏（万只） Sheep in Stock (10 000 heads)	山羊 Goats	年末生猪存栏（万头） Hogs in Stock at Year-end(10 000 heads)
全省	Province	335.56	334.01	413.23	412.69	2546.10
武汉市	Wuhan Municipality	20.93	20.89	3.84	3.84	170.93
黄石市	Huangshi Municipality	7.81	7.80	4.25	4.25	72.22
十堰市	Shiyan Municipality	26.20	25.93	68.95	68.95	152.35
荆州市	Jingzhou Municipality	18.61	18.36	6.00	5.97	288.46
宜昌市	Yichang Municipality	15.25	15.24	74.30	74.29	406.91
襄樊市	Xiangfan Municipality	95.69	95.68	107.74	107.45	420.08
鄂州市	Ezhou Municipality	3.42	3.41	1.00	1.00	62.10
荆门市	Jingmen Municipality	20.85	20.71	26.52	26.52	229.54
孝感市	Xiaogan Municipality	43.97	43.71	21.19	21.19	240.22
黄冈市	Huanggang Municipality	74.66	74.63	47.54	47.54	311.22
咸宁市	Xianning Municipality	12.12	12.10	11.11	11.11	133.88
随州市	Suizhou Municipality	21.71	21.71	31.66	31.62	118.72
恩施自治州	Enshi Prefecture	33.48	33.12	47.46	47.44	390.57
仙桃市	Xiaotao Municipality	3.24	3.22	0.22	0.07	64.71
天门市	Tianmen Municipality	6.21	6.09	0.77	0.77	69.09
潜江市	Qianjiang Municipality	3.92	3.92	1.52	1.52	46.59
神农架林区	Shennongjia Forest Zone	0.88	0.88	2.45	2.45	4.72

STATISTICS ON LARGE LIVE ANIMALS, SHEEP, HOGS IN STOCK AND OUT OF STOCK AT YEAR-END AND OUTPUT OF MEAT OF CITIES AND PREFECTURES(2009)

年内出栏肉猪 (万头) Hogs out of Stock at Year-end(10 000 heads)	年内出栏羊 (万只) Sheep out of Stock at Year-end(10 000 heads)	出笼禽 (万只) Poultry out of Stock at Year-end(10 000 heads)	肉类总产量 (万吨) Total Output of Meat (10 000 tons)	猪肉产量 Output of Pork	羊 肉 Mutton	禽蛋产量 (万吨) Output of Eggs (10 000 tons)
3735.49	551.37	43551.10	367.01	279.90	7.84	144.09
248.77	6.13	4763.04	29.17	19.94	0.12	14.43
102.59	3.76	1968.13	10.92	7.61	0.06	3.19
150.72	66.37	1669.60	15.59	11.30	1.09	3.45
397.19	7.00	5947.12	41.20	31.38	0.11	14.73
543.07	108.85	2884.48	51.99	44.14	2.00	4.72
542.99	117.79	7255.15	65.54	41.42	2.12	20.31
90.03	1.71	1215.72	8.39	6.50	0.02	3.60
346.64	36.45	3903.75		25.99	0.61	11.09
305.41	16.34	9784.39	38.74	24.16	0.27	25.67
389.98	48.15	3891.06	50.01	34.73	0.76	21.72
188.64	12.45	3388.62	18.29	14.05	0.19	2.49
187.86	42.98	2367.68	19.96	14.98	0.63	6.06
405.38	43.26	868.67	36.94	33.47	0.77	2.01
113.00	0.28	825.70	9.42	8.48		3.78
83.19	0.86	1126.12	7.72	6.24	0.01	4.78
90.58	2.06	1422.36	9.15	6.79	0.03	2.35
5.73	1.43	27.43	0.48	0.40	0.03	0.03

7–26 市、州主要土特产品产量（2009）
OUTPUT OF LOCAL SPECIALITY OF CITIES AND PREFECTURES(2009)

市、州	Municipalities and Prefecrures	茶叶		蚕茧		园林水果				白木耳	黑木耳
		(万吨) Tea (10 000 tons)	绿毛茶 Green Tea	(吨) Silkworm Coccons (ton)	桑蚕茧 Mulbeery Silkworm Coccons	(万吨) Fruits (10 000 tons)	桃子 Peaches	柑桔 Citrus	苹果 Apples	(吨) White Fungus (ton)	(吨) Jew's Ear (ton)
全省	Province	14.42	11.98	10154	10053	402.15	55.66	274.70	1.14	14951	41
武汉市	Wuhan Municipality	0.18	0.11			7.23	1.70	2.85		8	
黄石市	Huangshi Municipality	0.03	0.03	1	1	3.50	0.13	3.10		6	
十堰市	Shiyan Municipality	0.87	0.87	409	409	28.65	0.56	26.65	0.08	1706	
荆州市	Jingzhou Municipality					32.63	0.63	25.14	0.01	16	
宜昌市	Yichang Municipality	3.40	2.91	2954	2954	181.56	2.29	176.68	0.06	326	
襄樊市	Xiangfan Municipality	0.69	0.68	858	858	51.34	29.86	5.21	0.34	1751	20
鄂州市	Ezhou Municipality	0.01	0.01			2.22	0.38	1.33			
荆门市	Jingmen Municipality	0.02	0.02			35.54	3.92	13.56		1984	
孝感市	Xiaogan Municipality	0.26	0.26			12.95	6.88	0.65	0.13	198	
黄冈市	Huanggang Municipality	3.00	3.00	5727	5727	8.06	1.89	4.54	0.17	306	3
咸宁市	Xianning Municipality	1.82	0.71			4.42	0.57	2.20		65	
随州市	Suizhou Municipality	0.17	0.17	101		10.28	5.93	0.57	0.15	8541	18
恩施自治州	Enshi Prefecture	3.96	3.20	104	104	17.25	0.28	10.79	0.14		
仙桃市	Xiaotao Municipality					2.73	0.38	0.96	0.06		
天门市	Tianmen Municipality					1.34	0.07	0.25			
潜江市	Qianjiang Municipality					2.39	0.18	0.22			
神农架林区	Shennongjia Forest Zone	0.01	0.01			0.06	0.01			44	

7-27　市、州人平粮、棉、油、猪、水产品生产水平（2009）

AVERAGE PRODUCTION LEVEL OF GRAIN,COTTON,OIL,POHC AND AQUATIC PRODUCTS PER CAPITA OF CITIES AND PREFECTURES(2009)

单位:千克　　(kg)

市、州	Municipalities and Prefecrures	粮食 Grain	棉花 Cotton	油料 Oil Bearing Crops	肉类 Meat	水产品 Aquatic Products	禽蛋 Eggs
按常住人口平均	**Average of Total Population**						
全省	Province	403.69	8.41	54.90	64.16		25.19
武汉市	Wuhan Municipality	148.33	3.54	20.93	32.05		15.86
黄石市	Huangshi Municipality	254.07	2.51	31.70	45.01		13.15
十堰市	Shiyan Municipality	355.48	0.03	30.73	48.10		10.64
荆州市	Jingzhou Municipality	632.82	22.48	92.26	70.38		25.16
宜昌市	Yichang Municipality	390.56	7.32	57.05	128.51		11.67
襄樊市	Xiangfan Municipality	804.70	8.34	60.02	120.34		37.29
鄂州市	Ezhou Municipality	329.11	5.41	56.04	81.07		34.79
荆门市	Jingmen Municipality	882.01	1.42	127.18	12.03		38.91
孝感市	Xiaogan Municipality	488.65	6.92	49.51	82.71		.54.81
黄冈市	Huanggang Municipality	471.34	10.66	71.64	74.79		32.48
咸宁市	Xianning Municipality	447.12	1.07	32.83	72.69		9.90
随州市	Suizhou Municipality	678.45	6.75	29.30	90.39		27.44
恩施自治州	Enshi Prefecture	460.18		22.86	105.81		5.76
仙桃市	Xiaotao Municipality	577.53	21.49	96.43	76.40		30.66
天门市	Tianmen Municipality	437.91	34.42	81.67	56.30		34.86
潜江市	Qianjiang Municipality	414.57	43.09	120.63	97.59		25.06
神农架林区	Shennongjia Forest Zone	280.00		5.33	64.00		4.00
按农业人口平均	**Average of Agricultural Population**						
全省	Province	576.11	11.99	78.35	91.57		35.95
武汉市	Wuhan Municipality	516.22	12.23	72.37	110.81		54.82
黄石市	Huangshi Municipality	433.32	4.20	54.06	75.18		21.96
十堰市	Shiyan Municipality	458.16	0.04	39.61	62.00		13.72
荆州市	Jingzhou Municipality	887.80	31.18	127.98	97.63		34.90
宜昌市	Yichang Municipality	582.45	10.91	85.08	191.65		17.40
襄樊市	Xiangfan Municipality	1199.40	12.43	89.47	179.37		55.58
鄂州市	Ezhou Municipality	448.45	7.37	76.37	110.47		47.40
荆门市	Jingmen Municipality	1340.37	21.59	193.27	18.29		59.13
孝感市	Xiaogan Municipality	576.63	8.16	58.43	97.60		64.67
黄冈市	Huanggang Municipality	614.70	12.48	83.85	87.54		38.02
咸宁市	Xianning Municipality	532.74	1.28	39.11	86.60		11.79
随州市	Suizhou Municipality	766.87	7.68	33.33	102.83		31.22
恩施自治州	Enshi Prefecture	475.02		23.60	109.23		5.94
仙桃市	Xiaotao Municipality	613.83	22.84	102.49	79.82		32.58
天门市	Tianmen Municipality	465.18	36.56	86.76	59.80		37.03
潜江市	Qianjiang Municipality	578.16	60.09	168.23	136.10		34.95
神农架林区	Shennongjia Forest Zone	425.96		8.11	97.36		6.09

7-28 市、州农业机械、用电、化肥、水利情况（2009）

AGRICULTURAL MACHINERY, ELECTRICITY CONSUMPTION, CHEMICAL FERTILIZERS AND IRRAGATION IN CITIES AND PREFECTURES(2009)

市、州	Municipalities and Prefecrures	农业机械总动力（万千瓦特） Total Power of Agricultural Machinery (10 000kW)	当年实际机耕面积（千公顷） Actual Sown Areas (1 000 hectares)	农村用电量（万千瓦小时） Rural Electricity Consumption (1 000kW/h)	化肥施用量（折纯量）(万吨) Consumption of Chemical Fertilizers (pure) (10 000tons)	有效灌溉面积（千公顷） Effective Irrigation Area (1 000 hectares)
全省	Province	3057.24	4099.40	1040885.0	340.26	2132.92
武汉市	Wuhan Municipality	207.40	203.87	134697.0	16.26	159.00
黄石市	Huangshi Municipality	64.86	91.13	84644.2	4.36	37.98
十堰市	Shiyan Municipality	124.16	71.83	34599.2	11.93	37.29
荆州市	Jingzhou Municipality	403.57	719.64	112210.0	37.68	392.34
宜昌市	Yichang Municipality	231.45	193.22	62691.3	35.43	103.51
襄樊市	Xiangfan Municipality	474.17	628.32	61677.4	52.07	231.95
鄂州市	Ezhou Municipality	49.73	36.30	25560.0	11.79	28.73
荆门市	Jingmen Municipality	326.53	432.32	57918.5	26.08	179.67
孝感市	Xiaogan Municipality	195.96	341.38	67274.6	21.91	223.73
黄冈市	Huanggang Municipality	208.79	356.13	228817.2	46.94	221.57
咸宁市	Xianning Municipality	127.98	138.57	35389.0	11.18	84.60
随州市	Suizhou Municipality	160.75	294.39	26367.8	16.14	125.95
恩施自治州	Enshi Prefecture	155.88	88.64	33703.3	24.02	52.75
仙桃市	Xiaotao Municipality	107.01	192.00	37766.0	7.23	87.21
天门市	Tianmen Municipality	130.18	199.50	17567.9	7.52	108.30
潜江市	Qianjiang Municipality	82.01	111.80	19066.8	9.37	58.22
神农架林区	Shennongjia Forest Zone	6.80	0.36	935.0	0.35	0.12

主要统计指标解释

农林牧渔业总产值　指以货币表现的农、林、牧、渔业全部产品和对农林牧渔业生产活动进行的各种支持性服务活动的价值总量，它反映一定时期内农林牧渔业生产总规模和总成果。1957 年以前的农林牧渔业总产值中包括了厩肥和农民自给性手工业(如农民自制衣服、鞋、袜，自己从事粮食初步加工等)。1958 年及以后，林业中增加了村及村以下竹木采伐产值；牧业中取消了厩肥产值；副业中取消了农民自给性手工业产值，增加了村及村以下办的工业产值；渔业中增加了海洋捕捞水产品产值。1980 年及以后，在副业中增加了农民家庭兼营工业商品部分的产值。从 1984 年起村及村以下工业产值划归工业。从 1993 年起取消副业，将野生动物的捕猎划入牧业，野生植物采集和农民家庭兼营商品性工业划归农业。从 2003 年起，执行新的国民经济行业分类标准，农林牧渔业总产值中包括了农林牧渔服务业产值。林业中增加了森林采运业产值。农业中取消了家庭兼营商品性工业产值，将野生林产品的采集划归林业。第一次农业普查以后，由于畜牧业产品年报数据与普查数据之间存在一定的差距，国家统计局农调总队对畜牧业年报数据与普查数据进行衔接，对畜牧业产值进行相应调整。

农林牧渔业总产值的计算方法通常是按农、林、牧、渔业产品及其副产品的产量分别乘以各自单位产品价格求得；少数生产周期较长，当年没有产品或产品产量不易统计的，则采用间接方法匡算其产值；然后将四业产品产值相加即为农林牧渔业总产值。

粮食产量　指全社会的产量。包括国有经济经营的、集体统一经营的和农民家庭经营的粮食产量，还包括工矿企业办的农场和其他生产单位的产量。粮食除包括稻谷、小麦、玉米、高粱、谷子及其他杂粮外，还包括薯类和豆类。其产量计算方法，豆类按去豆荚后的干豆计算；薯类(包括甘薯和马铃薯，不包括芋头和木薯)1963 年以前按每 4 公斤鲜薯折 1 公斤粮食计算，从 1964 年开始改为按 5 公斤鲜薯折 1 公斤粮食计算。城市郊区作为蔬菜的薯类(如马铃薯等)按鲜品计算，并且不作粮食统计。其他粮食一律按脱粒后的原粮计算。1989 年以前全国粮食产量数据主要靠全面报表取得，1989 年开始使用抽样调查数据。

棉花产量　指全社会的产量。包括春播棉和夏播棉。产量按皮棉计算。不包括木棉。

油料产量　指全部油料作物的生产量。包括花生、油菜籽、芝麻、向日葵籽、胡麻籽（亚麻籽）和其他油料。不包括大豆、木本油料和野生油料。花生以带壳干花生计算。

水产品产量　指人工养殖的水产品和天然生长的水产品的捕捞量。包括海水的鱼类、虾蟹类、贝类和藻类以及内陆水域的鱼类、虾蟹类和贝类，不包括淡水生植物。水产品产量是通过各级水产和统计部门逐级上报取得数据。1995 年及以前，贝类中牡　按鲜肉计算；　、蛤、蚌按 5 斤鲜品折 1 斤计算。1996 年以后则统一按鲜品计算。

猪、牛、羊肉产量　指当年出栏并已屠宰、除去头蹄下水后带骨肉(即　体重)的重量。包括全社会范围内的产量。1996 年前为各级逐级上报数据。1996 年第一次农业普查以后，由于畜牧业产品年报数据与普查数据之间存在一定的差距，国家统计局农调总队对畜牧业年报数据与普查数据进行衔接。1999 年以后，国家统计局开展了猪、牛、羊、禽等主要畜禽品种的抽样调查，并用抽样数据作为国家定案数据使用。未开展抽样调查的品种，仍使用各级统计部门逐级上报数据。

期初(末)畜禽存栏头(只)数　指报告期初(末)农村各种合作经济组织和国营农场、农民个人、机关、团体、学校、工矿企业、部队等单位以及城镇居民饲养的大牲畜、猪、羊、家禽等畜禽的存栏数。数据上报方式及数据调整情况同猪、牛、羊肉产量。

常用耕地　是指耕地总资源中专门种植农作物并经常进行耕种、能够正常收获的土地。包括当年实际耕种的熟地；弃耕、休闲不满三年，随时可以复耕的地；开荒利用三年以上的土地。在统计口径上包括南方小于 1 米、北方小于 2 米宽的沟、渠、路和田埂。不包括临时种植农作物的坡度在 25 度以上的陡坡地；在河套、湖畔、库区临时开发的成片或零星土地；也不包括已列为国家和省（区、市）退耕计划但临时耕种的土地。常用耕地是国家需要重点保护的耕地，是反映我国农业综合生产能力的一个重要指标。

农作物播种面积 指实际播种或移植有农作物的面积。凡是实际种植有农作物的面积，不论种植在耕地上还是种植在非耕地上，均包括在农作物播种面积中。在播种季节基本结束后，因遭灾而重新改种和补种的农作物面积，也包括在内。它是反映我国耕地面积利用情况的一个重要指标。目前，农作物播种面积主要包括粮食、棉花、油料、糖料、麻类、烟叶、蔬菜和瓜类、药材和其他农作物九大类。

有效灌溉面积 指具有一定的水源，地块比较平整，灌溉工程或设备已经配套，在一般年景下，当年能够进行正常灌溉的耕地面积。在一般情况下，有效灌溉面积应等于灌溉工程或设备已经配备，能够进行正常灌溉的水田和水浇地面积之和。它是反映我国耕地抗旱能力的一个重要指标。

农用化肥施用量 指本年内实际用于农业生产的化肥数量，包括氮肥、磷肥、钾肥和复合肥。化肥施用量要求按折纯量计算数量。折纯量是指把氮肥、磷肥、钾肥分别按含氮、含五氧化二磷、含氧化钾的百分之百成份进行折算后的数量。复合肥按其所含主要成分折算。公式为：

折纯量=实物量×某种化肥有效成份含量的百分比

农业机械总动力 指主要用于农、林、牧、渔业的各种动力机械的动力总和。包括耕作机械、排灌机械、收获机械、农用运输机械、植物保护机械、牧业机械、林业机械、渔业机械和其他农业机械〔内燃机按引擎马力折成瓦(特)计算、电动机按功率折成瓦(特)计算〕。不包括专门用于乡、镇、村、组办工业、基本建设、非农业运输、科学试验和教学等非农业生产方面用的动力机械与作业机械。这个指标的统计数据主要来源于农机部门。

乡村从业人员 指乡村人口中劳动年龄在 16 周岁以上实际参加生产经营活动并取得实物或货币收入的人员，包括劳动年龄内经常参加劳动的人员，也包括超过劳动年龄但经常参加劳动的人员，但不包括户口在家的在外学生、现役军人和丧失劳动能力的人，也不包括待业人员和家务劳动者。从业人员按从事主业时间最长（时间相同按收入）分为农林牧渔业从业人员、工业从业人员、建筑业从业人员、交通运输业、仓储及邮电通信业从业人员、批零贸易业、餐饮业从业人员、其他非农行业从业人员。

Explanatory Notes on Main Statistical Indicators

Gross Output Value of Farming, Forestry, Animal Husbandry and Fishery refers to the total value of products of farming, forestry, animal husbandry and fishery, and total value of services rendered to support farming, forestry, animal husbandry and fishery activities. It reflects the total scale and results of agricultural production during a given period. Prior to 1957, Chinas gross agricultural output value included barnyard manure and handicraft products for self-consumption (clothes, shoes, stockings, and initial grain processing undertaken by peasants). Since 1958, cutting and felling of bamboo and trees by villages and other cooperative organizations under villages have been included in forestry; value of barnyard manure has been excluded from animal husbandry; self consumed handicrafts has been excluded from sideline occupations, while the output value of industries run by villages and cooperative organizations under village had been included in sideline occupations and the output value of fish catches by motor fishing boats has been added to fishery. Since 1980, the value of handicraft products made for sale by individuals in households had been added to sideline occupations. Since 1984, industries run by villages and under villages have been included in the sector of industry. Since 1993, the subdivision of sideline occupations has been canceled, and the hunting of wild animals has been classified into animal husbandry, and the gathering of wild plants and commodity industry run by rural household have been included in farming. A new industrial classification of economic activities was introduced in 2003. Under the new classification, value of services to farming, forestry, animal husbandry and fishery is included in the gross output value of agriculture, value of wood felling and transport is included in forestry, value of industrial output by rural households is not included in agriculture, and the collection of wild forest products is taken from agriculture and included in the forestry. The first agriculture census of China revealed some discrepancy between the production of animal products from the annual reports and that from the census. Efforts were made by the Rural Socio-economic Survey Organization of NBS to adjust the output value of animal husbandry to make the figures from the annual reports consistent with the census data.

Gross output value of agriculture is obtained by first multiplying the output of each product or by product by its price, resulting in the output value of each single item. For a small number of products, annual output of which is not available or difficult to get due to the long production (growing) process involved, the output value is estimated through an indirect approach. The sum of output value of all products of farming, forestry, animal husbandry and fishery is then equal to the gross output value of agriculture.

Grain Output refers to the total output in the whole country including grains produced by state farms, collective units, rural households, as well as by farms affiliated to industrial and mining enterprises and other production units. Grain includes rice, wheat, corn, sorghum, millet and other miscellaneous grains as well as tubers and bean. Output of beans refers to dry beans without pods. The output of tubers (sweet potatoes and potatoes, not including taros and cassava) was converted into that of grain at the ratio 4:1, i.e. 4 kilograms of fresh tubers was equivalent to 1 kilogram of grain up to 1963. Since 1964 the ratio for conversion has been 5:1. Tubers supplied as vegetables (such as potatoes) in cities and suburbs are calculated as fresh vegetables and their output is not included in the output of grain. Output of all other grains refers to husked grain. Data on grain production before 1989 were obtained through Comprehensive Statistical Reporting System. Since 1989, data from sample surveys are used.

Cotton Output refers to the cotton production in the whole country including cotton sown in spring and in autumn. Output is measured as the weight of ginned cotton. Ceiba is not included.

Output of Oil-bearing Crops refers to the total production of oil-bearing crops of various kinds, including peanuts, (dry, in shell) rapeseeds, sesame, sunflower seeds, flax seeds, and other oil-bearing crops. Soybeans, oil-bearing woody plants, and wild oil-bearing crops are not included.

Output of Aquatic Products refers to catches of both artificially cultured and naturally grown aquatic products, including fish, shrimps, crabs and shellfish in sea and inland water as well as seaweed. Freshwater plants are not included. Data on output of aquatic products are reported by aquatic product and statistical agencies level by level. Before 1995, among the shellfish, the oyster was counted as fresh meat; 5 kilograms of ark shell, clams and frogs are equivalent to 1 kilogram of fresh aquatic products; they are all counted as fresh aquatic products since 1996.

Output of Pork, Beef, and Mutton refers to the meat of slaughtered hogs, cattle, sheep and goats with head, feet, and offal taken away. Data refers to the production of the whole country. The first agriculture census of China in 1996 revealed some discrepancy between the production of animal products from the annual reports and that from the census. Efforts were made by the Rural Socio-economic Survey Organization of NBS to adjust the output value of animal husbandry to make the figures from the annual reports consistent with the census data. Since 1999, NBS conducted sample survey for the major animal husbandry products, such as hogs, cattle, sheep and goats and fowls, and the data from sample surveys are used as national finalized data. Those products, which are not covered by the sample survey, are still reported by statistical agencies level by level.

Number of Livestock or Poultry in Stock at Beginning (or End) refers to the total number of large animals, pigs, sheep, fowls, etc. raised by rural cooperative organizations, state farms, rural individuals, government agencies, schools, industrial and mining enterprises, army, and urban residents at the beginning (or end) of the reference period. Data reporting system and data adjustment are the same as that in the output of pork, beef and mutton.

Regularly Cultivated Land refers to farmland among the total land resources, which is exclusively used for farming and is under regular cultivation with harvest in normal years. Included are currently cultivated land, land that has been abandoned or put in idle for less than 3 years and could be re-used for cultivation at any time, and new-claimed land that has been put into cultivation for more than 3 years. According to statistical coverage, it includes the gouges, dykes, roads and ridges of field with 1 meter wide in Southern areas and 2 meters wide in Northern areas. Excluded under this category are steep slope land over 25 degrees under temporary cultivation, land (large or small plots) that is claimed along river bends, lake sides or banks of reservoirs, as well as land that has been designated under the "Green for Grain" programme of the state and provincial governments but is still temporarily under cultivation. The regularly cultivated land is the key protection land of the nation, an important indicator reflecting the comprehensive productivity of agriculture of China.

Sown Area of Crops refers to area of land sown or transplanted with crops regardless of being in cultivated area or non-cultivated area. Area of land re-sown due to natural disasters is also included. This is an important indicator that can reflect the utilization condition of the cultivated land in China. At present, the sown area of crops mainly include the following 9 categories of crops: grain, cotton, oil-bearing crops, sugar crops, fiber crops, Tobacco, Vegetables and melons, medicinal materials and other farm crops.

Irrigated Area refers to areas that are effectively irrigated, i.e. level land, which has water source and complete sets of irrigation facilities to lift and move adequate water for irrigation purpose under normal conditions. Under normal conditions, irrigated area is the sum of watered fields and irrigated fields where irrigation systems or equipment have been installed for regular irrigation purpose. This important indicator reflects drought resistance capacity of the cultivated land in China.

Consumption of Chemical Fertilizers in Agriculture refers to the quantity of chemical fertilizers applied in agriculture in the year, including nitrogenous fertilizer, phosphate fertilizer, potash fertilizer, and compound fertilizer. The consumption of chemical fertilizers is required in calculation to convert the gross weight into weight containing 100% effective component (e.g. 100% nitrogen content in nitrogenous fertilizer, 100% phosphorous pent oxide contents in phosphate fertilizer, 100% potassium oxide contents in potash fertilizer). Compound fertilizer is converted with its major component. The formula is :

Volume of effective component= physical quantity x effective component of certain chemical fertilizer (%)

Total Power of Farm Machinery refers to total mechanical power of machinery used in farming, forestry, animal husbandry, and fishery, including ploughing, irrigation and drainage, harvesting, transport, plant protection, stock breeding, forestry and fishery. The power of internal combustion engines is required to convert horsepower into watts and the power of electric motors is required to be converted into watts. Machinery employed for non-agricultural purposes, such as the machines used in township run and village-run industry, construction, non-agricultural transport, scientific experiments and teaching, is excluded. Data are mainly from agricultural machinery agencies.

Rural Employed Persons refer to rural labor forces aged over 16 years old who are engaged in real production and management activities and receive payment in kind or wages, including those covered within the age frame and regularly participating in production activities, and those who are out of the range of age frame and also participating in production activities regularly. Excluding students studying in other places with their permanent residence registered in local areas, servicemen and persons incapable of working; also excluding those who are waiting for jobs and those engaged in household work. Persons employed are classified as persons engaged in agriculture, forestry, animal husbandry or fishery activities; persons engaged in industrial activities; persons engaged in construction activities; persons engaged in transport, storage and telecommunications activities; persons engaged in whole sales and retail sales trade and catering activities; and persons engaged in other non-agriculture activities, depending upon the longest period of employment in major activities (or using income indicator when period of employment is the same).

8 工业、能源

Industry and Energy

资料整理：潘天曙　付春晖

工　业 、能　源

INDUSTRY 、ENERGY
2009

规模以上工业企业	Industrial Enterprises Above Designated Size	
工业总产值(现价)	Total Output Value (at current price)	15567.02（亿元）
#轻工业	Light Industry	4234.52（亿元）
重工业	Heavy Industry	11332.50（亿元）
#大型企业	Large Scale Enterprises	6418.90（亿元）
中型企业	Medium Scale Enterprises	3916.33（亿元）
资产总计	Total Assets	19221.02（亿元）
负债合计	Total Liability	10381.23（亿元）
主营业务收入	Income from Major Business	15331.62（亿元）
利税总额	Total Revenue	1987.88（亿元）
从业人员年平均人数	Annually Average number of Employment	272.39（万人）
工业原煤消费量	Consumption of Coal	6681.74（万吨）
工业原油消费量	Consumption of Crude Oil	947.28（万吨）

规模以上工业总产值构成（%）
Composition of Industry above desginated size

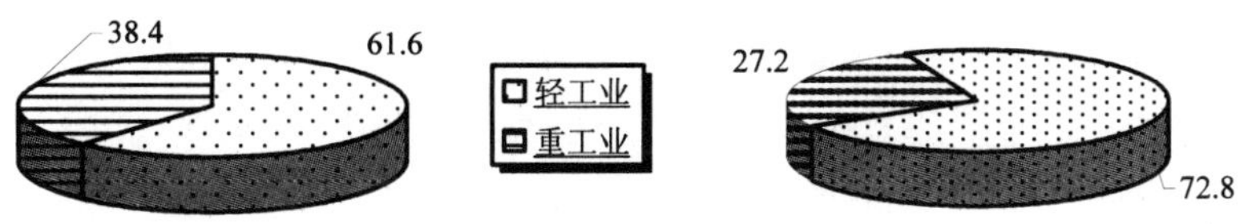

2000年　　2009年

规模以上工业增加值（上年＝100）
Value Added of Industry Above Desingnated (preceding year=100)

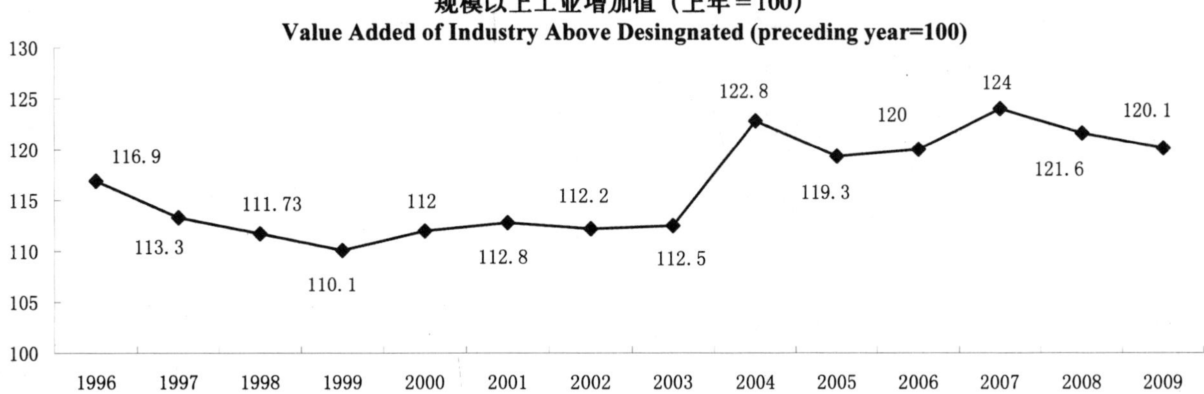

注：规模工业增加值指数为快报数。

Note:Value Added of Industry Above Desingnated are preliminary statistics.

8-1 工业发展基本情况

THE BASIC SITUATION OF INDUSTRIAL DEVELOPMENT

年份 Year	工业企业单位数（个）Number of Industrial Enterprises（unit）	轻工业 Light industry	重工业 Heavy industry	工业总产值（当年价）（亿元）Total Output Value（currentprice）（100 million yuan）	轻工业 Light industry	重工业 Heavy industry
1978	15929	10022	5907	167.21	78.71	88.50
1979	16073	10100	5973	220.82	93.45	107.37
1980	16609	10582	6027	228.02	110.14	117.88
1981	17032	11192	5840	249.72	131.13	118.59
1982	18066	11960	6106	272.08	137.66	134.42
1983	18926	12325	6637	319.21	157.33	161.88
1984	22713	14664	8049	371.93	182.57	189.36
1985	25011	15309	9702	467.22	216.47	250.75
1986	27697	16890	10807	538.28	256.06	282.22
1987	26294	15528	10766	659.19	315.49	343.70
1988	26016	15279	10737	834.84	405.13	429.71
1989	25999	15035	10964	976.93	463.35	513.58
1990	25913	14885	11028	1008.20	476.76	531.44
1991	25204	14317	10887	1136.02	531.26	604.76
1992	23985	13428	10557	1373.66	605.11	768.55
1993	22600	11958	10642	1992.31	770.20	1222.11
1994	23275	12096	11179	3024.72	1360.78	1663.94
1995	27815	14827	12988	3697.91	1870.12	1827.79
1996	25986	13618	12368	4836.33	2470.90	2365.43
1997	24498	12723	11775	5977.00	3158.47	2818.53
1998	7399	3581	3818	6731.31	3534.67	3196.64
1999	6874	3308	3566	2831.70	1109.92	1721.78
2000	6282	3026	3256	3064.43	1177.24	1887.18
2001	6197	2981	3216	3239.51	1194.90	2044.61
2002	6183	2947	3236	3589.26	1184.78	2404.48
2003	6271	2789	3482	3631.29	1192.46	2438.82
2004	6232	2632	3600	4960.25	1180.07	3780.17
2005	6813	2953	3860	6066.96	1503.00341	4563.95
2006	7546	3272	4274	7454.07	1898.34	5555.73
2007	8996	3808	5188	9601.52	2492.88	7108.64
2008	12067	4806	7261	13454.94	3344.80	10110.14
2009	14027	5515	8512	15567.02	4234.52	11332.50

注：1.本表规模以上工业1997年及以前统计范围为乡及乡以上工业。1998—2006年为全部国有工业及年销售收入500万元以上非国有工业企业；2007年起为主营业务收入500万元以上工业。

2."国有及国有控股经济"一栏，1998年以前统计范围为国有工业。

Note: 1. The table above-scale industrial statistics of 1997 and before the range of Fixed Assets. 1998-2006 for all state-owned industries and 5 million yuan in sales revenue.

2. "State-owned and state-controlled economy" a column, prior to 1998 statistics the range of state-owned industries.

8-1 续表 continued

单位:亿元 (100 million yuan)

年份 Year	主营业务收入 (亿元) Main business income (100 million yuan)	利润总额 (亿元) Total profit (100 million yuan)	利税总额 (亿元) Total profits and taxes (100 million yuan)	职工人数 (万人) Number of employees (1000 persons)
1978		17.71	29.51	160.16
1979	163.52	20.70	34.19	161.98
1980	197.52	25.45	41.54	173.29
1981	210.15	25.71	43.53	185.80
1982	239.64	27.50	47.82	197.62
1983	268.98	31.77	53.46	202.80
1984	308.66	37.33	62.38	292.49
1985	381.43	43.64	80.82	306.83
1986	438.95	40.22	82.14	333.63
1987	526.95	48.54	96.16	343.43
1988	654.72	58.85	117.28	356.43
1989	706.99	50.99	112.12	360.88
1990	705.97	26.73	88.40	358.65
1991	800.01	31.79	103.46	367.41
1992	1041.66	43.19	127.15	357.74
1993	1500.71	67.00	167.92	357.97
1994	1690.94	74.06	190.29	381.45
1995	2066.38	52.26	181.57	379.84
1996	2305.57	43.93	181.41	369.80
1997	2681.36	57.71	221.53	362.50
1998	2433.92	44.71	195.96	274.43
1999	2602.26	68.82	232.24	250.07
2000	2870.36	106.47	29.36	230.36
2001	3043.82	134.49	335.36	212.48
2002	3378.31	175.60	404.23	205.82
2003	3993.99	194.40	444.96	198.60
2004	4832.43	270.98	559.28	176.70
2005	5962.54	371.84	727.48	188.30
2006	7314.81	454.00	897.19	190.85
2007	9390.43	647.85	1229.16	200.35
2008	13081.90	909.03	1761.47	235.90
2009	15331.62	1092.47	1987.88	272.39

8-2 规模以上工业企业单位数和产销总值 (2009)

单位:亿元

项 目	Item	企业单位数(个) Number of Enterprises (unit)
总 计	Total	14027
一、按登记注册类型分组:	Grouped by Type of Registration	
内资企业	Inner Funded Enterprises	13136
国有企业	State Owned Enterprises	407
中央企业	Central Enterprises	103
地方企业	Local Enterprises	304
集体企业	Collective-owned Enterprise	331
股份合作企业	Share Holding Cooperative Enterprises	171
联营企业	Joint Owned Enterprise	37
国有联营企业	State Joint Ownership	3
集体联营企业	Collective Joint Ownership	10
国有与集体联营企业	Joint State- Collective Ownership	3
其他联营企业	Other Joint Owned Enterprise	21
有限责任公司	Responsibility Co. Ltd	3624
国有独资公司	State Solely Funded Co.	40
其他有限责任公司	Others	3584
股份有限公司	Share Holding Co.Ltd.	590
私营企业	Private - owned enterprises	7875
私营独资企业	Solely Private - owned enterprises	1756
私营合作企业	Private Joint Venture	670
私营有限责任公司	Private Responsibility Co. Ltd	4804
私营股份有限公司	Private Share Holding Co.Ltd.	645
其他企业	Others	101
港、澳、台商投资企业	Hongkong, Macao and Taiwan Funded Enterprises	421
合资经营企业(港或澳、台资)	Joint Venture with Hongkong, Macao and Taiwan	199
合作经营企业(港或澳、台资)	Cooperate with Hongkong, Macao and Taiwan Funded	10
港澳台商独资经营企业	Enterprises Solely Funded by Hongkong, Macao and Taiwan Businessmen	189
港澳台商投资股份有限公司	Share Holding Co.Ltd. With Hongkong, Macao and Taiwan Investment	23
外商投资企业	Foreign Funded Enterprises	470
中外合资经营企业	Sino - Foreign Joint Funded Enterprises	273
中外合作经营企业	Sino - Foreign Cooperative Funded Enterprises	10
外资企业	Foreign Solely Funded Enterprises	169
外商投资股份有限公司	Foreign Funded Share Holding Co.Ltd.	18
二、在总计中:亏损企业	Of the Total: enterprises running under deficit	1826
在总计中:国有控股企业	Of the Total: State-Owned Share Holding Enterprises	864
在总计中:农村工业	Of the Total: Rural Industry	390
在总计中:轻工业	Of the Total: Light Industry	5515
重工业	Heavy Industry	8512
在总计中:大型企业	Of the Total: Large Scale Enterprises	104
中型企业	Medium Scale Enterprises	1120
小型企业	Small Enterprises	12803

THE NUMBER OF UNITS OF INDUSTRIAL ENTERPRISES ABOVE DESIGNATED SIZE AND GROSS SALES (2009)

(100 million Yuan)

工业总产值（当年价格） Total Output Value (current price)	新产品产值 Output Value of New Products	工业销售产值（当年价格） Output Value of Industrial Products Sales (current price)	出口交货值 Delivery Value for Export
15567.02	1554.85	15164.52	653.47
12489.23	1045.47	12158.07	418.9
3505.01	462.26	3480.92	121.43
2867.34	368.68	2855.71	103.96
637.67	93.59	625.21	17.46
157.53	0.83	150.86	0.65
84.42	3.19	81.04	2.65
17.48	0.01	17.13	0.09
6.47		6.31	
4.90	0.01	4.82	
1.67		1.73	0.09
4.45		4.27	
3174.30	217.61	3068.39	124.84
535.67	74.16	522.58	18.6
	143.44	2545.81	106.24
1885.64	265.20	1813.61	61.37
3587.61	95.42	3468.74	107.36
595.09	5.34	576.82	14.27
241.18	1.05	233.04	1.62
2392.89	81.85	2317.16	76.38
358.45	7.18	341.72	15.09
77.24	0.95	77.39	0.51
709.68	40.92	685.49	162.86
343.65	28.10	330.35	33.75
14.77	1.32	14.69	
330.60	11.49	320.56	128.89
20.66		19.89	0.22
2368.11	468.47	2320.96	71.71
1924.61	452.36	1892.88	36.73
25.76	0.19	25.56	
306.90	7.79	293	32.97
110.83	8.13	109.52	2
1733.03	63.37	1683.13	54.17
6534.21	1095.54	6421.9	172.46
112.33	1.43	107.69	0.57
4234.52	213.99	4087.47	227.35
11332.50	1340.86	11077.05	426.11
6418.90	1101.24	6341.96	280.59
3916.33	348.76	3782.53	200.83
5231.79	104.85	5040.03	172.04

8-2 续表 continued

单位:亿元

项 目	Item	企业单位数（个） Number of Enterprises(unit)
按行业分	Grouped by sector	
采矿业	**Mining and Qarrying**	
煤炭开采和洗选业	Coal Mining and Processing	244.00
石油和天然气开采业	Petroleum and Natural Gas Extraction	5.00
黑色金属矿采选业	Ferrous Metals Mining and Processing	165.00
有色金属矿采选业	Non-ferrous Metals Mining and Processing	59.00
非金属矿采选业	Non-metal Minerals Mining and Processing	471.00
其他采矿业	Other Minerals Mining and Processing	5.00
制造业	**Manufacturing**	
农副食品加工业	Food Processing	1491.00
食品制造业	Food Production	347.00
饮料制造业	Beverage Production	378.00
烟草制品业	Tobacco Processing	12.00
纺织业	Textile Industry	1055.00
纺织服装、鞋、帽制造业	Textile,Garments, Shoes and Hats Products	492.00
皮革、毛皮、羽毛(绒)及其制品业	Leather, Furs,Down and Related Products	54.00
木材加工及木、竹、藤、棕、草制品业	Timber Processing, Wood, Bamboo, Cane, Palm and Sraw Products	240.00
家具制造业	Furniture Manufacturing	80.00
造纸及纸制品业	Papermaking and Paper Products	270.00
印刷业和记录媒介的复制	Printing and Record Processing	201.00
文教体育用品制造业	Stationery, Education and Sports Goods	21.00
石油加工、炼焦及核燃料加工业	Petroleum Processing, Coking Products and Nuclear Fuel Processing	40.00
化学原料及化学制品制造业	Raw Chemical Material and Chemical Products	1009.00
医药制造业	Medical and pharmaceutical Products	316.00
化学纤维制造业	Chemical Fibers	18.00
橡胶制品业	Rubber Products	95.00
塑料制品业	Plastic Products	514.00
非金属矿物制品业	Nonmetal Material Products	1584.00
黑色金属冶炼及压延加工业	Smelting and Pressing of Ferrous Metals	155.00
有色金属冶炼及压延加工业	Smelting and Pressing of Nonferrous Metals	184.00
金属制品业	Metal Products	576.00
通用设备制造业	Ordinary Machinery Manufacturing	915.00
专用设备制造业	Special Purpose Equipment Manufacturing	531.00
交通运输设备制造业	Transportation Equipment Manufacturing	1174.00
电气机械及器材制造业	Electric Machinery and Equipment	463.00
通信设备、计算机及其他电子设备制造业	Telecommunication Equipment, Computer and Other Electronic Equipment Manufacturing	258.00
仪器仪表及文化、办公用机械制造业	Instruments, Meters, Cultural and Official Machinery	132.00
工艺品及其他制造业	Handicraft Article and Other Manufacturing	104.00
废弃资源和废旧材料回收加工业	Waste Resources and Junk Material Recycled	28.00
电力、燃气及水的生产和供应业	**Electric Power, Gas and Water Production and Supply**	
电力、热力的生产和供应业	Electric Power, Steam and Hot Water Production and Supply	200.00
燃气生产和供应业	Gas Production and Supply	37.00
水的生产和供应业	Tap Water Production and Supply	104.00

(100 million Yuan)

工业总产值 (当年价格) Total Output Value(current price)	新产品产值 Output Value of New Products	工业销售产值 (当年价格) Output Value of Industrial Products Sales(current price)	出口交货值 Delivery Value for Export
47.04		44.49	
133.10	11.10	132.91	7.72
154.33		150.48	0.02
37.15	0.07	36.93	
152.39	0.23	145.52	0.04
0.75		0.42	
1086.63	21.18	1040.58	27.14
256.76	2.58	247.88	17.18
388.65	31.14	376.19	2.18
300.66		300.50	0.11
698.16	12.79	678.50	61.29
271.20	11.96	261.87	54.23
18.53	0.54	17.14	3.54
99.75	1.44	95.76	0.88
22.94	0.97	22.35	2.67
184.04	1.67	180.04	1.25
92.95	2.40	88.60	2.28
8.25		7.42	0.64
465.98		459.70	
1170.22	47.43	1136.87	54.29
314.22	39.55	300.00	29.04
20.40	1.26	20.47	1.46
66.58	2.52	64.37	5.46
251.63	24.23	244.36	1.37
781.53	10.99	760.54	8.00
1710.67	324.13	1699.96	33.07
378.90	66.20	373.44	5.43
366.42	30.53	339.97	7.47
564.52	66.34	534.48	11.33
253.16	15.57	243.39	4.76
2609.48	657.21	2552.26	88.79
520.98	96.54	504.08	24.91
622.05	49.26	596.66	190.17
60.42	7.92	59.16	3.49
60.74	16.51	58.01	3.22
21.51		21.32	
1246.19		1242.71	0.04
45.08	0.15	45.08	
83.06	0.43	80.12	

8-3 规模以上工业企业主要经济指标 (2009)

单位:亿元

项 目	Item	企业单位数(个) Number of Enterprises (unit)
总 计	Total	14027
一、按登记注册类型分组:	Grouped by Type of Registration	
内资企业	Inner Funded Enterprises	13136
国有企业	State Owned Enterprises	407
中央企业	Central Enterprises	103
地方企业	Local Enterprises	304
集体企业	Collective-owned Enterprise	331
股份合作企业	Share Holding Cooperative Enterprises	171
联营企业	Joint Owned Enterprise	37
国有联营企业	State Joint Ownership	3
集体联营企业	Collective Joint Ownership	10
国有与集体联营企业	Joint State- Collective Ownership	3
其他联营企业	Other Joint Owned Enterprise	21
有限责任公司	Responsibility Co. Ltd	3624
国有独资公司	State Solely Funded Co.	40
其他有限责任公司	Others	3584
股份有限公司	Share Holding Co.Ltd.	590
私营企业	Private - owned enterprises	7875
私营独资企业	Solely Private - owned enterprises	1756
私营合作企业	Private Joint Venture	670
私营有限责任公司	Private Responsibility Co. Ltd	4804
私营股份有限公司	Private Share Holding Co.Ltd.	645
其他企业	Others	101
港、澳、台商投资企业	Hongkong, Macao and Taiwan Funded Enterprises	421
合资经营企业(港或澳、台资)	Joint Venture with Hongkong, Macao and Taiwan	199
合作经营企业(港或澳、台资)	Cooperate with Hongkong, Macao and Taiwan Funded	10
港澳台商独资经营企业	Enterprises Solely Funded by Hongkong, Macao and Taiwan Businessmen	189
港澳台商投资股份有限公司	Share Holding Co.Ltd. With Hongkong, Macao and Taiwan Investment	23
外商投资企业	Foreign Funded Enterprises	470
中外合资经营企业	Sino - Foreign Joint Funded Enterprises	273
中外合作经营企业	Sino - Foreign Cooperative Funded Enterprises	10
外资企业	Foreign Solely Funded Enterprises	169
外商投资股份有限公司	Foreign Funded Share Holding Co.Ltd.	18
二、在总计中:亏损企业	Of the Total: enterprises running under deficit	1826
在总计中:国有控股企业	Of the Total: State-Owned Share Holding Enterprises	864
在总计中:农村工业	Of the Total: Rural Industry	390
在总计中:轻工业	Of the Total: Light Industry	5515
重工业	Heavy Industry	8512
在总计中:大型企业	Of the Total: Large Scale Enterprises	104
中型企业	Medium Scale Enterprises	1120
小型企业	Small Enterprises	12803

MAJOR ECONOMIC INDICATORS OF INDUSTRIAL ENTERPRISES ABOVE DESIGNATED SCALE (2009)

(100 million Yuan)

资产总计 Total Assets	流动资产合计 Circulating Funds	应收帐款净额 Net Value of Account Received	存货 Stock	产成品 Finished Products	固定资产合计 Total Fixed Assets
19221.02	7498.25	1938.52	1795.85	630.56	9210.24
15334.88	5061.89	948.30	1482.49	519.90	7994.01
4608.81	1610.15	217.91	578.46	137.25	2359.56
3921.85	1272.01	170.76	484.79	110.19	2068.05
686.96	338.14	47.15	93.68	27.05	291.51
82.39	37.70	10.83	9.63	5.26	32.71
50.09	22.21	6.20	8.33	4.55	25.27
14.25	5.69	2.00	0.98	0.67	7.92
4.42	1.85	0.29	0.10	0.03	2.46
1.37	0.73	0.13	0.22	0.13	0.63
1.33	1.06	0.34	0.20	0.09	0.28
7.13	2.05	1.24	0.45	0.42	4.54
3492.03	1370.85	336.48	358.72	143.25	1799.71
888.36	280.94	61.75	59.44	10.16	527.37
2603.67	1089.91	274.74	299.28	133.08	1272.34
4919.53	1045.89	160.37	245.46	90.89	2785.10
2111.94	942.29	209.11	272.37	134.60	961.84
254.88	109.16	24.02	32.48	19.16	128.90
103.44	42.90	9.39	10.08	6.19	54.18
1530.42	691.84	154.01	198.00	95.34	681.53
223.20	98.39	21.69	31.80	13.91	97.22
55.84	27.11	5.38	8.55	3.44	21.90
1304.70	972.95	777.37	86.65	25.99	275.93
1047.70	861.72	737.50	59.38	14.01	152.61
13.16	6.67	1.51	1.09	0.26	5.34
219.50	93.80	36.08	22.08	8.91	107.15
24.35	10.76	2.28	4.10	2.81	10.82
2581.44	1463.42	212.85	226.71	84.66	940.31
2097.71	1253.40	147.71	182.17	67.97	726.66
41.76	4.86	2.32	1.24	0.36	27.97
287.11	145.23	47.70	33.38	12.16	117.84
154.87	59.93	15.13	9.92	4.17	67.83
2254.46	633.21	154.08	176.74	68.47	1439.07
12399.78	4317.97	1217.08	974.02	273.37	6375.75
57.50	24.84	5.79	7.99	3.68	27.07
3064.59	1436.98	249.24	509.06	189.26	1245.20
16156.43	6061.27	1689.28	1286.79	441.30	7965.04
10489.05	3301.63	415.99	846.65	222.96	5524.00
5138.89	2627.74	1122.89	504.45	185.65	2042.57
3593.09	1568.88	399.64	444.74	221.95	1643.67

8-3 续表 1 continued

单位:亿元

项 目	Item	企业单位数(个) Number of Enterprises(unit)
按行业分	**Grouped by Sector**	
采矿业	**Mining and Qarrying**	
煤炭开采和洗选业	Coal Mining and Processing	244
石油和天然气开采业	Petroleum and Natural Gas Extraction	5
黑色金属矿采选业	Ferrous Metals Mining and Processing	165
有色金属矿采选业	Non-ferrous Metals Mining and Processing	59
非金属矿采选业	Non-metal Minerals Mining and Processing	471
其他采矿业	Other Minerals Mining and Processing	5
制造业	**Manufacturing**	
农副食品加工业	Food Processing	1491
食品制造业	Food Production	347
饮料制造业	Beverage Production	378
烟草制品业	Tobacco Processing	12
纺织业	Textile Industry	1055
纺织服装、鞋、帽制造业	Textile,Garments, Shoes and Hats Products	492
皮革、毛皮、羽毛(绒)及其制品业	Leather, Furs,Down and Related Products	54
木材加工及木、竹、藤、棕、草制品业	Timber Processing, Wood, Bamboo, Cane, Palm and Sraw Products	240
家具制造业	Furniture Manufacturing	80
造纸及纸制品业	Papermaking and Paper Products	270
印刷业和记录媒介的复制	Printing and Record Processing	201
文教体育用品制造业	Stationery, Education and Sports Goods	21
石油加工、炼焦及核燃料加工业	Petroleum Processing, Coking Products and Nuclear Fuel Processing	40
化学原料及化学制品制造业	Raw Chemical Material and Chemical Products	1009
医药制造业	Medical and pharmaceutical Products	316
化学纤维制造业	Chemical Fibers	18
橡胶制品业	Rubber Products	95
塑料制品业	Plastic Products	514
非金属矿物制品业	Nonmetal Material Products	1584
黑色金属冶炼及压延加工业	Smelting and Pressing of Ferrous Metals	155
有色金属冶炼及压延加工业	Smelting and Pressing of Nonferrous Metals	184
金属制品业	Metal Products	576
通用设备制造业	Ordinary Machinery Manufacturing	915
专用设备制造业	Special Purpose Equipment Manufacturing	531
交通运输设备制造业	Transportation Equipment Manufacturing	1174
电气机械及器材制造业	Electric Machinery and Equipment	463
通信设备、计算机及其他电子设备制造业	Telecommunication Equipment, Computer and Other Electronic Equipment Manufacturing	258
仪器仪表及文化、办公用机械制造业	Instruments, Meters, Cultural and Official Machinery	132
工艺品及其他制造业	Handicraft Article and Other Manufacturing	104
废弃资源和废旧材料回收加工业	Waste Resources and Junk Material Recycled	28
电力、燃气及水的生产和供应业	**Electric Power, Gas and Water Production and Supply**	
电力、热力的生产和供应业	Electric Power, Steam and Hot Water Production and Supply	200
燃气生产和供应业	Gas Production and Supply	37
水的生产和供应业	Tap Water Production and Supply	104

(100 million Yuan)

资产总计 Total Assets	流动资产合计 Circulating Funds	应收帐款净额 Net Value of Account Received	存货 Stock	产成品 Finished Products	固定资产合计 Total Fixed Assets
40.16	12.10	1.62	2.69	1.35	24.44
214.80	56.94	22.52	26.04	7.20	157.85
48.79	18.65	4.65	4.80	2.79	27.62
36.62	17.84	3.91	2.41	1.29	9.92
127.67	57.42	12.11	9.22	5.96	52.62
0.46	0.16	0.04	0.04	0.01	0.30
504.95	212.45	32.92	87.41	44.13	245.72
191.88	81.44	14.79	27.12	14.91	90.55
335.55	188.08	22.10	43.48	14.77	115.37
238.60	165.76	14.96	113.18	11.41	46.40
456.67	200.52	31.56	79.47	39.54	195.89
171.83	84.80	18.57	20.41	11.79	70.70
10.54	5.51	1.22	2.21	1.24	3.29
69.00	26.78	4.18	8.09	4.02	33.74
19.01	8.28	1.39	2.45	0.97	8.20
147.45	64.85	16.33	15.73	5.23	66.20
81.10	37.94	9.85	12.37	6.52	33.57
7.06	4.25	1.09	1.37	0.38	1.04
141.73	54.31	11.33	27.18	4.65	82.26
998.54	395.43	57.34	97.84	36.62	459.43
389.41	160.16	28.36	40.12	15.90	138.23
22.99	8.45	0.82	2.04	0.75	8.55
41.42	21.18	5.92	6.33	3.16	16.71
173.26	91.33	21.75	34.01	18.74	63.03
770.78	271.47	48.96	69.02	31.44	403.64
2158.40	661.62	49.20	258.44	49.93	995.06
249.61	156.22	23.52	58.87	11.02	86.58
382.48	159.67	34.99	42.32	16.77	152.77
677.07	387.77	94.65	88.86	31.07	213.53
268.58	166.31	45.59	39.81	15.57	75.55
3308.71	1883.45	301.29	327.85	111.89	1250.84
433.48	225.46	78.81	56.04	23.20	165.91
934.82	412.49	116.74	119.21	75.50	473.06
88.28	51.46	13.86	13.22	3.27	31.79
44.45	27.26	4.53	12.79	4.80	13.83
15.86	9.36	2.32	1.54	1.31	5.99
4387.25	303.63	71.09	9.60	1.00	3205.63
806.45	753.79	707.24	25.45	0.40	45.10
225.30	53.67	6.40	6.83	0.06	139.32

8-3 续表 2 continued

单位:亿元

项目	Item	固定资产原价 Original Price of Fixed Assets
总计	Total	9210.24
一、按登记注册类型分组:	Grouped by Type of Registration	
内资企业	Inner Funded Enterprises	7994.01
国有企业	State Owned Enterprises	2359.56
中央企业	Central Enterprises	2068.05
地方企业	Local Enterprises	291.51
集体企业	Collective-owned Enterprise	32.71
股份合作企业	Share Holding Cooperative Enterprises	25.27
联营企业	Joint Owned Enterprise	7.92
国有联营企业	State Joint Ownership	2.46
集体联营企业	Collective Joint Ownership	0.63
国有与集体联营企业	Joint State- Collective Ownership	0.28
其他联营企业	Other Joint Owned Enterprise	4.54
有限责任公司	Responsibility Co. Ltd	1799.71
国有独资公司	State Solely Funded Co.	527.37
其他有限责任公司	Others	1272.34
股份有限公司	Share Holding Co.Ltd.	2785.10
私营企业	Private - owned enterprises	961.84
私营独资企业	Solely Private - owned enterprises	128.90
私营合作企业	Private Joint Venture	54.18
私营有限责任公司	Private Responsibility Co. Ltd	681.53
私营股份有限公司	Private Share Holding Co.Ltd.	97.22
其他企业	Others	21.90
港、澳、台商投资企业	Hongkong, Macao and Taiwan Funded Enterprises	275.93
合资经营企业(港或澳、台资)	Joint Venture with Hongkong, Macao and Taiwan	152.61
合作经营企业(港或澳、台资)	Cooperate with Hongkong, Macao and Taiwan Funded	5.34
港澳台商独资经营企业	Enterprises Solely Funded by Hongkong, Macao and Taiwan Businessmen	107.15
港澳台商投资股份有限公司	Share Holding Co.Ltd. With Hongkong, Macao and Taiwan Investment	10.82
外商投资企业	Foreign Funded Enterprises	940.31
中外合资经营企业	Sino - Foreign Joint Funded Enterprises	726.66
中外合作经营企业	Sino - Foreign Cooperative Funded Enterprises	27.97
外资企业	Foreign Solely Funded Enterprises	117.84
外商投资股份有限公司	Foreign Funded Share Holding Co.Ltd.	67.83
二、在总计中:亏损企业	Of the Total: enterprises running under deficit	1439.07
在总计中:国有控股企业	Of the Total: State-Owned Share Holding Enterprises	6375.75
在总计中:农村工业	Of the Total: Rural Industry	27.07
在总计中:轻工业	Of the Total: Light Industry	1245.20
重工业	Heavy Industry	7965.04
在总计中:大型企业	Of the Total: Large Scale Enterprises	5524.00
中型企业	Medium Scale Enterprises	2042.57
小型企业	Small Enterprises	1643.67

(100 million Yuan)

资产总计 Total Assets		负债合计	流动负债合计	应付账款
累计折旧 Accumulated Depreciation	固定资产净值 Net Fixed Assets	Total Liability	Total Circulating Liability	Account Payable
3583.92	8025.03	10381.23	7463.72	1698.35
3029.95	7027.86	7889.87	5283.55	1190.56
1392.01	2074.77	2847.15	2101.83	391.50
1094.70	1821.83	2380.26	1774.78	335.39
297.32	252.94	466.89	327.05	56.11
23.03	27.69	45.41	30.24	11.62
9.83	23.04	21.75	16.62	5.17
2.24	7.58	6.49	5.07	1.29
1.14	2.29	2.92	1.83	0.56
0.19	0.60	0.95	0.76	0.18
0.27	0.27	0.69	0.69	0.21
0.64	4.42	1.93	1.78	0.33
618.80	1579.27	2062.36	1369.03	364.00
137.41	413.62	557.92	316.11	72.40
481.39	1165.65	1504.45	1052.92	291.60
627.94	2405.46	1814.52	935.92	196.66
344.85	889.91	1061.07	800.37	210.89
60.73	118.51	108.87	76.16	20.28
15.77	50.96	44.17	32.10	18.73
232.66	631.68	795.30	605.41	151.10
35.70	88.76	112.74	86.71	20.78
11.24	20.15	31.12	24.49	9.43
88.25	253.90	1015.36	896.51	71.86
42.62	144.28	898.13	810.49	34.84
3.00	3.93	5.56	5.18	1.22
39.56	95.11	100.91	73.26	33.19
3.06	10.58	10.76	7.58	2.60
465.72	743.27	1476.00	1283.65	435.93
362.90	540.60	1154.23	1057.97	366.68
9.41	25.88	20.79	8.05	1.00
38.56	111.31	157.53	128.86	44.90
54.86	65.48	143.46	88.78	23.35
701.79	1312.27	1493.28	1010.60	282.99
2413.62	5445.89	6804.71	4708.32	890.86
18.67	23.84	27.87	20.03	5.75
581.47	1126.63	1575.41	1247.74	275.14
3002.45	6898.41	8805.82	6215.97	1423.20
2047.35	4669.34	5231.85	3628.92	866.74
894.31	1869.75	3292.84	2487.83	439.85
642.25	1485.94	1856.54	1346.96	391.75

8-3 续表 3 continued

单位:亿元

项 目	Item	固定资产原价 Original Price of Fixed Assets
按行业分	Grouped by Sector	
采矿业	**Mining and Qarrying**	
煤炭开采和洗选业	Coal Mining and Processing	28.09
石油和天然气开采业	Petroleum and Natural Gas Extraction	252.30
黑色金属矿采选业	Ferrous Metals Mining and Processing	38.20
有色金属矿采选业	Non-ferrous Metals Mining and Processing	17.33
非金属矿采选业	Non-metal Minerals Mining and Processing	50.11
其他采矿业	Other Minerals Mining and Processing	0.47
制造业	**Manufacturing**	
农副食品加工业	Food Processing	328.55
食品制造业	Food Production	129.22
饮料制造业	Beverage Production	162.32
烟草制品业	Tobacco Processing	81.66
纺织业	Textile Industry	277.04
纺织服装、鞋、帽制造业	Textile,Garments, Shoes and Hats Products	94.24
皮革、毛皮、羽毛(绒)及其制品业	Leather, Furs,Down and Related Products	4.05
木材加工及木、竹、藤、棕、草制品业	Timber Processing, Wood, Bamboo, Cane, Palm and Sraw Products	49.82
家具制造业	Furniture Manufacturing	10.40
造纸及纸制品业	Papermaking and Paper Products	93.26
印刷业和记录媒介的复制	Printing and Record Processing	51.95
文教体育用品制造业	Stationery, Education and Sports Goods	1.36
石油加工、炼焦及核燃料加工业	Petroleum Processing, Coking Products and Nuclear Fuel Processing	131.05
化学原料及化学制品制造业	Raw Chemical Material and Chemical Products	655.10
医药制造业	Medical and pharmaceutical Products	164.12
化学纤维制造业	Chemical Fibers	14.88
橡胶制品业	Rubber Products	26.00
塑料制品业	Plastic Products	115.74
非金属矿物制品业	Nonmetal Material Products	531.25
黑色金属冶炼及压延加工业	Smelting and Pressing of Ferrous Metals	1587.06
有色金属冶炼及压延加工业	Smelting and Pressing of Nonferrous Metals	197.27
金属制品业	Metal Products	182.32
通用设备制造业	Ordinary Machinery Manufacturing	267.37
专用设备制造业	Special Purpose Equipment Manufacturing	104.06
交通运输设备制造业	Transportation Equipment Manufacturing	1011.21
电气机械及器材制造业	Electric Machinery and Equipment	222.19
通信设备、计算机及其他电子设备制造业	Telecommunication Equipment, Computer and Other Electronic Equipment Manufacturing	544.25
仪器仪表及文化、办公用机械制造业	Instruments, Meters, Cultural and Official Machinery	36.89
工艺品及其他制造业	Handicraft Article and Other Manufacturing	22.31
废弃资源和废旧材料回收加工业	Waste Resources and Junk Material Recycled	7.97
电力、燃气及水的生产和供应业	**Electric Power, Gas and Water Production and Supply**	
电力、热力的生产和供应业	Electric Power, Steam and Hot Water Production and Supply	3925.56
燃气生产和供应业	Gas Production and Supply	50.50
水的生产和供应业	Tap Water Production and Supply	141.44

(100 million Yuan)

资产总计 Total Assets		负债合计 Total Liability	流动负债合计 Total Circulating Liability	应付账款 Account Payable
累计折旧 Accumulated Depreciation	固定资产净值 Net Fixed Assets			
5.52	22.58	21.69	17.17	4.22
109.03	143.26	109.20	99.01	25.70
13.28	24.92	24.94	19.14	8.49
8.23	9.11	23.81	18.75	1.44
11.52	38.59	71.37	50.57	8.52
0.22	0.25	0.19	0.16	0.05
104.83	223.72	223.72	177.49	37.68
45.34	83.88	92.48	75.38	15.44
56.72	105.60	203.48	178.57	24.78
41.78	39.88	130.18	119.94	26.94
95.12	181.92	241.37	173.48	29.59
29.98	64.25	106.47	82.10	19.74
0.89	3.16	6.35	5.13	2.24
17.91	31.91	26.43	16.28	2.98
3.27	7.13	9.78	6.72	2.27
34.30	58.96	71.97	62.75	14.43
20.43	31.52	44.14	32.27	10.16
0.39	0.97	4.23	3.57	1.39
68.60	62.45	79.04	69.71	12.52
245.90	409.20	547.47	398.19	117.40
42.26	121.86	154.84	117.82	21.75
6.38	8.50	9.80	8.19	2.58
11.62	14.38	23.62	18.22	6.63
62.91	52.83	83.95	65.75	17.90
156.18	375.07	459.61	278.93	73.65
666.78	920.29	1345.53	1069.43	175.97
113.67	83.60	152.07	129.11	16.29
48.04	134.28	164.41	133.14	37.25
88.15	179.22	436.08	346.50	84.00
35.29	68.77	149.91	129.28	33.43
416.42	594.79	1851.52	1636.57	546.11
66.39	155.80	223.67	196.53	64.71
84.27	459.97	342.14	285.95	89.49
8.59	28.31	35.15	31.71	9.25
9.63	12.68	25.11	19.97	6.29
2.31	5.66	10.44	9.92	2.80
810.37	3115.19	1999.20	587.50	130.59
9.66	40.84	756.93	723.04	4.46
31.70	109.73	118.94	69.78	9.22

8-3 续表 4 continued

单位:亿元

项　目	Item	长期负债合计 Total Long term Liability	所有者权益合计 Total Rights of Owners
总　　计	Total	2547.00	8673.39
一、按登记注册类型分组:	Grouped by Type of Registration		
内资企业	Inner Funded Enterprises	2266.76	7356.28
国有企业	State Owned Enterprises	651.05	1754.20
中央企业	Central Enterprises	539.91	1534.63
地方企业	Local Enterprises	111.15	219.57
集体企业	Collective-owned Enterprise	7.86	36.27
股份合作企业	Share Holding Cooperative Enterprises	1.95	28.23
联营企业	Joint Owned Enterprise	1.27	7.76
国有联营企业	State Joint Ownership	1.09	1.51
集体联营企业	Collective Joint Ownership	0.03	0.42
国有与集体联营企业	Joint State- Collective Ownership		0.64
其他联营企业	Other Joint Owned Enterprise	0.15	5.20
有限责任公司	Responsibility Co. Ltd	625.06	1420.43
国有独资公司	State Solely Funded Co.	234.83	328.72
其他有限责任公司	Others	390.23	1091.71
股份有限公司	Share Holding Co.Ltd.	824.13	3054.62
私营企业	Private - owned enterprises	149.72	1032.48
私营独资企业	Solely Private - owned enterprises	19.03	142.86
私营合作企业	Private Joint Venture	4.43	57.55
私营有限责任公司	Private Responsibility Co. Ltd	107.21	723.13
私营股份有限公司	Private Share Holding Co.Ltd.	19.05	108.95
其他企业	Others	5.71	22.29
港、澳、台商投资企业	Hongkong, Macao and Taiwan Funded Enterprises	108.83	288.44
合资经营企业(港或澳、台资)	Joint Venture with Hongkong, Macao and Taiwan	81.11	149.11
合作经营企业(港或澳、台资)	Cooperate with Hongkong, Macao and Taiwan Funded	0.39	7.59
港澳台商独资经营企业	Enterprises Solely Funded by Hongkong, Macao and Taiwan Businessmen	25.87	118.17
港澳台商投资股份有限公司	Share Holding Co.Ltd. With Hongkong, Macao and Taiwan Investment	1.47	13.57
外商投资企业	Foreign Funded Enterprises	171.41	1028.68
中外合资经营企业	Sino - Foreign Joint Funded Enterprises	82.84	868.08
中外合作经营企业	Sino - Foreign Cooperative Funded Enterprises	12.74	20.14
外资企业	Foreign Solely Funded Enterprises	23.86	129.15
外商投资股份有限公司	Foreign Funded Share Holding Co.Ltd.	51.96	11.31
二、在总计中:亏损企业	Of the Total: enterprises running under deficit	449.48	745.31
在总计中:国有控股企业	Of the Total: State-Owned Share Holding Enterprises	1927.12	5504.89
在总计中:农村工业	Of the Total: Rural Industry	5.21	29.35
在总计中:轻工业	Of the Total: Light Industry	229.05	1470.41
重工业	Heavy Industry	2317.95	7202.99
在总计中:大型企业	Of the Total: Large Scale Enterprises	1490.30	5141.75
中型企业	Medium Scale Enterprises	680.97	1821.02
小型企业	Small Enterprises	375.73	1710.63

(100 million Yuan)

所有者权益合计 Total Rights of Owners					
实收资本 Assets Recevied	国家资本 National Assets	集体资本 Collective Assets	法人资本 Corperative Assets	个人资本 Individual Assets	港澳台资本 Assets from Hongkong, Maco and Taiwan Funded Enterprises
4610.04	2186.47	58.36	1187.37	708.55	119.29
3877.28	2069.81	55.56	1025.59	686.57	23.36
553.53	372.35	0.48	175.01	5.69	
413.99	291.04	0.18	122.57	0.19	
139.54	81.30	0.29	52.44	5.50	
20.57	0.25	12.23	4.64	3.33	0.09
11.01	0.01	1.53	4.92	4.55	
4.12	1.47	0.52	0.68	0.83	
1.27	1.17		0.10		
0.37		0.25		0.12	
0.51	0.30	0.14	0.08		
1.97		0.13	0.51	0.71	
733.58	134.70	26.52	366.14	174.49	18.35
142.18	104.57		36.77	0.84	
591.41	30.14	26.52	329.37	173.65	18.35
1975.47	1558.27	5.36	260.95	149.18	1.53
564.05	2.69	5.30	206.33	344.18	3.38
81.81	0.01	0.30	30.04	50.90	0.10
38.97	0.01	0.48	18.18	20.30	
380.24	2.57	3.33	134.90	235.46	2.80
63.03	0.09	1.19	23.20	37.51	0.48
14.94	0.08	3.62	6.92	4.32	
159.79	6.78	1.08	47.81	13.19	80.84
78.21	4.56	1.02	35.75	7.96	27.17
3.10			1.35	0.19	0.42
70.58		0.03	8.98	4.11	52.59
7.88	2.22	0.03	1.73	0.92	0.66
572.97	109.88	1.73	113.97	8.79	15.09
458.31	108.78	1.46	96.52	5.21	10.69
12.39	0.42	0.26	5.74	0.11	0.10
91.22	0.67		9.15	2.04	3.28
11.05			2.56	1.44	1.02
470.06	134.57	11.14	198.08	78.75	16.98
2976.43	2146.77	17.47	577.14	101.19	2.43
19.76	0.02	3.98	6.47	8.87	
708.10	58.76	14.41	274.54	250.73	38.99
3901.95	2127.71	43.95	912.83	457.82	80.30
2631.48	1998.18	7.20	317.36	104.09	19.01
940.58	138.28	24.18	452.16	193.19	51.99
1037.98	50.01	26.98	417.84	411.28	48.29

8-3 续表 5 continued

单位:亿元

项 目	Item	长期负债合计 Total Long term Liability	所有者权益合计 Total Rights of Owners
按行业分	Grouped by Sector		
采矿业	**Mining and Qarrying**		
煤炭开采和洗选业	Coal Mining and Processing	3.73	18.40
石油和天然气开采业	Petroleum and Natural Gas Extraction	10.04	105.60
黑色金属矿采选业	Ferrous Metals Mining and Processing	4.95	23.46
有色金属矿采选业	Non-ferrous Metals Mining and Processing	4.36	12.73
非金属矿采选业	Non-metal Minerals Mining and Processing	19.31	55.66
其他采矿业	Other Minerals Mining and Processing	0.03	0.28
制造业	**Manufacturing**		
农副食品加工业	Food Processing	28.41	275.13
食品制造业	Food Production	12.33	97.86
饮料制造业	Beverage Production	18.31	131.16
烟草制品业	Tobacco Processing	10.24	106.10
纺织业	Textile Industry	41.93	211.92
纺织服装、鞋、帽制造业	Textile,Garments, Shoes and Hats Products	16.27	64.77
皮革、毛皮、羽毛(绒)及其制品业	Leather, Furs,Down and Related Products	0.86	4.16
木材加工及木、竹、藤、棕、草制品业	Timber Processing,Wood,Bamboo,Cane,Palm and Straw Products	8.59	41.89
家具制造业	Furniture Manufacturing	2.60	9.13
造纸及纸制品业	Papermaking and Paper Products	6.74	74.96
印刷业和记录媒介的复制	Printing and Record Processing	10.21	36.72
文教体育用品制造业	Stationery, Education and Sports Goods	0.57	2.79
石油加工、炼焦及核燃料加工业	Petroleum Processing, Coking Products and Nuclear Fuel Processing	4.85	62.55
化学原料及化学制品制造业	Raw Chemical Material and Chemical Products	122.03	439.83
医药制造业	Medical and pharmaceutical Products	28.70	232.63
化学纤维制造业	Chemical Fibers	1.30	13.19
橡胶制品业	Rubber Products	4.81	17.72
塑料制品业	Plastic Products	14.36	88.43
非金属矿物制品业	Nonmetal Material Products	166.44	303.49
黑色金属冶炼及压延加工业	Smelting and Pressing of Ferrous Metals	272.27	810.46
有色金属冶炼及压延加工业	Smelting and Pressing of Nonferrous Metals	17.67	96.95
金属制品业	Metal Products	24.34	182.61
通用设备制造业	Ordinary Machinery Manufacturing	74.40	240.06
专用设备制造业	Special Purpose Equipment Manufacturing	13.83	116.76
交通运输设备制造业	Transportation Equipment Manufacturing	141.60	1380.06
电气机械及器材制造业	Electric Machinery and Equipment	22.84	209.16
通信设备、计算机及其他电子设备制造业	Telecommunication Equipment, Computer and Other Electronic Equipment Manufacturing	52.89	592.50
仪器仪表及文化、办公用机械制造业	Instruments, Meters, Cultural and Official Machinery	2.87	53.03
工艺品及其他制造业	Handicraft Article and Other Manufacturing	2.88	19.32
废弃资源和废旧材料回收加工业	Waste Resources and Junk Material Recycled	0.45	5.42
电力、燃气及水的生产和供应业	**Electric Power, Gas and Water Production and Supply**		
电力、热力的生产和供应业	Electric Power, Steam and Hot Water Production and Supply	1311.41	2381.15
燃气生产和供应业	Gas Production and Supply	32.41	49.52
水的生产和供应业	Tap Water Production and Supply	35.18	105.84

(100 million Yuan)

实收资本 Assets Recevied	国家资本 National Assets	所有者权益合计 Total Rights of Owners			
		集体资本 Collective Assets	法人资本 Corperative Assets	个人资本 Individual Assets	港澳台资本 Assets from Hongkong, Maco and Taiwan Funded Enterprises
11.75	1.51	0.62	4.30	4.97	0.34
90.79	68.56		22.13	0.10	
20.57	9.17	1.61	5.42	4.34	
5.66	1.81	0.08	1.64	1.83	0.26
31.30	0.53	2.21	12.76	15.33	0.44
0.18		0.03	0.04	0.11	
120.60	2.94	5.86	48.63	52.00	0.86
48.15	3.04	0.34	24.11	13.96	3.04
68.54	4.10	1.19	16.40	16.23	8.20
23.76	0.36		23.28	0.11	
118.99	2.79	1.40	46.22	58.89	7.36
39.71	0.74	0.34	18.49	16.70	2.73
3.25		0.01	1.11	1.23	0.81
20.70	0.41	1.40	7.39	8.98	2.50
4.38	0.01	0.02	1.79	1.68	0.66
34.14	0.60	0.78	13.23	12.43	1.74
20.78	4.54	1.28	6.91	6.42	1.45
1.46		0.01	0.23	0.36	0.38
49.46	35.64		1.09	2.11	0.19
187.65	18.64	4.27	96.49	50.37	4.06
88.66	5.52	0.53	32.92	39.51	7.58
6.72		0.01	1.74	2.97	0.36
9.50	0.43	0.15	4.59	3.41	0.15
48.90	2.36	1.95	16.36	23.56	1.92
218.25	9.34	4.24	94.34	86.48	6.69
241.97	157.24	0.60	20.69	19.14	9.47
48.06	16.20	0.90	17.16	10.24	0.30
95.07	2.21	1.91	58.45	23.80	7.04
139.01	40.46	1.48	53.70	37.27	0.79
63.87	8.73	0.95	33.25	17.52	1.28
664.04	179.63	8.84	231.45	77.19	2.06
104.84	6.00	3.02	46.85	25.27	3.31
152.17	46.28	0.87	56.40	15.62	22.26
17.40	1.43	0.14	10.33	3.44	0.87
9.87	1.58	0.38	2.92	4.37	0.57
1.48	0.23	0.23	0.71	0.32	
1735.72	1520.22	2.51	144.81	46.16	16.61
18.05	2.54	8.00	1.44	1.14	3.02
44.62	30.67	0.23	7.62	2.99	

8-3 续表 6 continued

单位:亿元

项　目	Item	所有者权益合计 Total owner 外商资本 Total Rights of the Owners Foreign Assets
总　　计	Total	350.00
一、按登记注册类型分组:	Grouped by Type of Registration	
内资企业	Inner Funded Enterprises	16.41
国有企业	State Owned Enterprises	0.01
中央企业	Central Enterprises	
地方企业	Local Enterprises	0.01
集体企业	Collective-owned Enterprise	0.03
股份合作企业	Share Holding Cooperative Enterprises	
联营企业	Joint Owned Enterprise	0.62
国有联营企业	State Joint Ownership	
集体联营企业	Collective Joint Ownership	
国有与集体联营企业	Joint State- Collective Ownership	
其他联营企业	Other Joint Owned Enterprise	0.62
有限责任公司	Responsibility Co. Ltd	13.39
国有独资公司	State Solely Funded Co.	
其他有限责任公司	Others	13.39
股份有限公司	Share Holding Co.Ltd.	0.19
私营企业	Private - owned enterprises	2.18
私营独资企业	Solely Private - owned enterprises	0.45
私营合作企业	Private Joint Venture	
私营有限责任公司	Private Responsibility Co. Ltd	1.17
私营股份有限公司	Private Share Holding Co.Ltd.	0.56
其他企业	Others	
港、澳、台商投资企业	Hongkong, Macao and Taiwan Funded Enterprises	10.08
合资经营企业(港或澳、台资)	Joint Venture with Hongkong, Macao and Taiwan	1.74
合作经营企业(港或澳、台资)	Cooperate with Hongkong, Macao and Taiwan Funded	1.15
港澳台商独资经营企业	Enterprises Solely Funded by Hongkong, Macao and Taiwan Businessmen	4.87
港澳台商投资股份有限公司	Share Holding Co.Ltd. With Hongkong, Macao and Taiwan Investment	2.32
外商投资企业	Foreign Funded Enterprises	323.51
中外合资经营企业	Sino - Foreign Joint Funded Enterprises	235.65
中外合作经营企业	Sino - Foreign Cooperative Funded Enterprises	5.75
外资企业	Foreign Solely Funded Enterprises	76.08
外商投资股份有限公司	Foreign Funded Share Holding Co.Ltd.	6.03
二、在总计中:亏损企业	Of the Total: enterprises running under deficit	30.55
在总计中:国有控股企业	Of the Total: State-Owned Share Holding Enterprises	131.43
在总计中:农村工业	Of the Total: Rural Industry	0.42
在总计中:轻工业	Of the Total: Light Industry	70.66
重工业	Heavy Industry	279.34
在总计中:大型企业	Of the Total: Large Scale Enterprises	185.64
中型企业	Medium Scale Enterprises	80.78
小型企业	Small Enterprises	83.58

(100 million Yuan)

主营业务收入 Revenue of Major Business	主营业务成本 Cost of Major Business	主营业务税金及附加 Tax of Major Business	其他业务收入 Revenue of Other Business	其他业务利润 Profit from Other Business	营业费用 Operation Expenses
15331.62	12641.04	406.64	341.56	42.46	464.97
12342.67	10260.68	359.01	198.81	23.27	341.11
3783.05	3156.41	194.08	105.75	-0.41	51.58
3050.82	2519.15	184.58	91.51	-3.66	40.27
732.22	637.26	9.50	14.25	3.25	11.32
145.71	122.10	2.80	1.34	0.26	3.37
77.59	64.39	1.43	0.12	0.03	2.37
16.98	14.75	0.09	0.07	0.04	0.50
5.63	5.07	0.03	0.03	0.02	0.25
4.66	3.85	0.02	0.02	0.01	0.08
1.49	1.32	0.01			0.05
5.20	4.52	0.04	0.01	0.01	0.12
3029.37	2591.14	37.89	32.88	7.70	83.20
533.76	489.36	10.14	5.22	1.06	6.21
2495.61	2101.79	27.75	27.67	6.64	76.99
1817.17	1370.51	70.59	44.89	12.88	83.24
3396.22	2871.89	51.68	13.36	2.67	113.34
571.25	481.36	9.06	0.70	0.22	17.38
233.57	197.17	6.12	0.34	0.16	4.84
2264.46	1916.19	33.51	7.33	2.01	81.31
326.94	277.17	2.99	5.00	0.29	9.81
76.59	69.48	0.46	0.39	0.12	3.51
678.94	585.46	3.39	6.45	0.80	25.93
322.53	269.03	1.86	4.71	0.43	14.62
14.46	11.89	0.25	0.53	0.02	0.76
321.61	289.69	0.97	0.97	0.22	9.78
20.34	14.85	0.31	0.24	0.12	0.76
2310.01	1794.90	44.24	136.31	18.39	97.94
1884.64	1460.77	40.43	128.97	15.04	71.09
25.17	20.06	0.02	0.14	0.10	0.50
299.96	236.11	2.58	5.90	2.68	24.52
100.24	77.96	1.21	1.29	0.57	1.84
1689.20	1545.89	20.17	48.94	5.62	45.52
6751.31	5540.12	278.62	234.61	15.93	146.82
106.12	89.35	2.22	0.06	0.02	3.18
4049.24	3190.43	187.85	80.11	2.66	209.03
11282.38	9450.60	218.78	261.45	39.79	255.94
6544.02	5359.22	287.35	254.85	22.60	180.26
3850.23	3130.88	54.12	50.46	10.62	139.39
4937.38	4150.94	65.17	36.25	9.23	145.33

8-3 续表 7 continued

单位:亿元

项 目	Item	所有者权益合计 Total owner 外商资本 Total Rights of the Owners Foreign Assets
按行业分	Grouped by Sector	
采矿业	**Mining and Qarrying**	
煤炭开采和洗选业	Coal Mining and Processing	
石油和天然气开采业	Petroleum and Natural Gas Extraction	
黑色金属矿采选业	Ferrous Metals Mining and Processing	0.03
有色金属矿采选业	Non-ferrous Metals Mining and Processing	0.04
非金属矿采选业	Non-metal Minerals Mining and Processing	0.03
其他采矿业	Other Minerals Mining and Processing	
制造业	**Manufacturing**	
农副食品加工业	Food Processing	10.30
食品制造业	Food Production	3.66
饮料制造业	Beverage Production	22.43
烟草制品业	Tobacco Processing	
纺织业	Textile Industry	2.33
纺织服装、鞋、帽制造业	Textile,Garments, Shoes and Hats Products	0.71
皮革、毛皮、羽毛(绒)及其制品业	Leather, Furs,Down and Related Products	0.09
木材加工及木、竹、藤、棕、草制品业	Timber Processing, Wood, Bamboo, Cane, Palm and Straw Products	0.02
家具制造业	Furniture Manufacturing	0.23
造纸及纸制品业	Papermaking and Paper Products	5.37
印刷业和记录媒介的复制	Printing and Record Processing	0.18
文教体育用品制造业	Stationery, Education and Sports Goods	0.48
石油加工、炼焦及核燃料加工业	Petroleum Processing, Coking Products and Nuclear Fuel Processing	10.44
化学原料及化学制品制造业	Raw Chemical Material and Chemical Products	13.82
医药制造业	Medical and pharmaceutical Products	2.60
化学纤维制造业	Chemical Fibers	1.65
橡胶制品业	Rubber Products	0.76
塑料制品业	Plastic Products	2.75
非金属矿物制品业	Nonmetal Material Products	17.16
黑色金属冶炼及压延加工业	Smelting and Pressing of Ferrous Metals	34.83
有色金属冶炼及压延加工业	Smelting and Pressing of Nonferrous Metals	3.27
金属制品业	Metal Products	1.65
通用设备制造业	Ordinary Machinery Manufacturing	5.31
专用设备制造业	Special Purpose Equipment Manufacturing	2.15
交通运输设备制造业	Transportation Equipment Manufacturing	164.87
电气机械及器材制造业	Electric Machinery and Equipment	20.39
通信设备、计算机及其他电子设备制造业	Telecommunication Equipment, Computer and Other Electronic Equipment Manufacturing	10.75
仪器仪表及文化、办公用机械制造业	Instruments, Meters, Cultural and Official Machinery	1.20
工艺品及其他制造业	Handicraft Article and Other Manufacturing	0.05
废弃资源和废旧材料回收加工业	Waste Resources and Junk Material Recycled	
电力、燃气及水的生产和供应业	**Electric Power, Gas and Water Production and Supply**	
电力、热力的生产和供应业	Electric Power, Steam and Hot Water Production and Supply	5.42
燃气生产和供应业	Gas Production and Supply	1.92
水的生产和供应业	Tap Water Production and Supply	3.12

(100 million Yuan)

主营业务收入 Revenue of Major Business	主营业务成本 Cost of Major Business	主营业务税金及附加 Tax of Major Business	其他业务收入 Revenue of Other Business	其他业务利润 Profit from Other Business	营业费用 Operation Expenses
50.20	40.30	1.14	0.05	-0.04	1.12
157.84	143.34	5.30	22.72	0.22	2.78
153.97	129.11	7.14	0.20	0.05	3.27
36.70	24.83	0.63	0.97	-0.01	0.49
144.33	106.05	5.76	0.71	0.09	5.48
0.68	0.57	0.01			0.03
1031.31	895.51	14.10	8.05	3.54	27.63
248.65	195.86	2.66	1.18	0.32	21.09
355.75	244.29	13.90	5.13	1.87	59.29
306.62	93.14	133.53	42.54	-8.50	10.40
659.05	578.35	5.82	2.01	0.21	15.08
253.57	215.64	3.08	0.58	0.34	9.23
16.64	14.05	0.19	0.01	0.01	0.56
91.84	76.88	1.25	0.12	0.04	3.02
21.98	17.18	0.32			1.50
174.87	152.69	1.82	2.32	0.31	5.61
87.22	71.57	0.86	0.97	0.26	2.61
7.54	6.20	0.06	0.06	0.01	0.25
465.10	354.51	75.25	3.68	0.31	1.50
1143.30	979.86	12.29	17.44	5.07	48.33
306.38	230.93	4.07	0.83	0.23	22.04
21.26	19.74	0.07	0.01		0.36
60.12	49.99	0.87	0.16	0.09	1.92
241.76	202.58	5.12	1.24	0.26	7.88
721.65	598.27	11.65	2.61	1.02	26.59
1853.41	1681.60	20.03	29.06	1.47	18.31
482.75	455.52	1.28	12.05	1.36	3.95
325.95	274.02	3.59	2.12	0.64	9.66
536.21	440.61	5.67	3.75	0.95	16.97
245.28	201.17	2.72	1.76	0.56	7.88
2515.19	2011.45	43.31	141.38	25.69	82.52
508.70	414.18	2.91	9.82	1.87	16.21
620.42	527.73	6.54	1.71	0.66	20.09
52.34	38.52	0.66	0.74	0.19	2.53
62.52	53.21	2.80	1.76	0.20	1.12
21.26	18.81	0.43	0.26	0.03	0.32
1245.91	1006.58	8.39	20.21	1.77	1.71
52.34	41.35	1.17	1.27	0.63	3.89
50.98	34.84	0.25	2.07	0.72	1.72

8-3 续表 8 continued

单位:亿元 (100 million Yuan)

项 目	Item	管理费用 Management Expense	税金 Tax	财务费用 Financial Expense	利息支出 Interest Expense
总 计	Total	799.69	81.08	212.79	194.34
一、按登记注册类型分组:	Grouped by Type of Registration				
内资企业	Inner Funded Enterprises	641.82	63.34	187.02	174.73
国有企业	State Owned Enterprises	195.50	13.86	55.22	60.39
中央企业	Central Enterprises	161.22	10.76	46.59	51.43
地方企业	Local Enterprises	34.28	3.10	8.63	8.96
集体企业	Collective-owned Enterprise	10.14	0.71	1.25	0.83
股份合作企业	Share Holding Cooperative Enterprises	3.01	0.26	0.75	0.55
联营企业	Joint Owned Enterprise	0.72	0.01	0.14	0.10
国有联营企业	State Joint Ownership	0.27		0.02	0.02
集体联营企业	Collective Joint Ownership	0.16		0.04	0.04
国有与集体联营企业	Joint State- Collective Ownership	0.13			
其他联营企业	Other Joint Owned Enterprise	0.17	0.01	0.08	0.04
有限责任公司	Responsibility Co. Ltd	173.66	15.78	50.68	46.42
国有独资公司	State Solely Funded Co.	48.69	5.58	10.39	10.49
其他有限责任公司	Others	124.97	10.20	40.28	35.93
股份有限公司	Share Holding Co.Ltd.	116.72	14.50	38.33	39.26
私营企业	Private - owned enterprises	138.45	18.14	39.38	26.11
私营独资企业	Solely Private - owned enterprises	16.61	1.45	6.45	3.95
私营合作企业	Private Joint Venture	6.37	0.77	2.07	1.25
私营有限责任公司	Private Responsibility Co. Ltd	103.41	15.10	26.89	18.19
私营股份有限公司	Private Share Holding Co.Ltd.	12.05	0.83	3.97	2.72
其他企业	Others	3.62	0.07	1.28	1.06
港、澳、台商投资企业	Hongkong, Macao and Taiwan Funded Enterprises	22.80	1.31	8.07	6.44
合资经营企业(港或澳、台资)	Joint Venture with Hongkong, Macao and Taiwan	11.73	0.83	4.52	4.27
合作经营企业(港或澳、台资)	Cooperate with Hongkong, Macao and Taiwan Funded	0.72	0.04	0.16	0.15
港澳台商独资经营企业	Enterprises Solely Funded by Hongkong, Macao and Taiwan Businessmen	8.54	0.40	3.16	1.82
港澳台商投资股份有限公司	Share Holding Co.Ltd. With Hongkong, Macao and Taiwan Investment	1.81	0.04	0.22	0.20
外商投资企业	Foreign Funded Enterprises	135.07	16.43	17.69	13.17
中外合资经营企业	Sino - Foreign Joint Funded Enterprises	107.54	13.98	12.61	8.69
中外合作经营企业	Sino - Foreign Cooperative Funded Enterprises	0.90	0.02	1.16	1.14
外资企业	Foreign Solely Funded Enterprises	17.84	2.38	2.47	1.91
外商投资股份有限公司	Foreign Funded Share Holding Co.Ltd.	8.79	0.05	1.45	1.44
二、在总计中:亏损企业	Of the Total: enterprises running under deficit	91.55	5.40	30.06	28.73
在总计中:国有控股企业	Of the Total: State-Owned Share Holding Enterprises	427.35	44.78	118.02	125.70
在总计中:农村工业	Of the Total: Rural Industry	4.60	0.32	1.23	0.63
在总计中:轻工业	Of the Total: Light Industry	199.06	23.96	47.23	32.72
重工业	Heavy Industry	600.63	57.12	165.56	161.63
在总计中:大型企业	Of the Total: Large Scale Enterprises	364.91	39.42	87.35	92.83
中型企业	Medium Scale Enterprises	223.24	25.66	69.02	60.20
小型企业	Small Enterprises	211.54	16.00	56.41	41.32

8-3 续表 9 continued

单位:亿元 (100 million Yuan)

项 目	Item	管理费用 Management Expense	税金 Tax	财务费用 Financial Expense	利息支出 Interest Expense
按行业分	Grouped by Sector				
采矿业	**Mining and Qarrying**				
煤炭开采和洗选业	Coal Mining and Processing	4.51	0.19	0.49	0.36
石油和天然气开采业	Petroleum and Natural Gas Extraction	15.15	0.79	1.57	1.53
黑色金属矿采选业	Ferrous Metals Mining and Processing	6.69	1.40	1.35	0.74
有色金属矿采选业	Non-ferrous Metals Mining and Processing	3.47	0.27	0.26	0.31
非金属矿采选业	Non-metal Minerals Mining and Processing	9.29	1.18	2.09	1.33
其他采矿业	Other Minerals Mining and Processing	0.06			
制造业	**Manufacturing**				
农副食品加工业	Food Processing	37.98	11.10	9.94	7.89
食品制造业	Food Production	9.85	0.66	2.20	1.71
饮料制造业	Beverage Production	20.00	1.99	7.97	2.36
烟草制品业	Tobacco Processing	25.45	0.77	0.98	0.94
纺织业	Textile Industry	26.97	3.74	9.90	6.68
纺织服装、鞋、帽制造业	Textile,Garments, Shoes and Hats Products	11.52	0.59	2.74	1.96
皮革、毛皮、羽毛(绒)及其制品业	Leather, Furs,Down and Related Products	0.85	0.12	0.30	0.18
木材加工及木、竹、藤、棕、草制品业	Timber Processing, Wood, Bamboo, Cane, Palm and Straw Products	3.69	0.13	0.94	0.78
家具制造业	Furniture Manufacturing	1.38	0.04	0.36	0.26
造纸及纸制品业	Papermaking and Paper Products	6.54	0.74	1.72	1.37
印刷业和记录媒介的复制	Printing and Record Processing	8.96	0.29	0.92	0.80
文教体育用品制造业	Stationery, Education and Sports Goods	0.44	0.03	0.11	0.08
石油加工、炼焦及核燃料加工业	Petroleum Processing, Coking Products and Nuclear Fuel Processing	11.37	0.21	1.28	1.31
化学原料及化学制品制造业	Raw Chemical Material and Chemical Products	45.51	3.90	16.30	14.75
医药制造业	Medical and pharmaceutical Products	20.77	1.52	3.16	2.88
化学纤维制造业	Chemical Fibers	0.83	0.07	0.24	0.21
橡胶制品业	Rubber Products	3.39	0.19	0.77	0.64
塑料制品业	Plastic Products	9.98	0.98	2.94	2.22
非金属矿物制品业	Nonmetal Material Products	29.77	1.99	9.72	7.61
黑色金属冶炼及压延加工业	Smelting and Pressing of Ferrous Metals	90.56	10.52	27.39	27.61
有色金属冶炼及压延加工业	Smelting and Pressing of Nonferrous Metals	10.54	0.88	3.16	2.50
金属制品业	Metal Products	14.37	0.94	7.10	8.37
通用设备制造业	Ordinary Machinery Manufacturing	37.91	2.23	6.52	5.79
专用设备制造业	Special Purpose Equipment Manufacturing	20.51	1.10	2.50	1.97
交通运输设备制造业	Transportation Equipment Manufacturing	194.25	27.07	11.33	13.26
电气机械及器材制造业	Electric Machinery and Equipment	25.32	1.87	4.23	2.76
通信设备、计算机及其他电子设备制造业	Telecommunication Equipment, Computer and Other Electronic Equipment Manufacturing	40.59	0.50	4.01	2.93
仪器仪表及文化、办公用机械制造业	Instruments, Meters, Cultural and Official Machinery	4.90	0.15	0.56	0.34
工艺品及其他制造业	Handicraft Article and Other Manufacturing	2.84	0.05	0.42	0.27
废弃资源和废旧材料回收加工业	Waste Resources and Junk Material Recycled	0.90	0.01	0.16	0.13
电力、燃气及水的生产和供应业	**Electric Power, Gas and Water Production and Supply**				
电力、热力的生产和供应业	Electric Power, Steam and Hot Water Production and Supply	36.02	2.29	63.84	66.66
燃气生产和供应业	Gas Production and Supply	1.20	0.02	0.90	0.57
水的生产和供应业	Tap Water Production and Supply	5.36	0.55	2.44	2.29

8-3 续表 10 continued

单位:亿元

项 目	Item	营业利润 Operating Profit
总 计	Total	1072.60
一、按登记注册类型分组:	Grouped by Type of Registration	
内资企业	Inner Funded Enterprises	794.63
国有企业	State Owned Enterprises	100.43
中央企业	Central Enterprises	71.63
地方企业	Local Enterprises	28.79
集体企业	Collective-owned Enterprise	11.06
股份合作企业	Share Holding Cooperative Enterprises	7.16
联营企业	Joint Owned Enterprise	2.77
国有联营企业	State Joint Ownership	1.86
集体联营企业	Collective Joint Ownership	0.46
国有与集体联营企业	Joint State- Collective Ownership	0.01
其他联营企业	Other Joint Owned Enterprise	0.44
有限责任公司	Responsibility Co. Ltd	187.06
国有独资公司	State Solely Funded Co.	11.40
其他有限责任公司	Others	175.66
股份有限公司	Share Holding Co.Ltd.	230.20
私营企业	Private - owned enterprises	245.53
私营独资企业	Solely Private - owned enterprises	44.63
私营合作企业	Private Joint Venture	18.23
私营有限责任公司	Private Responsibility Co. Ltd	161.37
私营股份有限公司	Private Share Holding Co.Ltd.	21.31
其他企业	Others	10.40
港、澳、台商投资企业	Hongkong, Macao and Taiwan Funded Enterprises	52.34
合资经营企业(港或澳、台资)	Joint Venture with Hongkong, Macao and Taiwan	32.72
合作经营企业(港或澳、台资)	Cooperate with Hongkong, Macao and Taiwan Funded	1.94
港澳台商独资经营企业	Enterprises Solely Funded by Hongkong, Macao and Taiwan Businessmen	14.98
港澳台商投资股份有限公司	Share Holding Co.Ltd. With Hongkong, Macao and Taiwan Investment	2.70
外商投资企业	Foreign Funded Enterprises	225.63
中外合资经营企业	Sino - Foreign Joint Funded Enterprises	190.60
中外合作经营企业	Sino - Foreign Cooperative Funded Enterprises	2.84
外资企业	Foreign Solely Funded Enterprises	28.68
外商投资股份有限公司	Foreign Funded Share Holding Co.Ltd.	3.51
二、在总计中:亏损企业	Of the Total: enterprises running under deficit	-78.29
在总计中:国有控股企业	Of the Total: State-Owned Share Holding Enterprises	383.02
在总计中:农村工业	Of the Total: Rural Industry	6.11
在总计中:轻工业	Of the Total: Light Industry	327.01
重工业	Heavy Industry	745.58
在总计中:大型企业	Of the Total: Large Scale Enterprises	398.88
中型企业	Medium Scale Enterprises	316.83
小型企业	Small Enterprises	356.89

(100 million Yuan)

投资收益 Income from Investment	补贴收入 Income from Subsidy	营业外收入 Non-operating Income	利润总额 Total Profit	应交所得税 Income Tax	亏损企业 亏损总额 Total Loss of Enterprises Running under Deficit
-82.36	40.52	78.33	1092.47	153.57	75.90
14.22	36.80	68.83	805.59	117.10	62.47
13.77	1.91	16.89	104.66	15.23	16.88
15.88	1.35	14.98	78.87	13.89	13.39
-2.10	0.57	1.91	25.79	1.34	3.49
0.04	0.19	0.21	11.01	1.69	0.45
	0.27	0.16	7.16	0.42	0.27
0.12	0.02	0.03	2.67	0.09	0.05
0.16		0.01	1.83	0.06	0.04
			0.46	0.02	
	0.02	0.01	0.03		
-0.04			0.36		0.01
0.87	4.64	13.79	186.78	20.18	22.55
1.48	0.46	4.70	14.41	4.38	7.99
-0.61	4.18	9.09	172.37	15.80	14.56
1.37	23.46	30.87	253.09	63.50	13.09
-1.99	6.13	6.82	230.15	15.54	8.74
0.58	1.11	0.59	40.60	2.08	0.71
0.17	0.41	0.13	12.62	1.12	0.46
-2.48	4.06	5.48	156.08	11.07	6.40
-0.26	0.55	0.62	20.85	1.27	1.17
0.04	0.18	0.06	10.07	0.45	0.44
-64.15	1.59	2.01	53.70	4.78	2.56
0.31	1.47	0.74	33.31	3.19	1.79
0.07	0.01	0.01	1.92	0.12	
-64.74	0.10	1.24	15.81	1.35	0.71
0.22	0.02	0.02	2.66	0.11	0.06
-32.43	2.13	7.49	233.17	31.69	10.88
-31.28	1.01	4.88	196.18	27.16	2.15
0.01	0.02	0.05	2.89	0.14	0.06
-1.17	0.11	1.28	29.48	3.05	3.91
0.01	0.99	1.29	4.61	1.35	4.74
-12.90	2.64	8.04	-75.90	0.92	75.90
18.63	25.62	54.99	420.50	89.44	41.65
0.03	0.05	0.27	5.99	0.53	0.14
-23.47	5.08	13.73	317.67	28.37	15.95
-58.89	35.44	64.61	774.80	125.20	59.95
-50.37	23.73	49.62	432.96	98.63	34.39
-16.62	6.96	17.04	320.93	28.48	18.48
-15.36	9.83	11.67	338.58	26.46	23.03

8-3 续表 11 continued

单位:亿元

项 目	Item	营业利润 Operating Profit
按行业分	Grouped by Sector	
采矿业	**Mining and Qarrying**	
煤炭开采和洗选业	Coal Mining and Processing	2.89
石油和天然气开采业	Petroleum and Natural Gas Extraction	-10.13
黑色金属矿采选业	Ferrous Metals Mining and Processing	12.91
有色金属矿采选业	Non-ferrous Metals Mining and Processing	6.91
非金属矿采选业	Non-metal Minerals Mining and Processing	16.98
其他采矿业	Other Minerals Mining and Processing	0.01
制造业	**Manufacturing**	
农副食品加工业	Food Processing	102.94
食品制造业	Food Production	19.62
饮料制造业	Beverage Production	34.34
烟草制品业	Tobacco Processing	22.07
纺织业	Textile Industry	38.50
纺织服装、鞋、帽制造业	Textile,Garments, Shoes and Hats Products	20.58
皮革、毛皮、羽毛(绒)及其制品业	Leather, Furs,Down and Related Products	1.00
木材加工及木、竹、藤、棕、草制品业	Timber Processing, Wood, Bamboo, Cane, Palm and Straw Products	7.69
家具制造业	Furniture Manufacturing	1.37
造纸及纸制品业	Papermaking and Paper Products	10.92
印刷业和记录媒介的复制	Printing and Record Processing	7.30
文教体育用品制造业	Stationery, Education and Sports Goods	0.35
石油加工、炼焦及核燃料加工业	Petroleum Processing, Coking Products and Nuclear Fuel Processing	22.97
化学原料及化学制品制造业	Raw Chemical Material and Chemical Products	82.35
医药制造业	Medical and pharmaceutical Products	34.07
化学纤维制造业	Chemical Fibers	0.48
橡胶制品业	Rubber Products	4.64
塑料制品业	Plastic Products	18.44
非金属矿物制品业	Nonmetal Material Products	61.79
黑色金属冶炼及压延加工业	Smelting and Pressing of Ferrous Metals	39.06
有色金属冶炼及压延加工业	Smelting and Pressing of Nonferrous Metals	10.55
金属制品业	Metal Products	19.93
通用设备制造业	Ordinary Machinery Manufacturing	35.17
专用设备制造业	Special Purpose Equipment Manufacturing	21.47
交通运输设备制造业	Transportation Equipment Manufacturing	211.73
电气机械及器材制造业	Electric Machinery and Equipment	47.44
通信设备、计算机及其他电子设备制造业	Telecommunication Equipment, Computer and Other Electronic Equipment Manufacturing	37.00
仪器仪表及文化、办公用机械制造业	Instruments, Meters, Cultural and Official Machinery	5.72
工艺品及其他制造业	Handicraft Article and Other Manufacturing	4.58
废弃资源和废旧材料回收加工业	Waste Resources and Junk Material Recycled	1.16
电力、燃气及水的生产和供应业	**Electric Power, Gas and Water Production and Supply**	
电力、热力的生产和供应业	Electric Power, Steam and Hot Water Production and Supply	110.14
燃气生产和供应业	Gas Production and Supply	7.29
水的生产和供应业	Tap Water Production and Supply	0.37

(100 million Yuan)

投资收益 Income from Investment	补贴收入 Income from Subsidy	营业外收入 Non-operating Income	利润总额 Total Profit	应交所得税 Income Tax	亏损企业亏损总额 Total Loss of Enterprises Running
0.07		0.08	2.90	0.68	0.52
0.22		0.96	-9.72	0.74	9.73
0.37		0.09	12.29	0.36	0.35
0.04	0.31	0.04	6.65	1.54	0.16
-1.04	0.36	1.18	16.00	1.67	0.38
			0.01		0.01
-2.11	1.21	2.18	96.23	4.67	1.31
-0.36	0.29	1.07	19.94	2.30	1.23
-6.89	0.52	1.51	28.87	5.01	1.03
0.09	0.03	0.08	19.70	4.86	0.17
0.03	0.50	1.47	38.62	1.95	3.05
-0.11	0.54	0.39	20.46	1.28	0.48
0.01	0.03	0.02	1.05	0.09	0.15
0.03	0.68	0.15	7.49	0.72	0.17
0.01		0.02	1.37	0.10	0.11
0.09	0.23	0.43	11.10	0.70	0.55
0.20	0.37	0.22	7.17	0.63	0.47
		0.02	0.34	0.04	0.08
0.16	0.05	0.13	22.66	4.86	0.06
0.18	1.69	3.58	79.47	8.86	7.77
1.55	0.67	1.01	33.63	2.97	2.05
1.77	0.06	0.05	2.37	0.26	
	0.23	0.39	4.71	0.21	0.10
0.09	0.27	0.48	17.67	1.95	0.58
0.68	2.29	2.72	61.00	5.96	2.53
9.99	0.63	7.86	43.60	5.75	1.23
0.45	0.34	0.72	10.72	0.65	2.11
0.83	0.30	0.58	18.74	1.98	1.13
0.59	1.31	3.07	35.24	4.17	7.35
1.11	0.55	2.60	23.38	1.91	1.12
-5.00	2.63	11.03	219.83	30.25	7.59
-20.76	0.65	1.52	43.12	4.04	1.68
-70.60	0.86	3.67	40.20	1.79	1.19
-0.03	0.40	0.50	5.93	0.27	0.26
0.04	0.10	0.11	4.61	0.13	0.03
-0.01	0.74	0.02	1.92	0.12	0.14
6.25	21.58	24.30	131.73	49.56	17.27
0.01	0.03	0.09	7.16	0.36	0.08
-0.31	0.06	4.01	4.29	0.18	1.68

8-3 续表 12 continued

单位:亿元 (100 million Yuan)

项 目	Item	利税总额 Total Profit	本年应付工资总额 Total Sum of Wages Payable this Year
总 计	Total	1987.88	971.15
一、按登记注册类型分组:	Grouped by Type of Registration		
内资企业	Inner Funded Enterprises	1551.09	831.15
国有企业	State Owned Enterprises	436.02	270.92
中央企业	Central Enterprises	378.00	219.95
地方企业	Local Enterprises	58.02	50.97
集体企业	Collective-owned Enterprise	17.97	11.95
股份合作企业	Share Holding Cooperative Enterprises	10.42	5.13
联营企业	Joint Owned Enterprise	3.24	1.10
国有联营企业	State Joint Ownership	2.11	0.42
集体联营企业	Collective Joint Ownership	0.61	0.22
国有与集体联营企业	Joint State- Collective Ownership	0.08	0.14
其他联营企业	Other Joint Owned Enterprise	0.44	0.32
有限责任公司	Responsibility Co. Ltd	311.91	201.12
国有独资公司	State Solely Funded Co.	36.69	35.42
其他有限责任公司	Others	275.22	165.71
股份有限公司	Share Holding Co.Ltd.	388.34	121.87
私营企业	Private - owned enterprises	370.73	213.27
私营独资企业	Solely Private - owned enterprises	62.22	32.82
私营合作企业	Private Joint Venture	27.07	11.95
私营有限责任公司	Private Responsibility Co. Ltd	249.31	143.38
私营股份有限公司	Private Share Holding Co.Ltd.	32.14	25.13
其他企业	Others	12.47	5.79
港、澳、台商投资企业	Hongkong, Macao and Taiwan Funded Enterprises	75.65	37.47
合资经营企业(港或澳、台资)	Joint Venture with Hongkong, Macao and Taiwan	46.05	22.31
合作经营企业(港或澳、台资)	Cooperate with Hongkong, Macao and Taiwan Funded	2.53	0.67
港澳台商独资经营企业	Enterprises Solely Funded by Hongkong, Macao and Taiwan Businessmen	23.47	12.70
港澳台商投资股份有限公司	Share Holding Co.Ltd. With Hongkong, Macao and Taiwan Investment	3.60	1.79
外商投资企业	Foreign Funded Enterprises	361.13	102.54
中外合资经营企业	Sino - Foreign Joint Funded Enterprises	306.12	72.57
中外合作经营企业	Sino - Foreign Cooperative Funded Enterprises	4.40	0.41
外资企业	Foreign Solely Funded Enterprises	42.27	22.12
外商投资股份有限公司	Foreign Funded Share Holding Co.Ltd.	8.34	7.43
二、在总计中:亏损企业	Of the Total: enterprises running under deficit	-8.44	160.56
在总计中:国有控股企业	Of the Total: State-Owned Share Holding Enterprises	953.32	439.48
在总计中:农村工业	Of the Total: Rural Industry	11.33	6.61
在总计中:轻工业	Of the Total: Light Industry	638.02	284.42
重工业	Heavy Industry	1349.86	686.74
在总计中:大型企业	Of the Total: Large Scale Enterprises	953.84	401.32
中型企业	Medium Scale Enterprises	499.48	305.07
小型企业	Small Enterprises	534.55	264.76

8−3 续表 13 continued

单位:亿元 (100 million Yuan)

项 目	Item	利税总额 Total Profit	本年应付工资总额 Total Sum of Wages Payable this Year
按行业分	Grouped by Sector		
采矿业	**Mining and Qarrying**		
煤炭开采和洗选业	Coal Mining and Processing	8.24	8.00
石油和天然气开采业	Petroleum and Natural Gas Extraction	1.85	23.26
黑色金属矿采选业	Ferrous Metals Mining and Processing	24.87	6.85
有色金属矿采选业	Non-ferrous Metals Mining and Processing	9.09	2.59
非金属矿采选业	Non-metal Minerals Mining and Processing	29.67	9.26
其他采矿业	Other Minerals Mining and Processing	0.05	0.13
制造业	**Manufacturing**		
农副食品加工业	Food Processing	127.81	41.40
食品制造业	Food Production	30.63	21.60
饮料制造业	Beverage Production	57.92	30.03
烟草制品业	Tobacco Processing	187.48	10.65
纺织业	Textile Industry	60.81	62.03
纺织服装、鞋、帽制造业	Textile,Garments, Shoes and Hats Products	29.36	28.49
皮革、毛皮、羽毛(绒)及其制品业	Leather, Furs,Down and Related Products	1.89	1.48
木材加工及木、竹、藤、棕、草制品业	Timber Processing, Wood, Bamboo, Cane, Palm and Straw Products	11.52	7.68
家具制造业	Furniture Manufacturing	2.16	2.08
造纸及纸制品业	Papermaking and Paper Products	17.40	10.73
印刷业和记录媒介的复制	Printing and Record Processing	10.47	9.04
文教体育用品制造业	Stationery, Education and Sports Goods	0.51	0.89
石油加工、炼焦及核燃料加工业	Petroleum Processing, Coking Products and Nuclear Fuel Processing	113.49	7.53
化学原料及化学制品制造业	Raw Chemical Material and Chemical Products	118.25	65.91
医药制造业	Medical and pharmaceutical Products	49.88	21.77
化学纤维制造业	Chemical Fibers	2.78	0.82
橡胶制品业	Rubber Products	7.58	4.02
塑料制品业	Plastic Products	29.66	18.45
非金属矿物制品业	Nonmetal Material Products	96.92	49.23
黑色金属冶炼及压延加工业	Smelting and Pressing of Ferrous Metals	118.72	106.88
有色金属冶炼及压延加工业	Smelting and Pressing of Nonferrous Metals	18.85	22.66
金属制品业	Metal Products	29.15	25.36
通用设备制造业	Ordinary Machinery Manufacturing	57.21	46.23
专用设备制造业	Special Purpose Equipment Manufacturing	31.71	19.32
交通运输设备制造业	Transportation Equipment Manufacturing	359.72	143.02
电气机械及器材制造业	Electric Machinery and Equipment	57.76	28.33
通信设备、计算机及其他电子设备制造业	Telecommunication Equipment, Computer and Other Electronic Equipment Manufacturing	50.92	38.43
仪器仪表及文化、办公用机械制造业	Instruments, Meters, Cultural and Official Machinery	7.95	5.15
工艺品及其他制造业	Handicraft Article and Other Manufacturing	8.60	5.08
废弃资源和废旧材料回收加工业	Waste Resources and Junk Material Recycled	3.27	1.18
电力、燃气及水的生产和供应业	**Electric Power, Gas and Water Production and Supply**		
电力、热力的生产和供应业	Electric Power, Steam and Hot Water Production and Supply	197.41	77.43
燃气生产和供应业	Gas Production and Supply	10.31	1.99
水的生产和供应业	Tap Water Production and Supply	5.98	6.14

8-3 续表 14 continued

单位:亿元

项　目	Item	本年应付福利费总额 Total Sum of Welfare Expense Payable of the Current Year of the Current Year
总　　计	Total	49.18
一、按登记注册类型分组:	Grouped by Type of Registration	
内资企业	Inner Funded Enterprises	42.07
国有企业	State Owned Enterprises	8.96
中央企业	Central Enterprises	6.67
地方企业	Local Enterprises	2.30
集体企业	Collective-owned Enterprise	0.85
股份合作企业	Share Holding Cooperative Enterprises	0.29
联营企业	Joint Owned Enterprise	0.10
国有联营企业	State Joint Ownership	0.02
集体联营企业	Collective Joint Ownership	0.01
国有与集体联营企业	Joint State- Collective Ownership	0.04
其他联营企业	Other Joint Owned Enterprise	0.03
有限责任公司	Responsibility Co. Ltd	11.93
国有独资公司	State Solely Funded Co.	1.73
其他有限责任公司	Others	10.20
股份有限公司	Share Holding Co.Ltd.	6.52
私营企业	Private - owned enterprises	13.18
私营独资企业	Solely Private - owned enterprises	2.00
私营合作企业	Private Joint Venture	1.04
私营有限责任公司	Private Responsibility Co. Ltd	8.92
私营股份有限公司	Private Share Holding Co.Ltd.	1.22
其他企业	Others	0.24
港、澳、台商投资企业	Hongkong, Macao and Taiwan Funded Enterprises	1.69
合资经营企业(港或澳、台资)	Joint Venture with Hongkong, Macao and Taiwan	0.94
合作经营企业(港或澳、台资)	Cooperate with Hongkong, Macao and Taiwan Funded	0.03
港澳台商独资经营企业	Enterprises Solely Funded by Hongkong, Macao and Taiwan Businessmen	0.58
港澳台商投资股份有限公司	Share Holding Co.Ltd. With Hongkong, Macao and Taiwan Investment	0.14
外商投资企业	Foreign Funded Enterprises	5.42
中外合资经营企业	Sino - Foreign Joint Funded Enterprises	4.35
中外合作经营企业	Sino - Foreign Cooperative Funded Enterprises	0.01
外资企业	Foreign Solely Funded Enterprises	0.89
外商投资股份有限公司	Foreign Funded Share Holding Co.Ltd.	0.17
二、在总计中:亏损企业	Of the Total: enterprises running under deficit	5.28
在总计中:国有控股企业	Of the Total: State-Owned Share Holding Enterprises	17.51
在总计中:农村工业	Of the Total: Rural Industry	0.58
在总计中:轻工业	Of the Total: Light Industry	16.34
重工业	Heavy Industry	32.84
在总计中:大型企业	Of the Total: Large Scale Enterprises	14.96
中型企业	Medium Scale Enterprises	13.80
小型企业	Small Enterprises	20.42

(100 million Yuan)

本年应交增值税 Value Added Payable of the Current Year	本年进项税额 Input Tax of Current Year	本年销项税额 Output Tax of the Current Year	全部从业人员年平均人数(万人) Average Number of Empolyment of the Current Year (10000 persons)
488.77	1552.98	1954.59	272.39
386.48	1202.68	1538.59	235.45
137.28	490.94	646.77	44.79
114.56	422.18	565.38	31.68
22.73	68.76	81.39	13.11
4.17	8.09	11.20	5.57
1.83	3.90	4.92	1.73
0.48	1.36	1.68	0.47
0.25	0.71	0.88	0.10
0.13	0.34	0.41	0.12
0.05	0.19	0.24	0.08
0.04	0.13	0.15	0.17
87.24	288.38	344.10	64.74
12.14	75.69	84.29	7.03
75.10	212.70	259.81	57.71
64.66	173.51	239.98	33.19
88.89	228.46	281.26	83.09
12.56	29.67	35.83	13.90
8.33	8.86	11.76	5.94
59.72	168.87	208.75	54.53
8.30	21.07	24.91	8.72
1.93	8.03	8.68	1.89
18.56	51.42	60.90	12.44
10.89	31.35	38.17	6.56
0.35	1.01	1.31	0.29
6.69	18.43	20.61	4.94
0.63	0.63	0.81	0.65
83.72	298.88	355.09	24.50
69.50	255.79	302.47	16.60
1.49	2.47	3.92	0.16
10.21	32.98	39.74	6.01
2.52	7.65	8.96	1.72
47.30	149.64	232.45	43.39
254.20	877.00	1124.23	84.40
3.12	7.29	9.13	3.79
132.50	319.00	409.02	99.85
356.27	1233.98	1545.57	172.54
233.53	891.29	1141.30	73.44
124.44	324.48	395.91	82.73
130.81	337.21	417.38	116.21

8-3 续表 15 continued

单位:亿元

项 目	Item	本年应付福利费总额 Total Sum of Welfare Expense Payable of the Current Year
按行业分	Grouped by Sector	
采矿业	**Mining and Qarrying**	
煤炭开采和洗选业	Coal Mining and Processing	0.52
石油和天然气开采业	Petroleum and Natural Gas Extraction	0.63
黑色金属矿采选业	Ferrous Metals Mining and Processing	0.73
有色金属矿采选业	Non-ferrous Metals Mining and Processing	0.19
非金属矿采选业	Non-metal Minerals Mining and Processing	0.66
其他采矿业	Other Minerals Mining and Processing	0.02
制造业	**Manufacturing**	
农副食品加工业	Food Processing	2.61
食品制造业	Food Production	0.96
饮料制造业	Beverage Production	2.41
烟草制品业	Tobacco Processing	0.95
纺织业	Textile Industry	2.74
纺织服装、鞋、帽制造业	Textile,Garments, Shoes and Hats Products	1.29
皮革、毛皮、羽毛(绒)及其制品业	Leather, Furs,Down and Related Products	0.08
木材加工及木、竹、藤、棕、草制品业	Timber Processing, Wood, Bamboo, Cane, Palm and Straw Products	0.48
家具制造业	Furniture Manufacturing	0.18
造纸及纸制品业	Papermaking and Paper Products	0.56
印刷业和记录媒介的复制	Printing and Record Processing	0.58
文教体育用品制造业	Stationery, Education and Sports Goods	0.04
石油加工、炼焦及核燃料加工业	Petroleum Processing, Coking Products and Nuclear Fuel Processing	0.16
化学原料及化学制品制造业	Raw Chemical Material and Chemical Products	4.32
医药制造业	Medical and pharmaceutical Products	1.01
化学纤维制造业	Chemical Fibers	0.02
橡胶制品业	Rubber Products	0.30
塑料制品业	Plastic Products	1.16
非金属矿物制品业	Nonmetal Material Products	2.99
黑色金属冶炼及压延加工业	Smelting and Pressing of Ferrous Metals	3.67
有色金属冶炼及压延加工业	Smelting and Pressing of Nonferrous Metals	0.53
金属制品业	Metal Products	1.54
通用设备制造业	Ordinary Machinery Manufacturing	2.25
专用设备制造业	Special Purpose Equipment Manufacturing	0.93
交通运输设备制造业	Transportation Equipment Manufacturing	8.49
电气机械及器材制造业	Electric Machinery and Equipment	1.40
通信设备、计算机及其他电子设备制造业	Telecommunication Equipment, Computer and Other Electronic Equipment Manufacturing	1.48
仪器仪表及文化、办公用机械制造业	Instruments, Meters, Cultural and Official Machinery	0.31
工艺品及其他制造业	Handicraft Article and Other Manufacturing	0.26
废弃资源和废旧材料回收加工业	Waste Resources and Junk Material Recycled	0.06
电力、燃气及水的生产和供应业	**Electric Power, Gas and Water Production and Supply**	
电力、热力的生产和供应业	Electric Power, Steam and Hot Water Production and Supply	2.07
燃气生产和供应业	Gas Production and Supply	0.21
水的生产和供应业	Tap Water Production and Supply	0.39

(100 million Yuan)

本年应交增值税 Value Added Payable of the Current Year	本年进项税额 Input Tax of Current Year	本年销项税额 Output Tax of the Current Year	全部从业人员年平均人数(万人) Average Number of Empolyment of the Current Year (10000 persons)
4.20	1.91	5.63	3.29
6.27	23.26	28.74	3.79
5.43	5.10	8.52	2.23
1.80	1.72	3.31	0.98
7.92	4.89	9.98	4.54
0.03		0.03	0.05
17.47	59.94	66.70	13.56
8.03	20.53	26.32	6.53
15.15	32.11	44.21	6.67
34.25	22.82	52.42	1.25
16.37	65.12	75.92	26.60
5.82	17.11	19.37	12.20
0.64	1.15	1.43	0.91
2.78	5.21	7.21	2.88
0.48	0.91	0.81	0.82
4.49	16.37	19.49	4.47
2.44	7.08	8.38	3.05
0.11	0.53	0.62	0.32
15.58	34.22	44.15	1.11
26.49	71.97	79.68	18.04
12.17	24.04	31.89	6.63
0.35	1.37	1.67	0.57
2.00	4.57	6.15	1.51
6.87	18.92	23.35	6.47
24.27	49.12	65.93	19.87
55.09	383.21	428.87	15.24
6.86	57.49	67.29	4.09
6.82	28.18	31.60	8.56
16.29	43.02	53.04	13.05
5.62	15.76	21.41	6.19
96.59	353.75	417.39	37.28
11.73	58.25	64.45	9.44
4.18	31.57	33.11	9.63
1.36	3.17	3.99	2.20
1.19	4.55	5.01	1.78
0.92	1.52	3.29	0.47
57.29	79.43	188.17	12.54
1.97	2.78	3.71	0.64
1.44	0.30	1.38	2.90

8-4 国有控股工业企业单位数和主要经济指标 (2009)

单位:亿元

项 目	Item	企业单位数(个) Number of Enterprises(unit)	工业总产值(当年价格) Total Output Value(current price)
总 计	Total	864	6534.21
在总计中:	Of the Total		
亏损企业	Enterprises running under Deficit		
在总计中:	Of the Total:		
中央企业	Central Enterprises	103	2867.34
地方企业	Local Enterprises	304	637.67
在总计中:	Of the Total:		
轻工业	Light Industry	275	632.99
重工业	Heavy Industry	589	5901.22
在总计中:	Of the Total:		
大型企业	Large Scale Enterprises	59	5029.14
中型企业	Medium Scale Enterprises	263	1193.57
小型企业	Small Enterprises	542	311.51
按行业分	Grouped by Sector		
采矿业	**Mining and Qarrying**		
煤炭开采和洗选业	Coal Mining and Processing	6	9.55
石油和天然气开采业	Petroleum and Natural Gas Extraction	3	132.88
黑色金属矿采选业	Ferrous Metals Mining and Processing	3	53.78
有色金属矿采选业	Non-ferrous Metals Mining and Processing	5	6.88
非金属矿采选业	Non-metal Minerals Mining and Processing	14	7.30
其他采矿业	Other Minerals Mining and Processing		
制造业	**Manufacturing**		
农副食品加工业	Food Processing	58	80.27
食品制造业	Food Production	13	29.97
饮料制造业	Beverage Production	15	21.74
烟草制品业	Tobacco Processing	9	299.09
纺织业	Textile Industry	23	32.36
纺织服装、鞋、帽制造业	Textile,Garments, Shoes and Hats Products	11	14.83
皮革、毛皮、羽毛(绒)及其制品业	Leather, Furs,Down and Related Products	1	0.09
木材加工及木、竹、藤、棕、草制品业	Timber Processing, Wood, Bamboo, Cane, Palm and Sraw Products	4	3.11
家具制造业	Furniture Manufacturing	3	0.41
造纸及纸制品业	Papermaking and Paper Products	7	19.92
印刷业和记录媒介的复制	Printing and Record Processing	25	16.63
文教体育用品制造业	Stationery, Education and Sports Goods		
石油加工、炼焦及核燃料加工业	Petroleum Processing, Coking Products and Nuclear Fuel Processing	7	403.01
化学原料及化学制品制造业	Raw Chemical Material and Chemical Products	52	317.53
医药制造业	Medical and pharmaceutical Products	15	28.12
化学纤维制造业	Chemical Fibers		
橡胶制品业	Rubber Products	3	20.30
塑料制品业	Plastic Products	5	18.93
非金属矿物制品业	Nonmetal Material Products	71	110.02
黑色金属冶炼及压延加工业	Smelting and Pressing of Ferrous Metals	12	1376.30
有色金属冶炼及压延加工业	Smelting and Pressing of Nonferrous Metals	9	154.15
金属制品业	Metal Products	26	46.36
通用设备制造业	Ordinary Machinery Manufacturing	56	180.63
专用设备制造业	Special Purpose Equipment Manufacturing	39	54.48
交通运输设备制造业	Transportation Equipment Manufacturing	110	1505.54
电气机械及器材制造业	Electric Machinery and Equipment	33	104.70
通信设备、计算机及其他电子设备制造业	Telecommunication Equipment, Computer and Other Electronic Equipment Manufacturing	33	224.18
仪器仪表及文化、办公用机械制造业	Instruments, Meters, Cultural and Official Machinery	14	12.89
工艺品及其他制造业	Handicraft Article and Other Manufacturing	6	12.38
废弃资源和废旧材料回收加工业	Waste Resources and Junk Material Recycled	1	0.05
电力、燃气及水的生产和供应业	**Electric Power, Gas and Water Production and Supply**		
电力、热力的生产和供应业	Electric Power, Steam and Hot Water Production and Supply	97	1183.74
燃气生产和供应业	Gas Production and Supply	5	28.48
水的生产和供应业	Tap Water Production and Supply	70	23.60

THE NUMBER OF STATE-OWNED SHARE HOLDING INDUSTRIAL ENTERPRISES AND THEIR TOTAL OUTPUT OF PRODUCTION AND SALES (2009)

(100 million yuan)

工业销售产值(当年价格) Output Value of Industrial Products Sales (current price)	出口交货值 Delivery Value for Export	资产总计 Total Assets	流动资产合计 Circulating Funds	固定资产合计 Total Fined Assets	固定资产原价 Original Value of Fixed Assets	主营业务收入 Revenue of Major Business	全部从业人员年平均人数(万人) Average Number of Empolyment of the Curreat Year(10 000 Bersons)
6421.90	172.46	12399.78	4317.97	6375.75	7859.51	6751.31	84.40
2855.71	103.96	3921.85	1272.01	2068.05	2916.52	3050.82	31.68
625.21	17.46	686.96	338.14	291.51	550.26	732.22	13.11
616.00	16.70	709.33	370.16	265.77	382.18	637.01	12.24
5805.90	155.77	11690.45	3947.81	6109.99	7477.33	6114.30	72.16
4969.99	132.30	9302.37	2702.16	5111.94	6104.81	5202.73	54.56
1156.40	37.20	2670.03	1460.11	1028.17	1429.14	1244.60	22.16
295.51	2.96	427.38	155.70	235.64	325.56	303.99	7.68
7.47		10.06	3.12	5.59	6.36	13.81	0.44
132.70	7.72	214.44	56.75	157.68	252.11	157.63	3.79
53.54		14.26	4.17	10.08	15.24	56.41	0.36
6.96		13.61	3.66	3.09	7.83	7.34	0.29
6.65		8.89	3.29	4.07	4.27	6.91	0.22
73.93	0.07	47.01	15.42	27.07	36.74	73.71	0.88
27.68	4.90	43.05	15.85	23.18	35.16	35.46	0.74
21.53		22.74	11.83	8.84	16.66	18.94	0.70
298.94	0.11	237.26	165.13	45.93	80.62	305.09	1.20
31.67	1.59	41.78	23.43	13.94	24.34	33.34	1.65
14.79	4.86	35.70	26.86	6.03	9.46	15.08	1.26
0.09		0.08	0.06	0.02	0.03	0.09	0.01
2.74		1.98	1.27	0.70	1.68	2.62	0.08
0.40		0.39	0.19	0.19	0.21	0.39	0.03
20.09		33.86	12.54	13.97	23.08	19.85	0.36
16.25		19.27	8.43	8.63	16.62	14.40	0.79
406.11		104.06	35.84	67.43	111.07	414.45	0.82
314.58	26.62	384.00	139.24	186.65	269.57	335.98	3.97
26.49	2.83	47.50	25.27	13.44	17.36	33.52	0.77
19.77	3.87	17.88	9.07	7.74	11.58	16.45	0.29
19.17	0.09	31.24	22.44	6.22	18.19	18.61	0.32
107.10	1.33	209.28	64.41	111.16	133.58	105.11	2.56
1374.66	28.02	1954.05	548.71	915.18	1454.09	1533.04	11.82
153.21	2.15	124.68	98.39	26.27	110.48	262.79	1.81
44.80	2.49	58.79	40.23	17.10	21.88	43.48	0.85
164.63	4.70	264.37	164.26	74.69	104.87	170.98	3.47
52.07	1.76	109.32	69.56	28.33	39.76	63.85	1.61
1460.06	69.65	2514.76	1376.61	1041.34	712.97	1384.27	22.32
101.19	2.63	126.05	61.74	58.73	78.59	123.90	1.40
208.18	5.72	577.13	235.31	315.93	360.19	219.88	3.69
12.06	0.95	16.99	10.82	4.59	7.52	12.38	0.64
11.89	0.35	22.75	16.02	5.73	10.15	11.07	0.69
0.05		0.13	0.01			0.05	
1181.07	0.04	4180.89	270.60	3044.46	3732.90	1187.49	11.81
28.48		774.49	741.15	29.29	32.81	32.67	0.22
20.90		137.04	36.26	92.45	101.53	20.24	2.55

8–5 集体工业企业单位数和主要经济指标 (2009)

单位：亿元

项 目	Item	企业单位数(个) Number of Enterprises (unit)	工业总产值(当年价格) Total Output Value (current price)
总 计	Total	331	157.53
在总计中：	Of the Total:		
亏损企业	Enterprises running under Deficit		
在总计中：	Of the Total:		
农村工业	Rural Industry	53	23.04
在总计中：	Of the Total:		
轻工业	Light Industry	69	40.31
重工业	Heavy Industry	262	117.22
在总计中：	Of the Total:		
大型企业	Large Scale Enterprises		
中型企业	Medium Scale Enterprises	21	54.42
小型企业	Small Enterprises	310	103.11
按行业分	Grouped by Sector		
采矿业	**Mining and Qarrying**		
煤炭开采和洗选业	Coal Mining and Processing	26	7.48
石油和天然气开采业	Petroleum and Natural Gas Extraction		
黑色金属矿采选业	Ferrous Metals Mining and Processing	7	10.35
有色金属矿采选业	Non-ferrous Metals Mining and Processing	5	1.56
非金属矿采选业	Non-metal Minerals Mining and Processing	33	17.66
其他采矿业	Other Minerals Mining and Processing	1	0.42
制造业	**Manufacturing**		
农副食品加工业	Food Processing	8	15.17
食品制造业	Food Production	5	7.23
饮料制造业	Beverage Production	15	3.11
烟草制品业	Tobacco Processing		
纺织业	Textile Industry	8	5.35
纺织服装、鞋、帽制造业	Textile,Garments, Shoes and Hats Products	3	0.42
皮革、毛皮、羽毛(绒)及其制品业	Leather, Furs,Down and Related Products	1	0.06
木材加工及木、竹、藤、棕、草制品业	Timber Processing, Wood, Bamboo, Cane, Palm and Sraw Products	5	4.56
家具制造业	Furniture Manufacturing	1	0.09
造纸及纸制品业	Papermaking and Paper Products	10	3.66
印刷业和记录媒介的复制	Printing and Record Processing	4	3.06
文教体育用品制造业	Stationery, Education and Sports Goods		
石油加工、炼焦及核燃料加工业	Petroleum Processing, Coking Products and Nuclear Fuel Processing		
化学原料及化学制品制造业	Raw Chemical Material and Chemical Products	21	6.13
医药制造业	Medical and pharmaceutical Products	1	0.16
化学纤维制造业	Chemical Fibers		
橡胶制品业	Rubber Products	1	0.08
塑料制品业	Plastic Products	7	2.59
非金属矿物制品业	Nonmetal Material Products	52	25.11
黑色金属冶炼及压延加工业	Smelting and Pressing of Ferrous Metals	3	0.33
有色金属冶炼及压延加工业	Smelting and Pressing of Nonferrous Metals	7	4.62
金属制品业	Metal Products	17	5.81
通用设备制造业	Ordinary Machinery Manufacturing	32	9.00
专用设备制造业	Special Purpose Equipment Manufacturing	7	5.87
交通运输设备制造业	Transportation Equipment Manufacturing	27	11.92
电气机械及器材制造业	Electric Machinery and Equipment	7	2.57
通信设备、计算机及其他电子设备制造业	Telecommunication Equipment, Computer and Other Electronic Equipment Manufacturing	1	0.23
仪器仪表及文化、办公用机械制造业	Instruments, Meters, Cultural and Official Machinery	3	0.73
工艺品及其他制造业	Handicraft Article and Other Manufacturing	1	0.08
废弃资源和废旧材料回收加工业	Waste Resources and Junk Material Recycled	1	0.23
电力、燃气及水的生产和供应业	**Electric Power, Gas and Water Production and Supply**		
电力、热力的生产和供应业	Electric Power, Steam and Hot Water Production and Supply	2	1.14
燃气生产和供应业	Gas Production and Supply		
水的生产和供应业	Tap Water Production and Supply	9	0.75

THE NUMBER OF COLLECTIVE-OWNED INDUSTRIAL ENTERPRISES

(100 million yuan)

工业销售产值(当年价格) Output Value of Industrial Products Sales (current price)	出口交货值 Delivery Value for Export	资产总计 Total Assets	流动资产合计 Circulating Funds	流动资产年平均余额 Average Balance of Circulating Funds	固定资产合计 Total Fined Assets	固定资产原价 Original Value of Fixed Assets	主营业务收入 Revenue of Major Business	全部从业人员年平均人数(万人) Average Number of Empolyment of the Curreat Year (10 000 Bersons)
150.86	0.65	82.39	37.70		32.71	50.71	145.71	5.57
22.17	0.07	12.12	4.49		5.83	11.41	21.47	0.82
39.09	0.56	21.87	8.65		9.19	16.82	35.33	1.01
111.77	0.08	60.52	29.04		23.52	33.90	110.37	4.56
52.55	0.38	31.53	16.47		12.90	20.15	52.74	1.98
98.31	0.27	50.86	21.22		19.82	30.56	92.97	3.59
7.35		3.80	1.29		2.33	2.91	7.27	0.58
9.66		2.32	0.76		1.57	3.24	10.15	0.30
1.42		0.70	0.08		0.62	0.70	1.42	0.04
16.89		8.54	2.93		4.09	4.76	16.75	0.70
0.09		0.13	0.10		0.03	0.03	0.36	0.02
14.81	0.31	7.51	3.73		3.64	4.91	13.98	0.15
7.01		3.01	0.63		1.59	3.83	6.87	0.21
2.98	0.15	2.25	0.60		1.13	1.11	3.13	0.11
5.02		3.59	0.41		0.83	0.83	2.45	0.11
0.40	0.09	0.15	0.05		0.02	0.03	0.46	0.02
0.06		0.06	0.06			0.01	0.06	
4.50		3.08	1.11		1.91	3.20	4.51	0.19
0.08		0.04	0.03		0.01	0.02	0.08	
3.60		1.19	0.76		0.36	4.03	3.16	0.09
3.04		2.56	2.08		0.45	0.59	3.04	0.21
5.69		3.53	1.54		1.82	1.86	5.26	0.25
0.16		0.07	0.02		0.05	0.06	0.16	
0.08		0.09	0.01				0.08	
2.49		1.54	0.51		1.02	1.32	2.97	0.10
24.45	0.07	8.76	4.28		2.93	4.01	24.37	0.84
0.33		0.69	0.51		0.08	0.14	0.38	0.05
4.52		3.06	1.31		1.36	1.57	4.10	0.11
4.97		2.81	1.80		0.95	1.79	5.58	0.14
8.76		6.82	3.87		1.62	2.58	7.67	0.48
5.12		3.51	2.67		0.65	1.39	5.15	0.23
11.82		8.42	4.97		1.63	3.47	10.79	0.36
2.49		0.65	0.23		0.24	0.36	2.43	0.08
0.18	0.02	0.33	0.21		0.01	0.02	0.26	0.01
0.73		0.90	0.52		0.36	0.05	0.57	0.02
0.07		0.04	0.03		0.01	0.03	0.07	
0.23		0.33	0.15		0.06	0.12	0.30	0.05
1.13		0.71	0.27		0.36	0.55	1.15	0.01
0.74		1.21	0.18		1.01	1.21	0.74	0.07

8-6 外商投资和港澳台商投资工业企业单位数和主要经济指标（2009）

单位：亿元

项 目	Item	企业单位数(个) Number of Enterprises (unit)
总计		891
在总计中：	Of the Total:	
亏损企业	Enterprises running under Deficit	
在总计中：	Of the Total:	
港、澳、台商投资企业	Hongkong, Macao and Taiwan Funded Enterprises	421
合资经营企业(港或澳、台资)	Joint Venture with Hongkong, Macao and Taiwan	199
合作经营企业(港或澳、台资)	Cooperate with Hongkong, Macao and Taiwan Funded	10
港澳台商独资经营企业	Enterprises Solely Funded by Hongkong, Macao and Taiwan Businessmen	189
港澳台商投资股份有限公司	Share Holding Co.Ltd. With Hongkong, Macao and Taiwan Investment	23
外商投资企业	Foreign Funded Enterprises	470
中外合资经营企业	Sino - Foreign Joint Funded Enterprises	273
中外合作经营企业	Sino - Foreign Cooperative Funded Enterprises	10
外资企业	Foreign Solely Funded Enterprises	169
外商投资股份有限公司	Foreign Funded Share Holding Co.Ltd.	18
在总计中：	Of the Total:	
国有控股企业	State-Owned Share Holding Enterprises	51
在总计中：	Of the Total:	
农村工业	Rural Industry	3
在总计中：	Of the Total:	
轻工业	Light Industry	424
重工业	Heavy Industry	467
在总计中：	Of the Total:	
大型企业	Large Scale Enterprises	19
中型企业	Medium Scale Enterprises	199
小型企业	Small Enterprises	673
按行业分	Grouped by Sector	
采矿业	Mining and Qarrying	
煤炭开采和洗选业	Coal Mining and Processing	1
石油和天然气开采业	Petroleum and Natural Gas Extraction	
黑色金属矿采选业	Ferrous Metals Mining and Processing	
有色金属矿采选业	Non-ferrous Metals Mining and Processing	2
非金属矿采选业	Non-metal Minerals Mining and Processing	9
其他采矿业	Other Minerals Mining and Processing	
制造业	Manufacturing	
农副食品加工业	Food Processing	43
食品制造业	Food Production	37
饮料制造业	Beverage Production	27
烟草制品业	Tobacco Processing	
纺织业	Textile Industry	85
纺织服装、鞋、帽制造业	Textile,Garments, Shoes and Hats Products	57
皮革、毛皮、羽毛(绒)及其制品业	Leather, Furs,Down and Related Products	14
木材加工及木、竹、藤、棕、草制品业	Timber Processing, Wood, Bamboo, Cane, Palm and Straw Products	7
家具制造业	Furniture Manufacturing	8
造纸及纸制品业	Papermaking and Paper Products	24
印刷业和记录媒介的复制	Printing and Record Processing	12
文教体育用品制造业	Stationery, Education and Sports Goods	6
石油加工、炼焦及核燃料加工业	Petroleum Processing, Coking Products and Nuclear Fuel Processing	5
化学原料及化学制品制造业	Raw Chemical Material and Chemical Products	50
医药制造业	Medical and pharmaceutical Products	47
化学纤维制造业	Chemical Fibers	2
橡胶制品业	Rubber Products	15
塑料制品业	Plastic Products	25
非金属矿物制品业	Nonmetal Material Products	48
黑色金属冶炼及压延加工业	Smelting and Pressing of Ferrous Metals	9
有色金属冶炼及压延加工业	Smelting and Pressing of Nonferrous Metals	6
金属制品业	Metal Products	34
通用设备制造业	Ordinary Machinery Manufacturing	40
专用设备制造业	Special Purpose Equipment Manufacturing	25
交通运输设备制造业	Transportation Equipment Manufacturing	121
电气机械及器材制造业	Electric Machinery and Equipment	43
通信设备、计算机及其他电子设备制造业	Telecommunication Equipment, Computer and Other Electronic Equipment Manufacturing	43
仪器仪表及文化、办公用机械制造业	Instruments, Meters, Cultural and Official Machinery	12
工艺品及其他制造业	Handicraft Article and Other Manufacturing	8
废弃资源和废旧材料回收加工业	Waste Resources and Junk Material Recycled	1
电力、燃气及水的生产和供应业	Electric Power, Gas and Water Production and Supply	
电力、热力的生产和供应业	Electric Power, Steam and Hot Water Production and Supply	6
燃气生产和供应业	Gas Production and Supply	14
水的生产和供应业	Tap Water Production and Supply	5

THE NUMBER OF FOREIGN FUNDED AND HONGKONG MACO AND TAIWAN FUNDED INDUSTRIAL ENTERPRISES AND THEIR TOTAL OUTPUT OF PRODUCTION AND SALES (2009)

(100 million yuan)

工业总产值(当年价格) Total Output Value (current price)	工业销售产值(当年价格) Output Value of Industrial Products Sales (current price)	出口交货值 Delivery Value for Export	资产总计 Total Assets	流动资产合计 Circulating Funds	固定资产合计 Total Fined Assets	固定资产原价 Original Value of Fixed Assets	主营业务收入 Revenue of Major Business	全部从业人员年平均人数(万人) Average Number of Empolyment of the Curreat Year (10 000 Bersons)
3077.79	3006.45	234.57	3886.14	2436.36	1216.23	1551.14	2988.95	36.94
709.68	685.49	162.86	1304.70	972.95	275.93	342.14	678.94	12.44
343.65	330.35	33.75	1047.70	861.72	152.61	186.90	322.53	6.56
14.77	14.69		13.16	6.67	5.34	6.94	14.46	0.29
330.60	320.56	128.89	219.50	93.80	107.15	134.67	321.61	4.94
20.66	19.89	0.22	24.35	10.76	10.82	13.64	20.34	0.65
2368.11	2320.96	71.71	2581.44	1463.42	940.31	1208.99	2310.01	24.50
1924.61	1892.88	36.73	2097.71	1253.40	726.66	903.50	1884.64	16.60
25.76	25.56		41.76	4.86	27.97	35.29	25.17	0.16
306.90	293.00	32.97	287.11	145.23	117.84	149.87	299.96	6.01
110.83	109.52	2.00	154.87	59.93	67.83	120.34	100.24	1.72
942.72	929.73	4.13	2115.63	1548.94	509.52	575.11	908.66	8.36
2.19	1.80		2.38	2.14	0.23	0.58	1.92	0.04
784.15	748.09	60.30	656.36	286.84	288.94	378.05	723.46	16.50
2293.64	2258.35	174.27	3229.78	2149.52	927.30	1173.09	2265.49	20.43
1537.67	1527.49	75.82	1661.18	1030.97	541.95	652.29	1447.22	12.39
942.10	906.71	83.58	1666.10	1156.55	425.31	575.26	980.36	15.35
598.02	572.25	75.16	558.86	248.84	248.97	323.59	561.37	9.20
1.00	1.00		0.72	0.40	0.32	0.59	1.00	0.05
3.22	3.86		3.03	2.21	0.81	0.46	3.96	0.07
1.19	1.11	0.02	0.84	0.42	0.41	0.57	1.07	0.03
125.94	113.45	3.01	111.01	42.64	60.53	69.05	116.28	0.95
75.14	73.62	2.64	54.13	21.48	26.68	36.67	69.50	1.42
111.32	106.31	0.01	99.96	37.55	51.46	77.51	94.21	1.19
103.82	99.89	18.38	58.68	23.93	27.25	37.76	99.11	3.60
42.05	40.34	14.31	29.16	15.13	11.75	15.34	37.61	1.91
5.01	4.91	2.67	3.30	1.78	0.48	0.60	4.59	0.39
6.34	6.06		6.43	2.54	3.63	6.47	6.04	0.15
4.35	3.97	2.62	5.32	3.13	1.49	1.92	4.04	0.23
53.48	54.50	1.18	68.55	33.22	26.25	37.16	55.12	1.24
15.65	15.21	0.26	19.38	11.20	5.20	8.84	16.34	0.40
3.12	2.60	0.43	5.78	3.51	0.65	0.82	2.80	0.17
46.53	37.28		30.75	15.59	11.47	15.90	33.40	0.15
105.53	100.03	9.95	60.98	29.35	21.52	33.23	97.20	2.16
84.53	80.10	6.50	104.05	44.09	37.96	40.45	75.50	1.58
1.44	1.44		4.88	1.81	2.35	2.53	2.52	0.03
9.83	9.13	0.53	7.75	4.37	3.06	4.48	9.09	0.27
28.53	28.38	0.87	24.20	12.88	7.64	11.54	26.37	0.46
115.48	114.12	1.73	165.15	50.21	92.02	138.43	102.46	1.73
101.59	102.39	5.05	90.28	52.52	32.46	70.05	94.73	0.80
28.04	26.82	2.30	24.86	7.24	16.43	22.92	25.55	0.29
49.57	45.55	1.25	49.15	18.42	26.34	31.54	43.61	0.63
75.01	74.34	4.95	99.51	60.76	29.48	55.03	80.75	1.13
13.28	13.08	1.55	14.42	10.71	2.92	3.41	13.81	0.33
1377.29	1367.73	14.23	1574.64	1030.35	469.16	521.06	1372.50	10.62
161.75	160.11	15.28	166.38	71.16	84.88	109.71	175.41	2.78
229.38	220.79	123.60	84.15	65.87	12.86	18.86	228.57	1.28
2.31	2.27	0.79	3.41	2.11	1.24	1.44	2.25	0.16
2.60	2.54	0.47	1.65	0.47	1.12	1.34	2.47	0.07
0.34	0.34		0.25	0.08	0.16	0.16	0.31	0.01
48.31	48.31		99.24	11.44	85.10	108.42	47.72	0.10
19.53	19.53		771.49	734.44	33.90	35.21	26.07	0.49
25.30	25.32		42.68	13.32	27.24	31.68	17.01	0.09

8-7 私营工业企业单位数和主要经济指标 (2009)

单位:亿元

项　目	Item	企业单位数(个) Number of Enterprises (unit)	工业总产值(当年价格) Total Output Value (current price)
总计		7875	3587.61
在总计中:	Of the Total:		
亏损企业	Enterprises running under Deficit		
在总计中:	Of the Total:		
轻工业	Light Industry	3297	1577.37
重工业	Heavy Industry	4578	2010.24
在总计中:	Of the Total:		
大型企业	Large Scale Enterprises	9	180.04
中型企业	Medium Scale Enterprises	291	747.66
小型企业	Small Enterprises	7575	2659.92
按行业分	Grouped by Sector		
采矿业	**Mining and Qarrying**		
煤炭开采和洗选业	Coal Mining and Processing	139	16.51
石油和天然气开采业	Petroleum and Natural Gas Extraction	1	0.16
黑色金属矿采选业	Ferrous Metals Mining and Processing	102	51.43
有色金属矿采选业	Non-ferrous Metals Mining and Processing	27	15.23
非金属矿采选业	Non-metal Minerals Mining and Processing	296	74.32
其他采矿业	Other Minerals Mining and Processing	4	0.33
制造业	**Manufacturing**		
农副食品加工业	Food Processing	1058	546.57
食品制造业	Food Production	189	76.79
饮料制造业	Beverage Production	231	82.74
烟草制品业	Tobacco Processing	1	0.10
纺织业	Textile Industry	638	358.37
纺织服装、鞋、帽制造业	Textile,Garments, Shoes and Hats Products	306	141.44
皮革、毛皮、羽毛(绒)及其制品业	Leather, Furs,Down and Related Products	30	9.35
木材加工及木、竹、藤、棕、草制品业	Timber Processing, Wood, Bamboo, Cane, Palm and Sraw Products	160	50.91
家具制造业	Furniture Manufacturing	53	16.02
造纸及纸制品业	Papermaking and Paper Products	148	69.87
印刷业和记录媒介的复制	Printing and Record Processing	107	33.97
文教体育用品制造业	Stationery, Education and Sports Goods	10	3.19
石油加工、炼焦及核燃料加工业	Petroleum Processing, Coking Products and Nuclear Fuel Processing	21	13.70
化学原料及化学制品制造业	Raw Chemical Material and Chemical Products	559	359.94
医药制造业	Medical and pharmaceutical Products	118	77.33
化学纤维制造业	Chemical Fibers	10	8.57
橡胶制品业	Rubber Products	51	25.10
塑料制品业	Plastic Products	337	130.19
非金属矿物制品业	Nonmetal Material Products	1026	325.27
黑色金属冶炼及压延加工业	Smelting and Pressing of Ferrous Metals	90	136.59
有色金属冶炼及压延加工业	Smelting and Pressing of Nonferrous Metals	108	84.06
金属制品业	Metal Products	337	158.74
通用设备制造业	Ordinary Machinery Manufacturing	494	175.88
专用设备制造业	Special Purpose Equipment Manufacturing	261	90.31
交通运输设备制造业	Transportation Equipment Manufacturing	529	261.61
电气机械及器材制造业	Electric Machinery and Equipment	185	91.53
通信设备、计算机及其他电子设备制造业	Telecommunication Equipment, Computer and Other Electronic Equipment Manufacturing	62	28.38
仪器仪表及文化、办公用机械制造业	Instruments, Meters, Cultural and Official Machinery	49	15.45
工艺品及其他制造业	Handicraft Article and Other Manufacturing	61	20.49
废弃资源和废旧材料回收加工业	Waste Resources and Junk Material Recycled	13	16.10
电力、燃气及水的生产和供应业	**Electric Power, Gas and Water Production and Supply**		
电力、热力的生产和供应业	Electric Power, Steam and Hot Water Production and Supply	41	13.92
燃气生产和供应业	Gas Production and Supply	9	3.72
水的生产和供应业	Tap Water Production and Supply	14	3.41

THE NUMBER OF PRIVATE-OWNED INDUSTRIAL ENTERPRISES AND THEIR MAJOR ECONOMIC INDICATORS (2009)

(100 million yuan)

工业销售产值(当年价格) Output Value of Industrial Products Sales(current price)	出口交货值 Delivery Value for Export	资产总计 Total Assets	流动资产合计 Circulating Funds	固定资产合计 Total Fined Assets	固定资产原价 Original Value of Fixed Assets	主营业务收入 Revenue of Major Business	全部从业人员年平均人数(万人) Average Number of Empolyment of the Curreat Year (10 000 Bersons)
3468.74	107.36	2111.94	942.29	961.84	1234.77	3396.22	83.09
1528.83	82.64	813.77	366.48	362.90	481.19	1505.83	41.01
1939.91	24.72	1298.17	575.81	598.94	753.58	1890.39	42.08
170.68	7.02	133.71	84.27	27.86	41.50	171.14	2.91
724.30	35.82	571.41	250.75	265.33	347.76	691.39	18.87
2573.76	64.52	1406.82	607.27	668.65	845.50	2533.69	61.31
16.25		15.97	3.69	11.28	12.01	15.97	1.29
0.16		0.10	0.10			0.16	
49.30		16.25	5.72	8.99	10.03	49.87	0.81
14.55		14.94	9.59	3.80	5.52	13.92	0.37
71.60		48.14	21.89	20.97	24.54	71.43	2.31
0.33		0.33	0.06	0.27	0.44	0.33	0.03
529.04	14.10	206.71	95.27	92.93	126.05	523.19	7.91
73.87	3.09	38.32	15.25	19.47	26.43	71.59	2.05
80.53	0.95	90.67	60.18	23.41	29.61	79.49	1.95
0.10		0.07	0.03	0.03	0.03	0.10	
350.46	34.15	190.58	80.60	90.48	116.59	341.70	13.11
137.13	18.13	65.63	26.63	32.08	39.34	133.71	5.70
8.72	0.88	4.37	1.93	2.06	2.27	8.92	0.32
48.33	0.81	28.61	9.98	12.83	16.85	47.43	1.51
15.84	0.05	11.41	4.07	5.91	7.56	15.42	0.48
68.39	0.08	34.44	15.03	15.59	23.45	66.24	1.63
33.14	0.23	22.86	9.75	11.46	14.47	32.56	1.11
3.12	0.18	0.79	0.39	0.26	0.36	3.07	0.11
13.69		5.54	2.12	2.86	3.26	14.67	0.10
345.19	9.26	222.68	74.55	128.18	161.90	336.44	5.63
73.85	2.74	64.66	22.50	32.73	38.13	70.33	1.34
8.43	0.10	2.31	0.85	1.32	1.89	8.36	0.15
24.27	0.66	9.67	4.53	3.66	4.56	23.79	0.59
125.60	0.39	64.80	30.06	27.25	40.61	125.93	3.66
315.29	2.81	216.66	80.16	117.31	145.47	305.68	9.16
132.61		65.15	33.75	26.47	33.22	133.48	1.30
81.50	0.10	48.18	17.97	27.42	34.18	79.44	0.98
149.19	1.92	89.39	44.15	33.83	50.11	144.35	3.73
169.33	0.80	114.03	61.40	44.09	54.39	165.84	3.83
88.41	0.85	53.44	26.83	20.23	30.36	84.76	2.06
254.04	2.38	176.06	101.85	53.74	70.45	247.80	5.13
87.38	3.23	62.73	32.38	23.78	31.67	86.48	2.15
27.21	5.46	24.11	12.73	9.11	12.31	25.16	0.56
15.18	1.73	16.80	12.14	3.51	3.89	14.63	0.81
19.88	2.29	9.49	3.39	4.42	7.69	19.50	0.71
16.06		11.89	7.45	4.35	5.02	16.01	0.09
13.75		53.05	9.81	39.52	44.53	11.76	0.26
3.72		5.01	1.62	2.15	2.24	3.33	0.04
3.31		6.08	1.92	4.08	3.35	3.38	0.12

8-8 大中型工业企业单位数和产销总值（2009）

单位:亿元

项 目	Item	企业单位数(个) Number of Enterprises(unit)
总 计	Total	1224
一、按登记注册类型分组:	Grouped by Type of Registration	
内资企业	Inner Funded Enterprises	1006
国有企业	State Owned Enterprises	145
中央企业	Central Enterprises	65
地方企业	Local Enterprises	80
集体企业	Collective-owned Enterprise	21
股份合作企业	Share Holding Cooperative Enterprises	9
联营企业	Joint Owned Enterprise	2
国有联营企业	State Joint Ownership	1
集体联营企业	Collective Joint Ownership	
国有与集体联营企业	Joint State- Collective Ownership	1
其他联营企业	Other Joint Owned Enterprise	
有限责任公司	Responsibility Co. Ltd	344
国有独资公司	State Solely Funded Co.	28
其他有限责任公司	Others	316
股份有限公司	Share Holding Co.Ltd.	177
私营企业	Private - owned enterprises	300
私营独资企业	Solely Private - owned enterprises	27
私营合作企业	Private Joint Venture	12
私营有限责任公司	Private Responsibility Co. Ltd	227
私营股份有限公司	Private Share Holding Co.Ltd.	34
其他企业	Others	8
港、澳、台商投资企业	Hongkong, Macao and Taiwan Funded Enterprises	90
合资经营企业(港或澳、台资)	Joint Venture with Hongkong, Macao and Taiwan	51
合作经营企业(港或澳、台资)	Cooperate with Hongkong, Macao and Taiwan Funded	3
港澳台商独资经营企业	Enterprises Solely Funded by Hongkong, Macao and Taiwan Businessmen	31
港澳台商投资股份有限公司	Share Holding Co.Ltd. With Hongkong, Macao and Taiwan Investment	5
外商投资企业	Foreign Funded Enterprises	128
中外合资经营企业	Sino - Foreign Joint Funded Enterprises	82
中外合作经营企业	Sino - Foreign Cooperative Funded Enterprises	
外资企业	Foreign Solely Funded Enterprises	39
外商投资股份有限公司	Foreign Funded Share Holding Co.Ltd.	7
二、在总计中:亏损企业	Of the Total: enterprises running under deficit	163
在总计中:国有控股企业	Of the Total: State-Owned Share Holding Enterprises	322
在总计中:农村工业	Of the Total: Rural Industry	9
在总计中:轻工业	Of the Total: Light Industry	498
重工业	Heavy Industry	726
在总计中:大型企业	Of the Total: Large Scale Enterprises	104
中型企业	Medium Scale Enterprises	1120
按行业分	Grouped by Sector	
采矿业	**Mining and Qarrying**	

NUMBER OF LARGE AND MEDIUM SCALE INDUSTRIAL ENTERPRISES AND THEIR TOTAL VALUE OF PRODUCTION AND SALES (2009)

(100 million yuan)

工业总产值(当年价格) Total Output Value(current price)	新产品产值 Output Value of New Products of New Products	工业销售产值(当年价格) Output Value of Industrial Products Sales(current price)	出口交货值 Delivery Value for Export
10335.22	1450.00	10124.49	481.42
7855.45	952.85	7690.29	322.02
3398.35	460.94	3380.77	121.11
2838.17	368.43	2829.18	103.73
560.18	92.51	551.59	17.37
54.42	0.50	52.55	0.38
36.71	1.34	34.80	1.55
6.05		6.11	
5.69		5.69	
0.36		0.42	
1753.35	181.66	1705.51	104.62
526.27	74.07	513.70	18.60
1227.08	107.59	1191.81	86.01
1632.29	245.81	1567.96	51.25
927.70	62.55	894.98	42.84
59.73	0.08	58.22	3.16
19.74		19.47	
715.93	56.13	693.93	27.55
132.29	6.34	123.35	12.13
46.58	0.05	47.61	0.27
443.81	38.60	426.12	111.53
202.75	26.46	192.94	25.70
9.42	1.04	9.44	
216.96	11.10	209.42	85.83
14.68		14.32	
2035.97	458.55	2008.08	47.87
1744.03	444.15	1721.44	23.49
188.56	6.35	184.15	22.40
103.38	8.05	102.50	1.98
1279.67	54.34	1254.22	40.47
6222.70	1087.63	6126.39	169.50
20.59	0.49	18.99	0.07
2124.57	182.43	2058.24	123.42
8210.65	1267.57	8066.25	358.00
6418.90	1101.24	6341.96	280.59
3916.33	348.76	3782.53	200.83

8-8 续表 continued

单位:亿元

项　目	Item	企业单位数(个) Number of Enterprises(unit)
煤炭开采和洗选业	Coal Mining and Processing	8
石油和天然气开采业	Petroleum and Natural Gas Extraction	3
黑色金属矿采选业	Ferrous Metals Mining and Processing	6
有色金属矿采选业	Non-ferrous Metals Mining and Processing	6
非金属矿采选业	Non-metal Minerals Mining and Processing	12
其他采矿业	Other Minerals Mining and Processing	
制造业	**Manufacturing**	
农副食品加工业	Food Processing	54
食品制造业	Food Production	40
饮料制造业	Beverage Production	32
烟草制品业	Tobacco Processing	5
纺织业	Textile Industry	152
纺织服装、鞋、帽制造业	Textile,Garments, Shoes and Hats Products	47
皮革、毛皮、羽毛(绒)及其制品业	Leather, Furs,Down and Related Products	1
木材加工及木、竹、藤、棕、草制品业	Timber Processing, Wood, Bamboo, Cane, Palm and Straw Products	10
家具制造业	Furniture Manufacturing	3
造纸及纸制品业	Papermaking and Paper Products	19
印刷业和记录媒介的复制	Printing and Record Processing	17
文教体育用品制造业	Stationery, Education and Sports Goods	2
石油加工、炼焦及核燃料加工业	Petroleum Processing, Coking Products and Nuclear Fuel Processing	8
化学原料及化学制品制造业	Raw Chemical Material and Chemical Products	84
医药制造业	Medical and pharmaceutical Products	50
化学纤维制造业	Chemical Fibers	2
橡胶制品业	Rubber Products	5
塑料制品业	Plastic Products	29
非金属矿物制品业	Nonmetal Material Products	89
黑色金属冶炼及压延加工业	Smelting and Pressing of Ferrous Metals	29
有色金属冶炼及压延加工业	Smelting and Pressing of Nonferrous Metals	16
金属制品业	Metal Products	37
通用设备制造业	Ordinary Machinery Manufacturing	72
专用设备制造业	Special Purpose Equipment Manufacturing	35
交通运输设备制造业	Transportation Equipment Manufacturing	163
电气机械及器材制造业	Electric Machinery and Equipment	62
通信设备、计算机及其他电子设备制造业	Telecommunication Equipment, Computer and Other Electronic Equipment Manufacturing	45
仪器仪表及文化、办公用机械制造业	Instruments, Meters, Cultural and Official Machinery	11
工艺品及其他制造业	Handicraft Article and Other Manufacturing	7
废弃资源和废旧材料回收加工业	Waste Resources and Junk Material Recycled	2
电力、燃气及水的生产和供应业	**Electric Power, Gas and Water Production and Supply**	
电力、热力的生产和供应业	Electric Power, Steam and Hot Water Production and Supply	47
燃气生产和供应业	Gas Production and Supply	4
水的生产和供应业	Tap Water Production and Supply	10

(100 million yuan)

工业总产值(当年价格) Total Output Value	新产品产值 Output Value of New Products	工业销售产值(当年价格) Output Value of Industrial Products Sales(current price)	出口交货值 Delivery Value for Export
14.73		12.67	
132.88	11.10	132.70	7.72
75.70		74.77	
13.15		13.54	
24.99		23.90	0.01
381.59	12.06	360.70	14.67
128.09	1.86	123.37	12.09
262.44	29.31	261.66	0.01
293.29		293.66	0.11
316.19	10.78	307.87	17.43
109.29	11.07	104.04	35.54
0.99		0.99	
33.63		32.70	0.59
7.19	0.96	6.92	2.29
77.97		76.63	0.13
37.72	1.64	35.98	1.62
2.04		1.69	0.10
437.58		431.62	
709.29	41.24	688.76	44.61
165.41	30.31	157.06	23.29
7.69		7.89	1.36
26.02	1.14	25.97	3.87
89.58	23.14	87.59	0.59
343.97	6.68	336.18	4.06
1594.92	323.21	1591.01	33.07
221.60	54.41	220.63	3.13
140.90	29.08	127.83	5.27
300.28	56.32	280.27	8.12
99.62	5.20	95.75	2.07
2155.30	643.03	2118.46	81.47
344.20	88.97	334.55	22.64
504.50	46.40	480.76	152.40
28.48	5.89	27.60	2.62
33.63	16.20	31.71	0.53
14.08		14.08	
1162.34		1160.01	
29.36		29.36	
14.58		13.61	

8-9 规模以上工业企业产品产量、生产能力及能力利用率综合表（2009）

产品名称		Item		企业单位数（个） Number of Enterprises
原煤	（万吨）	Raw coal	(10 000 tons)	226
天然原油	（万吨）	Natural oil	(10 000 tons)	2
卷烟	（亿支）	Cigarette	(10 000 units)	1
棉纺锭/纺纱量	（万锭/万吨）	Cotton spindles / spinning capacity	(10 000 /10 000 tons)	273
气流纺锭/纺纱量	（万头/万吨）	Air spindle / spinning capacity	(10 000 /10 000 tons)	63
棉布织机/布	（万台/亿米）	Cotton weaving / cloth	(Million / 100 million meters)	244
原油加工能力/原油加工量	（万吨/万吨）	Crude oil processing capacity / crude oil processing capacity	(10 000 tons)	3
焦炭	（万吨）	Coke	(10 000 tons)	7
碳化钙(电石，折300升/千克)	（万吨）	Calcium carbide(calcium carbide, off 300 liters/kg)	(10 000 tons)	12
农用氮、磷、钾化学肥料总计(折纯)	（万吨）	Agricultural nitrogen, phosphorus and potassium fertilizer Total (off net)	(10 000 tons)	144
化学纤维	（万吨）	Chemical fiber	(10 000 tons)	13
水泥熟料	（万吨）	Cement clinker	(10 000 tons)	95
其中：窑外分解窑熟料	（万吨）	Of which: Cement Kiln Clinker	(10 000 tons)	38
立窑熟料	（万吨）	Shaft kiln clinker	(10 000 tons)	50
预热器窑熟料	（万吨）	Preheater kiln clinker	(10 000 tons)	8
湿法窑熟料	（万吨）	Wet kiln clinker	(10 000 tons)	1
中空窑熟料	（万吨）	Kiln clinker	(10 000 tons)	2
水泥	（万吨）	Cement	(10 000 tons)	152
平板玻璃	（万重量箱）	Plate glass	(Million boxes)	11
其中：浮法玻璃	（万重量箱）	Of which: Float Glass	(Million boxes)	4
平拉玻璃	（万重量箱）	Ping Perlis	(Million boxes)	7
生铁	（万吨）	Pig iron	(10 000 tons)	18
粗钢	（万吨）	Crude steel	(10 000 tons)	12
钢材	（万吨）	Steel	(10 000 tons)	56
铁合金	（万吨）	Ferroalloy	(10 000 tons)	19
原铝(电解铝)	（万吨）	Primary aluminum (aluminum)	(10 000 tons)	6
金属切削机床	（万台）	Metal cutting machine tools	(10 000 sets)	14
汽车	（万辆）	Car	(10 000 sets)	14
其中：基本型乘用车(轿车)	（万辆）	Of which: basic passenger vehicles (cars)	(10 000 sets)	4
家用电冰箱	（万台）	Household Refrigerators	(10 000 sets)	1
房间空气调节器	（万台）	Room air conditioners	(10 000 sets)	3
家用洗衣机	（万台）	Household washing machines	(10 000 sets)	1
移动通信手持机(手机)	（万台）	Mobile handset (cell phone)	(10 000 sets)	1
电子计算机整机	（万台）	Computer machine	(10 000 sets)	2
其中：微型计算机设备	（万台）	Including: micro-computer equipment	(10 000 sets)	2
彩色电视机	（万台）	Color TV	(10 000 sets)	
发电设备容量总计/发电量	（千瓦/亿千瓦小时）	Total capacity of power equipment / power generation	(KW/ billion KW hours)	187
其中：火电设备容量/发电量	（千瓦/亿千瓦小时）	Of which: thermal power equipment capacity / power generation	(KW/ billion KW hours)	46
水电设备容量/发电量	（千瓦/亿千瓦小时）	Hydropower Equipment capacity / power generation	(KW/ billion KW hours)	133
核电设备容量/发电量	（千瓦/亿千瓦小时）	Capacity of nuclear power equipment / power generation	(KW/ billion KW hours)	
风电设备容量/发电量	（千瓦/亿千瓦小时）	Capacity of wind power equipment / power generation	(KW/ billion KW hours)	1

OUTPUT OF MAJOR PRODUCTS OF INDUSTRY ABOVE DESIGNATED SIZE (2009)

本年生产量 Production this year	年初生产能力 Early production	年末生产能力 At the end of production capacity	能力利用率(%) Capacity Utilization
1087.66	1388.14	1477.64	75.91
80.89	79.96	80.60	100.76
1278.58	1428.60	1712.83	81.40
133.46	740.88	774.75	
20.01	21.10	20.94	
31.95	15.33	15.94	
935.52	1307.60	1307.60	71.54
838.10	964.00	906.60	89.61
78.02	87.82	88.82	88.33
862.78	1132.44	1212.08	73.60
12.69	16.25	16.75	76.89
4236.89	5401.34	6208.15	72.99
3017.66	3756.30	4152.80	76.31
615.39	999.04	1035.85	60.48
364.53	391.50	541.50	78.14
0.19		77.50	0.50
165.92	213.00	359.00	58.01
6744.51	8491.18	9838.43	73.59
3528.15	3318.56	3679.47	100.83
2858.49	2629.22	2844.24	104.45
669.66	689.34	835.23	87.85
1924.04	2088.60	2345.24	86.79
1981.03	2364.24	2631.24	79.31
2122.68	2651.04	2969.00	75.54
21.39	27.83	28.03	76.59
28.18	41.30	44.30	65.83
0.49	0.70	0.70	70.26
117.61	114.87	146.85	89.87
49.50	64.00	84.00	66.89
39.51	52.50	52.50	75.25
514.28	782.00	782.00	65.76
36.00	55.00	54.40	65.80
831.52	890.00	1040.00	86.17
87.38	77.97	77.97	112.07
87.38	77.97	77.97	112.07
1783.10	0.45	0.45	45.09
569.13	0.13	0.13	50.16
1163.84	0.31	0.31	42.41
0.23			19.51

8-10 规模以上工业主要产品产量（2009）
SCALE INDUSTRIAL OUTPUT OF MAIN PRODUCTS （2009）

名　称	计量单位	name		产品产量
原煤	(吨)	Original Coal	(ton)	10632701.78
1.无烟煤	(吨)	Anthracite	(ton)	5503476.15
2.烟煤	(吨)	Bituminous coal	(ton)	5129225.63
一般烟煤	(吨)	General bituminous coal	(ton)	5129225.63
洗煤	(吨)	Coal washing	(ton)	40800.00
其中：洗精煤	(吨)	Washed coal	(ton)	40800.00
天然原油	(吨)	Natural oil	(ton)	808872.00
天然气	(万立方米)	Natural gas	(10 000 cu.m)	16717.00
铁矿石原矿	(吨)	Iron ore	(ton)	12885415.22
铜金属含量	(吨)	Copper content	(ton)	63116.84
锑金属含量	(吨)	Antimony metal content	(ton)	255.00
钨精矿折合量(折三氧化钨65%)	(吨)	Tungsten equivalent amount (65% off tungsten trioxide)	(ton)	577.00
钼精矿折合量(折纯钼45%)	(吨)	Equivalent amount of molybdenum concentrate (45% off pure Mo)	(ton)	23.10
硫铁矿石(折含硫35%)	(吨)	Pyrite Stone (off 35% sulfur)	(ton)	159863.00
磷矿石(折含五氧化二磷30%)	(吨)	Phosphate rock (containing phosphorus pentoxide 30% off)	(ton)	21181990.20
原盐	(吨)	Crude salt	(ton)	5286187.00
小麦粉	(吨)	Wheat flour	(ton)	2310693.78
大米	(吨)	Rice	(ton)	8382258.60
饲料	(吨)	Feed	(ton)	4092774.92
精制食用植物油	(吨)	Refined edible vegetable oil	(ton)	2147919.42
鲜、冷藏肉	(吨)	Fresh, chilled meat	(ton)	459882.23
冻肉	(吨)	Frozen meat	(ton)	46162.00
冷冻水产品	(吨)	Frozen Seafood	(ton)	33338.77
糕点	(吨)	Cake	(ton)	24492.90
饼干	(吨)	Biscuit	(ton)	470339.30
糖果	(吨)	Candy	(ton)	109707.20
速冻米面食品	(吨)	Frozen rice flour food	(ton)	2350.30
方便面	(吨)	Instant noodles	(ton)	111650.00
乳制品	(吨)	Dairy products	(ton)	519027.10
其中:液体乳	(吨)	Of which: Liquid dairies	(ton)	474963.10
乳粉	(吨)	Milk powder	(ton)	36716.00
罐头	(吨)	Can	(ton)	393641.80
味精(谷氨酸钠)	(吨)	MSG (monosodium glutamate)	(ton)	30216.51
酱油	(吨)	Soy sauce	(ton)	55240.00
冷冻饮品	(吨)	Frozen drinks	(ton)	49667.03
发酵酒精(折96度,商品量)	(千升)	Fermentation of alcohol (off 96 degrees, the amount of goods)	(1000 L.)	51037.00
饮料酒	(千升)	Alcoholic beverage	(1000 L.)	3027715.60
其中:白酒(折65度,商品量)	(千升)	Where: Liquor (off 65 degrees, the amount of goods)	(1000 L.)	435368.83
软饮料	(吨)	Soft drinks	(ton)	4528638.98
精制茶	(吨)	Refined tea	(ton)	89809.34
卷烟	(万支)	Cigarette	(10 000 Pieces)	12785840.00
纱	(吨)	Yarn	(ton)	1493569.03
印染布	(万米)	Dyeing cloth	(mym)	32139.06
绒线(俗称毛线)	(吨)	Wool (commonly known as wool)	(ton)	277.00
毛机织物(呢绒)	(万米)	Wool fabric (wool fabric)	(mym)	123.60

8-10 续表-1 continued

名　称	计量单位	name		产品产量
苎麻布(含苎麻≥55%)	(万米)	Ramie fabric (including ramie ≥ 55%)	(mym)	922.50
生丝	(吨)	Raw silk	(ton)	598.37
棉被	(万米)	Quilt	(mym)	219.90
蚕丝被	(万米)	Silk	(mym)	8.00
帘子布	(吨)	Cord	(ton)	1157.00
无纺布(无纺织物)	(吨)	Non-woven (nonwoven fabric)	(ton)	16032.15
服装	(万件)	Clothing	(10 000 Pieces)	51460.77
轻革	(平方米)	Light Leather	(sq.m)	1109534.69
皮革鞋靴	(万双)	Leather footwear	(10 000 Pairs)	226.95
天然皮革制手提包(袋)、背包	(万个)	Natural leather handbags (bags), backpacks	(10 000 set)	3.10
鞣制毛皮(折羊毛皮)	(张)	Tanning fur (discount Yangmao Pi)	(set)	370000.00
天然毛皮服装	(件)	Natural fur garments	(Pieces)	51328.00
人造板	(立方米)	Wood-based Panel	(cu.m)	2719420.02
人造板表面装饰板	(平方米)	Plywood surface decoration board	(sq.m)	3162420.32
复合木地板	(平方米)	Composite wood flooring	(sq.m)	5447876.00
家具	(件)	Furniture	(Pieces)	1740799.80
纸浆(原生浆及废纸浆)	(吨)	Pulp (original pulp and waste paper pulp)	(ton)	46520.00
机制纸及纸板(外购原纸加工除外)	(吨)	Mechanism of paper and paperboard (excluding processing outsourcing base paper)	(ton)	1765834.57
纸制品	(吨)	Paper products	(ton)	1047424.00
单色印刷品	(令)	Monochrome Print	(order)	3121508.82
多色印刷品	(对开色令)	Multi-color print	(Off-color orders)	7034805.41
本册	(万本)	This book	(10 000 book)	79194.70
室内训练健身器材	(台)	Indoor training fitness equipment	(set)	507.00
原油加工量	(吨)	Crude oil processing capacity	(ton)	9355208.39
汽油	(吨)	Gasoline	(ton)	2164895.73
煤油	(吨)	Kerosene	(ton)	235158.93
柴油	(吨)	Diesel fuel	(ton)	3600798.72
润滑油	(吨)	Lubricating oil	(ton)	169014.00
燃料油	(吨)	Fuel Oil	(ton)	159690.00
润滑脂	(吨)	Grease	(ton)	403.00
液化石油气	(吨)	LPG	(ton)	641920.41
石油沥青	(吨)	Petroleum pitch	(ton)	195958.00
焦炭	(吨)	Coke	(ton)	8381040.00
硫酸(折100%)	(吨)	Sulfuric acid (100% discount)	(ton)	7337988.26
盐酸(氯化氢,含量31%)	(吨)	Hydrochloric acid (hydrogen chloride, content 31%)	(ton)	546411.50
烧碱(折100%)	(吨)	Caustic soda (100% discount)	(ton)	645862.56
纯碱(碳酸钠)	(吨)	Soda ash (sodium carbonate)	(ton)	1376071.54
碳化钙(电石,折 300升/千克)	(吨)	Calcium carbide (calcium carbide, off 300 liters / kg)	(ton)	804255.63
纯苯	(吨)	Benzene	(ton)	34126.00
精甲醇	(吨)	Purified methanol	(ton)	298900.22
黄磷	(吨)	Yellow phosphorus	(ton)	118980.20
浓硝酸(折100%)	(吨)	Concentrated nitric acid (100% discount)	(ton)	49375.00
合成氨(无水氨)	(吨)	Ammonia (anhydrous ammonia)	(ton)	3700183.65
农用氮、磷、钾化学肥料总计(折纯)	(吨)	Agricultural nitrogen, phosphorus and potassium fertilizer Total (off net)	(ton)	8525811.18

8-10 续表-2 continued

名　称	计量单位	name		产品产量
1.氮肥(折含N100%)	(吨)	1. N (off with N100%)	(ton)	4120353.19
其中：尿素(折含N100%)	(吨)	Of which: Urea (off with N100%)	(ton)	1165531.10
2.磷肥(折五氧化二磷100 %)	(吨)	2. P (off 100% of phosphorus pentoxide)	(ton)	4394029.32
3.钾肥(折氧化钾100%)	(吨)	3. potash (potassium hydroxide 100% discount)	(ton)	11428.67
磷酸铵肥(实物量)	(吨)	Ammonium phosphate fertilizer (physical quantity)	(ton)	3451050.00
硝酸磷肥(实物量)	(吨)	Nitrate fertilizer (physical quantity)	(ton)	111011.00
化学农药原药(折有效成分100%)	(吨)	Chemicals and pesticides (active ingredient 100% discount)	(ton)	105552.54
涂料	(吨)	Paint	(ton)	149782.20
其中：建筑涂料	(吨)	Including: architectural coatings	(ton)	45979.00
油墨	(吨)	Ink	(ton)	2639.00
颜料	(吨)	Pigment	(ton)	22351.20
染料	(吨)	Dye	(ton)	40063.00
初级形态的塑料	(吨)	Primary form of plastic	(ton)	641446.20
其中:聚乙烯树酯	(吨)	Of which: PE resin	(ton)	12120.00
聚丙烯树脂	(吨)	Polypropylene Resin	(ton)	286705.00
聚氯乙烯树脂	(吨)	PVC resin	(ton)	324266.00
合成橡胶	(吨)	Synthetic Rubber	(ton)	198.99
化学试剂	(吨)	Chemical Reagent	(ton)	35895.65
催化剂	(吨)	Catalyst	(ton)	9286.50
肥(香)皂	(吨)	Fertilizer (Hong) soap	(ton)	3911.00
合成洗涤剂	(吨)	Synthetic detergent	(ton)	219424.00
牙膏(折65克标准支)	(万支)	Toothpaste (pack 65 g standard support)		302.00
香精	(吨)	Essence	(ton)	1988.00
火柴(折50支标准盒)	(吨)	Match (off 50 standard boxes)	(ton)	267355.00
化学药品原药	(吨)	Original drug chemicals	(ton)	54996.65
中成药	(吨)	Chinese patent medicine	(ton)	179412.93
化学纤维用浆粕	(吨)	Chemical Fiber Pulp	(ton)	90427.00
化学纤维	(吨)	Chemical fiber	(ton)	120813.70
橡胶轮胎外胎	(条)	Tire tire	(item)	6396544.00
其中：子午线轮胎外胎	(条)	Of which: radial tire tire	(item)	4633311.00
胶鞋类	(吨)	Shoes class	(ton)	330.22
塑料制品	(吨)	Plastic Products	(ton)	1204579.91
其中:塑料薄膜	(吨)	Of which: plastic film	(ton)	57529.80
其中：农用薄膜	(吨)	Of which: agricultural film	(ton)	7095.00
塑料板、片	(吨)	Plastic plates, sheets	(ton)	104126.86
塑料管及其附件	(吨)	Plastic pipe and accessories	(ton)	239324.30
塑料条、棒、型材	(吨)	Plastic strip, rods, profiles	(ton)	19941.50
塑料丝、绳及编织品	(吨)	Plastic wire, rope and woven goods	(ton)	284025.93
泡沫塑料	(吨)	Foam	(ton)	17579.00
塑料人造革、合成革	(吨)	Plastic leather, synthetic leather	(ton)	11934.14
塑料包装箱及容器	(吨)	Plastic boxes and containers	(ton)	90520.13
日用塑料制品	(吨)	Household Plastic Products	(ton)	283674.81
水泥熟料	(吨)	Cement clinker	(ton)	41842093.94
其中:窑外分解窑水泥熟料	(吨)	Of which: Cement Kiln Clinker	(ton)	26177862.80
水泥	(吨)	Cement	(ton)	69837720.17
其中:强度等级42.5水泥(含R型)	(吨)	Of which: strength grade 42.5 cement (including the R-type)	(ton)	7141896.00
强度等级52.5水泥(含R型)	(吨)	Strength grade 52.5 cement (including the R-type)	(ton)	63327.00

8-10 续表-3 continued

名　称	计量单位	name		产品产量
商品混凝土	(立方米)	Concrete	(cu.m)	8346408.35
水泥混凝土排水管	(千米)	Concrete drainage pipes	(Km)	7351.99
水泥混凝土压力管	(千米)	Concrete pressure pipe	(Km)	183.95
水泥混凝土电杆	(根)	Cement Concrete Poles	(Root)	221488.00
预应力混凝土桩	(米)	Prestressed concrete piles	(M)	7326435.00
石膏板	(万平方米)	Gypsum board	(10 000M^2)	4153.91
砖	(万块)	Brick		1837079.21
瓦	(万片)	Tile		74884.62
瓷质砖	(平方米)	Tile	(M^2)	127366015.00
陶质砖	(平方米)	Ceramic tiles	(M^2)	20208259.00
天然大理石建筑板材	(平方米)	Natural marble building boards	(M^2)	3425229.27
天然花岗石建筑板材	(平方米)	Natural granite building boards	(M^2)	3229024.00
沥青和改性沥青防水卷材	(平方米)	Asphalt and modified bitumen membrane	(M^2)	10036803.00
平板玻璃	(重量箱)	Plate glass		35281462.90
钢化玻璃	(平方米)	Tempered glass	(M^2)	2522978.40
夹层玻璃	(平方米)	Laminated Glass	(M^2)	212381.04
中空玻璃	(平方米)	Insulating glass	(M^2)	461482.77
日用玻璃制品	(吨)	Daily Glass Products	(ton)	261435.50
玻璃包装容器	(吨)	Glass containers	(ton)	145837.80
玻璃纤维纱	(吨)	Glass fiber yarn	(ton)	6482.00
卫生陶瓷制品	(件)	Sanitary ceramics products		6503829.00
日用陶瓷制品	(万件)	Ceramics Products		509.00
耐火材料制品	(吨)	Refractory Products	(ton)	438238.77
石墨及炭素制品	(吨)	Graphite and carbon products	(ton)	99741.71
生铁	(吨)	Pig iron	(ton)	19567029.00
粗钢	(吨)	Crude steel	(ton)	19852994.00
钢材	(吨)	Steel	(ton)	21723266.24
1.铁道用钢材	(吨)	1. Railway with steel	(ton)	770516.00
其中：轻轨	(吨)	Of which: Light Rail	(ton)	9511.00
重轨	(吨)	Heavy Rail	(ton)	761005.00
2.大型型钢	(吨)	2. Large-scale steel	(ton)	41143.82
3.中小型型钢	(吨)	3. Small and medium steel	(ton)	477424.00
4.棒材	(吨)	4. Bar	(ton)	2270432.97
5.钢筋	(吨)	5. Reinforced	(ton)	2778445.04
6.线材(盘条)	(吨)	6. Wire (coil)	(ton)	1818648.00
7.特厚板	(吨)	7. Special Plate	(ton)	189899.00
8.厚钢板	(吨)	8. Thick steel plate	(ton)	421602.00
9.中板	(吨)	9. The board	(ton)	1615526.00
10.热轧薄板	(吨)	10. Hot-rolled sheet	(ton)	115024.00
11.冷轧薄板	(吨)	11. Cold-rolled sheet	(ton)	682743.00
12.中厚宽钢带	(吨)	12. In the thick wide strips	(ton)	2592440.00
13.热轧薄宽钢带	(吨)	13. Hot rolled thin wide strips	(ton)	1191330.00
14.冷轧薄宽钢带	(吨)	14. Cold rolled wide strip	(ton)	1271446.00
15.热轧窄钢带	(吨)	15. Hot rolled narrow strip	(ton)	483559.00
16.冷轧窄钢带	(吨)	16. Cold rolled narrow strip	(ton)	47193.00

8-10 续表-4 continued

名 称	计量单位	name		产品产量
17.镀层板(带)	(吨)	17. Coated plate (with)	(ton)	1389682.00
18.涂层板(带)	(吨)	18. Coated plate (with)	(ton)	287054.00
19.电工钢板(带)	(吨)	19. Electrical Steel (band)	(ton)	1331796.00
20.无缝钢管	(吨)	20. Seamless	(ton)	683597.00
21.焊接钢管	(吨)	21. Welded steel pipe	(ton)	515088.41
22.其它钢材	(吨)	22. Other steel products	(ton)	748677.00
用外购国产钢材再加工生产的钢材	(吨)	With the outsourcing of domestic steel production steel reprocessing	(ton)	349803.00
铁合金	(吨)	Ferroalloy	(ton)	217013.64
其中：硅铁(折合含硅75%)	(吨)	Of which: ferrosilicon (U.S. silicon 75%)	(ton)	74207.49
锰硅合金	(吨)	Silicon manganese alloy	(ton)	105685.00
十种有色金属	(吨)	10 kinds of nonferrous metals	(ton)	667692.36
精炼铜(电解铜)	(吨)	Refined copper (electrolytic copper)	(ton)	271565.00
铅	(吨)	Lead	(ton)	108041.09
锌	(吨)	Zinc	(ton)	2594.00
锑品	(吨)	Antimony	(ton)	1591.51
原铝(电解铝)	(吨)	Primary aluminum (aluminum)	(ton)	281769.76
镁	(吨)	Magnesium	(ton)	2131.00
黄金	(千克)	Gold	(Kg)	11729.88
白银(银锭)	(千克)	Silver (silver bullion)	(Kg)	284752.00
铝合金	(吨)	Aluminum	(ton)	42019.77
铜材	(吨)	Copper	(ton)	66021.05
铝材	(吨)	Aluminum	(ton)	199348.56
其中：铝型材	(吨)	Of which: Aluminum	(ton)	79528.00
铝板材	(吨)	Aluminum Sheet	(ton)	19994.26
铝带材	(吨)	Aluminum Strip	(ton)	954.00
铝箔材	(吨)	Aluminum foil timber	(ton)	1053.00
金属切削工具	(万件)	Metal Cutting Tools		209.03
金属集装箱	(立方米)	Metal Container	(cu.m)	4509.00
钢丝	(吨)	Wire	(ton)	53517.14
钢丝绳	(吨)	Wire Rope	(ton)	33066.00
钢绞线	(吨)	Strand	(ton)	333687.05
锁具	(万把)	Lock		638.00
搪瓷制品	(吨)	Enamel products	(ton)	1461.62
不锈钢日用制品	(吨)	Stainless steel household products	(ton)	2250.77
电站锅炉	(蒸发量吨)	Boiler		10685.00
工业锅炉	(蒸发量吨)	Industrial boiler		2676.00
发动机	(千瓦)	Engine	(KW)	35060571.00
其中：汽车用发动机	(千瓦)	Of which: Automotive Engine	(KW)	33710000.00
电站用汽轮机	(千瓦)	Power Plant Steam Turbine	(KW)	1839000.00
电站水轮机	(千瓦)	Turbine	(KW)	171200.00
数控系统设备	(台)	CNC Equipment		152.00
金属切削机床	(台)	Metal cutting machine tools		3769.00
其中:数控金属切削机床	(台)	Of which: CNC metal cutting machine tools		791.00
金属成形机床	(台)	Metal forming machine tools		1701.00

8-10 续表-5 continued

名　称	计量单位	name		产品产量
其中：数控金属成形机床(数控锻压设备)	(台)	Where: NC metal forming machine tools (NC forging equipment)		266.00
铸造机械	(台)	Casting Machine		24392.00
起重机	(吨)	Crane	(ton)	33713.12
电动车辆(电动叉车)	(台)	Electric vehicles (electric forklift)		28231.00
内燃叉车	(台)	Internal combustion forklift		345.00
输送机械(输送机和提升机)	(吨)	Transportation machinery (conveyors and elevators)	(ton)	53734.26
泵	(台)	Pump		50200.00
气体压缩机	(台)	Gas compressor		436781.00
阀门	(吨)	Valve	(ton)	30796.00
液压元件	(件)	Hydraulic Components	(piece)	2213428.00
气动元件	(件)	Pneumatic components	(piece)	21963.00
滚动轴承	(万套)	Rolling		5334.89
齿轮	(吨)	Gear	(ton)	23641.17
风机	(台)	Fans		20835.00
其中：鼓风机	(台)	Of which: Blower		11852.00
电动手提式工具	(台)	Electric Portable Tools		1938.00
包装专用设备	(台)	Special equipment package		540.00
衡器(秤)	(台)	Scale (scale)		13709.00
减速机	(台)	Reducer		210546.00
弹簧	(吨)	Spring	(ton)	17467.00
铸铁件	(吨)	Cast Iron	(ton)	365389.71
铸钢件	(吨)	Steel Castings	(ton)	146391.72
锻件	(吨)	Forging	(ton)	70429.00
粉末冶金零件	(吨)	Powder Metallurgy Parts	(ton)	22572.39
采矿专用设备	(吨)	Mining special equipment	(ton)	22120.64
混凝土机械	(台)	Concrete Machinery		492.00
金属冶炼设备	(吨)	Metal smelting equipment	(ton)	7295.00
金属轧制设备	(吨)	Metal rolling equipment	(ton)	1841.00
炼油、化工生产专用设备	(吨)	Oil refining, chemical production special equipment	(ton)	257402.00
塑料加工专用设备	(台)	Plastics Processing Special Equipment		438.00
模具	(套)	Mold		2936.00
粮食加工机械	(台)	Food processing machinery	(set)	656141.00
饲料生产专用设备	(台)	Equipment for feed production	(set)	114.00
印刷专用设备	(吨)	Printing special equipment	(ton)	2239.00
中型拖拉机	(台)	Medium-sized tractors	(set)	2649.00
小型拖拉机	(台)	Small tractor	(set)	11175.00
棉花加工机械	(台)	Cotton processing machinery	(set)	1764.00
环境污染防治专用设备	台(套)	Equipment for Environmental Pollution Control	(set)	592.00
其中:大气污染防治设备	(台)	Of which: Air pollution control equipment	(set)	406.00
水质污染防治设备	台(套)	Water Pollution Control Equipment	(set)	62.00
固体废弃物处理设备	(台)	Solid waste handling equipment	(set)	115.00
铁路货车	(辆)	Freight	(set)	5475.00
汽车	(辆)	Car	(set)	1196671.00
其中：基本型乘用车(轿车)	(辆)	Of which: basic passenger vehicles (cars)	(set)	495008.00

8-10 续表-6 continued

名　称	计量单位	name		产品产量
(1)1升<排量≤1.6升	(辆)	(1) 1 1 liter <Displacement ≤ 1.6 liter	(set)	266588.00
(2)1.6升<排量≤2.0升	(辆)	(2) 1.6 liter <Displacement ≤ 2.0 liter	(set)	107083.00
(3)2.0升<排量≤2.5升	(辆)	(3) 2.0 liter <Displacement ≤ 2.5 liter	(set)	120626.00
(4)2.5升<排量≤3.0升	(辆)	(4) 2.5 liter <Displacement ≤ 3.0 liter	(set)	711.00
运动型多用途乘用车(SUV)	(辆)	Sport utility vehicles (SUV)	(set)	103500.00
客车	(辆)	Bus	(set)	195944.00
(1)大型客车(车长>10米)	(辆)	(1) Large Passenger (car length> 10 m)	(set)	1212.00
(2)中型客车(7米<车长≤10米)	(辆)	(2) Medium Passenger (7 m <car length ≤ 10 m)	(set)	17621.00
(3)轻型客车(车长≤7米)	(辆)	(3) light buses (drivers ≤ 7 m)	(set)	177111.00
载货汽车	(辆)	Lorry	(set)	402219.00
改装汽车	(辆)	Modified cars	(set)	106565.00
低速载货汽车	(辆)	Low speed truck	(set)	871.00
(1)中型客车(7米<车长≤10米)	(辆)	(1) Medium Passenger (7 m <car length ≤ 10 m)	(set)	17621.00
(2)轻型客车(车长≤7米)	(辆)	(2) light buses (drivers ≤ 7 m)	(set)	177111.00
载货汽车	(辆)	Lorry	(set)	402219.00
改装汽车	(辆)	Modified cars	(set)	106565.00
低速载货汽车	(辆)	Low speed truck	(set)	871.00
民用钢质船舶	(载重吨)	Civil Steel Ships	(Dwt)	1077080.00
船舶修理	(载重吨)	Ship repair	(Dwt)	26060.00
发电机组(发电设备)	(千瓦)	Generating units (power equipment)	(KW)	2060000.00
其中：水轮发电机组	(千瓦)	Of which: Generator Group	(KW)	75500.00
汽轮发电机	(千瓦)	Turbo	(KW)	1984500.00
交流电动机	(千瓦)	Motors	(KW)	1737543.68
变压器	(千伏安)	Transformer		8725827.00
互感器	(台)	Transformer	(set)	26800.00
高压开关板	(面)	High-voltage switch board		578.00
低压开关板	(面)	Low-voltage switch board		4615.00
高压开关设备(11万伏以上)	(台)	High Voltage Switchgear (11 KV and above)	(set)	12000.00
通信及电子网络用电缆	(对千米)	Communication and electronic networks Cables		56725.16
电力电缆	(千米)	Power cable	(Km)	460655.22
光缆	(芯千米)	Cable		9855145.23
绝缘制品	(吨)	Insulation Products		6919.00
铅酸蓄电池	(千伏安时)	Lead-acid batteries		10538014.13
碱性蓄电池	只(自然只)	Alkaline batteries		357992.00
锂离子电池	只(自然只)	Lithium ion battery		3650000.00
原电池及原电池组(折R20标准只)	(万只)	Primary cells and primary batteries (off R20 standard only)	(10 000)	26672.20
家用电冰箱	(台)	Household Refrigerators	(set)	395085.00
家用冷柜(家用冷冻箱)	(台)	Household Refrigerator (household freezers)	(set)	882221.00

8-10 续表-7 continued

名　称	计量单位	name		产品产量
房间空气调节器	(台)	Room air conditioners	(set)	5142816.00
家用吸排油烟机	(台)	Home range hood	(set)	5665.00
家用洗衣机	(台)	Household washing machines	(set)	359957.00
家用电热水器	(台)	Water heater	(set)	1155238.00
家用燃气灶具	(台)	With domestic gas	(set)	4040925.00
家用燃气热水器	(台)	Gas Water Heater	(set)	23993.00
电光源	(万只)	Light Sources	(10 000)	39095.48
其中:荧光灯	(万只)	Fluorescent	(10 000)	2066.00
灯具及照明装置	套(台、个)	Lamps and lighting fittings		16447723.00
程控交换机	(线)	PBX	(Line)	590.00
电话单机	(部)	Phone Single		210124.00
移动通信手持机(手机)	(台)	Mobile handset (cell phone)	(set)	8315172.00
电子计算机整机	(台)	Computer machine	(set)	873800.00
其中:微型计算机设备	(台)	Micro-computer equipment	(set)	873800.00
其中：笔记本计算机	(台)	Of which: Notebook Computers	(set)	4800.00
显示器	(台)	Monitor	(set)	11529436.00
其中：平板显示器	(台)	Of which: flat panel displays	(set)	238544.00
半导体分立器件	(万只)	Semiconductor discrete devices	(10 000)	8506.40
集成电路	(万块)	IC		68.50
光电子器件	万只(片、套)	Optoelectronic devices		353541.50
其中:发光二极管(LED)	(万只)	Of which: Light-emitting diode (LED)	(10 000)	348948.00
电子元件	(万只)	Electronic component	(10 000)	91438.74
其中:片式元件	(万只)	Of which: chip components	(10 000)	19618.30
射频元器件	(万只)	RF Components	(10 000)	1777.00
工业自动调节仪表与控制系统	台(套)	Automatic adjustment of industrial instrumentation and control system	(set)	10694.00
电工仪器仪表	(台)	Electric Instruments	(set)	103714.00
分析仪器及装置	台(套)	Analytical instruments and devices	(set)	28.00
试验机	(台)	Testing Machine	(set)	212.00
环境监测专用仪器仪表	(台)	Dedicated instrumentation for environmental monitoring	(set)	538.00
汽车仪器仪表	(台)	Automotive Instrumentation	(set)	3257.00
光学仪器	台(个)	Optical Instruments	(set)	284616.00
照相机	(台)	Camera	(set)	5524000.00
其中：数码照相机	(台)	Including: Digital cameras	(set)	5524000.00
伞类制品	(把)	Umbrellas Products	(set)	671000.00
发电量	(万千瓦小时)	Power generation	(Million kWh)	17817499.24
其中：火力发电量	(万千瓦小时)	Amony:Thermal capacity	(Million kWh)	6060697.90
水力发电量	(万千瓦小时)	Hydroelectricity	(Million kWh)	11696116.49
煤气生产量	(万立方米)	Gas production	(10 000 cu.m)	3709.00
自来水生产量	(万立方米)	Water Production	(10 000 cu.m)	151176.71
产品销售率	(%)	Products Sold	(%)	97.43
能源生产总量	(吨)	Total Energy Production	(ton)	53704225.55

8-11 规模以上工业企业主要经济效益指标 (2009)

项 目	Item	企业亏损面(%) Loss Making Rateof Enterprises
总 计	Total	13.02
一、按登记注册类型分组:	Grouped by Type of Registration	
内资企业	Inner Funded Enterprises	12.56
国有企业	State Owned Enterprises	24.82
中央企业	Central Enterprises	20.39
地方企业	Local Enterprises	26.32
集体企业	Collective-owned Enterprise	11.78
股份合作企业	Share Holding Cooperative Enterprises	14.04
联营企业	Joint Owned Enterprise	10.81
国有联营企业	State Joint Ownership	33.33
集体联营企业	Collective Joint Ownership	10.00
国有与集体联营企业	Joint State- Collective Ownership	
其他联营企业	Other Joint Owned Enterprise	9.52
有限责任公司	Responsibility Co. Ltd	17.19
国有独资公司	State Solely Funded Co.	17.50
其他有限责任公司	Others	17.19
股份有限公司	Share Holding Co.Ltd.	13.73
私营企业	Private - owned enterprises	9.65
私营独资企业	Solely Private - owned enterprises	3.59
私营合作企业	Private Joint Venture	4.93
私营有限责任公司	Private Responsibility Co. Ltd	12.39
私营股份有限公司	Private Share Holding Co.Ltd.	10.70
其他企业	Others	17.82
港、澳、台商投资企业	Hongkong, Macao and Taiwan Funded Enterprises	19.00
合资经营企业(港或澳、台资)	Joint Venture with Hongkong, Macao and Taiwan	16.58
合作经营企业(港或澳、台资)	Cooperate with Hongkong, Macao and Taiwan Funded	23.28
港澳台商独资经营企业	Enterprises Solely Funded by Hongkong, Macao and Taiwan Businessmen	
港澳台商投资股份有限公司	Share Holding Co.Ltd. With Hongkong, Macao and Taiwan Investment	13.04
外商投资企业	Foreign Funded Enterprises	20.43
中外合资经营企业	Sino - Foreign Joint Funded Enterprises	19.78
中外合作经营企业	Sino - Foreign Cooperative Funded Enterprises	10.00
外资企业	Foreign Solely Funded Enterprises	21.89
外商投资股份有限公司	Foreign Funded Share Holding Co.Ltd.	22.22
二、在总计中:亏损企业	Of the Total: enterprises running under deficit	100.00
在总计中:国有控股企业	Of the Total: State-Owned Share Holding Enterprises	21.06
在总计中:农村工业	Of the Total: Rural Industry	7.44
在总计中:轻工业	Of the Total: Light Industry	11.97
重工业	Heavy Industry	13.70
在总计中:大型企业	Of the Total: Large Scale Enterprises	15.38
中型企业	Medium Scale Enterprises	13.13
小型企业	Small Enterprises	12.99

MAJOR ECONOMIC INDICATORS OF INDUSTRIAL ENTERPRISES ABOVE DESIGNATED SIZE (2009)

总资产贡献率(%) Contributing Rate of Total Assets	资产负债率(%) Assets Liability Ratio	成本费用利润率(%) Ratio of Profits to Industrial Cost	产品销售率(%) Rate of Products Sold
11.35	54.01	7.74	97.41
11.25	51.45	7.05	97.35
10.77	61.78	3.03	99.31
10.95	60.69	2.85	99.59
9.75	67.96	3.73	98.05
22.83	55.12	8.04	95.77
21.90	43.42	10.15	96.00
23.44	45.53	16.59	97.95
48.08	65.90	32.66	97.48
47.60	69.51	11.14	98.27
6.36	52.12	1.71	103.68
6.71	27.07	7.31	96.15
10.26	59.06	6.44	96.66
5.31	62.80	2.60	97.56
11.95	57.78	7.35	96.48
8.69	36.88	15.73	96.18
18.79	50.24	7.28	96.69
25.96	42.71	7.78	96.93
27.37	42.70	6.00	96.62
17.48	51.97	7.34	96.84
15.62	50.51	6.88	95.33
24.23	55.74	12.93	100.19
6.29	77.82	8.36	96.59
4.80	85.72	11.11	96.13
20.38	42.28	14.19	99.42
11.52	45.98	5.08	96.96
15.61	44.16	15.07	96.28
14.50	57.18	11.40	98.01
15.01	55.02	11.88	98.35
13.27	49.78	12.80	99.23
15.39	54.87	10.49	95.47
6.31	92.63	5.12	98.81
0.90	66.24	-4.43	97.12
8.70	54.88	6.75	98.28
20.79	48.47	6.09	95.86
21.89	51.41	8.71	96.53
9.36	54.50	7.40	97.75
9.98	49.88	7.23	98.80
10.89	64.08	9.01	96.58
16.03	51.67	7.42	96.33

8-11 续表 continued

项 目	Item	企业亏损面(%) Loss Making Rateof Enterprises
按行业分	**Grouped by Sector**	
采矿业	**Mining and Qarrying**	
煤炭开采和洗选业	Coal Mining and Processing	16.39
石油和天然气开采业	Petroleum and Natural Gas Extraction	40.00
黑色金属矿采选业	Ferrous Metals Mining and Processing	10.30
有色金属矿采选业	Non-ferrous Metals Mining and Processing	11.86
非金属矿采选业	Non-metal Minerals Mining and Processing	7.86
其他采矿业	Other Minerals Mining and Processing	20.00
制造业	**Manufacturing**	
农副食品加工业	Food Processing	6.17
食品制造业	Food Production	8.93
饮料制造业	Beverage Production	7.41
烟草制品业	Tobacco Processing	8.33
纺织业	**Textile Industry**	15.92
纺织服装、鞋、帽制造业	Textile,Garments, Shoes and Hats Products	15.24
皮革、毛皮、羽毛(绒)及其制品业	Leather, Furs,Down and Related Products	20.37
木材加工及木、竹、藤、棕、草制品业	Timber Processing, Wood, Bamboo, Cane, Palm and Straw Products	8.75
家具制造业	Furniture Manufacturing	8.75
造纸及纸制品业	Papermaking and Paper Products	15.93
印刷业和记录媒介的复制	Printing and Record Processing	14.93
文教体育用品制造业	Stationery, Education and Sports Goods	14.29
石油加工、炼焦及核燃料加工业	Petroleum Processing, Coking Products and Nuclear Fuel Processing	15.00
化学原料及化学制品制造业	Raw Chemical Material and Chemical Products	14.27
医药制造业	Medical and pharmaceutical Products	14.87
化学纤维制造业	Chemical Fibers	5.56
橡胶制品业	Rubber Products	11.58
塑料制品业	Plastic Products	11.09
非金属矿物制品业	Nonmetal Material Products	9.85
黑色金属冶炼及压延加工业	Smelting and Pressing of Ferrous Metals	19.35
有色金属冶炼及压延加工业	Smelting and Pressing of Nonferrous Metals	17.93
金属制品业	Metal Products	13.37
通用设备制造业	Ordinary Machinery Manufacturing	14.64
专用设备制造业	Special Purpose Equipment Manufacturing	14.31
交通运输设备制造业	Transportation Equipment Manufacturing	16.18
电气机械及器材制造业	Electric Machinery and Equipment	14.69
通信设备、计算机及其他电子设备制造业	Telecommunication Equipment, Computer and Other Electronic Equipment Manufacturing	15.50
仪器仪表及文化、办公用机械制造业	Instruments, Meters, Cultural and Official Machinery	19.70
工艺品及其他制造业	Handicraft Article and Other Manufacturing	5.77
废弃资源和废旧材料回收加工业	Waste Resources and Junk Material Recycled	25.00
电力、燃气及水的生产和供应业	**Electric Power, Gas and Water Production and Supply**	
电力、热力的生产和供应业	Electric Power, Steam and Hot Water Production and Supply	26.50
燃气生产和供应业	Gas Production and Supply	16.22
水的生产和供应业	Tap Water Production and Supply	42.31

总资产贡献率(%) Contributing Rate of Total Assets	资产负债率(%) Assets Liability Ratio	成本费用利润率(%) Ratio of Profits to Industrial Cost	产品销售率(%) Rate of Products Sold
21.42	54.00	6.25	94.57
1.58	50.84	-5.97	99.86
52.49	51.11	8.75	97.50
25.65	65.01	22.92	99.40
24.28	55.90	13.01	95.49
10.65	40.54	1.31	56.35
26.87	44.31	9.91	95.76
16.85	48.20	8.71	96.54
17.96	60.64	8.71	96.80
78.97	54.56	15.16	99.95
14.78	52.85	6.13	97.18
18.23	61.97	8.56	96.56
19.61	60.30	6.67	92.53
17.83	38.31	8.86	96.00
12.74	51.43	6.71	97.44
12.73	48.81	6.66	97.83
13.89	54.43	8.53	95.32
8.34	60.00	4.92	90.01
81.00	55.77	6.15	98.65
13.32	54.83	7.29	97.15
13.55	39.76	12.15	95.48
13.02	42.63	11.19	100.33
19.86	57.02	8.41	96.69
18.40	48.45	7.91	97.11
13.56	59.63	9.18	97.31
6.78	62.34	2.40	99.37
8.55	60.92	2.27	98.56
9.81	42.98	6.14	92.78
9.30	64.41	7.02	94.68
12.54	55.82	10.07	96.14
11.27	55.96	9.56	97.81
13.96	51.60	9.38	96.76
5.76	36.60	6.79	95.92
9.39	39.81	12.75	97.91
19.96	56.48	8.00	95.49
21.44	65.83	9.49	99.12
6.02	45.57	11.89	99.72
1.35	93.86	15.13	100.00
3.67	52.79	9.66	96.45

8-12 规模以上工业企业产销总值及主要经济指标(分地区) (2009)

单位:亿元

地区	Region	企业单位数(个) Number of Enterprises(unit)	亏损企业 Enterprises Running under Deficit
全省	Province	14027	1826
武汉	Wuhan Municipality	2517	544
黄石	Huangshi Municipality	624	125
十堰	Shiyan Municipality	828	184
宜昌	Yichang Municipality	1095	128
襄樊	Xiangfan Municipality	1299	173
鄂州	Ezhou Municipality	466	9
荆门	Jingmen Municipality	1030	75
孝感	Xiaogan Municipality	1068	81
荆州	Jingzhou Municipality	1139	168
黄冈	Huanggang Municipality	1367	110
咸宁	Xianning Municipality	719	111
恩施	Suizhou Municipality	472	62
随州	Enshi Municipality	490	16
仙桃	Xiantao Municipality	394	17
潜江	Qianjiang Municipality	239	13
天门	Tianmen Municipality	264	2
林区	Shennongjia Forest Zone	16	8

8-12 续表 1 continued

单位:亿元

地区	Region	出口交货值 Export delivery value	资产总计 Total Assets	流动资产合计 Circulating Funds	应收帐款净额 Net Account Received
全省	Province	653.47	19221.02	7498.25	1938.52
武汉	Wuhan Municipality	305.94	7672.08	3471.33	1255.41
黄石	Huangshi Municipality	24.29	717.75	404.50	56.01
十堰	Shiyan Municipality	5.22	1660.99	804.45	99.88
宜昌	Yichang Municipality	66.15	4092.27	686.30	112.53
襄樊	Xiangfan Municipality	26.45	1160.37	653.11	103.50
鄂州	Ezhou Municipality	4.58	319.71	108.40	11.37
荆门	Jingmen Municipality	18.76	582.28	214.23	35.33
孝感	Xiaogan Municipality	18.59	570.12	212.15	49.92
荆州	Jingzhou Municipality	34.50	526.81	273.14	77.00
黄冈	Huanggang Municipality	13.35	420.87	150.77	31.72
咸宁	Xianning Municipality	14.98	293.31	116.20	20.93
恩施	Suizhou Municipality	2.78	335.84	60.59	8.39
随州	Enshi Municipality	26.86	152.38	78.41	20.75
仙桃	Xiantao Municipality	46.02	186.72	74.71	15.32
潜江	Qianjiang Municipality	26.46	345.69	111.02	30.56
天门	Tianmen Municipality	18.56	157.61	70.95	9.21
林区	Shennongjia Forest Zone		26.22	8.00	0.69

TOTAL VALUE OF PRODUCTION AND SALES AND MAJOR ECONOMIC INDICATORS OF INDUSTRIAL ENTERPRISES ABOVE DESIGNATED SIZE (BY REGIONS) (2009)

(100 million yuan)

工业总产值(当年价格) Total Output Value(current price)	新产品产值 Output Value of New Products	工业销售产值(当年价格) Output Value of Industrial Products(current price)	出口交货值 Delivery Value for Export
15567.02	1554.85	15164.52	653.47
5798.88	779.20	5705.66	305.94
860.99	158.01	841.98	24.29
821.47	206.38	793.72	5.22
1531.12	64.67	1482.08	66.15
1490.06	144.48	1434.09	26.45
423.03	9.64	414.19	4.58
883.23	15.67	867.26	18.76
688.14	59.15	678.05	18.59
669.92	40.58	635.95	34.50
570.90	20.72	547.30	13.35
443.14	16.31	421.35	14.98
139.76	0.61	136.08	2.78
320.37	23.96	310.87	26.86
348.97	1.12	338.29	46.02
365.15	13.57	352.04	26.46
206.10	0.77	200.47	18.56
5.79		5.14	

(100 million yuan)

存货 Goods in Stock	产成品 Completed Products	固定资产合计 Total Value of Fixed Assets	固定资产原价 Original Price of Fixed Assets	资产总计 Total Assets	
				累计折旧 Accumulated	固定资产净值 Net Value of Fixed Assets Fixed Assets
1795.85	630.56	9210.24	11608.95	3583.92	8025.03
825.86	232.65	3271.67	4462.49	1418.85	3043.64
116.55	36.00	246.01	487.48	241.60	245.88
113.96	59.85	798.02	362.01	137.91	224.10
148.99	53.78	2442.04	2819.81	450.30	2369.51
134.10	52.07	404.91	665.92	283.87	382.05
27.97	8.12	194.31	180.83	79.14	101.69
74.82	26.30	304.31	393.98	126.95	267.03
62.75	26.31	260.64	447.86	216.27	231.59
95.76	47.16	203.52	377.82	206.64	171.18
53.48	24.40	228.56	253.89	44.52	209.38
36.03	15.83	139.01	179.74	56.59	123.15
10.16	4.97	254.30	308.36	76.17	232.18
20.97	11.15	60.68	70.60	14.97	55.64
19.31	9.40	98.73	116.73	19.20	97.53
39.86	12.89	212.52	327.75	131.84	195.91
14.24	8.90	74.18	143.72	76.29	67.42
1.06	0.76	16.84	9.97	2.81	7.16

8-12 续表 2 continued

单位:亿元

地区	Region	负债合计 Total Liability	流动负债合计 Total Circulating Liability	应付账款 Account	长期负债合计 Total Long term Liability	所有者权益合计 Total Rights of Owners
全省	Province	10381.23	7463.72	1698.35	2547.00	8673.39
武汉	Wuhan Municipality	4663.73	3807.28	763.45	813.31	3006.85
黄石	Huangshi Municipality	552.17	421.94	92.06	118.89	164.13
十堰	Shiyan Municipality	808.14	682.18	219.59	80.75	776.43
宜昌	Yichang Municipality	1632.62	712.43	153.34	868.70	2450.04
襄樊	Xiangfan Municipality	674.62	518.42	133.89	107.54	478.33
鄂州	Ezhou Municipality	187.58	124.70	37.06	54.89	128.33
荆门	Jingmen Municipality	318.85	217.80	41.11	54.94	255.77
孝感	Xiaogan Municipality	240.44	169.72	49.93	61.56	292.83
荆州	Jingzhou Municipality	285.60	227.33	61.57	42.55	236.39
黄冈	Huanggang Municipality	227.11	129.07	32.05	84.90	189.99
咸宁	Xianning Municipality	133.41	90.83	18.28	39.94	156.84
恩施	Suizhou Municipality	222.47	58.74	11.66	143.74	109.40
随州	Enshi Municipality	71.42	59.71	20.63	9.27	79.52
仙桃	Xiantao Municipality	95.34	62.14	15.41	6.06	91.16
潜江	Qianjiang Municipality	172.33	143.11	39.07	19.35	172.55
天门	Tianmen Municipality	75.52	31.68	8.09	27.40	78.50
林区	Shennongjia Forest Zone	19.88	6.63	1.17	13.20	6.33

8-12 续表 3 continued

单位:亿元

地区	Region	所有者权益合计 Total Rights of the Owners: 外商资本 Foreign Assets	主营业务收入 Revenue of Major Business	主营业务成本 Cost of Major Business
全省	Province	350.00	15331.62	12641.04
武汉	Wuhan Municipality	149.48	5980.68	4891.77
黄石	Huangshi Municipality	53.64	936.79	824.52
十堰	Shiyan Municipality	85.18	779.36	686.46
宜昌	Yichang Municipality	8.23	1444.54	1116.90
襄樊	Xiangfan Municipality	3.87	1314.37	1054.49
鄂州	Ezhou Municipality	2.17	414.09	350.55
荆门	Jingmen Municipality	6.83	893.93	719.10
孝感	Xiaogan Municipality	5.32	664.68	561.72
荆州	Jingzhou Municipality	12.56	625.22	531.26
黄冈	Huanggang Municipality	7.70	526.76	449.55
咸宁	Xianning Municipality	1.36	400.57	332.33
恩施	Suizhou Municipality	0.65	135.41	102.85
随州	Enshi Municipality	1.15	305.23	254.51
仙桃	Xiantao Municipality	8.49	337.10	272.44
潜江	Qianjiang Municipality	3.22	365.98	323.46
天门	Tianmen Municipality	0.14	201.55	165.70
林区	Shennongjia Forest Zone		5.36	3.44

(100 million Yuan)

实收资本 Assets Recevied	国家资本 National Assets	所有者权益合计 Total Rights of Owners			
		集体资本 Collective Assets	法人资本 Corperative Assets	个人资本 Individual Assets	港澳台资本 Assets from Hongkong,Maco and Taiwan
4610.04	2186.47	58.36	1187.37	708.55	119.29
981.49	296.17	22.17	362.96	105.17	45.53
176.37	25.03	4.13	40.83	51.86	0.87
396.71	152.19	7.26	90.12	61.20	0.76
1761.23	1488.21	1.62	166.53	83.96	12.68
190.17	30.86	4.06	103.58	45.02	2.78
110.81	60.04	0.42	30.80	14.50	2.89
154.26	16.86	4.58	80.01	43.96	2.03
190.46	10.48	5.06	50.84	104.92	13.84
122.47	11.10	0.97	44.08	50.63	3.14
121.27	4.80	3.37	47.16	46.39	11.86
79.73	5.71	1.11	27.71	27.55	16.29
71.45	17.02	1.15	37.81	14.59	0.23
53.30	0.79	0.32	25.24	24.06	1.75
51.13	0.05	0.33	24.94	13.90	3.43
114.20	66.75	0.11	29.58	13.34	1.20
30.50	0.04	1.23	23.41	5.68	
4.49	0.36	0.50	1.79	1.83	

(100 million Yuan)

主营业务税金及附加 Tax of Major Business	其他业务收入 Revenue of Other Business	其他业务利润 Profit from Other Business	营业费用 Operation Expenses	管理费用 Management Expense	税金 Tax
406.64	341.56	42.46	464.97	799.69	81.08
236.69	107.33	6.76	155.51	299.60	12.04
5.84	41.06	3.83	27.82	31.34	1.69
4.62	93.51	7.28	26.18	67.20	3.35
20.52	18.12	4.66	54.73	64.36	3.85
12.38	23.51	10.04	32.98	132.50	42.15
30.58	2.36	0.19	4.26	22.92	6.60
43.76	7.79	3.30	27.27	31.95	1.57
10.65	5.22	0.89	22.54	26.16	1.63
8.56	7.64	1.49	28.84	24.65	3.30
7.08	2.23	0.68	16.59	16.22	0.84
3.33	1.91	0.36	10.53	13.44	0.92
5.93	2.54	0.59	4.40	8.92	0.24
5.11	1.14	0.08	11.34	13.27	0.46
1.60	3.85	1.94	27.83	16.55	1.26
8.00	23.36	0.36	6.71	19.66	0.99
1.45			7.33	10.45	0.14
0.53			0.12	0.51	0.03

8-12 续表 4 continued

单位:亿元

地区	Region	财务费用 Financial Expense	利息支出 Interest Expense	营业利润 Operating Profit	投资收益 Income from Investment
全省	Province	212.79	194.34	1072.60	-82.36
武汉	Wuhan Municipality	71.66	69.29	281.27	-93.27
黄石	Huangshi Municipality	8.12	6.60	33.05	1.47
十堰	Shiyan Municipality	10.25	8.62	41.43	10.99
宜昌	Yichang Municipality	46.12	47.33	200.50	-9.16
襄樊	Xiangfan Municipality	10.66	9.52	128.42	3.49
鄂州	Ezhou Municipality	1.79	1.85	31.27	0.29
荆门	Jingmen Municipality	9.28	8.50	100.53	0.44
孝感	Xiaogan Municipality	11.04	6.27	37.90	0.80
荆州	Jingzhou Municipality	6.11	4.81	35.33	0.23
黄冈	Huanggang Municipality	7.22	5.88	42.13	0.55
咸宁	Xianning Municipality	5.01	4.39	33.22	0.24
恩施	Suizhou Municipality	8.77	8.12	5.28	0.50
随州	Enshi Municipality	4.91	2.94	25.76	0.58
仙桃	Xiantao Municipality	4.35	4.03	40.05	0.05
潜江	Qianjiang Municipality	3.53	2.97	17.98	0.44
天门	Tianmen Municipality	3.46	2.87	18.26	0.01
林区	Shennongjia Forest Zone	0.49	0.38	0.24	

8-12 续表 5 continued

单位:亿元

地区	Region	本年应付工资总额 Total Sum of Wages Payable this Year	本年应付福利费总额 Total Sum of Welfare Expense Payable of the Current Year
全省	Province	971.15	49.18
武汉	Wuhan Municipality	369.27	15.22
黄石	Huangshi Municipality	50.39	2.06
十堰	Shiyan Municipality	62.51	3.50
宜昌	Yichang Municipality	94.02	6.84
襄樊	Xiangfan Municipality	66.04	2.70
鄂州	Ezhou Municipality	20.08	1.47
荆门	Jingmen Municipality	37.61	2.31
孝感	Xiaogan Municipality	66.12	2.63
荆州	Jingzhou Municipality	43.99	3.72
黄冈	Huanggang Municipality	27.84	2.29
咸宁	Xianning Municipality	26.80	0.94
恩施	Suizhou Municipality	9.92	0.78
随州	Enshi Municipality	21.62	1.96
仙桃	Xiantao Municipality	25.31	1.40
潜江	Qianjiang Municipality	33.61	0.91
天门	Tianmen Municipality	15.86	0.46
林区	Shennongjia Forest Zone	0.14	

(100 million Yuan)

补贴收入 Income from Subsidy	营业外收入 Non-operating Income	利润总额 Total Profit	应交所得税 Income Tax	亏损企业 亏损总额 Total Loss of Enterprises Running under Deficit	利税总额 Total Profit
40.52	78.33	1092.47	153.57	75.90	1987.88
4.07	24.93	296.44	42.49	34.95	715.84
1.83	2.94	34.82	5.85	3.89	61.19
0.74	5.42	49.49	9.67	5.31	88.54
21.20	27.85	204.41	56.75	2.83	282.17
3.39	4.91	132.55	9.25	2.81	194.86
0.02	0.38	24.41	1.33	0.46	75.20
0.81	1.62	93.90	6.60	2.44	156.23
0.55	1.88	37.89	2.03	2.80	65.11
1.22	1.63	35.23	3.07	2.89	59.88
1.99	0.93	44.00	2.41	1.19	67.38
4.42	0.72	32.99	2.65	1.04	48.28
0.05	0.89	5.57	0.96	1.52	17.27
0.06	0.29	25.94	1.47	0.17	43.19
0.14	0.24	39.98	3.89	2.65	52.20
0.03	3.41	20.84	1.47	10.58	38.92
	0.26	13.74	3.63	0.09	20.04
	0.05	0.26	0.02	0.26	1.59

(100 million Yuan)

本年应交增值税 Value Added Payable of the Current Year	本年进项税额 Input Tax of Current Year	本年销项税额 Output Tax of the Current Year	全部从业人员年平均人数(万人) Average Number of Empolyment of the Current Year (10000 persons)
488.77	1552.98	1954.59	272.39
182.71	697.42	916.71	76.02
20.53	111.26	133.39	14.60
34.43	160.88	167.24	18.94
57.23	118.06	169.86	22.90
49.92	121.62	149.95	23.39
20.20	41.99	53.49	6.49
18.58	37.21	40.79	13.31
16.56	49.58	57.62	22.17
16.09	60.64	70.05	16.34
16.30	30.95	41.30	15.71
11.97	24.81	32.88	9.27
5.76	8.15	12.98	4.51
12.14	15.81	16.55	6.51
10.62	36.21	45.99	9.15
10.09	37.97	45.09	8.15
4.85	0.15	0.13	4.77
0.79	0.26	0.55	0.14

8-13 分市州规模以上工业企业主要经济效益指标分地区（2009）

单位：%

地 区	Item	企业亏损面 Loss Making Rate of Enterprises
全省	**Province**	13.02
武汉市	Wuhan Municipality	21.61
黄石市	Huangshi Municipality	20.03
十堰市	Shiyan Municipality	22.22
宜昌市	Yichang Municipality	11.69
襄樊市	Xiangfan Municipality	13.32
鄂州市	Ezhou Municipality	1.93
荆门市	Jingmen Municipality	7.28
孝感市	Xiaogan Municipality	7.58
荆州市	Jingzhou Municipality	14.75
黄冈市	Huanggang Municipality	8.05
咸宁市	Xianning Municipality	15.44
恩施州	Suizhou Municipality	13.14
随州市	Enshi Prefecture	3.27
仙桃市	Xiantao Municipality	4.31
潜江市	Qianjiang Municipality	5.44
天门市	Tianmen Municipality	0.76
神农架林区	Shennongjia Forest Zone	50.00

8-14 规模以上工业能源生产量

产品	单位	Item	Unit	2000	2001
一次能源生产量	（万吨标煤）	Primary Energy Output	（10000 tons standardized coal）	1343.66	1255.52
原煤	（万吨）	Coal	（10000 ton）	389.34	338.86
原油	（万吨）	Crude Oil	（10000 ton）	75.11	77.20
天然气	（万立方米）	Natural Gas	（10000 cu.m）	0.91	0.76
水电	（亿千瓦时）	Water and Electricity	（100 million K W/h）	269.86	254.69

注：水电采用等价值核算。

Note: The value of water use such as accounting.

MAJOR INDICATORS OF ECONOMIC BENEFITS OF ABOVE DESIGNATED SIZE INDUSTRIAL ENTERPRISES BY REGION(2009)

总资产贡献率 Contributing Rate of Total Assets	资产负债率 Assets Liability Ratio	成本费用利润率 Ratio of Profits to Industrial Cost	产品销售率 Proportion of Products Sold
11.35	54.01	7.74	97.41
10.23	60.79	5.47	98.39
9.44	76.93	3.90	97.79
5.85	48.65	6.26	96.62
8.05	39.90	15.94	96.80
17.61	58.14	10.77	96.24
24.10	58.67	6.43	97.91
28.29	54.76	11.92	98.19
12.52	42.17	6.10	98.53
12.28	54.21	5.96	94.93
17.41	53.96	8.99	95.87
17.96	45.48	9.13	95.08
7.56	66.24	4.46	97.36
30.27	46.87	9.13	97.03
30.11	51.06	12.45	96.94
12.12	49.85	5.90	96.41
14.54	47.92	7.35	97.27
7.49	75.85	5.73	88.74

OUTPUT OF ENERGY PRODUCTION OF INDUSTRY ABOVE DESGINATED SIZE

2002	2003	2004	2005	2006	2007	2008	2009
1345.78	1719.44	287.09	3294.35	3134.35	3806.39	4860.41	5018.72
372.55	366.40	395.62	478.07	541.34	609.98	727.1	1083.00
78.30	77.53	78.20	78.11	79.73	85.54	83.92	80.89
0.91	0.94	0.98	1.11	1.16	1.16	2.85	1.67
272.58	380.64	689.71	805.64	746.35	921.48	1192.75	1169.61

8-15 规模以上工业能源消费量

产品	计量单位	Item	Unit	2000	2001
能源消费量合计	万吨标煤	Total	10000 tons standardized coal	5023.67	5118.15
原煤	万吨	Coal	10000 ton	2866.27	2989.88
洗精煤	万吨	Cleaned Coal	10000 ton	555.85	569.77
其他洗煤	万吨	Other Washed Coal	10000 ton	4.13	6.56
型煤	万吨	Moulded Coal	10000 ton	1.89	0.47
焦炭	万吨	Coke	10000 ton	456.84	457.05
其他焦化产品	万吨	Other Coked Products	10000 ton	6.04	4.58
焦炉煤气	亿立方米	Coke-oven Gas	100 million cu.m	16.65	15.39
高炉煤气	亿立方米	Bblast Furnace Gas	100 million cu.m	12.34	14.45
其他煤气	亿立方米	Other Gases	100 million cu.m	0.03	0.46
天然气	亿立方米	Natural Gas	100 million cu.m	0.2	0.29
原油	万吨	Crude Oil	10000 ton	660.31	573.98
汽油	万吨	Gasoline	10000 ton	11.34	12.87
煤油	万吨	Kerasene	10000 ton	1.14	1.37
柴油	万吨	Diesel Oil	10000 ton	28.57	24.09
燃料油	万吨	Fuel Oil	10000 ton	49.92	51.71
液化石油气	万吨	LPG	10000 ton	4.33	3.92
炼厂干气	万吨	Dry Gas	10000 ton	15.08	20.16
其他石油制品	万吨	Other Petroleum Products	10000 ton	100.33	152.74
热力	万百万千焦	Heat	10 billion kilo-joule	4456.06	5122.64
电力	亿千瓦时	Electricity	100 million kW/h	401.75	384.07
其他燃料	万吨标准煤	Other Fuels	10000 tons standardized coal	9.42	49.89

注：能源消费量包括加工转换投入量，且为当量值。

ENERGY CONSUMPTION OF INDUSTRY ABOVE DESIGNATED SIZE

2002	2003	2004	2005	2006	2007	2008	2009
5727.43	5923.43	7111.78	9105.67	9810.86	9849.85	9831.64	10312.48
3582.8	3838.87	4726.04	6629.10	6927.79	6549.55	6342.84	6681.74
567.61	603.17	712.24	956.93	914.29	1134.86	1137.75	1218.19
1.76	10.2	3.1	2.94	1.02	5.20	20.05	6.42
0.3	1.06	2.88	13.58	6.46	32.08	2.81	2.71
478.46	532.69	643.79	800.82	789.95	810.30	952.27	904.60
1.4	1.86	3.5	6.57	8.29	9.97	12.00	19.57
16.85	16.22	21.79	29.00	28.07	28.37	31.36	36.65
12.01	15.72	3.28	12.74	210.16	243.32	282.72	286.76
1.97	2.18	2.32	6.15	23.76	22.16	22.50	21.64
0.12	0.1	0.64	3.94	7.65	5.43	6.79	6.90
597.99	637.53	759.83	824.44	851.49	907.94	838.66	947.28
12.8	13.08	11.54	26.55	34.27	14.12	16.92	15.94
1.26	1.57	1.87	5.41	2.34	1.02	0.85	1.27
34.43	49.11	27.65	52.21	51.67	42.89	42.76	42.51
54.99	65.86	59.72	56.47	36.03	29.95	25.48	17.35
4.49	11.71	6.46	4.81	5.49	6.43	5.32	3.01
19.71	22.21	26.63	31.83	34.78	34.92	32.93	33.58
218.22	66.33	61.19	35.10	68.31	74.10	58.13	92.16
5318.78	4846.12	5156.11	5013.59	7675.22	7360.56	7646.08	7330.85
410.52	439.5	555.51	641.21	610.73	728.19	841.33	829.51
30.04	34.33	81.7	121.50	38.50	64.00	52.69	74.60

Note: The conversion of energy consumption, including processing input, and when the money is.

8-16 规模以上工业分行业原煤消费量

单位:万吨

行　业	Item	2000
合　　计	Total	2866.27
煤炭开采和洗选业	Coal Mining and Processing	36.48
石油和天然气开采业	Petroleum and Natural Gas Extraction	12.19
黑色金属矿采选业	Ferrous Metals Mining and Processing	0.06
有色金属矿采选业	Non-ferrous Metals Mining and Processing	0.23
非金属矿采选业	Non-metal Minerals Mining and Processing	43.03
其他采矿业	Other Minerals Mining and Processing	
农副食品加工业	Food Processing	32.06
食品制造业	Food Production	22.55
饮料制造业	Beverage Production	22.63
烟草制品业	Tobacco Processing	10.03
纺织业	Textile Industry	44.52
纺织服装、鞋、帽制造业	Textile Garments, Shoes and Hats Products	5.26
皮革、毛皮、羽毛(绒)及其制品业	Leather, Furs Down and Related Products	0.44
木材加工及木、竹、藤、棕、草制品业	Timber Processing and Wwood, Bamboo, Rattan, Palm and Straw Works	4.36
家具制造业	Furniture Manufacturing	0.19
造纸及纸制品业	Papermaking and Paper Products	51.59
印刷业和记录媒介的复制	Printing and Record Processing	0.27
文教体育用品制造业	Stationery, Education and Sports Goods	0.18
石油加工、炼焦及核燃料加工业	Petroleum Processing, Coking Products and Nuclear Fuel Processing	1.11
化学原料及化学制品制造业	Raw Chemical Material and Chemical Products	405.81
医药制造业	Medical and pharmaceutical Products	35.31
化学纤维制造业	Chemical Fibers	30.05
橡胶制品业	Rubber Products	10.45
塑料制品业	Plastic Products	3.19
非金属矿物制品业	Nonmetal Material Products	449.75
黑色金属冶炼及压延加工业	Smelting and Processing of ferrous Metals	201.11
有色金属冶炼及压延加工业	Smelting and Processing of Nonferrous Metals	11.87
金属制品业	Metal Products	7.23
通用设备制造业	Ordinaryly Machinery Manufacturing	16.38
专用设备制造业	Special Purpose Equipment Manufacturing	3.78
交通运输设备制造业	Transportation Equipment Manufacturing	113.3
电气机械及器材制造业	Electric Machinery and Equipment	1.18
通信设备、计算机及其他电子设备制造业	Telecommunication Equipment, Computer and Other Electronic Equipment Manufacturing	3.58
仪器仪表及文化、办公用机械制造业	Instruments, Meters, Cultural and Official Machinery	1.33
工艺品及其他制造业	Handicraft Article and Other Manufacturing	0.67
废弃资源和废旧材料回收加工业	Waste Resources and Junk Material Recycled	0.29
电力、热力的生产和供应业	Electric Power, Heat Production and Supply	1267.21
燃气生产和供应业	Gas Production and Supply	16.53
水的生产和供应业	Tap Water Production and Supply	0.07

COAL CONSUMPTION OF INDUSTRY ABOVE DESIGNATED SIZE BY SECTOR

(10000 tons)

2003	2004	2005	2006	2007	2008	2009
3838.87	4726.04	6629.10	6927.93	6549.55	6342.84	6681.74
10.23	12.96	1.48	1.14	3.30	9.10	7.64
15.24	16.63	22.18	14.53	16.16	22.62	25.38
0.11	0.69	1.26	14.95	56.06	89.55	102.06
0.71	0.39	0.35	0.33	0.53	0.73	0.91
28.66	34.53	85.39	90.70	90.28	34.79	40.40
				0.22		0.98
20.58	25.39	34.71	46.77	63.11	82.11	98.25
70.27	80.7	77.73	79.45	81.88	131.95	105.44
24.03	25.87	33.54	41.67	42.67	44.74	43.74
6.19	6.63	6.60	6.70	5.05	2.94	2.41
36.99	45.92	125.79	67.72	58.24	59.89	72.50
6.93	7.75	6.84	7.79	8.71	10.47	11.32
0.32	0.46	0.44	0.97	1.26	1.73	1.24
6.93	8.84	72.37	12.57	15.62	12.97	11.00
0.07	0.3	0.28	0.79	0.49	0.43	0.57
71.77	88.37	112.61	123.78	95.72	85.35	90.25
0.25	0.7	8.99	10.44	11.97	8.20	2.20
		1.09	0.26	0.27	0.31	0.45
3.24	4.4	14.75	3.78	2.78	3.18	8.34
632.93	679.53	1506.94	1437.65	1069.77	1060.66	1240.56
53.59	47.18	78.77	72.00	81.45	89.28	83.98
24.25	31.94	71.89	51.97	33.96	36.73	4.44
8.34	6.96	4.74	9.07	6.04	6.69	8.91
3.86	2.88	8.89	8.77	11.81	13.63	19.47
500.37	559.53	1013.31	914.59	885.48	1034.30	1081.86
224.53	242.85	336.31	388.46	398.73	439.64	445.28
12.23	75.52	122.08	85.44	86.09	91.93	76.00
6.75	5.81	7.91	14.27	18.06	19.90	22.04
19.14	20.55	43.75	34.50	35.94	39.34	49.95
3.33	2.55	5.82	10.37	9.42	11.22	13.21
198.63	202.43	108.72	188.65	129.38	128.72	139.47
3.72	2.95	6.16	14.34	9.26	12.81	15.31
2.71	0.45	0.49	1.17	0.44	0.65	0.46
0.22	0.59	0.76	2.86	1.81	1.79	1.84
1.06	0.6	2.68	6.08	7.46	8.95	8.75
0.98	0.05	0.39	0.26	0.26	0.17	0.33
1822.35	2463.23	2644.92	3119.75	3209.83	2745.27	2844.45
17.31	19.86	58.13	43.38			
0.05	0.05	0.04	0.02	0.01	0.12	0.34

8-17 规模以上工业分行业汽油消费量

单位：万吨

行业	Item	2000
总计	Total	11.33
煤炭开采和洗选业	Coal Mining and Processing	0.04
石油和天然气开采业	Petroleum and Natural Gas Extraction	0.85
黑色金属矿采选业	Ferrous Metals Mining and Processing	1.13
有色金属矿采选业	Non-ferrous Metals Mining and Processing	0.03
非金属矿采选业	Non-metal Minerals Mining and Processing	
其他采矿业	Other Minerals Mining and Processing	0.01
农副食品加工业	Food Processing	0.6
食品制造业	Food Production	0.38
饮料制造业	Beverage Production	0.07
烟草制品业	Tobacco Processing	0.05
纺织业	Textile Industry	0.2
纺织服装、鞋、帽制造业	Textile Garments, Shoes and Hats Products	0.31
皮革、毛皮、羽毛(绒)及其制品业	Leather, Furs Down and Related Products	0.01
木材加工及木、竹、藤、棕、草制品业	Timber Processing and Wwood, Bamboo, Rattan, Palm and Straw Works	0.05
家具制造业	Furniture Manufacturing	0.07
造纸及纸制品业	Papermaking and Paper Products	0.07
印刷业和记录媒介的复制	Printing and Record Processing	0.01
文教体育用品制造业	Stationery, Education and Sports Goods	
石油加工、炼焦及核燃料加工业	Petroleum Processing, Coking Products and Nuclear Fuel Processing	0.11
化学原料及化学制品制造业	Raw Chemical Material and Chemical Products	0.57
医药制造业	Medical and pharmaceutical Products	0.18
化学纤维制造业	Chemical Fibers	0.04
橡胶制品业	Rubber Products	0.1
塑料制品业	Plastic Products	0.12
非金属矿物制品业	Nonmetal Material Products	1.26
黑色金属冶炼及压延加工业	Smelting and Processing of ferrous Metals	0.88
有色金属冶炼及压延加工业	Smelting and Processing of Nonferrous Metals	0.27
金属制品业	Metal Products	0.17
通用设备制造业	Ordinaryly Machinery Manufacturing	0.2
专用设备制造业	Special Purpose Equipment Manufacturing	0.22
交通运输设备制造业	Transportation Equipment Manufacturing	2.81
电气机械及器材制造业	Electric Machinery and Equipment	0.01
通信设备、计算机及其他电子设备制造业	Telecommunication Equipment, Computer and Other =SUM(B9)	0.1
仪器仪表及文化、办公用机械制造业	Instruments, Meters, Cultural and Official Machinery	0.04
工艺品及其他制造业	Handicraft Article and Other Manufacturing	0.02
废弃资源和废旧材料回收加工业	Waste Resources and Junk Material Recycled	
电力、热力的生产和供应业	Electric Power, Heat Production and Supply	0.25
燃气生产和供应业	Gas Production and Supply	0.02
水的生产和供应业	Tap Water Production and Supply	0.08

GASOLINE CONSUMPTION OF INDUSTRY ABOVE DESIGNATED SIZE

(10000 tons)

2003	2004	2005	2006	2007	2008	2009
13.08	11.54	26.55	34.27	14.12	16.92	15.94
0.03	0.03	0.03	0.03	0.06	0.11	0.11
0.68	2.02	2.65	0.70	1.22	1.45	1.44
0.24	0.14	0.10	0.04	0.06	0.06	0.04
0.03	0.04	0.03	0.02	0.03	0.04	0.04
0.13	0.78	0.09	0.15	0.15	0.15	0.11
				0.00		
0.14	0.08	0.17	0.35	0.37	0.37	0.75
0.07	0.09	0.23	0.60	0.19	0.25	0.22
0.08	0.06	0.16	0.70	0.30	0.37	0.34
0.03	0.01	0.02	0.13	0.01	0.03	0.03
0.16	0.61	0.50	0.53	0.24	0.36	0.34
1.05	1.06	0.21	0.61	0.26	0.59	0.76
0.04	0.33	0.02	0.03	0.03	0.04	0.03
0.01	0.01	0.71	0.03	0.04	0.06	0.06
0.03	0.02	0.01	0.03	0.09	0.09	0.08
0.08	0.06	0.87	0.33	0.20	0.10	0.11
0.08	0.08	0.12	0.45	0.16	0.22	0.21
		0.01	0.02	0.01	0.01	0.01
0.02	0.33	0.17	0.19	0.20	0.09	0.06
0.73	0.68	0.95	1.11	0.99	1.41	1.80
0.3	0.26	0.58	0.71	0.90	0.74	0.78
0.01	0.02	0.07	0.01	0.01	0.03	0.00
0.08	0.06	0.18	0.35	0.07	0.07	0.08
0.07	0.06	0.17	0.43	0.27	0.30	0.21
0.58	0.52	1.00	1.70	1.28	1.49	1.22
1.58	0.65	0.78	0.56	0.59	0.66	0.59
0.16	0.11	0.24	0.23	0.31	0.23	0.11
0.13	0.1	0.69	1.05	0.46	0.81	0.82
0.24	0.36	0.80	2.24	0.79	0.96	0.80
0.2	0.16	0.34	0.72	0.83	0.43	0.51
5.06	1.87	12.25	16.87	2.43	2.90	2.74
	0.24	1.10	0.97	0.37	0.54	0.51
0.24	0.05	0.29	1.16	0.39	0.42	0.24
0.08	0.04	0.21	0.27	0.05	0.04	0.04
0.08	0.03	0.08	0.10	0.06	0.03	0.03
0.02	0.48	0.03	0.03	0.03	0.02	0.03
0.49	0.01	0.50	0.58	0.49	1.27	0.54
0.01	0.01	0.01	0.09	0.03	0.04	0.04
0.12	0.08	0.22	0.13	0.14	0.14	0.11

8-18 规模以上工业分行业柴油消费量

单位:万吨

行业	Item	2000
合　　计	Total	28.57
煤炭开采和洗选业	Coal Mining and Processing	0.03
石油和天然气开采业	Petroleum and Natural Gas Extraction	2.73
黑色金属矿采选业	Ferrous Metals Mining and Processing	0.18
有色金属矿采选业	Non-ferrous Metals Mining and Processing	0.09
非金属矿采选业	Non-metal Minerals Mining and Processing	1.1
其他采矿业	Other Minerals Mining and Processing	
农副食品加工业	Food Processing	0.35
食品制造业	Food Production	0.12
饮料制造业	Beverage Production	0.12
烟草制品业	Tobacco Processing	0.41
纺织业	**Textile Industry**	0.21
纺织服装、鞋、帽制造业	Textile,Garments, Shoes and Hats Products	0.33
皮革、毛皮、羽毛(绒)及其制品业	Leather, Furs,Down and Related Products	0.83
木材加工及木、竹、藤、棕、草制品业	Timber Processing, Wood, Bamboo, Cane, Palm and Straw Products	0.65
家具制造业	Furniture Manufacturing	0.01
造纸及纸制品业	Papermaking and Paper Products	0.11
印刷业和记录媒介的复制	Printing and Record Processing	0.03
文教体育用品制造业	Stationery, Education and Sports Goods	0.02
石油加工、炼焦及核燃料加工业	Petroleum Processing, Coking Products and Nuclear Fuel Processing	0.21
化学原料及化学制品制造业	Raw Chemical Material and Chemical Products	1.17
医药制造业	Medical and pharmaceutical Products	0.11
化学纤维制造业	Chemical Fibers	0.04
橡胶制品业	Rubber Products	0.05
塑料制品业	Plastic Products	0.19
非金属矿物制品业	Nonmetal Material Products	6.91
黑色金属冶炼及压延加工业	Smelting and Pressing of Ferrous Metals	1.69
有色金属冶炼及压延加工业	Smelting and Pressing of Nonferrous Metals	0.73
金属制品业	Metal Products	0.33
通用设备制造业	Ordinary Machinery Manufacturing	0.78
专用设备制造业	Special Purpose Equipment Manufacturing	0.23
交通运输设备制造业	Transportation Equipment Manufacturing	2.53
电气机械及器材制造业	Electric Machinery and Equipment	0.01
通信设备、计算机及其他电子设备制造业	Telecommunication Equipment, Computer and Other Electronic Equipment Manufacturing	0.24
仪器仪表及文化、办公用机械制造业	Instruments, Meters, Cultural and Official Machinery	0.08
工艺品及其他制造业	Handicraft Article and Other Manufacturing	
废弃资源和废旧材料回收加工业	Waste Resources and Junk Material Recycled	
电力、热力的生产和供应业	Electric Power, Steam and Hot Water Production and Supply	5.89
燃气生产和供应业	Gas Production and Supply	0.04
水的生产和供应业	Tap Water Production and Supply	0.02

DIESEL CONSUMPTION OF INDUSTRY ABOVE DESGINATED SCALE BY SECTOR

(10000 tons)

2003	2004	2005	2006	2007	2008	2009
25.41	27.65	52.21	51.67	42.89	42.76	42.51
0.03	0.06	0.06	0.10	0.16	0.29	0.46
2.76	4.86	4.90	3.13	5.49	7.76	9.03
0.03	0.3	0.75	2.80	0.99	1.10	1.31
0.03	0.06	0.03	0.04	0.06	0.12	0.12
1.04	1.34	7.43	1.36	1.96	1.78	3.14
		0.00	0.00	0.01	0.01	0.00
0.96	0.72	0.58	1.32	1.41	1.44	1.38
0.26	0.17	0.20	0.97	0.56	0.46	0.57
0.09	0.19	0.48	1.09	0.54	0.82	0.81
0.74	0.87	0.44	0.28	0.22	0.22	0.21
0.17	0.37	1.61	1.20	1.94	1.44	1.48
0.41	0.42	0.63	1.95	0.59	0.57	0.55
0.01	0.01	0.01	0.04	0.02	0.03	0.02
0.14	0.07	0.36	0.28	0.33	1.23	0.41
0.01	0.02	0.01	0.09	0.24	0.07	0.09
0.17	0.22	0.82	0.43	0.36	0.26	0.31
0.03	0.14	0.20	0.18	0.14	0.14	0.08
0.01		0.00	0.00	0.01	0.00	0.00
0.13	0.49	0.20	0.30	0.21	0.19	0.08
1.99	1.34	7.41	2.50	2.58	3.69	4.08
0.11	0.62	0.37	0.61	0.32	0.44	0.83
0.02	0.04	0.03	0.02	0.02	0.02	0.01
0.1	0.03	0.10	0.26	0.03	0.04	0.21
0.31	0.21	0.63	0.43	0.50	0.30	0.29
1.84	2.3	3.90	3.41	3.72	4.35	4.77
2.85	2.43	2.74	2.16	4.12	2.66	2.43
0.69	1.1	1.96	1.52	1.06	0.69	0.62
0.28	0.25	0.70	1.23	0.85	0.80	0.79
1.16	0.97	1.40	2.42	1.22	1.25	1.31
0.21	0.1	0.35	0.43	1.74	0.43	0.57
2.2	5.2	9.30	14.96	7.12	5.32	4.10
		1.10	1.37	0.84	0.93	0.81
0.28	0.15	0.28	1.92	0.44	0.33	0.06
						0.00
0.09	0.01	0.15	0.26	0.10	0.04	0.04
0.06	0.04	0.06	0.08	0.04	0.05	0.02
		0.14	0.13	0.20	0.19	0.13
6.05	2.43	2.72	1.89	2.57	3.12	1.24
0.07	0.08	0.09	0.27	0.04	0.04	0.04
0.08	0.04	0.04	0.21	0.11	0.12	0.10

8-19 规模以上工业分行业电力消费量

单位:亿千瓦时

行业	Item	2000
合　　计	Total	401.75
煤炭开采和洗选业	Coal Mining and Processing	1.49
石油和天然气开采业	Petroleum and Natural Gas Extraction	4.43
黑色金属矿采选业	Ferrous Metals Mining and Processing	0.66
有色金属矿采选业	Non-ferrous Metals Mining and Processing	1.01
非金属矿采选业	Non-metal Minerals Mining and Processing	2.21
其他采矿业	Other Minerals Mining and Processing	0.03
农副食品加工业	Food Processing	3.82
食品制造业	Food Production	17.84
饮料制造业	Beverage Production	1.78
烟草制品业	Tobacco Processing	1.46
纺织业	Textile Industry	21.79
纺织服装、鞋、帽制造业	Textile,Garments, Shoes and Hats Products	4.19
皮革、毛皮、羽毛(绒)及其制品业	Leather, Furs,Down and Related Products	0.26
木材加工及木、竹、藤、棕、草制品业	Timber Processing, Wood, Bamboo, Cane, Palm and Straw Products	1.68
家具制造业	Furniture Manufacturing	0.2
造纸及纸制品业	Papermaking and Paper Products	4.98
印刷业和记录媒介的复制	Printing and Record Processing	0.67
文教体育用品制造业	Stationery, Education and Sports Goods	0.04
石油加工、炼焦及核燃料加工业	Petroleum Processing, Coking Products and Nuclear Fuel Processing	4.81
化学原料及化学制品制造业	Raw Chemical Material and Chemical Products	55.11
医药制造业	Medical and pharmaceutical Products	5.46
化学纤维制造业	Chemical Fibers	3.96
橡胶制品业	Rubber Products	1.16
塑料制品业	Plastic Products	2.16
非金属矿物制品业	Nonmetal Material Products	26
黑色金属冶炼及压延加工业	Smelting and Pressing of Ferrous Metals	62.23
有色金属冶炼及压延加工业	Smelting and Pressing of Nonferrous Metals	25
金属制品业	Metal Products	6.39
通用设备制造业	Ordinary Machinery Manufacturing	5.41
专用设备制造业	Special Purpose Equipment Manufacturing	23.43
交通运输设备制造业	Transportation Equipment Manufacturing	21.33
电气机械及器材制造业	Electric Machinery and Equipment	0.29
通信设备、计算机及其他电子设备制造业	Telecommunication Equipment, Computer and Other Electronic Equipment Manufacturing	2.53
仪器仪表及文化、办公用机械制造业	Instruments, Meters, Cultural and Official Machinery	1.89
工艺品及其他制造业	Handicraft Article and Other Manufacturing	0.55
废弃资源和废旧材料回收加工业	Waste Resources and Junk Material Recycled	0.3
电力、热力的生产和供应业	Electric Power, Steam and Hot Water Production and Supply	76.14
燃气生产和供应业	Gas Production and Supply	2.25
水的生产和供应业	Tap Water Production and Supply	6.81

ELECTRICITY CONSUMPTION OF INDUSTRY ABOCE DESGINATED SIZE BY SECTOR

10000 KW/h

2003	2004	2005	2006	2007	2008	2009
439.38	551.51	641.21	610.73	728.19	841.33	829.51
2.14	2.31	2.20	2.03	2.24	3.04	3.31
4.69	6.15	7.78	7.60	8.21	11.62	11.89
0.58	3.17	1.19	2.56	3.99	4.39	5.34
1.55	1.25	1.23	1.78	2.06	2.96	3.51
1.76	3.02	2.93	5.36	5.95	5.65	6.51
0.01		0.00	0.00	0.01	0.01	0.01
20.56	15.11	5.98	9.53	10.44	13.48	17.72
4.26	4.96	7.28	6.61	6.75	8.96	9.57
2.24	3.02	7.62	4.78	5.50	5.59	6.74
0.99	1.2	1.54	1.61	1.32	1.42	1.52
25.04	28.52	35.73	36.24	43.44	45.36	45.26
1.71	1.4	3.87	2.71	2.37	3.00	2.97
0.17	0.16	0.32	0.35	0.33	0.29	0.30
3.57	3.31	3.92	3.45	4.17	4.95	5.73
0.31	0.22	0.19	0.17	0.24	0.29	0.29
7.29	12.75	10.18	11.22	10.83	11.87	13.09
1.05	0.93	5.22	2.36	2.30	1.96	1.84
0.04	0.05	0.17	0.23	0.32	0.20	0.15
5.31	8.6	9.17	7.12	8.22	7.76	8.80
77.8	85.32	139.48	124.89	145.51	166.90	182.27
4.85	5.42	13.52	9.31	9.95	10.62	11.01
2.06	3.61	1.96	3.04	3.24	2.91	1.98
1.1	0.83	1.33	1.13	1.32	1.51	1.87
3.31	10.25	9.14	6.60	8.05	9.97	11.23
30.36	39.02	52.20	52.08	60.42	80.92	91.61
76.38	125.93	104.05	107.11	142.47	146.71	152.37
35.47	48.41	60.74	64.69	74.50	74.29	56.40
4.92	5.03	8.28	7.62	8.15	9.52	10.97
7.51	8.04	16.75	13.79	13.06	16.80	20.36
2.39	2.06	2.84	2.40	2.37	4.03	4.54
26.44	46.75	59.18	49.33	39.68	44.36	49.88
3.77	2.85	7.33	5.10	6.60	9.35	15.38
1.34	1.18	4.52	3.44	2.23	3.17	3.41
0.33	0.72	0.77	0.57	0.54	0.62	0.61
0.21	0.09	0.64	0.69	0.55	1.05	1.19
		0.18	0.23	0.43	0.34	0.52
71.58	68.3	45.01	46.37	84.31	118.72	61.85
0.24	0.3	0.49	0.13	0.13	0.27	0.36
6.05	5.27	6.27	6.53	6.02	6.48	7.15

8-20 全社会综合能源平衡表(等价值)

BALANCE SHEET OF DOMESTIC ENERGY (EQIVALENCE PRICE)

单位:万吨标准煤 (10000 tons standardized coal)

行业	Item	2005	2006	2007	2008	2009
一.可供量	Quantity Available	10082	11049	12143	12845	13708
一次能源生产量	Primary Energy Production	4370	3838	4116	5336	5019
回收能	Recuperated Energy			54	424	489
外省(区、市)调入量	Engery moblized from other Province	8118	9135	10399	9863	10965
进 口 量	Import Volume					
我轮.机在外国加油量	Volume of Fuel Charged Abroad					
本省(区、市)调出量(-)	Engery moblized to other Province	2315	2042	2348	2711	2912
出 口 量(-)	Output Volume					
外轮.机在我国加油量(-)	Volume of Fuel Charged at Home					33
年初年末库存差额	Storage Balance Difference between the	-91	118	-77	-67	181
	Beginning and the End of the Year	377	493	401	485	814
年初库存量	Storage Volume at the Beginning of the Year	468	375	478	551	633
年末库存量(-)	Storage Volume by the End of the Year	10082	11049	12143	12845	13708
二.消费量	Consumption	10076	11086	12142	12834	13662
消费量分组一	Consumption Group 1.	462	410	422	438	460
1.农.林.牧.渔业	Agriculture, Forestry, Animal Husbandary, Fishing	7077	7860	8574	8827	9304
2.工 业	Industry	143	170	190	189	230
3.建 筑 业	Construction	881	1073	1112	1291	1259
4.交通运输.仓储和邮政业	Transport communication, Storage, Post Service	254	331	369	459	647
5.批发、零售业和住宿、餐饮业	Wholesale,Retail Sale, Hotel and Catering Industry	194	203	288	291	345
6.其他	Others	1065	1040	1187	1338	1418
7.生活消费	Living Consumption	10082	11049	12143	12845	13708
消费量分组二	Consumption Group 2.	9974	10925	11976	12799	13525
1. 终端消费	Terminal Consumption	6974	7739	8411	8792	9166
#工业	Industry	101	117	160	38	88
2. 加工转换损失	Loss in Processing	4	1	1	3	
火力发电损失	Loss in Thermal Power Generation	2				1
供热损失	Loss in Heating		1			
洗选煤损失	Loss in Coal Seperation	7		107	1	7
炼焦损失	Loss in Coke Making	73	73	23	4	71
炼油损失	Loss in Oil Refining	15	42	29	30	6
制气损失	Loss in Gas Drying					3
煤制品加工损失	Loss in Coal Products Processing	7	7	7	8	95
3. 损 失 量	Loss in Processing					
三.平衡差额	Balance					

8-21 全社会煤炭平衡表

BALANCE SHEET OF DOMESTIC COAL CONSUMPTION

单位:万吨 (10 000 tons)

行业	Item	2005	2006	2007	2008	2009
一、可供量	Quantity Available	8873	9910	10792	10196	11100
生产量	Production Capacity	778	1230	1084	1205	1087
外省(区、市)调入量	Engery moblized from other Province	8278	8545	9891	9189	9794
进口量	Import Volume					
本省(区、市)调出量(-)	Engery moblized to other Province					
出口量(-)	Output Volume					
年初年末库存差额	Storage Balance Difference between the Beginning and the End of the Year	-183	135	-184	-198	219
年初库存量	Storage Volume at the Beginning of the Year	333	516	272	456	854
年末库存量(-)	Storage Volume by the End of the Year	516	382	456	654	635
二、消费量	Consumption	8873	9910	10792	10196	11100
消费量分组一	Consumption Group 1.	8873	9910	10792	10196	11100
1.农.林.牧.渔业	Agriculture, Forestry, Animal Husbandary, Fishing	96	106	89	89	121
2.工业	Industry	8006	8863	9685	8983	9705
3.建筑业	Construction	70	77	91	98	98
4.交通运输.仓储和邮政业	Transport communication, Storage, Post Service	106	116	139	175	174
5.批发、零售业和住宿、餐饮业	Wholesale,Retail Sale, Hotel and Catering Industry	109	163	184	201	410
6.其他	Others	17	20	61	68	77
7.生活消费	Living Consumption	468	565	543	583	516
消费量分组二	Consumption Group 2.	8873	9910	10792	10196	11100
1. 终端消费	Terminal Consumption	4894	5384	5847	5797	6691
#工业	Industry	4028	4337	4741	4584	5296
2. 用于加工转换	Coal Used for Processing	3979	4526	4944	4399	4405
火力发电	Thermal Power Generation	2732	3180	3480	2852	2888
供热	Heating	297	285	310	396	334
洗煤损耗	Loss in Washing Coal		5		1	1
炼焦	Coke Making	930	1005	1118	1111	1146
制气	Air Drying	20	51	37	38	32
型煤加工损耗	Loss in Standardlized Coal Processing					4
3. 损失量	Loss					4
三、平衡差额	Balance					

8–22 全社会石油平衡表

BALANCE SHEET OF DOMESTIC PETROLEUM

单位:万吨 (10 000 tons)

行业	Item	2005	2006	2007	2008	2009
一.可供量	Quantity Available	1172	1449	1689	1808	1914
生产量	Production Capacity	78	80	86	84	81
外省(区、市)调入量	Engery moblized from other Province	1064	1352	1560	1670	1836
进 口 量	Import Volume					
我轮.机在外国加油量	Volume of Fuel Charged Abroad					
本省(区、市)调出量(–)	Engery moblized to other Province					
出 口 量(–)	Output Volume					
外轮.机在我国加油量(–)	Volume of Fuel Charged at Home					
年初年末库存差额	Storage Balance Difference between the Beginning and the End of the Year	29	17	44	54	20
年初库存量	Storage Volume at the Beginning of the Year	81	70	129	90	119
年末库存量(–)	Storage Volume by the End of the Year	52	52	86	37	100
二.消费量	Consumption	1172	1449	1689	1808	1914
消费量分组一	Consumption Group 1.	1172	1449	1689	1802	1885
1.农.林.牧.渔业	Agriculture, Forestry, Animal Husbandary, Fishing	111	133	151	168	169
2.工　业	Industry	452	523	554	538	534
3.建 筑 业	Construction	39	51	62	59	85
4.交通运输.仓储和邮政业	Transport communication, Storage, Post Service	509	641	660	753	741
5.批发、零售业和住宿、餐饮业	Wholesale,Retail Sale, Hotel and Catering Industry	18	41	68	70	94
6.其他	Others		5	59	60	50
7.生活消费	Living Consumption	42	56	136	154	214
消费量分组二	Consumption Group 2.	1172	1449	1689	1808	1914
1. 终端消费	Terminal Consumption	1094	1368	1633	1783	1906
#工业	Industry	374	444	500	520	557
2. 加工转换损失	Coal Used for Processing	73	76	51	19	16
火力发电	Thermal Power Generation	8	4	5	6	3
供　热	Heating	2	8	23	10	9
炼油损耗	Loss in Oil Refining	64	64	24	3	5
制　气	Gas Making					
3. 损 失 量	Loss	5	5	5	6	8
三.平衡差额	Balance					0

8-23 全社会电力平衡表
BALANCE SHEET OF DOMESTIC ELECTRICITY

单位:万千瓦时 (10 000 KW/h)

行业	Item	2005	2006	2007	2008	2009
一、可供量	Quantity Available	1369	1331	1561	1769.9	1797.77
生产量	Production Capacity	1369	1331	1561	1769.9	1797.77
火力发电	Thermal Power Generation	446	567	651	543.96	615.87
水力发电、核发电、其它发电	Hydroelectricity Generation, Nuclearpower Generation, and others	923	764	910	1225.94	1181.9
外省(区、市)调入量	Engery moblized from other Province	78	115	115	76.25	228.53
进 口 量	Import Volume					
本省(区、市)调出量(-)	Engery moblized to other Province	580	551	667	769.91	843.26
出 口 量(-)	Output Volume					
二、消费量	Consumption	867	895	1009	1076.24	1183.04
消费量分组一	Consumption Group 1.	867	895	1009	1076.24	1183.04
1.农.林.牧.渔业	Agriculture, Forestry, Animal Husbandary, Fishing	57	37	38	35.84	36.84
2.工　业	Industry	563	618	728	772.827	829.481
3.建 筑 业	Construction	8	10	9	8.29	10.37
4.交通运输.仓储和邮政业	Transport communication, Storage, Post Service	14	14	12	10.86	12.71
5.批发、零售业和住宿、餐饮业	Wholesale,Retail Sale, Hotel and Catering Industry	26	33	37	44.3	51.7
6.其他	Others	45	50	44	43.55	62.91
7.生活消费	Living Consumption	154	134	141	160.57	179.03
消费量分组二	Consumption Group 2.	867	895	1009	1076.24	1183.04
1. 终端消费	Terminal Consumption	867	895	1009	1076.24	1153.06
#工业	Industry	563	618	728	772.83	799.50
2. 输配电损失量	Distribution Loss					29.98
三、平衡差额	Balance					

8-24 单位GDP能耗、单位GDP电耗和单位工业增加值能耗(2009)
UNIT GDP ENERGY CONSUMPTION, UNIT GDP POWER CONSUMPTION AND UNIT ENERGY CONSUMPTION OF INDUSTRIAL VALUE ADDED

地区	Regions	单位GDP能耗 Unit GDP energy consumption		单位工业增加值能耗 Energy consumption per unit of industrial added value		单位GDP电耗 Unit GDP power consumption	
		指标值 (吨标准煤/万元) Index value	上升或下降 (±%) Up or down	指标值 (吨标准煤/万元) Index value	上升或下降 (±%) Up or down	指标值 (千瓦时/万元) Index value	上升或下降 (±%) Up or down
全省	**Total**	**1.23**	**-5.97**	**2.35**	**-12.30**	**1018.45**	**-5.52**
武汉市	Wuhan	1.11	-6.04	1.74	-18.62	790.06	-4.71
黄石市	Huangshi	1.92	-6.45	2.18	-8.79	1588.53	-9.80
十堰市	Shiyan	1.63	-5.83	1.05	-11.53	1425.87	-8.48
宜昌市	Yichang	1.94	-6.20	1.69	-8.81	1518.82	-6.17
襄樊市	Xiangfan	1.57	-6.15	1.49	-18.58	818.84	-7.21
鄂州市	Ezhou	2.05	-6.11	3.09	-16.21	1511.18	-4.89
荆门市	Jingmen	1.57	-5.50	3.14	-11.80	1222.10	-5.16
孝感市	Xiaogan	1.59	-5.82	2.19	-16.74	1168.49	1.23
荆州市	Jingzhou	1.06	-6.92	1.86	-18.06	1049.89	-5.69
黄冈市	Huanggang	1.32	-6.50	1.51	-13.49	949.84	-3.39
咸宁市	Xianning	1.47	-6.07	2.14	-22.13	1113.64	-4.72
随州市	Suizhou	0.86	-5.05	0.84	-9.01	469.00	5.75
恩施州	Enshi Prefecture	1.09	-6.20	1.79	-9.04	822.57	-4.62
仙桃市	Xiantao	1.10	-5.81	0.70	-11.78	479.25	-2.26
潜江市	Qianjiang	1.61	-6.87	1.76	-13.04	1272.07	-15.19
天门市	Tianmen	0.92	-5.62	1.26	-12.87	393.88	2.92
神农架	Shennongjia	1.40	-5.80	1.78	-12.65	2508.22	-23.36

主要统计指标解释

工业 指从事自然资源的开采，对采掘品和农产品进行加工和再加工的物质生产部门。具体包括：(1)对自然资源的开采，如采矿、晒盐等(但不包括禽兽捕猎和水产捕捞)；(2)对农副产品的加工、再加工，如粮油加工、食品加工、 丝、纺织、制革等；(3)对采掘品的加工、再加工，如炼铁、炼钢、化工生产、石油加工、机器制造、木材加工等，以及电力、自来水、煤气的生产和供应等；(4)对工业品的修理、翻新，如机器设备的修理、交通运输工具(如汽车)的修理等。

工业统计调查单位为独立核算法人工业企业。

独立核算法人工业企业指从事工业生产经营活动的单位。独立核算法人工业企业应同时具备以下条件：①依法成立，有自己的名称、组织机构和场所，能够承担民事责任；②独立拥有和使用资产，承担负债，有权与其他单位签订合同；③独立核算盈亏，并能够编制资产负债表。

本年鉴中涉及的企业登记注册类型：

国有及国有控股企业 指国有企业加上国有控股企业。国有企业(即原全民所有制工业或国营工业)指企业全部资产归国家所有，并按《中华人民共和国企业法人登记管理条例》规定登记注册的非公司制的经济组织。包括国有企业、国有独资公司和国有联营企业。1957年以前的公私合营和私营工业，后均改造为国营工业，1992年改为国有工业，这部分工业的资料不单独分列时，均包括在国有企业内。国有控股企业是对混合所有制经济的企业进行的“国有控股”分类。它是指这些企业的全部资产中国有资产(股份)相对其他所有者中的任何一个所有者占资(股)最多的企业。该分组反映了国有经济控股情况。

集体企业 指企业资产归集体所有，并按《中华人民共和国企业法人登记管理条例》规定登记注册的经济组织。是社会主义公有制经济的组成部分。包括城乡所有使用集体投资举办的企业，以及部分个人通过集资自愿放弃所有权并依法经工商行政管理机关认定为集体所有制的企业。

股份合作企业 指以合作制为基础，由企业职工共同出资入股，吸收一定比例的社会资产投资组建，实行自主经营，自负盈亏，共同劳动，民主管理，按劳分配与按股分红相结合的一种集体经济组织。

联营企业 指两个及两个以上相同或不同所有制性质的企业法人或事业单位法人，按自愿、平等、互利的原则，共同投资组成的经济组织。联营企业包括：

国有联营企业指国有企业与国有企业间的联营；

集体联营企业指集体企业与集体企业间的联营；

国有与集体联营企业指国有企业与集体企业间的联营。

有限责任公司 指根据《中华人民共和国公司登记管理条例》规定登记注册，由两个以上，五十个以下的股东共同出资，每个股东以其所认缴的出资额对公司承担有限责任，公司以其全部资产对其债务承担责任的经济组织。

有限责任公司包括国有独资公司以及其他有限责任公司。

股份有限公司 指根据《中华人民共和国企业法人登记管理条例》规定登记注册，其全部注册资本由等额股份构成并通过发行股票筹集资本，股东以其认购的股份对公司承担有限责任，公司以其全部资产对其债务承担责任的经济组织。

私营企业 指由自然人投资设立或由自然人控股，以雇佣劳动为基础的营利性经济组织。包括按照《公司法》、《合伙企业法》、《私营企业暂行条例》规定登记注册的私营有限责任公司、私营股份有限公司、私营合伙企业和私营独资企业。

港、澳、台商投资企业 指企业注册登记类型中的港、澳、台资合资、合作、独资经营企业和股份有限公司之和。

外商投资企业 指企业注册登记类型中的中外合资、合作经营企业、外资企业和外商投资股份有限公司之和。

“三资”企业系指港、澳、台商投资企业和外资企业的简称。

轻工业 指主要提供生活消费品和制作手工工具的工业。按其所使用的原料不同，可分为两大类：(1)以农产品为原料的轻工业，是指直接或间接以农产品为基本原料的轻工业。主要包括食品制造、饮料制造、烟草加工、纺织、缝纫、皮革和毛皮制作、造纸以及印刷等工业；(2)以非农产品为原料的轻工业，是指以工业品为原料的轻工业。主要包括文教体育用品、化学药品制造、合成纤维制造、日用化学制品、日用玻璃制品、日用金属制品、手工工具制造、医疗器械制造、文化和办公用机械制造等工业。

重工业 指为国民经济各部门提供物质技术基础的主要生产资料的工业。按其生产性质和产品用途，可以分为下列三类：(1)采掘(伐)工业，是指对自然资源的开采，包括石油开采、煤炭开采、金属矿开采、非金属矿开采等工业；(2)原材料工业，指向国民经济各部门提供基本材料、动力和燃料的工业。包括金属冶炼及加工、炼焦及焦炭、化学、化工原料、水泥、人造板以及电力、石油和煤炭加工等工业；(3)加工工业，是指对工业原材料进行再加工制造的工业。包括装备国民经济各部门的机械设备制造工业、金属结构、水泥制品等工业，以及为农业提供的生产资料如化肥、农药等工业。

根据上述划分原则，修理业中以重工业产品为修理作业对象的划为重工业，反之划为轻工业。

工业总产值

(1)定义：

工业总产值是以货币形式表现的，工业企业在一定时期内生产的工业最终产品或提供工业性劳务活动的总价值量。它反映一定时间内工业生产的总规模和总水平。

(2)计算原则：

工业生产的原则，即凡是企业在报告期生产的经检验合格的产品，不管是否在报告期销售，均包括在内。

最终产品的原则，即凡是计入工业总产值的产品，必须是本企业生产的经检验合格的，不需要再进行任何加工的最终产品。如果企业有中间产品(半成品)对外销售，则对外销售的中间产品应视为企业的最终产品。

工厂法原则，即工业总产值是以工业企业作为基本计算(核算)单位，即按企业的最终产品计算工业总产值。按这种方法计算的工业总产值，不允许同一产品价值在企业内部重复计算，不能把企业内部各个车间(分厂)生产的成果相加，但允许企业间的重复计算。

(3)内容及计算方法：

1995 年全国工业普查对工业总产值(原规定)的内容及计算原则和方法做了某些修订，修订后的工业总产值(新规定)包括三项内容：即本期生产成品价值、对外加工费收入、在制品半成品期末期初差额价值三部分。

本期生产成品价值：指企业本期生产，并在报告期内不再进行加工，经检验、包装入库的全部工业成品(半成品)价值合计，包括企业生产的自制设备及提供给本企业在建工程、其他非工业部门和福利部门等单位使用的成品价值。本期生产成品价值为按自备原材料生产的产品的数量乘以本期不含增值税(销项税额)的产品实际销售平均单价计算；会计核算中按成本价格转帐的自制设备和自产自用的成品，按成本价格计算生产成品价值。生产成品价值中不包括用定货者来料加工的成品(半成品)价值。

对外加工费收入：指企业在报告期内完成的对外承接的工业品加工(包括用定货者来料加工产品)的加工费收入和对外工业修理作业所取得的加工费收入。对外加工费收入按不含增值税(销项税额)的价格计算，可根据会计“产品销售收入”科目的有关资料取得。

对于本企业对内非工业部门提供的加工修理、设备安装的劳务收入，如果企业会计核算基础较好，能取得这部分资料，而且这部分价值所占比重较大，应包括在对外加工费收入中。

自制半成品在制品期末期初差额价值：指企业报告期在制品期末减期初的差额价值，本指标一般可以从会计核算资料中取得。如果会计产品成本核算中不计算半成品、在制品的成本，则总产值中也不包括这部分价值，反之则包括。

(4)工业总产值统计范围变化和计算方法修订情况：

1984 年以前工业总产值不包括村办工业，村办工业总产值划归农业。1984 年以后工业总产值包括村办工业。

1995 年工业普查对工业总产值计算方法做了修订，即从 1995 年始按新修订(新规定)方法计算工业总产值。新规定与原规定的区别如下：

全价与加工费的计算原则不同：新规定为凡自备原材料，不论其生产繁简程度如何，一律按全价计算工业总产值；凡来料加工，允许按加工费计算工业总产值。原规定则视生产加工的繁简程度不同，规定哪些行业按全价，哪些行业按加工费计算工业总产值。

自制半成品、在产品期末期初差额价值的计算原则不同：新规定要求，凡会计产品成本核算时计算了成本的差额价值，总产值中就应包括，否则可不包括；原规定则按生产周期六个月的界限区分，凡生产周期六个月以上的企业，总产值计算中应包括这部分差额价值，否则可不包括。

计算价格不同：新规定按不含增值税(销项税额)的价格计算；原规定则按含增值税(销项税额)的价格计算。

工业增加值 指工业企业在报告期内以货币表现的工业生产活动的最终成果。

工业增加值有两种计算方法：一是生产法，即工业总产出减去工业中间投入加上应交增值税；二是收入法，即从收入的角度出发，根据生产要素在生产过程中应得到的收入份额计算，具体构成项目有固定资产折旧、劳动者报酬、生产税净额、营业盈余，这种方法也称要素分配法。本年鉴中的工业增加值是以生产法计算的。

生产法工业增加值的计算方法为：

工业增加值=工业总产出−工业中间投入+应交增值税

(1)工业总产出：指工业企业在一定时期内工业生产活动的总成果。工业总产出包括：成品生产价值，对外加工费收入，自制半成品、在产品期末期初差额价值。1995年后用新规定计算的工业总产值代替。

(2)工业中间投入：指工业企业在工业生产活动中消耗的外购物质产品和对外支付的服务费用。服务费用包括支付给物质生产部门(工业、农业、批发零售贸易业、建筑业、运输邮电业)的服务费用和支付给非物质生产部门(如保险、金融、文化教育、科学研究、医疗卫生、行政管理等)的服务费用。工业中间投入的确定须遵循以下原则：必须从外部购入的，并已计入工业总产出的产品和服务价值；必须是本期投入生产，并一次性消耗掉(包括本期摊销的低值易耗品等)的产品和服务价值。

工业中间投入包括直接材料费用、制造费用中的工业中间投入、管理费用中的工业中间投入、销售费用中的工业中间投入和利息支出五部分。

资产总计 指企业拥有或控制的能以货币计量的经济资源，包括各种财产、债权和其他权利。资产按流动性分为流动资产、长期投资、固定资产、无形资产、递延资产和其他资产。该指标根据企业会计“资产负债表”中“资产总计”项目的期末数增列。

流动资产 指企业可以在一年内或者超过一年的一个生产周期内变现或者耗用的资产，包括现金及各种存款、短期投资，应收及预付款项、存货等。

流动资产平均余额 指企业在报告期内全部流动资产的平均余额。

固定资产原价 指企业在建造、购置、安装、改建、扩建、技术改造某项固定资产时所支出的全部货币总额。它一般包括买价、包装费、运杂费和安装费等。

固定资产净值年平均余额 指固定资产净值在报告期内余额的平均数。计算公式为：

$$固定资产净值年平均余额=\frac{1至12月各月月初、月末固定资产净值之和}{24}$$

该指标根据“资产负债表”中“固定资产原价”、“累计折旧”指标的期初、期末数计算填列。

固定资产净值指固定资产原价减去历年已提折旧额后的净额。计算公式为：

固定资产净值=固定资产原价−累计折旧

负债合计 指企业所承担的能以货币计量，将以资产或劳务偿付的债务，偿还形式包括货币、资产或提供劳务。负债一般按偿还期长短分为流动负债和长期负债。根据会计“资产负债表”中“负债合计”的年末数填列。

所有者权益 指企业投资人对企业净资产的所有权。企业净资产等于企业全部资产减去全部负债后的余额，包括企业投资人对企业的最初投入的实际到位的资产及资本公积金、盈余公积金和未分配利润。所有者权益合计数小于零，表示企业资不抵债。

主营业务收入 指会计“利润表”中对应指标的本年累计数。未执行2001年《企业会计制度》的企业，用“产品销售收入”的本期累计数代替。

主营业务成本 指会计“利润表”中对应指标的本年累计数。未执行2001年《企业会计制度》的企业，用“产品销售成本”的本期累计数代替。

主营业务税金及附加 指会计“利润表”中对应指标的本年累计数。未执行 2001 年《企业会计制度》的企业，用“产品销售税金及附加”的本期累计数代替。

利润总额 指企业生产经营活动的最终成果，是企业在一定时期内实现的盈亏相抵后的利润总额(亏损以“–”号表示)，它等于营业利润加上补贴收入加上投资收益加上营业外净收入再加上以前年度损益调整。

本年应交增值税 指企业在报告期内应交纳的增值税额。它等于本年销项税额加上出口退税加上进项税额转出数减去本年进项税额。小规模纳税企业直接按全年计税销售额乘以征收率计算取得。

从业人员平均人数 是指报告期内每天拥有的从业人员人数。其计算公式为：

$$\text{季平均人数}=\frac{\text{季内各月平均人数之和}}{3}$$

$$\text{月平均人数}=\frac{\text{报告月内每天实有人数之和}}{\text{报告月日历日数}}$$

$$\text{年平均人数}=\frac{\text{年内各月平均人数之和}}{12}$$

总资产贡献率 反映企业全部资产的获利能力，是企业经营业绩和管理水平的集中体现，是评价和考核企业盈利能力的核心指标。计算公式为：

$$\text{总资产贡献率（\%）}=\frac{\text{利润总额+税金总额+利息支出}}{\text{平均资金总额}}\times 100\%$$

公式中：税金总额为产品销售税金及附加与应交增值税之和；平均资产总额为期初期末资产之和的算术平均值。

资产负债率 该指标既反映企业经营风险的大小，也反映企业利用债权人提供的资金从事经营活动的能力。计算公式为：

$$\text{资产负债率（\%）}=\frac{\text{负债总额}}{\text{资产总额}}\times 100\%$$

资产与负债均为报告期期末数。

流动资产周转次数 指一定时期内流动资产完成的周转次数，反映投入工业企业流动资金的周转速度。计算公式为：

$$\text{流动资产周转资转}=\frac{\text{产品销售收入}}{\text{全部流动资产平均余额}}$$

公式中：全部流动资产平均余额为期初和期末的流动资产之和的算术平均值。

成本费用利润率　反映企业投入的生产成本及费用的经济效益，同时也反映企业降低成本所取得的经济效益。计算公式为：

$$成本费用利润（\%）=\frac{利润总额}{成本费用总额}\times 100\%$$

公式中：成本费用总额为产品销售成本、销售费用、管理费用、财务费用之和。

全员劳动生产率　该指标反映企业的生产效率和劳动投入的经济效益。计算公式为：

$$全员劳动生产率（元/人）=\frac{工业增加值}{全部从业人员平均人数}$$

产品销售率　该指标反映工业产品已实现销售的程度，是分析工业产销衔接情况，研究工业产品满足社会需求的指标。计算公式为：

$$产品销售率（\%）=\frac{工业销售产值}{工业总产值（现价）}\times 100\%$$

能源生产总量　指一定时期内，一次能源生产量的总和。该指标是观察能源生产水平、规模、构成和发展速度的总量指标。一次能源生产量包括原煤、原油、天然气、水电、核能及其他动力能(如风能、地热能等)发电量，不包括低热值燃料生产量、生物质能、太阳能等的利用和由一次能源加工转换而成的二次能源产量。

能源消费总量　指一定时期内，物质生产部门、非物质生产部门和生活消费的各种能源的总和。该指标是观察能源消费水平、构成和增长速度的总量指标。能源消费总量包括原煤和原油及其制品、天然气、电力，不包括低热值燃料、生物质能和太阳能等的利用。能源消费总量分为终端能源消费量、能源加工转换损失量和能源损失量三部分。

(1)终端能源消费量：指一定时期内，生产和生活消费的各种能源在扣除了用于加工转换二次能源消费量和损失量以后的数量。

(2)能源加工转换损失量：指一定时期内，投入加工转换的各种能源数量之和与产出各种能源产品之和的差额。该指标是观察能源在加工转换过程中损失量变化的指标。

(3)能源损失量：指一定时期内，能源在输送、分配、储存过程中发生的损失和由客观原因造成的各种损失量，不包括各种气体能源放空、放散量。

能源生产弹性系数　是研究能源生产增长速度与国民经济增长速度之间关系的指标。计算公式：

$$能源生产弹性系数=\frac{能源生产总量年平均增长速度}{国民经济年平均增长速度}$$

国民经济年平均增长速度，可根据不同的目的或需要，用国民生产总值、国内生产总值等指标来计算，本年鉴是采用国内生产总值指标计算的。

电力生产弹性系数 是研究电力生产增长速度与国民经济增长速度之间关系的指标。一般来说，电力的发展应当快于国民经济的发展，也就是说电力应超前发展。计算公式为：

$$电力生产弹性系数=\frac{电力生产量年平均增长速度}{国民经济年平均增长速度}$$

能源消费弹性系数 反映能源消费增长速度与国民经济增长速度之间比例关系的指标。计算公式为：

$$能源消费弹性系数=\frac{能源消费量年平均增长速度}{国民经济年平均增长速度}$$

电力消费弹性系数 反映电力消费增长速度与国民经济增长速度之间比例关系的指标。计算公式为：

$$电力消费弹性系数=\frac{电力消费量年平均增长速度}{国民经济年平均增长速度}$$

能源加工转换效率 指一定时期内，能源经过加工、转换后，产出的各种能源产品的数量与同期内投入加工转换的各种能源数量的比率。该指标是观察能源加工转换装置和生产工艺先进与落后、管理水平高低等的重要指标。计算公式为：

$$能源加工转换效率=\frac{能源加工转换产出量}{能源加工转换投入量}\times 100\%$$

单位国内生产总值能耗 指一定时期内，一个国家或地区每生产一个单位的国内生产总值所消耗的能源。计算公式为：

$$单位国内生产总值能耗=\frac{能源消费总量}{国内生产总值}$$

单位国内生产总值电耗 指一定时期内，一个国家或地区每生产一个单位的国内生产总值所消耗的电力。计算公式为：

$$单位国内生产总值电耗=\frac{全社会用电量}{国内生产总值}$$

单位工业增加值能耗 指一定时期内，一个国家或地区每生产一个单位的工业增加值所消耗的能源。计算公式为：

$$单位工业增加值能耗=\frac{工业能源消费量}{工业增加值}$$

Explanatory Notes on Main Statistical Indicators

Industry refers to the material production sector which is engaged in extraction of natural resources and processing and reprocessing of minerals and agricultural products, including (1) extraction of natural resources, such as mining, salt production (but not including hunting and fishing); (2) processing and reprocessing of farm and sideline produces, such as rice husking, flour milling, wine making, oil pressing, silk reeling, spinning and weaving, and leather making; (3) manufacture of industrial products, such as steel making, iron smelting, chemicals manufacturing, petroleum processing, machine building, timber processing; water and gas production and electricity generation and supply; (4)repairing of industrial products such as the repairing of machinery and means of transport (including cars).

Units of industrial statistics survey corporate industrial enterprises with independent accounting system.

Corporate industrial enterprises with independent accounting system refer to enterprises engaging in industrial production activities, which meet the following requirements: (1)They are established legally, having their own names, organizations, location, able to take civil liability; (2)They possess and use their assets independently, assume liabilities, and are entitled to sign contracts with other units; (3)They are financially independent and compile their own balance sheets.

Enterprises covered in the industrial statistics in the Yearbook include following categories by their registration:

State-owned and State-holding Enterprises refer to state-owned enterprises plus state-holding enterprises. State-owned enterprises (originally known as state-run enterprises with ownership by the whole society) are non-corporate economic entities registered in accordance with the Regulation of the People's Republic of China on the Management of Registration of Legal Enterprises, where all assets are owned by the state. Included in this category are state-owned enterprises, state-funded corporations and state-owned joint-operation enterprises. Joint state-private industries and private industries, which existed before 1957, were transformed into state-run industries since 1957, and into state-owned industries after 1992. Statistics on those enterprises are included in the state-owned industries instead of grouping them separately. State-holding enterprises is a sub-classification of enterprises with mixed ownership, referring to enterprises where the percentage of state assets (or shares by the state) is larger than any other single share holder of the same enterprise. This sub-classification illustrates the control of the state over a particular industry.

Collective-owned Enterprises refer to economic entities registered in accordance with the Regulation of the People's Republic of China on the Management of Registration of Legal Enterprises, where assets are owned by collectively. Collective enterprises constitute an integral part of the socialist economy with public ownership. They include urban and rural enterprises invested by collectives, and some enterprises registered in industrial and commercial administration agency as collective units where funds are pulled together by individuals who voluntarily give up their right of ownership.

Share-holding Cooperative Enterprises refer to economic units set up on cooperative basis, with funding partly from members of the enterprise and partly from outside investment, where the operation and management is decided by the members who also participate in the production, and the distribution of income is based both on work (labour input) and on shares (capital input).

Joint-operation enterprises refer to economic units that are established by joint investment by two or more corporate enterprises or institutions of the same or different types of ownership on voluntary, equal and mutual-beneficial basis. They include:

a) state-owned joint-operation enterprises (joint operation between state-owned enterprises);

b) collective joint-operation enterprises (joint operation between collective enterprises; and

c) state-collective joint-operation enterprises (joint operation between state and collective enterprises).

Limited Liability Corporations refer to economic units registered in accordance with the Regulation of the People's Republic of China on the Management of Registration of Corporations, with capitals from 2 to 49 investors, each investor bears limited liability to the corporation depending on his/her holding of shares, and the corporation bears liability to its debt to the maximum of its total assets.

Share-holding Corporations Ltd. refer to economic units registered in accordance with the Regulation of the People's Republic of China on the Management of Registration of Corporate Enterprises, with total registered capitals divided into equal shares and raised through issuing stocks. Each investor bears limited liability to the corporation depending on the holding of shares, and the corporation bears liability to its debt to the maximum of its total assets.

Private Enterprises refer to economic units invested or controlled (by holding the majority of the shares) by natural persons who hire labours for profit-making activities. Included in this category are private limited liability corporations, private share-holding corporations Ltd., private partnership enterprises and private sole investment enterprises registered in accordance with the Corporation Law, Partnership Enterprise Law and Tentative Regulation on Private Enterprises.

Enterprises with Funds from Hong Kong, Macao and Taiwan refers to all industrial enterprises registered as the joint-venture, cooperative, sole (exclusive) investment industrial enterprises and limited liability corporations with funds from Hong Kong, Macao and Taiwan.

Foreign Funded Enterprises refers to all industrial enterprises registered as the joint-venture, cooperative, sole (exclusive) investment industrial enterprises and limited liability corporations with foreign funds.

Enterprise with Hong Kong, Macao, Taiwan and foreign fund refer to all the enterpries with funds from Hong Kong Macao and Taiwan and foreign funded enterprises.

Light Industry refers to the industry that produces consumer goods and hand tools. It consists of two categories, depending on the materials used:

(1) Industries using farm products as raw materials. These are branches of light industry which directly or indirectly use farm products as basic raw materials, including the manufacture of food and beverages, tobacco processing, textile, clothing, fur and leather manufacturing, paper making, printing, etc.

(2) Industries using non farm products as raw materials. These are branches of light industry which use manufactured goods as raw materials, including the manufacture of cultural, educational articles and sports goods, chemicals, synthetic fiber, chemical products for daily use, glass products for daily use, metal products for daily use, hand tools, medical apparatus and instruments, and the manufacture of cultural and clerical machinery.

Heavy Industry refers to the industry which produces capital goods, and provides various sectors of the national economy with necessary material and technical basis. It consists of the following three branches according to the purpose of production or the use of products:

(1) Mining, quarrying and logging industry refers to the industry that extracts natural resources, including extraction of petroleum, coal, metal and non-metal ores.

(2) Raw materials industry refers to the industry that provides various sectors of the national economy with raw materials, fuels and power. It includes smelting and processing of metals, coking and coke chemistry, chemical materials and building materials such as cement, plywood, and power, petroleum refining and coal dressing.

(3) Manufacturing industry refers to the industry that processes raw materials. It includes machine-building industry which equips sectors of the national economy, industries of metal structure and cement products, industries producing means of agricultural production, such as chemical fertilizers and pesticides.

According to the above principle of classification, the repairing trades, which are engaged primarily in repairing products of heavy industry are classified into heavy industry while these engaged in repairing products of light industry are classified into light industry.

Gross Industrial Output Value

(1) Definition: Gross industrial output value is the total volume of final industrial products produced and industrial services provided during a given period. It reflects the total achievements and overall scale of industrial production during a given period.

(2) Principles for calculation:

Statistics on industrial production follow the principle that all products produced by the enterprises and accepted during the reference period are to be included no matter whether they are sold or not during the reference period.

Determination of final products follow the principle that all products that are included in the calculation of grow industrial output value are the final products of the enterprise which have been accepted through quality check and require no further processing. If an enterprise has intermediate (semi-finished) products to sell, these intermediate products are considered as the final products of the enterprise.

Gross industrial output value is calculated following the principle of factory approach, i.e. industrial enterprise is used as the basic accounting unit in calculating the gross industrial output value. By this approach, value of the same product is not to be double counted, and the output value of different workshops (branch factories) should not be added. However, this approach does not exclude the possibility of double counting between enterprises.

(3) Content and calculation method: The old definition of gross industrial output value was modified during the national industrial census in 1995. The revised (new) definition of gross industrial output value consists of 3 components: value of the finished products during the reference period, income from external processing, and value of change in semi-finished products at the end and at the beginning of the reference period.

Value of the finished products during the reference period: refers to the value of all finished (semi-finished) industrial products that are produced during the reference period without the need for further processing, checked for acceptance, packed and put into the warehouse of the enterprise, including the value of own-produced equipment and the value of products provided to the projects under construction of the enterprise, and to other non-industrial or welfare units. Value of finished products during the reference period is calculated by the quantity of products produced using own materials multiplied by the average unit prices at which products are sold (excluding value-added tax). Own-produced equipment and products produced for own use are value at cost prices as in the case of enterprise accounting. Value of finished products does not include the value of finished products (semi-finished products) that are produced using the materials from the clients who make the orders.

Income from external processing: refers to income from contracted external processing of industrial products (including processing of industrial products using materials from the clients), and the income from industrial repairing work provided to other units. Income from external processing is calculated using information from the item “products sales income” in the enterprise accounting at the prices excluding value-added tax.

For income from services such as processing, repairing and installation of equipment provided to non-industrial units within the enterprise, if the accounting work of the enterprise is good enough to separate it from other records, and the share of such services is significant, it should also be included in the income from external processing.

Value of change in semi-finished products at the end and at the beginning of the reference period: refers to the value of change in semi-finished products at the end and at the beginning of the reference period, which generally can be obtained from accounting records of enterprises. If the enterprise accounting excludes the cost of semi-finished products, then it should not be included in the gross industrial output value, and vice versa.

(4) Changes in the coverage and method of calculation of gross industrial output value

Prior to 1984, the value of rural industry run by villages was classified into agriculture instead of industry. Since 1984, it has been included in the gross industrial output value. Method of calculation for the gross industrial output value was modified in the industrial census in 1995. The difference in the new method as compared with the old one is outlined below:

Principle in using full value vs. processing fee: The new method stipulates that all products produced using own materials are to be calculated with full value in reporting the gross industrial output value irrespective of sophistication of production, and for external processing, it allows calculation using processing fee. In the old method, however, the use of full value or processing fee was determined by the degree of sophistication of production in different branches of industries.

Principle in determining the value of change in semi-finished products: The new method requires that value of the change in semi-finished products should be included in the gross industrial output value if it is included in the accounting record of the enterprise, otherwise it should not be included. By the old method, it is determined by the type of enterprises in terms of production cycle. If the production cycle is over 6 months, the value of change in semi-finished products is included in the gross industrial output value, otherwise it is excluded.

Difference in prices: The new method uses prices excluding value-added tax in the calculation of gross industrial output value, while the old method used prices including value-added tax.

Value-added of Industry refers to the final results of industrial production of industrial enterprises in money terms during the reference period.

Industrial value-added can be calculated by two approaches: the production approach, i.e. gross industrial output value minus intermediate input plus value-added tax, and the income approach, i.e. income for various factors used in the course of production, including depreciation of fixed assets, remuneration of labourers, net of production tax, and operating surplus. Value-added of industry in the Yearbook is calculated by production approach as following:

Value-added of industry = gross industrial output industrial intermediate input + value-added tax

(1) Gross industrial output: refers to the total achievements of industrial production during a given period. Gross industrial output includes value of finished products, income from external processing, and value of change in semi-finished products at the end and at the beginning of the reference period. Since 1995, it was substituted by the gross industrial output value by new method.

(2) Industrial intermediate input: refers to purchased goods and paid services consumed during the industrial production of enterprises. Fees paid for services include fees paid for the services provided by material production sectors (industry, agriculture, wholesale and retail trade, construction, transport, post and telecommunications) and by non-material production sectors (insurance, banking, culture, education, scientific research, health and medical care, public administration, etc.). The determination of industrial intermediate input follows the principle that the goods and services must be purchased from outside and included in the gross industrial output, and that the goods and services are inputted into production and consumed (include low-value consumables) during the reference period.

Industrial intermediate input includes 5 components, namely direct consumption of materials, industrial intermediate input in manufacturing cost, industrial intermediate input in management cost, industrial intermediate input in marketing cost and expenditure on interest.

Total Assets refer to all economic resources, in monetary terms, that is owned or controlled by enterprises, including properties, creditors equity and other economic rights of all forms. Classified by the degree of equitability, total assets include circulating assets, long-term investment, fixed assets, intangible assets and deferred assets, and other assets. Data on this indicator can be obtained by the year-end figures of total assets in the Assets and Liability Table of accounting records of enterprises.

Working Capitals refer to capitals that an enterprise can cash or use during one year or one production cycle that may exceeds one year, including cash and savings deposits of various forms, short-term investment, money receivable and prepaid money, inventories, etc.

Annual Average Value of Working Capitals refers to the average value of all working capitals of the enterprise during the reference period.

Original Value of Fixed Assets refers to the total value, in monetary terms, that an enterprise spent on fixed assets, through construction, purchase, installation, transformation, expansion or technical upgrading. Generally, it covers cost of purchase, packing, transportation and installation, etc.

Annual Average of Net Value of Fixed Assets refer to average of the net value of fixed assets during the reference period, calculated with the following formula:

Annual Average of Net Value of Fixed Assets = sum of net value of fixed assets at the beginning and at the end of each month

from January to December / 24.

Information on this indicator can be obtained from the beginning and ending figures of the original value of fixed assets and cumulative depreciation from the Assets and Liability Table of enterprises.

Net value of fixed assets refers to the original value of fixed assets minus depreciation over the years, i.e.:

Net value of fixed assets = original value of fixed assets cumulative depreciation

Total Liabilities refer to payable liabilities of enterprises that have to repay in terms of money, assets or labour services. In terms of payment, it can be divided into liquid liabilities and long-term liabilities. Data on this item is obtained from the ending figures on total liabilities from the Assets and Liability Table from the enterprises.

Owner's Equity refers to the ownership of net assets of enterprise by its investors. The net assets equal the total assets minus total liabilities of the enterprise, including the actual assets invested into the enterprise by investors, accumulation of capitals and operating surplus and non-distributed profits. The enterprise's assets is less than its liabilities if the sum of owner's equity is smaller than zero.

Revenue from Principal Business refers to the annual accumulation of corresponding item in the "profit table" of the accountant. For enterprises that do not follow the 2001 Enterprise Accounting Standards, the year-end accumulation of revenue from the sales of products is used as a substitute.

Cost of Principal Business refers to the annual accumulation of corresponding item in the "profit table" of the accountant. For enterprises that do not follow the 2001 Enterprise Accounting Standards, the year-end accumulation of cost for the sales of products is used as a substitute.

Tax and Extra Charges from Principal Business refer to the annual accumulation of corresponding item in the "profit table" of the accountant. For enterprises that do not follow the 2001 Enterprise Accounting Standards, the year-end accumulation of tax and extra charges from the sales of products is used as a substitute.

Total Profits refer to the final achievements of production and operation of the enterprises, represented by the total profits after deducting losses (loss is expressed by the negative figure). It is the sum of profits from operation, income from subsidies, investment earnings, net income from activities other than operation, and adjustment of profits and losses of previous years.

Value-added Tax Payable refers to the amount of the value-added tax which should be paid by the enterprises during the reference period. It is the sum of tax on sales, export rebate, and transferred tax on purchases of the current year, minus the tax on purchases of the current year. Value-added tax payable of small-size enterprises is determined by the taxable sales of the year multiplied by the tax rate.

Average Annual Number of Employed Persons Employed persons refer to all those who are employed in enterprises and receive remunerations therefrom, including currently working employees, retirees who are re-employed, teachers of local-run schools, as well as foreigners, staff from Hong Kong, Macao and Taiwan, part-time employees and persons with second job who are employed by the enterprise, and employees of other units temporarily working in the enterprises, but excluding former employees who left the enterprise with their employment records still kept by the enterprises.

Average number of employed persons refers to the number of employees everyday during the reference period, calculated with the following formula:

Monthly average number = sum of actual employees everyday in reference month/number of calendar dates in reference month

Quarterly average number = sum of monthly average number in reference quarter/3

Annual average number = sum of monthly average number in reference year/12

Ratio of Profits, Taxes and Interests to Average Assets reflects the profit-making capability of all assets of the enterprise and is a key indicator manifesting the performance and management and evaluating the profit-making potential of the enterprise. It is calculated as follows:

Ratio of Profits, Taxes and Interests to Average Assets (%) = [(total profits + total taxes + interest payment) / average assets]×100%

In the above formula, total taxes is the sum of tax and extra charges on the sales of products and value-added tax payable; and average assets is the arithmetic mean of the sum of beginning assets and ending assets.

Ratio of Debts to Assets reflect both the operation risk and the capability of the enterprise in making use of the capital from the creditors. It is calculated as follows:

Ratio of Debts to Assets (%) = (total debts / total assets)×100%

Both assets and debts are figures at the end of the reference period.

Turnover of Working Capitals refers to the number of times of turnover of working capital in a given period of time, which reflects the speed of the turnover of working capital of industrial enterprises, and is calculated as follows:

Turnover of Working Capital=(sales revenue of products) / (average balance of total working capital)

In the above formula, average balance of total working capital refers to the arithmetic mean of the sum of working capital at the beginning and at the end of the reference period.

Ratio of Profits to Total Industrial Costs refers to the ratio of profits realized in a given period to the total costs in the same period, which reflects the economic efficiency of input cost and is calculated as follows:

Ratio of Profits to Total Industrial Cost (%)=(total profits/ total costs)×100%

Total costs in the above formula is the sum of cost of products sold, marketing cost, management cost and financial cost.

Overall Labour Productivity is an indicator reflecting the production efficiency of an enterprise and the economic efficiency of its labour input, calculated by the formula:

Overall Labour Productivity (yuan/person) = industrial value-added / average of all persons engaged

Sales Ratio of Products is an indicator reflecting the actual sale of industrial products, analyzing the production-selling and supply-demand relations. It is calculated as:

Sales Ratio of Products (%) = value of industrial sales / gross industrial output value (current prices) * 100%

Total Energy Production refers to the total production of primary energy by all energy producing enterprises in a given period of time. It is a comprehensive indicator to show the capacity, scale, composition and development of energy production. The production of primary energy includes that of coal, crude oil, natural gas, hydro-power and electricity generated by nuclear energy and other means such as wind power and geothermal power. However, it excludes the production of fuels of low calorific value, bio-energy, solar energy and the secondary energy converted from the primary energy.

Total Domestic Energy Consumption refers to the total consumption of energy of various kinds by material production sectors, non material production sectors and households in a given period of time. It is a comprehensive indicator to show the scale, composition and development of energy consumption. The total energy consumption includes that of coal, crude oil and their products, natural gas and electricity, However, it excludes the consumption of fuel of low calorific value, bio-energy and solar energy. Total domestic energy consumption can be divided into three parts: final energy consumption, loss during the process of energy conversion, and energy loss.

(1)Final Energy Consumption: It refers to the total energy consumption by material production sectors, non material production sectors and households in a given period of time, but excludes the consumption in conversion of the primary energy into the secondary energy and the loss in the process of energy conversion.

(2)Loss During the Process of Energy Conversion: It refers to the total input of various kinds of energy for conversion, minus the total output of various kinds of energy in a given period of time. It is an indicator to show the loss that occurs during the process of energy conversion.

(3)Energy Loss: It refers to the total of the loss of energy during the course of energy transport, distribution and storage and the loss caused by any objective reason in a given period of time. The loss of various kinds of gas due to gas discharges and stocktaking is excluded.

Elasticity Ratio of Energy Production is an indicator to show the relationship between the growth rate of energy production and the growth rate of the national economy. The formula is:

Elasticity Ratio of Energy Production = Average Annual Growth Rate of Energy Production / Average Annual Growth Rate of National Economy

Elasticity Ratio of Electricity Production is an indicator to show the relationship between the growth rate of electricity production and the growth rate of the national economy. Generally speaking, the growth rate of electricity production should be higher than that of the national economy.

Its formula is:

Elasticity Ratio of Electricity Production = Average Annual Growth Rate of Electricity Production / Average Annual Growth Rate of National Economy

Elasticity Ratio of Energy Consumption is an indicator to show the relationship between the growth rate of energy consumption and the growth rate of the national economy. The formula is:

Elasticity Ratio of Energy Consumption = Average Annual Growth Rate of Energy Consumption / Average Annual Growth Rate of National Economy

Elasticity Ratio of Electricity Consumption is an indicator to show the relationship between the growth rate of electricity consumption and the growth rate of the national economy. The formula is:

Elasticity Ratio of Electricity Consumption = Average Annual Growth Rate of Electricity / Average Annual Growth Rate of National Economy

Efficiency of Energy Processing and Conversion refers to the ratio of the total output of energy products of various kinds after processing and conversion and the total input of energy of various kinds for processing and conversion in the same reference period. It is an important indicator to show the current conditions of energy processing and conversion equipment, production technique and management. The formula is:

Efficiency of Energy Processing & Conversion = (Output of Energy After Processing & Conversion / Input of Energy for Processing & Conversion)×100%

Energy Consumption per Unit of GDP refers to the energy consumption per unit of gross domestic production in a country or the gross region production in a region in the same reference period. The formula is:

Energy Consumption per Unit of GDP = Total Energy Consumption / Gross Domestic Production

Electricity Consumption per Unit of GDP refers to the electricity consumption per unit of gross domestic production in a country or the gross region production in a region in the same reference period. The formula is:

Electricity Consumption per Unit of GDP = Total Electricity Consumption / Gross Domestic Production

Energy Consumption per Unit of Industrial Value-added refers to the energy consumption per unit of industrial value-added in a country or region in the same reference peroid. The formula is:

Energy Consumption per Unit of Industrial Value-added = Total Energy Consumption / Industrial Value-added

9 建筑业

Construction

资料整理：樊喜珍

建 筑 业

Construction
2009

建筑施工企业个数	Number of construction enterprises	2878（个）
建筑施工企业职工平均人数	Average number of employees of construction enterprise	146.02（万人）
建筑业总产值	Gross Output Value	3421.89（亿元）
房屋建筑竣工面积	Building Completed	10280.7（万平方米）
建筑业全员劳动生产率	Construction Labor Productivity	240792.10（万元/人）
建筑业技术装备率	Rate of construction technology and equipment	16851.25（元/人）

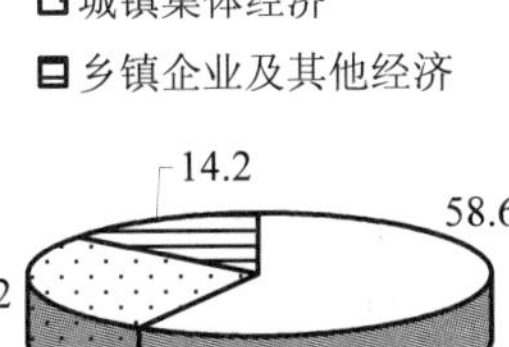

2000

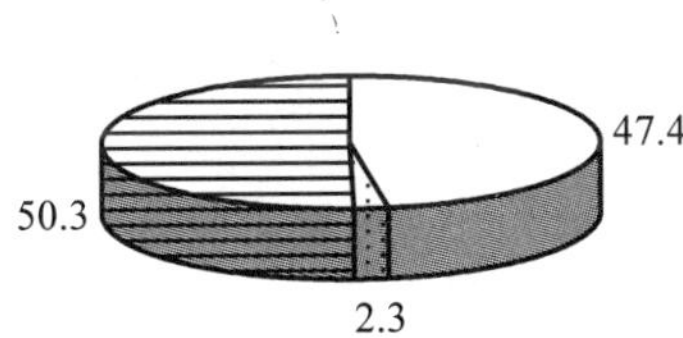

2009

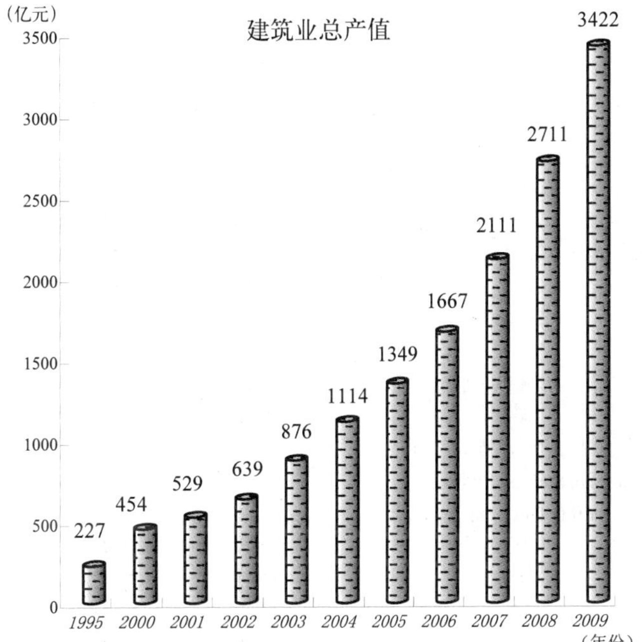

附：建筑业产值构成（%）

	2000	2001	2002	2003	2004	2005	2006	2007	2008	2009
国有经济	58.6	52.8	47.2	61.1	60.7	57.6	32.7	50.5	49.2	47.4
城镇集体经济	27.2	22.4	15.5	9.5	6.0	5.2	4.3	3.2	2.1	2.3
乡镇企业及其他经济	14.2	24.8	37.3	29.4	33.3	37.2	63	46.3	51.3	50.3

9-1 建筑施工企业概况

BASIC STATISTICS ON CONSTRUCTION ENTERPRISES

项 目 Item	总 计 Total	国有经济 State-Owned	地 方 Local - Owned	中 央 Central- Owned	城镇集体经济 Urban Collective- Owned	其他经济 Others
企业单位个数(个) Number of Enterprises (unit)						
1985	514	157	119	38	357	
1989	571	173	132	41	398	
1990	570	174	132	42	396	
1991	575	179	137	42	396	
1992	603	184	142	42	419	
1993	898	241	208	40	642	15
1994	823	307	268	39	492	24
1995	912	323	277	46	539	50
1996	1696	403	250	53	1198	95
1997	1761	429	378	51	1207	125
1998	1838	433	379	54	1206	199
1999	2120	491	432	59	1297	332
2000	2070	488	440	48	1175	409
2001	1661	393	350	43	809	459
2002	1625	363	327	36	480	782
2003	1808	558	488	70	344	906
2004	2357	433	378	55	358	2566
2005	2114	524	448	76	268	1322
2006	2238	320	279	41	223	1695
2007	2516	449	383	66	191	1876
2008	2975	440	374	66	161	2374
2009	2878	396	331	65	152	2330
全部职工平均人数(万人) Average Staff and Workers (10000 persons)						
1985	39.49	27.49	13.60	13.89	12.00	
1989	43.51	30.95	14.35	16.60	12.56	
1990	41.88	29.35	13.97	15.38	12.53	
1991	43.08	30.34	14.52	15.82	12.74	
1992	46.13	30.92	14.89	16.03	15.21	
1993	55.75	36.41	19.65	16.76	19.15	0.19
1994	52.66	36.83	19.07	17.76	15.43	0.40
1995	57.28	38.05	18.86	19.19	16.62	2.61
1996	76.51	36.83	18.58	18.25	36.20	3.48
1997	76.09	36.36	18.60	17.76	35.96	3.77
1998	82.63	38.22	19.22	19.00	38.82	5.59
1999	85.72	39.57	22.57	17.00	36.69	9.46
2000	82.76	36.58	21.73	14.83	35.36	10.82
2001	83.11	36.16	19.99	16.44	29.30	17.65
2002	93.50	34.20	21.25	12.95	23.50	35.80
2003	108.82	50.20	30.72	19.48	16.98	41.64
2004	105.30	44.40	28.10	16.30	12.20	48.70
2005	110.09	41.70	22.85	18.85	11.60	56.79
2006	114.25	27.26	15.18	12.08	10.28	76.71
2007	136.14	39.73	19.52	20.21	9.44	86.97
2008	137.61	38.51	18.40	20.11	6.61	92.49
2009	146.02	41.68	18.76	22.92	7.22	97.12

9-1 续表 1 continued

项 目 Item	总 计 Total	国有经济 State-Owned	地 方 Local - Owned	中 央 Central- Owned	城镇集体经济 Urban Collective- Owned	其他经济 Others
建筑业总产值(亿元) Gross Output Value of Construction Enterprises (100 million yuan)						
1985	28.01	21.22	10.33	10.89	6.78	
1989	45.73	36.22	15.61	20.61	9.51	
1990	49.30	38.92	16.34	22.58	10.38	
1991	57.56	44.19	19.16	25.03	13.37	
1992	78.44	59.51	25.03	34.47	18.93	
1993	119.90	90.27	36.17	54.10	29.10	0.53
1994	169.28	140.29	56.95	83.34	27.75	1.24
1995	227.41	178.51	58.96	119.55	33.70	15.19
1996	284.43	187.00	60.83	126.17	79.14	18.29
1997	305.97	199.53	63.59	135.94	84.70	21.75
1998	343.65	223.80	73.98	149.82	93.15	26.70
1999	399.02	246.58	88.07	158.51	107.32	45.13
2000	454.35	266.03	106.76	159.27	123.46	64.86
2001	529.02	279.39	112.32	167.07	117.70	131.93
2002	639.11	301.93	143.90	158.03	98.90	238.29
2003	876.26	535.71	227.72	307.99	82.99	257.56
2004	1114.33	676.45	285.29	391.16	67.25	370.63
2005	1349.32	776.70	268.77	507.92	69.92	502.71
2006	1667.00	545.64	184.87	360.77	72.44	1048.92
2007	2110.80	1065.26	234.03	831.23	68.69	976.85
2008	2710.80	1333.87	241.63	1092.24	57.52	1319.41
2009	3421.89	1621.66	191.86	1429.80	77.86	1722.37
施工房屋面积(万平方米) Floor Space of Buildings Under Construction (10000 sq.m)						
1985	955.7	955.7	497.2	458.5		
1989	1834.2	1167.0	820.7	346.3	677.2	
1990	1684.9	1061.4	746.1	315.3	623.5	
1991	1839.9	1103.3	758.1	345.2	736.6	
1992	2128.4	1190.4	829.9	360.5	938.1	
1993	2579.1	1439.3	989.1	450.2	1131.2	8.6
1994	2843.5	1894.5	1319.1	575.4	922.3	26.7
1995	3284.3	2122.8	1185.2	937.6	867.6	293.9
1996	4548.8	2224.6	1203.3	1021.3	2008.4	315.8
1997	4604.2	2330.6	1226.9	1103.7	1885.3	388.3
1998	5310.0	2488.8	1288.8	1200.0	2247.5	573.7
1999	5797.0	2703.4	1578.4	1125.0	2329.4	764.2
2000	6256.5	2889.1	1564.5	1324.6	2448.2	919.2
2001	6662.6	2792.5	1480.2	1312.3	2053.0	1817.1
2002	7215.9	2836.0	1452.0	1384.0	1742.0	2637.9
2003	8933.4	3817.5	2102.6	1714.9	1574.8	3541.1
2004	11772.3	5089.1	2522.6	2566.5	1348.9	5334.3
2005	12091.2	4568.9	1993.3	2575.6	1264.8	6257.5
2006	14478.2	3811.2	1016.2	2795.0	1021.6	9545.4
2007	16679.7	5503.8	1666.4	3837.4	1036.1	10139.8
2008	18376.5	5703.9	1060.4	4643.5	752	11920.6
2009	20499.3	5672.4	522.5	5149.9	799.4	14027.5

续表 2 continued

项　目 Item	总　计 Total	国有经济 State-Owned	地　方 Local - Owned	中　央 Central- Owned	城镇集体经济 Urban Collective- Owned	其他经济 Others
竣工房屋面积(万平方米) Floor Space of Buildings Completed (10000 sq.m)						
1985	425.7	425.7	326.3	99.4		
1989	817.3	433.5	344.4	89.1	383.8	
1990	785.9	455.9	351.6	104.3	330.0	
1991	852.4	474.9	338.7	136.2	377.5	
1992	1002.8	508.4	378.5	129.9	494.4	
1993	1114.9	481.0	384.4	96.1	632.9	1.0
1994	1070.9	577.5	485.2	92.3	481.6	11.8
1995	1175.9	622.2	466.9	155.3	484.3	69.4
1996	1880.7	653.3	501.3	152.0	1123.5	103.9
1997	1982.3	765.3	522.1	243.2	1124.5	92.5
1998	2374.0	836.0	624.0	212.0	1298.6	239.4
1999	2873.0	1023.1	776.1	247.0	1484.3	365.6
2000	3150.1	1096.3	836.1	260.2	1572.0	481.8
2001	3673.4	1237.0	828.3	408.7	1334.1	1102.3
2002	4146.6	1261.8	889.3	372.5	1146.0	1738.8
2003	4840.8	1578.8	1143.4	435.4	993.7	2268.3
2004	6647.1	2561.3	1563.2	998.1	820.5	3265.3
2005	6896.9	2125.6	923.7	1201.9	791.5	3979.8
2006	7376.2	1137.1	450.4	686.7	678.8	5560.3
2007	8425.0	1620.9	858.6	762.3	608.8	5895.3
2008	9256.1	1386.0	537.9	848.1	476.1	7394.0
2009	10280.7	1587.1	255.9	1331.2	494.7	8198.9
房屋建筑面积竣工率(%) Rate of Floor Space of Buildings Completed (%)						
1985	44.6	44.6	46.8	21.7		
1989	44.6	37.2	40.8	25.7	56.8	
1990	46.6	43.0	47.1	33.1	52.9	
1991	46.3	43.0	44.7	39.5	51.2	
1992	47.1	42.7	45.6	36.0	52.7	
1993	43.2	33.9	38.9	21.3	56.0	11.6
1994	37.7	30.5	36.8	16.0	52.2	44.2
1995	35.8	41.2	39.4	16.6	55.8	23.6
1996	41.3	29.4	41.7	14.9	55.9	32.9
1997	43.1	32.7	42.6	22.0	59.6	23.8
1998	44.7	33.6	48.4	17.7	57.8	41.7
1999	49.6	37.8	49.2	22.0	63.7	47.8
2000	50.3	37.9	53.4	19.6	64.2	52.4
2001	55.1	44.3	56.0	31.1	65.0	60.7
2002	57.5	44.5	61.2	26.9	65.8	65.9
2003	54.2	41.3	51.1	25.4	63.1	64.1
2004	56.5	50.3	62.0	38.9	60.8	61.2
2005	57.0	46.5	46.3	46.7	60.8	63.6
2006	50.9	29.8	44.3	24.6	66.4	58.3
2007	50.5	29.5	51.5	19.9	58.8	58.1
2008	50.4	24.3	50.7	18.3	63.3	62.0
2009	50.2	28.0	49.0	25.8	61.9	58.4

注：本表资料包括施工总承包和专业承包企业，不含劳务分包企业(下同)。

Note: In this table, the data including general contract and specilized contract enterprises under construction, excluding labor divided contract (the same as the following tables)

9-2 按行业分建筑业主要经济指标（2009）

MAJOR ECONOMIC INDICATORS OF CONSTRUCTION ENTRPRISES BY SECTOR(2009)

指 标	Item	房屋和土木工程建筑业 Housing and Civil Engineering Construction	房屋工程 Housing Construction	土木工程 Civil Engineering	建筑安装业 Construction and Installation	建筑装饰业 Building Decorative Construction
施工企业个数（个）	Number of Construction Enterprises (unit)	1639	1112	527	451	480
建筑业总产值（亿元）	Gross Output Value of Construction Enterprises (100 million yuan)	3061.19	1638.22	1422.96	209.65	65.32
#建筑工程	Construction	2783.15	1454.64	1328.51	124.15	22.98
安装工程	Construction and Installation	190.50	145.36	45.14	60.10	21.60
固定资产折旧	Depreciation on Fixed Assets	39.05	13.01	26.04	3.18	0.58
本年应付工资总额	Wages Payable of This Year	229.75	146.03	83.73	19.52	5.23
本年应付福利费总额	Welfare Costs Payable of This Year	17.41	11.52	5.90	1.15	0.36
工程结算税金及附加	Taxes abd Added Taxes of Settle Accounts	103.67	55.40	48.27	5.51	2.09
竣工产值（亿元）	Building Completed Output Value (100 million yuan)	1648.09	1077.60	570.50	146.84	37.63
房屋建筑施工面积（万平方米）	Floor Space Of Buildings under Construction (10000 sq.m)	19414.74	18852.45	562.28	952.70	7.06
#本年新开工	Beginning Projects inThis Year	10854.06	10518.66	335.41	750.68	2.99
投标承包面积	Floor Space of Bidding System	15013.76	14622.49	391.27	885.48	0.98
房屋建筑竣工面积（万平方米）	Floor Space of Buildings Completed (10000 sq.m)	9848.78	9601.95	246.83	347.61	0.40
自有机械设备总台数（万台）	Number of Machinery and Equipment Owned (10000 units)	48.59	32.11	16.47	3.26	2.02
自有机械设备总功率（万千瓦）	Total Power of Machinery and Equipment Owned (10000 Kw)	1111.92	472.28	439.64	51.41	17.82
自有机械设备净值（亿元）	Net Value of Machinery and Equipment Owned (100 million yuan)	214.23	87.75	126.48	10.13	2.92
职工平均人数（万人）	Annual Average Number of Staff and Workers (10000 person)	127.13	91.35	35.78	9.85	3.76
全员劳动生产率（元/人）	Overall Labor Productivity (yuan/person)	240792.10	179334.43	397697.04	212842.64	173723.40
技术装备率（元/人）	Value of Machines Per Laborer (yuan/person)	16851.25	9605.91	35349.36	10284.26	7765.96
动力装备率（千瓦/人）	Motive Power Per Labor (kW/person)	8.75	5.17	17.88	5.22	4.74
利润总额（亿元）	Total Profits (100 million yuan)	110.97	51.24	59.73	9.30	2.24

9-3 按登记注册类型分建筑业主要经济指标（2009）

指 标		tem		合 计 Total	内资企业 Domestic Funded	#国 有 State - Owned
施工企业个数	（个）	Number of Construction Enterprises	(unit)	2878	2852	291
建筑业总产值	（亿元）	Gross Output Value of Construction Enterprises	(100 million yuan)	3421.89	3413.99	1080.97
#建筑工程		Construction		2984.40	2980.49	964.45
安装工程		Construction and Installation		279.33	278.24	76.71
固定资产折旧		Depreciation on Fixed Assets		44.01	43.91	20.85
本年应付工资总额		Wages Payable of This Year		261.60	261.25	63.68
本年应付福利费总额		Welfare Costs Payable of This Year		19.42	19.39	4.47
工程结算税金及附加		Taxes abd Added Taxes of Settle Accounts		113.58	113.38	36.16
竣工产值	（亿元）	Building Completed Output Value	(100 million yuan)	1890.73	1886.57	422.97
房屋建筑施工面积	（万平方米）	Floor Space Of Buildings under Construction	(10000 sq.m)	20499.33	20491.33	4220.46
#本年新开工		Beginning Projects inThis Year		11696.37	11688.37	1365.52
#投标承包面积		Floor Space of Bidding System		15984.60	15984.60	2988.21
房屋建筑竣工面积	（万平方米）	Floor Space of Buildings Completed	(10000 sq.m)	10280.72	10272.72	1419.20
自有机械设备总台数	（万台）	Number of Machinery and Equipment Owned	(10000 units)	55.36	55.21	13.82
自有机械设备总功率	（万千瓦）	Total Power of Machinery and Equipment Owned	(10000 Kw)	1215.40	1214.31	498.34
自有机械设备净值	（亿元）	Net Value of Machinery and Equipment Owned	(100 million yuan)	234.11	234.03	89.24
职工平均人数	（万人）	Annual Average Number of Staff and Workers	(10000 person)	146.02	145.71	29.06
全员劳动生产率	（元/人）	Overall Labor Productivity	(yuan/person)	234343.93	234300.32	371978.66
技术装备率	（元/人）	Value of Machines Per Laborer	（yuan/person)	16032.74	16061.35	30708.88
动力装备率	（千瓦/人）	Motive Power Per Labor	(kW/person)	8.32	8.33	17.15
利润总额	（亿元）	Total Profits	(100 million yuan)	126.39	125.67	46.11

MAJOR ECONOMIC INDICATORS OF CONSTRUCTION ENTRPRISES BY REGISTRATION STATUS(2009)

#集 体 Collective - Collective - Owned	#股份合作 ShareHolding Cooperative Enterprises	#联 营 Joint - Owned Enterprises	#有限责任 Limited Liability Enterprises	#股份有限 Limited ShareHolding Enterprises	#私 营 Private - Owned Enterprises	#其 他 Others	港澳台商投资企业 Hongkong, Macao and Taiwan Funded Enterprises	外商投资企业 Foreign Funded Enterprises
152	18	10	917	171	1285	8	21	5
77.86	11.18	5.87	1437.40	205.02	580.15	15.59	4.34	3.56
70.67	10.49	5.23	1257.04	191.36	480.19	1.06	2.83	1.08
5.09	0.01	0.34	129.32	10.83	54.96	1.00	1.08	
0.74	0.14	0.05	14.64	1.38	5.92	0.20	0.07	0.20
9.24	1.54	1.05	107.81	15.35	62.05	0.53	0.26	0.10
0.71	0.12	0.13	7.74	1.24	4.94	0.04	0.01	0.01
2.70	0.37	0.20	47.74	6.86	19.17	0.20	0.09	0.10
46.33	7.72	5.35	829.92	146.09	415.10	13.09	3.10	1.06
799.43	113.61	71.22	7770.85	1763.46	5740.46	11.86	8.00	
543.64	85.87	39.50	4629.33	1110.62	3906.65	7.23	8.00	
582.46	113.40	63.25	6097.38	1451.76	4676.27	11.86		
494.71	51.44	46.03	3920.39	1015.23	3313.86	11.86	8.00	
2.31	0.23	0.15	19.76	2.87	15.88	0.20	0.05	0.10
30.94	3.83	2.25	330.31	120.70	226.73	1.23	0.92	0.16
4.79	1.02	0.48	78.69	11.44	47.58	0.80	0.04	0.04
7.22	0.94	0.69	54.60	11.44	41.57	0.20	0..23	0.08
107839.34	118936.17	85072.46	263260.07	179213.29	139559.78			445000.00
6634.35	10851.06	6956.52	14412.09	10000.00	11445.75			5000.00
4.29	4.07	3.26	6.05	10.55	5.45			2.00
3.00	0.21	0.21	42.63	6.81	26.17	0.52	0.64	0.08

9-4 按登记注册类型分建筑业财务状况（2009）

单位：亿元

指　标	Item	合　计 Total	内资企业 Domestic Funded	#国　有 State - Owned
资本金合计	Total Capital Assets	562.63	559.11	128.68
流动资产合计	Circulating Funds	2109.56	2099.41	817.75
#存货	Stock	690.79	689.06	291.55
固定资产合计	Total Fixed Assets	592.10	589.77	273.83
固定资产原价合计	Total Original Value of Fixed Assets	750.20	747.32	343.28
#生产经营用	Used By Production	512.98	510.68	210.78
累计折旧	Total Depreciation Drawn Accumulated	249.82	249.02	121.99
#本年折旧	Depreciation Drawn This Year	44.01	43.91	20.85
在建工程	Projets Under Construction	71.12	71.04	49.54
资产总计	Total Assets	3114.01	3101.08	1408.42
流动负债合计	Total Circulating Liability	1759.79	1752.18	772.02
长期负债合计	Total Long-Term Liability	416.74	416.74	329.37
所有者权益合计	Creditor's Equity	937.47	932.16	307.03
工程结算收入	Projets Settlement Revenue	3594.94	3586.71	1226.12
工程结算成本	Cost of Projets Settlement Accounts	3186.11	3179.07	1084.65
工程结算税金及附加	Tax and Extra Charges on Projets Settlement Accounts	113.58	113.38	36.16
工程结算利润	Profits of Projets Settlement Accounts	262.94	262.33	94.77
其他业务利润	Other Profits	7.94	7.18	3.56
管理费用	Management Expenses	120.29	119.96	40.89
#税金	Taxes	5.68	5.67	1.28
利润总额	Total Profits	126.39	125.67	46.11
应交所得税	Payable Income Taxes	23.13	22.92	7.31
应付利润	Payable Profits	39.73	39.70	9.00
本年应付工资总额	Payable Total Wages This Year	261.60	261.25	63.68
本年应付福利费	Payable Total Welfare This Year	19.42	19.39	4.47
亏损企业个数(个)	Number of Lossing-Making Enterprises	310	315	27

FINANCIAL INDICATORS OF CONSTRUCTION BY REGISTERATION STATUS (2009)

(100 million yuan)

#集 体 Collective - Owned	#股份合作 ShareHolding Cooperative Enterprises	#联 营 Joint - Owned Enterprises	#有限责任 Limited y Liabilit Enterprises	#股份有限 Limited ShareHolding Enterprises	#私营 Private - Owned Enterprises	#其他 Others	港澳台商投资企业 Hongkong, Macao and Taiwan Funded Enterprises	外商投资企业 Foreign Funded Enterprises
15.55	2.71	1.25	208.53	36.26	164.19	1.96	2.95	0.56
21.63	4.82	1.23	906.78	79.27	250.86	17.05	8.92	1.23
8.65	1.39	0.34	285.40	19.75	80.22	1.75	1.43	0.31
13.56	1.69	1.15	161.61	29.99	105.29	2.65	2.02	0.31
14.12	2.82	1.34	223.76	33.63	125.00	3.36	2.39	0.50
8.92	2.00	0.77	173.64	23.96	87.96	2.66	2.11	0.19
4.04	1.21	0.30	78.07	8.57	34.05	0.78	0.60	0.20
0.74	0.14	0.05	14.64	1.38	5.92	0.20	0.07	0.20
1.81	0.02	0.08	7.99	2.81	8.74	0.06	0.07	0.01
36.92	6.99	2.52	1135.41	114.59	375.78	20.45	11.31	0.91
14.79	3.56	0.77	746.13	53.51	144.53	16.87	6.98	0.64
1.97	0.11	0.10	70.77	4.61	9.81			
20.16	3.32	1.65	318.51	56.47	221.44	3.58	4.33	0.99
65.14	11.17	5.31	1572.36	180.09	509.06	17.46	4.98	3.25
54.53	10.00	4.57	1419.13	158.10	432.23	15.85	4.07	2.97
2.70	0.37	0.20	47.74	6.86	19.17	0.20	0.09	0.10
7.01	0.67	0.52	94.31	13.16	50.51	1.38	0.44	0.17
0.13	0.01		2.57	0.40	0.45	0.07	0.76	
3.30	0.39	0.30	49.22	4.85	20.43	0.58	0.24	0.09
0.26	0.04	0.01	1.93	0.56	1.56	0.04	0.01	
3.00	0.21	0.21	42.63	6.81	26.17	0.52	0.64	0.08
0.45	0.06	0.02	8.62	1.02	5.31	0.12	0.19	0.02
0.80	0.02	0.08	18.43	1.18	10.10	0.08	0.02	0.01
9.24	1.54	1.05	107.81	15.35	62.05	0.53	0.26	0.10
0.71	0.12	0.13	7.74	1.24	4.94	0.04	0.01	0.01
8	1		88	8	180	3	9	2

9-5 按行业分建筑业财务状况（2009）

FINANCIAL INDICATORS OF CNSTRUCTION BY SECTOR (2009)

单位：亿元 (100 million yuan)

指 标	Item	房屋和土木工程建筑业 Housing and Civil Engineering Construction	房屋工程 Housing Construction	土木工程 Civil Engineering	建筑安装业 Construction and Installation	建筑装饰业 Building Decorative Construction
资本金合计	Total Capital Assets	453.47	262.43	191.04	58.13	24.45
流动资产合计	Circulating Funds	1863.71	726.00	1137.71	151.12	46.32
#存货	Stock	628.60	244.66	383.94	37.78	13.75
固定资产合计	Total Fixed Assets	498.49	188.26	310.23	62.42	12.19
固定资产原价合计	Total Original Value of Fixed Assets	637.74	225.94	411.79	76.07	13.37
#生产经营用	Used By Production	443.70	161.75	281.95	45.32	8.44
累计折旧	Total Depreciation Drawn Accumulated	213.51	61.36	152.15	24.41	4.07
#本年折旧	Depreciation Drawn This Year	39.05	13.01	26.04	3.18	0.58
在建工程	Projets Under Construction	58.86	12.71	46.15	7.95	1.69
资产总计	Total Assets	2755.26	971.07	1784.20	226.86	60.84
流动负债合计	Total Circulating Liability	1575.94	536.04	1039.90	120.41	28.80
长期负债合计	Total Long-Term Liability	400.04	56.24	343.80	12.99	1.00
所有者权益合计	Creditor's Equity	779.29	378.80	400.49	93.47	31.05
工程结算收入	Projets Settlement Revenue	3269.91	1500.17	1769.74	193.63	56.30
工程结算成本	Cost of Projets Settlement Accounts	2914.06	1323.85	1590.21	162.24	46.71
工程结算税金及附加	Tax and Extra Charges on Projets Settlement Accounts	103.67	55.40	48.27	5.51	2.09
工程结算利润	Profits of Projets Settlement Accounts	225.54	104.77	120.77	22.05	6.45
其他业务利润	Other Profits	7.06	1.83	5.23	0.55	0.20
管理费用	Management Expenses	100.26	45.67	54.59	11.17	4.00
#税金	Taxes	4.87	3.20	1.66	0.49	0.14
利润总额	Total Profits	110.97	51.24	59.73	9.30	2.25
应交所得税	Payable Income Taxes	20.39	11.46	8.93	1.68	0.47
应付利润	Payable Profits	34.03	19.62	14.42	3.28	1.08
本年应付工资总额	Payable Total Wages This Year	229.75	146.03	83.73	19.52	5.23
本年应付福利费	Payable Total Welfare This Year	17.41	11.52	5.90	1.15	0.36
亏损企业个数(个)	Number of Lossing-Making Enterprises	87	51	36	94	98

9-6 分市州建筑业企业生产情况（2009）

STATISTICS ON PRODUCTION OF CONSTRUCTION ENTERPRISES OF CITIES AND PREFECTURE(2009)

单位：亿元 (100 million yuan)

项目	Item	建筑业总产值 Total Output Value of Construction Industry	建筑工程产值 Output Value of Construction Projects	安装工程产值 Output Value of Installation Projects	其他产值 Output Value of Other Projects	竣工产值 Output Value of Projects Completed
湖北省	Hubei Province	3421.89	2984.40	279.33	158.17	1890.73
武汉市	Wuhan Municipality	1967.84	1701.97	163.57	102.27	1062.25
黄石市	Huangshi Municipality	100.44	89.77	8.96	1.72	73.78
十堰市	Shiyan Municipality	158.60	152.76	4.30	1.54	32.99
宜昌市	Yichang Municipality	316.97	286.05	21.48	9.43	87.26
襄樊市	Xiangfan Municipality	126.87	106.06	19.25	1.56	63.72
鄂州市	Ezhou Municipality	49.22	38.42	9.27	1.53	29.38
荆门市	Jingmen Municipality	63.52	56.65	4.15	2.72	44.09
孝感市	Xiaogan Municipality	107.48	98.14	6.73	2.60	78.78
荆州市	Jingzhou Municipality	89.95	83.46	3.96	2.53	75.53
黄冈市	Huanggang Municipality	267.74	219.48	22.72	25.55	204.04
咸宁市	Xianning Municipality	41.26	37.34	1.53	2.39	33.74
随州市	Suizhou Municipality	29.35	25.10	2.58	1.67	22.36
恩施自治州	Enshi Prefecture	32.17	29.99	1.49	0.69	28.08
仙桃市	Xiantao Municipality	22.47	20.68	1.35	0.44	21.97
潜江市	Qianjiang Municipality	33.69	26.07	6.71	0.92	25.29
天门市	Tianmen Municipality	12.09	10.50	1.26	0.33	5.53
神农架林区	Shennongjia Forest Zone	2.23	1.96	0.02	0.27	1.94

9–7 分市州建筑业企业财务状况（2009）

单位：亿元

项目	Item	资产合计 Total Assets	流动资产合计 Total Circulating Assets	固定资产合计 Total Fixed Assets
湖北省	Hubei Province	3114.01	2109.56	592.10
武汉市	Wuhan Municipality	1974.69	1436.49	305.07
黄石市	Huangshi Municipality	74.23	55.89	15.94
十堰市	Shiyan Municipality	90.96	67.30	17.57
宜昌市	Yichang Municipality	523.64	275.32	108.16
襄樊市	Xiangfan Municipality	71.92	46.54	19.59
鄂州市	Ezhou Municipality	24.06	15.11	7.13
荆门市	Jingmen Municipality	49.26	33.34	11.46
孝感市	Xiaogan Municipality	50.79	31.50	17.32
荆州市	Jingzhou Municipality	51.40	25.90	19.31
黄冈市	Huanggang Municipality	86.58	51.06	31.19
咸宁市	Xianning Municipality	24.53	14.16	9.37
随州市	Suizhou Municipality	15.08	8.73	4.65
恩施自治州	Enshi Prefecture	27.00	16.09	9.52
仙桃市	Xiantao Municipality	8.45	5.27	2.74
潜江市	Qianjiang Municipality	29.78	19.61	9.23
天门市	Tianmen Municipality	8.17	4.77	2.98
神农架林区	Shennongjia Forest Zone	3.48	2.49	0.88

FINANCIAL INDICATORS OF CONSTRUCTION ENTERPRISES BY CITIES AND PREFECTURE (2009)

(100 million yuan)

流动负债合计 Total Circulating Liability	长期负债合计 Total Long-Term Liability	所有者权益合计 Creditor's Equity	工程结算收入 Projects Settlement Revenue	营业利润 Operating Profits	利润总额 Total Profits
1759.79	416.74	937.47	3594.94	124.51	126.39
1213.82	246.80	514.06	2229.77	67.31	66.63
44.32	0.54	29.37	94.85	2.95	2.90
68.29	1.38	21.29	152.09	3.34	3.11
244.11	151.46	128.06	352.84	15.03	19.79
34.84	3.86	33.22	101.10	5.31	4.67
9.15	0.81	14.10	45.21	2.79	2.80
31.47	0.65	17.13	61.63	1.72	1.69
17.31	3.12	30.36	98.67	5.83	5.72
14.75	2.50	34.15	86.23	3.11	2.68
30.94	2.84	52.81	199.87	10.41	9.93
10.55	0.87	13.11	39.25	1.92	1.90
5.84	0.30	8.95	26.25	0.95	0.87
9.98	0.99	16.03	32.97	1.39	1.36
3.29	0.04	5.12	17.16	0.61	0.55
14.99	0.51	14.27	42.72	1.10	1.08
4.05	0.03	4.09	12.17	0.69	0.65
2.09	0.06	1.32	2.14	0.06	0.05

9-8 分市州建筑业企业工程完成情况（2009）

STATISTICS ON PROJECTS COMPLETION OF CONSTRUCTION ENTERPRISES BY CITIES AND PREFECTURES (2009)

单位：万平方米 (10 000 sq.m)

项 目	Item	房屋建筑施工面积 Floor Space of Housing Construction	本年新开工面积 Beginning projects in This Year	实行投标承包面积 Actual Floor Space by Contracts and Bids	房屋建筑竣工面积 Floor Space of Housing Projects Completed	#住 宅 Residential Buildings	#办公用房 Office Buildings
湖北省	Hubei Province	20499.3	11696.4	15984.6	10280.7	6454.8	773.7
武汉市	Wuhan Municipality	11121.1	5392.1	8222.3	4659.8	2999.5	303.1
黄石市	Huangshi Municipality	841.2	529.6	674.4	396.2	243.1	11.0
十堰市	Shiyan Municipality	437.9	280.6	286.0	204.1	144.8	8.8
宜昌市	Yichang Municipality	755.4	404.3	617.5	458.1	232.1	42.9
襄樊市	Xiangfan Municipality	662.3	479.6	565.2	344.0	223.1	21.9
鄂州市	Ezhou Municipality	547.7	434.1	513.1	312.9	229.1	8.6
荆门市	Jingmen Municipality	339.6	226.1	246.2	256.2	140.8	15.1
孝感市	Xiaogan Municipality	1164.5	791.0	923.5	731.0	528.1	38.9
荆州市	Jingzhou Municipality	755.3	515.0	599.4	484.1	230.9	40.0
黄冈市	Huanggang Municipality	2119.0	1645.7	1987.3	1396.8	804.2	173.6
咸宁市	Xianning Municipality	414.6	253.9	296.4	315.5	218.5	18.1
随州市	Suizhou Municipality	324.9	200.0	255.8	229.8	158.7	21.8
恩施自治州	Enshi Prefecture	345.4	170.5	184.9	146.5	79.5	24.6
仙桃市	Xiantao Municipality	287.7	159.5	270.3	171.0	112.5	21.9
潜江市	Qianjiang Municipality	238.1	131.0	220.5	111.1	73.9	9.8
天门市	Tianmen Municipality	133.9	75.5	113.3	54.7	31.1	11.4
神农架林区	Shennongjia Forest Zone	10.6	7.8	8.5	8.7	4.7	2.4

主要统计指标解释

建筑业统计单位 指从事房屋、构筑物建造和设备安装活动的法人企业。建筑业法人企业应具有建筑业资质并能够独立核算，同时其应具备以下条件：①依法成立，有自己的名称、组织机构和场所，能够承担民事责任；②独立拥有和使用资产，承担负债，有权与其他单位签订合同；③独立核算盈亏，能够编制资产负债表。

建筑业总产值 是以货币形式表现的建筑业企业在一定时期内生产的建筑业产品和提供的服务的总和。建筑业总产值包括：

⑴建筑工程产值：指列入建筑工程预算内的各种工程价值。

⑵安装工程产值：指设备安装工程价值，不包括被安装设备本身的价值。

⑶其他产值：建筑业总产值中除建筑工程、安装工程以外的产值。包括房屋构筑物修理产值、非标准设备制造产值、总包企业向分包企业收取的管理费以及不能明确划分的施工活动所完成的产值。

a.房屋构筑物修理产值：指房屋和构筑物修理所完成的产值，但不包括被修理房屋、构筑物本身价值和生产设备的修理产值。

b.非标准设备制造产值：指加工制造没有定型的非标准生产设备的加工费和原材料价值(如化工厂、炼油厂用的各种罐、槽，矿井生产统一使用的各种漏斗、三角槽、阀门等)以及附属加工厂为本企业承建工程制作的非标准设备的价值。

建筑业增加值 指建筑业企业在报告期内以货币形式表现的建筑业生产经营活动的最终成果。

从 2004 年第一次全国经济普查开始，建筑业现价增加值按生产法和分配法(收入法)两种方法计算，以收入法的计算结果为准，即从收入的角度出发，根据生产要素在生产过程中应得的收入份额计算。具体计算方法：经济普查年度建筑业增加值按照《经济普查年度 GDP 核算方案》计算，非经济普查年度建筑业增加值按照《非经济普查年度 GDP 核算方案》计算。

房屋建筑施工面积 指在报告期内施过工的全部房屋建筑面积，包括本期新开工的房屋面积、上期施工跨入本期继续施工的房屋面积、上期停缓建在本期恢复施工的房屋面积、本期竣工的房屋面积及本期施工后又停缓建的房屋面积。

房屋建筑竣工面积 指在报告期内房屋建筑按照设计要求全部完工，达到了使用条件，经验收鉴定合格，正式移交使用单位的房屋建筑面积。

Explanatory Notes on Main Statistical Indicators

Statistical Unit in Construction refers to corporate enterprise engaged in the construction of buildings and structures and in the installation of equipment. A corporate construction enterprise should have qualification certificates with independent accounting system, and should meet the following 3 requirements: a) being set up in line with relevant legal basis, having its full name, organization and location, and capable of taking civil liabilities; b) independently possessing and using its assets and assuming its liabilities, and entitled to sign contracts with other institutions; and c) making independent accounts of its profits and losses, and capable of compiling its own balance sheet.

Gross Output Value of Construction refers to total of construction products and services, expressed in money terms, produced or rendered by construction and installation enterprises during a given period of time. It includes:

(1) Output value of construction projects, that is the value of projects covered by the project budgets;

(2) Output value of installation projects, that is the value of the installation of equipment, (excluding the value of the equipment

to be installed);

(3) Output value of others, that is the output value of construction industry excluding that of construction projects and installation projects. It includes: output value of repair of buildings and structures; output value of non-standard equipment manufacturing; overhead expenses received by contracted enterprises to the sub-contracted enterprises and the completed output value of construction activities that have no clear definition.

a. Output value of repair of buildings and structures, that is the value created through the repairs of buildings or structures, but does not include the value of buildings or structures being repaired and the value of the repair of production equipment;

b. Output value of manufactured non-standard equipment, that is the value of non-standard production equipment including raw materials and manufacturing cost made for the construction project (i.e., chemical plant; kettles or tanks used by refineries; various fillers, triangle tanks, valves used by mines), and the output value of equipment manufactured by subsidiary workshops.

Value-added of Construction refers to the final result of the activities of production and management of construction industry in monetary terms in the reference period.

Starting from the 2004 economic census, value-added of construction is calculated by both production approach and income approach, with the income approach as the final approach, where the calculation is based on the share of production factor in the production process. Specifically, value-added of construction for census years is calculated in accordance with the Programme of Compilation of GDP and National Accounts for the Year of Economic Census, and value-added of construction for other years is calculated in accordance with the Programme of Compilation of GDP and National Accounts for the Non Economic Census Years.

Floor Space of Buildings Under Construction refers to floor space of buildings under construction during the reference period, including newly started buildings, buildings started earlier and continued during the reference period, and buildings suspended earlier but restarted during the reference period, buildings completed during the reference period, and buildings under construction and then suspended during the reference period.

Floor Space of Buildings Completed refers to the floor space of buildings that are completed in the reference period in accordance with the requirements of the design, up to the standard for putting them into use, and have been checked and accepted by concerned departments as qualified ones.

10 交通运输、邮电

Transportation, Postal and Telecommunications Services

资料整理：李文强

交通运输、邮电

Transportation and communication,Post service
2009

全社会客运量	Passenger Capacity of The Whole Society	96219(万人)
#公路	Public Road	88703(万人)
全社会货运量	Volume of Freight Traffic	82714(万吨)
#公路	Public Road	59563(万吨)
邮电业务总量	Postal Service Portfolio	839.18(亿元)
#函件	Letters	1.45(亿件)
年末市内电话用户	Local Telephone Subscriber End of Year	1088.3(万户)
年末移动电话用户	Mobile Phone Subscriber End of Year	3136.9(万户)

全 社 会 客 货 运 量
Passenger Capactity of The Whole Society

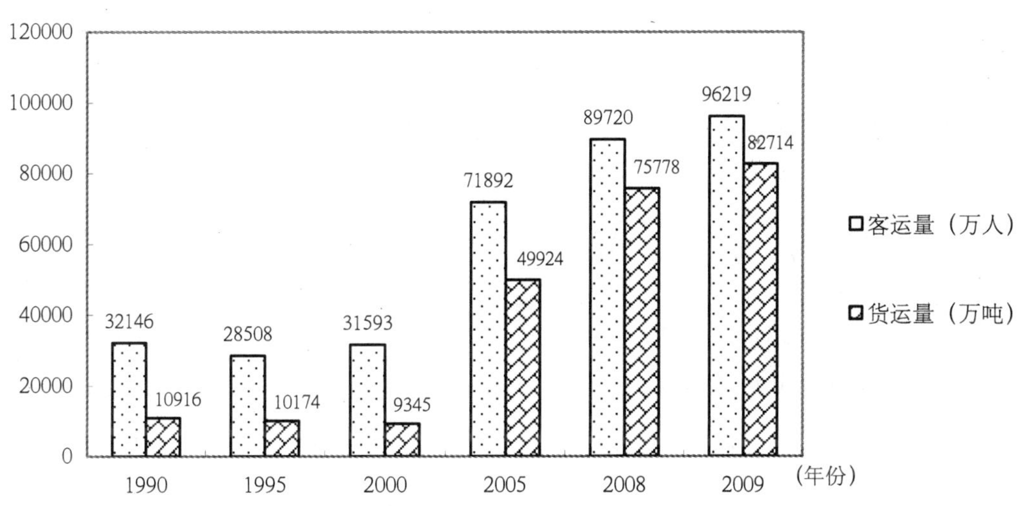

附：全社会客货运量
Passenger Capacity of The Whole Society

	客运量（万人） Passenger Capacity (10 000 persons)	货运量（万吨） volume of freight traffic (10 000 tons)
1990	32146	10916
1995	28508	10174
2000	31593	9345
2005	71892	49924
2007	84088	58523
2008	89720	75778
2009	96219	82714

10-1 交通运输业基本情况

指标		Item		1990	1995
运输线路长度	(公里)	Length of Transportation Routes	(km)		
铁路营业里程		Total Railway's Length in Operation		1634.00	1940.00
铁路正线延展长度		Mainline Railway's Length Completed			
公路通车里程		Total Highway in Operation		47511.00	48728.00
#等级公路里程		Length of Expressway and Class I to IV Highway		24532.00	30910.00
#高速公路		Expressway			
一级公路		Class I Highway		196.00	641.00
二级公路		Class II Highway		1973.00	4967.00
内河航道里程		Navigable Inland Waterways		8960.00	8969.00
公路桥梁	(座)	Highway Bridges	(unit)		
	(米)		(m)		
客运量总计	(万人)	Total Passenger Traffic	(10 000 persons)	32145.93	28508.20
铁路		Railway		2107.00	2300.00
公路		Highway		27333.00	24315.00
水运		Waterway		2693.00	1745.00
民用航空		Civil Aviation		12.93	150.00
旅客周转量	(亿人公里)	Turnover Volume of Passenger Traffic	(100 million persons-km)	225.85	285.29
货物运输量总计	(万吨)	Total Freight Traffic	(10 000 tons)	10916.10	10173.62
铁路		Railway		3901.00	3986.00
公路		Highway		2941.00	2600.00
水运		Waterway		3784.00	3585.00
货物周转量	(亿吨公里)	Turnover Volume of FreightTraffic	(100 million tons-km)	670.53	776.44
民用车辆拥有量	(万辆)	Civil Moto Vehicles			
#民用汽车拥有量		Civil Vehicles		20.32	34.89
#载客汽车		Passenger Vehicles		6.08	14.96
载货汽车		Trucks		13.04	18.61
#营运汽车		Moto Vehicles in Operation			
#私人汽车		Private Vehicles			
民用运输船舶拥有量	(艘)	Civil Transpot Vessels	(10 000 units)		
机动船		Moto Vessels			
驳船		Barges			
港口货物吞吐量	(万吨)	Cargo Handled at Ports	(10 000 tons)		

TRANSPORTATION

2000	2004	2005	2006	2007	2008	2009
2025.00	2166.00	2758.00	2759.00	2102.80	2826.00	2990.00
			3117.60	3198.20	4545.60	4587.80
57850.00	89673.00	91131.00	181791.00	183780.00	188366.00	197196.00
48062.00	72757.00	76075.00	135828.00	147152.00	153665.40	168833.90
569.00	1353.00	1649.00	1747.00	2365.00	2718.70	3283.20
611.00	973.00	1092.00	1278.00	1371.00	1566.40	1725.10
7911.00	14200.00	15225.00	15560.00	15732.00	16042.50	16261.20
8309.00	8988.00	8988.00	8988.00	8988.00	8988.00	8988.00
8222.00	10186.00	21076.00	20997.00	23389.00	23865.00	28809.00
324124.00	495368.00	802132.00	833725.00	1021418.00	1093302.00	1353397.01
31593.00	67362.11	71892.00	75440.00	84088.00	89720.00	96219.00
3469.00	3267.00	4615.00	4850.00	5125.00	6026.50	6440.00
27184.00	63127.00	66183.00	69335.00	77514.00	82532.00	88703.00
679.00	522.00	601.00	706.00	736.00	388.00	371.00
261.00	446.11	494.00	549.00	712.70	773.50	705.00
398.32	703.95	803.90	847.42	947.71	1077.70	1096.31
9345.19	43291.82	49923.52	52600.00	58523.47	75778.00	82714.00
3857.00	4442.00	8491.00	8990.00	9728.50	10202.00	9839.00
2228.00	31584.00	33481.00	35361.00	39568.00	52759.00	59563.00
3255.00	7259.00	7944.00	8242.00	9027.00	12681.00	13305.00
831.64	1628.88	1682.48	1726.10	1902.17	2699.97	2808.46
	406.08	39.39	437.37	497.06	573.10	760.97
47.55	94.37	103.04	117.82	135.74	156.42	187.03
24.69	46.25	53.40	65.39	78.62	94.41	119.81
21.72	29.79	30.96	30.96	33.92	38.54	46.07
	18.05	20.33	21.17	23.65	26.87	32.20
41.72	51.09	59.66	70.85	86.12	102.35	131.56
5905.00	4484.00	5362.00	5459.00	5241.00	5557.00	5460.00
4188.00	3697.00	4158.00	4290.00	4338.00	4270.00	4175.00
1717.00	787.00	1204.00	1169.00	903.00	1287.00	1285.00
4113.46	11659.37	13992.51	14556.70	15442.23	15970.58	16671.77

10-2 客 运 量

PASSENGER TRAFFIC

单位:万人 (10 000 persons)

年份 Year	总计 Total	铁路 Railway	公路 Highway	水运 Waterway	民用航空 Civil Aviation
1978	12009.20	2854.00	7429.00	1722.00	4.20
1980	16629.26	3217.00	11282.00	2123.00	7.26
1985	28178.22	3353.00	22378.00	2433.00	14.22
1986	31576.50	2905.00	25597.00	3055.00	19.50
1987	33452.98	2910.00	27575.00	2942.00	25.98
1988	35233.96	3214.00	28908.00	3096.00	15.96
1989	34682.13	2806.00	28794.00	3069.00	13.13
1990	32145.93	2107.00	27333.00	2693.00	12.93
1991	33982.62	2016.00	29279.00	2654.00	33.62
1992	34726.00	2077.00	29635.00	2894.00	120.00
1993	30152.00	2265.00	25116.00	2665.00	106.00
1994	29607.00	2358.00	24819.00	2210.00	120.00
1995	28508.20	2300.00	24315.00	1743.00	150.00
1996	29045.40	2248.00	25180.00	1449.00	168.00
1997	29503.08	2127.00	25684.00	1538.00	154.08
1998	28208.00	2218.00	24540.00	1306.00	144.00
1999	29360.14	2545.00	25596.00	1080.00	139.14
2000	63306.00	3469.00	58897.00	679.00	261.00
2001	62696.00	3632.00	58018.00	767.00	279.00
2002	63382.00	3813.00	58623.00	638.00	308.00
2003	62880.00	3602.00	58371.00	573.00	334.42
2004	68167.00	4072.00	63127.00	522.00	446.11
2005	71892.00	4615.00	66183.00	601.00	494.00
2006	75440.00	4850.00	69335.00	706.00	549.00
2007	84088.00	5125.00	77514.00	736.00	712.70
2008	89720.00	6027.00	82532.00	388.00	774.00
2009	96219.00	6440.00	88703.00	371.00	705.00

注:2003年以后为全社会口径

Note: after the whole society with a

10–3 旅 客 周 转 量
TURNOVER VOLUME OF PASSENGER TRAFFIC

单位:亿人公里 (100 million person-kms)

年份 Year	总计 Total	铁路 Railway	公路 Highway	水运 Waterway	民用航空 Civil Aviation
1978	69.38	30.72	24.85	13.54	0.17
1980	95.88	41.79	36.20	17.52	0.37
1985	185.25	84.00	81.33	19.40	0.52
1989	260.61	104.16	119.50	36.05	0.90
1990	225.85	82.83	112.83	29.28	0.91
1991	257.68	98.09	126.70	30.19	2.70
1992	286.35	104.89	135.61	34.72	11.13
1993	281.28	113.60	123.64	33.50	10.54
1994	283.98	121.91	121.40	28.71	11.96
1995	285.29	129.47	117.76	22.71	15.35
1996	285.04	121.17	124.97	21.09	17.81
1997	282.53	118.62	123.39	24.14	16.38
1998	278.66	126.68	118.51	18.79	14.68
1999	300.38	146.54	124.46	14.09	15.29
2000	563.78	232.00	297.46	8.84	25.48
2001	574.24	248.00	293.35	5.87	27.02
2002	633.6.9	283.00	317.02	3.60	30.07
2003	617.68	271.00	309.00	4.00	33.68
2004	703.95	322.80	334.00	3.20	43.95
2005	803.90	389.40	358.00	4.20	52.30
2006	847.42	408.10	374.80	5.10	59.42
2007	947.71	440.80	423.80	5.30	77.81
2008	1077.68	474.01	522.57	2.30	78.80
2009	1096.31	466.70	562.34	2.49	64.78

10–4 货 运 量

FREIGHT TRAFFIC

单位:万吨 (10 000 tons)

年份 Year	总计 Total	铁路 Railway	公路 Highway	水运 Waterway	#内河 Inland Waterway	#海运 Seashipping
1978	10199.08	3513.00	3556.00	3130.00		
1980	8420.17	3211.00	2199.00	3110.00		
1985	11059.25	2659.00	3852.00	3463.00		
1989	11608.16	4148.00	3164.00	4062.00		
1990	10916.10	3901.00	2941.00	3784.00		
1991	11217.38	3957.00	2999.00	3996.00		
1992	11565.41	4018.00	2828.00	4364.00		
1993	11183.58	4029.00	2734.00	4248.00		
1994	10662.73	3964.00	2666.00	3641.00		
1995	10173.62	3986.00	2600.00	3585.00		
1996	9927.74	3779.00	2537.00	3268.00		
1997	9389.06	3882.00	2280.00	3119.00		
1998	10153.79	3999.00	2009.00	4040.00		
1999	10517.39	3964.00	2141.00	4313.00		
2000	40948.50	6558.00	27863.30	6270.00	6202.00	68.00
2001	41475.82	7093.50	29851.00	4275.00	4198.36	76.80
2002	42063.55	7400.00	28777.00	5630.00	5389.80	240.30
2003	44661.05	7825.00	30348.00	6195.00	5830.10	364.80
2004	47073.05	7871.60	31584.00	7259.00	6823.00	436.00
2005	50316.82	8491.00	33481.00	7944.00	7466.00	478.00
2006	52884.55	8990.00	35361.00	8242.00	7679.00	536.00
2007	58523.47	9728.50	39568.00	9027.00	7765.00	1262.00
2008	75777.94	10202.00	52759.00	12681.00	8182.00	4499.00
2009	82714.00	9839.00	59563.00	13305.00	8108.00	5197.00

10–5 货物周转量

TURNOVER VOLUME OF FREIGHT TRAFFIC

单位:亿吨公里 (100 million ton-km)

年份 Year	总计 Total	铁路 Railway	公路 Highway	水运 Waterway	#内河 Inland Waterway	#海运 Seashipping
1978	281.09	191.72	9.22	80.15		
1980	326.85	206.14	9.85	110.85		
1985	507.57	320.37	16.59	169.94		
1989	710.01	425.31	17.05	262.33		
1990	670.53	415.17	14.72	235.04		
1991	720.23	455.00	14.67	245.41		
1992	757.00	461.81	13.89	272.70		
1993	753.52	477.64	11.99	259.90		
1994	743.21	505.57	10.23	222.32		
1995	776.44	544.40	9.62	222.20		
1996	775.79	552.32	9.93	208.05		
1997	725.34	501.77	8.72	212.21		
1998	696.62	465.81	7.59	220.63		
1999	696.27	457.70	8.25	227.76		
2000	1156.57	618.37	227.16	305.29	295.07	10.22
2001	1097.60	634.90	218.97	237.31	226.15	11.16
2002	1212.82	680.00	211.49	313.60	271.30	42.29
2003	1313.13	703.80	224.00	377.00	315.38	61.61
2004	1485.76	781.83	235.60	461.08	395.75	65.33
2005	1689.86	987.60	251.00	443.20	391.05	105.00
2006	1730.93	1021.40	266.10	437.90	379.81	58.10
2007	1902.17	1138.20	302.09	458.00	361.93	95.83
2008	2699.97	1096.90	789.37	810.46	416.17	394.29
2009	2808.46	1032.40	930.10	845.18	402.82	442.36

10-6 全省民用车辆拥有量（2009）
NUMBER OF CIVIL MOTOR VEHICLES OWNED BY WHOLE PROVINCE(2009)

单位:辆 (coach)

指标	Item	总计 Total	营运 Working	非营运 Non-Working	#进口 Import
合计	Total	7609682	632358	5950424	51957
汽车	Civil Vehicles	1870251	522775	1347476	42714
载客汽车	Passenger Vehicles	1198070	98947	1099123	41662
#大型	Lage Scale	41568	30781	10787	220
中型	Medium Scale	52159	20014	32145	1214
小型	Small Scale	1072568	46010	1026558	40180
#轿车	Cars	753512	36123	717389	23295
载货汽车	Trucks	460673	321952	138721	594
#重型	Heavy Scale	70191	64543	5648	190
中型	Medium Scale	124436	100781	23655	105
轻型	Light Scale	258841	153954	104887	293
#普通载货	Ordinary Trucks	228633	128793	99840	300
其他汽车	Other Vehicles	211508	101876	109632	458
#三轮汽车	Tricycle Motocars	87239	39770	47469	
低速汽车	Low Speed Vehicles	99822	57727	42095	2
摩托车	Motorear	4693557	92765	4600792	9206
#普通	Ordinary Motor	4592684	92611	4500073	8421
轻便	Light Motor	100873	154	100719	785
拖拉机	Tractors	1026900			
大中型	Large	118600			
小型方向盘式	Small Scale	908300			
挂车	Freight Trailers	17314	16270	1044	30
其他类型车	Other Motor Vehicles	1404	373	1031	7

注:本表“其他汽车”中，包括三轮和四轮农用运输车。
Notes:Tricycles and four-wheel farming vehiles are induded "Others"

10–7 私人车辆拥有量
NUMBER OF PRIVATE - OWNED VEHICLES

单位：辆 (coach)

指　标	Item	2000	2005	2006	2007	2008	2009
民用汽车	Civil Vehicles	475500	596601	708477	861160	1084444	1315569
载客汽车	Passenger Vehicles	245500	297095	380005	492974	629791	865582
#大型	Lage Scale	29200	3312	2842	2905	3120	3078
轿车	Cars		177650	242495	324616	423215	581163
载货汽车	Ordinary Trucks	211400	135352	143655	166099	197129	263129
#重型	Heavy Scale		8766	10203	12195	14366	25130
其它汽车	Others		164154	184817	202087	196601	186858
摩托车	Motors	1241000	2853113	3141644	3379278	4117488	4663593
载货挂车	Freight Trailers	4400	1714	1983	2922	3720	4935
拖拉机	Tractors	17600	504503	641900	834100		

10–8 全省公路运输汽车拥有量
NUMBER OF TRANSPORT MOTOR VEHICLES OWNED BY WHOLE PROVINCE

单位：辆 (coach)

指标	Item	2000	2005	2006	2007	2008	2009
合计	Total	179382	265399	281555	287441	308078	382066
载客汽车	Passenger Vehicles	36907	64358	66360	68185	69311	72801
客位　(万客位)	Seats　(10000 seats)	62.25	83.02	85.27	89.01	92.00	97.90
载货汽车	Trucks	142475	201041	215195	219256	238767	309265
#普通载货汽车	Ordinary Trucks	140391	192631	197792	209099	230157	249197
吨位　(万吨)	Tonnages　(10000 tons)		65.58	69.40	69.70	78.77	135.05

10−9 全社会运输船舶拥有量

指标	Item	2005			2006		
		艘 Number (unit)	载客量 (客位) Passenger Capacity (seat)	净载重量 (万吨位) Dead Weight Tonnages 10000	艘 Number (unit)	载客量 (客位) Passenger Capacity (seat)	净载重量 (万吨位) Dead Weight Tonnages 10000
机动船	Motor Vessels	4158		177.79	4290		206.59
内河船舶	Inland Waterways Vessels	3986		135.35	4098		157.29
客船	Passenger Ships	712	36580		702	37872	
货船	Cargo Ships	3117		177.74	3249		206.59
#油轮	Oil Tankers	62		5.54	103		9.23
拖轮	Tugboats	321			337		
驳船	Cargo Barges	1204		107.90	1169		114.65
海洋、海运船舶	Seaging Vessels	172		42.45	192		49.30

NUMBER OF TRANSPOT VESSELS OWND BY WHOLE PROVINCE

2007			2008			2009		
艘 Number (unit)	载客量 (客位) Passenger Capacity (seat)	净载重量 (万吨位) Dead Weight Tonnages 10000	艘 Number (unit)	载客量 (客位) Passenger Capacity (seat)	净载重量 (万吨位) Dead Weight Tonnages 10000	艘 Number (unit)	载客量 (客位) Passenger Capacity (seat)	净载重量 (万吨位) Dead Weight Tonnages 10000
4338	36779	232.4	4270	37705	3274338	4175	35248	3780697
4134	35554	175.89	4009	37705	1952686	3909	35248	2255156
745	35554		759	36930		645	34418	
3238		232.4	3101		327	3168		377.72
130		10.58	96		10	116		10.31
353			409			358		
903		108.68	1287		165.75	1285		170.08
204		56.5	261		132.17	266		152.55

10—10 邮电业务基本情况
BASIC CONDITIONS OF THE POST AND TELECOMMUNICATION SERVICES

指　　标	Item	2000	2005	2007	2008	2009
邮电业务总量 (亿元)	Total Volume of Post and Telecommunication Services (100 million yuan)		373.63	588.40	713.80	839.18
邮政业务总量	Postal Services	21.50	23.40	30.95	38.70	41.29
电信业务总量	Telecommunication Services		350.20	550.00	678.10	797.89
函件 (亿件)	Letters (100 million pcs)	3.60	1.30	1.27	1.37	1.45
包件 (万件)	Parcels (10000 pcs)	473	320	294	234	197
特快专递 (万件)	Special Express (10000 pcs)	428	685	986	3407	3840
报刊期发数 (万份)	Newspaper and Magzines Circulation (10000 pcs)		643	561	555	564
固定电话用户	Urban Telephone Subscribers at Year-end	726	1236	1279	1179	1088
年末城市电话 (万户)	(10000 subscribers)	546	900	864	777	710
年末农村电话 (万户)	Rural Telephones (10000 subscribers)	180	336	415	402	378
年末移动电话用户 (万户)	Mobile Telephone Subscribers at Year-end (10000 subscribers)		1401	1941	2529	3137
互联网宽带接入用户 (万户)	Internet Users (10000 subscribers)		128	269	286	361
邮电局所、服务网点合计 (处)	Post and Telecommunication Offices	2047	1933	1919	2134	1910
邮路总长度(单程) (公里)	Length of Postal Routes and Rural Delivery			90327	79223	83796
邮路线路总条数	Routes (10000 km)			555	414	413
农村投递线路条数 (条)	Highway Routes			3573	4487	4297
农村投递线路长度(单程:公里)	Railway Routes			169610	190582	195327
邮电通信工具拥有量	Telecommunication Facilities					
固定电话局用交换机容量 (万门)	City Swicthboard Capacity (10000 unit)		1587.0	1748.1	1795.0	1732.8
移动电话交换机容量 (万户)	Mobile Telephone Swicthboard Capacity (10000 unit)				4296.0	5447.7
固定长途电话交换机容量 (万路端)	Capacity of Long Distance Telephone Switchborad (circuit)		46.6	61.4	66.2	64.7
长途光缆线路长度 (万公里)	Length of Long Distance Optical Cable (km)			2.3	2.8	2.9

注：从2008年起特快专递数为全社会规模以上快递公司发送的数。

Note: From 2008 onwards the number of EMS over the scale of the whole society to send the number of courier companies.

10-11 邮电通信水平

LEVEL OF POST AND TELECOMMUNICATION SERVICES

指　　标	Item	2000	2005	2006	2007	2008	2009
邮电通信水平	Level of Postal and Telecommunication						
每百人平均函件量　（件/百人）	Average Number of Letters Mailed Per 100 Persons (unit/100 person)	638.8	228	263	209	240	253
每百人平均订阅报刊量（份/百人）	Average Number of Newspaper and Magzines Subscribed Per 100 Persons (unit/100 person)		978	888	727	888	893
每百人平均包件　（件/百人）	Average Number of Parcels Per 100 Persons (unit/100 person)	8.3	5.6	5.7	4.8	4.1	3.4
电话普及率　（部/百人）	Rate of Popularization of Telephone (unit/100 person)		43.9	52.7	58.7	65.1	.74.0
移动电话普及率　（部/百人）	Rate of Popularization of Mobile Phones (unit/100 person)		23.3	29.5	32	44.3	54.9

主要统计指标解释

铁路营业里程 又称营业长度(包括正式营业和临时营业里程)，指办理客货运输业务的铁路正线总长度。凡是全线或部分建成双线及以上的线路，以第一线的实际长度计算；复线、站线、段管线、岔线和特殊用途线以及不计算运费的联络线都不计算营业里程。该指标可以反映铁路运输业基础设施的发展水平，也是计算客货周转量、运输密度和机车车辆运用效率等指标的基础资料。

铁路电气化里程 指在全部铁路营业里程中已安装了供电线路及设备，可以供电力机车牵引列车运行的区段的总里程。

铁路自动、半自动闭塞里程 指装有列车自动或人工完成闭塞状态的铁路设备里程。为保证列车安全运行，在一个区间、同一时间内，一般只允许一列列车运行，这种保证列车在这个区间安全间隔运行的技术方法称为“闭塞”。自动或半自动闭塞里程占铁路营业里程的比重是反映铁路现代化的重要标志之一。

公路里程 指在一定时期内实际达到《公路工程[WTBZ]技术标准 JTJ01－88》规定的等级公路，并经公路主管部门正式验收交付使用的公路里程数。包括大中城市的郊区公路以及通过小城镇街道部分的公路里程和桥梁、渡口的长度，不包括大中城市的街道、厂矿、林区生产用道和农业生产用道的里程。两条或多条公路共同经由同一路段，只计算一次，不得重复计算里程长度。该指标可以反映公路建设的发展规模，也是计算运输网密度等指标的基础资料。

内河航道里程 也称内河通航里程，指在一定时期内，能通航运输船舶及排筏的天然河流、湖泊水库、运河及通航渠道的长度。包括全年季节性通航累计三个月以上的航道，不包括仅供零散流放竹、木排的河道。该指标可以反映内河水运网的规模、水平和发展情况。

民用航空航线里程 指民航运输定期班机飞行的航线长度的总和。航线长度按机场之间的距离计算，通常有两种计算方法：一是将每条航线长度相加称为重复计算航线里程；一是将两线或两条以上航线经过同一区段里程，只计算一次航线长度称为不重复计算航线里程。一般常用的是后者，该指标可以确切反映民航运输网的规模，是表明民航事业为国民经济服务和方便人民生活程度的主要指标。

输油(气)管道长度 也称输油(气)里程，指油品(或天然气)的实际输送距离，一般按输油(气)管道的单线长度计算。若包括复线和备用线长度则称为输油(气)管道延展长度，是指管道铺设的实际长度。我们通常使用的是不包括复线的“输油(气)管道里程”，该指标可以反映管道运输的发展规模和水平。

货(客)运量 指在一定时期内，各种运输工具实际运送的货物(旅客)数量。该指标是反映运输业为国民经济和人民生活服务的数量指标，也是制定和检查运输生产计划、研究运输发展规模和速度的重要指标。货运按吨计算，客运按人计算。货物不论运输距离长短、货物类别，均按实际重量统计。旅客不论行程远近或票价多少，均按一人一次客运量统计；半价票、小孩票也按一人统计。

货(客)运密度 指在一定时期内某种运输方式在营运线路的某一区段平均每公里线路通过的货物(旅客)运输周转量。计算公式为：

$$货（客）运密度=\frac{货物（旅客）周转量}{营业线路长度}$$

该指标可以反映交通运输线路上的货物(旅客)运输量运输繁忙程度，是平衡运输线路运输能力和通过能力，规划线路建设及改造、配备技术设备，研究运输网布局的重要依据。

货物(旅客)周转量 指在一定时期内，由各种运输工具运送的货物(旅客)数量与其相应运输距离的乘积之总和。该指标可以反映运输业生产的总成果，也是编制和检查运输生产计划，计算运输效率、劳动生产率以及核算运输单位成本的主要基础资料。计算货物周转量通常按发出站与到达站之间的最短距离，也就是计费距离计算。计算公式为：

货物（旅客）周转量=Σ（货物（旅客）运输量×运输距离）

民用汽车拥有量 指报告期末，在公安交通管理部门按照《机动车注册登记工作规范》，已注册登记领有民用车辆牌照的全部汽车数量。汽车拥有量统计的主要分类：根据汽车结构分为载客汽车、载货汽车及其他汽车；根据汽车所有者不同分

为个人(私人)汽车、单位汽车；根据汽车的使用性质分为营运汽车、非营运汽车；根据汽车大小规格不同载客汽车分为大型、中型、小型和微型，载货汽车分为重型、中型、轻型和微型。

邮电业务总量 指以价值量形式表现的邮电通信企业为社会提供各类邮电通信服务的总数量。邮电业务量按专业分类包括函件、包件、汇票、报刊发行、邮政快件、特快专递、邮政储蓄、集邮、公众电报、用户电报、传真、长途电话、出租电路、无线寻呼、移动电话、分组交换数据通信、出租代维等。计算方法为各类产品乘以相应的平均单价(不变价)之和，再加上出租电路和设备、代用户维护电话交换机和线路等的服务收入。该指标综合反映了一定时期邮电业务发展的总成果，是研究邮电业务量构成和发展趋势的重要指标。计算公式为：

邮电业务总量=Σ（各类邮电业务量×不变单价）+出租代维及其他业务收入

=邮政业务总量+电信业务总量

无线寻呼用户 无线寻呼是指电话用户通过无线寻呼中心，在规定范围内向携带小型寻呼机的用户发出声音、数字或文字显示信息。在寻呼台办理登记手续携带小型寻呼机的用户，称为无线寻呼用户。

移动电话用户 指通过移动电话交换机进入移动电话网、占用移动电话号码的各类电话用户。包括签约用户和智能网预付费用户。一个移动电话号码统计为一户。

互联网上网人数 指平均每周使用互联网至少 1 小时的中国公民人数。

本地电话用户 指接入本地电信运营商固定电话网上的电话用户。包括：住宅用户、单位用户、公用电话用户等。按电话用户位置又分为市内电话用户和农村电话用户。1997 年以前，“市内电话用户”是指接入县城及县以上城市的电话网上的电话用户；“农村电话用户”是指接入县邮电局农话台及县以下农村电话交换点，以县城为中心(除市话用户外)联通县、乡(镇)、行政村、村民小组的用户。从 1997 年起，电话用户数分组调整为以用户所在区域划分为“城市电话用户”和“乡村电话用户”，与过去的按市内电话和农村电话划分方法不同。而电话用户总数、电话机总部数统计范围不变。

城市电话用户 指直辖市、省辖市、地级市、县级市的市区、市郊区及县城(包括县人民政府所在地的县城关区或行政建制相当于县人民政府所在地的镇)范围内接入局用交换机的电话用户数，包括分布在农村地区的独立工矿区、林区、驻军等电话用户数。

农村电话用户 指按行政区划属于城市范围以外的乡(镇)、村的电话用户数。

住宅电话用户 指安装在居民住宅或农民家里并按照住宅电话用户登记注册和收费的电话用户。包括私人付费、单位付费和按规定免费安装的住宅电话用户。

长途电话交换机容量 指用于接入长途电话网的电话交换机设备的额定容量，包括国际电话交换机容量。

局用交换机容量 指安装在电信运营企业内用于接续本地固定电话的电话交换机容量，包括现用和备用的人工或自动交换机的全部容量。不包括用户交换机容量。

移动电话交换机容量 指移动电话交换机根据一定话务模型和交换机处理能力计算出来的最大同时服务用户的数量。

Explanatory Notes on Main Statistical Indicators

Length of Railways in Operation refers to the total length of the trunk line under passenger and freight transportation (including both full operation and temporary operation). The calculation is based on the actual length of the first line even if this line has a full or partial double track or more tracks, excluding double tracks, station sidings, tracks under the charge of stations, branch lines, special-purpose lines and the non-payable connecting lines. The length of railways in operation is an important indicator to show the development of the infrastructure for the railway transport, and also the essential data to calculate volume of passenger freight transport, traffic density and utilization efficiency of the locomotives and carriages.

Length of Electrified Railways refers to the length of the section of railways in operation in which the power supply lines and other equipment are installed for the running of electrified locomotives. The proportion of the length of electrified railways to the total length of railways in operation is an important indicator to show the modernization of railways.

Automatic-blocking and Semi-automatic-blocking Length of Railways refer to length of railways installed with equipment to perform automatic or manual blocking of trains. Blocking is a spacing technique by which a section of the railway only allows one train to pass at a time in the aim of ensuring the traffic safety. the proportion of automatic/semi-automatic blocking length to the total length of railways in operation is an important indicator to show the modernization of railways.

Length of Highways refers to the length of highways which are built in conformity with the grades specified by the highway engineering standard formulated by the Ministry of Communications, and have been formally checked and accepted by the departments of highways and put into use. The length of highways includes that of the suburb highways at large and medium-sized cities, highways passing through streets at small cities and towns, and also the length of bridges and ferries. It does not include the length of streets in big and medium-sized cities and highways built for the production purpose at factories, mines, forest areas and agricultural areas. If two or more highways go the same section of the way, the length of the section is only calculated for once and no duplication is allowed. The length of highways is an important indicator to show the development of the highway construction and to provide essential information to calculate the transport network density.

Length of Navigable Inland Waterways it is an indicator reflecting the size and development of inland water network, it refers to the length of the natural rivers, lakes, reservoirs, canals, and ditches open to navigation during a given period, which enables the transport by ships and rafts. It includes the channels open to navigation for over an accumulative 3 months in a year, yet this does not include the river courses, which are only used to float odd logs and bamboo rafts. This indicator can reflect the scale, level and development situation of the inland waterway network.

Length of Civil Aviation Routes refers to the length of all routes for regular civil aviation flights. There are usually two ways to calculate the distance between airports connected by the route length: One is to put the length of all air routes together, called duplicated calculation of the length of the routes; the other is not to allow the duplication in calculation when two or more routes passing the same section of aviation routes. The latter is usually used, as it can precisely show the size of the civil aviation network and indicate the extent of civil aviation serving the national economy and the people.

Length of Oil (Gas) Pipelines used as an indicator to show the development, scale and level of the pipeline transportation, it refers to the actual transport distance of oil (or gas) products, and is in general calculated in the length of single pipeline. If the length of the double pipelines and alternate pipeline are included, it is called the extension length of the oil (gas) pipelines, which indicates the actual length of the pipelines built, excluding double pipelines.

Freight (Passenger) Traffic refers to the volume of freight (passenger) transported with various means. Freight transport is calculated in tons and passenger traffic is calculated in the number of persons. Despite the type of freight and traveling distance, the freight transport is calculated in the actual weight of the goods: and despite the traveling distance and ticket price, the passenger traffic is calculated by the principle that one person can be counted only once in one travel. The passengers who travel with a half price ticket or a child ticket is also calculated as one person. The freight (passenger) traffic provides a quantitative measure to show how the transport industry serves the national economy and people, and is also an important indicator for planning the transport industry and for studying the development scale and speed of the transport industry.

Freight (Passenger) Traffic Density refers to the freight (passenger) traffic volume carried by a particular means of transportation during a given period through one kilometer of a specific section of transportation route. The formula is as follows:

Freight (Passenger) traffic density=[freight ton-kilometers (passenger-kilometers)] / (length of route in operation)

Freight (passenger) traffic density reflects the degree of business of freight (passenger) traffic on transportation routes, and therefore provides important information for balancing transport capability, planning construction and upgrading of transport routes and studying the distribution of transport network.

Freight Ton-kilometers (Passenger-kilometers) refer to the sum of the products of the volume of transported cargo (passengers) multiplying by the transport distance. It is an important indicator to reflect the achievement of transportation industry. Normally, the shortest distance between the departure station and the destination station (i.e., the payable distance) is the basis to calculate the freight ton-kilometers. This is an important indicator to show the total results of the transport industry, to prepare and examine the transport plan and to measure the efficiency, the labour productivity and the unit cost of transport.

The formula is as follows:

Freight ton-kilometers (passenger-kilometers) = Σ {freight (passenger) traffic × distance of transportation}

Possession of Civil Motor Vehicles refer to the total numbers of vehicles that are registered and received vehicles license tags according to the Work Standard for Motor Vehicles Registration formulated by transport management office under department of public security at the end of reference period. They are divided into following categories according to the structure of motor vehicles: passenger vehicles, trucks and others; and private vehicles and vehicles for units use according to ownerships; working vehicles and non-working vehicles according to kind of usage; large passenger vehicles, medium passenger vehicles, small passenger vehicles and mini passenger vehicle, heavy trucks, light-heavy trucks, light trucks and mini trucks according to sizes of vehicles.

Business Volume of Post and Telecommunications refers to the total amount of post and telecommunication services, expressed in value terms, provided by the post and telecommunications departments for the society. Post and telecommunication services can be classified as letters, parcels, remittance, issue of newspapers and magazines, fast mail service, express mail service,

savings deposits, stamps for collection, public and individual telegraph service, facsimiles, long-distance telephone service, leasing of telephone lines, urban paging service, mobile telephone service, data transfer and transmission, etc. The accounting approach is to multiply the service products of all types with their average unit price (constant price) to get sum of business value, plus income from other services such as leasing of telephone lines and equipment, maintenance of telephone switchboards and lines on behalf of customers. This indicator reflects the overall results of post and telecommunications service during a given period, and is important to study the composition of business service and the development of post and telecommunications service.

The formula is as follows:

Business volume of post and telecommunications= Σ (Transaction of post and telecommunication service x constant price) + Income from leasing, maintenance and other services = business volume of postal service + business volume of telecommunications service

Subscribers of Wireless Paging Services Wireless paging service refers the service by which telephone users send audio, digital or character signals to persons carrying small-size pagers within the designated areas through wireless paging centers. The page carriers who have registered in paging centers are counted as paging subscribers.

Mobile Telephone Subscribers refer to the persons who own mobile telephone numbers and are connected with the mobile telephone communication network through the mobile telephone switchboards, including contracted subscribers and pre-paid subscribers for intelligent network. One mobile telephone is taken as a subscriber.

Internet Users refer to the number of Chinese citizens who use Internet at least for one hour each week.

Local Telephone Subscribers refer to subscribers that are connected to the local telecommunication service provider through fix line network, including household subscribers, institutional subscribers and public telephones. They are also classified as city subscribers and rural subscribers according to locations. Before 1997, city subscribers referred to those connected to city telephone networks in county towns and cities, while village subscribers referred to those connected to village telephone stations at and below counties. Since 1997, the classification of telephone subscribers was modified on the basis of physical location of the subscribers as urban telephone subscribers and rural telephone subscribers, which is different from the previous classification of categorizing local telephones and rural telephones, while the definition of total subscribers and total number of telephones remain unchanged.

Urban Telephone Subscribers refer to number of telephone subscribers, located at municipalities, cities under the jurisdiction of province, cities at prefecture level, downtown and suburb of city at county level town and county towns (including country towns where county government located, and towns of county level according to the administrative organizational system), that are connected to the public line telephone network, including rural mineral area, forest area, military area.

Rural Telephone Subscribers refer to telephone subscribers, located at counties (towns) and villages outside the range of cities according to administrative jurisdiction.

Household Telephone Subscribers refer to telephone sets installed in the dwelling units of urban or rural residents, and registered as residence subscribers for payment, including 3 types of payment for the service: private payment, public payment and free service.

Capacity of Long Distance Telephone Exchanges refers to the rated capacity of telephone exchanges to connect long distance telephone network, including capacity of international telephone exchanges.

Capacity of Office Telephone Exchanges refers to the capacity (measured in gate) of telephone exchanges installed in the offices of telecommunication service providers for communication between fixed telephones. It includes the capacity of both manual and automatic exchanges in use and for stand-by purpose, excluding the capacity of subscribers exchanges.

Capacity of Mobile Telephone Exchanges refers to the capacity of the maximum services provided to subscribers at one time basing on a certain model and transacting capacity of the mobile telephone exchanges.

11 国内贸易 Domestic Trade

资料整理：陶红莹

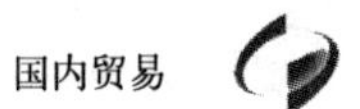

国 内 贸 易

Domestic Trade

2009

社会消费品零售总额	Total Retail Sales of Consumption Goods	5928.41 （亿元）
批发零售贸易业	Wholesales and retail Trade	4879.21 （亿元）
住宿和餐饮业	Hotel and Catering Industry	795.18 （亿元）
其他	Others	254.03 （亿元）

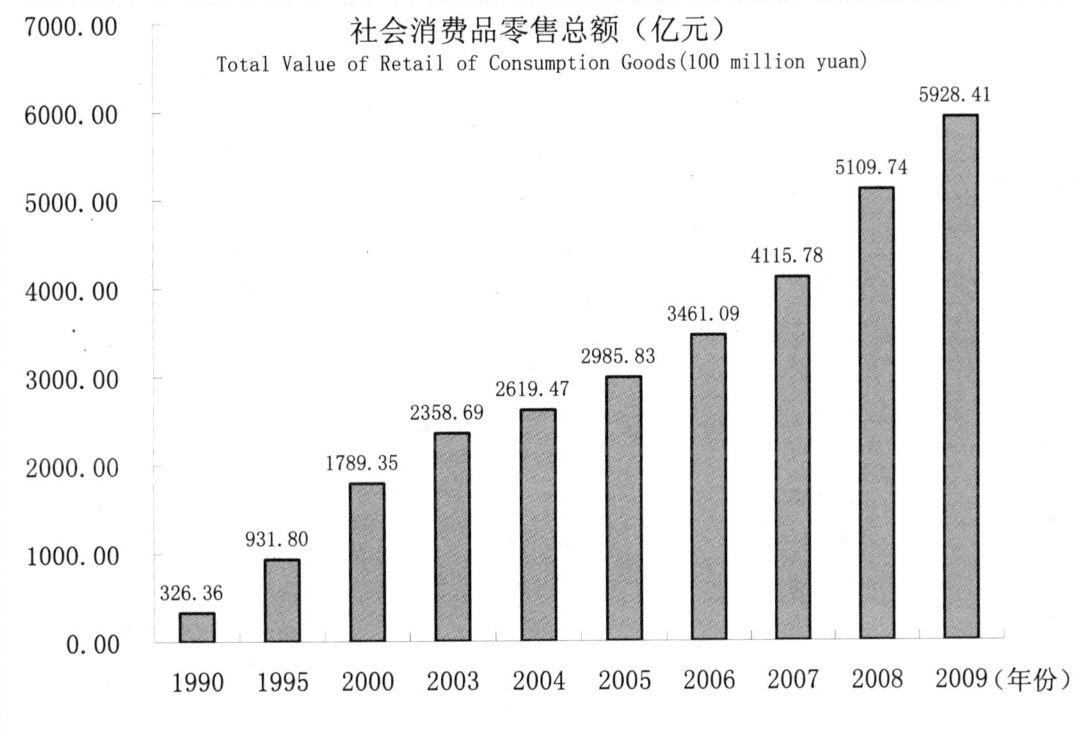

社会消费品零售总额（亿元）

Total Value of Retail Sales of Consumption Goods(100 million yuan)

年份	1990	1995	2000	2003	2004	2005	2006	2007	2008	2009
社会消费品零售总额	326.36	931.80	1789.35	2358.69	2619.47	2985.83	3461.09	4115.78	5109.74	5928.41

11-1 按地区分社会消费品零售总额

TOTAL RETAIL SALES OF CONSUMER GOODS BY REGION

单位:亿元 (100 million yuan)

年份 Year	零售额 Total Retail Sales of Consumer Goods	市 City	县 County	县以下 Below County Level
1978	59.84	19.24	16.56	24.04
1979	67.98			
1980	81.91	28.98	17.01	35.92
1981	89.90			
1982	99.83			
1983	112.44			
1984	137.34			
1985	181.17	75.26	31.64	74.17
1986	200.20	81.83	35.54	82.83
1987	234.06	103.21	38.23	92.62
1988	295.80	142.49	42.08	111.23
1989	320.68	159.89	43.78	117.01
1990	326.36	166.44	45.62	114.30
1991	362.26	190.65	50.04	121.57
1992	411.52	221.59	55.04	134.89
1993	521.35	293.82	68.88	158.65
1994	723.75	411.63	101.74	210.38
1995	931.80	539.79	127.76	264.25
1996	1145.73	688.40	130.28	327.05
1997	1345.34	802.37	146.61	396.36
1998	1481.38	896.08	156.07	429.23
1999	1617.14	1019.58	150.95	446.61
2000	1789.35	1128.47	177.65	483.23
2001	1975.16	1267.09	194.21	513.86
2002	2129.38	1429.83	200.69	498.86
2003	2358.69	1603.34	222.86	587.66
2004	2619.47	1819.80	246.21	277.44
2005	2985.83	2081.31	279.43	625.09
2006	3461.09	2430.05	325.66	705.38
2007	4115.78	2889.08	393.38	833.33
2008	5109.74	3587.49	491.44	1030.80
2009	5928.41	4128.16	586.81	1213.45

注：1.1996年及以后社会消费品零售总额及各分组指标中不含售给城乡居民生活用住房的零售额。

2.2004、2008年为经普数据，2005-2007年为按国家统计局制定的修订方法修订数据，1993-2003年原则根据原各年环比发展速度和2004年经济普查数据调整。

a) Since 1996, the residential house was exclued in the total retail sales of consumer goods and all the targets by groups.

b) The figures of 2004 and 2008 were from general economic Survey, that of the 2005-2007 were from statistics according to the reqirment of general economic survey; while the figures of 1993-2003 were from each year's indices (previous year =100) and readjusted according to the fata of general economic survey.

11-2 批发和零售业商品销售总额和分类销售额（2009）

SALE VALUES OF ENTERPRISES ABOVE DESIGNATED SIZE OF WHOLESALE AND RETAIL TRADES BY CATEGORY OF COMMODITIES (2009)

单位：万元 (10 000 yuan)

指标名称	Item	销售合计 Total Sales	批发额 Volume of Wholesales	零售额 Volume of Retail Sales
限额以上企业(单位)分类合计	**Total Number of Enterprises Above Designated Scale**	**56301865.5**	**42472104.2**	**13829761.3**
1.粮油.食品.饮料.烟酒类	**Foods, Beverage and Tobacco**	**7992264.7**	**5221771.7**	**2770493**
(1)粮油、食品类	Grain and Oil, Food	3490394.6	1563018.6	1927376
其中：粮油类	Among these:Oils	770888.6	392738.7	378149.9
肉禽蛋类	Meat, Poultry, Eggs	520553.5	114100.6	406452.9
水产品类	Aquatic Products	87758.7	25784.9	61973.8
蔬菜类	Vegetables	99024	21507.9	77516.1
干鲜果品类	Dry and fresh fruit category	130943.8	23310.5	107633.3
(2)饮料类	Beverages	464457.3	190442.8	274014.5
(3)烟酒类	Tobacco	4037412.8	3468310.3	569102.5
2.服装.鞋帽.针纺织品类	Clothing, Shoes, Hats and Textile Products	2421861.5	288510.6	2133350.9
(1)服装类	Clothing	1713913.3	210426.5	1503486.8
(2)鞋帽类	Shoes, Hats	393078.1	25879.7	367198.4
(3)针、纺织品类	Knitwear and Textiles	314870.1	52204.4	262665.7
3.化妆品类	Cosmetics	478420.2	73087.8	405332.4
4.金银珠宝类	Gold, Silver and Jewellery	303570.7	18529.1	285041.6
5.日用品类	Daily used Commodities	866949.1	211133	655816.1
其中：洗涤用品类	#Washing Articles	271875.3	81643.3	190232
儿童玩具类	#Children' Toys	36749.7	3803.7	32946
6.五金.电料类	Hardware and Electronic Products	89042.7	40252.1	48790.6
7.体育.娱乐用品类	Sports and Cultural Goods	73112.5	1987.4	71125.1
8.书报杂志类	Books, Newspaper, Magazines	294930.4	164787	130143.4
9.电子出版物及音像制品类	Electronic Publication and Audio Products	12978.3	3848	9130.3
10.家用电器和音像器材类	Household Appliances and Video Products	1937520	742079	1195441
11.中西药品类	Chinese Traditional Medicine and Western Medicine	2308274.1	1967264.8	341009.3
其中：西药类	#Western Medicine	1959560.4	1709133.2	250427.2
中草药及中成药类	#Chinese Herbal Medicine and Chinese Patent Drug	242897.8	178454.5	64443.3
12.文化办公用品类	Office Supplies	966426.6	844187.1	122239.5
13.家具类	Furnitures	29144.5	3194.2	25950.3
14.通讯器材类	Telecommunication Equipments	133184.9	29976.2	103208.7
15.煤炭及制品类	Coal and Coal-Made Products	1543614.5	1535176.3	8438.2
16.木材及制品类	Timber and Woody Products	1361.7	1361.7	
17.石油及制品类	Petroleum and Petroleum- Products	21121992.3	18355719.5	2766272.8
18.化工材料及制品类	Chemical Products	783713.6	783713.6	
其中：化肥类	#Chemical Fertilizers	228575.2	228575.2	
19.金属材料类	Metal Products	7738960.6	7738960.6	
20.建筑及装潢材料类	Construction and Decorative Materials	182345.6	89639.2	92706.4
21.机电产品及设备类	Machinery Products and Equipment	1253087.3	1220767.6	32319.7
其中：农机类	#Agricultural Machines	12809	12809	
22.汽车类	Automobiles	4183925.7	1694004.6	2489921.1
23.种子饲料类	Seeds Feedstuff	47262.2	47262.2	
24.棉麻类	Cotton and Fibre Plants	1000712.8	1000255.8	457
25.其他类	Others	537209	394635.1	142573.9

11-3 批发和零售业连锁经营情况
BASIC CONDITIONS OF WHOLESALES, RETAIL SALES, CATERING CHAIN STORES INDUSTRIES

指标名称	Item	合计 Total		直营店 Direct Sales Store		加盟店 League Store	
		2008	2009	2008	2009	2008	2009
一、门店总数 (个)	Number of Stores (unit)	5189	5449	3033	3337	2156	2112
其中:批发业 (个)	Number of Stores (unit)	237	249	176	188	61	61
零售业 (个)	Number of Stores (unit)	4952	5200	2857	3149	2095	2051
二、营业面积 (百平方米)	Floor Space of Business (100 sq.m)	41511	48542	39754	46404	1757	2138
其中:批发业 (百平方米)	Floor Space of Business (100 sq.m)	465	767	455	757	10	10
零售业 (百平方米)	Floor Space of Business (100 sq.m)	41047	47775	39299	45647	1747	2128
三、从业人员 (人)	Person Engaged (person)	90146	94069	80344	85317	9802	8752
其中:批发业 (人)	Person Engaged (person)	3368	3496	3168	3295	200	201
零售业 (人)	Person Engaged (person)	86778	90573	77176	82022	9602	8551
四、商品购进总额 (亿元)	Total Value of Commodities Purchaesd (100 000 000 yuan)	548.14	679.21	542.60	671.76	5.54	7.46
#统一配送商品购进额	#Total Purchasing Value	424.39	527.71	419.06	520.67	5.33	7.05
#自有配送中心配送商品购进额	#Commodities Purchased From Dispatching Center	373.99	437.38	370.03	431.54	3.96	5.84
#非自有配送中心配送商品购进额	#Commodities Purchased From Nondispatching Center	24.03	49.85	23.48	49.31	0.54	0.54
五、商品销售额 (亿元)	Sales Amount (100 000 000 yuan)	651.80	761.99	645.49	752.98	6.31	9.01
#零售额	#Retail Sales	522.86	593.23	516.56	584.37	6.31	8.85

注：2008年数据修改为限额以上企业数据。
Note:2008 data was revised to limit over enterprise data.

11-4 限额以上批发零售业基本情况（2009）

BASIC CONDITIONS OF ENTERPRISES ABOVE DESIGNATED SIZE IN WHOLESALES AND RETAILSALES TRADE (2009)

(按登记注册类型分)

(Grouped by Registration Type)

登记注册类型	Type of Registration	法人企业数(个) Number of Corperations (unit)	年末从业人数(人) Person Engaged at Year-end (person)	零售营业面积(万平方米) Floor Space of Retail Business (10 000 sq.m)
总 计	**Total**	**2123**	**288047**	**1019**
一、批发业	**Wholesales**	**933**	**93825**	**29**
#国有及国有控股	#State-owned and State Share Holding	190	54175	23
按登记注册类型分组	Grouped by Registration Type			
内资	**Domestic Funded Enterprises**	**912**	**90878**	**29**
国有	State-owned Enterprises	150	48135	6
集体	Collective-owned Enterprises	15	927	
股份合作	Cooperative Enterprises	26	1877	
联营企业	Joint Ownership Enterprises	5	728	
国有联营	State Joint Ownership Enterprises	2	52	
集体联营	Collective Joint Ownership Enterprises	1	13	
国有与集体联营	Joint State-collective Enterprises			
其他联营	Other Joint Ownership Enterprises	2	663	
有限责任公司	Limited Liability Corporations	275	16210	4
国有独资公司	State Sole Funded Corporations	2	176	
其他有限责任公司	Other Limited Liability Corporations	273	16034	4
股份有限公司	Share-holding Corporations Ltd.	62	8563	17
私营企业	Private Enterprises	377	14402	2
私营独资	Private-funded Enterprises	20	554	
私营合伙	Private Partnership Enterprises	7	105	
私营有限责任公司	Private Limited Liability Corporations	324	12723	2
私营股份有限公司	Private Share-holding Corporations Ltd.	26	1020	
其他	Other Enterprises	2	36	
港澳台商投资企业	**Enterprises with Funds from Hongkong, Macao and Taiwan**	**8**	**1748**	
合资经营	Joint-venture Enterprises	4	560	
合作经营	Cooperative Enterprises	1	810	
独资经营	Enterprises with Sole Investment	3	378	
独资股份有限公司	Sole Investment Co. Ltd. With Investment			
外商投资企业	**Foreign Funded Enterprises**	**13**	**1199**	
中外合资经营	Sino-foreign Joint-venture Enterprises	10	975	
中外合作经营	Sino-foreign Cooperative Enterprises	1	201	
外资企业	Enterprises with Sole Foreign Investment	2	23	
外商投资股份有限公司	Share-holding Co. Ltd. with Foreign Investment			

11-4 续表 continued

登记注册类型	Type of Registration	法人企业数（个）Number of Corperations (unit)	年末从业人数(人) Person Engaged at Year-end (person)	零售营业面积（万平方米）Floor Space of Retail Business (10 000 sq.m)
二、零售业	**Retail Trade**	**1190**	**194222**	**990**
#国有及国有控股	#State-owned and State Share Holding	219	65437	434
按登记注册类型分组	Grouped by Registration Type			
内资	**Domestic Funded Enterprises**	**1153**	**180988**	**937**
国有	State-owned Enterprises	160	16500	71
集体	Collective-owned Enterprises	42	9652	35
股份合作	Cooperative Enterprises	15	2017	5
联营企业	Joint Ownership Enterprises			
国有联营	State Joint Ownership Enterprises			
集体联营	Collective Joint Ownership Enterprises			
国有与集体联营	Joint State-collective Enterprises			
其他联营	Other Joint Ownership Enterprises			
有限责任公司	Limited Liability Corporations	339	48289	212
国有独资公司	State Sole Funded Corporations	4	327	3
其他有限责任公司	Other Limited Liability Corporations	335	47962	209
股份有限公司	Share-holding Corporations Ltd.	82	56284	391
私营企业	Private Enterprises	504	47119	221
私营独资	Private-funded Enterprises	80	4222	15
私营合伙	Private Partnership Enterprises	27	2114	7
私营有限责任公司	Private Limited Liability Corporations	355	37557	186
私营股份有限公司	Private Share-holding Corporations Ltd.	42	3226	13
其他	Other Enterprises	11	1127	2
港澳台商投资企业	**Enterprises with Funds from Hongkong, Macao and Taiwan**	**18**	**6028**	**25**
合资经营	Joint-venture Enterprises	4	980	3
合作经营	Cooperative Enterprises			
独资经营	Enterprises with Sole Investment	13	5025	22
独资股份有限公司	Sole Investment Co. Ltd. With Investment	1	23	
外商投资企业	**Foreign Funded Enterprises**	**19**	**7206**	**27**
中外合资经营	Sino-foreign Joint-venture Enterprises	10	4569	19
中外合作经营	Sino-foreign Cooperative Enterprises	1	185	1
外资企业	Enterprises with Sole Foreign Investment	8	2452	7
外商投资股份有限公司	Share-holding Co. Ltd. with Foreign Investment			

11-5 限额以上批发零售业基本情况（2009）
BASIC CONDITIONS OF ENTERPRISES ABOVE DESIGNATED SIZE IN WHOLESALES AND RETAILSALES TRADE (2009)

（按国民经济行业分）

(Grouped by Sector)

		法人企业数(个) Number of Corperations (unit)	年末从业人数(人) Person Engaged at Year-end (person)	零售营业面积(万平方米) Floor Space of Retail Business (10 000 sq.m)
总　计	**Total**	**2123**	**288047**	**1019**
一、批发业	**Wholesales**	**933**	**93825**	**29**
农畜产品批发业	Wholesales of Agricultrual and Animal Products	65	5692	3
食品、饮料及烟草制品批发业	Wholesales of Foods, Beverage and Tobacco	112	25531	2
米、面制品及食用油批发业	Wholesales of Rice, Noodles and Edible Oil	12	733	
烟草制品批发业	Wholesales of Tobacco	47	15759	1
纺织、服装及日用品批发业	Wholesales of Textile Products, Garments and Daily Used Articles	52	3014	
服装批发业	Wholesales of Garments	24	939	
文化、体育用品及器材批发业	Wholesales of Cultural and Sports Goods and Equipments	14	1225	
医药及医疗器材批发业	Wholesales of Medicnes and Medical Appliances	140	11278	4
矿产品、建材及化工产品批发业	Wholesales of Mineral Products, Building Materials and Chemical Products	323	33772	20
煤炭及制品批发业	Wholesales of Coal and Coal-made Products	30	899	
石油及制品批发业	Wholesales of Petroleum Products	42	25970	17
非金属矿及制品批发	Wholesales of Non-metal and Non-metal Mines	5	86	
金属及金属矿批发业	Wholesales of Metal and Metal Mines	165	3975	
建材批发业	Wholesales of Construction Materials	18	497	
化肥批发业	Wholesales of Chemical Fertilizers	14	565	2
机械设备、五金交电及电子产品批发	Wholesales of Machinery Equipment, Hardware, Transport and Electronic Products	199	9668	
汽车、摩托车及零配件批发业	Wholesales of Cars, and Motorcars Parts	107	2940	
家用电器批发业	Wholesales of Home Appliances	15	2923	
计算机、软件及辅助设备批发业	Wholesales of Computers, Softwares and Assisted Equipments	9	562	
贸易经纪与代理	Trade Agent	9	2179	
其他批发业	Other Wholesales	19	1466	
二、零售业	**Retail Sales**	**1190**	**194222**	**990**
综合零售业	Retail Sales of Department	315	121092	683
百货零售业	Department Stores	119	51292	285
超级市场零售业	Supermarkets	164	65485	382
食品、饮料及烟草制品专门零售业	Monopoly Retail of Foods, Beverage and Tobacco	68	6430	11
纺织、服装及日用品专门零售业	Monopoly Retail of Textile, Garments,and Daily Used Articles	75	13234	31
服装零售业	Retail Sales of Garments	48	9544	22
文化、体育用品及器材专门零售业	Monopoly Retail of Cultural, Sports Products and Equipments	89	5176	14
体育用品零售业	Retail Sales of Sports Products	2	99	1
图书零售业	Retail Sales of Books	67	4010	11
医药及医疗器材专门零售业	Monopoly Retail of Medicine and Medical Appliances	91	9235	28
药品零售业	Retail Sales of Medicine	86	9092	28
汽车、摩托车、燃料及零配件专门	Monopoly Retail of Cars, and Motorcars Parts	340	23827	125
汽车零售业	Retail Sales of Cars	252	13922	61
机动车燃料零售业	Retail Sales of Motor Vehicles Fuels	55	9131	61
家用电器及电子产品专门零售业	Monopoly Retail of Home Appliances and Electronic Products	161	11853	70
家用电器零售业	Retail Sales of Home Appliances	115	9955	67
计算机、软件及辅助设备零售业	Retail Sales of Computers, Softwares and Assisted Equipments	31	1023	1
通讯设备零售业	Retail Sales of Communication Equipments	12	741	1
五金、家具及室内装修材料专门零售业	Monopoly Retail of Hardware, Furnitures and Decorative Materials	27	1531	12
无店铺及其他零售业	Retail Sales of Storeless and Others	24	1844	17
邮购及电子销售业	Mail Order and Electronic Sales	1	75	

11-6 限额以上住宿和餐饮业基本情况（2009）
BASIC CONDITIONS OF ENTERPRISES ABOVE DESIGNATED SIZE IN HOTELS AND CATERING SERVICES (2009)

（按登记注册类型分）

(Grouped by Registeration Type)

指　标	Item	法人企业数（个） Number of Corperations (unit)	年末从业人数(人) Person Engaged at Year-end (person)	餐饮营业面积（万平方米） Floor Space of Catering Business (10 000 sq.m)
总　计	**Total**	**1133**	**129789**	**188**
一、住宿业	**Hotel Trade**	**476**	**59089**	**60**
#国有及国有控股	#State-owned and State Share Holding	113	16425	13
按登记注册类型分组	Grouped by Registration Type			
内资	**Domestic Funded Enterprises**	**456**	**53359**	**57**
国有	State-owned Enterprises	107	15076	11
集体	Collective-owned Enterprises	21	2172	2
股份合作	Cooperative Enterprises	11	1599	2
联营企业	Joint Ownership Enterprises	2	440	
国有联营	State Joint Ownership Enterprises			
集体联营	Collective Joint Ownership Enterprises			
国有与集体联营	Joint State-collective Enterprises	1	100	
其他联营	Other Joint Ownership Enterprises	1	340	
有限责任公司	Limited Liability Corporations	103	12676	12
国有独资公司	State Sole Funded Corporations	2	387	
其他有限责任公司	Other Limited Liability Corporations	101	12289	12
股份有限公司	Share-holding Corporations Ltd.	19	2504	3
私营企业	Private Enterprises	187	18336	25
私营独资	Private-funded Enterprises	47	4299	5
私营合伙	Private Partnership Enterprises	24	1559	3
私营有限责任公司	Private Limited Liability Corporations	101	10353	13
私营股份有限公司	Private Share-holding Corporations Ltd.	15	2125	4
其他	Other Enterprises	6	556	
港澳台商投资企业	**Enterprises with Funds from Hongkong, Macao and Taiwan**	**14**	**4357**	**2**
合资经营	Joint-venture Enterprises	6	2275	1
合作经营	Cooperative Enterprises	1	390	
独资经营	Enterprises with Sole Investment	6	1356	1
投资股份有限公司	Share-holding Co. Ltd. With Investment	1	336	
外商投资企业	**Foreign Funded Enterprises**	**6**	**1373**	
中外合资经营	Sino-foreign Joint-venture Enterprises	3	1098	
中外合作经营	Sino-foreign Cooperative Enterprises			
外资企业	Enterprises with Sole Foreign Investment	3	275	
外商投资股份有限公司	Share-holding Co. Ltd. with Foreign Investment			
二、餐饮业	**Catering Trade**	**657**	**70700**	**128**
#国有及国有控股	#State-owned and State Share Holding	27	2479	4
按登记注册类型分组	Grouped by Registration Type			
内资	**Domestic Funded Enterprises**	**631**	**60340**	**117**
国有	State-owned Enterprises	21	1819	3
集体	Collective-owned Enterprises	9	565	1
股份合作	Cooperative Enterprises	5	369	1
联营企业	Joint Ownership Enterprises			
国有联营	State Joint Ownership Enterprises			
集体联营	Collective Joint Ownership Enterprises			
国有与集体联营	Joint State-collective Enterprises			
其他联营	Other Joint Ownership Enterprises			
有限责任公司	Limited Liability Corporations	137	19054	36
国有独资公司	State Sole Funded Corporations			
其他有限责任公司	Other Limited Liability Corporations	137	19054	36
股份有限公司	Share-holding Corporations Ltd.	13	2582	3
私营企业	Private Enterprises	432	34974	71
私营独资	Private-funded Enterprises	126	7672	19
私营合伙	Private Partnership Enterprises	22	1722	3
私营有限责任公司	Private Limited Liability Corporations	261	23933	45
私营股份有限公司	Private Share-holding Corporations Ltd.	23	1647	4
其他	Other Enterprises	14	977	2
港澳台商投资企业	**Enterprises with Funds from Hongkong, Macao and Taiwan**	**14**	**2205**	**3**
合资经营	Joint-venture Enterprises	3	463	1
合作经营	Cooperative Enterprises			
独资经营	Enterprises with Sole Investment	9	1612	2
投资股份有限公司	Share-holding Co. Ltd. With Investment	2	130	
外商投资企业	**Foreign Funded Enterprises**	**12**	**8155**	**8**
中外合资经营	Sino-foreign Joint-venture Enterprises	5	320	
中外合作经营	Sino-foreign Cooperative Enterprises			
外资企业	Enterprises with Sole Foreign Investment	7	7835	8
外商投资股份有限公司	Share-holding Co. Ltd. with Foreign Investment			

11-7 限额以上住宿和餐饮业基本情况（2009）

BASIC CONDITIONS OF ENTERPRISES ABOVE DESIGNATED SIZE IN HOTELS AND CATERING SERVICES (2009)

(按国民经济行业分)

(Grouped by Sector)

指 标	Item	法人企业数（个）Number of Corperations (unit)	年末从业人数(人) Person Engaged at Year-end (person)	餐饮营业面积（万平方米）Floor Space of Catering Business (10 000 sq.m)
总 计	**Total**	**1133**	**129789**	**188**
一、住宿业	**Hotel**	**476**	**59089**	**60**
按国民经济行业分组	Grouped by Sector			
旅游饭店	Tourist Hotel	336	47005	
一般旅馆	Regular Hotel	123	9767	
其他住宿服务	Other Accomodation Service	17	2317	
二、餐饮业	**Catering**	**657**	**70700**	**128**
按国民经济行业分组	Grouped by Sector			
正餐服务业	Dinner	631	61158	118
快餐服务业	Fast Food	9	7949	8
饮料及冷饮服务业	Beverage and Cold Drink Services	2	67	
其他餐饮服务业	Others	15	1526	2

11-8 限额以上住宿和餐饮业经营情况（2009）

BUSINESS OF ENTERPRISES ABOVE DESIGNATED SIZE OF HOTELS AND CATERING SERVICES (2009)

(按国民经济行业分)

(Grouped by Sector)

指 标	Item	营业额（亿元）Turn-over (100 million yuan)	客房收入 Revnue from Guest Rooms	餐费收入 Revenue from Catering Bills	商品销售收入 Revenue from Commo-dity Sales	其他收入 Revenue from Others	年末住宿和餐饮企业拥有床位数(万个) Number of Beds owned by Hotels and Catering Enterprises at Year-end (10 000 units)	年末住宿和餐饮企业拥有餐位数(万位) Number of Seats owned by Hotels and Catering Enterprises at Year-end (10 000 units)
总 计	**Total**	**129.2**	**30.5**	**91.2**	**3.4**	**4.2**	**14.1**	**53.2**
一、住宿业	**Hotel**	**47.8**	**24.7**	**18.5**	**1.2**	**3.4**	**11.6**	**18.5**
按国民经济行业分组	Grouped by Sector							
旅游饭店	Tourist Hotel	38.7	20.0	15.1	0.8	2.8	9.5	14.6
一般旅馆	Regular Hotel	8.0	4.1	2.9	0.4	0.6	1.8	3.2
其他住宿服务	Other Accomodation Service	1.2	0.5	0.5		0.1	0.3	0.7
二、餐饮业	**Catering**	**81.4**	**5.8**	**72.7**	**2.2**	**0.7**	**2.5**	**34.7**
按国民经济行业分组	Grouped by Sector							
正餐服务业	Dinner	64.6	5.4	56.4	2.1	0.7	2.4	31.6
快餐服务业	Fast Food	14.8		14.8				2.5
饮料及冷饮服务业	Beverage and Cold Drink Services	0.1		0.1				
其他餐饮服务业	Others	2.0	0.4	1.4	0.1		0.1	0.5

11-9 限额以上住宿和餐饮业经营情况（2009）

(按登记注册类型分)

单位：亿元

指 标	Item	营业额 Turnover	客房收入 Revnue from Guest Rooms
总 计	**Total**	**129.2**	**30.5**
一、住宿业	**Hotels**	**47.8**	**24.7**
#国有及国有控股	#State-Owned and State Share Holding	14.0	7.0
按登记注册类型分组	Grouped by Registration Type		
内资	**Domestic Funded Enterprises**	**41.6**	**21.6**
国有	State-Owned Enterprises	12.4	6.3
集体	Collective-owned Enterprises	2.2	0.9
股份合作	Cooperative Enterprises	1.2	0.7
联营企业	Joint Ownership Enterprises	0.4	0.2
国有联营	State Joint Ownership Enterprises		
集体联营	Collective Joint Ownership Enterprises		
国有与集体联营	Joint State-collective Enterprises		
其他联营	Other Joint Ownership Enterprises	0.4	0.2
有限责任公司	Limited Liability Corporations	10.4	6.0
国有独资公司	State Sole Funded Corporations	0.4	0.2
其他有限责任公司	Other Limited Liability Corporations	10.0	5.8
股份有限公司	Share-holding Corporations Ltd.	2.1	1.0
私营企业	Private Enterprises	12.4	6.1
私营独资	Private-funded Enterprises	2.8	1.3
私营合伙	Private Partnership Enterprises	1.3	0.6
私营有限责任公司	Private Limited Liability Corporations	7.3	3.5
私营股份有限公司	Private Share-holding Corporations Ltd.	1.1	0.6
其他	Other Enterprises	0.5	0.3
港澳台商投资企业	**Enterprises with Funds from Hongkong, Macao and Taiwan**	**4.3**	**2.2**
合资经营	Joint-venture Enterprises	2.4	1.1
合作经营	Cooperative Enterprises	0.6	0.3
独资经营	Enterprises with Sole Investment	1.0	0.6
投资股份有限公司	Share-holding Co. Ltd. With Investment	0.3	0.1
外商投资企业	**Foreign Funded Enterprises**	**1.9**	**0.9**
中外合资经营	Sino-Foreign Joint-venture Enterprises	1.6	0.7
中外合作经营	Sino-Foreign Cooperative Enterprises		
外资企业	Enterprises with Sole Foreign Investment	0.2	0.2
外商投资股份有限公司	Share-holding Co. Ltd. with Foreign Investment		
二、餐饮业	**Catering Trade**	**81.4**	**5.8**
#国有及国有控股	#State-Owned and State Share Holding	3.7	1.4
按登记注册类型分组	Grouped by Registration Type		
内资	**Domestic Funded Enterprises**	**63.6**	**5.6**
国有	State-Owned Enterprises	2.7	1.0
集体	Collective-owned Enterprises	0.4	0.1
股份合作	Cooperative Enterprises	0.4	0.1
联营企业	Joint Ownership Enterprises		
国有联营	State Joint Ownership Enterprises		
集体联营	Collective Joint Ownership Enterprises		
国有与集体联营	Joint State-collective Enterprises		
其他联营	Other Joint Ownership Enterprises		
有限责任公司	Limited Liability Corporations	19.2	1.6
国有独资公司	State Sole Funded Corporations		
其他有限责任公司	Other Limited Liability Corporations	19.2	1.6
股份有限公司	Share-holding Corporations Ltd.	2.8	0.1
私营企业	Private Enterprises	37.4	2.6
私营独资	Private-funded Enterprises	8.0	0.6
私营合伙	Private Partnership Enterprises	1.5	
私营有限责任公司	Private Limited Liability Corporations	26.7	1.8
私营股份有限公司	Private Share-holding Corporations Ltd.	1.3	0.2
其他	Other Enterprises	0.8	0.1
港澳台商投资企业	**Enterprises with Funds from Hongkong, Macao and Taiwan**	**2.8**	**0.1**
合资经营	Joint-venture Enterprises	0.7	
合作经营	Cooperative Enterprises		
独资经营	Enterprises with Sole Investment	1.9	
投资股份有限公司	Share-holding Co. Ltd. With Investment	0.2	
外商投资企业	**Foreign Funded Enterprises**	**15.0**	**0.1**
中外合资经营	Sino-Foreign Joint-venture Enterprises	0.3	0.1
中外合作经营	Sino-Foreign Cooperative Enterprises		
外资企业	Enterprises with Sole Foreign Investment	14.7	
外商投资股份有限公司	Share-holding Co. Ltd. with Foreign Investment		

BUSINESS OF ENTERPRISES ABOVE DESIGNATED SIZE OF HOTELS AND CATERING SERVICES (2009)

(Grouped by Registeration Type)

(100 million yuan)

餐费收入 Revenue from Catering Bills	商品销售收入 Revenue from Commodity Sales	其他收入 Revenue from Others	年末床位数 (万个) Number of Beds at Year-end (10 000 units)	年末餐位数 (万位) Number of Seats at Year-end (10 000 units)
91.2	**3.4**	**4.2**	**14.1**	**53.2**
18.5	**1.2**	**3.4**	**11.6**	**18.5**
5.3	0.5	1.2	2.7	4.2
16.2	**1.1**	**2.7**	**10.9**	**17.6**
5.0	0.4	0.8	2.5	3.6
1.0		0.2	0.3	0.5
0.4		0.1	0.2	0.5
0.1		0.2	0.1	0.1
0.1		0.2		
3.5	0.3	0.6	2.5	2.8
0.2			0.1	0.1
3.4	0.2	0.6	2.4	2.8
0.9	0.1	0.1	0.4	0.9
5.2	0.3	0.7	4.9	8.8
1.3	0.1	0.1	2.2	3.6
0.6			0.4	0.6
2.9	0.3	0.5	2.1	4.1
0.4			0.3	0.6
0.1			0.1	0.3
1.5		**0.6**	**0.5**	**0.6**
0.8		0.5	0.2	0.3
0.3				
0.3		0.1	0.2	0.2
0.2				0.1
0.8		**0.1**	**0.2**	**0.4**
0.7		0.1	0.1	0.3
0.1			0.1	0.1
72.7	**2.2**	**0.7**	**2.5**	**34.7**
2.1	0.1		0.3	1.5
55.2	**2.1**	**0.7**	**2.4**	**31.2**
1.6	0.1		0.2	1.3
0.3				0.2
0.3				0.2
17.1	0.3	0.2	0.7	9.8
17.1	0.3	0.2	0.7	9.8
2.5	0.1			0.8
32.9	1.5	0.4	1.3	18.4
7.0	0.3		0.3	4.0
1.4				1.3
23.4	1.1	0.4	0.9	12.2
1.0	0.1		0.1	0.9
0.6			0.1	0.6
2.7			**0.1**	**0.9**
0.7				0.2
1.8				0.7
0.2				0.1
14.8				**2.6**
0.3				0.1
14.6				2.5

11-10 限额以上批发和零售业商品购、销、存总额（2009）
TOTAL PURCHASES, SALES AND STOCK OF ENTERPRISES ABOVE DESIGNATED SIZE OF WHOLESALE AND RETAIL TRADES(2009)

（按登记注册类型分）

(Grouped by Registeration Type)

单位：亿元 (100 million yuan)

指标	Item	购进总额 Total Purchasing Value	销售总额 Total Sales Value	批发 Whole-sales	零售 Retail Sales	年末库存总额 Total Value of Inventory at Year-end
总计	**Total**	**4984.6**	**5776.1**	**4353.1**	**1423.0**	**348.8**
一、批发业	**Wholesales**	**3704.3**	**4259.0**	**4152.2**	**106.8**	**222.4**
#国有及国有控股	#State-owned and State Share Holding	1729.7	2011.5	1944.6	66.8	114.4
按登记注册类型分组	Grouped by Registration Type					
内资	**Domestic Funded Enterprises**	**3596.8**	**4126.2**	**4019.4**	**106.8**	**206.8**
国有	State-owned Enterprises	1599.5	1833.5	1809.9	23.6	107.0
集体	Collective-owned Enterprises	19.0	21.4	20.9	0.5	4.7
股份合作	Cooperative Enterprises	68.4	90.6	90.0	0.6	1.2
联营企业	Joint Ownership Enterprises	36.1	35.7	35.7		1.8
国有联营	State Joint Ownership Enterprises	9.4	9.5	9.5		0.2
集体联营	Collective Joint Ownership Enterprises	0.5	0.5	0.5		
国有与集体联营	Joint State-collective Enterprises					
其他联营	Other Joint Ownership Enterprises	26.2	25.7	25.7		1.6
有限责任公司	Limited Liability Corporations	458.1	518.2	507.3	10.9	38.4
国有独资公司	State Sole Funded Corporations	4.2	4.3	4.3		
其他有限责任公司	Other Limited Liability Corporations	454.0	513.9	503.0	10.9	38.4
股份有限公司	Share-holding Corporations Ltd.	1029.4	1194.5	1132.6	61.9	15.3
私营企业	Private Enterprises	384.7	430.6	421.3	9.4	38.4
私营独资	Private-funded Enterprises	12.3	12.8	12.8	0.1	0.5
私营合伙	Private Partnership Enterprises	3.2	3.4	3.4		0.4
私营有限责任公司	Private Limited Liability Corporations	331.6	375.9	368.8	7.1	28.3
私营股份有限公司	Private Share-holding Corporations Ltd.	37.6	38.4	36.3	2.2	9.1
其他	Other Enterprises	1.4	1.6	1.6		
港澳台商投资企业	**Enterprises with Funds from Hongkong, Macao and Taiwan**	**47.8**	**62.0**	**62.0**		**5.1**
合资经营	Joint-venture Enterprises	34.1	48.0	48.0		4.9
合作经营	Cooperative Enterprises	3.7	3.9	3.9		
独资经营	Enterprises with Sole Investment	10.0	10.2	10.2		0.2
投资股份有限公司	Share-holding Co. Ltd. With Investment					
外商投资企业	**Foreign Funded Enterprises**	**59.6**	**70.8**	**70.8**		**10.6**
中外合资经营	Sino-foreign Joint-venture Enterprises	44.1	47.3	47.3		6.2
中外合作经营	Sino-foreign Cooperative Enterprises	2.2	3.3	3.3		4.2
外资企业	Enterprises with Sole Foreign Investment	13.3	20.2	20.2		0.2
外商投资股份有限公司	Share-holding Co. Ltd. with Foreign Investment					
二、零售业	**Retail Trade**	**1280.3**	**1517.1**	**200.9**	**1316.1**	**126.4**
#国有及国有控股	#State-owned and State Share Holding	565.2	706.2	123.2	583.0	28.1
按登记注册类型分组	Grouped by Registration Type					
内资	**Domestic Funded Enterprises**	**1174.7**	**1406.3**	**195.0**	**1211.3**	**95.7**
国有	State-owned Enterprises	173.2	218.1	43.4	174.7	7.4
集体	Collective-owned Enterprises	33.7	35.0	2.8	32.3	4.1
股份合作	Cooperative Enterprises	8.6	8.8	2.0	6.7	0.6
联营企业	Joint Ownership Enterprises					
国有联营	State Joint Ownership Enterprises					
集体联营	Collective Joint Ownership Enterprises					
国有与集体联营	Joint State-collective Enterprises					
其他联营	Other Joint Ownership Enterprises					
有限责任公司	Limited Liability Corporations	338.2	392.0	34.5	357.5	36.1
国有独资公司	State Sole Funded Corporations	31.7	38.2	7.1	31.0	2.4
其他有限责任公司	Other Limited Liability Corporations	306.5	353.8	27.3	326.5	33.7
股份有限公司	Share-holding Corporations Ltd.	425.9	529.4	97.3	432.1	22.6
私营企业	Private Enterprises	187.9	214.3	13.3	200.9	24.4
私营独资	Private-funded Enterprises	20.8	21.6	0.2	21.4	3.4
私营合伙	Private Partnership Enterprises	4.6	6.1	0.2	5.8	0.8
私营有限责任公司	Private Limited Liability Corporations	145.7	168.5	11.8	156.7	18.1
私营股份有限公司	Private Share-holding Corporations Ltd.	16.8	18.2	1.1	17.0	2.0
其他	Other Enterprises	7.3	8.7	1.6	7.1	0.5
港澳台商投资企业	**Enterprises with Funds from Hongkong, Macao and Taiwan**	**31.4**	**49.8**	**3.7**	**46.0**	**3.5**
合资经营	Joint-venture Enterprises	1.7	2.3	0.2	2.1	0.6
合作经营	Cooperative Enterprises					
独资经营	Enterprises with Sole Investment	29.5	47.2	3.5	43.7	2.9
投资股份有限公司	Share-holding Co. Ltd. With Investment	0.2	0.3	0.1	0.2	
外商投资企业	**Foreign Funded Enterprises**	**74.2**	**61.0**	**2.2**	**58.8**	**27.1**
中外合资经营	Sino-foreign Joint-venture Enterprises	59.0	43.6	2.2	41.4	25.7
中外合作经营	Sino-foreign Cooperative Enterprises	1.3	1.3		1.3	0.1
外资企业	Enterprises with Sole Foreign Investment	14.0	16.0		16.0	1.4
外商投资股份有限公司	Share-holding Co. Ltd. with Foreign Investment					

11-11 限额以上批发和零售业商品购、销、存总额（2009）
TOTAL PURCHASES, SALES AND STOCK OF ENTERPRISES ABOVE DESIGNATED SIZE OF WHOLESALE AND RETAIL TRADES (2009)

（按国民经济行业分）

(Grouped by Sector)

单位：亿元 (100 million yuan)

指标	Item	购进总额 Total Purchasing Value	销售总额 Total Sales Value	批发 Whole-sales	零售 Retail Sales	年末库存总额 Total Value of Inventory at Year-end
总计	**Total**	**4984.6**	**5776.1**	**4353.1**	**1423.0**	**348.8**
一、批发业	**Wholesales**	**3704.3**	**4259.0**	**4152.2**	**106.8**	**222.4**
农畜产品批发业	Wholesales of Agricultrual and Animal Products	61.8	72.0	68.2	3.8	31.5
食品、饮料及烟草制品批发业	Wholesales of Foods, Beverage and Tobacco	361.3	479.5	465.3	14.2	24.5
米、面制品及食用油批发业	Wholesales of Rice, Noodles and Edible Oil	15.4	14.9	13.8	1.1	3.5
烟草制品批发业	Wholesales of Tobacco	266.9	361.1	354.7	6.5	14.6
纺织、服装及日用品批发业	Wholesales of Textile Products, Garments and Daily Used Articles	37.2	41.7	40.6	1.2	3.1
服装批发业	Wholesales of Garments	17.3	17.7	17.7	0.1	1.5
文化、体育用品及器材批发业	Wholesales of Cultural and Sports Goods and Equipments	24.5	24.8	24.1	0.7	3.9
医药及医疗器材批发业	Wholesales of Medicnes and Medical Appliances	199.9	207.1	203.4	3.7	21.2
矿产品、建材及化工产品批发业	Wholesales of Mineral Products, Building Materials and Chemical Products	2231.0	2515.5	2453.9	61.6	88.4
煤炭及制品批发业	Wholesales of Coal and Coal-made Products	36.2	44.4	43.7	0.7	1.1
石油及制品批发业	Wholesales of Petroleum Products	1611.7	1845.8	1791.3	54.6	32.6
非金属及金属矿批发业	Wholesales of Non-metellic Mineral and Metal Industry	1.5	2.1	1.7	0.4	0.2
金属及金属矿批发业	Wholesales of Metal and Metal Mines	475.8	509.9	507.9	2.0	41.5
建材批发业	Wholesales of Construction Materials	10.9	11.1	10.2	0.9	1.5
化肥批发业	Wholesales of Chemical Fertilizers	21.0	23.3	20.5	2.8	6.0
机械设备、五金交电及电子产品批发	Wholesales of Machinery Equipment, Hardware, Transport and Electronic Products	310.1	367.5	358.8	8.7	26.3
汽车、摩托车及零配件批发业	Wholesales of Cars, and Motorcars Parts	141.5	172.0	167.3	4.7	17.8
家用电器批发业	Wholesales of Home Appliances	56.7	57.6	55.2	2.4	2.9
计算机、软件及辅助设备批发业	Wholesales of Computers, Softwares and Assisted Equipments	67.0	86.5	86.4	0.1	0.8
贸易经纪与代理	Trade Agent	465.7	510.6	510.6		22.7
其他批发业	Other Wholesales	12.7	40.3	27.3	13.0	0.8
二、零售业	**Retail Sales**	**1280.3**	**1517.1**	**200.9**	**1316.1**	**126.4**
综合零售业	Retail Sales of Department	596.5	695.2	94.4	600.8	65.6
百货零售业	Department Stores	288.3	366.9	24.6	342.4	18.8
超级市场零售业	Supermarkets	293.0	310.8	66.6	244.1	45.8
食品、饮料及烟草制品专门零售业	Monopoly Retail of Foods, Beverage and Tobacco	23.0	27.8	3.9	23.8	2.6
纺织、服装及日用品专门零售业	Monopoly Retail of Textile, Garments,and Daily Used Articles	34.0	45.4	4.4	41.0	7.6
服装零售业	Retail Sales of Garments	21.3	28.2	4.2	24.0	5.4
文化、体育用品及器材专门零售业	Monopoly Retail of Cultural, Sports Products and Equipments	19.4	20.0	2.0	18.0	5.1
体育用品零售业	Retail Sales of Sports Products	0.7	0.9	0.2	0.7	0.1
图书零售业	Retail Sales of Books	13.8	13.6	1.3	12.3	3.7
医药及医疗器材专门零售业	Monopoly Retail of Medicine and Medical Appliances	31.9	36.9	6.1	30.8	7.5
药品零售业	Retail Sales of Medicine	30.7	35.6	6.1	29.6	7.4
汽车、摩托车、燃料及零配件专门	Monopoly Retail of Cars, and Motorcars Parts	422.9	535.1	72.3	462.8	23.9
汽车零售业	Retail Sales of Cars	263.3	298.0	16.6	281.4	20.6
机动车燃料零售业	Retail Sales of Motor Vehicles Fuels	152.9	229.4	53.3	176.1	2.4
家用电器及电子产品专门零售业	Monopoly Retail of Home Appliances and Electronic Products	121.5	122.7	16.5	106.2	12.7
家用电器零售业	Retail Sales of Home Appliances	111.8	111.6	13.0	98.5	12.0
计算机、软件及辅助设备零售业	Retail Sales of Computers, Softwares and Assisted Equipments	6.0	6.2	1.2	5.0	0.6
通讯设备零售业	Retail Sales of Communication Equipments	3.5	4.6	2.2	2.3	0.2
五金、家具及室内装修材料专门零售业	Monopoly Retail of Hardware, Furnitures and Decorative Materials	5.3	7.2	0.5	6.7	0.6
无店铺及其他零售业	Retail Sales of Storeless and Others	25.9	26.7	0.8	25.9	0.7
邮购及电子销售业	Mail Order and Electronic Sales	0.2	0.3		0.3	

11-12 限额以上批发和零售业企业资产及负债（2009）
ASSETS AND LIABILITIES OF ENTERPRISES ABOVE DESIGNATED SIZE OF WHOLESALE AND RETAIL TRADES (2009)

单位：亿元 (100 million yuan)

指 标	Item	流动资产合计 Total Circulating Funds	固定资产原价 Original Price of Fixed Assets	资产总计 Total Assets	负债合计 Total Liabilities	所有者权益合计 Total Creditor's Equity
总 计	**Total**	**1388.1**	**319.6**	**1975.7**	**1443.4**	**532.2**
一、批发业	**Wholesales**	**1010.0**	**157.4**	**1323.6**	**985.7**	**337.9**
#国有及国有控股	#State-owned and State Share Holding	419.5	122.1	626.1	417.0	209.0
1.按登记注册类型分组	Grouped by Registration Type					
内资	**Domestic Funded Enterprises**	**980.7**	**152.5**	**1287.7**	**960.5**	**327.2**
国有	State-owned Enterprises	413.2	106.3	597.0	398.4	198.6
集体	Collective-owned Enterprises	17.3	1.5	20.5	18.0	2.5
股份合作	Cooperative Enterprises	13.3	0.7	14.9	11.8	3.1
联营企业	Joint Ownership Enterprises	16.4	0.1	16.6	15.6	1.1
国有联营	State Joint Ownership Enterprises	0.9	0.1	1.0	0.6	0.4
集体联营	Collective Joint Ownership Enterprises	0.2		0.2	0.2	
国有与集体联营	Joint State-collective Enterprises					
其他联营	Other Joint Ownership Enterprises	15.3		15.4	14.8	0.6
有限责任公司	Limited Liability Corporations	259.7	12.2	309.5	256.5	53.0
国有独资公司	State Sole Funded Corporations	1.2	0.1	1.5	1.2	0.3
其他有限责任公司	Other Limited Liability Corporations	258.5	12.0	308.0	255.3	52.7
股份有限公司	Share-holding Corporations Ltd.	53.0	21.0	87.6	61.5	26.1
私营企业	Private Enterprises	207.3	10.8	241.0	198.4	42.7
私营独资	Private-funded Enterprises	4.2	0.2	4.8	3.8	1.0
私营合伙	Private Partnership Enterprises	1.0		1.2	0.9	0.2
私营有限责任公司	Private Limited Liability Corporations	186.7	9.6	217.3	179.9	37.4
私营股份有限公司	Private Share-holding Corporations Ltd.	15.4	0.9	17.8	13.8	4.0
其他	Other Enterprises	0.5		0.5	0.4	0.1
港澳台商投资企业	**Enterprises with Funds from Hongkong, Macao and Taiwan**	**8.5**	**4.4**	**13.4**	**9.5**	**3.9**
合资经营	Joint-venture Enterprises	5.8	0.1	6.0	4.5	1.5
合作经营	Cooperative Enterprises	0.1		0.1	0.3	-0.1
独资经营	Enterprises with Sole Investment	2.6	4.3	7.2	4.7	2.6
投资股份有限公司	Share-holding Co. Ltd. With Investment					
外商投资企业	**Foreign Funded Enterprises**	**20.8**	**0.5**	**22.6**	**15.8**	**6.8**
中外合资经营	Sino-foreign Joint-venture Enterprises	14.2	0.1	14.5	12.2	2.4
中外合作经营	Sino-foreign Cooperative Enterprises	3.8	0.4	5.3	2.0	3.3
外资企业	Enterprises with Sole Foreign Investment	2.8		2.8	1.6	1.2
外商投资股份有限公司	Share-holding Co. Ltd. with Foreign Investment					
2.按国民经济行业分组	Grouped by Sector					
农畜产品批发业	Wholesales of Agricultrual and Animal Products	69.2	8.1	80.5	72.3	8.2
食品、饮料及烟草制品批发业	Wholesales of Foods, Beverage and Tobacco	140.6	32.0	188.0	85.1	102.9
米、面制品及食用油批发业	Wholesales of Rice, Noodles and Edible Oil	5.6	1.9	8.5	5.7	2.8
烟草制品批发业	Wholesales of Tobacco	141.9	141.9	141.9	55.7	86.2
纺织、服装及日用品批发业	Wholesales of Textile Products, Garments and Daily Used Articles	14.0	1.0	16.4	13.4	3.0
服装批发业	Wholesales of Garments	8.0	0.5	9.3	7.5	1.8
文化、体育用品及器材批发业	Wholesales of Cultural and Sports Goods and Equipments	9.8	3.3	16.3	10.7	5.6
医药及医疗器材批发业	Wholesales of Medicnes and Medical Appliances	101.0	5.8	127.0	95.1	31.9
矿产品、建材及化工产品批发业	Wholesales of Mineral Products, Building Materials and Chemical Products	382.1	98.9	556.8	429.5	127.3
煤炭及制品批发业	Wholesales of Coal and Coal-made Products	16.6	1.1	20.8	15.7	5.2
石油及制品批发业	Wholesales of Petroleum Products	62.9	87.8	197.2	117.0	80.2
非金属及金属矿批发业	Wholesales of Non-metellic Mineral and Metal Industry	0.9	0.1	1.0	0.6	0.4
金属及金属矿批发业	Wholesales of Metal and Metal Mines	254.7	7.4	282.4	248.9	33.5
建材批发业	Wholesales of Construction Materials	5.4	0.5	6.3	5.2	1.2
化肥批发业	Wholesales of Chemical Fertilizers	14.7	1.1	17.5	15.2	2.3
机械设备、五金交电及电子产品批发	Wholesales of Machinery Equipment, Hardware, Transport and Electronic Products	127.8	3.4	144.2	124.3	20.0
汽车、摩托车及零配件批发业	Wholesales of Cars, and Motorcars Parts	67.7	1.7	74.7	65.0	9.7
家用电器批发业	Wholesales of Home Appliances	20.0	0.1	24.9	22.4	2.6
计算机、软件及辅助设备批发业	Wholesales of Computers, Softwares and Assisted Equipments	7.6		8.5	6.6	2.0
贸易经纪与代理	Trade Agent	160.3	1.8	184.5	148.6	35.9
其他批发业	Other Wholesales	5.3	3.1	9.8	6.7	3.1

11-12 续表 continued

单位：亿元 (100 million yuan)

指 标	Item	流动资产合计 Total Circulating Funds	固定资产原价 Original Price of Fixed Assets	资产总计 Total Assets	负债合计 Total Liabilities	所有者权益合计 Total Creditor's Equity
二、零售业	**Retail Trade**	**378.1**	**162.2**	**652.0**	**457.8**	**194.3**
#国有及国有控股	#State-owned and State Share Holding	112.5	78.8	234.6	156.8	77.8
1.按登记注册类型分组	Grouped by Registration Type					
内资	**Domestic Funded Enterprises**	**325.4**	**136.3**	**552.4**	**390.9**	**161.5**
国有	State-owned Enterprises	17.3	30.0	53.0	29.6	23.4
集体	Collective-owned Enterprises	13.9	5.8	21.7	16.6	5.0
股份合作	Cooperative Enterprises	3.8	0.4	4.7	4.0	0.7
联营企业	Joint Ownership Enterprises					
国有联营	State Joint Ownership Enterprises					
集体联营	Collective Joint Ownership Enterprises					
国有与集体联营	Joint State-collective Enterprises					
其他联营	Other Joint Ownership Enterprises					
有限责任公司	Limited Liability Corporations	118.5	26.3	167.3	130.2	37.1
国有独资公司	State Sole Funded Corporations	6.3	1.0	8.9	8.4	0.5
其他有限责任公司	Other Limited Liability Corporations	112.2	25.3	158.4	121.8	36.6
股份有限公司	Share-holding Corporations Ltd.	94.9	55.9	195.1	131.6	63.5
私营企业	Private Enterprises	75.4	16.8	107.6	77.6	30.0
私营独资	Private-funded Enterprises	8.5	2.3	11.8	7.7	4.1
私营合伙	Private Partnership Enterprises	2.0	0.7	2.9	0.9	2.0
私营有限责任公司	Private Limited Liability Corporations	56.3	12.1	81.4	60.1	21.2
私营股份有限公司	Private Share-holding Corporations Ltd.	8.7	1.7	11.6	8.9	2.7
其他	Other Enterprises	1.5	1.2	3.0	1.2	1.8
港澳台商投资企业	**Enterprises with Funds from Hongkong, Macao and Taiwan**	**19.4**	**8.8**	**33.1**	**22.1**	**11.0**
合资经营	Joint-venture Enterprises	0.6	0.1	0.8	1.1	-0.3
合作经营	Cooperative Enterprises					
独资经营	Enterprises with Sole Investment	18.9	8.7	32.3	21.0	11.3
投资股份有限公司	Share-holding Co. Ltd. With Investment			0.1		0.1
外商投资企业	**Foreign Funded Enterprises**	**33.2**	**17.1**	**66.5**	**44.8**	**21.7**
中外合资经营	Sino-foreign Joint-venture Enterprises	30.3	15.9	61.6	40.6	21.0
中外合作经营	Sino-foreign Cooperative Enterprises	0.2	0.1	0.6	1.3	-0.7
外资企业	Enterprises with Sole Foreign Investment	2.7	1.1	4.3	2.9	1.4
外商投资股份有限公司	Share-holding Co. Ltd. with Foreign Investment					
2.按国民经济行业分组	Grouped by Sector					
综合零售业	Retail Sales of Department	173.2	93.9	337.3	238.0	99.3
百货零售业	Department Stores	79.5	48.3	168.2	120.9	47.3
超级市场零售业	Supermarkets	89.6	43.3	161.9	113.8	48.1
食品、饮料及烟草制品专门零售业	Monopoly Retail of Foods, Beverage and Tobacco	5.5	3.7	10.3	5.0	5.3
纺织、服装及日用品专门零售业	Monopoly Retail of Textile, Garments,and Daily Used Articles	15.4	3.5	24.5	18.1	6.4
服装零售业	Retail Sales of Garments	10.7	2.8	18.6	14.2	4.4
文化、体育用品及器材专门零售业	Monopoly Retail of Cultural, Sports Products and Equipments	9.7	8.5	21.4	12.1	9.3
体育用品零售业	Retail Sales of Sports Products	0.4		0.6	0.6	
图书零售业	Retail Sales of Books	6.6	8.1	17.5	8.8	8.7
医药及医疗器材专门零售业	Monopoly Retail of Medicine and Medical Appliances	25.6	2.9	32.8	20.7	12.1
药品零售业	Retail Sales of Medicine	25.2	2.9	32.4	20.3	12.1
汽车、摩托车、燃料及零配件专门零售业	Monopoly Retail of Cars, and Motorcars Parts	95.0	34.8	152.7	109.8	42.8
汽车零售业	Retail Sales of Cars	83.8	12.4	113.5	87.7	25.9
机动车燃料零售业	Retail Sales of Motor Vehicles Fuels	6.6	22.1	33.9	18.1	15.7
家用电器及电子产品专门零售业	Monopoly Retail of Home Appliances and Electronic Products	50.3	8.2	62.0	47.4	14.6
家用电器零售业	Retail Sales of Home Appliances	47.2	7.8	58.4	44.9	13.5
计算机、软件及辅助设备零售业	Retail Sales of Computers, Softwares and Assisted Equipments	1.5	0.2	1.9	1.1	0.7
通讯设备零售业	Retail Sales of Communication Equipments	1.2		1.3	1.1	0.2
五金、家具及室内装修材料专门零售业	Monopoly Retail of Hardware, Furnitures and Decorative Materials	2.0	1.5	3.6	3.2	0.4
无店铺及其他零售业	Retail Sales of Storeless and Others	1.5	5.4	7.4	3.4	4.0
邮购及电子销售业				1.4	0.1	

11-13 限额以上批发和零售业企业主要财务指标（2009）
MAIN FINANCIAL INDICATORS OF ENTERPRISES ABOVE DESIGNATED SIZE OF WHOLESALE AND RETAIL TRADES (2009)

单位：亿元 (100 million yuan)

指标	Item	主营业务收入 Revenue of Major Business	主营业务成本 Cost of Major Business	主营业务利润 Profits of Major Business	其他业务利润 Profits of Other Business	利润总额 Total Profits
总计	**Total**	**5003.4**	**4532.9**	**406.1**	**25.7**	**159.9**
一、批发业	**Wholesales**	**3764.0**	**3441.4**	**272.9**	**5.0**	**125.9**
#国有及国有控股	#State-owned and State Share Holding	1753.8	1605.3	154.0	2.5	62.8
1.按登记注册类型分组	Grouped by Registration Type					
内资	**Domestic Funded Enterprises**	**3643.8**	**3331.1**	**263.0**	**4.7**	**124.2**
国有	State-owned Enterprises	1587.2	1444.2	147.5	2.3	63.4
集体	Collective-owned Enterprises	20.2	19.8	0.4		-0.1
股份合作	Cooperative Enterprises	79.0	74.8	4.1	0.1	1.5
联营企业	Joint Ownership Enterprises	31.5	30.0	1.5		0.7
国有联营	State Joint Ownership Enterprises	8.2	8.0	0.1		0.1
集体联营	Collective Joint Ownership Enterprises	0.5	0.5	0.1		0.1
国有与集体联营	Joint State-collective Enterprises					
其他联营	Other Joint Ownership Enterprises	22.8	21.4	1.3		0.6
有限责任公司	Limited Liability Corporations	475.5	442.9	31.3	1.8	6.0
国有独资公司	State Sole Funded Corporations	4.4	3.6	0.8		0.3
其他有限责任公司	Other Limited Liability Corporations	471.0	439.3	30.5	1.8	5.7
股份有限公司	Share-holding Corporations Ltd.	1043.5	936.3	56.2	0.1	49.6
私营企业	Private Enterprises	405.7	382.0	22.0	0.3	3.1
私营独资	Private-funded Enterprises	12.2	11.6	0.5		0.1
私营合伙	Private Partnership Enterprises	3.3	3.0	0.2		0.1
私营有限责任公司	Private Limited Liability Corporations	357.8	337.8	18.6	0.3	2.2
私营股份有限公司	Private Share-holding Corporations Ltd.	32.3	29.5	2.7		0.8
其他	Other Enterprises	1.3	1.2			
港澳台商投资企业	**Enterprises with Funds from Hongkong, Macao and Taiwan**	**57.4**	**54.8**	**2.7**	**0.3**	**0.4**
合资经营	Joint-venture Enterprises	44.8	43.3	1.5		0.2
合作经营	Cooperative Enterprises	3.7	3.4	0.3		
独资经营	Enterprises with Sole Investment	8.9	8.1	0.8	0.3	0.2
投资股份有限公司	Share-holding Co. Ltd. With Investment					
外商投资企业	**Foreign Funded Enterprises**	**62.8**	**55.5**	**7.3**		**1.2**
中外合资经营	Sino-foreign Joint-venture Enterprises	44.5	41.9	2.6		0.7
中外合作经营	Sino-foreign Cooperative Enterprises	3.0	2.9	0.2		0.1
外资企业	Enterprises with Sole Foreign Investment	15.3	10.8	4.5		0.4
外商投资股份有限公司	Share-holding Co. Ltd. with Foreign Investment					
2.按国民经济行业分组	Grouped by Sector					
农畜产品批发业	Wholesales of Agricultrual and Animal Products	66.9	61.9	4.6	0.2	1.3
食品、饮料及烟草制品批发业	Wholesales of Foods, Beverage and Tobacco	436.4	335.7	111.1	2.0	51.3
米、面制品及食用油批发业	Wholesales of Rice, Noodles and Edible Oil	14.6	13.0	1.7	0.1	0.5
烟草制品批发业	Wholesales of Tobacco	329.0	246.8	93.4	1.6	49.6
纺织、服装及日用品批发业	Wholesales of Textile Products, Garments and Daily Used Articles	39.5	36.3	3.1	0.2	0.1
服装批发业	Wholesales of Garments	17.1	15.9	1.2		0.1
文化、体育用品及器材批发业	Wholesales of Cultural and Sports Goods and Equipments	18.5	16.6	1.8	0.1	0.4
医药及医疗器材批发业	Wholesales of Medicnes and Medical Appliances	187.3	175.5	10.9	1.3	2.8
矿产品、建材及化工产品批发业	Wholesales of Mineral Products, Building Materials and Chemical Products	2232.7	2061.1	114.2	0.7	61.7
煤炭及制品批发业	Wholesales of Coal and Coal-made Products	41.8	39.8	1.7	0.1	0.3
石油及制品批发业	Wholesales of Petroleum Products	1604.4	1460.7	88.0	0.4	57.9
非金属及金属矿批发业	Wholesales of Non-metellic Mineral and Metal Industry	2.0	1.8	0.2		
金属及金属矿批发业	Wholesales of Metal and Metal Mines	471.2	450.8	19.8	0.2	3.1
建材批发业	Wholesales of Construction Materials	11.4	10.4	1.0		0.2
化肥批发业	Wholesales of Chemical Fertilizers	23.5	22.9	0.4		
机械设备、五金交电及电子产品批发	Wholesales of Machinery Equipment, Hardware, Transport and Electronic Products	332.4	312.7	18.8	0.3	4.7
汽车、摩托车及零配件批发业	Wholesales of Cars, and Motorcars Parts	156.2	148.2	7.7	0.1	1.4
家用电器批发业	Wholesales of Home Appliances	49.5	46.2	3.2		0.5
计算机、软件及辅助设备批发业	Wholesales of Computers, Softwares and Assisted Equipments	75.0	71.9	3.0		1.3
贸易经纪与代理	Trade Agent	412.0	405.3	6.5	0.2	2.4
其他批发业	Other Wholesales	38.3	36.2	2.0		1.0

11-13 续表 continued

单位：亿元 (100 million yuan)

指 标	Item	主营业务收入 Revenue of Major Business	主营业务成本 Cost of Major Business	主营业务利润 Profits of Major Business	其他业务利润 Profits of Other Business	利润总额 Total Profits
二、零售业	**Retail Trade**	**1239.4**	**1091.6**	**133.2**	**20.7**	**34.1**
#国有及国有控股	#State-owned and State Share Holding	499.6	438.8	53.8	12.8	15.4
1.按登记注册类型分组	Grouped by Registration Type	1142.6	1013.0	115.3	18.5	29.3
内资	**Domestic Funded Enterprises**	**203.1**	**185.0**	**14.5**	**0.3**	**5.1**
国有	State-owned Enterprises	29.6	27.0	2.4	0.5	0.1
集体	Collective-owned Enterprises	8.4	7.6	0.7	0.1	0.3
股份合作	Cooperative Enterprises					
联营企业	Joint Ownership Enterprises					
国有联营	State Joint Ownership Enterprises					
集体联营	Collective Joint Ownership Enterprises					
国有与集体联营	Joint State-collective Enterprises					
其他联营	Other Joint Ownership Enterprises	357.6	324.1	31.3	4.4	9.8
有限责任公司	Limited Liability Corporations	32.7	31.9	0.7		
国有独资公司	State Sole Funded Corporations	325.0	292.1	30.6	4.4	9.8
其他有限责任公司	Other Limited Liability Corporations	328.2	281.6	43.4	12.6	9.9
股份有限公司	Share-holding Corporations Ltd.	206.2	179.9	21.8	0.6	3.8
私营企业	Private Enterprises	22.0	19.3	2.3		0.7
私营独资	Private-funded Enterprises	5.9	5.1	0.7		0.1
私营合伙	Private Partnership Enterprises	161.0	139.6	17.4	0.6	2.9
私营有限责任公司	Private Limited Liability Corporations	17.4	15.8	1.4		
私营股份有限公司	Private Share-holding Corporations Ltd.	9.5	7.8	1.2		0.4
其他	Other Enterprises	45.7	37.2	8.3	0.6	2.3
港澳台商投资企业	**Enterprises with Funds from Hongkong, Macao and Taiwan**	**2.8**	**2.3**	**0.5**		**-0.1**
合资经营	Joint-venture Enterprises					
合作经营	Cooperative Enterprises	42.7	34.7	7.8	0.6	2.4
独资经营	Enterprises with Sole Investment	0.3	0.3			
投资股份有限公司	Share-holding Co. Ltd. With Investment	51.1	41.3	9.6	1.6	2.4
外商投资企业	**Foreign Funded Enterprises**	**35.0**	**29.5**	**5.5**	**1.3**	**0.9**
中外合资经营	Sino-foreign Joint-venture Enterprises	1.4	1.2	0.1		-0.3
中外合作经营	Sino-foreign Cooperative Enterprises	14.7	10.6	4.0	0.3	1.7
外资企业	Enterprises with Sole Foreign Investment					
外商投资股份有限公司	Share-holding Co. Ltd. with Foreign Investment	475.1	399.1	67.6	16.8	14.8
2.按国民经济行业分组	Grouped by Sector	237.9	197.7	38.4	7.1	9.2
综合零售业	Retail Sales of Department	220.2	189.5	27.1	9.6	5.1
百货零售业	Department Stores	28.2	22.7	4.8	0.1	2.4
超级市场零售业	Supermarkets	43.3	31.8	10.9	0.2	2.1
食品、饮料及烟草制品专门零售业	Monopoly Retail of Foods, Beverage and Tobacco	27.1	21.6	5.0	0.1	0.2
纺织、服装及日用品专门零售业	Monopoly Retail of Textile, Garments,and Daily Used Articles	18.2	14.3	3.5	0.2	0.6
服装零售业	Retail Sales of Garments	0.9	0.8	0.1		
文化、体育用品及器材专门零售业	Monopoly Retail of Cultural, Sports Products and Equipments	11.9	9.0	2.6	0.2	0.6
体育用品零售业	Retail Sales of Sports Products	34.1	29.1	4.8	0.2	1.2
图书零售业	Retail Sales of Books	32.9	28.1	4.6	0.2	1.2
医药及医疗器材专门零售业	Monopoly Retail of Medicine and Medical Appliances	497.3	464.1	30.1	0.1	9.6
药品零售业	Retail Sales of Medicine	286.9	267.6	17.5	0.3	5.2
汽车、摩托车、燃料及零配件专门零售业	Monopoly Retail of Cars, and Motorcars Parts	202.9	189.7	11.9	-0.3	4.4
汽车零售业	Retail Sales of Cars	108.3	98.2	9.1	2.5	3.7
机动车燃料零售业	Retail Sales of Motor Vehicles Fuels	98.2	89.1	8.3	2.4	3.4
家用电器及电子产品专门零售业	Monopoly Retail of Home Appliances and Electronic Products	6.1	5.6	0.5		0.2
家用电器零售业	Retail Sales of Home Appliances	3.4	3.1	0.3	0.1	
计算机、软件及辅助设备零售业	Retail Sales of Computers, Softwares and Assisted Equipments	7.2	6.0	1.0	0.2	-0.2
通讯设备零售业	Retail Sales of Communication Equipments	27.7	26.2	1.4	0.3	-0.2
五金、家具及室内装修材料专门零售业	Monopoly Retail of Hardware, Furnitures and Decorative Materials	0.2	0.2			
无店铺及其他零售业	Retail Sales of Storeless and Others					
邮购及电子销售业						

11-14 限额以上餐饮业企业资产及负债（2009）

ASSETS AND LIABILITIES OF ENTERPRISES ABOVE DESIGNATED SIZE OF CATERING SERVICES (2009)

单位：亿元 (100 million yuan)

指 标	Item	流动资产合计 Total Circulating Funds	固定资产原价 Original Price of Fixed Assets	资产总计 Total Assets	负债合计 Total Liabilities	所有者权益合计 Total Creditor's Equity
总 计	**Total**	**22.4**	**37.4**	**77.0**	**52.2**	**24.8**
#国有及国有控股	#State-Owned and State Share Holding	21.2	35.0	69.5	46.5	23.0
1.按国民经济行业分组	Grouped by Sector	0.7	2.1	6.2	4.9	1.3
正餐服务业	Dinner			0.1		0.1
快餐服务业	Fast Food	0.5	0.2	1.2	0.7	0.5
饮料及冷饮服务业	Beverage and Cold Drink Services	20.6	34.0	67.7	44.9	22.8
其他餐饮服务业	Others	0.7	2.9	4.1	2.9	1.2
2.按登记注册类型分组	Grouped by Registration Type	0.2	0.6	0.8	0.8	
内资	**Domestic Funded Enterprises**	**0.1**	**0.2**	**0.4**	**0.5**	**-0.1**
国有	State-Owned Enterprises					
集体	Collective-owned Enterprises					
股份合作	Cooperative Enterprises					
联营企业	Joint Ownership Enterprises					
国有联营	State Joint Ownership Enterprises					
集体联营	Collective Joint Ownership Enterprises	6.7	13.7	25.0	14.9	10.1
国有与集体联营	Joint State-collective Enterprises					
其他联营	Other Joint Ownership Enterprises	6.7	13.7	25.0	14.9	10.1
有限责任公司	Limited Liability Corporations	0.5	0.8	1.9	1.7	0.2
国有独资公司	State Sole Funded Corporations	12.3	14.6	34.0	22.9	11.0
其他有限责任公司	Other Limited Liability Corporations	2.5	2.7	6.1	2.7	3.4
股份有限公司	Share-holding Corporations Ltd.	0.3	0.5	0.9	0.5	0.4
私营企业	Private Enterprises	9.1	10.5	25.1	19.0	6.1
私营独资	Private-funded Enterprises	0.5	0.9	1.9	0.7	1.1
私营合伙	Private Partnership Enterprises	0.2	1.2	1.5	1.1	0.3
私营有限责任公司	Private Limited Liability Corporations	0.9	0.7	2.1	1.5	0.6
私营股份有限公司	Private Share-holding Corporations Ltd.	0.1	0.3	0.4	0.4	
其他	Other Enterprises					
港澳台商投资企业	**Enterprises with Funds from Hongkong, Macao and Taiwan**	**0.7**	**0.4**	**1.5**	**1.0**	**0.5**
合资经营	Joint-venture Enterprises	0.1		0.2	0.1	
合作经营	Cooperative Enterprises	0.9	2.7	7.2	5.8	1.4
独资经营	Enterprises with Sole Investment	0.1	0.4	0.7	0.5	0.2
投资股份有限公司	Share-holding Co. Ltd. With Investment					
外商投资企业	**Foreign Funded Enterprises**	**0.8**	**2.3**	**6.5**	**5.3**	**1.2**
中外合资经营	Sino-Foreign Joint-venture Enterprises					
中外合作经营	Sino-Foreign Cooperative Enterprises	1.2	6.5	9.4	3.9	5.5
外资企业	Enterprises with Sole Foreign Investment					
外商投资股份有限公司	Share-holding Co. Ltd. with Foreign Investment					

11-15 限额以上餐饮业企业主要财务指标（2009）
MAIN FINANCIAL INDICATORS OF ENTERPRISES ABOVE DESIGNATED SIZE OF CATERING SERVICES (2009)

单位：亿元 (100 million yuan)

指 标	Item	主营业务收入 Revenue of Major Business	主营业务成本 Cost of Major Business	主营业务利润 Profits of Major Business	其他业务利润 Profits of Other Business	利润总额 Total Profits
总 计	**Total**	**80.7**	**40.4**	**36.6**	**0.1**	**2.6**
1.按国民经济行业分组	Grouped by Sector	64.0	34.4	26.8	0.1	1.5
正餐服务业	Dinner	14.6	4.9	9.0		1.1
快餐服务业	Fast Food	0.1				
饮料及冷饮服务业	Beverage and Cold Drink Services	2.0	1.0	0.8		0.1
其他餐饮服务业	Others	62.9	33.7	26.4	0.1	1.6
2.按登记注册类型分组	Grouped by Registration Type	2.7	2.5	1.1		0.1
内资	**Domestic Funded Enterprises**	**0.4**	**0.2**	**0.2**		
国有	State-Owned Enterprises	0.4	0.2	0.2		
集体	Collective-owned Enterprises					
股份合作	Cooperative Enterprises					
联营企业	Joint Ownership Enterprises					
国有联营	State Joint Ownership Enterprises					
集体联营	Collective Joint Ownership Enterprises					
国有与集体联营	Joint State-collective Enterprises	18.8	9.1	8.7		0.2
其他联营	Other Joint Ownership Enterprises					
有限责任公司	Limited Liability Corporations	18.8	9.1	8.7		0.2
国有独资公司	State Sole Funded Corporations	2.8	1.2	1.4		
其他有限责任公司	Other Limited Liability Corporations	37.0	20.1	14.6	0.1	1.2
股份有限公司	Share-holding Corporations Ltd.	7.9	4.9	2.6		0.8
私营企业	Private Enterprises	1.5	0.9	0.5		0.1
私营独资	Private-funded Enterprises	26.3	13.7	10.9		0.3
私营合伙	Private Partnership Enterprises	1.3	0.7	0.5		0.1
私营有限责任公司	Private Limited Liability Corporations	0.8	0.4	0.4		
私营股份有限公司	Private Share-holding Corporations Ltd.	2.9	1.7	1.1		
其他	Other Enterprises	0.7	0.4	0.3		
港澳台商投资企业	**Enterprises with Funds from Hongkong, Macao and Taiwan**					
合资经营	Joint-venture Enterprises	2.0	1.2	0.7		
合作经营	Cooperative Enterprises	0.2	0.1	0.1		
独资经营	Enterprises with Sole Investment	14.9	5.0	9.1		1.0
独资股份有限公司	Sole Investment Co. Ltd. With Investment	0.3	0.1	0.2		
外商投资企业	**Foreign Funded Enterprises**					
中外合资经营	Sino-Foreign Joint-venture Enterprises	14.5	4.9	8.9		1.0
中外合作经营	Sino-Foreign Cooperative Enterprises					
外资企业	Enterprises with Sole Foreign Investment	3.7	2.9	1.6		0.1
外商投资股份有限公司	Share-holding Co. Ltd. with Foreign Investment					

主要统计指标解释

社会消费品零售总额 指批发和零售业、餐饮业、新闻出版业、邮政业和其他服务业等，售予城乡居民用于生活消费的商品和社会集团用于公共消费的商品之总量。社会消费品零售总额包括：

一、批发和零售业企业（单位）：

1.售予城乡居民的各种生活消费品；

2.售予入境旅游的外国人、华侨、港澳台同胞的各类商品；

3.售予行政事业单位、社会团体、军队和武警等机构的商品，以及以零售方式售予各类企业的商品。具体包括：用于非生产和社会交往的办公用品，如通讯设备、计算器具和设备、电讯网络设备、文印设备、音像视听器材和设备、纸张、本册、文具及装订文印材料、家具、日用电器、针纺织品、清洁卫生用品、文体用品、奖品、纪念品、礼品等；供内部人员乘坐的交通工具和燃料；用于办公设施修缮的各类配件、材料、工具等；用于取暖和防暑降温的设备、燃料、材料及食品等；专用于教学的用品和设备；非营利医疗机构的中、西药品、中药材和医疗设备器材；非专用的劳动保护用品；不对外营业的内部食堂用的餐具、炊具、设备、清洁卫生工具和食品、燃料等；军队、武警用于其人员生活的衣着品和个人用品；其他各类非生产性设备和用品。

二、餐饮业出售的主食、菜肴、烟酒饮料和其他商品。

三、新闻出版业、邮政业售予城乡居民、企事业单位、军队和武警等机构的书报杂志、音像制品、邮品等。

四、其他服务业出售的食品、烟酒饮料、服装鞋帽、日常生活用品、医药保健用品、艺术品、工艺美术品、玩具、殡葬用品以及其他消费品。

批发零售业商品购、销、存总额 指各种登记注册类型的批发、零售业企业(单位)以本企业(单位)为总体的，从国内、国外市场购进的商品总量，销售和出口的商品总量、库存商品总量等情况。该指标可以反映商品流转过程中商品的购进、销售、库存之间的比例关系和存在的问题。

商品购进总额 指从本企业(单位)以外的单位和个人购进(包括从境外直接进口)作为转卖或加工后转卖的商品总额。它反映批发零售贸易业从国内、国外市场上购进商品的总量。商品购进总额包括：(1)从工农业生产者购进的商品；(2)从出版社、报社的出版发行部门购进的图书、杂志和报纸；(3)从各种登记注册类型的批发零售贸易企业(单位)购进的商品；(4)从其他单位购进的商品，如从机关、团体、企业等单位购进的剩余物资，从餐饮业、服务业购进的商品，从海关、市场管理部门购进的缉私和没收的商品，从居民手中收购的废旧商品等；(5)从国(境)外直接进口的商品。不包括企业(单位)为自身经营用和未通过买卖行为而收入的商品以及销售退回、商品升溢等。

商品销售总额 指对本企业(单位)以外的单位和个人出售(包括对境外直接出口)的商品总额。它反映批发零售贸易业在国内市场上销售商品以及出口商品的总量。商品销售总额包括：(1)售给城乡居民和社会集团消费用的商品；(2)售给工业、农业、建筑业、运输邮电业、批发零售贸易业、餐饮业、服务业等作为生产、经营使用的商品；(3)售给批发零售贸易业作为转卖或加工后转卖的商品；(4)对国(境)外直接出口的商品。不包括出售本企业(单位)自用的废旧包装用品、未通过买卖行为付出的商品、经本单位介绍，由买卖双方直接结算，本单位只收取手续费的业务、购货退出的商品以及商品损耗和损失等。

批发零售业库存 指报告期末各种登记注册类型的批发零售贸易企业(单位)已取得所有权的商品。它反映批发零售贸易企业(单位)的商品库存情况和对市场商品供应的保证程度。期末库存包括：(1)存放在批发零售贸易业经营单位(如门市部、批发站、经营处)仓库、货场、货柜和货架中的商品；(2)挑选、整理、包装中的商品；(3)已记入购进而尚未运到本单位的商品，即发货单或银行承兑凭证已到而货未到的部分；(4)寄放他处的商品，如因购货方拒绝承付而暂时存放在购货方的商品和已办完加工成品收回手续而未提回的商品；(5)委托其他单位代销(未作销售或调出)尚未售出的商品；(6)代其他单位购进尚未交付的商品。不包括所有权不属于本单位的商品、拨付除批发零售贸易业以外的其他行业所属独立核算加工厂等加工生产尚未收回成品的商品、代国家物资储备部门保管的商品等。

库存总额采用的计算价格是：农副产品采购单位按购进价计算；批发单位按进货价计算；零售单位按核算价格计算，即按什么价格核算就按什么价格计算。

住宿餐饮业营业额 指住宿和餐饮业法人企业、产业活动单位在经营活动中因提供服务或销售商品等取得的收入，包括客房收入、餐费收入、商品销售收入和其他收入。客房收入指住宿和餐饮业法人企业、产业活动单位在经营活动中因提供住宿服务取得的客房收入。餐费收入指住宿和餐饮业法人企业、产业活动单位因为顾客提供就餐服务取得的收入，包括经烹饪、调制加工后出售的各种食品，如主食、炒菜、凉拌菜等的收入。商品销售收入指住宿和餐饮业法人企业、产业活动单位伴随服务而出售商品所取得的收入。其他收入指营业收入中除客房收入、餐费收入、商品销售收入以外的其他收入，包括娱乐、健身和商务服务等。

亿元商品交易市场成交额 指年成交额达到亿元以上，经工商部门批准、专门从事商品批发、零售业务活动的市场。其市场所有摊位成交总额称为商品交易市场成交额。

连锁企业（或称连锁店、连锁公司） 指在核心企业或总店的领导下，由分散的、经营同类商品或服务的企业或活动单位，采取共同方针，实行集中采购和分散销售的有机结合，通过规范化经营，实现规模效益的经济联合组织形式。一般连锁店应由若干个分店组成。其经营特征：(1)经营同类商品；(2)使用统一商号；(3)统一采购配送，采购与销售相分离（部分商品可根据物流合理和保质保鲜原则，由供应商直接送货到门店，其余均由总部统一配送）。

连锁门店包括下列三种形式：

直营连锁：也叫正规连锁。连锁门店均由总部独资或控股开设，在总部的直接领导下统一经营。总部采取纵深似的管理方式，直接下令掌管所有的零售门店，零售门店也必须完全接受总部指挥。他是大型垄断商业资本通过吞并、兼并或独资、控股等途径，发展壮大自身实力和规模的一种形式。

特许连锁：各连锁门店（被特许人）通过合同形式，取得使用总部（特许人）商标、商号、经营技术和销售总部开发的商品的特许权，各加盟连锁门店为独立法人，在总部指导下统一经营。

自由连锁：也称自愿连锁。连锁公司的门店均为独立法人，各自的资产所有权关系不变，在公司总部的指导下共同经营。各成员店使用共同的店名，与总部订阅有关购、销、宣传等方面的合同，并按合同开展经营活动。在合同规定的范围之外，各成员店可以自由活动。根据自愿原则，各成员店可自由加入连锁体系，也可自由退出。

特许连锁加上自由连锁等于加盟连锁。

Explanatory Notes on Main Statistical Indicators

Total Retail Sales of Consumer Goods refer to the sum of retail sales of commodities sold by wholesale, retail, catering, publishing, post and telecommunications and other service industries to urban and rural households for private consumption and to social institutions for public consumption. Retail sales of consumer goods include:

1) Sales by wholesale and retail units:

a) of consumer goods sold to urban and rural households

b) of commodities sold to foreigners, overseas Chinese and Chinese compatriots from Hong Kong, Macao and Taiwan visiting in China

c) of commodities sold to government agencies, institutions, social organizations, military and armed police units, and commodities sold to enterprises in the form of retail sales. More specifically, they include: office facilities and articles for non-production purposes such as communications equipment, computing equipment and instruments, TV and network equipment, printing and copying equipment, audio-visual equipment and instruments, paper, notebooks, stationeries, furniture, electric appliances, knitwear, sanitation and cleaning articles, cultural and sport articles, articles for prizes, souvenirs, etc.; transport vehicles and fuels for employees; materials, spare parts and tools for the maintenance of office facilities; equipment, fuels, materials and food for winter heating or summer cooling purposes; articles and equipment for teaching purpose; Chinese and western medicines and medical equipment and facilities purchased by non profit-making medical institutes; non-specialized work safety articles; cooking utensils, tableware, equipment, cleaning articles, food and fuels purchased by internal cafeterias; clothes and personal articles purchased by military or armed police units for their officials and soldiers; and other equipment and articles for non-production purposes.

2) Sales of stable food, cooked dishes, beverages, tobaccos and other articles by catering units.

3) Sales of books, newspapers, magazines, audio-visual products and post products by publishing, post and telecommunications departments to urban and rural households and to enterprises, institutions, military and armed police units.

4) Sales of food, beverages, tobaccos, clothing, hats, footwear, articles for daily use, medicines, medical and health articles, work of art, handicrafts, toys, funeral articles and other articles by other service industries.

Purchase, Sales and Stock of Commodities by Wholesale and Retail Trades refer to the total volume of commodities purchased, total volume of sales and exports, and the stock of commodities by wholesale and retail enterprises (establishments) of different status of registration from domestic and overseas markets. This indictor reflects the relationship among purchase, sales and stock of commodities in the circulation of goods and reveals the existing problems.

Total Purchases of Commodities refer to the total value of purchases of commodities by the enterprises (establishments) from other establishments or individuals (including direct import from abroad) for the purpose of re-selling, either with or without further processing of the commodities purchased. This indicator is used to show the total value of purchases of commodities by wholesale and retail establishments from domestic and overseas markets. The total purchases include: (1) agricultural and industrial products purchased from producers; (2) books, magazines and newspapers purchased from distribution departments of the publishers; (3) commodities purchased from wholesale and retail establishments of different status of registration; (4) commodities purchased from other units, such as surplus materials purchased from government agencies, enterprises or institutions, commodities purchased from catering and service establishments, confiscated goods purchased from customs authorities or market management agencies, second-hand goods and wastes purchased from residents; and (5) commodities directly imported from abroad. Excluded are commodities purchased by enterprises (establishments) for use in their own business operation, commodities obtained without buying or selling procedures, rejected commodities, etc.

Total Sales of Commodities refer to value of commodities sold by the establishments to other establishments and individuals (including direct export). This indicator is used to show the total value of sales of commodities at domestic markets and export. The total sales include: (1) commodities sold to urban and rural residents and social groups for their consumption; (2) commodities sold to establishments in industry, agriculture, construction, transportation, post and telecommunications, wholesale and retail trades, catering trade and public utility for their production and operation; (3) commodities sold to wholesale and retail establishments for re selling, with or without further processing; and (4)commodities for direct export to other countries. Excluded are selling of waste packaging materials used by the establishments (units) themselves, commodities transferred without buying or selling procedures, commission income from brokerage in transactions whose settlement is directly handled by buyers and sellers, rejected commodities in the purchase, loss in commodities, etc.

Commodity Stock of Wholesale and Retail Enterprises refers to total commodities possessed by wholesale and retail enterprises (units) of various types of registration status at the end of the reference period, which reflects the commodity stock level of various wholesale and retail enterprises and the potential for market supply. It includes: (1) commodities located in storage, garages, counters, and shelves of operating units (such as sale stores, wholesale centers, and operating offices) of wholesale and retail enterprises; (2) commodities in the process of selecting, sorting, and packing; (3) commodities not arrived but recorded as purchase in the account, i.e. commodities not arrived but payment receipts for the commodities from the sellers or the banks arrived; (4) commodities deposited in other places rather than places mentioned above, for instance: commodities in the hold of purchasers temporarily due to the refusal of payment and commodities not taken back after going through the formalities; (5) commodities entrusted to other units to sell but not sold yet; (6) commodities purchased for other units but not delivered yet. Commodities not included as stock are those not owned by the enterprises (units), those allocated to financially independent factories rather than wholesale and retail enterprises for processing but not taken back yet, and finally those put in stock by wholesale and retail enterprises on behalf of the state material reserves units.

For the calculation of the value of commodities stock, the value is calculated at purchasing prices in agricultural goods purchasing units and wholesale units, and at the accounting prices in retail units.

Business Revenue of Hotels and Catering Services refer to revenue received from providing services or selling commodities by corporate enterprises and establishments engaged in hotel and catering services, including income from hotel rooms, from catering services, from selling of commodities and from other services. Income from hotel rooms refers to income of corporate enterprises and establishments by providing lodging services. Income from catering services refers to income of corporate enterprises and establishments by providing catering services, including selling of cooked or prepared foods such as stable food, cooked dishes or cold dishes. Income from selling of commodities refers to income of corporate enterprises and establishments by selling commodities that accompany the services they provide. Income from other activities refers to income received other than income from hotel rooms, catering services or selling of commodities, such as income from providing recreation, fitness or business services.

Volume of Transaction at Large Commodity Markets (with transaction value over 100 million yuan) refers to markets approved by the industrial and commercial administration departments, which specialize in wholesale and retail of commodities with an annual transaction of over 100 million yuan. The sum of sales of all sellers in the markets makes up the transaction value of the markets.

Chain Enterprises (also called chain stores or chain corporations) refer to a form of joint economic entities under which scattered enterprises or establishments engaged in providing homogeneous commodities or services, with the central leadership of core enterprise or headquarters and guided by common policies, conduct centralized purchase and distributed selling of commodities, in order to gain better efficiency through standardized operation. Consisting of a number of branch stores, the chain stores have in general following features: 1) homogeneous commodities, 2) unique name of stores, 3) centralized purchase and delivery which is separated from distributed selling operation (most commodities are delivered from the headquarters except some items which, from logistics, quality or freshness considerations, might be delivered by the suppliers directly).

Chain stores have 3 categories:

a) Chain stores under direct management: These are formal chain stores invested or controlled by the headquarters. They operate under the direct and unified management from the headquarters. Adopting a direct management approach, the headquarters give orders and control all retail stores, which follow completely the directives from the headquarters. Large monopolized commercial companies develop and expand their business through purchasing, merging, direct investment and controlling of shares.

b) Chain stores through special permit: Through contracts, chain stores (or their owners) obtain licenses from the headquarters to use designated trade marks, names, operation know-how, and to sell the commodity developed by the headquarters. Under this arrangement, each store in the chain is an independent legal entity and operates under the guidance from the headquarters.

c) Chain stores through voluntary arrangement: Under this arrangement, all stores operate together under the guidance of the headquarters, while maintaining their status of independent legal entities with full ownership of their assets. They use the same store name, sign contracts with the headquarters concerning purchase, sale, publicity, etc. and operate under the contract. They are free to engage in other activities which are not bounded in the contract. They could join or leave the chain on voluntary basis.

Chain stores through special permit and those through voluntary arrangement make up chain stores through license arrangement.

12 对外经济贸易和旅游

Foreign Economy, Trade and Tourism

资料整理：丁卫国

12-1 对外经济主要指标

MAJOR INDICATORS OF FOREIGN TRADE AND ECONOMY

单位：万美元 (USD 10 000)

指 标	Item	1995	2000	2005	2006	2007	2008	2009
进出口总额	**Total Inports and Exports**	**340920**	**321031**	**909188**	**1173841**	**1485828**	**2056673**	**1722867**
进口总额	Total Imports	142484	127941	464203	547976	668449	897464	725028
出口总额	Total Exports	198435	193090	444985	625864	817379	1159209	997840
合同外商直接投资项目(个)	**Contracted Projets of Foreign Direct Investment (uint)**	**881**	**331**	**520**	**460**	**420**	**343**	**268**
合同外商直接投资	**Contracted Value of Foreign Direct Investment**	**108847**	**106583**	**211023**	**200646**	**349212**	**433742**	**204916**
实际外商直接投资	**Actual Value of Foreign Direct Investment**	**62253**	**94368**	**218475**	**244853**	**276622**	**324481**	**365766**
对外经济合作	**Economic and Technical Cooperation with Foreign Countries**							
合同金额	Contracted Value	7300	36706	35953	63704	195692	331419	532879
#对外承包工程	#Contracted Projects			27952	56930	183749	318872	526671
对外劳务合作	Labor Services			5568	6331	6520	6016	6208
完成营业额	Value of Business Fulfilled	4100	15815	31843	41097	62267	152116	263356
#对外承包工程	#Contracted Projects			28852	36266	54416	142456	256368
对外劳务合作	Labor Services			2601	4379	5340	6856	6988

12-2 对外贸易进出口总额

TOTAL IMPORTS AND EXPORTS

单位：万美元 (USD 10 000)

年 份 Year	合 计 Total	进 口 Imports	出 口 Exports
1988	148045	50088	97957
1989	135161	38862	96299
1990	121342	26852	94490
1991	152188	39185	113003
1992	174533	58696	115837
1993	222912	100170	122743
1994	274880	103035	171845
1995	340920	142484	198435
1996	286287	133684	152603
1997	320668	128583	192084
1998	283189	112478	170711
1999	268107	116729	151378
2000	321031	127941	193090
2001	357801	178030	179771
2002	395457	185561	209896
2003	511047	245474	265573
2004	677151	338764	338386
2005	909188	464203	444985
2006	1173841	547977	625864
2007	1485825	668449	817379
2008	2070567	899676	1170891
2009	1722869	725028	997840

注：根据海关统计有关文件规定2008年年终数据部分调整。

Note:According to the provisions of the relevant documents to customs statistics data portion of the 2008 year-end adjustments.

12-3 按贸易方式和经济类型分的进出口额

单位：万美元

项 目	Item	2000		2004	
		进口 Imports	出口 Exports	进口 Imports	出口 Exports
总 计	**Total**	**127942**	**193090**	**338764**	**338386**
按贸易方式分	**Grouped by Type of Trade**				
一般贸易	General Trade	91576	138907	266081	261040
来料加工装配贸易	Processing and Assembling Trade	20136	13265	14824	22063
进料加工贸易	Raw Material Input Processing Trade	32803	14154	30268	53792
来料加工装配进口的设备	Processing and Assembling Import Equipment Provided With Material	6		16	
外商作为投资进口的设备	Goods as Invested for Import Equipments	8602		19289	
租赁贸易	Leasing Trade				
出料加工贸易	Raw Material Output Processing Trade				
易货贸易	Repalce Goods with Goods				
保税仓库进出境货物	Import and Export Goods of Protcetive Tariff Storage	105		7701	23
按经济类型分	**Grouped by Ownership**				
#国有企业	#State-Owned Enterprises	64805	140826	163522	168579
集体企业	Collective-Owned Enterprises	1255	9124	5704	20796
外商投资企业	Foreign-funded Enterprises	61691	42901	135704	98520
民营企业	Private-Owned Enterprises	111	240	33317	50465

TOTAL IMPORTS AND EXPORTS BY TYPE OF TRADE AND OWNERSHIP

(USD 10 000)

2005		2006		2007		2008		2009	
进 口 Imports	出 口 Exports	进 口 Imports	出 口 Exports	进 口 Imports	出 口 Exports	进 口 Imports	出 口 Exports	进 口 Imports	出 口 Exports
464203	**444985**	**547976**	**625864**	**668449**	**817379**	**897464**	**1159209**	**725028**	**997840**
340768	350354	399112	445104	506648	578657	673547	813895	520937	604915
15428	22381	26162	22285	33951	24492	30677	29376	25255	33081
54328	71920	61009	154351	65589	205579	101574	269084	124410	300408
18		7		793		1307		173	
45087		47661		37840		57325		35285	
114				19613		9738		4930	
		48	24	196	141	5265	463	245	95
					2				
8028	33	997	573	2743	704	16669	7325	12347	9382
221963	213955	224155	273834	317296	321892	456213	456685	292224	366163
5719	20033	6876	20636	7066	19889	11774	24169	2209	15168
190170	130579	262971	202851	278723	276891	351294	378960	363956	338730
45839	80397	53178	128543	64098	198631	71553	299162	64949	277567

12-4 进出口商品主要国别和地区

IMPORTS AND EXPORTS VALUE BY COUNTRIES AND REGIONS

单位：万美元 (USD 10 000)

国家(地区)	Countries (Regions)	2008			2009		
		进出口 Imports and Exports	进口 Imports	出口 Exports	进出口 Imports and Exports	进口 Imports	出口 Exports
亚　洲	**Asia**	**904402**	**363119**	**541283**	**801902**	**328226**	**473677**
#香港	#Hongkong	146342	52679	93663	114257	2598	111659
印度	India	65753	15300	50452	51795	10834	40960
日本	Japan	207036	152159	54876	220447	158400	62046
新加坡	Singapore	26445	7349	19096	25544	5138	20406
韩国	Korea, Rep.	145306	41093	104213	83270	42265	41005
台湾省	Taiwan Province	60667	47958	12708	57413	44655	12758
非　洲	**Afria**	**79281**	**19633**	**59647**	98836	23807	75029
#南非	#South Africa	31028	19352	11676	34737	22545	12192
欧　洲	**European**	**537645**	**234477**	**303168**	430204	195817	234388
#比利时	#Belgium	40612	16073	24538	18577	7115	11462
英国	United Kingdom	40365	8492	31872	38557	7902	30654
德国	Germany	138354	85804	52550	100556	69290	31265
法国	France	70047	58718	11328	60395	48505	11890
意大利	Italy	44246	18127	26119	31788	17347	14442
荷兰	Netherland	72828	24784	48044	61514	6495	55018
西班牙	Spanish	19519	3990	15529	13935	3214	10721
芬兰	Finland	3209	1197	2012	6545	5647	898
拉丁美洲	**Latin America**	**208994**	**105238**	**103755**	117427	41428	76000
#巴西	#Brazil	90012	64455	25557	29138	13512	15626
智利	Chile	35997	26810	9187	19720	13571	6149
北美洲	**North America**	**218374**	**86088**	**132286**	173057	58327	114730
#加拿大	#Canada	24806	15869	8937	20511	13078	7434
美国	United States of America	193568	70219	123349	152467	45243	107223
大洋洲	**Occeania**	**107977**	**88908**	**19069**	101442	77424	24017
#澳大利亚	#Australia	105447	88864	16582	91543	77097	14446
附：东南亚国家联盟	**Association of Southeast-Asia Nations**	**140335**	**20186**	**120149**	143471	32825	110646
欧洲联盟	European Union	476374	226377	249997	387862	184466	203395
亚太经济合作组织	**Asia-Pacific Economic Cooperation**	**1121718**	**528929**	**592789**	965948	470712	495239

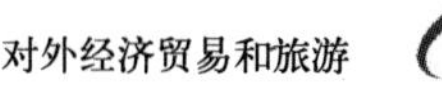

12-5 合同外商直接投资项目
NUMBER OF CONTRACTED PROJECTS OF FOREIGN DIRECT INVESTMENT

单位：个 (unit)

指 标	Item	1990	1995	2000	2005	2006	2007	2008	2009
合 计	**Total**	**99**	**881**	**331**	**520**	**460**	**420**	**343**	**268**
合资经营企业	Joint Venture	17	577	156	203	197	137	131	86
合作经营企业	Cooperative Operation	75	44	16	29	22	27	15	16
独资经营企业	Foreign Solely Funded Enterprises	7	260	158	285	240	255	197	165
外商投资股份制企业	Share Holding Enterprises With Foreign Investment			1	3	1	1		1

12-6 合同外商直接投资金额
VALUE OF CONTRACTED PROJECTS OF FOREIGN DIRECT INVESTMENT

单位：万美元 (USD 10 000)

指 标	Item	1990	1995	2000	2005	2006	2007	2008	2009
合 计	**Total**	**3947**	**108847**	**106583**	**211023**	**200646**	**349212**	**433742**	**365766**
合资经营企业	Joint Venture	1364	68923	27936	51010	81849	76631	150500	122227
合作经营企业	Cooperative Operation	2464	7899	48711	24480	9039	28143	26418	21117
独资经营企业	Foreign Solely Funded	119	32025	29936	132897	104431	240958	253900	198474
外商投资股份制企业	Share Holding Enterprises With Foreign Investment				2636	3453	3480	2924	23948

12-7 实际外商直接投资金额

ACTUAL VALUE OF FOREIGN DIRECT INVESTMENT

单位：万美元 (USD 10 000)

指　标	Item	1990	1995	2000	2002	2003
合　计	**Total**	**2900**	**62253**	**94368**	**140151**	**155702**
合资经营企业	Joint Venture	2492	40259	59879	53628	104622
合作经营企业	Cooperative Operation	85	5012	2789	27731	5513
独资经营企业	Foreign Solely Funded	323	16982	31700	58068	45139
外商投资股份制企业	Share Holding With Foreign Investment					

12-7 续表 continued

单位：万美元 (USD 10 000)

指　标	Item	2004	2005	2006	2007	2008	2009
合　计	**Total**	**207126**	**218475**	**244853**	**276622**	**324481**	**365766**
合资经营企业	Joint Venture	130048	65472	52367	43946	101474	122227
合作经营企业	Cooperative Operation	11741	5089	2990	6077	16665	21117
独资经营企业	Foreign Solely Funded	62155	75305	64184	81762	180960	198474
外商投资股份制企业	Share Holding Enterprises With Foreign Investment		2739	1885	1650	25382	23948

12-8 按行业分外商直接投资（2009）
FOREIGN DIRECT INVESTMENT GROUPED BY SECTOR (2009)

行 业	Item	项目(个) Number of Projects (unit)	合同外资 (万美元) Contracted Foreign Capital (USD 10 000)	实际投资 (万美元) Actual Foreign Investment (USD 10 000)
总 计	**Total**	**267**	**204916**	**365766**
农、林、牧、渔业	Farming, Forestry, Animal Husbandry and Fishery	19	18488	7649
采矿业	Mining and Quarrying	2	2707	2718
制造业	Manufactruring	128	112000	233583
电力、燃气及水的生产和供应业	Power, Gas and Water Production and Supply	9	7252	8291
建筑业	Construction	3	10887	2145
交通运输、仓储和邮政业	Transportaation, Storage and Post	7	4767	6561
信息传输、计算机服务和软件业	Information Trnsmmision, Computer Service and software	7	420	561
批发和零售业	Wholesale and Retail sale	24	3768	6532
住宿和餐饮业	Hotel and Catering	10	867	4937
金融业	Finance			1000
房地产业	Real Estate	3	16120	71780
租赁和商务服务业	Leasing and Commerical Service	32	14720	10897
科学研究、技术服务和地质勘查业	Scietific research, Polytechnical Service and Geological Prospecting	12	3332	541
水利、环境和公共设施管理业	Water Conservancy, Environment and Public Facility Management	8	9376	8085
居民服务和其他服务业	Resident Service and Others	1	26	27
教育	Education	1	1	1
卫生、社会保障和社会福利业	Health Care, Social Security and Social Welfare		-54	
文化、体育和娱乐业	Culture, Sports and Recreation	1	239	458
公共管理和社会组织	Public Management and Social Organizations			

12-9 年末登记外商投资企业行业分布情况（2009）
SECTOR DISTRIBUTION OF FOREIGN-FUNDED ENTERPRISES REGISTERED AT YEAR-END (2009)

单位：个 (unit)

行 业	Item	企业数 Number of Enterprises
总 计	**Total**	**267**
农、林、牧、渔业	Farming, Forestry, Animal Husbandry and Fishery	19
采矿业	Mining and Quarrying	2
制造业	Manufactruring	128
电力、燃气及水的生产和供应业	Power, Gas and Water Production and Supply	9
建筑业	Construction	3
交通运输、仓储和邮政业	Transportation, Storage and Post	7
信息传输、计算机服务和软件业	Information Trnsmmision, Computer Service and software	7
批发和零售业	Wholesale and Retail sale	24
住宿和餐饮业	Hotel and Catering	10
金融业	Finance	
房地产业	Real Estate	3
租赁和商务服务业	Leasing and Commerical Service	32
科学研究、技术服务和地质勘查业	Scietific research, Polytechnical Service and Geological Prospecting	12
水利、环境和公共设施管理业	Water Conservancy, Environment and Public Facility Management	8
居民服务和其他服务业	Resident Service and Others	1
教育	Education	1
卫生、社会保障和社会福利业	Health Care, Social Security and Social Welfare	
文化、体育和娱乐业	Culture, Sports and Recreation	1
其他	Others	

12-10 对外承包工程和劳务合作

CONTRACTED PROJECTS AND LABOR SERVICES CO-OPERATION WITH FOREIGN COUNTRIES

年 份 Year		合同金额 (万美元) Contracted Value (USD 10 000)	实际完成营业额 (万美元) Value of Business Fulfilled (USD 10 000)	年末在外人数(人) Number of Persons Working Abroad at Year-end (person)
1995		7300	4100	2460
1996		8800	5100	3919
1997		18100	6800	4338
1998		17400	9500	4933
1999		18100	12200	5718
2000		36706	15815	6584
2001		12019	14653	7058
2002		29469	15863	7102
2003		29882	20333	4923
2004		31141	27384	5854
2005		35953	31843	7599
2006		63704	41097	10363
2007		195692	62267	15115
2008		331419	152116	15406
2009		532879	263356	15148
对外承包工程	**Contracted Projects**			
2001		8663	9029	1569
2002		12515	27295	1535
2003		17900	28552	1759
2004		28027	25334	2199
2005		27952	28852	2365
2006		56930	36266	2671
2007		183749	54416	5950
2008		318872	142456	9145
2009		526671	256368	10546
对外劳务合作	**Labor Cooperation**			
2001		2997	4589	5461
2002		1633	3081	5525
2003		823	1783	3136
2004		1565	1597	3583
2005		5568	2601	5143
2006		6331	4379	7602
2007		6520	5340	8704
2008		6016	6856	6239
2009		6208	6988	4602
对外设计咨询	**Design Consulting**			
2002		541	267	42
2003		507	650	28
2004		475	1517	72
2005		390	2433	91
2006		983	452	90
2007		5423	2511	461
2008		6531	2804	22

注:2009年起“对外设计咨询”指标数并入“对外承包工程”中；“年末在外人数(人)”修订为“劳务外派人数(人)”

Note:From 2009, "design and consultation," index number into the "International Contractors" in; "at the end of outer (person)" to "manning (person)".

12-11 湖北旅游主要指标

MAJOR INDICATORS OF HUBEI TOURISM

年 份 Year	旅游总收入 (亿元) Total Earnings of Tourism (100 million yuan)	国内旅游收入 (亿元) Earnings from Domestic Tourism (100 million yuan)	国内旅游人数 (万人次) Number of Domestic Tourists (10 000 persons-time)	外汇收入 (万美元) Foreign Exchange Earnings (USD 10 000)	入境旅游人数 (万人次) Number of Tourists Received (10 000 persons-time)
1980				221.00	1.40
1981				297.20	1.60
1982				299.60	2.00
1983				355.30	2.40
1984				731.30	5.40
1985				1008.60	8.50
1986	3.47	2.50	1262	1166.00	10.50
1987	3.67	2.40	1184	1545.00	12.20
1988	3.56	2.40	1208	1411.80	11.30
1989	3.99	3.10	1034	1085.50	8.20
1990	4.56	2.70	890	2263.20	15.60
1991	5.83	3.90	984	2350.00	17.00
1992	9.03	5.40	1071	4432.20	26.30
1993	13.26	9.50	1350	4588.90	23.10
1994	18.09	13.00	1500	6211.40	24.70
1995	24.00	18.00	1700	7316.90	27.10
1996	163.28	153.00	3152	12545.60	36.90
1997	193.92	180.00	3600	16977.50	58.00
1998	217.24	210.00	4044	8831.40	29.60
1999	247.11	238.50	4659	10498.50	30.50
2000	282.26	270.30	5478	14572.10	45.10
2001	353.66	337.20	6064	20075.20	66.80
2002	407.48	384.20	6670	28390.90	102.40
2003	342.77	331.60	5684	13626.90	40.50
2004	410.00	394.20	6849	19240.40	61.20
2005	473.15	450.80	7630	27636.30	82.60
2006	539.74	514.24	8460	32000.38	105.57
2007	640.87	609.40	10135	41264.00	131.81
2008	744.19	713.43	11678	44255.31	118.75
2009	1004.48	969.63	15065	51020.22	133.46

12-12 接待入境旅游人数

NUMBER OF TOURISTS RECEIVED IN HUBEI

单位:人次 (person-times)

年 份 Year	总计 Total	外国人 Foreigners	港澳台同胞 Compatroits from Hongkong, Maco and Taiwan	#港澳同胞 #Compatroits from Hongkong, Macao	#台湾同胞 #Compatroits from Taiwan
1980	13800	8086	5714		
1981	16390	10916	5474		
1982	19775	15126	4649		
1983	24200	18903	5297		
1984	53800	40496	13304		
1985	84598	68103	16495		
1986	105300	83570	21730		
1987	122390	82029	40361		
1988	113051	78206	34845	19725	15120
1989	81781	49511	32270	13908	18362
1990	155734	36374	119360	11560	107800
1991	170121	53055	117066	12645	104421
1992	263401	72691	190323	14054	176269
1993	230883	84552	146331	28460	117871
1994	247212	133343	113869	56417	57452
1995	270890	172869	98021	42785	55236
1996	368877	243595	125282	58949	66333
1997	580223	359700	220523	64466	156057
1998	295643	209402	86241	30337	55904
1999	305408	224748	80660	30935	49725
2000	450805	357352	93453	42928	53162
2001	667818	542737	125081	48417	76664
2002	1024312	755718	268594	49113	219481
2003	405214	323151	82063	40294	41769
2004	611859	501873	109986	57086	52900
2005	825700	626805	198895	107141	91754
2006	1055752	857028	198724	110246	88478
2007	1318179	1077189	240990	140384	100606
2008	1187549	926625	260924	152631	108293
2009	1334634	1017620	317014	182616	134698

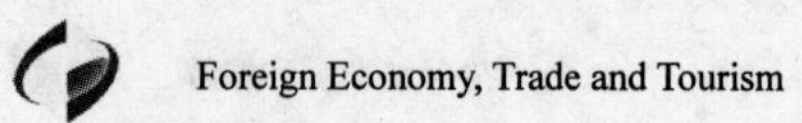

12-13 入境旅游外汇收入

FOREIGN EXCHANGE REVENUE FROM ENTRANCE TOURIST

年 份 Year	外汇收入(万美元) Foreign Exchange Earnings (USD 10 000)	发展指数(1978年为100) Development Index (year1978=100)	同比 Comparision Percentage (±%)	人均花费(美元) Expenditures Per Capita (USD)	
				全国 The Whole Nation	湖北 Hubei
1979	230.75	100.00			
1980	221.00	95.77	-4.23		
1981	297.20	128.80	34.48		
1982	299.64	129.85	82.00		
1983	355.30	153.98	18.58		
1984	731.30	316.92	105.83		
1985	1008.58	327.69	37.92		
1986	1166.00	505.31	15.61		
1987	1545.00	669.56	32.50		
1988	1411.75	611.81	-8.62		
1989	1085.45	470.40	-23.11		
1990	2263.18	980.79	108.50		
1991	2350.00	1018.42	3.84		
1992	4432.16	1920.76	88.60		
1993	4588.88	1988.68	3.54		
1994	6211.42	2691.84	35.36	125.10	125.10
1995	7316.86	3170.90	17.80	141.10	155.70
1996	12545.60	5436.88	71.46	131.16	167.04
1997	16977.51	7357.53	35.33	135.11	168.52
1998	8831.43	3827.27	-47.98	133.87	162.87
1999	10498.49	4549.72	18.88	135.00	166.31
2000	14572.13	6315.12	38.80	136.85	166.58
2001	20075.16	8699.96	37.76	138.76	164.25
2002	28390.95	12303.77	41.42	140.09	160.57
2003	13626.93	5905.50	-52.00	140.09	160.57
2004	19240.41	8338.21	51.00	156.84	169.92
2005	27636.30	11976.73	43.64	154.16	170.14
2006	32000.38	13867.99	15.79	164.29	177.16
2007	41264.00	17882.56	28.95	179.79	181.68
2008	44255.31	19178.90	7.25	186.18	197.56
2009	51020.22	22110.60	15.29	180.77	193.43

12-14 接待入境旅游人天数

DAYS OF THE ENTRANCE TOURISTS STAYED IN HUBEI

单位：人天 (person/day)

年 份 Year	总计 Total	外国人 Foreigners	港澳台同胞 Compatroits from Hongkong, Maco and Taiwan	#港澳同胞 #Compatroits from Hongkong, Macao	#台湾同胞 #Compatroits from Taiwan
1978	15690	7202	8488		
1979	17313	10461	6852		
1980	20700	12130	8570		
1981	22946	15282	7664		
1982	29016	24188	4828		
1983	29830	25298	4532		
1984	107600	37806	69794		
1985	143815	115774	28041		
1986	186379	139677	46702		
1987	167035	115219	51816		
1988	190486	132301	58185	35505	22680
1989	127891	79217	48674	20862	27812
1990	178737	49487	129250	11960	117290
1991	235595	74913	160682	17450	143232
1992	351591	101878	249713	18973	230740
1993	324350	142240	182110	49959	132151
1994	472467	231716	240751	117889	122862
1995	501038	317246	183792	86910	96882
1996	729968	477152	252816	131993	120823
1997	949661	591127	358534	111291	247243
1998	513569	366348	147221	61491	85730
1999	622037	478486	143551	57765	85786
2000	852455	676130	176325	81432	94893
2001	1208938	891787	317151	93376	223775
2002	1712230	1232818	479412	86427	392985
2003	799824	603001	196823	98230	98593
2004	1069442	849071	220371	118234	102137
2005	1513678	1135995	377683	194122	183561
2006	1824387	1502277	322110	176901	145209
2007	2342786	1926484	416302	233946	182356
2008	1187549	926625	260924	152631	108293
2009	1334634	1017620	317014	182616	134398

注：2000年国家不再设“华侨”指标，“华侨”人数含在“外国人”中。

Note:The item of "overseas Chinese" is cancled by state since 2000, The number of "Overseas Chinese" is included in the number of "Foreigner".

12-15 湖北国内旅游接待人数及收入

NUMBER OF DOMESTIC TOURISTS RECEIVEDAND EARNINGS

年 份 Year	接待人数(万人次) Number of Tourists Received (10 000person-times)	同比(±%) Comparision Percentage (±%)	旅游收入(亿元) Earnings (100 million yuan)	同比(±%) Comparision Percentage (±%)	人均天花费(元) Expenditures Per Capita a day (yuan) 全国 The Whole Nation	湖北 Hubei
1986	1262		2.52			
1987	1184	-6.18	2.37	-5.95		
1988	1208	2.03	2.42	2.11		
1989	1034	-14.40	3.10	28.10		
1990	890	-13.92	2.67	-13.87		
1991	984	10.56	3.93	47.19		
1992	1071	8.84	5.36	36.39		
1993	1350	26.05	9.50	77.24		
1994	1500	11.11	13.00	36.84		
1995	1700	13.33	18.00	38.46		
1996	3152	85.41	152.95	-	256	485
1997	3600	14.21	180.00	17.69	328	500
1998	4044	12.33	210.03	16.68	344	519
1999	4659	15.21	238.50	13.56	394	511
2000	5478	17.58	270.31	13.34	427	493
2001	6064	10.70	337.18	24.74	450	556
2002	6670	9.99	384.24	13.96	441	576
2003	5684	-14.78	331.60	-13.70	395	583
2004	6849	20.50	394.22	18.88	550	576
2005	7630	11.40	450.76	14.34	436	591
2006	8460	10.88	514.24	14.08	447	607
2007	10135	19.80	609.40	18.50	482	601
2008	11678	15.23	713.43	17.07	511	610
2009	15065	29.00	969.63	35.91	535	644

12-16 湖北旅游总收入及占全省GDP比重
THE RATIO OF TOTAL EARNINGS OF HUBEI TOURISM IN PROVINCIAL GDP

年 份 Year	旅游总收入 Total Earnings of Tourism		占GDP及三产比重 Percentage in GDP and Three Industries	
	绝对额(亿元) (100 million yuan)	同比(±%) Comparision Percentage (±%)	GDP(%)	三产增加值(%) Value Added of Three Industries (%)
1996	163.24		5.50	17.95
1997	193.92	18.79	5.62	18.03
1998	217.27	12.04	5.87	18.06
1999	247.11	13.73	6.41	18.78
2000	282.26	14.22	6.60	18.94
2001	353.64	24.93	7.59	21.35
2002	407.52	15.24	8.19	22.36
2003	342.77	-15.89	6.35	16.95
2004	410.00	19.61	6.49	17.78
2005	473.15	15.54	7.30	20.64
2006	539.74	14.07	7.20	18.03
2007	640.87	18.74	7.00	17.64
2008	744.19	16.12	6.57	16.22
2009	1004.48	34.98	7.83	20.06

12-17 分地区接待国内旅游者人数

NUMBER OF DOMESTIC TOURISTS RECEIVED BY REGION

单位:万人次 (10 000 person-time)

		2003	2004	2005	2006	2007	2008	2009
全　省	**Province**	**5684.17**	**6849.22**	**7630**	**8459.78**	**10134.53**	**11678.28**	**15065.18**
武汉市	Wuhan Municipality	2098.17	2607.05	2901	3283.05	3889.07	4612.79	6359.99
黄石市	Huangshi Municipality	69.78	100.90	140	198.22	312.47	426.84	517.6
十堰市	Shiyan Municipality	421.03	540.30	595	666.70	737.53	921.45	1123.71
宜昌市	Yichang Municipality	602.99	790.70	862	901.81	1000.05	970.00	1197.22
襄樊市	Xiangfan Municipality	496.11	569.89	626	690.22	750.10	820.05	993.51
鄂州市	Ezhou Municipality	96.90	112.07	115	125.99	140.26	161.98	212.43
荆门市	Jingmen Municipality	305.14	340.58	380	437.76	507.71	543.30	662.14
孝感市	Xiaogan Municipality	183.04	192.61	310	312.14	429.13	508.07	643.46
荆州市	Jingzhou Municipality	305.61	365.55	387	434.05	512.56	564.02	649.78
黄冈市	Huanggang Municipality	254.34	288.44	300	323.91	465.42	515.05	667.81
咸宁市	Xianning Municipality	267.52	301.36	332	334.04	430.25	560.09	715.74
随州市	Suizhou Municipality	291.12	307.19	322	323.94	334.15	398.57	481.69
恩施州	Enshi Prefecture	150.79	176.48	200	225.73	429.55	450.10	505.53
仙桃市	Xiantao Municipality	38.56	40.52	41	47.62	49.13	49.24	88.19
潜江市	Qianjiang Municipality	34.45	36.75	36	36.57	29.21	29.31	38.09
天门市	Tianmen Municipality	27.48	29.77	30	30.95	28.27	29.31	41.87
神农架林区	Shennongjia Forest Zone	40.81	49.05	51	87.07	89.67	118.09	166.42

12-18 分地区接待国内旅游收入

EARNINGS FROM RECEIVNG DOMESTIC TOURISTS BY REGION

单位:亿元 (100 million yuan)

		2003	2004	2005	2006	2007	2008	2009
全　　省	**Province**	**331.60**	**394.22**	**450.76**	**514.24**	**609.40**	**744.19**	**969.63**
武 汉 市	Wuhan Municipality	151.96	192.24	221.22	250.70	296.98	373.68	486.18
黄 石 市	Huangshi Municipality	3.41	3.98	5.98	8.45	12.50	18.55	26.68
十 堰 市	Shiyan Municipality	16.86	19.91	24.40	28.02	29.12	43.10	62.32
宜 昌 市	Yichang Municipality	34.83	45.02	53.80	65.09	67.52	65.09	75.95
襄 樊 市	Xiangfan Municipality	20.26	24.46	28.70	34.54	39.51	47.82	60.94
鄂 州 市	Ezhou Municipality	6.49	6.72	7.10	7.86	8.85	10.56	12.98
荆 门 市	Jingmen Municipality	8.68	8.98	13.40	15.89	18.34	21.88	29.86
孝 感 市	Xiaogan Municipality	14.64	14.79	11.72	12.59	23.15	29.10	37.39
荆 州 市	Jingzhou Municipality	18.26	19.25	19.60	22.05	27.20	31.75	34.77
黄 冈 市	Huanggang Municipality	13.95	14.61	14.80	16.75	27.70	28.20	34.35
咸 宁 市	Xianning Municipality	10.94	11.58	8.40	9.55	15.06	20.46	33.9
随 州 市	Suizhou Municipality	8.33	8.38	12.80	13.22	14.30	18.62	26.54
恩 施 州	Enshi Prefecture	14.44	15.28	16.70	20.61	21.23	26.17	29.21
仙 桃 市	Xiantao Municipality	2.18	2.26	2.30	2.91	3.37	3.01	5.57
潜 江 市	Qianjiang Municipality	2.43	2.43	2.44	2.51	1.40	1.52	2.31
天 门 市	Tianmen Municipality	1.31	1.33	1.40	1.60	1.12	1.25	2.42
神农架林区	Shennongjia Forest Zone	2.63	3.00	6.00	1.94	2.05	3.43	8.25

主要统计指标解释

进出口总额 指实际进出我国国境的货物总金额。包括对外贸易实际进出口货物，来料加工装配进出口货物，国家间、联合国及国际组织无偿援助物资和赠送品，华侨、港澳台同胞和外籍华人捐赠品，租赁期满归承租人所有的租赁货物，进料加工进出口货物，边境地方贸易及边境地区小额贸易进出口货物(边民互市贸易除外)，中外合资企业、中外合作经营企业、外商独资经营企业进出口货物和公用物品，到、离岸价格在规定限额以上的进出口货样和广告品(无商业价值、无使用价值和免费提供出口的除外)，从保税仓库提取在中国境内销售的进口货物，以及其他进出口货物。该指标可以观察一个国家在对外贸易方面的总规模。我国规定出口货物按离岸价格统计，进口货物按到岸价格统计。

商品经营单位所在地进、出口额 指所在地海关注册登记的有进出口经营权的企业实际进、出口额。

商品目的地进口额和商品货源地出口额 目的地进口额指进口货物的消费、使用或最终抵运地的实际进口额；货源地出口额指出口货物的产地或原始发货地的实际出口额。

利用外资 指我国各级政府、部门、企业和其他经济组织通过对外借款、吸收外商直接投资以及用其他方式筹措的境外现汇、设备、技术等。

对外借款 指通过对外正式签订借款协议，从境外筹措的资金，包括外国政府贷款、国际金融组织贷款、外国银行商业贷款、出口信贷以及对外发行债券等。1996 年及以前还包括对外发行股票。该指标是我国利用外资的重要部分。

外商直接投资 指外国企业和经济组织或个人(包括华侨、港澳台胞以及我国在境外注册的企业)按我国有关政策、法规，用现汇、实物、技术等在我国境内开办外商独资企业、与我国境内的企业或经济组织共同举办中外合资经营企业、合作经营企业或合作开发资源的投资(包括外商投资收益的再投资)，以及经政府有关部门批准的项目投资总额内企业从境外借入的资金。

外商其他投资 指除对外借款和外商直接投资以外的各种利用外资的形式。包括企业在境内外股票市场公开发行的以外币计价的股票（目前主要是在香港证券市场发行的H股和在境内证券市场发行的B股）发行价总额，国际租赁进口设备的应付款，补偿贸易中外商提供的进口设备、技术、物料的价款，加工装配贸易中外商提供的进口设备、物料的价款。

对外直接投资 指我国国内投资者以现金、实物、无形资产等方式在国外及港澳台地区设立、购买国（境）外企业，并以控制该企业的经营管理权为核心的经济活动。

对外承包工程 指各对外承包公司以招标议标承包方式承揽的下列业务：(1)承包国外工程建设项目；(2)承包我国对外经援项目；(3)承包我国驻外机构的工程建设项目；(4)承包我国境内利用外资进行建设的工程项目；(5)与外国承包公司合营或联合承包工程项目时我国公司分包部分；(6)对外承包兼营的房屋开发业务。对外承包工程的营业额是以货币表现的本期内完成的对外承包工程的工作量，包括以前年度签订的合同和本年度新签订的合同在报告期内完成的工作量。

对外劳务合作 指以收取工资的形式向业主或承包商提供技术和劳动服务的活动。我国对外承包公司在境外开办的合营企业，中国公司同时又提供劳务的，其劳务部分也纳入劳务合作统计。劳务合作营业额按报告期内向雇主提交的结算数(包括工资、加班费和奖金等)统计。

对外设计咨询 指以服务成果向业主收费的技术服务项目。包括承担地形地貌测绘，地质资源勘探与普查，建设区域规划，提供设计文件、图纸、生产工艺技术资料和工程技术经济咨询，工程项目的可行性考察、研究和评估，进行技术指导和培训人员等；也包括承担国(境)内利用外资建设工程项目中的设计咨询项目内收取外币部分。

旅游者人数

(1)入境国际旅游者人数：指来中国参观、访问、旅行、探亲、访友、休养、考察、参加会议和从事经济、科技、文化、教育、宗教等活动的外国人、华侨、港澳同胞和台湾同胞的人数。不包括外国在我国的常驻机构，如使领馆、通讯社、企业办事处的工作人员；来我国常住的外国专家、留学生以及在岸逗留不过夜人员。

(2)出境居民人数：指大陆居民因公务活动或私人事务短期出境的人数。公务活动出境居民人数包括在国际交通工具上的中国服务员工，因私出境居民人数不包括在国际交通工具上的中国服务员工。

(3)国内旅游者人数：指我国大陆居民和在我国常住 1 年以上的外国人、华侨、港澳台同胞离开常住地在境内其他地方的旅游设施内至少停留一夜，最长不超过 6 个月的人数。

国际旅游(外汇)收入　指入境旅游的外国人、华侨、港澳同胞和台湾同胞在中国大陆旅游过程中发生的一切旅游支出，其对于国家来说就是国际旅游(外汇)收入。

国际旅行社　指经营对外招徕并接待外国人、华侨、港澳同胞和台湾同胞来中国、归国或回内地旅游业务的旅行社。

国内旅行社　指负责经营招徕、组团、接待国内旅客的旅游业务，以及不对外招徕，负责经营接待国际旅行社或其它涉外部门组织的外国人、华侨、港澳同胞和台湾同胞来中国、归国或回内地的旅游业务的旅行社。

星级饭店　指已评定星级的饭店。

Explanatory Notes on Main Statistical Indicators

Total Imports and Exports at Customs refer to the real value of commodities imported into and exported from the boundary of China. They include the actual imports and exports through foreign trade, imported and exported goods under the processing and assembling trades and materials, supplies and gifts as aid given gratis between governments and by the United Nations and other international organizations, and contributions donated by overseas Chinese, compatriots in Hong Kong and Macao and Chinese with foreign citizenship, leasing commodities owned by tenant at the expiration of leasing period, the imported and exported commodities processed with imported materials, commodities trading in border areas (excluding mutual exchange goods), the imported and exported commodities and articles for public use of the Sino-foreign joint ventures, cooperative enterprises and ventures exclusively with foreign own investment. Also included are import or export of samples and advertising goods for whose CIF or FOB value are beyond the permitted ceiling (excluding goods of no trading or use value and free commodities for export), imported goods sold in China from bonded warehouses and other imported or exported goods. The indicator of the total imports and exports at customs can be used to observe the total size of external trade in a country. In accordance with the stipulation of the Chinese government, imports are calculated at CIF, while exports are calculated at FOB.

Import Export Value by Location of China' s Foreign Trade Managing Units refers to actual value of imports and exports carried out by corporations which have been registered by the local customhouse and are vested with right to run import export business.

Import Value of Commodities by the Places of their Destination and Export Value of Commodities by the Places of their Origin in China The former indicator refers to the value of import commodities of the places of their consumption, utilization or the places of their final destination. The latter indicator refers to the value of export commodities of the places of their origin or the places of the commodities dispatched.

Utilization of Foreign Capitals refers to remittance, equipment and technology financed from abroad, by loans, foreign direct investment and other forms undertaken by the Chinese governments at all levels, by various departments, enterprises and other economic units.

Foreign Borrowings refer to funds borrowed from abroad through formal signing of borrowing agreements with foreign institutions, including loans of foreign governments, loans of international financial institutions, commercial loans of foreign banks, export credit, and funds raised by Chinese bonds (and shares before 1996) issued abroad. It is an important part of China's utilization of foreign capitals.

Foreign Direct Investment refers to the investments inside China by foreign enterprises and economic organizations or individuals (including overseas Chinese, compatriots from Hong Kong, Macao and Taiwan, and Chinese enterprises registered abroad), following the relevant policies and laws of China, for the establishment of ventures exclusively with foreign own investment, Sino-foreign joint ventures and cooperative enterprises or for co-operative exploration of resources with enterprises or economic organizations in China. It includes the re investment of the foreign entrepreneurs with the profits gained from the investment and the funds that enterprises borrow from abroad in the total investment of projects which are approved by the relevant department of the government.

Overseas Direct Investment refers to enterprises set up or bought by domestic investors in foreign countries and in Hong Kong, Macao and Taiwan, and the economic activities centering on operation and management of those enterprises are under the control of domestic investors. The statistical scope covers various corporation type enterprises and non-corporation type enterprises receiving direct investment from domestic investment entities.

Other Investment by Foreign Entrepreneurs refers to all forms of utilization of foreign capitals other than foreign borrowings and foreign direct investment. It includes the total value of stock shares in foreign currencies issued by enterprises at domestic or foreign stock exchanges (now mainly consisting of H shares issued at Hong Kong Security Market and B shares issued at domestic security markets), rent payable for the imported equipment through international leasing arrangement, cost of imported equipment, technology and materials provided by foreign counterparts in compensation trade and processing and assembly trade.

Contracted Projects with Foreign Countries refer to projects undertaken by Chinese contractors (project contracting companies) through bidding process. They include: (1) overseas civil engineering construction projects financed by foreign investors; (2) overseas projects financed by the Chinese government through its foreign aid programs; (3) construction projects of Chinese diplomatic missions, trade offices and other institutions stationed abroad; (4) construction projects in China financed by foreign investment; (5) sub-contracted projects to be taken by Chinese contractors through a joint umbrella project with foreign contractor(s); (6) housing development projects. The business income from international contracted projects is the work volume of contracted projects completed during the reference period, expressed in monetary terms, including completed work on projects signed in previous years.

Service Cooperation with Foreign Countries refers to the activities of providing technology and labor services to employers or contractors in the forms of receiving salaries and wages. Labor services providing by contractual joint ventures of Chinese international contracting corporations should be included in the statistics of service co-operation with foreign countries. The business income of labor service cooperation is the income in the form of wages and salaries, overtime pay, bonuses and other remuneration received from the employers during the reference period.

Overseas Design and Consultation Service refers to projects with charges for technical services from overseas operators. It includes geographic and topographic mapping, geological resource prospecting and survey, planning of construction areas, provision of design documents, blueprints, materials on production process and techniques, as well as engineering, technical and economic consultation, and feasibility study, research and evaluation of projects. Also included under this category are the above-mentioned services of foreign-financed projects in China that are paid in foreign currencies.

Number of Tourists

(1) International tourists refer to foreigners, overseas Chinese, Chinese compatriots from Hong Kong, Macao and Taiwan coming to China for sight-seeing, visits, tours, family reunions, vacations, study tours, conferences and other activities of a business, scientific and technological, cultural, educational and religious nature. It does not include representatives and employees of resident institutions of foreign countries in China such as embassies, consulates, news agencies and offices of foreign companies and organizations, nor does it include long-term foreign experts or students residing in China, or persons in transition without spending a night in China.

(2) Chinese residents going abroad refer to Chinese residents going abroad for short terms for either public business or private purposes. Chinese employees working on international transport carriers are included in those going abroad for public business purpose, not in those for private purpose.

(3) Domestic tourists refer to residents of the mainland of China who stay for one night at least but no more than 6 months at tourist facilities in other places than their permanent residence within the territory of the mainland China, including foreigners, overseas Chinese and Chinese compatriots from Hong Kong, Macao and Taiwan who have resided in China for over one year.

Foreign Exchange Earnings from International Tourism refer to the total expenditures of foreigners, overseas Chinese, Chinese compatriots from Hong Kong, Macao and Taiwan during their stay in the mainland of China, which are earnings of foreign exchange from international tourism from the point of view from China.

International Travel Agencies refer to travel agencies engaged in the promotion, solicitation, organization and reception of tours to the mainland of China by foreigners, overseas Chinese, Chinese compatriots from Hong Kong, Macao and Taiwan.

Domestic Travel Agencies refer to travel agencies engaged in the promotion, solicitation, organization and reception of domestic tourists, and in the reception of foreigners, overseas Chinese, Chinese compatriots from Hong Kong, Macao and Taiwan organized by international travel agencies or other departments concerned, without their own promotion and solicitation programmes.

Star-Hotels refer to hotels rated with stars.

13 财政、金融、保险

Government Finance, Banking and Insurance

资料整理：陶　萍　杨　旸

财政、金融、保险
GOVERNMENT FINANCE, BANKING AND INSURANCE
2009

地方财政一般预算收入	Local Budgetary Revenue(100 million yuan)	814.87 (亿元)
地方财政一般预算支出	Local Budgetary Expenditure(100 million yuan)	2090.92 (亿元)
金融机构（含外资）人民币存款年末余额	Balance of RMB Deposits of Financial Organizations (including Foreign Funded Enterprises) By the End of 2009(100 million yuan)	17505.9 (亿元)
#居民储蓄存款	#People's Savings Deposit	8163.46 (亿元)
金融机构（含外资）人民币贷款年末余额	Balance of RMB Loans of Financial Organizations (including Foreign Funded Enterprises) By the End of 2009(100 million yuan)	11659.4 (亿元)

地方财政一般预算收支（亿元）

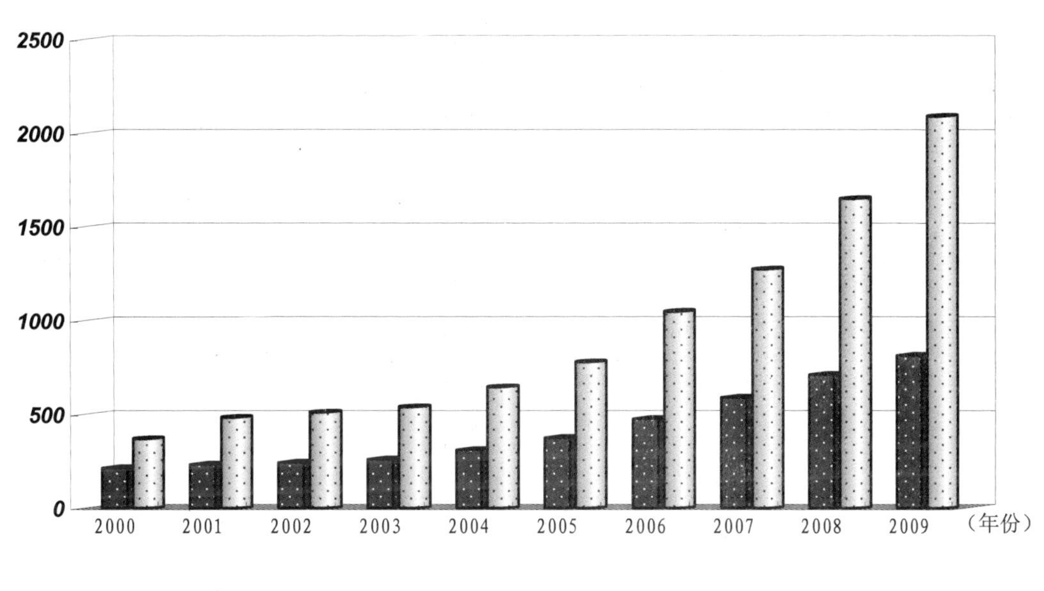

地方财政一般预算收支（亿元）
Local Budgetary Revenue and Expenditure(100 million yuan)

年份(Year)	1995	2000	2001	2002	2003	2004	2005	2006	2007	2008	2009
地方财政一般预算收入 (Local Budgetary Revenue)	100	214	232	243	260	311	376	476	590	711	815
地方财政一般预算支出 (Local Budgetary Expenditure)	162	369	484	511	540	646	779	1047	1274	1650	2091

13-1 历年地方财政收支额及指数

FINANCIAL REVENUE AND EXPENDITURE OVER THE YEARS

单位:亿元 (100 million yuan)

年份 Year	地方一般预算收入 Local Budgetary Revenue	地方财政支出 Local Financial Expenditure	指数(上年=100) Index (previous year=100)	
			收入 Revenue	支出 Expenditure
1952	3.81	1.96	100.00	100.00
1957	6.27	3.55	109.80	96.70
1965	11.26	6.85	97.40	105.20
1970	15.20	15.73	170.60	158.10
1975	24.05	17.52	139.50	103.90
1978	31.38	29.98	149.00	148.60
1980	34.01	26.53	107.60	94.50
1985	50.26	43.60	119.30	137.50
1990	77.85	84.82	100.80	106.10
1991	95.09	99.53	122.20	117.30
1992	94.14	98.97	99.00	99.40
1993	115.07	114.58	122.20	115.80
1994	77.46	137.20		119.70
1995	99.69	162.43	128.70	118.40
1996	124.51	197.44	124.90	121.60
1997	139.89	223.70	112.40	113.30
1998	168.95	280.12	120.80	125.20
1999	194.44	336.46	115.09	120.10
2000	214.35	368.77	110.20	109.60
2001	231.94	484.40	108.20	131.40
2002	243.44	511.39	105.00	105.60
2003	259.76	540.44	106.70	105.70
2004	310.45	646.29	119.50	119.60
2005	375.52	778.72	121.00	120.50
2006	476.08	1047.00	126.80	134.50
2007	590.36	1274.27	124.00	121.70
2008	710.85	1650.28	120.41	129.51
2009	814.87	2090.92	114.60	126.70

注：财政收入为地方一般预算收入。

Note:The financial Revenue refers to Local Budgetary Revenue.

13-2 财政收支
FINANCIAL REVENUE AND EXPENDITURE

单位：亿元 (100 million yuan)

指标	Item	2008	2009
一般预算收入	**General Budgetary Revenue**	**710.85**	**814.87**
税收收入	Revenue	537.21	616.06
#增值税25%	#25% Taxes on Value Added	106.74	113.96
营业税	Run Taxes	169.89	206.79
企业所得税	Enterprise Income Taxes	88.54	86.79
个人所得税	Individual Income Taxes	28.06	29.41
城市维护建设税	Taxes on City Maintenance and Construction	41.57	43.49
房产税	Real Estate Taxews	16.18	18.6
耕地占用税	Taxes on Use of Cultivated Land	7.03	19.05
一般预算支出	**General Budgetary Expenditure**	**1650.28**	**2090.92**
1.一般公共服务	General Public Service	265.8	308.4
2.外交	Foreign Affairs		
3.国防	National Defence	1.07	1.71
4.公共安全	Public Security	125.65	137.57
5.教育	Education	284.19	317.29
6.科学技术	Science and Technology	23.06	25.33
7.文化体育与传媒	Culture, Sports and Media	25.25	36.03
8.社会保障和就业	Social Security and Employment	281.3	343.98
9.医疗卫生	Medical Care	95.08	139.24
10.环境保护	Environmental Protecction	40.92	74.15
11.城乡社区事务	Community Service in Urban and Rural Community	85.22	112.34
12.农林水事务	Water Affairs of Agriculture and Forestry	176.7	254.92
13.交通运输	Transportation	38.31	84.92
14.工业商业金融等事务	Industrial and Commercial Finance Affairs	125.47	
15.地震灾后恢复重建支出	Post-earthquake Reconstruction	2.34	6.95
16.其它支出	Others	79.92	248.09

13-3 财政收入占地区生产总值的比重

FINANCIAL REVENUE AS PERCENTAGE TO GROSS DOMESTIC PRODUCT

年 份 Year	地方财政一般预算收入(亿元) Local Financial Revenue (100 million yuan)	地区生产总值(亿元) Gross Domestic Product (100 million yuan)	地方一般预算收入占地区生产总值的比重(%) Percentage of Local Financial Revenue to GDP (%)
1978	29.98	151.00	19.85
1979	28.07	188.46	14.89
1980	26.53	199.38	13.31
1981	23.60	219.75	10.74
1982	25.47	241.55	10.54
1983	28.32	262.58	10.79
1984	31.72	328.22	9.66
1985	43.50	396.26	10.98
1986	58.04	442.04	13.13
1987	60.98	517.77	11.78
1988	68.66	626.52	10.96
1989	79.07	717.08	11.03
1990	84.82	824.38	10.29
1991	95.09	913.38	10.41
1992	94.14	1088.39	8.65
1993	115.07	1325.83	8.68
1994	77.46	1700.92	4.55
1995	99.69	2109.38	4.73
1996	124.51	2499.77	4.98
1997	139.89	2856.47	4.90
1998	168.95	3114.02	5.43
1999	194.44	3229.29	6.02
2000	214.35	3545.39	6.05
2001	231.94	3880.53	5.98
2002	243.44	4212.82	5.78
2003	259.76	4757.45	5.46
2004	310.45	5633.24	5.51
2005	375.52	6590.19	5.70
2006	476.08	7617.47	6.25
2007	590.36	9333.40	6.33
2008	710.85	11328.92	6.27
2009	814.87	12961.10	6.29

13-4 市州财政收入

FINANCIAL REVENUE OF CITIES AND PREFECTURE

单位：亿元 (100 million yuan)

市、州	Municipalities and Prefecrure	2001	2002	2003	2004	2005	2006	2007	2008	2009
全　　省	**Whole Province**	**231.94**	**243.44**	**259.76**	**310.45**	**375.52**	**476.08**	**590.36**	**710.85**	**814.87**
省　　级	Provinial Level	23.10	59.28	57.33	72.71	94.59	131.60	161.83	174.37	184.06
武 汉 市	Wuhan Municipality	78.23	70.23	80.44	104.02	138.82	178.60	221.68	277.32	316.07
黄 石 市	Huangshi Municipality	8.23	7.43	8.09	9.72	11.96	15.33	19.71	24.09	26.03
十 堰 市	Shiyan Municipality	8.22	8.08	8.47	10.17	11.37	13.20	15.59	19.89	25.76
荆 州 市	Jingzhou Municipality	14.35	12.69	13.28	13.45	12.05	12.86	15.24	18.71	22.36
宜 昌 市	Yichang Municipality	18.24	15.73	16.74	19.13	22.53	27.37	35.57	44.27	54.94
襄 樊 市	Xiangfan Municipality	18.65	15.10	16.90	17.85	18.40	20.62	24.02	30.06	37.02
鄂 州 市	Ezhou Municipality	4.30	3.20	3.58	3.97	4.93	6.46	8.51	10.70	13.02
荆 门 市	Jingmen Municipality	8.03	8.01	8.58	9.29	9.34	10.17	12.06	14.92	18.14
孝 感 市	Xiaogan Municipality	10.75	8.89	9.53	10.13	10.78	12.73	16.63	21.46	26.97
黄 冈 市	Huanggang Municipality	15.54	12.60	12.37	13.11	13.14	15.35	19.93	26.21	32.17
咸 宁 市	Xianning Municipality	6.60	5.30	5.68	6.40	7.43	8.71	11.10	14.33	18.14
恩施自治州	Enshi Prefecture	6.34	5.73	6.02	7.85	8.35	10.03	13.05	15.40	18.28
随 州 市	Suizhou Municipality	3.43	3.60	4.41	4.48	4.25	4.76	5.47	6.68	7.60
仙 桃 市	Xiantao Municipality	3.60	2.92	3.15	3.18	2.81	2.80	3.31	4.21	5.05
天 门 市	Tianmen Municipality	1.85	1.89	2.12	1.82	1.37	1.67	2.18	2.80	3.53
潜 江 市	Qianjiang Municipality	2.32	2.62	2.87	2.94	3.02	3.29	3.85	4.71	4.86
神农架林区	Shennongjia Forest Zone	0.16	0.14	0.18	0.25	0.42	0.50	0.60	0.73	0.87

13-5 市州财政支出

FINANCIAL EXPENDITURE OF CITIES AND PREFECTURE

单位：亿元 (100 million yuan)

市、州	Municipalities and Prefecrure	2001	2002	2003	2004	2005	2006	2007	2008	2009
全　　省	**Whole Province**	**484.4**	**511.39**	**540.44**	**646.29**	**778.73**	**1047.00**	**1274.27**	**1650.28**	**2090.92**
省　　级	Provinial Level	156.13	158.3	148.51	183.98	205.75	284.30	312.94	388.90	258.00
武 汉 市	Wuhan Municipality	104.81	105.58	117.78	142.62	176.88	257.81	307.23	377.88	503.64
黄 石 市	Huangshi Municipality	12.31	13.48	15.26	18.34	23.47	31.43	40.9	53.06	80.85
十 堰 市	Shiyan Municipality	16.69	19.66	21.23	26.9	33.42	42.83	54.24	73.97	118.50
荆 州 市	Jingzhou Municipality	23.36	26.48	29.44	34.14	39.51	52.57	65.8	90.41	130.35
宜 昌 市	Yichang Municipality	28.07	31.54	34.3	38.92	47.63	62.76	79.78	105.86	156.50
襄 樊 市	Xiangfan Municipality	28.49	28.26	32.44	36.38	49.19	56.78	71.52	96.64	148.16
鄂 州 市	Ezhou Municipality	6.09	6.06	7.02	7.98	10.38	13.55	17.85	23.97	35.67
荆 门 市	Jingmen Municipality	12.63	14.41	16.26	19.47	24.58	29.33	38.65	49.18	81.66
孝 感 市	Xiaogan Municipality	18.9	21.11	23.68	26.23	32.5	41.89	54.6	74.64	109.79
黄 冈 市	Huanggang Municipality	27.29	28.84	31.77	37.1	44.4	57.13	76.23	104.47	155.09
咸 宁 市	Xianning Municipality	12.3	13.07	14.26	17.33	21.41	27.72	37.87	56.50	84.97
恩施自治州	Enshi Prefecture	17.79	20.53	22.03	26.19	32.12	41.92	54.89	71.04	102.25
随 州 市	Suizhou Municipality	7.34	8.81	10.33	11.45	14.11	18.08	23.1	31.73	46.11
仙 桃 市	Xiantao Municipality	4.77	5.67	6.4	7.44	8.29	9.81	13.3	17.03	26.25
天 门 市	Tianmen Municipality	3.03	3.84	4.09	5.18	6.22	8.11	10.79	15.14	23.44
潜 江 市	Qianjiang Municipality	3.35	3.99	4.37	5.34	6.99	8.62	11.43	15.36	23.03
神农架林区	Shennongjia Forest Zone	1.07	1.77	1.24	1.32	1.86	2.37	3.13	4.26	6.66

13-6 金融机构(含外资)人民币存款年末余额

BALANCE OF RMB DEPOSITS IN FINANCIAL ORGANIZATIONS (INCLUDING FOREIGN FUNDED ENTERPRISES) BY THE END

单位：亿元 (100 million yuan)

指 标	Item	2000	2005	2006	2007	2008	2009
各项存款	**Deposits**	**3572.33**	**8184.96**	**9570.97**	**11093.03**	**13439.52**	**17505.86**
企业存款	Deposits of Enterprises	1343.00	2503.60	2915.40	3628.25	4307.28	5720.69
活期存款	Demand	921.59	1821.88	2090.62	2686.77	2958.65	4095.15
定期储蓄	Time	421.41	681.72	824.79	941.48	1348.63	1625.54
财政存款	Treasurry Deposits	53.73	208.12	273.55	466.80	529.17	766.45
机关团体存款	Deposits of Government Agency and Organizations	45.20	304.43	389.42	420.68	515.58	680.03
储蓄存款	Saving Deposits	1908.80	4465.79	5103.43	5430.81	6745.44	8163.46
活期存款	Demand	591.06	1544.58	1846.35	2142.79	2486.35	3213.06
定期储蓄	Time	1317.75	2921.22	3257.08	3288.01	4259.09	4950.40
农业存款	Agricultural Deposits	49.32	138.26	182.28	249.02	281.65	385.97
信托存款	Trusted Deposits	9.99					
委托存款	Entrusted Deposits	29.64	105.37	159.76	228.44	284.46	665.85
其他存款	Others	132.65	459.39	547.13	669.03	775.95	1123.41

注：从2007年开始金融机构人民币存款年末余额为含外资数。
Note:RMB balance of financial organiztions began to include that of foreign funded enterprises' since 2007.

13-7 金融机构(含外资)人民币贷款年末余额

BALANCE OF RMB LOANS OF FINANCIAL ORGANIZTIONS (INCLUDING FOREIGN FUNDED ENTERPRISES) BY THE END

单位：亿元 (100 million yuan)

指 标	Item	2000	2005	2006	2007	2008	2009
各项贷款	**Loans**	**3493.91**	**5649.67**	**6430.44**	**7496.46**	**8465.64**	**11659.37**
短期贷款	Short-term Loans	2198.73	2381.77	2527.20	2876.34	2983.72	3576.50
工业贷款	Industrial Loans	680.19	508.61	583.18	687.57	794.79	867.71
商业贷款	Commercial Loans	833.86	767.76	753.33	832.89	750.51	775.24
建筑业贷款	Construction Loans	27.43	114.98	150.93	147.91	130.09	86.92
农业贷款	Agricultural Loans	130.43	246.71	342.07	387.16	388.94	480.21
乡镇企业贷款	Loans to Township Enterprises	87.18	93.36	0.59	0.07	0.02	0.46
三资企业贷款	Loans to Sino-foreign Joint Venture, Cooperative Enterprises and Foreign-funded Enterprises	53.10	19.72	19.78	25.91	35.67	21.04
私营企业及个体贷款	Loans to Private Enterprises and Individuals	12.89	37.78	38.73	44.60	58.64	134.57
其他短期贷款	Other Short-term Loans	373.65	592.84	638.59	750.22	825.06	1210.35
中长期贷款	Medium-term and Long-term Loans	1057.71	2787.77	3363.10	4150.47	4857.82	6908.65
信托贷款	Credit Loans	10.03	0.99				
融资租赁	Loans for Accomodation and Rent	0.23	0.09	0.02		15.50	12.08
委托贷款	Entrusted Loans	39.47	95.46	133.32	154.26	219.32	555.55
票据融资	Bill Financing		380.19	404.00	313.22	386.50	600.61
各项垫款	Money Advanced Payment for Others		3.40	2.80	2.16	2.78	5.98

注：从2007年开始金融机构人民币贷款年末余额为含外资数。
Note: Balance of RMB loans of financial organiztions began to include that of foreign funded enterprises' since 2007.

13-8 国有商业银行人民币存款年末余额
DEPOSITS BALANCE (RMB) OF STATE-OWNED AND STATE FUNDED COMMERCIAL BANK (YEAR-END)

单位：亿元 (100 million yuan)

指 标	Item	2005	2006	2007	2008	2009
各项存款	**Deposit**	**4452.80**	**5025.14**	**5527.17**	**6778.73**	**8398.80**
#企业存款	#Deposits of Enterprises	1215.14	1384.83	1695.64	1974.14	2528.40
活期存款	Demand	902.94	1028.32	1284.63	1431.56	1926.21
定期储蓄	Time	312.20	356.51	411.01	542.58	602.19
储蓄存款	Saving Deposits	2800.32	3145.73	3255.96	4078.43	4906.12
活期存款	Demand	1019.19	1178.18	1316.58	1553.65	1988.06
定期储蓄	Time	1781.13	1967.52	1939.38	2524.78	2918.06
农业存款	Agricultural Deposits	9.28	1.46	1.47	1.81	4.27
其他存款	Others	188.52	230.23	244.61	301.59	399.86

13-9 国有独资商业银行人民币贷款年末余额
LOANS BALANCE (RMB) OF STATE-OWNED AND STATE FUNDED COMMERCIAL BANK (YEAR-END)

单位：亿元 (100 million yuan)

指 标	Item	2005	2006	2007	2008	2009
各项贷款	**Loans**	**2498.77**	**2757.21**	**3143.37**	**3322.29**	**4500.08**
#短期贷款	#Short-term Loans	710.68	728.52	845.48	694.16	911.33
工业贷款	Industrial Loans	262.65	325.29	372.45	390.51	391.31
商业贷款	Commercial Loans	180.43	155.97	166.46	59.02	71.27
建筑业贷款	Construction Loans	22.91	42.02	47.46	40.45	30.84
农业贷款	Agricultural Loans	30.61	45.99	44.59	3.94	8.16
乡镇企业贷款	Loans to Township Enterprises	28.98				
三资企业贷款	Loans to Sino-foreign Joint Venture, Cooperative Enterprises and Foreign-funded Enterprises	6.55	6.48	7.24	10.77	7.45
私营企业及个体贷款	Loans to Private Enterprises and Individuals	10.67	13.49	16.92	15.28	62.16
其他短期贷款	Other Short-term Loans	167.88	139.27	190.37	174.18	340.13
中长期贷款	Medium-term and Long-term Loans	1531.82	1797.82	2145.47	2426.67	3280.05
#基本建设贷款	#Loans for Capital onstruction	755.02	964.38	963.04	1149.62	1560.67
技术改造贷款	Loans for Technical Transformation	48.67	38.48	38.35	46.07	35.43

13-10 农村信用社存贷款年末余额
RURAL CREDIT ASSOCIATION DEPOSITS AND LOANS BALANCE (YEAR-END)

单位：亿元 (100 million yuan)

指　标	Item	2005	2006	2007	2008	2009
各项存款	**Deposits**	**750.08**	**881.21**	**1070.59**	**1293.57**	**1122.18**
#企业存款	#Enterprises Depsits	58.59	58.39	65.08	87.45	56.93
农业存款	Agricultural Depsits	128.86	180.45	247.47	278.11	154.92
储蓄存款	Saving Deposits	554.63	622.62	731.84	900.92	885.83
各项贷款	**Loans**	**449.75**	**519.97**	**630.05**	**744.83**	**683.85**
#乡镇企业贷款	#Enterprises Loans	64.10	0.46			
农业贷款	Agricultural Loans	215.61	295.38	340.48	381.20	371.00

13-11 保险业务主要指标

MAJOR INDICATORS OF INSURANCE BUSINESS

项　目	Item	2008	2009
一、保险密度 (元/人)	Density of Insurance (yuan/person)	555.33	652.11
二、保险深度 (%)	Depth of Insurance (%)	2.8	2.9
三、保费收入 (亿元)	Premium (100 million yuan)	317.15	372.42
(一)财产保险 (亿元)	Property Insurnce (100 million yuan)	54.99	68.97
1.财产险	Property Insurnce	4.65	4.93
2.机动车辆保险	Machine Driving Cars Insurnce	37.86	52.44
3.责任险	Responsibility Insurance	2.29	2.45
4.信用保证险	Credit Guarantee Insurance	0.86	0.39
5.其它	Others	9.34	8.76
(二)人身保险 (亿元)	Life Insurance (100 million yuan)	262.16	303.45
1.人身意外伤害保险	Accident Insurance	5.97	7.09
团体保险	Group Insurance	1.97	2.59
个人保险	Individual Insurance	4	4.50
2.健康险	Healthy Insurance	15.49	17.71
团体保险	Group Insurance	3.63	4.58
个人保险	Individual Insurance	11.86	13.13
3.寿险	Personal Insurance	240.71	278.65
团体保险	Group Insurance	6.65	5.67
个人保险	Individual Insurance	234.06	272.98
四、各项赔款和给付 (亿元)	Claim and Payment	85.89	82.63
(一)财产保险	Property Insurnce (100 million yuan)	39.42	42.88
1.财产险	Property Insurnce	4.53	2.16
2.机动车辆保险	Machine Driving Cars Insurnce	28.3	33.29
3.责任险	Responsibility Insurance	1.35	1.50
4.信用保证险	Credit Guarantee Insurance	0.14	0.17
5.其它	Others	5.09	5.76
(二)人身保险 (亿元)	Life Insurance (100 million yuan)	46.47	39.75
1.人身意外伤害保险	Accident Insurance	2.26	2.55
团体保险	Group Insurance	0.72	0.85
个人保险	Individual Insurance	1.53	1.70
2.健康险	Healthy Insurance	7.14	7.09
团体保险	Group Insurance	4.4	4.19
个人保险	Individual Insurance	2.74	2.90
3.寿险	Personal Insurance	37.08	30.11
团体保险	Group Insurance	3.05	1.25
个人保险	Individual Insurance	34.03	28.86

主要统计指标解释

财政收入 指国家财政参与社会产品分配所取得的收入，是实现国家职能的财力保证。财政收入所包括的内容几经变化，目前主要包括:

(1)各项税收：包括增值税、营业税、消费税、土地增值税、城市维护建设税、资源税、城市土地使用税、企业所得税、个人所得税、关税、证券交易印花税、车辆购置税、农牧业税和耕地占用税等。

(2)专项收入：包括排污费收入、城市水资源费收入、矿产资源补偿费收入、教育费附加收入等。

(3)其他收入：包括利息收入、基本建设贷款归还收入、基本建设收入、捐赠收入等。

(4)国有企业亏损补贴：此项为负收入，冲减财政收入。主要包括对工业企业、商业企业、粮食企业的补贴。

财政支出 国家财政将筹集起来的资金进行分配使用，以满足经济建设和各项事业的需要，主要包括:

(1)基本建设支出：指按国家有关规定，属于基本建设范围内的基本建设有偿使用、拨款、资本金支出以及经国家批准对专项和政策性基建投资贷款，在部门的基建投资额中统筹支付的贴息支出。

(2)企业挖潜改造资金：指国家预算内拨给的用于企业挖潜、革新和改造方面的资金。包括各部门企业挖潜改造资金和企业挖潜改造贷款资金，为农业服务的县办“五小”企业技术改造补助，挖潜改造贷款贴息资金。

(3)地质勘探费用：指国家预算用于地质勘探单位的勘探工作费用，包括地质勘探管理机构及其事业单位经费、地质勘探经费。

(4)科技三项费用：指国家预算用于科技支出的费用，包括新产品试制费、中间试验费、重要科学研究补助费。

(5)支援农村生产支出：指国家财政支援农村集体(户)各项生产的支出。包括对农村举办的小型农田水利和打井、喷灌等的补助费，对农村水土保持措施的补助费，对农村举办的小水电站的补助费，特大抗旱的补助费，农村开荒补助费，扶持乡镇企业资金，支援农村合作生产组织资金、农村农技推广和植保补助费，农村草场和畜禽保护补助费，农村造林和林木保护补助费，农村水产补助费，发展粮食生产专项资金。

(6)农林水利气象等部门的事业费用：指国家财政用于农垦、农场、农业、畜牧、农机、林业、森工、水利、水产、气象、乡镇企业的技术推广、良种推广(示范)、动植物(畜禽、森林)保护、水质监测、勘探设计、资源调查、干部训练等项费用，园艺特产场补助费，中等专业学校经费，飞播牧草试验补助费，营林机构、气象机构经费，渔政费以及农业管理事业费等。

(7)工业交通商业等部门的事业费：指国家预算支付给工交商各部门用于事业发展的人员和公用经费支出，包括勘探设计费、中等专业学校经费、技术学校经费、干部训练费。

(8)文教科学卫生事业费：指国家预算用于文化、出版、文物、教育、卫生、中医、公费医疗、体育、档案、地震、海洋、通讯、电影电视、计划生育、党政群干部训练、自然科学、社会科学、科协等项事业的人员和公用经费支出以及高技术研究专项经费。主要包括工资、补助工资、福利费、离退休费、助学金、公务费、设备购置费、修缮费、业务费、差额补助费。

(9)抚恤和社会福利救济费：指国家预算用于抚恤和社会福利救济事业的经费。包括由民政部门开支的烈士家属和牺牲病残人员家属的一次性、定期抚恤金，革命伤残人员的抚恤金，各种伤残补助费，烈军属、复员退伍军人生活补助费，退伍军人安置费，优抚事业单位经费，烈士纪念建筑物管理、维修费，自然灾害救济事业费和特大自然灾害灾后重建补助费等。

(10)行政事业单位离退休支出：指实行归口管理的行政事业单位离退休经费。

(11)社会保障补助支出：指国家预算用于社会保障的补助支出，包括对社会保险基金的补助、促进就业补助、国有企业下岗职工补助、补充全国社会保障基金等。

(12)国防支出：指国家预算用于国防建设和保卫国家安全的支出，包括国防费、国防科研事业费、民兵建设以及专项工程支出等。

(13)行政管理费：包括行政管理支出，党派团体补助支出，外交支出，公安安全支出，司法支出，法院支出，检察院支出和公检法办案费用补助。

(14)政策性补贴支出：指经国家批准，由国家财政拨给用于粮棉油等产品的价格补贴支出。主要包括粮、棉、油差价补贴，平抑物价和储备糖补贴，农业生产资料价差补贴，粮食风险基金，副食品风险基金，地方煤炭风险基金等。

(15)债务利息支出：指国家预算中用于偿还国内外债务利息的支出。

信贷资金　指金融机构以信用方式积聚和分配的货币资金。金融机构信贷资金的来源有各项存款、金融债券发行、应付及暂收款、对国际金融机构负债、流通中货币、各项准备、所有者权益和其他项目等；信贷资金的运用有各项贷款、有价证券及投资、应收及预付款、委托投资、金银占款、外汇占款、库存现金、财政借款及在国际金融机构中的资产等。

存款　指企业、机关、团体或居民根据资金必须收回的原则，把货币资金存入银行或其他信贷机构保管并取得一定利息的一种信用活动形式。根据存款对象或性质的不同可划分为企业存款、财政存款、机关团体存款、基本建设存款、储蓄存款、农村存款、委托存款、其他存款等科目。它是银行信贷资金的主要来源。

贷款　指银行或其他信贷机构根据资金必须归还的原则，按一定利率，为企业、个人等提供资金的一种信用活动形式。我国银行贷款分为短期贷款、中期流动资金贷款、中长期贷款、信托贷款、融资租赁、委托贷款、票据融资、各项垫款等。

保险公司　在中国境内的、经过保险监督管理部门批准设立，并依法登记注册的各类商业保险公司。

保险金额　指保险人承担赔偿或者给付保险金责任的最高限额。

保费　指投保人为取得保险人在约定范围内所承担赔偿责任而支付给保险人的费用。

赔款　指保险人根据保险合同的规定，向被保险人支付的赔偿保险责任损失的金额。

给付　包括死伤医疗给付和满期给付。死伤医疗给付是指保险人根据人寿保险及长期健康保险合同的规定，因被保险人在保险期内发生保险责任范围内的保险事故支付给被保险人(或受益人)的金额。满期给付是指被保险人生存期满，保险人按人寿保险合同规定支付给被保险人的满期保险金额。

Explanatory Notes on Main Statistical Indicators

Government Revenue refers to the revenue of the government finance by means of participating in the distribution of the social products, which is the financial resources for ensuring the government to function. The contents of government revenue have been changed several times. Now it includes the following main items:

(1) Various tax revenues, including value added tax, business tax, consumption tax, land value added tax, tax on city maintenance and construction, resources tax, tax on use of urban land, enterprise income tax, personal income tax, tariff, stamp tax on security transactions, tax on purchase of motor vehicles, tax on agriculture and animal husbandry and tax on occupancy of cultivated land, etc.

(2) Special revenues, including revenues from the fee on sewage treatment, fee on urban water resources, fee for the compensation of mineral resources and extra-charges for education, etc.

(3) Other revenues, including revenue from interest, revenue from the repayment of capital construction loan, revenue from capital construction projects, and donations and grants.

(4) Subsidies for the losses of the state-owned enterprises. This is an item of negative revenue, consisting of subsidies to industrial, commercial and grain purchasing and supply enterprises.

Government Expenditure refers to the distribution and use of the funds the government finance has raised, so as to meet the needs of economic construction and various causes. It includes the following main items:

(1) Expenditure for capital construction: It refers to the non-gratuitous use and appropriation of funds for capital construction in

the range of capital construction, outlay of capital as well as the loans on capital construction approved by the government for special purpose or policy purpose and the expenditure with discount paid in an overall way within the amount of the funds appropriated to the departments for capital construction.

(2) Innovation funds of the enterprises: They refer to the funds appropriated from the government budget for the enterprises to tap the latent power, upgrade the technology and carry out innovation, including the innovation fund of the departments, loan of the enterprises for innovation, subsidies on the innovation of the small fertilizer plant, small cement plant, small coal mines, small machinery plant and small steel plant, the expenditure of interest for the loan for innovation.

(3) Geological prospecting expenses: They refer to the expenses appropriated from the government budget to the geological prospecting units for the expenditure of the prospecting work, including the expenditures of the administrative agencies for geological prospecting and their institutional units as well as the geological prospecting expenditure.

(4) Expenditures for science and technology promotion: They refer to the expenses appropriated from the government budget for the scientific and technological expenditure, including new products development expenditure, expenditure for intermediate trial and subsidies on important scientific researches.

(5) Expenditure for supporting rural production: It refers to the expenditures appropriated from the government budget for supporting the various expenditures of the rural collective units or households for production, including the subsidies to the small water conservancy projects and well drilling, sprinkling irrigation projects run by the villages; subsidies on the rural water and soil conserving measures; subsidies to the small power stations run by the villages; subsidies to the expenditure for fighting against particularly severe draughts; subsidies on the rural waste land exclamation; fund for supporting the township enterprises; fund for supporting rural cooperative production organizations, subsidies to the expenditure for popularization of the agricultural technologies and plant protection in the rural areas; subsidies to the expenditure for the protection of grasslands and cattle and fowls; subsidies on afforestation and forest protection in rural areas; subsidies on the rural aquatic products industry; special fund for developing grain production.

(6) Operating expenses of the departments of farming, forestry, water conservancy and meteorology etc.: They refer to the expenses appropriated from the government budget for the expenditures of agricultural exclamation, farms, agriculture, animal husbandry, agricultural machinery, forestry, timber industry, water conservancy, aquatic products industry, meteorology, technology popularization in township enterprises, popularization (demonstration) of improved varieties, plant (cattle and fowls, forest) protection, water quality monitoring, prospecting and designing, resources investigation, cadres training, subsidies to horticulture gardens, expenditure of specialized secondary schools, subsidies on the experiments of sowing herbage seeds by flights, expenditures of afforestation agencies and meteorology agencies, expenses for fishery administration and operating expenses for agricultural administration, etc.

(7) Operating expenses of the departments of industry, transport and commerce: They refer to the expenses appropriated from the government budget to cover the expenditure on salaries and operational expenditure of the departments of industry, transport and commerce for the expenditure of business development, including expenses for prospecting and designing, expenditures of specialized secondary schools, expenditures of the technical training schools and expenditures for cadres training, etc.

(8) Operating expenses of the departments of culture, education, science and public health: They refer to the expenses appropriated from the government budget for the expenditures on salaries and operational expenditure of the causes of culture, publication, cultural relics, education, public health, traditional Chinese medical science, free medical services, sports, archives, earthquake, ocean, communications, broadcasting, film and television, family planning; expenditure for training of cadres of government, party and mass organization; expenditures for natural sciences, social sciences, associations for science and technology and the special expenditure for the high-tech researches. They include mainly wages, extra wages, welfare funds, pension for the

retirees, stipend, expenses for official business, expenses for equipment purchases, expenses for repairs, business expenses and subsidies to the units which are unable to support their expenditures by their own earnings.

(9) Pension for the disabled or for the families of the bereaved and relief funds for social welfare: They refer to the funds appropriated from the government budget for the expenditures of pension for the disabled or for the families of the bereaved and relief funds for social welfare, including the lump-sum or regular pension paid by the departments of civil affairs to the members of martyrs families and families of those who died for the public interest, pension to the revolutionary disabled, subsidies for permanent disability of various kinds, subsidies to the military martyrs dependents and the demobilized servicemen, expenditure for settling down the demobilized servicemen, operating expenses of the consoling institutions, expenses for management and repair of the commemorative buildings for the martyrs, the expenses managed by the departments of civil affairs for the retirees and those who have quitted their work, expenses for social relief in rural and urban areas, operating expenses for providing relief to the areas of natural calamity and subsidies on the reconstruction after the particularly severe natural calamities, etc.

(10) Expenditure on retirees: It refers to the expenditure on retirees of government agencies and institutions that are covered by the state budget.

(11) Expenses on subsidies to social security system: It refers to expenditure from the state budget for subsidies to social security system, including subsidies to the social insurance fund, subsidies to promoting employment, subsidies to laid-off workers of state-owned enterprises, supplement to national social security funds, etc.

(12) Expenditures for national defence: They refer to the security, including expenses of national defence, expenses of scientific researches on national defence, expenses for building up peoples militia and expenditure for special projects, etc.

(13) Administrative expenses: They include expenditure for administration, subsidies to the parties and mass organizations, diplomatic expenditure, expenditure for public security, judicial expenditure, law court expenditure, procuratorial expenditure and subsidies to the expenses for treating the cases by the public security departments, procuratorial organs and law courts.

(14) Expenditure on policy-related subsidies: It refers to the expenditure appropriated, with the approval of the government, from the state budget for price subsidies on such products as grain, cotton and edible oil. More specifically, it includes subsidies to the difference between the selling prices and purchasing prices of grains, cotton and edible oil, subsidies for curtaining prices and for sugar reserve, subsidies to the difference between the selling prices and purchasing prices of means pf agricultural production, risk fund for grains, risk fund for non-staple food, risk fund for local production of coal, etc.

(15) Expenditure on interest of debts: It refers to expenses from the state budget on paying interest of domestic and foreign debts.

Credit Funds refer to the funds issued as loans by banking institutions. The sources of credit funds of the banking institutions included deposits, issue of financial bonds, account-payable and temporary gathering, liabilities to international financial institutions, currency in circulation, various reserves, owners' rights and interests and other items. The credit funds can be used in forms of loans, securities and investment, account receivable and advance payment, entrusted investment, gold, foreign exchange, cash on hand, government debt and assets in the international financial institutions.

Deposit is a form of credit by which enterprises, institutions, organizations or households can put money into banks and other credit institutions for safekeeping and interest earning under the principle of free withdrawal. According to different depositors, deposits are divided into enterprise deposits, treasury deposits, deposits of government agencies and organizations, capital construction deposits, savings deposits, rural saving deposits, entrusted deposits and other deposits. Deposits are major sources of the credit funds of banks.

Loan is a form of credit by which banks and other credit institutions provide funds at certain interest rate to enterprises and individuals in the light of the principle of unconditional repayment. Loans from Chinese banks include circulating capital loans, fixed assets loans, loans to urban and rural individuals engaged in industrial and commercial business and agricultural loans.

Insurance Companies refer to commercial insurance companies of various forms registered by law and established in China with the approval of insurance regulatory agencies.

Amount Insured refers to the maximum that the insurant will get for the claim of the case insured.

Premium is the fee paid by the insurant to the insurer to obtain the obligation of compensation from the insurance within the agreed terms.

Settled Claim is the compensation paid by the insurer to the insurant in accordance with the insurance contract.

Payment includes payment for death, injury or medical treatment and mature payment. Payment for death, injury or medical treatment refers to the money paid to the insurant (or the beneficiary) in accordance with the life or health insurance contract when the insurant encounters accidents within the insured period covered in the contract. Mature payment refers to the mature payment to the insurant in accordance with the life insurance contract at the end of the insured period.

14 科技、教育

Science, Technology and Education

资料整理：谢余强　陈　晓

14-1 科技活动基本情况

BASIC STATISTICS ON PERSONEL ENGAGED IN SCIENTIFIC AND TECHNICAL ACTIVITIES

项 目	Item	2003	2004	2005	2006	2007	2008
科技活动人员 (人)	Personels Engaged in Scientific and Technical Activities (person)	192724	168548	191276	195984	197301	210911
科学家和工程师	Scientists and Engieerings	143410	125618	146692	149861	150941	160560
R&D人员 (人)	R & D Personels	51901	48074	65309	62616	67902	73042
科技经费筹集额 (万元)	Funding for Scientific and Technical Research (10 000 yuan)	1182487	1363286	1716672	1908685	2309623	3120569
政府资金	Government Funds	352133	349391	493027	544224	718538	819721
企业资金	Enterprises Funds	692952	810443	1048591	1116836	1320199	2006339
科技经费支出 (万元)	Expenditures of Scientific and Technical Research Funds (10 000 yuan)	1147325	1305311	1739892	1894829	2286837	3017439
内部支出	Inner Expenditures	1081258	1240147	1643187	1808784	2168513	2858106
R&D经费内部支出 (万元)	Inner Expenditures for R & D Funds (10 000 yuan)	548173	567558	841514	947512	1124990	1490636
基础研究	Basic Research	24462	33532	38615	51294	49617	54136
应用研究	Practical Research	120400	153664	168669	158098	196931	204439
实验发展	Experiment Development	325902	347573	600035	692012	813899	1141009

注：由于2009年开展全国第二次R&D资源清查，全省汇总数据已报国家，正处于审核调整阶段，暂不能提供省级数据，因此此表中2009年资料空缺。

Note:The data of 2009 is not availeble because the second national R&D survey was conducted in 2009, and the data of the province submitted to the national level is at the stage of evalution.

14-2 科技活动项目、成果与机构情况

BASIC STATISTICS ON SCIENTIFIC AND TECHNICAL PROJECTS, ACHIEVEMENT AND INSTITUTIONS

项 目	Item	2004	2005	2006	2007	2008
发表科技论文 (篇)	Scientific Research Papers Published (piece)	61925	65268	73059	79511	77207
出版科技专著数 (种)	Scientific and Techincal Books Published (kind)	1914	2077	2271	2413	2485
科技项目(课题)数 (个)	Number of Scientific Projects (unit)	23238	28997	31981	37490	43928
科技项目经费支出 (万元)	Expenses for Scientific Projects (10 000 yuan)	636283	1076845	1313380	1531019	2041625
科学研究与开发机构数 (个)	Number of Scientific Research Institutions and Development Organizations (unit)	1158	1378	1364	1341	1493
科研机构科技活动人员数 (人)	Number of Personels Engaged in Scientific Research and Activities (person)	49337	54107	62900	64284	69960
科研机构科技经费内部支出(万元)	Inner Expenditures for R & D Funds (10 000 yuan)	503119	633487	880961	1139004	1316824
科研机构年末固定资产原价(万元)	Original Price of Fixed Assets at Year-end of Scientific Research Institutions and Organizations (10 000 yuan)	671492	801700	828395	1013264	1185224

注：由于2009年开展全国第二次R&D资源清查，全省汇总数据已报国家，正处于审核调整阶段，暂不能提供省级数据，因此此表中2009年资料空缺。

Note:The data of 2009 is not availeble because the second national R&D survey was conducted in 2009, and the data of the province submitted to the national level is at the stage of evalution.

14-3　政府部门所属科学研究与开发机构科技活动情况
BASIC STATISTICS ON STATE-OWNED RESAEARCH AND DEVELOPMENT INSTITUTIONS

项　目	Item	机构(个) Number of Institu-tions (unit)	科技活动人员(人) Persons Engaged (person)	#科学家与工程师 Scientists and Engieers	#R&D人员 Research and Development Persons	收费收入(万元) Revenue (10 000 yuan)	#政府拨款 Government Appropriations
2008年总计	**Total of 2008**	**293**	**9210**	**6528**	**3388**	**200862**	**147810**
一、自然科学和技术领域	Natural Science and Technology	272	8280	5764	4177	221334	135498
县级政府部门属	Department of County	149	1357	457		15722	2532
市、州级政府部门属	Department of Cities and Prefecture	87	2639	1815	528	36887	20626
省政府部门属	Department of Province	25	2081	1615	850	55402	25999
国务院部门属	Department of State Council	11	2203	1877	2799	113323	86341
#中科院武汉分院属	#Chinese Academy of Science Wuhan Branch	6	991	901	2289	56723	48259
二、社会、人文科学领域	Sosiety, Humanities	10	423	359	53	7269	6635
2009年总计	**Total of 2009**	**287**	**9713**	**5728**	**4713**	**220902**	**171813**
一、自然科学和技术领域	Natural Science and Technology	266	8815	4960	4695	206882	159070
县级政府部门属	Department of County	144	1326	768		45230	2849
市、州级政府部门属	Department of Cities and Prefecture	75	3080	3080	532	20346	30006
省政府部门属	Department of Province	30	2548	1854	993	64133	41822
国务院部门属	Department of State Council	13	2759	2097	3170	143904	107734
#中科院武汉分院属	#Chinese Academy of Science Wuhan Branch	7	1310	1111	2666	65963	54507
二、社会、人文科学领域	Society, Humanities	10	409	334	18	6276	6105

14-3 续表 continued

项　　目	Item	经费支出(万元) Expenditures (10 000 yuan)	#科技经费支出 Expenditure on Science & Technology	#R&D经费内部支出 Inner Expenditure for R & D	研究课题数(个) Number of Projects	课题经费投入(万元) Investment on Subject Study (10 000 Yuan)	参加课题组(人年) Number of persons engaged in Subjects Study (person/year)
2008年总计	**Total of 2008**	**204430**	**175728**	**68675**	**1607**	**61645**	**4714**
一、自然科学和技术领域	Natural Science and Technology						
县级政府部门属	Department of County	17475	4724		57	878	171
市、州级政府部门属	Department of Cities and Prefecture	33953	26555	3297	351	4886	1067
省政府部门属	Department of Province	53459	36653	8653	419	10350	977
国务院部门属	Department of State Council	102633	98546	55804	1483	45548	2341
#中科院武汉分院属	#Chinese Academy of Science Wuhan Branch	47854	47577	38538	1041	27972	1552
二、社会、人文科学领域	Sosiety, Humanities	7064	7033	920	53	96	102
2009年总计	**Total of 2009**	**235605**	**183396**	**89609**	**2676**	**78186**	**5167**
一、自然科学和技术领域	Natural Science and Technology						
县级政府部门属	Department of County	19873	4338		60	686	254
市、州级政府部门属	Department of Cities and Prefecture	43579	31028	3514	420	6519	1199
省政府部门属	Department of Province	62098	42563	16461	535	12467	1285
国务院部门属	Department of State Council	129927	109804	69633	1721	59200	2684
#中科院武汉分院属	#Chinese Academy of Science Wuhan Branch	60040	49878	45580	1215	34516	1866
二、社会、人文科学领域	Society, Humanities	13547	10705	480	45	572	115

注：1.本表数据没有包括科技情报文献机构数据，但包括了县政府所属科技综合服务机构数。
2.科技部门的课题数包括生产性活动课题。

Notes:a)The data of intelligence literature is not included in this table.
b)The number of projects in science and technology department includes projects of production activities.

14-4 科学情报文献机构情况
STATISTICS ON SCIENTIFIC INTELLIGENCE LITERATURE ORGANIZATIONS

项 目	Item	1995	2000	2005	2006	2007	2008	2009
机构 (个)	Institutions (unit)	12	14	12	11	11	11	11.0
职工总数 (人)	Total Number of Employees (person)	609	564	546	535	525	542	539.0
从事科技活动人员	Persons engaged in Scientific Activities	158	511	456	457	458	507	489.0
#科学家与工程师	#Scientists and Engieers	329	337	306	310	354	369	336.0
经费收入总额 (万元)	Funds (10 000 yuan)	1529.2	2629.3	6676.8	6368.9	7086.5	7671.6	7743.6
#政府拨款	#Government Appropriations	934.5	1679.2	5209.6	4503.8	5102.8	5675.4	6637.3
经费支出总额 (万元)	Expendtitures (10 000 yuan)	1480.0	2339.9	6778.2	6460.0	6599.0	7320.0	8292.3
#劳务费	#Service Charge	448.2	970.2	1178.8	1599.6	2017.6	2130.9	2272.0

14-5 高等院校科技活动情况
BASIC STATISTICS ON SCIENTIFIC AND TECHNICAL ACTIVITIES OF INSTITUTIONS OF HIGHER EDUCATION

项 目	Item	2008			2009		
		合 计 Total	自然科学和技术领域 Natural Science and Technology	社会、人文科学领域 Sosiety, Humanities	合 计 Total	自然科学和技术领域 Natural Science and Technology	社会、人文科学领域 Sosiety, Humanities
科学研究与开发机构数 (个)	Institutions of Research and Development (unit)	297	239	58	414	298	116
科技活动人员数 (人)	Number of Personels in Scientific and Technical Activities (person)	52216	43584	8632	65999	45120	20879
#科学家和工程师	Scientists and Engieers	49915	41502	8413	51856	43369	8487
科技经费筹集额 (万元)	Funds (10 000 yuan)	411119	376362	34757	476137	437420	38717
#政府资金	Government Appropriations	221508	203444	18064	267295	245852	21443
科技经费支出 (万元)	Expenditures (10 000 yuan)	353635	322827	30808	423321	388138	35183
#研究与发展经费内部支出	Inner Expenditures for Research and Development	184996	154866	30130	270363	235772	34591
研究课题数 (个)	Number of Research Projects (unit)	29301	20387	8914	32157	22082	10075
项目(课题)经费投入 (万元)	Funds Invested in Research Projects (10 000 yuan)	301874	283391	18483	366091	339024	27067
项目(课题)参加人员 (人)	Number of Persons Engaged in Projects (10 000 persons)	14537	11085	3452	15160	11785	3375

14-6 大中型工业企业科技活动情况
STATISTICS ON SCIENTIFIC AND TECHNICAL ACTIVITIES OF LAREGE AND MEDIUM-SIZED INDUSTRIAL ENTERPRISES

单位：万元 (10 000 yuan)

项　目	Item	1990	1995	2000	2005	2007	2008	2009
科技活动经费筹集额	Volume of Funds Raised for Scientific and Technical Activities	60882	229905	398463	648423	979291	1603181	
政府部门资金	Government Funds	2588	11830	15253	21055	43395	55829	
金融机构贷款	Loans from Financial Organizations	10075	48029	37137	15943	49605	32425	
企业资金	Enterprises Funds	44029	165390	313576	604596	878731	1477531	
其他	Others	4190	4655	32497	6830	7560	37396	
科技活动经费支出总额	Total Expendirures for Scientific and Technical Activities	57133	208682	374166	758613	1090272	1807913	
#研究与发展经费支出	#Expenditures for Research and Development			140828	307880	525193	772287	1056576
新产品开发费支出	Expenditures for Develop New Products	23572	87157	162302	354130	614461	923529	1355946
技术改造经费支出	Expenditures for Technical Innovation	89966	535621	323734	1253563	2502039	3683065	
技术引进经费支出	Expenditures for Technology Introduction	103227		106801	83022	60190	95030	
消化吸收经费支出	Expenditures for Utilization	1248		9092	16312	24747	32923	
购买国内技术经费支出	Expenditures for Purchasing Domestic Technology	1144		12919	7387	10233	13947	

14-6 续表 continued

项　目	Item	1990	1995	2000	2005	2007	2008	2009
大中型企业个数 (个)	Large and Medium Enterprises (unit)	551	922	848	803	930	1053	1174
有科技活动的企业数 (个)	Number of Enterprises with Scientific Activities (unit)			484	303	348	435	
从事科技活动人员数 (个)	Number of Persons Engaged in Scientific Activities (person)	36289	63340	69678	60811	73450	84035	102909
#科学家和工程师	#Scientists and Engieers	13491	25602	38762	39639	47593	54783	
研究与发展人员数 (个)	Persons Engaged in Research and Development (person)			26614	32005	37894	42914	65580
企业办科技开发机构数 (个)	Number ofScientific development Organizations Opened by Enterprises (unit)	396	587	306	253	278	320	418
技术开发项目数 (个)	Number of Technical Development Projects (unit)	1525	5414	5482	4306	5693	7233	
开发项目经费支出 (万元)	Expenses for Development Projects (10 000 yuan)	25222	208682	217040	462619	848952	1226957	

注：由于2009年进行全国第二次R&D资源清查，指标体系有很大调整，多项指标数据不能提供。
Note:As the second in 2009 for national R & D resources, inventory, greatly adjusted index system, a number of indicator data can not provide.

14-7 有科技活动的大中型工业企业主要分组指标

指 标	Item	有R&D活动企业(个) Number of Enterprises with R & D Activities (unit)	
		2008	2009
总 计	**Total**	**317**	**373**
一、按登记注册类型分	**Grouped by Type of Registration**		
内资企业	Domestic Enterprises	264	302
国有企业	State-owned Enterprises	48	57
集体企业	Collective-owned Enterprises	1	4
股份合作企业	Cooperative Enterprises	3	5
国有联营企业	State-owned Enterprises		
国有与集体联营企业	State-owned And Collective Enterprises		
国有独资公司	Owned Company	15	14
其他有限责任公司	Other Limited Liability Company	91	103
股份有限公司	Share Co., Ltd.	71	69
私营独资企业	Private Enterprise	2	1
私营合伙企业	Private Partnership Enterprises		2
私营有限责任公司	Private Limited Liability Company	25	38
私营股份有限公司	Private Limited	7	8
其他内资企业	Other Domestic-funded Enterprises	1	1
港、澳、台商投资企业	Hongkong, Maco and Taiwan-invested Enterprises	11	21
合资经营企业(港或澳、台资)	Joint Ventures (Hongkong, Maco or Taiwan Invested Enterprises)	9	12
合作经营企业(港或澳、台资)	Cooperative Ventures(Hongkong, Maco or Taiwan Invested Enterprises)		2
港、澳、台商独资经营企业	Enterprises Solely Funded by hongkong, Maco and Taiwan Businessmen	2	5
港、澳、台商投资股份有限公司	Hongkong, Maco and Taiwan Funded Share Holding Co.Ltd.		2
外商投资企业	Foreign-invested Enterprises	42	50
中外合资经营企业	Sino-Foreign Joint Ventures	33	38
外资企业	Foreign Funded Enterprises	6	9
外商投资股份有限公司	Foreign Funded Share Holding Co.Ltd.	3	3
二、按行业分	**Grouped by Sector**		
煤炭开采和洗选业	Coal Mining and Processing	1	
石油和天然气开采业	Petroleum and Natural Gas Extraction	2	1
黑色金属矿采选业	Ferrous Metals Mining and Processing		
有色金属矿采选业	Non-ferrous Metals Mining and Processing	2	1
非金属矿采选业	Non-metal Minerals Mining and Processing	2	1
农副食品加工业	Primary Products, Food, Process Industry	4	12

MAJOR INDIENTORS OF LARGE AND MEDIUM-SIZED INDUSTRIAL ENTERPRISES WITH SCIENTIFIC AND TECHNOLOGICAL ACTIVITIES

科技活动人员合计(人) Number of Persons Engaged in Scientific and Technical Activities (person)		R&D人员合计(人) R & D Personels (person)		R&D经费支出(万元) Funding for R & D Expenditure (10 000 yuan)		新产品开发经费支出(万元) Funding for New Product Development Expenditures (10 000 yuan)		新产品销售收入(万元) Revenue of New Product Sales (10 000 yuan)	
2008	2009	2008	2009	2008	2009	2008	2009	2008	2009
84035	**102909**	**42914**	**65580**	**772287.4**	**1056575.9**	**923528.9**	**1355945.8**	**16573052.1**	**16505431**
68937	86156	34054	55045	565221.1	868153	672228.5	1080114.9	9857044.7	9896818.5
26555	31921	12213	20234	250311.6	423145.5	313540.4	525678.4	4898653.1	5404212
73	184	22	157	305.8	824.4	353.3	659.4		
261	374	129	258	3919.1	2932.4	4829.3	4485.3	58333.9	48261.2
6689	8598	3672	5775	75850	69828.2	84688.4	82814.1	1614438.1	662206.3
12741	17347	5915	10972	73119.8	145257.7	97048.8	168960.7	897873.7	1166734.9
17740	21699	9963	14545	129153.7	191177.1	135497.8	249230.6	2016279.6	2085084
58	56	28	26	616	32.7	598.2	32.7	3101.4	696.8
	84		84		2580		2580		
3790	4532	1914	2336	28946.1	25885.1	32515.5	36200.8	333060.7	361494.5
974	1273	176	633	2238.7	6440.9	2375.8	9415.7	25891.8	168030.8
56	88	22	25	760.3	49	781	57.2	9412.4	98
2186	3327	1091	2320	11100.5	33014.3	20117.4	55446.2	413526	984267.6
1487	2340	1010	1580	9925.7	9585.7	16303.2	27187.1	341710	490521.2
35	166		115		3846.6	176.9	1454.8	5794.8	10026.5
418	542	81	458	1174.8	17180.3	2837.3	26697.4	64358.5	475295.5
246	279		167		2401.7	800	106.9	1662.7	8424.4
12912	13426	7769	8215	195965.8	155408.6	231183	220384.7	6302481.4	5624344.9
11081	11443	7019	6689	190501.2	132288.9	224568.3	193578.9	6204421.9	5539551.3
560	783	244	719	3187.5	5844.3	4090.4	4750.2	84761.8	29554.4
1198	1200	506	807	2277.1	17275.4	131	22055.6	11945.8	55239.2
24		22		305.8					
2066	1997	826	1712	2876	10479.8	2410	9268.3	127225.4	9748
12									
397	257	295	12	715.5	83	394.9	4531.6		
107	43	83	31	610	1200.5	849.7		231.5	
203	1072	73	549	774	3646.4	1888.5	7602.5	45857.9	190658.2

14-7 续表 continued

指　　标	Item	有R&D活动企业(个) Number of Enterprises with R & D Activities (unit)	
		2008	2009
食品制造业	Food Production	1	1
饮料制造业	Beverage Production	6	
烟草加工业	Tobacco Processing	1	1
纺织业	Textile Industry	14	
纺织服装、鞋、帽制造业	Textile Garments, Shoes and Hats Products	2	3
皮革、毛皮、羽毛(绒)及其制品业	Leather, Furs Down and Related Products		2
木材加工及木、竹、藤、棕、草制品业	Timber Processing and Wwood, Bamboo, Rattan, Palm and Sraw Works		
家具制造业	Furniture Manufacturing		2
造纸及纸制品业	Papermaking and Paper Products	3	26
印刷业和记录媒介的复制	Printing and Record Processing	1	26
文教体育用品制造业	Stationery, Education and Sports Goods		1
石油加工、炼焦及核燃料加工业	Petroleum Processing, Coking Products and Nuclear Fuel Processing	2	2
化学原料及化学制品制造业	Raw Chemical Material and Chemical Products	30	5
医药制造业	Medical and pharmaceutical Products	21	15
化学纤维制造业	Chemical Fibers	3	9
橡胶制品业	Rubber Products	4	7
塑料制品业	Plastic Products	7	11
非金属矿物制品业	Nonmetal Material Products	11	38
黑色金属冶炼及压延加工业	Smelting and Processing of ferrous Metals	7	17
有色金属冶炼及压延加工业	Smelting and Processing of Nonferrous Metals	5	85
金属制品业	Metal Products	11	30
通用设备制造业	Ordinaryly Machinery Manufacturing	27	28
专用设备制造业	Special Purpose Equipment Manufacturing	16	8
交通运输设备制造业	Transportation Equipment Manufacturing	74	5
电气机械及器材制造业	Electric Machinery and Equipment	20	
通信设备、计算机及其他电子设备制造业	Telecommunication Equipment, Computer and Other Electronic	21	5
	Equipment Manufacturing	7	
仪器仪表及文化办公用机械制造业	Instruments, Meters, Cultural and Official Machinery	4	
工艺品及其他制造业	Handicraft Article and Other Manufacturing		
废弃资源和废旧材料回收加工业	Waste Resources and Junk Material Recycled	7	
电力、热力的生产和供应业	Electric Power, Steam and Hot Water Production and Supply		
煤气生产和供应业	Gas Production and Supply	1	
水的生产和供应业	Tap Water Production and Supply		

科技活动人员合计(人) Number of Persons Engaged in Scientific and Technical Activities (person)		R&D人员合计(人) R & D Personels (person)		R&D经费支出(万元) Funding for R & D Expenditure (10 000 yuan)		新产品开发经费支出(万元) Funding for New Product Development Expenditures (10 000 yuan)		新产品销售收入(万元) Revenue of New Product Sales (10 000 yuan)	
2008	2009	2008	2009	2008	2009	2008	2009	2008	2009
299	443	160	209	1801	3714	5044	8629	22457	89568
911	1260	633	407	4372	5068	1905	7620	27329	103447
786	1055	468	421	14326	14962	14873	18219	813550	60277
1655	2132	857	923	7486	12422	11704	18417	115256	157421
560	22	296	22	3373	81	4100		19264	800
	61		32		11		1041		10080
859	903	476	286	341	3534	876	1693	20148	18531
391	467	74	218	46	2357	1517	1019	3583	13604
	20								456
606	713	395	448	1406	2217	1767	1381	23000	
5908	7061	2662	4358	46198	92896	71489	116519	652269	809302
4100	4667	2324	3142	20409	25248	22334	41908	320496	641836
883	386	476	156	2715	510	1815	510	36216	
287	201	150	170	1217	1362	1536	1532	33382	11424
1394	1358	774	1209	5566	7096	6236	3108	83104	166222
2069	2434	832	1604	10103	23880	11983	28255	118530	143935
9925	10192	4367	6033	129871	253354	213033	285589	3776630	3269644
1487	1030	702	602	24254	19470	3872	3971	423812	566826
3590	3859	1265	3242	17420	19901	14412	13425	386196	361477
5777	7047	2490	4841	33316	62840	44748	79229	571526	548751
3349	4321	1565	2958	16460	22999	17207	30914	196863	266182
22692	27250	13196	16663	303062	231760	326497	361254	7189822	6538322
3007	5187	1390	2835	35574	57768	42518	67278	879116	1140999
6837	10522	3701	7617	69304	154167	76275	213189	559752	1013046
1169	1202	634	1007	4209	10697	7817	11710	106018	344272
1347	1002	1074	965	11256	7234	11196	6881	20437	28064
1213	4620	649	2908	2868	5620	3220	11255	983	540
125	125	5		56		14			

14-8 全省高新技术产业发展情况
STATISTICS ON NEW AND HIGH TECHNIC INDUSTRY DEVELOPMENT IN THE WHOLE PROVINCE

单位:亿元 (100 million yuan)

		2000	2001	2002	2003	2004	2005	2006	2007	2008	2009
总产值	**Total Output Value**	**618.6**	**782.9**	**937.1**	**1117.8**	**1290.6**	**1617.9**	**2093.0**	**2598.2**	**3351.8**	**4062.4**
增加值	Value Added	237.5	277.8	316.6	376.7	431.8	533.2	685.7	873.5	1108.1	1331.0
1.电子信息	Electronic Information		63.8	43.8	57.8	74.7	90.5	119.1	130.4	189.6	253.1
2.生物技术与新医药	Bio-technology and New Medicine		32.9	35.5	42.9	39.4	51.1	63.6	79.2	82.2	98.8
3.新材料	New Materials		47.9	63.0	86.7	114.5	147.0	160.9	231.7	311.4	292.0
4.先进制造	Advanced Manufacturing		55.8	94.7	111.3	138.1	134.0	209.5	277.3	333.6	473.0
产品出口交货值	Value of Delivery for Export	46.7	41.5	41.0	48.1	60.2	85.2	175.7	205.2	279.0	251.3
产品销售收入	Sales Revenue of Products	575.7	707.5	863.4	1059.2	1219.0	1520.9	195.8	2428.9	3077.3	4102.1
利税总额	Total Value of Profits and Taxes	80.5	116.2	122.6	134.5	148.5	174.8	223.2	256.3	362.1	376.5

14-9 市州高新技术产业发展情况（2009）
STATISTICS ON THE DEVELOPMENT OF HIGH AND NEW TECHNOLOGY INDUSTRIE IN CITIES AND PREFECTURE (2009)

单位:万元 (10 000 yuan)

		总产值 Total Output Value	增加值 Value Added	产品出口交货值 Value of Delivery for Export	产品销售收入 Sales Revenue of Products	利税总额 Total Value of Profits and Taxes
全省合计	**Total of the Province**	**40623852**	**13310987**	**2513250**	**41021088**	**3764658**
武 汉 市	Wuhan Municipality	20287174	7110270	1284882	22113027	2174430
黄 石 市	Huangshi Municipality	2234641	706595	138657	2195013	195644
十 堰 市	Shiyan Municipality	949696	272136	21817	951081	39090
宜 昌 市	Yichang Municipality	3234791	959323	348995	2778171	232829
襄 樊 市	Xiangfan Municipality	6277894	1847002	149610	6086920	485534
鄂 州 市	Ezhou Municipality	842680	320841	26917	809576	81993
荆 门 市	Jingmen Municipality	1210122	339355	64199	1206651	92658
孝 感 市	Xiaogan Municipality	1560680	541220	64551	1448583	130368
荆 州 市	Jingzhou Municipality	1266445	376823	183278	990653	120188
黄 冈 市	Huanggang Municipality	994487	322255	72861	869288	45806
咸 宁 市	Xianning Municipality	464336	143408	28323	379333	31594
随 州 市	Suizhou Municipality	516587	135153	36729	510668	51772
恩 施 州	Enshi Prefecture	35477	12788	1991	30353	428
仙 桃 市	Xiantao Municipality	422108	115051	6542	340942	12415
潜 江 市	Qianjiang Municipality	152225	52327	62045	143444	9875
天 门 市	Tianmen Municipality	157248	56440	8327	150480	3025
神农架林区	Shennongjia Forest Zone					

14-10 申报登记省、部级以上成果分类及经济效益
CASSIFICATION AND ECONOMIC BENEFITS OF SCIENTIFIC ACHIEVEMENTS APPLIED AND REGISTERED ABOVE PROVINCIAL AND MINISTRIAL LEVEL

单位：项 (unit)

项　目	Item	1990	1995	2000	2005	2006	2007	2008	2009
成果总类	**Total Calsses of Achievement**	**480**	**500**	**571**	**717**	**778**	**881**	**800**	**740**
一、按成果水平分类	Grouped by Level								
国际首创/领先	International Innovation/ Leading	2	4	19	28	52	65	73	56
国际先进	Internationl Advanced Technology	48	48	97	172	171	238	214	217
国内首创/领先	Domestic Innovation/ Leading	159	236	276	394	434	445	393	353
国内先进	Domestic Advanced Technology	222	212	84	72	77	74	64	60
其它	Others	49		18	3	3	5	6	7
二、按成果类型分类	Grouped by Type								
基础理论研究	Basic Theory Research	33	30	37	15	14	7	19	20
应用开发研究	Applicable Development	442	446	494	669	737	827	750	693
其它	Others	5	24	40	33	27	47	31	27
三、按成果产业属性分类	Grouped by Sector Property								
工业类成果	Industrial Achievements	250	207	145	225	170	220	179	178
农业类成果	Agricultural Achievements	79	71	79	129	139	120	142	113
医学类成果	Medical Achievements	113	147	199	291	183	229	263	214
其他类成果	Others	38	21	148	74	286	312	216	235
四、按成果完成单位分类	Grouped by Units								
高等院校完成	Institutions of Higher Education	152	163	149	169	172	235	174	144
研究单位完成	Scientific Research Institutions	121	92	92	92	79	75	74	70
厂矿企业完成	Industrial and Mineral Enterprises	139	101	137	176	208	258	259	272
其他单位完成	Others	68	144	193	280	319	313	293	267
五、经济效益　（亿元）	Economic Benefits　(100 million yuan)								
本年度新增产值	Newly Added Output Value	1.98	8.58	78.33	199.5	143.3	215.6		
本年度节约资金	Capital Saved in This Year	0.02	1.77	6.33	28.28	48.75	34.82	36.54	

注：1993年以后的“按成果产业属性分类”改为“按成果应用行业分类”。
Note: "Grouped by Sectors" has ben changed into "Grouped by Applied Sector" scince 1993.

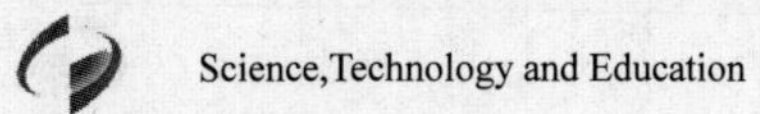

14-11 科学技术协会组织与活动
ORGANIZATIONS AND ACTIVITIES OF SCIENTIFIC AND TECHNOLOGICAL ASSOCIATION

项目	Item	1995	2000	2005	2007	2008	2009
一、机构与人员	Organizations and Personels						
1.省直学会 (个)	Provincal Institute (unit)	101	119	128	128	127	127
会员 (人)	Members (person)	198641	166066	144837	169456	141380	138859
#高级(资深)会员 (人)	#Senoir Members (person)			27306	29056	26633	26448
外国会员 (人)	Foreign Members (person)	3	28	4	3	7	6
2.地、市、州学人会 (个)	Local, city, and Prefecture Institute (unit)	434	368			574	633
3.省科协 (个)	Provincial Scientific Assosiations (unit)	1	1	1	1	1	1
地、市科协 (个)	Local, city Scientific Assosiations (unit)	12	12	13	13	13	13
县(区)科协 (个)	County Scientific Assosiations (unit)	89	100	101	100	101	101
二、省级学会、科协学术活动	Provincial Institutes and Scientific and Academic Activities						
国内学术会议 (次)	Domestic Academic Conference (time)	477	286	257	343	262	379
国际学术会议 (次)	International Academic Conference (time)	17	15	25	22	7	14
参加人数 (人次)	Number of Person Participated (person-time)	30865	51588	26056	37055	19919	34425
论文数 (篇)	Number od Scholary Paper (piece)	13971	7696	8393	9959	6916	9891
三、科普活动	Science and Technology Popularization Activities						
省学会及县以上科协举办	Organized by Institutes Above Provincial and County Level						
科普讲座 (次)	Science and Technology Popularization Lectures (time)			3206	3346	3730	4353
听讲人数 (万人次)	Number of People Participated (10 000 person-time)			176.0	180	352	278
科普展览 (次)	Science and Technology Popularization Expo (time)			1794	1857	2492	3097
参观人数 (万人次)	Number of People Participated (10 000 person-time)			445	595	567	655
科普宣传 (次)	Science and Technology Popularization Promotion (time)			1469	2627		
四、社会、科技服务	Social and Scientific Services						
省学会及县以上科协举办	Organized by Institutes Above Provincial and County Level						
无偿科技咨询 (项)	Free Science and Technology Consultation (unit)			2337	8384		
完成科技咨询合同数(项)	Contracts Signed in Science and Technology Consultation (unit)			590	1105	1460	1574
咨询合同实现金额(千元)	Value of Contracts (1000 yuan)			12518	195296	627818	448230
#技术交易额 (千元)	#Value of Technology Transactions (1000 yuan)			5265	723072	206373	146083
举办培训班 (个)	Training Class (unit)			1037	1060	2132	1649
培训人数 (万人次)	Unmber of People Participated Training (10 000 person-time)			39	24	36	17
五、科技下乡	Spreading Scientific and Technological Knowledge to Rural Areas						
省学会及县以上科协举办	Organized by Institutes Above Provincial and County Level						
组织科技下乡 (次)	Number of Times Going to Rural Organized			1121	1943	2843	2708
举办科普讲座 (次)	Science and Technology Popularization Lectures (time)			643	614	723	678
开展科普咨询 (次)	Science and Technology Consultation (time)			821	1505	7075	2982
举办实用技术培训 (次)	Practical Technology Training (time)			1535	2662	2736	2258

14-12 专利受理量、批准量及分布状况

NUMBER OF PATENT APPLICATIONS EXAMINATION, APPROVAL AND DISTRITUTION

单位：项 (unit)

项 目	Item	受理量 Number of Patent Applications Examined						批准量 Number of Patent Applications approved					
		1995	2000	2005	2007	2008	2009	1995	2000	2005	2007	2008	2009
合 计	**Total**	**2004**	**3486**	**11534**	**17376**	**21147**	**27206**	**2228**	**2198**	**3860**	**6616**	**8374**	**11357**
发 明	Creations and Inventions	384	771	2038	3705	4616	6065	107	156	733	886	1152	1478
实用新型	Utility Models	1430	2102	4835	7168	8793	10579	1628	1573	2238	4400	5732	6285
外观设计	Designs	190	613	4661	6503	7738	10562	493	469	889	1330	1490	3594
在合计中	**Of This Total**												
个 人	Individual	1472	2411	7400	8306	9199	10013	1503	1502	2189	3535	3792	3782
大专院校	Universities and Colleges	117	205	1365	2054	1968	2364	84	92	574	934	1227	1351
科研单位	Insitutions of Scientific Research	84	128	182	614	1101	21272	76	82	101	180	239	285
工矿企业	Industrial and Mineral Enterprises	229	721	2305	5761	8774	13999	543	509	901	1783	3032	5872
机关团体	Government Agencies and Organizations	102	21	283	641	105	138	22	13	98	184	83	67

14-13 按市州分三种专利申请与授权状况

THREE KINDS OF PATENT APPICATION AND AUTHORIZATION BY MUNICIPALITIES AND PREFECTURE

单位：项 (unit)

市、州	Municipalities and Prefecture	申请 当年累计 Patent Application Total of 2009	发明 Invention	实用新型 New type of practicial Utility	外观设计 Design	授权 当年累计 Authorization Total of 2009	发明 Invention	实用新型 New type of practicial Utility	外观设计 Design
全省合计	**Total of the Province**	**21147**	**4616**	**8793**	**7738**	**8374**	**1152**	**5732**	**1490**
武 汉	Wuhan	14600	3927	5767	4906	6853	1262	3749	1842
黄 石	Huangshi	1822	83	224	1515	433	13	161	259
十 堰	Shiyan	987	75	514	398	444	19	244	181
荆 州	Jingzhou	1087	227	681	179	439	28	295	116
宜 昌	Yichang	2371	527	725	1119	657	54	457	146
襄 樊	Xiangfan	2302	490	841	971	965	26	594	345
鄂 州	Ezhou	556	114	144	298	133	7	46	80
荆 门	Jingmen	895	154	372	369	195	10	125	60
孝 感	Xiaogan	559	123	357	79	271	22	190	59
黄 冈	Huanggang	628	76	310	242	343	8	134	201
咸 宁	Xianning	409	52	100	257	234	5	61	168
随 州	Suizhou	277	48	175	54	111	7	78	26
恩施州	Enshi	131	34	78	19	56	8	29	19
仙 桃	Xiantao	184	44	84	56	65	3	30	32
潜 江	Qianjiang	146	21	104	21	67	2	49	16
天 门	Tianmen	205	65	103	37	63	2	42	19
神农架林区	Shennongjia Forest District	47	5		42	28	2	1	25

14-14 各类技术合同签定及执行情况

SIGNING AND IMPEMENTATION OF VARIOUS TECHNICAL CONTRACTS

项 目	Item	合同数(项) Number of Contracts (unit)	合同金额(万元) Value of Contracts (10 000 yuan)
2005		**11131**	**501823**
技术开发合同	Technology Development Contracts	3438	183631
技术转让合同	Technology Transfer Contracts	2351	126141
技术咨询合同	Technology Consultation Contracts	1698	14223
技术服务合同	Technology Service Contracts	3644	177829
2006		**5327**	**444943**
技术开发合同	Technology Development Contracts	2273	151848
技术转让合同	Technology Transfer Contracts	512	19951
技术咨询合同	Technology Consultation Contracts	482	19357
技术服务合同	Technology Service Contracts	2060	253786
2007		**8298**	**525216**
技术开发合同	Technology Development Contracts	3317	284859
技术转让合同	Technology Transfer Contracts	234	44577
技术咨询合同	Technology Consultation Contracts	1305	37977
技术服务合同	Technology Service Contracts	3442	157803
2008		**7147**	**628971**
技术开发合同	Technology Development Contracts	3703	379092
技术转让合同	Technology Transfer Contracts	235	45101
技术咨询合同	Technology Consultation Contracts	1237	42571
技术服务合同	Technology Service Contracts	1972	162207
2009		**5694**	**779700**
技术开发合同	Technology Development Contracts	2391	337341
技术转让合同	Technology Transfer Contracts	216	239272
技术咨询合同	Technology Consultation Contracts	1144	42747
技术服务合同	Technology Service Contracts	1943	160339

14-15 全省技术买卖情况（2009）

PURCHASE AND SELLING OF TECHNOLOGY IN THE WHOLE PROVINCE (2009)

卖方类别 买方类别	Type of the Seller Type of the Buyer	合 计 Total		事业法人 Institutions Corporations		社团法人 Associations Corporations	
		合同数(项) Number of Contracts	成交额(万元) Contracted Value (10 000 yuan)	合同数(项) Number of Contracts	成交额(万元) Contracted Value (10 000 yuan)	合同数(项) Number of Contracts	成交额(万元) Contracted Value (10 000 yuan)
总计	**Total**	**5694**	**779700**	**3430**	**180581**	**4**	**139**
机关法人	Departments	277	20311	94	4680		
事业法人	Institutions	979	30737	799	19022		
社团法人	Social Groups	13	1730	6	32		
企业法人	Corporations	4300	721213	2501	156480	4	139
自然人	Natural Person	61	2127	7	14		
其他组织	Other Organizations	64	3582	23	353		

14-15 续表 continued

卖方类别 买方类别	Type of the Seller Type of the Buyer	企业法人 Corporations		自然人 Natural Person		其他组织 Other Organizations	
		合同数(项) Number of Contracts	成交额(万元) Contracted Value (10 000 yuan)	合同数(项) Number of Contracts	成交额(万元) Contracted Value (10 000 yuan)	合同数(项) Number of Contracts	成交额(万元) Contracted Value (10 000 yuan)
总计	**Total**	**2236**	**578388**	**1**	**45**	**23**	**20547**
机关法人	Departments	182	15595			1	36
事业法人	Institutions	169	11566			11	149
社团法人	Social Groups	7	1698				
企业法人	Corporations	1783	544187	1	45	11	20362
自然人	Natural Person	54	2113				
其他组织	Other Organizations	41	3229				

14-16 地震观测及地方地震工作情况
STATISTICS ON EARTHQUAKE OBSERCATION AND LOCAL EFFERTS ON EARTHQUAKE WORKS

项 目	Item	2000	2005	2007	2008	2009
职工总数 （人）	Total Number of Staff and Workers (person)	589	528	483	452	465
专业技术人员 （人）	Professtional Technical Personel (person)	386	295	305	294	307
高级技术人员 （人）	Senior Technical Personel (person)	107	91	90	89	82
市州级地震局 （个）	Number of Earthquake Agency (unit)	12	17	17	17	17
重点县地震办公室 （个）	Number of Earthquake Offices in key Counties (unit)	52	35	35	35	35
地方地震工作人员 （人）	Local Staff on Earthquake Efforts (person)	255	267	267	267	267
地震观测台(网)人员 （人）	Number of Staff in Earthquake Observation Station (person)	74	70	70	68	68
#观测技术人员 （人）	#Technical Personel (person)	64	60	60	50	50
地震台站 （个）	Earthquake Observation Station (unit)	11	9	10	10	10
基准台	Norm Station	4	1	1	1	1
基本台	Basic Station		4	4	4	4
省级台	Provincial Station		4	5	5	5
GPS测量 （千米/点）	GPS Measurement (km/point)		75000/85	88000/170	110000/300	12000/425
流动重力测量 （千米/点）	Flow Gravity Measurement (km/point)		40000/300	50000/150	10000/100	9000/80

14-17 气象部门基本情况

BASIC CONDITIONS OF METEOROLOGICAL DEPARTMENT

项目	tem	1990	1995	2000	2005	2007	2008	2009
一、气象观测人员总数 （人）	Total Number of Staff in Meteorological Depaartment (person)	511	400	333	375	389	409	455
地面观测	Groud Observation	440	343	285	320	351	339	350
高空观测	Upper Air Observation	46	31	24	18	18	18	20
雷达观测	Radar Observation	25	26	24	20	20	23	25
特种观测	Special Observation						29	60
二、气象台站总数 （个）	Total Number of Meteorological Obervatory (unit)	85	86	85	87	87	87	87
气象台	Meteorological Obervatory	10	10	13	14	15	14	14
气象站	Weather Station	73	74	70	71	71	71	71
独立农试站	Independent Agricultural Station	2	2	2	2	2	2	2
三、卫星云图接收站点数（个）	Number of Stations Receiving Satellite Image (unit)	2	2	11	25	15	17	15
极轨卫星	Polar Orbiting Meteorological Satellite	1	1	2	23	5	3	5
同步卫星	Geostationary Satellite	1	2	9	7	10	14	10
接收卫星云图图片数	Number of Satellite Image Pictures Received	3500	14000					
使用云图单位数	Number of Pictures Used	4	22	144				
四、拥有计算机数 （台）	Number of Computer (unit)	279	421	1 019	1695	2185	2377	2408
中小型机	Small and Medium-size	5	8	8	1	1	1	1
微型机	Microcomputer	90	279	950	1694	2185	2376	2407
袖珍机	Pocket-computer	184	134	61				
五、拥有雷达数 （部）	Number of Radar Owned (unit)	12	11	11	12	12	12	14
701测风	701 Wind Sensing	4	4	4	4	2	1	
3厘米	3 cm	5	3	2	2		1	1
5厘米	5 cm	1	2	2	1	1	1	1
10厘米	10 cm	2	2	3	5	7	7	9
l波段	l Wave Band					2	2	3

14-18 质量技术监督检查情况

STATISTICS ON SUPERVISION AND EXAMINATION OF QUALITY TECHNOLOGY

年 份 Year	机构 (个) Institu-tions (unit)	职工人数(人) Number of Staff and Workers (person)	#专业技术人员 #Professional Technic Personel	经费收入 (万元) Revenue (10 000 yuan)	经费支出 (万元) Expenditures (10 000 yuan)	固定资产 (万元) Fixed Assets (10 000 yuan)	#仪器设备 #Equipment and Devices	计量器具检定台(万套件) Number of Measuring Equip-ment Tested (10 000 units)	#衡 具 #Measuring Instrument	#强制检定 #Complorsy Test
1980	88	1211	327	308	306	1667	512	60		
1985	107	1668	356	640	515	3234	1402	146	36	
1990	105	3299	1409	3063	2610	7994	3760	136	68	118
1991	107	3433	1458	3051	2774	8425	3971	153	64	120
1992	105	4161	1692	3976	3680	9607	4070	150	67	112
1993	104	4169	1755	4150	4010	14043	4183	144	63	106
1994	103	4879	2006	6165	6154	13368	4531	136	55	113
1995	167	6275	2121	10095	10374	21213	6327	150	64	140
1996	102	2265	1252	3237	3177	6985	3261	136	61	108
1997	101	2337	1337	3491	3418	6751	3680	150	62	110
1998	106	2479	1439	4 079	4034	6314	3810	126	50	100
1999	105	2531	1446	4 515	4532	6732	3713	120	43	103
2000	104	2790	1478	4 568	4853	8829	5286	150	43	105
2001	91	1632	911	3005	2899	6537	3881	132	33	65
2002	360	9583	4059	36371	34024	39461	9806	165	40	138
2003	403	9137	3960	44450	41317	47323	12114	154	45	118
2004	376	9034	4703	50520	48383	53579	14549	128	23	114
2005	398	9046	3953	59089	56152	62607	19986	120	22	98
2006	398	9050	4094	67864	64078	72440	23840	119	22	110
2007	393	9065	4072	79698	75988	81822	26984	119	19	102
2008	392	9055	3732	93140	89653	94547	27832	109	16	96
2009	395	9077	3718	111477	10965	111627	35047	128	18	107

14-19 标准事业基本情况
BASIC STATISTICS ON STANDARD ENTERPRISES

项目	Item	1990	1995	2000	2005	2007	2008	2009
质量监督机构 (个)	Quality Supervision Institution (unit)	57	85	86	99	99	99	99
固定人员 (人)	Fixed Personel (person)		1 019	1 007				
制定标准 (项)	Standard Established (unit)	47	15	29	36	41	89	72
修定标准 (项)	Standard Revised (unit)							15
废止标准 (项)	Standard Abolished (unit)							
当年采用国际标准(项)	International Norm Adopted in 2007 (unit)	261		4	129	162	232	190
受检产品质量监督(种)	Number of Products under Quality Supervision (kind)	389	92	99				
质量监督检测 (批次)	Quality Supervision Test (batch)	15579	29105	20093	26548	30171	34520	45582
标准文件馆藏 (万件)	Standard Document Collection (10 000 units)	17	21	25	22	23	28	29

14-20 档案事业基本情况
BASIC STATISTICS ON ARCHIVES

项　　目	Item	1990	1995	2000	2005	2007	2008	2009
1.机构数 (个)	Number of Institution (unit)	212	230	553	988	964	1201	11636
#档案馆	#Archives	112	135	148	150	147	143	157
2.专职人员数 (人)	Number of Full-time Personel (person)	3064	3325	3597	4166	3678	3644	8327
#副研究馆员以上	#Associate Research Fellow of Archives Above	36	136	136	257	211	140	178
馆员	Research Fellow of Archives	479	924	911	964	752	638	995
助理馆员	Assistant Research Fellow of Archives	699	980	707	573	456	404	942
管理员	Administors	747	323	268	263	177	209	1025
3.馆藏档案卷宗 (个)	Volumes Stored In Archives (unit)	8907	14258	13005	14206	13444	13650	13457.0
案卷 (万个)	Files (10 000 unit)	369	527	837	1178	1697	1726	1224.0
案卷总长度 (万米)	Total Length of Volume (10 000 m)	5	8	13	34	26	29	39.0
零散文件长度 (米)	Total Length of Scattered Files (m)	442	339	1 234	200	2744	454	539.0
馆藏资料册数 (万册)	Number of Material Stored (10 000 Volumes)	96	145	201	255	246	227	206.6
举办展览 (个)	Display Organized (unit)					12164	143	397.0
接待参观 (万人次)	Visitors (10 000 person-times)					29	39	64.9
4.本年度利用档案人次(万人次)	Use of Material This Year (10 000 times)	46	27	11	18	27	31	42.6
利用档案卷次 (万卷次)	Number of Archives Used (10 000 volume-times)	88	55	40	74	110	122	101.2
利用资料册数 (万册数)	Number of Data Used (10 000 volume-times)		36	6	6	11	12	4.3
5.本年编研档案资料	Materials Editored This Year							
公开出版种数 (种)	Number of Materials Open Pbulished (kind)	47	31	507	140	56	57	58
公开出版字数 (万字)	Number of Words Open Published (10 000 wordds)	1076	452	1259	993	1488	2104	2223
内部参考种数 (种)	Number of Materials for Inner Reference (kind)	746	362	218	197	231	145	132
内部参考字数 (万字)	Number of Words For Inner Reference(10 000 words)	2576	1828	909	1762	5344	15024	1712
库房面积 (万平方米)	Floor Space of Storehouse (10 000 sq.m)	11	17	22	12	12	10	9

14-21　各级各类学校数
NUMBER OF SCHOOLS OF VARIOUS LEVELS

单位：所　　(unit)

学校分类	Type of Shool	1990	2000	2002	2003	2004	2005	2006	2007	2008	2009
普通高等学校	Regular Institutions of Higher Education	63	54	75	76	85	85	86	86	87	120
#地方院校	#Local Schools	36	45	67	68	77	77	78	78	79	112
中等职业学校	Secondary Vocation Schools	222	203	168	390	401	437	455	478	462	402
#中师	#Secondary Teachers School	35	23							10	7
普通中学	Regular Middle School	4737	3 261	3295	3305	3282	3231	3198	3108	3011	2897
#初中	#Junior Middle Schools	4091	2 678	2696	2679	2651	2578	2509	2440	2356	2275
城市	Urban	510	757	720	696	687	465	400	435	431	383
县镇	Township	348	189	650	451	416	487	504	539	564	622
农村	Rural	3233	1 732	1326	1532	1548	1635	1605	1466	1361	1270
高中	Senior High School	646	583	599	626	631	653	689	668	655	622
城市	Urban	280	371	334	347	335	306	295	292	295	267
县镇	Township	149	111	201	188	203	235	285	289	271	268
农村	Rural	217	101	64	91	93	112	109	87	89	87
职业中学	Vocational School	451	290	224							
#初中	#Junior Schools	126	53	38	43	37	31	29	26	18	13
城市	Urban	5	5	1	6	6	6				2
县镇	Township	5	4	8	7	4	4	3	7	6	2
农村	Rural	116	44	29	30	27	21	26	19	12	9
高中	Senior School	325	237	186							
城市	Urban	117	168	120							
县镇	Township	73	33	51							
农村	Rural	135	36	15							
小学	Primary School	32309	23 372	17994	15746	14085	12631	11422	10210	9302	8544
城市	Urban	2 067	3 319	2283	1926	1799	949	763	831	845	722
县镇	Township	1 822	1 155	874	585	553	627	615	693	715	847
农村	Rural	28420	18 898	14837	13235	11733	11055	10044	8686	7742	6975
特殊教育学校	Special Education School	34	74	76	76	77	77	77	76	76	76
幼儿园	Kindergarden	3914	3 748	2153	2258	2256	2336	2546	2572	2880	2995
技工学校	School of Technology	160	204	204	204	204	208	208	208	208	
民办学校	Private Schools									2868	3016
#普通高等学校	#Regular Institutions of Higher Education									11	42
#独立设置的普通高校	#Independent Set Colleges and Universities									11	11
独立学院	Independent Colleges										31
中等职业学校	Secondary Vocation Schools									118	111
普通中学	Regular Middle School									290	271
#初中	#Junior Middle Schools									140	132
高中	Senior High School									150	139
职业初中	Professional Junior school									1	
小学	Primary School									93	70
幼儿园	Kindergarden									2054	2209

14-22 各级各类学校在校学生数

ENROLLMENT IN SCHOOLS OF VARIOUS LEVELS

单位：人 (person)

学校分类	Type of Shool	2000	2002	2003	2004	2005	2006	2007	2008	2009
普通高等学校	Regular Institutions of Higher Education	346568	585023	721513	892018	1012665	1092274	1163686	1184915	1249061
#地方院校	#Local Schools	205615	406787	533797	697919	824960	905242	973037	991819	1053341
中等职业学校	Secondary Vocation Schools	278602	188729	364276	458459	606014	799509	936192	1037294	1041759
#中师	#Secondary Teachers School	26431								
普通中学	Regular Middle School	4E+06	4166154	4414715	4517196	4466879	4358461	4169098	3934445	3650102
#初中	#Junior Middle Schools	3E+06	3224319	3341801	3319842	3172392	3010769	2840700	2612455	2363351
城市	Urban	772160	780301	753752	720712	494739	443969	499232	515470	452518
县镇	Township	232916	958581	700641	688191	750903	810338	857005	821270	811217
农村	Rural	2E+06	1485437	1887408	1910939	1926750	1756462	1484463	1275715	1099616
高中	Senior High School	698409	941835	1072914	1197354	1294487	1347692	1328398	1321990	1286751
城市	Urban	424406	465253	532077	582479	541404	504309	504312	536578	512139
县镇	Township	171592	387960	403795	455902	553411	663507	666697	625120	608803
农村	Rural	102411	88622	137042	158973	199672	179876	157389	160292	165809
职业中学	Vocational School	148770	174946							
#初中	#Junior Schools	40110	38279	37227	34003	26524	22639	13553	7678	4788
城市	Urban	3246	429	1270	1096	497				
县镇	Township	2606	9551	6314	6048	5947	4000	2442	1408	63
农村	Rural	34258	28299	29643	26859	20080	18639	11111	6270	4725
高中	Senior School	108660	136667							
城市	Urban	79268	88832							
县镇	Township	20705	38666							
农村	Rural	8687	9169							
小学	Primary School	7E+06	5799930	5281177	4749500	4291881	3913276	3703434	3607744	3592629
城市	Urban	2E+06	1264795	1150591	1108833	787812	691437	715805	748768	717749
县镇	Township	457132	722056	548735	528919	593090	632459	697890	705023	812990
农村	Rural	5E+06	3813079	3581851	3111748	2910979	2589380	2289739	2153953	2061890
特殊教育学校	Special Education School	9739	9283	7908	7808	9444	9232	13972	13374	13959
幼儿园	Kindergarden	726712	590405	597841	587973	594481	642216	655408	742531	831399
技工学校	School of Technology	55812	74328	97186	110376	136000	180000	252532	245246	

14-23 各级各类学校招生数
NEW ENROLLMENT IN SCHOOLS OF VARIOUS LEVELS

单位：人 (person)

学校分类	Type of Shool	1990	2000	2003	2004	2005	2006	2007	2008	2009
普通高等学校	Regular Institutions of Higher Education	38024	139666	250198	295763	315560	343877	339174	375512	395929
#地方院校	#Local Schools	15904	94524	202207	246313	269042	296394	290754	326845	346525
中等职业学校	Secondary Vocation Schools	48931	62418	151838	196821	273789	369156	387065	390641	367161
#中师	#Secondary Teachers School	9467	4724							
普通中学	Regular Middle School	785143	1E+06	1560675	1515616	1469777	1419561	1309571	1214750	1120047
#初中	#Junior Middle Schools	666252	1E+06	1164538	1085882	1011186	964018	869778	775634	696261
城市	Urban	134913	281648	239231	217161	162324	152148	161033	159646	139712
县镇	Township	73696	89106	256894	232638	241579	262665	261063	244207	240542
农村	Rural	457643	704773	668413	636083	607283	549205	447682	371781	316007
高中	Senior High School	118891	277065	396137	429734	458591	455543	439793	439116	423786
城市	Urban	44835	168541	198287	208432	187976	170039	164673	175774	169309
县镇	Township	35709	68314	146255	161140	197496	221800	221310	209698	199571
农村	Rural	38347	40210	51595	60162	73119	63704	53810	53644	54906
职业中学	Vocational School	54592	52411							
#初中	#Junior Schools	17089	15178	13789	10993	7294	6750	2879	1823	1311
城市	Urban	649	1319	431	390	138				
县镇	Township	818	986	2374	2070	1646	965	38	33	15
农村	Rural	15622	12873	10984	8533	5510	5785	2841	1790	1296
高中	Senior School	37503	37233							
城市	Urban	15329	24548							
县镇	Township	9907	8725							
农村	Rural	12267	3960							
小学	Primary School	1003126	904559	651856	599698	567411	570100	610762	626247	642190
城市	Urban	143680	239984	157477	147815	113284	108988	115092	123171	117466
县镇	Township	84105	75192	67009	68173	81622	94990	115709	117355	144972
农村	Rural	775341	589383	427370	383710	372505	366122	379961	385721	379752
特殊教育学校	Special Education School	859	1655	1118	966	1038	1316	1988	2183	2167
幼儿园	Kindergarden		523542	425259	406781	396082	440486	441792	497716	537579
技工学校	School of Technology	32823	23052	53884	65460	73000	97000	115633	110338	

14-24 各级各类学校毕业生数

NUMBER OF GRADUATES FROM SCHOOLS OF VARIOUS LEVELS

单位：人 (person)

学校分类	Type of Shool	1990	2000	2003	2004	2005	2006	2007	2008	2009
普通高等学校	Regular Institutions of Higher Education	36979	51932	119118	143246	187920	262591	276005	351854	328202
#地方院校	#Local Schools	13850	26461	82169	100670	144529	215846	232990	306770	282718
中等职业学校	Secondary Vocation Schools	39548	125593	108936	104687	129436	168598	220461	264826	307813
#中师	#Secondary Teachers School	10213	14908							
普通中学	Regular Middle School	639910	883828	1188795	1316041	1438503	1472566	1440766	1410673	1373676
#初中	#Junior Middle Schools	517078	718015	916054	993151	1055083	1061845	997673	960997	923759
城市	Urban	105100	198402	218953	235732	169257	143767	157380	170316	161959
县镇	Township	56172	61909	186793	184521	239870	277674	290997	297268	319137
农村	Rural	355806	457704	510308	572898	645956	640404	549296	493413	442663
高中	Senior High School	122832	165813	272741	322890	383420	410721	443093	449676	449917
城市	Urban	41997	98353	136620	153222	161281	154718	170285	184590	181546
县镇	Township	38742	41382	102923	127896	164517	201779	223002	212750	208682
农村	Rural	42093	26078	33198	41772	57622	54224	49806	52336	59689
职业中学	Vocational School	36179	52549							
#初中	#Junior Schools	8745	11465	11682	10219	8951	8967	7342	4654	4000
城市	Urban	545	1328	224	451	265				70
县镇	Township	815	701	1377	1619	1997	1756	1775	1674	1214
农村	Rural	7385	9436	10081	8149	6699	7211	5567	2980	2716
高中	Senior School	27434	41084							
城市	Urban	9545	31396							
县镇	Township	6863	6790							
农村	Rural	11026	2898							
小学	Primary School	899610	1E+06	1186986	1099308	1020710	946634	832908	715128	646753
城市	Urban	140827	281706	232227	210932	149766	138783	144778	136872	126806
县镇	Township	80501	84207	124185	121395	134340	140840	146001	128750	143354
农村	Rural	678282	794290	830574	766981	736604	667011	542129	449506	376593
特殊教育学校	Special Education School	89	1310	774	730	1498	898	1286	1530	1675
技工学校	School of Technology	25637	24848	23374	32826	45000	59000	89604	87271	

14-25 各级各类学校教职工数

NUMBER OF FACULTIES AT SCHOOLS OF VARIOUS LEVELS

单位：人 (person)

学校分类	Type of Shool	1990	2000	2003	2004	2005	2006	2007	2008	2009
普通高等学校	Regular Institutions of Higher Education	63315	72265	94215	105249	107459	114485	119736	120816	123693
#地方院校	#Local Schools	16386	35120	59269	70243	73079	78473	83921	86217	89339
中等职业学校	Secondary Vocation Schools	28323	28816	32750	33091	36658	39907	43120	44847	42244
#中师	#Secondary Teachers School	5957	3384							
普通中学	Regular Middle School	199516	237500	263879	269895	273146	275389	275150	271629	267265
教育部门和集体办	Run by Ministry of Education and	165630	216338	245411	250772	253955	256244	255743	251185	247068
	Collective Run									1488
其他部门办	Run Other Department	21957	15483	11082	9513	6585	2551	2434	1528	18709
社会力量办	Run by Non-Governmental Sectors	11929	2316	7386	9610	12606	16594	16973	18916	
私立	Private Owned		3363							
城市	Urban Owned	55270	97054	90790	92287	75581	68866	74017	78734	74103
县镇	Township Owned	30572	28889	65713	66286	78027	89136	95674	95035	99653
农村	Rural Owned	113674	111557	107376	111322	119538	117387	105459	97860	93509
职业中学	Vocational Secondary Schools	16297	15105	1973	1748	1446	1396	961	615	449
教育部门和集体办	Run by Ministry of Education and Collective Run	12724	11722	1896	1629	1391	1347	937	599	433
其他部门办	Run Other Department	2395	2819	11	91		15	13	13	16
社会力量办	Run by Non-Governmental Sectors	1178	69	66	28	55	34	11	3	
城市	Urban Owned	5643	9255	104	142	55				2
县镇	Township Owned	3399	2665	313	286	300	224	184	109	16
农村	Rural Owned	7255	3185	1556	1320	1091	1172	777	506	431
小学	Primary Schools	334985	299994	252645	239549	232888	225803	220326	216119	213347
城市	Urban Owned	52992	84877	66445	66154	47727	42074	45260	47349	43738
县镇	Township Owned	30368	23515	29726	29113	33532	35368	38324	38615	44738
农村	Rural Owned	251625	191602	156474	144282	151629	148361	136742	130155	124871
特殊教育学校	Special Education School	635	1676	1633	1660	1679	1626	1670	1694	1708
幼儿园	Kindergarden	47838	40484	28905	31335	33094	35833	37366	41920	46867
技工学校	School of Technology	18003	13070	8903	10142	9934	12146	12023	12884	

14-26 各级各类学校专任教师数

NUMBER OF FULL-TIME TEACHERS AT SCHOOLS OF VARIOUS LEVELS

单位：人 (person)

学校分类	Type of Shool	1990	2000	2003	2004	2005	2006	2007	2008	2009
普通高等学校	Regular Institutions of Higher Education	24624	30363	46947	55683	59009	65164	68117	70617	73159
#地方院校	#Local Schools	7129	15995	32015	39945	43240	48100	51533	53797	56013
中等职业学校	Secondary Vocation Schools	14407	15549	20263	21460	24036	26857	29355	30689	29148
#中师	#Secondary Teachers School	3424	2161							
普通中学	Regular Middle School	154388	198486	223751	229649	233517	235681	236040	233878	231452
#初中	#Junior Middle Schools	124998	154543	167211	169315	169084	167572	166540	163666	160662
城市	Urban	29020	49752	43667	43731	31803	28227	31976	34487	31574
县镇	Township	14479	13138	35440	34371	39851	43954	48427	50178	54203
农村	Rural	81499	91653	88104	91213	97430	95391	86137	79001	74885
高中	Senior High School	29390	43943	56540	60334	64433	68109	69500	70212	70790
城市	Urban	11501	27663	29262	30620	28330	27215	28079	30242	29754
县镇	Township	8882	10336	20846	22489	27235	32579	33974	32372	32913
农村	Rural	9007	5944	6432	7225	8868	8315	7447	7598	8123
职业中学	Vocational School	11306	11047							
#初中	#Junior Schools	3043	2292	1749	1539	1308	1253	873	556	396
城市	Urban	114	238	79	107	36				1
县镇	Township	204	156	298	271	300	224	179	105	11
农村	Rural	2725	1898	1372	1161	972	1029	694	451	384
高中	Senior School	8263	8755							
城市	Urban	3696	6185							
县镇	Township	2018	1775							
农村	Rural	2549	795							
小学	Primary School	295710	274979	233902	221763	215693	209342	204899	201356	198188
城市	Urban	45167	75377	58881	58769	42127	37204	40224	42413	39274
县镇	Township	27057	21459	27422	26611	30351	32127	35173	35653	41273
农村	Rural	223486	178143	147599	136383	143215	140011	129502	123290	117641
特殊教育学校	Special Education School	411	1231	1243	1267	1317	1337	1383	1427	1444
幼儿园	Kindergarden	29622	29889	17815	19202	20018	21482	22254	24795	27440
技工学校	School of Technology	8182	6182	8800	8668	7064	8692	10456	10561	

14–27 各级各类学校专任教师学历分类

STATISTICS ON ACADEMIC DEGREE OF FULL-TIME TEACHERS AT SCHOOLS OF VARIOUS LEVELS

单位：人 (person)

学历分类	Type of School	2003	2004	2005	2006	2007	2008	2009
一、中等职业学校	Secondary Vocational School	20174	21460	24036	26857	29355	30689	29148
高等学校本科毕业及以上	Bachlor Degree and Above	13604	14793	17261	20161	22126	23626	22922
高等学校专科毕业	Graduated from Colleges	5878	6079	6063	5960	6354	6573	5803
高等学校本专科肆业未满两年的	Undergraduate from Colleges within Two Years							
高中阶段及以下	Degree Below Senior High School	692	588	712	736	875	490	423
二、技工学校	Technical School	8800	8668					
高等学校本科毕业及以上	Bachlor Degree and Above	2041	2865					
高等学校专科及本科肆业、中专、技校、高中及其他	Others	6759	5803					
三、职业中学	Vocational School	1749	1539	1308	1253	873	556	396
高等学校本科毕业及以上	Bachlor Degree and Above	245	271	200	254	254	162	138
高等学校专科毕业	Graduated from Colleges	1260	1052	941	852	546	360	244
中专、高中毕业的	Others	232	201	155	139	71	34	14
四、普通中学	Regular Secondary Schools	223751	229649	233517	235681	236040	233878	231452
高等学校本科毕业及以上	Bachlor Degree and Above	87097	100926	112254	125748	134970	139997	146936
高等学校专科毕业	Graduated from Colleges	119115	113883	108594	99509	92372	86191	78549
中专、高中毕业的	Others	17046	14499	12388	10110	8464	7515	5819
五、小学	Primary School	233902	221763	215693	209342	204899	201356	198188
中师、高中毕业及以上的	Graduate from Teachers Schools and Degrees Above	227366	216881	211473	206160	202564	199444	196647
六、幼儿园(不包括园长)	Kindergarden (President is excluded)	17815	19202	20018	21482	22254	24795	27440
中师、高中毕业及以上的	Graduate from Teachers Schools and Degrees Above	17132	18556	19532	20826	21678	24064	26658

14-28 高等学校分类别情况

单位：所、人

学校分类	Type of School	2000				2005			
		学校数 Number of Colleages and Universities	在校生数 Students Enrollment in Schools	招生数 New Enrollment	毕业生数 Graduates	学校数 Number of Colleages and Universities	在校生数 Students Enrollment in Schools	招生数 New Enrollment	毕业生数 Graduates
总　计	**Total**	**54**	**346568**	**139666**	**51932**	**85**	**989754**	**306775**	**184706**
综合大学	Comprehensive Universities	6	79303	28489	13871	10	196454	48591	48617
理工院校	Colleages and Universities of Science	11	124501	47724	18603	49	545277	181363	92857
农业院校	Colleages and Universities of Agriculture	2	13111	4311	1775	1	15715	3999	2763
医药院校	Colleages and Universities of Medicine	4	10770	4095	1068	1	1678	1062	121
师范院校	Colleages and Universities of Techer-Training	7	39694	17186	5950	3	26534	7686	5238
财经院校	Colleages and Universities of Finance	4	26218	9923	4466	5	52581	15687	12960
政法院校	Colleages and Universities of Politics and Law	1	2482	974	448	6	93524	30319	12771
体育院校	Colleages and Universities of Physical Education	1	2787	915	515	3	12389	3416	2369
艺术院校	Colleages and Universities of Art	2	2255	749	318	1	8837	2735	1154
民族院校	Colleages and Universities of Minority Groups	2	12719	4298	2584	4	8834	4378	814
短期职大	Short-Time Vocational Colleages	14	32728	21002	2334	2	27931	7539	5042

注：1999年“在校生数”、“招生数”总计中含成人高校招收的新高职学生数1535人。

INSTITUTIONS OF HIGHER EDUCATION BY TYPE

(Unit,Person)

2007				2008				2009			
学校数 Number of Colleages and Universities	在校生数 Students Enrollment in Schools	招生数 New Enrollment	毕业生数 Graduates	学校数 Number of Colleages and Universities	在校生数 Students Enrollment in Schools	招生数 New Enrollment	毕业生数 Graduates	学校数 Number of Colleages and Universities	在校生数 Students Enrollment in Schools	招生数 New Enrollment	毕业生数 Graduates
86	**1147140**	**334698**	**271458**	**87**	**1184915**	**375512**	**351854**	**120**	**1238713**	**394140**	**322688**
10	174707	48424	44060	8	156834	43144	41084	8	160943	46193	41425
49	675787	198751	159135	52	698188	228922	220498	74	743701	244636	197936
1	16706	4300	3648	1	17468	4504	3507	1	17812	4550	3918
1	3125	1344	713	3	34282	11005	8309	1	5162	2014	1087
3	29860	9300	8485	5	68871	21688	17827	4	37309	12150	8666
5	62791	18365	14525	6	109582	35249	35805	7	73116	23708	20556
6	110118	31519	25428	4	12232	4285	4493	12	116417	36503	29208
4	12489	4287	4113	1	12495	3843	2268	4	12664	4177	3637
1	11052	3294	2287	4	22982	7236	3604	2	13662	3872	2646
4	19524	7138	1456	2	32480	8573	7367	5	25232	7856	5499
2	30981	7976	7608					2	32695	8481	8110

Note:Total number of "Students enrollment in school" and "New Enrollment" in 1999 include the 1535 students enrolled in new vocational-technological school.

14-29 大学、中专专任教师职称情况
STATISTICS ON RANKS AND TITLES OF FULL-TIME TEACHERS AT SCHOOLS OF VARIOUS LEVELS

单位：人 (person)

职称	Ranks and Titles	1990	2000	2003	2004	2005	2006	2007	2008	2009
普通高等学校专任教师数	**Number of Full-Time Teachers of Regular Institutions of Higher Education**	**24624**	**30363**	**46947**	**55683**	**59009**	**65164**	**65975**	**70617**	**73159**
正高级	Senoir	932	3253	5036	5933	6434	7371	7353	7707	8297
副高级	Associate Senoir	5215	9448	15145	17126	17843	19623	19675	20623	21608
中　级	Junior	9077	9847	15626	18878	19169	20585	21091	23380	24978
初　级	Primary	902	5741	7784	9314	10311	12043	13133	14402	13817
无职称	No Title	8498	2074	3356	4432	5252	5542	4723	4505	4459
中等专业学校专任教师数	**Number of Full-Time Teachers of Specialized Schools**	**14407**	**15549**	**20263**	**21460**	**24036**	**26857**	**29355**	**30689**	**29148**
副高级	Associate Senoir	1463	3523	4362	4659	5152	5890	6422	6752	6541
中　级	Junior	4493	7229	9751	10237	11467	12560	13847	14460	13366
初　级	Primary	4419	4399	5276	5300	5889	6479	7344	7564	7403
无职称	No Title	4032	398	874	1264	1528	1928	1742	1913	1838

14-30 各级各类学校校舍建筑面积情况
STATISTICS ON FLOOR SPACE OF SCHOOL HOUSES UNDER CONSTRUCTION IN SCHOOLS OF VARIOUS LEVELS

单位：万平方米 (10 000 sq.m)

项　目	Item	1990	2000	2003	2004	2005	2006	2007	2008	2009
中等职业学校	**Secondary Vocational School**	**319.52**	**736.78**	**734.27**	**732.44**	**833.01**	**859.51**	**951.81**	**999.97**	**899.28**
中等技术学校	Secondary School of Technology	248.20	647.55							
中等师范学校	Secondary Normal School	66.46	89.23							
普通中学	**Regular Middle School**	**1509.29**	**3140.54**	**3472.14**	**3598.25**	**3745.41**	**3941.88**	**3941.49**	**4004.21**	**3991.6**
城市	Urban	424.21	1251.43	1246.51	1280.72	1121.26	1048.98	1116.26	1240.22	1175.05
县镇	Township	247.29	381.35	868.02	907.29	1083.29	1324.50	1391.64	1381.34	1484.82
农村	Rural	877.79	1507.76	1357.61	1410.24	1540.86	1568.40	1433.59	1382.65	1331.73
职业中学	**Vocational Middle School**	**147.74**	**235.91**	**27.10**	**23.81**	**20.51**	**18.70**	**12.89**	**11.38**	**6.71**
城市	Urban	48.40	149.14	2.70	3.47	3.34				0.1
县镇	Township	36.03	44.53	4.45	3.22	3.21	2.36	2.44	3.36	0.08
农村	Rural	63.31	42.24	19.95	17.12	13.96	16.34	10.45	8.01	6.52
小学	**Primary School**	**2400.12**	**3603.03**	**3132.71**	**3019.71**	**2926.92**	**2888.81**	**2781.65**	**2690.59**	**2648.74**
城市	Urban	311.13	781.80	628.74	620.53	414.55	361.86	411.24	432.74	400.48
县镇	Township	192.48	251.07	267.37	271.37	319.56	353.28	379.51	379.31	469.32
农村	Rural	1896.51	2570.17	2236.60	2127.81	2192.81	2173.67	1990.9	1878.53	1778.94

14-31 初中毕业生升入高中和小学毕业生升入初中的升学率
STATISTICS ON PROPORTION OF MIDDLE-SCHOOL STUDENTS ENTERING TO HIGH SCHOOL AND PROPORTION OF PRIMARY-SCHOOL STUDENTS ENTERING TO MIDDLE SCHOOL

年份 Year	初中毕业生升入高中升学率 Proportion of Middle-School Students Entering into High-School			小学毕业生升学率 Proportion of Primary-School Students Entering into Middle-School		
	初中毕业生数(万人) Number of Middle-School Graduates (10 000 persons)	高中招生数(万人) Number of High-School Graduates (10 000 persons)	升学率(%) proportion of students entering schools of a higher level(%)	初中毕业生数(万人) Number of Middle-School Graduates (10 000 persons)	高中招生数(万人) Number of High-School Graduates (10 000 persons)	升学率(%) proportion of students entering schools of a higher level(%)
1957	3.67	1.64	44.8	18.32	6.45	35.2
1965	7.60	3.75	49.4	29.60	24.95	84.3
1975	49.25	31.26	63.5	116.05	110.11	94.9
1978	98.80	43.33	43.9	132.37	119.46	90.3
1980	52.23	25.04	47.7	107.64	88.93	82.6
1985	49.92	19.13	38.3	104.89	69.21	66.0
1990	51.71	16.78	32.5	89.96	66.63	74.1
1991	46.10	16.76	33.0	91.77	69.85	78.1
1992	49.40	17.93	36.3	95.47	72.51	78.2
1993	52.49	19.61	37.4	94.00	75.75	80.5
1994	53.20	16.70	31.4	91.32	78.02	85.4
1995	57.85	19.88	34.4	90.76	80.53	88.7
1996	59.33	19.86	33.5	90.19	83.59	92.7
1997	64.70	21.29	32.9	95.35	89.30	93.7
1998	69.23	24.53	35.4	103.75	96.10	92.6
1999	69.60	27.20	39.1	111.24	101.40	91.2
2000	71.80	31.43	43.8	116.02	109.06	94.0
2001	76.34	35.31	46.3	121.00	113.49	93.8
2002	82.93	42.45	51.2	122.17	120.07	98.3
2003	91.61	39.61	43.2	118.70	117.83	99.3
2004	99.32	42.97	43.3	109.93	109.69	99.8
2005	105.51	45.86	43.5	102.07	101.85	99.8
2006	106.18	45.55	42.9	94.66	97.07	102.6
2007	99.77	43.98	44.1	83.29	87.27	104.8
2008	96.10	43.91	45.7	71.51	77.75	108.7
2009	92.38	42.38	45.9	64.68	69.63	107.7

14-32 小学学龄儿童入学率

STATISTICS ON PROPORTION OF CHILDREN AT SCHOOLING AGE ENTERING TO PRIMARY SCHOOLS

年份 Year	学龄儿童数(万人) Number of Children at Schooling Age (10 000 person)	已入学学龄儿童数(万人) Number of Children Entered School (10 000 persons)	入学率(%) proportion of students entering schools of a higher level (%)
1952			47.4
1957			57.6
1965	545.42	481.32	87.8
1975	629.50	611.00	97.1
1978	616.86	597.73	96.9
1980	594.80	576.86	97.0
1985	496.69	489.38	98.5
1990	485.00	480.32	99.0
1991	556.39	549.35	98.7
1992	571.44	563.44	98.6
1993	574.54	566.84	98.7
1994	599.47	593.88	99.1
1995	637.12	632.34	99.2
1996	661.72	658.38	99.5
1997	681.52	678.95	99.6
1998	685.87	682.53	99.5
1999	669.16	665.88	99.5
2000	641.60	638.57	99.5
2001	585.99	583.29	99.5
2002	538.02	535.98	99.6
2003	490.29	488.68	99.7
2004	440.03	438.66	99.7
2005	397.52	396.11	99.7
2006	363.99	362.14	99.5
2007	345.49	344.77	99.8
2008	340.59	340.08	99.9
2009	343.63	342.74	99.7

14-33 各级各类学校服务的人口及每万人口中在校学生数
STATISTICS ON THE NUMBER OF POPULATION SERVED BY SCHOOLS OF VARIOUS LEVELS AND THE NUMBER OF STUDENTS AT SCHOOL PER 10000 PERSONS

项 目	Item	1990	2000	2003	2004	2005	2006	2007	2008	2009
每一学校服务的人口数（万人）	**Number of Population Served by Each School (10 000 persons)**									
普通高等学校	Regular Institutions of Higher Education	86.34	111.63	78.97	70.78	70.95	70.35	70.58	65.64	47.67
成人高等学校	Adults Higher Education	63.25	188.37	272.80	353.89	354.76	378.13	404.67	380.73	408.57
普通中等专业学校	Specialized Secondary School	24.50	29.69	15.39	15.00	13.80	13.30	12.70	12.36	14.23
成人中等专业学校	Specialized Secondary School for Adults	18.01	33.86							
普通中学	Regualr Secondary School	1.45	1.85	1.82	1.83	1.87	1.89	1.95	1.90	1.97
职业中学	Vocational Middle-School	12.06	20.79						317.28	440.00
小学	Primary School	0.16	0.26	0.38	0.43	0.48	0.53	0.59	0.61	0.67
幼儿园	Kindergarden	1.39	1.61	2.66	2.67	2.58	2.38	2.36	1.98	1.91
每万人口中的学生数（人）	**Number of Students at School Per (person)**									
普通高等学校	Regular Institutions of Higher Education	23.97	57.49	120.22	148.27	167.91	180.54	191.71	207.48	218.37
成人高等学校	Adults Higher Education	21.22	35.94	58.98	40.08	37.05	46.81	46.66	49.89	48.27
普通中等专业学校	Specialized Secondary School	26.81	46.22	60.70	76.21	100.48	132.15	154.23	181.63	182.13
成人中等专业学校	Specialized Secondary School for Adults	21.29	12.08							
普通中学	Regualr Secondary School	388.95	582.19	735.58	750.85	740.65	720.41	686.84	688.92	638.13
职业中学	Vocational Middle-School	23.72	24.68	6.20	5.65	4.40	3.74	2.23	1.34	0.84
小学	Primary School	1145.48	1107.77	879.95	789.46	711.64	646.82	610.12	631.72	628.08
幼儿园	Kindergarden	140.54	120.56	99.61	97.73	98.57	106.15	107.97	130.02	145.35

14-34 各级各类学校每个专任教师负担的学生数
STATISTICS ON STUDENS-TEACHERS RATIO BY LEVEL OF SCHOOL

单位：人 (person)

项 目	Item	1990	2000	2003	2004	2005	2006	2007	2008	2009
普通高等学校	Regular Institutions of Higher Education	5.30	11.41	16.15	15.11	15.86	15.30	15.35	15.29	15.70
中等职业学校	Secondary Vocation School	10.10	17.92	17.98	21.36	25.21	29.77	31.89	33.8002	35.74
#中师	#Secondary Teachers School	8.90	12.23							
普通中学	Regular Middle School	13.70	17.68	19.73	19.67	19.13	18.49	17.66	16.8226	15.77
#初中	#Junior Middle Schools	14.20	18.19	18.98	19.61	18.76	17.97	17.06	15.9621	14.71
高中	Senior High School	11.70	15.89	19.99	19.85	20.09	19.79	19.11	18.8285	18.18
职业中学	Vocational Secondaryl School	11.40	13.47	21.28	22.09	20.28	18.07	15.52	13.8094	
#高中	#Senior School	10.80	12.41							
小学	Primary School	21.10	24.28	22.58	21.42	19.90	18.69	18.07	17.9172	12.09
幼儿园	Kindergarden	25.80	24.31	33.56	30.62	29.70	29.90	29.45	29.9468	18.13

14–35 各级学校女学生和女教师数

NUMBER OF FEMALE STUDENTS AND FEMALE TEACHERS AT SCHOOL OF VARIOUS LEVELS

单位：万人 (10 000 persons)

项目	Item	1990	2000	2003	2004	2005	2006	2007	2008	2009
一、女学生数	Number of Female Students	387.79	506.2	494.08	483.39	473.27	462.45			
普通高等学校	Regular Institutions of Higher Education	3.53	11.93	30.10	37.11	44.11	48.46	53.32	55.00	58.9
中等专业学校	Specialized Secondary School	6.10	14.33	17.90	22.07	29.14	38.01	44.56	49.13	49.73
普通中学	Regualr Secondary School	83.22	155.7	200.73	205.49	203.98	199.04	189.92	178.81	166.26
职业中学	Vocational Middle-School	5.28	6.80	1.69	1.56	1.19	1.01	0.59	0.33	0.21
小学	Primary School	289.66	317.5	243.66	217.16	194.85	175.93	166.01	161.74	161.82
二、女学生占学生总数%	Percentage of Female Students in School to Total Students	44.1	46.2	45.7	45.5	45.5				
普通高等学校	Regular Institutions of Higher Education	27.06	34.42	41.69	41.6	43.56	44.37	45.82	46.417	47.16
中等专业学校	Specialized Secondary School	41.84	51.44	49.14	48.14	48.08	47.54	47.6	47.364	47.74
普通中学	Regualr Secondary School	39.34	44.36	45.47	45.49	45.66	45.67	45.55	45.447	45.55
职业中学	Vocational Middle-School	40.96	45.7	45.43	45.88	44.87	44.61	43.53	42.98	43.48
小学	Primary School	46.49	47.54	46.14	45.72	45.4	44.96	44.83	44.831	45.04
三、女教师数	Number of Female Teachers	16.39	20.33	20.81	21.24	21.58	21.92			
普通高等学校	Regular Institutions of Higher Education	0.64	1.02	1.77	2.17	2.34	2.62	2.82	2.94	3.07
中等专业学校	Specialized Secondary School	0.48	0.6	0.78	0.83	0.94	1.06	1.15	1.23	1.19
普通中学	Regualr Secondary School	3.84	6.26	7.42	7.73	7.94	8.17	8.29	8.31	8.37
职业中学	Vocational Middle-School	0.24	0.38	0.05	0.05	0.04	0.04	0.02	0.02	0.01
小学	Primary School	11.19	12.07	10.79	10.46	10.32	10.03	9.88	9.79	9.71
四、女教师占教师总数%	Percentage of Female Teachers in School to Total Teachers	32.4	38.3	38.1	39.4	40.4				
普通高等学校	Regular Institutions of Higher Education	26.04	33.55	37.74	38.97	39.65	40.21	41.40	41.63	42.01
中等专业学校	Specialized Secondary School	33.30	38.50	38.42	38.68	39.11	39.47	39.18	40.08	40.67
普通中学	Regualr Secondary School	24.86	31.54	33.15	33.66	34.00	34.67	35.12	35.53	36.14
职业中学	Vocational Middle-School	21.62	34.55	29.41	32.49	30.58	31.92	22.91	35.971	30.56
小学	Primary School	37.82	43.89	46.13	47.17	47.85	47.91	48.22	48.62	49

14-36 各级各类成人学校在校学生数
NUMBER OF STUDENTS ENROLLED AT SCHOOLS FOR ADULTS OF VARIOUS LEVELS

单位：万人 (10 000 persons)

各类学校	Items	1990	2000	2003	2004	2005	2006	2007	2008	2009
成人高等学校	Adult Higher Education	11.54	21.66	34.36	24.11	22.34	28.32	28.61	28.49	27.61
广播电视大学	Radio and TV Universities	2.26	2.78	3.08	3.01	2.52	2.10	1.70	1.29	0.76
职工大学	Schools of Higher Education for Staff	0.77	1.36	0.61	0.27	0.22	0.15	0.36	0.33	0.30
管理干部学院	Colleges for Management and Caders	0.25	0.90	1.19	0.77	0.60	0.82	0.83	0.71	0.48
教育学院	Pedagogical College	1.54	0.94	1.14	0.71	0.89	1.21	0.44	0.36	0.42
普通高等学校办函授部、夜大学	Correspondence and Evening College Run by Regualr High Education	6.31	15.16	28.34	19.35	18.11	24.05	25.28	25.81	25.64
成人中等学校	Secondary Schools for Adults	60.42	139.75	53.67	23.43	35.90	31.78	76.99	85.83	64.40
中学	Middle School	1.22	0.61	0.50	1.63	2.42	1.96	8.39	4.71	3.00
技术培训学校	Technical Training Schools	47.76	131.86	53.17	21.80	33.48	29.82	68.60	81.12	55.28
成人初等学校	Primary Schools for Adults	45.59	12.50	6.28	6.72	2.20	0.77	2.38	1.10	0.81
#扫盲班	#Class for Illiteracy	14.22	6.43	2.26	3.58	0.82	0.63	1.46	0.15	0.34

注：1.成人高等学校学生数是本、专科学生数。
2.1999年成人高等学校在校学生数总计中，减去了成人高校招收的新高职学生1535人。

Notes:a)The number of students in Adults Higher Education refers to the number of undergraduates and students in vocational schools.
b)The total number of students in Adult Higher Education in 1999 dose not include in the 1535 students enrolled in new vocational school.

14-37 教育事业经费
STATISTICS ON FUNDS FOR EDUCATION

单位：万元 (10 000 yuan)

项 目	Item	1990	2000	2003	2004	2005	2006	2006	2007	2008	2009
教育事业经费支出总计	Total Expenditures for Education	114540	536915	840699	974340	1202624	1454124	1464678	2098316	2431136	3148057
#高教支出	#Expenditures from Institutions of Higher Education	13457	72912	128362	136371	171579	225702	229229	236381	279807	361943
普教支出	Expenditures from Regular Schools	101084	464003	712336	837969	933877	1101045	1105809	1598055	1858698	2426595

注：1.该表不包括中央属院校教育情况。
2.该表为地方财政预算内教育经费。

Notes:a) Statistics on Education expenditures from Central Colleges and Universities were Excluding from this table.
b) Statistics on this table for education was educational expenditures within local financial bugdet.

14-38 成人教育基本情况

BASIC CONDTIONS ABOUT ADULT EDUCATION

项　目	Item	1990	2000	2003	2004	2005	2006	2007	2008	2009
成人高等学校数（个）	Number of Institutes for Adults Higher Education (unit)	72	32	22	17	17	16	15	15	14
在校学生数（人）	Students Enrollment in Schools (person)	52271	216618	343646	241143	223431	283214	286129	284903	276100
招生数　（人）	New Students Enrollment (person)	13612	89937	130803	129615	104051	115099	114217	88873	99590
毕业生数　（人）	Graduates (person)	28071	54957	95190	103544	116062	60715	86098	88850	102562
教职员工数(人)	Nuber of Faculties (person)	10076	9771	6697	6095	5680	3008	4574	2294	2037
#专任教师数(人)	#Number of Full-Time Teachers (person)	4739	5036	3657	3575	3231	1842	2908	1576	1384
成人中学学校数（个）	Number of Secondary Schools for Adults (unit)	134	33	81	65	60	64	101	77	144
在校学生数(人)	Students Enrollment in Schools (person)	12183	6081	4971	16327	24179	19618	83885	47075	29971
招生数　（人）	New Students Enrollment (person)	9969	8512							
毕业生数　（人）	Graduates (person)	6950	13613	9454	14874	17924	31696	82709	69268	54962
教职员工数(人)	Nuber of Faculties (person)	612	476	778	1012	592	218	738	793	785
#专任教师数(人)	#Number of Full-Time Teachers (person)	405	344	189	443	481	166	566	615	530
成人技术培训学校数（个）	Number of Technical Training Schools for Adults (unit)	1221	12304	4155	2253	2337	2954	3911	3109	2465
在校学生数(人)	Students Enrollment in Schools (person)	477588	1318555	531722	217990	334825	298221	686021	811196	552793
招生数　（人）	New Students Enrollment (person)	423858	1815629							
毕业生数　（人）	Graduates (person)	459999	2294247	955303	471259	703613	605036	673101	799211	515647
教职员工数(人)	Nuber of Faculties (person)	4461	18685	8532	3844	6018	9114	13026	12941	8665
#专任教师数(人)	#Number of Full-Time Teachers (person)	2858	10242	4863	2331	3681	5909	9890	9325	5942
成人初等学校数（个）	Primary Schools for Adults (unit)	2595	6010	1344	1344	375	305	353	216	465
在校学生数(人)	Students Enrollment in Schools (person)	455917	125004	62797	67218	21977	7720	23807	10962	8084
招　生　数(人)	New Students Enrollment (person)	341128	134645							
毕业生数　（人）	Graduates (person)	410793	143090	66164	72568	11631	6856	19982	43132	65905
教职员工数(人)	Nuber of Faculties (person)	3205	5450	1532	2460	1249	396	1021	387	672
#专任教师数(人)	#Number of Full-Time Teachers (person)	1691	2540	400	2007	870	197	719	223	490

14-39 研究生基本情况

BASIC CONDTIONS ABOUT POST-GRADUATES

单位：人 (person)

项 目	Item	1990	2000	2003	2004	2005	2006	2007	2008	2009
高等学校在校研究生数	Number of Post-graduates at School in Institutions of Higher Education	6411	23745	50994	64747	71303	73736	75352	80388	88416
攻读博士学位研究生	Post-graduate Studying for Doctor's Degree	628	4803	10413	12889	14315	15594	16647	17861	18207
攻读硕士学位研究生	Post-graduate Studying for Master's Degree	5721	18942	40581	51858	56988	58142	58705	62527	70209
招收研究生数	New Students Enrollment	2116	9942	21642	25423	25554	27239	28261	29242	33978
攻读博士学位研究生	Post-graduate Studying for Doctor's Degree	215	1688	4067	4412	4105	4202	4361	4386	4478
攻读硕士学位研究生	Post-graduate Studying for Master's Degree	1857	8254	17575	21011	21449	23037	23900	24856	29500
毕业研究生数	Number of Graduates	2346	4955	8874	11688	14441	23094	25100	23419	24963
攻读博士学位研究生	Post-graduate Studying for Doctor's Degree	125	648	1313	1681	1838	2677	3099	3033	3938
攻读硕士学位研究生	Post-graduate Studying for Master's Degree	2144	4287	7561	10007	12603	20417	22001	20386	21025
科研单位在学研究生数	Number of Post-graduates Studying in Research Institutions	309	630	1303	1622	1948	2173	2227	2271	2303
攻读博士学位研究生	Post-graduate Studying for Doctor's Degree	46	191	426	521	630	667	681	673	687
攻读硕士学位研究生	Post-graduate Studying for Master's Degree	263	439	877	1101	1318	1506	1546	1598	1616
招收研究生数	New Students Enrollment	76	266	549	678	734	759	737	767	773
攻读博士学位研究生	Post-graduate Studying for Doctor's Degree	12	80	163	190	192	189	175	178	189
攻读硕士学位研究生	Post-graduate Studying for Master's Degree	64	186	386	488	542	570	562	589	584
毕业研究生数	Number of Graduates	126	120	205	257	295	427	609	584	601
攻读博士学位研究生	Post-graduate Studying for Doctor's Degree	4	38	64	85	76	150	211	174	171
攻读硕士学位研究生	Post-graduate Studying for Master's Degree	122	82	141	172	219	277	398	410	430

主要统计指标解释

科技活动 指在自然科学、农业科学、医药科学、工程与技术科学、人文与社会科学领域(简称科学技术领域)中，与科技知识的产生、发展、传播和应用密切相关的有组织的活动。可分为研究与试验发展(R&D)、研究与试验发展成果应用及相关的科技服务三类活动。该定义是联合国教科文组织考虑成员国特别是发展中国家开展科技统计工作的需要，而对科技活动所作的统计界定。

科技活动人员 指直接从事科技活动、以及专门从事科技活动管理和为科技活动提供直接服务，累计的实际工作时间占全年制度工作时间10%及以上的人员。(1)直接从事科技活动的人员包括：在独立核算的科学研究与技术开发机构、高等学校、各类企业及其他事业单位内设的研究室、实验室、技术开发中心及中试车间(基地)等机构中从事科技活动的研究人员、工程技术人员、技术工人及其它人员；虽不在上述机构工作，但编入科技活动项目(课题)组的人员；科技信息与文献机构中的专业技术人员；从事论文设计的研究生等。(2)专门从事科技活动管理和为科技活动提供直接服务的人员，包括：独立核算的科学研究与技术开发机构、科技信息与文献机构、高等学校、各类企业及其他事业单位主管科技工作的负责人，专门从事科技活动的计划、行政、人事、财务、物资供应、设备维护、图书资料管理等工作的各类人员，但不包括保卫、医疗保健人员、司机、食堂人员、茶炉工、水暖工、清洁工等为科技活动提供间接服务的人员。该指标用来反映投入科技活动人力的规模。

科学家与工程师 指科技活动人员中具有高、中级技术职称(职务)的人员和不具有高、中级技术职称(职务)的大学本科及以上学历人员。该指标用来反映投入科技活动人力的素质。

研究与试验发展(R&D) 指在科学技术领域，为增加知识总量，以及运用这些知识去创造新的应用进行的系统的创造性的活动，包括基础研究、应用研究、试验发展三类活动。国际上通常采用 R&D 活动的规模和强度指标反映一国的科技实力和核心竞争力。

专业技术人员 指从事专业技术工作和专业技术管理工作的人员，即企事业单位中已经聘任专业技术职务从事专业技术工作和专业技术管理工作的人员，以及未聘任专业技术职务，现在专业技术岗位上工作的人员。包括工程技术人员，农业技术人员，科学研究人员，卫生技术人员，教学人员，经济人员，会计人员，统计人员，翻译人员，图书资料、档案、文博人员，新闻出版人员，律师、公证人员，广播电视播音人员，工艺美术人员，体育人员，艺术人员及企业政治思想工作人员，共十七个专业技术职务类别。用来反映科技人力资源情况。

科技活动经费筹集 指从各种渠道筹集到的计划用于科技活动的经费，包括政府资金、企业资金、事业单位资金、金融机构贷款、国外资金和其他资金等。反映各社会经济主体对促进科技进步所做的努力。

新产品 指采用新技术原理、新设计构思研制、生产的全新产品，或在结构、材质、工艺等某一方面比原有产品有明显改进，从而显著提高了产品性能或扩大了使用功能的产品。既包括政府有关部门认定并在有效期内的新产品，也包括企业自行研制开发，未经政府有关部门认定，从投产之日起一年之内的新产品。用来反映科技产出及对经济增长的直接贡献。

专利 是专利权的简称，是对发明人的发明创造经审查合格后，由专利局依据专利法授予发明人和设计人对该项发明创造享有的专有权。包括发明、实用新型和外观设计。反映拥有自主知识产权的科技和设计成果情况。

发明 指对产品、方法或者其改进所提出的新的技术方案。是国际通行的反映拥有自主知识产权技术的核心指标。

普通高等学校 指按照国家规定的设置标准和审批程序批准举办的，通过全国普通高等学校统一招生考试，招收高中毕业生为主要培养对象，实施高等教育的全日制大学、独立设置的学院和高等专科学校、高等职业学校和其他机构。

大学、独立设置的学院主要实施本科层次以上教育，高等专科学校、高等职业学校实施专科层次教育，其他机构是承担国家普通招生计划任务不计校数的机构。包括普通高等学校分校和批准筹建的普通高等学校等。

成人高等学校 指按照国家规定的设置标准和审批程序批准举办的，通过全国成人高等学校统一招生考试，招收具有高中毕业或同等学历的在职从业人员为主要培养对象，利用函授、业余、脱产等多种形式对其实施高等学历教育的学校。包括职工高等学校、农民高等学校、管理干部学院、教育学院、独立函授学院、广播电视大学、其他机构等。其他机构是承担国家成人招生计划任务不计校数的机构。

小学学龄儿童净入学率 指调查范围内已入小学学习的学龄儿童占校内外学龄儿童总数(包括弱智儿童，不包括盲聋哑儿童)的比重。计算公式为:

$$\text{小学学龄儿童净入学率}=\frac{\text{已入学的小学学龄儿童数}}{\text{校内外小学学龄儿童总数}}\times 100\%$$

Explanatory Notes on Main Statistical Indicators

Scientific and Technological Activities (S&T Activities) refer to organized activities which are closely related with the creation, development, dissemination and application of the scientific and technical knowledge in the fields of natural sciences, agricultural science, medical science, engineering and technological science, humanities and social sciences (referred to as scientific and technological fields). S&T activities can be classified in to 3 categories: research and development (R&D) activities, application of R&D results, and related S&T services. This statistical definition is made by UNICHIEF for scientific and technological activities to meet the need of carrying out statistical work in this field for its member countries in particular those developing countries.

Personnel Engaged in S&T Activities refer to personnel directly engaged in S&T activities, in the management of S&T activities, and in providing direct service to S&T activities, who spend over 10% of the total working hours in a year in S&T activities. (1) Personnel directly engaged in S&T activities include researchers, engineers, technicians and other related personnel engaged in S&T activities in independent-accounting R&D institutions, institutions of higher learning, and in research institutes, laboratories, technology development centers and central experiment workshops under enterprises and institutions. Also included are people working in S&T research project teams, professional and technical personnel working in S&T information archiving institutes, and graduate students working on the design of their thesis. (2) Personnel engaged in the management of S&T activities and in providing direct service to S&T activities include senior management people responsible for S&T activities in independent-accounting R&D institutions, S&T information archiving institutes, institutions of higher learning, and in enterprises and institutions where S&T activities are undertaken. Also included are people responsible for the planning, administration, personnel management, financial management, logistics supply, equipment maintenance, information and library management that are related with S&T activities. People providing indirect services are excluded, such as security, medical service, drivers, plumbers, cleaners and those providing catering and related service. This indicator reflects the size of personnel engaged in S&T activities.

Scientists and Engineers refer to persons engaged in S&T activities who have obtained titles of senior and middle level professional positions, and those without such position but have completed university or higher education. This indicator reflects the quality of personnel engaged in S&T activities.

Research and Development (R&D) refers to systematic and creative activities in the field of science and technology aiming at increasing the knowledge and using the knowledge for new application. R&D includes 3 categories of activities: basic research, applied research and experiments and development. The scale and intensity of R&D are widely used internationally to reflect the strength of S&T and the core competitiveness of a country in the world.

Professional and Technical Personnel refer to persons engaged in professional and technical work or in the management of professional and technical activities, i.e., people with professional or technical positions who are engaged in professional and technical work or in the management of professional and technical activities, and people without professional or technical positions but are working on professional or technical posts. They include professionals and technicians working in 17 categories of technical occupations including engineering, agriculture, scientific researches, medical service, teaching, economic research and application, accounting, statistics, translation, libraries, archives, cultural and museum service, journalism and publication, lawyers, notarization service, radio and television broadcasting, handicraft and fine arts, sports, performing art, and political workers in enterprises. This indicator reflects the condition of human resources in S&T.

Funding for S&T Activities refers to funds obtained from various sources for S&T activities, including government funds, self-raised funds by enterprises, self-raised funds by institutions, loans from financial institutions, foreign funds and other funds. This indicator reflects the efforts made by various social economic entities in promoting the development of S&T.

New Products refer to new products produced with new technology and new design, or products that represent noticeable improvement in terms of structure, material, or production process so as to improve significantly the character or function of the older versions. They include new products certified by relevant government agencies within the period of certification, as well as new products designed and produced by enterprises within a year without certification by government agencies. This indictor reflects the direct contribution of S&T output to economic growth.

Patent is an abbreviation for the patent right and refers to the exclusive right of ownership by the inventors or designers for the creation or inventions, given from the patent offices after due process of assessment and approval in accordance with the Patent Law. Patents are granted for inventions, utility models and designs. This indicator reflects the achievements of S&T and design with independent intellectual property.

Inventions refer to the new technical proposals to the products or methods or their modifications. This is universal core indicator reflecting the technologies with independent intellectual property.

Regular Institutions of Higher Learning refer to educational establishments set up according to the government evaluation and approval procedures, enrolling graduates from senior secondary schools and providing higher education courses and training for senior professionals. They include full-time universities, colleges, high professional schools, high professional vocational schools and others.

Universities and colleges are mainly providing undergraduate courses; those high professional schools and high professional vocational schools are mainly providing professional trainings; and others refer to educational establishments, which are responsible for enrolling students but not covered in the total number of schools, including: branch schools of universities and colleges, and universities and colleges that have been proved and prepared to construct.

Institutions of Higher Learning for Adults refer to educational establishments, set up in line with relevant rules approved by the government, enrolling staff and workers with senior secondary school or equivalent education, and providing higher education courses in many forms of correspondence, spare time, or full time for adults. Professionals thus trained receive a qualification equivalent to graduates studying regular courses at regular universities, colleges and professional colleges. Institutions of higher learning for adults include schools of high education for staff and workers, schools of high education for peasants, colleges for management cadres, pedagogical colleges, independent correspondence colleges, Radio and TV universities and other educational establishments. Other educational establishments are responsible for enrolling adult students but not covered in the number of schools.

Enrollment Rate of Primary School Age Children refers to the proportion of school age children enrolled at schools to the total number of school age children both in and outside schools (including retarded children, but excluding blind, deaf and mute children). The formula is:

Enrollment Rate of Primary School-age Children = (Total Primary School-age Children at Schools)/(Total Primary School age Children Both at and Outside Schools) x 100%

15 文化、体育、卫生、环保

Culture, Sports, Public Health and Environmental Protection

资料整理：谢余强

15-1 文化事业机构、人员数

NUMBER OF CULTURAL INSTITUTIONS AND PERSONEL

单位：个、人 (unit, person)

项 目	Item	1990	2000	2003	2004	2005	2006	2007	2008	2009
艺术事业机构	Art Performing Institution	263	217	213	224	198	212	186	187	180
#剧团	#Troupes	108	99	98	98	99	98	98	100	100
#剧场	#Theater	90	78	69	72		58	58	59	58
文物事业机构	Historical Relics Institutions	121	144	157	163	148	149	149	168	171
#博物馆	#Museums	85	94	98	98	91	96	96	111	114
图书馆事业机构	Library Institutions	101	103	103	104	102	102	102	104	104
群众文化事业机构	Public Culture Institutions	1849	1695	1301	1296	1258	1335	1342	1356	1367
群众艺术馆	Public Art Center	16	18	18	18	18	18	18	17	17
文化馆(站)	Art Center	1833	1677	1283	1168		1317	1229	1339	1350
艺术事业人员数	Number of People Engaged in Art Performing	9668	8655	8677	8732	8102	8153	7378	7470	7799
#剧团人员	Staff in Troupes	6900	6381	6363	6275	6138	5924	5902	6013	6104
#剧场人员	Staff in Theater	2256	2274	1756	1736		1303	1303	1300	1478
文物事业人员数	Number of People Engaged in Historical Relics	1884	2924	3136	3497	3354	3585	3585	3623	3915
#博物馆人员	#umber of staff in Library	1140	1707	1864	1955	1728	1834	1834	2076	2281
图书馆事业人员数	Number of People Engaged in Library	1815	2299	2256	2285	2253	2243	2243	2233	2178
群众文化事业人员数	Number of People Engaged in Public Art	6101	5928	5529	5369	5269	4936	4968	4786	4951
群众艺术馆人员	Number of People in Public Art Center	662	776	677	684	673	722	722	594	610
文化馆(站)人员	Number of People in Cultural Station	5439	5152	4852	4685		4214	4246	4192	4341
#乡镇文化站	#Twnship Cultural Stations		2574	2524	2418		2542	2122	2013	2181

15-2 公共图书馆发展情况
DEVELOPMENT STATISTICS ON PUBLIC LIBRARIES

项目	Item	2000	2003	2004	2005	2006	2007	2008	2009
机构数 (个)	Number of Library (unit)	103	103	104	102	102	102	104	104
藏书数 (万册)	Total Collections (10 000 volumes)	1678	1819	1867	1923	1981	2037	2106	2181
书架单层总长度 (万米)	Total Length of Bookshelves (10 000 m)	109	101	103	101	101	106	103	104
发放借书证数 (万个)	Number of Library Cards (10 000 units)	41	70	84	72	75	79	96	129
图书流通情况	Number of Circulation								
人次 (万人次)	Person-time (10 000 person-time)	714	897	1025	1145	1200	1176	1215	1271
册次 (万册数)	Volume-time (10 000 volume-time)	949	916	824	927	1012	943	1039	1047
为读者服务举办各种活动	Serveive for Readers								
次数 (次)	Times (time)	1222	35191	1741	1621	2389	2136	2303	2777
参加人数 (万人次)	Number of Readers Involved (10 000 person-time)	115	209	242	176	192	156	150	111
当年新购图书 (万册)	New Books Purchaesd in 2009 (10 000 volume-time)	36	51	46	43	48	53	56	68
图书费 (万元)	Purchase Expenses (10 000 yuan)	699	1120	1075	1296	1520	1539	1802	1475

15-3 公共图书馆藏书及分类情况
STATISTICS ON BOOKS AND TYPE OF BOOKS IN PUBLIC LIBRARIES

单位：万册 (10 000 volumes)

年份 Year	合计 Total	#外文 #Forgein	#古籍 #Ancient	#新书籍 #New
1986	1096	156	88	1008
1990	1227	161	97	1125
1991	1319	84	97	1222
1992	1343	80	96	1247
1993	1372	83	97	1275
1994	1408	81	97	1311
1995	1445	82	97	1356
1996	1472	82	97	1375
1997	1533	81	97	1436
1998	1599	81	96	1503
1999	1643	81	96	1547
2000	1678	82	97	1581
2001	1709	83	98	1611
2002	1759	81	99	1660
2003	1819	83	98	1721
2004	1867		94	1773
2005	1923		97	1826
2006	1981		100	1881
2007	2037		96	1941
2008	2106		97	2009
2009	2181		96	2085

15-4 图书、报纸、期刊出版情况

STATISTICS ON PUBLICATION OF BOOKS, NEWSPAPERS AND PERIODICALS

项 目	Item	1990	2000	2004	2005	2006	2007	2008	2009
一、图书出版种数（种）	Number of Kind of Library Books Published (kind)	2546	4529	5633	6535	6335	7137	8137	9024
新出版 （种）	New Publication (kind)	1827	2443	3143	3739	3802	3523	4215	5241
总印数 （千册）	Total Prints (1000 volume)	402517	288416	225140	345510	210559	202813	138957	224409
总印张 （千印张）	Total Number of Paper Printed (1000 papers)	1418989	1552128	1615662	2495183	1545915	1317945	868799	1639309
1.书籍出版种数 （种）	Number of Kind of Library (kind)	2104	3620	3220	3988				
#新出版 （种）	#New Publication (kind)	1484	2177	2600	3289				
总印数 （千册）	Total Prints (1000 volume)	274427	118319	35750	131980				
总印张 （千印张）	Total Number of Paper Printed (1000 papers)	977116		441560	893203				
2.课本出版种数 （种）	Number of Kind of Textbooks Published (kind)	313	896	2163	2523				
#新出版 （种）	#New Publication (kind)	220	266	468	443				
总印数 （千册）	Total Prints (1000 volume)	121703	169953	189390	213525				
总印张 （千印张）	Total Number of Paper Printed (1000 papers)	421465	926553	1174099	1601975				
3.图片 （种）	Picyures (kind)	129	13	250	24	26	26		
#新出版 （种）	#New Publication (kind)	123			7				
总印数 （千册）	Total Prints (1000 volume)	639	64		5				
总印张 （千印张）	Total Number of Paper Printed (1000 papers)	1357	236		6				
4.活页小件印品(千印张)	Loose Sheet Prints (1000 papers)	684	9	44					
二、杂志出版种数 （种）	Number of Kind of Magazines Published (kind)	254	391	397	407	402	402	404	404
平均期印数 （千册）	Printing Number of Average Peroid (1000 volume)	6078	12273	8935	11576				
总印数 （千册）	Total Prints (1000 volume)	73456	220280	142945	196800	208110	204230	229260	298504
总印张 （千印张）	Total Number of Paper Printed (1000 papers)	119523	746145	484503	745526	1072152	796297	1026240	1252739
三、报刊出版种数 （种）	Number of Kind of Newspapers and Periodicals Published (kind)	84	164	131	193	131	131	130	130
平均期印数 （千份）	Printing Number of Average Peroid (1000 volume)	4454	5693	6289	6736	6300	5860		
总印数 （千份）	Total Prints (1000 copies)	623820	1342282	1552438	1956980	1844240	1637220	188011	1736026
总印张 （万印张）	Total Number of Paper Printed (10 000 papers)	44247	339434	445537	520833	6143233	4759324	8796774	7959427

15-5 电影、艺术活动、群众文化活动、图书馆及博物馆活动情况

STATISTICS ON MOVIE, ART ACTIVITIES, PUBLIC CULTURE ACTIVITIES, LIBRARY AND MUSEUM

项　目	Item	1990	2000	2004	2005	2006	2007	2008	2009
电影活动	Movie								
放映场次数　(万场)	Times Projected　(10 000 times)	130.0	7.6	24.2	29.3	32	39	56	
群众人数　(千人次)	Number of People Participated (1000 person-time)	559940	2940	45296	88120	83920	94966	138980	
年人均观看次数　(次)	Annual Times of Watching Per Capita　(time)	10.42	0.05	0.75	1.45	1.35	1.58	2.43	
艺术活动	Art Activities								
年表演场次　(场)	Annual Times of Performing (time)	13100	15000	16467	16000	20667	22000	22000	22679
观众人数　(千人次)	Number of Spectators (1000 person-times)	10620	21211	17580	16939	22418	24599	26699	26390
年人均观看次数　(次)	Annual Times of Watching Per Capita　(time)	0.20	0.36	0.29	0.28	0.36	0.41	0.47	0.46
群众文化活动	Public Culture Activities								
举办展览个数　(个)	Number of Expo Displayed　(unit)	1166	2785	2648	2653	3795	3262	3771	3908
举办训练班结业人数(万人次)	Number of Trained (10 000 person-times)	4.90	9.90	12.69	13.00	13.00	13.0	46.0	45.8
图书馆活动	Library Activities								
图书流通人次　(千人次)	Number of Circulation (1000 person-times)	5480	7138	10245	11453	12004	11762	12153	12711
图书流通册次　(千册)	Number of Circulation (1000 volumes)	9600	9485	8236	9267	10126	9429	10387	10468
人均年借阅册数　(册)	Number of Books Borrowed Per Capita Annually　(volume)	0.18	0.16	0.14	0.15	0.16	0.16	0.18	0.18
人均年借阅人数(次)	Number of People Borrowing Anuualy　(person)	0.10	0.12	0.17	0.19	0.19	0.19	0.20	0.22
博物馆活动	Museum Activities								
现有陈列展览个数　(个)	Number of Displaying at Present (unit)	145	210	175	218	160	200	388	510
参观人数　(千人次)	Visitors　(1000 persons)	2089	1819	2050	2194	2947	3313	11084	13183
人均年参观次数　(次)	Number of Visit Time Per Capia Annually　(time)	0.04	0.03	0.03	0.04	0.05	0.05	0.19	0.23

15-6　艺术表演团体、群众艺术馆、文化馆经费情况

STATISTICS ON EXPENSES OF ART TROUPES, PUBLIC ART CENTERS AND CULTURE ACTIVITIES CENTERS

单位：万元　　　　(10 000 yuan)

项　目	Item	1990	2000	2003	2004	2005	2006	2007	2008	2009
艺术表演团体	Art Troupes									
补贴团体　(个)	Subsidy Troupes　(unit)	107	99	97	4	4	4	4	4	4
国家经费补贴	National Subsidy	1962	6609	3210	2938	3568	5496	5598	7015	8374
业务及其他收入	Revenue from Business and From tothers	941	2989	2622	875	1474	1047	1587	1467	1709
#演出收入	#From Performing	427	1610	2010	464	534	331	654	694	474
总支出	Total Exppenditures	2774	9808	14206	3785	4945	6481	7127	8402	9953
第三产业增加值	Value Added of Tertiart Industry	1549	4827	6526	2866	3170	3436	4752	6131	7013
经费自给率　(%)	Percentage of Self-Supply Expenses　(%)	33.9	32.6	27.9	23.0	29.0	16.0	22	17	16
群众艺术馆、文化馆(站)	Mass Art Galleries and Culture Galleries									
总支出	Total Expenditures	1487	7841	7889	385	463	523	714	822	994
#预算内	#Within Budget	895	7104	7335	265	337	454	571	661	850
#业务费	#Business Fees	286	1382	1735	153	155	138	154	103	104
修缮费	Maintainnace Fees	219	713	326	15	4	19	9	2	
第三产业增加值	Value Added of Tertiart Industry	684	4357	5062	284	320	344	307	441	372

注：本表各项指标仅指文化厅系统内的。
Note:The items in this table refers to those within culture bureau system.

15-7　文化、文物事业经费支出及基本建设情况

BASIC CONDITIONS ABOUT EXPENDITURES ON CULTURE AND HISTORICAL RELICS AND ITS CONDTRUCTION

单位：万元　　　　(10 000 yuan)

项　目	Item	1990	2000	2003	2004	2005	2006	2007	2008	2009
文化、文物事业经费支出总计	**Total Expenditures on Culture and Historical Relics**	**10923**	**43079**	**57904**	**69052**	**80952**	**197018**	**129905**	**156358**	**198651**
文化事业	Culture	9908	33256	46491	57105	66111	173425	100548	123434	161906
艺术表演团体	Art Performing Groups	2774	9808	14206	16672	19185	24418	28023	30873	35968
艺术表演场所	Art Performing Places	1525	3268	3261	3669	2835	3508	4547	4310	5431
图书馆	Library	1109	3952	6745	7292	8120	9120	11587	16596	24833
群众文化	Public Culture	1706	7841	7890	9322	10072	24878	20851	20981	25284
中等专业学校	Secondary Vocation School	218	2244	2652	2789	1523	2851	12638	8656	2184
干部训练	Cadre Taining	80	38	339	204	86				
其他文化事业	Others	2496	8348	14050	17257	21721	28684	22901	42018	68206
文物事业	Historical Relics	1015	7579	8760	11947	14841	18734	29357	32924	36745
博物馆	Museum	573	3104	4661	6686	6774	10922	10922	21509	23628
文物事业机构	Institutions of Historical Relics	305	2460	2419	2000	3453	6819	6819	6144	5134
其它文物事业	Others	137	397	495	3261	4614	993	993	5271	7983
文化、文物基本建设完成投资	Investment in Culture & Historical Relics Cause Construction	2407	28849	6184	22024	26708	27516	132440	73022	56901
文化事业	Culture Cause	1887	24760	2175	9096	20211	22658	121892	45206	43374
文物事业	Historical Relics Cause	516	4089	4009	12928	6497	4858	10548	27816	13527

15-8 广播电视从业人员基本情况（2009）
BASIC STATISTICS ON PERSONEL ENGAGED IN BROADCASTING AND TELEVISION (2009)

单位：人 (person)

		全省合计 Total of the Province	省级 Provincial Level	市州级 Municiple, Prefecture Level	县级 County Level
从业人员	Personel	32947	11720	8063	13164
#长期职工	#Long-time Staff and Workers	31907	11090	7912	12905
按学历划分	Classified According to Academic Qualifications				
#研究生及以上	Graduate and Above	438	250	149	39
本科及大专	Undergraduate and Post-secondary	19255	6443	6034	6778
高中及以下	High School and Below	13254	5027	1880	6347
按职业划分	Grouped by Career				
管理人员	Management Personel	5282	1693	1137	2452
专业技术人员	Professional Technical Personel	19093	6996	4984	7113
#高级	#Senior	1294	654	533	107
中级	Medium	5909	1767	1988	2154
初级及以下	Primary and Below	11890	4575	2463	4852
其他人员	Others	8572	3031	1942	3599
编辑、记者	Editors and Reporters	5533	997	2241	2295
#高级	#Senior	559	230	288	41
中级	Medium	2056	272	928	856
初级及以下	Primary and Below	2918	495	1025	1398
播音员、主持人	Announcers and Hosts	1010	243	380	387
#高级	#Senior	47	23	24	
中级	Medium	288	43	131	114
初级及以下	Primary and Below	675	177	225	273
工程技术人员	Engineering and Technical Personnel	9452	3950	1872	3630
#高级	#Senior	336	168	129	39
中级	Medium	2471	836	735	900
初级及以下	Primary and Below	6645	2946	1008	2691

15-9 广播电视传输覆盖与经济效益
STATISTICS ON BROADCASTING AND TV COVERAGE RATING AND ECONOMIC BENEFITS

项 目	Item	2004	2005	2006	2007	2008	2009
广播覆盖率 (%)	Broadcasting Coverage Rate (%)	95.69	95.99	96.29	96.31	96.81	97.41
电视覆盖率 (%)	TV Coverage Rate (%)	96.61	96.71	96.76	96.96	97.31	97.49
有线电视用户 (万)	Cable Television Users (10 000 household)	466.21	508.13	576.26	649.7	730.45	803.43
中短波发射转播台/机(座/部)	Medium and Short-Wave Transmitters Stations (set)	31/ 44	27/ 43	28 /67	26/ 72	25/69	24/70
中短波发射转播台功率 (千瓦	Power of Medium and Short-Wave Transmitters (kw)	620	646	1109	1199	1212	1256
调频发射转播台 (座/部)	FM Transmitters Stations (set)	189/ 261	189/ 266	420/ 519	431/ 537	436/569	428/575
调频发射机功率 (千瓦)	Power of FM Transmitters (kw)	257.096	272.998	418.732	449.838	460.638	496.888
电视发射转播台 (座/部)	Television Transmitters Station (set)	078/ 1365	068/ 1399	1053/ 1267	010/ 1215	1009/1280	1000/1272
电视发射转播台功率 (千瓦)	Power of Television Transmitters (kw)	319.018	335.621	399.836	462.796	556.616	569.866
卫星地面站 (万座)	Satellite Groud Station (10 000 sets)	18.36	17.98	17.96	142	137.59	150.87
微波线路站数/长度(座/公里)	Length of Micro-Wave Route Per Station (set/km)	199/ 5400	186/ 4894	187/ 4086	173/ 3995	142/3263	120/2911
广播喇叭 (万只)	Loudspeaker (10 000 sets)	26.75	19.93				
创收收入 (亿元)	Revenue (100 million yuan)	19.1	21.86	24.63	29.94	34.83	42.45
固定资产原值 (亿元)	Original Price of Fixed Assets(100 million yuan)	43.52	46.91	52.08	61.13	62.43	75.66

15-10 广播电视宣传和节目制作
BROADCASTING PUBLICITY AND PROGRAM PRODUCTION

项目	Item	2000	2004	2005	2006	2007	2008	2009
广播电台 (座)	Broadcasting Station (unit)	13	11	11	11	11	11	11
电视台 (座)	TV Station (unit)	14	12	12	12	12	12	12
广播电视台 (座)	Radiated TV Station (unit)	65	47	71	71	71	71	71
广播节目套数 (套)	Number of Radio Programs (unit)	82	79	81	83	84	84	85
广播平均日播音时间 (小时)	Average Broadcasting Hour per Week (h)	821.70	901.97	1040.40	1103.84	1163.87	1186.10	1217.78
广播节目年制作能力 (万小时)	Annual Capacity of Radio Program Production (10 000 h)	21.18	20.57	20.59	21.55	22.90	23.40	23.46
电视节目套数 (套)	Number of TV Programs (unit)	70	107	113	115	115	115	114
电视平均周播出时间 (万小时)	Average TV Hour per Week (10 000 h)	0.42	0.90	1.05	1.12	1.13	1.18	1.24
电视节目年制作能力 (万小时)	Annual Capacity of TV program Production (10 000 h)	6.74	6.90	7.93	8.76	8.28	8.52	8.97
电视剧制作 (部/集)	Production of TV Series (episod)	16/ 280	14/ 321	11/ 208	5/ 142	9/ 167	5/110	8/206

15-11 体委系统职工人数

NUMBER OF STAFF AND WORKERS IN SPORTS COMMISSIONS

单位：人 (person)

人员分类	Type	1990	2000	2002	2003	2004	2005	2006	2007	2008	2009
总 计	**Total**	**4716**	**6 673**	**5754**	**5563**	**1613**	**5654**	**5247**	**5022**	**5140**	**6391**
#教练员	#Coach	951	917	988	956	885	881	908	872	887	866
等级裁判员	Referees in Grades	1652	2544	3090	3766	881	3439	1212	974	866	1467
运动员	Athletes	878	745	782	872	710	763	646	701	896	652
科技人员	Scientific and Technical Personel	31	38	16	4	18	24	24	18	34	36

15-12 等级裁判员、运动员情况

NUMBER OF ATHLETES AND REFEREES IN GRADES

单位：人 (person)

项　目	Item	1990	2000	2002	2003	2004	2005	2006	2007	2008	2009
等级裁判员合计	Number of Referees in Grades	843	1195	3371	4066	881	787	1212	974	866	1467
国际裁判	International Referees			57	57						
国家级裁判	National Referees		29	332	351	41	25	25	13	12	10
一级裁判	First Grade	357	143	1042	1118	117	115	178	251	208	492
二级裁判	Second Grade	486	1023	1940	2540	723	647	1009	710	646	965
等级运动员合计	Number of Athletes in Grade	123	418	661	1262	686	1171	1576	1335	1644	1507
国际运动健将	International Master of Sports		6	29	35	7	2	3	4	1	6
运动健将	Master of Sports		36	88	121	52	36	37	52	57	51
一级运动员	First Grade	35	10	414	484	114	267	187	190	188	179
二级运动员	Second Grade	88	366	130	622	513	866	1349	1089	1398	1271

15-13 体育竞赛成果情况
STATISTICS ON ACHIEVEMENT IN SPORTS COMPETITION

项 目	Item	1990	2000	2002	2003	2004	2005	2006	2007	2008	2009
世界比赛获奖牌数(枚)	Number of Metals Won in International Games (unit)	10	13	7	13	12	5	13	12	19	49
金牌	Gold Metal	9	4	2	5	4	3	11	8	8	12
银牌	Silver Metal	1	6	2	6	3	2	1	3	4	10
铜牌	Bronze Metal		3	3	2	5		1	1	7	12
亚洲比赛获奖牌数(枚)	Number of Metals Won in Asia Games(unit)	51	5	12	6	2	7	23	1	5	34
金牌	Gold Metal	37	4	6	2	2	5	16			5
银牌	Silver Metal	7		4	1		2	3	1	1	9
铜牌	Bronze Metal	7	1	2	3			4		4	9
全国比赛获前六名(人)	First Six Places in National Games (person)			164	133	139	155	83	85	270	315
第一名	The First Place	52	35	29	15	15	24	5	12	31	49
第二名	The Second Place	50	22	22	19	15	23	5	16	31	53
第三名	The Third Place	40	21	31	29	28	27	4	17	48	51
第四名	The Fourth Place	29	35	17	26	30	24	23	10	39	44
第五名	The Fifth Place	31	29	38	22	30	31	28	23	32	66
第六名	The Sixth Place	38	26	27	22	21	26	18	7	31	52

15-14 群众体育活动情况（2009）
MASS SPORTS ACTIVITIES (2009)

项 目	Item	合计 Total	现代体育项目活动 Modern Sports Activities	民间传统体育活动 Traditional Sports Activities
省级	Provincial			
年活动次数 (次)	The Number of Activities (times)	32	22	10
每次活动平均参与人数 (人)	The Average Number of Participants for Each Event (person)	9376	9092	10000
年活动总人数 (人)	The Total Number of Year (person)	300020	200020	100000
地市级	Municipal			
年活动次数 (次)	The Number of Activities (times)	752	455	297
每次活动平均参与人数 (人)	The Average Number of Participants for Each Event (person)	1200	1054	1425
年活动总人数 (人)	The Total Number of Year (person)	902752	479557	423195
县区级	County			
年活动次数 (次)	The Number of Activities (time)	3524	2046	1478
每次活动平均参与人数 (人)	The Average Number of Participants for Each Event (person)	913	1014	772
年活动总人数 (人)	The Total Number of Year (person)	3215929	2075330	1140599

15-15 卫生机构数
NUMBER OF HEALTH CARE INSTIUTIONS

单位：个 (unit)

年 份 Year	总 计 Total	医 院 Hospitals	#县及县以上医院 #Hospitals Above County Level	疗养院、所 Sanatoriums	门诊部、所 Clinics	专科防治所、站 Specialized Prevention & Treatment Stations or Centers
1952	2198	104	103	8	1770	5
1957	11566	158	137	17	9381	287
1965	10863	789	202	27	9613	201
1970	7847	16003	234	10	1500	104
1975	5381	1834	347	2	3079	39
1978	5940	1817	355	6	3626	42
1980	6146	1827	376	12	3785	52
1985	9885	1853	417	12	7486	67
1990	10472	2024	483	11	7878	70
1991	10509	2111	502	11	7824	74
1992	10590	2115	507	11	7903	73
1993	10268	2139	523	12	7526	73
1994	9762	2147	516	12	7002	84
1995	9744	2119	523	11	7020	84
1996	9167	2105	514	10	6453	82
1997	11562	2078	523	10	8867	86
1998	11584	2082	526	10	8885	88
1999	11311	2077	532	11	8631	85
2000	11065	2041	524	11	8430	83
2001	10941	1924	519	10	8500	73
2002	9946	555		2	7687	168
2003	9983	552		3	7690	177
2004	9285	566		2	6949	166
2005	9459	574		1	7215	120
2006	10052	575			7687	116
2007	11089	580			7585	118
2008	10832	592			7397	107
2009	10362	614			6770	88

15-15 续表 continued

单位:个 (unit)

年 份 Year	卫生防疫站 Sanitation and Antiepidemic Station	妇幼保健所、站 Maternity and Child Care Centers	药品检验所、室 Institute for Drug Control	医学科学研究机构 Institutions of Medical Science Research	其他卫生机构 Others
1952	7	10	1		293
1957	21	542	1	1	1 158
1965	86	80	2		65
1970	106	54	5	2	63
1975	99	85	83	6	154
1978	107	92	88	6	156
1980	110	97	88	7	168
1985	111	96	87	7	166
1990	120	96	87	9	177
1991	122	98	87	7	175
1992	119	96	86	8	179
1993	149	96	87	8	178
1994	149	97	87	8	176
1995	151	95	85	8	171
1996	156	95	84	8	174
1997	158	96	84	8	175
1998	158	96	85	8	172
1999	156	94	83	7	167
2000	155	94	81	7	163
2001	130	91	53	7	153
2002	107	12	87		1328
2003	110	32	92		1327
2004	110	39	92		1359
2005	113	63	96		1366
2006	114	72	95		1393
2007	113	100	59	1	2533
2008	111	99		1	2525
2009	111	98		1	2680

15-16 卫生机构人员数

NUMBER OF PERSONS ENGAGED IN HEALTH CARE INSTITUTIONS

单位：万人 (10 000 persom)

年 份 Year	总 计 Total	卫生技术人员 Medical Technical Personel	#医生 #Doctorss	中 医 Chinese Traditional Medicine Doctors	西 医 师 Western Medicine Doctors	西 医 士 Wertern Medical Assistant	#护师、护士 #Nurses	每千人口医生数(人) Number of Doctors per 1000 Population (person)
1952	3.57	3.46	1.74	1.31	0.26	0.17	0.20	0.63
1957	6.42	5.33	2.64	1.84	0.33	0.47	0.40	0.86
1965	8.60	7.13	3.48	1.76	0.85	0.87	1.32	0.99
1970	10.30	8.33	4.15	1.86	1.22	1.07	1.83	1.03
1975	15.05	11.85	4.91	1.74	1.63	1.55	2.05	1.11
1978	17.84	14.06	5.82	1.88	2.02	1.92	2.24	1.27
1980	19.94	15.59	6.32	1.82	2.59	1.91	3.09	1.35
1985	23.58	18.48	7.27	2.22	3.09	1.95	3.77	1.47
1990	26.75	20.92	8.68	2.19	5.09	1.40	5.66	1.62
1991	27.51	21.55	8.79	2.18	5.11	1.50	5.97	1.62
1992	28.24	22.15	9.02	2.20	5.18	1.65	6.25	1.64
1993	28.91	22.46	9.16	2.12	5.48	1.57	6.49	1.64
1994	29.31	22.84	9.38	2.04	5.64	1.65	6.64	1.66
1995	29.55	23.20	9.58	1.98	5.79	1.76	6.83	1.68
1996	29.65	23.47	9.72	1.93	5.92	1.90	7.00	1.67
1997	30.38	23.90	9.96	1.84	6.09	1.90	7.21	1.70
1998	30.31	23.96	10.11	1.84	6.30	1.90	7.29	1.71
1999	30.40	24.05	10.31	1.81	6.58	1.85	7.41	1.74
2000	30.14	23.88	10.30	1.76	6.76	1.74	7.53	1.74
2001	29.48	23.41	10.21	1.63	6.91	1.63	7.51	1.72
2002	25.30	20.59	8.63	1.14			6.35	1.43
2003	25.62	20.83	8.72	0.94	1.73	0.13	6.38	1.45
2004	26.06	21.38	8.99				6.62	1.49
2005	26.22	21.50	8.98				6.94	1.49
2006	26.53	21.80	9.01				7.06	1.49
2007	27.80	22.70	9.20				7.69	1.52
2008	28.63	23.52	9.27				8.12	1.52
2009	29.45	24.30	9.43				8.69	1.54

15-17 卫生机构床位数

NUMBER OF BEDS IN HEALTH CARE INSTITUTIONS

单位：万张 (10 000 beds)

年 份 Year	总 计 Total	医 院 Hospitals	#县及县以上医院 #Hospitals Above County Level	疗养院、所 Sanatoriums	其他卫生机构 Other Health Care Institutions	每千人口医院床位数(张) Number of Hospital Beds Per 10 000 Population (bed)
1952	0.90	0.52	0.52	0.18		0.19
1957	2.10	1.38	1.35	0.17		0.45
1965	4.14	3.13	2.45	0.31		0.89
1970	6.14	5.56	2.84	0.18		1.38
1975	9.90	9.02	4.33	0.02		2.05
1978	11.52	10.34	4.94	0.07		2.26
1980	12.59	11.22	5.41	0.20		2.40
1985	14.70	11.52	6.80	0.20	2.98	2.34
1990	16.34	13.16	8.27	0.19	2.99	2.45
1991	16.52	13.43	8.50	0.21	2.88	2.47
1992	16.62	13.46	8.58	0.22	2.84	2.44
1993	16.30	13.48	8.71	0.21	2.61	2.41
1994	16.13	13.40	8.73	0.21	2.52	2.36
1995	15.78	13.08	8.58	0.20	2.50	2.29
1996	14.42	13.08	8.63	0.15	1.19	2.24
1997	15.30	13.08	8.76	0.16	2.05	2.24
1998	15.09	13.03	8.77	0.17	1.89	2.21
1999	14.90	12.91	8.76	0.16	1.83	2.07
2000	14.96	12.99	8.80	0.16	1.81	2.18
2001	14.62	12.91	8.80	0.16	0.60	2.18
2002	12.72	8.53		0.03	4.16	2.12
2003	13.59	9.39		0.04	4.16	2.26
2004	13.78	9.52		0.02	4.24	2.29
2005	13.96	9.67		0.01	4.28	2.31
2006	14.24	9.81			4.43	2.35
2007	15.06	10.36			4.70	2.48
2008	16.73	11.32			5.41	2.75
2009	18.72	12.66			6.06	2.82

15-18 各类卫生工作人员数

NUMBER OF SARITARY TECHNICAL PERSONELS OF VARIOUS TYPE

单位：人 (person)

人员分类	Type	1990	1998	2000	2004	2005	2006	2007	2008	2009
合　计	**Total**	**267548**	**303083**	**301415**	**260569**	**262263**	**265298**	**277946**	**286332**	**294539**
医院	Hospitals	182490	141044	140720	136308	138843	139462	148305	153150	161631
县及县以上医院	Hospitals Above County Level	118718	140689	140355						
中医院	Hospitals of Chinese Medicines	11386	16612	17442	19159	19274	19324	18559	18856	20805
乡镇卫生院	Commune Hospitals	58518	74062	54500	67190	69626	68857	67606	69035	69304
疗养院、所	Sanatoriums	1271	1287	1387	241	60				
门诊部、所	Clinics	44450	36411	34020	20666	17940	22344	20280	20004	16300
专科防治所、站	Specialized Prevention & Treatment Stations or Centers	6218	7964	7830	6035	4352	4039	2220	3429	3119
卫生防疫站	Sanitation and Antiepidemic Station	7602	9767	10388	8729	9149	9142	8642	8667	8094
妇幼保健所、站	Maternity and Child Care Centers	4139	6539	6874	8537	8796	8762	9454	9931	10640
药品检验所、室	Institute for Drug Control	1098	1358	1373						
其他卫生事业机构	Others	6376	3980	4087						
医学科研机构	Medical Science Institutions	810	714	746						
高等医院院校	Institutions of Higner Education	6489	7069	6154						
中等卫校	Secondary Health School	3762	6724	6043						
个体开业	Individual Run	2843	3288	4252						

15-19 县及县以上医院业务工作开展情况

BASIC STATISTICS ON HOSPITAL BUSINESS AT AND ABOVE COUNTY LEVEL

项 目	Item	1990	1995	2000	2005	2007	2008	2009
机构数 (个)	Number of Institutions (unit)	474	523	507	574	580	592	614
诊疗总人次数 (万人次)	Number of Clients (10 000 person-times)	6287.20	5764.80	4616.20	5452.11	11078.35	6537.45	7303.81
#门、急诊人次数(万人次)	#Number of Pacients(10 000 person-times)	6018.00	5460.20	4396.10	5107.19	10688.35	6320.79	7158.39
出院人数 (万人)	Number of Clients Leaving Hospital (10 000 persons)	145.65	147.71	158.93	219.45	393.83	312.44	377.13
#出院病人数 (万人)	Number of Paciences Leaving Hospital (10 000 persons)	129.03	135.11	147.94				
#治愈 (万人)	Cure (10 000 persons)	97.44	95.19	89.25	104.94	218.7	148.15	178.69
死亡 (万人)	Death (10 000 persons)	1.68	1.56	1.59	2.28	2.76	2.78	2.89
治愈率 (%)	Rate of Cure (%)	75.60	70.50	60.33	54.52	61.99	54.31	53.91
病死率 (%)	Rate of Death from Illness (%)	1.40	1.20	1.08	1.04	0.70	0.89	0.77
病床平均周转次数 (次)	Average times of Beds Used (time)	18.50	17.80	18.66	23.99	27.00	29.60	31.20
病床平均工作日 (日)	Average Number of Days Beds Used (day)	286.40	247.50	218.79	268.24	269.00	285.20	338.20
病床使用率 (%)	Utilization Rate of Beds (%)	78.50	67.80	59.94	73.49	73.62	49.29	92.67
出院者平均住院日 (日)	Average Number of Days Paciences Living in Hospitals (day)	15.20	13.30	11.12	10.71	9.00	9.20	10.50

15-20 农村村级卫生组织情况

STATISTICS ON HEALTH CARE INSTITUTIONS AT VILLAGE LEVEL

项　　目	Item	1990	1995	2000	2005	2007	2008	2009
行政村数　（个）	Number of Villages　(unit)	32579	32661	31980				
无卫生室的村　（个）	Number of Villages without Health Care Offices　(unit)	5246	4249	3917				
村设置的医疗点数　（个）	Medical care Station Set by Villages　(unit)	30036	31817	26879	21136	23714	22707	22405
#村或集体办	#Set by Villages or Collective Set	6995	13230	14666	11207	1020	14184	14135
乡村医生或卫生员联合办	Set by Village Doctors	3670	7313	4640	3777		3047	2560
乡卫生院设点	Set by Township Hospital	888	1526	2403	2410	17661	3309	3230
体办	Set by Individual	6523	8178	4344	2907	1884	1655	1832
其他	Others	354	1570	826	835	1553	512	648
乡村医生和卫生员人数（人）	Number of Village Doctors and Medical Working Personel　(person)	59760	61324	57511	34417	33913	38411	41054
#乡村医生	#Village Doctors	33429	43288	44490	33375	37095	37535	40065
卫生员	Medical Working Personel	26331	18036	13021	1042	13159	876	989
#会接生	Of This Number : Those can Delivery	19369	8411	16769				
农村接生员数　（人）	Number of Those Can Delivery　(person)	221171	15747	11303	3040			

15-21　全省法定报告传染病的发病及死亡情况

病　名	Name of Disease	2005			2006		
		发病率 (1/10万) Incidence (1/100 thousand)	死亡率 (1/10万) Mortality Rate (1/100 thousand)	病死率(%) Rate of Death from Illness (1/100 thousand)	发病率 (1/10万) Incidence (1/100 thousand)	死亡率 (1/10万) Mortality Rate (1/100 thousand)	病死率(%) Rate of Death from Illness (1/100 thousand)
总　计	**Total**	**267.27**	**0.98**	**0.36**	**284.96**	**0.99**	**0.35**
#病毒性肝炎	#Viral Hepatitis	109.78	0.24	0.21	122.13	0.24	0.20
痢疾	Dysentery	23.12	0.01	0.03	29.28		0.01
伤寒副伤寒	Typhoid and Paralyhoid	1.23		0.13	0.99		
艾滋病	Aids	0.39	0.13	32.20	0.42	0.15	36.10
淋病	Gonorhea	7.36			7.02		
梅毒	Syhilis	2.93	0.01	0.17	4.64	0.01	0.15
脊髓灰质炎	Poliomyelitis						
百日咳	Pertussis	0.15			0.14		
白喉	diphtheria						
流脑	Epidemic Encephalitis	0.08	0.01	10.87	0.03	0.01	0.22
猩红热	Scarlet Fever	0.40			0.40		
出血热	Hemorrhage Fever	0.36	0.02	5.12	0.50	0.02	3.16
狂犬病	Hydrophobia	0.31	0.31	100.00	0.38	0.38	100.00
钩端螺旋体病	Leplospirosis	0.06	0.01	11.11	0.04		
乙脑	Encephalitis B	0.20			0.25	0.02	6.99
疟疾	Malaria	2.52			3.07		
肺结核	TB	113.44	0.23	0.20	108.23	0.15	0.14

LEGAL REPORT ON INFECTIONS DISEASE INCIDENCE AND DEATH

2007			2008			2009		
发病率 (1/10万) Incidence (1/100 thousand)	死亡率 (1/10万) Mortality Rate (1/100 thousand)	病死率(%) Rate of Death from Illness (1/100 thousand)	发病率 (1/10万) Incidence (1/100 thousand)	死亡率 (1/10万) Mortality Rate (1/100 thousand)	病死率(%) Rate of Death from Illness (1/100 thousand)	发病率 (1/10万) Incidence (1/100 thousand)	死亡率 (1/10万) Mortality Rate (1/100 thousand)	病死率(%) Rate of Death from Illness (1/100 thousand)
310.33	**0.90**	**0.29**	**428.49**	**0.83**	**0.19**	**318.62**	**0.88**	**0.28**
143.16	0.20	0.14	149.16	0.14	0.09	160.17	0.11	0.07
26.79	0.00	0.01	25.27			22.51	0.00	0.01
0.83			0.84			0.97		
0.42	0.25	59.34	0.47	0.36	76.69	0.51	0.36	69.86
5.89			6.11			5.25		
6.17			10.97			13.85		
0.11			0.10			0.05		
0.04	0.00	4.00	0.03	0.00	10.53	0.04	0.01	18.18
0.49			0.46			0.34		
0.40	0.01	1.75	0.29	0.01	3.07	0.44	0.01	3.20
0.27	0.27	100.00	0.16	0.16	100.00	0.21	0.21	100.00
0.09	0.00	2.00	0.17	0.00	2.11	0.03	0.00	5.88
0.10	0.01	5.36	0.09	0.01	7.84	0.22	0.01	3.94
3.11			1.90	0.00	0.09	1.25		
112.43	0.15	0.13	107.55	0.14	0.13	90.70	0.15	0.17

15-22 部分城市十种主要疾病死亡构成及顺位

顺位 order	1995		2000		2005		2006
	死亡原因 Cause of Death	占死亡总数% Number of Death in Total Deaths %	死亡原因 Cause of Death	占死亡总数% Number of Death in Total Deaths %	死亡原因 Cause of Death	占死亡总数% Number of Death in Total Deaths %	死亡原因 Cause of Death
1	脑血管病 Cerebrovascular Disease	29.70	脑血管病 Cerebrovascular Disease	28.21	恶性肿瘤 Malignant Tumor	23.58	恶性肿瘤 Malignant Tumor
2	恶性肿瘤 Malignant Tumor	10.80	恶性肿瘤 Malignant Tumor	21.28	脑血管病 Cerebrovascular Disease	21.29	脑血管病 Cerebrovascular Disease
3	心脏病 Heart Disease	12.80	心脏病 Heart Disease	15.07	心脏病 Heart Disease	15.60	心脏病 Heart Disease
4	呼吸系统疾病 Respiratory System Disease	12.50	呼吸系统疾病 Respiratory System Disease	11.24	呼吸系统疾病 Respiratory System Disease	9.39	呼吸系统疾病 Respiratory System Disease
5	损伤和中毒 Injury and Poisoning	7.60	损伤和中毒 Injury and Poisoning	7.12	损伤和中毒 Injury and Poisoning	6.56	损伤和中毒 Injury and Poisoning
6	消化系统疾病 Digestive Disease	3.40	消化系统疾病 Digestive Disease	3.48	内分泌、营养、代谢 Endocrine System, Nutritional Disease and Disease of Metabolism	3.62	内分泌、营养、代谢 Endocrine System, Nutritional Disease and Disease of Metabolism
7	内分泌系统 Endocrine System	1.60	内分泌系统 Endocrine System	2.47	消化系统疾病 Digestive Disease	3.36	消化系统疾病 Digestive Disease
8	泌尿生殖系统 Urogenital System	1.47	传染病 Communicable Disease	1.82	泌尿生殖系统 Urogenital System	1.68	其他疾病小计 Others
9	精神病 Mental DiSease	1.34	泌尿生殖系统 Urogenital System	1.51	精神障碍 Psychonosema	1.50	泌尿生殖系统 Urogenital System
10	新生儿病 New Born Baby Disease	1.20	精神病 Mental DiSease	1.49	传染病和寄生虫病 Communicable and parasitic Disease	1.45	精神障碍 Psychonosema
	合 计 Total	**89.61**	**合 计 Total**	**93.69**	**合 计 Total**	**88.03**	**合 计 Total**

STATISTICS ON TEN MAJOR DEATH-CAUSING DESEASES IN PARIAL CITIES

	2007		2008		2009	
占死亡总数% Number of Death in Total Deaths %	死亡原因 Cause of Death	占死亡总数% Number of Death in Total Deaths %	死亡原因 Cause of Death	占死亡总数% Number of Death in Total Deaths %	死亡原因 Cause of Death	占死亡总数% Number of Death in Total Deaths %
24.78	恶性肿瘤 Malignant Tumor	25.85	恶性肿瘤 Malignant Tumor	25.88	恶性肿瘤 Malignant Tumor	26.36
22.03	脑血管病 Cerebrovascular Disease	22.62	脑血管病 Cerebrovascular Disease	23.32	脑血管病 Cerebrovascular Disease	23.49
15.57	心脏病 Heart Disease	14.41	心脏病 Heart Disease	16.07	心脏病 Heart Disease	16.29
8.91	呼吸系统疾病 Respiratory System Disease	9.29	呼吸系统疾病 Respiratory System Disease	9.06	呼吸系统疾病 Respiratory System Disease	8.74
6.96	损伤和中毒 Injury and Poisoning	7.34	损伤和中毒 Injury and Poisoning	6.84	损伤和中毒 Injury and Poisoning	7.53
3.66	内分泌，营养和代谢疾病 Endocrine System, Nutritional Disease and Disease of Metabolism	3.63	内分泌，营养和代谢疾病 Endocrine System, Nutritional Disease and Disease of Metabolism	3.69	内分泌，营养和代谢疾病 Endocrine System, Nutritional Disease and Disease of Metabolism	4.14
3.29	其他疾病 Digestive Disease	3.51	消化系统疾病 Digestive Disease	3.1	消化系统疾病 Digestive Disease	3.27
2.57	消化系统疾病 Others	3.10	传染病和寄生虫病 Communicable and parasitic Disease	1.62	传染病和寄生虫病 Communicable and parasitic Disease	1.33
1.70	泌尿生殖系统疾病 Urogenital System	1.75	精神障碍 Psychonosema	1.56	精神障碍 Psychonosema	1.27
1.61	传染病和寄生虫病 Communicable and parasitic Disease	1.44	泌尿生殖系统 Urogenital System	1.5	泌尿生殖系统 Urogenital System	1.24
91.08	**合 计 Total**	**92.94**	**合 计 Total**	**92.64**	**合 计 Total**	**93.66**

15-23 部分农村十种主要疾病死亡构成及顺位

顺位 Order	1995 死亡原因 Cause of Death	1995 占死亡总数% Number of Death in Total Deaths %	2000 死亡原因 Cause of Death	2000 占死亡总数% Number of Death in Total Deaths %	2005 死亡原因 Cause of Death	2005 占死亡总数% Number of Death in Total Deaths %	2006 死亡原因 Cause of Death
1	呼吸系统疾病 Respiratory System Disease	22.70	脑血管病 Cerebrovascular Disease	24.92	脑血管病 Cerebrovascular Disease	24.51	心脏病 Heart Disease
2	脑血管病 Cerebrovascular Disease	21.98	呼吸系统疾病 Respiratory System Disease	19.52	心脏病 Heart Disease	24.42	脑血管病 Cerebrovascular Disease
3	损伤和中毒 Injury and Poisoning	15.59	恶性肿瘤 Malignant Tumor	16.74	恶性肿瘤 Malignant Tumor	18.23	恶性肿瘤 Malignant Tumor
4	恶性肿瘤 Malignant Tumor	11.08	损伤和中毒 Injury and Poisoning	12.17	损伤和中毒 Injury and Poisoning	11.07	损伤和中毒 Injury and Poisoning
5	心脏病 Heart Disease	9.84	心脏病 Heart Disease	11.80	呼吸系统疾病 Respiratory System Disease	8.43	呼吸系统疾病 Respiratory System Disease
6	消化系统疾病 Digestive Disease	6.29	消化系统疾病 Digestive Disease	4.26	消化系统疾病 Digestive Disease	3.62	消化系统疾病 Digestive Disease
7	新生儿病 New Born Baby Disease	1.88	传染病 Communicable Disease	1.73	泌尿生殖系统疾病 Urogenital System	1.64	泌尿生殖系统疾病 Urogenital System
8	泌尿生殖系统疾病 Urogenital System	1.60	高血压病 High Blood Pressure	1.64	传染病和寄生虫病 Communicable and parasitic disease	1.01	传染病和寄生虫病 Communicable and parasitic disease
9	肺结核 Tuberculosis	1.53	泌尿生殖系统疾病 Urogenital System	1.62	起源于围生期的某些情况小计 Others	0.77	精神障碍 Psychonosema
10	传染病 Communicable Disease	1.47	新生儿病 New Born Baby Disease	1.48	精神障碍 Psychonosema	0.71	内分泌、营养和代谢 Endocrine System, Nutritional Disease and Disease of Metabolism
	合 计 Total	**93.96**	**合 计 Total**	**95.88**	**合 计 Total**	**94.41**	**合 计 Total**

STATISTICS ON TEN MAJOR DEATH-CAUSING DESEASES IN PARTIAL COUNTRIES

	2007		2008		2009	
占死亡总数% Number of Death in Total Deaths %	死亡原因 Cause of Death	占死亡总数% Number of Death in Total Deaths %	死亡原因 Cause of Death	占死亡总数% Number of Death in Total Deaths %	死亡原因 Cause of Death	占死亡总数% Number of Death in Total Deaths %
23.05	恶性肿瘤 Malignant Tumor	20.28	脑血管病 Cerebrovascular Disease	20.8	脑血管病 Cerebrovascular Disease	28.9
22.25	心脏病 Heart Disease	18.84	心脏病 Heart Disease	20.5	心脏病 Heart Disease	18.99
19.97	脑血管病 Cerebrovascular Disease	16.91	恶性肿瘤 Malignant Tumor	20.35	恶性肿瘤 Malignant Tumor	22.57
11.99	损伤和中毒 Injury and Poisoning	12.12	损伤和中毒 Injury and Poisoning	10.69	损伤和中毒 Injury and Poisoning	9.98
7.81	呼吸系统疾病 Respiratory System Disease	10.91	呼吸系统疾病 Respiratory System Disease	9.34	呼吸系统疾病 Respiratory System Disease	7.97
3.47	消化系统疾病 Digestive Disease	2.67	消化系统疾病 Digestive Disease	2.96	消化系统疾病 Digestive Disease	2.25
1.65	泌尿生殖系统疾病 Urogenital System	1.65	泌尿生殖系统疾病 Urogenital System	1.27	泌尿生殖系统疾病 Urogenital System	1.2
1.33	传染病和寄生虫病 Communicable and parasitic disease	1.20	传染病和寄生虫病 Communicable and parasitic disease	1.03	传染病和寄生虫病 Communicable and parasitic disease	0.98
0.78	内分泌，营养和代谢疾病 Endocrine System, Nutritional Disease and Disease of Metabolism	1.06	内分泌，营养和代谢疾病 Endocrine System, Nutritional Disease and Disease of Metabolism	0.89	内分泌，营养和代谢疾病 Endocrine System, Nutritional Disease and Disease of Metabolism	0.69
0.73	起源于围生期的某些情况 Others	0.52	起源于围生期的某些情况 Others	0.67	起源于围生期的某些情况 Others	0.46
93.03	合计 **Total**	**86.16**	合计 **Total**	**88.5**	合计 **Total**	**93.99**

15-24 “三废”排放和处理综合利用情况

分类	Item	1990	1995	2000
一、废水排放总量 （万吨）	Total Volume of Waste Water Discharged (10 000 ton)	259699	300598	233086
工业废水排放总量	Total Volume of Industrial Waste Water Discharged	162302	139938	106733
#符合排放标准的	#Qualified Dsicharge	85709	86342	80 591
排放达标率 （%）	Percentage of Satndarized Discharge (%)	52.8	61.7	75.5
二、废气排放总量 （亿标立方米）	Total Volume of Waste Gas Discharged (100 million cu.m)	3416	4485	5 674
1.燃料燃烧废气排放量	Volume of Waste Gas in the Process of Fuel and Borning	1955	2394	2 468
2.生产工艺过程中废气排放量	Volume of Waste Gas in the Process of Production	1461	2042	3 206
三、废气中污染物排放量 （万吨）	Pollutants Discharged in Waste Gas (10 000 ton)			
二氧化硫	Sulfur Dioxide	55.60	54.00	56.04
#工业二氧化硫	#Industrial Sulfur Dioxide			50.82
烟尘	Soot	47.20	43.20	36.34
四、工业粉尘 （万吨）	Industrial Dust (10 000 ton)			
1.已去除的	Discharged	108.00	124.40	233.20
工业粉尘去除率 （%）	Discharged Percentage (%)	77.7	83.9	85.0
2.工业粉尘排放量	Volume of Industrial Dust Emission	31.00	23.80	41.00
五、工业固体废物产生量 （万吨）	Volume of Industrial Solid Wastes Producced (10 000 ton)	1799	2063	2818
已处置的	Teated	254	267	128
工业固体废物处置率 （%）	Percentage of Industrial Solid Waste Being Treated (%)	14.1	12.8	4.5
已综合利用的	Utilized In a Comprehensive Way	763	1158	1 514.3
工业固体废物综合利用率 （%）	Percentage of Industrial Solid Waste Being Utilized In a Comprehensive Way (%)	42.4	55.5	53.7
已贮存的	Stored	731	666	791
工业固体废物贮存率 （%）	Percentage of Industrial Solid Waste Being Stored (%)	40.6	32.3	28.1
工业固体废物排放量	Volume of Industrial Solid Wastes Emission	91	16	16
六、锅炉总数 （台）	Total Number of Boiler (unit)	10880	3994	2661
#已达标的	#Standarized	4605	3335	2442
锅炉蒸吨数 （蒸吨）	Steam Tons of Boiler (steam ton)	33820	31697	37565
#烟尘排放达标的	#Standarized Soot Discharge	19893	28250	36622
七、工业炉窑 （座）	Number of Industrial Kiln Stove (unit)	3356	2980	2 349
烟尘排放达标的	Standarized Soot Discharge	1662	1904	1698
八、三废综合利用产品产值 （万元）	Total Output Value of Wastes Utilized In a Comprehensive Way (10 000 yuan)	28416	97058	128351

"THREE WASTES" DISCHARGE AND TREATMENT UTILIZATION SITUATION

2001	2002	2003	2004	2005	2006	2007	2008	2009
222995	232347	230578	232629	237368	239670	246019	258873	265757
97714	98481	96498	97451	92432	91146	90437	93687	91324
78736	82930	80848	83591	80926	82930	84942	87753	87594
80.6	84.2	83.8	85.8	87.6	91.0	93.92	93.67	95.92
5820	6440	6707	8838	9404	11015	10213	11558	1253
2695	2963	3248	3626	3958	4040	4284	4192	5958
3125	3476	3459	5212	5446	6974	6029	7367	6565
54.05	53.92	53.06	69.24	70.00	76.02	70.00	66.98	64.38
48.44	47.28	46.48	60.84	60.85	65.36	60.00	56.23	52.74
30.82	29.63	29.34	30.62	33.02	30.74	25.30	22.87	21.67
240.09	257.50	251.90	313.47	378.10	416.20	344.00	362.12	408.26
87.2	88.5	88.3	90.1	91.8	92.7	92.70	94.33	95.71
35.30	33.50	33.49	34.42	33.81	32.61	27.26	21.75	18.31
2694	2977	3112	3266	3692	4315	4683.43	5014.17	5561.45
190	110	91	150	110	303	426.79	1023.43	1164.44
7.0	3.7	2.9		3.0	7.0	9.11	20.41	20.94
1733	2004	2277	2358	2748	3150	3621.06	3853.41	4210.15
62.2	66.4	72.5	72.0	73.3	72.3	74.92	74.72	74.81
861	893	764	758	874	891	782.96	291.75	251.43
31.9	30.0	24.6		23.7	20.7	16.72	5.82	4.52
12	12	9	9	17	12	8.00	5.82	5.12
2587	2470	2395	2291	2117	1805	1826	1950	1897.00
2237	2170	2096	2007	1887				
36302	37130	35441	36736	42623	42997	43998	48718	56271
33982	35780	34046	3578	1887	1615	42685	47803	55922
2431	2422	2368	2094	2167	2242	2237	2235	2258
1772	2058	1980	1783	1911	2001	2015	2048	2112
150186	334565	375175	432037		559119	613942	648622	699428

15-25 工业污染治理情况

项　　　目	Item	Unit	1990
一、汇总工业企业单位数	(个) Total Number of Industrial Enterprises	(unit)	991
二、污染治理项目本年投资来源合计	(万元) Total Resource of Investment in Pollutant Treatment Proje	(10 000 yuan)	18051.0
国家预算内资金	(万元) State Budgetary Funds	(10 000 yuan)	5568.0
环境保护补助资金	(万元) Environmental Protection Subsidy Funds	(10 000 yuan)	2531.0
环保贷款	(万元) Environmental Protection Loans	(1 0000 yuan)	2149.0
其　　他	(万元) Others	(10 000 yuan)	1372.0
三、污染治理项目本年完成投资合计	(万元) Total Investment in Pollutant Treatment Projects	(10 000 yuan)	
治理废水	(万元) Waste Water	(10 000 yuan)	5637.0
治理废气	(万元) Waste Gas	(10 000 yuan)	9891.0
治理固体废物	(万元) Solid Waste	(10 000 yuan)	1371.0
治理噪声	(万元) Noise Abatement	(10 000 yuan)	534.0
其　　他	(万元) Others	(10 000 yuan)	618.0
四、本年施工项目数	(个) Projects Carried Out in This Year	(unit)	1 545
治理废水	(个) Waste Water	(unit)	450
治理废气	(个) Waste Gas	(unit)	758
治理固体废物	(个) Solid Waste	(unit)	119
治理噪声	(个) Noise Abatement	(unit)	139
其　　他	(个) Others	(unit)	79
五、本年竣工项目	(个) Projects Completed in This Year	(unit)	1312
治理废水	(个) Waste Water	(unit)	353
治理废气	(个) Waste Gas	(unit)	662
治理固体废物	(个) Solid Waste	(unit)	99
治理噪声	(个) Noise Abatement	(unit)	126
其　　他	(个) Others	(unit)	72

STATISTICS ON TREATMENT OF INDUSTRIAL POLLITION

1995	2000	2002	2003	2004	2005	2006	2007	2008	2009
613	583	293	244	254	336	354	342	307	225
27433.0	85237.9	71079.1	94314.3	98256.9	148096.5	148872.8	169404.7	161453.3	281332.3
3540.0	962.0	2590.9	6406.1	3584.8	7590.8	9039.5	4433.5	4243.8	5602.0
5430.0	1282.4	3704.8	3710.9	4535.2	7384.5	2941.6	5543.0	3713.0	4092.0
3143.0	7579.4	1553.3		90136.9		9574.0		3487.2	
7966.0	61880.5	63230.1	7882.7		133121.2	127317.7	159428.2	153496.5	271638.3
	85237.9	71079.1	94314.3	98256.9	148096.5	148872.8	169404.7	161453.3	281332.3
12042.0	45653.4	22487.1	29743.2	35561.0	48067.7	59631.7	78246.1	82634.8	54001.6
9164.0	26667.7	27539.7	55718.8	30140.4	40007.5	65821.7	74455.1	60834.4	213918.3
5293.0	6072.3	9440.9	724.5	1889.8	11408.1	10240.6	2004.3	3959.9	5969.7
583.0	644.0	366.5	239.3	198.9	440.1	13178.8	1411.2	1041.1	674.8
351.0	6200.5	11244.9	7888.5	29661.3	48173.1	649.8	13288.0	12983.1	6767.9
939	851	449	422	380	473	447	504	406	318
305	384	169	165	152	191	199	224	178	126
367	361	180	180	158	176	188	188	139	132
121	27	33	19	21	15	29	21	23	11
109	31	20	23	13	20	17	21	15	11
37	48	47	35	33	71	44	50	51	38
832	692	372	320	329	428	403	442	345	273
256	316	139	128	128	174	165	197	152	108
339	286	150	136	137	160	167	168	115	111
96	22	28	18	21	11	22	18	19	10
106	26	17	19	11	18	15	20	14	9
35	42	38	19	32	65	34	39	45	35

15-26 排污费征收、使用和污染赔（罚）款情况

STATISTICS ON COLLECTION, REPARATIONS AND FINES ON POLLUTION DSICHARGES

项　目	Item	1990	1995	2000	2005	2006	2007	2008	2009
交纳排污费单位（个）	Number of Enterprises (unit)	4072	9409	32581			25700	19607	15584
本年征收排污费数（万元）	Volume of Pollutant Discharge Fees Collected in This Year (10 000 year)	7823.0	13870.4	20092.3			3981.45	40600	38176
超标排污费	Fees on Over-Standard Pollutant Discharge	6430.0	9609.7	8921.0					2974
治理污染源(环保治理基金)	Pollution Resources Treatment (Environ-ment Protection Treatment Funds)	4037.0	5384.5	7209.2					
综合治理补助	Comprehensive Treatment Subsidy	676.0	232.6	241.2					
购置仪器设备	Equipment and Devices Purchased	287.0	487.9	374.0					
其他	Others	1430.0	4477.7						
污染事故（次）	Pollution Cases (time)	98	62	30					
污染赔款总额（万元）	Total Volume of Reparation on Pollution (10 000 yuan)	362.0	77.7	22.7					
污染罚款总额（万元）	Total Volume of Fines on Pollution (10 000 yuan)	45.00	7.60	0.50					

注：据国统函[04]95号，此表已调。排污使用总额11777.1万，其中污染治理项目无偿拨款5278.6万元。

Note:Pollution discharge totally costed 117.771 million yuan, among which 52.786 million yuan has been appropriated to the projects of pollution. treatment without compensaion.

15-27 工业企业废水处理设施情况

STATISTICS ON INDUSTRIAL WASTE WATER TREATMENT FACILITES

项　目	Item	2000	2005	2006	2007	2008	2009
汇总企业单位数（个）	Total Number of Enterprises (unit)	2172	2313	2225	2422	2541	2552
治理设施数量（套）	Number of Treatment Facilities	2120	2163	2050	2102	2050	2068
处理能力（万吨/日）	Treatment Capacity (10 000 ton/day)		912.45	858.87	878.78	930.27	950.88
运行费用（万元）	Operation Fees (10 000 yuan)	46650.70	77930.60	101505.00	94014.00	138820.80	134206.60
污染物去除量	Quantities of Pollutants Removed						
酚(挥发酚)（吨）	Phenol (Volatilized) (ton)	1761.27	2311.15	1948.44	2010.76	1468.51	1532.47
氰化物（吨）	Cyanide (ton)	1 193.56	213.95	183.28	131.26	128.52	117.84
石油类（吨）	Petroleum (ton)	1.34	1.18	0.56	0.75	0.38	0.39
氨氮（吨）	Ammonia Nitrogen (ton)		12936.80	9401.72	7490.26	11216.03	13455.17

15-28 全省当年建成投产的建设项目“三同时”执行情况

STATISTICS ON IMPLEMENTATION OF "THREE MEANWHILE" OF CONSTRUCTION PROJECTS IN HUBEI PROVINCE

项 目	Item	1990	1995	2000	2003	2004	2005	2006	2007	2008	2009
一、建设项目 (个)	Number of Construction Projects (unit)	306	245	359	1180	1015	1437	2050	4206	1498	2150
二、建设项目投资总额 (亿元)	Total investmentin Construction Projects (100 million yuan)	12.72	33.6	69.61	147	153.21	1603.1	366.5	2140.5	315.73	2085.8
#环保工程投资	#Investment in Environmental Protection Projects	0.32	1.5	2.37	4.45	7.9	11.22	17.35	139.8	25.647	51.89
三、“三同时”执行情况 (个)	Implementation of "Three Meanwhile" (unit)										
实际执行项目数	Number of Projects Actually Being Implemented	221	227	356	1099	969	1336	1958	1706	1491	2148
执行项目中合格的	Qualified	217	211	356	1032	900	1191	1814	1705	1481	2135
四、新增处理利用“三废”能力	Capacity of "Three Wastes" Treatment										
废水 (万吨/日)	Waste Water (10 000 ton/day)	6.34	31.45		22.79	373.37	541.82	207.4	59.51		
废气 (万标立方米/时)	Waste Gas (10 000 cu.m/h)	2979	265	113	367	22450	132462	24741	1317332		

主要统计指标解释

文化事业机构 指从事专业文化工作和为专业文化工作服务的独立建制的单位。不包括这些单位另外举办独立核算的其他机构和各部门的业余文化组织。该指标主要反映文化事业机构发展规模水平。

艺术表演团体 指从事戏曲、音乐、舞蹈、杂技等专业艺术表演，有独立帐户的单位，不包括半工半艺、半农半艺和民间职业剧团。该指标主要反映全国专业艺术表演团体发展规模水平。

艺术表演观众人数(人次) 指售票、包场演出或民族地区免费演出的艺术表演观众人次数，不包括彩排审查和内部观摩演出的观看人次数。该指标主要反映全国观看专业艺术表演团体演出的效益规模。

卫生机构 包括医疗机构、疾病预防控制中心(防疫站)、采供血机构、卫生监督及监测(检验)机构、医学科研和在职培训机构、健康教育所等。

医疗机构 包括医院、社区卫生服务中心(站)、疗养院、卫生院、门诊部、诊所(卫生所、医务室)、妇幼保健院(所、站)、专科疾病防治院(所、站)、急救中心(站)和临床检验中心。医疗机构分为非赢利性医疗机构和赢利性医疗机构。

医院 包括综合医院、中医医院、中西医结合医院、民族医院、各类专科医院和护理院。

卫生技术人员 指卫生机构中医生、护理人员 、药剂人员、检验人员等卫生技术人员。

医生 指在医疗、预防保健机构工作且取得《执业医师证书》的执业医师和执业助理医师。

卫生服务总费用 反映全国当年用于医疗卫生保健服务所消耗的资金总额，用筹资来源法测算。政府预算卫生支出指各级政府用于卫生事业的财政预算拨款。社会卫生支出指政府预算外的卫生资金投入，主要表现为社会医疗保险。其中包括如企事业单位和乡村集体经济单位举办医疗卫生机构设施建设费，企业职工医疗卫生费，行政事业单位负担的职工公费医疗超支部分等。居民个人卫生支出指城乡居民用自己可支配的经济收入支付的各项医疗卫生费用和医疗保险费用。

工业废水排放量 指经过企业厂区所有排放口排到企业外部的工业废水量。包括生产废水、外排的直接冷却水、超标排放的矿井地下水和与工业废水混排的厂区生活污水，不包括外排的间接冷却水(清污不分流的间接冷却水应计算在内)。

工业废水排放达标量 指报告期内废水中各项污染物指标都达到国家或地方排放标准的外排工业废水量，包括未经处理外排达标的，经废水处理设施处理后达标排放的，以及经污水处理厂处理后达标排放的。

工业废水排放达标率 指工业废水排放达标量占工业废水排放量的百分率，计算公式为:

$$\text{工业废水排放达标率}=\frac{\text{工业废水排放达标量}}{\text{工业废水排放量}}\times 100\%$$

工业废气排放量 指报告期内企业厂区内燃料燃烧和生产工艺过程中产生的各种排入大气的含有污染物的气体的总量，以标准状态(273K，101325Pa)计算。测算公式为:

工业废气排放量 = 燃料燃烧过程中废气排放量 + 生产工艺过程中废气排放量

工业烟尘排放量 指企业厂区内燃料燃烧过程中产生的烟气中夹带的颗粒物排放量。

工业粉尘排放量 指企业在生产工艺过程中排放的能在空气中悬浮一定时间的固体颗粒物排放量。如钢铁企业的耐火材料粉尘、焦化企业的筛焦系统粉尘、烧结机的粉尘、石灰窑的粉尘、建材企业的水泥粉尘等。不包括电厂排入大气的烟尘。

工业固体废物产生量 指报告期内企业在生产过程中产生的固体状、半固体状和高浓度液体状废弃物的总量，包括危险废物、冶炼废渣、粉煤灰、炉渣、煤矸石、尾矿、放射性废物和其他废物等；不包括矿山开采的剥离废石和掘进废石(煤矸石和呈酸性或碱性的废石除外)。酸性或碱性废石指采掘的废石其流经水、雨淋水的pH值小于4或pH值大于10.5者。

工业固体废物综合利用量 指报告期内企业通过回收、加工、循环、交换等方式，从固体废物中提取或者使其转化为可以利用的资源、能源和其他原材料的固体废物量(包括当年利用往年的工业固体废物贮存量)，如用作农业肥料、生产建筑材料、筑路等。综合利用量由原产生固体废物的单位统计。

工业固体废物综合利用率 指工业固体废物综合利用量占工业固体废物产生量(包括综合利用往年贮存量)的百分率。计算公式为:

$$\text{工业固体废物综合利用率}=\frac{\text{工业固体废物综合利用量}}{\text{工业固体废物产生量+综合利用往年贮存量}}\times 100\%$$

生活垃圾无害化处理率 指报告期生活垃圾无害化处理量与生活垃圾产生量比率。在统计上，由于生活垃圾产生量不易取得，可用清运量代替。计算公式为:

$$\text{生活垃圾无害化处理率}=\frac{\text{生活垃圾无害化处理量}}{\text{生活垃圾产生量}}\times 100\%$$

Explanatory Notes on Main Statistical Indicators

Cultural Institutions refer to units, which have their own organizational system and independent accounting system and specialize in or serve cultural development. They exclude other establishments run by these cultural institutions and amateur cultural groups established by various departments. This indicator reflects the development of cultural units.

Art Troupe refers to the troupe which is engaged in drama, opera, music, dance, acrobatics or other art performance, opens independent accounts with banks and has self-supporting accounting system; excluding the troupes which are engaged partly in industrial or agricultural activities, partly in art performance and the professional troupes organized by the people. This indicator reflects the development of national professional art troupes.

Number of Audience at Art Performance refers to the number of attendants at commercial shows, completely booked shows or free shows given in minority national areas, and does not include the number of spectators at rehearsals for examination and internal shows for study.

Health Care Institutions include medical institutions, disease prevention and control centers (epidemic prevention stations), blood gathering and supplying institutions, health supervision and inspection (check up) institutions, medicinal scientific research and on-job training institutions, health education and so on.

Medical Organizations include hospitals, health service centers (stations) of communities, nursing homes, health centers, clinics, clinics (health stations and infirmaries), maternity and child care agencies (centers and stations), special disease prevention and curing agencies (centers and stations), first aid centers (stations) and clinical inspection centers. Medical organizations are grouped by two types: profit-making and non-profit-making medical organizations.

Hospitals include polyclinics, traditional Chinese medical hospitals, hospitals integrated with traditional Chinese therapeutics and western therapeutics, ethical hospitals, various specialties hospitals and nursing hospitals.

Medical Technical Personnel refers to doctors, assistant nurses, pharmacists, and laboratory technicians working in medical institutions.

Doctors refer to certified physicians and certified assistant physicians with certifications working in medical and health care and prevention agencies.

Total Cost of Health Services reflects the total expenditures on medical and health care services for the whole country, calculated on basis of sources of funding. Health expenditure from government budget refers to budgetary allocation for health undertakings by governments at all levels. Social health expenditure refers to non-government budgetary capital input, mainly the health insurance. It includes expenditure on health institutions run by enterprises and rural collective entities, expenditure on medical and health care of employees of enterprises, and excessive health expenditure of government employees that could be covered by the government health care system. Health expenditure on individuals refers to expenditure on health service and health insurance paid by residents from their disposable income.

Waste Water Discharged by Industry refers to the volume of waste water discharged by industrial enterprises through all their outlets, including waste water from production process, directly cooled water, groundwater from mining wells which does not meet discharge standards and sewage from households mixed with waste water produced by industrial activities, but excluding indirectly cooled water discharged (It should be included if the discharge is not separated with waste water).

Industrial Waste Water Meeting Discharge Standards refers to volume of industrial waste water discharge which, with or without treatment, reaches national or local standards with regard to all pollutants.

Ratio of Industrial Waste Water Meeting Discharge Standards refers to percentage of industrial waste water meeting discharge standards over total industrial waste water discharge. It is calculated as:

Ratio of industrial waste water meeting discharge standards = industrial waste water meeting discharge standards / total industrial waste water discharge

Industrial Waste Air Emission refers to discharge into atmosphere of waste air containing pollutants generated from fuel burning and production process in enterprises within a given period of time. It is calculated at standard status (273K, 101325Pa) as:

Industrial waste air emission = emission through fuel burning + emission through production process

Industrial Soot Emission refers to volume of soot in smoke emitted in process of fuel burning in premises of enterprises.

Industrial Dust Emission refers to volume of dust emitted by production process of enterprises and suspended in the air for a given period of time, including dust from refractory material of iron and steel works, dust from coke-screening systems and sintering machines of coke plants, dust from lime kilns and dust from cement production in building material enterprises, but excluding soot and dust emitted from power plants.

Industrial Solid Wastes Produced refers to total volume of solid, semi-solid and high concentration liquid residues produced by industrial enterprises from production process in a given period of time, including hazardous wastes, slag, coal ash, gangue, tailings, radioactive residues and other wastes, but excluding stones stripped or dug out in mining (gangue and acid or alkaline stones not included). A stone is acid or alkaline depending on the pH value of the water below 4 or above 10.5 when the stone is in, or soaked by, the water.

Industrial Solid Wastes Utilized refers to volume of solid wastes from which useful materials can be extracted or which can be converted into usable resources, energy or other materials by means of reclamation, processing, recycling and exchange (including utilizing in the year the stocks of industrial solid wastes of the previous year). Examples of such utilizations include fertilizers, building materials and road materials. The information shall be collected by the producing units of the wastes.

Ratio of Industrial Solid Wastes Utilized refers to the percentage of industrial solid wastes utilized over industrial solid wastes produced (including stocks of the previous years). It is calculated as:

Ratio of industrial solid wastes utilized = volume of industrial solid wastes utilized / (industrial solid wastes produced + stock of previous years) ×100%

Ratio of Consumption Wastes Treated refers to consumption wastes treated over that produced. In practical statistics, as it is difficult to estimate, the volume of consumption wastes produced is replaced with that transported. It is calculated as:

Ratio of consumption wastes treated = consumption wastes treated / consumption wastes produced×100%

16 其他社会活动

Other Social Activities

资料整理：谢余强

16-1 工会组织情况

BASIC STATISTICS ON LABOR UNION

年 份 Year	工会基层组织数(个) Number of Grassroot Labor Union Organizations (unit)	全省已建工会的基层单位职工与会员人数(万人) Number of Grassroot Staff and Workers and Members of Established Labor Union in the Province(10 000 persons)				工会专职工作人员人数(万人) Number of Full-time Workers in Labor Union (10 000 persons)
		职工人数		会员人数		
		Number of Staff and Workers	#女职工 #Women Workers	Number of Members	#女会员 #Women Members	
1952	3667	6.27	1.43	35.98	7.20	0.17
1957	7758	103.11	23.48	69.90	13.99	0.33
1970	14952	210.72	57.18	135.52	38.64	0.72
1975	18872	280.22	83.18	174.72	56.24	0.87
1978	21224	32 298	99.74	197.24	78.80	0.96
1980	22802	387.95	139.20	299.41	94.91	1.04
1985	25286	484.68	192.32	404.58	156.62	2.76
1990	33990	559.00	227.00	498.00	198.00	3.40
1991	34270	569.01	231.91	513.62	204.92	3.96
1992	33972	545.00	226.00	492.00	201.00	3.47
1993	33441	537.47	221.48	480.60	193.06	3.72
1994	28459	582.84	243.52	511.84	208.05	2.86
1995	28461	564.34	230.90	511.11	207.49	1.81
1996	28459	584.30	238.16	527.09	213.08	2.88
1997	20151	472.60	192.65	419.72	168.89	2.68
1998	17488	445.80	183.90	400.90	163.90	2.30
1999	18976	442.97	178.21	396.90	155.03	3.18
2000	45251	532.31	197.81	475.57	176.87	2.45
2001	111309	728.94	218.68	660.82	198.25	2.45
2004	50391	755.90	276.69	721.46	262.74	2.95
2005	54893	856.07	298.78	771.95	279.94	3.09
2006	61627	904.15	314.67	856.95	296.39	3.76
2007	69886	1004.92	358.44	972.30	345.64	3.94
2008	79048	1099.78	382.72	1073.22	377.43	4.48
2009	83436	1160.45	418.82	1127.68	411.12	4.75

注：1．因文革期间工会统计中断，表中1970、1975、1978年数据根据年平均增长值推算

2．1994年工会基层组织数不包括“双停”企业数。

Notes:a)The datas in 1970, 1975, 1978 were calculated by the average growth rate, because Labor Union statistics had been broken in the period of "The Great Cultural Revolution".

b)The number of basic Level Labor Union organizations in 1994 doesn't include the enterprises which stopped production.

16-2 基层政权和村（居）委会情况

BASIC STATISTICS ON GRASSROOT REGIME AND VILLAGE COMMITTEES

单位：个 (unit)

年份 Year	镇 Township	乡 Villages	街道办事处 Regional Office	居委会个数 Number of Committees	村委会个数 Number of Village Committees
1984	592	3997	285	3051	32582
1985	858	3829	308	3141	32303
1986	859	3700	178	3257	32796
1987	836	1257	186	3394	32738
1988	828	1260	215	3483	32354
1989	840	1143	298	3545	32094
1990	849	1123	293	3573	32703
1991	849	1121	307	3709	32595
1992	852	1117	297	3830	32716
1993	857	1097	214	3921	32674
1994	864	1092	218	3998	32636
1995	865	1038	236	4110	32547
1996	823	567	252	4170	32486
1997	840	552	252	4287	32393
1998	847	543	253	4364	32293
1999	850	488	271	4425	32187
2000	860	466	283	3619	32001
2001	735	228	250	3468	31191
2002	738	224	272	3265	27667
2003	735	224	273	3351	27127
2004	738	224	274	3356	26470
2005	733	217	277	3465	29534
2006	737	210	277	3545	25828
2007	734	210	279	3653	25722
2008	735	207	285	3794	25551
2009	740	204	283	3882	25517

16-3 社会福利事业、企业单位机构及人员数

BASIC STATISTICS ON NUMBER OF SOCIAL WELFARE ENTERPRISES AND PERSONS ENGAGED

单位：个 (unit)

项 目	Item	机 构 Number of Institutions				
		2000	2005	2007	2008	2009
全省合计	**Total of the Province**	**4027**	**4358**	**61335**	**4266**	**4255**
一、事业单位	Institution	2949	3425	26140	3512	3473
(一)收养性事业单位	Adoptive Institutions	2459	2755	17157	2553	2504
1.优抚休(疗)养院	Special Care Nursing Home	121	99	2767	91	91
2.社会福利收养院	Welfare Homes	2338	2656	14390	2462	2413
(二)非收养性事业单位	Non-Adoptive Institutions	490	670	8983	959	969
1.烈士纪念建筑物管理单位	Units Managing Architectures in Honor of the Revolutionary Martyrs	39	45	630	45	45
2.军队离退休干部管理机构	Units Managing Veteran	90	97	851	103	103
3.军供站	Military Supply Station	8	8	317	9	9
4.社区服务中心	Community Service Centre	175	278	2234	369	441
(收容遣送站)	Asylum and Dispatching Station	20	38			
5.救助管理站	Home for Beggers and Vegrant			53	54	54
6.流浪儿童救助保护中心	Funeral Units			13	13	13
7.殡葬事业单位	Funeral Units	105	131	125	127	128
#殡仪馆	#Funeral Home	78	81	81	82	82
8.福利彩票发行单位	Units Issuing Lottery Tickets	50	54	49	52	52
9.慈善团体	Philantropy Groups	3	19	46	63	
10.婚姻登记服务中心	Marrage Register Center			86	90	90
11.救灾储备单位	Relief Unit			28	34	34
二、社会福利企业	Social Welfare Enterprises	1 078	933	761	754	782
#国有	#State-Owned	92	38			

16-3 续表 continued

单位：人 (person)

项 目	Item	人 员 Number of Persons Engaged in				
		2000	2005	2007	2008	2009
全省合计	**Total of the Province**	**55 845**	**51625**	**61335**	**65684**	**66815**
一、事业单位	Institution	21 342	25899	26140	27542	27463
(一)收养性事业单位	Adoptive Institutions	14 203	18132	17157	18395	18190
1.优抚休(疗)养院	Special Care Nursing Home	2 688	2999	2767	2738	2623
2.社会福利收养院	Welfare Homes	11 515	15133	14390	15657	15567
(二)非收养性事业单位	Non-Adoptive Institutions	7 139	7767	8983	9147	9273
1.烈士纪念建筑物管理单位	Units Managing Architectures in Honor of the Revolutionary Martyrs	645	699	630	628	590
2.军队离退休干部管理机构	Units Managing Veteran	770	844	851	837	853
3.军供站	Military Supply Station	322	283	317	354	257
4.社区服务中心	Community Service Centre	2 131	1940	2234	2329	2782
(收容遣送站)	Asylum and Dispatching Station	385	460			
5.救助管理站	Home for Beggers and Vegrant			667	513	541
6.流浪儿童救助保护中心	Funeral Units			130	174	175
7.殡葬事业单位	Funeral Units	2 661	3265	3307	3302	3247
#殡仪馆	#Funeral Home	2 264	2668	2767	2728	2670
8.福利彩票发行单位	Units Issuing Lottery Tickets	218	201	224	259	254
9.慈善团体	Philantropy Groups	7	75	144	203	
10.婚姻登记服务中心	Marrage Register Center			383	429	465
11.救灾储备单位	Relief Unit			96	119	109
二、社会福利企业	Social Welfare Enterprises	34 503	25726	35195	38142	39352
#国有	#State-Owned	6 609	1372			

16-4 社会保险基本情况
BASIC CONDITION ABOUT SOCIAL INSURANCE

年 份 year	失业保险 Unemployment Insurance		城镇职工基本养老保险 Basic Endowment Insurance for Urban and Rural Employees		工伤保险年末参保人数 (万人) Participants at Year-end (10 000 persons)	年末参加生育保险人数 (万人) Number of People Participated in Maternity Insurance at Year-end (10 000 persons)
	年末参保人 数 (万人) Participants at Year-end (10 000 persons)	全年发放失业保险金 (亿元) Unemployed Relief Released (10 000 yuan)	年末参保职工人数 (万人) Participants at Year-end (10 000 persons)	年末参保退休人员 (万人) Retirees (10 000 persons)		
1995	377.7		338.5		162.0	120.5
1996	392.9	0.4	353.2		177.6	137.8
1997	381.2	0.5	355.8		188.5	165.5
1998	378.2	0.5	413.1	107.4	190.0	168.8
1999	517.6	0.6	455.3	122.4	183.8	189.0
2000	459.6	1.6	465.6	130.4	185.0	191.3
2001	420.8	3.2	474.4	136.6	182.3	182.1
2002	416.1	5.4	532.7	154.5	183.2	182.7
2003	390.1	5.6	554.5	167.5	189.2	182.1
2004	391.3	4.0	586.1	194.7	187.2	179.9
2005	391.5	4.0	597.6	206.4	230.3	175.9
2006	395.5	3.7	630.2	220.5	275.5	194.5
2007	405.4	3.8	651.4	235.3	328.0	225.0
2008	422.6	3.6	671.7	252.4	350.7	315.4
2009	437.0	3.6	701.9	273.7	396.5	350.6

16-5 参加基本养老保险人数
NUMBER OF PRESONS PARTICIPATED IN BASIC ENDOEMENT INSURANCE

单位：万人 (10 000 persons)

年份 Year	合计 Total	职工 Number of Employees	企业(含其他) Enterprises (including others)	离退休人员 Number of Retirees	企业(含其他) Enterprises (including others)
1995	338.5	338.5	338.5		
1996	353.2	353.2	353.2		
1997	355.8	355.8	355.8		
1998	520.5	413.1	413.1	107.4	107.4
1999	577.7	455.3	455.3	122.4	122.4
2000	596.0	465.6	465.6	130.4	130.4
2001	611.0	474.4	474.4	136.6	136.6
2002	687.2	532.7	481.5	154.5	147.2
2003	722.0	554.5	501.1	167.5	158.6
2004	780.8	586.1	530.6	194.7	184.5
2005	804.0	597.6	539.8	206.4	195.1
2006	850.7	630.2	570.0	220.5	207.5
2007	886.7	651.4	602.6	235.3	223.0
2008	924.1	671.7	628.7	252.4	238.7
2009	975.6	701.9	660.54	273.7	259.2

16-6 城乡各种福利院基本情况

BASIC CONDITIONS OF WELFARE HOUSES IN URBAN AND RURAL AREAS

年份 Year	单位数(个) Number (unit)	职工人数(人) Number of Staff and Workers (person)	床位数(张) Number of Beds (unit)	收养人数(人) Number of People Adopted (person)
1980	367	2995	9430	8194
1985	3033	9716	39458	35652
1986	3955	12373	52912	46818
1987	3655	12360	57698	49356
1988	3300	11901	57356	47448
1989	3285	11759	57022	47075
1990	3252	11854	57878	48017
1991	3130	11966	57839	47684
1992	3114	12361	61878	50885
1993	3101	12955	61389	51638
1994	3066	13280	63451	52866
1995	2977	13607	64417	53662
1996	2907	13664	65853	54987
1997	2715	14163	69970	57471
1998	2650	14392	72284	59753
1999	2603	14552	76203	63326
2000	2459	14203	77871	63901
2001	2191	14173	78119	62590
2002	2145	14414	79522	65564
2003	2123	14856	117511	103320
2004	2359	16344	156461	144042
2005	2755	18132	189486	168800
2006	2770	17705	198458	179385
2007	2616	17157	206049	188308
2008	2553	18395	210342	180286
2009	2504	18190	216211	185933

16-7 婚姻登记和离婚情况

STATISTICS ON MARRIAGE REGISTERATION AND DIVORCE

年份 Year	准予登记结婚(对) Marriage Registeration Granted (couple)	初婚(人) First Marriage (person)	再婚(人) Digamist(person)	离婚(对) Divorce (couple)	离婚率(%) Rate of Divorce (%)
1980	348003	676633	19373	6129	0.26
1985	373015	730106	15924	6481	0.26
1986	402315	785319	19311	6322	0.25
1987	417552	809808	25296	6660	0.26
1988	362654	698447	26861	7389	0.29
1989	413460	801171	25749	9203	0.35
1990	408688	790477	26899	9477	0.35
1991	424708	820092	29324	9584	0.35
1992	463279	897899	28659	10793	0.39
1993	425276	822044	28508	11937	0.43
1994	457324	884817	29831	12910	0.46
1995	482063	930832	33294	13340	0.46
1996	442532	851577	33487	14590	0.50
1997	426460	820615	32305	21260	0.72
1998	399900	763163	36637	24711	0.84
1999	376961	716175	37747	19519	0.66
2000	353781	673294	34268	21255	0.71
2001	335421	632188	38654	22077	0.74
2002	321517	605055	37979	24003	0.80
2003	329256	614244	44268	29375	0.98
2004	381472	710633	52311	46369	1.54
2005	394093	717495	70691	53394	1.77
2006	445672	822294	69050	57682	1.91
2007	485278	896768	73788	65876	2.17
2008	542251	1025496	59006	76003	2.49
2009	565400	1058851	71949	81133	2.84

16-8 残疾人基本情况
BASIC STATISTICS ON THE DISABLED

单位：万人 (10 000 persons)

年份 Year	残疾人总数 Total Number of the Disabled	听力语言残疾人数 Number of Those with Hearing and Speaking Impairment	视力残疾人数 Number of Those with Sight Impairment	智力残疾人数 Number of Those with Intelligence Weakness	肢体残疾人数 Number of Those with Physical Handicapped	精神病残疾人数 Number of those with Mental Illness	综合残疾人数 Number of disabled
1952	177.53	64.68	34.25	28.34	21.51	3.55	25.20
1957	197.62	72.00	38.13	31.54	23.95	3.95	28.05
1965	226.15	82.39	43.63	36.10	27.41	4.52	32.10
1975	284.46	103.64	54.88	45.40	34.47	5.69	40.38
1978	295.23	107.56	56.96	47.12	35.78	5.90	41.91
1980	302.28	110.13	58.32	48.25	36.63	6.04	42.91
1981	305.91	111.45	59.02	48.83	37.07	6.12	43.42
1982	309.80	112.87	59.77	49.45	37.54	6.19	43.98
1983	313.99	114.39	60.58	50.12	38.05	6.28	44.57
1984	317.35	115.62	61.23	50.65	38.46	6.34	45.05
1985	321.37	117.08	62.00	51.30	38.95	6.42	45.62
1986	325.72	118.67	62.84	51.99	39.47	6.51	46.24
1987	330.42	120.38	63.75	52.74	40.04	6.61	46.90
1988	334.58	121.90	64.55	53.40	40.55	6.69	47.49
1989	339.35	123.64	65.47	54.17	41.12	6.78	48.17
1990	351.00	127.88	67.72	56.02	42.54	7.02	49.82
1991	355.71	129.59	68.63	56.78	43.11	7.11	50.49
1992	360.06	131.18	69.47	57.47	43.63	7.20	51.11
1993	364.82	132.91	70.39	58.23	44.21	7.29	51.79
1994	369.03	134.45	71.20	58.90	44.72	7.38	52.38
1995	372.47	135.70	71.86	59.45	45.14	7.45	52.87
1996	375.89	136.95	72.52	60.00	45.55	7.51	53.36
1997	378.95	138.06	73.11	60.49	45.92	7.58	53.79
1998	381.64	139.04	73.63	60.92	46.25	7.63	54.17
1999	383.00	139.68	73.68	61.20	46.42	7.68	54.35
2000	384.36	140.32	73.73	61.48	46.59	7.73	54.53
2001	388.58	141.53	74.85	62.17	47.08	7.74	55.21
2002	389.21	143.71	77.84	59.88	47.90	5.99	53.89
2003	390.11	144.04	78.07	60.02	48.01	6.00	54.02
2004	391.05	144.39	78.21	60.16	48.13	6.02	54.14
2005	392.01	144.83	78.39	60.30	48.26	6.04	54.19
2006	379.40	88.90	62.40	34.40	105.70	30.40	55.80
2007	379.40	88.90	62.40	34.40	105.70	30.40	55.80
2008	379.40	88.90	62.40	34.40	105.70	30.40	55.80
2009	379.40	88.90	62.40	34.40	105.70	30.40	55.80

注：1.本统计表根据1987年全国残疾人抽样调查资料推算。
2.精神病残疾人从15岁起算。

Notes:a)The figures in this table were caculated according to the national sample survey on the disabled in 1987.
b)The Metally disabled refers to those over 15.

16-9 刑事案件发、破案情况

STATISTICS ON OCCURANCE AND CLEARING UP CRIMINAL CASES

指 标	Item	1990	1995	2000	2003	2004	2005	2006	2007	2008	2009
刑事案件发案总数 (件)	Number of Criminal Cases Occurred (case)	166630	85876	114866	147210	143165	147004	154114	164415	173061	195836
刑事案件破案总数 (件)	Number of Criminal Cases Cleared (case)	99604	73831	72796	72223	69212	71455	67595	74833	79035	90916
刑事案件破案率 (%)	Rate of Criminal Cases Cleared (%)	59.8	86.0	63.4	49.1	48.3	48.6	43.9	45.5%	45.7%	46.4%

16-10 城市交通事故与火灾情况

BASIC STATISTICS ON TRAFFIC ACCIDENTS AND FIRE ACCIDENTS

指 标	Item	1990	1995	2000	2005	2006	2007	2008	2009
交通事故处理发生件数 (起)	Number of Traffic Accidents Being Dealt (case)	6862	8336	20148	9585	9590	8986	7696	6632
死亡人数 (人)	Deaths (person)	2267	3401	3792	2417	2304	2142	2023	1952
受伤人数 (人)	Injuries (person)	4937	5353	16492	10555	11979	11355	9561	8204
折合经济损失 (万元)	Losses Converted into Financial (10 000 yuan)	738	4460	7041	4958	4752	3428	2797	2850.5
火灾发生数 (起)	Fires Accsidents (case)	1757	1393	6780	9356	11842	11392	11805	11166
死亡人数 (人)	Deaths (person)	73	64	54	56	63	61	41	31
受伤人数 (人)	Injuries (person)	206	86	106	47	57	65	20	17
折合经济损失 (万元)	Losses Converted into Financial (10 000 yuan)	3368	3221	1754	1945	2678	3549	4376	4434

16-11 审查批捕、起诉情况

STATISTICS ON EXAMINATION, ARREST AND PROSECUTION

项 目	Item	1991	1995	2000	2003	2004	2005	2006	2007	2008	2009
受理批捕件数 (件)	Number of Cases (case)	27703	18870	20378	18032	18486	19846	20113	21790	22400	22915
受理批捕人数 (人)	Number of People Arrested (person)	50926	31122	31245	26381	27496	29427	30787	32698	33496	34545
批准逮捕 (人)	Number of Arrests Granted (person)	42700	25257	25114	24372	25347	27063	28239	30142	30751	31703
不批捕人数 (人)	Number of Non-Arrest (person)	2791	1545	4329	1015	1161	1522	1798	1892	2031	2185
受理审查起诉件数(件)	Number of Cases Received (case)	30116	21240	17660	19860	20056	21966	21931	24693	25218	26506
受理审查起诉人数(件)	Number of Prosecutions Being Dealt (case)	52916	33532	25416	29208	30098	33410	34228	37940	38748	41393
起诉人数 (人)	Prosecutor (person)	42587	24404	22396	23178	24386	26926	28368	31577	32143	34575
不起诉人数 (人)	Non-prosecutor (person)	221	43	1019	995	943	982	882	1158	1190	1048

16-12 检察机关查办职务犯罪情况

STATISTICS ON CRIMES COMMITTED BY TAKING ADVANTAGE OF DUTY BY PROCURATORIAL ORGAN

项 目	Item	1991	1995	2000	2003	2004	2005	2006	2007	2008	2009
受理案件件数(件)	Number of Cases Dealt (case)	9555	10906	8343	4194	3917	3125	2716	2431	2227	2081
立案件数 (件)	Registered Cases (case)	4316	3640	2034	1687	1643	1552	1557	1644	1628	1593
立案人数 (人)	Registered Offenders (person)	4961	4290	2312	1833	1791	1682	1708	1805	1808	1868
贪污贿赂件数(件)	Number of Corruption and Bribe Cases (case)	3736	3081	1821	1481	1446	1363	2231	1410	1382	1330
渎职侵权件数(件)	Number of Malversation Cases (case)	580	559	213	206	197	189	485	234	246	263
查办大案件数(件)	Large Cases (case)	263	824	882	857	852	887	869	1035	1015	1050
#5万元以上件数	#Money Involved Above 50000 yuan	189	685	850	801	813	839	822	965	942	938
查办要案人数(人)	Number of Offender Involved in Large Cases (person)	46	110	108	180	193	139	158	164	170	153
#厅局级人数	#Number of Offenders at Bureau Level	1	4	11	21	15	17	13	12	13	16
提起公诉人数(人)	Number of Prosecutors (person)	2402	1738	1490	1385	1395	1265	1321	1490	1484	1494

16-13 律师、公证、调解工作基本情况
BASIC STATISTICS ON LAWYERS, NOTARIZATION AND MEDITATION

项 目	Item	1990	1995	2000	2005	2006	2007	2008	2009
一、律师工作	Lawyers								
律师事务所 (个)	Number of Lawyer Office (person)	150	281	350	387	389	387	415	441
律师工作人员 (人)	Number of Lawyer (person)	1624	3190	4568	5238	5497	1475	1600	839
专职律师	Number of Full-Time Lawyer	622	1593	2383	3722	3984	4353	4612	4870
兼职律师	Number of Part-Time Lawyer	157	297	472	165	174	181	219	239
担任法律顾问 (家)	Number of Units with Legal Advisors (unit)	5535	12763	9727	9565	9923	10126	11009	11554
民事案件诉讼代理 (件)	Agent of Civil Cases (case)	15452	13190	21412	27079	27359	44143	44978	44600
经济案件诉讼代理 (件)	Agent of Economic Cases (case)		18689	18931	13799	14151			
刑事诉讼辩护及代理 (件)	Defender and Agent of Crriminal Cases (case)	15326	8836	10078	11341	11388	11504	12158	17269
非诉讼法律事务 (件)	Agent of Non-Litigious Legal Affairs (case)	5406	35542	25142	34674	35027	37395	40168	37600
涉外及港澳台法律事务(件)	Agent of Foreign, Hogkong, Maco and Taiwan Affairs (case)	273	582	305	5994	97			
解答法律咨询 (万人次)	Agent of Legal Advisory Services (10 000 (person-times)	13.07	9.91	11.37	15.23	15.69	15.70	9.06	7.71
代写法律事务文件 (万件)	Agent of Legal Document Written on Behalf of Clients (10 000 case)	2.07	2.38	3.44	3.49	3.58	3.60	1.81	2.38
二、公证工作	Notarization								
公证机构 (个)	Number of Notary Offices (unit)	101	116	117	118	118	118	116	116
公证人员 (人)	Notarial Pesonel (person)	659	746	769	689	619	665	672	657
#公证员	#Notaries	386	404	506	455	421	422	385	371
公证员助理	Assistant Notaries	105	144	108	62	51	146	123	286
办理公证文件 (万件)	Number of Domestic Notarized Document (10 000 cases)	22.12	25.68	36.30	31.04	31.57	31.24	33.60	33.77
#涉外公证 (件)	#Foreign Notarized Documents (case)	7134	22915	63993	65498	65932	66099	71672	70482
三、人民调解工作	People's Mediation								
司法助理员 (人)	Judicial Assistant (person)	2608	2652	1732	2210	2328	2383	2464	2826
#专职司法助理员	#Full-Time Judicial Assistant	1790	1788	1589	2157	2298	2333		2516
人民调解委员会 (万个)	Number of People's Mediation Committees (10 000 units)	4.88	5.09	4.90	3.70	3.52	3.53	3.52	3.47
调解人员 (万人)	Number of Mediators (10 000 persons)	37.33	55.87	38.53	17.20	17.44	17.21	17.82	20.87
调解纠纷总数 (万件)	Number of Disputes Mediated (10 000 cases)	40.91	32.53	26.47	21.62	21.01	27.89	23.96	26.42
调解成功总数 (万件)	Number of Successful Mediation (10 000 cases)	38.69	31.36	25.77	21.13	20.62	27.42	23.53	25.79

16-14 涉外公证文书分类情况
FOREIGN-RELATED NOTARIAL DOCUMENTS BY TYPE

单位：件 (case)

分类	Item	1990	1995	2000	2003	2004	2005	2006	2007	2008	2009
合 计	**Total**	**7134**	**22915**	**63993**	**64348**	**65400**	**65498**	**65932**	**66099**	**71672**	**70482**
出生	Births	1349	3302	9748	7214	7242	7243	7358	7630	8254	6874
学历	Academic Degree	819	2742	9134	9776	10069	10078	10169	11779	16682	9078
经历	Personal Expirments	738	654	1015	1196	804	806	811	950	347	289
生存和居住	Survival and Residence	8	183	74	55	97	102	135	182	48	61
死亡	Death	29	101	83	109	101	109	122	107	139	126
收养子女	Children Adoption	30	331	683	263	537	539	542	574	929	707
亲属关系	Kinship	813	1929	3225	3819	3956	3962	4026	5795	7665	6598
婚姻状况	Marital Status	814	1920	4228	3266	3682	3691	3701	3968	5979	5274
继承权	Rights of Inheritance	6	13	14	26	31	28	25	81	52	1003
遗嘱	Testament	2	31	18	261	19	18	19	26	35	43
职称	Title		337	438	140	142	141	239	282	231	21
国籍	Nationality		49	69	154	152	150	142	307	73	58
法人资格	Corperate Capacity		46	30	14	12	16	20	17	18	44
委托书	Trust Deeds	124	359	133	226	290	293	298	316	298	31
公司章程	Chapter of Company		9	22	19	22	24	21	18	21	159
副本与原本相符	Confirmation of Copy and Photo-Offset Copies to Originals		2672	11532	9866	7852	7861	7702	8202	4389	3954
营业证书	Operation Document		25	139	163	184	186	181	143	32	202
声明书	Declarations	56	136	384	3849	3970	3972	4011	4378	1039	33
其他经济合同	Other Economic Contracts		142	16	28	363	372	380	652	43	37
受、未受刑事处分	Criminal Record & Uncriminal Record	765	2267	6646	5779	6115	6126	6209	9149	7857	6470
其他	Others	1675	5667	16362	8579	9913	9916	9987	2092	9059	14868

16-15 履行法律监督情况

SUPERVISION ON LAW ENFORCEMENT

单位：人、件 (person, case)

项　目		1991	1995	2000	2003	2004	2005	2006	2007	2008	2009
监督公安机关立案件数	Number of Cases Registered by Public Security			247	739	653	554	554	778	889	951
监督追捕人数	Number of criminals hunted under Supervision	775	272	300	174	201	204	204	257	559	578
监督追诉人数	Number of People being Prosecuted	468	132	61	47	51	78	78	207	295	520
刑事抗诉件数	Number of cases Against Crimnal Prosecutions	252	78	192	122	129	123	123	85	88	124
监督刑罚执行纠错人次	Error Correction of Execution of Punishment Person-time	2788	3005	3546	817	127	51	51	37	83	345
民事行政监督抗诉件数	Number of Counterappeal Civil Cases		260	894	536	587	514	514	486	447	409

16-16 调解民间纠纷分类

CIVIL DISPUTES MEDIATED BY TYPE

项　目	Item	调解纠纷(件) Number of Disputes Mediated (case)				各种纠纷所占比重(%) Proportion (%)			
		2006	2007	2008	2009	2006	2007	2008	2009
合计	**Total**	**45834**	**51398**	**55047**	**57600**	**100**	**100**	**100**	**100**
婚姻	Marriage	18337	21612	22252	23038	40.01	42.05	40.42	40
继承	Rghts of Inheritance	182	260	265	324	0.4	0.51	0.48	0.56
房地产开发	Real Estate Development	550	904	643	989	1.2	1.76	1.17	1.72
运输合同	Transportation Contracts	116	164	143	175	0.25	0.32	0.26	0.3
买卖合同	Selling and Purchasing Contracts	3703	3783	4099	3963	8.08	7.36	7.45	6.88
借款合同	Loans Contracts	8656	8938	9370	9116	18.89	17.39	17.02	15.83
劳动争议	Labor Disputes	562	727	1634	2017	1.23	1.41	2.97	3.5
人身权	Personal Right	5277	6064	6594	7172	11.51	11.8	11.98	12.45
所有权	Right of Ownership	1856	2388	2208	2005	4.05	4.65	4.01	3.48
其他	Others	6595	6558	7839	8801	14.39	12.76	14.24	15.28

16-17 人民法院审理一审案件情况

STATISTICS ON FIRST TRIAL CASES IN PEOPLE'S COURT

单位：件 (case)

年 份 Year	收案 Cases Received	刑事 Criminal Cases	民事 Civil Cases	经济纠纷 Economic Disputes	行政 Administration	海事海商 Martial Commerce
1985	63079	12709	40660	9710		26
1990	227618	29086	166960	31004	568	
1995	257312	21391	174908	56654	4359	456
1996	279640	23332	188929	60796	6583	542
1997	280064	17134	191273	63768	7889	516
1998	252403	17763	171025	57247	6368	606
1999	238715	19598	151191	61679	6247	647
2000	228804	19204	146838	56008	6754	618
2001	22162	21741	14429	48882	6560	745
2002	211464	19548	188163		3753	525
2003	193780	18943	171282		3555	488
2004	172889	18833	150682		3374	592
2005	155478	19672	132585		3221	745
2006	156885	19914	133584		3387	606
2007	161728	21719	137328		2681	459
2008	165099	22364	140072		2663	746
2009	173032	23481		147319	2232	710

注：一审案件指人民法院按照诉讼级别管辖按第一审程序审理的案件。
Note:First try cases refer to cases in the first try process in People's Court.

16-18 人民法院刑事一审案件收结案情况

END OF FIRST TRY CASES IN PEOPLE'S COURT OF CRIMINAL LAWSUITS

单位：件 (case)

项 目	Item	收案 Cases Received					结案 Cases Ended				
		2005	2006	2007	2008	2009	2005	2006	2007	2008	2009
合 计	**Total**	**19672**	**19914**	**21719**	**22364**	**23481**	**19760**	**19897**	**21928**	**22313**	**23395**
危害公共安全罪	Crimes Harming Public Security	1972	2044	2298	2460	2606	1988	2026	2315	2448	2591
破坏社会主义市场经济秩序罪	Crimes Harming Sosialism Market Economy Order	481	573	700	720	778	470	572	702	717	771
侵害公民人生权利民主权利罪	Crimes against Rights in Human Life and Democratic Rights	6056	5360	5305	5349	5869	6111	5390	5465	5340	5846
侵犯财产罪	Property Inviolability	7899	8484	9376	9497	9161	7918	8443	9416	9486	9154
妨害社会管理秩序罪	Crimes Hampering Social Management Order	2157	2306	2772	3063	3911	2155	2307	2767	3068	3882
危害国防利益罪	Crimes Harimg National Defense Interests	1	7	10	5	2	1	7	10	5	2
贪污贿赂罪	Corruption and Bribe	1024	1065	1144	1145	1038	1031	1073	1151	1119	1028
渎职罪	Malversation	79	69	109	120	115	83	73	97	125	120
其他	Others	3	6	5	5	1	3	6	5	5	1
合计中含自诉案件	Self-Suing Cases	1641	1086	878	703	569	1691	1130	1000	714	582

16-19 人民法院刑事案件中青少年犯罪情况
STATISTICS ON JUVENILE DELINQUENCY IN PEOPLE'S COURT OF CRIMINAL LAWSUITS

单位：人 (person)

年份 Year	刑事犯罪总数 Total Number of Criminal Cases	青少年犯罪 Juvenile Delinquency	不满18岁 Juvenile Age under 18	18-25岁 Age 18-25	青少年罪犯刑事罪犯率% Percentage of Juvenile Delinquency in Criminal Cases %
1997	18822	6064	1121	4943	32.22
1998	18423	6593	1356	5237	35.79
1999	20534	6836	1302	5534	33.30
2000	20076	5922	1279	4643	29.50
2001	22911	6597	1774	4823	28.79
2002	20868	5669	1901	3768	27.17
2003	20908	6207	2328	3879	29.69
2004	20429	5838	2633	3205	28.58
2005	21669	6283	2939	3344	29.00
2006	22876	6933	2945	3988	30.31
2007	17368	7459	3131	4328	42.95
2008	26682	6810	3030	3780	25.52
2009	28507	7700	2930	4770	27.01

16-20 人民法院民事一审案件收结案情况（2009）
STATISTICS ON END OF FIRST TRIAL CASES IN PEOPLE'S COURT OF CIVIL LAWSUITS (2009)

单位：件 (case)

项　目	Item	收案 Cases Received	结案 Cases Ended	调解 Mediated	判决 Judgement	驳回 Cases Turned Town	撤诉 Cases Dropped	其他 Others
合　计	**Total**	**147319**	**148087**	**57600**	**50803**	**1536**	**32691**	**5457**
婚姻家庭	Marriage	45288	45755	23038	13826	134	8393	364
继承	Rights of Inheritance	795	771	324	297	4	138	8
知识产权	Intelligence Property Rights	858	811	314	158	8	254	77
房地产开发	Real Estate Development	3041	3025	989	1040	155	726	115
运输合同	Transportation Contracts	444	439	175	175	4	78	7
买卖合同	Selling and Purchasing Contracts	11901	11931	3963	3796	111	3815	246
借款合同	Loans Contracts	24533	24492	9116	8306	200	6509	361
劳动争议	Labor Disputes	6514	6539	2017	2764	428	1218	112
海事海商	Martial Commerce	503	506	225	175	5	94	7
人身权	Personal Right	19207	19325	7172	9108	91	2684	270
特别程序	Special Procedure	3891	4031	14	661	53	247	3056
破产	Bnakruptcy	193	308		26	3	1	278
所有权及与其相关合同	Rights of Ownership and Relevant Contracts	6524	6685	2005	2746	67	1740	127
其他	Others	23627	23469	8248	7725	273	6794	429

注：结案中含上年旧存。

Note:The statistics of ended cases include statistics of last year.

16-21 人民法院行政一审案件收结案情况（2009）
STATISTICS ON END OF FIRST TRY CASES IN PEOPLE'S COURT OF ADMINISTRATION (2009)

单位：件 (case)

项目	Item	收案 Cases Received	结案 Cases Ended	维持 Cases Maintained	撤消 Cases Cancled	驳回 Cases Turned Town	撤诉 Cases Dropped	单独赔偿 Sole Compensation	其他 Others
合计	**Total**	**2232**	**2278**	**255**	**177**	**198**	**752**	**8**	**888**
土地	Land	259	265	20	23	20	97		105
公安	Public Security	225	229	44	11	14	106	2	52
城建	City Construction	574	585	42	57	94	187	5	200
交通运输	Transportation	60	58	2	3	1	28	1	23
工商	Industry and Commerce	84	97	15	6	1	36		39
环保	Environment	66	65	1		17	10		37
林业	Forestry	59	63	11	10	3	25		14
税务	Taxes	10	10			1	6		3
卫生	Sanitary and Hygiene	37	36	1		2	4		29
其他	Others	858	870	119	67	45	253		386

注：结案中含上年旧存。

Note:The statistics of ended cases include statistics of last year.

主要统计指标解释

社会福利事业单位 指集中收养社会孤老、残、幼的机构，包括由民政部门管理的社会福利院、儿童福利院、精神病人福利院和城镇集体举办的福利院及农村集体举办的敬老院以及优抚医院和具有收养能力的社区服务中心等。该指标主要反映我国在社会福利性单位投入的水平。

社会福利事业单位收养人数 包括民政部门管理和城镇、农村集体举办的社会福利事业单位中收养的老人、少年儿童、缺乏生活自理能力的残疾人员和精神病人。该指标主要反映收养性社会福利单位的收养能力。

社会福利企业单位 指以安置城镇有一定劳动能力的盲、聋、哑和肢体残疾人员就业为目的，享受国家减免税待遇的国有或集体企业。包括福利工厂、福利商业和服务业、假肢厂和安置农场等单位。该指标主要反映我国对残疾人照顾的特殊政策。

农村五保户 指农村中既无劳动能力，又无经济来源的老、弱、孤、残的农民，其生活由集体供养，实行保吃、保穿、保住、保医、保葬(孤儿保教)，简称“五保”，享受五保待遇的家庭叫五保户。该指标主要反映农村弱势群体的人员数量。

粗离婚率 指当年离婚对数占年平均人口的比重，计算公式为:

$$粗离婚率=\frac{当年离婚对数}{年平均人口数}\times 1000‰$$

律师 指依法取得律师执业证书，担任法律顾问，民事(刑事、行政)案件代理人、刑事案件辩护人、办理非诉讼业务，解答法律询问，代写法律事务文书等，为社会提供法律服务的人员。

公证人员 指在公证处工作的人员总称，包括公证处主任、副主任、公证员、公证员助理(助理公证员)和其他从事辅助性工作的人员。

公证文书 指公证处根据当事人申请，依照事实和法律，按照法定程序制作的，具有法律效力的司法证明文书。根据公证书用途和使用地，公证书分为国内公证书、国内经济公证书、涉外民事公证书、涉外经济公证书四类。

调解员 指在人民调解委员会担负调解民间纠纷工作的人员，包括调解委员会的委员和调解小组的调解员。该指标主要反映从事人民调解工作的人员数量。

调解民间纠纷 指调解委员会按照法律规定，根据自愿原则，用说服教育的方法调解民间发生的有关民事权利和义务争执的件数，包括调解成功数和调解未成功数。该指标主要反映人民调解委员会的工作量。

立案 指人民检察院对受理的报案、控告、举报或自首及自行发现的犯罪线索、犯罪嫌疑人进行初步调查后，认为存在职务犯罪事实和应追究刑事责任，并决定作为刑事案件进行侦查的诉讼活动，是追究犯罪的开始。该指标主要反映人民检察院依法将职务犯罪线索作为刑事案件进行侦查的诉讼活动。

大案 指贪污、贿赂案数额在 5 万元以上，挪用公款案数额在 10 万元以上，集体私分、巨额财产来源不明、隐瞒境外存款案数额在 50 万元以上以及按照《人民检察院直接受理的渎职、侵权重、特大案件标准(试行)》认定的案件。该指标主要反映人民检察院立案查办的职务犯罪案件中经济损失大、社会危害严重的案件。

要案 指县、处级以上干部的犯罪案件。该指标主要反映国家工作人员中县、处级以上干部因职务犯罪被人民检察院依法立案侦查的情况。

决定逮捕 指人民检察院对直接受理、自行侦查的案件，认为需要逮捕犯罪嫌疑人时，依据法律做出的逮捕决定。该指标主要反映人民检察院对直接受理的案件行使决定逮捕权的情况。

批准逮捕 指人民检察院对公安机关、国家安全机关、监狱管理机关提出逮捕的犯罪嫌疑人进行审查，根据事实，依法做出逮捕决定。该指标主要反映人民检察院对提请逮捕机关提请逮捕犯罪嫌疑人进行审查后依法做出批准逮捕决定的情况。

决定起诉 指人民检察院对公安机关、国家安全机关、监狱管理机关和检察机关内设机构反贪污贿赂部门等移送起诉的案件进行审查，根据事实，做出提起公诉的案件。该指标主要反映人民检察院对各种刑事案件向人民法院提起公诉的情况。

申诉 指经检察机关信访部门审查处理后，移送到检察机关申诉部门的申诉案件，包括不服检察机关处理决定和不服法院刑事判决和裁定的申诉的案件。

受理劳动争议案件数 指劳动争议仲裁委员会根据国家有关规定，对劳动争议当事人的申请予以审查，符合受理条件而正式立案、准备处理的劳动争议案件数。

基本养老保险

1.（参保）职工人数：指报告期末按照国家法律、法规和有关政策规定参加基本养老保险并在社保经办机构已建立缴费记录档案的职工人数，包括中断缴费但未终止养老保险关系的职工人数，不包括只登记未建立缴费记录档案的人数。

2.（参保）离退休人员人数：指报告期末参加基本养老保险的离休、退休和退职人员的人数。

3.基本养老保险基金收入：指根据国家有关规定，由纳入基本养老保险范围的缴费单位和个人按国家规定的缴费基数和缴费比例缴纳的养老保险基金，以及通过其他方式取得的形成基金来源的收入。包括单位和职工个人缴纳的基本养老保险费、基本养老保险基金利息收入、上级补助收入、下级上解收入、转移收入、财政补贴和其他收入。

4.基本养老保险基金支出：指按照国家政策规定的开支范围和开支标准从养老保险基金中支付给参加基本养老保险的离休、通休、退职人员个人的养老金、丧葬抚恤补助，以及由于保险关系转移、上下级之间调剂资金等原因而发生的支出。包括离休金、退休金、退职金、各种补贴、医疗费、死亡丧葬补助费、抚恤救济费、社会保险经办机构管理费、补助下级支出、上解上级支出、转移支出、其他支出等。

5.基本养老保险基金累计结余：指截止报告期末基本养老保险基金收支相抵后的累计余额。

离休、退休、退职人员 指正式办理了离休、退休、退职手续，并享受相应的离休、退休、退职待遇的人员。

基本医疗保险

1.参保人数：指报告期末按国家有关规定参加基本医疗保险的人数。包括参加保险的职工人数和退休人员人数。

2.基金收入：指根据国家有关规定，由纳入基本医疗保险范围的缴费单位和个人，按国家规定的缴费基数和缴费比例缴纳的基金，以及通过其他方式取得的形成基金来源的款项，包括：单位缴纳的社会统筹基金收入、个人缴纳的个人账户基金收入、财政补贴收入、利息收入、其他收入。

3.基金支出：指按照国家政策规定的开支范围和开支标准从社会统筹基金中支付给参加基本医疗保险的职工和退休人员的医疗保险待遇支出，和从个人帐户基金中支付给参加基本医疗保险的职工和退休人员的医疗费用支出，以及其他支出。包括：住院医疗费用支出、门急诊医疗费用支出、个人账户基金支出、其他支出。

4.基金累计结余：指截止报告期末基本医疗保险的社会统筹和个人帐户基金累计结余金额。包括银行存款、财政专户、债券投资和其他。

失业保险

1.参保人数：指报告期末按照国家法律、法规和有关政策规定参加了失业保险的城镇企业事业单位的职工及地方政府规定参加失业保险的其他人员的人数。

2.失业保险基金收入：指按照规定从企业、事业及其他单位筹集的失业保险费及其他并入失业保险基金收入的总额。包括单位和个人缴纳的失业保险费、失业保险基金利息收入、上级补助收入、下级上解收入、转移收入、财政补贴和其他收入。

3.失业保险基金支出：指报告期内为保障失业人员和下岗职工基本生活、促进其再就业等支出的基金总额。包括失业救济金、医疗费、死亡丧葬补助费、抚恤救济费、转业训练费支出、失业保险经办机构管理费、补助下级支出、上解上级支出、转移支出和其他支出。

4.基金累计结余：指截止报告期末失业保险基金收支相抵后的累计余额。

工伤保险

1.参加保险人数：指报告期末依据国家有关规定参加工伤保险的职工人数。

2.享受保险待遇人数：指劳动者因工负伤致残、死亡或因患职业病致残，根据有关规定享受工伤保险待遇职工或供养直系亲属人数。包括伤残人数、职业病人数、因工死亡人数、供养直系亲属人数。

3.基金收入：指根据国家有关规定，由参加工伤保险的单位按国家规定的缴费基数和缴费比例缴纳的工伤保险基金，以及通过其他形式取得的形成基金来源的款项。包括：单位缴纳的社会统筹基金收入、财政补贴收入、利息收入、其他收入。

4.基金支出：指按照国家政策规定的开支范围和开支标准从工伤保险基金中支付给参加工伤保险的人员及供养直系亲属工伤保险待遇支出及其他支出。包括工伤医疗费、伤残补助金、工亡补助金、护理费、丧葬补助费、工伤预防费用、职业康复费用和其他支出。

5.基金累计结余：指截止报告期末工伤保险基金累计结余金额。包括银行存款、财政专户、债券投资和其他。

生育保险

1.参保人数：指报告期末依据有关规定参加生育保险的职工人数。

2.基金收入：指根据国家有关规定，由参加生育保险的单位按照国家规定的缴费基数和缴费比例缴纳的生育保险基金，以及通过其他方式取得的形成基金来源的款项，包括：单位缴纳的基金收入、利息收入和其他收入。

3.基金支出：指按照国家政策规定的开支范围和开支标准，从生育保险基金中支付给参加生育保险的职工，因妊娠、分娩和计划生育手术而享受的待遇及其他支出。包括：生育津贴、医疗费用支出及其他支出。

4.基金累计结余：指截止报告期末生育保险基金累计结余金额。包括银行存款、财政专户、债券投资和其他。

离休、退休、退职人员保险福利费用　指离休、退休、退职人员实际得到的生活费用总额，包括从社会保险经办机构和单位得到的费用。

1.离休金：指按规定支付给离休人员的生活费用。

2.退休金：指按规定支付给退休人员的生活费用。

3.退职生活费：指按规定支付给退职人员的生活费用。

4.医疗卫生费：指单位直接支付给离休、退休、退职人员的医疗费、住院费以及住院伙食补助等费用。

5.其他：指离休金、退休金、退职生活费和医疗卫生费以外的其他保险福利费用，如丧葬抚恤救济费、生活补贴、物价补贴、冬季取暖补贴等。

Explanatory Notes on Main Statistical Indicators

Social Welfare Institutions refer to institutions taking care of old people without children, handicapped people and orphans. They include social welfare institutions run by civil affairs departments, children welfare institutions, social welfare institutions for mental patients, collective-owned old people's homes in rural areas, convalescent homes and community service centers with the capacity of receiving those people. This indicator reflects the input in social welfare institutions.

Number of People Taken in by Social Welfare Institutions refers to the number of old people, children, totally dependent handicapped people and mental patients taken in by social welfare institutions run by civil affairs departments and those run by collective units in urban and rural areas. This indicator reflects the capacity of social welfare institutions.

Social Welfare Enterprises are collective owned enterprises which employ the blind, deaf-mute, and other handicapped people who are able to work in cities and towns and enjoy exemption from state taxes, including welfare plants, welfare commercial services, artificial limb plants and farms, etc. This indicator reflects the preferential policies toward disabled persons.

Rural Households with Livelihood Guaranteed in Five Aspects refer to the households in which there are old people without child, orphans and handicapped people who are unable to work and without financial resources in rural areas. They are taken care of by the collective units and their food, clothing, housing, medical care, funeral expenses (or schooling for orphans) are guaranteed to be provided for. This indicator reflects the total number of disadvantageous groups of rural population.

Crude Divorce Rate refers to proportion of divorced people to the annual average population for the reference year, the formula is:

Crude Divorce rate= number of couples divorced for the reference year/annual average population x 1000 per thousand

Lawyers are certified legal workers according to law, and who are employed by legal counseling firms to act as legal advisers, agents in criminal or civil lawsuits, or defenders in criminal lawsuits, or to handle non-litigious legal affairs, to advise on matters of law or to write legal papers for others, and provide service to the public.

Notary Personnel refers to people working for notary offices including: directors, deputy director, notaries, assistant notaries, and other people providing assistance.

Notary Documents refer to the judicatory notary documents drawn up by the request of the party and are in accordance with facts and laws and following certain legal proceedings. According to usage and locality, the notary documents are divided into following 4 types: domestic notary documents, domestic economic notary documents, foreign-related civil notary documents and foreign-related economic notary documents.

Mediators refer to workers on peoples mediation committees responsible for mediating in civil disputes and cases of slight infraction of the law. They include members of the mediation committees and mediators of mediation groups. This indicator reflects the number of people engaged in meditation.

Mediation of Civil Disputes refers to number of cases made by mediation committees in mediating in civil disputes concerning civil rights and duties through persuasion and education in accordance with the provisions of law on a voluntary basis, so as to solve disputes by helping the parties involved come to an agreement and understanding, including those unsuccessful ones. This indicator reflects the workload of the mediation committees.

Acceptance of Case refers to the decision made by the people's procuratorate office on reported cases, prosecution, impeachment, surrender, self-found criminal clues or suspects after initial investigation to confirm the act of crime and to start legal proceedings of the case as criminal case.

Large Cases refer to cases involving a corruption or bribery of over 50,000 yuan, or a misappropriation of over 100,000 yuan. Cases of collectively illegal possession of public funds, unstated sources of large properties, or disguised overseas savings deposits involving 500,000 yuan, or a case that has been defined by the "Standard on Serious and Large Cases of Misconduct and Tortious that Directly Accepted by People's Procurators Office (trial)". This indicator mainly reflects number of accepted cases of job-related criminals that caused serious economic losses or extremely harmful to the society.

Key Cases refer to cases committed by government officials with a ranking of division director or county administrator. This indicator mainly reflects the recorded and spied on cases by the people's procurators offices toward government official with a ranking of division director or county administrator.

Decision on Arrest refers to decision made by people's procurators office, in accordance with laws, to arrest the suspect(s) in the cases that are accepted and to be investigated by procurators office. This indicator mainly reflects the implementation of the decision on arrest by people's procurators office.

Approval for Arrest refers to the decision made by people's procurators office, in accordance with laws and relevant facts, to approve the arrest of the suspect(s) that is proposed by the public security departments, state security departments or authority of prisons. This indicator reflects approved arrests made by people's procurators office that are proposed by related departments.

Decision on Prosecution refers to the decision made by people's procurators office, in accordance with laws and relevant facts, to institute proceedings to the people's court against the suspect(s) of criminal cases handed over by the public security departments, state security departments or authority of prisons, or by the anti-corruption departments within the procurators office. This indicator reflects the condition of the prosecutions made by people's procurators office toward the people's court.

Appeals refer to cases transferred to the appeal departments of procurator's offices after initial review by departments dealing with complaint letters and calls of the public. Included are appeals against decisions made by procurator's offices and appeals against court rules and verdicts.

Number of Labor Dispute Cases Accepted refers to the number of cases of labor dispute submitted that, after being reviewed by the labor dispute arbitration committees in line with the relevant national regulations, are accepted and registered for treatment.

Basic Pension Insurance

1.Number of staff and workers covered refer to staff and workers participating in basic pension insurance programme in line with national laws, regulations and related policies by the end of reference period, who have already had payment records in social security management agencies, including those who interrupt payment without terminating the insurance programme. Those who have registered in the programme with no payment records are not included.

2. Number of retirees participating in basic pension insurance programme refer to number of retirees participating in basic pension insurance programme by the end of reference period.

3. Revenue of basic pension insurance refer to payments made by employers and individuals participating in pension insurance

programs in accordance with the basis and proportion stipulated in state regulations, and income from other sources that become source of pension insurance fund, including the premium paid by employers and staff and works, interest income, subsidies from higher level agencies, income as transfer from subordinate agencies, transferred income, government financial subsidies and other income.

4. Expenses of basic pension insurance refer to payment made to those retired and resigned people covered in pension insurance program in terms of pension or compensation within the scope and standards of expenditure according to related national policies, and expenditure occurred due to shift of the insurance relationship or adjustment of funds among agencies, including pension for resigned people, pension for retired people, pension for people quitting jobs, various subsidies, medical fees, funeral subsidies, compensation pension, management fees for social security agencies, expenses on subsidies to lower subordinates, expenses as transfer to agencies at higher level, transferred expenditure and other expenditure.

5. Balance of basic pension insurance refers to the balance of basic pension insurance at the end of the reference period after deducting expenses from revenue.

Retired or Resigned Personnel refers to people who have formally completed formalities for their retirement or quitting work and enjoy the corresponding retirement treatments.

Basic Medical Care Insurance:

1. Number of people participating in the insurance programme refers to people participating in the basic medical care insurance programme according to related regulations by the end of reference period, including number of staff and workers and retirees participating in this insurance programme.

2. Revenue of insurance programme refer to payments made by employers and individuals participating in medical care insurance programs in accordance with the basis and proportion stipulated in state regulations, and income from other sources that become source of medical insurance fund, including income of social comprehensive funds paid by employers, income from individual accounts, government financial subsidies, interest income and other income.

3. Expenses of insurance programme refer to payment made from social comprehensive funds to those retired and resigned people covered in basic medical care insurance within the scope and standards of expenditure according to related national policies, and medical care payment made from individual accounts to staff and workers and retirees, and other expenses, including medical expenses of hospital inpatients, medical expenses for outpatients and emergency patients, payment from individual accounts and other expenditure.

4. Balance of basic medical care insurance refer to the balance of medical care insurance of social comprehensive funds and individual accounts at the end of the reference period, including bank savings, special fiscal accounts, investment in bonds and others.

Unemployment Insurance

1. Number of people covered refers to staff and workers in urban enterprises or institutions who have participated in unemployment insurance programme in line relevant policies and regulations, and other people who have participated according to local government regulations, by the end of reference period.

2. Revenue of unemployment insurance refer to payments made by employers and individuals participating in unemployment insurance programme in accordance with relevant regulations and other income contributed to this programme, including unemployment insurance premium made by employers and individuals, interest income, subsidies from higher level agencies, income as transfer from subordinate agencies, transferred income, government financial subsidies and other income.

3. Expenses of unemployment insurance refer to total expenses during the reference period to guarantee the basic livelihood of unemployed people and laid-off staff and workers and to encourage their re-employment. Included are unemployment relief, medical fees, funeral subsidies, compensation pension, training expenses, management fees for unemployment insurance agencies, subsidies to lower level agencies, expenses as transfer to higher level agencies, transferred expenditure and other expenditure.

4. Balance of unemployment insurance refer to the balance of unemployment revenue deducting unemployment expenses at the end of the reference period.

Work Injury Insurance

1. Number of people covered refers to staff and workers who have participated in work injury insurance programme in line with relevant national regulations.

2. Number of beneficiaries refers to staff and workers and their direct dependents who can, in line with relevant regulations, benefit from work injury insurance, as a result of work injury leading to disability or death of the staff/worker, or occupational disease leading to disability. Included in this category are number of injured and disabled people, number of people with occupational diseases, number of deaths at work places, and number of direct dependents.

3. Revenue of work injury insurance refer to payments made by employers participating in work injury insurance programs in accordance with the basis and proportion stipulated in state regulations, and income from other sources that become source of work injury insurance fund, including income of social comprehensive funds paid by employers, government financial subsidies, interest income and other income.

4. Expenses of work injury insurance refer to payments made from work injury insurance funds to those who participated in the work injury insurance programme and their direct dependents within the scope and standards of expenditure according to related national policies, and other expenditure, including medical fees for work injury, injury and disability subsidies, death subsidies, nursing fees, funeral subsidies, injury prevention fees, rehabilitation fees for occupational diseases and other expenditure.

5. Balance of work injury insurance refer to the balance of the work injury funds at the end of the reference period, including bank savings, special fiscal account, investment in bonds and others.

Maternity Insurance

1. Number of people covered refers to staff and workers who have participated in maternity insurance programme according to relevant regulation at the end of the reporting period.

2. Revenue of maternity insurance refers to payments made by employers participating in maternity insurance programs in accordance with the basis and proportion stipulated in state regulations, and income from other sources that become source of maternity insurance fund, including income of funds paid by employers, interest income and other income.

3. Expenses of maternity insurance refer to payments made from maternity insurance funds to staff and workers who participated in maternity insurance programme within the scope and standards of expenditure according to related national policies, expenses paid for pregnancy, child delivery or surgeries related to family planning, and other expenditure, including allowance for child bearing, medical fees and other expenditure.

4. Balance of the maternity insurance refers to the balance of the maternity insurance funds at the end of reference period, including bank savings, special fiscal account, investment in funds and others.

Insurance and Welfare Funds for Retirees refer to the total payment for living expenses actually received by retirees, including payment received from social insurance management agencies and units.

1. Pensions for retired veteran cadres refer to living expenses paid to retired veteran cadres according to related regulations.

2. Pensions for retirement refer to living expenses paid to retired staff and workers according to related regulations.

3. Living allowances for resigned staff and workers refer to living expenses paid to resigned staff and workers according to related regulation.

4. Medical care expenses refer to medical fees, hospitalization cost and per diem subsidies during hospitalizations paid by employers directly to retirees.

5. Others refer to insurance and welfare payments other than the above-mentioned payments, including funeral subsidies, living allowances, price subsidies and heating subsidies during winter.

17 城市经济与建设

Urban Economy and Construction

资料整理：刘　超　张金兰

17-1 主要城市土地面积、人口情况（2009）

LAND AREA AND PPULATION OF MAJOR MUNICIPALITIES (2009)

城市	Municipalities	土地面积 (平方公里) Land Area (sq.m)	年末总人口(万人) Total Population at Year-end (10 000 persons)	当年出生人口 (人) Births (persons)	当年死亡人口 (人) Deaths (persons)	人口密度 (人/平方公里) Population Desity (person/sq.m)
武 汉	Wuhan Municipality	8494	835.55	68285	36779	983.69
黄 石	Huangshi Municipality	237	71.54	3966	3209	3018.56
十 堰	Shiyan Municipality	1193	52.78	4867	1926	442.41
宜 昌	Yichang Municipality	4248	124.79	8791	6987	293.76
襄 樊	Xiangfan Municipality	3672	221.75	25318	8929	603.89
鄂 州	Ezhou Municipality	1504	107.24	9359	6113	713.03
荆 门	Jingmen Municipality	2171	67.92	5427	1844	312.85
孝 感	Xiaogan Municipality	946	96.82	9415	3029	1023.47
荆 州	Jingzhou Municipality	1576	116.85	8717	4576	741.43
黄 冈	Huanggang Municipality	353	36.80	3122	1217	1042.49
咸 宁	Xianning Municipality	1500	59.78	6455	2120	398.53
随 州	Suizhou Municipality	1322	64.68	6852	2041	489.26

17-2 主要城市就业情况（2009）

EMPLOYMENT OF MAJOR MUNICIPALITIES (2009)

单位：万人 (10 000 persons)

城市	Municipalities	年末单位从业人数 Employment (year-end)	#在岗职工人数 #Staff and Workers Employed	#城镇私营和个体人数 #Employment in Private Enterprises and Self-employed Individuals of Urban Areas	从业人员按三次产业分 Employment Grouped by Type of Industry		
					第一产业 Primary Industry	第二产业 Secondary Industry	第三产业 Tertiary Industry
武 汉	Wuhan Municipality	175.74		128.56	0.92	88.58	86.24
黄 石	Huangshi Municipality	19.41	18.87	14.29	0.08	11.94	7.39
十 堰	Shiyan Municipality	24.36	24.00	14.71	0.06	15.10	9.20
宜 昌	Yichang Municipality	21.62	21.30	27.80	0.06	11.81	9.75
襄 樊	Xiangfan Municipality	21.13	16.68	23.50	0.36	8.65	12.12
鄂 州	Ezhou Municipality	16.74	16.12	9.06	0.03	10.58	6.13
荆 门	Jingmen Municipality	11.75	7.57	3.53	0.15	5.14	6.46
孝 感	Xiaogan Municipality	13.22	11.64	9.35	0.86	7.35	5.01
荆 州	Jingzhou Municipality	16.15	13.51	8.97	2.34	7.82	5.99
黄 冈	Huanggang Municipality	5.46	5.12	3.13	0.05	2.21	3.20
咸 宁	Xianning Municipality	6.25	6.54	5.17		1.46	4.79
随 州	Suizhou Municipality	5.06	4.80	20.54		2.24	2.82

17-3 主要城市地区生产总值及指数（2009）
GROSS DOMESTIC PRODUCTS OF MAJOR MUNICIPALITIES (2009)

城 市	Municipalities	地区生产总值(亿元) Gross Domestic Product (100 million yuan)	第一产业 Primary Industry	第二产业 Secondary Industry	第三产业 Tertiary Industry	人均地区生产总值(元) Per Capita GDP(yuan)	地区生产总值指数(上年=100) GDP Index (preceding year=100)	人均地区生产总值指数(上年=100) Per Capita Index (preceding year=100)
武 汉	Wuhan Municipality	4620.86	149.06	2142.14	2329.66	51144	116.69	115.48
黄 石	Huangshi Municipality	303.84	2.55	184.64	116.65	37336	104.64	104.50
十 堰	Shiyan Municipality	327.04	2.61	171.73	152.70	63616	112.10	122.48
宜 昌	Yichang Municipality	649.93	29.59	409.59	210.75	48593	121.40	137.31
襄 樊	Xiangfan Municipality	712.32	59.40	350.95	301.97	32284	122.59	121.12
鄂 州	Ezhou Municipality	323.71	43.98	179.21	100.52	31310	119.98	119.77
荆 门	Jingmen Municipality	211.00	19.73	118.59	72.68	37190	117.85	121.52
孝 感	Xiaogan Municipality	140.08	16.37	65.58	58.13	16324	119.52	123.02
荆 州	Jingzhou Municipality	249.06	32.59	124.74	91.73	20265	117.88	108.22
黄 冈	Huanggang Municipality	80.17	7.85	40.65	31.67	23414	110.17	132.64
咸 宁	Xianning Municipality	109.28	14.90	47.90	46.48	17969	110.12	98.50
随 州	Suizhou Municipality	144.80	12.14	69.85	62.81	22457	115.56	115.56

17-4 主要城市固定资产投资（2009）
INVESTMENT IN FIXED ASSETS OF MAJOR MUNICIPALITIES (2009)

单位：亿元 (100 million yuan)

城市	Municipalities	城镇固定资产投资 Urban Investment in Fixed Assets	房地产开发投资 Investment in Real Estate	#住宅 #Residential Buildings	新增固定资产 Newly Increased Fixed Assets	商品房屋销售建筑面积(万平方米) Construction Floor Space of Commercial House Sold (10 000 sq.m)	#住宅 #Residential Buildings
武 汉	Wuhan Municipality	2921.76	778.59	498.04	1882.39	1086.99	1041.39
黄 石	Huangshi Municipality	173.08	17.56	12.10	121.32	61.36	57.78
十 堰	Shiyan Municipality	104.06	27.02	15.71	56.32	112.59	109.69
宜 昌	Yichang Municipality	370.15	66.14	42.11	217.06	150.73	143.07
襄 樊	Xiangfan Municipality	308.48	37.60	25.80	180.37	144.70	123.55
鄂 州	Ezhou Municipality	213.00	8.10	7.20	115.20	48.75	48.43
荆 门	Jingmen Municipality	105.42	19.08	14.84	75.10	67.13	65.22
孝 感	Xiaogan Municipality	82.10	12.91	11.59	62.18	69.59	65.39
荆 州	Jingzhou Municipality	178.15	19.46	16.92	114.32	66.53	66.74
黄 冈	Huanggang Municipality	76.14	10.14	7.46	77.83	36.78	34.31
咸 宁	Xianning Municipality	90.52	17.13	13.26	77.66	50.14	47.42
随 州	Suizhou Municipality	76.68	14.14	10.42	91.06	90.56	84.55

17-5 主要城市工业基本情况（2009）
BASIC STATISTICS ON INDUSTRY OF MAJOR MUNICIPALITIES (2009)

单位：亿元 (100 million yuan)

城市	Municipalities	工业企业单位数(个) Number of Industrial Enterprises (unit)	工业增加值 Value Added of Industry	主营业务收入 Major Business Income	利润总额 Total Profits
武 汉	Wuhan Municipality	2517	1772.14	5980.68	296.44
黄 石	Huangshi Municipality	301	170.84	658.83	24.04
十 堰	Shiyan Municipality	365	160.40	618.84	107.13
宜 昌	Yichang Municipality	338	372.64	729.97	161.02
襄 樊	Xiangfan Municipality	545	311.72	818.74	45.93
鄂 州	Ezhou Municipality	466	158.42	414.09	24.41
荆 门	Jingmen Municipality	337	111.17	462.82	25.45
孝 感	Xiaogan Municipality	174	56.69	90.74	6.36
荆 州	Jingzhou Municipality	473	112.78	303.97	15.03
黄 冈	Huanggang Municipality	131	31.45	69.45	4.01
咸 宁	Xianning Municipality	197	45.64	126.68	10.38
随 州	Suizhou Municipality	166	64.83	146.46	17.82

17-6 主要城市工业总产值（2009）
GROSS OUTPUT VALUE OF INDUSTRY OF MAJOR MUNICIPALITY (2009)

单位：亿元 (100 million yuan)

城市	Municipalities	工业总产值 Total Value of Industry	内资企业 Inner Funded Enterprises	外商港澳台投资企业 Foreign, Hongkong, Macao and Taiwan Funded Enterprises	#国有企业 #State-owned Enterprise
武 汉	Wuhan Municipality	5798.88	4378.83	1420.05	2549.65
黄 石	Huangshi Municipality	569.87	343.54	226.33	154.69
十 堰	Shiyan Municipality	639.77	330.67	309.10	62.22
宜 昌	Yichang Municipality	747.08	693.86	53.22	160.26
襄 樊	Xiangfan Municipality	1001.91	637.12	364.79	142.76
鄂 州	Ezhou Municipality	423.03	399.00	24.03	65.89
荆 门	Jingmen Municipality	439.05	427.40	11.66	28.72
孝 感	Xiaogan Municipality	93.53	70.08	23.44	20.16
荆 州	Jingzhou Municipality	328.59	263.90	64.69	40.26
黄 冈	Huanggang Municipality	72.71	62.82	9.89	19.90
咸 宁	Xianning Municipality	138.02	108.97	29.05	4.22
随 州	Suizhou Municipality	156.93	126.07	30.86	8.08

17-7 主要城市财政收支（2009）
GOVERNMENT REVENUE AND EXPENDITURES OF MAJOR MUNICIPALITIES (2009)

单位：亿元 (100 million yuan)

城市	Municipalities	地方财政一般预算收入 Local Financial General Budgetary Revenue	#各项税收 #Taxes	地方财政一般预算支出 Local Financial General Budgetary Expenditures	#文教科卫事业费 #Expenditures for Culture, Education, Science & Technology and Health Care	#社会保障和就业支出 #Subsides Expenditures for Social Security	#城乡社区事务支出 #Expenditures for City Maintenance
武 汉	Wuhan Municipality	316.07	247.95	503.64	115.94	86.60	55.99
黄 石	Huangshi Municipality	15.42	11.15	40.92	6.83	3.14	1.30
十 堰	Shiyan Municipality	14.42	13.00	31.49	8.22	5.74	2.10
宜 昌	Yichang Municipality	30.18	25.62	68.20	15.81	8.91	6.46
襄 樊	Xiangfan Municipality	23.01	19.28	69.74	15.16	16.18	5.09
鄂 州	Ezhou Municipality	13.60	10.40	35.67	8.52	4.55	4.10
荆 门	Jingmen Municipality	9.58	7.10	29.75	5.63	4.94	0.88
孝 感	Xiaogan Municipality	8.37	5.60	29.18	6.70	5.63	1.87
荆 州	Jingzhou Municipality	11.64	8.92	24.39	6.55	2.28	1.33
黄 冈	Huanggang Municipality	5.59	3.22	19.98	5.51	2.56	0.57
咸 宁	Xianning Municipality	7.21	4.69	26.32	5.38	2.09	0.58
随 州	Suizhou Municipality	4.30	3.08	22.07	4.87	4.82	0.50

17-8 主要城市金融机构存贷款余额（2009）
DEPOSITS AND LOANS BALANCE OF BANKING INSTITUTIONS OF MAJOR MUNICIPALITIES (2009)

单位：亿元 (100 million yuan)

城市	Municipalities	存款余额 Deposit Balance	#居民储蓄存款 #Savings Deposits from Residents	贷款余额 Loans Balance
武 汉	Wuhan Municipality	8761.62	3010.11	7535.32
黄 石	Huangshi Municipality	372.39	187.53	278.27
十 堰	Shiyan Municipality	399.58	221.80	198.52
宜 昌	Yichang Municipality	1182.79	328.60	1064.41
襄 樊	Xiangfan Municipality	627.88	375.43	351.26
鄂 州	Ezhou Municipality	202.51	121.09	99.56
荆 门	Jingmen Municipality	266.27	205.02	160.29
孝 感	Xiaogan Municipality	222.76	129.76	116.94
荆 州	Jingzhou Municipality	359.52	241.80	214.90
黄 冈	Huanggang Municipality	123.77	72.85	68.24
咸 宁	Xianning Municipality	122.83	67.10	83.15
随 州	Suizhou Municipality	245.78	173.25	97.12

17-9 主要城市贸易、外经（2009）
DOMESTIC TRADE AND FOREIGN TRADE AND ECONOMY OF MAJOR MUNICIPALITIES (2009)

城市	Municipalities	社会消费品零售总额(亿元) Total Retail Sales of consumer Goods (100 million yuan)	进出口总额全市(亿美元) Total Import and Export (USD 100 million)	出口 Imports	进口 Exports	实际外商直接投资(亿美元) ActualForeign Direct Investment (USD 100 million)
武 汉	Wuhan Municipality	2164.09	114.72	58.25	56.47	29.35
黄 石	Huangshi Municipality	133.23	11.46	4.73	6.73	3.10
十 堰	Shiyan Municipality	135.94	2.09	1.89	0.20	0.38
宜 昌	Yichang Municipality	253.75	10.34	7.76	2.58	1.16
襄 樊	Xiangfan Municipality	278.84	4.33	3.29	1.04	1.54
鄂 州	Ezhou Municipality	126.68	1.69	0.74	0.95	1.05
荆 门	Jingmen Municipality	83.65	2.29	1.73	0.56	0.57
孝 感	Xiaogan Municipality	57.66	2.23	1.92	0.31	0.43
荆 州	Jingzhou Municipality	286.99	5.74	4.48	1.26	0.44
黄 冈	Huanggang Municipality	50.71	4.79	4.06	0.73	0.71
咸 宁	Xianning Municipality	47.69	1.22	0.94	0.28	0.59
随 州	Suizhou Municipality	80.81	5.60	4.65	0.95	0.28

17-10 主要城市邮电、电力（2009）
POST AND TELECOMMUNICATIONS SERVICES AND POWER CONSUMPTION OF MAJOR MUNICIPALITIES (2009)

城市	Municipalities	邮电业务收入(全市)(亿元) Revenue from Posts and Telecommunication Services(100 million yuan)	本地电话用户(万户) Telephones (10 000 Subscribers)	移动电话用户(万户) Mobile Telephones (10 000 Subscribers)	国际互联网用户(万户) Internet Service (10 000 Subscribers)	全年用电量(亿千瓦小时) Power Consumption (100 million kWh)	#居生活用电 #Urban and Rural Residents Power Consumption
武 汉	Wuhan Municipality	112.40	339.00	1037.00	166.00	310.27	56.76
黄 石	Huangshi Municipality	27.99	38.50	94.20	12.50	49.66	3.90
十 堰	Shiyan Municipality	12.56	27.26	96.47	9.28	27.98	3.88
宜 昌	Yichang Municipality	20.63	32.70	97.01	14.94	64.04	5.89
襄 樊	Xiangfan Municipality	19.62	27.88	129.04	19.19	33.89	8.05
鄂 州	Ezhou Municipality	5.36	18.12	63.27	7.19	38.77	3.41
荆 门	Jingmen Municipality	11.13	13.73	48.41	7.66	22.87	2.33
孝 感	Xiaogan Municipality	11.20	15.36	49.41	3.95	4.45	2.21
荆 州	Jingzhou Municipality	24.96	28.16	82.26	12.46	25.19	5.15
黄 冈	Huanggang Municipality	17.98	9.11	24.10	2.40	5.50	1.78
咸 宁	Xianning Municipality	9.37	13.05	33.72	5.35	11.89	2.15
随 州	Suizhou Municipality	9.50	9.40	86.30	5.87	10.92	3.27

17-11 主要城市环境保护（2009）
ENVIRONMENTAL PROTECTION OF MAJOR MUNICIPALITIES (2009)

城市	Municipalities	工业废水排放达标量(亿吨) Industrial Waste Water Discharged (100 million tons)	工业二氧化硫排放量(万吨) Industrial Sulphur Dioxide Emission (100 million tons)	城市环境基础设施建设本年投资(亿元) Investment on City Environmental Infrastruction Construction (100 million yuan)	“三废”综合利用产品产值(亿元) Output Value of Products Made from Comprehensive Utilization of Waste Water Solid Wasted (100 million yuan)
武汉	Wuhan Municipality	2.23	11.46	366.52	21.18
黄石	Huangshi Municipality	0.76	8.36	6.90	10.94
十堰	Shiyan Municipality	0.27	2.51	6.31	3.74
宜昌	Yichang Municipality	1.22	3.49	13.04	7.29
襄樊	Xiangfan Municipality	1.07	6.48	3.01	4.72
鄂州	Ezhou Municipality	0.30	3.43	6.00	5.21
荆门	Jingmen Municipality	0.59	4.21	1.14	9.73
孝感	Xiaogan Municipality	0.49	4.17	1.48	2.37
荆州	Jingzhou Municipality	0.51	3.16	1.38	2.42
黄冈	Huanggang Municipality	0.43	1.17	1.38	2.35
咸宁	Xianning Municipality	0.27	1.38	6.87	1.16
随州	Suizhou Municipality	0.15	0.79	0.51	0.39

17-12 主要城市居民收支情况（2009）
INCOME AND EXPENDITURES OF MAJOR MUNICIPALITY HOUSEHOLDS (2009)

单位：元 (yuan)

城市	Municipalities	在岗职工平均工资 Average Wages of Employed Staff and Workers	城镇居民人均可支配收入 Per Capita Disposable Income of Urban Residents	城镇居民人均消费性支出 Per Capita Living Expenditure of Urban Residents	#食品 #Food	#衣着用品 #Clothing Articles	#家庭设备、用品及服务 #Households Facilities, Articles and Servicess
武汉	Wuhan Municipality		18385	12710	5110	1420	1052
黄石	Huangshi Municipality	17145	13897	10179	4081	1144	657
十堰	Shiyan Municipality	22970	14454	11028	3867	1590	766
宜昌	Yichang Municipality	22164	14058	10577	3735	1294	781
襄樊	Xiangfan Municipality	23629	13409	10145	3993	1220	695
鄂州	Ezhou Municipality	12721	13408	10056	4085	1265	781
荆门	Jingmen Municipality	25575	13857	10595	3585	1258	661
孝感	Xiaogan Municipality	18316	13562	9953	3889	1322	420
荆州	Jingzhou Municipality	21318	13304	9181	4070	941	563
黄冈	Huanggang Municipality	17558	13636	8865	3041	1157	647
咸宁	Xianning Municipality	20991	12589	10042	3752	1060	684
随州	Suizhou Municipality	23170	12349	8113	3363	1302	385

17-13 主要城市居民消费支出、物价（2009）

LIVING EXPENDITURES AND PRICE OF MAJOR MUNICIPALITY HOUSEHOLDS (2009)

单位：元 (yuan)

城市	Municipalities	城镇居民人均消费性支出 Per Capita Living Expenditures for Consumption of Urban Residents				人均住房建筑面积(平方米) Per Capita Utility Floor Space of Residential Buildings (sq.m)	居民消费价格指数(上年=100) Consumer Price Index (preceding year=100)
		#医疗保健 #Medicine and Medicine and Medical Service	#交通和通讯 #Transport and Telecom-munication	#娱乐、教育、文化服务 #Recreation,Education and Cultural Services	#居住 #Residence		
武汉	Wuhan Municipality	889	1283	1407	1150	26.00	99.40
黄石	Huangshi Municipality	558	824	1695	849	30.03	99.53
十堰	Shiyan Municipality	673	1129	1722	837	28.72	100.84
宜昌	Yichang Municipality	630	1510	1520	796	28.03	100.10
襄樊	Xiangfan Municipality	872	704	1172	1147	28.85	98.74
鄂州	Ezhou Municipality	487	784	1125	1327	32.13	100.50
荆门	Jingmen Municipality	1079	1571	1286	891	39.40	100.10
孝感	Xiaogan Municipality	547	1140	1739	582	33.60	99.20
荆州	Jingzhou Municipality	851	558	915	1032	28.65	98.80
黄冈	Huanggang Municipality	605	1037	1621	612	43.00	100.50
咸宁	Xianning Municipality	573	1614	1051	959	35.48	99.30
随州	Suizhou Municipality	315	678	999	854	40.50	101.20

17-14 主要城市文教、科技、卫生（2009）

CULTURE, EDUCATION, SCIENCE AND TECHNOLOGY AND PUBLIC HEALTH OF MAJOR MUNICIPALITIES (2009)

城市	Municipalities	高等学校在校学生数(万人) Number of Students Enrolled in Institutions of Higher Education (10 000 persons)	从事科技活动人员数(人) Number of Scientific and technical Personel (person)	公共图书馆图书藏量(万册) Total Volume of Collection of Public Libraries (10 000 volumes)	医院、卫生院数(个) Number of Health Care Institutions (unit)	医院、卫生院数床位数(万张) Number of Beds In Health Care Intitutions (10 000 units)	执业(助理)医师(万人) Practioner Doctors (Assitant) (10 000 persons)
武汉	Wuhan Municipality	84.63	71000	997.90	227	4.29	2.40
黄石	Huangshi Municipality	3.22	15090	83.70	33	0.60	0.23
十堰	Shiyan Municipality	3.25	44221	58.20	29	0.56	0.20
宜昌	Yichang Municipality	4.91	5408	88.70	45	0.67	0.40
襄樊	Xiangfan Municipality	3.68	15890	74.80	68	0.83	0.39
鄂州	Ezhou Municipality	0.93	1149	35.80	43	0.36	0.26
荆门	Jingmen Municipality	1.84	1901	29.70	29	0.39	0.18
孝感	Xiaogan Municipality	3.17	10167	36.60	25	0.28	0.16
荆州	Jingzhou Municipality	11.74	16895	54.60	41	0.64	0.26
黄冈	Huanggang Municipality	3.83	400	46.00	18	0.22	0.11
咸宁	Xianning Municipality	2.54	1405	19.40	15	0.18	0.09
随州	Suizhou Municipality	0.66	696	121.90	42	0.21	0.13

主要统计指标解释

供水综合生产能力 指按供水设施取水、净化、送水、出厂输水干管等环节设计能力计算的综合生产能力。包括在原设计能力的基础上，经挖、革、改增加的生产能力。计算时，以四个环节中最薄弱的环节为主确定能力。

年末供水管道长度 指从送水泵至用户水表之间所有管道的长度。不包括新安装尚未使用的管道。

全年供水总量 指报告期供水企业(单位)供出的全部水量。包括有效供水量和漏损水量。

生活用水量 包括公共服务用水和居民家庭用水。公共服务用水指为城市社会公共生活服务的用水。包括行政事业单位、部队营区和公共设施服务、社会服务业、批发零售贸易业、旅馆饮食业以及其他公共服务业等单位的用水。居民家庭用水指城市范围内所有居民家庭的日常生活用水。包括城市居民、农民家庭、公共供水站用水。

用水普及率 指城市用水人口数与城市人口总数的比率。计算公式:

$$用水普及率=\frac{城市用水人口数}{城市人口总数}\times 100\%$$

供气管道长度 指报告期末从气源厂压缩机的出口或门站出口至各类用户引入管之间的全部已经通气投入使用的管道长度。不包括煤气生产厂、输配站、液化气储存站、灌瓶站、储配站、气化站、混气站、供应站等厂(站)内的管道。

全年供气总量 指全年燃气企业(单位)向用户供应的燃气数量。包括销售量和损失量。

用气普及率 指报告期末使用燃气的城市人口数与城市人口总数的比率。计算公式为:

$$用气普及率=\frac{城市用气人口数}{城市人口总数}\times 100\%$$

城市供热能力 指供热企业(单位)向城市热用户输送热能的设计能力。

城市供热总量 指在报告期供热企业(单位)向城市热用户输送全部蒸汽和热水的总热量。

城市供热管道长度 指从各类热源到热用户建筑物接入口之间的全部蒸汽和热水的管道长度。不包括各类热源厂内部的管道长度。

年末道路长度 指年末道路长度和与道路相通的广场、桥梁、隧道的长度，按车行道中心线计算。在统计时只统计路面宽度在3.5米(含3.5米)以上的各种铺装道路，包括开放型工业区和住宅区道路在内。

城市桥梁 指为跨越天然或人工障碍物而修建的构筑物。包括跨河桥、立交桥、人行天桥以及人行地下通道等。包括永久性桥和半永久性桥。

城市排水管道长度 指所有排水总管、干管、支管、检查井及连接井进出口等长度之和。

城市污水日处理能力 指污水处理厂(或处理装置)每昼夜处理污水量的设计能力。

年末运营车数 指年末公交企业(单位)用于运营业务的全部车辆数。以企业(单位)固定资产台帐中已投入运营的车辆数为准。

城市园林绿地面积 指报告期末用作园林和绿化的各种绿地面积。包括公共绿地、居住区绿地、单位附属绿地、防护绿地、生产绿地、道路绿地和风景林地面积。不包括:

1.屋顶绿化、垂直绿化、阳台绿化和室内绿化。

2.以物质生产为主的林地、耕地、牧草地、果园和竹园等。

3.城市总体规划中不列入绿地的水域。

公共绿地　指向公众开放的市级、区级、居住区级各类公园、街旁游园，包括其范围内的水域。其中居住区级公园应不小于 1 万平方米，街旁游园的宽度不小于 8 米，面积不小于 400 平方米。

Explanatory Notes on Main Statistical Indicators

Production Capacity of Water Supply refers to the designed comprehensive production capacity of water facilities, covering the 4 links of water collection, purification, conveyance, and outflow through trunk pipelines. Increase capacity through transformation and innovation projects are included as well. The capacity is determined mainly on the weakest of the above-mentioned 4 links.

Length of Water Supply Pipelines at the Year-end refers to the total length of all the pipelines between the water pumps and the user 扭 water meters, excluding pipelines newly installed but not used yet.

Annual Volume of Water Supply refers to the total volume of water supplied by water-works (units) during the reference period, including both the effective water supply and loss during the water supply.

Consumption of Water for Residential Use refers to the water consumption of households for daily life and the water consumption of public service facilities. The latter refers to water consumption for urban public services, including the consumption of government agencies and public institutions, military barracks, public facilities, wholesale and retail outlets, restaurants, hotels, and other units providing public services. Household water consumption refers to consumption of water for daily life of all households in the boundary of cities, including households of urban residents and farmers, and public water supply stations.

Percentage of Urban Population with Access to Tap Water refers to the ratio of the urban population with access to tap water to the total urban population. The formula is:

Percentage of population with access to tap water= (Urban population with access to tap water) / (Urban population)×100%

Length of Gas Pipelines refers to the total length of pipelines in use between the outlet of the compressor of gas-work or outlet of gas stations and the leading pipe of users, excluding pipelines within gasworks, delivery stations, LPG storage stations, refilling stations, gas-mixing stations and supply stations.

Volume of Gas Supply refers to the total volume of gas provided to users by gas-producing enterprises (units) in a year, including the volume sold and the volume lost.

Percentage of Urban Population with Access to Gas refers to the ratio of the urban population with access to gas to the total urban population at the end of the reference period. The formula is:

Percentage of population with access to gas = (Urban population with access to gas / Urban population) x 100%

Heating Capacity in Urban Area refers to the designed capacity of heating enterprises (units) in supplying heating energy to urban users during the reference period.

Quantity of Heat Supplied in Urban Area refers to the total quantity of heat from steam and hot water supplied to urban users by heating enterprises (units) during the reference period.

Length of Heating Pipelines refers to the total length of steam or hot water pipelines for sources of heat to the leading pipelines of the buildings of the users, excluding internal pipelines in heat generating enterprises.

Length of Paved Roads at the Year-end refers to the length of roads with paved surface including squares bridges and tunnels connected with roads by the end of the year. Length of the roads is measured by the central lines for vehicles for paved roads with a width of 3.5 meters and over, including roads in open-ended factory compounds and residential quarters.

Urban Bridges refer to bridges built to cross over natural or man-made barriers, including bridges over rivers, overpasses for traffic and for pedestrian, underpasses for pedestrian, etc. Both permanent and semi-permanent bridges are included.

Length of Urban Sewage Pipes refers to the total length of general drainage, trunks. branch and inspection wells, connection wells, inlets and outlets, etc.

Daily Disposal Capacity of Urban Sewage refers to the designed 24 hour capacity of sewage disposal by the sewage treatment works or facilities.

Number of Vehicles under Operation at the Year-end refers to the total number of vehicles under operation by public transport enterprises (units) at the end of the year, based on the records of operational vehicles by the enterprises (units).

Area of Urban Gardens and Green Areas refers to the total area occupied for green projects at the end of the reference period, including public green land, green land in residential quarters, green land attached to institutions, protection green land, production green land, roadside green land and forest in scenic spots. It does not include the following:

(1) Greenery and plants on roofs, balconies, indoors and vertical green areas;

(2) Forest, cultivated land, grassland, orchards and bamboo grooves that are for production purpose; and

(3) Water areas that are not included in urban master plan as green land.

Public Green Area refers to green areas open to the public such as municipal, community and neighborhood parks and roadside parks, including waters within parks. Neighborhood parks should occupy an area larger than 10,000 square meters, and the width of roadside parks should occupy an area larger than 400 square meters, with a width of more that 8 meters.

18 企业景气及重点企业集团

General Operating Situation of Enterprises and Dey Enterprise Groups

资料整理：彭　刚　叶祯祥　蔡利平

18-1 企业家信心指数
ENTERPRENEUR EXPECTATION INDICES

指 标	Item	2007			
		一季度 the First Quarter	二季度 the Second Quarter	三季度 the Third Quarter	四季度 the Fourth Quarter
企业家信心指数	**Enterpreneur Expectation Indices**	**139.28**	**140.46**	**142.64**	**139.51**
一、按行业门类分	Grouped by Sector				
(一)工业	Industry	139.79	143.07	146.32	140.26
#采掘业	#Mining and Quarrying	119.73	140.35	137.78	156.14
制造业	Manufacturing	142.63	145.84	148.67	143.15
电力、煤气及水生产供应	Electric Power,Gas and Water	120.15	122.02	133.65	117.58
(二)建筑业	Construction	137.88	136.86	141.5	140.84
(三)交通运输、仓储及邮电通信业	Transportation, Storage and Post	135.89	127.54	131.69	130.71
(四)批发和零售业	Wholesale and Retail Sales	147.27	147.04	146.67	153.14
(五)房地产业	Real Estate	140.83	147.13	152.61	139.55
(六)社会服务业	Social Service	144.83	144.83	132.14	132.14
(七)信息传输、计算机服务和软件	Information Transmmision, Service and Catering	109.84	109.44	103.46	105.32
(八)住宿和餐饮业	Service and Software	135.47	131.97	139.62	141.95
二、按企业登记注册类型分	Grouped by Type of Registration				
(一)国有企业	State-owned	140.6	140.81	141.78	142.64
(二)集体企业	Collective-owned	108.4	122.9	108.39	114.11
(三)股份合作企业	Share Holding Cooperative	100	131.58	136.84	136.84
(四)有限责任公司	Responsibility Co. Ltd.	132.75	132.72	132.91	127.36
(五)股份有限公司	Share Holding Co. Ltd.	143.91	151.69	148.06	145.14
(六)私营企业	Private	144.16	146.46	142.13	148.28
(七)外商及港、澳、台投资企业	Foreign and Hongkong, Macao, Taiwan Funded	139.89	136.42	169.27	162.03
三、按企业规模分	Grouped by Scale of Enterprises				
特大型及大型	Oversize and Large	154.99	162.65	171.67	167.52
中小型	Medium and Small	133.79	133.14	133.47	130.09
中 型	Medium	136.73	133.22	133.64	130.5
小 型	Small	130.15	133.04	133.26	129.59
附：国家重点联系企业	Major Enterprises Related with the State	178.6	181.99	188.2	190.36
国家试点企业集团成员	Member of Experimental Unit of Enterprise Groups	163.59	163.59	200	200
乡镇企业	Town-owned Enterprises	134.74	140.48	136.2	133.27
上市公司	Enterprises in the Stock Market	142.83	173.69	173.72	175.64
国有控股企业	State Share Holding	144.23	147.5	149.1	145.66

18-1 续表 1 continued

指 标	Item	2008			
		一季度 the First Quarter	二季度 the Second Quarter	三季度 the Third Quarter	四季度 the Fourth Quarter
企业家信心指数	**Enterpreneur Expectation Indices**	**133.1**	**133.8**	**124.6**	**96.7**
一、按行业门类分	Grouped by Sector				
(一)工业	Industry	137.1	137.8	125.3	83.7
#采掘业	#Mining and Quarrying	158.8	157.8	130.3	65.2
制造业	Manufacturing	138.8	139.8	126.5	84.4
电力、煤气及水生产供应	Electric Power,Gas and Water	124.3	124.8	122.6	89.5
(二)建筑业	Construction	148	133.4	133.7	125.3
(三)交通运输、仓储及邮电通信业	Transportation, Storage and Post	130.8	122.5	119	107.4
(四)批发和零售业	Wholesale and Retail Sales	111.1	126.5	124.9	120.3
(五)房地产业	Real Estate	140.3	128.5	109	81
(六)社会服务业	Social Service	117.9	134.5	126.7	127.6
(七)信息传输、计算机服务和软件	Information Transmmision, Service and Catering	115.5	125.4	115.4	109
(八)住宿和餐饮业	Service and Software	141.5	133.8	134	113.5
二、按企业登记注册类型分	Grouped by Type of Registration				
(一)国有企业	State-owned	125.4	124.2	126.1	100
(二)集体企业	Collective-owned	119.5	113.4	108.2	102.3
(三)股份合作企业	Share Holding Cooperative	106.7	106.3	98.9	85.4
(四)有限责任公司	Responsibility Co. Ltd.	134.8	126.9	116.7	95
(五)股份有限公司	Share Holding Co. Ltd.	132.5	151.2	139.6	94.9
(六)私营企业	Private	147	147.1	132.9	119.8
(七)外商及港、澳、台投资企业	Foreign and Hongkong, Macao, Taiwan Funded	156.6	149.1	128.7	82.8
三、按企业规模分	Grouped by Scale of Enterprises				
特大型及大型	Oversize and Large	137.6	146.4	135.9	82.3
中小型	Medium and Small	131.7	128.5	120.5	101
中 型	Medium	133.3	131.8	121.5	100.4
小 型	Small	129.7	124.3	119.2	101.9
附：国家重点联系企业	Major Enterprises Related with the State	165.1	160.1	146.1	89
国家试点企业集团成员	Member of Experimental Unit of Enterprise Groups	148.1	148.1	148.1	116.2
乡镇企业	Town-owned Enterprises	133.3	130	124.8	104.7
上市公司	Enterprises in the Stock Market	153.9	177.4	165.1	101.2
国有控股企业	State Share Holding	130.3	135.4	132.9	99.8

18-1 续表 2 continued

指 标	Item	2009			
		一季度 the First Quarter	二季度 the Second Quarter	三季度 the Third Quarter	四季度 the Fourth Quarter
企业家信心指数	**Enterpreneur Expectation Indices**	**105**	**109**	**121.7**	**122.8**
一、按行业门类分	Grouped by Sector				
(一)工业	Industry	97	102.4	116.4	117
#采掘业	#Mining and Quarrying	65.2	67.8	94.4	122.2
制造业	Manufacturing	98.5	102.7	117.7	117.5
电力、煤气及水生产供应	Electric Power,Gas and Water	96.9	109.4	108.1	110.1
(二)建筑业	Construction	128.4	128.2	135.5	142.7
(三)交通运输、仓储及邮电通信业	Transportation, Storage and Post	112.1	107.5	123	116.5
(四)批发和零售业	Wholesale and Retail Sales	114.7	120.9	128.8	135.2
(五)房地产业	Real Estate	90.8	110.6	122.3	132.2
(六)社会服务业	Social Service	131	127.6	137.9	124.1
(七)信息传输、计算机服务和软件	Information Transmmision, Service and Catering	110.7	107.6	121.1	111.5
(八)住宿和餐饮业	Service and Software	116.3	108.4	128.6	137.2
二、按企业登记注册类型分	Grouped by Type of Registration				
(一)国有企业	State-owned	104.1	111.3	118.5	122.8
(二)集体企业	Collective-owned	102	85.3	99.9	99.9
(三)股份合作企业	Share Holding Cooperative	98.9	85.7	78.6	78.6
(四)有限责任公司	Responsibility Co. Ltd.	107.1	106	117.2	120.6
(五)股份有限公司	Share Holding Co. Ltd.	106.6	111.9	129.5	131.3
(六)私营企业	Private	114.5	116.5	124.9	126.3
(七)外商及港、澳、台投资企业	Foreign and Hongkong, Macao, Taiwan Funded	93	106.6	145.8	126
三、按企业规模分	Grouped by Scale of Enterprises				
特大型及大型	Oversize and Large	89.4	94.7	130	113.6
中小型	Medium and Small	109.2	109.5	119.8	123.4
中 型	Medium	111.1	116.4	126.5	131.4
小 型	Small	106.6	102.3	112.9	115
附：国家重点企业	Major Enterprises Related with the State	91.1	92.9	129.6	99.2
国家试点企业集团成员	Member of Experimental Unit of Enterprise Groups	81.5	81.5	144.7	81.5
乡镇企业	Town-owned Enterprises	99.2	90.6	111.8	113.2
上市公司	Enterprises in the Stock Market	86.5	93.7	133.3	133.8
国有控股企业	State Share Holding	106.8	112.6	123.4	128.4

18-2 企业景气指数

BUSINESS CLIMATE INDICES

指 标	Item	2007			
		一季度 the First Quarter	二季度 the Second Quarter	三季度 the Third Quarter	四季度 the Fourth Quarter
企业景气指数	**Business Clemate Indices**	**133.72**	**138.1**	**136.11**	**138.12**
一、按行业门类分	Grouped by Sector				
(一)工业	Industry	132.56	140.97	137.78	138.85
#采掘业	#Mining and Quarrying	103.07	155.26	139.54	155.33
制造业	Manufacturing	134.94	142.54	139.06	140.72
电力、煤气及水生产供应	Electric Power,Gas and Water	121.2	127.8	132.16	122.51
(二)建筑业	Construction	127.26	131.86	132.08	144.56
(三)交通运输、仓储及邮电通信业	Transportation, Storage and Post	130.21	131.58	121.28	124.95
(四)批发和零售业	Wholesale and Retail Sales	150.34	152.23	152.93	154.6
(五)房地产业	Real Estate	134.61	136.89	138.96	138.74
(六)社会服务业	Social Service	124.14	131.03	135.71	132.14
(七)信息传输、计算机服务和软件	Information Transmmision, Service and Catering	135.06	104.6	109.57	105.08
(八)住宿和餐饮业	Service and Software	126.05	116.86	117.33	124.15
二、按企业登记注册类型分	Grouped by Type of Registration				
(一)国有企业	State-owned	134.88	140.33	141.7	141.63
(二)集体企业	Collective-owned	106.93	118.84	100.6	110
(三)股份合作企业	Share Holding Cooperative	115.79	126.32	115.79	121.05
(四)有限责任公司	Responsibility Co. Ltd.	127.61	130.43	130.97	129.39
(五)股份有限公司	Share Holding Co. Ltd.	149.09	152.54	141.7	138.51
(六)私营企业	Private	131.69	138.06	133.66	137.27
(七)外商及港、澳、台投资企业	Foreign and Hongkong, Macao, Taiwan Funded	132.07	135.85	131.73	161.85
三、按企业规模分	Grouped by Scale of Enterprises				
特大型及大型	Oversize and Large	163.73	168.4	163.89	170.7
中小型	Medium and Small	122.91	127.78	126.22	126.1
中 型	Medium	124.43	129.51	126.62	125.88
小 型	Small	121.04	125.65	125.74	126.38
附：国家重点联系企业	Major Enterprises Related with the State	179.3	196.98	191.83	198.17
国家试点企业集团成员	Member of Experimental Unit of Enterprise Groups	163.59	172.57	172.57	200
乡镇企业	Town-owned Enterprises	130.7	137.64	131.88	136.04
上市公司	Enterprises in the Stock Market	168.45	179.66	175.29	152.96
国有控股企业	State Share Holding	142.17	147.69	145.1	144.15

18-2 续表 1 continued

指 标	Item	2008			
		一季度 the First Quarter	二季度 the Second Quarter	三季度 the Third Quarter	四季度 the Fourth Quarter
企业景气指数	**Business Clemate Indices**	**130.6**	**133.4**	**129.0**	**104.9**
一、按行业门类分	Grouped by Sector				
(一)工业	Industry	131.2	134.7	128.2	91.6
#采掘业	#Mining and Quarrying	122.5	151.8	112.1	70.5
制造业	Manufacturing	133.1	135.8	129.7	89.5
电力、煤气及水生产供应	Electric Power,Gas and Water	122.6	129.0	129.8	116.0
(二)建筑业	Construction	134.4	134.4	136.9	137.2
(三)交通运输、仓储及邮电通信业	Transportation, Storage and Post	131.8	113.6	115.5	94.3
(四)批发和零售业	Wholesale and Retail Sales	130.9	145.4	145.8	142.9
(五)房地产业	Real Estate	143.5	138.3	122.0	98.2
(六)社会服务业	Social Service	121.4	127.6	113.3	124.1
(七)信息传输、计算机服务和软件	Information Transmmision, Service and Catering	108.3	129.1	124.8	117.7
(八)住宿和餐饮业	Service and Software	123.9	113.8	128.7	113.0
二、按企业登记注册类型分	Grouped by Type of Registration				
(一)国有企业	State-owned	126.1	132.6	133.9	117.9
(二)集体企业	Collective-owned	119.5	105.7	108.0	114.2
(三)股份合作企业	Share Holding Cooperative	125.5	100.0	92.7	91.6
(四)有限责任公司	Responsibility Co. Ltd.	124.9	120.2	118.1	102.6
(五)股份有限公司	Share Holding Co. Ltd.	139.4	152.1	142.1	97.6
(六)私营企业	Private	135.7	139.6	132.1	108.8
(七)外商及港、澳、台投资企业	Foreign and Hongkong, Macao, Taiwan Funded	153.8	145.2	146.4	87.6
三、按企业规模分	Grouped by Scale of Enterprises				
特大型及大型	Oversize and Large	150.1	155.8	160.6	106.2
中小型	Medium and Small	123.3	124.0	118.0	103.4
中 型	Medium	123.2	125.8	118.0	104.2
小 型	Small	123.5	121.7	118.0	102.4
附：国家重点联系企业	Major Enterprises Related with the State	165.6	143.9	157.0	76.1
国家试点企业集团成员	Member of Experimental Unit of Enterprise Groups	148.1	148.1	148.1	89.3
乡镇企业	Town-owned Enterprises	126.0	127.1	119.4	103.2
上市公司	Enterprises in the Stock Market	175.4	177.5	166.7	97.9
国有控股企业	State Share Holding	133.6	138.6	138.6	113.2

18-2 续表 2 continued

指 标	Item	2009			
		一季度 the First Quarter	二季度 the Second Quarter	三季度 the Third Quarter	四季度 the Fourth Quarter
企业景气指数	**Business Clemate Indices**	**106.4**	**113.5**	**120.2**	**129.4**
一、按行业门类分	Grouped by Sector				
(一)工业	Industry	100	109.4	116.5	126.8
#采掘业	#Mining and Quarrying	61.4	73.4	96.8	111.1
制造业	Manufacturing	101.5	109.7	117.2	128.3
电力、煤气及水生产供应	Electric Power,Gas and Water	102.7	116.8	114.4	115
(二)建筑业	Construction	128.9	132.3	133.4	142.8
(三)交通运输、仓储及邮电通信业	Transportation, Storage and Post	105.5	111.9	110.8	107.2
(四)批发和零售业	Wholesale and Retail Sales	124.6	130.4	136	148.3
(五)房地产业	Real Estate	112.9	104.6	117.7	135.9
(六)社会服务业	Social Service	100	110.3	117.2	124.1
(七)信息传输、计算机服务和软件	Information Transmmision, Service and Catering	111.2	115	130.7	135
(八)住宿和餐饮业	Service and Software	90.9	98	113.3	115.5
二、按企业登记注册类型分	Grouped by Type of Registration				
(一)国有企业	State-owned	103.6	115.1	120.1	128.4
(二)集体企业	Collective-owned	102.6	85.3	94.6	113.5
(三)股份合作企业	Share Holding Cooperative	106	92.9	85.7	92.9
(四)有限责任公司	Responsibility Co. Ltd.	107.2	105.4	114.4	125.1
(五)股份有限公司	Share Holding Co. Ltd.	118.5	120.7	130.7	139.2
(六)私营企业	Private	109.1	117.9	113.7	125.3
(七)外商及港、澳、台投资企业	Foreign and Hongkong, Macao, Taiwan Funded	93.7	125.9	134.3	135.3
三、按企业规模分	Grouped by Scale of Enterprises				
特大型及大型	Oversize and Large	100.1	131.3	144.6	150.5
中小型	Medium and Small	106.2	108.5	115	124.3
中 型	Medium	106.4	117.4	124.1	135.6
小 型	Small	105.9	99.1	105.4	112.6
附：国家重点企业	Major Enterprises Related with the State	88.6	125.4	145.2	156.1
国家试点企业集团成员	Member of Experimental Unit of Enterprise Groups	70.8	144.7	178.6	178.6
乡镇企业	Town-owned Enterprises	97.8	93.9	99.8	113
上市公司	Enterprises in the Stock Market	122.6	122.8	133.9	142.2
国有控股企业	State Share Holding	110.5	120.5	126.8	133.7

18-3 企业生产营运主要景气观察指标

INDICATORS OF ENTERPRISES' PRODUCT AND WORK

单位:% (%)

				生产总量 Total Production	盈利(亏损)变化 Change of Profit	流动资金 Circulating Fund	货款拖欠 Payment Defaulted
2008	**一季度**	偏好	Partiality	39.82	38.03	24.52	25.29
	the	持平	Keep Balance	32.95	34.9	45.16	54.22
	First	偏差	Warp	27.23	27.07	30.32	20.49
	Quarter	景气指数	Climate Indices	112.59	110.96	94.2	104.8
	二季度	偏好	Partiality	49.46	39.16	20.13	20.06
	the	持平	Keep Balance	33.05	36.97	49.82	57.9
	Second	偏差	Warp	17.49	23.86	30.05	22.04
	Quarter	景气指数	Climate Indices	131.97	115.3	90.08	98.01
	三季度	偏好	Partiality	40.75	32.27	21.88	21.96
	the	持平	Keep Balance	36.44	39.92	46.54	55.86
	Third	偏差	Warp	22.81	27.81	31.58	22.18
	Quarter	景气指数	Climate Indices	117.95	104.45	90.3	99.79
	四季度	偏好	Partiality	29.25	27.27	14.83	21.96
	the	持平	Keep Balance	29.21	32.31	46.12	51.6
	Fourth	偏差	Warp	41.54	40.42	39.05	26.44
	Quarter	景气指数	Climate Indices	87.71	86.86	75.78	95.52
2009	**一季度**	偏好	Partiality	30.39	27.24	17.47	20.94
	the	持平	Keep Balance	29.69	34.23	46.97	57.23
	First	偏差	Warp	39.93	38.54	35.56	21.83
	Quarter	景气指数	Climate Indices	90.47	88.7	81.91	99.11
	二季度	偏好	Partiality	44.21	33.79	17.31	20.13
	the	持平	Keep Balance	29.33	35.42	47.81	57.63
	Second	偏差	Warp	26.46	30.8	34.88	22.24
	Quarter	景气指数	Climate Indices	117.75	102.99	82.44	97.89
	三季度	偏好	Partiality	46.39	39.49	20.1	21.86
	the	持平	Keep Balance	32.54	35.4	47.2	56.11
	Third	偏差	Warp	21.07	25.11	32.7	22.03
	Quarter	景气指数	Climate Indices	125.32	114.38	87.4	99.82
	四季度	偏好	Partiality	45.45	41	21.03	21.24
	the	持平	Keep Balance	33.56	35.23	50.58	58.81
	Fourth	偏差	Warp	20.99	23.77	28.38	19.96
	Quarter	景气指数	Climate Indices	124.46	117.23	92.65	101.28

18-3 续表 continued

				劳动力需求 Labour Demand	固定资产投资 Investment	产品订货 Order Goods	企业融资 Enterprise Financing
2008	一季度	偏好	Partiality	33.13	27.36	35.02	13.22
	the	持平	Keep Balance	53.72	53.6	49.15	59.29
	First	偏差	Warp	13.14	19.04	15.82	27.49
	Quarter	景气指数	Climate Indices	119.99	108.31	119.2	85.73
	二季度	偏好	Partiality	29.55	33.72	35.29	9.43
	the	持平	Keep Balance	61.77	56.5	49.14	60.5
	Second	偏差	Warp	8.69	9.79	15.57	30.08
	Quarter	景气指数	Climate Indices	120.86	123.93	119.71	79.35
	三季度	偏好	Partiality	23.45	30.22	29.07	10.82
	the	持平	Keep Balance	62.78	58.81	52.03	57
	Third	偏差	Warp	13.77	10.97	18.89	32.18
	Quarter	景气指数	Climate Indices	109.68	119.25	110.18	78.64
	四季度	偏好	Partiality	15.34	27.01	17.99	9.1
	the	持平	Keep Balance	57.23	52.78	46.51	55.91
	Fourth	偏差	Warp	27.43	20.22	35.5	34.99
	Quarter	景气指数	Climate Indices	87.92	106.79	82.49	74.1
2009	一季度	偏好	Partiality	18.13	20.44	19.24	13.89
	the	持平	Keep Balance	57.24	55.17	50.71	55.44
	First	偏差	Warp	24.63	24.39	30.05	30.67
	Quarter	景气指数	Climate Indices	93.5	96.06	89.19	83.22
	二季度	偏好	Partiality	21.75	23.84	23.08	12.75
	the	持平	Keep Balance	59.13	58.26	53.2	54.93
	Second	偏差	Warp	19.11	17.9	23.71	32.32
	Quarter	景气指数	Climate Indices	102.64	105.94	99.37	80.42
	三季度	偏好	Partiality	25.56	26.18	31.61	13.57
	the	持平	Keep Balance	59.97	58.01	51.1	56.67
	Third	偏差	Warp	14.48	15.81	17.3	29.75
	Quarter	景气指数	Climate Indices	111.09	110.36	114.31	83.82
	四季度	偏好	Partiality	24.79	30.49	34.45	12.83
	the	持平	Keep Balance	60.56	57.75	48.79	60.39
	Fourth	偏差	Warp	14.65	11.75	16.75	26.79
	Quarter	景气指数	Climate Indices	110.14	118.73	117.7	86.05

主要统计指标解释

520 户国家重点企业 指 1999 年 10 月经国务院批准确定的 520 户国家重点企业。

重组为集团的原 512 户 指经国务院批准确定的原 512 户重点企业中，经过重组，已成为某个企业集团的母公司或子公司的企业。

省级重点企业 指各省、自治区、直辖市人民政府及主管部门确定的省(自治区、直辖市)级重点企业。

现企原国家百户试点企业 指经国务院 1994 年批准确定的建立现代企业制度百户试点企业。现企原省级试点企业 指各省、自治区、直辖市人民政府及主管部门于 1994 年至 1997 年批准确定的省(自治区、直辖市)级建立现代企业制度原试点企业。

试点企业集团母公司 指国务院批准成立的国家试点企业集团的母公司(核心企业)。

国务院审批企业集团 指由国务院批准组建的国家试点企业集团。

国务院主管部门审批企业集团 指由国务院授权的部门批准组建的企业集团。

省级人民政府审批企业集团 指由各省、自治区、直辖市政府批准组建的企业集团。不包括各省、自治区、直辖市政府的主管部门批准组建的企业集团。

省级政府主管部门审批企业集团 指由省级人民政府授权的部门批准组建的企业集团。

企业景气指数 亦称企业综合生产经营景气指数，是根据企业家对本企业当前综合生产经营情况的判断及对未来的预期(选择“好”、“一般”、“不佳”)而编制的指数，用以综合反映调查总体范围内企业生产经营景气状况。企业景气指数介于 0 和 200 之间，100 为景气指数的临界值：当企业景气指数大于 100 时，表明企业生产经营状况趋于上升或改善，处于景气状态；当企业景气指数小于 100 时，表明企业生产经营状况趋于下降或恶化，处于不景气状态。

Explanatory Notes on Main Statistical Indicators

520 State Major Enterprises refer to the enterprises which were approved and defined as the 520 state major enterprises by the state council in October 1999.

Reorganized As Groups (Original 512 Units) refer to the original 512 enterprises which were permitted and defined by the state council，had become the parent companies or branch companies of certain enterprise group.

Provincial Level Major Enterprises refer the enterprises which were defined by the government of provinces，autonomous areas and manipulates direct under the central government and responsible departments as the provincial major enterprises(autonomous areas，municipalities direct under the central government).

100 Experimental Enterprises (Original State-owned) refer the 100 experimental enterprises of modern enterprises system. which were established through the permission and definition of the state council in 1994.

Experimental Enterprises (Original Provincial Units) refer to the enterprises which were establishment through the permission and definition of the government of the provinces，autonomous areas and municipalities directly under the central government and responsible departments in 1994—1997 as the original experimental enterprises of modern enterprise system under the jurisdiction of minces，autonomous areas and municipalities directly under the central government.

Parent Companies of the Experimental Enterprise Groups refer the parent companies of enterprise groups which were established through the examination and permission of the state council as the parent companies(core enterprises)of the national experimental enterprise groups.

Enterprise Groups Examined and Approved by the State Council refer to the national experimental enterprise groups which were established through the examination and permission of the state council.

Enterprise Groups Examined and Approved by the Responsible Department Of the State Council refer the enterprise groups which were established through the examination and permission of the responsible department according to the authorization of the state council.

Enterprise Groups Examined and Permitted by the Provincial Government refer to the enterprise groups which were established through the examination and permission of the government of the provinces autonomous areas and municipalities direct under the state, excluding the enterprise groups which were established through the examination and permission of responsible department of the government of the provinces, autonomous areas and municipalities directly under the central government.

Enterprise Groups Examined and Approved by the Responsible Departments of the Provincial Government refer the enterprise groups which were established through the permission of the departments authorized by the provincial government.

Index of Operating Situation of the Enterprises which is also called as the index of general operating situation. It is the index working out by entrepreneurs of these enterprises according to the current determination and future expectation(choosing good, regular and bad)of the operating condition of production and management of the enterprises to comprehensive reflect the operating situation of production and management in the scope of the investigative units. The index of operating situation of the enterprises is situated between 2--200, of which 100 is the critical value. When the index is larger than 100, it indicates that the operating condition is growing and taking a turn for the better, and at the manner of operating situation, when the index is smaller than 100, it indicates that the operating condition is decreasing and at the manner of non-operating situation.

19 开发区主要经济指标

Major Economic Indicators of Development Zone

资料整理：陈昌华

19-1 湖北省开发区经济发展基本情况（2009）

BASIC INDICATORS OF ECONOMIC DEVELOPMENT OF DEVELOPMAENT ZONE IN HUBEI PROVINCE(2009)

指 标		Item		2008	2009	增幅(%) Percentage of Increase (%)
基本情况		**Basic condition**				
开发区批准规划面积	(平方公里)	Floor Areas Approved in Development Zone	(Sq.km.)	1192.4	1449.9	21.6
开发区实际占地面积	(平方公里)	Actual Land Areas of Development Zone	(Sq.km.)	777.6	906.1	16.5
企业个数	(个)	Number of Enterprises	(unit)	46379	50968	9.9
其中：工业企业	(个)	Among Them, Those Belong to Industrial Enterprises	(unit)	13980	16070	14.9
其中：规模以上	(个)	Among Which, Enterprises above Designated Scale	(unit)	5578	6843	22.7
高新技术企业	(个)	High and New Technological Enterprises	(unit)	2998	3332	11.1
外商投资企业	(个)	Foreign Invested Enterprises	(unit)	1146	1282	11.9
第三产业	(个)	Tertiary Industry	(unit)	21937	23758	8.3
从业人员	(万人)	Population of Employment	(10 000 persons)	210	245.22	16.8
其中：工业企业	(万人)	Among Them, Those Belong to Industrial Enterprises	(10 000 persons)	144.21	181.19	25.6
其中：规模以上	(万人)	Among Them, Those Engaged in Enterprises above Designated Scale	(10 000 persons)	114.79	147.99	28.9
主要经济指标		**Major Economic Indicators**				
规模以上工业总产值	(亿元)	Total Output Value of Enterprises above Designated Scale	(100 million Yuan)	7130.98	9464.87	32.7
规模以上工业增加值	(亿元)	Value-added of Enterprises above Designated Scale	(100 million Yuan)	2228.92	2940.07	29.3
其中：高新技术产业	(亿元)	Among Which, Value-added of High and New Technological Enterprises	(100 million Yuan)	1159.88	1483.39	27.9
规模以上工业主营业务收入	(亿元)	Total Income From Major Business of Enterprises above Designated Scale	(100 million Yuan)	6722.89	8972.63	33.5
其中：高新技术产业	(亿元)	Among Which, Those Belong to High and New Technological Enterprises	(100 million Yuan)	3426.22	4284.15	25.0
固定资产投资总额	(亿元)	Total Value of Investment in Fixed Assets	(100 million Yuan)	1626.9	2493.63	53.3
其中：基础设施建设投资	(亿元)	Among Which, Infrastructure Investment	(100 million Yuan)	392.38	622.14	58.6
施工项目个数	(个)	Number of Projects under Construction	(unit)	4416	5806	31.5
其中:亿元以上项目	(个)	Among Which, the Value of the Projects is Worth More Than 100 million Yuan	(unit)	716	991	38.4
新开工项目	(个)	Newly Opened Projects	(unit)	2679	3351	25.1
外商投资项目	(个)	Foreign Invested Projects	(unit)	312	334	7.1
省外内资项目	(个)	Foreign-funded Projects	(unit)	1092	1493	36.7
开发区税收总额	(亿元)	Total Tax Revenue of Development Zone	(100 million Yuan)	413.50	542.30	31.2
招商引资总额	(亿元)	The Total Investment	(100 million yuan)	1205.61	1670.98	38.6
其中：外商投资金额	(亿美元)	Total Value of Foreign Investment	(100 million dollars)	21.89	27.14	24.0
出口总额	(亿美元)	Total Value of Export	(100 million dollars)	50.83	49.96	-1.7

19-2 湖北省130家开发区主要指标（2009）

开发区名称	Name of Development Zone	实际开发面积(公顷) Actual Land Areas of Development Zone (hectare)	
		2008	2009
湖北省	**Hubei Province**	**77762.8**	**90614.42**
武汉市	**Wuhan**	**16011.03**	**17338.9**
武汉江岸经济开发区	Wuhan Jiang'an Economic Development Zone	34.73	34.73
武汉江汉经济开发区	Wuhan Jiang Han Economic Development Zone	70	70
武汉硚口经济开发区	Wuhan Qiao Kou Economic Development Zone	64.5	64.5
武汉汉阳经济开发区	Wuhan Han Yang Economic Development Zone	413	413
武汉武昌经济开发区	Wuhan Wu Chang Economic Development Zone	502	502
武汉青山经济开发区	Wuhan Qing Shan Economic Development Zone	90.13	121
武汉洪山经济开发区	Wuhan Hong Shan Economic Development Zone	26.67	26.67
武汉吴家山台商工业园区	Wuhan Wu Jiashan Taiwanese businessman Invested Industrial Park	1000	1000
武汉汉南经济开发区	Wuhan Han Nan Economic Development Zone	274	800
武汉蔡甸经济开发区	Wuhan Cai Dian Economic Development Zone	435	436
武汉江夏经济开发区	Wuhan Jiang Xia Economic Development Zone	2354	235.6
武汉盘龙城经济开发区	Wuhan Pan Longcheng Economic Development Zone	750	1130
武汉阳逻经济开发区	Wuhan Yang Luo Economic Development Zone	1321	1594
武汉经济技术开发区	Wuhan Economic and Technological Development Zone	5976	5976
武汉东湖新技术产业开发区	Wuhan East Lake Technology Industrial Development Zone	2700	2815
黄石市	**Huangshi**	**4503.11**	**5625.11**
湖北黄石港工业园区	Hubei Huang Shi Gang Industrial Park		122
湖北西塞山工业园区	Hubei Xi Saishan Industrial Park	1000	1000
湖北黄石经济开发区	Hubei Huang Shi Economic Development Zone	1528.11	1548.11
湖北阳新工业园区	Hubei Yang Xin Industrial Park	450	600
湖北大冶经济开发区	Hubei Da Ye Economic Development Zone	1265	1970
大冶灵成工业园	Daye Ling Cheng Industrial Park	260	385
十堰市	**Shiyan**	**2329.87**	**2679.12**
湖北十堰经济开发区	Hubei Shiyan Economic Development Zone	795	795
湖北十堰东城经济开发区	Hubei Shi Yan Dongcheng Economic Development Zone	472.17	472.17
湖北十堰西城经济开发区	Hubei Shi Yan Xicheng Economic Development Zone	297	297
湖北郧县经济开发区	Hubei Yun County Economic Development Zone	286.7	475.9
湖北郧西工业园区	Hubei Yun West Industrial Park	53	73.05
湖北竹山经济开发区	Hubei Zhu Shan Economic Development Zone	71	104
湖北竹溪工业园区	Hubei Zhu Xi Industrial Park	31	31
湖北房县工业园区	Hubei Fang County Industrial Park	84	151
湖北丹江口经济开发区	Hubei Dan Jiangkou Economic Development Zone	240	280
宜昌市	**Yichang**	**5556**	**6804**
湖北西陵经济开发区	Hubei Xi Ling Economic Development Zone	425	425
湖北伍家岗工业园区	Hubei Wu Jiagang Industrial Park	240	240
湖北点军工业园区	Hubei Dian Jun Industrial Park	50	50
湖北夷陵经济开发区	Hubei Yi Ling Economic Development Zone	365	450
湖北远安工业园区	Hubei Yuan An Industrial Park	260	270
湖北秭归经济开发区	Hubei Zi Gui Economic Development Zone	235	327
湖北长阳经济开发区	Hubei Chang Yang Economic Development Zone	130	140
湖北五峰工业园区	Hubei Wu Feng Industrial Park	210	230
湖北宜昌经济开发区	Hubei Yi Chang Economic Development Zone	1460	1720
湖北宜都工业园区	Hubei Yi Du Industrial Park	675	730
湖北当阳经济开发区	Hubei Dang Yang Economic Development Zone	680	1200
湖北枝江经济开发区	Hubei Zhi Jiang Economic Development Zone	760	950
枝江安福寺工业园	Zhi Jiang Anfu Temple Industrial Park	66	72

MAIN INDICATORS OF 130 DEVELOPMENT ZONE IN HUBEI(2009)

企业个数(个) Number of Enterprises (unit)		其中：规模以上工业企业(个) Among which, Industrial Enterprises above Designated Size(unit)		高新技术企业(个) Number of High and New Technological Enterprises (unit)		从业人员(万人) Population of Employment (10 000 persons)	
2008	2009	2008	2009	2008	2009	2008	2009
46379	**50968**	**5578**	**6843**	**2998**	**3332**	**210**	**245.22**
25755	**28037**	**1693**	**1929**	**2381**	**2566**	**63.31**	**74.29**
40	38	3	4	5	3		
375	385	27	26	42	45	2.08	2.17
217	221	130	137	29	9	3.5	3.9
492	654	99	100			1.06	1.6
248	272	95	98	47	47	1.73	1.75
108	159	40	50	6	6	1.24	1.32
83	125	48	49	25	25	0.51	0.68
8252	8252	165	203	11	14	11.2	11.6
63	329	63	82	4	4	0.8	2.57
122	139	42	56	4	3	0.9	2.3
462	502	115	119	36	37	4.56	4.68
150	220	28	32			1.25	1.75
66	78	19	32	3	2	1.36	1.55
2293	2744	217	251	37	31	9.84	14.29
12784	13919	602	690	2132	2340	23.28	24.13
2959	**3314**	**217**	**281**	**39**	**51**	**9.85**	**11.72**
	22		13		5		0.29
213	246	69	98			1.5	1.9
659	913	61	70	34	40	4.53	5.12
44	50	17	20	1	2	0.51	0.53
1995	2033	26	36	4	4	2.92	3.32
48	50	44	44			0.39	0.56
1990	**2097**	**272**	**318**	**53**	**63**	**6.28**	**7.51**
1304	1337	70	83	39	41	2.2	2.6
150	168	62	72	3	10	1.5	1.58
77	79	27	30	2	2	0.44	0.43
38	64	12	17	2	2	0.35	0.68
9	11	7	9			0.1	0.12
54	65	30	38	2	2	0.27	0.3
16	20	8	10	1	2	0.2	0.25
42	45	24	25	1	1	0.22	0.25
300	308	32	34	3	3	1	1.3
2798	**3007**	**445**	**523**	**67**	**86**	**19.96**	**22.2**
132	154	8	14	6	10	0.42	0.51
90	90	22	29	6	6	1.8	1.56
15	15	13	13	3	3	0.32	0.32
251	259	34	38	8	8	2.4	2.68
30	52	25	28	1	1	1.1	1.2
125	137	33	41	3	3	1.41	1.44
40	49	24	33	2	2	0.55	0.61
493	511	9	13	2	3	0.8	0.9
732	750	39	45	14	29	3.7	4.23
185	193	100	108	9	9	2.42	2.5
263	298	59	71	6	6	1.53	2.3
422	473	67	77	7	6	3.07	3.48
20	26	12	13			0.44	0.47

19-2 续表 1 continued

开发区名称	Name of Development Zone	实际开发面积(公顷) Actual Land Areas of Development Zone (hectare)	
		2008	2009
襄樊市	**Xianfan**	**13193**	**14402**
湖北襄樊高新技术产业开发区	Hubei Xiang Fan High and New Technology Industrial Development Zone	9600	9600
襄樊鱼梁州经济开发区	Xiang Fan Yu Liangzhou Economic Development Zone		200
湖北襄城经济开发区	Hubei Xiang Cheng Economic Development Zone	264	752
湖北樊城经济开发区	Hubei Fan Cheng Economic Development Zone	197	213
湖北襄阳经济开发区	Hubei Xiang Yang Economic Development Zone	334	334
襄阳工业园	Xiang Yang Industrial Park	89	95
湖北南漳经济开发区	Hubei Nan Zhang Economic Development Zone	158	281
湖北谷城经济开发区	Hubei Gu Cheng Economic Development Zone	686	712
谷城石花经济开发区	Gu Cheng Shi Hua Economic Development Zone	428	439
湖北保康经济开发区	Hubei Bao Kang Economic Development Zone	233	427
湖北老河口经济开发区	Hubei Lao Hekou Economic Development Zone	253	307
湖北枣阳济开发区	Hubei Zao Yang Economic Development Zone	526	582
枣阳吴店工业园	Zao Yang Wu Dian Industrial Park	140	160
湖北宜城经济开发区	Hubei Yi Cheng Economic Development Zone	285	300
鄂州市	**Ezhou**	**2592**	**2862**
湖北鄂州花湖经济开发区	Hubei E'Zhou Hua Hu Economic Development Zone	720	760
湖北鄂州葛店经济开发区	Hubei E'Zhou Ge Dian Economic Development Zone	872	902
湖北鄂州经济开发区	Hubei E'Zhou Economic Development Zone	1000	1200
荆门市	**Jingmen**	**5774.9**	**7494.9**
湖北东宝工业园区	Hubei Dong Bao Industrial Park	130	130
湖北荆门经济开发区	Hubei Jing Men Economic Development Zone	1500	1600
湖北京山经济开发区	Hubei Jing Shan Economic Development Zone	420	470
湖北沙洋经济开发区	Hubei Sha Yang Economic Development Zone	280	380
湖北钟祥经济开发区	Hubei Fan Zheng Economic Development Zone	395	1000
钟祥胡集经济开发区	Zhong Xiang Hu Ji Economic Development Zone	324.9	334.9
孝感市	**Xiaogan**	**6812**	**7694**
湖北孝感经济开发区	Hubei Xiao Gan Economic Development Zone	1300	1300
湖北孝南经济开发区	Hubei Xiao Nan Economic Development Zone	982	1094
湖北孝昌经济开发区	Hubei Xiao Chang Economic Development Zone	600	600
湖北大悟经济开发区	Hubei Da Wu Economic Development Zone	450	650
湖北云梦经济开发区	Hubei Yun Meng Economic Development Zone	1000	1000
湖北应城经济开发区	Hubei Ying Cheng Economic Development Zone	800	1200
湖北安陆经济开发区	Hubei An Lu Economic Development Zone	500	600
湖北汉川经济开发区	Hubei Han Chuan Economic Development Zone	1180	1250
荆州市	**Jingzhou**	**4300**	**5154**
湖北沙市经济开发区	Hubei Sha Shi Economic Development Zone	400	500
湖北荆州城南经济开发区	Jing Zhou Cheng Nan Economic Development Zone	998	1158
湖北荆州经济开发区	Hubei Jing Zhou Economic Development Zone	750	750
湖北公安经济开发区	Hubei Gong An Economic Development Zone	323	663
湖北监利经济开发区	Hubei Jian Li Economic Development Zone	192	214
湖北江陵工业园区	Hubei Jiang Ling Industrial Park	231	308
湖北石首经济开发区	Hubei Shi Shou Economic Development Zone	350	400
湖北洪湖经济开发区	Hubei Hong Hu Economic Development Zone	618	693
洪湖府场经济开发区	Honghu Fuchang Economic Development Zone	200	200
湖北松滋经济开发区	Hubei Song Zi Economic Development Zone	238	268
黄冈市	**Huanggang**	**6196.13**	**6607.83**
湖北黄冈经济开发区	Hubei huang Gang Economic Development Zone	1023.33	1023.33

企业个数(个) Number of Enterprises (unit)		其中：规模以上工业企业(个) Among which, Industrial Enterprises above Designated Size(unit)		高新技术企业(个) Number of High and New Technological Enterprises (unit)		从业人员(万人) Population of Employment (10 000 persons)	
2008	2009	2008	2009	2008	2009	2008	2009
3218	**3680**	**541**	**811**	**65**	**108**	**20.92**	**24.58**
1668	1795	134	159	10	37	5.4	5.8
78	52					0.1	0.1
42	96	10	25		2	0.23	0.52
121	170	71	106	10	16	0.98	1.7
117	154	40	48	6	8	2.82	3.54
37	45	14	18			0.5	0.6
42	52	42	48	6	8	0.52	0.76
526	549	51	78	6	4	3.79	3.98
146	157	26	36	5	5	1.37	1.63
5	9	5	9			0.25	0.3
75	148	48	109	5	6	1.5	1.61
198	236	41	68	6	6	1.69	1.98
90	95	18	19			1	1.1
73	122	41	88	11	16	0.77	0.96
1006	**1163**	**129**	**151**	**18**	**31**	**8.31**	**8.76**
106	126	14	19			0.52	0.66
738	849	81	84	16	29	7.1	7.4
162	188	34	48	2	2	0.69	0.7
1099	**1337**	**489**	**643**	**60**	**72**	**10.26**	**13.7**
54	58	24	33	1	1	0.3	0.71
225	259	128	163	20	23	1.95	2.8
171	197	24	31	1	1	1.27	1.31
35	66	19	23	1	4	0.53	0.68
54	78	41	63	7	7	0.99	1.24
21	21	17	17			0.18	0.22
980	**1158**	**277**	**353**	**71**	**83**	**12.82**	**15.21**
330	342	48	60	24	27	2.5	2.5
138	156	35	48	15	15	2.8	3.2
74	95	13	24	4	7	0.48	0.75
26	34	9	9	2	2	0.8	1.2
33	48	15	26	4	6	0.82	0.92
89	101	53	61	9	12	2.17	2.62
109	166	14	14	4	5	0.45	0.57
181	216	90	111	9	9	2.8	3.45
1588	**1742**	**459**	**570**	**46**	**49**	**17.83**	**20.89**
34	40	23	28	1	1	0.31	0.42
473	501	67	85	3	3	4.92	5.03
578	596	150	167	18	18	5.6	5.69
66	71	36	37	3	3	0.68	1.41
50	65	10	30			0.75	1.05
42	71	26	40			0.4	0.6
35	40	34	40	9	10	0.86	1.25
134	155	28	31	2	3	1.84	2.16
118	126	40	43	6	6	0.87	1.13
58	77	45	69	4	5	1.6	2.15
2194	**2309**	**340**	**395**	**45**	**59**	**11.7**	**14.19**
910	934	89	93	13	13	2.13	2.37

19-2 续表 2 continued

开发区名称	Name of Development Zone	实际开发面积(公顷) Actual Land Areas of Development Zone (hectare)	
		2008	2009
湖北黄州火车站经济开发区	Huang Zhou Railway Station Economic Development Zone	210	210
黄州工业园	Huang Zhou Industrial Park	133	133
湖北龙感湖工业园区	Hubei Long Gan Hu Industrial Park	450	450
湖北团风经济开发区	Hubei Tuan Feng Economic Development Zone	605	693
湖北红安经济开发区	Hubei Hong An Economic Development Zone	300	400
湖北罗田经济开发区	Hubei Luo Tian Economic Development Zone	333	366
湖北英山经济开发区	Hubei Ying Shan Economic Development Zone	200	243
湖北浠水经济开发区	Hubei Xi Shui Economic Development Zone	472.3	500
湖北蕲春李时珍医药工业园区	Qi Chun Li Shizhen Medicine Industrial Park	320	320
蕲春经济开发区	Qi Chun Economic Development Zone	1000	1050
湖北黄梅经济开发区	Hubei Huang Mei Economic Development Zone	544.5	544.5
湖北麻城经济开发区	Hubei Ma Cheng Economic Development Zone	400	460
湖北武穴经济开发区	Hubei Wu Xue Economic Development Zone	205	215
咸宁市	**Xianning**	**2827.67**	**4455.67**
湖北咸安经济开发区	Hubei Xian'an Economic Development Zone	296	321
湖北嘉鱼经济开发区	Hubei Jia Yu Economic Development Zone	666.67	666.67
湖北通城经济开发区	Hubei Tong Cheng Economic Development Zone	150	178
湖北崇阳工业园区	Hubei Chong Yang Industrial Park	320	683
湖北通山经济开发区	Hubei Tong Shan Economic Development Zone	100	200
湖北咸宁经济开发区	Hubei Xian Ning Economic Development Zone	875	1142
湖北赤壁经济开发区	Hubei Chi Bi Economic Development Zone	420	465
湖北赤壁蒲纺工业园区	Hubei Chi Bi Puqi Textile Industrial Park		800
随州市	**Suizhou**	**1535**	**1836**
湖北随州经济开发区	Hubei Sui Zhou Economic Development Zone	900	1000
湖北曾都经济开发区	Hubei Zeng Dou Economic Development Zone	135	276
湖北广水经济开发区	Hubei Guang Shui Economic Development Zone	500	560
恩施州	**Enshi**	**2386.7**	**2506.3**
湖北恩施经济开发区	Hubei En Shi Economic Development Zone	1470	1470
湖北利川经济开发区	Hubei Li Chuan Economic Development Zone	208	231
湖北建始工业园区	Hubei Jian Shi Industrial Park	100	100
湖北巴东经济开发区	Hubei Ba Dong Economic Development Zone	110	165
湖北宣恩工业园区	Hubei Xuan En Industrial Park	281	281
湖北咸丰工业园区	Hubei Xian Feng Industrial Park	77.7	89.3
湖北来凤经济开发区	Hubei Lai Feng Economic Development Zone	126	156
湖北鹤峰经济开发区	Hubei He Feng Economic Development Zone	14	14
仙桃市	**Xiantao**	**1599.6**	**1683.3**
湖北仙桃经济开发区	Hubei Xian Tao Economic Development Zone	555.6	604.3
仙桃高新技术产业园	Xian Tao High and New Technology Industrial Park	346	346
仙桃工业园	Xian Tao Industrial Park	600	600
仙桃彭场工业园	Xian Tao Pengchang Industrial Park	98	133
潜江市	**Qianjiang**	**1382**	**1382**
湖北潜江经济开发区	Hubei Qian Jiang Economic Development Zone	466	466
潜江张金经济开发区	Qian Jiang Zhangjin Economic Development Zone	256	256
潜江园林经济开发区	Qian Jiang Yuanlin Economic Development Zone	660	660
天门市	**Tianmen**	**763.8**	**2089.3**
湖北天门经济开发区	Hubei Tian Men Economic Development Zone	227.8	529.3
天门岳口工业园	Tian Men Yuekou Industrial Park	266	300
天门仙北工业园	Tian Men Xianbei Industrial Park	270	1260

企业个数(个) Number of Enterprises (unit)		其中：规模以上工业企业(个) Among which, Industrial Enterprises above Designated Size (unit)		高新技术企业(个) Number of High and New Technological Enterprises (unit)		从业人员(万人) Population of Employment (10 000 persons)	
2008	2009	2008	2009	2008	2009	2008	2009
129	129	7	7	1	1	0.24	0.25
26	26	20	20	1	1	0.57	0.62
		25	28	1	1	0.52	0.61
56	58	34	36	2	3	0.65	0.78
37	53	17	31	6	8	1.75	2
5	14	5	14		5	0.05	0.17
14	19	10				0.13	0.23
248	270	28	33	6	9	1.5	1.8
12	17	3	6		1	0.36	0.85
35	40	10	14	1	1	0.4	0.75
335	348	43	49	4	4	1.5	1.7
288	296	20	31	6	8	1.1	1.19
99	105	29	33	4	4	0.8	0.87
514	**626**	**223**	**307**	**33**	**38**	**6.28**	**7.59**
27	63	13	39	4	7	0.64	1.02
102	110	34	42	2	2	1.29	1.36
63	67	33	35	5	5	0.62	0.65
57	58	31	39	1	1	0.45	0.53
19	19	8	11	1	1	0.4	0.46
183	203	41	53	12	14	1.48	1.61
63	68	63	68	8	8	1.4	1.6
	38		20				0.36
584	**662**	**92**	**91**	**17**	**17**	**3.18**	**3.77**
356	397	48	44	7	7	2.24	2.35
57	92	30	32	6	6	0.56	0.93
171	173	14	15	4	4	0.38	0.49
377	**413**	**87**	**116**	**8**	**9**	**4.04**	**4.07**
192	210	41	53	3	3	2.3	2
89	96	8	10	1	1	0.85	0.87
10	10	8	10	1	1	0.2	0.3
16	22	7	12		1	0.11	0.17
23	25	6	12	1	1	0.1	0.2
15	15	4	4	1	1	0.03	0.05
23	26	11	12			0.33	0.35
9	9	2	3	1	1	0.12	0.13
654	**725**	**150**	**166**	**20**	**20**	**6.5**	**7.4**
324	356	51	57	5	5	2.3	2.5
94	96	39	42	9	9	0.9	1.1
50	55	27	29	4	4	0.8	1
186	218	33	38	2	2	2.5	2.8
502	**511**	**93**	**99**	**62**	**64**	**6.97**	**7.27**
211	213	48	50	35	35	1.2	1.35
148	150	18	20	18	20	1.96	2
143	148	27	29	9	9	3.81	3.92
161	**187**	**71**	**90**	**13**	**16**	**1.79**	**2.07**
83	85	33	43	9	9	0.66	0.73
50	57	33	40	2	5	0.53	0.59
28	45	5	7	2	2	0.6	0.75

19-2 续表 3 continued

开发区名称	Name of Development Zone	其中：规模以上工业企业(万人) Among which, Industrial Enterprises above Designated Size (10 000 persons)	
		2008	2009
湖北省	**Hubei Province**	**114.79**	**147.99**
武汉市	**Wuhan**	**34.78**	**40.86**
武汉江岸经济开发区	Wuhan Jiang'an Economic Development Zone	0.11	0.12
武汉江汉经济开发区	Wuhan Jiang Han Economic Development Zone	0.42	0.45
武汉硚口经济开发区	Wuhan Qiao Kou Economic Development Zone	3	3.3
武汉汉阳经济开发区	Wuhan Han Yang Economic Development Zone	0.6	0.76
武汉武昌经济开发区	Wuhan Wu Chang Economic Development Zone		
武汉青山经济开发区	Wuhan Qing Shan Economic Development Zone	1.07	1.08
武汉洪山经济开发区	Wuhan Hong Shan Economic Development Zone	0.41	0.45
武汉吴家山台商工业园区	Wuhan Wu Jiashan Taiwanese businessman Invested Industrial Park	2.7	2.8
武汉汉南经济开发区	Wuhan Han Nan Economic Development Zone	0.8	0.86
武汉蔡甸经济开发区	Wuhan Cai Dian Economic Development Zone	0.8	2.08
武汉江夏经济开发区	Wuhan Jiang Xia Economic Development Zone	2.12	2.73
武汉盘龙城经济开发区	Wuhan Pan Longcheng Economic Development Zone	0.53	0.55
武汉阳逻经济开发区	Wuhan Yang Luo Economic Development Zone	1.08	1.23
武汉经济技术开发区	Wuhan Economic and Technological Development Zone	7.67	9.48
武汉东湖新技术产业开发区	Wuhan East Lake Technology Industrial Development Zone	13.47	14.97
黄石市	**Huangshi**	**3.54**	**4.33**
湖北黄石港工业园区	Hubei Huang Shi Gang Industrial Park		0.07
湖北西塞山工业园区	Hubei Xi Saishan Industrial Park	0.75	0.9
湖北黄石经济开发区	Hubei Huang Shi Economic Development Zone	0.89	1.02
湖北阳新工业园区	Hubei Yang Xin Industrial Park	0.42	0.43
湖北大冶经济开发区	Hubei Da Ye Economic Development Zone	1.12	1.41
大冶灵成工业园	Daye Ling Cheng Industrial Park	0.36	0.5
十堰市	**Shiyan**	**3.69**	**4.37**
湖北十堰经济开发区	Hubei Shiyan Economic Development Zone	0.93	0.95
湖北十堰东城经济开发区	Hubei Shi Yan Dongcheng Economic Development Zone	1.22	1.3
湖北十堰西城经济开发区	Hubei Shi Yan Xicheng Economic Development Zone	0.35	0.33
湖北郧县经济开发区	Hubei Yun County Economic Development Zone	0.23	0.65
湖北郧西工业园区	Hubei Yun West Industrial Park	0.1	0.12
湖北竹山经济开发区	Hubei Zhu Shan Economic Development Zone	0.12	0.15
湖北竹溪工业园区	Hubei Zhu Xi Industrial Park	0.1	0.15
湖北房县工业园区	Hubei Fang County Industrial Park	0.13	0.17
湖北丹江口经济开发区	Hubei Dan Jiangkou Economic Development Zone	0.51	0.55
宜昌市	**Yichang**	**12.09**	**13.82**
湖北西陵经济开发区	Hubei Xi Ling Economic Development Zone	0.05	0.09
湖北伍家岗工业园区	Hubei Wu Jiagang Industrial Park	0.9	0.66
湖北点军工业园区	Hubei Dian Jun Industrial Park	0.31	0.31
湖北夷陵经济开发区	Hubei Yi Ling Economic Development Zone	1.5	1.56
湖北远安工业园区	Hubei Yuan An Industrial Park	1	1.1
湖北秭归经济开发区	Hubei Zi Gui Economic Development Zone	0.78	0.81
湖北长阳经济开发区	Hubei Chang Yang Economic Development Zone	0.51	0.57
湖北五峰工业园区	Hubei Wu Feng Industrial Park	0.25	0.3
湖北宜昌经济开发区	Hubei Yi Chang Economic Development Zone	1.6	2.36
湖北宜都工业园区	Hubei Yi Du Industrial Park	1.92	1.99
湖北当阳经济开发区	Hubei Dang Yang Economic Development Zone	1.28	1.72
湖北枝江经济开发区	Hubei Zhi Jiang Economic Development Zone	1.64	1.98
枝江安福寺工业园	Zhi Jiang Anfu Temple Industrial Park	0.35	0.37

规模以上工业增加值(亿元) Above-scale Industrial Added Value (100 million Yuan)		规模以上工业主营业务收入(亿元) Scale Industrial Core Business Revenue (100 million Yuan)		固定资产投资总额(亿元) Total Investment In Fixed Assets (100 million Yuan)		施工项目个数(个) Number of Construction Project (unit)	
2008	2009	2008	2009	2008	2009	2008	2009
2228.92	**2940.07**	**6722.9**	**8972.63**	**1626.9**	**2493.63**	**4416**	**5806**
1071.89	**1314.84**	**3218.91**	**4032.03**	**510.68**	**758.66**	**623**	**1056**
5.24	4.96	12.4	15.98	2.66	3.06	4	4
7.81	8.33	23.84	25.04	5.6	3.69	4	10
29.9	32.6	104.8	105.4	6	11	5	4
33.6	49.46	106.53	144.92	25.89	49.32	26	37
28.5	31	102	131.2	4.01	6.5	12	8
7.29	7.84	25.6	27.34	5.2	7.49	11	9
9	9.91	25	26.55	1.01	1.57	15	16
61.2	74.8	213.4	250.9	75.7	106.9	177	276
10	13.43	33	48.23	5.4	13.41	12	20
36	45.45	119	123.25	12	16.9	32	43
53.44	65.66	130.67	168.14	58	99.15	48	35
7.4	12.5	23.7	39.9	12.8	16.1	30	28
28.69	33.01	88.58	101.25	44.87	62.13	32	53
285.82	332.89	865	1082.64	96.24	147.04	137	348
468	593	1345.39	1741.29	155.3	214.4	78	165
58.14	**84.44**	**164.87**	**248.7**	**72.51**	**130.63**	**184**	**287**
	0.78		2.12		4.3		12
9.8	10.5	23.4	25.6	16.77	18.25	39	40
23.63	32.24	73.5	100.53	29.1	54.68	76	88
7.44	10.35	23.83	30.4	4.13	5	11	10
10.77	23.16	30.41	69.85	13.68	37.41	37	107
6.5	7.41	13.73	20.2	8.83	10.99	21	30
56.9	**71.28**	**177.35**	**234.06**	**40.06**	**64.59**	**169**	**214**
25.3	28.5	77.78	94.54	9.4	12.26	21	32
14.9	19.2	49.6	65.9	6.8	15.2	32	36
4.94	6.59	12.43	20.12	1.58	2.91	5	9
2.71	4.37	7.85	12.88	2.23	6.89	30	47
0.29	0.69	0.7	2.2	1.31	6	4	5
2.54	3.42	6.09	8.34	0.6	0.7	35	25
1.64	2.15	4.4	5.46	3.85	1.49	13	13
1.44	2.06	5.27	5.92	3.67	5.74	9	24
3.14	4.3	13.23	18.7	10.62	13.4	20	23
202.52	**278.05**	**593.03**	**832.02**	**194.18**	**300.78**	**601**	**790**
0.38	1.2	1.48	3.76	3.97	6.41	29	43
7.1	8.09	18.89	21.31	3.93	5.53	14	22
8.14	5.78	27.4	22.99	1.55	1.97	3	8
31.3	39.75	77	112.55	16	32.42	42	62
7.81	14.08	20.5	37.16	9.16	19.97	16	41
6.89	8.58	15.88	22.68	7.01	7.76	36	33
4.1	5.36	13.1	14.05	5.38	5.71	11	11
1.44	2.2	3.69	5.09	1.96	4.97	21	37
39.9	62.5	139	204.82	42.5	67.57	78	64
42.76	60.49	110.57	164.9	41.05	64.29	137	146
23.23	30.99	67.26	84.94	18.11	29.73	47	103
27.49	35.69	89.85	126.16	40.04	49.73	159	206
1.98	3.34	8.41	11.61	3.52	4.72	8	14

19-2 续表 4 continued

开发区名称	Name of Development Zone	其中：规模以上工业企业(万人) Among which, Industrial Enterprises above Designated Size (10 000 persons)	
		2008	2009
襄樊市	**Xianfan**	**11.96**	**14.35**
湖北襄樊高新技术产业开发区	Hubei Xiang Fan High and New Technology Industrial Development Zone	4.1	4.2
襄樊鱼梁州经济开发区	Xiang Fan Yu Liangzhou Economic Development Zone		
湖北襄城经济开发区	Hubei Xiang Cheng Economic Development Zone	0.2	0.4
湖北樊城经济开发区	Hubei Fan Cheng Economic Development Zone	0.87	0.9
湖北襄阳经济开发区	Hubei Xiang Yang Economic Development Zone	1.7	2.05
襄阳工业园	Xiang Yang Industrial Park		
湖北南漳经济开发区	Hubei Nan Zhang Economic Development Zone	0.52	0.75
湖北谷城经济开发区	Hubei Gu Cheng Economic Development Zone	1.1	1.3
谷城石花经济开发区	Gu Cheng Shi Hua Economic Development Zone	0.93	0.98
湖北保康经济开发区	Hubei Bao Kang Economic Development Zone	0.25	0.3
湖北老河口经济开发区	Hubei Lao Hekou Economic Development Zone	0.61	1.45
湖北枣阳济开发区	Hubei Zao Yang Economic Development Zone	0.75	0.86
枣阳吴店工业园	Zao Yang Wu Dian Industrial Park	0.28	0.31
湖北宜城经济开发区	Hubei Yi Cheng Economic Development Zone	0.65	0.85
鄂州市	**Ezhou**	**2.69**	**2.93**
湖北鄂州花湖经济开发区	Hubei E'Zhou Hua Hu Economic Development Zone	0.28	0.35
湖北鄂州葛店经济开发区	Hubei E'Zhou Ge Dian Economic Development Zone	2.3	2.35
湖北鄂州经济开发区	Hubei E'Zhou Economic Development Zone	0.11	0.23
荆门市	**Jingmen**	**7.36**	**10.54**
湖北东宝工业园区	Hubei Dong Bao Industrial Park	0.23	0.61
湖北荆门经济开发区	Hubei Jing Men Economic Development Zone	1.4	2.2
湖北京山经济开发区	Hubei Jing Shan Economic Development Zone	0.71	0.75
湖北沙洋经济开发区	Hubei Sha Yang Economic Development Zone	0.38	0.5
湖北钟祥经济开发区	Hubei Fan Zheng Economic Development Zone	0.89	1.12
钟祥胡集经济开发区	Zhong Xiang Hu Ji Economic Development Zone	0.14	0.18
孝感市	**Xiaogan**	**7.92**	**9.41**
湖北孝感经济开发区	Hubei Xiao Gan Economic Development Zone	1.85	1.86
湖北孝南经济开发区	Hubei Xiao Nan Economic Development Zone	1.08	1.2
湖北孝昌经济开发区	Hubei Xiao Chang Economic Development Zone	0.28	0.49
湖北大悟经济开发区	Hubei Da Wu Economic Development Zone	0.5	0.8
湖北云梦经济开发区	Hubei Yun Meng Economic Development Zone	0.74	0.82
湖北应城经济开发区	Hubei Ying Cheng Economic Development Zone	1.18	1.43
湖北安陆经济开发区	Hubei An Lu Economic Development Zone	0.24	0.25
湖北汉川经济开发区	Hubei Han Chuan Economic Development Zone	2.05	2.56
荆州市	**Jingzhou**	**8.22**	**11.38**
湖北沙市经济开发区	Hubei Sha Shi Economic Development Zone	0.17	0.27
湖北荆州城南经济开发区	Jing Zhou Cheng Nan Economic Development Zone	1.68	1.93
湖北荆州经济开发区	Hubei Jing Zhou Economic Development Zone	2.08	2.17
湖北公安经济开发区	Hubei Gong An Economic Development Zone	0.42	1.3
湖北监利经济开发区	Hubei Jian Li Economic Development Zone	0.35	0.63
湖北江陵工业园区	Hubei Jiang Ling Industrial Park	0.3	0.5
湖北石首经济开发区	Hubei Shi Shou Economic Development Zone	0.85	1.25
湖北洪湖经济开发区	Hubei Hong Hu Economic Development Zone	0.83	0.97
洪湖府场经济开发区	Honghu Fuchang Economic Development Zone	0.44	0.51
湖北松滋经济开发区	Hubei Song Zi Economic Development Zone	1.1	1.85
黄冈市	**Huanggang**	**6.3**	**7.93**
湖北黄冈经济开发区	Hubei huang Gang Economic Development Zone	1.22	1.24

规模以上工业增加值(亿元) Above-scale Industrial Added Value (100 million Yuan)		规模以上工业主营业务收入(亿元) Scale Industrial Core Business Revenue (100 million Yuan)		固定资产投资总额(亿元) Total Investment In Fixed Assets (100 million Yuan)		施工项目个数(个) Number of Construction Project (unit)	
2008	2009	2008	2009	2008	2009	2008	2009
260.43	**392.7**	**892.84**	**1285.31**	**165.34**	**293.69**	**640**	**886**
140	185	530	665	76.27	115.54	201	251
				0.11	0.34		4
12.13	24.11	24.32	53.66	3.6	10.51	6	33
20.3	28.4	63.6	89.3	8.62	16.04	33	53
9.38	18.15	35.13	58.43	17.53	36.06	53	56
5.1	7.6	18.7	28.7	1.14	1.97	11	33
4.07	7.44	13.26	21.86	6.99	11.59	19	27
10.81	17.57	29.66	47.99	10.57	22.45	88	113
10.98	15.45	36.98	53.75	3.5	5.28	33	38
1.08	2.64	3.1	5.89		2.55	5	13
12.05	26.8	33.99	82.3	10.69	20	67	83
12.44	25.94	43.68	84.58	16.34	27.2	75	124
3.49	5.4	11.62	15.77	2.4	6.37	20	16
18.6	28.2	48.8	78.08	7.58	17.79	29	42
35.78	**48.45**	**95.26**	**125.32**	**44.07**	**67.7**	**99**	**115**
1.65	2.81	5.42	8.7	8.33	10.69	36	38
32.33	40.95	84.36	103.52	30.59	46.5	51	64
1.8	4.69	5.48	13.1	5.15	10.51	12	13
101.89	**137.88**	**288.62**	**423.44**	**94.59**	**132.5**	**311**	**377**
4.41	5.17	9.96	12.96	3.27	2.2	14	11
19.6	24.72	54.5	75.66	20.05	31.06	50	55
13	15.85	33.77	48.96	11.5	13.69	38	38
4.1	5.2	11.1	17	3.84	7.73	13	29
7.85	15	27.69	46.96	6.2	9.1	27	42
3.97	6	14.58	20.36	4.87	4.94	27	27
63.43	**102.2**	**188.21**	**295.91**	**82.78**	**124.47**	**242**	**305**
15.45	20.17	40.37	49.51	10.37	16.78	36	55
6.39	7.22	23.82	25.1	15.25	26.6	32	55
1.77	3.16	3.75	9.13	4.63	12.41	26	38
0.7	1.1	2.9	4.2	4.2	4.8	7	5
8.16	9.02	28.68	31.45	5.79	6.65	16	16
8.31	24.01	22.17	68.57	9.05	11.62	41	42
3.45	4.4	8.73	10.04	8.13	12.6	25	27
19.2	33.12	57.79	97.91	25.36	33.01	59	67
90.8	**129.18**	**269.99**	**379.37**	**106.26**	**149.38**	**450**	**423**
4.12	6.18	10.85	16.49	6	10	16	12
18.31	25.03	55	77.74	15.95	25.67	70	59
24.16	33.01	73.03	93.83	42	59	157	137
6.2	10.6	19.9	29.7	13.9	12.2	51	30
0.8	5.3	2.65	17.52	1.93	8.9	12	18
2.69	3.47	8.22	10.82	4.8	6.28	22	27
17.1	22.57	47.3	61.2	6.2	9.8	15	15
5.57	7.2	20.23	23.83	4.39	6.23	47	55
6.5	7.2	16.8	21.5	1.9	2.32	28	35
5.35	8.62	16.01	26.74	9.19	8.98	32	35
55.66	**86.39**	**159.59**	**240.76**	**90.99**	**147.39**	**317**	**387**
16.45	21.43	45.49	65.56	12.42	36.6	40	44

19-2 续表 5 continued

开发区名称	Name of Development Zone	其中：规模以上工业企业(万人) Among which, Industrial Enterprises above Designated Size (10 000 persons)	
		2008	2009
湖北黄州火车站经济开发区	Huang Zhou Railway Station Economic Development Zone	0.1	0.04
黄州工业园	Huang Zhou Industrial Park	0.57	0.5
湖北龙感湖工业园区	Hubei Long Gan Hu Industrial Park	0.4	0.45
湖北团风经济开发区	Hubei Tuan Feng Economic Development Zone	0.62	0.75
湖北红安经济开发区	Hubei Hong An Economic Development Zone	0.44	0.9
湖北罗田经济开发区	Hubei Luo Tian Economic Development Zone	0.05	0.17
湖北英山经济开发区	Hubei Ying Shan Economic Development Zone	0.1	0.15
湖北浠水经济开发区	Hubei Xi Shui Economic Development Zone	0.5	0.55
湖北蕲春李时珍医药工业园区	Qi Chun Li Shizhen Medicine Industrial Park	0.28	0.7
蕲春经济开发区	Qi Chun Economic Development Zone	0.1	0.3
湖北黄梅经济开发区	Hubei Huang Mei Economic Development Zone	1.2	1.4
湖北麻城经济开发区	Hubei Ma Cheng Economic Development Zone	0.32	0.37
湖北武穴经济开发区	Hubei Wu Xue Economic Development Zone	0.4	0.41
咸宁市	**Xianning**	**4.95**	**6.24**
湖北咸安经济开发区	Hubei Xian'an Economic Development Zone	0.5	0.89
湖北嘉鱼经济开发区	Hubei Jia Yu Economic Development Zone	0.82	0.88
湖北通城经济开发区	Hubei Tong Cheng Economic Development Zone	0.58	0.6
湖北崇阳工业园区	Hubei Chong Yang Industrial Park	0.42	0.5
湖北通山经济开发区	Hubei Tong Shan Economic Development Zone	0.35	0.41
湖北咸宁经济开发区	Hubei Xian Ning Economic Development Zone	0.88	1.03
湖北赤壁经济开发区	Hubei Chi Bi Economic Development Zone	1.4	1.6
湖北赤壁蒲纺工业园区	Hubei Chi Bi Puqi Textile Industrial Park		0.33
随州市	**Suizhou**	**1.96**	**2.5**
湖北随州经济开发区	Hubei Sui Zhou Economic Development Zone	1.28	1.32
湖北曾都经济开发区	Hubei Zeng Dou Economic Development Zone	0.44	0.86
湖北广水经济开发区	Hubei Guang Shui Economic Development Zone	0.24	0.32
恩施州	**Enshi**	**1.71**	**1.85**
湖北恩施经济开发区	Hubei En Shi Economic Development Zone	1	0.8
湖北利川经济开发区	Hubei Li Chuan Economic Development Zone	0.12	0.14
湖北建始工业园区	Hubei Jian Shi Industrial Park	0.19	0.3
湖北巴东经济开发区	Hubei Ba Dong Economic Development Zone	0.04	0.11
湖北宣恩工业园区	Hubei Xuan En Industrial Park	0.1	0.2
湖北咸丰工业园区	Hubei Xian Feng Industrial Park	0.02	0.03
湖北来凤经济开发区	Hubei Lai Feng Economic Development Zone	0.12	0.15
湖北鹤峰经济开发区	Hubei He Feng Economic Development Zone	0.12	0.12
仙桃市	**Xiantao**	**4.15**	**13.5**
湖北仙桃经济开发区	Hubei Xian Tao Economic Development Zone	1.1	1.2
仙桃高新技术产业园	Xian Tao High and New Technology Industrial Park	0.8	9.9
仙桃工业园	Xian Tao Industrial Park	0.75	0.8
仙桃彭场工业园	Xian Tao Pengchang Industrial Park	1.5	1.6
潜江市	**Qianjiang**	**2.13**	**2.35**
湖北潜江经济开发区	Hubei Qian Jiang Economic Development Zone	0.8	0.87
潜江张金经济开发区	Qian Jiang Zhangjin Economic Development Zone	0.9	1
潜江园林经济开发区	Qian Jiang Yuanlin Economic Development Zone	0.43	0.48
天门市	**Tianmen**	**1.34**	**1.63**
湖北天门经济开发区	Hubei Tian Men Economic Development Zone	0.57	0.71
天门岳口工业园	Tian Men Yuekou Industrial Park	0.47	0.52
天门仙北工业园	Tian Men Xianbei Industrial Park	0.3	0.4

规模以上工业增加值(亿元) Above-scale Industrial Added Value (100 million Yuan)		规模以上工业主营业务收入(亿元) Scale Industrial Core Business Revenue (100 million Yuan)		固定资产投资总额(亿元) Total Investment In Fixed Assets (100 million Yuan)		施工项目个数(个) Number of Construction Project (unit)	
2008	2009	2008	2009	2008	2009	2008	2009
0.98	1.08	2.21	2.51	1.24	2.71	12	8
3.55	3.66	4.54	5.76	1.01	2.33	13	14
3.79	5.17	13.18	16.5	3.14	6.18		
2.65	4.35	8.94	15.12	9.08	11.15	22	26
5.5	11.99	14.65	27.99	4.26	8.71	23	36
0.02	4.3	0.6	12.9	1.2	3.5	5	14
0.3	1.43	1.2	2.63	2.56	1.78	12	27
3.8	4	9.9	11.5	6.5	7.5	50	60
2.5	5.6	9.8	13.1	1.65	3.1	8	9
0.6	1.25	2.03	3.14	5.7	8.5	15	29
5.15	6.95	15.32	19.7	10.85	15.68	39	74
6.24	10.41	18.86	29.42	23.88	32.45	46	26
4.13	4.77	12.87	14.93	7.5	7.2	32	20
68.44	**90.83**	**170.77**	**235.37**	**76.26**	**96.98**	**233**	**254**
4.68	7.79	12.45	21.22	6.79	10.45	21	26
14.47	19.11	42.55	54	13.93	18.68	32	30
7.01	7.82	16.89	17.54	6.26	7.05	36	18
3.81	4.82	9.08	12.38	2.06	6.02	32	36
4	4.3	11	12.8	4.5	5.3	10	14
15.96	20.81	29.45	44.46	27.84	33.86	60	79
18.51	24.48	49.35	66.64	14.88	15.1	42	43
	1.7		6.33		0.52		8
26.95	**35.34**	**85.08**	**115.72**	**17.94**	**30.43**	**69**	**83**
13.95	17.6	50.7	59.1	9.31	14.77	39	43
8.44	12	19.56	39.3	5.59	10.87	10	22
4.56	5.74	14.82	17.32	3.04	4.79	20	18
8.65	**18.01**	**23.67**	**45.46**	**26.61**	**43.49**	**151**	**237**
5.12	10.8	13.1	27.6	13.18	24.54	59	108
0.86	1.22	1.98	2.69	3.24	3.63	17	18
0.09	1.63	2.21	4.1	2.6	2.59	4	17
0.47	1.2	0.75	2.1	1.45	4.49	16	31
0.75	1.09	1.87	2.87	0.73	2.13	8	15
0.18	0.39	0.52	1.11	0.97	1.75	9	13
0.92	1.41	2.28	3.48	3.71	3.5	27	19
0.26	0.27	0.96	1.51	0.73	0.72	11	14
59.45	**73.68**	**175.65**	**227.56**	**39.87**	**60.58**	**118**	**162**
21.3	26.5	63.4	83.1	10.1	15.36	55	85
17.36	20.5	52.64	64.33	16.65	20	26	28
10	14	30	42	10	20	22	27
10.79	12.68	29.61	38.13	3.12	5.22	15	22
44.6	**47.85**	**149.18**	**159.84**	**38.53**	**51.7**	**148**	**151**
28.3	29.5	87.5	94.5	12.1	17.5	29	12
12.7	14	52.3	54	4.5	5	26	15
3.6	4.35	9.38	11.34	21.93	29.2	93	124
23.39	**28.95**	**69.88**	**91.76**	**26.23**	**40.66**	**61**	**79**
13.1	15.2	33.5	43.8	16.8	23.2	28	30
8	11	32.4	36.6	3.4	9.2	18	19
2.29	2.75	3.98	11.36	6.03	8.26	15	30

19-2 续表 6 continued

开发区详细名称	Name of Development Zone	其中:亿元以上项目(个) Number of Projects above 100 million yuan (unit)	
		2008	2009
湖北省	**Hubei Province**	**716**	**991**
武汉市	**Wuhan**	**192**	**174**
武汉江岸经济开发区	Wuhan Jiang'an Economic Development Zone	2	2
武汉江汉经济开发区	Wuhan Jiang Han Economic Development Zone	1	2
武汉硚口经济开发区	Wuhan Qiao Kou Economic Development Zone	3	3
武汉汉阳经济开发区	Wuhan Han Yang Economic Development Zone	9	10
武汉武昌经济开发区	Wuhan Wu Chang Economic Development Zone		
武汉青山经济开发区	Wuhan Qing Shan Economic Development Zone		1
武汉洪山经济开发区	Wuhan Hong Shan Economic Development Zone	1	
武汉吴家山台商工业园区	Wuhan Wu Jiashan Taiwanese businessman Invested Industrial Park	48	22
武汉汉南经济开发区	Wuhan Han Nan Economic Development Zone	4	3
武汉蔡甸经济开发区	Wuhan Cai Dian Economic Development Zone	1	4
武汉江夏经济开发区	Wuhan Jiang Xia Economic Development Zone	19	5
武汉盘龙城经济开发区	Wuhan Pan Longcheng Economic Development Zone	28	25
武汉阳逻经济开发区	Wuhan Yang Luo Economic Development Zone	18	28
武汉经济技术开发区	Wuhan Economic and Technological Development Zone	32	32
武汉东湖新技术产业开发区	Wuhan East Lake Technology Industrial Development Zone	26	37
黄石市	**Huangshi**	**58**	**76**
湖北黄石港工业园区	Hubei Huang Shi Gang Industrial Park		4
湖北西塞山工业园区	Hubei Xi Saishan Industrial Park	5	5
湖北黄石经济开发区	Hubei Huang Shi Economic Development Zone	37	42
湖北阳新工业园区	Hubei Yang Xin Industrial Park	5	5
湖北大冶经济开发区	Hubei Da Ye Economic Development Zone	5	12
大冶灵成工业园	Daye Ling Cheng Industrial Park	6	8
十堰市	**Shiyan**	**24**	**41**
湖北十堰经济开发区	Hubei Shiyan Economic Development Zone	5	4
湖北十堰东城经济开发区	Hubei Shi Yan Dongcheng Economic Development Zone	4	15
湖北十堰西城经济开发区	Hubei Shi Yan Xicheng Economic Development Zone	1	1
湖北郧县经济开发区	Hubei Yun County Economic Development Zone	4	10
湖北郧西工业园区	Hubei Yun West Industrial Park	3	3
湖北竹山经济开发区	Hubei Zhu Shan Economic Development Zone	2	1
湖北竹溪工业园区	Hubei Zhu Xi Industrial Park	1	
湖北房县工业园区	Hubei Fang County Industrial Park	2	4
湖北丹江口经济开发区	Hubei Dan Jiangkou Economic Development Zone	2	3
宜昌市	**Yichang**	**84**	**122**
湖北西陵经济开发区	Hubei Xi Ling Economic Development Zone	5	5
湖北伍家岗工业园区	Hubei Wu Jiagang Industrial Park	1	6
湖北点军工业园区	Hubei Dian Jun Industrial Park	1	
湖北夷陵经济开发区	Hubei Yi Ling Economic Development Zone	12	17
湖北远安工业园区	Hubei Yuan An Industrial Park	3	10
湖北秭归经济开发区	Hubei Zi Gui Economic Development Zone	4	6
湖北长阳经济开发区	Hubei Chang Yang Economic Development Zone	3	5
湖北五峰工业园区	Hubei Wu Feng Industrial Park	1	3
湖北宜昌经济开发区	Hubei Yi Chang Economic Development Zone	22	25
湖北宜都工业园区	Hubei Yi Du Industrial Park	7	7
湖北当阳经济开发区	Hubei Dang Yang Economic Development Zone	9	11
湖北枝江经济开发区	Hubei Zhi Jiang Economic Development Zone	15	25
枝江安福寺工业园	Zhi Jiang Anfu Temple Industrial Park	1	2

新开工项目(个) Number of Newly Opened Projects (unit)		开发区税收总额(万元) Total Tax Revenue of Development (10 000 yuan)		外商投资金额(万美元) Total Value of Foreign Investment (10 000 US dollors)		出口总额(万美元) Total Value of Export (10 000 US dollors)	
2008	2009	2008	2009	2008	2009	2008	2009
2679	**3351**	**4134961**	**5423036**	**218866**	**271419**	**508345**	**499650**
336	**361**	**2509457**	**3357224**	**101809**	**110427**	**244645**	**219701**
3	1	6808.6	11107.7				
		52000	57500			3760	3760
2	1	61470	70000	1211	285	12661	10349
9	10	110838	127319			18.7	400
10	5	35062	43338	1025	300	3026	860
6	4	33597	35000	100	242		
9	15	10423	16720	150	100	1537	1430
115	125	342288	456884	14133.5	15124.8	11701	9374
8	7	15300	19440	1706	2161	7000	5906
9	14	40288	49470	743	817	1765	265
19	29	118200	128340	2699	3465	3216	3182.14
6		38700	38887			2200	1120
9	15	46182	51118	5931	5786	5016	4981
95	95	735900	1003500	11726	12546	123774	103074
36	40	862400	1248600	62384	69600	68970	75000
89	**163**	**110123**	**148697**	**8530**	**12900**	**15325**	**19859**
	10		500				170
12	10	14973	15340	6000		410	320
36	40	34648	41069	2000	6500	13082	17100
8	5	11059	12862	100	3000	583	984
25	82	47228	74500		500	1164	1085
8	16	2215	4426	430	2900	86	200
90	**129**	**48548**	**64623**	**1487**	**700**	**3489.3**	**5167**
5	19	25192	30192	929	500	1017	1099
14	15	7780	12200	558	200	800	1988.1
	4	565	1044				
28	33	3961	5268			587.3	785.9
1	3	500	1200				
15	16	1100	2000			255	88
8	5	610	750			100	150
6	17	1310	2769			730	1056
13	17	7530	9200				
426	**546**	**282548.31**	**336060**	**11217**	**34659.9**	**39746**	**38435**
11	26	3493	7401	604	507		364
	7	11172	8462			787	661
3	1	7807	6183	378	210	5071	2350
16	44	25104	31098	1507	160	1347	347
13	32	6094	13948			610	850
11	13	10622	14051	342	370	1006	1413
6	4	13128	14173			703	1334
10	20	4136.3	4485		327.9	104	110
51	33	80211	86365	3951	24431	12326	6900
126	80	51300	56336	2333	5900	11135	15478
33	91	21961	27277	1028	1200	412	686
139	182	45266	63549	792	1263	2573	3452
7	13	2254	2732	282	291	3672	4490

19-2 续表 7 continued

开发区详细名称	Name of Development Zone	其中:亿元以上项目(个) Number of Projects above 100 million yuan (unit)	
		2008	2009
襄樊市	**Xianfan**	**55**	**112**
湖北襄樊高新技术产业开发区	Hubei Xiang Fan High and New Technology Industrial Development Zone	15	25
襄樊鱼梁州经济开发区	Xiang Fan Yu Liangzhou Economic Development Zone		1
湖北襄城经济开发区	Hubei Xiang Cheng Economic Development Zone	1	10
湖北樊城经济开发区	Hubei Fan Cheng Economic Development Zone	2	4
湖北襄阳经济开发区	Hubei Xiang Yang Economic Development Zone	7	16
襄阳工业园	Xiang Yang Industrial Park		
湖北南漳经济开发区	Hubei Nan Zhang Economic Development Zone	3	9
湖北谷城经济开发区	Hubei Gu Cheng Economic Development Zone	5	9
谷城石花经济开发区	Gu Cheng Shi Hua Economic Development Zone	4	5
湖北保康经济开发区	Hubei Bao Kang Economic Development Zone		5
湖北老河口经济开发区	Hubei Lao Hekou Economic Development Zone	5	12
湖北枣阳济开发区	Hubei Zao Yang Economic Development Zone	3	3
枣阳吴店工业园	Zao Yang Wu Dian Industrial Park		1
湖北宜城经济开发区	Hubei Yi Cheng Economic Development Zone	10	12
鄂州市	**Ezhou**	**24**	**37**
湖北鄂州花湖经济开发区	Hubei E'Zhou Hua Hu Economic Development Zone	8	8
湖北鄂州葛店经济开发区	Hubei E'Zhou Ge Dian Economic Development Zone	14	27
湖北鄂州经济开发区	Hubei E'Zhou Economic Development Zone	2	2
荆门市	**Jingmen**	**58**	**99**
湖北东宝工业园区	Hubei Dong Bao Industrial Park	1	5
湖北荆门经济开发区	Hubei Jing Men Economic Development Zone	10	12
湖北京山经济开发区	Hubei Jing Shan Economic Development Zone	7	9
湖北沙洋经济开发区	Hubei Sha Yang Economic Development Zone	2	5
湖北钟祥经济开发区	Hubei Fan Zheng Economic Development Zone	6	15
钟祥胡集经济开发区	Zhong Xiang Hu Ji Economic Development Zone	6	7
孝感市	**Xiaogan**	**54**	**87**
湖北孝感经济开发区	Hubei Xiao Gan Economic Development Zone	11	22
湖北孝南经济开发区	Hubei Xiao Nan Economic Development Zone	13	25
湖北孝昌经济开发区	Hubei Xiao Chang Economic Development Zone	3	4
湖北大悟经济开发区	Hubei Da Wu Economic Development Zone		
湖北云梦经济开发区	Hubei Yun Meng Economic Development Zone	2	2
湖北应城经济开发区	Hubei Ying Cheng Economic Development Zone	3	8
湖北安陆经济开发区	Hubei An Lu Economic Development Zone	4	5
湖北汉川经济开发区	Hubei Han Chuan Economic Development Zone	18	21
荆州市	**Jingzhou**	**31**	**32**
湖北沙市经济开发区	Hubei Sha Shi Economic Development Zone	3	1
湖北荆州城南经济开发区	Jing Zhou Cheng Nan Economic Development Zone	2	5
湖北荆州经济开发区	Hubei Jing Zhou Economic Development Zone	11	5
湖北公安经济开发区	Hubei Gong An Economic Development Zone	3	2
湖北监利经济开发区	Hubei Jian Li Economic Development Zone	1	2
湖北江陵工业园区	Hubei Jiang Ling Industrial Park	2	5
湖北石首经济开发区	Hubei Shi Shou Economic Development Zone	3	4
湖北洪湖经济开发区	Hubei Hong Hu Economic Development Zone	4	6
洪湖府场经济开发区	Honghu Fuchang Economic Development Zone		
湖北松滋经济开发区	Hubei Song Zi Economic Development Zone	2	2
黄冈市	**Huanggang**	**33**	**61**
湖北黄冈经济开发区	Hubei huang Gang Economic Development Zone	8	11

新开工项目(个) Number of Newly Opened Projects (unit)		开发区税收总额(万元) Total Tax Revenue of Development (10 000 yuan)		外商投资金额(万美元) Total Value of Foreign Investment (10 000 US dollors)		出口总额(万美元) Total Value of Export (10 000 US dollors)	
2008	2009	2008	2009	2008	2009	2008	2009
421	**626**	**395868**	**529491**	**16198**	**24490**	**41110**	**40226**
95	159	280000	320000	6935	10008	24000	18000
	4	1073	2246				
5	21	13670	42707		708		722
25	41	14900	38900	3208	4570	5800	8200
37	25	23121	28716	1100		1310	1025
4	15	8120	8440			930	960
17	18	3294	4996	1012	1210	1100	1209
65	88	10568	15135	414	469	487	220
23	27	6130	11674	42	250	268	256
4	9	5500	6810			63	642
47	68	11358	19131	962	1807	852	1622
65	112	8170	16189	1025	1067	1200	1628
13	9	1584	1650				
21	30	8380	12897	1500	4401	5100	5742
52	**63**	**42282.07**	**45296.3**	**4689**	**5279.6**	**14324**	**15093**
18	16	4948.07	6506.3			396	700
26	37	33334	33730	4039	4279.6	13433	13933
8	10	4000	5060	650	1000	495	460
177	**235**	**96712**	**128056**	**15422**	**18392**	**20164**	**22272**
11	11	5316	8817			600	600
30	30	20107	25139	2704	3196	4256	5145
23	20	11598	16379	7		2550	1387
5	27	2587	1895	3000	3000	1020	1832
18	28	5498	8298	2000	3000	1656	2172
3	3	6500	7000				
125	**180**	**99212**	**133999**	**9485**	**9885**	**11767.9**	**9884**
17	33	11099	16750	700	900	2700	2900
22	38	13169	22018	2032	1607	3369	2639.7
8	15	1200	3468	780	870	480	510
3	1	10873	11870	420	543	245	285
9	16	7200	12000	1687	2210	794.9	486.3
13	15	14823	19270	960	1205	583	812
8	10	4259	5498	582		415	618
45	52	36589	43125	2324	2550	3181	1633
287	**230**	**137179.91**	**179177.2**	**10105**	**11376**	**33240**	**31239.6**
12	2	1760	2033			2503	5160
51	38	17116	21530	404	859	11417	8162
112	88	50187	61269	5500	6050	5773	6288
41	6	13000	17153				
11	13	972	5892				
13	18	1772.9	3039.2				4.6
8	9	21000	23000	3200	3300	10197	8158
23	25	6814	7876	621	617	1850	2187
1	7	4500	5880	380	550	1500	1280
15	24	20058	31505				
158	**234**	**119393**	**147769**	**11498**	**12268**	**20282.1**	**21677.61**
20	31	29802	33882	2852	3392	3580	3963

19-2 续表 8 continued

开发区详细名称	Name of Development Zone	其中:亿元以上项目(个) Number of Projects above 100 million yuan (unit)	
		2008	2009
湖北黄州火车站经济开发区	Huang Zhou Railway Station Economic Development Zone		
黄州工业园	Huang Zhou Industrial Park	3	1
湖北龙感湖工业园区	Hubei Long Gan Hu Industrial Park	2	6
湖北团风经济开发区	Hubei Tuan Feng Economic Development Zone	5	9
湖北红安经济开发区	Hubei Hong An Economic Development Zone	2	3
湖北罗田经济开发区	Hubei Luo Tian Economic Development Zone		3
湖北英山经济开发区	Hubei Ying Shan Economic Development Zone		
湖北浠水经济开发区	Hubei Xi Shui Economic Development Zone	1	3
湖北蕲春李时珍医药工业园区	Qi Chun Li Shizhen Medicine Industrial Park		2
蕲春经济开发区	Qi Chun Economic Development Zone	6	8
湖北黄梅经济开发区	Hubei Huang Mei Economic Development Zone	3	3
湖北麻城经济开发区	Hubei Ma Cheng Economic Development Zone	1	10
湖北武穴经济开发区	Hubei Wu Xue Economic Development Zone	2	2
咸宁市	**Xianning**	**51**	**73**
湖北咸安经济开发区	Hubei Xian'an Economic Development Zone	4	8
湖北嘉鱼经济开发区	Hubei Jia Yu Economic Development Zone	17	15
湖北通城经济开发区	Hubei Tong Cheng Economic Development Zone		3
湖北崇阳工业园区	Hubei Chong Yang Industrial Park	2	4
湖北通山经济开发区	Hubei Tong Shan Economic Development Zone		1
湖北咸宁经济开发区	Hubei Xian Ning Economic Development Zone	23	34
湖北赤壁经济开发区	Hubei Chi Bi Economic Development Zone	5	6
湖北赤壁蒲纺工业园区	Hubei Chi Bi Puqi Textile Industrial Park		2
随州市	**Suizhou**	**13**	**18**
湖北随州经济开发区	Hubei Sui Zhou Economic Development Zone	8	13
湖北曾都经济开发区	Hubei Zeng Dou Economic Development Zone	4	4
湖北广水经济开发区	Hubei Guang Shui Economic Development Zone	1	1
恩施州	**Enshi**	**15**	**30**
湖北恩施经济开发区	Hubei En Shi Economic Development Zone	8	22
湖北利川经济开发区	Hubei Li Chuan Economic Development Zone	1	1
湖北建始工业园区	Hubei Jian Shi Industrial Park	1	1
湖北巴东经济开发区	Hubei Ba Dong Economic Development Zone	3	3
湖北宣恩工业园区	Hubei Xuan En Industrial Park		
湖北咸丰工业园区	Hubei Xian Feng Industrial Park	1	1
湖北来凤经济开发区	Hubei Lai Feng Economic Development Zone	1	2
湖北鹤峰经济开发区	Hubei He Feng Economic Development Zone		
仙桃市	**Xiantao**	**14**	**14**
湖北仙桃经济开发区	Hubei Xian Tao Economic Development Zone	4	3
仙桃高新技术产业园	Xian Tao High and New Technology Industrial Park	6	7
仙桃工业园	Xian Tao Industrial Park	4	4
仙桃彭场工业园	Xian Tao Pengchang Industrial Park		
潜江市	**Qianjiang**	**6**	**5**
湖北潜江经济开发区	Hubei Qian Jiang Economic Development Zone	4	3
潜江张金经济开发区	Qian Jiang Zhangjin Economic Development Zone	1	2
潜江园林经济开发区	Qian Jiang Yuanlin Economic Development Zone	1	
天门市	**Tianmen**	**4**	**10**
湖北天门经济开发区	Hubei Tian Men Economic Development Zone	3	4
天门岳口工业园	Tian Men Yuekou Industrial Park	1	1
天门仙北工业园	Tian Men Xianbei Industrial Park		5

新开工项目(个) Number of Newly Opened Projects (unit)		开发区税收总额(万元) Total Tax Revenue of Development (10 000 yuan)		外商投资金额(万美元) Total Value of Foreign Investment (10 000 US dollors)		出口总额(万美元) Total Value of Export (10 000 US dollors)	
2008	2009	2008	2009	2008	2009	2008	2009
6	8	1880	2095	100	100	1100	1100
9	3	1209	1980			1000	1200
10	30	2300	3400	87	85	1864	2100
7	8	1600	2100	400		1500	1800
9	23	34562	40140	2000	2300	250	350
	9	320	1000				900
3	8	2600	2931	1300	700	0.1	0.61
25	20	4500	5000	2000	3000	4000	4500
4	5	2500	4100	1600	1850	400	687
14	20	4411	5954				121
28	42	5841	8401		400	566	720
5	13	11512	19966	1100	441	77	81
18	14	16356	16820	59		5945	4155
127	**124**	**108824**	**134747**	**8764**	**9575**	**9866**	**9864.3**
10	10	5826	10654	380	390	2902	2810
11	8	4521	5718	265	321	263.7	298.9
25	13	8981	8665	49	60	1379	1434
17	24	3180	4200	550		427.8	510
10	5	4600	6928	350	200	350	110
39	39	51073	66503	3408	3624	2375.5	1791.4
15	22	30643	30879	3762	4850	2168	2250
	3		1200		130		660
50	**51**	**26934**	**33524**	**3222**	**1839**	**23401**	**36989**
29	28	17289	20502	1870	1839	11242	19642
4	8	7909	10392	962		10979	15389
17	15	1736	2630	390		1180	1958
83	**117**	**31159.4**	**48463.01**	**240**	**520**	**2511**	**2751.31**
31	51	23412	37010		100	860	1152
8	9	3360	3939			16	21
4	13	444	1421.8		40	1321	945.7
14	13	56.4	2059.3		180		
7	10	97	152				50
7	4	418	717	240	200		
3	5	2554	2629			60	174.61
9	10	818	434.91			254	408
93	**111**	**51158**	**60835**	**7000**	**9800**	**14330**	**16980**
46	70	10739	13230		1200	2672	3870
16	17	23796	25340	1500	2000	696	860
19	6	10000	15000	1000	2000	3500	3000
12	18	6623	7265	4500	4600	7462	9250
134	**139**	**61813**	**56726**	**5500**	**3300**	**10242**	**5689**
27	42	28775	21577			6912	4489
24	14	11838	10133	3000		2430	
83	83	21200	25016	2500	3300	900	1200
31	**42**	**13750**	**18348**	**3700**	**6008**	**3902**	**3822**
9	8	8490	8911	3700	3700	1642	1132
17	17	4560	8218		470	2260	2680
5	17	700	1219		1838		10

主要统计指标解释

开发区批准面积　指国土部门核定的开发区规划面积。

开发区占地面积　指开发区实际开发占用的面积。

企业个数　指报告期末已在工商行政管理机关登记注册、并在开发区管理机构进行统计登记的法人单位数，包括内资企业、港澳台投资企业和外商投资企业。不含个体企业。

高新技术企业　指生产高新技术产品经省科学技术厅授牌的企业。

工业企业　包括采矿业、制造业、电力、燃气及水的生产和供应业。

规模以上工业企业　是指企业所在地在开发区内的全部年主营收入500万元及以上的法人工业企业。即无论企业是否在开发区注册，也无论企业隶属何行政级别或部门，只要所在地在开发区的所有规模以上企业都在本制度规定的统计范围以内。反之，所在地不在开发区，尽管其在开发区注册的规模以上企业也不在本制度规定的统计范围之内。

从业人员　指报告期末在开发区企业、行政和事业单位中工作，取得工资或其他形式的劳动报酬的全部人员数。包括在岗职工，再就业的离退休人员、民办教师及在企业工作的外方人员和港澳台方人员、兼职人员、借用的外单位人员和第二职业者。不包括离开本单位但仍保留劳动关系的职工。

技工贸总收入　指企业全年的产品销售收入、技术性收入和与本企业产品相关的商品的销售收入、其它业务收入、营业外收入等各种收入的总和。

技术收入　指支书转让、技术承包、技术咨询与服务、技术入股、中试产品收入以及接受外单位委托的科研收入等。

技术承包收入　包括技术项目设计承包、技术工程设计和承包所获得的收入。

技术咨询与服务收入　指企业利用自己的人力、物力和数据系统等为社会和用户提供技术情报、技术资料、技术咨询、测试分析及其它类型的技术性服务所获得的收入。

接受委托研究开发收入　指企业承担社会各方面委托研究，开发新产品所获得的收入。

工业总产值(现价)　是以货币形式表现的，工业企业在一定时期内生产的工业最终产品或提供工业性劳务活动的总价值量。

工业总产值包括本期生产成品价值、对外加工费收入，在制品半成品期末期初差额价值三部分。

①本期生产成品价值　是指企业本期生产，并在报告期内不再进行加工，经检验、包装入库的全部工业成品(半成品)价值合计，包括企业生产的自制设备及提供给本企业在建工程、其他非工业部门和生活福利部门等单位使用的成品价值，本期生产成品价值按自备原材料生产的产品的数量乘以本期不含增值税(销项税额)的产品实际销售平均单价计算;会计核算中按成本价格转帐的自制设备和自产自用的成品，按成本价格计算生产成品价值。生产成品价值中不包括用定货者来料加工的成品(半成品)价值。

②对外加工费收入　是指企业在报告期内完成的对外承接的工业品加工(包括用定货者来料加工产品)的加工费收入和对外工业修理作业所取得的加工费收入。对外加工费收入按不含增值税(销项税额)的价格计算，可根据会计“产品销售收入”科目的有关资料取得。

对于本企业对内非工业部门提供的加工修理、设备安装的劳务收入，如果企业会计核算基础比较好，能取得这部分资料，而且这部分价值所占比重较大，应包括在对外加工费收入中。

③自制半成品在制品期末期初差额价值　是指企业报告期自制半成品、在制品期末减期初的差额价值，本指标一般可从会计核算资料中取得。如果会计产品成本核算中不计算半成品、在制品的成本，则总产值中也不包括这部分价值，反之则包括。

高新技术产值 高新技术产品指高新技术领域的产品。即满足下列条件之一的产品：①首次应用新科学原理生产的最新产品；②首次应用最新工艺生产并使产品质量、成本和劳动效率有显著改进的产品；③技术水平达到90年代国际先进水平的产品。高新技术产值指报告期省科技厅认定的高新技术企业和非高新技术企业中的高新技术产品的产值两部分。

工业增加值 指工业企业在报告期内以货币形式表现的工业生产活动的最终成果，是企业全部生产活动的总成果扣除了在生产过程中消耗或转移的物质产品和劳务价值后的余额，是企业生产过程中新增加的价值。

计算工业增加值通常采用两种方法。一是“生产法”，二是“收入法”，目前工业统计主要采用“生产法”计算工业增加值。

“生产法”，即从工业生产过程中产品和劳务价值形成的角度入手，剔除生产环节中间投入的价值，从而得到新增价值的方法。公式为:

工业增加值=工业总产值—工业中间投入+本期应交增值税

上述公式中，本期应交增值税的企业为负数时，综合部门汇总时按零处理。

“收入法”，即从工业生产过程中创造的原始收入初次分配的角度，对工业生产活动最终成果进行核算的一种方法，其计算公式为:

工业增加值=固定资产折旧+劳动者报酬+生产税净额+营业盈余

工业中间投入 1. 定义：指企业在报告期内用于工业生产活动所一次性消耗的外购原材料、燃料、动力及其他实物产品和对外支付的服务费用。

2. 计算原则：计算工业中间投入须遵循以下三条原则：（1）必须是从企业外部购入的产品和服务的价值，不包括生产过程中回收的废料以及自制品的价值。（2）必须是本期投入生产，并一次性消耗的产品和服务的价值，不包括固定资产转移价值：（3）中间投入的计算口径必须与总产值的计算口径相一致：即计入工业中间投入的产品和服务价值必须已经计入了工业总产值中。

3. 分类：工业中间投入按企业支付对象可以分为中间物质投入和中间劳务投入。中间物质投入是指生产过程中所消耗的外购原材料、燃料、动力以及其它实物产品和支付给物质生产部门(工业、农业、批发零售贸易业、建筑业、货物运输及邮电业)的服务费用，中间劳务投入指支付给非物质生产部门(如金融、保险、文化教育、科学研究、医疗卫生、行政管理)的服务费用。

工业中间投入按照具体内容分为直接材料、制造费用中的中间投入、管理费用中的中间投入、销售费用中的中间投入和利息支出五大项。

日常统计中计算中间投入是按第二种分类计算的。

4. 计算方法：计算工业中间投入的具体方法可以分为二种。一是正算法，即将制造费用、管理费用、销售费用中属于中间投入的部分分别相加，再加上直接材料和利息支出，得出工业中间投入合计。二是倒算法，即分别用制造费用、管理费用、销售费用合计减去其中属于增加值的项目(大体包括工资、福利费、折旧、劳动保险费、职工待业保险费等)，倒算出三项费用中的中间投入，再加上直接材料和利息支出，得出工业中间投入合计。在实算操作过程中，采用倒算法计算比较简便易行。

5. 资料来源：计算中间投入的资料来源，可分别根据企业“产品成本表”、“管理费用”、“财务费用”、“销售费用”明细表归纳整理填报。

高新技术增加值 增加值是指报告期内企业在生产活动中新创造的价值。有两种计算方法：一是“生产法”；二是“收入法”，亦称要素分配法。计算方法为:

（1）按生产法计算的工业增加值=工业总产值—工业中间投入+本期应交增值税；（2）按分配法计算的工业增加值=固定资产折旧+劳动者报酬+生产税净额+营业盈余。

高新技术增加值指报告期省科技厅认定的高新技术企业的增加值和非高新技术企业中的高新技术产品的增加值两部分。

主营业务收入 指企业经常性的、主要业务所产生的收入。不同行业的企业主营业务收入包括的内容不同。工业企业的主营业务收入主要包括销售产品、自制半成品、提供工业性劳务等收入；商品流通企业的主营业务收入主要包括销售商品取得的收入。主营业务收入一般占企业收入的比重较大，对企业的经济效益产生较大的影响。在会计核算中单独设置“主营业务收入”科目核算经常性的、主要业务所产生的收入。

固定资产投资总额　指开发区所有单位报告期内以货币表示的建造和购置固定资产活动的工作量以及与此有关的费用总称。报告期内固定资产投资总额按实际完成投资额（包括实际完成的建筑安装工程价值，设备、工具、器具的购置费，以及实际发生的其他费用）计算。

施工项目个数　指报告期内曾进行建筑或安装工程施工活动的建设项目个数，包括报告期内新开工项目、报告期以前开工跨入报告期继续施工的项目以及报告期施过工并在报告期内全部建成投产或停缓建的项目个数。

税收总额　指开发区全口径税收收入。包含国税收入、地税收入。主要有增值税、营业税、所得税、城市维护建设税、城镇土地使用税、房产税、印花税、资源税、土地增值税等。

外商投资金额　指外国企业和经济组织或个人(包括华侨、港澳台胞以及我国在境外注册的企业)按我国有关政策、法规，用现汇、实物、技术等在我国境内开办外商独资企业、与我国境内的企业或经济组织共同举办中外合资经营企业、合作经营企业或合作开发资源的投资(包括外商投资收益的再投资)，以及经政府有关部门批准的项目投资总额内企业从境外借入的资金。

出口总额　指实际出口的货物总金额。我国规定出口货物按离岸价格统计。

Explanatory Notes on Main Statistical Indicators

Land Area Approved for Development Zone refers to the land area of development zone ratified for program by the state department of territory.

Floor Area of Development Zone refers to the land area of development zone that is practically exploited and occupied.

The Number of Enterprise refers to the number of impersonal entity that has registered at industrial organs and commerce administration at the end of report period and that has been counted and registered. Included in this catogary are domestic—funded enterprises, enterprises with funds from Hong kong,Macao,Taiwan and foreign—funded enterprises. Private enterprises are excluded.

Enterprises of High and New Technology refer to enterprises verified by provincial office of science and technology that produce hi-tech products.

Industrial Enterprises include mining, manufacturing, and manufacturing and supply of power, gas and water.

Industrial enterprises above designated size refer to entity industrial enterprises whose main annual turnover exceeds 5 million in the circle of development zone where enterpriese are located. That is to say,no matter enterprises has registered or not, what department enterprises belong to, all the enterprises whose location are in the development zone are counted which are above designated size. Otherwise, enterprises above designated size whose location is not in the development zone are not counted although they have registered at development zone.

Employees refer to all the workers working in enterprises in development zone,administrative unit and public institution who have got their income or payment of labour in other forms at the end of report period. Included in this category are workers on guard, re—employed laid—off workers and retirees, citizen-managed teachers; foreign workers in enterprises,workers of Hong Kong, Macao and Taiwan, part—time workers, borrowed workers from external enterprises and second—job workers. Workers having left enterprises who reserve labour relations are excluded.

Total turnover of technology, industry and trade refers to the total sum of product sales proceeds, technological gain and goods sales proceeds that are related to our products,other business gain,external—business gain in one year,and the like.

Technological turnover refers to the gain of technology transferrance, technology contract, technology advisory and service, technology share,products of pilotscale experiment and the gain of external-entrusted scientific research.

Technology contract turnover refers to the gain from contract of technology program design,design and contract of technology project.

Technology advisory and service turnover refers to the income from technical intellegence, technilcal information,technical advisory and test analysis provided availing enterprises themselves of human resources,physical resources and data system, and other kinds of technical service.

Revenue of entrusted reserch and development refers to the revenue from reserch and development of new products contracted provided to various social units.

Gross Industrial Output Value (at current price) refers to the total volum of final industrial products produced and industrial services provided in money terms during a given period .

Gross Industrial Output Value consists of 3 components: value of the finished products during the reference period, income from external processing, and value of change in semi-finished products at the end of and at the beginning of the reference period.

①value of the finished products during the reference period refers to the value of all finished(semi-finished) industrial products that are produced during the reference period without the need for further processing, checked for accepatance, packed and put into the warehouse of the enterprise, including the value of own-produced equipment and the value of products provided to the projects under construction of the enterprise, and to other non-industrial or welfare units. Value of finished products during the reference period is calculated by the quantity of products produced using own materials multiplied by the average unit prices at which products are sold(exculding value-added tax). Own-produced equipment and products for own use are value at cost prices as in the case of enterprise accounting. Value of finished products does not include the value of finished products(semi-finished products) that are produced using the materials from the clients who make the ordres.

②Income from external processing refers to income from contracted external processing of industrial products(including processing of industrial products using materials from the clients), and the income from industrial repairing work provided to other units. Income from external processing is calculated using information from the item "products sales income" in the enterprise accounting at the prices excluding value-added tax.For income from external services such as processing, repairing and installation of equipment provided to non-industrial units within the enterprise, if the accounting work of the enterprise is good enough to separate it from other records, and the share of such services is significant, it should also be included in the income from external processing.

③value of change in semi-finished products at the end of and at the beginning of the reference period refers to the value of change in semi-finished products at the end and at the beginning of the reference period, which generally can be obtained from accounting records of enterprises. If the enterprise accounting excludes the cost of semi-finished products, then it should not be inculded in the gross industrial output value,and vice versa.

High and new technology value High and new technology products refer to products in the area of high and new technology, namely any kind of products meeting following standars: ① the latest products using latest scientific principles the first time; ②the products that are produced by the latest technology and have noticeably improved the quality, cost and work efficiency; ③ products whose technical merit has reached advanced international standards of 1990s. High and new technology value refers to 2 components: the value of high and new technology enterprises designated by provincial Science and Technology Office in reference period, and value of high and new technology products of non-high-and-new technology enterprises.

Industrial value added refers to the final results of industrial production enterprises in money terms during the the reference period.

Industrial value added can be usually calculated by two approaches:the production approach,and the income approach.Industrial stastics mainly adopts the production approach to calculate the industrial value added at present.

The production approach is the approach that newly-increased value is gained by eliminating the value indulged in the production link in terms of value formation of products and labor in the process of industrial prodution. The formula is: Industrial value added= total industrial value-industrial intermediate input

+ current value added tax receivable

In this formula,when current value added tax receivale is minus, the Integration Department will treat it as zero.

The income approach is an approach that final results of industrial production activities are checked in terms of the primary distribution of original income created in the indusrial production. Here is its formula: Industrial value added= depreciation of fixed assets+remuneration of labourers+net of produce tax+ operating surplus

Industrial intermediate input:

1.Definition: It refers to the service cost for purchased raw material,gas,power and other physical products,and external-paid services consumed during the reference period for the industrial production of enterprises.

2.Calculating principles:Calculating industrial intermediate input must follow the three principles:(1)The value must be the value of goods and services that are purchased from outside,exculding the value of reclaimed waste materials in the production and that of own products.(2) The value must be the value of goods and services that are inputted into production consumed during the reference period,excluding transfer value of fixed assets.(3)The calculating units of the intermediate input must be in correspondence with that of total value, namely the value of products and service reckoned in industrial intermediate input has been reckoned in industrial value.

3.Category: Industrial intermediate input in terms of pay objectcan be classified as intermediate material input and intermediate labor input . Intermediate material input refers to the the purchased raw material, gas,power and other physical products consumed in the production, and the cost of service paid to departments of material production(industry,agriculcuture, wholesales and retail trade,construction goods transportation and post). Intermediate labor input refers to cost of service paid to departments of nonmaterial production(finance,insurance,cultural education,scientific research,medical health and administration)

Industrial intermediate input in terms of concrete content can be classified into 5 components , namely direct consumption of materials,industrial intermediate input in manufacturing cost, industrial intermediate input in management cost, industrial intermediate input in marketing cost and expenditure on interest.

Intermediate input in common calculating is calculated by the second category.

4.Calculating approaches:the calculating approaches to industrial intermediate input have two approaches. Positive calculating, namely add respectively the manufacuring cost, management cost,sales cost that belong to intermediate input, then add direct material and interest expense.The final result is reconed into the total. Negative calculating, namely manufacturing cost, management cost, sale cost that belong to value-added items(generally included are sallary, welfarism, depreciation,labor insurance, employee's job-waiting insurance,ect)is substracted respectively from the total.The result is the its intermediate input respectively. Then direct material and interest expense are added. The final result is reconed into the total. Negative calculating is easier to carry out in pratical calculating.

5.Information source: The information source in calculating intermediate input can be obtained from product Cost Table, tables of Management Cost, Financial Expense and Sales Cost.

Value added of high and new technology value added refers to the newly created value in the production in the reference period. There are two approaches to calculting, the production approach, and the income approach,also factor distribution approach. The calculation methods are: (1)industrial value added by the production approach=total industrial value-industrial intermediate input+ current value added tax receivable; (2) industrial value added by distribution approach=depreciation of fixed assets+ remuneration of labourers+net of produce tax+ operating surplus

Value added of high and new technology refers to the value added of high and new technology enterprises designated by provincial Science and Technology Office in reference period, and value added of high and new technology products of non-high-and-new technology enterprises.

Income from major business refers to the income of regular and major bussiness of enterprises. The content of the income from major business differs from enterprise to enterprise. The income from major business of industrial enterprises mainly includes the income from product sales,own semi-finished products,industrial labor; the income from major business of commodity circulation enterprises mainly includes the incoome from commodity sales.Income from major business generally takes a big share in the income of enterprise,and has a great influence on the economic benefit.The "income from major business" item is set individually to check income from regular and major business in accounting.

Total investment in fixed assets refers to the generic term for operation capacity of building up and purchasing fixed assets in money terms during the reference period and related cost. Total investment in fixed assets in reference period is calculated by actual investment(including value of actual finish constructive installation engineering,purchasing cost of equipment,tools and devices,and other actual cost)

The number of projects under construction:refers to number of projects that has carried out construction or installation engineering in reference period, including the number of newly-opened projects during reference period,projects opened before reference period and constructed over reference period,and projects that have been constructed in reference period and completed or delayed within reference period.

Total tax revenue refers to tax revenue in all units of development zone.Included in this category are national and local tax revenue.They are mainly value added tax, turnover tax, income tax, city maintenance construction tax, use tax of town land, house tax, stamp tax, resource tax, land value increment tax, ect.

Value of foreign investment refers to the investment made by the soley foreign-owned enterprises opened according to the relevant policies and regulations and by means of convertible foreign exchange, physical goods,and technology,ect ; sino-foreign joint venture run by foreign enterprises,ecnomic organizations or individuals(including overseas Chinese,fellow citizens of Hongkong,Macao and Taiwan and Sino-enterprises registered in foreign countries) with Chinese enterprises or Chinese ecnomic organizations. And capital borrow from abroad and within the total value of investment in projects approved by the relevant department of Government.

Total value of export refers to total value of pratical outward cargoes . Our country stipulates that outward cargoes are calculated on FOB basis.

20 武汉城市圈

Wuhan Urban Circle

资料整理：陶　红

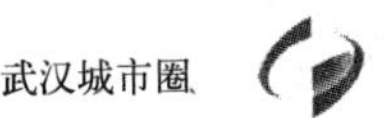

20-1 武汉城市圈主要经济指标

MAIN ECONOMIC INDICATORS OF WUHAN URBAN CIRCLE

指标	Item	土地面积(平方公里) Land Area (sq.km)	常住人口(万人) Total Population (year-end) (10 000 persons)	地区生产总值(亿元) Gross Regional Product(100 million yuan)	第一产业(亿元) Primary Industry (100 million yuan)	第二产业(亿元) Secondary Industry (100 million yuan)	#工业(亿元) #Industry (100 million yuan)	第三产业(亿元) Tertiary Industry (100 million yuan)	人均地区生产总值(元) Per Capita Gross Regional Prduct (yuan/person)
合计	**Total**	**58052**	**2999**	**8000.41**	**822.53**	**3702.56**	**3147.39**	**3475.32**	**26698**
武汉市	Wuhan Municipality	8494	910	4620.18	149.06	2142.14	1772.14	2328.98	51136
黄石市	Huangshi Municipality	4583	243	571.59	45.26	314.12	290.02	212.21	23580
鄂州市	Ezhou Municipality	1594	103	323.71	43.98	179.21	158.42	100.52	31308
孝感市	Xiaogan Municipality	8910	468	672.88	145.17	292.20	256.31	235.51	14378
黄冈市	Huanggang Municipality	17446	669	730.19	215.39	273.46	216.91	241.33	10930
咸宁市	Xianning Municipality	9861	252	418.45	87.02	179.18	161.56	152.24	16644
仙桃市	Xiantiao Municipality	2538	123	242.55	47.50	115.57	105.90	79.48	18759
潜江市	Qianjiang Municipality	2004	94	234.01	41.19	121.09	109.14	71.73	24980
天门市	Tianmen Municipality	2622	137	186.86	47.96	85.58	76.98	53.32	13653

20-1 续表 1 continued

指标	Item	就业人员(万人) Employed Persons (10 000 persons)	第一产业(万人) Primary Industry (10 000 persons)	第二产业(万人) Secondary Industry (10 000 persons)	第三产业(万人) Tertiary Industry (10 000 persons)	全社会固定资产投资(亿元) Investment in Fixed Assets (100 million yuan)	城镇固定资产投资(亿元) Investment in Urban Area (100 million yuan)	#房地产开发投资完成额(亿元) #Investment in Real Estate Development (100 million yuan)	地方一般预算财政收入(亿元) Revenue of Local Governments (100 million yuan)
合计	**Total**	**1618.49**	**442.68**	**515.19**	**659.62**	**5177.40**	**4857.66**	**935.91**	**445.83**
武汉市	Wuhan Municipality	456.00	79.57	156.00	220.43	3001.10	2921.76	778.59	316.07
黄石市	Huangshi Municipality	139.80	29.40	55.80	54.60	343.05	321.96	25.30	26.03
鄂州市	Ezhou Municipality	62.10	21.20	19.50	21.40	220.60	213.40	8.11	13.02
孝感市	Xiaogan Municipality	282.60	91.60	93.70	97.30	397.26	341.47	32.40	26.97
黄冈市	Huanggang Municipality	343.00	128.00	93.00	123.00	553.29	484.61	37.33	32.16
咸宁市	Xianning Municipality	140.80	42.50	35.60	62.70	301.58	249.10	39.55	18.14
仙桃市	Xiantiao Municipality	84.70	14.40	33.60	34.70	120.05	106.81	4.79	5.05
潜江市	Qianjiang Municipality	43.19	16.21	12.89	14.09	123.96	112.69	3.57	4.86
天门市	Tianmen Municipality	66.30	19.80	15.10	31.40	116.51	105.86	6.27	3.53

20-1 续表 2 continued

指标	Item	#各项税收(亿元) #Taxes (100 million yuan)	地方财政支出(亿元) Expenditures of Local Governments (100 million yuan)	农村居民人均纯收入(元) Annual Per Capita Disposable Income of Rural Households (yuan)	城镇居民人均可支配收入(元) Annual Per Capita Disposable Income of Urban Households (yuan)	农林牧渔业总产值(亿元) Gross Output Value of Agriculture (100 million yuan)	粮食产量(万吨) Output of Grain (10 000 tons)
合计	**Total**	**326.87**	**2107.31**	**5153**	**16795**	**1352.80**	**1058.26**
武汉市	Wuhan Municipality	247.95	445.10	7161	18389	251.79	135.89
黄石市	Huangshi Municipality	18.28	73.30	4811	13119	72.17	61.64
鄂州市	Ezhou Municipality	9.45	34.29	5718	13408	79.54	34.06
孝感市	Xiaogan Municipality	16.66	105.89	5131	12507	260.60	228.87
黄冈市	Huanggang Municipality	14.91	121.02	4130	11336	325.82	315.16
咸宁市	Xianning Municipality	10.85	78.99	4873	11626	140.18	112.51
仙桃市	Xiantiao Municipality	3.47	23.00	5856	11783	83.20	71.21
潜江市	Qianjiang Municipality	3.40	21.03	5531	12571	67.00	38.87
天门市	Tianmen Municipality	1.90	20.12	5326	11243	72.50	60.05

棉花产量(万吨) Output of Cotton (tons)	油料产量(万吨) Output of Oil-bearing Crops (10 000 tons)	工业企业单位数(个) Number of Enterprises (unit)	大型企业(个) Large Enterprises (unit)	中型企业(个) Medium Enterprises (unit)	小型企业(个) Small Enterprises (unit)	工业总产值(亿元) Gross Industrial Output Value (100 million yuan)	工业企业资产总计(亿元) Total Assets (100 million yuan)	工业企业利润总额(亿元) Total Profits (100 million yuan)
26.44	**146.29**	**7527**	**62**	**677**	**6549**	**9705.36**	**10683.86**	**579.11**
3.22	19.05	2538	40	285	2192	5798.88	7672.08	296.44
0.61	7.69	602	8	54	562	860.99	717.75	34.82
0.56	5.80	454	2	21	43	423.03	319.71	24.41
3.24	23.19	1004	6	102	960	688.14	570.12	37.89
7.13	47.90	1317	1	59	1307	570.96	420.87	44.00
0.27	8.26	726		53	666	443.14	293.31	32.99
2.65	11.89	359	2	46	376	348.97	186.72	39.98
4.04	11.31	255	3	28	208	365.15	345.69	24.84
4.72	11.20	272		29	235	206.10	157.61	43.74

20-1 续表 3 continued

指标	Item	房屋建筑竣工面积(万平方米) Floor Space Completed of Buildings (10 000 sq.m)	民用汽车拥有量(辆) Possession of Civil Vehicles (unit)	邮电业务总收入(亿元) Business Volume of Post Services(100 million yuan)	社会消费品零售总额(亿元) Total Retail Sales(100 million yuan)	进出口总额(亿美元) Imp. and Exp. Value of Commodities (USD 10 000)	出口额(亿美元) Export Value of Commodities (USD 10 000)	实际利用外资(万美元) Actually Foreign Direct Investments (USD 10 000)
合计	**Total**	**5052.96**	**1213625**	**381.71**	**3629.14**	**140.90**	**75.01**	**297571**
武汉市	Wuhan Municipality	1968.49	668523	293.82	2164.09	114.73	58.25	212175
黄石市	Huangshi Municipality	277.54	64153	13.64	256.09	11.50	4.73	27650
鄂州市	Ezhou Municipality	147.67	196885	22.51	126.68	1.69	0.74	9514
孝感市	Xiaogan Municipality	892.67	70474	1.39	326.89	2.23	1.92	13840
黄冈市	Huanggang Municipality	771.62	90010	17.48	340.07	4.79	4.05	12479
咸宁市	Xianning Municipality	477.42	65932	9.37	165.88	1.22	0.94	11235
仙桃市	Xiantiao Municipality	178.29	14742	3.89	127.87	2.74	2.51	4748
潜江市	Qianjiang Municipality	127.89	22646	17.48	86.36	1.65	1.56	2693
天门市	Tianmen Municipality	211.37	20260	2.13	135.21	0.35	0.31	3237

入境旅游者人数(万人次) Number of International Tourists (10 000 person-times)	国际旅游外汇收入(万美元) Foreign Exchange Earnings (USD 10 000)	金融机构人民币存款(亿元) State Bank Deposits (100 million yuan)	城乡居民储蓄存款(亿元) Urban & Rural Savings Deposits (100 million yuan)	金融机构人民币贷款(亿元) State Bank Loans(100 million yuan)	普通高等学校数(所) Schools on Regular Institutions of Higher Education (unit)	普通高等学校在校学生数(万人) Enrollment on Regular Institutions of Higher Education (10 000 persons)	卫生机构床位数(张) Number of Beds in Health Care Institutions (bed)	#卫生技术人员(人) #Medical and Technical Personnel (person)
72.37	**34942.65**	**11658.50**	**5016.35**	**8486.40**	**94**	**99.43**	**100648**	**133329**
66.90	32902.22	8575.56	2963.66	7069.38	78	84.63	48061	60038
0.82	348.66	576.17	312.87	356.06	3	3.2	9029	12063
0.62	233.57	202.51	121.09	99.56	1	0.9	3579	4663
1.34	495.14	625.95	428.24	318.26	2	3.2	10077	15044
1.06	285.43	773.45	553.03	317.19	4	3.8	14382	21259
1.03	315.94	347.19	222.55	171.52	3	2.5	6769	9465
0.26	243.43	183.43	137.35	55.37	1	0.8	2825	2714
0.19	73.43	207.06	142.34	52.64	2	0.4	2919	4854
0.15	44.83	167.18	135.22	46.42			3007	3229

21 鄂西生态文化旅游圈

Exi Ecological and Cultural Tourism Circle

资料整理：陶　红

21 鄂西生态文化旅游圈主要经济指标完成情况及占全省比重（2009）

ECOLOGICAL CULTURE IN WESTERN HUBEI ABOVE COMPLETION AND MAIN ECONOMIC INDICATORS OF PROPORTION(2009)

指标	单位	Item	Units	绝对值 Absolute value	比上年增长(%) Growth than last year(%)	占全省比重(%) Proportion(%)
土地面积	(平方公里)	The Land Area	(sq.km)	127847		68.8
#宜昌市	(平方公里)	#Yichang Municipality	(sq.km)	21084		11.3
襄樊市	(平方公里)	Xiangfan Municipality	(sq.km)	19724		10.6
常住人口	(万人)	The Resident Population	(10000persons)	2721.07	0.2	47.6
#宜昌市	(万人)	#Yichang Municipality	(10000persons)	404.55	0.2	7.1
襄樊市	(万人)	Xiangfan Municipality	(10000persons)	544.61	0.2	9.5
生产总值	(亿元)	Gross Regional Product	(100 million yuan)	4980.44	14.4	38.4
#宜昌市	(亿元)	#Yichang Municipality	(100 million yuan)	1272.33	15.1	9.8
襄樊市	(亿元)	Xiangfan Municipality	(100 million yuan)	1201.01	15.0	9.2
第一产业增加值	(亿元)	Primary Industry	(100 million yuan)	931.39	5.0	51.9
#宜昌市	(亿元)	#Yichang Municipality	(100 million yuan)	150.70	5.3	8.4
襄樊市	(亿元)	Xiangfan Municipality	(100 million yuan)	200.21	3.0	11.1
第二产业增加值	(亿元)	Second Industrial	(100 million yuan)	2287.84	18.9	37.9
#宜昌市	(亿元)	#Yichang Municipality	(100 million yuan)	705.00	17.6	11.7
襄樊市	(亿元)	Xiangfan Municipality	(100 million yuan)	575.32	19.9	9.5
#工业增加值	(亿元)	Industrial	(100 million yuan)	2088.56	18.8	40.3
#宜昌市	(亿元)	#Yichang Municipality	(100 million yuan)	650.10	18.0	12.5
襄樊市	(亿元)	Xiangfan Municipality	(100 million yuan)	530.10	20.0	10.2
第三产业增加值	(亿元)	Tertiary Industry	(100 million yuan)	1761.26	19.6	34.4
#宜昌市	(亿元)	#Yichang Municipality	(100 million yuan)	416.63	14.4	8.1
襄樊市	(亿元)	Xiangfan Municipality	(100 million yuan)	425.48	14.4	8.3
全社会固定资产投资	(亿元)	Investment in Fixed Assets	(100 million yuan)	2757.30	46.8	33.6
#宜昌市	(亿元)	#Yichang Municipality	(100 million yuan)	750.27	43.3	9.1
襄樊市	(亿元)	Xiangfan Municipality	(100 million yuan)	574.79	53.8	7.0
地方一般预算收入	(亿元)	Revenue of Local Governments	(100 million yuan)	368.95	13.2	45.3
#宜昌市	(亿元)	#Yichang Municipality	(100 million yuan)	54.94	24.1	6.7
襄樊市	(亿元)	Xiangfan Municipality	(100 million yuan)	37.02	23.2	4.5
城乡居民储蓄存款余额	(亿元)	Urban & Rural Savings Deposits	(100 million yuan)	3207	20.2	39.0
#宜昌市	(亿元)	#Yichang Municipality	(100 million yuan)	608.85	20.6	7.4
襄樊市	(亿元)	Xiangfan Municipality	(100 million yuan)	687.58	19.6	8.4
社会消费品零售总额	(亿元)	Total Retail Sales	(100 million yuan)	2299.27	26.7	38.8
#宜昌市	(亿元)	#Yichang Municipality	(100 million yuan)	470.41	21.1	7.9
襄樊市	(亿元)	Xiangfan Municipality	(100 million yuan)	500.56	22.0	8.7
海关进出口总额	(亿美元)	Total Import & Export	(100 million dollars)	31.39	-14.3	18.2
#宜昌市	(亿美元)	#Yichang Municipality	(100 million dollars)	10.35	-24.5	6.0
襄樊市	(亿美元)	Xiangfan Municipality	(100 million dollars)	4.34	-17.3	2.5
#出　口	(亿美元)	#Export	(100 million dollars)	24.77	-5.5	24.8
#宜昌市	(亿美元)	#Yichang Municipality	(100 million dollars)	7.76	-14.3	7.8
襄樊市	(亿美元)	Xiangfan Municipality	(100 million dollars)	3.29	-12.3	3.3
实际外商直接投资	(亿美元)	Actual Foreign Direct Investmen	(100 million dollars)	68195	21.8	18.6
#宜昌市	(亿美元)	#Yichang Municipality	(100 million dollars)	18136	13.3	5.0
襄樊市	(亿美元)	Xiangfan Municipality	(100 million dollars)	25073	48.1	6.9

22 三峡工程湖北库区

Hubei Area of The Three Gorges Project

资料整理：陶　红

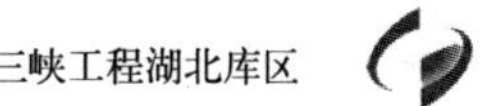

22 三峡工程湖北库区社会经济统计指标（2009）
HUBEI AREA OF THE THREE GORGES PROJECT SOCIAL AND ECONOMIC ATATISTICS(2009)

指 标	单 位	Item	Units	四县合计 Total	夷陵区 Yiling District	秭归县 Zigui County	兴山县 Xingshan County	巴东县 Badong County
一、资源、环境与基础条件		**Resources Environment and Basic Conditions**						
土地总面积	(平方公里)	The Land Area	(sq.km)	11532	3424	2427	2327	3354
常用耕地面积	(公顷)	Common Cultivated Area	(hectares)	92349	24369	19054	12976	35950
森林面积	(平方公里)	Forest Area	(sq.km)	5641	1630	1209	1291	1511
水土流失治理面积	(平方公里)	Soil Erosion Control Area	(sq.km)	75	37	16	12	11
公路通车里程	(公里)	Highway Traffic Mileage	(km)	11838	3659	2344	1528	4307
移动电话年末用户	(万户)	At The End of Mobile Phone Users	(10 000 units)	84	31	15	6	32
农村安全饮用水人口	(万人)	Rural Population of Safe Drinking Water	(10 000 persons)	69	31	16	6	17
全年用电量	(万千瓦时)	Annual Electricity Consumption	(10 000 kWh)	192515	56423	42057	71243	22792
二、人口与就业		**Population and Employment**						
年末总人口	(万人)	At The End of Population	(10 000 persons)	158	52	38	18	49
城镇人口(非农业人口)	(万人)	The Urban Population(non-agricultural population)	(10 000 persons)	30	13	7	5	5
乡村人口(农业人口)	(万人)	Rural Population (agricultural population)	(10 000 persons)	128	39	32	13	44
劳动力资源总人数	(万人)	Total Workforce	(10 000 persons)	102	37	23	11	30
城镇	(万人)	Town	(10 000 persons)	21	10	4	3	4
乡村	(万人)	Rural	(10 000 persons)	82	28	19	8	27
社会从业人员数	(万人)	Social Workers	(10 000 persons)	89	30	20	11	27
第一产业	(万人)	The First Industry	(10 000 persons)	43	10	11	6	15
第二产业	(万人)	The Second Industry	(10 000 persons)	15	6	4	1	3
第三产业	(万人)	The Third Industry	(10 000 persons)	32	14	5	4	9
城镇登记失业人数	(人)	Urban Unemployment Is Registered	(person)	7968	1953	1290	3807	918
三、经济发展		**The Economic development**						
国内生产总值	(万元)	GDP	(10 000 yuan)	2662947	1455382	437622	369742	400201
第一产业	(万元)	The First Industry	(10 000 yuan)	493617	224258	92956	59702	116701

22-1 续表 1 continued

指 标	单位	Item	Units	四县合计 Total	夷陵区 Yiling District	秭归县 Zigui County	兴山县 Xingshan County	巴东县 Badong County
第二产业	(万元)	The Second Industry	(10 000 yuan)	1229734	761172	128052	198405	142105
第三产业	(万元)	The Third Industry	(10 000 yuan)	939596	469952	216614	111635	141395
社会劳动生产率	(元)	Social Labour Productivity	(yuan)	29191	48032	21452	32721	14558
第一产业	(元)	The First Industry	(yuan)	11973	21986	8128	10119	7658
第二产业	(元)	The Second Industry	(yuan)	94971	126862	30488	180368	42168
第三产业	(元)	The Third Industry	(yuan)	34699	33330	45128	44414	15923
全社会固定资产投资	(万元)	The Social Investment in Fixed Assets	(10 000 yuan)	1613890	888363	288597	200117	236813
社会消费品零售总额	(万元)	Total Retail Sales of Consumer Goods	(10 000 yuan)	918433	501094	168039	124215	125085
出口总额	(万美元)	Total Exports	(10 000 dollars)	19832	1800	1509	15017	1506
地方财政收入	(万元)	Local Fiscal Revenue	(10 000 yuan)	122368	66058	17418	16871	22021
地方财政支出	(万元)	Local Fiscal Expenditure	(10 000 yuan)	487278	189578	100105	71059	126536
年末金融机构人民币存款余额	(万元)	Year-end Financial Institutions RMB Deposit Balance	(10 000 yuan)	2288080	1050857	448144	339757	449322
年末金融机构人民币贷款余额	(万元)	At The End of The Loan Balance of Financial Institutions	(10 000 yuan)	1038948	552382	147224	207165	132177
工业总产值	(万元)	Gross Industrial Output	(10 000 yuan)	3286269	2069383	353551	662962	200373
工业产品销售收入	(万元)	Sales Revenue of Industrial Products (advocate business wu income)	(10 000 yuan)	3044129	1886753	251291	714363	191722
工业实现利税总额	(万元)	Industrial Realized Profit Tax Amoun	(10 000 yuan)	360320	246815	15535	63127	34843
全社会货物运输量	(万吨)	Total Social Freight Traffic	(10 000 ton)	1812	768	466	267	311
#公路	(万吨)	#Highway	(10 000 ton)	1329	741	326	96	166
水运	(万吨)	Water	(10 000 ton)	483	27	140	171	145

22-1 续表 2 continued

指　标	单位	Item	Units	四县合计 Total	夷陵区 Yiling District	秭归县 Zigui County	兴山县 Xingshan County	巴东县 Badong County
全社会客运总量	(万人)	The Total Social Passenger	(10 000 persons)	2366	1176	741	155	295
#公路	(万人)	#Highway	(10 000 persons)	2244	1133	710	155	246
水运	(万人)	Water	(10 000 persons)	122	43	31		49
邮电业务总量	(万元)	Postal Business Volume	(10 000 yuan)	51543	21553	11655	2671	15664
四、社会发展		**The Social Development**						
小学学龄儿童入学率	(%)	Primary School-age Children	(%)		100	100	100	100
医院、卫生院技术人员数	(人)	Hospitals and Clinics Technical Personne	(person)	4507	1731	1113	494	1169
医院、卫生机构床位数	(张)	Hospitals and Health Care Institutions	(unit)	3948	1020	924	437	1567
公共图书馆藏书	(万册)	The Public Library	(10 000 units)	45	14	11	13	8
电视人口覆盖率	(%)	TV Population Coverage	(%)		99	98	96	97
刑事案件发案数	(件)	Total Criminal Cases	(unit)	2458	998	451	244	765
城镇居民最低生活保障人数	(人)	Urban Subsistence Security	(person)	29670	9288	7510	5428	7444
五、人民生活		**The People's Life**						
城镇职工工资总额	(万元)	Town Worker Total Wages	(10 000 yuan)	166403	80369	36211	22713	27110
城镇居民人均可支配收入	(元)	Urban per Capita Disposable Income	(yuan)	11386	12691	10514	10748	9977
城镇居民人均生活消费支出	(元)	Urban per Capita Expenditure	(yuan)	8568	9161	8090	8531	7794
农村居民人均纯收入	(元)	Per Capita net Income of Rural Residents	(yuan)	3999	6048	3177	3851	2790
农村居民人均消费性支出	(元)	Rural per Capita Consumer Spending	(yuan)	3338	4263	3259	3340	2561
城乡居民储蓄存款余额	(万元)	Savings Deposit Balance Urban and Rural Residents	(10 000 yuan)	1288940	623716	253109	159231	252884
城镇居民人均住宅使用面积	(平方米)	Urban per Capita Residential Area	(sq.m)	28.23	29	28	27	28
农村居民人均住宅使用面积	(平方米)	Rural per Capita Residential Area	(sq.m)	40.15	35	44	46	40
六、移民		**Immigration**						
移民工程本年计划投资	(万元)	The Project Plan to Invest in This Year	(10 000 yuan)	69453	4127	30772	22179	12375
移民工程本年完成投资	(万元)	This Project Completed Investment	(10 000 yuan)	72667	10682	21142	25920	14924
本年移民工程资金到位率	(%)	The Arrival Rate of Project Fund Immigrants	(%)		73	76	48	100
本年实迁城乡人口	(人)	The Rural Population Move Reality	(person)	4939	546	1872	360	2161
城镇实迁人口	(人)	Urban Real Moved Population	(person)	485		8	12	465
乡村实迁人口	(人)	Rural Reality Moved Population	(person)	4454	546	1864	348	1696

23 县域经济

Economy of Cities and Counties

资料整理：章　玲

23-1 县市主要经济指标
MAIN ECONOMIC INDICATORS OF COUNTIES

指标名称	Item	行政区域土地面积(平方公里) Land Area(Sq. km)	常住人口(万人) The Resident (10 000 person)		#城镇人口(万人) #Urban Population (10 000 persons)		#乡村人口(万人) #Rural Population (10 000 persons)	
		2009	2009	2008	2009	2008	2009	2008
蔡甸区	Caidian District	1094	43.65	43.00	12.27	11.35	31.38	31.65
江夏区	Jiangxia District	2009	64.35	63.40	23.01	22.05	41.34	41.35
黄陂区	Huangpi District	2261	89.10	92.20	26.77	27.61	62.33	64.59
新洲区	Xinzhou District	1501	85.16	86.80	39.34	39.49	45.82	47.31
汉南区	Hannan District	287	12.90	12.28	6.91	6.26	5.99	6.02
阳新县	Yangxin County	2783	75.47	80.38	18.41	19.53	57.06	60.85
大冶市	Daye City	1566	80.70	80.55	32.93	32.70	47.77	47.85
郧县	Yun County	3863	57.71	57.02	13.80	12.35	43.91	44.67
郧西县	Yunxi County	3509	42.84	47.31	6.03	6.02	36.81	41.29
竹山县	Zhushan County	3586	42.72	42.68	6.96	6.55	35.76	36.13
竹溪县	Zhuxi County	5110	33.46	32.40	4.91	4.94	28.55	27.46
房县	Fang County	5110	42.15	43.10	3.98	3.63	38.17	39.47
丹江口市	Danjiangkou City	3121	48.13	48.16	19.37	20.75	28.76	27.41
夷陵区	Yiling District	3424	52.00	52.00	12.73	12.58	39.27	39.42
远安县	Yuanan County	1752	18.60	18.60	3.87	3.86	14.73	14.74
兴山县	Xingshan County	2327	17.50	17.50	4.31	4.26	13.19	13.24
秭归县	Zigui County	2427	37.60	37.60	6.73	6.64	30.87	30.96
长阳县	Changyang Tujia A.C.	3430	40.50	40.50	6.58	6.55	33.92	33.95
五峰县	Wufeng Tujia A.C.	2072	19.60	19.60	2.69	2.70	16.91	16.90
宜都市	Yidu City	1357	38.95	38.80	11.56	11.62	27.39	27.18
当阳市	Dangyang City	2159	48.05	47.90	12.53	12.42	35.52	35.48
枝江市	Zhijiang City	1310	49.85	49.80	13.78	13.72	36.07	36.08
襄阳区	Xiangyang District	2306	90.90	90.70	45.48	44.30	45.42	46.40
南漳县	Nanzhang County	3859	53.30	53.20	11.38	11.36	41.92	41.84
谷城县	Gucheng County	2553	50.50	50.50	10.86	10.76	39.64	39.74
保康县	Baokang County	3225	26.20	26.10	5.33	4.88	20.87	21.22
老河口市	Laohekou City	1032	48.30	48.20	24.35	23.83	23.95	24.37
枣阳市	Zaoyang City	3277	102.20	102.00	50.34	47.63	51.86	54.37
宜城市	Yicheng City	2115	51.50	51.40	22.20	23.15	29.30	28.25
梁子湖区	Liangzihu District	500	17.61	16.62	2.13	1.87	15.48	14.75
华容区	Huarong District	493	26.01	25.09	2.76	2.68	23.25	22.41
鄂城区	Echeng District	600	59.87	59.69	31.09	30.19	28.78	29.50
东宝区	Dongbao District	1645	36.26	36.09	19.07	18.77	17.19	17.32
京山县	Jingshan County	3520	57.09	57.12	17.11	15.47	39.98	41.65
沙洋县	Shayang County	2044	56.42	59.18	7.57	7.38	48.85	51.80
钟祥市	Zhongxiang City	4488	100.92	100.75	22.20	21.93	78.72	78.82
孝南区	Xiaonan District	1020	88.48	88.32	34.51	34.15	53.97	54.17
孝昌县	Xiaochang County	1217	58.61	58.51	13.61	12.36	45.00	46.15
大悟县	Dawu County	1979	56.88	56.78	14.71	14.41	42.17	42.37
云梦县	Yunmeng County	604	51.96	51.91	12.56	12.46	39.40	39.45
应城市	Yingcheng City	1103	57.57	57.47	23.66	22.30	33.91	35.17
安陆市	Anlu City	1355	55.99	55.92	14.84	14.21	41.15	41.71
汉川市	Hanchuan City	1663	98.88	98.69	39.45	34.90	59.43	63.79
荆州区	Jingzhou District	1046	55.02	54.90	25.01	24.02	30.01	30.88
江陵县	Jiangling County	1048	36.79	36.52	6.32	6.26	30.47	30.26
公安县	Gongan County	2257	91.76	91.51	18.22	18.00	73.54	73.51
监利县	Jianli County	3460	128.80	128.58	26.17	25.90	102.63	102.68
石首市	Shishou City	1427	56.81	57.16	15.99	15.73	40.83	41.43
洪湖市	Honghu City	2519	82.65	83.35	17.77	17.64	64.89	65.71
松滋市	Songci City	2177	76.79	76.48	16.04	15.72	60.75	60.76
黄州区	Huangzhou District	353	34.24	34.11	20.68	20.43	13.56	13.68
团风县	Tuanfeng County	833	28.49	33.46	3.86	4.41	24.63	29.05
红安县	Hongan County	1789	51.25	60.19	10.24	10.71	41.01	49.48
罗田县	Luotian County	2129	46.73	54.91	6.72	7.85	40.01	47.06
英山县	Yingshan County	1449	30.61	35.95	6.01	6.96	24.60	28.99
浠水县	Xishui County	1949	80.48	94.54	12.95	14.93	67.53	79.61
蕲春县	Qichun County	2398	75.89	89.13	22.01	24.96	53.88	64.17
黄梅县	Huangmei County	1701	74.49	90.94	14.05	14.73	60.44	76.21
麻城市	Macheng City	3747	91.05	106.96	26.06	29.51	64.99	77.45
武穴市	Wuxue City	1246	57.30	62.31	22.99	26.13	34.31	36.18
咸安区	Xian'an District	1504	55.00	54.40	24.31	24.87	30.69	29.53
嘉鱼县	Jiayu County	1017	32.60	32.65	10.57	10.48	22.03	22.17
通城县	Tongcheng County	1141	40.28	40.78	10.77	9.56	29.51	31.22
崇阳县	Chongyang County	1968	40.70	40.65	7.54	7.46	33.16	33.19
通山县	Tongshan County	2680	37.45	37.39	9.60	9.19	27.85	28.20
赤壁市	Chibi City	1723	45.60	45.33	16.43	16.24	29.17	29.09
曾都区	Zengdu District	1316	56.50	54.19	15.03	12.57	41.47	41.62
随县	Sui Country	5763	85.66	76.48	10.84	9.18	74.82	67.30
广水市	Guangshui City	2641	78.65	73.50	17.95	16.59	60.70	56.91
恩施市	Enshi City	3972	75.59	75.09	20.31	20.34	55.28	54.75
利川市	Lichuan City	4607	73.51	73.04	12.81	12.42	60.71	60.62
建始县	Jianshi County	2666	45.39	45.19	4.24	4.20	41.15	40.99
巴东县	Badong County	3354	43.93	43.62	5.49	5.30	38.44	38.32
宣恩县	Xuanen County	2730	31.19	31.08	2.53	2.52	28.66	28.56
咸丰县	Xianfeng County	2550	31.14	32.80	2.95	2.94	28.19	29.86
来凤县	Laifeng County	1345	28.20	28.07	4.57	4.48	23.63	23.59
鹤峰县	Hefeng County	2872	19.75	19.61	2.19	2.19	17.56	17.42
仙桃市	Xiantiao City	2538	123.30	135.30	41.50	40.92	81.80	94.38
潜江市	Qianjiang City	2004	93.76	93.60	31.02	30.64	62.74	62.96
天门市	Tianmen City	2622	137.13	136.90	44.02	43.53	93.11	93.37

23-1 续表 1 continued

指标名称	Item	从业人员(万人) Employed Persons (10 000 persons) 2009	2008	第一产业 Primary Industry 2009	2008	第二产业 Secondary Industry 2009	2008	第三产业 Tertiary Industry 2009	2008
蔡甸区	Caidian District	22.16	21.87	7.29	7.30	6.53	5.66	8.34	8.91
江夏区	Jiangxia District	29.62	28.68	7.57	8.48	9.58	8.29	12.47	11.91
黄陂区	Huangpi District	60.72	64.53	18.94	19.30	24.87	25.34	16.91	19.89
新洲区	Xinzhou District	53.81	53.74	16.20	16.15	16.73	16.74	20.88	20.85
汉南区	Hannan District	8.08	7.68	1.96	1.89	4.57	4.27	1.55	1.52
阳新县	Yangxin County	54.13	53.38	11.05	11.02	10.12	9.95	32.96	32.41
大冶市	Daye City	58.26	52.55	13.50	13.37	17.70	14.17	27.06	25.01
郧县	Yun County	31.24	31.22	14.53	14.54	7.87	7.86	8.83	8.82
郧西县	Yunxi County	23.46	23.42	8.50	8.70	3.10	2.86	11.86	11.86
竹山县	Zhushan County	22.20	21.70	8.70	9.60	4.30	3.50	9.20	8.60
竹溪县	Zhuxi County	26.50	20.67	8.61	7.36	6.98	2.85	10.91	7.34
房县	Fang County	26.50	26.45	8.61	10.69	6.98	6.07	10.91	9.69
丹江口市	Danjiangkou City	25.42	24.45	9.11	9.03	3.72	3.92	12.59	11.50
夷陵区	Yiling District	30.30	30.10	10.20	10.20	6.00	5.90	14.10	14.00
远安县	Yuanan County	11.38	11.80	3.81	4.08	4.22	4.42	3.35	3.30
兴山县	Xingshan County	11.30	11.60	5.90	6.00	1.10	1.10	4.30	4.50
秭归县	Zigui County	20.40	20.50	11.40	11.70	4.20	4.10	4.80	4.70
长阳县	Changyang Tujia A.C.	24.21	24.10	10.80	11.09	4.75	3.82	8.66	9.19
五峰县	Wufeng Tujia A.C.	12.55	12.24	6.29	6.14	1.58	1.55	4.68	4.55
宜都市	Yidu City	21.98	21.58	4.29	5.21	8.56	7.34	9.13	9.03
当阳市	Dangyang City	28.35	32.09	8.25	7.20	5.72	6.89	14.38	18.00
枝江市	Zhijiang City	28.30	27.70	6.90	8.10	7.60	6.90	13.80	12.70
襄阳区	Xiangyang District	54.80	54.20	10.41	20.81	12.29	11.49	22.10	21.90
南漳县	Nanzhang County	32.38	30.45	10.39	12.00	8.67	7.18	13.32	11.27
谷城县	Gucheng County	26.44	25.73	8.48	8.20	6.50	6.20	11.46	11.30
保康县	Baokang County	18.32	17.55	6.60	6.60	3.80	0.60	7.92	5.30
老河口市	Laohekou City	30.14	29.17	9.06	9.64	9.03	8.72	12.05	10.81
枣阳市	Zaoyang City	53.20	52.60	13.50	15.10	18.50	15.70	21.20	19.80
宜城市	Yicheng City	33.61	33.93	11.94	12.18	7.28	7.45	14.39	14.30
梁子湖区	Liangzihu District	10.03	9.97	4.89	4.91	3.91	3.86	1.23	1.20
华容区	Huarong District	15.25	15.11	6.26	6.27	6.67	6.56	2.32	2.28
鄂城区	Echeng District	37.14	20.60	9.91	7.25	9.18	8.24	18.05	5.11
东宝区	Dongbao District	23.02	22.98	4.68	4.00	4.36	4.22	13.98	14.76
京山县	Jingshan County	37.60	37.46	8.27	9.37	9.62	9.57	19.71	18.52
沙洋县	Shayang County	28.35	29.66	14.98	11.02	4.2	5.77	9.17	12.87
钟祥市	Zhongxiang City	45.40	44.50	11.50	14.00	12.70	11.10	21.20	19.40
孝南区	Xiaonan District	50.16	57.00	11.83	13.40	16.18	19.22	22.16	24.38
孝昌县	Xiaochang County	39.10	38.60	10.90	11.20	11.40	11.00	16.80	16.40
大悟县	Dawu County	36.70	36.45	12.50	8.40	15.15	12.45	9.05	15.60
云梦县	Yunmeng County	36.85	36.48	9.14	8.95	12.55	12.53	15.16	15.00
应城市	Yingcheng City	34.42	31.03	11.87	9.97	10.60	9.23	11.95	11.83
安陆市	Anlu City	37.78	36.10	9.32	9.20	11.31	10.50	17.15	16.40
汉川市	Hanchuan City	69.30	68.05	19.42	19.56	19.08	18.29	30.80	30.20
荆州区	Jingzhou District	25.98	25.29	6.11	6.21	5.72	5.24	14.15	13.84
江陵县	Jiangling County	21.40	21.20	12.77	13.10	3.19	2.86	5.44	5.24
公安县	Gongan County	48.42	50.03	22.90	22.89	8.70	6.50	16.82	20.64
监利县	Jianli County	69.72	66.52	24.48	28.34	16.81	11.35	28.43	26.83
石首市	Shishou City	35.12	35.03	7.03	7.01	9.77	9.74	18.32	18.28
洪湖市	Honghu City	38.11	37.90	22.36	12.03	8.28	12.29	7.47	13.58
松滋市	Songci City	46.38	45.52	13.00	13.47	3.65	3.04	29.73	29.01
黄州区	Huangzhou District	21.01	20.42	3.40	3.30	7.85	7.51	9.76	9.61
团风县	Tuanfeng County	16.75	16.75	6.32	6.67	5.58	5.28	4.85	4.80
红安县	Hongan County	35.80	35.74	16.60	16.73	5.51	5.47	13.69	13.54
罗田县	Luotian County	35.84	35.39	11.02	11.10	13.86	11.52	10.95	12.77
英山县	Yingshan County	27.19	26.52	7.01	6.91	5.23	5.11	14.95	14.50
浠水县	Xishui County	52.10	49.45	18.82	17.50	16.68	15.60	16.60	16.35
蕲春县	Qichun County	48.37	48.40	12.72	14.52	9.30	8.08	26.35	25.80
黄梅县	Huangmei County	47.80	47.50	15.38	15.35	14.42	14.32	18.00	17.83
麻城市	Macheng City	60.24	58.95	22.97	23.48	10.54	9.94	26.73	25.53
武穴市	Wuxue City	43.17	42.94	12.96	13.11	18.03	17.73	12.18	12.10
咸安区	Xian'an District	35.37	34.51	9.78	9.87	9.38	9.03	16.21	15.61
嘉鱼县	Jiayu County	22.70	22.60	6.01	6.09	7.03	6.95	9.66	9.56
通城县	Tongcheng County	24.89	22.62	6.78	6.16	6.43	5.84	11.68	10.62
崇阳县	Chongyang County	25.40	23.95	7.53	7.46	6.64	5.76	11.23	10.73
通山县	Tongshan County	22.40	21.20	6.50	5.80	5.60	5.50	10.30	9.90
赤壁市	Chibi City	23.04	22.99	6.11	6.23	6.54	6.53	10.39	10.23
曾都区	Zengdu District	33.37	81.43	10.18	26.03	10.95	25.87	12.24	29.53
随县	Sui Country	49.45	48.85	17.19	14.53	14.80	14.62	16.12	15.93
广水市	Guangshui City	60.94	58.18	20.24	20.00	14.36	13.68	26.34	24.50
恩施市	Enshi City	41.32	40.85	17.35	16.71	7.93	6.99	16.04	17.15
利川市	Lichuan City	46.76	45.09	20.66	19.75	4.94	3.41	21.40	21.93
建始县	Jianshi County	29.73	29.28	10.98	13.27	5.98	3.30	12.77	12.71
巴东县	Badong County	27.49	26.49	15.24	14.03	3.37	3.50	8.88	8.96
宣恩县	Xuanen County	19.92	19.40	9.13	9.02	1.48	1.40	9.31	8.98
咸丰县	Xianfeng County	25.03	24.66	7.55	9.31	8.02	7.16	9.46	8.19
来凤县	Laifeng County	20.72	19.10	7.52	7.44	1.78	1.63	11.42	10.03
鹤峰县	Hefeng County	14.03	12.66	6.21	5.95	3.58	3.14	4.24	3.57
仙桃市	Xiantiao City	85.73	84.65	16.37	16.42	33.61	33.56	35.75	34.67
潜江市	Qianjiang City	45.45	62.10	17.03	14.28	13.57	18.53	14.85	29.29
天门市	Tianmen City	77.55	66.30	20.98	19.80	17.36	15.10	39.21	31.40

23-1 续表 2 continued

指标名称	Item	地区生产总值(亿元) Gross Regional Product(100 million yuan)		第一产业 Primary Industry		第二产业 Secondary Industry		#工业 #Industry		第三产业 Tertiary Industry	
		2009	2008	2009	2008	2009	2008	2009	2008	2009	2008
蔡甸区	Caidian District	115.88	96.39	16.22	15.97	66.96	56.71	57.06	47.26	32.70	23.71
江夏区	Jiangxia District	199.06	162.20	33.16	31.49	93.74	77.63	84.05	69.59	72.17	53.08
黄陂区	Huangpi District	215.50	161.40	41.61	39.79	88.84	68.12	61.84	47.58	85.05	53.49
新洲区	Xinzhou District	201.56	147.59	29.96	29.02	95.02	77.70	65.62	53.10	76.58	40.87
汉南区	Hannan District	44.86	38.01	7.45	6.77	28.17	23.39	14.67	11.81	9.24	7.85
阳新县	Yangxin County	97.15	96.47	22.02	19.93	36.02	42.34	32.52	38.87	39.11	34.20
大冶市	Daye City	170.60	169.73	20.69	19.00	93.46	92.15	86.66	76.12	56.45	58.58
郧县	Yun County	36.45	31.05	11.77	9.88	12.54	10.41	11.62	9.69	12.14	10.76
郧西县	Yunxi County	26.51	23.89	8.84	8.20	6.56	5.75	5.76	5.13	11.11	9.94
竹山县	Zhushan County	30.41	26.27	9.62	9.66	10.87	8.06	8.81	6.98	9.92	8.55
竹溪县	Zhuxi County	25.57	24.49	10.47	9.09	9.48	6.99	9.02	6.47	5.62	8.41
房县	Fang County	29.13	24.49	11.10	9.09	8.54	6.99	7.86	6.47	9.49	8.41
丹江口市	Danjiangkou City	75.71	67.63	11.29	9.80	35.28	32.12	31.36	28.78	29.14	25.71
夷陵区	Yiling District	140.44	111.23	22.43	19.97	76.08	51.84	70.25	45.39	41.94	39.42
远安县	Yuanan County	53.05	40.70	7.92	7.66	34.07	23.58	33.41	22.42	11.06	9.46
兴山县	Xingshan County	38.55	31.48	5.97	5.68	19.96	16.17	19.60	15.49	12.62	9.63
秭归县	Zigui County	43.96	36.97	9.30	8.34	14.04	9.79	12.00	8.91	20.63	18.84
长阳县	Changyang Tujia A.C.	47.45	40.18	14.24	12.96	11.97	9.41	10.25	8.01	21.25	17.81
五峰县	Wufeng Tujia A.C.	24.92	21.07	8.00	7.03	7.04	5.71	6.58	5.39	9.88	8.34
宜都市	Yidu City	145.50	109.43	16.85	14.30	82.11	56.15	77.86	51.34	46.54	38.98
当阳市	Dangyang City	133.05	106.06	30.00	28.15	60.60	42.53	53.96	37.98	42.46	35.38
枝江市	Zhijiang City	128.58	109.34	28.85	25.43	60.27	44.47	57.21	40.87	39.46	39.44
襄阳区	Xiangyang District	175.88	151.29	36.49	34.31	67.81	50.70	63.06	48.20	71.58	66.28
南漳县	Nanzhang County	62.06	50.18	21.97	18.31	19.66	14.26	18.26	12.86	20.43	17.61
谷城县	Gucheng County	85.41	60.42	15.85	15.20	48.02	27.98	44.76	23.88	21.53	17.23
保康县	Baokang County	29.66	23.94	9.81	8.06	9.32	6.99	7.22	6.09	10.53	8.89
老河口市	Laohekou City	84.98	63.03	22.01	19.51	45.64	24.07	41.77	21.27	17.33	19.46
枣阳市	Zaoyang City	153.94	122.81	44.81	42.44	63.71	33.47	58.72	29.17	45.42	46.90
宜城市	Yicheng City	85.00	64.43	22.91	19.83	39.20	25.54	36.00	23.43	22.89	19.06
梁子湖区	Liangzihu District	24.71	19.89	12.61	14.06	7.27	2.95	1.62	2.85	4.83	2.88
华容区	Huarong District	78.46	66.17	13.96	17.58	54.46	42.09	49.14	40.19	10.05	6.50
鄂城区	Echeng District	220.53	183.73	17.41	9.88	117.48	103.05	107.66	93.90	85.64	70.80
东宝区	Dongbao District	115.37	100.79	11.47	11.39	55.68	44.39	52.34	40.96	48.22	45.01
京山县	Jingshan County	129.30	105.09	32.93	29.27	62.33	46.55	59.24	43.41	34.05	29.27
沙洋县	Shayang County	96.02	88.29	32.60	33.97	33.14	26.29	30.55	23.19	30.27	28.03
钟祥市	Zhongxiang City	163.01	140.93	42.64	42.27	73.10	55.73	67.52	50.15	47.27	42.93
孝南区	Xiaonan District	140.08	117.20	16.37	14.77	65.57	53.58	46.88	38.43	58.13	48.85
孝昌县	Xiaochang County	49.16	42.41	16.49	14.43	13.87	11.38	9.42	7.59	18.81	16.60
大悟县	Dawu County	57.69	51.93	16.33	14.33	18.41	16.07	13.22	12.21	22.95	21.53
云梦县	Yunmeng County	86.89	75.09	18.49	17.33	36.80	31.47	33.85	28.91	31.59	26.29
应城市	Yingcheng City	93.18	89.80	24.11	22.13	43.77	37.50	42.23	36.25	25.30	30.17
安陆市	Anlu City	73.62	63.99	19.90	17.80	23.45	19.75	20.53	17.23	30.28	26.44
汉川市	Hanchuan City	165.04	143.05	32.63	30.93	86.17	72.07	82.31	68.53	46.24	40.05
荆州区	Jingzhou District	100.13	75.40	21.33	19.67	43.88	29.70	39.02	27.60	34.93	26.03
江陵县	Jiangling County	29.51	27.02	13.72	13.15	5.98	5.07	5.21	4.34	9.81	8.80
公安县	Gongan County	90.92	83.50	33.77	29.83	28.65	25.94	26.69	23.75	28.51	27.73
监利县	Jianli County	108.59	95.40	51.26	43.90	24.48	22.10	22.79	20.41	32.85	29.43
石首市	Shishou City	68.13	65.07	18.96	17.33	25.57	26.42	23.91	24.42	23.60	21.31
洪湖市	Honghu City	90.12	81.43	34.95	33.31	24.32	18.79	20.49	16.33	30.86	29.33
松滋市	Songzi City	80.55	69.15	22.11	20.87	24.69	22.91	19.67	18.71	33.75	25.37
黄州区	Huangzhou District	82.51	72.77	7.85	6.99	43.58	37.37	34.38	28.47	31.08	28.41
团风县	Tuanfeng County	33.95	29.58	8.47	7.48	17.23	14.45	8.78	6.09	8.25	7.65
红安县	Hongan County	58.27	48.89	16.31	14.16	24.57	20.28	21.13	16.86	17.40	14.15
罗田县	Luotian County	53.47	39.97	13.12	11.56	22.70	15.81	18.81	14.53	17.65	12.60
英山县	Yingshan County	39.72	35.56	16.88	10.00	12.23	13.61	8.95	9.53	10.60	11.95
浠水县	Xishui County	89.56	78.06	32.84	28.98	28.79	23.91	21.08	17.85	27.93	25.17
蕲春县	Qichun County	84.77	74.77	23.08	19.23	29.08	25.63	22.62	19.60	32.61	29.91
黄梅县	Huangmei County	77.55	67.70	28.06	25.30	26.74	22.90	23.74	20.10	22.75	19.50
麻城市	Macheng City	99.34	83.63	36.58	32.83	30.48	21.56	27.62	18.16	32.27	29.24
武穴市	Wuxue City	100.11	87.79	28.42	25.76	41.58	37.21	33.96	34.54	30.10	24.82
咸安区	Xian'an District	109.18	99.24	14.90	14.23	53.52	43.38	49.10	41.29	40.76	41.63
嘉鱼县	Jiayu County	66.07	59.92	19.28	19.26	28.58	23.75	27.24	22.64	18.21	16.91
通城县	Tongcheng County	48.22	43.97	10.09	13.13	17.34	14.90	15.27	13.28	20.79	15.94
崇阳县	Chongyang County	47.00	42.00	11.82	11.63	16.68	14.11	14.43	12.59	18.50	16.26
通山县	Tongshan County	37.64	37.41	6.69	6.69	10.42	10.79	8.92	9.29	20.53	19.93
赤壁市	Chibi City	110.43	102.16	17.98	17.15	56.07	52.57	52.28	49.39	36.38	32.44
曾都区	Zengdu District	149.60	131.39	12.14	11.73	70.10	58.27	61.90	50.98	67.36	61.39
随县	Sui Country	77.02	72.39	34.66	32.87	27.92	25.30	27.52	25.00	14.44	14.22
广水市	Guangshui City	117.00	106.42	28.11	25.96	52.36	48.64	45.16	38.00	36.53	31.82
恩施市	Enshi City	72.63	58.80	17.36	16.37	24.49	18.11	20.89	13.72	30.77	24.32
利川市	Lichuan City	47.86	38.98	20.84	19.30	9.66	6.81	7.97	5.71	17.36	12.88
建始县	Jianshi County	33.04	28.49	12.06	11.38	8.68	6.72	7.51	5.83	12.29	10.39
巴东县	Badong County	40.72	35.68	11.67	10.94	14.61	12.49	12.92	11.82	14.44	12.25
宣恩县	Xuanen County	24.31	21.50	9.42	8.74	5.19	4.66	4.51	3.59	9.70	8.10
咸丰县	Xianfeng County	28.78	23.63	10.62	9.94	6.48	5.15	5.18	4.04	11.68	8.54
来凤县	Laifeng County	25.05	19.53	7.62	7.12	6.06	5.01	5.31	4.10	11.36	7.40
鹤峰县	Hefeng County	21.54	18.17	6.40	5.64	8.10	6.49	7.23	5.49	7.04	6.04
仙桃市	Xiantiao City	242.55	233.50	47.50	44.77	115.57	108.51	105.90	99.51	79.48	80.22
潜江市	Qianjiang City	234.01	212.82	41.19	35.71	121.09	112.71	109.14	104.41	71.73	64.40
天门市	Tianmen City	186.86	168.15	47.96	44.87	85.58	73.94	76.98	66.44	53.32	47.34

23-1 续表 3 continued

指标名称	Item	全社会固定资产投资完成额(万元) Investment in Fixed Assets (10 000 yuan)		地方财政一般预算收入(万元) Revenue of Lacal Governments (10 000 yuan)		#各项税收(万元) Taxes (10 000 yuan)		地方财政支出(万元) Expenditures of Local Governments (10 000 yuan)	
		2009	2008	2009	2008	2009	2008	2009	2008
蔡甸区	Caidian District	746138	477132	67461	54658	51387	46496	193471	156347
江夏区	Jiangxia District	1376723	1005694	128728	72609	58585	47942	291282	210740
黄陂区	Huangpi District	1355527	954092	98309	70522	61516	51603	339153	236923
新洲区	Xinzhou District	1213175	851582	75742	62415	44770	35928	181463	167492
汉南区	Hannan District	355516	253578	25000	20246	22311	18435	56407	42722
阳新县	Yangxin County	698552	465272	36076	28435	21669	16975	191641	129450
大冶市	Daye City	1000442	660510	70089	62285	49728	46064	207490	153675
郧县	Yun County	238045	114699	18289	12048	12689	7404	158542	90691
郧西县	Yunxi County	153800	125017	9300	8078	5397	4566	60000	49300
竹山县	Zhushan County	398926	188344	13666	10276	9455	8010	129766	83558
竹溪县	Zhuxi County	233433	169144	12987	10051	6495	5734	151600	86800
房县	Fang County	300285	156932	13966	10717	8049	6193	151600	86800
丹江口市	Danjiangkou City	397285	304138	45158	30444	37289	23070	183822	104785
夷陵区	Yiling District	831030	577907	66058	50619	49142	40479	189578	120516
远安县	Yuanan County	329100	184980	25498	18226	19147	14170	83210	52834
兴山县	Xingshan County	200117	124765	16871	13111	13059	10667	71059	47936
秭归县	Zigui County	288597	201108	17418	14236	12790	10085	100105	66108
长阳县	Changyang Tujia A.C.	197845	140696	19354	16841	14187	13035	110720	73549
五峰县	Wufeng Tujia A.C.	101797	66222	7000	6002	5535	4410	69144	47064
宜都市	Yidu City	1004097	636449	68509	49803	49621	35744	157367	107279
当阳市	Dangyang City	564278	396975	46076	34128	33696	23863	150749	103587
枝江市	Zhijiang City	812289	618448	46910	37458	32331	24599	140674	92525
襄阳区	Xiangyang District	968805	583022	30002	22485	19758	14508	162641	106842
南漳县	Nanzhang County	337104	219949	12979	10072	9228	7280	123620	78498
谷城县	Gucheng County	362863	210487	20289	15880	12668	9911	120112	78246
保康县	Baokang County	255890	161532	14002	10622	10264	7673	45228	33475
老河口市	Laohekou City	400649	230008	28596	22730	12245	9217	124600	87553
枣阳市	Zaoyang City	609137	380250	36447	29087	17823	14221	203209	129075
宜城市	Yicheng City	412489	253676	27811	21689	14171	10858	125777	88145
梁子湖区	Liangzihu District	143080	98500	6747	5415	4237	3893	20670	17048
华容区	Huarong District	838787	563338	14019	10624	10312	7970	45819	36855
鄂城区	Echeng District	1224143	838231	44973	33359	33397	27300	290223	185633
东宝区	Dongbao District	636215	407122	28314	20855	23582	17300	67525	59519
京山县	Jingshan County	743538	452200	34146	24526	20574	17187	84167	71798
沙洋县	Shayang County	379916	253092	15116	11809	7934	6394	125113	76743
钟祥市	Zhongxiang City	949205	574239	41108	32586	21330	16123	251144	119098
孝南区	Xiaonan District	874397	591208	31586	23638	18981	13873	179015	140575
孝昌县	Xiaochang County	430170	276064	19448	13111	10790	6923	67319	55518
大悟县	Dawu County	439821	282297	23072	17074	12807	8754	75669	60105
云梦县	Yunmeng County	501818	330891	29430	24138	17808	14359	72687	57640
应城市	Yingcheng City	564716	458851	41742	34244	25558	20586	139327	97199
安陆市	Anlu City	489250	336774	22095	18878	13036	11962	131681	80594
汉川市	Hanchuan City	672412	450495	50199	42168	30550	25762	125636	100416
荆州区	Jingzhou District	611996	383491	30122	17347	22910	13721	52782	34163
江陵县	Jiangling County	128259	100535	5776	4817	2856	2351	60157	38172
公安县	Gongan County	544277	331546	24710	21240	14876	11947	66379	62506
监利县	Jianli County	506878	353965	14169	12455	11070	9431	234423	139659
石首市	Shishou City	442006	296174	20735	20060	11429	11597	114682	80966
洪湖市	Honghu City	408266	290374	17570	14990	9747	7868	66812	62803
松滋市	Songci City	512507	355996	24200	20929	14106	12016	160104	105261
黄州区	Huangzhou District	770520	512180	20110	16070	11560	9572	199758	142576
团风县	Tuanfeng County	268931	206842	14108	11387	7962	6586	87463	57193
红安县	Hongan County	355909	249522	26007	20931	11927	9199	148040	95470
罗田县	Luotian County	770956	450045	18315	14657	8153	6799	127419	89025
英山县	Yingshan County	295300	262975	13306	10874	6183	4963	59941	52777
浠水县	Xishui County	439906	289356	29457	24246	12314	10697	188282	125109
蕲春县	Qichun County	753693	491079	36839	29270	14136	11379	85282	81024
黄梅县	Huangmei County	489152	324371	38057	31424	12958	10071	96271	114170
麻城市	Macheng City	831306	510058	40514	34117	19930	16449	203890	140458
武穴市	Wuxue City	567238	373600	45332	36022	20277	15553	151298	109554
咸安区	Xian'an District	955325	643316	25341	18791	15614	11882	263178	186941
嘉鱼县	Jiayu County	470229	323181	21953	17420	12109	8785	71571	52842
通城县	Tongcheng County	306242	203078	16046	12938	7368	5601	100525	67458
崇阳县	Chongyang County	305920	177667	13366	10738	6328	4331	104610	73223
通山县	Tongshan County	299136	193741	13493	10119	8739	5584	103350	71088
赤壁市	Chibi City	678953	460619	44398	36147	27104	20392	146645	106376
曾都区	Zengdu District	821992	519767	21465	17595	17464	13751	139723	133870
随县	Sui Country	444336	393238	4386	3584	2560	2016	77094	
广水市	Guangshui City	820675	557727	30910	25007	16260	13699	163278	105062
恩施市	Enshi City	496505	401070	41837	36329	33836	31610	172484	127013
利川市	Lichuan City	274111	189604	31388	25089	23505	18624	180599	115593
建始县	Jianshi County	236748	161585	17388	15807	13089	11693	134480	92688
巴东县	Badong County	236813	154831	22021	18117	16022	13171	127465	85554
宣恩县	Xuanen County	117104	95086	8200	6820	6420	5532	83276	58376
咸丰县	Xianfeng County	132637	105282	10709	9119	8148	7341	84482	63951
来凤县	Laifeng County	130523	99141	8208	7580	6551	6142	86863	57340
鹤峰县	Hefeng County	155579	105600	9458	8129	7900	6929	82345	51572
仙桃市	Xiantiao City	1100492	852622	50518	42129	34698	28742	262468	170863
潜江市	Qianjiang City	1239616	883547	48593	47126	34053	34343	295153	203317
天门市	Tianmen City	1195077	861006.484	35281	28000	18973	15803	201176	151410

23-1 续表 4 continued

指标名称	Item	城镇居民人均可支配收入(元) Annual Per Capita Disposable Income of Urban (yuan)		农村居民人均纯收入(元) Annual Per Capita Disposable Income of Rural Households(yuan)		农村居民人均消费性支出(元) Annual Per Capita Consumption Expenditure of Rural Households(yuan)		年末金融机构各项存款余额(万元) State Bank Deposits (10 000 yuan)	
		2009	2008	2009	2008	2009	2008	2009	2008
蔡甸区	Caidian District	11726	10423	7033	6318	4592	4511	811105	648858
江夏区	Jiangxia District	11852		7128	6361	5242	4663	1325054	1113970
黄陂区	Huangpi District	11615	10391	6753	6026	4023	3873	1336625	1009395
新洲区	Xinzhou District	11211	10004	6682	6001	4255	4582	1064802	862773
汉南区	Hannan District	11865	10847	7265	6441	4667	4489	245675	190794
阳新县	Yangxin County	9983	8982	4029	3660	3593	3171	698125	556302
大冶市	Daye City	12035	10872	5604	4997	4763	4220	1339657	1092604
郧县	Yun County	7682	6909	3021	2741	1782	2237	546707	434065
郧西县	Yunxi County	8997	8101	2931	2705	2112	2025	419738	341428
竹山县	Zhushan County	8901	8099	3026	2740	2916	2818	354558	259908
竹溪县	Zhuxi County	9997	9024	3072	2801	2880	2288	455029	335136
房县	Fang County	9997	9024	2945	2671	2880	2288	455029	335136
丹江口市	Danjiangkou City	10805	10005	3657	3374	3203	2686	895046	741256
夷陵区	Yiling District	12691	11611	6048	5426	4263	4415	1050857	836615
远安县	Yuanan County	11788	10786	5815	5220	3837	3412	350835	294903
兴山县	Xingshan County	8531	7701	3851	3483	1538	1543	339757	249427
秭归县	Zigui County	10514	9679	3177	2875	3259	3387	448144	372968
长阳县	Changyang Tujia A.C.	8650	8400	3282	2969	1595	1622	425875	346513
五峰县	Wufeng Tujia A.C.	7952	7758	2968	2664	1781	1693	216500	172315
宜都市	Yidu City	8460	8307	6516	5846	1838	1956	714462	552472
当阳市	Dangyang City	10135	8581	6514	5815	2251	2030	832942	698725
枝江市	Zhijiang City	12052	11054	6559	5932	4569	3935	865241	695612
襄阳区	Xiangyang District	9934	9075	6154	5504	3596	3069	1153057	929323
南漳县	Nanzhang County	10540	9643	5011	4499	4476	4401	559865	469610
谷城县	Gucheng County	9578	8749	5106	4573	3083	3042	790095	626335
保康县	Baokang County	8410	7679	3425	3063	3508	3241	293380	229693
老河口市	Laohekou City	11044	10115	6059	5446	3662	3554	675188	569471
枣阳市	Zaoyang City	10392	9520	5795	5200	3527	3504	1269253	1085223
宜城市	Yicheng City	10269	9380	6063	5452	4028	3806	652890	526611
梁子湖区	Liangzihu District	11408	10455	4779	4275	2624	3623	60907	42544
华容区	Huarong District	12960	11694	5792	5121	2710	2603	244501	165492
鄂城区	Echeng District	13408	12244	5887	5257	2793	2684	1719731	1371739
东宝区	Dongbao District	13857	12690	5996	5367	3490	2528	2162675	1716350
京山县	Jingshan County	10554	9589	5991	5362	3726	3717	990125	825737
沙洋县	Shayang County	10108	8949	5799	5192	3873	4112	659373	546577
钟祥市	Zhongxiang City	10015	8785	6032	5400	4840	4435	1442907	1166092
孝南区	Xiaonan District	13562	12419	5710	5134	3485	3429	2220454	1720795
孝昌县	Xiaochang County	10571	9686	3709	3366	3600	3555	413682	338708
大悟县	Dawu County	3913	3781	3844	3452	354	377	554997	463930
云梦县	Yunmeng County	12137	11117	5998	5417	4051	3796	575712	378308
应城市	Yingcheng City	12170	11165	6050	5495	4030	3916	815171	683844
安陆市	Anlu City	12084	11073	5031	4560	3787	3572	709716	602403
汉川市	Hanchuan City	12330	11406	5598	5058	3805	3459	958974	737372
荆州区	Jingzhou District	13240	12130	6011	5350	4486	3656		
江陵县	Jiangling County	10709	9867	4837	4378	2898	2001	326365	279238
公安县	Gongan County	10691	9725	5512	4917	4047	4036	1097051	897332
监利县	Jianli County	11369	10129	5331	4867	3058	3128	1037555	824729
石首市	Shishou City	10709	9752	5453	4932	4173	4053	794004	655408
洪湖市	Honghu City	9945	9165	5525	4975	3267	3168	791512	630443
松滋市	Songci City	10700	9735	5441	4883	4018	4011	990495	832334
黄州区	Huangzhou District	13634	11860	5399	4896	4143	3941	1237685	972028
团风县	Tuanfeng County	9927	8618	3287	2994	2768	2505	295065	237627
红安县	Hongan County	11360	9663	3387	3096	2745	2818	536527	449339
罗田县	Luotian County	11135	9657	3875	3524	3582	3316	585196	502543
英山县	Yingshan County	11048	9480	3668	3356	3889	4162	424767	336636
浠水县	Xishui County	11159	9738	4529	4083	3802	3922	946325	781712
蕲春县	Qichun County	11110	9685	3898	3578	3072	3356	967015	765535
黄梅县	Huangmei County	10866	8935	4542	4088	3525	3519	932358	735058
麻城市	Macheng City	11279	9910	3746	3460	3362	4050	953053	762705
武穴市	Wuxue City	12031	10526	5100	4621	4034	3592	856460	707419
咸安区	Xian'an District	12589	11529	5116	4629	3604	3466	1228304	959863
嘉鱼县	Jiayu County	11980	10980	5841	5280	3767	2915	338718	281917
通城县	Tongcheng County	10822	9838	4809	4364	4260	3801	446939	364206
崇阳县	Chongyang County	9801	8927	4312	3913	2987	3616	428787	338536
通山县	Tongshan County	9249	8406	3141	2852	2360	2418	362863	281847
赤壁市	Chibi City	11985	10955	6120	5528	3898	4235	666326	559616
曾都区	Zengdu District	13461	11594	5662	5175	3839	3613	2455328	1949672
随县	Sui Country	12349	11298	5365	4943	3839	3613		
广水市	Guangshui City	12308	10258	5162	4665	3987	3924	1045268	853736
恩施市	Enshi City	11875	10903	2815	2520	3047	3078	1340228	1137325
利川市	Lichuan City	9477	8551	2814	2555	2663	2454	525787	425144
建始县	Jianshi County	9989	9165	2807	2490	2373	2125	319015	273964
巴东县	Badong County	9977	9196	2790	2482	2561	2519	449322	365378
宣恩县	Xuanen County	9952	9212	2804	2486	2649	2548	198349	146626
咸丰县	Xianfeng County	9214	7998	2807	2522	2534	2317	266157	206764
来凤县	Laifeng County	10169	9335	2798	2543	2521	2500	255590	191138
鹤峰县	Hefeng County	10309	9428	2848	2555	2322	2232	203025	154096
仙桃市	Xiantiao City	7236	6985	5856	5248	1645	1457	1834277	1435138
潜江市	Qianjiang City	8518	7589	5531	4929	1405	1432	2070563	1768601
天门市	Tianmen City	11243	10488	5326	4761	3784	3768	1671771	1370230

23-1 续表 5 continued

指标名称	Item	居民储蓄存款(万元) Urban & Rural Savings Deposits(10 000 yuan)		年末金融机构各项贷款余额(万元) State Bank Loans (10 000 yuan)		常用耕地面积(千公顷) Area of Cultivated Land(1000 hectare)		农村用电量(万千瓦小时) Electricity Consumed in Rural Area(10 000 kwh)	
		2009	2008	2009	2008	2009	2008	2009	2008
蔡甸区	Caidian District	487508	411181	335711	262239	25.75	25.72	19294	16814
江夏区	Jiangxia District	784244	669676	519702	421362	40.08	39.80	9796	10202
黄陂区	Huangpi District	840561	674676	579242	402177	54.00	53.93	58085	54016
新洲区	Xinzhou District	721190	582785	765698	701567	48.97	48.89	16033	15375
汉南区	Hannan District	125222	103924	84121	55794	10.46	10.46	3638	3615
阳新县	Yangxin County	461667	380422	198800	142297	52.01	49.91	28785	30108
大冶市	Daye City	791725	689334	579086	328504	36.92	35.41	50363	53014
郧县	Yun County	343821	267598	119266	82833	35.41	34.67	7803	4456
郧西县	Yunxi County	299370	243428	90561	63668	26.53	26.23	5517	4826
竹山县	Zhushan County	199299	162774	217199	102814	32.63	33.02	3338	4221
竹溪县	Zhuxi County	270094	222540	141719	88227	27.97	27.39	6348	4102
房县	Fang County	270094	222540	141719	88227	27.97	27.39	6348	4102
丹江口市	Danjiangkou City	583140	491599	450605	231039	20.13	19.53	5997	5863
夷陵区	Yiling District	623716	511202	552382	344694	24.37	23.54	11174	10238
远安县	Yuanan County	233603	200680	91513	58383	11.37	11.36	3144	2635
兴山县	Xingshan County	159231	126664	207165	160840	12.98	13.26	3123	2468
秭归县	Zigui County	253109	215867	147224	80481	19.05	19.59	5422	4463
长阳县	Changyang Tujia A.C.	294250	251060	205131	148545	31.64	31.55	4806	4415
五峰县	Wufeng Tujia A.C.	134207	1124456	74990	57422	17.69	17.69	3198	1787
宜都市	Yidu City	470961	407386	573933	387919	15.80	15.80	6994	6515
当阳市	Dangyang City	629875	549971	362981	292728	43.95	44.03	7687	7135
枝江市	Zhijiang City	628227	527795	287896	242245	45.14	44.83	7408	6728
襄阳区	Xiangyang District					97.22	95.92	10406	9878
南漳县	Nanzhang County	416219	350898	224096	182357	41.56	41.33	3356	3148
谷城县	Gucheng County	567470	462900	256266	185965	28.92	28.41	4431	3971
保康县	Baokang County	169978	136619	117455	84518	22.50	22.30	2453	2785
老河口市	Laohekou City	501707	436900	395248	323075	39.60	39.66	4152	3785
枣阳市	Zaoyang City	979200	845489	356904	273056	109.65	101.83	17060	14163
宜城市	Yicheng City	487473	412810	320041	227157	57.08	56.87	7522	7299
梁子湖区	Liangzihu District	55417	39025	27422	29540	12.78	12.37	7157	7110
华容区	Huarong District	183009	127553	136830	124019	15.29	15.78	5431	5624
鄂城区	Echeng District	972464	810310	831336	630282	13.18	13.08	12972	14864
东宝区	Dongbao District	1350158	1100632	1602870	1254540	16.70	16.58	4952	4769
京山县	Jingshan County	716081	610066	434219	311414	57.31	57.18	14135	11459
沙洋县	Shayang County	480916	409747	200259	168183	78.07	77.73	20308	18599
钟祥市	Zhongxiang City	1123751	950274	427081	329938	82.09	81.70	16324	13733
孝南区	Xiaonan District			1164802	875999	31.01	31.01	9525	11699
孝昌县	Xiaochang County	317420	259267	122459	101497	31.53	31.07	5748	5451
大悟县	Dawu County	400762	336506	157289	122737	36.68	36.68	8676	7452
云梦县	Yunmeng County	443226	305613	196052	179328	24.91	24.86	7625	6407
应城市	Yingcheng City	612042	527103	516130	359848	37.62	37.53	11341	9579
安陆市	Anlu City	547829	454423	384437	319664	33.56	33.37	4034	3319
汉川市	Hanchuan City	668226	544559	641449	499304	64.95	65.64	18010	15429
荆州区	Jingzhou District					34.90	34.90	10053	8688
江陵县	Jiangling County	211857	181265	144080	129391	37.99	38.21	4603	3854
公安县	Gongan County	857511	724178	346011	284213	80.38	80.38	20525	15797
监利县	Jianli County	745717	637200	436318	340053	137.69	137.18	22579	19831
石首市	Shishou City	580355	494043	244650	181134	34.91	34.91	8520	7722
洪湖市	Honghu City	565455	486553	291592	224727	64.19	64.19	18359	17352
松滋市	Songzi City	783620	680362	268619	179088	59.74	59.63	14033	13038
黄州区	Huangzhou District	728472	594510	682432	594179	10.61	10.22	12825	11847
团风县	Tuanfeng County	213818	180272	126876	103499	17.38	17.87	10744	11105
红安县	Hongan County	394738	331573	165300	130678	38.41	38.05	16095	13004
罗田县	Luotian County	416640	362011	229076	173887	25.21	25.09	8660	8160
英山县	Yingshan County	301981	253005	131191	100147	17.21	17.20	6473	5388
浠水县	Xishui County	719211	606243	280360	225163	43.99	43.58	12445	13778
蕲春县	Qichun County	771088	645888	277195	241365	39.07	38.89	26865	25751
黄梅县	Huangmei County	701096	595160	232724	185377	48.89	46.35	15695	19594
麻城市	Macheng City	673094	561791	710003	496083	54.12	52.93	20257	19198
武穴市	Wuxue City	610180	519153	336695	267185	35.20	34.85	14118	14990
咸安区	Xian'an District	671030	553259	831509	521943	35.53	35.37	5238	4936
嘉鱼县	Jiayu County	228109	189427	217555	148307	27.66	27.53	8122	7688
通城县	Tongcheng County	326696	279659	109386	76405	21.28	21.05	5135	4474
崇阳县	Chongyang County	318043	263301	103350	73060	23.07	22.90	4695	4399
通山县	Tongshan County	218637	183200	144540	93794	14.77	14.67	5384	4600
赤壁市	Chibi City	463009	390451	308867	307695	32.40	32.09	6815	6391
曾都区	Zengdu District	1731325	1427763	962228	614862	26.00	25.88	6394	4192
随县	Sui Country					73.05	72.13	10867	10113
广水市	Guangshui City	805843	701779	269596	194903	38.47	38.45	9107	7589
恩施市	Enshi City	583888	493233	1149512	910353	47.37	47.48	6531	6058
利川市	Lichuan City	379174	324402	177719	112036	58.89	58.06	7261	5816
建始县	Jianshi County	204922	176707	125846	91390	33.38	33.34	4166	3712
巴东县	Badong County	252884	209624	132177	100880	35.95	35.89	4797	4745
宣恩县	Xuanen County	118632	106464	80856	63400	24.90	24.86	2876	2716
咸丰县	Xianfeng County	175753	144777	114615	83415	23.26	23.00	3006	2388
来凤县	Laifeng County	162225	139758	120035	81132	17.26	17.26	1912	1776
鹤峰县	Hefeng County	136141	116848	168395	132786	15.87	15.43	3792	2735
仙桃市	Xiantiao City	1373475	1154870	553745	418940	90.84	90.14	37766	35901
潜江市	Qianjiang City	1423423	1244974	526357	357790	69.77	68.41	19067	16385
天门市	Tianmen City	1352247	1137920	464209	463513	108.30	106.98	17568	16676

23-1 续表 6 continued

指标名称	Item	粮食产量(万吨) Output of Grain (10 000 tons) 2009	2008	棉花产量(吨) Output of Cotton Cotton (tons) 2009	2008	油料产量(万吨) Output of Oil-bearing Crops (10 000 tons) 2009	2008	肉类总产量(吨) Output of Meat (tons) 2009	2008	水产品产量(吨) Output of Aquatic Products(tons) 2009	2008
蔡甸区	Caidian District	17.30	15.70	7465	8833	1.30	1.40	14710	15738	52639	50133
江夏区	Jiangxia District	29.21	25.90	557	757	4.67	4.77	66310	66181	85316	82646
黄陂区	Huangpi District	41.84	41.78	3449	3533	6.63	6.48	97382	99776	79216	75109
新洲区	Xinzhou District	32.91	32.42	9337	9538	4.87	4.67	20101	19019	92078	87654
汉南区	Hannan District	7.84	7.51	6598	7219	0.35	0.21	22426	20670	20675	19899
阳新县	Yangxin County	33.42	31.42	3351	2962	3.94	3.40	35412	32307	77433	75068
大冶市	Daye City	27.49	25.96	2598	802	3.60	3.59	38895	36938	58443	55646
郧县	Yun County	20.85	18.95	42	39	1.55	1.12	20649	19568	1670	1296
郧西县	Yunxi County	20.59	20.46			1.38	1.86	23767	23683	375	334
竹山县	Zhushan County	21.96	21.77	5	5	2.30	1.89	18134	18110	274	243
竹溪县	Zhuxi County	16.46	14.29	37	35	1.41	1.21	27940	26691	980	904
房县	Fang County	16.46	14.29	37	35	1.41	1.21	27940	26691	980	904
丹江口市	Danjiangkou City	12.97	12.09	1	4	0.85	0.81	22048	23113	53439	46005
夷陵区	Yiling District	21.49	20.86	19	18	2.41	2.10	76024	63862	7541	6945
远安县	Yuanan County	9.76	9.45	1	8	1.40	1.19	21354	21372	2260	2065
兴山县	Xingshan County	6.53	6.34			0.73	0.67	38968	21712		
秭归县	Zigui County	9.71	9.29			1.39	1.27	36799	33622	1545	1097
长阳县	Changyang Tujia A.C.	12.66	10.53			1.39	1.20	53772	47702		
五峰县	Wufeng Tujia A.C.	8.76	7.98			0.59	0.53	21314	14164		
宜都市	Yidu City	12.48	12.09	34	34	1.82	1.72	41160	37530		
当阳市	Dangyang City	43.96	42.48	7698	7859	7.37	6.83	59434	133293		
枝江市	Zhijiang City	31.30	30.20	21826	18858	5.65	5.34	72552	67410	62498	57850
襄阳区	Xiangyang District	120.07	110.07	13207	11443	10.27	9.17	127079	109213	38327	34885
南漳县	Nanzhang County	37.71	36.64	455	353	1.81	1.80	70453	63104	6085	5330
谷城县	Gucheng County	25.71	25.50	15	70	1.10	1.23	48990	36674	7350	6288
保康县	Baokang County	11.83	11.61			1.35	1.32	21408	18637	710	565
老河口市	Laohekou City	32.46	32.10	6313	6512	2.75	2.75	52035	31660	3329	30491
枣阳市	Zaoyang City	120.02	115.56	14290	14226	4.87	5.08	86881	77851	40100	36758
宜城市	Yicheng City	57.54	52.06	8510	7859	7.42	6.55	61604	55324	27953	22825
梁子湖区	Liangzihu District	11.05	10.21	437	434	1.91	1.56	24974	16099	121927	96603
华容区	Huarong District	10.72	10.61	3535	1753	2.01	2.00	18956	14185	93133	76105
鄂城区	Echeng District	13.03	12.01	3641	3012	2.09	1.75	23170	26916	121151	100292
东宝区	Dongbao District	16.12	15.73	1635	1630	3.07	2.77	94007	27852	23500	20878
京山县	Jingshan County	58.78	56.48	8787	8176	5.30	5.12	66717	61332	59012	53329
沙洋县	Shayang County	75.64	71.73	10567	12377	12.23	12.04	70280	61635	138151	125590
钟祥市	Zhongxiang City	81.65	79.33	14414	14365	12.07	11.59	90976	89261	110001	105222
孝南区	Xiaonan District	23.36	21.85	4436	3764	2.84	2.28	20912	17707	51304	46471
孝昌县	Xiaochang County	29.22	27.29	1063	1286	2.96	2.87	33246	23806	12483	9986
大悟县	Dawu County	31.49	29.87	218	221	5.40	4.44	39065	40102	20862	18141
云梦县	Yunmeng County	23.96	23.19	2341	1994	1.84	1.78	31691	32496	33845	33630
应城市	Yingcheng City	37.52	36.78	4741	4935	3.45	2.97	32546	29108	50977	46091
安陆市	Anlu City	36.77	35.31	1028	998	2.15	1.77	64983	59519	21353	17244
汉川市	Hanchuan City	46.04	42.75	18559	14509	4.50	3.56	34808	30293	129980	120351
荆州区	Jingzhou District	25.11	23.59	12467	13490	6.26	5.74	28939	21483	103184	85788
江陵县	Jiangling County	36.68	28.25	8866	15907	6.34	6.19	24138	21434	26521	22418
公安县	Gongan County	53.71	51.52	34588	36818	10.08	9.05	53106	54452	113235	97964
监利县	Jianli County	124.67	115.75	24456	27299	10.62	10.14	64395	46186	233341	180163
石首市	Shishou City	25.04	23.11	17382	18071	5.15	4.13	30129	24307	103076	88178
洪湖市	Honghu City	58.66	55.95	10673	17705	7.63	6.17	25254	21592	345121	301926
松滋市	Songci City	36.39	35.12	15718	13255	6.69	6.20	90756	82609	25178	21109
黄州区	Huangzhou District	7.01	6.56	6668	6705	0.62	0.65	7505	5214	40196	39466
团风县	Tuanfeng County	18.44	16.93	4721	3024	2.14	1.87	12820	7488	23018	18790
红安县	Hongan County	31.58	29.48	2907	2435	9.76	9.96	35354	31715	8863	7009
罗田县	Luotian County	22.49	21.62	251	185	2.38	2.26	20208	19483	6446	4157
英山县	Yingshan County	18.55	17.85	268	256	1.61	1.67	20969	16981	6819	6800
浠水县	Xishui County	44.03	43.46	12861	12300	6.74	6.56	64270	60285	87628	85145
蕲春县	Qichun County	43.91	41.27	5215	3394	4.33	3.00	60347	42387	61079	55800
黄梅县	Huangmei County	41.77	40.48	23303	21270	5.74	5.21	51384	26723	76500	70500
麻城市	Macheng City	50.06	50.85	9801	9226	8.71	6.92	81168	51648	21600	20416
武穴市	Wuxue City	37.30	32.77	10481	14000	6.85	5.86	110645	62087	51619	40300
咸安区	Xian'an District	19.63	17.00	201	251	3.71	3.59	16493	16182	25158	20211
嘉鱼县	Jiayu County	19.39	18.25	1032	917	0.90	0.85	12837	12071	73444	71190
通城县	Tongcheng County	20.67	20.11			0.39	0.38	53965	52945	3300	2500
崇阳县	Chongyang County	21.45	20.06	100	96	0.58	0.50	27327	24950	8102	7602
通山县	Tongshan County	8.76	7.01			0.43	0.45	14580	13823	7100	4530
赤壁市	Chibi City	22.61	20.36	1325	1523	2.25	2.16	19868	18829	73007	70471
曾都区	Zengdu District	26.58	25.70	2455	2661	0.58	0.54	39828	27174	11674	10711
随县	Sui Country	80.08	77.41	7235	7559	2.35	2.20	71207	59762	28554	26563
广水市	Guangshui City	43.19	43.18	5188	4288	3.54	3.22	47159	43575	25258	23570
恩施市	Enshi City	22.11	21.78	25	40	1.32	1.22	74308	69855	453	423
利川市	Lichuan City	37.47	34.81			0.93	0.72	60798	49868	2146	1965
建始县	Jianshi County	23.30	21.70			1.43	1.17	48837	50673	296	366
巴东县	Badong County	22.29	21.55			1.75	1.42	58502	53619	964	1165
宣恩县	Xuanen County	13.17	12.78			0.58	0.54	29731	24646	311	272
咸丰县	Xianfeng County	20.22	18.85			0.93	0.68	36493	27890	348	314
来凤县	Laifeng County	12.88	12.58			0.63	0.71	24687	20734	1272	1163
鹤峰县	Hefeng County	9.26	9.04			0.42	0.34	18416	17865	100	86
仙桃市	Xiantiao City	71.21	67.34	26511	27738	11.89	11.80	281963	255921		
潜江市	Qianjiang City	38.87	36.49	40383	47429	11.31	9.36	118281	107998		
天门市	Tianmen City	62.05	56.88	47193	43075	11.20	9.44	82222	79029	103609	98605

23-1 续表 7 continued

指标名称	Item	工业总产值(当年价)(万元) Gross Industrial Output Value(10 000 yuan)		#轻工业(万元) #Light Industry (10 000 yuan)		#重工业(万元) #Heavy Industry (10 000 yuan)		工业经济效益综合指数% Comprehensive Efficiency I For Industrial Economic	
		2009	2008	2009	2008	2009	2008	2009	2008
蔡甸区	Caidian District	2016627	1668083	435757	366643	1580870	1301440	260.50	248.72
江夏区	Jiangxia District	2491223	2021549	581321	422264	1908402	1599285		204.52
黄陂区	Huangpi District	1243173	935681	456300	383308	786800	551705	294.00	252.00
新洲区	Xinzhou District	1575613	1258447	287122	241036	1288491	1017411	224.10	143.90
汉南区	Hannan District	457206	365721	167982	195229	289224	170492	201.74	182.44
阳新县	Yangxin County	742880	659783	30760	26049	712120	633733	190.68	200.27
大冶市	Daye City	2340688	1888500	453095	316800	1887593	1571700	210.35	239.35
郧县	Yun County	319599	185773	19015	1405	300584	184368	112.50	110.20
郧西县	Yunxi County	72997	62496	8135	9229	64862	53267	169.49	137.99
竹山县	Zhushan County	155387	111824	26699	16293	129279	95534	157.21	188.57
竹溪县	Zhuxi County	150731	95104	67097	48175	83633	40382	150.30	133.00
房县	Fang County	150731	95104	67097	48175	83633	40382	150.30	133.00
丹江口市	Danjiangkou City		817952		91697		677064		163.03
夷陵区	Yiling District	2047176	1350104	924886	636974	1122290	713130	247.80	227.70
远安县	Yuanan County	953586	669613	44462	20420	909124	649193	210.76	223.54
兴山县	Xingshan County	662962	511626	542989	381756	188395	145491	288.25	280.05
秭归县	Zigui County		252960		104380		148580		143.70
长阳县	Changyang Tujia A.C.	206142	158468	157607	138545	75080	59627	127.31	164.84
五峰县	Wufeng Tujia A.C.	154010	129423	50981	50521	51661	42336	98.94	203.15
宜都市	Yidu City	1654949	1026343	1495836	1085041	695700	441712	277.26	243.41
当阳市	Dangyang City	1474324	1019398	896942	627814	483354	334203	116.20	202.10
枝江市	Zhijiang City	1706700	1346937	690300	812603	596800	534334	237.75	200.69
襄阳区	Xiangyang District	1314521	902820	873761	550720	440760	352100	200.22	219.96
南漳县	Nanzhang County	336000	221522	178016	117924	157984	103598	158.76	166.77
谷城县	Gucheng County	1265600	813522	650648	390532	614952	422990	198.68	169.94
保康县	Baokang County	142600	105167	17825	12620	124775	92547	140.40	139.00
老河口市	Laohekou City		655652		257301		398351		155.88
枣阳市	Zaoyang City		807522		323008		484514		280.00
宜城市	Yicheng City	1000700	688700	648453	425672	352247	263028	204.45	191.15
梁子湖区	Liangzihu District	26943	16150	8038	4471	18905	11679	131.68	112.07
华容区	Huarong District	1559578	1180390	546688	396835	1012890	783555	315.81	236.10
鄂城区	Echeng District	2866841	2676160	134550	115351	2732291	2539366	279.09	296.33
东宝区	Dongbao District	1604580	1145474	244658	174656	1359921	970818	329.84	292.76
京山县	Jingshan County	1761718	1214409	1028016	623251	733702	591158	229.00	228.80
沙洋县	Shayang County	667293	415374	459438	269877	207881	145498	210.22	212.14
钟祥市	Zhongxiang City	1956316	1341700	675956	416206	1280360	925494	264.47	288.56
孝南区	Xiaonan District	352651	265963	2288777	186714	1237733	79249	208.51	170.20
孝昌县	Xiaochang County	192697	126204	67370	36964	125327	89241	190.00	175.70
大悟县	Dawu County	275720	287077	114564	66591	161156	220476	114.91	204.58
云梦县	Yunmeng County	1166318	910220	655552	489313	510766	420907	191.00	192.00
应城市	Yingcheng City	1264897	1039056	328374	270870	936523	768186	245.62	211.00
安陆市	Anlu City	530614	417818	318125	249688	212489	168130	166.50	152.40
汉川市	Hanchuan City	2497720	1872504	1439355	1018329	1058365	854176	223.90	201.70
荆州区	Jingzhou District	128358	803210	513708	303088	429806	253586	262.00	226.00
江陵县	Jiangling County	133677	101659	95255	72440	38422	29220	108.90	113.40
公安县	Gongan County	792200	635146		288828		364318	220.00	188.00
监利县	Jianli County	704780	627333	493346	443967	211434	177849	204.10	228.50
石首市	Shishou City	625008	652563	114280	101482	510728	551081	176.40	179.50
洪湖市	Honghu City	553660	431060	278306	193029	275354	238031	156.30	152.10
松滋市	Songci City	595685	413359	470000	281091	125700	132268	161.30	146.20
黄州区	Huangzhou District	980609	778911	931309	726601	49300	52310	177.99	162.33
团风县	Tuanfeng County	284923	176546	114590	93962	170333	82584	198.00	195.00
红安县	Hongan County	234500	185200	140958	138100	77979	43400	360.00	295.60
罗田县	Luotian County	396705	299500	155842	135059	240863	164441	147.80	168.20
英山县	Yingshan County	314348	268215	136930	114426	177418	153789	258.35	194.80
浠水县	Xishui County	582800	461169	174427	119123	408373	342046	261.74	249.21
蕲春县	Qichun County	746700	541907	388284	281792	358416	260115		
黄梅县	Huangmei County	690900	465100	393900	273200	297000	191900	232.90	211.13
麻城市	Macheng City	700667	525413	63512	70539	637155	454874	136.80	121.60
武穴市	Wuxue City	858280	689533	275670	221470	582610	468063	188.19	238.24
咸安区	Xian'an District	1538400	1236654	685635	551153	852765	685501	240.22	200.30
嘉鱼县	Jiayu County	947223	724265	363158	305158	584065	419107	252.33	228.96
通城县	Tongcheng County	343985	259236	73521	54435	270464	204801	185.56	165.53
崇阳县	Chongyang County	218011	155036	87220	68176	130791	86860	145.91	145.90
通山县	Tongshan County	181545	132016	20740	16642	160805	115374	148.56	160.06
赤壁市	Chibi City	1380917	1091965	552853	440272	828064	651693	220.50	220.50
曾都区	Zengdu District	1569254	1337274	661911	550689	907343	786585	231.45	261.82
随县	Sui Country	723383	691180	435832	414821	287551	254597	268.86	
广水市	Guangshui City	1137961	853729	522079	424532	615883	429197	273.59	307.36
恩施市	Enshi City	471209	303620	201909	73144	269300	230476	272.90	174.10
利川市	Lichuan City	156417	109915	90205	40639	66211	68620	175.43	154.87
建始县	Jianshi County	131072	98529	57004	59236	74068	39293	133.95	139.90
巴东县	Badong County	200373	200967	52669	30264	147704	170703	189.92	400.88
宣恩县	Xuanen County	65310	50642	40815	26111	24495	24531	174.44	197.54
咸丰县	Xianfeng County	95932	71754	44241	26364	51691	45390	161.60	145.90
来凤县	Laifeng County	97959	70274	53146	36787	45813	33318	178.13	200.32
鹤峰县	Hefeng County	145676	105651	82005	64589	63671	41062	138.30	123.98
仙桃市	Xiantiao City	2738397	2096154	914801	692769	1023318	780649	201.58	270.01
潜江市	Qianjiang City	3316104	3271386	2553834	2485777	1172600	1020000	213.20	188.50
天门市	Tianmen City	2060400	1701930	1068900	818915	991400	883015	225.80	273.60

23-1 续表 8 continued

指标名称 Item	利税总额(万元) Total Pre-Tax Profits (10 000 yuan)		利润总额(万元) Total Profits (10 000 yuan)		邮电业务营业收入(万元) Business Volume of Post Services (10 000 yuan)		社会消费品零售总额(万元) Total Retail Sales (10 000 yuan)	
	2009	2008	2009	2008	2009	2008	2009	2008
蔡甸区 Caidian District	366514	382917	36691	45936	27838	21247	319794	269449
江夏区 Jiangxia District		159434		95573	69375	59652	573597	481551
黄陂区 Huangpi District	147900	83821	135100	70025	33061	28757	837950	683132
新洲区 Xinzhou District	48000	-22490	10900	-53637	11320	9090	789523	662653
汉南区 Hannan District	38344	17077	13894	8427	1724	1540	92010	77515
阳新县 Yangxin County	60810	65636	20075	28372	9405	8353	498717	390844
大冶市 Daye City	206400	222500	103000	121300	21399	19311	729890	585176
郧县 Yun County	11000	10586	5900	1260	4728	5858	238496	197594
郧西县 Yunxi County	79016	3763	3995	639	9196	7864	172198	143379
竹山县 Zhushan County	15662	10984	5781	5148	9200	7921	169074	139962
竹溪县 Zhuxi County	8123	5332	1864	1251	4490	4368	129802	107720
房县 Fang County	8123	5332	1864	1251	4490	4368	183262	151833
丹江口市 Danjiangkou City		76295		36563	13840	12591	290204	241033
夷陵区 Yiling District	197971	146034	160837	98555	21553	20044	501094	410694
远安县 Yuanan County	53184	54423	24754	40179	3657	2188	165679	136245
兴山县 Xingshan County	31721	25064	22		878	583	124215	134870
秭归县 Zigui County		15605		5359	11655	9757	168039	139956
长阳县 Changyang Tujia A.C.	5056	9688	3171	2011	1226	1406	192304	160411
五峰县 Wufeng Tujia A.C.	5066	7900	2009	1479	1133	616	86451	73275
宜都市 Yidu City	35081	40911	1234	2712	1052	1051	417246	342307
当阳市 Dangyang City	128945	63252	2254	968	1366	1261	476245	396871
枝江市 Zhijiang City	126100	120021	94300	48198	19386	18638	530827	437171
襄阳区 Xiangyang District	76127	71444	49197	46678		18499	551670	441690
南漳县 Nanzhang County	25565	21035	12063	10360	11726	10217	237767	191902
谷城县 Gucheng County	60800	43055	44400	21160	14021	12918	250012	200664
保康县 Baokang County	4100	21017	7000	10159	8752	6772	141661	116786
老河口市 Laohekou City		29253		13217		12201	454670	373293
枣阳市 Zaoyang City		163808		92337	24730	23265	712884	570764
宜城市 Yicheng City	30400	60000	37900	40200	16142	15187	420215	339431
梁子湖区 Liangzihu District	2088	1955	1578	719	3978	3501	98780	81857
华容区 Huarong District	136898	56734	69226	21729	7253	6559	195176	161436
鄂城区 Echeng District	440316	116268	233831	-11027	42355	37943	972833	805576
东宝区 Dongbao District	154113	110659	93011	59412			503974	419978
京山县 Jingshan County	118667	87644	70114	55161	21881	19134	617932	486561
沙洋县 Shayang County	17411	11613	9325	3662	17900	15793	379681	300618
钟祥市 Zhongxiang City	165496	172435	113300	109692	31245	26595	641655	505638
孝南区 Xiaonan District	45529	23103	37897	13442			576577	476904
孝昌县 Xiaochang County	9671	4103	7979	3463	29795	24485	220798	182616
大悟县 Dawu County	24800	37960	12816	27597			288611	238548
云梦县 Yunmeng County	75680	68764	26198	25061	14426	14101	420427	347748
应城市 Yingcheng City	151074	103685	73755	59550	6954	6186	510658	423000
安陆市 Anlu City	30846	22132	20108	12063	6885	4147	407460	337139
汉川市 Hanchuan City	239396	120692	143507	51494	23148	19101	844419	698444
荆州区 Jingzhou District	49500	37700	29100	23400	73443	47108	608763	485457
江陵县 Jiangling County	6828	3718	3000	1335	3465	2986	182659	158421
公安县 Gongan County	91100	43654	52000	23529	30626	26235	560338	481804
监利县 Jianli County	36610	37817	18842	16266	34951	30392	600092	496765
石首市 Shishou City	45374	32370	29480	16133	19361	19050	446019	371064
洪湖市 Honghu City	22627	19347	12977	10428	27902	24994	495959	411926
松滋市 Songzi City	57752	44944	22178	17454	24566	24667	507028	419378
黄州区 Huangzhou District	48500	32984	67100	16992	51210	49310	521368	402601
团风县 Tuanfeng County	10028	9774	8239	6357	9257	7821	114021	94995
红安县 Hongan County	25400	34600	29200	23200	13965	12469	238070	196639
罗田县 Luotian County	23303	24236	8546	8970	13800	11800	227333	187604
英山县 Yingshan County	16550	39957	15042	17174	9252	9404	136152	108835
浠水县 Xishui County	56000	61339	59300	29405	21135	16981	469566	394588
蕲春县 Qichun County	58300	34342	32800	17359	24506	19779	390416	319022
黄梅县 Huangmei County	30700	31400	41100	17000	9405	8260	424713	349015
麻城市 Macheng City	45516	20153	13404	2233	21553	18212	509568	411606
武穴市 Wuxue City	36331	68452	19668	40034	20671	18639	511551	387539
咸安区 Xian'an District	261300	137907	205500	96116	10590	9768	472936	387018
嘉鱼县 Jiayu County	76012	58749	61591	46289	8974	8372	192218	159568
通城县 Tongcheng County	20256	18119	11635	9043	24040	11249	252070	200560
崇阳县 Chongyang County	10236	6972	3367	2245	11808	10695	232981	176101
通山县 Tongshan County	8600	18339	2867	10433	13543	13056	146279	120308
赤壁市 Chibi City	107909	82187	61350	39827	27650	25130	392360	322372
曾都区 Zengdu District	183812	268833	130082	185050			667541	543777
随县 Sui Country	6328		249104				506264	457743
广水市 Guangshui City	155304	118586	71857	60881	22804	19602	646683	534670
恩施市 Enshi City	70575	31053	6393	13378	26013	23408	384304	328602
利川市 Lichuan City	16342	14308	10118	7530	21590	4470	166317	134583
建始县 Jianshi County	8465	6057	1841	1521	13707	11125	108634	87750
巴东县 Badong County	36692	45779	12139	13072	15664	13262	125085	100438
宣恩县 Xuanen County	6434	13803	3918	10952	7949	6877	87071	72559
咸丰县 Xianfeng County	9336	7341	4286	2937	10529	8671	100259	81666
来凤县 Laifeng County	13837	12843	8062	8525	8480	7555	88743	70431
鹤峰县 Hefeng County	4079	5821	3999	1287	8513	6660	80003	66696
仙桃市 Xiantiao City	119549	87095	37188	7585	11388	9448	1278741	1058460
潜江市 Qianjiang City	92100	119620	111200	21724	7176	5968	863561	723322
天门市 Tianmen City	195400	237378	131300	143297	35473	31673	1352108	1122215

附录

全国分省主要指标

Major Indicators by Region

资料整理：倪群峰

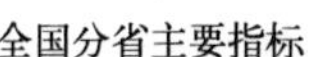

附录1-1 各地区按三次产业分法人单位数（2008）

REGIONS BY THE NUMBER OF UNITS THREE INDUSTRIES CORPORATE UNITS(2008)

单位：个 (unit)

地区	Region	法人单位数 Corporate Units	第一产业 Primary Industry	第二产业 Secondary Industry	#工业 #Industry	第三产业 Tertiary Industry
全 国	**National Total**	**7195210**	**98546**	**2200404**	**1973617**	**4896260**
北 京	Beijing	271800	3485	38483	29301	229832
天 津	Tianjin	146175	764	47226	41760	98185
河 北	Hebei	281329	2758	92175	87011	186396
山 西	Shanxi	166938	6205	35352	31149	125381
内蒙古	Inner Mongolia	115288	1784	23545	20439	89959
辽 宁	Liaoning	318936	3571	104572	89613	210793
吉 林	Jilin	126098	1695	31928	27836	92475
黑龙江	Heilongjiang	151788	1723	38108	32287	111957
上 海	Shanghai	361828	1913	100311	80999	259604
江 苏	Jiangsu	635411	4594	294670	269624	336147
浙 江	Zhejiang	568636	8544	261241	248305	298851
安 徽	Anhui	206990	1767	67180	57983	138043
福 建	Fujian	237115	4543	76258	70275	156314
江 西	Jiangxi	148337	556	44817	41790	102964
山 东	Shangdong	609297	5451	205876	182136	397970
河 南	Henan	360592	9570	123219	114136	227803
湖 北	**Hubei**	**294735**	**1407**	**74465**	**62012**	**218863**
湖 南	Hunan	265196	6765	73437	67878	184994
广 东	Guangdong	622083	4476	215779	201322	401828
广 西	Guangxi	158844	4306	26541	24212	127997
海 南	Hainan	31248	1941	4529	2811	24778
重 庆	Chongqing	142743	3723	39045	33480	99975
四 川	Sichuan	315390	5148	67846	59982	242396
贵 州	Guizhou	95622	1434	15886	14295	78302
云 南	Yunnan	126255	3715	23998	20273	98542
西 藏	Tibet	15344	21	741	490	14582
陕 西	Shaanxi	182179	3222	37908	32378	141049
甘 肃	Gansu	94739	643	15041	12983	79055
青 海	Qinghai	24660	424	3550	2829	20686
宁 夏	Ningxia	29987	683	5401	4515	23903
新 疆	Xinjiang	89627	1715	11276	9513	76636

注：附录2009年数据为初步统计数。
Note:The data of Appendix of 2009 are preliminary statistics.

附录1-2 各地区按行业分法人单位数（2008）

REGION NUMBER OF CORPORATE UNITS BY SECTOR(2008)

单位：个 (unit)

地 区	Region	法人单位数 Corporate Units	#农、林、牧、渔业 Agriculture, Forestry, Animal husbandry, Fishery	#采矿业 Mining Industry	#制造业 Manufacturing	#电力、煤气及水的生产和供应业 Electricity, Gas and Water Production and Supply	#建筑业 Construction	#交通运输、仓储及邮政业 Traffic, Transport, Storage and Postal Industry
全国总计	**National Total**	**7195210**	**98546**	**97314**	**1818380**	**57923**	**226787**	**157737**
北 京	Beijing	271800	3485	143	28799	359	9182	6152
天 津	Tianjin	146175	764	99	41354	307	5466	7416
河 北	Hebei	281329	2758	7794	78240	977	5164	4967
山 西	Shanxi	166938	6205	7969	22410	770	4203	2964
内蒙古	Inner Mongolia	115288	1784	4174	15279	986	3106	3212
辽 宁	Liaoning	318936	3571	5522	82603	1488	14959	8958
吉 林	Jilin	126098	1695	1877	24865	1094	4092	2901
黑龙江	Heilongjiang	151788	1723	2287	29131	869	5821	3124
上 海	Shanghai	361828	1913	1	80736	262	19312	13330
江 苏	Jiangsu	635411	4594	1145	265261	3218	25046	13813
浙 江	Zhejiang	568636	8544	1529	242892	3884	12936	10251
安 徽	Anhui	206990	1767	3162	52886	1935	9197	5015
福 建	Fujian	237115	4543	2466	61938	5871	5983	5763
江 西	Jiangxi	148337	556	3703	34665	3422	3027	3344
山 东	Shangdong	609297	5451	4581	175986	1569	23740	13025
河 南	Henan	360592	9570	7454	105315	1367	9083	4885
湖 北	**Hubei**	**294735**	**1407**	**4862**	**54633**	**2517**	**12453**	**6009**
湖 南	Hunan	265196	6765	7919	55536	4423	5559	3664
广 东	Guangdong	622083	4476	2330	191810	7182	14457	14804
广 西	Guangxi	158844	4306	2258	19683	2271	2329	3178
海 南	Hainan	31248	1941	223	2325	263	1718	632
重 庆	Chongqing	142743	3723	3389	28221	1870	5565	3691
四 川	Sichuan	315390	5148	5436	49258	5288	7864	5835
贵 州	Guizhou	95622	1434	4283	8889	1123	1591	1208
云 南	Yunnan	126255	3715	4681	13922	1670	3725	2206
西 藏	Tibet	15344	21	101	309	80	251	161
陕 西	Shaanxi	182179	3222	3643	27644	1091	5530	2930
甘 肃	Gansu	94739	643	1570	10550	863	2058	1323
青 海	Qinghai	24660	424	521	2077	231	721	409
宁 夏	Ningxia	29987	683	567	3810	138	886	444
新 疆	Xinjiang	89627	1715	1625	7353	535	1763	2123

附录1-2 续表 1 continued

单位：个 (unit)

地区	Region	#信息传输、计算机服务和软件业 Information Transmission, Computer Services and Software	#批发和零售业 Wholesale and Retail Trade	#住宿和餐饮业 Accommodation and Catering Services	#金融业 Financial Sector	#房地产业 Real Estate	#租赁和商务服务业 Leasing and Business Services
全国总计	**National Total**	**153289**	**1403143**	**145302**	**28133**	**214405**	**427005**
北京	Beijing	15776	85052	10672	1025	10969	45005
天津	Tianjin	1843	44056	3844	580	3825	9546
河北	Hebei	3993	46879	3947	880	5523	7816
山西	Shanxi	2603	28977	2866	731	3886	6615
内蒙古	Inner Mongolia	1630	23379	3047	983	3905	5776
辽宁	Liaoning	6330	72700	5658	1410	11379	20085
吉林	Jilin	1668	29534	2467	671	3361	6260
黑龙江	Heilongjiang	2214	33775	2330	938	4426	8342
上海	Shanghai	10745	118526	9281	175	11850	43380
江苏	Jiangsu	11692	134732	8366	2310	16970	33041
浙江	Zhejiang	11514	97126	6426	1961	13267	37945
安徽	Anhui	4880	31128	4025	1151	7130	8806
福建	Fujian	4949	42037	3695	1164	7725	13888
江西	Jiangxi	1310	15765	2955	556	4170	4568
山东	Shangdong	11451	129114	13190	1795	14013	26729
河南	Henan	4631	47473	8809	1076	6765	9821
湖北	**Hubei**	**6024**	**58526**	**7877**	**1074**	**10122**	**13630**
湖南	Hunan	7213	27809	6547	848	6004	8165
广东	Guangdong	14467	141359	13309	1969	28526	55996
广西	Guangxi	5040	21560	2152	636	5628	10535
海南	Hainan	715	5630	1033	200	2763	2698
重庆	Chongqing	3269	27425	4142	909	5363	8942
四川	Sichuan	8384	39561	5696	1503	8426	13675
贵州	Guizhou	1697	11236	1251	518	3722	3648
云南	Yunnan	2526	20283	2531	772	4298	6397
西藏	Tibet	141	668	281	105	94	192
陕西	Shaanxi	2822	27687	4964	698	4111	5938
甘肃	Gansu	804	14040	1884	525	2062	2911
青海	Qinghai	358	2878	517	175	713	924
宁夏	Ningxia	621	5682	493	190	778	1238
新疆	Xinjiang	1979	18546	1047	605	2631	4493

附录1-2　续表 2 continued

单位：个　　(unit)

地　区	Region	#科学研究、技术服务和地质勘查业 Research, Technical Service and Geological Prospecting	#水利、环境和公共设施管理业 Water, Environment and Public Facilities Management	#居民服务和其他服务业 Resident Services and Other Services	#教　育 Education	#卫生、社会保障和社会福利业 Health, Social Security and Social Welfare	#文化、体育和娱乐业 Culture, Sports and Entertainment	#公共管理和社会组织 Public Management and Social Organization
全国总计	**National Total**	**201696**	**57553**	**120466**	**335065**	**206517**	**81882**	**1364067**
北　京	Beijing	20460	1719	10239	6245	2307	7374	6837
天　津	Tianjin	4971	987	5566	3130	1505	1181	9735
河　北	Hebei	4140	1514	2814	18885	7105	1982	75951
山　西	Shanxi	3957	1720	2685	9003	5292	2299	51783
内蒙古	Inner Mongolia	3588	1584	1601	5296	4379	1602	29977
辽　宁	Liaoning	10705	2642	5711	11564	10138	3477	40036
吉　林	Jilin	4160	1276	2140	5638	3610	1758	27031
黑龙江	Heilongjiang	5236	1516	3233	7445	4743	1754	32881
上　海	Shanghai	14823	1906	12409	5186	2412	3692	11889
江　苏	Jiangsu	13009	4935	8560	14470	9660	5187	59402
浙　江	Zhejiang	12396	3580	5589	15711	7104	4703	71278
安　徽	Anhui	4341	1654	2647	13152	7048	2177	44889
福　建	Fujian	6279	1953	3433	11401	5970	3128	44929
江　西	Jiangxi	3294	1404	1929	9826	7448	1939	44456
山　东	Shangdong	11477	3169	9351	20484	15637	4213	124322
河　南	Henan	5266	2206	3700	22536	26057	3492	81086
湖　北	**Hubei**	**9841**	**3760**	**6022**	**16788**	**12213**	**4191**	**62786**
湖　南	Hunan	6378	2684	4445	14497	8136	3687	84917
广　东	Guangdong	16717	3979	12140	29205	8323	5764	55270
广　西	Guangxi	7141	2081	1607	16435	6207	2600	43197
海　南	Hainan	957	286	499	2092	749	547	5977
重　庆	Chongqing	3502	1203	2499	7393	5793	1904	23940
四　川	Sichuan	10348	3021	3394	19476	14255	4342	104480
贵　州	Guizhou	2900	1004	1144	9398	3852	1368	35356
云　南	Yunnan	4911	1764	1566	7271	4226	2139	37652
西　藏	Tibet	145	34	93	1035	506	160	10967
陕　西	Shaanxi	4287	1788	2465	14779	14223	2328	52029
甘　肃	Gansu	1963	821	1158	8974	3461	1121	38008
青　海	Qinghai	848	282	215	1185	757	373	11052
宁　夏	Ningxia	617	224	366	1344	791	298	10817
新　疆	Xinjiang	3039	857	1246	5221	2610	1102	31137

附录1-3 地区生产总值

GROSS DOMESTIC PRODUCT

单位：亿元 (100 million yuna)

地 区	Region	2003	2004	2005	2006	2007	2008	2009
北 京	Beijing	5023.8	6033.2	6969.5	8117.8	9846.8	11115.0	11865.9
天 津	Tianjin	2578.0	3111.0	3905.6	4462.7	5252.8	6719.0	7500.8
河 北	Hebei	6921.3	8477.6	10012.1	11467.6	13607.3	16012.0	17026.6
山 西	Shanxi	2855.2	3571.4	4230.5	4878.6	6024.5	7315.4	7365.7
内蒙古	Inner Mongolia	2388.4	3041.1	3905.0	4944.2	6423.2	8496.2	9725.8
辽 宁	Liaoning	6002.5	6672.0	8047.3	9304.5	11164.3	13668.6	15065.6
吉 林	Jilin	2662.1	3122.0	3620.3	4275.1	5284.7	6426.1	7203.2
黑龙江	Heilongjiang	4057.4	4750.6	5513.7	6211.8	7104.0	8314.4	8288.0
上 海	Shanghai	6694.2	8072.8	9247.7	10572.2	12494.0	14069.9	14900.9
江 苏	Jiangsu	12442.9	15003.6	18598.7	21742.1	26018.5	30982.0	34061.2
浙 江	Zhejiang	9705.0	11648.7	13417.7	15718.5	18753.7	21462.7	22832.4
安 徽	Anhui	3923.1	4759.3	5375.1	6112.5	7360.9	8851.7	10052.9
福 建	Fujian	4983.7	5763.4	6554.7	7583.8	9248.5	10823.0	11949.5
江 西	Jiangxi	2807.4	3456.7	4056.8	4820.5	5800.3	6971.1	7589.2
山 东	Shangdong	12078.1	15021.8	18366.9	21900.2	25776.9	30933.3	33805.3
河 南	Henan	6867.7	8553.8	10587.4	12362.8	15012.5	18018.5	19367.3
湖 北	**Hubei**	**4757.5**	**5633.2**	**6590.2**	**7617.5**	**9333.4**	**11328.9**	**12831.5**
湖 南	Hunan	4660.0	5641.9	6596.1	7688.7	9439.6	11555.0	12930.7
广 东	Guangdong	15844.6	18864.6	22557.4	26587.8	31777.0	36796.7	39081.6
广 西	Guangxi	2821.1	3433.5	3984.1	4746.2	5823.4	7021.0	7700.4
海 南	Hainan	693.2	798.9	898.0	1044.9	1254.2	1503.1	1646.6
重 庆	Chongqing	2272.8	2692.8	3467.7	3907.2	4676.1	5793.7	6528.7
四 川	Sichuan	5333.1	6379.6	7385.1	8690.2	10562.4	12601.2	14151.3
贵 州	Guizhou	1426.3	1677.8	2005.4	2339.0	2884.1	3561.6	3893.5
云 南	Yunnan	2556.0	3081.9	3461.7	3988.1	4772.5	5692.1	6168.2
西 藏	Tibet	185.1	220.3	248.8	290.8	341.4	394.9	441.4
陕 西	Shaanxi	2587.7	3175.6	3933.7	4743.6	5757.3	7314.6	8186.7
甘 肃	Gansu	1399.8	1688.5	1934.0	2276.7	2702.4	3166.8	3382.4
青 海	Qinghai	390.2	466.1	543.3	648.5	797.4	1018.6	1081.3
宁 夏	Ningxia	445.4	537.1	612.6	725.9	919.1	1203.9	1334.6
新 疆	Xinjiang	1886.4	2209.1	2604.2	3045.3	3523.2	4183.2	4273.6

注：本表按当年价格计算。

Note:The table at current prices.

附录1-4 地区生产总值指数

INDICES OF GROSS DOMESTIC PRODUCT

(上年=100) (last year=100)

地 区	Region	2003	2004	2005	2006	2007	2008	2009
北 京	Beijing	111.0	114.1	112.1	113.0	114.5	109.1	110.1
天 津	Tianjin	114.8	115.8	114.9	114.7	115.5	116.5	116.5
河 北	Hebei	111.6	112.9	113.4	113.4	112.8	110.1	110.0
山 西	Shanxi	114.9	115.2	113.5	112.8	115.9	108.5	105.5
内蒙古	Inner Mongolia	117.9	120.5	123.8	119.1	119.2	117.8	116.9
辽 宁	Liaoning	111.5	112.8	112.7	114.2	115.0	113.4	113.1
吉 林	Jilin	110.2	112.2	112.1	115.0	116.1	116.0	113.3
黑龙江	Heilongjiang	110.2	111.7	111.6	112.1	112.0	111.8	111.1
上 海	Shanghai	112.3	114.2	111.4	112.7	115.2	109.7	108.2
江 苏	Jiangsu	113.6	114.8	114.5	114.9	114.9	112.7	112.4
浙 江	Zhejiang	114.7	114.5	112.8	113.9	114.7	110.1	108.9
安 徽	Anhui	109.4	113.3	111.0	112.0	114.2	112.7	112.9
福 建	Fujian	111.5	111.8	113.7	115.7	122.0	117.0	112.0
江 西	Jiangxi	113.0	113.2	112.8	112.3	113.2	113.2	113.1
山 东	Shangdong	113.4	115.4	115.0	114.7	114.2	112.0	111.9
河 南	Henan	110.7	113.7	114.2	114.4	114.6	112.1	110.7
湖 北	**Hubei**	**109.7**	**111.2**	**112.1**	**113.2**	**114.6**	**113.4**	**113.2**
湖 南	Hunan	109.6	112.1	112.2	112.8	115.0	113.9	113.6
广 东	Guangdong	114.8	114.8	114.1	114.8	114.9	110.4	109.5
广 西	Guangxi	110.2	111.8	113.1	113.6	115.1	112.8	113.9
海 南	Hainan	110.6	110.7	110.5	113.2	115.8	110.3	111.7
重 庆	Chongqing	111.5	112.2	111.7	112.4	115.9	114.5	114.9
四 川	Sichuan	111.3	112.7	112.6	113.5	114.5	111.0	114.5
贵 州	Guizhou	110.1	111.4	112.7	112.8	114.8	111.3	111.2
云 南	Yunnan	108.8	111.3	108.9	111.6	112.2	110.6	112.1
西 藏	Tibet	112.0	112.1	112.1	113.3	114.0	110.1	112.4
陕 西	Shaanxi	111.8	112.9	113.7	113.9	115.8	116.4	113.6
甘 肃	Gansu	110.7	111.5	111.8	111.5	112.3	110.1	110.0
青 海	Qinghai	111.9	112.3	112.2	113.3	113.5	113.5	110.1
宁 夏	Ningxia	112.7	111.2	110.9	112.7	112.7	112.6	111.6
新 疆	Xinjiang	111.2	111.4	110.9	111.0	112.2	111.0	108.1

注：本表按不变价格计算。

Note:At constant prices, this table.

附录1-5 人均地区生产总值
GROSS DOMESTIC PRODUCT OF PER CAPITA

单位：元 (yuan)

地 区	Region	2003	2004	2005	2006	2007	2008	2009
北 京	Beijing	34892	41099	45993	52054	61274	66797	68788
天 津	Tianjin	25544	30575	37796	42141	47970	58656	62403
河 北	Hebei	10251	12487	14659	16682	19662	22986	24284
山 西	Shanxi	8642	10742	12647	14497	17805	21506	21544
内蒙古	Inner Mongolia	10039	12767	16371	20692	26777	35263	40225
辽 宁	Liaoning	14270	15835	19074	21914	26054	31736	34898
吉 林	Jilin	9854	11537	13348	15720	19383	23521	26319
黑龙江	Heilongjiang	10638	12449	14440	16255	18580	21740	21665
上 海	Shanghai	39128	46338	52535	58837	68024	75109	78225
江 苏	Jiangsu	16830	20223	24953	28943	34294	40497	44232
浙 江	Zhejiang	20444	24352	27661	31825	37358	42166	44335
安 徽	Anhui	6375	7681	8666	9996	12039	14447	16391
福 建	Fujian	14333	16469	18605	21384	25906	30122	33051
江 西	Jiangxi	6624	8097	9440	11145	13322	15900	17185
山 东	Shangdong	13268	16413	19934	23603	27604	32936	35796
河 南	Henan	7376	9201	11346	13172	16012	19181	20477
湖 北	**Hubei**	**8378**	**9898**	**11554**	**13360**	**16386**	**19858**	**22450**
湖 南	Hunan	7589	9165	10562	12139	14869	18147	20226
广 东	Guangdong	17795	20870	24647	28747	33890	38748	40748
广 西	Guangxi	6169	7461	8590	10121	12277	14652	15923
海 南	Hainan	8592	9812	11165	12810	14923	17691	19166
重 庆	Chongqing	8091	9624	12403	13940	16629	20490	22916
四 川	Sichuan	6623	7895	8721	10613	12963	15495	17339
贵 州	Guizhou	3701	4317	5119	5932	7273	9428	10258
云 南	Yunnan	5871	7012	7809	8929	10609	12570	13536
西 藏	Tibet	6893	8103	9036	10422	12083	13824	15295
陕 西	Shaanxi	7028	8587	10594	12724	15386	19480	21732
甘 肃	Gansu	5429	6566	7477	8757	10346	12110	12852
青 海	Qinghai	7346	8693	10045	11889	14506	18421	19454
宁 夏	Ningxia	7734	9199	10349	12099	15142	19609	21475
新 疆	Xinjiang	9828	11337	13108	15000	16999	19797	19926

注：本表按当年价格计算。
Note:The table at current prices.

附录1-6 地区生产总值构成（2009）

COMPOSITION OF GROSS DOMESTIC PRODUCT(2009)

（地区生产总值=100）

(GDP=100)

地区	Region	第一产业 Primary Industry	第二产业 Secondary Industry	工业 Industry	建筑业 Contruction	第三产业 Tertiary Industry	#交通运输、仓储和邮政业 #Transport, Storage and Post	#批发和零售业 #Wholesale and Retail Trade
北京	Beijing	1.0	23.1	18.5	4.7	75.9	3.9	13.2
天津	Tianjin	1.7	54.8	50.0	4.8	43.5	6.2	11.2
河北	Hebei	13.0	52.1	46.4	5.7	34.8	8.9	6.6
山西	Shanxi	6.5	54.6	48.2	6.4	38.9	7.0	7.6
内蒙古	Inner Mongolia	9.6	52.5	46.3	6.1	38.0	8.0	9.4
辽宁	Liaoning	9.4	51.9	45.4	6.5	38.7	5.2	9.5
吉林	Jilin	13.6	48.5	41.7	6.8	37.9	4.4	9.4
黑龙江	Heilongjiang	13.9	47.3	41.2	6.1	38.8	5.2	8.6
上海	Shanghai	0.8	39.9	35.9	4.0	59.4	4.3	14.7
江苏	Jiangsu	6.5	54.1	48.3	5.7	39.5	4.1	10.4
浙江	Zhejiang	5.1	51.9	45.8	6.1	43.0	3.8	9.5
安徽	Anhui	14.9	48.8	40.4	8.3	36.4	4.6	7.1
福建	Fujian	9.9	48.6	41.2	7.5	41.5	6.3	8.5
江西	Jiangxi	14.5	51.3	41.8	9.5	34.3	5.1	7.1
山东	Shangdong	9.5	56.3	50.4	5.9	34.1	5.3	8.7
河南	Henan	14.3	56.6	50.9	5.7	29.1	4.4	5.4
湖北	**Hubei**	**14.0**	**46.1**	**39.4**	**6.6**	**40.0**	**5.0**	**7.1**
湖南	Hunan	15.2	43.9	37.2	6.7	40.8	5.3	8.6
广东	Guangdong	5.1	49.3	45.9	3.4	45.6	4.4	10.0
广西	Guangxi	18.9	43.9	37.2	6.7	37.2	4.6	7.1
海南	Hainan	28.1	26.9	18.3	8.7	45.0	5.3	10.3
重庆	Chongqing	9.3	52.8	44.7	8.1	37.9	5.3	8.0
四川	Sichuan	15.8	47.4	40.1	7.3	36.7	3.7	6.1
贵州	Guizhou	14.2	37.9	32.2	5.7	47.9	10.2	7.5
云南	Yunnan	17.2	41.8	33.9	8.0	40.9	2.8	8.9
西藏	Tibet	14.5	30.9	7.4	23.5	54.6	4.7	6.1
陕西	Shaanxi	9.6	52.7	43.7	9.0	37.7	5.1	8.2
甘肃	Gansu	14.7	44.7	35.2	9.5	40.6	6.3	6.8
青海	Qinghai	9.9	53.3	43.6	9.7	36.8	4.6	6.1
宁夏	Ningxia	9.5	51.0	40.3	10.6	39.5	7.3	6.0
新疆	Xinjiang	17.8	45.7	37.0	8.7	36.5	4.4	5.9

注：本表按当年价格计算。

Note:At present year price, this table.

附录1-7 各地区年末总人口

THE END OF THE TOTAL POPULATION OF ALL REGIONS

单位：万人 (10 000 persons)

地 区	Region	2003	2004	2005	2006	2007	2008	2009
全 国	**National Total**	**129227**	**129988**	**130756**	**131448**	**132129**	**132802**	**133474**
北 京	Beijing	1456	1493	1538	1581	1633	1695	1755
天 津	Tianjin	1011	1024	1043	1075	1115	1176	1228
河 北	Hebei	6769	6809	6851	6898	6943	6989	7034
山 西	Shanxi	3314	3335	3355	3375	3393	3411	3427
内蒙古	Inner Mongolia	2380	2384	2386	2397	2405	2414	2422
辽 宁	Liaoning	4210	4217	4221	4271	4298	4315	4319
吉 林	Jilin	2704	2709	2716	2723	2730	2734	2740
黑龙江	Heilongjiang	3815	3817	3820	3823	3824	3825	3826
上 海	Shanghai	1711	1742	1778	1815	1858	1888	1921
江 苏	Jiangsu	7406	7433	7475	7550	7625	7677	7725
浙 江	Zhejiang	4680	4720	4898	4980	5060	5120	5180
安 徽	Anhui	6410	6461	6120	6110	6118	6135	6131
福 建	Fujian	3488	3511	3535	3558	3581	3604	3627
江 西	Jiangxi	4254	4284	4311	4339	4368	4400	4432
山 东	Shangdong	9125	9180	9248	9309	9367	9417	9470
河 南	Henan	9667	9717	9380	9392	9360	9429	9487
湖 北	**Hubei**	**6002**	**6016**	**5710**	**5693**	**5699**	**5711**	**5720**
湖 南	Hunan	6663	6698	6326	6342	6355	6380	6406
广 东	Guangdong	7954	8304	9194	9304	9449	9544	9638
广 西	Guangxi	4857	4889	4660	4719	4768	4816	4856
海 南	Hainan	811	818	828	836	845	854	864
重 庆	Chongqing	3130	3122	2798	2808	2816	2839	2859
四 川	Sichuan	8700	8725	8212	8169	8127	8138	8185
贵 州	Guizhou	3870	3904	3730	3757	3762	3793	3798
云 南	Yunnan	4376	4415	4450	4483	4514	4543	4571
西 藏	Tibet	270	274	277	281	284	287	290
陕 西	Shaanxi	3690	3705	3720	3735	3748	3762	3772
甘 肃	Gansu	2603	2619	2594	2606	2617	2628	2635
青 海	Qinghai	534	539	543	548	552	554	557
宁 夏	Ningxia	580	588	596	604	610	618	625
新 疆	Xinjiang	1934	1963	2010	2050	2095	2131	2159

注：1.全国数据包括中国人民解放军现役军人数，但不包括香港、澳门特别行政区和台湾省数据；分省数据中未包括中国人民解放军现役军人数。

2.2003-2004年部分地区数据不是常住人口口径。

Notes:a)The number of national data including military personnel, but not including Hong Kong and Macao Special Administrative Region and Taiwan Province; provincial data does not include active duty PLA.

b)2003-2004 resident population in parts of the data is not caliber.

附录1-8 各地区就业人员

EMPLOYMENT IN ALL REGIONS

单位：万人 （年底数） (End of Year) (10 000 persons)

地 区	Region	2002	2003	2004	2005	2007	2008	2009
全国总计	**National Total**	**73740**	**74432**	**75200**	**75825**	**76990**	**77480**	**77995**
北 京	Beijing	799	859	895	920	1111	1174	1255
天 津	Tianjin	403	420	422	427	433	503	507
河 北	Hebei	3386	3389	3416	3467	3567	3652	3900
山 西	Shanxi	1417	1469	1475	1476	1550	1583	1600
内蒙古	Inner Mongolia	1010	1005	1019	1041	1082	1103	1142
辽 宁	Liaoning	1842	1861	1952	1979	2071	2098	2190
吉 林	Jilin	1095	1045	1116	1099	1096	1144	1185
黑龙江	Heilongjiang	1626	1622	1623	1626	1660	1670	1687
上 海	Shanghai	743	772	812	856	877	896	929
江 苏	Jiangsu	3506	3610	3720	3878	4193	4384	4536
浙 江	Zhejiang	2835	2962	3092	3203	3615	3692	3825
安 徽	Anhui	3404	3416	3453	3485	3598	3595	3690
福 建	Fujian	1711	1757	1818	1868	1999	2080	2169
江 西	Jiangxi	1955	1972	2040	2107	2196	2223	2244
山 东	Shangdong	4752	4851	4940	5111	5262	5352	5450
河 南	Henan	5522	5536	5587	5662	5773	5835	5949
湖 北	**Hubei**	**2467**	**2537**	**2589**	**2676**	**2763**	**2876**	**3024**
湖 南	Hunan	3469	3516	3600	3658	3749	3811	3908
广 东	Guangdong	3967	4120	4316	4702	5293	5478	5643
广 西	Guangxi	2571	2601	2649	2703	2760	2807	2863
海 南	Hainan	342	354	367	378	415	412	431
重 庆	Chongqing	1640	1660	1689	1721	1790	1837	1878
四 川	Sichuan	4409	4450	4503	4604	4779	4874	4945
贵 州	Guizhou	2081	2118	2169	2216	2283	2302	2341
云 南	Yunnan	2341	2350	2401	2461	2601	2679	2730
西 藏	Tibet	129	131	135	140	154	160	169
陕 西	Shaanxi	1873	1911	1885	1883	1922	1947	1919
甘 肃	Gansu	1255	1304	1322	1348	1374	1389	1407
青 海	Qinghai	247	254	263	268	276	277	286
宁 夏	Ningxia	282	291	298	300	309	304	329
新 疆	Xinjiang	701	721	744	764	801	814	829

注：1.2001年起为人口变动抽样调查推算数，分地区数据相加不等于全国总计。

2.因2006年进行第二次全国农业普查，故各地区就业人员数据空缺。

Notes:a)2001 sample survey of population changes projected for the few, sub-regional data is not equal sum of the national total.

b)Because in 2006 the second national agricultural census, so data on employment in the area vacant.

附录1-9　各地区全社会固定资产投资
REGIONAL INVESTMENT IN FIXED ASSETS

单位：亿元　　(100 million yuan)

地　区	Region	2003	2004	2005	2006	2007	2008	2009
全国总计	**National Total**	**55566.6**	**70477.4**	**88773.6**	**109998.2**	**137323.9**	**172828.4**	**224845.6**
北　京	Beijing	2169.3	2528.2	2827.2	3296.4	3907.2	3814.7	4616.9
天　津	Tianjin	1039.4	1245.7	1495.1	1820.5	2353.1	3389.8	4738.5
河　北	Hebei	2478.0	3218.8	4139.7	5470.2	6884.7	8866.6	12267.0
山　西	Shanxi	1100.9	1443.9	1826.6	2255.7	2861.5	3531.2	4943.2
内蒙古	Inner Mongolia	1174.7	1788.0	2643.6	3363.2	4372.9	5475.4	7318.9
辽　宁	Liaoning	2076.4	2979.6	4200.4	5689.6	7435.2	10019.1	12292.6
吉　林	Jilin	969.0	1169.1	1741.1	2594.3	3651.4	5038.9	6411.3
黑龙江	Heilongjiang	1166.2	1430.8	1737.3	2236.0	2833.5	3656.0	5029.2
上　海	Shanghai	2499.1	3050.3	3509.7	3900.0	4420.4	4823.1	5143.7
江　苏	Jiangsu	5233.0	6557.1	8165.4	10069.2	12268.1	15300.6	18950.0
浙　江	Zhejiang	4740.3	5781.3	6520.1	7590.2	8420.4	9323.0	10741.6
安　徽	Anhui	1418.7	1935.2	2525.1	3533.6	5087.5	6747.0	8985.8
福　建	Fujian	1496.4	1892.9	2316.7	2981.8	4287.8	5207.7	6231.2
江　西	Jiangxi	1303.2	1713.2	2176.6	2683.6	3301.9	4745.4	6642.4
山　东	Shangdong	5315.1	6970.6	9307.3	11111.4	12537.7	15435.9	19034.5
河　南	Henan	2263.0	3099.4	4311.6	5904.7	8010.1	10490.6	13704.6
湖　北	**Hubei**	**1809.5**	**2264.8**	**2676.6**	**3343.5**	**4330.4**	**5647.0**	**7866.9**
湖　南	Hunan	1590.3	2072.6	2629.1	3175.5	4154.8	5534.0	7703.5
广　东	Guangdong	4813.2	5870.0	6977.9	7973.4	9294.3	10868.7	12941.5
广　西	Guangxi	921.3	1236.5	1661.2	2198.7	2939.7	3756.4	5237.2
海　南	Hainan	280.0	317.0	367.2	423.9	502.4	705.4	988.2
重　庆	Chongqing	1161.5	1537.0	1933.2	2407.4	3127.7	3979.6	5214.3
四　川	Sichuan	2336.3	2818.4	3585.2	4412.9	5639.8	7127.8	11387.3
贵　州	Guizhou	748.1	865.2	998.3	1197.4	1488.8	1864.5	2401.7
云　南	Yunnan	1000.1	1291.5	1777.6	2208.6	2759.0	3435.9	4526.4
西　藏	Tibet	134.0	162.4	181.4	231.1	270.3	309.9	379.4
陕　西	Shaanxi	1200.7	1508.9	1882.2	2480.7	3415.0	4614.4	6249.0
甘　肃	Gansu	619.8	733.9	870.4	1022.6	1304.2	1712.8	2363.0
青　海	Qinghai	255.6	289.2	329.8	408.5	482.8	583.2	798.3
宁　夏	Ningxia	318.0	376.2	443.3	498.7	599.8	828.9	1075.9
新　疆	Xinjiang	973.4	1147.1	1339.1	1567.1	1850.8	2260.0	2710.9
不分地区	**Irrespective of region**	**962.2**	**1182.5**	**1677.9**	**1947.6**	**2530.8**	**3734.9**	**5950.8**

附录1-10 各地区城镇固定资产投资

REGIONAL URBAN FIXED ASSET INVESTMENT

单位：亿元 (100 million yuan)

地 区	Region	2003	2004	2005	2006	2007	2008	2009
全国总计	**National Total**	**45811.70**	**59028.19**	**75095.10**	**93368.68**	**117464.47**	**148738.30**	**194138.62**
北 京	Beijing	1999.91	2333.00	2595.41	3012.40	3597.29	3520.95	4149.63
天 津	Tianjin	931.74	1128.68	1364.00	1678.98	2192.17	3175.14	4446.83
河 北	Hebei	1772.81	2441.98	3307.77	4403.23	5690.31	7463.77	10472.25
山 西	Shanxi	998.82	1315.21	1666.47	2055.69	2600.22	3194.57	4509.56
内蒙古	Inner Mongolia	1097.10	1707.50	2555.25	3264.86	4255.00	5327.04	7144.35
辽 宁	Liaoning	1771.23	2580.28	3666.52	4977.84	6576.05	8881.95	11605.17
吉 林	Jilin	872.91	1059.35	1581.26	2366.06	3340.19	4592.71	5958.62
黑龙江	Heilongjiang	1069.48	1316.97	1581.22	2040.41	2591.69	3354.82	4696.08
上 海	Shanghai	2245.54	2862.95	3198.57	3497.48	4045.10	4404.95	4718.76
江 苏	Jiangsu	4011.59	5008.21	6218.89	7479.60	9161.37	11609.71	14266.88
浙 江	Zhejiang	3198.51	3998.77	4784.68	5429.28	5996.93	6551.10	7453.64
安 徽	Anhui	1184.52	1613.01	2126.69	3050.15	4444.58	5948.61	7940.55
福 建	Fujian	1229.28	1594.54	1958.30	2692.36	3829.02	4601.50	5548.61
江 西	Jiangxi	1099.10	1477.89	1902.66	2375.39	2954.87	4325.38	6006.69
山 东	Shangdong	4163.90	5418.55	7275.06	8715.50	10153.56	12528.96	15439.10
河 南	Henan	1677.17	2434.88	3461.23	4840.80	6609.16	8721.19	11455.01
湖 北	**Hubei**	**1573.73**	**2005.15**	**2387.41**	**3038.49**	**3927.36**	**5148.76**	**7183.68**
湖 南	Hunan	1235.27	1679.39	2203.95	2718.44	3609.54	4879.96	6880.09
广 东	Guangdong	4145.12	5029.44	5890.11	6553.67	7368.69	8640.87	10238.46
广 西	Guangxi	791.26	1094.62	1480.92	1947.81	2596.74	3325.95	4689.88
海 南	Hainan	246.24	291.02	339.24	397.00	472.77	668.02	942.57
重 庆	Chongqing	1040.65	1400.58	1777.07	2251.98	2937.07	3715.90	4855.11
四 川	Sichuan	1835.07	2322.91	2991.77	3927.37	5043.42	6362.08	9061.43
贵 州	Guizhou	667.92	780.24	899.33	1052.79	1289.13	1609.34	2040.02
云 南	Yunnan	839.22	1112.97	1592.29	2001.80	2443.79	3106.33	4117.53
西 藏	Tibet	133.96	162.36	181.39	200.65	230.83	271.25	328.66
陕 西	Shaanxi	1071.04	1378.46	1740.86	2285.71	3168.82	4286.42	5890.47
甘 肃	Gansu	553.72	660.76	786.05	923.92	1177.46	1510.75	2076.38
青 海	Qinghai	236.94	272.74	310.84	384.61	443.69	514.05	689.12
宁 夏	Ningxia	263.14	316.83	381.99	438.73	527.69	735.71	964.16
新 疆	Xinjiang	892.59	1046.43	1210.01	1418.01	1659.19	2025.64	2418.51
不分地区	**Irrespective of region**	**962.22**	**1182.51**	**1677.90**	**1947.56**	**2530.77**	**3734.93**	**5950.85**

附录1-11 各地区房地产开发企业（单位）房屋施工、竣工面积和商品房销售面积

REGIONAL REAL ESTATE DEVELOPMENT ENTERPRISES(UNITS) HOUSING CONSTRUCTION, COMPLETION AND SALES OF COMMERCIAL SPACE AREA

单位：万平方米　　　　(10 000 sqm)

地 区	Region	房屋施工面积 Housing Construction Area		房屋竣工面积 Housing Completed Area		商品房销售面积 Sales of Commercial Area	
		2008	2009	2008	2009	2008	2009
全国总计	**National Total**	**283266.2**	**319649.5**	**66544.8**	**70218.8**	**65969.8**	**93713.0**
北 京	Beijing	10014.3	9719.1	2558.0	2678.6	1335.4	2362.3
天 津	Tianjin	5704.3	6052.2	1799.4	1902.1	1252.0	1590.0
河 北	Hebei	8958.1	12739.3	1663.6	1896.4	2231.8	2849.1
山 西	Shanxi	3895.9	5491.4	920.5	793.3	994.7	1014.4
内蒙古	Inner Mongolia	7099.1	8234.5	1981.4	2237.3	2396.4	2463.0
辽 宁	Liaoning	14904.6	18575.5	3826.1	4037.3	4091.2	5375.1
吉 林	Jilin	4965.1	5356.9	1549.1	1240.3	1583.9	1823.2
黑龙江	Heilongjiang	3611.1	4520.3	1404.7	1876.2	1486.6	2015.5
上 海	Shanghai	10784.2	9961.6	2570.7	2105.0	2339.3	3372.4
江 苏	Jiangsu	28963.3	29802.5	8265.5	7706.6	6091.9	9922.7
浙 江	Zhejiang	19273.3	19920.9	4458.3	3673.1	2992.2	5525.4
安 徽	Anhui	11729.4	14142.1	2541.1	2861.2	2785.8	4053.9
福 建	Fujian	11459.7	11681.2	1906.2	2240.3	1625.7	2723.2
江 西	Jiangxi	6344.7	6755.6	1586.7	1646.8	1727.6	2280.9
山 东	Shangdong	20098.7	21988.5	4535.1	4950.5	5507.6	6931.7
河 南	Henan	13906.2	16075.9	3026.0	3401.0	3192.0	4338.6
湖 北	**Hubei**	**7800.5**	**9546.5**	**2057.9**	**2312.1**	**1941.6**	**2718.3**
湖 南	Hunan	10715.5	13726.7	2393.8	2965.2	2655.5	3513.7
广 东	Guangdong	23683.0	24719.9	5063.9	4695.1	4852.3	7035.9
广 西	Guangxi	6877.0	8346.1	1253.5	1441.6	1768.0	2383.8
海 南	Hainan	1500.1	1992.8	308.8	368.5	372.4	560.3
重 庆	Chongqing	11639.3	13052.6	2367.9	2907.0	2872.2	4002.9
四 川	Sichuan	15589.3	17609.2	3348.6	4086.9	3501.3	5888.7
贵 州	Guizhou	5228.9	6062.3	720.7	1210.9	908.2	1619.2
云 南	Yunnan	5367.6	6837.9	1051.7	1680.6	1643.1	2230.0
西 藏	Tibet	144.6	8.3	54.6		66.5	14.2
陕 西	Shaanxi	5780.1	8260.9	875.7	917.0	1513.0	2087.0
甘 肃	Gansu	2310.3	2543.1	546.5	545.2	624.7	696.3
青 海	Qinghai	698.2	900.4	225.3	178.1	147.9	218.3
宁 夏	Ningxia	1580.7	1952.0	634.2	741.2	514.8	775.3
新 疆	Xinjiang	2639.1	3073.6	1049.3	923.5	954.3	1327.6

注：商品房销售面积包括期房。

Note:Sales of Commercial, including Forward House.

附录1-12 各地区房地产开发企业（单位）投资和商品房销售额

REGIONAL REAL ESTATE DEVELOPMENT COMPANY(UNITS) OF INVESTMENT AND COMMERCIAL HOUSING SALES

单位：亿元 (100 million yuan)

地 区	Region	房地产开发投资额 Real Estate Development Investment		商品房销售额 Commercial Housing Sales		#住宅 #Residential	
		2008	2009	2008	2009	2008	2009
全国总计	**National Total**	**31203.2**	**36231.7**	**25068.2**	**43994.5**	**21196.0**	**38157.2**
北 京	Beijing	1908.7	2337.7	1658.3	3259.7	1201.4	2486.8
天 津	Tianjin	653.7	735.2	753.2	1094.8	635.6	965.4
河 北	Hebei	1084.4	1517.2	620.2	941.8	583.9	881.6
山 西	Shanxi	326.8	477.3	234.3	275.8	201.2	242.6
内蒙古	Inner Mongolia	744.3	815.5	595.1	733.2	474.2	573.2
辽 宁	Liaoning	2060.8	2640.6	1537.6	2168.3	1333.9	1883.7
吉 林	Jilin	641.0	756.3	397.1	540.3	344.4	470.3
黑龙江	Heilongjiang	439.9	563.9	421.0	652.5	339.9	536.2
上 海	Shanghai	1435.7	1464.2	1917.1	4330.2	1629.1	3620.2
江 苏	Jiangsu	3304.6	3338.6	2466.7	4955.4	2008.8	4222.3
浙 江	Zhejiang	2023.1	2253.6	1873.7	4303.0	1524.1	3734.6
安 徽	Anhui	1362.7	1667.5	821.5	1378.4	714.0	1179.7
福 建	Fujian	1129.1	1136.3	712.6	1478.2	562.3	1299.1
江 西	Jiangxi	547.7	634.5	369.0	602.8	324.4	530.6
山 东	Shangdong	2038.5	2428.7	1635.7	2436.5	1436.9	2176.2
河 南	Henan	1206.7	1553.8	746.5	1156.6	629.4	1005.2
湖 北	**Hubei**	**892.7**	**1200.4**	**582.6**	**959.9**	**527.8**	**879.3**
湖 南	Hunan	955.9	1084.7	611.3	941.6	510.1	826.1
广 东	Guangdong	2949.3	2961.3	2888.4	4585.9	2495.6	4173.7
广 西	Guangxi	627.3	813.7	499.6	777.2	431.5	704.8
海 南	Hainan	199.4	287.9	202.7	351.0	195.2	343.0
重 庆	Chongqing	991.0	1238.9	800.0	1377.8	704.8	1231.7
四 川	Sichuan	1451.7	1586.8	1105.5	2074.9	996.0	1890.6
贵 州	Guizhou	311.3	369.7	212.5	467.8	179.9	400.5
云 南	Yunnan	557.7	737.5	440.3	653.5	360.8	555.6
西 藏	Tibet	13.7	15.7	21.3	4.7	19.3	4.3
陕 西	Shaanxi	762.2	943.7	446.7	672.7	402.2	621.3
甘 肃	Gansu	185.8	204.1	122.3	174.6	109.0	159.5
青 海	Qinghai	51.2	72.8	36.4	54.9	33.7	51.1
宁 夏	Ningxia	117.6	162.7	125.4	239.5	100.4	191.5
新 疆	Xinjiang	228.6	230.8	213.8	351.0	186.1	316.7

附录1-13 各地区货物进出口总额
TOTAL IMPORT AND EXPORT REGIONS

(按经营单位所在地分)

(Location of Points by Business Units)

单位：亿美元 (100 million US dollors)

地 区	Region	2003	2004	2005	2006	2007	2008	2009
全国总计	**National Total**	**8509.9**	**11545.5**	**14219.1**	**17604.0**	**21737.3**	**25632.6**	**22072.2**
北 京	Beijing	685.0	945.8	1255.1	1580.4	1930.0	2716.9	2148.7
天 津	Tianjin	293.4	420.3	532.8	644.6	714.5	804.0	638.4
河 北	Hebei	89.8	135.3	160.7	185.3	255.2	384.2	296.1
山 西	Shanxi	30.9	53.8	55.5	66.3	115.8	144.0	85.5
内蒙古	Inner Mongolia	28.3	37.2	48.8	59.6	77.4	89.2	67.7
辽 宁	Liaoning	265.1	344.1	410.1	483.9	594.7	724.3	629.3
吉 林	Jilin	61.5	67.9	65.3	79.1	103.0	133.3	117.5
黑龙江	Heilongjiang	53.3	67.9	95.7	128.6	173.0	231.3	162.2
上 海	Shanghai	1123.4	1600.1	1863.4	2275.2	2828.5	3220.6	2777.5
江 苏	Jiangsu	1136.2	1708.5	2279.2	2839.8	3494.7	3922.7	3388.3
浙 江	Zhejiang	614.1	852.0	1073.9	1391.4	1768.5	2111.3	1877.3
安 徽	Anhui	59.5	72.1	91.2	122.5	159.3	201.8	156.4
福 建	Fujian	353.3	475.3	544.1	626.6	744.5	848.2	796.6
江 西	Jiangxi	25.3	35.3	40.6	61.9	94.5	136.2	126.6
山 东	Shangdong	446.4	606.6	767.4	952.1	1224.7	1584.1	1389.7
河 南	Henan	47.1	66.2	77.2	97.9	127.9	174.8	134.4
湖 北	**Hubei**	**51.1**	**67.7**	**90.5**	**117.6**	**148.7**	**207.1**	**172.3**
湖 南	Hunan	37.3	54.4	60.0	73.5	96.9	125.5	101.5
广 东	Guangdong	2835.2	3571.3	4279.6	5272.0	6341.9	6849.7	6110.7
广 西	Guangxi	31.9	42.8	51.8	66.7	92.6	132.4	142.3
海 南	Hainan	22.7	34.0	25.4	28.5	35.1	45.3	48.1
重 庆	Chongqing	25.9	38.6	42.9	54.7	74.4	95.2	77.1
四 川	Sichuan	56.3	68.7	79.0	110.2	143.8	221.1	242.3
贵 州	Guizhou	9.8	15.1	14.0	16.2	22.7	33.7	23.0
云 南	Yunnan	26.7	37.4	47.4	62.2	87.9	96.0	80.2
西 藏	Tibet	1.6	2.0	2.1	3.3	3.9	7.7	4.0
陕 西	Shaanxi	27.8	36.4	45.8	53.6	68.9	83.3	84.0
甘 肃	Gansu	13.3	17.6	26.3	38.2	55.2	61.0	38.2
青 海	Qinghai	3.4	5.8	4.1	6.5	6.1	6.9	5.9
宁 夏	Ningxia	6.5	9.1	9.7	14.4	15.8	18.8	12.0
新 疆	Xinjiang	47.7	56.3	79.4	91.0	137.2	222.2	138.3

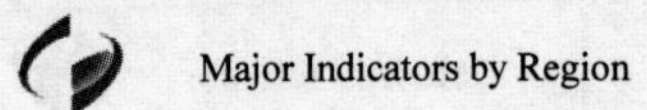

附录1-14 各地区货物进出口总额（2009）

TOTAL IMPORT AND EXPORT REGIONS(2009)

(单位：亿美元) (100 million US dollors)

地 区	Region	按经营单位所在地分 Location of Points by Business Units	
		出口额 Exports	进口额 Imports
全国总计	**National Total**	**12016.6**	**10055.6**
北 京	Beijing	483.8	1664.8
天 津	Tianjin	298.9	339.4
河 北	Hebei	156.9	139.2
山 西	Shanxi	28.4	57.2
内蒙古	Inner Mongolia	23.2	44.6
辽 宁	Liaoning	334.4	294.8
吉 林	Jilin	31.3	86.2
黑龙江	Heilongjiang	100.8	61.5
上 海	Shanghai	1418.8	1358.7
江 苏	Jiangsu	1992.4	1395.9
浙 江	Zhejiang	1330.2	547.1
安 徽	Anhui	88.9	67.5
福 建	Fujian	533.3	263.3
江 西	Jiangxi	73.6	53.0
山 东	Shangdong	795.0	594.7
河 南	Henan	73.5	60.9
湖 北	**Hubei**	**99.8**	**72.5**
湖 南	Hunan	54.9	46.6
广 东	Guangdong	3589.6	2521.2
广 西	Guangxi	83.8	58.6
海 南	Hainan	13.1	35.1
重 庆	Chongqing	42.8	34.3
四 川	Sichuan	141.5	100.8
贵 州	Guizhou	13.6	9.5
云 南	Yunnan	45.1	35.1
西 藏	Tibet	3.8	0.3
陕 西	Shaanxi	39.9	44.2
甘 肃	Gansu	7.4	30.9
青 海	Qinghai	2.5	3.3
宁 夏	Ningxia	7.4	4.6
新 疆	Xinjiang	108.2	30.0

附录1-15 各地区财政收入

REGIONAL REVENUE

单位：亿元 (100 million yuan)

地 区	Region	2008 指标值 Index Value	2008 位次 Precedence	2009 指标值 Index Value	2009 位次 Precedence
北 京	Beijing	1837.3	6	2026.8	6
天 津	Tianjin	675.5	16	821.4	15
河 北	Hebei	944.6	10	1066.2	10
山 西	Shanxi	747.9	12	805.8	17
内蒙古	Inner Mongolia	649.6	17	850.7	13
辽 宁	Liaoning	1356.1	7	1591.0	7
吉 林	Jilin	422.8	24	487.1	24
黑龙江	Heilongjiang	578.4	20	641.6	21
上 海	Shanghai	2358.7	3	2540.3	3
江 苏	Jiangsu	2731.1	2	3228.8	2
浙 江	Zhejiang	1933.1	5	2142.4	5
安 徽	Anhui	724.6	13	863.9	12
福 建	Fujian	833.3	11	932.3	11
江 西	Jiangxi	488.6	23	581.2	23
山 东	Shangdong	1956.9	4	2198.5	4
河 南	Henan	1009.1	9	1126.0	9
湖 北	**Hubei**	**710.2**	**15**	**814.8**	**16**
湖 南	Hunan	722.7	14	845.0	14
广 东	Guangdong	3310.0	1	3649.2	1
广 西	Guangxi	518.7	22	620.8	22
海 南	Hainan	145.0	28	178.2	28
重 庆	Chongqing	577.2	21	652.3	20
四 川	Sichuan	1041.7	8	1269.8	8
贵 州	Guizhou	349.5	26	416.5	25
云 南	Yunnan	613.6	18	698.3	19
西 藏	Tibet	24.9	31	29.4	31
陕 西	Shaanxi	591.3	19	743.8	18
甘 肃	Gansu	264.9	27	286.9	27
青 海	Qinghai	71.6	30	87.7	30
宁 夏	Ningxia	95.0	29	111.5	29
新 疆	Xinjiang	361.1	25	388.8	26

注：本表数据为地方财政本级收入。

Note:Data in this table for the local fiscal income level.

附录1-16 各地区居民消费价格指数

REGIONAL CONSUMER PRICE INDEX

(上年=100) (Preceding Year = 100)

地　区	Region	2003	2004	2005	2006	2007	2008	2009
全　国	**National Total**	**101.2**	**103.9**	**101.8**	**101.5**	**104.8**	**105.9**	**99.3**
北　京	Beijing	100.2	101.0	101.5	100.9	102.4	105.1	98.5
天　津	Tianjin	101.0	102.3	101.5	101.5	104.2	105.4	99.0
河　北	Hebei	102.2	104.3	101.8	101.7	104.7	106.2	99.3
山　西	Shanxi	101.8	104.1	102.3	102.0	104.6	107.2	99.6
内蒙古	Inner Mongolia	102.2	102.9	102.4	101.5	104.6	105.7	99.7
辽　宁	Liaoning	101.7	103.5	101.4	101.2	105.1	104.6	100.0
吉　林	Jilin	101.2	104.1	101.5	101.4	104.8	105.1	100.1
黑龙江	Heilongjiang	100.9	103.8	101.2	101.9	105.4	105.6	100.2
上　海	Shanghai	100.1	102.2	101.0	101.2	103.2	105.8	99.6
江　苏	Jiangsu	101.0	104.1	102.1	101.6	104.3	105.4	99.6
浙　江	Zhejiang	101.9	103.9	101.3	101.1	104.2	105.0	98.5
安　徽	Anhui	101.7	104.5	101.4	101.2	105.3	106.2	99.1
福　建	Fujian	100.8	104.0	102.2	100.8	105.2	104.6	98.2
江　西	Jiangxi	100.8	103.5	101.7	101.2	104.8	106.0	99.3
山　东	Shangdong	101.1	103.6	101.7	101.0	104.4	105.3	100.0
河　南	Henan	101.6	105.4	102.1	101.3	105.4	107.0	99.4
湖　北	**Hubei**	**102.2**	**104.9**	**102.9**	**101.6**	**104.8**	**106.3**	**99.6**
湖　南	Hunan	102.4	105.1	102.3	101.4	105.6	106.0	99.6
广　东	Guangdong	100.6	103.0	102.3	101.8	103.7	105.6	97.7
广　西	Guangxi	101.1	104.4	102.4	101.3	106.1	107.8	97.9
海　南	Hainan	100.1	104.4	101.5	101.5	105.0	106.9	99.3
重　庆	Chongqing	100.6	103.7	100.8	102.4	104.7	105.6	98.4
四　川	Sichuan	101.7	104.9	101.7	102.3	105.9	105.1	100.8
贵　州	Guizhou	101.2	104.0	101.0	101.7	106.4	107.6	98.7
云　南	Yunnan	101.2	106.0	101.4	101.9	105.9	105.7	100.4
西　藏	Tibet	100.9	102.7	101.5	102.0	103.4	105.7	101.4
陕　西	Shaanxi	101.7	103.1	101.2	101.5	105.1	106.4	100.5
甘　肃	Gansu	101.1	102.3	101.7	101.3	105.5	108.2	101.3
青　海	Qinghai	102.0	103.2	100.8	101.6	106.6	110.1	102.6
宁　夏	Ningxia	101.7	103.7	101.5	101.9	105.4	108.5	100.7
新　疆	Xinjiang	100.4	102.7	100.7	101.3	105.5	108.1	100.7

附录1-17　各地区城镇居民家庭人均可支配收入

THE AREA OF URBAN RESIDENTS PER CAPITA DISPOSABLE INCOME OF HOUSEHOLDS

单位：元　　(yuan)

地　区	Region	2003	2004	2005	2006	2007	2008	2009
全国总计	**National Total**	**8472.2**	**9421.6**	**10493.0**	**11759.5**	**13785.8**	**15780.8**	**17174.7**
北　京	Beijing	13882.6	15637.8	17653.0	19977.5	21988.7	24724.9	26738.5
天　津	Tianjin	10312.9	11467.2	12638.6	14283.1	16357.4	19422.5	21402.0
河　北	Hebei	7239.1	7951.3	9107.1	10304.6	11690.5	13441.1	14718.3
山　西	Shanxi	7005.0	7902.9	8913.9	10027.7	11565.0	13119.1	13996.6
内蒙古	Inner Mongolia	7012.9	8123.0	9136.8	10358.0	12377.8	14432.6	15849.2
辽　宁	Liaoning	7240.6	8007.6	9107.6	10369.6	12300.4	14392.7	15761.4
吉　林	Jilin	7005.2	7840.6	8690.6	9775.1	11285.5	12829.5	14006.3
黑龙江	Heilongjiang	6678.9	7470.7	8272.5	9182.3	10245.3	11581.3	12566.0
上　海	Shanghai	14867.5	16682.8	18645.0	20667.9	23622.7	26674.9	28837.8
江　苏	Jiangsu	9262.5	10481.9	12318.6	14084.3	16378.0	18679.5	20551.7
浙　江	Zhejiang	13179.5	14546.4	16293.8	18265.1	20573.8	22726.7	24610.8
安　徽	Anhui	6778.0	7511.4	8470.7	9771.1	11473.6	12990.4	14085.7
福　建	Fujian	9999.5	11175.4	12321.3	13753.3	15506.1	17961.5	19576.8
江　西	Jiangxi	6901.4	7559.6	8619.7	9551.1	11451.7	12866.4	14021.5
山　东	Shangdong	8399.9	9437.8	10744.8	12192.2	14264.7	16305.4	17811.0
河　南	Henan	6926.1	7704.9	8668.0	9810.3	11477.1	13231.1	14371.6
湖　北	**Hubei**	**7322.0**	**8022.8**	**8785.9**	**9802.7**	**11485.8**	**13152.9**	**14367.5**
湖　南	Hunan	7674.2	8617.5	9524.0	10504.7	12293.5	13821.2	15084.3
广　东	Guangdong	12380.4	13627.7	14770.0	16015.6	17699.3	19732.9	21574.7
广　西	Guangxi	7785.0	8690.0	9286.7	9898.8	12200.4	14146.0	15451.5
海　南	Hainan	7259.3	7735.8	8123.9	9395.1	10996.9	12607.8	13750.9
重　庆	Chongqing	8093.7	9221.0	10243.5	11569.7	12590.8	14367.6	15748.7
四　川	Sichuan	7041.9	7709.9	8386.0	9350.1	11098.3	12633.4	13839.4
贵　州	Guizhou	6569.2	7322.1	8151.1	9116.6	10678.4	11758.8	12862.5
云　南	Yunnan	7643.6	8870.9	9265.9	10069.9	11496.1	13250.2	14423.9
西　藏	Tibet	8765.5	9106.1	9431.2	8941.1	11130.9	12481.5	13544.4
陕　西	Shaanxi	6806.4	7492.5	8272.0	9267.7	10763.3	12857.9	14128.8
甘　肃	Gansu	6657.2	7376.7	8086.8	8920.6	10012.3	10969.4	11929.8
青　海	Qinghai	6745.3	7319.7	8057.9	9000.4	10276.1	11640.4	12691.9
宁　夏	Ningxia	6530.5	7217.9	8093.6	9177.3	10859.3	12931.5	14024.7
新　疆	Xinjiang	7173.5	7503.4	7990.2	8871.3	10313.4	11432.1	12257.5

注：本表绝对数按当年价格计算。
Note:In this table are at current prices.

附录1-18 各地区农村居民家庭人均纯收入
REGIONAL PER CAPITA EGIONAL PER CAPITA INCOME OF RURAL HOUSEHOLDS

单位：元 (yuan)

地区	Region	2003	2004	2005	2006	2007	2008	2009
全国总计	**National Total**	**2622.2**	**2936.4**	**3254.9**	**3587.0**	**4140.4**	**4760.6**	**5153.2**
北京	Beijing	5601.6	6170.3	7346.3	8275.5	9439.6	10661.9	11668.6
天津	Tianjin	4566.0	5019.5	5579.9	6227.9	7010.1	7910.8	8687.6
河北	Hebei	2853.4	3171.1	3481.6	3801.8	4293.4	4795.5	5149.7
山西	Shanxi	2299.2	2589.6	2890.7	3180.9	3665.7	4097.2	4244.1
内蒙古	Inner Mongolia	2267.7	2606.4	2988.9	3341.9	3953.1	4656.2	4937.8
辽宁	Liaoning	2934.4	3307.1	3690.2	4090.4	4773.4	5576.5	5958.0
吉林	Jilin	2530.4	2999.6	3264.0	3641.1	4191.3	4932.7	5265.9
黑龙江	Heilongjiang	2508.9	3005.2	3221.3	3552.4	4132.3	4855.6	5206.8
上海	Shanghai	6653.9	7066.3	8247.8	9138.7	10144.6	11440.3	12482.9
江苏	Jiangsu	4239.3	4753.9	5276.3	5813.2	6561.0	7356.5	8003.5
浙江	Zhejiang	5389.0	5944.1	6660.0	7334.8	8265.2	9257.9	10007.3
安徽	Anhui	2127.5	2499.3	2641.0	2969.1	3556.3	4202.5	4504.3
福建	Fujian	3733.9	4089.4	4450.4	4834.8	5467.1	6196.1	6680.2
江西	Jiangxi	2457.5	2786.8	3128.9	3459.5	4044.7	4697.2	5075.0
山东	Shangdong	3150.5	3507.4	3930.5	4368.3	4985.3	5641.4	6118.8
河南	Henan	2235.7	2553.2	2870.6	3261.0	3851.6	4454.2	4807.0
湖北	**Hubei**	**2566.8**	**2890.0**	**3099.2**	**3419.4**	**3997.5**	**4656.4**	**5035.3**
湖南	Hunan	2532.9	2837.8	3117.7	3389.6	3904.2	4512.5	4909.0
广东	Guangdong	4054.6	4365.9	4690.5	5079.8	5624.0	6399.8	6906.9
广西	Guangxi	2094.5	2305.2	2494.7	2770.5	3224.1	3690.3	3980.4
海南	Hainan	2588.1	2817.6	3004.0	3255.5	3791.4	4390.0	4744.4
重庆	Chongqing	2214.6	2510.4	2809.3	2873.8	3509.3	4126.2	4478.4
四川	Sichuan	2229.9	2518.9	2802.8	3002.4	3546.7	4121.2	4462.1
贵州	Guizhou	1564.7	1721.6	1877.0	1984.6	2374.0	2796.9	3005.4
云南	Yunnan	1697.1	1864.2	2041.8	2250.5	2634.1	3102.6	3369.3
西藏	Tibet	1690.8	1861.3	2077.9	2435.0	2788.2	3175.8	3531.7
陕西	Shaanxi	1675.7	1866.5	2052.6	2260.2	2644.7	3136.5	3437.6
甘肃	Gansu	1673.1	1852.2	1979.9	2134.1	2328.9	2723.8	2980.1
青海	Qinghai	1794.1	1957.7	2151.5	2358.4	2683.8	3061.2	3346.2
宁夏	Ningxia	2043.3	2320.1	2508.9	2760.1	3180.8	3681.4	4048.3
新疆	Xinjiang	2106.2	2244.9	2482.2	2737.3	3183.0	3502.9	3883.1

注：本表按当年价格计算。
Note:The table at current prices.

附录1-19 各地区农林牧渔业总产值及增长速度（2009）

REGIONAL FORESTYR,ANIMAL HUSBANDDRY AND FISHERY OUTPUT VALUE GROWTH RATE(2009)

地 区	Region	农林牧渔业总产值(亿元) Gross output Value of Farming, Forestry, Animal Husbandy and Fishery(100 million yuan)	#农业 #Agriculture	#林业 #Forestry	#牧业 #Animal Husbandry	#渔业 #Fishing	农林牧渔业总产值比上年增长(%) Grouth Rate of Gross Output Value of Farming, Forestry, Animal Husbandry and Fishery Over 2007 (%)
全国总计	**National Total**	**60361.0**	**30611.1**	**2359.4**	**19468.4**	**5626.4**	**4.6**
北 京	Beijing	315.0	140.4	22.9	136.1	10.3	5.5
天 津	Tianjin	281.7	139.7	2.2	83.6	47.5	3.7
河 北	Hebei	3640.9	1927.8	70.7	1350.1	108.4	3.2
山 西	Shanxi	908.7	556.3	66.7	230.9	5.3	4.4
内蒙古	Inner Mongolia	1570.6	731.9	78.2	721.4	12.7	2.4
辽 宁	Liaoning	2704.6	913.5	70.0	1171.4	441.9	3.3
吉 林	Jilin	1734.3	777.5	58.9	825.5	23.5	5.3
黑龙江	Heilongjiang	2251.1	1206.8	85.2	870.2	45.2	5.4
上 海	Shanghai	283.2	147.5	9.0	64.6	53.5	-0.5
江 苏	Jiangsu	3816.0	1948.2	70.8	874.0	719.2	4.6
浙 江	Zhejiang	1873.4	879.0	117.6	404.9	435.5	2.4
安 徽	Anhui	2569.5	1289.8	125.1	795.8	257.6	5.5
福 建	Fujian	2001.2	826.2	162.2	366.9	565.6	5.0
江 西	Jiangxi	1733.8	729.7	161.8	541.5	231.2	4.6
山 东	Shangdong	6003.1	3224.0	101.3	1683.8	747.4	4.3
河 南	Henan	4871.5	2833.3	134.1	1654.3	64.9	4.5
湖 北	**Hubei**	**2985.2**	**1511.5**	**57.7**	**881.8**	**413.1**	**5.4**
湖 南	Hunan	3207.9	1596.6	174.2	1100.4	188.5	5.2
广 东	Guangdong	3337.6	1551.0	88.3	917.1	661.2	5.0
广 西	Guangxi	2377.2	1135.0	129.0	812.5	216.9	5.4
海 南	Hainan	705.0	307.6	79.6	142.8	154.5	7.2
重 庆	Chongqing	913.1	522.8	34.1	319.4	24.3	6.4
四 川	Sichuan	3689.8	1806.1	112.5	1596.7	119.1	4.2
贵 州	Guizhou	875.2	501.5	36.9	281.5	11.1	4.6
云 南	Yunnan	1706.2	850.7	196.1	557.8	42.0	5.8
西 藏	Tibet	93.4	39.1	7.1	44.3	0.2	3.6
陕 西	Shaanxi	1337.2	823.6	45.6	387.9	6.5	5.0
甘 肃	Gansu	876.3	587.3	24.2	171.9	1.1	5.8
青 海	Qinghai	157.3	61.3	2.3	90.1	0.1	5.8
宁 夏	Ningxia	243.5	146.8	8.4	70.7	7.0	8.2
新 疆	Xinjiang	1297.6	898.6	26.6	318.4	11.1	5.1

注：本表绝对数按当年价格计算，增长速度按可比价格计算。

Note:In this table are at current prices, growth rates at constant prices.

附录1-20 各地区主要农产品产量（2009）

MAJOR AGRICULTURAL PRODUCTION REGIONS(2009)

单位：万吨 (10 000 tons)

地 区	Region	粮 食 Food	油 料 Oil feed	棉 花 Cotton	糖 料 Sugar	蔬 菜 Vegetables	水 果 Fruit
全国总计	**National Total**	**53082.1**	**3154.3**	**637.7**	**12276.6**	**61823.8**	**20395.5**
北 京	Beijing	124.8	1.8	0.1		317.1	120.1
天 津	Tianjin	156.3	0.5	7.1		373.9	67.0
河 北	Hebei	2910.2	143.3	60.5	30.7	6742.1	1578.6
山 西	Shanxi	942.0	17.0	8.4	15.4	893.1	449.2
内蒙古	Inner Mongolia	1981.7	119.6	0.1	109.6	1380.6	208.7
辽 宁	Liaoning	1591.0	55.3	0.1	6.2	2604.4	655.6
吉 林	Jilin	2460.0	50.4	0.2	6.6	968.4	253.5
黑龙江	Heilongjiang	4353.0	28.2		110.0	701.2	267.7
上 海	Shanghai	121.7	3.4	0.3	1.6	394.1	104.7
江 苏	Jiangsu	3230.1	162.2	25.5	11.6	3837.8	715.7
浙 江	Zhejiang	789.2	43.2	2.8	81.4	1764.8	712.4
安 徽	Anhui	3069.9	240.3	34.6	21.8	2028.1	745.8
福 建	Fujian	666.9	26.3		65.9	1521.5	645.0
江 西	Jiangxi	2002.6	102.0	12.5	62.2	1088.6	497.5
山 东	Shangdong	4316.3	334.5	92.1	0.06	8937.2	2728.3
河 南	Henan	5389.0	533.0	51.7	28.3	6370.4	2228.1
湖 北	**Hubei**	**2309.1**	**314.1**	**48.1**	**34.4**	**2979.6**	**725.8**
湖 南	Hunan	2902.7	179.2	21.2	78.2	2844.2	715.7
广 东	Guangdong	1314.5	84.6		1253.5	2567.2	1160.8
广 西	Guangxi	1463.2	42.1	0.2	7509.4	2063.1	1010.7
海 南	Hainan	187.6	9.1		479.2	410.0	350.4
重 庆	Chongqing	1137.2	40.5		11.6	1177.4	212.9
四 川	Sichuan	3194.6	261.8	1.5	94.1	3227.3	689.5
贵 州	Guizhou	1168.3	78.7	0.1	64.3	1079.5	119.7
云 南	Yunnan	1576.9	50.2		1761.4	1238.2	342.7
西 藏	Tibet	90.5	5.8			55.1	1.2
陕 西	Shaanxi	1131.4	54.4	8.6	0.2	1257.6	1366.1
甘 肃	Gansu	906.2	58.5	9.5	20.4	1145.4	459.9
青 海	Qinghai	102.7	36.6		0.1	118.9	3.3
宁 夏	Ningxia	340.7	13.6		0.01	354.0	202.4
新 疆	Xinjiang	1152.0	63.9	252.4	418.4	1383.2	1056.3

注：水果产量含果用瓜。

Note:Fruit production with fruit with a melon.

附录1-20 续表 continued

单位：万吨 (10 000 tons)

地区	Region	肉类 Meat	#猪肉 #Pork	#牛肉 #Beef	#羊肉 #Sheep Meat	奶类 Dairy
全国总计	**National Total**	**7649.9**	**4890.5**	**635.5**	**389.5**	**3734.6**
北京	Beijing	47.2	24.1	2.1	1.4	67.4
天津	Tianjin	39.5	25.7	3.6	1.5	68.7
河北	Hebei	426.6	253.6	55.3	28.0	461.0
山西	Shanxi	69.8	50.7	4.8	5.6	74.1
内蒙古	Inner Mongolia	234.0	68.6	47.4	88.2	934.0
辽宁	Liaoning	389.2	218.8	40.2	7.8	115.6
吉林	Jilin	226.2	113.2	41.8	3.6	44.5
黑龙江	Heilongjiang	187.6	108.2	36.8	11.6	534.7
上海	Shanghai	26.4	17.3		0.5	23.3
江苏	Jiangsu	344.4	204.5	3.3	7.5	55.4
浙江	Zhejiang	170.4	128.2	1.0	1.7	19.9
安徽	Anhui	362.5	229.8	17.5	13.8	20.1
福建	Fujian	175.1	142.9	2.2	1.7	15.6
江西	Jiangxi	276.0	210.8	10.9	1.1	11.2
山东	Shangdong	684.1	341.3	69.6	32.9	258.1
河南	Henan	615.0	389.6	84.0	25.9	301.3
湖北	**Hubei**	**367.0**	**279.9**	**17.0**	**7.8**	**28.3**
湖南	Hunan	476.3	395.4	15.7	11.0	7.7
广东	Guangdong	427.0	262.1	6.1	0.9	14.4
广西	Guangxi	371.3	232.3	13.4	3.2	8.1
海南	Hainan	66.0	39.7	2.3	1.1	0.4
重庆	Chongqing	187.7	146.5	5.9	2.1	7.9
四川	Sichuan	632.8	474.2	28.9	24.3	68.7
贵州	Guizhou	169.6	140.1	11.4	3.2	4.5
云南	Yunnan	304.6	230.8	28.0	12.1	105.9
西藏	Tibet	24.0	1.2	14.2	8.4	28.7
陕西	Shaanxi	98.7	75.0	7.8	7.3	185.8
甘肃	Gansu	82.9	45.8	15.1	15.6	37.7
青海	Qinghai	26.9	9.2	8.1	8.8	25.3
宁夏	Ningxia	25.6	9.2	7.3	6.8	81.1
新疆	Xinjiang	115.4	22.0	33.9	43.8	125.2

注：全国水产品产量包括中国农业发展集团总公司水产品产量24.8万吨，各地区数据中未包括。

Note:Aquatic products, including the National Agricultural Development Group Corporation output of aquatic products 248,000 tons, not included in the regional data.

附录1-21 各地区规模以上工业企业主要经济指标（2009）
REGIONAL-SCALE INDUSTRIAL ENTERPRISES MAIN ECONOMIC INDICATORS (2009)

单位：亿元 (100 million yuan)

地区	Region	主营业务收入 Main Business Income	主营业务成本 Main Business Costs	主营业务税金及附加 Business Tax And Additional	营业费用 Operating expenses	税金总额 Total Tax	利润总额 Total Profit
全国总计	**National Total**	**474608.6**	**403816.3**	**7292.8**	**11991.7**	**21129.2**	**25890.8**
北京	Beijing	10606.3	9096.2	149.6	402.7	451.9	561.1
天津	Tianjin	11470.2	10034.2	121.2	279.2	338.4	612.1
河北	Hebei	21213.0	18621.6	228.9	360.8	777.1	1112.7
山西	Shanxi	7968.8	6559.8	89.5	262.8	588.7	339.8
内蒙古	Inner Mongolia	9366.2	7644.1	133.8	225.7	534.2	653.2
辽宁	Liaoning	24322.9	21030.2	505.2	420.6	989.6	781.8
吉林	Jilin	8007.9	6921.1	195.4	240.7	432.2	455.5
黑龙江	Heilongjiang	6612.3	5072.7	204.9	156.0	556.2	761.4
上海	Shanghai	22271.9	18847.7	382.0	777.1	940.8	1246.0
江苏	Jiangsu	64061.9	56505.7	486.2	1356.3	2137.2	3198.2
浙江	Zhejiang	33972.0	29193.4	393.4	863.4	1283.6	1742.5
安徽	Anhui	10737.2	9179.0	190.2	328.0	516.2	416.4
福建	Fujian	14438.6	12439.1	164.9	374.6	451.4	652.2
江西	Jiangxi	8618.3	7371.8	121.9	163.6	392.9	402.6
山东	Shangdong	64463.1	55217.4	742.2	1259.9	2581.8	3936.7
河南	Henan	25153.6	21276.8	347.1	552.6	1212.5	2062.3
湖北	**Hubei**	**13235.1**	**11015.2**	**312.5**	**397.6**	**697.6**	**675.8**
湖南	Hunan	11141.0	8871.9	357.5	288.2	715.6	488.5
广东	Guangdong	56467.7	48160.1	540.7	1842.2	1789.5	2643.1
广西	Guangxi	5486.2	4691.8	91.5	151.5	299.2	196.8
海南	Hainan	886.7	668.6	68.4	26.6	119.1	85.3
重庆	Chongqing	5796.8	4834.9	87.6	194.9	267.4	269.7
四川	Sichuan	15299.5	12808.1	203.3	459.0	729.1	794.3
贵州	Guizhou	2727.4	2149.1	111.5	92.2	257.7	153.2
云南	Yunnan	4367.2	3257.5	417.8	124.4	676.3	265.4
西藏	Tibet	42.5	32.8	0.7	2.8	4.5	5.6
陕西	Shaanxi	6985.4	5271.1	263.8	188.0	616.8	679.6
甘肃	Gansu	3351.1	2778.8	163.6	61.0	294.0	140.8
青海	Qinghai	939.6	756.1	20.0	19.6	67.3	80.8
宁夏	Ningxia	1207.9	1008.5	25.1	42.8	71.2	57.3
新疆	Xinjiang	3390.4	2500.8	172.7	77.1	339.2	420.3

注：本表为2009年1-11月快报数据(下表同)。
Note:This table is from January to November 2009, Express Data (the same).

附录1-22　各地区主要工业产品产量（2009）

MAJOR INDUSTRIAL PRODUCTS BY REGION(2009)

地　区	Region	原煤(万吨) Coal (10 000 tons)	原油(万吨) Crude Oil (10 000 tons)	发电量 (亿千瓦小时) Power generation (Billion kilowatt hours)	生铁(万吨) Pig Iron (10 000 tons)	粗钢(万吨) Crude steel (10 000 tons)	钢材(万吨) Steel (10 000 tons)	水泥(万吨) Cement (10 000 tons)
全国总计	**National Total**	**297300.0**	**18949.0**	**37146.5**	**54374.8**	**56803.3**	**69626.3**	**165000.0**
北　京	Beijing	641.3		242.7	442.7	464.9	769.6	1077.4
天　津	Tianjin		2297.0	415.8	1763.4	2124.2	4079.5	690.2
河　北	Hebei	8494.6	599.1	1742.5	13084.9	13536.3	15134.5	10611.5
山　西	Shanxi	59354.0		1873.8	3127.5	2648.5	2288.4	2482.5
内蒙古	Inner Mongolia	60058.5		2242.4	1381.3	1261.9	1294.9	4275.5
辽　宁	Liaoning	6624.2	1000.0	1162.5	5061.3	4783.0	4937.3	4693.4
吉　林	Jilin	4401.5	639.9	541.8	648.3	792.6	856.0	3673.1
黑龙江	Heilongjiang	8748.7	4000.7	723.0	494.6	566.0	505.0	2598.0
上　海	Shanghai		9.1	778.2	1787.5	2032.2	2181.4	754.2
江　苏	Jiangsu	2397.4	184.0	2928.4	4590.2	5489.9	7859.7	14434.1
浙　江	Zhejiang	13.2		2246.3	536.0	1045.6	2359.4	10796.5
安　徽	Anhui	12848.6		1320.2	1661.6	1759.7	2112.0	7056.1
福　建	Fujian	2466.1		1170.7	552.9	765.0	1341.9	5446.5
江　西	Jiangxi	2982.5		532.9	1447.0	1620.9	1647.4	6153.2
山　东	Shangdong	14377.7	2828.2	2859.9	5273.2	4857.3	5854.3	14036.7
河　南	Henan	23018.1	474.5	2055.5	1944.6	2329.0	2882.5	11710.7
湖　北	**Hubei**	**1058.5**	**80.9**	**1818.1**	**1956.7**	**1985.3**	**2172.3**	**6983.8**
湖　南	Hunan	6572.9		1028.0	1380.5	1436.6	1503.6	7539.0
广　东	Guangdong		1345.1	2757.6	755.9	1126.6	2285.5	10028.9
广　西	Guangxi	519.7	2.9	944.5	967.7	1000.0	1174.9	6411.2
海　南	Hainan		18.4	127.6	2.1	23.2	10.7	925.7
重　庆	Chongqing	4290.8		474.3	324.9	333.8	477.4	3611.0
四　川	Sichuan	8997.3	21.7	1578.8	1532.6	1509.1	1830.6	8887.0
贵　州	Guizhou	13690.7		1380.0	374.8	343.1	337.6	2664.8
云　南	Yunnan	5571.3		1170.9	1280.9	1049.1	971.8	4868.4
西　藏	Tibet			18.0				187.7
陕　西	Shaanxi	29611.1	2695.9	908.9	512.5	522.5	887.3	4464.7
甘　肃	Gansu	3875.6	49.2	696.7	612.1	626.4	644.5	1816.1
青　海	Qinghai	1283.6	186.4	377.9	109.5	126.7	125.1	610.0
宁　夏	Ningxia	5509.5	3.1	479.9	36.2		38.0	1064.5
新　疆	Xinjiang	7646.0	2512.9	549.1	731.6	625.0	687.3	2029.3

附录1-22 续表 continued

地 区	Region	布(亿米) Cloth (100 million meters)	家用电冰箱(万台) Household Refrigerators (10 000 units)	农用化肥(万吨) Agricultural Fertilizers (10 000 Tons)	汽车(万辆) Car (10 000)	程控交换机(万线) PBX (10 000 lines)	移动通信手持机(万台) Mobile Handset (10 000 units)	微型计算机设备(万台) Micro-computer Equipment (10 000 units)
全国总计	**National Total**	**740.0**	**5930.5**	**6599.7**	**1379.5**	**4147.4**	**61924.5**	**18215.1**
北 京	Beijing	0.1		0.2	127.1	1508.8	21355.3	842.7
天 津	Tianjin	2.5	53.9	14.7	60.2	2.4	8558.7	1.5
河 北	Hebei	38.1		214.4	51.4	11.8		
山 西	Shanxi	0.3		375.2	0.2			0.1
内蒙古	Inner Mongolia	0.8		261.5	3.3			
辽 宁	Liaoning	4.3	96.2	82.1	50.9	37.8	46.7	0.2
吉 林	Jilin	0.4		20.3	110.6		49.8	
黑龙江	Heilongjiang	0.4		59.6	28.4			2.9
上 海	Shanghai	1.2	189.2	2.7	125.0	387.0	315.8	7320.2
江 苏	Jiangsu	79.0	667.1	317.2	50.6	4.7	2044.7	8180.9
浙 江	Zhejiang	139.2	761.8	46.2	28.2	110.3	2777.7	89.2
安 徽	Anhui	5.6	1565.8	284.9	86.3		12.1	0.0
福 建	Fujian	27.1		59.7	13.5	0.8	671.5	607.2
江 西	Jiangxi	6.8	91.3	48.7	28.5	0.9	590.9	5.3
山 东	Shangdong	129.3	825.1	864.9	55.8	274.3	5454.6	25.4
河 南	Henan	31.7	319.2	531.2	12.5			
湖 北	**Hubei**	**38.6**	**39.5**	**798.5**	**108.2**	**0.1**	**831.5**	**87.4**
湖 南	Hunan	4.9	15.6	365.8	12.0		0.1	
广 东	Guangdong	29.1	1058.5	61.7	113.1	1808.2	18091.8	1047.0
广 西	Guangxi	0.1		92.4	118.5			1.0
海 南	Hainan			60.6	9.2			
重 庆	Chongqing	7.9	0.2	150.4	118.7		374.9	0.2
四 川	Sichuan	10.9	51.9	463.0	7.6		630.5	
贵 州	Guizhou	0.2	168.2	347.3	0.2		118.2	
云 南	Yunnan	0.0		355.2	7.3	0.3		
西 藏	Tibet							
陕 西	Shaanxi	7.5	27.1	86.8	50.7			3.9
甘 肃	Gansu	0.2	0.1	81.0	1.9			
青 海	Qinghai			277.9				
宁 夏	Ningxia			91.8				
新 疆	Xinjiang	1.2		183.8	0.1			

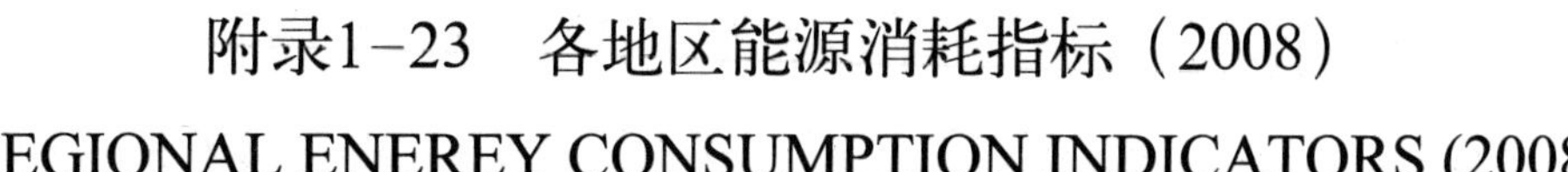

附录1-23　各地区能源消耗指标（2008）

REGIONAL ENEREY CONSUMPTION INDICATORS (2008)

地　区	Region	单位地区生产总值能耗(等价值) (吨标准煤/万元) Unit GDP Energy Consumption(such as value) (Tons of standard coal /10 000 yuan)	单位地区生产总值电耗(等价值) (千瓦小时/万元) Unit GDP Energy Consumption (such as value) (KWh /10 000 yuan)	单位工业增加值能耗(规模以上，当量值)(吨标准煤/万元) Energy Consumption Per Unit of Industrial Added Value (scale, when the money) (tons of standard coal /10 000 yuan)
北　京	Beijing	0.662	719.6	1.04
天　津	Tianjin	0.947	910.4	1.05
河　北	Hebei	1.727	1492.8	3.32
山　西	Shanxi	2.554	2288.9	4.89
内蒙古	Inner Mongolia	2.159	1887.3	4.19
辽　宁	Liaoning	1.617	1223.8	2.43
吉　林	Jilin	1.444	885.9	1.98
黑龙江	Heilongjiang	1.290	865.9	1.90
上　海	Shanghai	0.801	884.1	0.96
江　苏	Jiangsu	0.803	1149.4	1.27
浙　江	Zhejiang	0.782	1202.1	1.18
安　徽	Anhui	1.075	1106.8	2.34
福　建	Fujian	0.843	1098.6	1.18
江　西	Jiangxi	0.928	942.2	1.94
山　东	Shangdong	1.100	1001.1	1.70
河　南	Henan	1.219	1266.2	3.08
湖　北	**Hubei**	**1.314**	**1103.9**	**2.68**
湖　南	Hunan	1.225	975.5	1.98
广　东	Guangdong	0.715	1085.5	0.87
广　西	Guangxi	1.106	1254.2	2.34
海　南	Hainan	0.875	979.2	2.61
重　庆	Chongqing	1.267	1090.2	2.11
四　川	Sichuan	1.381	1156.4	2.48
贵　州	Guizhou	2.875	2452.2	4.32
云　南	Yunnan	1.562	1654.9	2.85
西　藏	Tibet			
陕　西	Shaanxi	1.281	1256.0	2.01
甘　肃	Gansu	2.013	2539.0	4.05
青　海	Qinghai	2.935	4061.6	3.24
宁　夏	Ningxia	3.686	5084.1	7.13
新　疆	Xinjiang	1.963	1331.2	3.00

注：地区生产总值和工业增加值按2005年价格计算。
Note:GDP and industrial output value at 2005 prices.

附录1-24 各地区社会消费品零售总额

TOTAL RETAIL SALES OF CONSUMER GOODS BY REGIONS

单位：亿元 (100 million yuan)

地 区	Region	2005	2006	2007	2008	2009	2009年比上年增长(%) Over the previous year (%)
全国总计	**National Total**	**68352.6**	**79145.2**	**93571.6**	**114830.1**	**132678.4**	**15.5**
北 京	Beijing	2911.7	3295.3	3835.2	4645.5	5309.9	14.3
天 津	Tianjin	1201.6	1383.1	1650.6	2078.7	2430.8	16.9
河 北	Hebei	2969.5	3435.7	4053.8	4991.1	5764.9	15.5
山 西	Shanxi	1410.7	1635.4	1953.3	2421.1	2809.0	16.0
内蒙古	Inner Mongolia	1358.1	1628.6	1964.0	2463.0	2855.3	15.9
辽 宁	Liaoning	3014.4	3471.6	4097.8	5032.4	5812.6	15.5
吉 林	Jilin	1470.3	1697.6	2038.3	2549.2	2957.3	16.0
黑龙江	Heilongjiang	1773.8	2029.0	2386.2	2928.3	3401.8	16.2
上 海	Shanghai	2979.5	3375.2	3873.3	4577.2	5173.2	13.0
江 苏	Jiangsu	5735.5	6706.2	7985.9	9905.1	11484.1	15.9
浙 江	Zhejiang	4645.9	5358.0	6271.3	7533.3	8622.3	14.5
安 徽	Anhui	1776.7	2056.5	2451.9	3045.2	3527.8	15.8
福 建	Fujian	2351.7	2717.6	3212.3	3866.7	4481.0	15.9
江 西	Jiangxi	1244.9	1448.2	1718.9	2142.0	2484.4	16.0
山 东	Shangdong	6166.9	7217.1	8607.5	10658.8	12363.0	16.0
河 南	Henan	3380.9	3932.6	4690.3	5815.4	6746.4	16.0
湖 北	**Hubei**	**2985.9**	**3461.1**	**4115.8**	**5109.7**	**5928.4**	**16.0**
湖 南	Hunan	2474.3	2869.4	3419.2	4222.6	4913.7	16.4
广 东	Guangdong	7915.5	9194.3	10731.3	12986.6	14891.8	14.7
广 西	Guangxi	1405.5	1620.3	1932.7	2395.8	2790.7	16.5
海 南	Hainan	270.8	313.4	370.9	463.2	537.5	16.0
重 庆	Chongqing	1227.8	1431.5	1711.1	2147.1	2479.0	15.5
四 川	Sichuan	3003.5	3472.5	4105.6	4944.8	5758.7	16.5
贵 州	Guizhou	615.7	710.0	858.2	1075.2	1247.3	16.0
云 南	Yunnan	1041.3	1204.8	1422.5	1764.7	2051.1	16.2
西 藏	Tibet	73.2	90.0	112.6	130.0	156.6	20.5
陕 西	Shaanxi	1331.3	1542.4	1837.3	2317.1	2699.7	16.5
甘 肃	Gansu	638.1	729.5	854.4	1023.6	1183.0	15.6
青 海	Qinghai	161.6	182.6	212.6	259.7	300.5	15.7
宁 夏	Ningxia	175.8	202.5	239.5	295.4	339.3	14.9
新 疆	Xinjiang	640.2	733.2	857.5	1041.5	1177.5	13.1

中国统计出版社最新图书简目

（仅供参考，以最后出书为准）

统计资料

中国统计年鉴－2010
2010 中国发展报告
中国劳动统计年鉴－2010
中国建筑业统计年鉴－2010
中国商品交易市场统计年鉴－2010
中国民政统计年鉴－2010
中国科技统计年鉴－2010
中国高技术产业统计年鉴－2010
全国农产品成本收益资料汇编－2010
第二次全国残疾人抽样调查资料系列
中国县（市）社会经济调查年鉴－2010
中国国内生产总值核算历史资料（1952－2004）
大中型批发零售和住宿餐饮企业统计年鉴－2010

中国统计摘要－2010
中国第三产业统计年鉴－2010
中国社会统计年鉴－2010
中国人口和就业统计年鉴－2010
中国房地产统计年鉴－2010
中国贸易外经统计年鉴－2010
中国农村统计年鉴－2010
中国教育经费统计年鉴－2009
中国科学技术协会统计年鉴－2010
中国棉花年鉴－2008/2009
中国农村住户调查年鉴－2010（中、英文）
中国季度国内生产总值核算历史资料（1992－2005）
国际统计年鉴－2010

中国区域经济统计年鉴－2010
中国城市统计年鉴－2009
中国工业经济统计年鉴－2010
中国能源统计年鉴－2010
2010 中国地区经济监测报告
中国农产品价格调查年鉴－2010
中国农村贫困监测报告－2010
工业企业科技活动资料－2010
中国城市（镇）生活与价格年鉴－2010
中国农村全面建设小康监测报告－2010
中国零售和餐饮业连锁企业统计年鉴－2010
2005 年中国 1% 人口抽样调查系列资料

2010 年省级综合统计年鉴系列

北京　天津　河北　山西　内蒙古　辽宁　吉林　黑龙江　上海　江苏　浙江　安徽　福建　江西　山东
河南　湖北　湖南　广东　广西　海南　重庆　四川　贵州　云南　西藏　陕西　甘肃　青海　宁夏
新疆　新疆生产建设兵团

2010 年市（县）级综合统计年鉴系列

天津滨海新区　石家庄　唐山　邯郸　太原　大同　长治　阳泉　晋城　朔州　晋中
运城　忻州　临汾　呼和浩特　包头　沈阳　大连　长春　吉林市　四平　延吉　哈尔滨　齐齐哈尔
黑龙江垦区　上海浦东新区　苏州　无锡　常州　徐州　南通　盐城　镇江　江阴　丹阳　杭州
宁波　绍兴　台州　舟山　温州　金华　嘉兴　衢州　安庆　福州　福州经济技术开发区
厦门经济特区　南昌　上饶　济南　青岛　潍坊　东营　郑州　洛阳　三门峡　南阳　武汉　宜昌
十堰　荆州　黄冈　长沙　广州　东莞　惠州　深圳　桂林　南宁　柳州　来宾　河池　海口　成都
贵阳　昆明　西安　庆阳　银川　乌鲁木齐　吐鲁番

“十一五”规划教材

非参数统计　医学统计学
多元统计分析　经济计量学教程
统计数据处理概论
企业经营管理统计
统计学：从数据到结论

概率论与数理统计　统计学
应用时间序列分析
质量管理统计方法　社会统计学
市场调查与预测
国民经济核算教程（国民经济统计学）

现代金融投资统计分析
统计指数理论及应用
多元统计分析实验
统计学原理（非统计专业使用）
概率论与数理统计（经济、管理类专业使用）

重点图书

新中国六十年　挑大学选专业 2010—高考志愿填报指南　挑大学选专业 2010—考研择校指南

中国统计出版社最新图书简目

（仅供参考，以最后出书为准）

统计资料

中国统计年鉴－2010
2010 中国发展报告
中国劳动统计年鉴－2010
中国建筑业统计年鉴－2010
中国商品交易市场统计年鉴－2010
中国民政统计年鉴－2010
中国科技统计年鉴－2010
中国高技术产业统计年鉴－2010
全国农产品成本收益资料汇编－2010
第二次全国残疾人抽样调查资料系列
中国县（市）社会经济调查年鉴－2010
中国国内生产总值核算历史资料（1952－2004）
大中型批发零售和住宿餐饮企业统计年鉴－2010
中国统计摘要－2010
中国第三产业统计年鉴－2010
中国社会统计年鉴－2010
中国人口和就业统计年鉴－2010
中国房地产统计年鉴－2010
中国贸易外经统计年鉴－2010
中国农村统计年鉴－2010
中国教育经费统计年鉴－2009
中国科学技术协会统计年鉴－2010
中国棉花年鉴－2008/2009
中国农村住户调查年鉴－2010（中、英文）
中国季度国内生产总值核算历史资料（1992－2005）
国际统计年鉴－2010
中国区域经济统计年鉴－2010
中国城市统计年鉴－2009
中国工业经济统计年鉴－2010
中国能源统计年鉴－2010
2010 中国地区经济监测报告
中国农产品价格调查年鉴－2010
中国农村贫困监测报告－2010
工业企业科技活动资料－2010
中国城市（镇）生活与价格年鉴－2010
中国农村全面建设小康监测报告－2010
中国零售和餐饮业连锁企业统计年鉴－2010
2005 年中国 1% 人口抽样调查系列资料

2010 年省级综合统计年鉴系列

北京　天津　河北　山西　内蒙古　辽宁　吉林　黑龙江　上海　江苏　浙江　安徽　福建　江西　山东
河南　湖北　湖南　广东　广西　海南　重庆　四川　贵州　云南　西藏　陕西　甘肃　青海　宁夏
新疆　新疆生产建设兵团

2010 年市（县）级综合统计年鉴系列

天津滨海新区　石家庄　唐山　邯郸　太原　大同　长治　阳泉　晋城　朔州　晋中
运城　忻州　临汾　呼和浩特　包头　沈阳　大连　长春　吉林市　四平　延吉　哈尔滨　齐齐哈尔
黑龙江垦区　上海浦东新区　苏州　无锡　常州　徐州　南通　盐城　镇江　江阴　丹阳　杭州
宁波　绍兴　台州　舟山　温州　金华　嘉兴　衢州　安庆　福州　福州经济技术开发区
厦门经济特区　南昌　上饶　济南　青岛　潍坊　东营　郑州　洛阳　三门峡　南阳　武汉　宜昌
十堰　荆州　黄冈　长沙　广州　东莞　惠州　深圳　桂林　南宁　柳州　来宾　河池　海口　成都
贵阳　昆明　西安　庆阳　银川　乌鲁木齐　吐鲁番

"十一五"规划教材

非参数统计　医学统计学
多元统计分析　经济计量学教程
统计数据处理概论
企业经营管理统计
统计学：从数据到结论
概率论与数理统计　统计学
应用时间序列分析
质量管理统计方法　社会统计学
市场调查与预测
国民经济核算教程（国民经济统计学）
现代金融投资统计分析
统计指数理论及应用
多元统计分析实验
统计学原理（非统计专业使用）
概率论与数理统计（经济、管理类专业使用）

重点图书

新中国六十年
挑大学选专业 2010—高考志愿填报指南
挑大学选专业 2010—考研择校指南